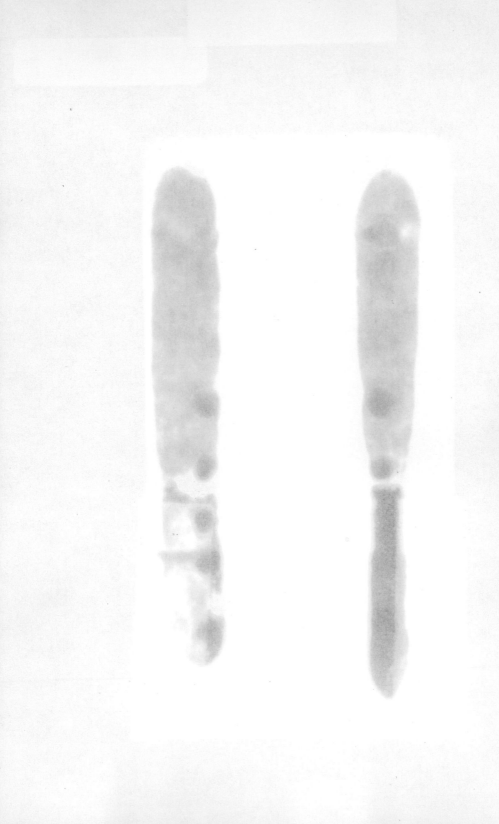

THE CAMBRIDGE HISTORY
OF THE BRITISH EMPIRE

General Editors:

E. A. BENIANS

J. R. M. BUTLER

P. N. S. MANSERGH

E. A. WALKER

VOLUME THREE

THE
CAMBRIDGE HISTORY
OF THE
BRITISH EMPIRE

Edited by

E. A. BENIANS

Sir JAMES BUTLER

C. E. CARRINGTON

VOLUME III

THE EMPIRE-COMMONWEALTH
1870–1919

CAMBRIDGE
AT THE UNIVERSITY PRESS
1967

PUBLISHED BY
THE SYNDICS OF THE CAMBRIDGE UNIVERSITY PRESS

Bentley House, 200 Euston Road, London, N.W.1
American Branch: 32 East 57th Street, New York, N.Y. 10022

©

CAMBRIDGE UNIVERSITY PRESS
1959

First published 1959
reprinted with corrections 1967

First printed in Great Britain at the University Press, Cambridge
Reprinted by lithography in Great Britain by
Halstan & Co., Amersham, Bucks.

PREFACE

THE publication of the present volume completes the original project set out by the editors of volume I. They envisaged eight volumes, of which the first three would relate the general history of British oversea expansion and imperial policy, two volumes, IV and V, the history of British India, and the remaining three the history of Canada and Newfoundland, Australia and New Zealand, and South Africa. The history of the various parts of the dependent Empire would be treated in the first three volumes in connection with the general story of the Empire's growth and policy.

Volume II, on the growth of the New Empire, was published in 1940. The delay in the appearance of volume III is due partly to the war, partly to the untimely death of Mr E. A. Benians, Master of St John's College, the editor in charge of it. Mr Benians was one of the three general editors who planned the series as a whole; he had in addition accepted the primary responsibility for the present volume; he planned the book and chose the contributors. His death in February 1952 was, therefore, a heavy blow to this History, as well as to his College and University. It was characteristic of him to treat his contributors with extreme forbearance and generosity, and uncomplainingly to take on himself work which others had felt compelled to lay down. The book which now appears is essentially his book, though several of the chapters were written and some of the contributors selected after his death, and the volume as a whole lacks his final editorial supervision. Fortunately Mr Benians had completed his own two chapters, the first of which, The Empire in the New Age, serves as an introduction to the volume, just as his chapter on The Beginnings of the New Empire stood as the opening chapter of volume II. It is appropriate that, of the remaining seventeen chapters of a book which owes so much to him, no less than five should have been contributed by members of his own College. The present editors would express their high appreciation of the privilege of having worked with Mr Benians and their sense of the loss which historical studies in the University have sustained by his death.

As originally planned, the volume was to have covered the period from 1870 to 1921. It has been found more convenient to bring it to a close in 1919, but one or two chapters take the story on to the later date, while chapter II starts with Gladstone's accession to power in 1868. If the later chapters on international relations and colonial policy seem to be in fact rather a history of British foreign policy, it may be urged that in this period colonial issues were so subordinate to other questions of foreign policy that they could not be kept, even in such a work as this, in the centre of the stage.

The editors wish to express their thanks to all the contributors, some of whom may perhaps feel that they have been hardly treated. The delay in publication has had the unfortunate result that several years have now elapsed since some of the chapters were written, and apologies are due to their authors if they now appear without the gloss of novelty and if works written subsequently by other historians have in certain respects anticipated them. Apologies are also due to writers recruited at a later date for pressure put upon them to hasten their contributions. In particular we have to thank Mr A. F. Madden for undertaking an important chapter at very short notice.

Professors V. T. Harlow and E. A. Walker, and the late Professor J. B. Brebner, kindly helped us with advice, and Mr Tunstall, the author of chapter xv, wishes to make special acknowledgment of assistance given by the late Mr L. S. Amery.

In the vacuum in the editorship caused by Mr Benians' death much labour which would naturally have fallen on the editor was cheerfully undertaken by the Staff of the University Press, and we should like to express our warm thanks to Mr R. J. L. Kingsford, Secretary to the Syndics.

Mr A. Taylor Milne not only undertook the compilation of the Bibliography but read all the chapters both in typescript and in print, co-ordinated the footnotes, and contributed the Index. The editors are greatly indebted to him and take this opportunity of expressing their thanks.

J. R. M. B.
C. E. C.

1957

ABBREVIATIONS OF TITLES OF WORKS AND SOURCES QUOTED IN THIS VOLUME

A.P.S.	Aborigines Protection Society.
A.S.S.	Anti-Slavery Society.
Adm.	Admiralty Records, Public Record Office, London.
B.D.	*British Documents on the Origins of the War*, 1898–1914.
B.F.S.P.	*British and Foreign State Papers.*
B.M. Add. MSS.	British Museum, Additional Manuscripts.
C.H.B.E.	*Cambridge History of the British Empire.*
C.H.B.F.P.	*Cambridge History of British Foreign Policy.*
C.J.	*Journals of the House of Commons.*
C.O.	Colonial Office Records, Public Record Office, London.
D.D.F.	*Documents diplomatiques français*, 1871–1914.
D.G.P.	*Die Grosse Politik der Europäischen Kabinette*, 1871–1914.
D.N.B.	*Dictionary of National Biography.*
E.H.R.	*English Historical Review.*
F.O.	Foreign Office Records, Public Record Office, London.
G.D.	Gifts and Deposits, Public Record Office, London.
H.O.	Home Office Records, Public Record Office, London.
Hansard	*Hansard's Parliamentary Debates.*
L.J.	*Journals of the House of Lords.*
P.R.O.	Public Record Office, London.
Parl. Pap.	Great Britain, Parliament, House of Commons, Parliamentary Papers.
W.O.	War Office Records, Public Record Office, London.

TABLE OF CONTENTS

CHAPTER I

THE EMPIRE IN THE NEW AGE, 1870–1919

By E. A. BENIANS

CHAPTER II

IMPERIAL QUESTIONS IN BRITISH POLITICS, 1868–1880

By J. R. M. BUTLER, M.A., Fellow of Trinity College, Cambridge

CHAPTER III

THE OPENING OF TROPICAL AFRICA, 1870–1885

By J. SIMMONS, M.A., Professor of History in the
University of Leicester

CHAPTER IV

INTERNATIONAL RIVALRY IN THE COLONIAL
SPHERE, 1869–1885

By F. H. HINSLEY, M.A., Fellow of St John's College, Cambridge;
Reader in the History of International Relations in the
University of Cambridge

CHAPTER V

IMPERIAL PROBLEMS IN BRITISH POLITICS, 1880–1895

By R. E. ROBINSON, M.A., Fellow of St John's College, Cambridge; Smuts Reader in the University of Cambridge

CHAPTER VI

FINANCE, TRADE AND COMMUNICATIONS
1870–1895

By E. A. BENIANS

CHAPTER VII

IMPERIAL DEFENCE, 1870–1897

By W. C. B. Tunstall, M.A.

CONTENTS

CHAPTER VIII

INTERNATIONAL RIVALRY, 1885–1895

By F. H. HINSLEY, M.A.

CHAPTER IX

THE BRITISH EMPIRE AND THE UNITED STATES OF AMERICA, 1870–1914

By ANTHONY STEEL, O.B.E., Litt.D., Fellow of Christ's College, Cambridge

CONTENTS

CHAPTER X

CHANGING ATTITUDES AND WIDENING RESPONSIBILITIES, 1895–1914

By A. F. MADDEN, M.A., B.Litt., Fellow of Nuffield College, Oxford; Reader in Commonwealth Government in the University of Oxford

CHAPTER XI

DEVELOPMENT OF THE IMPERIAL
CONFERENCE, 1887–1914

By J. E. TYLER

CHAPTER XII

IMPERIAL FINANCE, TRADE, AND
COMMUNICATIONS, 1895–1914

By G. S. GRAHAM, M.A., Rhodes Professor of Imperial
History in the University of London

CHAPTER XIII

BRITISH FOREIGN POLICY AND COLONIAL QUESTIONS, 1895–1904

By F. H. HINSLEY, M.A.

CHAPTER XIV

GREAT BRITAIN AND THE POWERS, 1904–1914

By F. H. HINSLEY, M.A.

CHAPTER XV

IMPERIAL DEFENCE, 1897–1914

By W. C. B. TUNSTALL, M.A.

1897–1905

1905–1914

CHAPTER XVI

THE EMPIRE AT WAR, 1914–1918

By C. E. CARRINGTON, M.A.

CHAPTER XVII

THE EMPIRE AND THE PEACE TREATIES
1918–1921

By K. C. WHEARE, M.A., Rector of
Exeter College, Oxford

CHAPTER XVIII
INTERNATIONAL LAW AND COLONIAL QUESTIONS, 1870–1914

By Sir H. LAUTERPACHT; and R. Y. JENNINGS, M.A., LL.B., Fellow
of Jesus College, Cambridge; Whewell Professor of International
Law in the University of Cambridge.

CHAPTER XIX
THE COLONIAL OFFICE, 1801–1925

By R. B. PUGH, M.A., Editor of the *Victoria History of the Counties of
England*; Fellow of St Edmund Hall, Oxford.

CONTENTS

CHAPTER I

THE EMPIRE IN THE NEW AGE, 1870–1919

"THE acquisition of self-government", wrote Sir Charles Adderley in his account of the British colonies in 1869, "is not so much the gift of an enlightened policy, as the natural tendency and necessity of English colonies."[1] Two groups of British colonies, the North American and the Australasian, by that time enjoyed self-government in internal matters nearly as complete as that in Britain—while the Cape Colony in Southern Africa was on the eve of acquiring like privileges and powers. These colonies were now so sharply differentiated from the other oversea dominions of the Queen that the colonial empire was fast assuming that dual character which was afterwards to find expression in the term Empire Commonwealth. Whatever future might have lain before Great Britain and her original American colonies had they remained united, some different destiny lay before the Second Empire from its very diversity of character and dispersion over all quarters of the world. The colonies under Crown government, or Crown colonies as they were now called, were the West African settlements, the Caribbean colonies, the Eastern possessions of Mauritius and Ceylon, the commercial stations around the Straits of Malacca, Labuan, Hong Kong, the Falkland Islands, St Helena and Heligoland, and the war and naval stations of Gibraltar, Malta and Bermuda. These dependencies, where the Governor ruled as the representative of the Crown, with no check on his action save the advice of the Council and the free expression of public opinion, were not at the time regarded as on their way to a normal state of self-government, but as necessarily remaining in an inferior political status, either because of the character of their population, or from other causes. "Stations merely occupied for war," writes Adderley, "depots of trade, and subjects of inferior race are fitly so governed." And he quotes the Duke of Wellington: "A Constitution for Malta! I should as soon think of elections in an army or a parliament on board ship"—and continues:

No one would ask for a representative Assembly to superintend the few settlers round the coal mines of Labuan. A community chiefly consisting of Cingalese, for another example, could hardly be first taken out of the custody of the Presidency of Madras, and then entrusted with free British citizenship.... The West India representative constitutions begin to recede, of necessity, towards Crown Government—I hope only *pour mieux sauter*. From smallness of area, absence of proprietary, social and generic incongruity, and the unfitness of the mass of the population—

[1] Adderley, Sir C. B. (Lord Norton), *Review of "The Colonial Policy of Lord J. Russell's Administration", by Earl Grey, 1853; and of subsequent colonial history* (1869), p. 14.

the result of slavery—to form electoral constituencies, these little islands, once preserves of patronage, are now unequal singly to furnish the materials for constitutional government.[1]

Nor did he see for such possessions any natural or necessary future within the Empire. The advantage to Britain of these dependencies lay in their assistance to commerce, encouragement of enterprise and furthering of imperial interests throughout the world. If they ceased to serve such purposes they might be abandoned or exchanged at any time, "only fulfilling engagements made, and reserving interests created". They were merely "occupations for use" and could be alienated without any national severance, unlike the national settlements which, if our policy were wise, "will retain a connection of nationality with us for ever". Nor was there any desire for the expansion of such possessions. Rather limitation and, if possible, diminution of such responsibilities, was our policy. With free trade in the ascendant and colonial rivalries abated, the British Empire seemed likely to resolve itself into a partnership of free nations having insignificant responsibilities outside their own borders except to guard the routes of ocean trade, and except for India.

India fitted into neither of the categories described. It was neither a national settlement nor an occupation for use. It was not yet seen as a partner in a commonwealth of nations, nor was it likely to be willingly abandoned. The Mogul Emperor and the East India Company had passed from the scene during the Indian Mutiny (1857–8), and British India other than the Indian States was now under the direct government of the Crown. Its political unity was established and peace and order prevailed within its bounds. The Crown was pledged to respect the rights of the Indian princes and the ancient usages and customs of India, to guarantee complete religious toleration and free and impartial employment to its subjects of whatever race and creed. Modern India was coming into sight, with great cities and westernised industries and economic organisation. A united India was being shaped for a new place in the world. The process had reached the stage at which Englishmen felt the maximum pride and confidence in their work. What Warren Hastings had said in 1785 remained true: "It is useless to enquire whether the Company or the nation has derived any substantial benefit from the change, since it is impossible to retrace the perilous and wonderful paths by which they have attained their present elevation and to redescend to the humble and undreaded character of trading adventurers." The process must continue—the association of East and West under the control of British policy, following the course of events, till some result emerged which would change the relations of Britain and India. As yet there seemed little prospect of their being rapidly changed so as to assimilate India politically to the self-governing parts of the Empire,

[1] Adderley, *op. cit.* p. 13.

and the nature and magnitude of the problem differentiated it from all others. The Indian Councils Act of 1861, which had added a non-official element to the Governor-General's Council and the Councils of Bombay and Madras for legislative purposes, made but a faint start on the road to the parliamentary system of the West. A self-governing India was no doubt the ultimate goal, but it was not yet upon the horizon.

Such in general was the character of the British Empire in the middle of Queen Victoria's reign. During the half-century whose history is the subject of the present volume a great transformation took place. In this phase of British imperial history the nations of the Commonwealth came into being as a group of Dominions; great dependencies were added, and, passing from indifference to their future save as it affected imperial interests, Great Britain became seized of a new policy, of a sense of duty to them as societies to be associated in due course on equal terms with other members of the British Commonwealth; and further, "the progressive realisation of responsible government in India as an integral part of the British Empire" was declared to be Britain's purpose. We may now sketch the causes which brought these changes to pass.

In British colonial policy three influences were always making themselves felt—Britain's own needs and sense of her own interests, the needs and opinions of her colonies, and the changing face of the world. In 1870 Great Britain was still leading the industrial movement. She alone was an industrial State, with an unquestioned superiority in manufactures, trade and finance. She lived by the products of her factories, and, though her agriculture was still pre-eminent, half her bread and corn was already being imported. Coal was cheap, and it was still the coal age; electricity was not yet power. Peace was her interest, and naval superiority was necessary to her survival in time of war. Thus she had come to concentrate on commercial and maritime strength, to adopt free trade, hoping to see the worldwide extension of a policy so favourable to her manufacturing and trading supremacy. Though the possession of her Empire gave her reputation and place in the world and the principal problems of her oversea policy, it was not to her Empire that she looked particularly for her livelihood, but to the profits of her trade, her investments and the services of her ships in all parts of the world. Her oversea investments were growing and the magnitude of her shipping relative to that of other countries was still increasing. The self-governing colonies asserted their right to the control of their own economic policies regardless of British opinion and advantage, but India was to some extent subordinated to free-trade orthodoxy in British interests, though on the other hand she profited by the connection to borrow capital on the London market at reasonable rates for her industries and railway system. The mistress of so great an empire, still growing richer, secure in her island strength and power at sea, stood high among the states of the world. If peace, liberal ideas and free trade prevailed in the world, Britain's position was invulnerable and might be long maintained. There must be limits to her further growth as compared with the under-populated lands and the new lands, but many of the latter lay within the Empire. So far as her own circumstances and prevailing ideas were to determine imperial policy, they still favoured extending freedom and not forming closer ties. But British policy was a web woven of separate strands. The relations of Britain with the young societies of European origin, with the mixed societies in some colonies, with the simple societies, and with India, were already very different, and each might be influenced by new developments.

Between Great Britain and the young nations sprung from Europe a mutual desire to preserve the unity of the Empire was already apparent. Colonial self-government might change the nature of the Empire, but was not to dissolve it. The consciousness of kinship and of common ideals and traditions, and a common pride in membership of a great State, were strong forces favouring its preservation. The colonies felt their incapacity to stand alone and also saw economic advantages in the imperial connection. Great Britain on her side was becoming conscious of a changing world, more militant, competitive and perhaps aggressive, in which her colonies would be a strength and not a weakness. *Laissez-faire* ideas had passed the zenith of their influence, and the discussion excited by the withdrawal of imperial garrisons from some colonies had shown the strength of imperial sentiment. All saw in the Empire a union of the forces of freedom. But the colonies wished to preserve the Empire in a form that would not diminish but rather enlarge their independence, while Great Britain wished to maintain the policy of free trade which had developed her economic strength and to share the burden of imperial defence. Lord Carnarvon in 1870 defined the Britannic question as being to preserve on the one hand the self-government of the colonies and on the other to add to it a more real connection. In the preceding year Sir Charles Adderley had written that "anything in the way of a Congress for discussing questions which might be called Imperial, was far too great an innovation to find any acceptance with Englishmen".[1] Nevertheless, before twenty years had passed, the Conservative leader, Lord Salisbury, made that innovation. Leaders in the colonies did not want too close a unity. John Macdonald, Prime Minister of Canada, had spoken before 1867 of the Empire as "an alliance of equal and autonomous states linked together by a common sovereign", and Henry Parkes, a leading politician in New South Wales, had said "the softer the cords the stronger will be the union". Parkes believed federation to be impossible because of the inequality between the partners—a true federa-

---

[1] Adderley, *op. cit.* p. 12.

tion must be an agreement between equals. The Imperial Federation League, which had a life of nine years (1884–93), served to advertise the question and bring to discussion the issue of imperial unity in various forms. But there was no agreement on the form federation might take. Discussion showed the difficulty of all the forms proposed, but dispelled the idea that the Empire must either federate or disintegrate. Parliamentary union had always appeared impractical and unacceptable, and, almost equally, an Imperial Council. It became clear that defence and economic questions were the centre of the matter, and what emerged from the discussions was the idea of periodical conferences to maintain contact and discuss practical problems. Voluntary association under the Crown would be the form, co-operation the object, and conference the method. Great Britain, so far as her policy was concerned, would follow the precedent already set in the case of the Canadian Confederation (1867–73) and promote the strength and national growth and spirit of her great colonies by encouraging the union of contiguous areas into larger unities, capable of organised existence and national life, and ceding to them the powers they required for this. From this policy came later the Commonwealth of Australia, 1901, and the Union of South Africa, 1910. So a Commonwealth of Nations began to form. The self-governing colonies clearly regarded themselves as members of a greater whole but meant to keep and enlarge their autonomy. A gradual process of definition was to determine relationships and make clear the nature of the association as the children became adult.

Among the self-governing colonies South Africa demanded and received, in this period, particular attention. It might seem in 1910, and even in 1919, that South Africa was following in the footsteps of Canada. In each vast area two peoples of European origin, having subdued the indigenous inhabitants, were settling down after long friction and some bloodshed into co-existence as a single nation. But there were in fact profound differences between the two cases. In South Africa there was a tough tradition of independence among the non-British white colonists, they were more numerous than the British, and they were capable of a far more effective armed resistance than the Canadian rebels of 1837. The native problem, too, was much more serious than in any of the other colonies ripe for self-government, and in relation to this problem, as well as to the economic future of their country, the customs and ideas of the two sections of the white population appeared in sharp and ominous contrast.

While the process of definition described above pursued its leisurely course, subject to the various pressures of events and the development of problems of defence and economic relations, and following usually the wishes of the colonies, an immense change took place in the character and extent of the dependent Empire for which the mother country was responsible. International relations were entering

upon a new phase. In 1870–1 the unity of Italy was completed and
the German Empire was founded. Power in Europe was now transferred from France to Germany, to a German Empire, united, flushed
with success, and confident in war as an instrument of policy. Both
Germany and Italy were soon to take part in the competition for
colonial expansion, which, since 1815, had been almost confined to
Great Britain and France, and had so much abated as to influence very
little the growth of the Empire. To protect our communications with
India had been for many years the principal motive of new acquisitions, but now the future of Africa and of the Pacific Islands came
into question. To have assumed control of immense areas of tropical
Africa and of groups of islands in the Pacific would have been repugnant to mid-Victorian statesmen, anxious to be rid of the responsibility and the cost of governing distant colonies and primitive peoples.
Nor did traders or missionaries generally favour such expansion.
But the industrial progress of the United States and Germany, Germany's vigorous entry into the competition for trade and colonies, and
the increasingly protective policy of many countries, confronted Great
Britain with a new situation. A general competition for markets and
for sources of supply of raw materials for industry had begun and
was rapidly intensified. She wished to keep open the great market of
Africa and to guard the routes to her oversea colonies. In the 'eighties
and 'nineties there followed the partition of Africa and the Pacific
Islands among various Powers. By successive agreements with other
powers Great Britain for her part annexed large areas of eastern,
western and southern Africa, where her merchants and colonists had
interests or expected to gain them, and where her existing settlements
gave her a door through which to penetrate the interior. British
South Africa was linked to Central Africa: the sources of the Nile and
the main course of the Niger passed under British control. In carrying out this process Great Britain reverted for a time to the old system
of chartered companies. Four great companies were chartered in the
'eighties and given commercial and political rights: in Borneo (1881),
Nigeria (1886), East Africa (1888) and Southern Africa (1889). One
by one they were later to surrender their political rights, and the
administration of these great dependencies was to become a direct
responsibility of the Crown.

This acquisition and subsequent transference to direct imperial
government of vast and diverse territories opened a new phase in
British imperial history. Though carried out under the stress of international competition and primarily for economic reasons, it was soon
seen to involve, in addition to problems of economic development,
new problems of government and of imperial policy. What kind of
responsibility was entailed by this expansion? On the economic side
Joseph Chamberlain, the Colonial Secretary, in vigorous speech drew
attention to the undeveloped estates of the Empire, while, on the

political and administrative side, the conception of indirect rule, already familiar to the British and Dutch colonial systems, was being applied. Britain's general policy would be to retain, so far as was practicable and beneficial, native rulers and institutions, and to carry on her administration through them. An imperialist power, it was urged, should recognise a dual mandate—on the one hand, the obligation to develop the dependent lands in the interests of world commerce, and, on the other, to preserve and promote the interests and welfare of their inhabitants. That expansion of Britain's power ought to serve some other purpose than her own commercial prosperity and military renown was an idea that went far back in British imperial tradition. Hakluyt and Raleigh had proclaimed it in Elizabethan days. Chatham had reminded Parliament that the hearts and good affections of the people of Bengal were of more worth than all the profits of ruinous and odious monopolies, and the House of Commons Committee on Aborigines (1835–7) had laid it down that the protection of the natives must be considered a duty belonging to government: "He who has made Great Britain what she is will enquire at our hands how we have employed our influence." The long-sustained effort to abolish slavery and the slave trade which Great Britain had made, illustrated the persistence of this moral sense in imperial policy. It had now to find new expression in new circumstances and vaster areas which the rapid expansion in the last quarter of the nineteenth century had brought under British control. The Empire must not be a machinery for the exploitation of weaker races. In what way, on what lines, and by what agency was their development to be influenced? It was no easy thing to mediate in the contacts of modern industrial civilisation with simple economies; of Western settlers, eager for profit, with primitive peoples. The responsibility had to be realised, assumed and translated into administrative action and political institutions. British rule had for a long time past represented peace, order, justice and toleration; it had now to achieve more—to bring western science and western moral and cultural ideas to aid and improve the simpler societies. *Laissez-faire* was no longer a possible attitude for a Western government in its dependencies. It could not in that way discharge its responsibilities to the native inhabitants. A simple protection was not enough; a more positive policy must be declared. This was done in 1923:[1] His Majesty's Government, said the Colonial Secretary, "regard themselves as exercising a trust on behalf of the native populations... the object of which may be defined as the protection and advancement of the native races...it is the mission of Great Britain to work continuously for the training and education of the African towards a higher intellectual, moral and economic level." How could effect be given to it? From policing to administration is a long road.

[1] See Memorandum on *Indians in Kenya, Parl. Pap.* 1923, XVIII [Cmd. 1922].

Educational advance and economic development were necessary before dependencies could look to the further objective of British policy—self-government. Financial independence and the capacity for democratic political life must precede this. But it lay in the logic of the policy now being worked out. The weaker members of the imperial society were not to be superannuated, but to move forward at such a rate as they might prove capable of to the common goal. Meanwhile, association in that international system which the Empire Commonwealth had become was to inure to their benefit. Protection, assistance and the same ultimate status were to be assured to them. The weaker side of Britain's imperial system, a product of national instincts and character—that the promotion of intellectual and economic development had hitherto been primarily left to voluntary agencies —was thus to be strengthened. That this change and quickening of British colonial policy came in the wake of the First World War was a result of the increasing economic competition between the nations, the focusing of attention upon colonial questions which the War had brought, and at the same time the changing ideas of the functions of government in Britain herself.

In the Covenant of the League of Nations the changing attitude to dependencies was expressed by the establishment of the mandatory system. President Wilson in his Fourteen Points had declared that in the adjustment of colonial claims "the interests of the populations concerned must have equal weight with the equitable claims of the Government whose title is to be determined".[1] General Smuts suggested that the government of these dependencies might be provided for in the Covenant, and Article XXII of the Covenant laid down the principle that the well-being and development of "peoples not yet able to stand by themselves under the strenuous conditions of the modern world" form "a sacred trust of civilisation".[2] A mandatory system was devised which provided for "national responsibility subject to international criticism and supervision". The Mandatory Power was to guarantee freedom of conscience and religion, to prohibit the slave trade, the arms traffic and the liquor traffic, to prevent the military training of the natives save for police purposes and home defence, and to secure equal opportunities in trade and commerce to all nations. These provisions embodied the practice of British colonial administration.

In addition to the African dependencies annexed to the Empire or held under mandate were other protectorates where British authority was less directly exercised. Of these the chief were the Malay States which were loosely bound together in a federation in 1895. The external affairs of these states were dealt with by the Imperial Government, which also appointed a Resident at the court of each of the

---

[1] Temperley, H. W. V., *A History of the Peace Conference of Paris*, I, 413.
[2] *Ibid.* VI, 500–2.

Sultans, whose business was to advise; but direct interference with internal affairs was reduced to a minimum. Here Britain followed the same general lines as in her dealings with the Princely States of India.

We may now resume the story as it relates to the self-governing parts of the Empire. The series of Colonial Conferences, which began in 1887 when Lord Salisbury's government, concerned about defence, raised the matter as an imperial question, was continued, and the Conference was recognised as a standing institution of the Empire. It became an assembly of Prime Ministers, meeting every four years, and in 1907 its name was changed to Imperial Conference. The greater colonies were styled Dominions, and the expression "Dominion status" described, without defining, their position. The idea of an Imperial Council, which Chamberlain had urged in 1897, was unacceptable to the other members, yet their part in the South African War (1899–1902) and their general attitude showed their sense of imperial unity. To the mother country the problem of defence seemed the most urgent, while the Dominions pressed for closer economic relations in the form of mutual trade preferences. Behind this difference were two not easily soluble problems. Defence was bound up with foreign policy, which Great Britain controlled; imperial preference ran counter to the free-trade tradition, to which she still held fast. She had passed the necessary legislation to set her self-governing colonies completely free in their commercial policy, which was in general protectionist. But faced with ever-increasing competition from Germany and the United States in the markets of the world, she was unwilling to surrender such advantages as free trade gave her in the maintenance of her industries and in export markets.

Successive elections in 1906 and 1910 showed that Chamberlain's campaign in favour of tariff reform and imperial preference had failed to convince the British people. Great Britain's industrial supremacy had now been successfully challenged. She was fighting a losing battle to hold her former place and already foresaw a hard struggle to maintain by her manufacturing, commercial and financial activities the high standard of life for her still-growing population which she had established in the nineteenth century. At the same time she felt her security endangered by the militant naval policy on which the German Empire embarked in the twentieth century. The South African War had shown her as isolated in an unfriendly and jealous world and, but for the naval supremacy she then had and the irreconcilable feud between Germany and France, she might have been prevented from bringing it to a successful issue. This menacing situation obliged her to re-examine her position and reconsider her foreign policy. Isolation was more splendid than safe. Europe was divided between two rival groups of Powers—the Dual and the Triple Alliance—to neither of which she was attached; in Asia she had liabilities and risks without friends to share them. So came about a considerable reorientation of her foreign policy. She sought to work with the United States, whose growing power and interest in external problems was not likely to be used against her; and between the two countries came an increasing harmony of views, facilitated by her withdrawal from competition with American interests in the New World. With Japan she had always been friendly, and an alliance (1902) offered to both countries some assurance against the possible aggressiveness of Russia. Rebuffed by Germany, she turned to France and found ways to compromise and remove old differences, and thus to place herself in friendly relations with the Dual Alliance (1904). This change, so unexpected by Germany, intensified the antagonism of the two groups of European Powers. Having taken her side by making the Anglo-French *entente*, Great Britain went on to improve her relations with Russia, settling long-standing differences in Central Asia and forming the Triple Entente (1907). In face of these developments German policy became more hostile and militant, and German naval preparations more challenging. In 1911 Great Britain found herself on the verge of war.

The line of policy followed by Great Britain had been her own choice and not an imperial policy, jointly conceived with the Dominions. They neither questioned nor fully understood it. It was forced on her for the defence of India, and by her inability to bear any longer the risk and cost of a policy of complete isolation. The Dominions welcomed the better understanding with the United States and even sympathised with the Anglo-Japanese alliance, but they had no wish to be involved in a European war concerning issues remote from them. The increasing tension in international relations could not however fail to be of concern to them, and in 1911 it was decided that, while Great Britain must control foreign policy, the Dominions were to be consulted as far as possible. At the Imperial Conference of that year Sir Edward Grey explained to them the anxieties and dangers of the position.

The First World War involved a struggle for existence. The members of the Empire stood together in defence of their common ideals and interests. The loose political structure bore the strain. Means were improvised to ensure united policy and action. Canadians, Australians, New Zealanders, South Africans and Indians fought in Europe for the first time. Once European Powers had fought each other in North America and India; now the future of these countries was settled on the plains of France and Belgium. "Australia", wrote Dilke in 1869, "would scarcely feel herself deeply interested in the guarantee of Luxemburg, nor Canada in the affairs of Serbia",[1] but this was precisely what happened. They recognised the struggle as their battle and their future as the stake, for the Empire-Commonwealth was the guardian of their ideals and must be preserved.

[1] Dilke, Sir C. W., *Greater Britain*, p. 395.

But the Dominions were no longer prepared to defend a purely British policy. During the war it was agreed that after the war the constitutional position and the status of a Dominion must be clarified. They asked now for independence and freedom of action in foreign relations. They claimed separate representation in the negotiation of peace and in the constitution of the League of Nations. In December 1918 Canada urged that "the unique character of the British Commonwealth, composed of a group of free nations under one sovereign", be recognised. It seemed as if the British Empire might well find its euthanasia in the League of Nations. And had that institution functioned as was intended, it might have served for all nations the purpose which the British Commonwealth had served for some.

Slowly, moving stage by stage, British political instinct had fashioned by experience a working league of nations, capable of collaboration, settling in peace their own differences, each free in its own life, strong and united in defence, and sharing common ideals. A long history lay behind it, which secured it a loyalty and gave it a strength and elasticity lacking in the vaster structure that was planned with so much hope, and planned in vain.

The course of events that followed the war—the independent assertion by the Dominions of their right to control their own foreign policy, to have their own representatives in foreign courts and to stand out of treaties negotiated by Great Britain if they wished; the settlement of the Irish question made in 1921 by the recognition of the Irish Free State; and the urgency of Canada and South Africa for a definition of Dominion status, brought the matter at last to a head. The Conference of 1926 took the question up and the Balfour definition of the British Commonwealth was accepted: the Dominions were described as "autonomous communities within the British Empire, equal in status, in no way subordinate to one another in any aspect of their domestic or external affairs, though united by a common allegiance to the Crown and freely associated as members of the British Commonwealth of Nations".[1] In 1930 it was decided that the Governor-General of a Dominion was to be appointed on the advice of ministers in the Dominions concerned and to represent His Majesty and not His Majesty's United Kingdom Government. The High Commissioners, appointed by the several Governments, would be the channel of communication between them. In the following year the Statute of Westminster embodied the necessary enactments for giving effect to these decisions. The Dominions were defined by enumeration. The Crown became the only common political institution of the Empire, the expression and means of its unity. The unity must be one of spirit, voluntarily expressed by each member in such manner as its circumstances made desirable.

The creation of the Dominions is the most significant process of this

[1] *Imperial Conference, 1926. Summary of Proceedings: Parl. Pap.* 1926, xi [Cmd. 2768], p. 14.

phase of British history thus briefly introduced. The events just narrated carry us beyond the scope of the present volume, but are mentioned to give precision to the developments which appeared by the end of the First World War. A Dominion was a new nation and a free state, freely associated with other members of the Commonwealth. It was born of self-government, the federal principle locally applied and the spirit of nationality. Self-government gave the political freedom; the federal principle, integrating contiguous territories in a common political life, ensured the necessary economic and political strength, and the spirit of nationality gave character and personality to each. To be the mother of new nations has been the destiny of most of the colonial powers of Europe; to be mother and member of a commonwealth of nations has been the destiny of Great Britain alone. Her political genius foreshadowed in this an international system, beginning in a family of nations.

The First World War, which, with its decisions and consequences, carried the Dominions on to assert their equality of status with the Mother Country, was even more fateful in its influence upon her relations with India. For the Dominions the final step had long been within their reach. They had but to find the form and fashion in which they wished to express the autonomy and equal status of each within the unity of all. But India had as yet made little progress on the road to self-government. The Government of India remained absolute. Parliament was supreme over the Government of India, and the Government of India over the local governments. Her Majesty's Government regarded themselves as being as much responsible to Parliament for the government of India as they were for any of the Crown colonies of the Empire. The executive officers of the Crown when sitting as members of a Legislative Council had no freedom of action, for the authority of the legislating body was derived from the Crown and not from the principle of popular representation. Changes made in 1892 and by the Morley-Minto reforms of 1907 brought the idea of election and of discussion and criticism into Indian politics, but gave no responsibility to the elector or the elected. The conception of a responsible executive was not yet admitted. Power remained with the government. The Government of India was still a benevolent despotism, more than ever conscious, as well it might be, of its immense responsibilities, willing to consult to a limited extent the wishes of its subjects, but unwilling to resign any fraction of its power. The remote democracy to which it was subject hesitated to interfere with matters outside its interest and knowledge. On the one hand Indians had received an increasing share in the administration of the country and increasing opportunities of influencing and criticising the government; on the other hand they had no real political power and consequently no reason for political responsibility. Official opinion, resentful of irresponsible criticism, became increasingly apprehensive of the danger of any further advance toward self-government. The Morley-Minto reforms had not been intended to lead on to the parliamentary government for which they excited the desire and to which, in the event, they did lead. Local self-government in town and country was still regarded as the sphere in which the Indians should exercise their capacity and obtain their experience in the management of public affairs. In these circumstances dissatisfaction was widespread. British rule was no longer generally regarded as having merits sufficient to offset its denial of political freedom. Most of the Indian political leaders were united against it. Racial discrimination was keenly felt and there was a rising demand for more liberal institutions. India and Britain were moving rapidly apart.

The outbreak of war in 1914 acted and reacted on these conditions. India responded loyally to the common cause. But the war and the feelings which it excited, the new importance which it gave to India, speedily produced a demand for political change. India felt herself worthy of a more liberal form of government. She had fought for the liberty of others and could not be denied her own. In August 1917 Edwin Montagu, the Secretary of State for India, announced in the House of Commons that the policy of His Majesty's Government was "the gradual development of self-governing institutions with a view to the progressive realisation of responsible government in India as an integral part of the British Empire" and "that substantial steps in this direction should be taken as soon as possible". The Parliamentary government of the West was to be transferred to the East; India was to become in due course a Dominion.

The Montagu-Chelmsford Report of 1918 broke away from the tradition of absolute government. It proposed by a great extension of local self-government to train the electorates who were to be the roots of Western political life and institutions in India; to provide at once for a substantial measure of self-government in the Provinces; to give better representation and more influence to Indian opinion in the Government of India, and to ensure for Parliament fuller knowledge of the affairs of India. Great as was this step, almost revolutionary, it was generally recognised as the least that could now be done to enable India to hold the place to which she had risen in world affairs and to realise the aspirations which her long association with the West had stirred in her. If the step was large and sudden, it was because shorter steps had been too long postponed. "Parliament's omission", wrote the authors of the Report, "to institute regular means of reviewing the Indian administration is as much responsible as any single cause for our failure in the face of growing nationalist feeling in India, to think out and to work out a policy of continuous advance."[1] If this censure was just, why had Parliament

[1] *Report on Indian Constitutional Reforms: Parl. Pap.* 1918, VIII [Cmd. 9109], p. 30.

failed? Why had not the British democracy insisted on placing India long before on the road to self-government? Those who governed India in India had had so much to do in establishing the unity of India and the justice and efficiency of its administration that they were far from ready to hand over their tasks, feeling so little done and so much to do; and those who governed her in England doubtless agreed with Sir Charles Adderley that self-government was not a general policy— although a necessity for British colonies. But now that the decision had been taken India embarked on the first stage of its progress, and in 1919 government by dyarchy was established in the great Indian provinces. From this step there could be no retreat, and it was likely that the pace would be quickened. Great Britain unhappily had not won the loyalty of the political classes. Indian self-esteem could no longer endure a foreign control. Some Indians might want to go forward; some to go back; but none were content to remain in tutelage. Politically and economically India was in a state of troubled transition. Population was growing rapidly; the problems of subsistence, of westernisation, of development of her resources, of the preservation or change of ancient custom, and of the relations of her communities under a new order, pressed hard upon her. While the British thought of a slow transition, an ordered progress to Dominion status, the conditions were such that the course and speed of change were at the mercy of events.

Meanwhile in Ireland a bitter conflict had broken out. In the 'seventies Irish discontent had found expression in the new policy of Home Rule formulated by Isaac Butt. In 1878 Charles Stewart Parnell had succeeded him as leader of the Irish Home Rule party and from this time the Irish question distorted the course of English politics. Was it soluble on colonial lines? On this issue Great Britain was divided and the moment for such a solution passed. The impatient nationalism of the Irish ceased to find expression in the Home Rule movement, and in 1914 that movement reached fruition too late—nor had it achieved a united Ireland. The excitement of the War gave the opportunity for an outbreak in Dublin, the Easter Rebellion of 1916, which, though suppressed for the moment, soon developed into a civil war waged by the nationalists for Irish independence. Irish leaders demanded now not Home Rule, not colonial self-government, but separation, on grounds of Ireland's historic national existence. The constitutional movement of the nineteenth century gave place to a revolutionary movement, determined to establish a republic. After a war for freedom the British could not engage with clear conscience in a struggle to suppress a small nation. They had no more will for this than for the War of the American Revolution. The struggle was ended in a Treaty (1921) which gave to Southern Ireland the same status in the British Empire as Canada and her sister Dominions. Ulster was as resolved to remain a part of the United

Kingdom as Southern Ireland to end that union. So Ireland was divided; Northern Ireland retained its attachment to Britain, and the remainder of the country became the Irish Free State—a Dominion loosely connected with the British Crown and Commonwealth. Irish nationalism had thus stretched still wider the elastic ties of the British Commonwealth.

If we contrast the half century whose history we have briefly surveyed with the half century that preceded it, we observe how great was the influence of the course of international affairs on the development of the Empire. The international rivalries, tension and wars that succeeded the relative peace and security of the earlier period had led to an immense growth of the Empire. They had also done much to ensure its continuance and unity and to influence the political form it assumed. They had brought to a climax many of its domestic questions and stimulated the expression of its ideal side in the extension of national freedom and the idea of trusteeship. Imperialism was forced to find and assume its responsibilities and had lost something of its egotism. In 1920 it was fifty years since Adderley had written the sentence with which this chapter begins, and self-government had now become a policy, for it had become a necessity in other than British colonies.

Great Britain's domestic development had less influence in this period. Her outlook was changing, but had not yet changed. Her economic position had lost something of its former strength. Her political position, with the vast extensions of her power in Africa, Asia and the Pacific, made her even more than before a world State. But her power was being slowly passed by the growth of the United States, and the future of her old Asiatic rival, Russia, was shrouded in uncertainty. How long would she have the wealth to sustain this mighty role?

"People are curious," wrote Adderley at the conclusion of his book, "to know what will be the nature of our future relations with the Colonies: as if anyone could foretell, or shape, either those future relations, or the coming condition of either side of them!" He distrusted "the idiosyncrasies of statesmanship", and would "let things take their natural way". He looked to a "common partnership", "the real secret of a lasting connection". He asserted "a firm faith in the future of this great Empire, now that its spirit of self-administration is freed from central interference beyond the reach of recall".[1] He wrote with the wisdom of the generation which made possible the transition of the Empire into a Commonwealth of Nations.

The point to which this volume brings us shows the British Empire taking the "natural way" as an association of states, in all stages of development—political, economic and cultural. Its Western-born members had almost completed the evolution of their relations into a league of nations. So quietly and easily had this transformation taken

[1] Adderley, *op. cit.* pp. 417-23.

place, like the progress of a well-ordered family, that the greatness of
the change and the achievement were hardly realised. Yet it was a
picture of hope for the world—a family of nations formed by growth,
a precedent for a world of nations. With them were associated, in
peaceful and ordered relations under a common head, societies in
various stages of development, from the simple societies of the Pacific
and tropical Africa to the proud and ancient peoples of the East. The
Asiatic States were moving uneasily either towards Dominion status
and the equal associations of Eastern and Western nations, or to
independence of the Empire. It remained yet to see in what form
they could best work out their political life, blending the aspirations
of Western communities with the rigidity of their own traditions and
their racial and religious divisions. Could Western political ideas take
root and guide their life? Or could they live in peace only under
authority? At least the Empire provided the theatre for this great
experiment, and in doing so was contributing something of vast
importance to the welfare of the world.

The simpler societies were further off from these issues. They had
yet to find the means of their livelihood in the modern world and to
form states in which Western political life could take root and function.
But there was more conscience now in their government and a watch-
ful world took account of our stewardship.

To the future belonged the outcome of these situations. But at the
time a vast part of the British Empire had grown and developed into
a system of states. It no longer existed solely for economic advantages,
or for mutual defence, but as a society of nations. It was no longer
the project of an Empire, but the project of a world state in the form
of a league of nations. The spirit of British politics had brought into
human relations a larger degree of tolerance and self-government
than any other Power had done. If the Empire had now a purpose, that
purpose was to enable states to live together in peace and co-operation.
Animating the group, particularly in this phase of its history, was the
movement towards national liberty. The distinguishing feature of the
British Empire was the elasticity of relationships, following from the
free spirit of the British Parliament. And this association of states in
various stages of development could still serve the interests of all
parties. The weaker could be protected and benefited and enabled to
exist without being exploited in the modern world. At the same time,
if the stronger power did its duty by them, and they by it, they could
be developed and make their contribution to the world's wealth and
welfare, with the hope of progress and control in due course of their
own life. They were not turned out of the school of freedom, nor made
its menials. Great states must serve some general purpose if they
are to survive, and the British Empire, by virtue of its free spirit and
consequent elasticity, was exploring a way towards an ordered system
of international relations which had become humanity's greatest need.

CHAPTER II

IMPERIAL QUESTIONS IN BRITISH POLITICS, 1868–1880

APART from India, to which other volumes of this History are devoted, the chief imperial question which troubled British politics in the eighteenth century and the first half of the nineteenth was that of the proper relationship between the mother country and its oversea colonists of European stock. The establishment of the Dominion of Canada in 1867, crowning the work of Grey and Elgin, pointed the way of progress in self-government in all internal matters, at least, for the North American and Australasian colonies. They were now, or would soon become, virtually independent states either within or without the Empire, and it remained only to work out the logical consequences, mainly the financial and military consequences, of their new status. The chief imperial question of the last third of the nineteenth century was a different one: the question of the nature of the responsibility of the mother country in respect of colonies where non-European peoples formed the majority, or at any rate a powerful element. Here the Jamaica rising and the surrender of the old Jamaican constitution in 1866 were landmarks, and almost created a presumption that where self-government meant the domination of a white oligarchy it must not be conceded, and where already conceded it should be withdrawn. There ran indeed through British politics in the nineteenth century a strong strand of philanthropic regard for native races, both in the matter of slavery and the slave-trade and in that of imported indentured labour, whether in the West Indies, or on the coasts and islands of the Indian Ocean, or the Pacific. This humanitarian feeling played an important part, more important perhaps than the commercial motive, and certainly than the strategic, in these years when the opening up of Africa and the appearance on the scene of other colonial Powers suggested the annexation of new territories. For the mere extension of the Empire there was hardly any desire except possibly in a narrow circle towards the very end of the period of which this chapter treats. Broadly speaking, the general wish was to diminish responsibilities rather than to increase them. Mid-Victorian statesmen had a profound sense of responsibility and duty. It was their duty to give the colonies good government, and this included justice for natives as well as protection of white men's commercial interests; but the desire for good government was perpetually restrained by the desire to keep down expenses. Nothing could be more apt than Carnarvon's warning to Shepstone: "Parliament does not like to be made to pay

2

even for what it approves.... Your object therefore must be to bear in mind these two opposite considerations—effective government and economy—and as far as possible to reconcile them."[1]

The period 1868–80 is divided almost equally between two parliaments, two administrations, two Prime Ministers and, some would add, two theories of colonial policy. How far the last antithesis is justified will appear later, but the two sections are sufficiently distinct to suggest separate treatment. Of the full period it may be said that, after a short spell of anxiety and controversy over the immediate destiny of the Empire as a whole, South Africa comes increasingly to fill the sky, in so far as colonial questions could fill it. For we need to remember that these were overshadowed throughout by domestic issues during Gladstone's premiership and by foreign affairs during Disraeli's.

1868–1874

Great things indeed were expected of the Liberal government by the new constituencies which returned them to power in November 1868 in the first general election held since the second Reform Act, and much was feared. John Bright in the Cabinet seemed a portent of a new age. But this alone does not explain why, within a few months, the approaching dissolution of the Empire was being seriously discussed at home and overseas and why the Government were widely believed to be intent on bringing this about. The answer is to be found partly in the general drift of feeling in Great Britain, partly in the antecedents of some prominent Liberals, and partly in the special circumstances of Canada and New Zealand.

The development of separatist feeling in the 'sixties and the reasons for it have been sketched in volume II.[2] At the root of it, no doubt, lay the analogies of the ripe fruit and the grown-up child, analogies apparently justified by the histories of North and South America. Next in importance may rank the abandonment of the old mercantile system with that central direction of commercial policy which for generations had seemed the main compensation for the cares and burdens of empire. Almost simultaneous with the abandonment of the old commercial system had come the grant of responsible government, which was shown in 1859 to include the right to impose tariffs. So that to the Tory's question "What is the use of colonies which we do not govern?" the Cobdenite might add, "and on whose fidelity to free trade we cannot count". Indeed, to the Cobdenite the possession of colonies seemed an actual obstacle to his nobler purpose, the maintenance of peace: during the 'sixties the long Canadian frontier threatened to prove an irresistible temptation to the new bellicose American nationalism, while in New Zealand and South

---

[1] 30 May 1877 (Private): P.R.O. 30–6/23.
[2] Pp. 698 *seqq.* See also Schuyler, R. L., in *Political Science Quarterly*, vol. xxxvi, reprinted as *The Fall of the Old Colonial System*; Bodelsen, C. A., *Studies in Mid-Victorian Imperialism.*

Africa no end to the prospect of bloody and expensive native wars was in sight. These misgivings were confirmed by British misunderstanding of colonial sentiments. The ruling classes at home had few links with the peoples of the colonies, except perhaps of New Zealand.[1] Colonial claims to fuller self-determination were interpreted as showing hostility to the mother country, and it was widely assumed— no doubt because colonies were usually thought of as dependencies— that the growth of colonial nationalism implied an intention to sever all political connection.[2] The result was often indifference, in some cases separatism, and these sentiments tended to reproduce themselves in the colonies. Sir Alexander Galt, visiting London from Canada in 1867, said bitterly: "I am more than ever disappointed at the tone of feeling here as to the colonies. I cannot shut my eyes to the fact that they want to get rid of us."[3] But the limits of separatism, also summarised in volume II, must not be forgotten. The ignorance and misunderstanding bred of ignorance were not universal. The classes which knew the colonies as partners in trade or as the homes of their emigrated children, rather than as a breeding-ground of angry Minutes, remained untroubled by the notion that they were bent on separation. Herman Merivale, too, realised that impatience of interference from Downing Street did not mean disloyalty.[4] And whatever individual politicians may have thought, separatism had never yet been an official policy.

But might it not become so now? Goldwin Smith, its "great apostle", had prophesied in 1863 that though Palmerston would never emancipate the colonies, his political successors might do so.[5] Palmerston had, in fact, under Gladstonian influence, in the very next year presented the Ionian Islands to Greece, and now Gladstone was in power: Gladstone, whom many regarded as "the disciple and organ" of the Manchester School.[6] Bright, an avowed separatist, was a member of his Cabinet, and Robert Lowe, the Chancellor of the Exchequer, who had learnt in Australia to dislike democracy, had publicly used language betraying no enthusiasm for the maintenance of the connection. The Prime Minister himself by no means held the crudely separatist views often ascribed to him, but while his general principles were clear enough it was often far from clear how in a set case he would interpret them.[7] As a former Colonial Secretary, a

[1] See Monsell, 22 July 1869, *Hansard*, 3rd ser. cxcviii, 479.
[2] See Lewis, Sir G. Cornewall, *On the Government of Dependencies* (1841).
[3] Skelton, O. D., *Life and Times of Sir A. T. Galt*, p. 410, cited Bodelsen, *op. cit.* p. 45.
[4] *Fortnightly Review*, Jan. 1870.
[5] So-called by R. R. Torrens in 1870, *Hansard*, 3rd ser. cc, 1818; Smith, G., *The Empire*, p. 10.
[6] Morley, J., *Life of Gladstone*, i, 805 (1905 edn.).
[7] See Knaplund, P., *Gladstone and Britain's Imperial Policy*, where the development of his views is traced and the important speech he made at Chester in Nov. 1855 is printed in full. See also Gladstone's evidence before the Select Committee on Colonial Military Expenditure, *Parl. Pap.* 1861, xiii (423), pp. 255 *seqq.*

passionate Hellenist and a champion of liberty, Gladstone was attracted by the principle of Greek colonisation which he summed up as "perfect freedom and perfect self-government", attaching much less importance to political connection than to "union in heart and character". He favoured the possession of colonies for two main reasons: the one material—the extension of trade—the other moral and social—the creation abroad of what Roebuck had called "so many happy Englands". He claimed that the adoption in the 'forties of "a rational mode of administering" colonial affairs "without gratuitous interference" had shown most encouraging results. In short, he believed firmly in the value of colonies so long as there was no element of compulsion in the tie. But alike as an advocate of self-reliance and as the fanatical protagonist for many years of the "battle for economy" in an indifferent Cabinet, as one who regarded public extravagance as "a great moral evil",[1] Gladstone also believed that "a rational mode" of administering colonial affairs implied that the colonies should provide for their own defence and be financially self-supporting. It was on these two matters of military and financial help from the mother country that trouble was to arise.

The policy of reducing the imperial garrisons in the colonies was nothing new. Accepting the recommendations of the Select Committee of the previous year, the Commons resolved in March 1862 "that this House, while it fully recognises the claims of all portions of the British Empire on Imperial aid against perils arising from the consequences of Imperial policy, is of opinion that Colonies exercising the rights of self-government ought to undertake the main responsibility of providing for their own internal order and security, and ought to assist in their own external defence".[2] The Derby government acted on this principle, and Cardwell was only carrying it further when, as part of his great scheme of army reorganisation, he obtained Gladstone's consent to reduce the numbers of the imperial troops in the colonies from 50,000 to 26,000 men.[3] The proposal involved the withdrawal of five battalions from Canada, and it was bitterly resented there: relations between the Dominion and the United States were still strained, and the Canadians were most unwilling to increase their own expenditure on defence. Nevertheless the Imperial Government adhered to its policy, and in February 1870 Granville informed the Governor-General that, apart from the city of Halifax, which would be garrisoned as an imperial station, it was proposed after a year's respite to withdraw the whole of the forces in Canada, except a small body of regular troops if these should be required for instructional purposes. This drastic decision reached Canada at a time when minds were agitated by the vaunts of American poli-

---

[1] Morley, *op. cit.* I, 676 *seqq.*   [2] *Hansard*, 3rd ser. CLXV, 1032.
[3] Biddulph, Sir R., *Lord Cardwell at the War Office*, pp. 26–8. Cf. Cardwell to Granville (Conf.), 25 Jan. 1869, P.R.O., C.O. 323/296.

ticians intent on pressing their *Alabama* claims, by Fenian threats, and by the outbreak in the Red River valley.[1] Protests were of no avail, despite the actual Fenian outbreak of May 1870; in November 1871, when the situation had been eased by the signature of the Washington Treaty, the last British battalion west of Halifax embarked for home. One concession, however, had been granted; a small force of imperial troops had been allowed to accompany the expedition under Colonel Wolseley which quelled the Red River rebellion in the summer of 1870. What the Dominion ministers valued most was not the additional protection of a few hundred rifles but the "visible symbol" of imperial unity and of the readiness of the United Kingdom to play its part in the defence of Canada.[2]

Another Canadian grievance was the Treaty of Washington itself.[3] It was something that one of the British Commissioners who negotiated it was a Canadian, no less a man than Sir John Macdonald, but his countrymen found it hard to forgive the sacrifice of Canada's rights in the matter of the inshore fisheries and the failure to secure compensation from the United States for allowing the Fenian raids to be organised on American soil.[4] Eventually Canadian feelings were soothed by an imperial guarantee of a Dominion loan of £2½ millions to build railways and canals. The concession was no slight one in view of the strong Liberal objection to such guarantees. Gladstone had defined his position in 1869 when defending the guarantee of another Canadian loan, to raise £300,000 to be paid to the Hudson's Bay Company in settlement of its claims to compensation for the surrender of Rupertsland to the Dominion. The Government, he said, were bound to promote the measure in order to fulfil pledges given in 1865, and though "such guarantees ought not to be given except for objects of broad imperial policy", the purpose of the loan in question was to enable the North American colonies to make a new start on the basis of financial independence. It "was not to be a beginning but an end".[5] Perhaps the most useful single service rendered by Granville during his short tenure of his office was in bringing the Dominion and the Company to an agreement.[6] The home Government gave its full approval and support to Canada's just ambition to extend her sway from sea to sea; while not

[1] The United States claimed damages for the negligence of the British Government in allowing the S.S. *Alabama* to sail from Liverpool in July 1862 to join the Confederate fleet. For Fenian raids and the Red River expedition see *C.H.B.E.* vi, 460, 471.

[2] See Stacey, C. P., *Canada and the British Army, 1846–51*; *Parl. Pap.* 1870, L [C. 207]; 1871, XLVIII [C. 298]; Lords debates of 14 Feb., 27 May and 22 July 1870, *Hansard*, 3rd ser. CXCIX, 193, CCI, 1462 and CCIII, 703.

[3] *Parl. Pap.* 1872, XLIII [C. 539]; 1873, XLIX [C. 702]. See debates in Lords, 12 June 1871, and Commons 4 Aug. 1871, *Hansard*, 3rd ser. CCVI, 1823 and CCVIII, 861.

[4] See Skelton, O. D., *op. cit.* pp. 458 *seqq.*

[5] House of Commons, 5 Aug. 1864, *Hansard*, 3rd ser. CXCVIII, 1330.

[6] Fitzmaurice, Lord E., *Life of Lord Granville*, II, 25; also Northcote in House of Commons, 1 June 1869, *Hansard*, 3rd ser. CXCVI, 1114.

forgetting the interests of the Red Indians it believed that the Dominion could be trusted to look after them.[1]

It is clear, however, that as long as the tension with the United States lasted British politicians felt uneasy as to the possible consequences on relations with Canada: this daughter nation was a hostage given to fortune. Nearly all the Cabinet, Kimberley tells us, were of opinion in May 1869 that Canada could not be successfully defended against the United States and that it was much to be desired that she should become independent: "we should be relieved from a continual source of weakness and danger, and the Canadians would have nothing to fear from the United States, whose ill-will to Canada arises from a desire to injure us."[2] Granville himself wrote privately that the best solution of our difficulties "would probably be that in the course of time and in the most friendly spirit the Dominion should find itself strong enough to proclaim her independence".[3] It was in the same mind, but in more guarded terms, that in June 1869 he conveyed the views of the Government to the Governor-General, Sir John Young (afterwards Lord Lisgar), in a confidential dispatch. After reciting the pronouncement made by Gladstone as Colonial Secretary in 1846, to the effect that the connection with Canada neither could nor should be maintained except by consent, he claimed that the policy of the mother country ever since had been in harmony with these opinions.

Nothing can be happier than the result of that policy. It has been more and more felt on both sides that Canada is part of the British Empire because she desires to be so; and under the influence of this conviction the attachment of the Colonists to Great Britain has grown with the growth of their independence. H.M. Government value the existing relation as the symbol and support of that attachment. They value it while it is valued by the Canadians, and while it is useful to the Canadians. They have no desire to maintain it for a single year after it has become injurious or distasteful to them. Nor do they consider that a Canadian statesman who at a proper time and place may think fit to question the expediency of continuing indefinitely the present form of connection or to propose measures to facilitate its modification or dissolution could on that account be charged with any unfriendly feelings towards Great Britain or disloyalty towards The Queen.[4] ... The greatness of England consists not in the geographical extent of her Empire, but in the spirit which animates those who inhabit it, and the traditional regard of her allies. It will be far more truly consulted by retaining Canada as an ancient, prosperous and cordial friend, than as a half-hearted dependency. H.M. Government believe that hereditary cordiality is best secured by not only treating the continuance of the imperial authority as dependent on the interest of Canada, but by holding the statesmen and people of the Dominion to be the proper judges of that interest.

[1] Monsell, W. (afterwards Lord Emly), in House of Commons, 1 June 1869, *Hansard*, 3rd ser. cxcvi, 1107 *seqq.*; see *C.H.B.E.* vi, ch. xix.
[2] "Kimberley's Diary", 8 May 1869, now being edited for the Royal Historical Society by Miss Ethel Drus.
[3] To Russell, 28 Aug. 1869; Fitzmaurice, *op. cit.* ii, 22.
[4] This sentence is relevant to Granville's offer of the K.C.M.G. to Galt, who held that Canada's "independent existence as a nation in the future" was desirable and possible; Skelton, *op. cit.* pp. 41 *seqq.*; *Hansard*, 3rd ser. cc, 324, 574.

If I do not direct you to communicate this dispatch to your advisers and other principal statesmen of Canada, it is from no want of confidence in them but because such an overture might be liable to misconstruction. Meantime your knowledge of the opinions of H.M. Government will enable you to speak with confidence to them and to encourage them to speak unreservedly to you. You will of course observe and keep me informed of the current of opinion.

To the draft of this dispatch Granville added a paragraph in his own hand: "You will also be good enough to bring to my notice any line of policy, or any measures which without implying on the part of H.M. Government any wish to change abruptly our relations, would gradually prepare both countries for a friendly relaxation of them."

Sir John Young in reply reported on his recent tour of the Dominion, in the course of which he had gathered from conversations with Canadians of various parties that the people valued and were proud of their connection with Great Britain; they had uniformly expressed themselves "averse to any change". Granville hailed this dispatch as affording "strong encouragement" to believe that whether the present connection "continues in precisely the same form or whether at some future time the strong but elastic bond between them should be further relaxed", feelings of the strongest attachment and mutual respect would endure.[1]

The Prime Minister was in close consultation with Granville and warmly approved his general policy; it is not certain, however, whether he saw his two dispatches before they were sent,[2] nor whether he ever contemplated, as Granville did, the possibility of the mother country taking the first step towards separation. In January 1870 he wrote down "without any special aim" a secret memorandum containing five points: Canada "and every person in Canada" ought to enjoy perfect liberty of thought and speech in regard to her future destiny; we ought however to hand over to her "with due regard to time and mode", the charge of her own defence, while ready to assist her in it. The fourth point asserted that, while Great Britain must be the judge of the manner and measure of such assistance, "in our belief, where this country was satisfied as to the cause, whether Canada were independent of us or not, such assistance would be freely accorded and would only be limited by our means". The fifth point was to the effect that "if and so long as Canada shall continue to desire, as we believe she now does, a political connection with this country upon the free and honourable footing which has been described, the connection should be upheld with the whole power of the Empire".

[1] Granville to Young, 14 June 1869 (Conf.), 10 Jan. 1870 (Conf.); Young to Granville, 11 Nov. 1869 (Conf.), P.R.O., C.O. 42/678; the copy of the first dispatch, from which Knaplund quotes (op. cit. pp. 98–100), is dated 16 June in the Letter-book (C.O. 43/156). I am indebted to Miss E. Drus for calling my attention to the original draft, which is bound out of place alongside that of Granville's second dispatch, as well as to several other documents.

[2] In a letter to Gladstone dated 25 Jan. 1870 Granville refers to his confidential dispatch in a way which suggests that Gladstone had not seen it: The Political Correspondence of Mr Gladstone and Lord Granville, 1868–1876, ed. A. Ramm (1952), I, 89.

The Colonial Secretary agreed with the Prime Minister's first three points but was alarmed by the fourth and fifth. "I see your object", he said—meaning, presumably, a caution to the United States—"in promising the unlimited assistance of this country, if Canada separates from us, but I am not sure of the prudence of pledging ourselves on such a contingency"; and on the last point, "May not circumstances arise, in which it would be politic for this country to say, 'You are now so rich and strong that we must take the initiative and ask you to agree to a friendly separation'?"[1]

Granville did not explain why the mother country should desire to separate from a rich and strong Dominion; but, if he toyed with the wish to promote separation, the thought that it was ultimately inevitable was probably father to the wish, and he placed the emphasis throughout on "friendly". Kimberley, who succeeded Granville as Secretary for the Colonies in July 1870, thought that it would be "premature and impolitic to do anything with a view to bringing about [Canadian independence] now". If it were true that for twenty-five years or so Canada would not be strong enough to avoid falling into the clutches of the United States, then "the question of independence ought not to be regarded as a practical one in our time. It is reduced to a mere speculation as to the future."[2] In any case this pessimism about Canada was due to special circumstances, and after the Treaty of Washington (8 May 1871) the cloud lifted. Lord Dufferin, who went out as Governor-General next year, did not accept Lowe's counsel that he should make it his "business to get rid of the Dominion";[3] on the contrary his supreme tact and ability did much to place relations on a firmer footing.

The colony, however, whose treatment provoked the fiercest controversy, was not Canada but New Zealand.[4] The recall of imperial troops from New Zealand in accordance with the new policy began in 1866, and by the next year only one battalion remained. In the summer of 1868 the long-drawn-out war with the Maoris flared up again, and the colonial ministers and legislature begged that the troops should be retained for the present. The new Governor, Sir George Bowen, supported the petition, but Granville upheld the recent decision of his Tory predecessor that they must go. The news of the massacre at Poverty Bay in November provoked renewed appeals from the colony, but Granville would grant no more than a temporary respite. Misunderstandings and poor communications detained the troops in New Zealand until February 1870, but the intervening months were filled with reiterated appeals and refusals.

---

[1] 19 Jan. 1870, *Gladstone Papers*, B.M. Add. MSS. 44759. Cf. *Political Corresp. of Gladstone and Granville*, I, 95.

[2] *Diary*, 22 July 1870.

[3] Lyall, Sir A., *Life of the Marquis of Dufferin and Ava*, I, 286: cited by Bodelsen, p. 47.

[4] See *C.H.B.E.* VII, pt. II, p. 140; *Parl. Pap.* 1868–9, XLIV (307), 1870, L [C. 83], 180; Bowen, Sir G. F., *Thirty Years of Colonial Government*, vol. I.

Granville's decisive dispatch of 21 May 1869 was sent after consultation with Gladstone and Cardwell;[1] in a later dispatch he maintained that the general objections to the employment of imperial troops in a self-governing colony were strengthened in the case of New Zealand by the distrust felt in London of the colonial policy.[2] "The present distress of the Colony", he wrote, "arises mainly from two circumstances: the discontent of the Natives, consequent on the confiscation of their land, and neglect of successive Governments to place on foot a force sufficiently formidable to overawe that discontent." The real safety of the colonists lay in "deliberately measuring their own resources, and, at whatever immediate sacrifice, adjusting their policy to them".

But the dispatch which set the Thames and the Seven Seas on fire was one in which, while refusing the Colonial Treasurer's request for a guarantee of a loan to meet war expenses, Granville indignantly rejected the assumptions on which the request was based. Mr Fitzherbert's presentation of the facts was all wrong. The difficulties of New Zealand were in no way due to the action of the mother country. No obligations had been imposed on the colonist "except that imposed on all of us by natural justice, not to appropriate the property of others". No part of the colonial expenditure had been in any degree for the benefit of the United Kingdom. The management of native affairs had not been imposed upon the colonial Government but conceded to their request, and it might well be thought that the present dangers of New Zealand were "due not to the punctual performance of their obligations to the Maori race, but rather to their adoption of a policy which, if not inconsistent with those obligations, was certain to appear so to the natives affected by it".[3] The lecture, as Granville called it, was inspired and drafted by Sir Frederick Rogers, but the consequences were borne by Granville and his colleagues. The publication of the dispatch at the end of May aroused a lively discussion in the London Press and in Parliament, and later a storm of protest in New Zealand, where papers went so far as to pronounce themselves now in favour of annexation to the United States. The Colonial Ministers, replying to the dispatch of 7 October, declared that its tone and purport were scarcely susceptible of any other explanation than a desire to abandon their country and to sever its connection with the Empire.

Perhaps the most curious result of the outburst was to impel a number of colonial gentlemen in London to circulate a letter to the Colonial Secretaries of the principal colonies expressing their concern at the present state of affairs, which might lead to the break-up

---

[1] Minutes in P.R.O., C.O. 209/210.
[2] Granville to Bowen, 7 Oct. 1869, *Parl. Pap.* 1870, L [C. 83], p. 195.
[3] Fitzherbert to Granville, 5 Feb. 1869; Granville to Bowen, 21 March 1869; *Parl Pap.* 1868–9, XLIV (218). See Minutes in P.R.O., C.O. 209/215, 214.

of the Empire, and suggesting that a conference of representatives of the self-governing colonies should be held in London to consider how relations might be improved.[1] This *démarche* caused a considerable stir, and Granville took it seriously enough to issue a counter-circular to the Governors of the colonies concerned. The replies on the whole were satisfactory. Nowhere was there any support for the proposed conference. The New Zealand Government went out of its way to protest its loyalty to the imperial connection.[2] Only the Victorian House of Assembly, moved by the eloquence of George Higinbotham, while rejecting the proposals of a "self-constituted and irresponsible body of absentee Colonists" and declaring their desire to remain an integral part of the Empire, seized the opportunity to protest against any interference in their domestic affairs by imperial legislation or instructions from Downing Street.[3]

Meanwhile the crisis in relations with New Zealand had passed. Granville's confidence that the colonists, who largely outnumbered the Maoris, could restore the situation without imperial help was justified, and, on the plane of sentiment, the two parties to the dispute realised that things had gone too far. Civil expressions were used on both sides, and, when commissioners arrived in England in the spring of 1870 to negotiate an amicable settlement, Granville persuaded the Cabinet, "as a proof of good will at a time of difficulty", to guarantee a New Zealand loan of a million to assist emigration and public works.[4] Henceforward all was roses, and Bowen was soon able to write of the "kindly and sympathetic language of the Secretary of State in his recent communications".[5]

The years 1869–70, in the opinion of two historians who have studied closely the movement of public opinion during the mid-Victorian epoch, form the turning-point of separatist feeling.[6] The withdrawal of the garrisons, the plaints of Canada and New Zealand, the known opinions of some members of the Cabinet and the publication of harshly-worded dispatches helped to create the belief that the Government cared little about the colonies and, so far from striving to prevent the threatened disintegration of the Empire, were actually promoting it. Lord Carnarvon, Conservative Colonial Secretary in 1866–7, opening a discussion in the Lords in February 1870, lamented that "within the last few months" a change had occurred in the feelings of the colonies towards Downing Street, for

[1] *Parl. Pap.* 1870, XLIX [C. 24], 13 Aug. 1869; *Annual Register* (1870), p. 113; Bodelsen, *op. cit.* p. 96.
[2] *Parl. Pap.* 1870, XLIX [C. 51].
[3] *Ibid.* [C. 24]. See Morris, E. E., *Memoir of George Higinbotham*, p. 160.
[4] *Parl. Pap.* 1870, L (298). The Granville Papers (P.R.O., G. & D. 29/25) contain copies of a paper controversy in which Lowe gives twenty-eight reasons for not guaranteeing a New Zealand loan and Granville on 9 May replies seriatim.
[5] Bowen to Kimberley, 23 Aug. 1870, *Thirty Years*, I, 401.
[6] Schuyler, *op. cit.* p. 276; Bodelsen, *op. cit.* p. 94.

which the Liberals were to blame.[1] "There are whispers abroad that there is a policy on foot to dismember the Empire." Similar views were expressed in a Commons debate in April.[2] For once, colonial matters attracted a good deal of attention. The *Quarterly*, the *Edinburgh*, the *Fortnightly* Reviews and *Fraser's Magazine* all had articles on the subject in their January numbers. But practically nowhere does any desire to be rid of the colonies appear. Even the *Edinburgh* reviewer, defending the refusal of Ministers to place the resources of this country at the disposal of colonial Governments and looking forward to "a union of coequal states" as his ideal, disclaims any desire "to see these great dependencies dissevered from the British Empire". "But it depends on the manner in which this union is understood and maintained, whether it can or ought to be perpetuated."[3] The *Quarterly*, admitting that for the last seventeen years one administration after another has been content to swim with the stream, believes that we have at last woken up to the slenderness of our ties with the colonies and the difficulty of strengthening them.[4] Herman Merivale, in the *Fortnightly*, notices a general feeling that the bonds which hold the Empire together are loosening and that "something ought to be done" not merely to arrest further disintegration but to consolidate and strengthen.[5]

Something, if only a little, had in fact been done. In 1868 a number of private individuals had founded a non-political body, the Royal Colonial Institute, "for the purpose of promoting in England a better knowledge of the colonies and of India"; a speech from the Prime Minister had graced its inaugural dinner.[6] Another small thing had been the trouble taken by Granville and his predecessor, the Duke of Buckingham, to expand the Order of St Michael and St George for the benefit of colonial notables and to increase its prestige.[7] More important were the books on colonial subjects by prominent men which had recently appeared: Dilke's *Greater Britain* (1868) and Adderley's *Review* of Lord Grey's well-known work on Colonial Policy (1869).[8] From 1870 a stream of articles poured forth in which a new note of emotion is to be heard, Froude attacking the Government for being separatists at heart and Edward Jenkins protesting against the dissolution of "this marvellous empire".[9] At length in

---

[1] 14 Feb. 1870, *Hansard*, 3rd ser. CXCIX, 193.
[2] 26 April 1870, *Hansard*, 3rd ser. CC, 1817. [3] *Edinburgh Review*, CXXXI, 99, 120, 105.
[4] *Quarterly Review*, CXXVIII, 134 *seqq.* [5] *Fortnightly Review*, new ser. VII, 153.
[6] Folsom, A., *The Royal Empire Society*; see also Bodelsen, *op. cit.* p. 94.
[7] See P.R.O., G. & D. 29/25.
[8] Charles Dilke entered Parliament in 1868 as a Radical. Sir Charles Adderley (later Lord Norton) was Under-Secretary for the Colonies in the Derby-Disraeli government, but his views, said the *Edinburgh* (Jan. 1870), showed "no tincture of Toryism". He complained in the House of Commons that "in our primary schools every geography was taught but that of our colonies" (*Hansard*, 3rd ser. CXCVI, 1122).
[9] *Fraser's Magazine*, Jan., Aug. 1870: see *Short Studies in Great Subjects* (1898 ed.), vol. II; Jenkins, *Discussions on Colonial Questions* (1872), p. 28. See Tyler, J. E., *The Struggle for Imperial Unity*, p. 3.

1873 the Poet-Laureate, addressing his Sovereign in the Epilogue to the *Idylls of the King*,[1] gave memorable expression to the new imperial pride.

According to Adderley, the three most important colonial questions of the day were Defence, Church Affairs and Emigration.[2] Of defence something has been said. The constitutional status of the colonial Churches had come under discussion in the dispute leading to the annulment by the Judicial Committee of the Privy Council in March 1865 of the sentence of deposition pronounced by the Bishop of Cape Town against Bishop Colenso of Natal: the Queen, it was held, had no authority to confer, by the prerogative, coercive ecclesiastical jurisdiction in a colony possessing a representative legislature.[3] In 1868 the late Government had decided no longer to subsidise the Establishment in the West Indies out of imperial funds,[4] and the Liberals, in accordance with their Irish policy, proceeded to encourage the authorities in colonies not enjoying responsible government to adopt the principle of religious equality. This implied the disestablishment of the Church of England and either disendowment or else the concurrent endowment of the various Christian denominations; colonial bishops would not henceforward be appointed by the Queen.[5] The principle was generally adopted, but not everywhere: Carnarvon was unwilling to apply it to Ceylon in 1875.[6]

Both Adderley and Froude were particularly interested in the idea of emigration to the colonies. It was fostered by the distress and unemployment resulting from the depression; and in 1869 and 1870 a good many articles were written and societies formed to promote state-aided emigration.[7] In February 1870 a petition to this effect signed by over 100,000 London working men was presented to the Home Secretary, and a fortnight later R. R. Torrens, a former Premier of South Australia, moved a resolution on the subject in the Commons.[8] His argument was the usual one that emigration was desirable as at once reducing unemployment at home and providing more consumers for British manufactured goods. State aid and control would supplement voluntary enterprise and select classes of emigrant, such as middle-aged parents with children, who would not go otherwise. Torrens proposed to finance his rather nebulous scheme out of the rates, assisted by proportionate grants from the Exchequer. Those who supported him in debate laid more stress than

---

[1] See Bodelsen, *op. cit.* p. 124.
[2] *Review*, etc., p. 379.
[3] See *C.H.B.E.*, viii, 416, and *Annual Register, 1865*, pp. 209 ff.
[4] *Review*, etc., p. 307.
[5] See *C.H.B.E.* ii, 737; *Parl. Pap.* 1871, xlviii (269), esp. Granville to Grant, 1 March 1869; 1873, xlviii (259); H. of C. 24 July 1871 and 15 July 1873, *Hansard*, 3rd ser. ccviii, 166 and ccxvii, 425; Todd, A., *Parliamentary Government in the British Colonies* (1880), p. 307.
[6] *Parl. Pap.* 1876, liv (154).   [7] Bodelsen, *op. cit.* p. 103.
[8] 1 Mar. 1870, *Hansard*, 3rd ser. cxcix, 1002 *seqq.*

he did on the political advantages of building up the strength of the colonies as "fortresses for ourselves in all parts of the world".[1] Monsell for the Government said that this was the first time the subject had been raised in the House for twenty-two years, for the good reason that experience since 1847 had shown the success which had attended voluntary emigration: state aid must kill it.[2] He and others used the dilemma that either paupers must be shovelled out, whom the colonies did not want and would not take, or else the best workmen would be sent, whom Great Britain could not spare. Finally Gladstone declared his doubts of the fundamental principle:[3] the proposal was one to support individuals "at the expense of the community, but not for duties done to the community",[4] and, even were the principle conceded, why should the poor be subsidised to go to the colonies rather than to other countries, should they so prefer, or why to go abroad at all if they would prefer maintenance at home? But while Her Majesty's Government could not approve any such grandiose scheme, they would continue to make inquiries and in some cases to provide facilities which would assist emigration on a small scale. The resolution was rejected on a division by 153 to 48, but the matter does not appear to have become a party question. The Government were supported by Murdoch of the Emigration Board in their belief that voluntary emigration had been strikingly successful and that State aid would dry up voluntary contributions.[5] The policy could hardly be effective without a good deal more planning than it was likely to secure in that age of *laissez-faire.*

The fullest statements of the Government's general position were made in the Lords in February and June, and in the Commons in April.[6] "I have no doubt your Colonial Policy will be discussed, and attacked, in Parliament," the Prime Minister had written to Granville, "I hope we shall all claim it as *ours* and give it no half-hearted defence. And it so happens that we are very strong in colonial men of different kinds: Cardwell, Childers, Lowe, Fortescue, Forster."[7] Winding up the debate in the Commons, Gladstone admitted that uneasiness prevailed, but asserted that it had existed for the last thirty years and was one of the necessary results of the development of policies under a free constitution.[8] It was the nature of colonies "to grow, and so to grow as to alter essentially, in obedience to laws stronger than the will of man, the conditions of their relation with the

---

[1] *Hansard,* 3rd ser. CXCIX, 1013.
[2] According to figures given by a speaker (*ibid.* 1012), while there had been a lull in emigration for the decade 1858–68, the number of English emigrants had risen from 58,268 in the latter years to 90,416 in 1869.
[3] *Ibid.* 1064 *seqq.*
[4] Dilke had described it as "one of a purely socialistic character", *ibid.* 1058.
[5] Memo. of 23 Oct. 1869;; P.R.O., G. & D. 29/25.
[6] *Hansard,* 3rd ser. CXCIX, 213; CC, 1876; CCII, 460.
[7] 1 Oct. 1869, *Polit. Corresp. of Gladstone and Granville,* I, 62.
[8] 26 April 1870, *Hansard,* 3rd ser. CC, 1898.

countries with which they were originally connected, until they arrive at that stage of their progress in which separation from the mother country inevitably takes place". But there was no reason why such a separation should not be the result of a peaceable and friendly transaction. "Surely it is a great object to place, if possible, our colonial policy on such a footing, not for the purpose of bringing about a separation, but of providing a guarantee that, if separation should occur, it should be in a friendly way. That is the sense, the principle and the secret of our policy, with regard to colonial reform." Such a policy did not, he believed, "tend to weaken the relations between the mother country and the colonies, but on the contrary, while securing the greatest likelihood of a perfectly peaceable separation, whenever separation may arrive, gives the best chance of an indefinitely long continuance of a free and voluntary connection". Even after this pronouncement the mover of the resolution might be forgiven for expressing regret that the Prime Minister "could not regard this connection as other than of a temporary character". But to the Gladstonian mind a connection which might be of indefinitely long continuance could not, even though eventual separation was inevitable, properly be regarded as temporary. "Mr Gladstone begged to say that he had not used the expression and did not entertain the idea."[1] Ambiguous as they were, the Prime Minister's words fairly expressed the views of most of his colleagues and his party, and perhaps of the majority of Englishmen. The debates of 1870 no doubt did much to clear the air, even if they did not dispel the suspicions of such enthusiasts as Froude. Year after year R. A. Macfie thought fit to move, in thin Houses, general resolutions on the subject of relations with the colonies;[2] he pleaded for more vigorous assertions by the Government of their confidence in the future of the Empire and advocated "a great federation", or at least an Imperial Council. E. H. Knatchbull-Hugessen,[3] who in each case answered him, maintained that there was no case for charging the Government with indifference; indeed he regretted these repeated "sentimental" debates and speeches which could only perturb opinion in the colonies. For himself, he boasted in 1874 that during his three years as Parliamentary Under-Secretary for the Colonies he had "insisted, he feared, *usque ad nauseam* on the doctrine of maintaining our colonial possessions intact".[4] The cause was most effectively pleaded by W. E. Forster in 1875. Admitting that there was then no cry more popular than the preservation of our colonial empire, he believed none the less that the prevalent feeling in both parties was that separation must eventually come. He wished to counteract this feeling by fostering the idea that a lasting associa-

[1] *Hansard*, 3rd ser. cc, 1906.
[2] *Ibid.* ccvi, 750; ccxi, 912; ccxiv, 1102.
[3] Afterwards Lord Brabourne.
[4] 4 Aug. 1874, *Hansard*, 3rd ser. ccxxi, 1295.

tion on equal terms could be achieved through some kind of federation which he did not elaborate. Recognising the widespread desire of the time for national unions, he urged that the British peoples should give an example of a vast peaceful union based not on standing armies but on the rapid communications now made possible by science.[1]

In July 1870, on Clarendon's death, Granville was transferred to the more congenial sphere of the Foreign Office. It is surprising that one renowned for his courteous and conciliatory bearing should have been charged with such opposite behaviour in colonial matters. Sir Frederick Rogers, his Permanent Under-Secretary, praised him as "the pleasantest and most satisfactory chief of those under whom I served".[2] On broad questions, though lacking his profound convictions and moral fervour, Granville no doubt shared the views of the Prime Minister, who trusted him completely.[3] In reply to dispatches he gave a free hand to the immense experience and ability of Rogers, and made no attempt to break away from the office tradition. Rogers had a good deal of the schoolmaster in him, and to this the asperity of the tone of some of Granville's dispatches was clearly due.[4] On more than one occasion during the controversy with New Zealand Granville, while approving an argumentative office draft, added in his own hand a sympathetic or conciliatory phrase. Rogers himself regretted that the office was "getting a character for snubbing New Zealand", but felt that misstatement or fallacies in incoming dispatches ought not to be let pass.[5]

Granville's successor, Lord Kimberley, a man whom John Morley ranked with Lord Spencer "at the top of the Whigs" that he had known, for "capacity, industry, probity, independence, entire single-mindedness", was to receive high praise from colonial Governors for his loyal support.[6] He had no special knowledge of the colonies, but he was sympathetic to them and had supported Granville in the matter of the New Zealand loan. He did not doubt, he wrote soon afterwards, that in due time Canada and the Australian colonies would become independent, but he could conceive "no greater folly than to drive them into separation". Unless the home Government were very wrong-headed collisions might be avoided; so long as they did not interfere in the internal affairs of the colonies, the connection

---

[1] *Our Colonial Empire* (Nov. 1875), pp. 24, 30. See Reid, T. W., *Life of W. E. Forster*.
[2] Marindin, G. E., *Letters of Lord Blachford*, p. 264.
[3] See *Reminiscences of Lord Kilbracken*, p. 104, for the impression made by Granville on his private secretary.
[4] There had been a sharp note in the corespondence with New Zealand long before Granville took office. See *Parl. Pap.* 1868–9, XLIV (307).
[5] Granville to Bowen, 21 Aug., 25 Nov. 1869, P.R.O., C.O. 209/211, 213. Rogers found the New Zealand politicians so provoking that he hardly trusted his own judgment where they were concerned: see C.O. 209/215, on draft of dispatch of 21 March 1869.
[6] *Recollections*, II, 247; Bowen, *Thirty Years of Colonial Government*, I, 403.

might be maintained indefinitely in peace; on the other hand, any attempt to draw the connection tighter would soon result in separation.[1] In May 1871 Rogers retired from the office, to become as Lord Blachford a useful critic of colonial matters in Parliament and in the Press. He was succeeded by Robert Herbert, who enjoyed the unusual distinction for an Under-Secretary of having served as Prime Minister of a colony. Herbert won respect as "the perfect permanent official"; his Minutes show him much less afraid of imperial responsibilities than Rogers and less favourable towards native claims.[2]

To vague or fanciful proposals for consolidating the Empire by incorporating the colonies in some way with the United Kingdom Gladstone replied with Burke's *Opposuit natura*. But his government showed no reluctance to promote the union of neighbouring colonies. In the West Indies Sir Benjamin Pine was instructed to prepare a scheme for the federation of the Leeward Islands, which had followed the example of Jamaica in abandoning their old elected assemblies. By the end of 1870 he was able to report that the Councils of all the islands had agreed to his proposals. The consequent imperial Act of the following year made provision for the voluntary inclusion of the Windward Islands also, but of this there seemed no immediate prospect.[3]

In Australia opinion was not yet ripe for federation, but the inconvenience caused by the differing tariff policies of the several colonies made some understanding desirable. Rejecting the home Government's suggestion of a customs union, the intercolonial conference held at Melbourne in June 1870 decided in favour of mutual preferences. These, however, were forbidden by articles in the Australian Colonies Government Act of 1850[4] and in some of the Constitutions prohibiting the levying of differential duties or duties contrary to a treaty with a foreign power. The colonies, including New Zealand, at once urged on Downing Street the removal of such restrictions.[5] Kimberley's advisers thought the demand of the colonies reasonable, in so far as it was confined to intercolonial preferences, and Kimberley himself was inclined to concession. But the Prime Minister and the Cabinet were not convinced, and Kimberley wrote a long circular dispatch raising objections.[6] At their conference of September 1871 the colonies resolved to press their demands. The question had become one of

---

[1] *Diary*, May 1870, 2 March 1872, 24 May 1873.
[2] Queensland; see *D.N.B. 2nd Suppl.* vol. II; Gwynn, S., and Tuckwell, G. M., *Life of Sir C. W. Dilke*, I, 288.
[3] *Parl. Pap.* 1871, XLVIII [C. 353]; Kimberley in House of Lords, 19 May 1871, *Hansard*, 3rd ser. CCVI, 1022. See Wrong, H., *Government of the West Indies*. Statute 34 and 35 Vict. c. 107.
[4] 13 and 14 Vict. c. 59.
[5] See *C.H.B.E.* VII, pt. I, pp. 319 *seqq.*; *Parl. Pap.* 1872, XLII [C. 576], 1873, XLIX [C. 703]; Knaplund, *Gladstone and Britain's Imperial Policy*, pp. 103 *seqq.*
[6] 13 July 1871 [C. 576].

status: they insisted that "imperial interference with intercolonial fiscal legislation should finally and absolutely cease", and Charles Gavan Duffy, the Premier of Victoria, protested that the colonists were naturally impatient of being treated as "persons who cannot be intrusted to regulate their own affairs at their own discretion".[1] Gladstone was seriously perturbed, both by the possibility that concession would involve a breach of treaty with international consequences, and by what he considered the extreme claims of the colonies to pursue their own courses regardless of imperial interests and principles.[2] The whole question was carefully considered by the Cabinet in the winter of 1871–2; complications were introduced by further demands on the part of New Zealand and by the passing of a Canadian law, which for special reasons the Government were not prepared to disallow, imposing discriminating duties on tea and coffee from the United States; but eventually the Cabinet felt constrained to yield, provided that the colonies limited the special preferences to imports from one another and remained bound by imperial treaties.[3]

In the debates on the bill which followed, Lord Grey expressed his now usual view that Responsible Government had gone too far: it had never been intended that the great principle of Free Trade should be sacrificed through the mother country's abdication of its function of imposing a common economic policy. Some of the colonial statesmen, he regretted to say, were "in such utter ignorance of the principles of political economy that of the writings of Adam Smith and Mr Ricardo they seemed never to have even heard". But Kimberley had the support of the House in holding that the principle of self-government was even more important than the principles of political economy.[4]

In turning to the other important issue on which the home government disagreed with the views of the Australasian colonies we cross to the second of the main fields of imperial interest in this age, that of relations with native races. The problems connected with the arrival of the European planter in the western Pacific have been discussed in another volume and need only be referred to here for the light they throw on British policy.[5] Though commercial and strategic issues were of course involved, the Government viewed the question mainly as one of the moral responsibility of Great Britain, as the leading

[1] *Ibid.* pp. 1, 19, 57.
[2] Knaplund, *op. cit.* pp. 109–13, 247.
[3] Australian Customs Duties Act, 1873, 36 and 37 Vict. c. 22.
[4] See House of Lords debates, 15, 20 May 1873, *Hansard*, 3rd ser. CCXV, 1998; CCXVI, 153.
[5] *C.H.B.E.* VII, pt. i, 345 *seqq.* See also Ward, J. M., *British Policy in the South Pacific* (1948) and, for Fiji, Drus, Ethel, "The Colonial Office and the Annexation of Fiji" in *Trans. Royal Hist. Soc.* 4th ser. vol. XXXII (1950), pp. 87–110, a communication based on the Gladstone and Kimberley papers, as well as on the C.O. records in the P.R.O.

imperial and naval power, for the prevention of wrong to the South Sea islanders. The murder of Bishop Patteson in September 1871 drew attention to the subject, but some time before this the conscience of British philanthropists had been touched by reports of the kidnapping which occurred in the course of the labour trade.[1] Then, in 1870, the annexation of Fiji was pressed on the Imperial Government by a resolution of the intercolonial conference at Melbourne, followed later on by an appeal from the Government of New South Wales. The result, in brief, was that the Gladstone Cabinet agreed to pass a measure to punish crimes committed by British subjects in Polynesia outside the Queen's dominions, but refused to annex Fiji or Samoa.[2] The prospect of becoming involved in the controversies of a second or a third New Zealand was not attractive; but the Government would not have objected to Fiji being annexed to New South Wales if the colony had been prepared to accept the responsibility.[3] The House of Commons was given an opportunity of discussing the whole matter in June 1872, on the day after Disraeli's famous speech at the Crystal Palace, on a resolution calling for the establishment of a British protectorate over Fiji.[4] William McArthur, the mover, asserted that "the course we had pursued of late years of refusing to extend our colonial empire had led us into many unfortunate wars". The Prime Minister in reply laid down the principle that "H.M. Government would not annex any territory, great or small, without the well-understood and expressed wish of the people to be annexed, freely and generously expressed, and authenticated by the best means the case would afford".[5] The motion was accordingly rejected, but Kimberley instructed a naval commodore and a consul to report on the whole question, including the various lines of action which Great Britain might adopt.[6] The Colonial Secretary was by February 1873 converted to the need of annexing Fiji; but the Prime Minister remained unconvinced.[7]

The only case in which the Gladstone administration appear to have seriously considered the abandonment of a colony was that of the Gambia. Here they were only accepting a policy bequeathed to them by their predecessors and later to be revived by their successors. In 1865 a Select Committee of the Commons had recommended that we should eventually withdraw from the West African settlements with the exception, perhaps, of Sierra Leone:[8] in view of the virtual suppression of the slave trade and of the small amount of our legitimate commerce there seemed little purpose in holding on to these

---

[1] For kidnapping, see *Parl. Pap.* 1868–9, XLIII (408); 1871, XLVIII (468), [C. 399]; 1872 XLIII [C. 496].
[2] For Fiji, see *Parl. Pap.* 1871, XLVII (435); Pacific Islanders Protection Act, 35 & 36 Vict. c. 19. See *C.H.B.E.* VII, pt. ii, 205 for New Zealand's interest.
[3] *Parl. Pap.* 1872, XLIII [C. 509]; 1873, XLIX (124). See Drus, *op. cit.* p. 99.
[4] 25 June 1872, *Hansard*, 3rd ser. CCXII, 193 *seqq.*
[5] *Ibid.* 217.   [6] *Parl. Pap.* 1874, XLV [C. 983].
[7] Drus, *loc. cit.* pp. 101–2.
[8] See *C.H.B.E.* II, 673; *Parl. Pap.* 1865, V (412).

"fatal shores", as Adderley called them.[1] "There is no care in this country for our African possessions", wrote Clarendon in October 1869 with reference to the west coast. "I believe that an announcement of intention to get rid of them would be popular."[2] The Governor of Sierra Leone himself recommended the cession of the Gambia to France against compensation elsewhere: the expense of maintaining the troops exceeded the whole mercantile profits; the place was useless as a military post and, while there was little prospect of promoting civilisation among the peculiar population, there was danger of collisions with neighbouring tribes.[3] The Government approved the cession, and but for the outbreak of the Franco-Prussian War it would probably have taken place.[4]

The government of the West African settlements was discussed by the Commons in a thin House in June 1871.[5] Hugessen, in reply to various criticisms, maintained that our occupation of these settlements was "rather in discharge of a moral obligation than any self-seeking policy for imperial interests". Our hope was that the native population would gradually learn lessons of self-government and make progress in civilisation and Christianity. Good government in these conditions was difficult, but we were doing our best. He was not in favour of withdrawal.

With regard to the Gold Coast, Granville did not much care whether we stayed or not, but he thought the time was inopportune for withdrawal and he was not prepared to consider it so long as the Dutch remained on the scene.[6] The Dutch settlements had been closely intermixed with the British until a partition was negotiated in 1867, and even then their existence alongside made good administration difficult.[7] The Dutch were now prepared to go, and terms were agreed on. The Government's objects, said Kimberley, were "not the acquisition of territory, nor the extension of British power, but the maintenance of tranquillity and the promotion of peaceful commerce on the Coast".[8] But satisfaction at the news of the friendly transfer of the Dutch base at Elmina was premature; Kimberley admitted later that, knowing nothing of the Gold Coast, he had neglected the possibility of trouble with the Ashantis arising out of this agreement.[9] In February 1873 it was learnt that the Ashanti king had invaded the British protectorate. Military considerations now dominated political. Sir Garnet Wolseley, with the laurels of the

---

[1] *Review*, etc., p. 218.
[2] Clarendon to Admiral Harris (Private), 21 Oct. 1869 (copy): P.R.O. 30–29/55.
[3] Kennedy to Rogers, 23 Sept. 1869; *Parl. Pap.* 1870, L (444), 3.
[4] House of Commons, 15 July 1870, *Hansard*, 3rd ser. CCIII, 351 *seqq.*; Kimberley to Kennedy, 23 July 1870, *Parl. Pap.* 1870, L (444).
[5] *Hansard*, 3rd ser. CCVI, 1806 *seqq.*
[6] Granville to Clarendon, 1 Dec. 1869 (copy), P.R.O. 30–29/55.
[7] See *C.H.B.E.* II, 675.
[8] Kimberley to Pope Hennessy 12 Feb. 1872. *Parl. Pap.* 1873, XLIX (266), p. 6.
[9] Diary, 6 July 1873.

Red River expedition not three years old, was sent out as Administrator of the Gold Coast as well as commander of the land forces. The Government's primary aim was to chastise the Ashantis and expel them from districts where their presence might threaten the British coastal settlements, but not to prevent them from peaceable intercourse with the seaboard.[1] Wolseley's prompt success in destroying King Coffee's power, and perhaps also the unusual cheapness of the campaign, might seem to mark him for further employment in a dual capacity.[2]

It was left for Kimberley's successor to exploit Wolseley's triumph in measures tending towards the abolition of slavery in West Africa; but on the east coast, where explorers' reports were bringing home to the European conscience horrors equal to those of the middle passage, the Gladstone government won an outstanding success.[3] In 1871, the year of the finding of Livingstone by Stanley, the accession of a new Sultan at Zanzibar encouraged the Government to appoint a Select Committee to inquire into "the whole question of the slave-trade on the East Coast of Africa". The Committee reported in favour of an attempt not merely to enforce the old restriction but to secure the abolition of the trade by intensified diplomatic and naval action.[4] Accordingly Granville, as Foreign Secretary, sent out Sir Bartle Frere, then at the height of his Indian fame, with a draft treaty on special mission.[5] At length, in June 1873, a few weeks after Livingstone's death in the heart of Africa, after Frere had returned as yet unsuccessful, Sultan Barghash yielded to a threat of blockade and agreed under duress that the sea-borne traffic in slaves should cease throughout his dominions and the slave-markets be closed.[6] This achievement was perhaps the most beneficent of Gladstone's first ministry; it was due largely to the influence which young Dr Kirk, the British political agent and Consul at Zanzibar, had established over the Sultan.

The British subjects with whom Kirk was chiefly concerned were Indian traders. India was also deeply interested in the conditions of indentured labour in Mauritius, British Guiana and the West Indies, and from 1874 onwards in Natal. For British Guiana, where Chinese coolies as well as Indians were employed, Granville was moved in March 1870 by the accusations of a former magistrate to appoint a small commission to inquire into their alleged maltreatment. The result was the dispatch from London of a revised Ordinance on immigrant labour; Kimberley urged the Court of Policy to pass "such

---

[1] Kimberley to Wolseley, 10 Sept., 6 Oct. 1873, *Parl. Pap.* 1874, XLVI [C. 891], [C. 892].
[2] See Maurice, Sir F., and Arthur, Sir G., *Life of Lord Wolseley*; Biddulph, *Lord Cardwell at the War Office*, pp. 221–4.
[3] See Coupland, Sir R., *The Exploitation of East Africa*, for this whole topic.
[4] *Parl. Pap.* 1871, XII (420); Coupland, *op. cit.* p. 169; see article in *Quarterly*, Oct. 1872.
[5] Martineau, J., *Life and Correspondence of Sir B. Frere*, II, 68 *seqq.*
[6] Coupland, *op. cit.* chap. x: text of the treaty is at p. 212.

measures as will remove all ground of complaint on the part of the Indian authorities and enable H.M. Government to maintain this system of emigration which has been of so great advantage to the Colonies and has also, I believe, conferred considerable benefits on the emigrants themselves".[1] Kimberley had shortly before appointed a Royal Commission under the same chairman, W. H. Frere, to report on the treatment of Indian immigrants in Mauritius. When their Report was received, the Conservatives were in office; it convinced Carnarvon that the existing vagrancy Ordinance, passed in 1867, must be radically revised as repugnant to the principles of liberty and that other reforms were needed.[2]

All these troubles, however, were child's play compared with the great issues calling for decision in South Africa: responsible government, withdrawal of troops, native policy, annexation and relations with foreign states were all intermingled here.[3] In Cape Colony the Gladstone administration inherited an unpopular and imperious Governor, a difficult parliamentary situation and a long-standing quarrel about responsibility for defence; in Natal a constitutional dispute and a grievance over an annexation refused; with the Orange Free State a grievance over an annexation effected;[4] with the Transvaal a controversy over suspected slave-dealing and expansionist ambitions; in South Africa as a whole a vast and menacing native question; and in Downing Street, but not only there, a feeling that the problems of the country could perhaps be solved only by the union of the whole country under British sovereignty.[5] Writing to Granville in July 1869 Sir Philip Wodehouse, the Governor of the Cape due for early retirement, urged that the time had "really arrived at which Her Majesty's Government should take into consideration the whole position of these territories, and declare upon what principle and by whom their general policy is to be directed".[6]

But Her Majesty's Government were less concerned with long-term policy than with the issues in which either Parliament as a whole or individual Members were interested. Such were the withdrawal of the imperial garrisons and the treatment of the natives by the Boers. The situation was superficially similar to that of New Zealand, but much more complicated and serious. In New Zealand it was easy to place financial and military responsibility on the local

---

[1] Kimberley to Scott, 16 May 1872, *Parl. Pap.* 1871, xx [C. 393]; 1872, xliii [C. 641], p. 14.

[2] *Parl. Pap.* 1875, liii [C. 1188]; House of Lords, 12 May 1876, *Hansard*, 3rd ser. ccxxix, 474. See article by Stanley, E. L., in *Fortnightly Review*, June 1875.

[3] See *C.H.B.E.* viii, chap. xvi and de Kiewiet, C. W., *British Colonial Policy and the South African Republics, 1848–72*, pp. x–xvi.

[4] Basutoland, when annexed to the Crown on 12 March 1868 against the wishes of the Orange Free State, was not made part of Natal as the Natal government had desired. See *C.H.B.E.* viii, 417–25.

[5] Buckingham to Wodehouse, 23 Nov. 1868, quoted de Kiewiet, *op. cit.* p. 269.

[6] 2 July 1869, *Parl. Pap.* 1870, xlix (181), p. 15.

administration. In South Africa neither the Cape nor Natal enjoyed responsible government; the Bantu peoples, then known as Kaffirs, were far more dangerous than the Maoris, and the manner of their treatment in one colony or state was bound to have repercussions in others.

In Cape Colony Wodehouse regarded his own position as pitiable. Economic depression and the hostility between the Western and Eastern Provinces added to the usual difficulties of a system where a representative assembly has the power of the purse but does not control the executive. Wodehouse wished to improve this constitution by abolishing the Legislative Council and adding some official members to the elected Assembly. The Governor needed more power.[1] Granville, while insisting on the withdrawal after 1872 of all imperial troops, except one battalion to be left at the naval base of Simonstown for imperial purposes, and dissociating himself from Wodehouse's objections to responsible government, gave him leave to introduce his bill for a single-chamber legislature before the Assembly. It was rejected, and soon afterwards Wodehouse left for home.[2] His successor, Sir Henry Barkly, was instructed to lay before the Cape legislature the choice of responsible or Crown colony government; the home authorities preferred the former and in the event of its adoption would make a partial concession in the matter of the troops.[3] In Natal, where danger from the natives was greater and troops were admittedly still required, Granville had refused to concede any constitutional change.[4]

But a statesman could not regard the natives merely as a source of danger. It had been Wodehouse's great argument against responsible government for the Cape that it was neither just nor humane to hand over the native population to a legislature whose interests were so different from theirs.[5] And there was a group of people in Great Britain whose main concern with South African affairs was the desire to check injustice and inhumanity to the natives on the part of the Boers of the two Republics.[6] Especially the charges—supported by the evidence at the Government's disposal—that the Transvaal system of apprenticeship amounted in fact to slavery aroused such indignation that it was decided in 1869 to allow natives as well as Boers to buy arms and ammunition. These feelings, ill-informed though they might often be, played no small part in determining the attitude of Englishmen to the controversial questions recently decided,

---

[1] Wodehouse to Granville, 17 Jan. 1870, *Parl. Pap.* 1870, XLIX (181), 17.
[2] Granville to Wodehouse, 9 Dec. 1869, *ibid.*; 24 March 1870, *Parl. Pap.* 1871, XLVII [C. 459].
[3] Kimberley to Barkly, 17 Oct., 17 Nov. 1870, *ibid.*
[4] de Kiewiet, *op. cit.* p. 277.
[5] Wodehouse to Granville, 17 Jan. 1870, *Parl. Pap.* 1870, XLIX (181).
[6] See *Parl. Pap.* 1868–9, XLIII [C. 4141]. Their chief spokesman was R. N. Fowler; e.g. House of Commons, 26 April 1870, *Hansard*, 3rd ser. CC, 1873. The Aborigines Protection Society were also active.

as in Basutoland, or now arising for decision in Griqualand, the westerly region between the Orange and the Vaal.[1]

Between the departure of Wodehouse and the arrival of his successor the Secretary of State was officially informed of the discovery of diamonds in this area and of a settlement of diggers rapidly growing round the places where the diamonds were to be got. For the next six years the rival claims to possession of this region bedevilled relations between the British Government and the Republics, and indirectly with the Cape, while the employment of natives at the diggings had important reactions in Natal.[2]

The position from which the Colonial Office first approached the question is set out in a dispatch of November 1870. They would deplore any encroachment on the Griqua territory by the Republics, which would open to the Boers an extended field for slave-dealing and probably lead to oppression of the natives and disturbance of the peace. At the same time they had no wish to increase the territories of the colonies, particularly in view of the unsatisfactory state of the government of the Cape. Should, however, the Cape accept full responsibility for governing and policing the disputed area and should both the new white as well as the old native inhabitants of the area consent, then, and only then, might annexation be considered. Later, it would seem, the anarchic state of the diggers' community strengthened the argument for annexation, and Kimberley gave conditional approval.[3] But the conditions had not been fulfilled, the Cape parliament had not given a firm consent to take over the government, when Barkly, fortified by the terms of the Keate award, rashly proclaimed the diamond fields British in October 1871.[4] Kimberley had felt bound to rely on the Governor's discretion and when presented with a *fait accompli* could not disown him, but he none the less regretted the fateful act.[5] It is true that Kimberley held out no expectation to Barkly that any further extension of frontiers would be sanctioned;[6] but the annexation of the diamond fields, following only three years after the annexation of Basutoland, showed that a new phase of imperial policy had begun. The resentment of the Republics and their sympathisers in the Cape marked a new phase

---

[1] See W. Monsell in House of Commons, 7 July 1869, Grey in House of Lords, 8 March 1873, *Hansard*, 3rd ser. CXCVII, 1342; CCIX, 1635; de Kiewiet, *op. cit.* p. 247. For the Basuto War and its settlement see *C.B.H.E.* VIII, 417–25.

[2] The early history of the dispute over the diamond fields is given in *C.H.B.E.* VIII, 430 *seqq.*

[3] Kimberley to Barkly, 17 Nov. 1870, 18 May 1871, *Parl. Pap.* 1871, XLVII [C. 459]; see minutes on Barkly to Kimberley, 8 March 1871, P.R.O., C.O. 48/454; also de Kiewiet, *op. cit.* pp. 284, 291; Gladstone was consulted. See also article in *Edinburgh Review*, Oct. 1871.

[4] See *C.H.B.E.* VIII, 446: Lt.-Gov. Keate of Natal had awarded the lands between the Harts and Vaal rivers to the independent chiefs contrary to Republican claims.

[5] Kimberley to Barkly, 8 Dec. 1871, *Parl. Pap.* 1872, XLIII [C. 508]; 27 July 1872, *ibid.* 1873, XLIX [C. 732]; and see minute cited by de Kiewiet, p. 299.

[6] Kimberley to Barkly, 3 Feb. 1872, *Parl. Pap.* 1872, XLIII [C. 508].

also in the relations between the Imperial Government and the Afrikaners, and the new relations were to prove fatal to the new policy.[1]

Meanwhile in Cape Colony Barkly, with Kimberley's approval, encouraged the measure for responsible government.[2] Rejected in July 1871, it was passed in the following June and in August received the assent of the Queen in Council. Henceforward Downing Street would have to reckon with a Prime Minister as well as a Governor at the Cape. Kimberley had also authorised Barkly to start discussions on the subject of federation, a subject which bore first on the divisions of Cape Colony itself and secondly on its relations with the Orange Free State and, more remotely, with Natal and the Transvaal.[3] Hugessen wrote enthusiastically of the great hope thus offered "of the full and satisfactory development of the resources of South Africa", while Kimberley saw in a self-governing and self-reliant confederation an authority to which the hated burden of direct military and financial responsibility might be transferred.[4] The subject was debated in the Commons on motions by Fowler in each of the three years 1871, 1872 and 1873; on the last occasion Adderley remarked that confederation of all the South African governments seems now "generally desired" at home, but it was "not for us to originate, still less to dictate, measures towards it".[5]

1874–1880

In February 1874 Disraeli and the Conservatives came into power. Colonial issues had played little part in the General Election. If suspicions that Gladstone might intend to dismember the Empire were expressed, they now referred to Ireland.[6]

The new Prime Minister's attitude to the Empire, as to everything else, was widely different from his predecessor's. Gladstone cared for it mainly as representing the principles of "freedom and voluntaryism"; in so far as government from Downing Street was necessary, the responsibility must not be refused, but it was certainly not welcomed. Disraeli thought less of *Libertas* than of *Imperium*, and *Imperium* meant power. His acquisition of Cyprus in 1878 conformed perfectly to the theme of his "prigs and pedants" speech of 1863: "a country, and especially a maritime country, must get possession of the strong places of the world if it wishes to contribute to its power".[7] Power expressed

---

[1] See Walker, E. A., *Lord de Villiers and his Times*, p. 54.
[2] P.R.O., C.O. 48/486 contains interesting minutes discussing the objections of Barkly's councillors to responsible government enclosed in his dispatch of 31 May 1871.
[3] Barkly to Kimberley, 30 Aug.; Kimberley to Barkly, 16 Nov. 1871; *Parl. Pap.* 1872, XLIII [C. 508].
[4] de Kiewiet, *op. cit.* p. 296.
[5] *Hansard*, 3rd ser. CCIV, 1275; CCXI, 806; CCXIV, 790.
[6] Buckle, G. E., *Life of Disraeli*, v, 275; Duke of Somerset in Lords, 19 March 1874, *Hansard*, 3rd ser. CCXXVIII, 43.
[7] Buckle, *op. cit.* IV, 335.

itself through government. Disraeli was therefore less interested in the settled colonies than in India and the other Eastern possessions. "Power and influence we should exercise in Asia; consequently in Eastern Europe, consequently also in Western Europe; but what is the use of these colonial deadweights which *we do not govern?*"[1] He had no wish to curtail the freedom of the colonies which already possessed it: "I cannot conceive how our distant Colonies can have their affairs administered except by self-government." But he regretted the whole process by which the change had come about: thanks to the Liberal obsession with finance, the process had been wholly negative, a loosening of ties, without regard for the positive measures for preserving union which should have accompanied it. Great opportunities had been lost. But the Liberal attempt to disintegrate the Empire had failed. How had it failed?

> Through the sympathy of the Colonies for the Mother Country. They have decided that the Empire shall not be destroyed; and in my opinion no Minister in this country will do his duty who neglects any opportunity of reconstructing as much as possible our colonial Empire, and of responding to those distant sympathies which may become the source of incalculable strength and happiness to this land.[2]

So spoke Disraeli in his famous address to his party at the Crystal Palace, from which, his biographer claims, "the modern conception of the British Empire largely takes its rise". Certainly it was a landmark in the history of the Conservative party, which had hitherto, with a few exceptions, not noticeably differed from the Whigs in its views on colonial subjects. Disraeli himself had written in 1866: "Leave the Canadians to defend themselves; recall the African squadron; give up the settlements on the West coast of Africa; and we shall make a saving which will at the same time enable us to build ships and have a good Budget."[3] But the revival of interest in the colonies and the determination to keep them which had shown themselves in the country since 1869 had evidently had their effect on Disraeli. He had learnt the warmth and force of the "distant sympathies", and now realised that whether we governed the colonies or not the connection might yet prove of supreme value in the future. Nor should we fail to reckon among the influences which changed his views that alteration in the balance of power in Europe in 1870 which Disraeli was among the first to appreciate.[4]

In everything he said and did to encourage pride in the Empire and to increase its strength Disraeli had the eager support of the Queen. It was she who pressed him in 1876 to introduce the Royal Titles Bill authorising the Sovereign to assume the style of Empress of India. By

---

[1] Disraeli to Derby, 30 Sept. 1866, Buckle, *op. cit.* IV, 476.
[2] Speech of 24 June 1872, Buckle, V, 195.
[3] Buckle, IV, 476.
[4] "Perhaps the most important war of this century"; House of Commons, 7 Feb. 1871, *Hansard*, 3rd ser. CCIV, 70. For an estimate of Disraeli's position see Bodelsen, *op. cit.* pp. 120–4.

1879, if not before, she had become convinced that under Gladstone the Liberals had been guilty of "letting down our Empire". The maintenance of the Empire implied the risk of constant attacks and wars, but the risk must be faced: "the *true economy* will be *to be always ready*."[1]

The views of Lord Salisbury, the new Secretary of State for India, resembled those of his chief. He stigmatised the Liberals as men "who disdained empire, who objected to colonies, and who grumbled even at the possession of India". It had been the purpose of the Conservatives, he claimed in 1878, "to pick up the broken thread of England's old Imperial traditions".[2] Like his chief he was a believer in strong government. While detesting the arrogance of race towards non-Europeans he thought despotic rule best for Asiatics and cautioned the Viceroy that there must be no "leaving go of the thin rope of power".[3] Even with regard to white settlers he had spoken scornfully of "the peculiar Liberal nostrum" of responsible government, and had been very doubtful of its suitability for the Cape, where the electorate would be dominated either by the Coloured people or, if these did not vote, by the Afrikaners.[4]

For the Colonial Office Disraeli's obvious selection was Carnarvon. He had filled the post with credit in 1866–7 and his interest and knowledge far exceeded those of any of his colleagues. He was a highminded idealist, imaginative, sanguine, courageous and courteous, but sometimes injudicious in his choice of men, methods and times, somewhat tempted to force things and play the autocrat. But he had the merit of being "not the least afraid of the House of Commons".[5] Disraeli admired his ability and enterprise, but was at times apt to find him "fidgety" and overfond of Liberal applause. However, by the spring of 1876 he was complaining of "little Carnarvon's" blunders and, though he assured him that he was a person in whom he had "much trust", South African developments confirmed his misgivings of Carnarvon's judgment and he did not regret his resignation, over the Eastern question, in January 1878.[6] Sir Michael Hicks Beach, who was transferred from the Irish Office to fill Carnarvon's place, had no colonial experience but was already distinguished for his administrative competence.

The Prime Minister gave both his Colonial Secretaries free hands and full support in their policies. But he was far less interested in

---

[1] To Lady Ely, 21 Sept.; to Beaconsfield, 28 July 1879; *Letters of Queen Victoria*, 2nd ser. III, 47, 37.
[2] Cecil, Lady G., *Life of Robert, Marquis of Salisbury*, II, 302.
[3] Cecil, *op. cit.* II, 67, 68; House of Lords, 11 March 1869, *Hansard*, 3rd ser. CXCIV, 1070.
[4] House of Lords, 8 March, 29 July 1872, *Hansard*, 3rd ser. CCIX, 1621, CCXIII, 24.
[5] Marindin, G. E. *Letters of Lord Blachford*, p. 263; also Hardinge, Sir A., *Life of the 4th Earl of Carnarvon*, III, 317 *seqq.*, which includes a sketch of Carnarvon at the Colonial Office by one of his private secretaries.
[6] Zetland, *Letters of Lord Beaconsfield to Lady Bradford and Lady Chesterfield*, I, 313; Buckle, V, 475, VI, 419; Hardinge, *op. cit.* II, 234.

purely colonial questions than in power politics, and was annoyed when the former threatened to prejudice the latter. He invited both Carnarvon and Hicks Beach at different times to leave the Colonial Office for other posts.[1] There was another prominent Conservative whose long-standing devotion to colonial matters and recent experience might have made his advice useful. But Adderley was placed at the Board of Trade and neither then nor later was he admitted to the Cabinet.[2]

Carnarvon's immediate problem was the future of the Gold Coast. Resisting demands from certain quarters that we should withdraw altogether, the Government decided that we had unwritten obligations to the friendly tribes not to abandon them and not to allow a relapse into barbarism. The authority of Livingstone could be quoted for the civilising influence of trade, "the handmaid of religion". Their policy was to unite the Gold Coast and Lagos as a single Crown colony, not to extend the area under direct British sovereignty, to rely henceforward on African troops alone under British officers, and to work towards the gradual abolition of the institution of slavery.[3] The amalgamation of the two colonies took place in July 1874, and after consulting the new Governor Carnarvon approved two Ordinances forbidding slave-dealing and providing for eventual emancipation in the Protectorate.[4]

Reporting good progress, both administrative and financial, next year, Carnarvon took occasion to call attention to the renewal of negotiations with France for an exchange of the Gambia enclave against a number of small French stations on the Guinea coast, the possession of which by another Power hampered control of slave-dealing and the arms traffic. The French had reopened the question in April 1874, but it was not handled skilfully on the British side: departmental delays, premature Press announcements, commercial protests and timidity on the part of the Cabinet let the opportunity pass, and a month after the Commons had agreed to refer the matter to a Select Committee Carnarvon had to announce that the French had reduced their offer and negotiations were at an end. Had these succeeded, the whole of the Ivory Coast and of Dahomey would presumably in due course have become British.[5]

In East Africa, as formerly on the West Coast, the main object of British endeavour, both official and popular, was still the extirpation

---

[1] Hardinge, *op. cit.* II, 94, 95; Hicks Beach, Lady V., *Life of Sir M. Hicks Beach*, 1, 84.
[2] See Childe-Pemberton, W. S., *Life of C. B. Adderley, 1st Lord Norton*, p. 1.
[3] House of Commons, 27 April, 4 May, 25, 29 June 1874; House of Lords, 12 May 1874; *Hansard*, 3rd ser. CCXVIII, 1204, 1592; CCXX 451, 607; CCXIX, 151.
[4] *Parl. Pap.* 1875, LII [C. 1139].
[5] *Parl. Pap.* 1876, LII [C. 1409]; House of Lords, 3 Aug. 1875, 17 Feb., 20 March 1876; *Hansard*, 3rd ser. CCXXVI, 436; CCXXVII, 374; CCXXVIII, 264; Hardinge, *op. cit.* II, 141–5.

of the slave-trade. The prohibition of the sea-borne traffic, extorted by British sea-power in 1873, had been evaded by the conveyance of slaves by land. The suggestion that this land traffic should be stopped by the British occupation of a post on the East Coast was rejected by the Government,[1] but in April 1876 Kirk induced Sultan Barghash to follow up his engagements under the Treaty of 1873 by prohibiting the conveyance of slaves by land either along the coast or to the coast from the interior.[2] These measures in due course killed the organised slave-trade, and their importance can hardly be exaggerated. In the last resort, as their historian points out, it was the determination of the British people which achieved this result.[3] Interest might vary in intensity from time to time, but it was none the less deep-seated and at any moment might express itself strongly.[4] An instance of this is the excitement caused over the unfortunate Fugitive Slave Circular, which in its original form unduly restricted the circumstances in which an escaping slave might claim protection from a ship of the Royal Navy; the controversy led to a two-night debate and a full division in February 1876.[5]

It is from the mid-'seventies that we are now to date the beginning of the "scramble" in East Africa.[6] Men from many countries took part in it from many motives, but these were not at first or in the main political. British influence, however, in the person of Kirk, remained dominant in Zanzibar for twelve years from the signing of the treaty in 1873, and it was natural that the Sultan, having persuaded himself that his mainland domains must be opened up and that European help was needed, should turn for this help to London. London was willing, and but for unnecessary delays, it would seem, a concession for the whole vast region between Somaliland and Mozambique and from the Great Lakes to the sea might have been granted to a British company, not only with the Sultan's acquiescence but actually on his invitation.[7] The chance was lost, and so in the next few years were several other opportunities of establishing British control of the area over which the Sultan claimed a suzerainty he was too weak to enforce.[8]

In the Pacific, in the case of Fiji, the opportunity, or the responsibility, was not refused.[9] By 1874 Kimberley's two Commissioners,

---

[1] 8 July 1875, 4 April 1876; *Hansard*, 3rd ser. ccxxv. 1165, 8, ccxxviii, 1217–25: suggestions for a British settlement on the East Coast, where liberated slaves could be received.

[2] Coupland, *op. cit.* chap. xi.

[3] *Ibid.* p. 233.

[4] See Bourke in House of Commons, *Hansard*, 3rd ser. ccxxviii, 1221.

[5] Hartington, House of Commons, 8 Feb. 1876, *Hansard*, 3rd ser. ccxxvii, 75; also debates of 22, 24 Feb. 1876. See Hardinge, *op. cit.* ii, 84–9.

[6] Keltie, J. S., *The Partition of Africa*, p. 119; Coupland, *op. cit.* p. 319.

[7] See Coupland, *op. cit.* chap. xiv for the Mackinnon negotiations, 1877–8, and below, p. 74.

[8] *Ibid.* pp. 371 *seqq.*

[9] For official views on the subject see Drus, Ethel, *Trans. Royal Hist. Soc.* 4th ser. xxxii (1950), 104 *seqq.*; see also Ward, J. M., *British Policy in the South Pacific*, chap. xxxii.

Commodore Goodenough and Consul Layard, had presented their report.[1] They declared that all the white settlers were in favour of the cession of the islands to Great Britain and they recommended their annexation as a Crown colony. Carnarvon could see no satisfactory alternative. While he hardly liked to say, so he told the Lords, that England had "a mission to extend her policy of colonisation" in the South Seas, he recognised "an indirect duty...to take under our protection a place into which English capital has overflowed, in which English settlers are resident, in which, it must be added, English lawlessness is going on, and in which the establishment of English institutions has been unsuccessfully attempted". There were positive advantages too: the climate and resources of the islands, their position as a possible station between America and Australia, and the facilities they would provide for suppressing the kidnapping trade. All things considered, the Government could not "decline the duty of accepting these islands". While welcoming the novel offer of New South Wales to bear a share of the burdens which annexation would entail, they were not prepared, as Gladstone's Cabinet had been, to encourage an Australian colony to administer the new possession. If Fiji came under the British flag it must be as a Crown colony "of a rather severe type", and the cession must be unconditional. They accordingly proposed to send Sir Hercules Robinson, the Governor of New South Wales, to visit Fiji, lay their conditions before the inhabitants, native and white, and take necessary action. Kimberley in the Lords, and Gladstone and Dilke in the Commons, were doubtful of the wisdom of annexing a second New Zealand with the inevitable difficulties over the land question and relations between natives and white men, but an amendment urging caution on the Government was rejected by 81 to 28.[2] In this debate, while disclaiming any desire for annexation regardless of the circumstances, James Lowther, the Under-Secretary, protested "against a doctrine which found favour in certain quarters, according to which all annexations or additions to British dominions would be sternly discouraged.... He ventured to hope not only that we should not abandon our Colonies, but that we should not abandon colonisation, for such abandonment had usually been, if he read history aright, the precursor of a period of national decay." Further, the responsibilities which a colonial empire entailed were not without their compensations; in case of a life and death struggle with another Power, the latter would have to reckon with "many other millions of the Anglo-Saxon race who looked on the mother-country with feelings of veneration and regard, and were by no means indisposed to accept the duties and obligations which

[1] *Parl. Pap.* 1874, XLV [C. 1011].
[2] House of Lords, 17 July 1874, *Hansard*, 3rd ser. CCXXI, 179 *seqq.* House of Commons, 4 Aug. 1874, *Hansard*, 3rd ser. CCXXI, 126 *seqq.* Kimberley himself admitted that "it would have been very difficult to avoid taking Fiji"; to Gladstone, 4 Nov. 1874, Drus, *loc. cit.* p. 109.

attached to them as members of a great Colonial Empire".[1] It was agreed on both sides of the House that the responsibility for the decision must rest not with Parliament but with the executive government, and that in this case meant Carnarvon.[2] So the requisite authority was given to Robinson, and in due course Carnarvon approved his action in proclaiming the annexation of Fiji.[3]

In the following year, as a further check on lawlessness in the Pacific, Carnarvon carried a bill to strengthen Kimberley's Act of 1872 by providing for the appointment of a British High Commissioner and the establishment of a court of law.[4] But this is as far as he was ready to go. He was not prepared, in deference to official and unofficial Australian desires, to add the eastern half of New Guinea to the British dominions, and Hicks Beach after him was of the same opinion.[5]

In the Malay peninsula the problem was different. The peace and the trade of the Straits Settlements colony were disturbed by anarchy in the adjoining Malay States and by endemic piracy.[6] The current disorders had been rife since 1872: the rivalries of Malayan potentates were complicated by the disputes of Chinese factions from Penang concerned in exploiting the tin mines. Both Granville and Kimberley had warned the Governor, Sir Henry Ord, that they would not be disposed to approve any step tending to increase British responsibilities in Malaya;[7] but in 1873 Kimberley had suggested to Sir Andrew Clarke, Ord's successor, that it might be desirable to appoint British officers to reside in the native states, subject to their rulers' consent.[8] In January 1874 Clarke reported that, as part of a settlement which he had just negotiated with the Malayan chieftains and the Chinese merchants, he had provisionally agreed to a request from the new Sultan of Perak for the appointment of a British Resident "whose advice must be asked and acted upon on all questions other than Malay religion and custom".[9] The scheme was welcomed by commercial interests in the colony and in London, and Carnarvon eventually sanctioned it with regard to both Perak and Selangor;[10] in this matter, however, as in others touching Malaya, he had to defend

---

[1] *Hansard*, 3rd ser. ccxxi, 1291.

[2] See Hardinge, *op. cit.* ii, 133, 73, for the reason why no Cabinet was held.

[3] On 10 Oct. 1874: *Parl. Pap.* 1875, lii [C. 1114]; for the proposal to change the name of the islands, see *Letters of Queen Victoria*, 2nd ser. ii, 358.

[4] Pacific Islanders Protection Act 1875, 38 and 39 Vict. c. 51; see Ward, *op. cit.* chap. xxiii.

[5] *Parl. Pap.* 1876, liv [C. 1566]; House of Commons, 3 April 1879, *Hansard*, 3rd ser. ccxlv, 262.

[6] *Parl. Pap.* 1874, xlv [C. 1111]; 1875, liii [C. 1320].

[7] *Parl. Pap.* 1874, xlv [C. 1111]; Granville to Ord, 10 Sept. 1869; Kimberley to Ord, 26 Aug. 1871, enclosed in Clarke to Kimberley, 24 Feb. 1874.

[8] 20 Sept. 1873 [C. 1111].

[9] 26 Jan. 1874, expanded 24 Feb. 1874 [C. 1111].

[10] Carnarvon to Clarke, 29 May, 4 Sept. 1874 [C. 1111].

his policy against the sharp criticisms of Lord Stanley of Alderley, who had a sharp nose for scandals in this part of the world.[1]

These criticisms gained force in November 1875 when news came, first, of the murder on the Perak river of one of the new Residents and, a few days later, of the high-handed revision on the part of the new Governor, Sir William Jervois, of the approved policy.[2] Jervois was convinced that the Residents, if they were to serve any purpose at all, must be more than mere advisers and apparently believed that despite the letter of the agreement the Colonial Office shared this view. Accordingly he had taken on himself, without awaiting Carnarvon's sanction, to extort the consent of the contemptible Sultan Abdullah to the elevation of the Residents into Commissioners, who should openly administer the country in the Sultan's name.[3] It was natural that Carnarvon should ascribe the murder of Birch to native resentment at the new policy, but the necessity of summoning troops from Hong Kong and India to establish British prestige in Perak and in the neighbourhood of Malacca forced forward the question of annexation. Carnarvon decided against it, however, whether under that name or in the disguised form which Jervois had attempted to introduce, and preferred to revert to the original policy; he retained the Residents as advisers only, but strengthened them by a Council consisting mainly of Malay chiefs and protected them by a bodyguard of police.[4] The Sultan, whom it had first been intended to keep on the throne on promise of good behaviour, was later found guilty of complicity in the murder on the Perak river and was deported to the Seychelles.

The notion of Residents was borrowed from the Native States of India, but the whole incident illustrated the difficulty of combining the protection of legitimate European economic enterprise with regard for the sovereignty of semi-barbarous Malay princelings; in the peninsula, unlike India, there was no preponderant military or political power close at hand to overawe opposition. Referring to our growing interests in the Far East, Merivale had pleaded in 1870 for some single authority to harmonise policy in Ceylon, Malaya, China and Japan, to stimulate British industry and to prevent aggression against native races.[5] It was difficult for a Resident to content himself with mere advice when faced with the scandals of debt-slavery, or

---

[1] E.g. House of Lords, 19 May 1874, *Hansard*, 3rd ser. ccxix, 467 *seqq.* Stanley also corresponded privately with Carnarvon. He is described in *D.N.B. 2nd Suppl.* as a diplomatist and orientalist; he had travelled widely and embraced Islam.

[2] *Parl. Pap.* 1876, liv [C. 1505], [C. 1510], [C. 1512]; 1877, lxi [C. 1709]: P.R.O. 30–6/40; Hardinge, *op. cit.* ii, 135–40; H. L. Hall, *The Colonial Office*, pp. 238–42.

[3] Jervois to Carnarvon, 16 Oct., 2 Dec. 1875; 10 Feb. 1876; [C. 1505], pp. 31, 159; [C. 1510], p. 1; also 18 Oct. 1875 (Private), P.R.O. 30–6/40. Jervois had explained his view to Carnarvon privately in July, but Carnarvon's reply deprecating immediate action reached him on the day after he had proclaimed British rule.

[4] Carnarvon to Jervois, 10 Dec. 1875, 20 May, 1 June 1876: [C. 1505], p. 64; [C. 1510], p. 21; [C. 1512], p. 98.

[5] *Fortnightly Review*, Jan. 1870, new ser. vii, 175.

for a Governor so far away to remember the need of not outstripping a public opinion at home fearful of increased commitments.[1]

In turning from Malaya to the West Indies, we leave one of the newest of British colonies for some of the oldest; here the native population whose plight stirs the Governor to embarrassing action are not the thralls of a foreign Sultan but British subjects of long standing. The trouble in Barbados in April 1876 arose directly from the belief of the planter oligarchy that the new Governor, J. Pope Hennessy, was inciting the Negroes to discontent and insubordination, indirectly from the instructions he had received from Carnarvon to promote the confederation of the Windward Islands, as contemplated by previous British governments.[2] But the proud and prosperous ruling class of Barbados were alarmed at the prospect of confederation with four islands in a lower constitutional and economic position.[3] Carnarvon might have learnt from his South African experiences in the previous year how little his disclaimers of any intention to coerce or hustle a colonial legislature would avail him when local pride and self-interest became involved. The West India interest in England demanded Hennessy's recall, and the issue was twice debated in both Houses.[4] When full information had reached them, the Government spokesmen expressed the general feeling of their hearers in exonerating Hennessy of all blame except for some injudicious remarks in a speech to the colonial legislature, and in consequently refusing to recall him; on the contrary they used severe language of the behaviour of some of his opponents and of the condition to which in certain respects the negligence of successive Assemblies had reduced the island. They did not however propose to deprive Barbados of its constitution, and it was left to be understood that it would before long receive another Governor.

Dealing with the charges against the Barbados planters, Lowther rejected the idea of interference with "the sacred right of freedom of contract", since the home Government's "influence for good would be seriously diminished if they were to be suspected of any sympathy with communism".[5] But Barbados did not import coolies. In colonies which relied on indentured labour the mother country felt a special responsibility, as we have seen in the cases of British Guiana and Mauritius. Similarly in Grenada Hicks Beach arranged in 1879 for the visit of an official from Trinidad to discover how far

[1] See Carnarvon to Jervois (Private), 13 Sept. 1875, Hardinge, II, 137.

[2] See *Parl. Pap.* 1876, LIII [C. 1539], [C. 1559]; 1877, LXI [C. 1679], [C. 1687]; 1880, XLIX [C. 2645]; Wrong, H., *Government of the West Indies*, pp. 82–6, 155–7.

[3] Grenada, St Vincent, Tobago, St Lucia. By 39 and 40 Vict. c. 47 the three former island colonies were in effect reduced (at their own request) to the Crown colony status of the latter.

[4] House of Lords, 28 April, 1 Aug. 1876; House of Commons, 5 May, 28 July 1876; *Hansard*, 3rd ser. CCXXVIII, 1819; CCXXIX, 144; CCXXXI, 42, 236.

[5] *Hansard*, 3rd ser. CCXXXI, 52.

the treatment of coolies had improved since the abuses reported in the previous year.[1] In Jamaica, where the financing of importation had broken down, the planters, supported by the West India Committee in London, asked for subvention from the general revenues of the Colony, such as was allowed in Trinidad and British Guiana. Carnarvon, determined to consider the case of each colony on its merits, proposed a scheme which he and the Governor thought equitable; a measure on these lines was enacted by the island legislature and confirmed by Hicks Beach.[2]

We must now return to South Africa. With the grant of responsible government to the Cape and the establishment of Griqualand with its diamond fields as a Crown colony a new phase had begun. In the autumn of 1873 the storm-centre, from the point of view of the Colonial Office, shifted to Natal, and Carnarvon was immediately faced with the native question and the clash of opinion which it provoked. After calling for full reports on the Langalibalele affair and hearing the views of Bishop Colenso and Theophilus Shepstone in person, Carnarvon was convinced that the decision of Sir Benjamin Pine and his irregular court could not be upheld. The insubordinate chieftain's sentence was commuted, Pine was recalled, and the indispensable Sir Garnet Wolseley was sent out to Natal. His mission was to revise the system of native administration and to stiffen up the constitution, as a temporary measure, by an addition to the nominated element in the Legislative Council.[3]

The affair aroused great interest in England, and Carnarvon was criticised in the Lords by Grey as well as Kimberley. In his forceful reply he insisted that ministers at home must have a conscience and a voice in such matters as these, where a local European minority had been led into injustice. "If the ties of Empire really will not bear that strain upon them, then I say the whole imperial theory becomes an absolute fiction."[4] By the stand which he took Carnarvon won the confidence of many Liberals and the approval of the Queen, who wished all her colonial Governors to know "her very strong feeling ...that the natives and coloured races should be treated with every kindness and affection".[5] In a later debate Carnarvon defended against Blachford's criticisms the revised constitution of Natal: the former Council with its elected majority had failed, but to strict Crown colony government Carnarvon preferred "a compromise which

---

[1] Parl. Pap. 1878–9, LI [C. 2249]; 1880, XLIX [C. 2602].
[2] Parl. Pap. 1878–9, LI [C. 2437]. See House of Lords, 3 Aug. 1875; Hansard, 3rd ser. CCXXVI, 440 (Stanley of Alderley and Carnarvon).
[3] See C.H.B.E. VIII, 454 seqq., 498 seqq; Parl. Pap. 1874, XLV [C. 1025]; 1875, LIII [C. 1119], [C. 1121], [C. 1141], [C. 1158], [C. 1187]; 1875, LII [C. 1342–1]; Hardinge, op. cit. II, 163 seqq.; Maurice and Arthur, Life of Lord Wolseley, pp. 76 seqq.
[4] 12 April 1875, Hansard, 3rd ser. CCXXIII, 664 seqq. For a strong condemnation of the Natal Government, see Westlake in Fortnightly Review, Dec. 1874.
[5] The Queen to Carnarvon, 24 Dec. 1874, Letters, 2nd ser. II, 361.

on the one hand strengthens the executive, while it does not take away the representative institutions which exist".[1]

Carnarvon's decision in the Langalibalele affair had brought him into conflict not only with the European population in Natal, but also with the ministry at the Cape.[2] The moment was thus not propitious for the reception of the important proposal which was now with high hopes launched from Downing Street. Kimberley, as we have seen,[3] had been in favour of South African confederation; Carnarvon was playing with the idea as early as May 1874, and he discussed the matter with Barkly during the summer, fully realising that success must depend upon "the circumstances and feelings of the time".[4] By the spring of 1875, despite the unresolved disputes with the two Republics over the diamond fields and the western borderlands, despite the strongly anti-Afrikaner feelings of the Queen's representatives at Cape Town and at Kimberley, Carnarvon decided that the time had come. In order to break the deadlock the Imperial Government must take the initiative and, while it could not impose, it could at least suggest federation.

The dispatch of 4 May 1875 was tactless in its detail as well as unlucky in its timing, but its tone was eminently courteous and anything but dictatorial.[5] In view of the urgent importance of securing uniformity or agreement on various matters—particularly native policy—of general concern to South Africa, Carnarvon proposed that delegates from all the states and provinces should meet in Cape Colony to deliberate and report; there was no restriction of subject, and while H.M. Government would welcome suggestions on "the all-important question of a possible union of South Africa in some form of confederation", no pressure was to be put on the delegates.

The notion of bringing under a single government at an early date, by their own free will, two independent republics, two Crown colonies and an ancient dependency newly rejoicing in freedom to order its own affairs was perhaps chimerical, even in the special circumstances of South Africa. But though Carnarvon was now dead set on confederation, this topic was not given pride of place in his dispatch, and there were other matters regarded by him as urgent which such a conference might well have discussed. The major blunder, which scotched the project, was his failure to win the confidence and support of the Government of the Cape, by far the most powerful of the five units concerned: a failure due to a lack of understanding of both the

---

[1] 23 July 1875, *Hansard*, 3rd ser. ccxxv, 1891. For Blachford's views on native policy, see *Edinburgh Review*, April 1877.

[2] See Molteno, P. A., *Life and Times of Sir J. C. Molteno*, i, chap. xi.

[3] See p. 40 above.

[4] Carnarvon to Barkly, 27 May, 22 Aug. 1874, Hardinge, *op. cit.* ii, 172 *seqq.* Carnarvon's private correspondence with Barkly is in P.R.O., 30–6/32. See also de Kiewiet, C. W., *The Imperial Factor in South Africa*, chap. ii; *C.H.B.E.* viii, chap. xviii.

[5] *Parl. Pap.* 1876, lii [C. 1399]. See *C.H.B.E.* viii, 460.

situation and the personalities.[1] It would seem that Barkly's disobedience and Froude's indiscretions were only secondary causes of Carnarvon's failure, compared with this initial mistake.[2] It is true that after Molteno's dismissal in February 1878 the Cape Government favoured confederation, but by this time the situation elsewhere had completely changed.

Encouraged by his settlement of the boundary dispute with the Orange Free State and undaunted by Molteno's sabotage and the fiasco of the London Conference, Carnarvon could still hope in August 1876 that confederation was "not far distant."[3] He was now chiefly concerned with the Afrikaner republics; as inducements to confederate he could offer them possible modifications of imperial policy regarding customs and extensions of their borders.[4] But in the Transvaal events occurred which rapidly altered the whole aspect of affairs and seemed to Carnarvon to offer a heaven-sent chance.[5] The iron was hot, so he struck, with Shepstone as his hammer. But again faulty appreciation of South African feeling led to disaster.

The award of Delagoa Bay to Portugal by the French President in July 1875 had aroused high hopes at Pretoria and alarm in Downing Street. To the Transvaal it offered access to the sea and an inlet for goods not subject to colonial tariffs; to the British, apart from unwelcome commercial competition, it threatened all sorts of complications, and hindrance to the future unity of the country, through the irruption of foreign influences into the enclosed garden of South African politics. The aspirations of the Transvaal were advertised by President Burgers's vain efforts in 1875 and 1876 to secure a loan for the building of a railway to connect Pretoria with Lourenço Marques.[6]

In May and August 1875, during Burgers's absence in Europe, the Transvaal Government took action likely to lead to trouble with the natives on their frontiers, both on the west in the lands covered by the Keate award and with Cetewayo, the Zulu King.[7] In January 1876 Carnarvon was perturbed by the prospect of fighting between Boers and Zulus and declared his determination not to allow any extension of the boundaries of the Transvaal so long as South Africa remained an agglomeration of disunited provinces: under present conditions "a war between the Republic and the Zulus would inevitably draw

[1] See *C.H.B.E.* VIII, 457 *seqq.*; Molteno, I, chaps. xiii, xiv; de Kiewiet, *The Imperial Factor in South Africa*, chap. iv; Hardinge, II, 181–200.

[2] The Froude agitation was of course the most obvious *gaffe*; both Disraeli (Buckle, VI, 419) and Blachford (*Letters*, p. 364) were critical of it. Froude's Report to Carnarvon is dated 10 Jan. 1876 in [C. 1399]; see his article in *Quarterly Review*, Jan. 1877, on "English policy in South Africa."

[3] *Parl. Pap.* 1876, LII [C. 1631]; 1877, LX [C. 1681]; Carnarvon to Northcote, 18 Aug. 1876, Hardinge, II, 212.

[4] Carnarvon to Barkly, 31 Aug. 1876 [C. 1681]; 25 Jan. 1876, *Parl. Pap.* 1877, LX [C. 1748].

[5] *C.H.B.E.* VIII, 462 *seqq.*

[6] See de Kiewiet, *Imperial Factor*, pp. 97 *seqq.*

[7] *Ibid.* pp. 21, 99; *Parl. Pap.* 1877, LX [C. 1748].

this country and its South African dependencies into serious complications". In July he obtained Cabinet approval for a warning to Burgers.[1]

Apparently it was fears aroused both by threats of Boer expansion towards the coast and by the danger of a general native war which induced Carnarvon to regard control of the Transvaal in some form as a pressing need in 1876; it was the report received in London on 14 September of a Boer reverse at the hands of Sekukuni's tribesmen and of a request from a meeting of Transvaalers for British intervention which convinced him that now was the time to act.[2] "My hope is", he wrote to the Prime Minister next day, "that by acting at once, we may prevent war and acquire at a stroke the whole of the Transvaal Republic, after which the Orange Free State will follow, and the policy in South Africa, for which we have been labouring, [will be] fully and completely justified." On 20 September he asked Beaconsfield's approval for his plan to send out "Shepstone—the man who has the most intimate knowledge of South African affairs and the greatest influence over natives and Dutch—with a secret dispatch empowering him to take over the Transvaal Government and country, and to become the first English Governor—if circumstances on his arrival render this in any way possible".[3] The Prime Minister's early confidence in Carnarvon's judgment, such as it was, had been shaken by the Froude episode, but he was now overwhelmed with Balkan affairs and he acquiesced in the present proposal. Carnarvon must do as he thought wisest.[4]

The development of Carnarvon's own views is not altogether clear, nor is it plain how his various statements on the subject can be reconciled. Undoubtedly, as he said, the war between the Transvaal and the Bapedi tribesmen under Sekukuni rapidly "ripened all South African policy".[5] A week after he learnt of the outbreak of this war he wrote to Northcote: "though the Transvaal Government have behaved scandalously, I am not sure that their action will not bring about, and perhaps quickly, all that I have been aiming at."[6] On 14 September came the excited telegram from Barkly. In forwarding it to Carnarvon, Herbert remarked that "our anticipations as to President Burgers's failure and the consequent desire of the Transvaal to come under British rule are being fulfilled very rapidly".[7] Next day Carnarvon wrote the message to the Prime Minister which has

---

[1] Carnarvon to Barkly, 25 Jan. 1876 [C. 1748], p. 15; see minutes by Shepstone, Herbert and Wolseley on Bulwer's dispatch of 26 Oct. 1875, P.R.O., C.O. 179/118, and comments by Uys, C. J., In the Era of Shepstone, p. 128; Hardinge, op. cit. II, 228–30.

[2] Barkly to Carnarvon, 25 Aug. 1876 [C. 1748], p. 100; See Uys, op. cit. p. 173 for the source of Barkly's telegram.

[3] Carnarvon to Beaconsfield, 15, 20 Sept. 1876, Buckle, VI, 414.

[4] Buckle, V, 475; Zetland, II, 75; Hardinge, II, 234.

[5] Carnarvon to Frere, 13 Oct. 1876; Martineau, J., Life and Correspondence of Sir B. Frere, II, 161.

[6] 18 Aug. 1876, Hardinge, II, 212.   [7] Hardinge, II, 232.

been quoted on page 52. On the 20th he asked his approval of his plan to send out Shepstone; this, he said, was not a hasty or ill-considered measure. On the same day he informed Barkly in a private letter that he attached "to a cession the greatest importance", and doubted not that "with skilful handling circumstances could be made greatly to contribute to the objects in view"; he was arranging further for a strong battalion to be dispatched "ostensibly to relieve the 32nd, but really to be available for all purposes and in the first instance to stop at Natal, where, with the complications that are possible in the case of Cetewayo and Zululand, its presence will be most useful".[1] Carnarvon was in these first few days clearly elated by the prospect of a "cession", but the ripe plum must be encouraged to drop. On the 22nd in an official dispatch he told Barkly that H.M. Government could not allow the prolongation of the Bapedi war with its threat to British lives and property throughout South Africa; the course of events might cause him to modify his inclination to co-operate with the Transvaal as a separate state, and British help would not be given except on terms securing closer co-operation for the future.[2] The Boers' extremity was Britain's opportunity.

In the next few days he seems to have considered further to what extent pressure was expedient: in a private letter of 4 October he pointed out to Shepstone that, while on the one hand it was of great consequence to secure the Transvaal, it was important to make the cession as far as possible the act of the Afrikaner part of the population.[3] "It is extremely desirable to have the consent of the Volksraad to a cession of the state, and it would be dangerous to take over the country *against* their desire except under circumstances so grave as to justify us on the ground of unquestionable safety. I hope you may secure this even if on your arrival you find that the vote is not what you desired. It may be possible to get a second and a more satisfactory resolution."[4] With regard to the troops which were being sent out, it would be imprudent to move them into Transvaal territory unless Shepstone saw his way "to take and proclaim it". And in Shepstone's secret Commission, dated 5 October, which in the first instance instructed him merely to make inquiry, but authorised him in case of urgent necessity to administer and provisionally to annex the territory, the condition was inserted that he must issue no such proclamation unless "satisfied that the inhabitants, or a sufficient number of them, or their Legislature desired to become British subjects".[5] "A sufficient number" gave a willing agent a loophole wide

[1] P.R.O. 30–6/32; part printed in Hardinge, *op. cit.* II, 234.
[2] Carnarvon to Barkly, 22 Sept. 1876 [C. 1748], p 103.   [3] P.R.O. 30–6/23.
[4] Carnarvon wrote to Sir H. Ponsonby on 3 Oct.: "It may be necessary in the last resort to use some compulsion: but it should only be when every other method has failed." P.R.O. 30–6/3. Cf. Salisbury in Oct. 1875, "I do not propose to send a mission to Afghanistan against the Ameer's wishes: but I propose to tell the Government of India to make the Ameer wish it." Buckle, *op. cit.* v, 434.
[5] Enclosed in Carnarvon to Bulwer, 9 Oct. 1876, *Parl. Pap.* 1877, LX [C. 1776].

enough; and, as time went on, reports from Shepstone and Barkly emphasising, and perhaps exaggerating, the military and financial helplessness of the Boers and the inhumanity of their methods of warfare, while minimising the extent of the dislike of annexation, conspired with Carnarvon's autocratic temperament and his eager desire for cession to prevent him from contemplating any other solution.[1] So when Shepstone reported the fateful events of 12 April 1877— the bloodless civilian annexation, the relief of the British inhabitants, the absence of effective protest from the Afrikaners, the willingness of nearly all the republican officials to continue at their posts, Carnarvon was overjoyed and sent Shepstone his hearty congratulations: "the work has been admirably done." He could have wished that the President and Volksraad had themselves proposed the annexation, but he could "well understand that this was impossible."[2]

In the face of these avowals and exhortations, what are we to make of Carnarvon's assertion in the Lords that he regretted what had occurred? "I had for some time feared that this event would come to pass."[3] Or of the statement in a letter from the Colonial Office to the Treasury that the annexation had been "neither coveted nor sought" by him?[4] Still more surprising is the assertion which he made in Parliament in March 1879: "In annexing the Transvaal the question of Confederation never entered my mind, still less was it a motive inducing me to such a policy. It was, on the contrary, opposed to my systematic efforts of the previous two years to conciliate the Dutch population in South Africa."[5] This statement is hard to reconcile with a passage in a letter to the Prime Minister, dated 15 October 1876: "The progress of events in South Africa seems to bring a possible annexation of the Transvaal Republic and the consequent confederation of the various Colonies and States within sight."[6] Both statements of Carnarvon's to his fellow peers show an economy of truth; perhaps they can be explained, if hardly excused, as meaning that annexation formed no part of his original plan and that he would have preferred confederation to come about by the spontaneous act of a number of self-determining governments and peoples.

Carnarvon's claim that he had tried to conciliate the Afrikaners was justified. He had met Burgers in London on friendly terms in May 1875 and he had settled the boundary question with President Brand of the Orange Free State in July 1876, just as later on he was civil enough to Kruger and Jorissen.[7] But he believed that the Boers had been the aggressors in 1876, and the sequel had convinced him of the hopelessness of their system of government, at once oppressive,

[1] See de Kiewiet, *Imperial Factor*, pp. 109, 110.
[2] 30 May 1877, P.R.O. 30–6/23.   [3] 7 May 1877, *Hansard*, CCXXXIV, 354.
[4] 8 June 1877, *Parl. Pap.* 1877, LX [C. 1814], p. 5.
[5] 25 March 1879, *Hansard*, 3rd ser. CCXLIV, 1653.   [6] Buckle, VI, 415.
[7] Carnarvon to Barkly, 12 May 1875, Hardinge, II, 187; but cf. Uys, *op. cit.* p. 200; *Parl. Pap.* 1876, LII [C. 1631], p. 47; Hardinge, II, 271.

meddlesome and factious, incompetent in peace and war and financially ruinous. By November he had lost patience with them: "The cruelty and baseness of this little wretched Government ought not to be allowed to continue to the misery of those whom they oppress, and the danger of their neighbours."[1] The prospects of peace, order and solvency when Shepstone arrived at Pretoria with his twenty-five policemen were bleak enough, and it is possible that the majority of the people and even of the Volksraad might have come in time of their own free will to ask for a closer connection with the British Empire. But these eager, forceful Englishmen erred as Durham erred in his estimate of the French Canadians a generation before; in their hearts they despised the uncouth, backward Boers and failed to appreciate the persistence of their love for their old free way of life. Accordingly, instead of trying to tide them without loss of status over the crisis which indeed they had brought on themselves, they chose to exploit it and to take away their independence.[2]

Anxious to lose no opportunity which this swift movement of events might offer, Carnarvon brought forward in the autumn of 1876 a permissive bill for a South African union. The bill was first submitted to the criticism of the colonial governments and then redrafted in the light of it before being laid before Parliament. Drawn largely on the lines of the Canadian Act of 1867, it differed vitally from it in being the product of imperial, not local initiative. In asking Parliament not, as in 1867, to ratify an agreement arrived at in the colonies but to approve a rough scheme which the colonial legislatures might later adopt, Carnarvon quoted the precedent of the Queensland constitution; he justified the measure by the dangers of delay and the need to remove doubts in South Africa as to the nature of the confederation or union which Parliament would sanction. Among its most important provisions were those by which native affairs were placed within the exclusive competence of the central authority and all such legislation was to be reserved for the Queen's decision. It was the native question, as he told the Lords, which was the real difference between Canada and South Africa.[3] It was the native question too which aroused most interest in Parliament, and it must be repeated that it was their reputation for treating their Kaffirs harshly which lost the Boers the sympathy of many liberal-minded people in Great Britain.

Some time had elapsed since Parliament had debated South African

---

[1] Carnarvon to Ponsonby, 12 Nov. 1876, Hardinge, II, 240.

[2] For Shepstone's defence of his action in forcing the issue, see his private letter to Carnarvon, 23 July 1877, P.R.O. 30–6/23. For an interpretation hostile to Carnarvon, see Uys, esp. chap. vii; de Kiewiet, *Imperial Factor*, chap. v, is more balanced. There is reassessment of responsibilities, with a Bibliographical Note, by A. F. Hattersley in *History*, xx, no. 81 (June 1936), pp. 41–7.

[3] *Parl. Pap.* 1877, LX [C. 1732], esp. Carnarvon to Barkly, 14 Dec 1876; also House of Lords, 23 April 1877. House of Commons, 9 July 1877, *Hansard*, 3rd ser. CCXXXIII, 1645 *seqq.*, CCXXXV, 974 *seqq.*

affairs. More or less by accident, it would seem, Carnarvon's first confederation dispatch and its sequel had received no full discussion at the time,[1] and in 1876 interest was concentrated on the Near East. When the Permissive Bill was introduced in the Lords in April 1877 it was blessed by all speakers, though Grey as usual declared his conviction that responsible government was unsuitable for South Africa. When it reached the Commons in July, the annexation of the Transvaal had become known, and the two topics were discussed together. The Bill passed its second reading in a thin House and neither then nor in Committee, where the Irish Nationalists gave a foretaste of parliamentary obstruction, was there much opposition. Carnarvon believed that the Act "would go out to the Cape with greater weight than had been attached to any former measure relating to the Colonies".[2] The annexation too was generally approved. Leonard Courtney, who henceforward became its chief critic, found only one other speaker to give him rather lukewarm support in the contrary resolution which he moved just before the end of the session.[3] Anthony Trollope admitted to Shepstone that his deed had satisfied both the Government and the Opposition,[4] and Carnarvon could flatter himself that his bold step had been justified by results.

In the twelve months following, the exciting developments in the Near East, which led to Carnarvon's resignation in January 1878, completely overshadowed events in South Africa—the Kaffir war on the north-east frontier of Cape Colony, Frere's dismissal of the Molteno ministry, and the growing discontent in the Transvaal. Debates in the Commons at the end of the 1878 session on native administration in Natal and on Boer grievances produced no division and no great interest.[5] Even Courtney did not as yet suggest that the annexation could be reversed. But the Prime Minister was losing confidence in Carnarvon's policy, and Carnarvon's successor, Sir Michael Hicks Beach, was losing confidence in Shepstone.[6] It is possible that the actual annexation might have been forgiven and acquiesced in if the expectations aroused by Shepstone at the time had been fulfilled. But he showed a lack of constructive ability and of sympathy for the Afrikaners, and the troops and money hoped for from England were not forthcoming.[7] Nor were the free institutions: the immediate opportunity was lost and, though Hicks Beach's intentions were liberal, Boer disaffection and caution in Downing Street (the latter due largely to a desire not to prejudice Confederation) formed a

---

[1] See Hugessen, 24 July 1877, *Hansard*, 3rd ser. CCXXXV, 1744.
[2] 9 Aug. 1877, *Hansard*, 3rd ser. CCXXXVI, 651.
[3] House of Commons, 7 Aug. 1877, *Hansard*, 3rd ser. CCXXXVI, 545; see Gooch, G. P., *Life of Lord Courtney*.
[4] Uys, p. 406; Trollope visited South Africa in 1877; see his *South Africa*, published 1878.
[5] House of Commons, 26 July, 15 Aug. 1878, *Hansard*, 3rd ser. CCXLII, 451, 2061.
[6] Corry to Ponsonby, 13 April 1878, Buckle, VI, 419; Hicks Beach to Frere, 11 July 1878, Worsfold, W. B., *Sir B. Frere*, p. 76.
[7] See de Kiewiet, *Imperial Factor*, chap. v.

vicious circle. Perhaps the situation might have been saved had Frere felt able to visit the Transvaal earlier or been allowed to follow up his overtures to the Boers in April 1879. But the last chance was lost when Wolseley superseded him.

Sir Bartle Frere was sent out by Carnarvon in March 1877 as a public servant of tried ability and loyalty to consummate the policy of Confederation.[1] Recommended to the Queen for his humanity and interest in native welfare,[2] distinguished within a few months by his dismissal of a colonial ministry with a parliamentary majority, he was hailed after two years by the colonists as their champion against the native peril. In the course of 1878 he convinced himself that a combined movement was afoot among the tribes to drive the white men into the sea, and that the only sure method of defence was to attack and break the murderous militarism of the Zulus. Not till this had been achieved were peace and Confederation possible for South Africa. In the measures which he took towards this end in the last months of the year, culminating in the ultimatum sent to King Cetewayo on 11 December, he outran the approval of the Cabinet, whose eyes were fixed on Russia and Central Asia. The Cabinet had dreaded the prospect of a Zulu war.[3] They had been ready enough to give the Colonial Secretary his head so long as his policies made no serious demand on the national resources. But the Galeka outbreak had been annoying and Frere's repeated requests for troops, received in October and November, most untimely. The Cabinet had not foreseen how the Zulus would react to the annexation of the Transvaal, and it is unlikely that they had digested the voluminous subsequent correspondence, to say nothing of the private letters, exchanged between South Africa and Downing Street. The absence of telegraphic communication prevented the Secretary of State and High Commissioner from keeping one another abreast of the quick movements of events and changes of mental atmosphere in both Europe and South Africa, while Hicks Beach's inexperience made him reluctant to dispute a view pressed by the masterful man on the spot.[4] "I cannot really control him without a telegraph. (I don't know that I could with one)", he lamented to Beaconsfield.[5] On the other hand politicians in England forgot how long it took for their instructions to reach Frere, and inferred that this Governor did not possess what Salisbury, sore about Lytton and the Kabul mission, had called "the eccentric quality of obeying orders".[6] Had things run smoothly after the dis-

---

[1] See Martineau, J., *op. cit.* ii, chaps. xviii-xx; Worsfold, W. B., *Sir B. Frere.*
[2] Carnarvon to the Queen, 23 Nov. 1876, *Letters of Queen Victoria*, 2nd ser. ii, 502 n.
[3] Hicks Beach to Frere, 7, 28 Nov. (Private), 1878; Worsfold, *op. cit.* pp. 128, 137.
[4] Until December 1879 messages from London were telegraphed to Madeira or St Vincent and thence forwarded by mail steamer to Cape Town; the telegraph between Cape Town and Natal was finished in November 1878; Worsfold, p. 56.
[5] 3 Nov. 1878; Buckle, vi, 421.
[6] To Hicks Beach, 10 Oct. 1878; Hicks Beach, Lady V., *Sir M. Hicks Beach*, i, 72.

patch of reinforcements in November, Frere would no doubt have
been forgiven for forcing the pace,[1] but one day's fatal issue brought
the whole conduct of South African affairs under the fierce criticism
of Parliament and people.[2]

The diplomatic triumph of the summer of 1878, crowned by the
acquisition of Cyprus, stood out against a background of severe
industrial depression at home, and when Parliament was unexpectedly
summoned before Christmas it was asked to approve the Government's policy which had led to the Afghan War.[3] The Commons gave
this approval by a majority of 100 in a full House, and after the
Christmas recess the Prime Minister could claim that the new frontier
rendered the Indian Empire invulnerable. But he was addressing a
parliament which had reassembled under the shadow of a "terrible
military disaster".[4] The news of Isandhlwana, received in England on
11 February, marked a turning-point not only in the fortunes of the
Beaconsfield government but in the course of British colonial policy.
Followed as it was by the death, in Zululand, of the Prince Imperial
in June and the Kabul catastrophe in September, and compelling the
dispatch of costly reinforcements, it drew attention to the less pleasant
aspects of a forward policy and helped to disgust the nation with such
adventures.

In the country the news of Isandhlwana came as a severe shock;
there had been nothing like it, said the *Annual Register*,[5] since the
Mutiny. Discussion in Parliament was postponed until adequate
information could be laid before Members and until the Cabinet
could determine its attitude towards Frere. Eventually it was decided
to censure him for his precipitancy but not to recall him. The consequent dispatches were published,[6] whereupon the phrasing of the
votes of censure in both Houses, drafted by Sir Charles Dilke, was
recast to run:

That this House...regrets that the ultimatum which was calculated to produce
immediate war should have been presented to the Zulu King without authority
from the responsible advisers of the Crown, and that an offensive war should have
been commenced without imperative and pressing necessity or adequate pre-

---

[1] Hicks Beach to Beaconsfield, 13 Jan. 1879, Buckle, VI, 423.
[2] The events leading to the war are described in de Kiewiet, *op. cit.* chap. x and in
C.B.H.E. VIII, chap. xviii; for the campaign, see Coupland, Sir R., *Zulu Battle-Piece
(Isandhlwana)*. The published correspondence is in *Parl. Pap.* 1878, LVI [C. 2079],
[C. 2100], [C. 2220]; 1878–9, LII [C. 2220]; large extracts from the private correspondence
of Frere and Hicks Beach are in Worsfold, where the case for Frere is strongly argued.
See also letters in Buckle, *Disraeli*, vol. VI, and Hicks Beach, vol. I. Worsfold surmises
(p. 174) that Hicks Beach's "more accurate and sympathetic" dispatch of 23 Jan. 1879
was drafted by Herbert; it was in fact "dictated by Sir M. Hicks Beach"; P.R.O., C.O.
48/487.
[3] See *C.H.B.E.* v, chap. xxiii.
[4] 13 Feb. 1879; *Hansard*, 3rd ser. CCXLIII, 1042.
[5] 1879, p. 13.
[6] Hicks Beach to Frere, 19, 20 March 1879; *Parl. Pap.* 1878–9, LIII [C. 2260], pp. 109,
110.

paration; and this House further regrets that after the censure passed upon the High Commissioner by H.M. Government in the dispatch of the 19th day of March 1879 the conduct of affairs in South Africa should be retained in his hands.

The addition of the last sentence invited a straight party vote, but the Government majority in the Commons dropped to 60; it was the first important division on a colonial matter in the 1874 parliament.[1]

Nearly every speaker in the Commons agreed that Frere had erred from excess of zeal in presenting his ultimatum, but there was a deep cleavage of opinion on the policy behind the ultimatum, whether in fact the war was a just war or had been forced on the Zulus aggressively. On this vital point, so the Opposition claimed, the Government had not declared themselves; as Gladstone asserted later, they had hedged, preferring to await the outcome.[2] The censure of Frere, some critics urged, had been a mere sop to public anger after Isandhlwana, whereas the real feelings of the Ministry were shown by his retention in office. Hartington later in the session expressed the view of other critics in saying that what was objectionable was not so much the policy of the Government as its execution being entrusted to men who did not believe in it or obey it.[3] In fact the Cabinet were incensed by Frere's high-handedness which landed them in such difficulties, and it was only the resistance of Beaconsfield and Hicks Beach, encouraged by the Queen, which prevented his recall.[4]

In May the Cabinet insisted, against the Queen's remonstrances, in sending out Wolseley as "dictator" over Natal and the Transvaal and the native territories to the north and east.[5] Public opinion had become impatient as the unpopular war dragged on and uneasy as to the terms which might be imposed on the Zulus. The Cabinet were now thoroughly frightened of annexations, even to the extent of approving Wolseley's partition of Zululand among thirteen semi-independent chiefs, an arrangement which postponed annexation, if it had no other merits.[6] Frere meanwhile was retained at the Cape, particularly with a view to the achievement of Confederation, on which Hicks Beach was still set[7] and to which a reference was included in the Queen's Speech at the opening of the 1880 session. But in fact the last hope of Afrikaner co-operation had been killed when authority to negotiate with the Transvaal Boers was transferred from Frere to Wolseley.[8]

[1] House of Lords, 25 March, House of Commons, 27, 28, 31 March 1879, *Hansard*, 3rd ser. CCXLIV, 1606, 1865; Gwynn, S. and Tuckwell, G. M., *Life of Sir C. W. Dilke*, I, 273.
[2] 25 Nov. 1879; *Political Speeches in Scotland*, I, 36.
[3] 26 May 1879; *Hansard*, 3rd ser. CCXLVI, 1263.
[4] Hicks Beach to Frere, 13 March 1879; Hicks Beach, *op. cit.* I, 128–30; *Letters of Queen Victoria*, 2nd ser. III, 11, 13.
[5] Beaconsfield to the Queen, 19, 23, 27 March 1879, Buckle, VI, 428–33; *Letters of Queen Victoria*, 2nd ser. III, 24–6; Hicks Beach, *op. cit.* I, 134–7; *Parl. Pap.* 1878–9, LIII [C. 2318], p. 83.
[6] See *C.H.B.E.*, VIII, p. 479.
[7] E.g. Hicks Beach to Wolseley, 19 Feb. 1880; *Parl. Pap.* 1880, L [C. 2505].
[8] *C.H.B.E.* VIII, 482; de Kiewiet, *Imperial Factor*, pp. 236–45.

As for the Transvaal, Hicks Beach had admitted privately in May that "we *could* not keep it by force of bayonets against the wish of a large majority of the white population";[1] the official attitude, however, was still the same: the annexation must stand, but the Boers could regain self-government under the South Africa Act. A provisional constitution was at length vouchsafed for the interval, but as its Legislative Assembly contained no elected members at all it made no appeal to the burghers.[2] On the Opposition side, while a Radical group encouraged the malcontent Boers by their sympathy, Hartington pronounced that the annexation should not be considered a settled question.[3]

As the thoughts of politicians were now centred on the impending general election, the issues at stake began to emerge clearly. The vivid external policy of the Government had aroused questionings as to the nature and purpose of Empire, and in 1877, 1878 and 1879 the Reviews were full of controversial articles on this topic, the Liberals accusing their rivals of a new aggressive spirit of aggrandisement. Blachford was anxious about native welfare: "A few men of superior intelligence, with an Anglo-Saxon desire to make fortunes, cannot, from the nature of the case, be trusted to take care of the often conflicting interests of an inferior race."[4] On the question of expansion he wrote privately in 1877: "I think it very likely that our resolute indisposition to annex up to 1871 was incapable of being maintained, and that we had run up a kind of arrear of necessity in that way. But I still look with a certain distrust on our accessions of responsibility in West Africa, Fiji, the Straits and South Africa."[5] Since then we had taken Cyprus, had broken up Zululand and Afghanistan, and had started on the Dual Control in Egypt. Gladstone dreaded a British occupation of Egypt, holding that "as a general rule, enlargements of the Empire are for us an evil fraught with serious, though possibly not with immediate danger", owing to their demands on our limited manpower. "The root and pith and substance", he declared in words that summed up the Little England creed, "of the material greatness of our nation lies within the compass of these islands, and is, except in trifling particulars, independent of all and every sort of political dominion beyond them." And on the less material side, true to his ancient faith that the glory of the British Empire lay in rearing up "free congenital communities" overseas, he scorned the value attached to "the administrative connection, and the shadow of political subordination", by the party "who at home as well as abroad

---

[1] To Frere, 29 May 1879; Hicks Beach, *op. cit.* I, 140.
[2] Hicks Beach to Wolseley, 20 Nov. 1879, enclosing Letters Patent, *Parl. Pap.* 1880, L [C. 2482], p. 378.
[3] House of Commons, 5 Feb. 1880, *Hansard*, 3rd ser. CCL, 92.
[4] *Edinburgh Review*, April 1877, p. 482.
[5] To Sir H. Taylor, 28 May 1877; Marindin, G. E., *Letters of Lord Blachford*, p. 380.

are striving to cajole or drive us into Imperialism".[1] The word was out and came rapidly into use.[2] It must indeed have been used already, since in September 1877 Gladstone's "anti-imperialist theory of English statecraft" was challenged eloquently by Edward Dicey.[3] Sir Julius Vogel, referring to the sudden *volte-face* of the Liberal Government in the spring of 1870 and asserting that the Liberals were still indifferent to the Empire, rejoiced that a new spirit had entered Downing Street since Herbert replaced Blachford, but he pleaded for practical measures which should prepare the way for imperial confederation.[4] Carnarvon, in an academic address on "Imperial Administration", spoke of the duty set by Imperialism to breathe "a common unity" into the mighty mass of the British peoples: to promote self-government in the Anglo-Saxon colonies and to help the races "struggling to emerge into civilization".[5]

The great debate reached its climax on the Liberal side in Gladstone's Scottish campaigns in the autumn of 1879 and the following spring, though it was the Government's foreign, rather than its colonial, policy which he most fiercely attacked.[6] But by now the country was sick of annexations, as the Cabinet realised. "You can hardly imagine", wrote Hicks Beach, "the reluctance to agree to anything that could by any possibility be twisted into a charge of extension of territory in South Africa."[7] A year before this he had remained deaf to Frere's exhortations to annex the whole coastline as far north as the Portuguese frontiers, east and west. "A South African Dominion, once firmly and strongly established," he wrote in 1880, "may shape, and bear the brunt of, its own policy—but would, I should think, for some time to come be rather in need of consolidation than extension."[8] He had not allowed, however, for Lüderitz and Bismarck.[9]

In the meantime the colonies with large populations of European stock continued their march towards complete self-government in domestic affairs, Canada leading the way. These colonies were not greatly affected by the play of parties at Westmister nor even by

[1] *Nineteenth Century*, August 1877, II, 151, 153; Sept. 1878, IV, 571.
[2] Lowe in the *Fortnightly Review* of October 1878, new ser. XXIV, 453, referred to "what in the language of our Secretaries of State is called 'Imperialism'", speaking also of "this new and most unacceptable addition to our vocabulary". Next year, in the debate on Dilke's Vote of Censure, Joseph Chamberlain protested against "this new Imperialism of the Government"; *Hansard*, 3rd ser. CCXLIV, 1916.
[3] *Nineteenth Century*, II, 293.
[4] *Ibid.* July 1877, April 1878, I, 809; III, 617; Vogel had till recently been Premier of New Zealand.
[5] *Fortnightly Review*, Dec. 1878.
[6] *Political Speeches in Scotland.*
[7] To Frere, 20 Nov. 1879, Hicks Beach, *op. cit.* I, 164.
[8] To Frere, 14 Nov. 1878 (Conf.), 15 Jan. 1880, *ibid.* I, 93, 162. See minutes in P.R.O., C.O. 48/486 on Frere's Confidential dispatches of 5 Sept. 1878.
[9] See *C.H.B.E.* VIII, 515.

changing personalities at Downing Street, and in turn their concerns, after 1870, hardly rippled the surface of politics at home. Imperial legislation for a colony was not passed against a colony's wish, but it was not always forthcoming at a colony's request. We have seen with what difficulty the Australasian colonies extorted from Gladstone the repeal of the restriction on differential duties; Hicks Beach was not disposed to submit to Parliament a contentious Bill to reform the constitution of Victoria as desired by the Lower House.[1] Disallowance was virtually a thing of the past, though Kimberley disallowed one Canadian Act as *ultra vires* and Carnarvon was prepared to disallow a Cape Act in the course of the Langalibalele dispute.[2] Hicks Beach told the Commons in 1879 that though the Government regretted Canada's increased tariff they considered that her fiscal policy was her own affair.[3] In other matters, too, Secretaries of State were reluctant to embroil themselves in colonial politics. Kimberley shrank from urging Dufferin to get rid of the discredited Macdonald ministry in 1873;[4] Carnarvon, while he aroused Molteno's wrath by taking the initiative in the matter of Confederation—a matter which, seeing that two independent republics besides other colonies were involved, might well seem to invite imperial initiative—was most unwilling to intervene unasked in Canadian politics in 1874, though his intervention proved of great value.[5] In 1876 Carnarvon was glad to meet Blake's proposals for whittling down the Governor-General's responsibilities in the reservation of Bills, and in both Canada and Australasia his rulings on the future exercise of the prerogative of mercy found general acceptance.[6]

The function of the Secretary of State had in fact reduced itself mainly to appointing and, in rare cases, removing Governors, to advising them, both officially and confidentially, to conveying private approval or rebuke, to supporting or censuring them in public.[7] Lord Dufferin, Whig magnate as he was, proved a model Governor-General. To succeed him in Canada Hicks Beach had the happy idea of proposing the Queen's son-in-law, the Marquess of Lorne.[8] Sir George Bowen, almost a professional Governor, who presided over five different colonies in succession, was blamed by Granville for pleading the New Zealand cause too partially and was thought by Hicks Beach to have yielded too far to his headstrong ministers

---

[1] *Parl. Pap.* 1878–9, LI [C. 2217], p. 20.
[2] An Act to enable committees of the Canadian legislature to examine witnesses on oath; Kimberley to Dufferin, 30 June 1873, *Parl. Pap.* 1874, XLV [C. 911]; Carnarvon to Barkly, 4 Dec. 1874, *Parl. Pap.* LIII [C. 1121].
[3] 20 March 1879, *Hansard*, 3rd ser. CCXLIV, 1312.
[4] To Ponsonby, 18 Nov. 1873, *Letters of Queen Victoria*, 2nd ser. II, 292.
[5] Molteno, P. A., *Life and Times of Sir J. C. Molteno*, I, 334; Hardinge, II, 114–23.
[6] *C.H.B.E.* VI, 487; Todd, A., *Parliamentary Government in the British Colonies* (1880), pp. 77–82, 255–74; *Parl. Pap.* 1875, LIII [C. 1202], [C. 1248].
[7] See Wilson, E. D. J., "What is a Colonial Governor?" in *Nineteenth Century*, Dec. 1878.
[8] Hicks Beach, *op. cit.* I, 64.

in Victoria.[1] Frere, the great Indian Civil Servant, was upheld by Hicks Beach, as well as by the Cape legislature and electorate, when he dismissed Molteno in February 1878 for his wrong-headed behaviour in the mismanagement of the Galeka war;[2] of his censure a year later enough has been said already.

In Frere's case imperial interests were clearly involved, and of these for another half-century the Governor was recognised as the guardian. In his other function, as spokesman for his colony to the mother country, he was now reinforced, particularly in economic affairs, by the Agent-General maintained (by several colonies) in London. It was part of these officials' duties to look after their colonies' interests when discussions with foreign countries were afoot, and in 1879 the Canadian Government proposed that their representative should be given the more honourable title of "Resident Minister" with a "quasi-diplomatic status".[3] The Government in London were willing enough to change the title, though preferring "Commissioner" to "Minister", but the Foreign Secretary saw difficulties in conceding the substance of the demand. It is true that Canada was officially represented on the Commission which negotiated the Treaty of Washington in 1871,[4] but Salisbury was averse to allowing the Dominion a formal right to participate in treaty-making or to allowing its agent any official connection with the Foreign Office. He was emphatic on the wholly disproportionate burdens of responsibility which a treaty then entailed to the colony and to the mother country.

> In any treaty we make with foreign States, in which Canada is interested, it is our influence that gets the treaty made, it is our strength that has to enforce it, it is we who must bear the brunt if Canada breaks it on her side. That in addition she should ask to have machinery constructed to enable her to decide on its terms, is a little too much.[5]

In the event a compromise was reached on "High Commissioner of Canada in London".

By such methods of give and take, of trial and error, and by force of circumstances new conventions and institutions were devised to fit new facts in the relations between the self-governing units of the Empire. The future meaning of the explosive words "nationality" and "independence" was left to the future to determine. The process was commended to some by an abstract love of liberty, to others by a desire to shed financial and military responsibility. The wish to share

---

[1] E.g. Granville to Bowen, 25 March 1879 (Conf.), C.O. 209/215; *Parl. Pap.* 1878, LVI [C. 2173], p. 99. Bowen weathered the storm and before he left could assure Hicks Beach that the colony was quiet and intent on amusements, especially "the cricket match played between the English XI, of which Lord Harris is Captain, and the Australian XI"; *Parl. Pap.* 1878–9, LI [C. 2339], p. 15.

[2] Hicks Beach to Frere, 21 March 1878; *Parl. Pap.* 1878, LVI [C. 2079], p. 124. Cf. Molteno, *op. cit.* II, chaps. xxviii, xxix.

[3] *Parl. Pap.* 1880, XLIX [C. 2594]. See Todd, *op. cit.* p. 184.

[4] See *Parl. Pap.* 1872, XLIII [C. 539].

[5] To Hicks Beach, 8 Aug. 1879; Hicks Beach, *op. cit.* I, 67.

burdens, as well as the wish to arrest disintegration and to pool resources, was strong in the movement for imperial federation which was beginning to find advocates not in one party only.[1]

The fact was that twenty years' drift had been challenged and checked: improved communications, economic pressure, rash words of politicians, changes in the Balance of Power had all played their part. Disraeli had pointed a more excellent way to Conservatives; on the other side Whigs, like Clarendon, were yielding to idealists, like Forster, not unworthy of the Durham tradition. Moreover, this new interest in the overseas territories had spread to include the colonies with non-European populations where the problems were so much more acute: it was excited by exploration, by gold and diamonds, by new markets, by the competition of other Powers and by a reluctant discovery that the responsibilities of government cannot be limited at will. But here there was less agreement. The views of "prancing proconsuls" such as Frere and Wolseley were hateful to large numbers of the Liberal party which triumphed at the polls in 1880.[2] Nevertheless in this matter, as in much else, the Queen was a true representative of her people when she sought to warn them: "Our position in India and the Colonies *must* be *upheld*. I wish to *trust my* Government whoever it is, but they should be *well aware* beforehand I never could if they intended to *try* and *undo* what has been done."[3]

[1] E.g. Forster, W. E., *Our Colonial Empire*, 1875; Vogel, J., *Nineteenth Century*, July 1877, April 1878. See Bodelsen, *Studies in Mid-Victorian Imperialism*, p. 114; Tyler, J. E., *The Struggle for Imperial Unity*, chap. x.
[2] W. V. Harcourt's phrase; Gardiner, A. G., *Life*, I, 350.
[3] The Queen to the Marchioness of Ely, 21 Sept. 1879, *Letters*, 2nd ser. III, 48.

CHAPTER III

THE OPENING OF TROPICAL AFRICA, 1870–1885

BETWEEN 1788 and 1870, the knowledge of Tropical Africa by Europeans made very great progress. Its coasts were carefully surveyed by Owen in 1821–6.[1] Inland, the courses of three of the four great rivers—the Niger, the Zambezi and the Nile—were traced, and much was learnt about their basins. Moreover, a good deal was now known of the northern and southern frontiers of Tropical Africa, the Sahara and the Kalahari Deserts, through the work of Barth, Livingstone and other travellers.[2]

Yet all this great effort amounted to no more than a beginning. Even in the regions that had been traversed and described by explorers, there were geographical problems that remained unsolved. It is strange to realise that Speke's claim, which we now know to be true, that he had found the main source of the Nile was doubted even by Livingstone,[3] who devoted much of his failing energy on his last journey to a search for the fountains described by Herodotus, in which he still believed the river rose. Away from the course taken by the travellers, everything was uncertain: the maps could show nothing but blank spaces, or dotted lines with question-marks. The outline of the structure of Tropical Africa was still known only in the most general terms; and even that statement is open to the great qualification that in 1870 nothing whatever was known of the basin of the Congo, which is geographically the heart of it all.

The 1866 edition of Stanford's *Library Map of Africa* makes this strikingly clear. It shows the centre of the continent as a complete blank, from the French settlements near the mouth of the Gaboon across to the incomplete outline of Lake Albert Nyanza, from Darfur southward to the upper reaches of the Kasai, which Livingstone had visited in 1854 and 1855. Again, in the west, the hinterland of Sierra Leone, Liberia and the Gold Coast is almost entirely white.

If one looks at a political map of Tropical Africa in 1870, this state of affairs will be less surprising. On the west coast a narrow strip of territory is variously coloured to indicate possession by Britain, France, the Netherlands, Spain and Portugal. The United States took a very remote interest in the Republic of Liberia. In East Africa the only European Power that pretended to any sovereignty was Portugal. But these claims hardly amounted to what we should now call an

[1] Owen, W. F., *Narrative of Voyages to Explore the Shores of Africa, Arabia and Madagascar* (1833).
[2] Cf. *C.H.B.E.* II, chap. xvii.
[3] *The Last Journals of David Livingstone* (1874), II, 50–1.

effective occupation. The Europeans might genuinely govern the towns or forts that were their bases. Outside them—within a mile or two of Cape Coast Castle or Lagos—the Africans retained full control, subject to no more than the most general supervision by Europeans, which became active only in case of affray or riot.

Economically, the situation was somewhat different. In this field, the opening and exploitation of Tropical Africa had already been seriously begun. The export trade in palm-products had developed rapidly in the first half of the nineteenth century, and by the 'fifties it had become firmly established. It then suffered a set-back, largely owing to the discovery of petroleum in Pennsylvania in 1860 and the appearance of India as a rival producer of oil-nuts and seeds. For the rest of the century, production remained stable at 40,000–50,000 tons a year and the price fell, until in 1896–1900 it was less than half what it had been in 1856–60.[1] None the less it was a valuable trade. Its statistics are uncertain, for the greater part of it went out by the ports in the "Oil Rivers", which were beyond the control of European customs officials; but taking only the fraction that passed through the British colony of Lagos, its value amounted in 1870 to £419,034, rising in the next year to £500,555.[2] Nor were palm-products the only new commodity that was being developed by Europeans, in place of the defunct slave trade. Driven by the American Civil War to look for new sources of supply of cotton, Europe had turned to West Africa, and in 1868–70 Lagos exported 1,000,000 lb. a year to Britain.[3]

The British West African colonies showed a favourable balance of trade in 1870: the combined value of their imports was £934,820, of their exports £1,243,093.[4] This trade was in the hands of a number of quite small firms, mainly of Liverpool and London, together with African "middlemen", whose power and importance were becoming increasingly great. Combination among these interests had not yet begun.

The volume of British trade with East Africa is harder to assess. On that coast, north of Cape Delgado, there were no ports under European control. The commercial centre of the whole of eastern Tropical Africa was Zanzibar, the capital of the Arab sultanate, and, as the British Vice-Consul there, John Kirk, wrote in 1871, "it is impossible to obtain accurate and reliable statistics of the trade of Zanzibar, every one being interested in representing the imports and exports as less than they actually are".[5] But one thing is clear beyond dispute. The volume of British trade with this region was rapidly increasing, and if the British Indian trade is added, it outstripped that of any other state, though German, American and French firms had also

---

[1] McPhee, A., *The Economic Revolution in British West Africa* (1926), p. 33.
[2] *Parl. Pap.* 1884–5, LXXXIII [C. 4520], pp. 242–3. Cf. Diké, K. O., *Trade and Politics in the Niger Delta, 1830–85* (1956) especially chap. VI.   [3] McPhee, *op. cit.* p. 45.
[4] *Parl. Pap.* 1884–5, LXXXIII [C. 4225], pp. 116–20.
[5] *Parl. Pap.* 1872, LIV [C. 657], p. 783.

an important share in it.[1] The largest item of import was always cotton goods; the biggest exports, of ivory, cloves and slaves—in that order. Here, again, the trade had not fallen into the hands of great combines, though some of the Indian *banyans* had built up very large fortunes out of East Africa. One firm was proved to have £430,000 invested in the country.[2]

Apart from the traders, the explorers, and a very small number of administrators, the only Europeans who visited Tropical Africa were missionaries. Christian missions had been established there since the sixteenth century. In British territory, apart from the efforts of a few isolated pioneers in the eighteenth century,[3] the work was begun by the Church Missionary Society, founded in 1799 under the title "the Society for Missions to Africa and the East".[4] Its first field of work had been Sierra Leone, but in 1846 it established the Yoruba Mission, in quite new territory, at Abeokuta, fifty miles inland from Lagos;[5] and in 1857 Bishop Crowther founded the Niger Mission with its principal stations at Onitsha and Lokoja.[6] The Wesleyans, the Baptists, the United Presbyterian Church of Scotland, the Basel and Bremen Missions, and the Roman Catholics also maintained small establishments in the British West African territories.[7] The London Missionary Society, after a brief and disastrous venture in Sierra Leone in 1797–8,[8] had confined its attention to Cape Colony, Bechuanaland and Matabeleland.

In mid-East Africa the pioneers of missionary effort were the three Germans Krapf, Rebmann and Ehrhardt, who worked from a base at Mombasa from 1844 onwards, under the auspices of the Church Missionary Society.[9] But though they did much to extend the geographical knowledge of that country in Europe, their success, judged from a strictly missionary point of view, was slight. The main impulse behind mission work in East Africa came not from them but from Livingstone.[10]

His great journey of 1852–6[11] and his Zambezi expedition of 1858–64[12] had revealed to him, and so to the world, the horrors of the slave trade in the interior. His appeal for missionaries to undertake the evangelisation of the country led to the founding of the Universities'

[1] Coupland, R., *The Exploitation of East Africa* (1939), pp. 77–81; Hieke, E., *Zur Geschichte des deutschen Handels mit Ostafrika*, 1 (1939), 233, 282.
[2] Coupland, *op. cit.* p. 202.
[3] Cf. Ward, W. E. F., *A History of the Gold Coast* (1948), pp. 193–6.
[4] Stock, E., *History of the Church Missionary Society* (1899), 1, 71.
[5] *Ibid.* 1, 458. Cf. Tucker, Miss S., *Abbeokuta; or, Sunrise within the Tropics* (1853).
[6] Stock, *op. cit.* 11, 450–60.
[7] Latourette, K. S. *A History of the Expansion of Christianity*, v (1943), 439, 446–7; Gray, J. M., *A History of the Gambia* (1940), pp. 384–5.
[8] Lovett, R., *The History of the London Missionary Society* (1899), 1, 477–80.
[9] Stock, *op. cit.* 1, 459–62; 11, 124–36.
[10] Cf. Oliver, R., *The Missionary Factor in East Africa* (1952), p. 7.
[11] *C.H.B.E.* 11, 628.   [12] *Ibid.* 11, 629–30.

Mission to Central Africa in 1858–9. Under Bishop Mackenzie, the Mission established itself on the Zambezi; but after his death in 1862 it was transferred by his successor, Bishop Tozer, to Zanzibar. This step was scornfully condemned by Livingstone, who underestimated the gravity of the difficulties that confronted the mission in its original territory. Yet, in the circumstances, it was probably the right decision to take.

Livingstone himself was soon obliged to leave the lower Zambezi, on the recall of his expedition by the Foreign Office. His third journey (1866–73) lay further to the north, in the country between Lake Tanganyika and the River Lualaba, which Livingstone believed to be the upper Nile. When he died by Lake Bangweulu on 1 May 1873, it was in the bitter knowledge that the Arab slave trade still flourished and that the geographical problems he had set out to solve remained unanswered.[1]

Yet his work did not really end in failure. His exposure of the horrors of the East African slave trade did more than anything else to bring it to an end. In the 1850's it was assumed, even by humanitarians in Britain, that the slave trade was being steadily abolished: that its total destruction depended solely on the full co-operation of the French and American Governments—and that appeared at length to be forthcoming.[2] This view, however, took in only the slave trade across the Atlantic. A few well-informed people were aware that another great branch of the slave trade was still in existence, running up the East African coast. But it was only when Livingstone, with his unique prestige and authority, drew the attention of his countrymen to it on his visits home in 1856–8 that its magnitude came to be generally realised. He was loyally and ably supported by the missionaries and by successive British consuls at Zanzibar. It was there, indeed, that the solution of the problem lay, for the Arab Sultan of Zanzibar was the political suzerain of the whole coast north of Cape Delgado, and the Zanzibar slave-market was the centre on which the entire trade converged. By treaties signed with the British Government in 1822 and 1845,[3] the Sultan had agreed to restrict the slave trade and to allow a British naval squadron to operate on the coast, supplementing his own forces, which were quite insufficient to police it. Under further British pressure, the Sultan issued decrees in 1862, 1864 and 1868, restricting the trade still further and expressly forbidding all transport of slaves during the four months of the southwest monsoon—the period when they were most easily shipped to the Arabian coast.[4]

[1] *C.H.B.E.* II, 630–1; Simmons, J., *Livingstone and Africa* (1955), pp. 118–52.
[2] For the ending of the Atlantic slave trade see *C.H.B.E.* II, 662–3, 670–1, 853–5; Mathieson, W. L., *Great Britain and the Slave Trade* (1929), chaps. v and vi; Coupland, R., *The British Anti-Slavery Movement* (1933), chap. vi.
[3] *C.H.B.E.* II, 576–8; Coupland, *East Africa and its Invaders* (1938), pp. 215, 514–15.
[4] Coupland, *The Exploitation of East Africa*, pp. 157–9.

These measures were, however, inadequate: they were imperfectly enforced, and they still left a considerable field within which the slave-traders could legally operate. In 1870 the British Government began to face the necessity of direct action, to destroy the whole trade. A new Sultan, Barghash, had just succeeded in Zanzibar, and he was at once invited to assent to much more stringent measures.[1] He refused. Thereupon the government appointed a Parliamentary Committee to inquire into the whole subject, and its report (dated 4 August 1871) recommended that "all legitimate means should be used to put an end altogether to the East African slave trade".[2] Sir Bartle Frere was then sent out to negotiate a treaty with the Sultan for its abolition. Barghash was very awkwardly placed. He wished to remain on good terms with the British government, following the traditional policy of his predecessors for two generations past. But the prohibition of the slave trade would be bitterly unpopular with his own subjects, to whom it was a part of the natural economic and social order; and it would mean a substantial loss in his own revenue, for slaves imported into Zanzibar were subject to customs duty. In the end he decided, once again, to refuse his signature to the treaty proposed by the British Government. "We cannot sign it", he wrote to Frere, "on account of the hardship which it involves to us; on account of dread of insurrection; and on account of the ruin which it would cause to the plantations of our subjects."[3]

Barghash's determination was partly influenced by clandestine support from the American and French consuls.[4] Less than a month after the news reached London, the British government decided to force the Sultan to sign the treaty, threatening him with a blockade of Zanzibar if he continued to refuse. On 5 June 1873 he gave way, and the treaty was concluded.[5] It was designed to prohibit the sea-borne trade in slaves entirely. The great Zanzibar slave-market was shut down the same day.

Having signed the treaty, under *force majeure*, Barghash loyally attempted to see that its provisions were observed. The main agency for enforcing them was the British naval squadron on the coast. The Sultan gave it his full support and three years later, on 18 April 1876, he completed the official banning of the slave trade by issuing two proclamations against the trade by land.[6] Thereafter, though an illicit traffic continued and the smuggling of slaves went on until slavery itself was abolished, under the British Protectorate, at Zanzibar in 1897, the East African slave trade was doomed.

It is not easy to estimate the importance of the economic change that this involved. The statistics of the slave trade are notoriously

[1] Coupland, *The Exploitation of East Africa*, p. 165.
[2] *Parl. Pap.* 1871, XII (420), p. 8.   [3] *Parl. Pap.* 1873, LXI [C. 820], p. 840.
[4] Coupland, *The Exploitation of East Africa*, pp. 193–7.
[5] *B.F.S.P.* LXIII (1872–3), 173–4.
[6] *Ibid.* LXVII (1875–6), 455–6; Coupland, *The Exploitation of East Africa*, pp. 211–26.

unreliable. This is true of those of the Atlantic trade even while it was still legitimate.[1] At Zanzibar, where the records were imperfectly kept and so many people had reason to conceal their share in the trade, our information is open to doubt at every point. But it was generally accepted by British observers that the slave-tax realised some £20,000 a year.[2] This did not go directly to the Sultan, for the customs revenue was farmed. But as in 1870 the whole farm stood at £72,842,[3] it can be seen that the slave-tax was an important factor in the Sultan's budget. Kirk, who studied the matter closely, assessed the value of the slaves brought into Zanzibar for sale in the financial year 1867–8 at £56,000,[4] and the profits of the slave-traders at the mainland port of Kilwa in 1873–6 at £120,000 a year.[5] Attempts to estimate the magnitude of the East African slave trade as a whole were bound to be guess-work,[6] and they must be treated with great caution. But if it is impossible to express the volume of the trade in valid statistics, its importance in the economy of the region can nevertheless be accurately appreciated. No one doubted that slaves ranked with ivory and cloves as the leading articles of export from Zanzibar. Now cloves, as an agricultural crop, were subject to the fluctuations of seasons and the varying demands of the market. And ivory, though it commanded a steadily high price, could be transported from the interior to the coast only by human porterage—since the tsetse-fly made it impossible to use beasts of burden, and no railways had yet been built. Slaves provided the only porterage that was cheap. The destruction of the slave trade meant, therefore, a direct threat to the ivory trade as well.

Its ending was due more to Livingstone than to anyone; and it is ironical that he should have died just too soon to see it—five weeks before the treaty of 1873 was signed. His geographical work, too, was completed by others. The last months of his life had been spent in a tenacious endeavour to regain the River Lualaba and explore its course: to find out if it rose in Herodotus's "fountains" and whether it turned itself into the Nile or the Congo lower down. The effort was beyond his strength: but it was the crucial problem of the time in Central African geography, and he pointed the way to its solution. V. L. Cameron, who was sent out by the Royal Geographical Society in 1872 to assist him, met Livingstone's dead body at Tabora as it was being conveyed by his African bearers to the coast.[7] He did not

---

[1] Some problems in handling the material that is available are discussed in Hyde, F. E., Parkinson, B. B., and Marriner, S., "The Nature and Profitability of the Liverpool Slave Trade", *Economic Hist. Rev.* 2nd ser. v (1953), pp. 368–77.
[2] *Parl. Pap.* 1871, XII (420), QQ.23, 360.
[3] *Ibid.* 1872, LIV [C. 657], p. 782.
[4] *Ibid.* 1871, XII (420) Q.361.
[5] Kirk to Derby, 18 May 1876: F.O. 84/1453.
[6] *Parl. Pap.* 1871, XII (420), pp. 5, 6, 139, QQ.23, 304, 360, 685.
[7] Cameron, V. L., *Across Africa* (1877), I, 165–8.

turn back with it, but made his way westward into the country towards which Livingstone was struggling when he died. He reached
the Lualaba at Nyangwe and, from the levels he obtained there, at
once rejected Livingstone's view that it was the upper Nile. Instead,
he expressed the strong opinion that it was the Congo.[1] But he could
get no canoes for further exploration from Nyangwe; and accordingly
he turned south, in company with the slave-trader Tipu Tib, towards
Katanga, the country of the copper mines. He did not actually
penetrate to Katanga, but passed to the west of it, climbing up to
cross the Angolan highlands. At Dilolo he struck the route Livingstone had taken, marching up from the Zambezi in 1854; but, rather
than follow in Livingstone's track to the west coast at Loanda, he
made for Benguela, much along the line now taken by the railway,
arriving there in November 1875. It was a great journey, made in
the teeth of constant difficulties, and the book in which it was described
won a justly high repute: "the most exact and unimpeachably accurate of African travellers" was the verdict passed on him by one of
his successors in the same field of exploration.[2]

Cameron's journey, then, was a consequence of Livingstone's
work. It furnished a valuable account of a large region hitherto quite
unvisited by Europeans. But the map that he himself published in
his book shows how little was yet known of the heart of Africa.
Neither Livingstone nor he had travelled down the Lualaba from
Nyangwe; and though Cameron hit upon the truth when he asserted
that it was the Congo or one of its affluents, he had no idea of the
course that the river took. He showed it as flowing a little south of
west, through a lake named Sankorra, of which he had heard at
Nyangwe, to run out into the Atlantic by the Congo, whose mouth
had been known to the Portuguese since the fifteenth century and
whose lower course had been explored by Tuckey in 1816.[3] Cameron's
"Lake Sankorra" was no more than what we know as the River
Sankuru, which flows into the Congo by way of the Kasai; and the
Lualaba in fact flows northward, not west, for more than 300 miles
from Nyangwe before it slowly wheels round in its great arc towards
the Atlantic.

Livingstone directly inspired the solution of the problem. At the
close of his life, in 1872, he had been relieved by H. M. Stanley, an
American journalist who had been sent to "find" him by the *New
York Herald*. Stanley's story was at first doubted when he arrived back
in Europe,[4] but his achievement quickly won generous recognition.
For a time he returned to the normal work of a journalist. He was
special correspondent for his paper with the British army in the

[1] *Ibid.* ii, 110.
[2] Bateman, C. J. L., *The First Ascent of the Kasai* (1889), p. 78.
[3] *C.H.B.E.* ii, 618-19.
[4] Coupland, *Livingstone's Last Journey* (1945), pp. 203-4.

Ashanti War of 1873–4. It was on his way back to the United States from that assignment that he heard the news of Livingstone's death. He changed his course for London, attended Livingstone's funeral in Westminster Abbey, and persuaded the *Daily Telegraph* and the *New York Herald*, acting jointly, to send him out to Central Africa again with the express object of completing Livingstone's work. The journey that resulted is the greatest, in point of mileage, ever undertaken by an African explorer. In the course of it, between November 1874 and August 1877, he travelled round the whole coast of Lake Victoria Nyanza, proving that it was a single great lake, as Speke had always maintained against Livingstone, Burton and others, who had argued that it was a chain of smaller ones; he completed the circumnavigation of Lake Tanganyika and then, following Livingstone across to Nyangwe, he sailed straight down the Lualaba-Congo to the sea.[1]

Stanley had triumphantly attained his object. He had completed Livingstone's geographical work, and much more. He had displayed great tenacity and fortitude, and an almost superhuman energy, which had enabled him to complete his task at a speed that even now seems incredible. But if, beside him, other African travellers appear to move at a snail's pace, it must be remembered that he had large funds at his disposal, where most others—Livingstone above all—were poor; that he had under him a great company of bearers—356 at the outset[2]—and that he was always ready to fight his way through as he encountered hostility, where most of his great predecessors had worked by patient and peaceful negotiation.

On his return to Europe, Stanley at once interested himself in the political and economic exploitation of his vast discovery. He turned first to the governments, the capitalists and the traders of Great Britain and the United States. But he found no warm or effective response in either country. The British refusal to sponsor Stanley's project is instructive. Political responsibility for it rests not on the Liberals but on the imperially-minded administration of Disraeli. It shows how strongly determined the Government and the Foreign Office were to adhere to the policy of 1865,[3] avoiding all new commitments in tropical Africa, while maintaining and defending those that had already been undertaken.

But the decision was not solely a political one. Stanley found no energetic financial or economic support either. He made his appeal at an unlucky moment: there was war in the Balkans, American railway shares had slumped, the agricultural depression was already causing alarm. The years 1876–9, in fact, marked the end of a long period during which Britain had had ample capital to spare for

---

[1] Cf. Stanley, H. M., *Through the Dark Continent* (1878).
[2] *Ibid.* 1, 83.
[3] *C.H.B.E.* II, 673. The policy is explicitly defined in the report of the 1865 Select Committee: *Parl. Pap.* 1865, v (412), p. 3.

foreign investment. Now "she could scarcely balance her requirements of food and raw materials, with the manufactures she could
export and the freights her merchant marine could collect. The export of a capital surplus was over".[1]

Stanley was deeply chagrined at the cool reception his project met
with in Britain—especially in Manchester, where he had looked for
support.[2] But if Britain was apathetic, King Leopold II of the
Belgians was eager to profit by his work and to secure his services. He
had begun to show his interest in Africa while Stanley was still on the
Congo, summoning explorers and scientists to a three-day conference
in Brussels in September 1876. The International African Association,
which developed out of this conference, concerned itself in the first
place with East Africa, sending out an expedition there in 1877,
which, after great initial difficulties, established a station at Karema,
140 miles south of Ujiji on Lake Tanganyika.[3] In the following year
the field of King Leopold's activities widened. On 25 November 1878
another international meeting was held in Brussels on his invitation,
at which a *Comité d'Études du Haut Congo* was founded, and Stanley
accepted the practical direction of its work.[4] With a modest capital
of £20,000 behind him, Stanley set out. In the course of the next five
years he founded and organised the Congo Free State, which secured
international recognition in 1885.

Stanley's proposal of 1877 was not the only one of its kind. In the
previous year Sultan Barghash of Zanzibar had told Lord Derby, the
Foreign Secretary, that he wished for the help of British capitalists in
the opening-up of his dominions and in the development of trade both
on the coast and in the interior of East Africa.[5] Sir William Mackinnon, chairman of the British India Steam Navigation Company,
had already begun to interest himself in the region, and Derby forwarded the Sultan's request to him. In the course of the winter of
1876–7, a scheme was prepared by Mackinnon and his associates,
providing for the establishment of a company that would in practice
take over the whole of the administration of the mainland dominions
of the Sultan, subject to financial guarantees for the maintenance of
his revenue from customs duties and for his participation in the profits
the Company might make.[6] The Sultan accepted the terms proposed,
with some minor amendments; the Foreign Office, while refusing its
"formal sanction" (which in any case was not required), stated that
the scheme "commends itself to such support as Her Majesty's

[1] Jenks, L. H., *The Migration of British Capital to 1875* (1939), p. 333. Cf. also Rostow,
W. W., *British Economy of the Nineteenth Century* (1948), chap. ix, esp. pp. 186, 206–7.
[2] Stanley, H. M., *The Congo and the Founding of its Free State* (1885), i, v, xiii. Cf. his
sarcastic references to "the clever practical people of Manchester", *ibid.* ii, 366, 369.
[3] Coupland, *The Exploitation of East Africa*, pp. 331–2.
[4] Stanley, *op. cit.* i, 25–8.
[5] Coupland, *The Exploitation of East Africa*, p. 305.
[6] *Ibid.* pp. 306–8.

Government can properly afford to such an undertaking".[1] Mackinnon expressed satisfaction at this assurance and then, at the last stage, negotiations broke down. They were not resumed.

The reasons for this failure will never be completely known. There is a hint of a "secret history".[2] The blame was generally placed on the British government: it was said to have been dilatory, even hostile to the whole scheme. But the Foreign Office records do not support these charges. It is much more probable that, as the discussions proceeded, Mackinnon and his friends came to realise, more completely than they had at first, the magnitude of the financial commitments ahead of them. During the very months in which they were negotiating, the economic situation in London was, as we have seen, markedly deteriorating. In the autumn of 1878, when the failure might still have been retrieved, two of the Glasgow banks crashed, involving Mackinnon (who had formerly been a director of one of them) in prolonged litigation. In short, the times were as unfavourable for Mackinnon's scheme as they were for Stanley's.

If these two great projects had materialised, Britain's economic and political position in Tropical Africa would have been vastly altered. The Scramble for Africa in the 'eighties, if it had come at all, would have taken a quite different form. It would be wrong, however, to conclude, because they failed, that British enterprise in Tropical Africa was dormant. The volume of trade in the British West African colonies as a whole rose strikingly in the 'seventies. The average annual value of imports and exports, taken together, was £1,272,000 in 1866–70: in 1876–80 it was £3,020,000.[3] Similarly, in the Sultan of Zanzibar's dominions in East Africa, where the average value of the trade had been about £1,000,000 a year in 1862–72, it rose to £2,200,000 in 1879.[4] And both in West and in East Africa the greatest share in this trade was British. Of the external trade of the Gold Coast in 1870, for example, 55 per cent was with Britain: by 1885 that figure had become 71 per cent.[5] The Zanzibar trade statistics being fragmentary, and unreliable in detail, the most satisfactory comparison there is in the volume of shipping. In 1871 British ships accounted for the largest proportion of the total tonnage of those calling at Zanzibar, but it was only 38 per cent: eight years later it had risen to 85 per cent.[6]

It is naturally impossible to secure any satisfactory account of the trade in districts not under British jurisdiction or supervision, but

[1] Coupland, The Exploitation of East Africa, p. 312.
[2] Ibid., p. 318; see also Perham, M., Lugard, vol. 1 (1956), pp. 135–6.
[3] See the table in McPhee, op. cit. p. 313.
[4] Coupland, The Exploitation of East Africa, p. 319.
[5] Parl. Pap. 1884–5, LXXXIII [C. 4520], pp. 288–9, 334–5; 1887, LXXXVII [C. 5176], p. 335.
[6] Coupland, op. cit. pp. 78, 322. These figures exclude British Indian shipping.

attempts were made to estimate the trade in the Niger Delta, from time to time, by the British Consuls for the Bights of Benin and Biafra. In 1871 Consul Charles Livingstone (brother of the great explorer) stated that there were sixty large trading establishments in the Delta, owned by some twenty British firms, and he estimated the value of their property at £1,000,000. Over 200 Englishmen were permanently employed in these trading stations, he said, and they had some 2000 Africans in their service, mainly recruited in the British territories but including some Kroo men from Liberia. Since the agents refused to make any official statement of the amount of palm-oil they exported, the consul could rely solely upon his own estimate. He put it at 25,000–30,000 tons a year, and quoted the prevailing price in England as £34–£44 a ton.[1] This was certainly a heavy exaggeration. In 1878 Consul Hopkins furnished the Foreign Office with a more precise and convincing statement. Four firms, he reported, were engaged in the Niger trade, and they had shipped about 5000 tons of palm-oil home that year, worth £195,000. The only other substantial item of trade was shea-butter (£58,500). The total trade amounted to £309,700.[2]

The accuracy of these estimates is open to question; but on one important point they are certainly correct. The number of British firms operating in the Niger Delta sharply declined in the 'seventies. Their work had developed to a point where the small company was no longer a viable economic unit. If they were to achieve prosperity, they must combine. The need became even more urgent at the same time for two other reasons. The competition of African traders was becoming increasingly severe: one of them, Jaja of Opobo, had built up a substantial fortune and much political power for himself out of the palm-oil trade, and others were following his example, not far behind. Moreover, up to this time the only European traders in the Niger Delta had been British. But French and German traders had now begun to take an interest in the country. French competition might at any moment become dangerous, not only commercially but also politically: for in these years France was beginning to extend her hold inland from Senegal to the upper Niger—she secured the cession of Cotonou from the King of Dahomey under agreements of 1868 and 1878,[3] she was already established in Gabon, just across the Gulf of Guinea, and De Brazza made his first journey up the Ogowe in 1875–9. The movement towards combination among the British firms developed further in 1877, when George Goldie[4] came out, for private

[1] Memorandum by Consul Livingstone (undated, but received 8 Dec. 1871): F.O. 84/1343. See also Livingstone's report on Old Calabar, 11 Jan. 1873: *Parl. Pap.* 1873, LXV [C. 828], pp. 3–10.
[2] Hopkins to Salisbury, 18 Nov. 1878: F.O. 84/1508.
[3] Hertslet, Sir E., *The Map of Africa by Treaty* (1911 ed.), p. 647.
[4] "Strictly speaking 'Goldie-Taubman' until 1887, when he assumed the surname Goldie"—*D.N.B.*

family reasons, to investigate the affairs of one of them.[1] He at once saw that, for their own protection, they should amalgamate into a single concern, and in 1879 he brought this about with the formation of the United African Company. But Goldie's plan did not end there. He wished from the beginning to secure a royal charter for the Company, to enable it to exercise powers of government. The first requisite was to secure a large capital. Within two years this was forthcoming, and the United African Company was transformed into the National African Company, with a capital of £1,000,000, in 1882. By that time a further difficulty had arisen. The foreign competition that had first threatened in the 'seventies had become serious with the launching of the *Compagnie française de l'Afrique équatoriale* in Paris and the *Compagnie du Sénégal et de la côte occidentale d'Afrique*, backed personally by Gambetta, in Marseilles.[2] The emergence of these French companies effectively prevented the English company from securing its charter for the time being: the British Government could not consider recognising it as a political entity, with jurisdiction over territory in which French stations were established. The French companies speedily collapsed after the death of Gambetta at the end of 1882 and passed under the control of their British rival. But the German irruption into West Africa in 1884 and the summoning of the Berlin Conference in 1885[3]—partly to deal with the question of freedom of trade on the Niger—again delayed the fulfilment of Goldie's ambition. It was at length attained in 1886 with the issue of a royal charter, as a consequence of which the National African Company formally became the Royal Niger Company.[4]

The long and complex negotiations that preceded the formation of the chartered company are themselves an indication of the high value now placed in Europe on the trade of the region it controlled. The economic importance of the Gold Coast, too, began to increase at the same time. It was in these years that the first steps were taken by Europeans to mine the metal from which the country had taken its name when the Portuguese first visited it in the fifteenth century.[5] Gold-working was observed and commented upon by British officers during the Ashanti War of 1873–4.[6] Until 1878 the whole of the trade was in gold dust, obtained mainly from streams. But in that year a French "African Gold Coast Company" began mining opera-

[1] Kingsley, M., *The Story of West Africa* (n.d.), pp. 154–6.
[2] Darcy, J., *France et Angleterre. Cent années de rivalité coloniale. L'Afrique* (1904), pp. 236–40.   [3] See p. 164 below.
[4] The history of the predecessors of the Royal Niger Company and of that company's formation is a confused and uncertain story, chiefly because Goldie destroyed his own papers and did his best to see that nobody ever attempted to write his biography: Wellesley, Lady D., *Sir George Goldie* (1934), p. ix. See also Geary, Sir W. M. N., *Nigeria under British Rule* (1927), pp. 174–86; Cook, A. N., *British Enterprise in Nigeria* (1943), pp. 81–9; and the documents in F.O. 84/1879, 1880.
[5] For the origins of this trade see Blake, J. W., *European Beginnings in West Africa* (1937), pp. 80–3.
[6] Brackenbury, H., *The Ashanti War* (1874), II, 351–2.

tions at Tarkwa, quickly followed by a number of others, mostly British. A very small "gold rush" took place to the colony in 1881–2. Among the prospectors were the explorers Burton and Cameron.[1] Burton described the goldfield in terms of extravagant eulogy: "I went to the Gold Coast with small expectations. I found the Wassaw country, Ancobra section, far richer than the most glowing descriptions had represented it. Gold and other metals were there in abundance, and there are good signs of diamonds, ruby, sapphire. Remains to be seen if England still has honesty and public spirit enough to work this old-new California as it should be worked."[2] The early excitement, however, soon died down, and the industry made slow permanent progress, chiefly owing to the difficulties of transport to and from the coast at Axim. A line for a railway was surveyed, but the cost of its construction appeared prohibitive. A good road could have been made for £17,500; but the government of the colony was unable to find that sum, even though the mining companies were willing to pay substantial tolls for the use of it, and an imperial grant-in-aid does not seem even to have been considered. Failing any satisfactory means of transport, the mining engineers were continually hampered by the lack of the heavy machinery they needed, and the companies by the high cost of production.[3] None the less, the industry maintained itself, and though the Gold Coast was never able to rival the Rand, its gold-production helped the colony to a valuable broadening of its economy.

Gold-mining was not the only wholly new economic activity to be developed in British Tropical Africa during this period. The first cocoa was grown in the Gold Coast, from beans smuggled away by an African from San Thomé, in 1879. And it was in 1884 that William Wallace, trading up the Benue River, discovered the tin-smelting industry of the Bauchi plateau. Tin had long been known to be in common use among the Hausa; but it had always been supposed that it was imported by the caravan routes across the Sahara. Wallace attempted to induce the Bauchi people to expand the trade, but they refused, fearing that this might lead to their subjection by the more powerful Fulani; and it was not until after the Fulani had been themselves subjected to British rule in 1902 that the tin trade could be developed.[4]

In East Africa, no permanently successful new products were exploited in these years, though for a time, immediately after the prohibition of the slave trade by land, a serious effort was made to develop the production of india-rubber near Kilwa.[5] By 1880 it was

---

[1] They described their experiences in *To the Gold Coast for Gold* (1883).
[2] *Ibid.* I, xii.
[3] Claridge, W. W., *A History of the Gold Coast and Ashanti* (1915), II, 203, 246–9.
[4] Calvert, A. F., *Nigeria and its Tin Fields* (1910), pp. 13–14.
[5] Kirk to Derby, 5 Feb. 1877, enclosing report from Bishop Steere of 27 July 1876: F.O. 84/1484.

said that 1000 tons were being shipped every year: the price had just risen from £140 to £250 a ton.[1]

Apart from these experimental new trades, the commercial staples of British Tropical Africa remained what they had long been. The total volume of the trade, as we have seen, was rising, and in general the economic position appeared satisfactory, even though the importance of these territories in relation to the British Empire as a whole was slight. But there was cause for disquiet, none the less. If Goldie's behaviour towards the British Government was often high-handed—sometimes comically outrageous[2]—there was a good deal in his complaints that it afforded very inadequate assistance, and no encouragement, to British enterprise in Africa. The promising development of gold-mining on the Gold Coast languished for want of £17,500 to build a road. In 1877 a scheme of sanitation for Bathurst, the need of which had been desperately demonstrated in the epidemics of yellow fever and cholera there in 1866 and 1869, was abandoned on the ground that the Gambia Government was in too weak a position financially to incur the expense of it: but when, three years later, a surplus of £19,000 had been scraped together, permission to undertake the work was still withheld, and the money applied instead to help balance the budget of the Gold Coast—with which at this time the Gambia was still administratively linked. Furthermore, as if to ensure that there should be no such surplus again, the government in London determined that the Gambia should become liable in future for a subsidy paid to the British and African Steamship Company to induce their ships to call at Bathurst: this had previously been a charge on imperial funds.[3]

It was a well-established principle that British colonies could expect only such amenities and economic assets as they could pay for out of their own revenue. The principle bore hardly on territories like those in West Africa, whose whole future depended on attracting European capital for their development. Where the government gave so little help, it was hardly to be expected that the traders should come forward with great schemes on their own.

Moreover, though Britain had a preponderant share in the external trade of both West and East Africa, foreign competition was at some points becoming strong. The United States and France had long been established in this field: American imports into the Gold Coast in this period averaged about £90,000 a year—between a quarter and a half those from Britain; in the late 'seventies France traded very substantially with Lagos, though this trade declined after 1879.[4] But Germany showed a steadily rising interest in the West

[1] Holmwood to Kirk, 30 Jan. 1880: F.O. 84/1574.
[2] Cf. Cook, op. cit. pp. 87-8.
[3] Gray, op. cit. pp. 444-6, 457-8.
[4] Parl. Pap. 1884-5, LXXXIII [C. 4520], pp. 286-9.

African market. In 1884 the value of exports from Lagos to Germany actually exceeded that to Britain by 14 per cent, and German imports were also growing fast.[1]

The greatest weakness of all in the British position in these territories was, however, the violent fluctuations to which their trade was subject. Consider, for instance, the figures of imports and exports for Lagos:[2]

	Imports	Exports
	£	£
1870	400,558	515,366
1873	258,884	406,986
1877	614,359	734,708
1881	333,659	460,007
1885	542,564	614,181

It has already been seen that the American Civil War stimulated the production of cotton in Lagos and its hinterland, and that it was still maintained at a high level in 1870. In the 'seventies the cotton export fell: from £51,618 in 1873 to £12,436 in 1877 and to £360 in 1880. The trade was not finished, however. By 1884 it had climbed back to £11,454, only to fall again to £5797 in 1885.[3]

But though the trade in individual commodities, and the share taken in it by different foreign states, might fluctuate, the total volume of external trade rose strikingly in these years, both in East and in West Africa. That can be assessed by an analysis of the shipping figures. The tonnage of ships entered and cleared at Lagos, excluding those employed in the coasting trade, more than doubled, rising from 198,737 in 1870 to 432,950 in 1885.[4] At Zanzibar the proportionate increase in the 'seventies was bigger—from 27,626 tons (excluding British Indian ships) in 1871 to 89,463 in 1879.[5] These figures also show how comparatively small the trade of East Africa with Europe still was. But as they do not include British Indian shipping, they give a misleading under-estimate of the total business done by the port. It should also be remembered that these increases took place at a time when technical improvements in the design of steamships were enabling them to carry bigger cargoes for the same shipping tonnage.[6]

There were two principal British shipping companies in the West African trade: the African Steamship Co., founded in 1852, and the British & African Steam Navigation Co. (1869). They were in close and unremitting competition with each other until the 'nineties, when

---

[1] *Parl. Pap.* 1884–5, LXXXIII [C. 4520], pp. 286–7. For the figures for 1885 see *Parl. Pap.* 1887, LXXXVII [C. 5176], p. 333.
[2] *Parl. Pap.* 1884–5, LXXXIII [C. 4520], pp. 242–3; 1887, LXXXVII [C. 5176], p. 289.
[3] *Ibid.*
[4] *Parl. Pap.* 1884–5, LXXXIII (39), p. 184.
[5] Coupland, *The Exploitation of East Africa*, p. 322.
[6] Cf. Knowles, L. C. A., *The Economic Development of the British Overseas Empire*, I (1928 ed.), p. 18.

they were both brought under the control of Elder Dempster and Company. Consul Livingstone reported in 1871 that five steamers then left Liverpool for his district every month (besides others from Glasgow), "the trade of the Oil Rivers being their principal support".[1] French and German shipping lines also maintained a regular service to the West Coast.

Almost as soon as the Suez Canal was opened, plans were put forward for a service of mail-steamers between London and Cape Town that should run alternately by the west and the east coasts of Africa. This project was never realised: it was only approximately fulfilled fifty years later, in 1922, when the Union Castle Line started its "Round Africa" service.[2] But at least it led, almost immediately, to the establishment of a monthly mail-service (assisted by a subsidy from the British government) by the Union Line and the British India Steam Navigation Co., running between Durban, Zanzibar and Aden, where it connected with the mailboats for Europe and India. The Union Line withdrew from the arrangement in 1881, leaving the British India Co. with the strongest position in the East African trade. The Messageries Maritimes and the Woermann Line from Hamburg, however, began to become serious competitors in 1885.[3]

The journeys of Livingstone, Cameron and Stanley, described above, mark the close of the "classical" age of African exploration. They filled in the map of the interior of the continent. Henceforward, the main need was no longer for great journeys of the earlier kind. The time had come for a more minute and scientific investigation of the topography of the country. The way was now open for the preparation of adequate maps and surveys. This did not necessarily mean that the later explorers, whose work now falls to be considered, faced an easier task than their predecessors. On occasion they showed equally remarkable endurance and tenacity; and, from a scientific point of view, their work was often of a higher quality. Their exploration was not inferior, but it was profoundly different. It had much less of the dramatic than the journeys of Livingstone or Stanley. The books in which it is described are not a record of heroically long journeys, represented by a coloured line on a map: rather, they are concerned with the slow, patient, unspectacular work of the botanist, the geologist and the economic geographer.

One other, equally important, change should be noted. From the 1870's onwards, African journeys of exploration begin to take on an increasingly political character. They are supported, with more and

[1] F.O. 84/1343 (as cited above p. 75, note 1).
[2] *Parl. Pap.* 1872, LIV [C. 657], pp. 833–40; Murray, M., *Union-Castle Chronicle* (1953), pp. 180–1.
[3] *Ibid.* pp. 63–72; Coupland, *The Exploitation of East Africa*, pp. 84–5, 322.

more vigour, by governments—and their allies, like the International African Association.[1] This was not in itself new: the British government, for example, had steadily assisted the exploration of the Niger for half a century past. But whereas the most powerful impulse behind the exploration of Tropical Africa had come hitherto from Britain, it now came from other countries in equal measure: so that the travellers we shall be concerned with here are an international company—British, French, German, Austrian, Italian, Portuguese, American.

It was in East Africa that the most important tasks still lay. Winwood Reade noted wryly in 1873: "Fifty years ago my journey to the Niger and Bouré would have made a sensation, but now it has not excited the slightest interest among English geographers. The basin of the Niger is deserted, and all minds are crowding to the basin of the Nile."[2] The work of Speke, Grant and Baker[3] had opened up entirely new problems. The most spectacular was that of the configuration of the great lakes and the ultimate source of the Nile, and that, as we have seen, was illuminated and largely settled by Stanley. But other work, as valuable, remained to be done. Speke had revealed the importance of Buganda and the neighbouring kingdoms. It was not long before other people interested in East Africa arrived to visit King Mtesa: the American Chaillé-Long and the Frenchman Linant de Bellefonds, who were on the staff of Gordon, Governor-General of Equatoria under the Khedive of Egypt; Stanley himself on his second African journey, in 1875. Buganda occupied a vital strategic position in north-east Africa. To the north, on the Upper Nile, Gordon was engaged in the formidable task of building up a settled administration: to the south lay the mainland dominions of the Sultan of Zanzibar, in which Europeans were beginning to take a keener interest than ever before. The Khedive and Gordon conceived the idea of opening up a line of communication between the upper Nile and the coast of the Indian Ocean, passing through Buganda, and in 1875 they sent an expedition to occupy a post at the mouth of the River Juba in Somaliland, which the Khedive claimed, somewhat airily, was under his sovereignty. The expedition came to nothing.[4] But its failure did not diminish the interest taken by Gordon and his associates in Buganda and the northern lakes. An Italian member of his staff, Romolo Gessi, was the first European to sail round Lake Albert, in the spring of 1876.[5] Gordon maintained diplomatic relations with Buganda: the first task he entrusted to Eduard Schnitzer, the Austrian who entered his service in 1876 and later became known as Emin Pasha, was to carry presents to King Mtesa.

Gordon's plans for the organisation of Equatoria were constantly

---

[1] See p. 73 above. [2] Reade, W., *The African Sketch-Book* (1873), II, 505.
[3] *C.H.B.E.* II, 625–7. [4] See Coupland, *The Exploitation of East Africa*, chap. xiii.
[5] Gessi, R., *Seven Years in the Soudan* (1892), chaps. xii–xvi.

frustrated, notably by his colleague the Governor-General of the Sudan at Khartoum, and in the autumn of 1876 he resigned his commission.[1] The Khedive persuaded him to remain in his service by making him Governor-General of the whole Sudan province from Wadi Halfa to Lake Albert, including Khartoum within his jurisdiction. Gordon made one more effort to secure the co-operation of Mtesa, and then, at the end of 1878, he decided to abandon all attempts to extend his power south of Mrooli, 100 miles north of Lake Victoria Nyanza.[2] Emin Pasha, however, remained, struggling to assert the authority of the Egyptian Government and maintaining contact with Buganda.[3] Thenceforward, for the next eight years, with one exception, the only Europeans to visit Buganda were the missionaries, who began to arrive in the country in June 1877. Their work will be touched on later. The exception was the great traveller Wilhelm Junker, who made his way up the Nile to explore the upper course of the Welle river—a tributary of the Ubangi, and so ultimately of the Congo—in 1880.[4] He intended to return as he had come, through Egypt, but found his way barred by the Mahdist revolt and determined therefore to strike up to the headwaters of the Nile and across to the east coast. He arrived at Bagamoyo in November 1886, after a series of journeys that had lasted altogether seven years.

In the country south of Lake Victoria Nyanza, the most important of the successors of Livingstone and Stanley was Joseph Thomson. His career illustrates very well the changing conditions under which exploration was now being carried on. He went out first in 1878, as geologist to an expedition financed by the Royal Geographical Society and led by Keith Johnston. Its task was to examine the country between Dar-es-Salaam and Lake Nyasa—that is, the region north-west of that crossed by Livingstone on his last journey in 1866; and this examination was intended to lead on to the establishment of a new route to the great lakes, better than those that had hitherto been found. Shortly after they left the coast Johnston died, and Thomson found himself in command of the expedition, at the age of twenty-one. Without hesitation he took over and carried the task through, reaching the northern end of Lake Nyasa, making his way through the entirely unknown tract of country between it and Lake Tanganyika, marching up the western side of that lake and then making a bold attempt to reach the Congo. This proved impracticable, and he was obliged to travel back to Tabora and so by the well-known Arab trade-route to the coast at Bagamoyo.[5]

[1] The best account of Gordon's work in this period is in Allen, B. M., *Gordon and the Sudan* (1931), Part I. [2] *Ibid.* p. 138.
[3] Schweitzer, G., *The Life and Work of Emin Pasha* (1898), vol. I; *Emin Pasha in Central Africa*, ed. Schweinfurth, G., etc. (1888).
[4] Junker, W., *Travels in Africa* (1890–2), II, chaps. vi–viii.
[5] The journey is described in Thomson's book *To the Central African Lakes and Back* (1881)

In 1881 Thomson accepted an invitation from the Sultan of Zanzibar to visit the River Rovuma and report on the deposits of coal that Livingstone thought he detected there in 1862.[1] It was a strictly business commission, and it proved only—to the Sultan's chagrin—that the coal was a bituminous shale, of no value as fuel.[2]

The most important of Thomson's journeys was the third (1883–4). It took him to the country we now know as the Kenya Highlands. Krapf had seen Mount Kenya from a great distance in 1849,[3] and Rebmann,[4] Von der Decken[5] and Charles New[6] had given some account of the lower slopes of Kilimanjaro. A German traveller, G. A. Fischer, made his way from Kilimanjaro to Lake Naivasha in 1883. He was the first European to enter the Kenya Highlands, and at once he proclaimed that the country was "well adapted for European settlement".[7] But he met with fierce opposition from the Masai, which prevented him from reaching his ultimate objective, Lake Baringo. Thomson's journey was begun only a month after Fischer's, and he succeeded where his predecessor had failed, travelling on beyond Lake Naivasha to visit Mount Kenya and Lake Baringo, and then turning westward through Kavirondo to Victoria Nyanza. The Masai and the Kikuyu—whom he found equally formidable[8]—continually threatened his passage, but he managed to avoid a major collision. This achievement was due to his steady, cool temper, sure judgment and unfailing restraint: a combination of qualities remarkable in any traveller and astonishing in a man of twenty-five.[9]

The work of Fischer and Thomson opened up a great new field for European enterprise: more tempting than any other in Tropical Africa because it offered a chance for European settlement. Their discoveries began to be exploited politically at once, by H. H. Johnston[10] and by Karl Peters and his colleagues of the *Gesellschaft für deutsche Kolonisation*.[11]

King Leopold's International Association did much to further the detailed knowledge of East Africa. The Belgian branch established a base at Karema on Lake Tanganyika, which Leopold was soon disposed to turn into a Belgian colony.[12] A long series of expeditions—

[1] Livingstone, D. and C., *Narrative of an Expedition to the Zambesi and its Tributaries* (1865), pp. 439–40.
[2] For this journey see Thomson's "Notes on the Basin of the River Rovuma", *Proc. R. Geog. Soc.*, new ser. IV (1882), pp. 65 *seqq.*
[3] Coupland, *East Africa and its Invaders*, p. 399.
[4] *Ibid.* pp. 396–7.
[5] Coupland, *The Exploitation of East Africa*, p. 112.
[6] New, C., *Life, Wanderings and Labours in Eastern Africa* (1883), chaps. xx and xxi.
[7] Coupland, *The Exploitation of East Africa*, p. 353.
[8] Thomson, J., *Through Masai Land* (1885), pp. 306–11, 319–24.
[9] For this journey see the work cited in the preceding footnote.
[10] Johnston, H. H., *The Kilimanjaro Expedition* (1886); Johnston, A., *The Life and Letters of Sir Harry Johnston* (1929), chap. iv.
[11] Peters, K., *Die deutsch-ostafrikanische Kolonie* (ed. 2, 1889) and *Die Gründung von Deutsch-Ostafrika* (1906); Kurtze, B., *Die deutsch-ostafrikanische Gesellschaft* (1913), pp. 1–7.
[12] Kirk to Salisbury, 8 March 1880: F.O. 84/1574.

French and German as well as Belgian—made their way inland from 1880 onwards; and most of them went under the Association's auspices.[1] By 1885, thanks largely to their work, building upon the foundations laid by their predecessors, the structure of Lake Tanganyika itself was well known, and the main routes to the east coast were charted. Similarly, Lake Nyasa and the Shiré valley were examined and described by members of the two British missionary parties stationed in that country from 1875 onwards, whose work will be considered later on.[2]

The journeys of Cameron and Stanley fired the Portuguese to an active exploration of the remote interior of their colonies of Mozambique and Angola. In 1877, for example, they sent two expeditions out to the west coast: one, under Serpa Pinto, travelling in a south-easterly direction from Benguela to Natal;[3] the other, under Capello and Ivens, examining a considerable part of the valley of the Coango and of north-eastern Angola, which no European traveller had ever before described.[4]

The principal field of exploration in West Africa in these years was what may loosely be called the Congo basin: the valley, that is, of the huge river itself and of its tributaries the Ubangi and the Kasai. The establishment of the Congo Free State under Stanley had its counterpart in the work of De Brazza on the Ogowé and Ubangi, building up—by methods somewhat different from Stanley's[5]—the great empire of French Equatorial Africa; and the Kasai was extensively and carefully examined by the German Hermann von Wissmann in a series of journeys, in the course of which he crossed the continent from west to east twice in the space of seven years (1880–7).[6]

The Muslim emirates of the western Sudan had been visited by a succession of European travellers from Denham and Clapperton onwards. In the 'forties and 'fifties, Barth had accumulated and published a massive store of knowledge about this country.[7] But thereafter, British enterprise had concentrated on the lower Niger, and the French had concerned themselves principally with Senegal. Some contact was maintained with the kingdom of Nupé, and in the 'seventies the British Government customarily sent up an annual present to its ruler, who "invariably befriended and encouraged" British traders.[8] In 1881–2 the United African Company gave him some assistance in putting down a rebellion.[9] The Company and its

---

[1] Coupland, *The Exploitation of East Africa*, chap. xv.
[2] See p. 91 below.   [3] Pinto, A. S., *How I Crossed Africa* (1881).
[4] Capello, H., and Ivens, R., *From Benguella to the Territory of Yacca* (1882).
[5] Cf. De Brazza's own comparison between himself and Stanley: *Conférences et Lettres* (1887), pp. 172–5; and Froment-Guieysse, G., *Brazza* (1945), pp. 9–17.
[6] Cf. Wissmann, H. von, *Unter deutscher Flagge quer durch Afrika von West nach Ost* (1889), and Perbandt, C. von, Richelmann, G., and Schmidt, R., *Hermann von Wissmann* (1906).
[7] *C.H.B.E.* II, 619, 621.
[8] Derby to Hartley, 13 July 1877: F.O. 84/1487.
[9] Cf. Nadel, S. F., *A Black Byzantium: the Kingdom of Nupe in Nigeria* (1942), p. 82.

successor became increasingly interested at this time in the country lying to the north-east of the lower Niger, and greatly concerned at the danger of French and German political annexation there. To forestall a German attempt, it commissioned Joseph Thomson to visit Sokoto and Gando and make treaties on its behalf with their rulers. He performed the task with his habitual competence and speed and so laid the foundation of the British protectorates in Northern Nigeria.[1]

The development of trade in Tropical Africa, and the exploration of the country, were linked at some points—more closely than is often realised—with the history of Christian missions.

In West Africa, as we have seen, the Church Missionary Society had long been established. It was unquestionably the senior mission in the British territories. The oldest of its bases was in Sierra Leone, where in 1872 the number of members of the Church of England was stated to be 14,000, 4500 of whom were communicants. 4000 children were then in attendance at its day-schools, and 2000 at its Sunday schools.[2] It was also responsible for Fourah Bay College, the only institution of higher education in Tropical Africa. That College made decisive progress at this time, when in 1876 it became affiliated to the University of Durham, with the privilege of presenting its students externally for Durham degrees in arts and licences in theology.[3]

The diocese of Sierra Leone was erected in 1852,[4] comprehending, besides Sierra Leone itself, the Gambia, the Gold Coast and Lagos.[5] In the first two of these territories, the work of the Anglican church was comparatively unimportant. But the C.M.S. exercised a powerful influence in Lagos and its neighbourhood through its Yoruba Mission. The most important of the early stations in this country were at Abeokuta (1846) and at its great rival, Ibadan (1851). But these towns were constantly fighting each other, and Abeokuta was exposed to two attacks by the army of Dahomey, in 1863 and 1864. In 1867 the chiefs of Abeokuta (there was no Alake at the time) suddenly forbade the missionaries to hold their services, and they were expelled. Though Townsend, the head of the mission, was allowed to return for short periods in 1871 and 1875, the station was not reestablished until 1880.[6] The C.M.S., nevertheless, continued to show a close interest in the welfare of Abeokuta—urging the British Government to take action, for example, to avert a third attack on the town from Dahomey in 1875.[7] The mission at Ibadan encountered similar

[1] Thomson, J., "Sketch of a Trip to Sokoto by the River Niger", *Jour. Manchester Geog. Soc.* (1886), pp. 1–18; Thomson, J. B., *Joseph Thomson, African Explorer* (1896), chap. vii; Hertslet, *op. cit.* pp. 122–4.

[2] Stock, *op. cit.* ii, 448.   [3] *Ibid.* iii, 377.
[4] *Ibid.* ii, 15.   [5] *Ibid.* iii, 380.
[6] *Ibid.* ii, 442–3; Walker, F. D., *The Romance of the Black River* (1930), pp. 121–4.
[7] C.M.S. to Carnarvon, 2 Dec. 1875, forwarded by C.O. to F.O. for consideration: F.O. 84/1464.

difficulties at the same time. But it deserves to be recalled that in 1870, when the political relations of the two towns were still hostile, visits were exchanged between delegates of the Christian communities in each. The message from Ibadan ran: "However great misunderstandings may be among the heathen of Abeokuta and Ibadan, let unity and peace be among us Christians of the two rival cities, for we are the followers of the Prince of Peace."[1]

The interruption of the work at Abeokuta and Ibadan caused the Society to move the headquarters of the Yoruba Mission to Lagos. In 1872 it claimed 4400 adherents.[2] In 1877 an African, the Rev. James Johnson, was appointed superintendent of the mission in the interior, and his work prepared the way for the resumption of full activity there from 1880 onwards.[3]

The C.M.S. had another important field of work in West Africa, in its Niger Mission. This sprang immediately from the work of the Niger expeditions of 1841 and 1854,[4] and it was directed from the outset (1857) by an African clergyman, Samuel Adjai Crowther, who was consecrated bishop in 1864.[5] Under him the work went forward steadily, greatly helped from 1878 onwards by the provision of a steamer for the use of the mission, and a substantially enlarged staff. Stations were established in the Niger delta at Bonny and Brass, and at Onitsha[6] and Lokoja higher up the river. Bishop Crowther concerned himself closely with technical instruction as well as with evangelisation, and he showed a quick, intuitive skill in adapting the teaching and practice of the mission to the nature of the people among whom it was at work.

Of the other Protestant bodies that maintained missions in West Africa, five were notably active in these years: the Wesleyans, the Basel and Bremen Missions, the Baptists and the Presbyterians. The Wesleyans had been established on the Gambia since 1821,[7] and their work had lain largely among the people of the interior.[8] When it was proposed to exchange the colony for French territory elsewhere in West Africa in 1870, the Wesleyan missionaries were among the vocal opponents of the scheme.[9] It could be argued that their opposition sprang partly from the knowledge that under a French administration their work would be likely to suffer. But they showed a disinterested understanding of the needs of the country when they urged the British Government at all costs to reach some decision in the matter. "Even the transfer," they wrote, "all but universally deprecated, would be a commercial advantage compared with the

[1] Stock, op. cit. ii, 444.   [2] Ibid. ii, 445.
[3] Ibid. iii, 381.   [4] C.H.B.E. ii, 620.
[5] For Crowther's life and work, see Stock, op. cit. ii, 450–65, iii, 383–97, and Page, J., The Black Bishop (1908).
[6] For an interesting short description of the station at Onitsha, see Whitford, J., Trading Life in Western and Central Africa (1877), pp. 176–9.
[7] Gray, op. cit. p. 313.   [8] Ibid. pp. 362, 434.
[9] Ibid. p. 438.

embarrassing uncertainty at present existing; and the ministers testify of what is within their knowledge when they affirm that a most injurious paralysing influence rests upon British enterprise."[1]

On the Gold Coast the Wesleyans produced a missionary of outstanding quality in Thomas Birch Freeman, who worked there continuously for more than half a century (1838–90). Freeman was a mulatto, which may help to explain how he managed to live so long where his European fellow-workers quickly died or went home, broken in health. That may also account, in part at least, for the unique standing he acquired in the country. In the troubles of 1867–8, consequent on rumours of the impending evacuation of the Dutch settlement in favour of Britain,[2] he was employed by the Gold Coast government as a peacemaker.[3] Like Robert Moffat, he had been trained as a gardener, and he did a great deal to improve the Africans' methods of husbandry, encouraging the growth of coffee, cinnamon, ginger and other crops that were new to the country.[4]

The work of the Basel Mission, established on the Gold Coast in 1827, and the Bremen Mission, which followed twenty years later, had an even more pronounced "industrial" character. A trading company was associated with the Basel Mission, one of whose objects was to develop substitutes for the trade in liquor and gunpowder. The Basel schools secured a high reputation: the practical nature of their teaching was greatly valued by the people.

The C.M.S. did not have a monopoly of the Bights. The English Baptists established themselves on Fernando Po in the 'forties, when the island was under British control; and when the Spaniards reasserted their authority over it, they moved to the opposite mainland, to a station (which they named Victoria) just below the Cameroon mountains. Their leader was Alfred Saker, who worked there from 1844 to 1876. It was there that George Grenfell began his career as a missionary and explorer in 1875.[5] When the Germans occupied the neighbouring country in 1884, the Baptists strongly supported Hewett in his efforts to retain the country for Britain. On the failure of this attempt, they handed over their station to the Basel Mission.[6]

The United Presbyterian Church of Scotland founded a mission at Old Calabar in 1846. From the outset it fought a resolute battle against certain of the social customs of the Efik people with whom it was working, especially the killing of the old and of twins. In 1876 the mission was joined by Mary Slessor, a factory-girl from Dundee, who spent the remaining thirty-nine years of her life in its service,[7]

---

[1] *Ibid.* p. 440.
[2] *C.H.B.E.* ii, 674.
[3] Claridge, *op. cit.* i, 569–70.
[4] Cf. Milum, J., *Thomas Birch Freeman* (n.d.).
[5] Johnston, Sir H. H., *George Grenfell and the Congo* (1908), i, chaps. ii and iii.
[6] Rudin, H. R., *Germans in the Cameroons* (1938), pp. 61–3, 69–73.
[7] Cf. Livingstone, W. P., *Mary Slessor of Calabar* (1915).

achieving what Mary Kingsley described as "an influence and a power among the negroes unmatched in its way by that of any other white".[1]

The West African missions of the Roman Catholics naturally established themselves primarily in French, Portuguese and Spanish territory. But their mission on the Gambia, founded in 1849, rendered fine service to the colony in its medical work;[2] and on the Gold Coast, though they did not arrive until 1881, they rapidly expanded their activities from their base at Elmina, to achieve what has been described as "more genuine success than perhaps all the other missions on the Coast combined".[3]

In East Africa, as in West, the Church Missionary Society was the oldest-established. The work of its first agents, the Germans Krapf, Rebmann and Ehrhardt, was important in the field of linguistics and in exploration: but the mission—based at Rabai, close to Mombasa—had no striking influence on the people. It must be remembered that on the East African coast it had to meet the challenge of Islam, a much more dynamic rival religion than any of the pagan faiths of West Africa. Krapf had returned to Europe in 1853, and Ehrhardt two years later. Rebmann toiled on alone, growing gradually blind. In the 'sixties there was a "virtual suspension" of the mission.[4] Its work was resumed, in a new form, as a consequence of Frere's visit to Zanzibar in 1873.[5] Under his influence the Society established a settlement for freed slaves on the mainland opposite Mombasa, which was named Freretown. Its work began in 1875, under the direction of the Rev. W. S. Price. In taking this step, the C.M.S. was making a serious attempt to solve the most difficult of all the problems consequent upon emancipation, affording the slaves protection and some training in the labour they would have to undertake as free men.

The establishment of Freretown brought difficult political problems in its train. The Arabs made constant complaints that the missionaries were harbouring runaway slaves, still their lawful possession, and more than once the settlement was threatened with attack.[6] The C.M.S. repeatedly urged the British Government to take possession of a stretch of the East African mainland,[7] and when that proposal was rejected it suggested that the lay superintendent at Freretown should at least be given vice-consular authority. Though Kirk was not unsympathetic to the missions and generously acknowledged the good work they were doing, he always advised the government against accepting this proposal;[8] and it was not adopted.

---

[1] *Travels in West Africa* (1897), p. 474.
[2] Gray, *op. cit.* pp. 384–5.   [3] Claridge, *op. cit.* II, 245.
[4] Stock, *op. cit.* II, 430.   [5] See above p. 69.
[6] Stock, *op. cit.* III, 91; Coupland, *The Exploitation of East Africa*, pp. 254, 359–60; Kirk to Granville, 19 Oct. 1880, F.O. 84/1575.
[7] Stock, *op. cit.* III, 75.
[8] Kirk to Derby, 7 June 1876, F.O. 84/1453; 30 March 1877, F.O. 84/1484.

The decision of the C.M.S. to appoint a "lay superintendent" for Freretown was undoubtedly right, in view of the practical and technical character of the work there; but the men chosen were not always equal to their difficult and delicate task.[1] The settlement remained small: there were only 400 freed slaves there in 1880.[2] But it proved its value, and the indirect influence of its example was, as with most mission stations, important beyond calculation in statistical terms.

The activity of the C.M.S. in East Africa was not confined to Freretown. On his visit to Buganda, Stanley wrote home, appealing for missionaries to work there and expressing confidence that they would be kindly received by King Mtesa, who welcomed the suggestion. His letter was published in the *Daily Telegraph* of 15 November 1875. At once, an anonymous offer of £5,000 was made to the C.M.S., on condition that it took up Stanley's challenge. £10,000 more was quickly forthcoming.[3] Of the first party sent out, all but two were soon dead; and the survivors, Alexander Mackay and C. T. Wilson, quickly discovered that, however warmly Mtesa might have entered into Stanley's project, his support for the mission was uncertain. What he really valued, naturally enough, was Mackay's competence as an engineer. Moreover, in 1879 two French Roman Catholic priests arrived, and at once an unedifying struggle began between the two Christian missions. Their quarrels soon became merged in the troubled politics of the Buganda kingdom. Mtesa played them off against each other, and Mwanga (who succeeded him in October 1884) set himself to persecute, first the Protestants and then all Christians alike. James Hannington, the first bishop of Eastern Equatorial Africa, was murdered, on Mwanga's instructions, on his way up to Buganda in October 1885. From this time until the establishment of the British protectorate in 1894 the missionaries and their converts were submitted to continual, and at times extremely savage, persecution.[4]

The London Missionary Society, under which Livingstone had served, adopted a plan in 1875–6 for a mission in the country between Lake Tanganyika and the coast, and in 1877 its work began. It was impeded at the start by over-elaborate equipment and radical defects in its planning: the historian of the Society calls it "a striking and instructive example of how great missionary enterprises ought not to be attempted".[5] Four subsequent expeditions were sent out, in

[1] Coupland, *The Exploitation of East Africa*, p. 360. The case of J. R. Streeter, discussed here, is referred to only in the most oblique terms by Stock, who says, rather inadequately, that Streeter "for some years did exceptionally good work, and won the confidence of the Society": *op. cit.* III, 90, 91.

[2] *Ibid.* III, 91.   [3] *Ibid.* III, 94–6.

[4] See *ibid.* III, chaps. lxxiv, xc, xci; Oliver, *op. cit.* pp. 73–8, 103–8, 128–62; Latourette, *op. cit.* v, 412–18; *The Last Journals of Bishop Hannington*, ed. Dawson, E. C. (1888); Ashe, R. P.. *Chronicles of Uganda* (1894); Thoonen, J. P., *Black Martyrs of Uganda* (1941).

[5] Lovett, *op. cit.* I, 649–50.

1879–84, to consolidate and develop the work. The layman of the first party, E. C. Hore, successfully established himself at Ujiji, acquiring a detailed knowledge of the shores of Lake Tanganyika through journeys made in small ships belonging to the mission. The L.M.S. also maintained a mission at Urambo, the headquarters of a chief named Mirambo, some fifty miles north-west of Tabora. In 1885 the station on the lake was removed from Ujiji to a healthier site at Kavala Island, off the western coast; and Hore's work was crowned with the launching of the steamer *Good News*—the first ever seen on Lake Tanganyika.[1]

Roman Catholic missionaries first appeared, in the wake of French political expansion, at Zanzibar in 1860.[2] Three years later a permanent station was established there by the French *Congrégation du Saint Esprit*.[3] In 1868 these Holy Ghost Fathers opened a settlement for freed slaves on the mainland, at Bagamoyo. It was notably successful and well run, though on one point it was open to serious criticism: the missionaries frankly bought slaves in order to free them, a practice that could give mild encouragement to the slave trade.[4] Roman Catholic activity developed rapidly with the work of the International African Association. It was inspired by Archbishop Lavigerie of Algiers, who had founded his missionary order of White Fathers (the *Société de Notre Dame d'Afrique*) in 1868 and went on to preach a crusade for the final destruction of the slave trade throughout Central Africa. He procured from Pope Leo XIII ten years later the creation of two East African vicariates, of Nyanza and Tanganyika. The first missionaries went out in the spring of 1878, one party travelling up into Buganda, the other eventually establishing itself in four stations on Lake Tanganyika, two of them side by side with those of the International African Association.[5]

The Universities Mission to Central Africa was removed from the Shiré Highlands to Zanzibar in 1863. Although it made some attempt to extend its work to the mainland in the 'sixties, it was not until Edward Steere was appointed bishop of Zanzibar in 1875 that a permanently successful establishment there was undertaken. Steere made a prospecting journey to the country between the Rovuma and Lake Nyasa, through which Livingstone had passed in 1866, and decided that a station should be set up at Masasi. In the following year it was founded, with sixty-five freed slaves under the charge of the Rev. W. P. Johnson and a lay superintendent. From Masasi

[1] Lovett, *op. cit.* 1, 650–62; Coupland, *The Exploitation of East Africa*, pp. 261, 263–4, 362–4; Hore, E. C., *Tanganyika* (1892).
[2] Coupland, *The Exploitation of East Africa*, pp. 33–4.
[3] Oliver, *op. cit.* p. 18.
[4] *Ibid.* pp. 21–3.
[5] *Ibid.* pp. 45–9; Coupland, *The Exploitation of East Africa*, pp. 356–7; Clarke, R. F., *Cardinal Lavigerie and the African Slave Trade* (1889); Goyau, G., *Un grand missionnaire: le Cardinal Lavigerie* (1925).

Johnson pressed forward westwards, and in 1885 the mission established itself on Lake Nyasa, with a steamer and a station at Likoma.[1]

Though Livingstone said many hard things about the removal of the U.M.C.A. from the Shiré to Zanzibar, he would have been gratified that, in the end, the mission he had done most to found established itself on Lake Nyasa, which he had discovered. It would have pleased him still more to know that the shores of the lake and the Shiré Highlands were to be settled by missionaries of his own people and communion, directly inspired by his life and work.

A month after Livingstone's funeral at Westminster, James Stewart (who had been out on the Zambezi with him in 1862)[2] proposed to the United Free Church of Scotland that it should establish a mission station "of an industrial as well as an educational nature" in Central Africa as a memorial to the great explorer. The first site chosen was at the southern end of Lake Nyasa, from which the mission gradually extended its work up the western shore, until in the end its headquarters were at Livingstonia, near the head of the lake. Stewart was assisted in the founding of the mission by E. D. Young, who had been in charge of the "search" expedition for Livingstone in 1867, and Robert Laws, a young doctor, who became the director of the work and developed at Livingstonia a comprehensive station of the kind envisaged from the start, at once mission, school, industrial settlement and hospital: closely similar in many respects to the famous institution that Stewart presided over at Lovedale.[3]

Very shortly after the foundation of the Free Church Mission, the Established Church of Scotland set up a station in the Shiré Highlands —the country in which, above all, Livingstone had desired to see missionaries at work. It was named Blantyre, after his birthplace, and, like the other Scottish mission, it bore an industrial character from the outset. The early history of Blantyre was chequered, but under the Rev. D. C. Scott, who assumed the direction of its work in 1881, it became soundly established.[4]

The Free Church mission was greatly helped from the start by the wise provision of a steamer for use on Lake Nyasa. But both missions were hampered by their unsatisfactory communications with the outside world. In order to overcome this difficulty, an effort was made (with the financial backing of Sir William Mackinnon) to build a road from the east coast to Lake Nyasa. It was never completed. Instead, the old approach used by Livingstone, by riversteamer up the Zambezi and the Shiré, now came back into favour.

[1] Anderson-Morshead, A. E. M., *The History of the Universities Mission to Central Africa* (1909); Wilson, G. H., *A History of the Universities Mission to Central Africa* (1936); Heanley, R. M., *A Memoir of Edward Steere* (3rd ed. 1898); Barnes, B. H., *Johnson of Nyasaland* (1933).
[2] Cf. *The Zambesi Journal of James Stewart*, ed. J. P. R. Wallis (1952).
[3] Young, E. D., *Nyassa* (1877); Laws, R., *Reminiscences of Livingstonia* (1934); Livingstone, W. P., *Laws of Livingstonia* (1921).
[4] Hetherwick, A., *The Romance of Blantyre* (n.d.).

It was clear, however, that the missionaries were in no position to organise this transport themselves; and accordingly, in 1878, the Livingstonia Central Africa Company was formed, in order to maintain the steamship service and to engage at the same time in the ivory trade, with the object of competing with the Arabs using slave labour. Two brothers, J. W. and F. L. M. Moir, were sent out as managers.[1]

From a business point of view, the Company was never a great success. It did not pay its first modest dividend of 2½ per cent until 1886.[2] It was too small and feeble to play the political role of the chartered companies on the Niger and in East Africa; and the attempt to maintain it in close association with the work of the missions led to inevitable difficulties on both sides. But the experiment was an interesting one, and it is peculiarly appropriate that it should have been made in the Shiré country; for it was a practical application of the principle that Livingstone had always urged so warmly—the union of Christianity and commerce.

In the political history of Tropical Africa the year 1885 is a clear and notable landmark. But in the fields of history treated in this chapter it has no special significance. The change in the character of African exploration, as we have seen, came in the 'seventies. It was in that decade, too, that the great expansion of the missions' work in East Africa began; while in West Africa the most important developments had already taken place in the middle years of the century. In the economic history of East Africa, again it is in the 'seventies, with the prohibition of the slave trade and the linking of Zanzibar with the rest of the world by a steamship service, that the great change is effected. In West Africa, a closely similar revolution had occurred thirty years earlier; and the next major development did not come until the later 'nineties.[3]

For all the great work that had been performed over the past century, Africa was still rightly called a "dark continent". Before it could be fully opened up, under European leadership, further changes were required, over and above the establishment of a settled political administration. Two of these may be indicated here.

Although the value of quinine as a prophylactic against malaria had been demonstrated on the Niger Expedition of 1854,[4] little progress was made in the understanding of that disease, or of the other dangerous African fevers. The health of the traders in the Niger delta probably benefited by their removal from the old "hulks", on which they had previously lived, to stations on land—a change that

[1] See Moir, F. L. M., *After Livingstone* (1923), and Hanna, A. J. *The Beginnings of Nyasaland and North-Eastern Rhodesia, 1859–95* (1956), p. 20.
[2] *Ibid.* p. 175.
[3] Cf. McPhee, *op. cit.* pp. 313–14.
[4] Baikie, W. B., *Narrative of an Exploring Voyage up the Rivers Kwora and Binue* (1856), pp. 328, 452–5. See also Hutchinson, T. J., *Impressions of Western Africa* (1858), pp. 212–50.

occurred in the 'seventies.[1] The National African Company allowed its employees frequent and generous leave, up to four or five months in the year, and it found the advantage of doing so: in 1885 Goldie claimed that out of a staff of seventy Europeans employed in West Africa, only one had died from the effects of the climate.[2] But this was plainly an expensive way of meeting the problem, and the government could not afford to maintain the large staffs in West Africa that such a method demanded. "*All* the men I have known there as consuls", wrote a senior official of the Foreign Office in the spring of 1885, "have died or broken down."[3] In the following November the position was that "out of a staff of four consular officers on the West Coast of Africa (of whom three were appointed this year), one is dead and the three others are in England on sick leave".[4] The Consular and Colonial Office correspondence of these years is full of such examples. They make it clear to us that before the great advances made by Manson and Ross in tropical medicine, from 1897 onwards, no efficient, continuous and economical administration by Europeans was possible in British West Africa.

An equally important obstacle to large-scale development in the 'eighties was the deficiency of mechanical transport. It is notable that really striking economic progress took place, during the period we are considering, in only two areas—on the Niger and the Congo. On these great rivers steamers could be used, freely and effectively, profiting by the experience acquired in West Africa from 1832 onwards.[5] In trades depending on land transport, progress was still very slow. It was plain that a great improvement could be effected only by railways. Some attempts were made to build roads.[6] But they were half-hearted; and, at this exact point in the history of mechanical transport, it is easy to see why. The development of the steam road motor, in a form suited to the conditions of the tropics, had begun in the 'sixties in Ceylon, Java and north-western India.[7] But no machine had yet been produced for this purpose that was at once economical and dependable. Until mechanical haulage was available, roads were of small value in Tropical Africa. Horses and oxen could be little used there, because of the tsetse-fly; and, in the forest country at least, a wide road was less well adapted for human porterage than the traditional narrow path, which furnished shelter from the sun and better protection from attack. At this time, therefore, the railway offered the greatest hope of progress.

[1] Geary, *op. cit.* p. 89. For a good account of a "hulk", see Whitford, *op. cit.* pp. 284–5.
[2] Minutes by C. L. Hill and Sir Percy Anderson on Hewett to Granville, 14 Feb. 1885: F.O. 84/1701.   [3] Hill's minute: *ibid.*
[4] Minute by Sir T. V. Lister on Johnston to Anderson, 24 Nov. 1885: F.O. 84/1702. Cf. also the comments of Acting Consul White on the Germans' difficulties from the same cause in his dispatch to Granville of 16 May 1885: F.O. 84/1701.
[5] Cf. *C.H.B.E.* II, 658.
[6] Cf. Claridge, *op. cit.* II, 247, and Coupland, *The Exploitation of East Africa*, pp. 302–3.
[7] See Kidner, R. W., *The First Hundred Road Motors* (1950), pp. 39, 45–8.

Further south, the first railways had already been built, in Natal (1860) and at the Cape (1863). To the north, the first railway in Egypt was opened in 1854, and more than 900 miles of line had been built by the end of the reign of Khedive Ismail in 1879.[1] Both in East and in West Africa, proposals for the building of railways were put forward in the 'seventies;[2] and Stanley made it clear from the start of his great enterprise that a railway would be an important adjunct to the exploitation of the Congo.[3] He declared in 1882 "that the Congo basin was not worth a two-shilling piece in its present state. To reduce it into profitable order, a railroad must be made between the Lower Congo and the Upper Congo, when with its accessibility will appear its value".[4] Yet by 1884 only a short stretch of local railway had been built;[5] and in British Tropical Africa not a single mile had even been surveyed. Again the reason was in part a technical one: the building of cheap light railways had not yet been fully developed. But the fundamental explanation was that the capital was not yet available. Railways in Tropical Africa were unlikely to make a commercial profit, at least for many years to come. If they were to be built, the money would have to be found by the government—either directly, or indirectly, by means of some kind of guarantee, after the fashion that had been adopted in India.[6] The British Government was not yet willing to shoulder any such additional burden.

At the time of the political partition of Tropical Africa, then, the economic development of the country, and what the Victorians compendiously called its "civilisation", were making slow, though important, headway. From 1885 onwards, if the rate of progress was to be quickened, the responsibility rested squarely upon the governments in Europe that had now assumed political control.

---

[1] Rifaat Bey, M., *The Awakening of Modern Egypt* (1947), p. 108.
[2] See, e.g., Cameron, *op. cit.* II, 332, and Whitford, *op. cit.* pp. 273–4.
[3] Stanley, *op. cit.* I, 25, 186–7.   [4] *Ibid.* I, 463.
[5] *Ibid.* II, 227.
[6] Cf. Anstey, V., *The Economic Development of India* (1929), pp. 131–3, and Macpherson, W. J., "Investment in Indian Railways, 1845–75", *Econ. Hist. Rev.* 2nd ser. VIII (1955–6), pp. 177–86.

CHAPTER IV

INTERNATIONAL RIVALRY IN THE
COLONIAL SPHERE, 1869–1885

I

THE Franco-Prussian War of 1870–1 was the end of a generation of rapid change in Europe. It put the last touches to a new territorial map of the Continent by depriving France of Alsace-Lorraine, by completing the unification of Germany and Italy and by confirming the relegation of the Austro-Hungarian Empire to south-eastern Europe. It was the last blow to the old balance of European power. Based for centuries on a weak German centre and strong French, Austrian and Russian wings, European politics were to rest in future on the predominance of the new Germany. Nor was it only the culmination of a series of territorial changes and of a revolution in the distribution of power. Germany emerged from the war as the strongest military force that Europe had ever known; the speed and extent of her defeat of France, paralleled only by her recent success against Austria, were the final proof that changes had also taken place in the organisation of some of the European states of a sort that were bound to alter the nature of relations between them all. Marking a further stage in the slow transition from the old days of professional armies and primitive supply to an age of universal conscription and modern military organisation, Prussia's victory, in addition to altering the balance of power, forced this transition on the attention of the whole of Europe.

The combined effect of these changes may be seen in the fact that the years from 1871 to the outbreak of the First World War were to be a period of armed peace. The new-found importance in war of speed of mobilisation and of mass in manœuvre emphasised, as never before, the need for military preparedness in time of peace. They increased, at the same time, the reluctance of the Powers to resort to war or to press policies beyond the lengths at which the risk of war arose. Given their increased hesitation to fight, the increased need of the Powers for war-readiness in time of peace produced, instead, a search for alliances and combinations of a more permanent nature and on a wider scale than Europe had hitherto experienced. The gradual evolution of alliance systems embracing all or nearly all the great states was to be another characteristic of the period. Germany's predominance in the new balance of power worked in the same direction. Germany did not determine that the situation between the Powers after 1870 should be one of deadlock: she was herself restrained by the deadlock that existed. But under Bismarck, influenced also by his flair for diplomacy, his conservative instincts and his determination to preserve the new Europe he had created, she made the deadlock more complete by accepting it and turning it to her purposes when she might have tried to resist it. It was Bismarck, anxious to keep France neutralised and to do so without further war, who set the pattern for the relations adopted by the Powers in the first twenty years after 1870. His determined answer to the French problem was friendship between Austria, Russia and Germany. As early as 1872, neither of the Eastern Powers being able to resist this programme, he had forced upon them the Three Emperors' League.

The pattern was not set firmly at once, however, nor was the effect of the changed situation on international relations as great at the outset as it was later to become. In one vital area of Europe, where things were far from being settled after 1870, there was still room for conflict and manœuvre; and another new feature, the national stirrings of the Balkan Slavs, made this area, the south-east, one in which developments were also passing beyond the control of the Powers. In 1875 revolts among Turkey's Christian populations in Bosnia and Herzegovina, coinciding with the collapse of Turkey's finances and spreading to Bulgaria in 1876, brought about a renewal of the Eastern Question when none of the Continental Powers wanted it to be renewed. Even then, the revolts forced compromise and co-operation on Austria and Russia, instead of bringing their natural and long-standing rivalry in this area to a head: each shrank from a collision, and Bismarck's determination to preserve the Three Emperors' League was another restraining influence. But Anglo-Russian rivalry in the Near East was as deep if not as long-standing as the rivalry of Austria and Russia; and this fact, together with British anxiety at the alignment into which the relations of the other Powers were falling, produced out of the revolts the great international crisis of 1876–8. There had already been a marked revival of anti-Russian feeling in Great Britain as a result of the Black Sea incident of 1870–1. Russia had then taken the opportunity provided by the Franco-Prussian War to declare that she would no longer be bound by those clauses of the Treaty of Paris which forbade her to maintain a fleet or build fortifications in the Black Sea. Gladstone's government, after rejecting Russia's declaration, had discovered that no other Power was prepared to join Great Britain in resisting it; and though obtaining the agreement of the Powers to the principle that the unilateral denunciation of treaties was contrary to the law of nations, it had finally acceded to Russia's demand and allowed her freedom of action in the Black Sea. As well as increasing British distrust of Russia, this incident had begun a change in Great Britain's outlook on Europe that was furthered by reflection on the formation of the Three Emperors' League. The contrast between Great Britain's isolation and Russia's membership of the League had been emphasised by an acceleration of Russia's expansion in Central Asia.[1] Anxiety at the contrast had joined with suspicion of Russia to help to bring about Gladstone's defeat and Disraeli's accession to power in the elections of 1874. And when Disraeli refused to co-operate with the other Powers in forcing reforms upon the Turkish Government in May 1876, but instead sent the British Fleet to Besika Bay, outside the Dardanelles, his motives were his suspicion that the reform programme would be used as a pretext for a Russian advance into Turkish territory[2] and his wish to destroy the Three Emperors' League by increasing the strain on Austro-Russian relations.[3]

Disraeli's decision precipitated the Near Eastern crisis. By leading Turkey to believe that Great Britain would support her in all circumstances against a Russian attack, it encouraged her to evade a reform programme drawn up by the Powers even after Disraeli's Cabinet had forced him to join the other Powers in what was virtually a return to the policy originally proposed by the Three Emperors' League.[4] Turkey's evasion tried Russia's patience too far: in April 1877, her prestige deeply involved by her earlier insistence that Turkey must obey or be coerced, she began the Russo-Turkish War. Coming on top of British disgust at Turkey's brutal suppression of the Bulgarian risings, which had generated the moral fervour of Gladstone's pamphlet on *The Bulgarian Horrors*, her action made it impossible for Disraeli to carry his Cabinet with him in taking measures that might, in the Cabinet's view, bring on an Anglo-Russian war.[5] Disraeli's object, however, was not to provoke war with Russia, but to restrain her from occupying Constantinople, even temporarily, and to place Great Britain in "a commanding position when the conditions of peace are discussed";[6] and after January 1878, when Turkish resistance collapsed and the occupation of Constantinople became a distinct possibility, the Cabinet began to agree with him that Russia would be a danger unless deterred. In March 1878 Russia, though nearly exhausted, imposed conditions on Turkey in the Treaty of San Stefano which seemed to confirm these fears. The treaty gave Montenegro, Serbia and Roumania their independence and increased their territories at Turkey's expense. It gave Russia Southern Bessarabia from Roumania, and Batum, Kars and large areas of Armenia from Turkey. Most important of all, it created an autonomous "big Bulgaria", whose frontiers stretched from the Danube to the Aegean and from the Black Sea to Albania, whose constitution was to be

---

[1] Below, pp. 100–7.
[2] Buckle, G. E., *Life of Disraeli*, VI, 34, 104–5, 120–2; *Letters of Queen Victoria*, 2nd ser. II, 455.
[3] Buckle, *op. cit.* VI, 13, 31, 104, 367.
[4] *Ibid.* pp. 103–6, 130–1; Cecil, Lady Gwendolen, *Life of Salisbury*, II, 93 *seqq.*
[5] Buckle, *op. cit.* VI, 142 *seqq.*; Cecil, *op. cit.* II, 139 *seqq.*
[6] Buckle, *op. cit.* VI, 139, 142, 146, 152, 176.

drawn up by a Russian commission and whose temporary occupation by Russia would further ensure its dependence on St Petersburg. The British Government, at last unanimous, decided that the treaty must be revised and that war must be declared if Russia insisted on her terms.[1]

The treaty had also affronted Austria; while Bismarck could not support Russia in going to such lengths. In seeking to undo it Lord Salisbury, who succeeded Lord Derby as Foreign Secretary at the end of March, exploited to the full both its unpopularity with the other Powers and the fact of Russia's exhaustion. But he still sought a compromise settlement by which Russia would retain some of her gains so long as she did not dominate the Balkans and Constantinople or Turkey-in-Asia, and even though this would involve Great Britain in a policy of strengthening Turkey in the areas that remained to her. In negotiations in the next two months, Russia agreed to exclude Macedonia from the "big Bulgaria" and to divide the rest of it into two provinces along the line of the Balkan mountains, only the northern provinces receiving complete autonomy from Turkey. She kept her conquests in Turkey-in-Asia, including Batum, but repudiated any intention of extending them. In order to secure German and Austrian support in insisting on these arrangements, Salisbury concluded an agreement with Austro-Hungary by which she was to receive a mandate for the occupation of Bosnia and Hercegovina at some date to be decided. To counterbalance the concessions to Russia, he forced the Turks to accept the additional loss of Cyprus, which was ceded to Great Britain as a *place d'armes* in return for a British guarantee of Turkey's remaining possessions in Asia, and to agree to British supervision of reforms in the Asian provinces.[2] All these arrangements were confirmed, though not without a more than formal show of resistance by Russia, at the Congress of Berlin in June 1878. At the Congress Salisbury provided further evidence of Great Britain's determination to resist Russian expansion in the Near East by declaring that, though continuing to uphold the Sultan's right to close the Straits to Russia, she would in future disregard his right to keep them closed against the passage of British warships into the Black Sea if she considered that he was acting under undue pressure from another Power.[3]

The chief consequence of the Near Eastern crisis and the chief feature of the 1878 settlement was thus the recognition that Turkey had ceased to be an effective neutral barrier between Russia and Great Britain. If these two Powers had previously, on account of the existence in Turkey of room for manœuvre, been less restrained than

---

[1] Buckle, *op. cit.* p. 257; Cecil, *op. cit.* II, 207, 211–12.
[2] Cecil, *op. cit.* II, 227 *seqq.*; Buckle, *op. cit.* VI, chap. viii.
[3] Cecil, *op. cit.* II, chap. viii; Buckle, *op. cit.* VI, chap. ix; Langer, *op. cit.* pp. 150 *seqq.*; Taylor, A. J. P., *The Struggle for Mastery in Europe*, pp. 251–2.

others, and had nearly clashed, they too were now brought up against the fact that Turkey could hardly suffer further dismemberment without the certainty of a major war between them. At the same time, Russia's gains increased Austrian latent suspicion of her designs in the Balkans even when Russia's exhaustion and Great Britain's new commitments made it less likely than before that Russia would pursue them; and this fact pushed Germany further than she had previously gone in the policy of restraining her neighbours by alignments and alliances. In concluding the Austro-German Alliance of 1879 Bismarck's object was not only to keep Austria apart from France, but to curb her restlessness towards Russia and to force her to accept reconciliation with Russia. By the middle of 1881 he had succeeded in reviving the Three Emperors' League. This completed the deadlock between the Powers on the subject of the Eastern Question. And if the Eastern Question became the source of less fierce but even more inconclusive rivalry after the Berlin settlement, this fact heightened the degree of stalemate existing throughout Europe. After 1878, even more than in the years since 1871, the European Powers shrank from serious European conflicts for more than thirty years, during which period they sought security against the complications of modern warfare and adjustments to the new balance of power in increasingly complicated systems of alliances and counter-alliances.

This was perhaps the main reason why, after 1878, the Powers began to exert themselves beyond Europe to a greater extent than they had done before: European rivalries and anxieties, restrained within the Continent, were projected on to the wider canvas of the outside and undeveloped world. It was not the sole reason for this development. In reaching out beyond Europe the Powers were also impelled by the forces of economic expansion and the need for new fields for financial investment. In the years immediately after the Congress of Berlin they were influenced, not to say overtaken, by the disintegrating effects upon Turkey's outlying provinces in North Africa of this futher evidence that Turkey's days were numbered as an effective Great Power. In subsequent years, colonial gains and losses bred further colonial rivalry of themselves. Yet deadlock in Europe was, if not the most immediate incentive, at least the chief underlying condition in the great phase of extra-European expansion that now began. From the beginning of the phase, the policies of the governments, if not of all elements in the states, were dominated by strategic rather than by economic and financial motives, by considerations of balance and relative position, in Europe no less than throughout the world, rather than by purely colonial interests; and these were the motives and considerations that always would be prominent. Against a background of stalemate and compromise in the Eastern Question, it was they which produced the first serious extra-European clash, that between Russia and Great Britain on the North-West Frontier of India in 1878. And they were still uppermost in the colonial issues of the twentieth century that immediately preceded the First World War.

II

It was natural enough that Russia should try to subdue the nomad tribes, the independent oases and the dying khanates east of the Caspian. She began the task as soon as she had completed, at the end of the 'fifties, the similar work of subjugating the Caucasian mountaineers; her extension into these undeveloped borderlands corresponded to that of other Powers in other backward areas. But it was equally to be expected that her advance should revive, in some British minds, the threat to British India, and especially when it became more intensive after the creation of the new province of Russian Turkestan in 1867.

Since the failure in the First Afghan War to establish direct British influence at Kabul, British policy had been to remain aloof from Afghanistan's internal affairs. Since the conquest, by way of compensation, of Sind in 1847 and of the Punjab in 1849, it had shown no interest in the expansion of British rule to other territories of the North-West Frontier. Each of these principles was challenged in the 'sixties by those who feared the consequences of Russia's southward progress. As early as 1865 Sir Henry Rawlinson, in *The Quarterly Review*, was pressing for the appointment of a British representative in Afghanistan and the provision of aid to the Amir.[1] In 1866 experts in India proposed the British occupation of Quetta, a position of great natural strength which dominates the Afghan approaches to the Indus valley.[2] Though these proposals went unheeded at the time, the Government in London, under Disraeli until 1868 no less than under Gladstone after him, refusing to take an alarmist view, and the Government of India remaining wedded to the traditional policy of "masterly inactivity", nevertheless there was growing uneasiness at Russia's advance, even in official circles, after 1867.

Requests for aid from the various pretenders to the Afghan throne were ignored in 1866; but what had been refused in 1866 the Viceroy advised the Cabinet to grant in 1867.[3] Requests from an increasingly anxious Afghanistan for an unconditional guarantee against Russia were rejected in 1869; but what the Amir was then offered—arms, ammunition and a money subsidy at the discretion of the Viceroy— was as significant as what he was denied.[4] The Amir repeated his request in 1873, when London and Calcutta again agreed on its

[1] Rawlinson, G., *A Memoir of Sir Henry Rawlinson*, pp. 257–8.
[2] *C.H.B.E.* v, 406–7.
[3] Davies, G. C., *The North-West Frontier, 1890–1908*, pp. 8–9.
[4] *Ibid.*; *C.H.B.F.P.* iii, 74, 76–7.

rejection. But on that occasion Lord Northbrook, a Viceroy of the traditional school, proposed instead that, in return for British control of her foreign policy, Afghanistan should be offered assistance at the discretion of the Cabinet against an unprovoked attack[1]. This proposal was rejected by the Gladstone government, together with the Amir's own demand. It still marked, however, another small inroad into the principles of non-interference and "masterly inactivity". And whether the inroads of 1867 and 1869 were due to the effect on official opinion of Rawlinson's campaign,[2] or to the fact that the Viceroy was forced to change his mind because Afghanistan began to turn to Russia for the help he refused,[3] the move of 1873 was due to the effect on the Government of India, if not on Gladstone's Cabinet, of Russia's conduct in her continued advance in Central Asia, as well as of the Black Sea incident of 1870–1.

If only because of the British reluctance to make these concessions to altered circumstances, it had become a necessary corollary of the traditional outlook since 1867 that the problem of the North-West Frontier must be settled by negotiation between London and St Petersburg.[4] Twice during Gladstone's first administration, in 1869 and 1873, when the fall of Samarkand and Bokhara in 1868 had made Russia a neighbour of Afghanistan in the south-east, talks were held with the Russian Government in an attempt to define the spheres of influence of the two Empires and establish a neutral zone between them.[5] But these negotiations and Russia's subsequent conduct had only emphasised that diplomacy could not achieve a stable settlement so long as there was no departure from the policy of "masterly inactivity" on the North-West Frontier itself. Russia had evaded the British proposal that the Oxus should be the northern boundary of the neutral zone.[6] In 1873 she had denied any intention of taking Khiva[7]; yet Khiva had been absorbed within the year. Samarkand, which she had occupied avowedly as a temporary measure, had been retained. In Afghanistan, despite assurances given in 1869 and 1873 that it would remain outside the Russian sphere of influence, there had been increasing evidence of her interference since 1872.[8]

It was not difficult to account for Russia's unreliability or for her refusal to be tied down. Inadequate communication between St Petersburg and the forward areas allowed free play to the enthusiasm of officers in the field. In St Petersburg itself there was a struggle between the expansionist school and the Court, between the War Ministry and the Foreign Office. Because of the unsettled nature of

---

[1] *C.H.B.E.* v, 409–11.
[2] Roberts, Lord, *Forty-One Years in India*, II, 45–8.
[3] *C.H.B.E.* v, 406–7.
[4] Lord Lawrence first suggested this in 1867, when Disraeli's government replied that Russia's movements caused no anxiety. *C.H.B.F.P.* III, 73.
[5] *C.H.B.F.P.* III, 75; *C.H.B.E.* v, 409.
[6] *Ibid.*   [7] *Ibid.* pp. 412–13.
[8] *Ibid.* p. 412.

the area, the nomadic habits of its people and the difficulty of its terrain, the extension of civilised power was often the only alternative to withdrawal; and some at least of Russia's broken promises were due to this dilemma.[1] But it was still impossible to overlook the fact that territory was fast changing hands. For all the mitigating circumstances—which were understood by all except the most Russophobe of British critics—a threat to Afghanistan, traditional gateway for India's invaders, India's "Achilles' heel", might still arise from local actions which St Petersburg could turn to advantage even if they had arisen from circumstances beyond St Petersburg's control. And while it seemed clear that Russia did not seriously contemplate the invasion of India, it was equally clear that she knew the value of the threat to India as an asset in political strategy—as "a basis of operations which, if need be, can be offensive",[2] as a "check on Great Britain in other directions".[3]

It was for these reasons that, even before Disraeli replaced Gladstone in power in 1874, the Government of India had begun to feel the need for a different regulation of Anglo-Afghan relations; and doubts about the traditional policy had been strengthened by the quicker gravitation of the Amir to Russia since Great Britain's refusal either to meet his demands or to accept the Northbrook proposal in 1873.[4] Gladstone's succession by Disraeli only confirmed that a shift in British policy would take place. Gladstone's government, lagging behind the Government of India, had continued to hope that the problem would be solved by the effect of time and persuasion on the Amir and in further negotiations with Russia. Disraeli, who had long regarded Great Britain as an Asiatic as well as a European Power and who was soon to be preoccupied with the visit of the Prince of Wales to India, the purchase of the Suez Canal shares and the legislation by which the Queen became Empress of India, was hoping for "an opportunity for settling and strengthening our frontiers" in India within a few months of coming to office.[5] But there was no immediate change of policy after the change of government; and the change that was eventually effected was only the logical outcome of the doubts about "masterly inactivity" that had been growing up since 1866.

It was not until January 1875 that Salisbury, the new Indian Secretary, on behalf of a Cabinet that was aware of the difficulties and dangers,[6] ordered the Viceroy to take measures to place a resident agent in Afghanistan.[7] This decision to pursue a more forward policy was not accompanied by increased impatience with Russia or a

---

[1] Meyendorff, Baron A. (ed.), *Correspondance diplomatique du Baron de Staal*, I, 42–3.
[2] The Russian Foreign Minister in 1883, quoted in Sumner, B. H., *Survey of Russian History*, p. 435.
[3] The Russian Foreign Minister in 1884, quoted in Meyendorff, *op. cit.* I, 26.
[4] *C.H.B.E.* v, 412.
[5] Buckle, *op. cit.* v, 416, 426; June 1874.
[6] *Ibid.* p. 427.
[7] *Parl. Pap.* 1878–9, LVI [C. 2190], p. 502; Cecil, *op. cit.* II, 71–2.

disposition to abandon negotiations with St Petersburg.[1] When Northbrook objected to the instructions the Cabinet allowed nearly a year to pass in argument and discussion before insisting that they should be obeyed.[2] Northbrook, as is evident from his proposal of 1873, recognised that the situation had changed in the past few years. "There is a point upon which I would fight," he admitted in January 1875, "and I would let the Russians know this very clearly."[3] But he could not agree with the London government that it had already proved "futile to base the safety of the North-West Frontier on any understanding, stipulation, convention or treaty with the imperial (Russian) Government".[4] He also opposed his instructions because he thought they would necessarily lead to British expansion and war in Afghanistan. In the light of this argument, his counter-proposal— that the change of policy should be delayed till Russia had occupied Merv[5]—reveals that he was chiefly anxious to put off the evil day. But he resigned rather than listen to the arguments which Salisbury addressed to this flaw in his case.[6]

Lord Lytton, his successor, arrived in India in March 1876 with orders to send a mission to the Amir, to obtain the Amir's consent to the establishment of a British resident agent in Afghanistan and to concede, in return, the Amir's demands of 1869 and 1873. He was also instructed to negotiate an agreement with Kalat, the Khanate on Afghanistan's southern frontier, for the British occupation of Quetta. He was given complete discretion as to when to carry out these orders.[7] But his arrival in India coincided with the outbreak of the Eastern Question, and this made the London government even more cautious than before about its decision to adopt a forward policy in Afghanistan. Lytton's orders were allowed to stand. His negotiations with Kalat were completed by the end of 1876. Quetta was occupied as a result in 1877. There was some strengthening of British influence, involving minor military operations, among the tribes on the Punjab frontier. But when the negotiations with the Amir proved difficult, and when the Peshawar Conference between British and Afghan delegations broke down in March 1877, no further pressure on Afghanistan was allowed for fear of widening the breach with Russia at a time when Great Britain and Russia were on the verge of war over Turkey.[8]

Neither Disraeli nor Salisbury had changed his views about the ultimate solution of the problem of the North-West Frontier. They still believed that Russia would make it a constant source of anxiety

[1] Buckle, op. cit. v, 416, 422; Letters of Queen Victoria, 2nd ser. III, 338, 391.
[2] Dispatch of 19 Nov. 1875; Parl. Pap. 1878–9, LVI [C. 2190], p. 521.
[3] C.H.B.F.P. III, 77.
[4] Lord Dufferin to Salisbury, quoted in C.H.B.E. v, 414.
[5] C.H.B.F.P. III, 79.
[6] For Salisbury's arguments, see Cecil, op. cit. II, 70, 72–3.
[7] Dispatch of 28 Feb. 1876; Parl. Pap. 1878–9, LVI [C. 2190], p. 530.
[8] Cecil, op. cit. II, 74–5, 124–5, 157–9.

unless she were stopped, and that only determined action in Afghanistan would stop her.[1] But Disraeli was preoccupied with the Eastern Question, and Salisbury was determined to delay the grasping of the Afghan nettle until the Eastern Question was settled. He took this view partly in the hope that some solution on the North-West Frontier could be incorporated in a general settlement with Russia when the Turkish question came to a head; and he made efforts in this direction at the Constantinople Conference. But he also felt that the situation in Afghanistan had been allowed to drift too long for a peaceful solution to be possible, and that, as force in Afghanistan would be necessary, it would be better to delay the issue.

The Government of India took a different view of the Turkish crisis and saw only the Indian aspects of the Russo-Turkish war. Crediting Russia in advance with the increased prestige that would result from a victory over Turkey, they argued the imminence of her attack through Afghanistan and requested London's approval in May and July 1877 for action to forestall it.[2] The Cabinet warned Russia that Great Britain must occupy Herat or Kandahar if Russia moved to Merv. But it rejected all other suggestions from India and refused to move a soldier beyond the Indian frontier.[3] Opinion in India accordingly crystallised into open opposition to London's cautious policy. It sought justification in the continued drift of the Amir to Russia's side. The Peshawar Conference had shown how much ground had already been lost in this respect by the beginning of 1877. The Amir had refused the British mission on the plea that to accept it would prevent him from refusing a mission from Russia. He had thus treated Russia as being on an equal footing with Great Britain, which had not been his attitude in 1873. The merits of the waiting policy, on the other hand, were not only that it succeeded in delaying a crisis in Afghanistan until the Berlin Congress had almost finished its work, but that, when the crisis came, it was provocation by the Amir and Russia that brought matters to a head and justified decisive action by Great Britain.

Early in June 1878 the Russian Government, frustrated in the Near East but emboldened like the Amir by British forbearance in the past eighteen months, and hoping also to influence the deliberations of the Berlin Congress, took the step that precipitated the Second Afghan War by sending a mission under Stolietoff to the Amir.[4] At the same time three columns of Russian troops were set on the march from Tashkent towards Afghanistan. Stolietoff, who was given only half-hearted warnings by the Amir to stay out of the country, was fêted on his arrival at Kabul; and this raised the ques-

---

[1] Cecil, op. cit. II, 153–4.
[2] Ibid. pp. 152, 157.   [3] Ibid. pp. 157–8.
[4] For further details of the crisis, see Parl. Pap. 1878, LXXXI [C. 1905] and 1881, XCVIII [C. 2798]; also C.H.B.E. V, 417 seqq.

tion of Anglo-Afghan relations in an acute form. The Government of India, refusing to regard the mission as merely a Russian reply to Great Britain's diplomatic success in the Eastern Question, insisted that, in view of his persistent refusal to receive a British envoy, its reception was an open breach of his obligations by the Amir. It demanded London's approval for the immediate dispatch of a British mission to Afghanistan. When this was given it sent a letter to Kabul announcing the mission and asking for a friendly reception. When no reply was received from the Amir it announced to the Cabinet on 8 September its determination to send the mission without further delay. The Cabinet split on the issue. Salisbury, still temporising, opened a direct correspondence with St Petersburg. Disraeli and the new Indian Secretary, Cranbrook, inclined to Lytton's view that his proposal was logically involved in the dispatch of the letter which the Cabinet had approved, and that it was essential to establish British ascendancy in Afghanistan.[1] Lytton felt bold enough, in these circumstances, to order the mission forward on 20 September on his own authority. When the mission was stopped on the Afghan frontier and forced to withdraw, Lytton was left with no alternative but to recommend to the Cabinet the declaration of war on the Amir. The Cabinet, after further discussion and more temporising,[2] was left with no alternative but to agree that an ultimatum should be sent and that the Government of India should be supported as if there had been no difference of opinion between London and Calcutta. No reply was received to the ultimatum, and British troops crossed the Afghan frontier at three points on 21 November.

The subsequent campaign was brilliant in its rapidity, in the small loss of life and in its completely successful results. Not only did Great Britain obtain all she had contended for in Afghanistan—the establishment of a mission at Kabul, the control of Afghan foreign policy, the cession of some frontier districts and the command over the Khyber and Michnee Passes. She obtained these things, as well as the withdrawal of the Russian mission, without running the risk of complications with Russia. Fortuitously or otherwise, Lytton and Cranbrook, the chief movers, had chosen to reassert British ascendancy in Afghanistan at the moment when the Amir's hostility was at its height and at the moment when Russia's freedom of action had been destroyed. Her intervention in the Second Afghan War would have involved tearing up the agreement so recently concluded at the Congress of Berlin; her resources were so depleted by the recent war with Turkey that she dared not take this step. Even before Stolietoff had arrived in Kabul he had been informed that a settlement had been reached at Berlin and warned against making positive promises to the Amir.[3]

---

[1] For details of the disagreement in the Cabinet, see Cecil, *op. cit.* II, 338 *seqq.* and Buckle, *op. cit.* VI, 379–82.

[2] Cecil, *op. cit.* II, 341–2; Buckle, *op. cit.* VI, 383–8.   [3] *C.H.B.E.* V, 417.

When the Amir applied to Kaufmann for assistance on the outbreak of war he was advised to make peace if he could.[1] The success of the campaign was dimmed and the favourable nature of the settlement was obscured by the massacre, in September 1879, of the British mission that had been established in Kabul, a setback which required the renewal of the Afghan War. But the war was renewed without complications from Russia and without prejudice to the settlement, the solidity of which was to be proved in after years.

In the light of Russia's discomfiture and inactivity, Lytton and Cranbrook have been criticised for taking an over-serious view of the Afghan situation and Disraeli for deliberately making the war in the interests of a "scientific" frontier and territorial aggression. What Lytton had to consider, however, was not whether a Russian invasion of India was intended, but the fact that there was a widespread belief in its possibility "in every assemblage of chiefs from Tabriz to Peshawar"[2] and the fact that this belief would continue to grow so long as the closer relations between Russia and Afghanistan remained undisturbed. As for the charge against Disraeli, it is true that the Afghan War was the fulfilment of the change of policy on which his government had decided in 1875 and which Lytton had been entrusted to carry out in 1876. He had publicly announced before the outbreak of the war that the North-West Frontier "is a haphazard and not a scientific frontier" and that "the time has arrived when we must terminate all this inconvenience".[3] But it would be difficult to deny the wisdom of this policy. Clarity and firmness are the only alternatives to friction between states in such uncertain circumstances as those which existed on the North-West Frontier; the lack of resources is the only justification for the lack of firmness. It was the Russian conquest of Turkestan which made firmness essential in the interests, not so much of the defence of India, as of settled relations with Russia. It was the conduct of Russia and the Amir which made it necessary to effect the change by ultimatum and war. And it was the earlier failure of British policy to adjust to new circumstances which had induced Russia and the Amir to behave as they did.

Nor was stability on the North-West Frontier the only consideration for the British Government. Russia's interest in the control of Afghanistan was not so much that it would enable her to invade India as that it would strengthen the threat to India for use in the wider field of relations between the Powers. Great Britain's interest in the defence of India had the same wider implications. None saw these more clearly than Disraeli. "It is not a question", he told the Lords on 11 December 1878, "of the Khyber Pass merely.... It is a question which concerns the character and influence of England in

[1] Parl. Pap. 1881, xcviii [C. 2798], pp. 353–5.
[2] Frere, Letter to Durand, p. 44, quoted in C.H.B.E. v, 418.
[3] Buckle, op. cit. vi, 390–1.

Europe.... The principle of peace at any price...has done more mischief than any I can well recall...."[1]

III

Coming on top of a similar disaster in Zululand, itself an incident in a series of unwelcome petty wars, the Kabul massacre and the renewal of the Afghan War created a profound revulsion against the policies of Disraeli's government and ensured its defeat in the elections of 1880. Gladstone's return to power, with his different views on foreign policy, came at a time when the centre of gravity in the relations between the Powers was shifting in any case. It was not only at its centre, and not only in its repercussions on Anglo-Russian rivalry at the Straits and in Central Asia, that the decline of the Ottoman Empire had become an international issue. By 1880, when Disraeli's policies, for all their unpopularity, had replaced friction by settlement in Anglo-Russian relations, this decline had reached an advanced stage in Egypt and Tunisia and was to involve the Mediterranean in the rivalries between the Powers.

Technically Turkish provinces, Egypt and Tunisia had in large measure obtained their independence of the Porte. To an even greater extent than Turkey itself, they had become fields for European investment and concessions. Whether it was the result of mismanagement by the Khedive and the Bey,[2] or of robbery by European financiers,[3] or of a general governmental inadequacy of which these other features were but the symptoms, they were, by 1870, already faced with financial collapse. The 'seventies saw further developments at a time when the financial problem was beginning to call for the more direct intervention of the Powers. Whereas France had so far been the only Power directly interested in the provinces, Italian agitation for the acquisition of Tunisia by Italy developed as a result of the growth in numbers of Italian colonists. Although Great Britain had long been determined that the provinces should not fall to France, her determination was strengthened in the case of Egypt by the rapid increase in the use of the Suez Canal by British shipping[4] and by her purchase of the Khedive's canal shares. On account of the strain it put on the relations between the Powers, the renewal of the Eastern Question also served to bring the problem of the future of the provinces into the forefront.

Between 1875 and 1877 the suggestion that France or Italy should take Tunis and that Great Britain should take Egypt was urged more than once by Germany, Austria or Russia in an attempt to reach a settlement favourable to themselves on the subject of Turkey.[5] These various suggestions were all ignored. France was suspicious of any proposal from Germany. Italy would not look at the Tunis bait for

---

[1] Buckle, *op. cit.* VI, 400–1.   [2] *C.H.B.F.P.* III, 154–5.
[3] Langer, *op. cit.* pp. 218–19, 252–6.   [4] Hoskins, *British Routes to India*, pp. 469–70.
[5] Langer, *op. cit.* pp. 53–4, 99, 121, 123–4, 160.

fear of abandoning her friendship with France. Largely for the same reason Disraeli, though he defended the Suez purchase "as a political transaction...calculated to strengthen the Empire", would neither follow up the purchase nor listen to Bismarck's hints about Egypt.[1] The fact that his policy in the Eastern Question involved insistence on the integrity of the Porte also deterred him from taking action, as did his conviction that the occupation of Egypt, far from being adequate compensation for Russian gains in the Balkans, would only be "an expensive encumbrance" so long as Russia, by dominating Constantinople, could at any time march to the Nile.[2] But though, for these reasons, the interested Powers made no move during the Turkish crisis, the Russo-Turkish War and the Berlin settlement involved so much interference with Turkey's sovereign rights and so much confirmation of Turkey's continued decline as to bring forward the time for decision about her outlying provinces; and negotiations at the Congress of Berlin reflected the recognition of this fact by the statesmen concerned. Bismarck renewed his proposal that France should take Tunis. Salisbury supported him by promising to approve of the acquisition, his motive being Great Britain's need to buy off French opposition to the Cyprus Convention.[3] At the same time, having previously been disposed to secure the sole control of Egypt in due course at the expense of friction with France, he accepted the policy of parity with France in Egypt.[4] He refused, however, to meet the French request that this should be put into the obligatory form of a convention, arguing that, in the event of further collapse in Turkey, "it may suit us at some future time to push ahead".[5]

These arrangements were the framework within which, in the next few years, the grip of France in Tunis and of France and Great Britain in Egypt gradually tightened. Continual disputes with Italy convinced a reluctant France, more anxious to deny Tunisia to other Powers than to acquire it herself, that action there was at last unavoidable. In April 1881, using one of the frequent raids by tribesmen into Algeria as a pretext, she sent a punitive expedition to Tunisia and quickly established a protectorate. Italy's appeals to the Powers were of no avail. The new Liberal government in Great Britain had only grudgingly recognised the commitments undertaken by Salisbury; it was irritated by the French action.[6] But it made no protest. Germany warned the Porte against retaliation.[7] In Egypt, meanwhile, the failure of earlier attempts to stabilise the finances by means of an international *Caisse de la Dette Publique* had led Great Britain and France to intervene directly. They first insisted on the establishment

---

[1] Buckle, *op. cit.* vi, 353.   [2] *Ibid.* pp. 83–4, 100, 102, 104.
[3] Cecil, *op. cit.* ii, 332.   [4] *Ibid.* pp. 329–32.
[5] *Ibid.* pp. 331–5.
[6] Lord Fitzmaurice, *Life of Granville*, ii, 234–5; Gwynn, S., and Tuckwell, G. M., *Life of Sir Charles Dilke*, i, 330; Newton, Lord, *Life of Lord Lyons*, ii, 241; Langer, *op. cit.* pp. 222–4.   [7] Langer, *op. cit.* p. 225.

of a responsible ministry containing a French and a British minister and committed to a programme of financial reform. In April 1879, when the Khedive dismissed this ministry and produced a financial scheme of his own, they secured the deposition of the Khedive by the Porte, his succession by his son, Tewfik, and the establishment of their joint control over the country.

In the chapter of accidents which led to the breakdown of the Franco-British Dual Control the chief feature was the development of unrest in Egypt which, though led by disaffected soldiers, was "national as well as military...anti-European and, above all,... anti-Turk".[1] Resenting the Khedive's deposition as foreign dictation, resenting the Dual Control on the same grounds and also because, by limiting domestic expenditure, it reduced the army and blocked the way to large-scale reforms, resenting also the fact that their seniors were all Turks or Circassians, the officers of several regiments under Colonel Ahmed Arabi forced the resignation of the Minister of War in January 1881. Joined by nationalist forces, they secured the dismissal of the entire ministry in September. In December, appealing to constitutionalism as well as to nationalism, the new Chamber demanded the reduction of foreign tutelage and the parliamentary right to control the expenditure of at least part of the revenue that was not appropriated for debt payments. The French Government disapproved of the nationalist movement; British officials in Egypt generally supported the French view that it was a threat to the Dual Control, which should be safeguarded at all costs.[2] The Liberal government in Great Britain adopted the same view when, under French pressure, it joined France in delivering the Gambetta Note to the Egyptian Government in January 1882. The Gambetta Note,[3] which declared that the two governments regarded the maintenance of the powers of the Khedive as "alone able to guarantee...the good order and development of general prosperity in Egypt", was a rejection of the demands of the Chamber. It specifically mentioned the Chamber as one of the dangers to the Khedive.

But Gladstone's government took this step reluctantly; and its policy or lack of policy in the next few months was chiefly responsible for making an already awkward situation even worse. Embarrassed at the outset by the incompatibility of the Dual Control with Gladstone's doctrine of national freedom and the ideal of "Egypt for the Egyptians",[4] it wavered between its own principles and French pressure, between its unwillingness to intervene and its reluctance to see France intervene without it. In its anxiety to accept as little responsibility as possible for the government of Egypt it would have preferred to call in Turkey to restore order there, overlooking the fact, which Gladstone later admitted,[5] that France and Great Britain

[1] Morley, *op. cit.* III, 73.   [2] Langer, *op. cit.* pp. 269–71.
[3] Langer, *op. cit.* p. 226.   [4] Morley, *op. cit.* III, 76–7.   [5] *Ibid.* p. 74.

had already assumed political responsibility in the strictest sense when establishing the Dual Control. In its anxiety to prevent unilateral action by France, it abandoned its preference for intervention by Turkey, as the suzerain, or, failing that, by France and Great Britain with a mandate from all the European Powers, when further action in Egypt became unavoidable and these proposals were opposed by the French. But no sooner had the Gladstone Government adopted the policy of the Gambetta Note than it went back on the pledge of conditional joint action in the Note, warned France that it wished to preserve the rights of sovereign and vassal as between the Sultan and the Khedive and opened negotiations for an international conference. One reason, in addition to its original reluctance, for this change of front was the fact that the Note produced a protest from the Porte, which saw an opportunity to re-establish its shattered sovereignty in Egypt, against the unauthorised action of the two Powers. More important, however, was the change of front by the other European Powers, under Bismarck's leadership, after the delivery of the Note.

The change in Bismarck's attitude was the third feature in the complicated situation which led to the British occupation of Egypt. Before the delivery of the Gambetta Note he had seemed to approve the course of action of the two Powers most concerned. It was, indeed, his unexpected action in publicly protesting against the Khedive's new finance scheme in 1879 that had induced Great Britain to insist on the Khedive's deposition.[1] Under his leadership, all the Powers had joined Great Britain and France in pressing this demand on the Sultan. At the same time he had assured the French and British Governments that he had no intention of infringing in any way the political field of the Anglo-French *entente*.[2] But when the Gambetta Note was issued, Germany, Russia, Austria and Italy at once met to discuss it and hinted that they disapproved. On 2 February 1882 they issued identical notes to the Sultan declaring that the *status quo* in Egypt should not be modified without previous understanding between the Great Powers and Turkey.[3] Developments in Europe made this change of policy possible. In June 1881 Bismarck at last managed to revive the Three Emperors' League—dissolved after the Congress of Berlin—by the signature of the Alliance of the Three Emperors.[4] Before that date he had needed to promote the collaboration of France and Great Britain in order to prevent France from becoming desperate and drifting into dependence on Russia. Having secured the Alliance, he felt free to oppose French initiative in Egypt; and, though he approved the French occupation of Tunis, he wanted Great Britain and not France to play the leading role in Egypt, probably in the hope of keeping the two Powers divided.[5]

---

[1] Langer, *op. cit.* pp. 260–1.
[2] *Documents diplomatiques français*, II, nos. 408, 430, 440; Langer, *op. cit.* p. 261.
[3] Langer, *op. cit.* pp. 267–8.   [4] *Ibid.* pp. 197–212.   [5] *Ibid.* pp. 267, 277–8.

In any event, his action encouraged the real preference of the British Government for an international rather than a dual solution, which was itself the beginning of the rift between Great Britain and France. But this rift was further deepened by the development of yet another complication: indecisiveness on the part of France. Gambetta had been determined on direct intervention by France and Great Britain, with France in the lead and the other Powers excluded. His fall from power, on a domestic issue, had coincided with the delivery of the notes of Germany, Russia, Austria and Italy to the Porte on 2 February. The return to the scene of the European Powers had as marked an effect on France as on Great Britain. If Freycinet, Gambetta's successor, had little of Gambetta's determination to keep the initiative it was because of this recent reminder of Bismarck's interest. The French Chamber was even more affected than Freycinet by a renewed anxiety to avoid risks outside Europe in order to meet those within it. Its policy in 1882 was "dominated by the German terror,...the direct outcome of our defeats in 1870 on the Continent".[1] In bringing about the final break between France and Great Britain this French fear of Germany was as important as the difference of view that had already developed between the two countries on the subject of intervention in Egypt.

Because of this fear the keynote of French, as of British, policy after the fall of Gambetta was the internationalisation of the Egyptian question. But because Great Britain wanted to secure a European mandate for Turkish intervention in Egypt while France, fearing the consequences of this course for her position in Algeria and Tunis, wanted to secure such a mandate for Franco-British intervention, this coincidence of policy failed to heal the Anglo-French breach. On the contrary, anxiety to conceal their differences led the two countries to drift into expedients which only conflicted with their desire to internationalise the problem and only made their relations even more strained. When the nationalists in Egypt, influenced by the Gambetta Note, forced a nationalist ministry on the Khedive in February 1882 and then began to demand his deposition, the two Powers sent warships to Alexandria and demanded the resignation of the ministry and the exile of Arabi. At the insistence of Great Britain, however, they agreed not to land troops, but to continue to work for the summoning of a conference at Constantinople at which the Powers would give Turkey a mandate for direct action, despite the fact that their action—a partial return to the policy of the Gambetta Note, and thus another blow to the dignity of the Porte—induced Turkey to delay the calling of a conference. By further inciting the nationalists in Egypt, moreover, the action precipitated anti-foreign riots, helped Arabi to become dictator of the country and made further action unavoidable before an international procedure could be arranged.

[1] Deschanel, Paul, *Gambetta* (Eng. edn.), p. 321.

Egypt was already in Arabi's power when the conference at last met at Constantinople on 23 June. On 3 July, while the conference was still debating the conditions on which Turkey would pacify the country, the British Government ordered the British admiral to destroy the fortifications that were being built at Alexandria, unless work stopped on them after due warning. This was yet another change of front by Great Britain, made under the pressure of events in Egypt and of fear for the Canal. In taking it, however, Gladstone, who without consulting the Cabinet, had already refused the Sultan's offer of the "control and administration of Egypt" to the exclusion of France,[1] was still determined to avoid the landing of troops as constituting "the assumption of authority" and as "disloyal" to Europe and the conference,[2] and was careful to ask France and Italy to co-operate. But Italy refused because the Powers had undertaken no separate action; and France withdrew her ships on the grounds that bombardment would be an act of war which the Government could not undertake without the consent of the Chamber. And when, after the bombardment of 11 July, Great Britain found herself forced to take the further decision to land troops, France again refused to co-operate. Freycinet was willing to do so provided action were limited to the defence of the Canal and a mandate were obtained by the two Powers to act in the name of Europe. But the other Powers refused to bind themselves so formally and the French Chamber, convinced that Bismarck was plotting to drag the country into a morass of foreign complications, overthrew the Government. Six weeks later, at Tel-el-Kebir on 13 September 1882, the British troops under Wolseley "in one rapid and well-delivered blow, crushed the rebellion".[3]

Thus it was that the British Government, which had all along set its face against Anglo-French intervention, let alone against isolated action by Great Britain, found itself in solitary occupation of Egypt, while the French, who had originally been more disposed to intervene, took no part in the action. In the last resort France owed this untoward and unexpected outcome to her own loss of nerve in the final stage. But it did not reduce her annoyance with Great Britain to see Gladstone's government, which had so far moved half-heartedly and without forethought at every step, handle the final stage with promptitude and decision. For all the earlier protestations and principles, only Bright had resigned from the Cabinet. Announcing the plan to send an army, Gladstone had declared in almost Disraelian terms that, though he would seek the co-operation of the European Powers, "if every chance of obtaining co-operation is exhausted the work will be undertaken by the single power of England".[3]

---

[1] C.H.B.F.P. III, 169–70; Morley, op. cit. III, 79–80.
[2] Langer, op. cit. p. 273.   [3] Cromer, Lord, Modern Egypt, I, 300.

The French occupation of Tunisia was the beginning of years of hostility between France and Italy. By emphasising the extent of her isolation it had already contributed to Italy's decision to ally with the Central Powers. Her accession to the Austro-German Alliance was signed in May 1882.[1] The British occupation of Egypt had still more important effects by shattering the good relations between France and Great Britain; for France, once excluded, blamed Great Britain for occupying Egypt and then for not withdrawing, with no less violence for the fact that she did not aim to replace her there. It is difficult to see that this result could have been avoided. The many factors that combined to produce it show "how impenetrable were the workings of the labyrinth".[2] It was only one of those factors that Gladstone's government, in its anxiety to uphold its principles and avoid intervention, followed events without understanding them. Nor would it have avoided the hostility of France if it had been less slow to see that, because Egypt had got beyond control, it must be taken over and that, on account of the Canal, Great Britain could not afford to let other Powers do the work.

More serious than its earlier lack of forethought, and less excusable, were the terms on which the British Government began its administration of Egypt. Gladstone, representing the occupation as a disinterested duty, insisted on "the maintenance of all established rights, whether they be those of the Sultan, those of the Khedive, those of the people of England or those of the foreign bondholders".[3] His government officially informed the Powers on 3 January 1883 that its army would be withdrawn "as soon as the state of the country and the organisation of the proper means for the maintenance of the Khedive's authority will admit of it";[4] and this pledge was often repeated. To Gladstone these were "specific and solemn pledges given to the world in the most solemn manner".[5] "Of all things in the world," he declared, referring to the permanent occupation of Egypt, "that is one thing we are not going to do."[6] When all the world was ready for Great Britain to declare annexation or a protectorate, he did not miss the opportunity to alter Egypt's status; he refused it. In doing so, he was partly acting from the highest motives and from faith in the Concert of Europe, partly seeking to salve his conscience; for he was never certain that the British intervention in Egypt could be justified. Perhaps he also hoped to avoid giving other Powers an excuse to partition the rest of the Ottoman Empire, though this was less important as a motive. But he was also ignoring Salisbury's warning that "you have not upheld the Khedive, you have picked up the Khedive", who "must be sustained by that which is the only thing

[1] Langer, op. cit. pp. 236–44.

[2] Morley, op. cit. III, 75.

[3] Hansard, 3rd ser. CCLXX, 150.

[4] C.H.B.F.P. III, 174–5.

[5] Hansard, 3rd ser. CCLXXXII, 2196 seqq.

[6] Ibid. 3rd ser. CCLXXIII, 1384 seqq.

left upright in the land—the power of Great Britain."[1] And the consequences of his continuing to refuse to face the facts were, first, a further series of blunders leading to the death of Gordon at Khartoum[2] and then, and far more serious, a situation in which, by insisting that Egypt remained technically sovereign, under the rule of an independent Khedive, he placed it legally and financially under the control of the European Powers. An international conference arising from the British Government's wish for international agreement on Egyptian finance met in June 1884; it broke down in August because of French opposition. A British proposal of November 1884 for the guarantee of a loan to Egypt by Great Britain fell through for the same reason. In the end, in the Convention of 1885, the loan was guaranteed by all the European Powers, all of whom obtained seats on the commission of debt. Thereafter Egypt could not be run without the commission's consent; and British governments were handicapped over a wider field than Egypt itself. Because France and Russia habitually opposed Great Britain, she could only govern Egypt by keeping the Triple Alliance, and Germany in particular, on her side. "Berlin and not Cairo", wrote Baring in 1886, "is the real centre of gravity in Egyptian affairs."[3] This situation was to limit Great Britain's power to exert an independent influence on international affairs right down to 1914.[4] Already by 1884 it had become a handicap to the Gladstone government itself in dealing with the problems that arose when the struggle for the heritage of the dying Ottoman Empire gave way to colonial rivalry in new and wider fields.

IV

Not the least of these problems were the result of Germany's sudden entry into the ranks of the colonial powers. The German colonial empire was virtually the work of a single year. The Cameroons were established in July 1884, German South-West Africa in August, New Guinea in December. Though its frontiers were not settled till 1890, German East Africa was begun in May 1885. Apart from the addition of Samoa in 1899 and minor adjustments to the frontiers of the Cameroons in 1911 the empire was then complete.

The occasion for this burst of expansion by Germany was the opening up of new areas to European enterprise after her rise to predominance in Europe. The extra-European rivalries of the Powers had so far been confined to areas and problems in which Germany, so recently united, had neither the wish nor the opportunity to play a major part. Her interest in Anglo-Russian rivalry on the North-West Frontier, in the Eastern Question, in the fate of Tunisia and Egypt

---

[1] Cecil, op. cit. III, 94–5.   [2] History of ' The Times', III, 19 seqq.
[3] Zetland, Lord, Lord Cromer, p. 128.
[4] Grey of Fallodon, Viscount, Twenty-Five Years, pp. 7–11.

had been only in the possible effects on the relations between the Powers and her own position in Europe; her opportunities for intervention in these struggles had been limited to diplomatic moves. But the hinterland of Africa and the islands of the Pacific were still unknown and virtually ownerless at the time of her accession to the ranks of the Great Powers. As late as 1880, though European commercial activity in these territories had begun by then, only one-tenth of Africa had been claimed; only the Mediterranean coast and the South African settlements were generally thought to be important; and interest in the Pacific was still more restricted. United now, and strong among the Powers, Germany could expect to participate directly in the arrangements for territories whose disposal had still to be decided. Her activity in these territories, moreover, was already as great as those of the other Powers. From 1870 onwards German merchants and traders had begun to appear on the coasts of Africa and in the Pacific; German missionaries had gone out in hundreds to the same areas. By 1880 about fifteen German firms had sixty factories on the African west coast, Germans enjoyed a practical monopoly of the Samoan trade and were also interested in Fiji and other Pacific islands.[1]

In the same period concerted agitation for the establishment of colonies had grown in Germany, as in other European countries; by 1882, with the establishment of the Colonial Society, it was perhaps stronger in Germany than elsewhere. But the attitude of the German Government to these activities and demands had so far been similar to that of most European Governments. King Leopold II of the Belgians, with his interest in the Congo, was a notable exception at a time when British[2] and French[3] statesmen were uninterested in, if not opposed to, colonial expansion and when Bismarck frequently expressed himself in the same terms.[4] Extensions of the French and British Empires were being made in these new areas. But they were being made by circumstances and initiative on the spot and not by Government policy. Bismarck was constantly asked for protection by German traders. But he would do no more than give them the assistance of the nearest German consul.

It was in 1883–4 that the first signs of a change in this attitude appeared. Several developments convinced public opinion in many countries that it had become "necessary to reconsider the whole colonial question".[5] Western European countries were at last beginning to experience the pressure of competition and over-production.

[1] Keltie, J. Scott, *The Partition of Africa*; Townsend, M. E., *The Origins of Modern German Colonialism, 1871–85*, and *The Rise and Fall of Germany's Colonial Empire*.
[2] Bodelsen, C. A., *Studies in Mid-Victorian Imperialism*.
[3] Roberts, S. H., *History of French Colonial Policy*.
[4] Busch, *Bismarck, Some Secret Pages*, I, 552; Taylor, A. J. P., *Germany's First Bid for Colonies*, pp. 4–5, 23, 67.
[5] Seeley, J. R., *The Expansion of England* (1883).

Already they had felt the need for protective policies; now they began to seek new outlets for surplus goods. At the same time the fear emerged, and was reinforced by the French occupation of Tunisia and the British occupation of Egypt, that if undeveloped areas were not taken by one Power they would be taken by another. Such considerations were not enough in themselves to alter previous governmental attitudes: Gladstone's government continued, though unsuccessfully, to resist their pressure, remaining opposed to expansion on principle and being anxious to avoid further expense and excitement after the events in Egypt. Elsewhere than in Great Britain, however, they combined with special circumstances to create the great outburst of deliberate colonial expansion of the years 1883–5. In France it was obsession with the weakness of her continental position, the new antagonism to Great Britain and the wish for compensation on the subject of Egypt that produced, against this background, the imperialist policies of Jules Ferry and the beginnings of French expansion in Africa, Madagascar and South-East Asia. In Germany, too, it was the joint effect of the underlying trends and of special circumstances that induced Bismarck to gratify the growing demand of German public opinion for colonies.

In this case the special circumstances were in part the result of the German internal situation. Though he was not one to succumb to public opinion against his will and though he remained personally unconvinced of the value of colonies as such,[1] Bismarck had good reasons of domestic policy for feeling that it would be an advantage to give way to the increasing public pressure.[2] He also felt that the colonial outlet would be less harmful for Germany than any other, and more easily reconciled with his conservative foreign policy in Europe.[3] But his sudden change of attitude on colonies, to be fully understood, must also be fitted into the special circumstances that existed after 1883 in the relations between the Powers. Germany's international position had become overwhelmingly strong. To her controlling position in the Triple Alliance and the League of the Three Emperors, which was to be renewed in 1884, there was now added the advantage of Great Britain's breach with France and dependence on Germany in Egypt. Diplomatic opportunity was as important as domestic considerations in Bismarck's decision to embark on a colonial policy, though both must be borne in mind if the precise motives behind the decision are to be appreciated. In this connection, it has been argued that he was as anxious to avoid driving France to despair as he was to prevent her from becoming too strong; that the Anglo-French breach over Egypt, far from being his aim, upset the balance of his policy; and that he went in for colonies in

[1] Eyck, E., *Bismarck and the German Empire*, p. 272.
[2] *Ibid.* pp. 273–5.
[3] Taylor, A. J. P., *The Course of German History*, p. 134.

order to quarrel with Great Britain so as to draw France closer to Germany.[1] This assumes that diplomatic considerations alone induced him to enter the colonial field and overlooks the fact that he had to face domestic pressure as well. But for that, it would have been altogether simpler, and much more effective, to align with France by picking a quarrel with Great Britain over Egypt. An alternative explanation argues that the diplomatic situation merely provided his opportunity: whereas he had previously avoided making colonial claims as a way of easing the pressure in Germany, for fear of antagonising other Powers, the new state of relations between the Powers destroyed the need for caution.[2] This assumes that his motives are to be found entirely in the German domestic situation. It also ignores, as does the previous argument, the extent to which, by first ruining the forward policy of France and by later facilitating the British occupation, Bismarck had deliberately helped to bring about the breach between France and Great Britain on the Egyptian issue.[3] If this is remembered, and if Germany's diplomatic position and Bismarck's domestic reasons are both given due weight, a more satisfactory explanation than either of these can be provided, and the key to it is the existence of yet another factor in the situation.

Bismarck helped to bring about the breach between France and Great Britain. But he cannot have been certain that it would arise, or that Gladstone's Cabinet would play into his hands to the extent that it did. Nor did he at once begin to exploit the breach in order to advance a colonial policy. He did not do so until he had been angered by Great Britain's inability to understand the advantages it had given him. This was the third factor; and it was this which fused Bismarck's domestic considerations and his diplomatic opportunity in such a way as to produce his colonial policy. During 1883 his attitude was that he would continue to support Great Britain in Egypt in return for a *quid pro quo*, but he had not decided what the *quid pro quo* should be. It was the hesitant, ignorant and sometimes niggling behaviour of Gladstone's government that altered his desire for, and anticipation of, general advantages into a specific determination to acquire colonies.

This process may be studied in the correspondence over the protection of German settlers at Angra Pequeña in South-West Africa.[4] Bismarck asked for British protection for the German settlers in February 1883. He had already asked for this in 1880 and had been refused. This second request went unanswered. When he made yet a third request in December 1883, in order to silence the German settlers, he received the reply that the area was not British but that

[1] Taylor, A. J. P., *Germany's First Bid for Colonies*, pp. 6, 17–23.
[2] Eyck, *op. cit.* p. 273; Townsend, *Rise and Fall of Germany's Colonial Empire*, p. 68.
[3] Langer, *op. cit.* pp. 277–8.
[4] Taylor, *op. cit.* pp. 23–9, 33–5; Langer, *op. cit.* pp. 292–3; Aydelotte, W. O., "The First German Colony and its Diplomatic Consequences", *Cambridge Hist. Jour.* vol. v, no. 3.

Great Britain would object to its belonging to any other Power. Even then he contented himself with pointing out the absurdity of the British reply and with asking for more information; he had not decided on a course of action, and certainly not on a policy of colonial acquisition. Both in South-West Africa and in Fiji, however, where he was already being similarly irritated by negotiations with Great Britain about compensation for German traders dispossessed by the recent British annexation, he had expected some "reciprocity of good offices...in consideration of the friendly attitude...he had maintained...in regard to the Eastern policy of Her Majesty's Government."[1] In Angra Pequeña itself, moreover, the German traders had not waited for a diplomatic settlement but had already hoisted the German flag, thus involving the prestige of the German Government and the nationalism of the German public. When, therefore, he had still received no reply to his December enquiry after four months' further delay, he at last announced the Angra Pequeña settlements to be under German protection on 24 April 1884. Bismarck had still not decided on a colonial policy, but this was the first step towards one. His loss of temper with the British Government was his most important reason for taking the step, though his annoyance fitted in with his need for popularity in Germany at that moment and coincided with the circumstance that British prevarication had inflamed the issue in the mind of the German public.

Further evidence of Great Britain's failure to respond to the obvious weakness of her position, and Bismarck's reflection on that fact, helped to widen the issue between the two countries and to turn the scale, so far as Bismarck was concerned, in the next few weeks. Fearing that the French might secure control of the mouth of the Congo and shut it to British trade, the British Government had been negotiating with Portugal since 1882 for a treaty that would recognise Portugal's nebulous claims to the area in return for a guarantee of free navigation of the river. The treaty was signed at the end of February 1884. When it was announced, its championing of the Portuguese claims aroused strong protests from France and further annoyance in Germany.[2] This was quickly followed by trouble between Germany and Great Britain elsewhere in Africa. In April 1884 Bismarck had asked Great Britain to assist Nachtigal, a German official, during his survey of trade in West Africa. Only in July, and only then because it feared that France might seize the area in her advance up the Congo, did the British Government take action. But when its consul arrived to proclaim British sovereignty he found that Nachtigal had already proclaimed German sovereignty and established the German Cameroons.[3] Meanwhile, misunderstanding had grown apace over the original dispute in South-West Africa. In June,

---

[1] Quoted in Taylor, *op. cit.* p. 29.
[2] Langer, *op. cit.* pp. 299–300.   [3] Taylor, *op. cit.* pp. 32–3.

following the German declaration of a protectorate at Angra Pequeña, the Cape Government had announced its intention to extend its sovereignty to the area. When Germany protested Great Britain recognised the German protectorate at Angra Pequeña. But, under the impression that the way was still clear for the Cape's annexation of the rest of the coast between the Cape frontier and the Portuguese frontier, she also announced her intention, at the end of July, to approve this step. Germany again protested and announced in return, at the end of August, that her own protectorate extended over the whole area.[1]

It would be distorting the facts to claim that Bismarck's loss of temper with Great Britain and the ineptitude of the British Government were the sole causes of this extension of the dispute and of Bismarck's final decision to acquire colonies. Apart from Bismarck's domestic motives, independent initiative by Germans on the spot played its part in this first outburst of German colonial expansion. Apart from the British Government's failure to understand the drift of affairs, it was embarrassed by the need to take colonial interests into account and consult colonial governments; and elements of sheer misunderstanding and irrepressible rivalry added their momentum to the growth of bad feeling between the two countries. Nor was Bismarck's annoyance entirely the fault of the British Government. Bismarck contributed to the misunderstandings by refusing, or at least by failing, to formulate his wishes clearly.[2] Yet Bismarck's annoyance with Great Britain, however it came about, was what sealed his determination to advance and press colonial claims after the first step in April 1884. It was, above all, Great Britain's apparent unconcern at the increased strength of Germany's diplomatic position that caused him to be annoyed. If the German public and traders felt, in view of Great Britain's behaviour, that she must be forced before she would ever concede colonies, Bismarck himself came to reflect that, even if colonies were valueless in themselves, they were at least the one field in which Great Britain could be made to be sensitive. He had been quick to appreciate the advantages of his position on the Continent and in Egypt. He had dropped hints to Great Britain. To block her possible escape he had begun, in March 1884, to encourage the French in their antagonism against Great Britain by offering them an *entente* with Germany.[3] Yet the British had still failed to respond to their obvious weakness and isolation. This is what led him on.

If, as seems probable, Bismarck acted in this mood, mainly with the object of bringing home to the British Government the dangers of isolation, he only partly succeeded. Great Britain's weakness was quickly brought home to the British Government. In the face of

[1] Taylor, *op. cit.* pp. 46–50.
[2] *Ibid.* pp. 26–7, 29, 33–8, 55; Langer, *op. cit.* pp. 293–6, 300; Eyck, *op. cit.* pp. 276–80.
[3] *Ibid.* pp. 29–31.

French and German opposition it had no alternative but to abandon the Anglo-Portuguese Congo treaty in June 1884. Though it protested that Nachtigal had acted under false pretences in West Africa, it at once recognised the German Cameroons. In September it surrendered in South-West Africa, recognising the German claim to the entire area between the Cape boundary and the Portuguese frontier. In making these retreats it acted with alacrity; it had no more had the will than it had had the position to quarrel with Germany in the first place. It also acted shamefacedly, having previously behaved, apparently if not intentionally, in the opinion of the British press and public as well as of the Germans,[1] as if its sole object had been to forestall German expansion. But its earlier behaviour had not been entirely due to its failure to understand either the consequences for its international position of its breach with France or the seriousness of the urge to expansion that was affecting the European Powers. It had been the result, as well, of the conflict between, on the one hand, the British Government's own reluctance to add to its expenses and responsibilities and, on the other, the pressure for expansion and against concessions to other Powers that was growing among the colonists abroad and affecting even its own supporters at home. And while the shamefacedness with which it surrendered to Germany increased its own irritation with Bismarck, the alacrity with which it made the concessions only swelled this pressure. Thus, Bismarck having tasted blood and received encouragement from Great Britain's retreat, and British circles feeling increased annoyance with Bismarck and increased determination to prevent further German acquisitions,[2] the colonial struggle was only widened and made more intense by Germany's first successes.

In the winter of 1884–5 the two countries vied with each other, as did France with Great Britain, in staking further claims. Both Governments descended to the same level, each trying to get ahead in the programme of acquisition, each bitterly accusing its rival of unfairness in the process, each succumbing to motives and emotions which led Gladstone to lament that "there is a wild and irrational spirit abroad"[3]. Herbert Bismarck warned Granville that the Germans would "prove to him how unpleasant we could make ourselves";[4] Joseph Chamberlain confessed to Dilke in the same mood that "I don't care about New Guinea and I am not afraid of German colonisation, but I don't like to be cheeked by Bismarck or anyone else".[5] It was with such motives, each also fearing the advantages that its rival might otherwise obtain, that Germany added parts of Togoland to the Cameroons, occupied a part of New Guinea and

[1] Langer, op. cit. pp. 300–1, 317.
[2] See, for example, Gwynn and Tuckwell, op. cit. II, chap. xxxvii.
[3] Taylor, op. cit. p. 71.　　　　[4] Die Grosse Politik, vol. IV, no. 101.
[5] Garvin, J. L., Joseph Chamberlain, I, 497.

began her extension into East Africa, while Great Britain took St Lucia Bay, Bechuanaland and a part of New Guinea and extended her control in Somaliland.

Great Britain's weakness as against Germany was emphasised during this further extension of the colonial conflict by her bad relations with France. French opposition in the colonial field was less unexpected than that of Germany, both because France had had extra-European interests already and because of the antagonism created by events in Egypt. It was also more inhibited than that which Bismarck displayed. France had been offended by the British occupation of Egypt, but she still hoped to secure a British withdrawal by peaceful settlement. She had also, in her first reaction to the Egyptian set-back, spread her net too widely. During 1884 her Government was meeting with difficulties and reaping much unpopularity at home in connection with its operations in Madagascar and its war against China in Tonkin. It could not afford to be too adventurous in North-West Africa, the Congo and the Sudan, where its activities clashed more directly with those of Great Britain. In these African areas, moreover, it was almost as anxious and jealous of German as of British expansion, while no amount of identity of interests with Germany could ever quite destroy its distrust of the old enemy. Yet a close, if temporary, identity of interests with Germany clearly existed; and though it was almost entirely due to Bismarck's initiative, and though France was always suspicious of Bismarck's proposals for a League of Neutrals which would settle African affairs to the exclusion of Great Britain and for a combination of the secondary maritime Powers which would balance British predominance at sea, diplomatic co-operation between the two Powers broadened out into an *entente* on the whole subject of colonial policy.[1] The two countries worked together to summon the Berlin Conference in November 1884. The French Government converted the Conference from being an anti-British instrument, as Bismarck had conceived it, into a project for establishing the Open Door in Africa with British agreement. The British Government had no real objection to the recognition of Leopold's International Association as a free-trade area. But the Conference was still convened with little reference to Great Britain; it met under Bismarck's presidency; and it killed any hope Great Britain may have had of controlling the Congo through the medium of Portuguese claims by recognising the neutrality of the International Association and the Congo State.[2]

The opening of the Berlin Conference followed soon after the defeat by France of the British proposals on the finances of Egypt. Before it closed, towards the end of February 1885, the news of the

---

[1] Taylor, *op. cit.* pp. 36-7, 46-53, 58-65; Langer, *op. cit.* pp. 301-4; *Documents diplomatiques français*, 1ere sér. nos. 404, 405, 407, 421, 468, 469, 471.
[2] Moon, *op. cit.* pp. 82-4.

death of Gordon in the Sudan had covered the Gladstone government with obloquy and forced it, against its will, to decide to continue the Sudan campaign. While it was in session a climax had also been reached in the rivalry between Germany and Great Britain in a quarrel over New Guinea, where the British attempt to annex the eastern half—the west already belonged to the Dutch—was met in December 1884 by the announcement of a German protectorate over some parts of the disputed territory.[1] All these circumstances conspired to force on Great Britain a secondary and isolated position during this first attempt at a settlement of Africa. It was Granville, on behalf of a British Government that was frustrated in Egypt, Africa and New Guinea, worried in the Sudan and anxious to break the Franco-German front, who brought the New Guinea quarrel to a head by announcing at the end of February 1885 that Bismarck had earlier encouraged Great Britain "to take Egypt".[2] But it was also the obvious weakness of Great Britain on many fronts and the resulting British anxiety for a reconciliation that brought about the general settlement of the following month. It was Gladstone and Granville who announced the settlement to the world.[3] And in the settlement Great Britain again yielded at all points. She agreed to explain away Granville's disclosure about Egypt and to partition eastern New Guinea between herself and Germany. She accepted the decisions of the Berlin Conference. In separate negotiations with France she fell in with Ferry's counter-proposals for the international control of Egypt's finances.[4]

V

It was not only in Africa and the Pacific that Great Britain's difficulties in Egypt and the Sudan had had their effect. The hostility of Germany and France in those areas was dangerous in itself. It had also contributed by February 1885 to the renewal of tension with Russia on the North-West Frontier of India.

During the renewed fighting in Afghanistan in 1879 Lord Lytton had proposed that Great Britain should permanently occupy Kandahar and let the rest of the country disintegrate into tribal areas. In the absence of any strong chief in Afghanistan Disraeli's government had come round to this solution for the North-West Frontier[5] until the emergence of Abdul Rahman, a nephew of Sher Ali, who seemed capable of uniting and controlling the country. Lytton's partition scheme was then dropped and negotiations with Abdul Rahman had begun when the Government fell and was replaced by Gladstone's. The new Government and the new Viceroy—Lytton resigned and

[1] Taylor, op. cit. pp. 66–79.
[2] Ibid. pp. 77–8; Langer, op. cit. pp. 307–8.
[3] Langer, op. cit. p. 308.
[4] Taylor, op. cit. pp. 78–9; Langer, op. cit. pp. 306–8.
[5] Buckle, op. cit. vi, 484–5.

was succeeded by Lord Ripon—conducted the negotiations from the point at which Lytton had left them and brought them to the conclusion at which Salisbury and Lytton had aimed.

In one respect there was not even an attempt to revert to the old policy of "masterly inactivity". Accepting the need to maintain Afghanistan as a friendly buffer state, Gladstone's government offered the new Amir, in return for control of his foreign policy, the annual subsidy and the guarantee against unprovoked aggression which it had refused to give in 1873. This offer was accepted at the Conference of Zimma in August 1880.[1] Nor was this the only compromise with the views of the "forward" school. The new Government soon yielded, though not without a struggle, the other main principle in its traditional attitude to the frontier. Ripon was sent out with instructions to effect the withdrawal of British forces from all recently acquired territory—from Baluchistan as well as from Kandahar—and even to consider retirement to the Indus line.[2] The evacuation of the Sibi and Pishin areas was promised in the Queen's speech at the opening session of 1881.[3] Overruling a vote in the Lords, the Cabinet insisted on the evacuation of Kandahar on financial grounds in March 1881.[4] By this time Ripon had already taken the first steps to carry out his orders. But he soon changed his mind. When called upon to explain himself he warned the Government that its orders were mistaken and would lead to another Afghan war in ten years, and hinted that he would resign rather than carry them out.[5] In the event, though Kandahar was evacuated, Baluchistan was retained, the railway through the Bolan, which Ripon had torn up, was reconstructed and the Cabinet preserved a convenient silence about its earlier withdrawal undertakings.[6]

Ripon had changed his mind because he realised that total withdrawal was unwise in view of Russia's continuing advance towards Afghanistan. The Russian ambassador had assured the new Government in May 1880 that the Tsar had "nothing more at heart than to see re-established those good relations which only misunderstandings or evil passions could have troubled".[7] Yet the Government of India was right to assume that Russia's consolidation of her position in Central Asia would proceed. In 1882 she avoided the renewed attempt of the Gladstone government to reach agreement on the delimitation of Afghanistan's northern boundary. Despite her assurances during these negotiations that she did not intend to occupy fresh territory, it soon became obvious that she still sought the submission of the Merv area.[8] In February 1884, when Great Britain was beginning to be faced with difficulties in the Sudan, she beguiled or coerced the

[1] Davies, G. C., The North-West Frontier, 1890–1908, pp. 156–7.
[2] Ibid. pp. 15–16.   [3] C.H.B.E. v, 421.
[4] Davies, op. cit. p. 15.   [5] C.H.B.E. v, 422.   [6] Davies, op. cit. p. 16.
[7] Seton-Watson, R. W., Britain in Europe, 1789–1914, p. 556.
[8] C.H.B.E. v, 423.

Merv chiefs into allegiance to the Tsar.[1] And when the British Government, alarmed at this development, took up once more and with increased energy the boundary negotiations of 1882, she again evaded the British proposals to the extent of delaying the meeting of the Russian and British boundary commissions from October 1884, as Granville had suggested, to February 1885.[2]

There were several reasons for Russia's unco-operative tactics. The old antagonism between civil and military authorities in St Petersburg played its part.[3] Russia disagreed with Great Britain about the principle on which the boundary should be drawn. While Great Britain pressed for a frontier corresponding to the existing political authority of the Amir, tribes owing him allegiance being *ipso facto* regarded as Afghan, Russia demanded a geographic and ethnic frontier on the mountains.[4] But she also sought from a delimitation favourable to herself a strong position against Afghanistan that would be used as a source of pressure on Great Britain in future clashes elsewhere;[5] and she hoped by her obstructiveness to dominate the disputed frontier by force before the boundary commissions began their negotiations. Even while delaying the meeting of the commissions she laid claim to Penjdeh and other positions which the British regarded as Afghan, complained of aggressive Afghan concentrations and sent a column of troops to the area.[6] She had no desire to precipitate a crisis, but she was determined to carry her points by threat of force, and, in view of British embarrassments on other fronts, she expected that she would do so.

Gladstone's government, however, always loath to impute such motives to other Powers, always disunited when faced with the need to act in foreign affairs, took an unexpectedly serious view of Russia's behaviour. It did so precisely because it had already lost so much face elsewhere. With its credit at stake abroad and its back to the wall at home, where public opinion insisted that it must at last be firm, it resorted to more drastic measures in this frontier dispute than Disraeli's government had needed to employ to safeguard British influence in Afghanistan altogether. In February 1885 it ordered the Indian Government to prepare to send an army corps to Herat in the event of war with Russia and instructed the British boundary commission to help the Afghan defence in the event of a Russian attack on Herat.[7] On 12 March it decided to assemble 20,000 men at Quetta and to regard a Russian attack on Herat as a *casus belli*.[8] The Russian Ambassador was informed of this last decision on 25 March.[9]

---

[1] *C.H.B.E.* v, 423.   [2] *Ibid.*
[3] Meyendorff, *op. cit.* pp. 115, 117, 160 *seqq.*
[4] Langer, *op. cit.* pp. 310–11.
[5] *D.D.F.* 1ere sér. VI, no. 23.
[6] *C.H.B.E.* v, 424; Seton-Watson, *op. cit.* p. 557.
[7] Gwynn and Tuckwell, *op. cit.* II, 111.   [8] *Ibid.* pp. 115–16.
[9] *Letters of Queen Victoria*, 2nd ser. III, 629–30.

War therefore seemed inevitable, to both London and St Petersburg, when it was learned that Russian troops had occupied Penjdeh on 30 March after driving out a body of Afghan troops. The news certainly placed Gladstone's government in a difficult situation. It was committed to firmness by its warnings to Russia and by its promise of assistance to the Afghan Government; its position at home could not have sustained another humiliation so soon after the news of the death of Gordon. On the other hand, it was without allies and completely out of favour with the other Powers. Whether or not the Russian behaviour was due to the encouragement of Bismarck,[1] it was widely believed in London that it was so inspired.[2] Even without assuming anti-British motives and action on Bismarck's part, it was obvious that he preferred Russia to be active in Central Asia rather than in the Balkans; it was known that he was bound to support her to some extent out of his wish to preserve the Alliance of the Three Emperors. It can have caused no surprise when he put pressure on Turkey to declare her neutrality in the event of a war and to refuse to open the Straits to British ships, and got France and Austria to give Turkey the same advice. Russia, for her part, had come to an understanding with Austria in the Balkans to ensure her neutrality during the quarrel with Great Britain, and had offered Turkey concessions in Asia Minor in return for the closing of the Straits.[3] Gladstone's government was thus forced to adopt a defiant attitude without having the will or the confidence to sustain it and to prepare for war with the knowledge that it was denied the obvious recourse of an attack on Russia in the Black Sea. Between 9 April, when the news of the Penjdeh incident was received, and 27 April it denounced the incident as "unprovoked aggression",[4] called up the reserves, moved for a vote of credit and decided to abandon operations in the Sudan. But even while making these preparations it suggested that the happening at Penjdeh should be reviewed by an arbitrator. And at the end of April and in early May 1885, when Russia had also shown a readiness to accept arbitration, the Gladstone Government made so many concessions in the negotiations as to lose any advantage it might have gained from its rare show of determination.

Having previously blamed the Russian commander for the incident, while Russia had attributed the clash to British encouragement of the Afghans, it now accepted Russia's refusal to permit an enquiry into the Russian commander's conduct, proposing instead that the arbitration should consider only how the misunderstanding had arisen. Having suggested the German Emperor as arbitrator, it then accepted the King of Denmark at the Tsar's insistence. It conceded that Afghanistan might abandon Penjdeh, which was important to

---

[1] There is not enough evidence to substantiate this claim. See Langer, op. cit. pp. 311–14; Taylor, op. cit. p. 81.   [2] Fitzmaurice, op. cit. II, 422.
[3] Cecil, op. cit. III, 136.   [4] Hansard, 3rd ser. CCXCVI, 1159 et seq.

Russia, provided she kept Zulfikar, which Russia regarded as of no value; and it represented Russia's agreement on this point as a graceful concession by Russia to Great Britain's wishes.[1] Thus encouraged, Russia not only ensured that the arbitration would never take place but increased her demands and strengthened her position in advance of the frontier settlement that was finally reached in September.

By that time Gladstone's government had fallen, deserted by its own supporters, in June 1885, and had been replaced by a Salisbury administration. Gladstone and Granville had regained some of their lost prestige by their firmness in the early stages of the Penjdeh crisis. But nothing could dispel the popular disapproval of their colonial policy and their mishandling of the situation in the Sudan; and not even the threat of war with Russia had healed the disunity of the Cabinet on foreign affairs.[2] Nor could the ministers hide from themselves or their opponents the straits to which, by their policy and their disunity, the country had been reduced in its foreign relations. "It is too dreadful," wrote Granville during the Penjdeh incident, "jumping from one crisis to another. Once at war with Russia we shall have to toady to Germany, France and Turkey."[3] "Every nation could do as it liked with us", argued Rosebery in defence of the decision to abandon the Sudan. "In all probability (if we had kept an army in the Sudan during the quarrel with Russia) we should have embarked on one of the greatest wars of the century; and with both our arms bound, one to Afghanistan, the other to Central Africa, we should have been exposed to endure what any Power might choose to lay upon us, and be compelled to forgo all voice or share in the destinies of the world."[4] "The Liberal Government"— this was Salisbury's comment—"have at last achieved their long desired 'Concert of Europe'. They have succeeded in uniting the continent of Europe—against England."[5]

---

[1] *C.H.B.E.* v, 424–5.
[2] Gwynn and Tuckwell, *op. cit.* II, 111–16.
[3] Quoted in Langer, *op. cit.* p. 313.
[4] *Letters of Queen Victoria*, 2nd ser. III, 640 *seqq.*
[5] Cecil, *op. cit.* III, 136.

CHAPTER V

IMPERIAL PROBLEMS IN BRITISH POLITICS, 1880–1895

OUTLOOKS ON EMPIRE

ON the threshold of the classic age of imperial expansion in the tropics, the British were still thinking almost entirely in mid-Victorian terms of reducing the burden of the Empire of White settlement. Even to imperialists, the Empire's future seemed to lie in closer union with the settled colonies, not in the acquisition of "new Indias" in Africa. In 1880 at Cambridge Professor John Seeley expressed this contemporary concentration of interest in the empire of British settlement when he described the Empire (with significant inaccuracies), as "four great groups of territory [Canada, Australasia, South Africa and the West Indian Islands], inhabited either chiefly or to a large extent by Englishmen...and a fifth great territory [India]...inhabited by a completely foreign race".[1] "When we inquire then into the Greater Britain of the future," he observed, "we ought to think much more of our Colonial than of our Indian Empire."[2]

From this standpoint the Empire seemed to present few problems which time and the application of well-tried precedents could not solve. The withdrawal of imperial garrisons from the "Great Colonies" and the devolution of local responsibility to their governments was almost completed, except in Natal and Western Australia. Colonial responsible governments, shielded from foreign interference by the Royal Navy, might now be expected to secure unaided the imperial spheres of influence in their respective continents. If the colonists could be induced to contribute to the Empire's general expenses, especially those for naval defence, the home taxpayer could be still further relieved of his imperial load.[3]

These developments had done much to reconcile the British at home to an Empire of settlement; but they still objected strongly to further acquisitions of territory directly dependent upon the United Kingdom. A textbook on the colonies published in 1883 made it plain that "the policy of England discourages any increase of territory in tropical countries already occupied by native races".[4] The mid-Victorians who survived frowned upon the idea of extending imperial rule to aid British trading and philanthropic enterprise beyond existing frontiers. Expenditure on military expeditions and

[1] Seeley, Sir J. R., *The Expansion of England*, pp. 11–12.   [2] *Ibid.* p. 13.
[3] Lucas, C. P., Introduction to Lewis, Sir G. C., *An Essay on the Government of Dependencies* (new ed. 1891), p. xlix.
[4] Cotton, J. S., and Payne, E. J., *Colonies and Dependencies*, pt. II, p. 114.

territorial responsibilities overseas was begrudged by the Commons and Treasury. The world's unappropriated regions, it seemed, would remain open to British commerce without the assumption of the unpopular liability of ruling them; and there was an instinctive dislike of advancing imperial land frontiers in Asia and Africa beyond the protective reach of British sea-power. The liberal traditions of limited, economical government and free trade still prevailed, and with them the mid-Victorian anti-expansionist[1] outlook on Empire which they inspired.

The "Midlothian elections" of 1880 seemed to the Liberal victors to reaffirm the nation's loyalty to that tradition.[2] In opposition the Liberals had denounced the extravagance and injustice of Beaconsfield's "Forward" policies abroad. Gladstone had stigmatised the acquisition of Cyprus and Fiji, the invasion of Zululand, the occupation of the Transvaal and Kandahar, and the purchase of Suez Canal shares as "gratuitious, dangerous, ambiguous, impracticable and impossible engagements".[3] With a majority of 106 in the new Parliament over the Conservatives in place of their previous minority of 101, Liberals congratulated themselves that they had deposed "King Jingo" and exorcised his "baleful spirit of domination".[4] Ministries were long to remember Midlothian and obey the canon of economy lest they should offer the Opposition such an opportunity as Beaconsfield had given Gladstone.

The Gladstone ministry (April 1880–June 1885) set out to restore economical government at home by reverting to the tradition of non-intervention and minimum responsibility abroad. This imperial policy of "Consolidation" was inspired partly by a doctrinal objection to dominion over foreign races but mainly by a limited financial approach to government. To the older generation of Liberals a reduction of public expenditure and a penny off the income tax was the hall-mark of sound policy. They opposed a Forward policy because it provoked foreign hostility, forced Britain into Continental alliances and drove up defence budgets. Liberals and Whigs alike feared that imperial commitments were already too heavy. To increase them might mean financial collapse, which would open the door to social revolution in the United Kingdom. Gladstone and most of his Cabinet agreed with Harcourt "that we have already as much Empire as the nation can carry. If you give the heart too much work to do by extending the limbs and the frame beyond measure you enfeeble its action, and it succumbs."[5]

---

[1] Throughout this chapter the term "anti-expansionist" describes opposition to the extension of British territorial rule; it does not include objection to British commercial or informal political expansion.

[2] Wilkinson, H. Spenser, *Thirty-Five Years, 1874–1909*, p. 52.

[3] Bassett, A. Tilney (ed.), *Gladstone's Speeches*, pp. 570–1.

[4] Bassett, *op. cit.* p. 562; Gardiner, A. G., *The Life of Sir William Harcourt*, I, 362.

[5] Sir William Harcourt to Lord Rosebery, 27 Sept. 1892, in Gardiner, *op. cit.* II, 196.

This anti-expansionist tradition was far more powerful in the Parliaments of the 'eighties than the rising expansionist movement. Most practical politicians in both parties agreed that existing imperial interests must be maintained; but they objected at the same time to increased expenditure on Empire.[1] Normally Parliaments were hostile to increased commitments. Members judged imperial questions upon expediency rather than principle. "Jingo" and "Little Englander" were largely myths of party polemics, truly descriptive only of two extremist and doctrinaire minorities. The Little Englander Liberals and Radicals opposed extensions of Empire on principle; and the Conservative extremists advocated the acquisition of territory without much regard to its value or cost.[2] But the controversies of the 'eighties centred upon the Forward and Consolidationist methods of securing existing imperial interests[3] rather than upon the principle of expansion as such.

The Forward school of opinion, represented by the Conservatives Salisbury and Carnarvon and the Liberals Forster, Goschen and Rosebery, tended to insist that imperial interests beyond the frontiers, if threatened by anarchy or foreign expansion, could only be protected effectively by formal extensions of imperial rule. Consolidationists, on the other hand, held that the same purpose could be achieved by means of international agreements and informal influence. The division of opinion cut across party lines. Nevertheless, the Liberal party, in deference to its Little Englander wing and in inflexible opposition to increased administrative responsibility, leaned more to Consolidation; while the Conservatives, more intimately connected with the Court[4] and the Imperial Services and more open to appeals to imperial prestige, were more susceptible to the persuasions of the Forward school.

The comfortable mid-Victorian imperial position in the world to which the old Consolidationist principle was fitted was already crumbling by the early 'eighties, though few in Whitehall and Westminster realised it. The Continental Powers had begun to challenge Britain's industrial, colonial and naval supremacy. Their colonial expansion appeared to menace at once the security of existing British frontiers and the larger spheres of imperial paramount influence in Africa, South-East Asia and the Western Pacific. Foreign protectionist tariffs and exclusive trade practices threatened to shut

---

[1] E.g. for Lord Hartington's views see Holland, Bernard, *Life of the Duke of Devonshire*, I, 250; for Gladstone's views, Gladstone to Queen Victoria, June 1880, Buckle, G. E. (ed.), *Letters of Queen Victoria*, 2nd ser. III, 110; Gwynn, Stephen and Tuckwell, G. M., *The Life of Sir Charles Dilke*, II, 86; for Kimberley's views, Kimberley's Minute, 6 April 1882, C.O. 806/203—App. I, p. 7; for Randolph Churchill's views, Commons, 31 Jan. 1887, *Hansard*, 3rd ser. CCCX, 296–8.

[2] Morley, John Viscount, *Recollections*, II, 78–80; cf. Oxford and Asquith, Earl of, *Fifty Years of Parliament*, I, 270–1.   [3] Cf. Seeley, *op. cit.* pp. 340–1.

[4] For Queen Victoria's Forward views, see Buckle, *op. cit.* 2nd ser. III, 47, 105, 113, 135, 137–9 and 157.

out British enterprise from hitherto unoccupied free trade areas beyond imperial dominion. Competition of Continental manufactures sharpened the rivalry for political control of overseas markets and sources of raw materials.

This Continental challenge confronted British ministries with a recurrent political dilemma during the period 1880–95. While the persisting economical spirit of the country still resisted increased imperial liabilities, there was a growing imperialist outcry against abandoning to foreign annexation unappropriated territories of colonial and commercial interest. The struggle between the Gladstonian upholders of the mid-Victorian anti-expansionist tradition and leaders of the Forward and expansionist movement is the greater part of the story of imperial problems in British politics between 1880 and 1895.

The imperialists of the early 'eighties were mostly federationists, not expansionists. From a sense of kinship with Greater Britain overseas and of insecurity, they were intent upon strengthening the unity of the settled colonies and the mother country.[1] Their racial conception of Empire excluded enthusiasm for acquisitions of non-settlement dependencies.[2] But the federationists' support of colonial demands for the extension of imperial rule to forestall foreign annexations made them leading advocates of the Forward school of frontier policy. Only a small minority of imperialists, represented by W. E. Forster and Sir Charles Dilke, favoured the extension and development of tropical dependencies. Since David Livingstone's death the anti-slavery and missionary societies, with the African merchants, had urged governments to bring new African regions under British administration, to end slavery and the slave trade and to prepare new fields for commercial enterprise.[3] But these humanitarians and imperialists, though they had gained the sympathy of the Court and the Imperial Services, made little headway in political circles until the mid-'eighties, as Dilke himself admitted.[4]

It was not until the late 'eighties that the struggle over methods of defending existing frontiers broadened into one between expansionists and anti-expansionists. By that time the old Forward school, the main body of federationists, the humanitarians and important business interests had combined to press for the acquisition of a new tropical Empire for future United Kingdom commercial and philanthropic development. Paradoxically, the mass of British opinion remained undecided or indifferent and accepted this expansionist philosophy of staking out claims for posterity only after the event.

[1] See. pp. 176–80 below.
[2] Seeley, *op. cit.* pp. 203–6; Bodelsen, C. A., *Studies in Mid-Victorian Imperialism*, p. 129.
[3] See *The Anti-Slavery Reporter*, 1870–95, *passim*; Livingstone in *Minutes of Evidence of the Select Committee on Africa (Western Coast)*, *Parl. Pap.* 1865, v (412), pp. 227–33; Waller, Horace, *Ivory, Apes and Peacocks* and *Title Deeds to Nyasa*.
[4] Dilke, Sir Charles W., *Problems of Greater Britain*, II, 164.

DOMESTIC FACTORS IN IMPERIAL POLICY

Dissensions within the Gladstone ministry and its parliamentary majority profoundly affected Liberal imperial policy. A moderate Liberal-Whig group of Gladstone's old colleagues formed the core of the Cabinet—Granville at the Foreign Office, Kimberley and, after 1882, Derby at the Colonial Office and Northbrook at the Admiralty. These balanced anxiously between the extreme Whigs (Lord Hartington at the India Office and Lord Chancellor Selborne) and the Radical ministers (John Bright, Joseph Chamberlain at the Board of Trade and Sir Charles Dilke, who entered the Cabinet in 1882). Although the Whigs held the high offices, the initiative in the Party and the country lay with the Radicals.[1] "This attempt to govern by a combination of Whigs and Radicals", Hartington lamented in 1880, "is to ride two horses."[2]

In the country the Radicals courted the newly enfranchised voters with popular reform programmes and attacks on privilege and property. In the Cabinet they concentrated on "dishing the Whigs"[3] no less assiduously than Randolph Churchill and the Fourth Party assailed the old Tory leaders of the Conservative Opposition. The agrarian-nationalist revolution in Ireland provided the central issue for the clashes between Radical and Whig. Radicals and moderate Liberals insisted upon liberal land and local government legislation to keep the peace and to relieve the distress of the Irish tenantry. The Whigs, Hartington, Spencer and Argyll, backed by the Tory majority in the Lords, demanded that order be restored and property protected by means of coercive emergency powers.

Until this dispute overthrew it in 1885, the ministry held together through a series of desperate Irish crises only by uneasy compromises and vacillations. The schism of the Liberal party on the Irish Home Rule issue in 1885-6 was foreshadowed from the beginning of Gladstone's second ministry.

In the politics of the day it was assumed with some reason that the party of concession in Ireland and constitutional reform was anti-imperialist, and that of conservatism and coercion imperialist. Whigs and Conservatives accused the Radicals, moderate Liberals and Parnellites of plotting to destroy the Empire along with constitutional privilege, property and order at home.[4] Radicals and Parnellites tended to include the Empire generally in their attacks on conservatism and social injustice in the United Kingdom. The Queen and

[1] Hartington to Gladstone, 12 Nov. 1882, in Holland, *op. cit.* 1, 378.
[2] Holland, *op. cit.* 1, 332.
[3] Gladstone to Rosebury, 16 Sept. 1880, in Morley, John, *The Life of William Ewart Gladstone* (Lloyd's Popular ed.), 11, 182-3.
[4] Buckle, *op. cit.* 2nd ser. 111, 163-7, 168; *ibid.* 3rd ser. 11, 172 *seqq.*; Ensor, R. C. K., "Some political and economic interactions in later Victorian England", *Trans. R. Hist. Soc.* 4th ser. xxxi (1948), 26-7.

elder statesmen like Gladstone and Salisbury feared the Radicals were stirring up class war, and pondered uneasily the results of rising democracy.[1] Were democracy and Empire compatible?[2] "Kings and aristocracies can govern empire," Derby observed, "but one people cannot govern another people."[3] Further extensions of the franchise after 1867 appeared inevitable. The political future seemed to belong to the Radicals, whose supremacy might bring about the dissolution of the Empire.

The collaboration between Radical Little Englanders and Irish Nationalists in the Commons seemed to confirm these fears.[4] Parnellites and Radicals declared that the Empire treated the Irish as unjustly as it did the Boers, Zulus, Afghans and Egyptians.[5] Old Radicals like John Bright represented pacifism and the pure Cobdenite anti-imperialist tradition.[6] The outlook on Empire of the new Radicals, Henry Labouchere and Charles Bradlaugh, was coloured by their animus against the Court, the aristocracy and the military services. They regarded the Empire as a vast system of outdoor relief for the upper classes—a stronghold of aristocratic patronage and nepotism, supported by public funds which should have been spent on social reform at home.[7] Together Irish Nationalists and Radical Little Englanders greatly reinforced the anti-expansionist resolutions of Liberal ministers, because their combined defection would have deprived the Government of a working majority.

Perhaps the most striking feature of the second Gladstone Cabinet was the extent to which imperial questions tended to be used as pawns in the domestic struggles of Parnellite and Radical against Whig and Tory. During 1880–2 the Radical ministers, Chamberlain and Dilke, opposed Hartington and Kimberley on the Transvaal issue to extract concessions on Irish policy, and to force Whig ministers out of the Cabinet. Similarly, Radicals used the Cameroons and Zanzibar issues to bring pressure against Whig policy in Egypt. With the occupation of Egypt and German intervention in South Africa and the Pacific the divergence of ministerial views on imperial policy partially coincided with the divisions on Irish questions. Gladstone,

[1] Salisbury, "Disintegration", *Quarterly Review*, CLVI (Oct. 1883), 559 *seqq.*; Gladstone to Queen Victoria, 27 Oct. 1892, in Buckle, *op. cit.* 3rd ser. II, 172 *seqq.*

[2] See Arnold-Forster, H. O., "The Liberal Idea and the Colonies", *Nineteenth Century*, XIV (Sept. 1883), 386–7.

[3] Bodelsen, *op. cit.* pp. 201–2.

[4] Memorandum by Mr Gladstone to Queen Victoria (Secret), 23 March 1886, in Buckle, *op. cit.* 3rd ser. I, 88–9; Queen Victoria to Hartington, 12 Dec. 1880, *ibid.* 2nd ser. III, 163–4.

[5] Commons, 3 Feb. 1893, *Hansard*, 4th ser. VIII, 455–8; Commons, 5 May 1881, *Hansard*, 3rd ser. CCLX, 1853–4.

[6] Commons, 29 April 1881 and 5 May 1881, *Hansard*, 3rd ser. CCLX, 1424–50 and 1853–70.

[7] Their attitude was typified by Will Crooks's response to the cliché about the Empire on which the sun never sets: "In our alley it never rises", quoted in Slesser, Sir Henry, *A History of the Liberal Party*, p. 132. See also Commons, 31 Jan. 1887, *Hansard*, 3rd ser. CCCX, 277.

Bright, Harcourt, Derby and, to a lesser extent, Granville, held fast
to pure Consolidationist doctrine and opposed extension of imperial
rule to forestall colonial expansion by foreign powers.[1] Hartington,
Selborne, Kimberley and, at times, Northbrook veered towards a
strong Forward policy in defence of British paramountcy wherever it
was menaced by foreign advances. After 1882 they were supported
unexpectedly on African and New Guinea issues by their bitter
opponents on domestic, Irish and Egyptian questions, Chamberlain
and Dilke. Under pressure of international rivalry, there was to
develop, among the very ministers who at the outset had seemed to be
unanimously opposed to it, a Liberal school in favour of a strong,
Forward foreign and imperial policy.

These interacting disputes imparted an almost accidental character
to the ministry's imperial policies. Its decisions were more often
dictated by the need to reconcile the factions than by any consistent
aim or method. The confusion of conflicts within the Liberal party,
as Dilke observed in his "Memoir" for 1881, "made it difficult to
act with anybody for long without being attacked by some section
with which it was necessary to act at other times".[2] Granville,
apologising for the Cabinet's vacillating Egyptian policy, explained:
"the objectors to whatever was decided were pretty sure to have the
best of it".[3] The ministry's embarrassment was increased by Opposition attempts to split the Liberal majority by exposing and widening
its disunity on imperial issues. The anti-expansionist Gladstone and
his ministers, unable to agree on a positive policy, drifted into compromises which led to extension of the Empire. Only Gladstone's
prestige in the country, his infinite resourcefulness and marvellous
ambiguity kept the ministry and party together.

South African Problems in British Politics, 1880–1885

The South African problem, already critical when the Liberals
took office, was thrust into the centre of British politics by the Boer
revolt in the Transvaal (December 1880) and the humiliating military
reverses culminating at Majuba Hill (February 1881).[4] Disputes
over South African policy almost immediately became involved in the
contemporary Radical-Whig clashes within the Cabinet over the
Irish Protection of Life and Property and the Irish Land Bills.

The Liberals, while in Opposition, had branded their predecessors'
Forward policy in South Africa as extravagant and immoral. Gladstone was all but pledged to restore self-government to the Transvaal.

---

[1] See Gladstone's defence of Derby in his letter to Queen Victoria, 23 Jan. 1885, in
Buckle, op. cit. 2nd ser. III, 593–4.
[2] Dilke, "Memoirs", in Gwynn and Tuckwell, op. cit. I, 364.
[3] Granville to Baring, 18 April 1884, in Cromer, Modern Egypt, I, 499.
[4] C.H.B.E. VIII, 483–5.

On coming into office, the Liberals found that the Zulu War and the annexation of the Transvaal had been essential elements in a policy of enforced confederation.[1] The Conservatives had borne the unpopularity of the expensive military campaigns; Gladstone's ministry could not resist the opportunity of consummating confederation. Early confederation was the imperial authorities' only safe escape from all direct responsibility for the turbulent, advancing colonial frontiers of the subcontinent. Otherwise, the task of maintaining order would be a heavy drain on the Treasury and the Army for decades to come. The Liberal ministry, therefore, decided (May 1880) to keep control of the Transvaal, overruling the Radical ministers, Bright and Chamberlain, who demanded immediate restoration of Boer self-government. This decision initiated a bitter controversy between Whigs and pro-Boer Radicals, although the Court and the Opposition naturally applauded such continuity of policy. Dilke asserted that the decision was made "on the ground that as we were retiring from Kandahar we had better not also retire from Pretoria"[2]—a nice insurance against the ambiguity of parliamentary opinion on the two issues; but it was a half-truth. Gladstone gave the real reason for continuing to occupy the Transvaal in defending his government from the criticism of the disappointed pro-Boers among his own followers. Confederation, he observed, "is so important...it eclipses and absorbs every other consideration".[3] In Canada relations between the colonies had attained that healthy state which led naturally to federation; conversely, confederation in South Africa, he asserted, was the only hope of bringing about healthy relations between the colonies and republics, Boers and Britons, colonists and natives. As formerly in New Zealand, the colonists would never deal with the native problem liberally and realistically, Gladstone continued, until they were deprived of imperial aid and forced to bear the consequences of their own actions.[4]

Withdrawal from direct responsibility for the security of colonial inland frontiers in South Africa had long been the ambition of both parties. The Cape naval base until 1884 was still thought of in the Colonial Office as the only major imperial interest in the subcontinent. Consequently, it appeared to imperial statesmen (as a Cabinet Note of 1879 states) that the British taxpayer had paid heavily for the acquisition and pacification of the interior solely for the colonists' benefit. He could not be expected to bear the charges of their future defence and administration.[5] The traditional aim of

---

[1] Sir Bartle Frere to Sir Michael Hicks Beach, 3 Dec. 1879, C.O. 806/149, p. 639; and Hicks Beach to Sir Garnet Wolseley, 20 Nov. 1879, C.O. 806/155, pp. 3–4. *Vide supra*, chap. ii, and De Kiewiet, C. W., *The Imperial Factor in South Africa*, pp. 259–60.

[2] Dilke, "Memoir", 24 May 1880, in Gwynn and Tuckwell, *op. cit.* 1, 319.

[3] Commons, 25 May 1880, *Hansard*, 3rd ser. CCLII, 461.

[4] *Ibid.* 459–64.

[5] Cabinet Note in form of Draft Dispatch, Colonial Office to Sir Bartle Frere, 1879; C.O. 806/131.

Colonial Office policy was to transfer these burdens to the colonial governments. All proposals for extension of imperial territorial commitments into the interior, Kimberley once more informed South African governors in 1880, would be firmly rejected. It was not part of their duty to protect or civilise the tribes beyond the borders. "The complications incident upon the contact of white colonists with native tribes must arise wherever the border line is drawn", Kimberley continued; if, nevertheless, further annexations became imperative, the colony on whose behalf they were made must be forced to undertake full responsibility without imperial aid.[1] Sir Henry Holland (later Lord Knutsford) endorsed this consolidationist frontier policy on behalf of the Opposition (August 1880).[2]

Nevertheless, individually the South African colonies were too weak to dispense with imperial assistance or to uphold British paramountcy and to keep the peace in the sub-continent. The conclusion reached in a Cabinet Paper of 1879 was generally accepted in London: "A confederation or union charged with the full responsibility of defence against the natives" is the only prospect of "avoiding the periodical recurrence of wars carried on at great cost to this country."[3] Frere had removed one obstacle to early confederation by breaking the Zulu military power; Shepstone's occupation of the Transvaal, it seemed, could be used to remove another. Self-government was to be restored to the Boers only if they consented to join a "united dominion" under the British flag.[4] Confederation would allow Natal to be entrusted safely with responsible government and the administration of Zululand. These were the arguments which led to the Liberal ministry's decision in May 1880 to continue the occupation of the Transvaal.

The Cabinet's hopes of enforcing an early confederation of South Africa were dispelled in July, only two months later. The Transvaal and Cape Boer leaders had foiled the imperial authorities.[5] Divorced from the confederation issue, the question of restoring self-government to the Transvaal divided the Liberal party and drove the Cabinet factions into stalemate.

From July 1880 until March 1881 the ministry was unable to agree upon a final decision as to the Transvaal. Ministers were distracted by a continuous crisis due to disputes over the Irish Coercion and Land Bills.[6] The divisions within the Cabinet on the Transvaal issue tended to coincide with those on Irish questions. Gladstone now inclined to support Chamberlain, Bright and the Radicals in insisting

---

[1] Kimberley to Frere, 18 May 1880, *Parl. Pap.* 1880, LI [C. 2586], p. 1.
[2] Commons, 31 Aug. 1880, *Hansard*, 3rd ser. CCLVI, 892–3.
[3] Cabinet Paper, "Future policy with regard to Zululand and South Africa generally" 10 March 1879; C.O. 806/123, p. 1.
[4] Frere to Hicks Beach, 3 Dec. 1879, C.O. 806/149, p. 639.
[5] *C.H.B.E.* VIII, 482–3, 538.
[6] See Dilke's "Confidential Political Diary" for this period, B.M. Add. MSS. 43934.

on withdrawal from the Transvaal.[1] They did not want to create "another Ireland in South Africa" which would have to be held by force against a hostile population.[2] At the same time the Radical ministers, with the sympathy of Gladstone and Bright, were attempting to force their Whig colleagues to agree to an Irish Land Bill which would concede the claims of the Irish National Land League.[3] But the Whigs, Kimberley and Hartington, and the imperialist Irish Secretary, Forster, backed by the Court and the humanitarians, proposed to hold the Transvaal. These same ministers resisted the Radicals' Irish land measures. To withdraw from the Transvaal, the Whigs and Conservatives protested, would be to abandon the native population to Boer oppression and weaken imperial prestige throughout South Africa. When the Transvaal rebellion broke out (16 December 1880) public opinion forced the ministry to act. "The question of reducing the Boers", Randolph Churchill observed, "will divide the Liberal party by a sharper and more insuperable line than any Irish question."[4]

A Whig policy of suppressing the Rebellion and of "vindicating" the Queen's authority in the Transvaal was announced in the Speech from the Throne.[5] The pro-Boer Radicals and Parnellites openly opposed this policy by moving a hostile amendment in the Commons.[6] The five Radical ministers abstained from voting in support of the Government.[7] On the admission of Dilke, who was one of them, this Radical revolt against the Whig faction was one of tactics as well as principle. Between January and March the Radical and Irish Nationalist leaders harassed the Whigs on the Transvaal question to force the Whigs to accept their Irish land policy, and to unseat the Colonial Secretary, Kimberley, and thus weaken the Whigs in the ministry.[8] The Radical manœuvre partially succeeded in that Argyll resigned over the Irish Land Bill, and Forster and Lord Cowper later left the Government in protest against the Radical-inspired Kilmainham Treaty. But Kimberley and the Whigs yielded momentarily on the Transvaal issue, and in the first week of February the Cabinet agreed to Radical demands to negotiate with the Boers.[9] The ministry feared the Transvaal War would spread to the Orange Free State and the Cape Colony.[10] National indignation against the

[1] *Ibid.* 21 Feb. and 2, 3, 7 and 15 March 1881.

[2] Lords, 15 June 1883, *Hansard*, 3rd ser. CCLXXX, 675.

[3] Dilke, "Diary", 2 March 1881, B.M. Add. MSS. 43934; Hartington to Gladstone, 19 Dec. 1880, and Gladstone to Hartington, 20 Dec. 1880, in Holland, *op. cit.* I, 333-7.

[4] Randolph Churchill to Sir Henry Wolff, 27 Dec. 1880, in Churchill, W. S., *Lord Randolph Churchill*, I, 195.

[5] Lords, 6 Jan. 1881, *Hansard*, 3rd ser. CCLVII, 4-5.

[6] Commons, 21 Jan. 1881, *Hansard*, 3rd ser. CCLVII, 1109 *seqq.*

[7] Dilke, "Memoir", in Gwynn and Tuckwell, *op. cit.* I, 366.

[8] Dilke, "Diary", 2-5, 14 and 19 March 1881, B.M. Add. MSS. 43934.

[9] *Ibid.* See also Kimberley's account in Lords, 31 March 1881, *Hansard*, 3rd ser. CCLX, 283.   [10] *Ibid.*

Boers after Majuba again strengthened Whig demands for suppression of the rebellion. But by March 3, after the Radical ministers' threatened resignation, their policy of conciliation prevailed.[1]

The Pretoria Convention[2] (August 1881) was partly a compromise designed to mollify Radical-Whig strife in the ministry and party. Whigs and humanitarians had to be content with imperial suzerainty and the appearance of control of Transvaal native and frontier policy; while the pro-Boers obtained restoration of Boer self-government. Conservatives in Parliament condemned the ministry's vacillations and criticised the Convention's safeguards for native interests as spurious.[3] Hicks Beach, however, admitted that the Conservatives also would have granted the Boers responsible government, but only after the revolt had been quelled.[4] The Convention appeared to reduce imperial commitments; but events in Bechuanaland after 1882 were to show, as Derby afterwards admitted, that it had only extended the United Kingdom's territorial responsibilities without reserving effective power to execute them.[5]

Imperial burdens were increasing elsewhere in South Africa. In deference to Radical-humanitarian agitation on behalf of the Basutos,[6] and in accordance with the traditional Colonial Office principle of protecting native land rights in order to forestall the spread of native unrest and revolt, Kimberley and Derby in 1883 resumed the administration of Basutoland from the Cape Colony.[7] "Her Majesty's Government", Derby warned the Cape ministers, "accept no permanent responsibility for the affairs of this part of South Africa."[8] Responsible government could not be conferred on Natal in 1882 because its legislature would not undertake responsibility for frontier defence without the aid of imperial troops.[9] But until 1887 British governments withstood strong pressure from the Natal legislature[10] and the humanitarians[11] to restore order in Zululand.[12]

While the attention of Parliament was focused on Egypt and the

[1] Dilke, "Diary", 21 Feb. and 15 March 1881, B.M. Add. MSS. 43934.
[2] *C.H.B.E.* VIII, 485–6. For Kimberley's defence, see Lords, 31 March 1881, *Hansard*, 3rd ser. CCLX, 279–90.
[3] Commons, 25 July 1881, *Hansard*, 3rd ser. CCLXIII, 1756–84; Lords, 31 March 1881, *Hansard*, 3rd ser. CCLX, 249–78.
[4] Commons, 25 July 1881, *Hansard*, 3rd ser. CCLXIII, 1760, 1765–6.
[5] Lords, 31 May 1883, *Hansard*, 3rd ser. CCLXXIX, 1287–8.
[6] Commons, 31 Aug. 1880, *Hansard*, 3rd ser. CCLVI, 880–4, 897–8; Kimberley to Frere, 20 May 1880, *Parl. Pap.* 1880, LI [C. 2569], pp. 49 *seqq.*; and Aborigines Protection Society to C.O., 17 April 1879, *ibid.* pp. 2–3.
[7] *C.H.B.E.* VIII, 480, 503–4.
[8] Derby to Sir Hercules Robinson, 14 June 1883, *Parl. Pap.* 1883, XLVIII [C. 3708], p. 40.
[9] Kimberley to Bulwer, 2 Jan. 1882, C.O. African (South) 244; Commons, 31 Aug. 1880, *Hansard*, 3rd ser. CCLVI, 863.
[10] Bulwer to Derby, 5 Aug. 1884, *Parl. Pap.* 1884, LVI [C. 4214], pp. 41–2.
[11] Memorials of Aborigines Protection Society and Members of Parliament, 26 March and 24 Sept. 1886, *Parl. Pap.* 1887, LXI [C. 4913], pp. 41–2, and [C. 4980], p. 19.
[12] Kimberley to Bulwer, 30 Nov. 1882, *Parl. Pap.* 1883, XLIX [C. 3466], pp. 216–18; Derby to Bulwer, 19 Aug. 1884, *Parl. Pap.* 1884, LVIII [C. 4191], p. 138; Dilke, "Diary", 25 March and 14 May 1884, B.M. Add. MSS. 43936A.

Sudan during the years 1882–5, the South African frontier and federation problem turned upon the future of Bechuanaland. The Transvaal controversy in British politics entered a new phase with the establishment of the Boer Republics of Stellaland and Goshen, and Boer freebooters' intervention in the Bechuana tribal wars.[1] The ministry's Irish disputes, in abeyance from the beginning of 1883 until the end of 1884, were replaced by dissensions over Egyptian policy. The Radical leaders, Chamberlain and Dilke, from the middle of 1882 onward now tended to act with the Whig leader, Hartington, in favour of a Forward imperial policy both in Egypt and elsewhere in Africa.

The Opposition, the anti-Boers who burned to avenge Majuba, the humanitarians and the Forward school of frontier policy, regardless of party, combined in the Commons (13 March 1883) to urge the Government to intervene between the Boers and the Bechuana. Gladstone and Chamberlain had justified the Pretoria Convention mainly by its provisions for imperial protection of native interests. The Conservatives, Sir Henry Holland, Sir John Gorst and Lord Randolph Churchill, in the Commons, seizing another chance to split the Liberals on the Transvaal issue, called upon the ministry to carry out its pledges.[2] One faction of Liberals, the humanitarian imperialists, led by Forster and Goschen,[3] supported the Conservatives; another, the Radical anti-imperialists, headed by John Morley,[4] insisted on withdrawing altogether from any responsibility for the Transvaal or its frontiers. Deputations and petitions from the Aborigines Protection Society, missions, South African merchants, shippers and investors at the end of 1883 and during 1884 urged the Colonial Office to intervene against the Boer expansion in Bechuanaland and Zululand.[5] But these sectional pressures alone were too weak to force the ministry from its Consolidationist resolutions.

Gladstone, Derby, Harcourt and other non-interventionist ministers still controlled the Cabinet on this issue. They rejected a proposal of Hartington, Chamberlain and Dilke in March 1883 to send troops to the rescue of the Bechuana chief, Montsiwa.[6] John Morley and the

---

[1] *C.H.B.E.* VIII, 508.

[2] Commons, 13 March 1883, *Hansard*, 3rd ser. CCLXXVII, 413 *seqq.* and 13 April 1883, CCLXXVIII, 202 *seqq.*; and Lords, 13 March 1883, *Hansard*, 3rd ser. CCLXXVIII, 315 *seqq.* and 15 June 1883, CCLXXX, 654 *seqq.*

[3] Commons, 16 March 1883, *Hansard*, 3rd ser. CCLXXVII, 703–20, and 13 April 1883, CCLXXVIII, 246–53.

[4] Commons, 13 March 1883, *Hansard*, 3rd ser. CCLXXVII, 425.

[5] Memorial to Lord Derby by Earls Shaftesbury and Grey, W. E. Forster, Sir J. Pease, Sir T. Fowell Buxton, J. E. Gorst, etc., 20 Nov. 1883, enclosed in Forster to Derby, 20 Nov. 1883, *Parl. Pap.* 1884, LVII [C. 3841], pp. 91–2; J. MacKenzie to C.O., 20 Nov. 1883, *ibid.* pp. 92 *seqq.* See also Sir Donald Currie to Gladstone, 1 and 21 Nov. 1884, C.O. 806/245, pp. 1, 5–8.

[6] Dilke, "Diary", 10 and 16 March 1883, B.M. Add. MSS. 43935; Dilke, "Memoir", 10 Nov. 1884, B.M. Add. MSS. 43930, p. 299; Garvin, J. L., *The Life of Chamberlain*, I, 489–92.

Radical Little Englander wing of the Party were exasperated already by the occupation of Egypt; and the Gladstonians feared another Transvaal war which would endanger the whole South African position and probably shatter party unity.[1] Derby expressed the Gladstonians' attitude towards the Bechuana question in the Lords: a settled administration, not merely an expedition, would be required to pacify Bechuanaland; the territory was useless for purposes of colonisation; and British opinion would not accept responsibility for a fresh province there. "Bechuanaland", Derby concluded, "is of no value to us for any English, or for any Imperial purposes... politically, it is of no consequence to us whether Boers or Native Chiefs are in possession."[2] Derby's insular, negative outlook was characteristic of the older generation of party leaders at this time.[3] At the end of June 1883 Derby was still hoping for the best solution—that the Bechuana would drive out the Boers without imperial or colonial aid.[4]

Fears of a German-Transvaal conspiracy to seize hegemony in South Africa were aroused at the Cape and in London as German annexation in South-west Africa advanced inland from Angra Pequeña (August 1883) and Damaraland-Namaqualand (August 1884)[5] towards Bechuanaland and the Transvaal western frontiers. The Bechuana question, as a result, became important in the general South African strategy of federation. British opinion noted the Afrikaner Bond's aspirations for a Boer-dominated South African Republican Federation linked closely with Germany, and the Transvaal Government's grant (April 1884) of a railway development monopoly to a German-Dutch company.[6] Paul Kruger's plans to link Pretoria with Angra Pequena and St Lucia Bay alarmed South African merchants, investors and shippers in the City.[7] They agreed with Cecil Rhodes and the Cape ministry that Boer control of Bechuanaland would shut out the Cape from the interior. Control of the "Road to the North" would determine whether the future South African federation was to be dominated by the Cape or the Transvaal; whether it was to be imperial or republican. The Cape ministry requested that the territory between the Transvaal border and Damaraland and Namaqualand be brought under an imperial protectorate;[8] while humanitarian and South African interests in London

---

[1] Commons, 16 March 1883, *Hansard*, 3rd ser. CCLXXVII, 729–30.
[2] Lords, 13 March 1883, *Hansard*, 3rd ser. CCLXXVII, 327–8.
[3] Garvin, *op. cit.* I, 491, note 3.
[4] Derby to Sir Henry Ponsonby, 29 June 1883, Buckle, *op. cit.* 2nd ser. III, 432.
[5] *C.H.B.E.* VIII, 515–17; Cape Minister's Minute of 17 Sept. 1884, *Parl. Pap.* 1884–5, LVII [C. 4252], pp. 6–7.
[6] *C.H.B.E.* VIII, pp. 491–501, 507–9, 515–18.
[7] Currie to Gladstone, 21 Nov. 1884, and Currie to Derby, 6 and 17 Jan. 1885, C.O. 806/245, pp. 11–15. See also Forster to Derby and J. McKenzie to C.O., 20 Nov. 1883, *Parl. Pap.* 1884, LVII [C. 3841], pp. 91–2.
[8] Minute of Cape Ministers to High Commissioner, 17 Sept. 1884, *Parl. Pap.* 1884, LVII [C. 4252], p. 7.

urged extensions of protectorate over Bechuanaland and Zululand. This sectional agitation towards the end of 1884 became caught up in the national indignation against the Franco-German *entente* (August 1884) which encroached upon imperial preserves elsewhere in Africa and the Pacific, and obstructed British policy in Egypt.[1] Granville observed to Gladstone (December 1884) regarding the reaction to the publication of the Angra Pequeña Blue Books: "there is a wild and irrational spirit abroad." Gladstone replied, "to which for one I do not feel at all disposed to give in".[2]

But the majority in the Cabinet, including Derby, now became sufficiently convinced of the importance of Bechuanaland to insure against Boer or German control provided this did not involve direct obligations and expenditure. Derby obtained a pledge from the Cape Scanlen ministry (November 1883) that, should a Bechuanaland protectorate become necessary, the Cape Government would share and eventually undertake responsibility for it.[3] But he refused the Cape ministry's request for an imperial protectorate over the whole region between Damaraland-Namaqualand and the Transvaal border.[4] No further imperial protectorate would be proclaimed in the interests of the responsible government colonies, he informed the Cape ministry, unless they accepted the resultant charges upon their own revenues.[5] The Colonial Secretary further made political and boundary concessions to the Transvaal Boers[6] in the London Convention (February 1884) in hopes of getting them voluntarily to accept exclusion from the North Road.[7]

Derby's attempted insurances against direct Colonial Office responsibility in Bechuanaland both failed. The Upington ministry at the Cape repudiated the Scanlen pledge (August 1884).[8] In the following month the South African Republic violated the London Convention by declaring a protectorate over the Goshen settlements.[9] The urgent need for some form of imperial administration in Bechuanaland was now recognised in London and Cape Town.[10]

The Cabinet decided to send the Warren Expedition to enforce the Convention upon the Boers (October 1884),[11] still hoping that the

[1] Dilke, *op. cit.* II, 190–1.
[2] Granville to Gladstone, 25 Dec. 1884, and Gladstone to Granville, 26 Dec. 1884, Fitzmaurice, Lord Edmond, *The Life of Lord Granville*, II, 371.
[3] Scanlen to Derby, 26 Nov. 1883, *Parl. Pap.* 1884, LVII [C. 3841], pp. 118–19.
[4] Derby to Robinson, 11 Nov. 1884, *Parl. Pap.* 1884–5, LVII [C. 4252], p. 37; Derby to Robinson, 28 Aug. 1884, *Parl. Pap.* 1884–5, LVII [C. 4213], p. 26.
[5] Derby to Robinson, 20 Aug. 1884, *Parl. Pap.* 1884–5, LVII [C. 4213], pp. 1 *seqq.*
[6] According to Chamberlain the Cape refused to participate in a Bechuanaland protectorate unless agreement was reached with the Transvaal, Commons, 6 Feb. 1884, *Hansard*, 3rd ser. CCLXXXIV, 149–50; for Derby's view of the Convention see Lords, 31 May 1883, *Hansard*, 3rd ser. CCLXXIX, 1288 and 15 June 1883, CCLXXX, 668–77.
[7] *C.H.B.E.* VIII, 509–10.
[8] Minute of Cape Ministers, 5 Aug. 1884, *Parl. Pap.* 1884–5, LVII [C. 4213], pp. 28–9.
[9] *C.H.B.E.* VIII, pp. 512–14.
[10] Lords, 1 May 1885, *Hansard*, 3rd ser. CCXCVII, 1281.
[11] See Chamberlain, Cabinet Minute, 1 Oct. 1884, in Garvin, *op. cit.* I, 492–3.

Cape could be persuaded to assume the projected protectorate.[1] But the colonial ministers would not accept it on Colonial Office terms. Exeter Hall and the humanitarian imperialists, led by Forster and Goschen as well as Warren himself, objected to tribal populations being placed under colonial governments.[2] Their agitation reinforced the Colonial Office's insistence on extensive tribal land reserves in the proposed Bechuana protectorate.[3] The Cape ministry supported Boer land claims and demanded a land settlement which would allow maximum White colonisation.[4]

These disputes, like those which had led the Colonial Office to resume charge of Basutoland in 1883, revealed the fundamental incompatibility of the dual imperial aims of administrative non-responsibility and of trusteeship for tribal rights. The Colonial Office in these circumstances had to choose between withdrawing from Bechuanaland and undertaking direct responsibility until the Cape could be persuaded to do so. The Colony and Protectorate of Bechuanaland were proclaimed in September 1885. Ten expensive years were to elapse before the administration could be transferred to the Cape with pre-requisite safeguards for tribal rights.

The dispatch of the Warren Expedition was the result of a change of balance in the ministry brought about by an outburst of nationalist sentiment in favour of a stronger foreign policy. During 1884, the struggles within the Cabinet over imperial policy turned upon the Egyptian problem. Granville, Derby and Northbrook were inclined to accede to German colonial claims in Africa and the Pacific in return for Bismarck's support against French obstruction in Egypt.[5] Chamberlain and Dilke insisted that Egypt should be evacuated, thus removing the need to appease Bismarck elsewhere in Africa and the Pacific.[6] Hartington favoured prolonged occupation of Egypt[7] but, like Chamberlain and Dilke, was anxious to restore British prestige abroad and Liberal popularity at home by more virile action overseas. These three ministers now revolted against Granville's continual appeasement of Germany and Derby's cautious colonial

---

[1] C.O. to Sir Charles Warren, 10 Nov. 1884, *Parl. Pap.* 1884–5, LV [C. 4227], pp. 4–5; Robinson to Derby, 5 Jan. 1885, C.O. African 295 in *Carnarvon Papers*, P.R.O. 30–6/130, p. 3; and Lords, 1 May 1885, *Hansard*, 3rd ser. CCXCVII, 1281.

[2] Warren to Derby, 23 May 1885, *Parl. Pap.* 1885, LVII [C. 4588], pp. 12–13.

[3] Sir H. Robinson, Minute to Cape Ministers, 15 Oct. 1884, *Parl. Pap.* 1884–5, LVII [C. 4252], p. 31; F. A. Stanley to Robinson, 13 Aug. 1885, *Parl. Pap.* 1885, LVII [C. 4588], p. 118.

[4] Minute of Cape Ministers, 7 July 1885, *Parl. Pap.* 1885, LVII [C. 4588], pp. 31–2; Cabinet Paper: "Bechuanaland Affairs" (F. A. Stanley), C.O. African 301 in *Carnarvon Papers*, P.R.O. 30–6/130.

[5] E.g. Granville's instructions in T. V. Lister, Minute of Kirk to Granville, 31 Dec. 1884, F.O. 84/1679. See also Fitzmaurice, *op. cit.* II, 354–5, 360–2, 366–73; Crowe, S. E., *The Berlin West African Conference*, p. 26.

[6] Dilke, "Diary", 5 July, 5 and 9 Aug., 6 and 31 Oct. 1884, B.M. Add. MSS. 43936A; Dilke, "Memoir", Nov. 1884–Jan. 1885, B.M. Add. MSS. 43930–1. See also Garvin, *op. cit.* I, 450–6, 494–545.

[7] Holland, *op. cit.* II, 2–6.

policy.[1] They urged a strong policy in defence of imperial interests in Africa and the Pacific regardless of Germany's attitude.[2] Gladstone and Harcourt held the extreme anti-expansionist position, wishing with the Radicals to evacuate Egypt and with Granville to acquiesce in Germany's colonial ambitions.[3] Until mid-1884 the Gladstone-Granville view usually had prevailed. The German annexations of Angra Pequeña and the Cameroons had been recognised.[4]

Towards the end of 1884 Gladstone was ill and seemed about to resign, with the result that the anti-expansionist faction in the Cabinet was weakened. Hartington, who would have succeeded him, was contemplating reforming the Cabinet in the direction of a Forward policy abroad with Dilke at the Foreign Office and Chamberlain at the Treasury.[5] From August 1884 to February 1885 this Forward school of foreign policy gained ascendancy in the Government. The Wolseley Expedition was sent to the Sudan; St Lucia Bay, Tembuland, Bomvanaland and Galekaland, as well as Bechuanaland, were brought under imperial or colonial control; the Middle Niger Territories were secured at the Berlin Conference; and the New Guinea Protectorate was proclaimed. All these measures were defensive in intention, being designed to restore British prestige in Europe and to counteract the Franco-German *entente* directed against imperial paramountcy in Africa and the Pacific.[6] They did not originate in an expansionist ambition to acquire territory.[7]

But the Forward school's hold on the Cabinet was temporary. Gladstone did not resign at this time; the agreement between Hartington and the Radical ministers upon African and Pacific questions was upset by their deeper disagreement on Irish and Egyptian policies;[8] and the two succeeding Salisbury governments inclined to resume Gladstone's and Granville's appeasement of France and Germany on the imperial issues.

AUSTRALASIAN QUESTIONS

German and French intervention in the Western Pacific Islands and Australasian colonial reaction to it during the early 'eighties posed problems similar in some ways to those of the South African

[1] Garvin, *op. cit.* 1, 497–8; Gwynn and Tuckwell, *op. cit.* II, 81–99; Holland, *op. cit.* II, 24–5.

[2] Chamberlain, Cabinet Note, 28 Sept. 1884, *Granville Papers*, P.R.O. 30–29/120.

[3] Gardiner, *op. cit.* 1, 516–19; Harcourt's Memorandum on Egypt of 16 Nov. 1884, *ibid.* App. II.

[4] Dilke, "Diary", 21 June 1884, B.M. Add. MSS. 43936A. See also Fitzmaurice, *op. cit.* chaps. ix–xi.

[5] Dilke, "Memoir", 5 Jan. 1885, B.M. Add. MSS. 43931, p. 19.

[6] *Ibid.* 4 and 7 Jan. 1885, B.M. Add. MSS. 43931, pp. 17 and 26. See also Dilke, *Problems*, II, 191.

[7] Chamberlain to Dilke, 29 Dec. 1884, in Garvin, *op. cit.* 1, 497–8.

[8] Dilke, "Memoir", 9 Jan. 1885, B.M. Add. MSS. 43931, pp. 24–5. *Vide infra*, pp. 154–5.

interior.[1] In both regions the Gladstone ministry pursued four scarcely compatible aims: to prevent foreign annexations which would embitter colonial feeling towards the Empire;[2] to avoid imbroglios with foreign powers over minor colonial issues which might provoke retaliation against major imperial interests in the Mediterranean, Egypt and India; and to protect native interests in deference to humanitarian opinion. At the same time, further territorial liabilities were to be avoided.

Queensland's attempted annexation of Eastern New Guinea (April 1883) was intended to force London into responsibility for meeting the danger of foreign expansion. Other Australasian colonies urged annexation of the New Hebrides and Samoa and the exclusion of foreign governments from all islands from New Guinea eastwards to Fiji.[3]

These colonial aspirations in the Pacific exasperated the Gladstonians in the Cabinet[4] as much as those of the Cape Colony in Bechuanaland. Derby rebuffed them similarly. New Guinea, he explained to the Australians, had not been colonised and the Imperial Government would not risk another war by attempting to rule several million natives who had no desire to be ruled.[5] Assured by Granville that Germany had no designs on New Guinea, Derby made light of this danger. However, he warned the colonies that should a protectorate become necessary, they would have to pay the cost of administration.[6] As in the case of Bechuanaland there seemed at first to be no direct Empire or United Kingdom interest which would justify imperial expenditure. In Australia as in South Africa the imperial authority looked to confederation for relief from colonial importunity. Derby urged the Australasian colonies to confederate in order to protect their own interests without relying on imperial aid.[7] The colonists and their sympathisers, the imperialist and humanitarian societies at home, clamoured for a New Guinea protectorate despite Derby's rebuke. The humanitarians, however, were opposed to a colonial government administering New Guinea's native population.[8] From July 1884 onwards the Pacific Island question, like that of the Bechuana, became a pawn in the Cabinet's internal struggles over the major policy issue of Egypt.[9] Despite Granville's appeasement of Germany in South Africa, Bismarck remained hostile and did not

[1] C.H.B.E. VII, pt. I, 351–9 and pt. II, pp. 206, 209–11.
[2] C.O. to F.O., 18 June 1883, C.O. 808/45, pp. 23–4.
[3] C.H.B.E. VII, pt. I, 356–60.
[4] Derby to Ponsonby, 29 June 1883, in Buckle, op. cit. 2nd ser. III, 432–3; Harcourt to Kimberley, 8 Dec. 1894, in Gardiner, op. cit. II, 326.
[5] Derby to Sir A. H. Palmer, 11 July 1883, Parl. Pap. 1883, XLVII [C. 3691], pp. 22–3.
[6] C.O. to F.O., 18 June 1883, C.O. 808/45, pp. 23–4.
[7] Derby to Palmer, 11 July 1883, Parl. Pap. 1883, XLVII [C. 3691], pp. 23–4.
[8] Memorandum of Bishop Selwyn, 2 July 1883, C.O. 808/45, pp. 66–7.
[9] Derby to Granville, 18 Sept., 11 Dec. 1884, 6 March 1885, Granville Papers, P.R.O. 30–29/120; Dilke, "Memoir", July 1884–Jan. 1885, B.M. Add. MSS. 43930–1.

support Britain at the London Conference on Egypt (July 1884). Aided by anti-German feeling in the country, the Forward party of Hartington, Kimberley, Chamberlain and Dilke, having converted Derby, overcame the opposition of Gladstone, Selborne and Harcourt, and persuaded the Cabinet to agree to a New Guinea protectorate (August 1884).[1] This victory was the easier because the colonies at the Sydney Convention (July 1884) had already agreed to bear most of the cost.[2] But in the autumn Granville heard that Bismarck would oppose Britain's policy if Germany's New Guinea claims were not met.[3] To obtain Bismarck's co-operation, the Foreign Secretary persuaded Derby, when he proclaimed the New Guinea Protectorate (October 1884), to limit it to the south-eastern shores of the island.[4] It was a half-hearted compromise between the Consolidationists' objection to increased responsibility, Hartington's and the Radical ministers' support of the colonists' claims, and Granville's fear of upsetting Bismarck.[5] A German protectorate over the northern shores followed.

Angered by United Kingdom toleration of foreign colonisation, several Australian responsible governments looked to a federation as a stronger champion of their Pacific ambitions than the Colonial Office. Nothing could have been more welcome to Gladstonians and imperialists alike. The first intrusions of foreign governments in Australasia as in South Africa had accentuated the need of intercolonial federations able to defend themselves and uphold British paramountcy without further demands on the United Kingdom Treasury. While confederation could not be forced in South Africa even by conquest and stratagem, in Australia it emerged spontaneously as a colonial self-help movement. The Imperial Parliament, without dividing, passed a Bill authorising an Australasian Federal Council[6] in which the several colonial governments could begin to unite for external action. Derby in moving the Bill recommended it as "the scheme on which the Australian community has decided for itself";[7] and this was characteristic of the constitutional convention by which the Parliament at Westminster exercised its supreme imperial authority to make laws for the great colonies only with their governments' consent. During the debate, Lord Norton described the origins of the Bill: first it had been discussed in the colonial legislatures, then between the colonial agents and the Secretary of State; it had been endorsed by a colonial convention and now came to the

---

[1] Dilke, "Memoir", in Gwynn and Tuckwell, op. cit. II, 82.
[2] Sir W. F. Stanwell to Derby, 11 July 1884, Parl. Pap. 1884, LIV [C. 4217], p. 7.
[3] Granville to Gladstone, 30 Sept. 1884, in Fitzmaurice, op. cit. II, 371–2.
[4] Ibid. See also Derby to Granville, 18 Sept. 1884. Granville Papers, P.R.O. 30–29/120; and Garvin, op. cit. I, 497–8.
[5] On New Guinea policy generally see Ward, J. M., British Policy in the South Pacific, 1786–1893, chap. xxviii.
[6] C.H.B.E. VII, pt I, 431–2.
[7] Lords, 23 April 1885, Hansard, 3rd ser. CCXCVII, 435.

Imperial Parliament for final approval. This process, he declared, "illustrated exactly the kind of imperial consultation and co-action which alone was practicable and effective".[1]

The Federal Council was designed by colonial leaders to make up for imperial deficiencies and help to maintain "the supremacy of Australian influences in adjoining seas".[2] Delegates to the Council's first meeting called upon the imperial authorities to conduct Pacific affairs in consultation with the colonial governments;[3] and ministers in London in fact already tended to follow this practice. There was some truth in Rosebery's observation that the policy of the Empire was beginning to be dictated from its extremities.[4] Although United Kingdom ministries refused to make the further annexations requested by the colonial governments, they attempted by diplomacy to restrict extension of foreign administration in the Pacific.[5] For the sake of imperial harmony the Foreign Office prevented German rule in Samoa[6] and French control of the New Hebrides,[7] and declared protectorates over the Cook Islands (1888) and the southern Solomon Islands (1893). The Australian governments' promotion of their own Pacific interests also enabled London to shed most of the burden of the New Guinea territory annexed in 1887. Its administration, with safeguards for native land and labour rights, was transferred to the Queensland Government;[8] as Derby had planned, most of its charges were assumed by the Colonial Government.[9]

PROBLEMS OF INDIAN SECURITY

Imperial interests in the Pacific and South Africa were regarded in Whitehall as merely peripheral in importance compared with the security of the Indian Empire and its Suez lifeline. Concentration of United Kingdom military, financial and diplomatic strength upon these vital objectives often dictated diffident imperial policies elsewhere.[10] The Indian Empire seemed to be endangered by Russian expansion in Central Asia towards the North-West Frontier, and on the North-East by French designs upon Burma, Siam and Indo-

---

[1] Ibid. 441–2.
[2] Memorandum of Sir Thomas McIlwraith, July 1883, C.O. 808/45, p. 93.
[3] Proceedings of First Session of the Federal Council of Australia, 1886, C.O. 808/66, pp. 24–5.
[4] Rosebery, Speech, 23 March 1892, in Crewe, op. cit. I, 315.
[5] Ward, op. cit. chap. xxvii.
[6] C.O. to F.O., 11 Nov. 1885, C.O. 808/62, pp. 79–81; C.O. to F.O. 23 Nov. 1886, C.O. 808/69, p. 151.
[7] C.O. to F.O., 9 June 1886, C.O. 808/68, p. 50; C.O. 808/67, pp. 4–5; Crewe, op. cit. I, 267–8; C.O. Memorandum on the New Hebrides, 23 April 1887, Parl. Pap. 1887, LVI [C. 5091], II, pp. 165–6.
[8] See Ripon to Gladstone, 10 Dec. 1892, Gladstone Papers, B.M. Add. MSS. 44287.
[9] C.O. to Scratchley, 17 Nov. 1884, Parl. Pap. 1885, LIV [C. 4273], pp. 29–30.
[10] Parl. Pap. 1887, LVI [C. 5091], II, 169 seqq.

China. Suez, "the spinal cord of the Empire",[1] was threatened by possible Franco-Russian naval hegemony in the Eastern Mediterranean and by Egyptian anarchy, which invited the interposition of the Continental Powers across the road to India.

The Liberals came into office in 1880 determined to reverse the Conservative Forward policy on the Indian North-West Frontier as in the Transvaal, and to revert to their Consolidationist policy of 1868–74. Its principles had been to maintain the Afghan kingdom intact as a buffer between Russia and the Indian Empire, but to avoid formal commitments to defend it.[2] Argyll and Northbrook, the Secretary of State and Viceroy of that time, survived into Gladstone's second ministry to insist upon this strategy as if time had stood still in Afghanistan. The new Government had been outraged by its Conservative predecessor's large expenditure of Indian revenue on the Afghan War and by the occupation of Kandahar.[3] The Queen's Speech (6 January 1881) announced the Liberals' decision to withdraw from Afghanistan. There ensued an acrimonious *post mortem* on the Conservative party's frontier policy which illustrates well the differences between the Consolidationist and Forward psychologies. Salisbury and the ex-Viceroy, Lord Lytton, defended themselves by asserting that even more than the security of the Indian Empire was at stake. Russia, they feared, planned by external pressure and internal sedition "to cripple the action or embarrass the policy of England in Europe, by disturbing the security of England in India. And to do this, moreover, without even employing her own troops. . . . but simply by creating a diversion on the North-West Frontier of India, through an alliance with the Cabul Power."[4] The military occupation of Kandahar, they concluded, must be maintained to exclude Russian influence and keep the Amir faithful to the British interest. India, the most precious jewel in the imperial crown, Lytton argued, was worth more than the few pieces of silver, the occupation cost.[5] The Queen and Indian Army strategists supported this Conservative view.[6] Ministerial spokesmen replied that the Indian Empire was endangered more by ruinous expenditure than by Russian threats.[7] "To impoverish India by expending our money on Afghanistan would clearly be to play our enemies' game", Dilke declared.[8] Another characteristic Liberal belief was expressed by Ripon, the

---

[1] Bismarck's phrase: Busch, J. A. M., *Bismarck*, iii, 52.

[2] *C.H.B.E.* v, 23, 406–14.

[3] Commons, 11 Feb. 1880, *Hansard*, 3rd ser. ccl, 466 *seqq.*

[4] Lytton, Lords, 10 Jan. 1881, *Hansard*, 3rd ser. cclvii, 288.

[5] *Ibid.* 287 *seqq.*, 1594–621; Commons, 24 March 1881, *Hansard*, 3rd ser. cclix, 1831 *seqq.*

[6] Ponsonby to Hartington, 8 Sept. 1880, in Buckle, *op. cit.* 2nd ser. iii, 138–9; Queen Victoria to Gladstone, 13 May 1880, *ibid.* p. 105.

[7] Commons, 7 June 1880, *Hansard*, 3rd ser. cclii, 1342–3; and Lords, 28 Jan. 1881, cclvii, 1594–621, *passim.* See also Hartington to Queen Victoria, 6 Nov. 1880, in Buckle, *op. cit.* 2nd ser. iii, 154–5.

[8] Commons, 24 March 1881, *Hansard*, 3rd ser. cclix, 1863.

Liberal Viceroy: "good government and the development of the Indian resources" was a more effective counter to Russia "...than the fortification of all the frontier towns of Afghanistan".[1]

Withdrawal from the Sibi and Pishin districts, as well as from Kandahar, was unanimous Cabinet policy until April 1881.[2] But Ripon doubted whether the Afghan kingdom, undermined by invasion and British and Russian factions, could be restored as an effective buffer simply by withdrawing imperial troops. This would lead rather to anarchy, inviting restoration of the Russian influence over the Amir which the Afghan War had been fought to remove. The Viceroy insisted on maintaining the Sibi and Pishin garrisons as an indispensable safeguard. Fearful of Radical accusations of continuing Lytton's Forward policy, and more concerned with the cost than the object of garrisoning Sibi and Pishin, the Cabinet at first rejected Ripon's advice. But slowly it was persuaded that some modification of its mid-Victorian concepts was required. Argyll's resignation in May 1881 weakened the strict traditionalists. Hartington was converted to continuing the occupation of Sibi and Pishin.[3] With Dilke's aid,[4] Hartington undermined Northbrook's influence sufficiently to shelve the issue in the Cabinet and to permit the Viceroy on his own responsibility to retain those garrisons.[5] Radicals in the Commons, who had objected to continued occupation of the Transvaal, now protested against the failure to withdraw completely from Afghanistan.

Until the Liberal government fell in June 1885 it was forced, step by step, as the Russians advanced their control to Merv, Herat and Penjdeh, to undertake new responsibilities for the Afghan frontiers.[6] As events made it plain that inexorable Russian pressure, not Beaconsfield's Jingoism, had advanced the Indian Empire's strategic frontier to the northern Afghan borders, old Liberal prejudices faded. The North-West Frontier was ceasing to be a party issue.[7]

Radicals, Liberals and Conservatives, nevertheless, continued to disagree upon how to deal with the unrest stirred in India by the intensification of Western influences and the Indian National Congress's demands for greater representation in government.[8] Ripon discerned in this question "the great coming difficulty of our rule here".[9] The difficulty foreshadowed the problems of non-European nationalism awaiting the Empire in the twentieth century and pro-

[1] Ripon to Hartington, 29 April 1882, in Wolf, Lucien, *Life of the First Marquess of Ripon*, II, 59.
[2] Dilke, "Diary", 7, 9, 20 and 30 Aug. 1880, B.M. Add. MSS. 43934.
[3] Holland, *op. cit.* I, 313.
[4] Dilke, "Memoir", 26 July 1881, B.M. Add. MSS. 43926, p. 274.
[5] *C.H.B.E.* v, 421–2; Wolf, *op. cit.* II, 44–9.
[6] *Vide infra*, chap. vii.
[7] R. Churchill to Queen Victoria, 11 July 1885, in Churchill, *op. cit.* I, 485–6. Cf. Commons, 13 March 1888, *Hansard*, 3rd ser. CCCXXIII, 1093 *seqq*.
[8] *C.H.B.E.* v, chap. xxix.
[9] Ripon to T. Hughes, 16 June 1883, in Wolf, *op. cit.* II, 103.

voked one of the few major disputes upon the administration of the Dependencies in the politics of this period.

Different Radical, Liberal and Conservative attitudes to this particular issue were each characteristic of their different approaches to imperial problems in general, including the Irish question. Radical Little Englanders·(the pro-Parnellites, pro-Boers and pro-Arabists of the 'eighties) supported the claims of the Indian Congress;[1] and Sir David Wedderburn and Charles Bradlaugh pressed in the Commons for elected Indian representation on provincial councils.[2] They welcomed every opportunity of lessening imperial responsibilities and some regarded this as a first step towards Home Rule for India.[3] Gladstone, Ripon, Kimberley and Dufferin, the Liberal Irish Home Rulers, always inclined to limited concessions in the form of devolutions of authority as a means of preserving the Empire. They favoured the introduction of elected Indians into local councils as part of a gradual Indianisation of government which would achieve administrative economies.[4] Salisbury and other Conservative Unionists held that representative forms of government were unsuited to non-European peoples, and they resisted the Liberal proposals for India as they had the Dufferin Constitution in Egypt.[5] Salisbury feared that the elective principle would undermine British rule and betray the Indian peasantry into the hands of a westernised Indian oligarchy.[6] The Conservative Cabinet's Indian Councils Bill (1890–2) increased nominated, but omitted elective, Indian representatives on the councils,[7] although the latter were introduced by the succeeding Liberal ministry.

Parliament otherwise left India "to pursue its destiny alone",[8] casting its authority generally against expenditure and strong frontier policies. But the Forward school in times of international crisis sometimes escaped these shackles. Salisbury and Randolph Churchill during the Conservative minority government (June 1885–January 1886) took advantage of the backwash of nationalist feeling from the

---

[1] Commons, 20 Feb. 1888, *Hansard*, 3rd ser. CCCXXII, 926 *seqq.*; Dilke, *op. cit.* II, 94, 104–5; Cotton and Payne, *op. cit.* pt. I, pp. 70–81.

[2] Commons, 13 Feb. 1880, *Hansard*, 3rd ser. CCL, 593 *seqq.*, and 9 Aug. 1888, CCCXXX, 148 *seqq.*

[3] Cotton and Payne, *op. cit.* pt. I, India, pp. 82–7, 175. Cf. Labouchere, Commons, 8 Feb. 1893, *Hansard*, 4th ser. VIII, 457.

[4] Ripon to Gladstone, 24 March and 18 Aug. 1883, Gladstone Papers, B.M. Add. MSS. 44287; Commons, 17 Aug. 1880, *Hansard*, 3rd ser. CCLV, 1385 *seqq.*, 23 Aug. 1883, CCLXXXIII, 1818–19, and 6 March 1890, CCCXLII, 61 *seqq.*

[5] Lords, 12 Feb. 1884, *Hansard*, 3rd ser. CCLXXXIV, 582–3; Commons, 5 Feb. 1884, *Hansard*, 3rd ser. CCLXXXIV, 64 *seqq.*

[6] Salisbury, Cabinet Memorandum, 31 Dec. 1888, in Cecil, *op. cit.* IV, 194–6. See also Commons, 22 Aug. 1883, *Hansard*, 3rd ser. CCLXXXIII, 1649–80, and 9 Aug. 1888, CCCXXX, 164–7; Lords, 6 March 1890, 3rd ser. CCCXLII, 100.

[7] *C.H.B.E.* V, 543–5; Commons, 28 March 1892, *Hansard*, 4th ser. III, 52 *seqq.*, and 9 Feb. 1892, *ibid.* I, 81 *seqq.*

[8] R. Churchill, Commons, 6 Aug. 1885, *Hansard*, 3rd ser. CCC, 1314. See also Lord Norton, "Democracy and England", *Nineteenth Century*, XVII (Feb. 1885), p. 333.

Penjdeh Crisis and of confused party bidding for Parnellite support to annex Upper Burma (January 1886). The Gladstonians and Radicals waited impotently for the new Parliament to protest, when the Parnellites, having sold their support to the Home Rulers, joined in the attack.[1] But when French penetration through the Siam-Mekong Valley once again menaced the Indian North-East frontier in Burma (1893), Rosebery, the Liberal Foreign Secretary, admitted that neither Parliament nor his Gladstonian colleagues would tolerate another war to secure it.[2]

The second Gladstone ministry, which had deviated reluctantly from its Consolidationist path to meet Russian expansion towards Afghanistan, also chartered the British North Borneo Company (December 1882) to forestall Spanish claims to the Sulu and Brunei Sultanates.[3] Granville, Kimberley and Selborne towards the end of 1881 persuaded the Cabinet to authorise the Company to rule the northern coasts of the Island. The Radical ministers, Chamberlain, Bright, Dilke, and Harcourt objected; but Gladstone absentmindedly approved the plan and when it was too late turned against it.[4] The Fourth Party Conservatives moved in the Commons to amend or withdraw the Charter, a motion which many Radicals would be bound to support to the Government's embarrassment (March 1882). Together they attacked the Charter as a veiled means of annexation and "filibustering by proxy".[5] Gladstone defended the Charter as a means of reducing the burden thrust upon the Government by the "irrepressible tendency of British enterprise to carry our commerce and the range and area of our Settlements beyond the limits of our Sovereignty".[6] The Charter, Granville assured the Lords, did not mean imperial dominion in North Borneo, nor did it oblige the Government to aid the Company or take over the territory.[7] The Whigs, unlike Gladstone and the Radicals, by no means disdained to promote British commercial interests overseas if it could be done, as Granville said, "with an absence of reasonable ground for apprehending military or financial burdens".[8] These assurances rang hollow to many Liberals already uneasy at the dangers of increased responsibility inherent in the use of chartered companies. Only ministers and Conservative leaders like Sir Henry Holland spoke in defence of the Charter, and the motion was carried in the Commons against the Government.

[1] Commons, 30 Aug. 1886, *Hansard*, 3rd ser. cccviii, 797 *seqq.*
[2] Rosebery to Queen Victoria, 26 July 1893, in Crewe, *op. cit.* ii, 425-77; Gardiner, *op. cit.* ii, 333.   [3] *Parl. Pap.* 1882, lxxxi [C. 3108-9], *passim.*
[4] Dilke, "Diary", 11 Jan. 1882, B.M. Add. MSS. 43934; Gardiner, *op. cit.* i, 414.
[5] Commons, 17 March 1882, *Hansard*, 3rd ser. cclxvii, 1148-52.   [6] *Ibid.* 1191.
[7] Lords, 13 March 1882, *Hansard*, 3rd ser. cclxvii, 715-16; Granville to Morier, 7 Jan. 1882, *Parl. Pap.* 1882, lxxxi [C. 3108], pp. 202-5.
[8] Lords, 13 March 1882, *Hansard*, 3rd ser. cclxvii, 715. See also Kimberley to Granville, 10 Dec. 1881, and Granville to Kimberley, 7 Jan. 1882, in Granville Papers, P.R.O. 30—29/135.

Dissensions over Egypt

Within a year of its withdrawals from Kandahar and the Transvaal, the Gladstone ministry had drifted into far more dangerous responsibilities in Egypt. Policy towards Egypt and the Sudan was the central issue in the growing controversy between Forward and Consolidationist schools of thought in British politics after 1882.

A cardinal imperial aim was to prevent foreign powers achieving such influence in Egypt as would enable them to command the road to India. This had been possible hitherto by means of Anglo-French agreement to intervene when necessary in Egypt on a basis of equality of influence.[1] During 1881 the Arabist Revolution there threatened to sweep aside the Anglo-French Financial Control which protected the interests of foreign bondholders. Anglo-French co-operation in restoring the Khedive's power and maintaining foreign rights finally broke down with the fall of the de Freycinet Cabinet and the French Chamber's rejection of an interventionist policy (29 July 1882). Gladstone's ministry tried to eliminate the need for British intervention by persuading the Turkish Sultan and the "Concert of Europe" to act.[2] But by mid-1882 the Liberals faced the prospect of restoring order alone and the accompanying opportunity of establishing imperial supremacy in Egypt.

British leaders until 1888 were more concerned with the dangers than the opportunity. Gladstone had opposed Disraeli's purchase of Suez Canal shares, fearing they would prove to be "the almost certain egg of a North African Empire".[3] Salisbury in 1878, while recognising the advantages of British control in Egypt, thought it not worth the risk of war with France.[4] Eight years earlier Gladstone had observed that it would be better to seize the Canal in war time if the need arose than to provoke a war by anticipating that need in peace time.[5] The hostility of the Continental powers, the "incalculable burdens" of an occupation and responsibility for the Egyptian debt, and the prevailing anti-expansionist feeling in Parliament led Gladstone and Granville in June 1882 to reject, out of hand, a Turkish invitation to accept what amounted to an Egyptian protectorate.[6]

The question of sending an expedition to Egypt to restore order, reassert the Financial Control, and safeguard the Canal caused a Cabinet crisis (June–July 1882).[7] Hartington, the Whig leader,

[1] Cromer, op. cit. 1, 91–3.
[2] Lords, 24 July 1882, Hansard, 3rd ser. CCLXXII, 1493; Fitzmaurice, op. cit. II, 244 seqq.
[3] Gladstone, W. E., "Aggression on Egypt and Freedom in the East", Nineteenth Century, II (Aug. 1877), pp. 149–66.
[4] Salisbury to Beaconsfield, 5 Sept. 1878, and Salisbury to Lyons, 10 Aug. 1878, in Cecil, Lady Gwendolen, Life of Robert Marquis of Salisbury, II, 334–5.
[5] Gladstone to Granville, 13 Nov. 1870, in Fitzmaurice, op. cit. II, 252.
[6] Dilke, "Memoir", in Gwynn and Tuckwell, op. cit. 1, 463.
[7] Garvin, op. cit. 1, 446–50.

and the Radicals and Dilke, threatened to resign if the Arabists were not suppressed.[1] British bondholders, and shipping and mercantile associations interested in the Canal, urged the Government to intervene.[2] Gladstone and Bright opposed intervention on principle.[3] These disputes were resolved by a compromise policy of "Rescue and Retire", designed to concede the demands of the Forward school in the Liberal Party, while reassuring the Radical anti-expansionists and foreign powers that no permanent extension of the Empire was intended. The Cabinet sent an expedition under Wolseley to restore a stable Egyptian government under the Khedive's power; this done, the ministry declared its determination to withdraw from further responsibility.[4] Following this plan, evolved hastily out of little more than ministerial disagreements, the Liberal government drifted into the prolonged occupation it was intent on avoiding. The results of its dissension and Granville's indecision and carelessness[5] impressed the French as "British perfidy", and John Morley as "rashness and hurry". John Bright resigned in protest against the intervention and Gladstone thought of going with him.[6] The Radicals and the Fourth Party, who believed that the Canal could be secured by more limited measures,[7] attacked the Government for suppressing a "genuine nationalist revolution" and "fighting a bondholders' war".[8] But the Commons accepted Gladstone's assurances that Egyptian anarchy threatened the security of the Canal[9] as well as the bondholders' interests, and voted supplies by 275 to 19.

Wolseley's victory at Tel-el-Kebir (13 September 1882) restored to the ministry the prestige lost at Majuba. Anglo-French Financial Control was replaced by a single British "Adviser". Occupation of Egypt enabled the ministry to obtain reductions in Canal charges and increased British representation in its management, and to press for international guarantees of free navigation and neutralisation of the country. Gladstone told Harcourt in September 1882 that "the great question of British interest is the Canal, and this turns on neutralisation aye, or no".[10] But the policy of "Rescue and Retire,"

---

[1] Dilke, "Diary", 17–25 June 1882, B.M. Add. MSS. 43935.
[2] For the shippers' agitation see Commons, 30 July 1883, Hansard, 3rd ser. CCLXXXII, 962 seqq. and 1028–30.
[3] Dilke, "Diary", 7 July 1882, B.M. Add. MSS. 43935; Morley, Life of Gladstone, II, 242–3.
[4] Cromer, op. cit. I, 332–4; Granville to Gladstone, 29 Nov. 1882, in Fitzmaurice, op. cit. II, 303–4, 306–7; and Dilke, "Diary", 18 Sept. 1882 and 25 Oct. 1883, B.M. Add. MSS. 43935.
[5] Dilke, "Diary", 14 Feb. 1884, B.M. Add. MSS. 43935.
[6] Ibid. 7, 18 and 22 July 1882, B.M. Add. MSS. 43935; Fitzmaurice, op. cit. II, 266; and Crewe, op. cit. I, 161–2.
[7] Commons, 25 July 1882, Hansard, 3rd ser. CCLXXII, 1687.
[8] Commons, 24–26 July 1882, ibid. 1701–10, 1766–93, 1862–5. See also Commons, 2 March 1883, Hansard, 3rd ser. CCLXXVI, 1300–21.
[9] Commons, 24 July 1882, Hansard, 3rd ser. CCLXXII, 1586 seqq.; Dilke, "Memoir", in Gwynn and Tuckwell, op. cit. I, 468.
[10] Gladstone to Harcourt, 17 Sept. 1882, in Gardiner, op. cit. I, 459.

at first so expedient in Westminster, proved impracticable in Egypt.[1] Prospects of early withdrawal faded when the military basis of Khedival authority was destroyed at Tel-el-Kebir and the Mahdist Revolt broke out in the Sudan. Futile attempts to suppress the Mahdi reduced the already mortgaged Egyptian Government to bankruptcy. The occupying power became in fact, if not in form, responsible for the defence and the debts of the country. Gladstone gloomily summed up the perverse effect of Liberal policy to his Cabinet on 2 April 1884: "We have done our Egyptian business and we are an Egyptian Government."[2]

The questions of the abandonment of the Sudan, the mission and the relief of General Gordon at Khartoum and measures to remedy Egyptian bankruptcy became involved in a bitter controversy (1883–5) between partisans of prolonged occupation and advocates of early withdrawal. Again, the Liberals were divided and the Opposition exploited their dissensions by moving votes of censure. Successive disasters exposed the fallacies of the compromise policy of 1882 and discredited Gladstonian consolidationist methods of maintaining imperial interests.

Evacuation of the Sudan, announced on 4 January 1884, was intended to lessen the British liability in Egypt and to reconcile the Radicals in the Commons. Earlier the Radical Little Englanders had censured the Government for the Egyptian War.[3] The pro-Arabist Randolph Churchill had asserted that control of Suez would be a burden rather than an asset in time of war. He warned against placing "any reliance on transcontinental communication, where, at any time, you may have to encounter gigantic military hosts".[4] Although abandonment of the Sudan pacified the Radicals, it antagonised the Forward wing of the Liberal party. Forster, the spokesman of the humanitarian and anti-slavers, and Goschen, who had close connections with the Egyptian bondholders, supported Conservative censures on the Government's Sudan policy.[5] *The Times* and *The Pall Mall Gazette* criticised abandonment of the Sudan as shirking the imperial mission of civilisation. In the City demands were made for an Egyptian protectorate.[6] The Cabinet's inability to carry out its reiterated promises of early withdrawal from Egyptian

---

[1] Sir Evelyn Baring to Granville, 9 Oct. 1883, in Cromer, *op. cit.* II, 362–5; *ibid.* chap. xliv.

[2] Dilke, "Diary", 2 April 1884, B.M. Add. MSS. 43936A.

[3] Commons, 2 March 1883, *Hansard*, 3rd ser. CCLXXVI, 1300 *seqq.*; 12 Feb. 1884, CCLXXXIV, 744–7, 890–912, 1025–35; and 15 March 1884, CCLXXXV, 1662–70.

[4] Lord Randolph Churchill's speech at Edinburgh, 18 Dec. 1883, in Churchill, *op. cit.* I, 280.

[5] Commons, 5 Feb. 1884, *Hansard*, 3rd ser. CCLXXXIV, 58 *seqq.*, and 12 Feb. 1884, *ibid.* 684 *seqq.*; Lords, 12 Feb. 1884, *ibid.* 567 *seqq.*; and Commons, 15 March 1884, *Hansard*, 3rd ser. CCLXXXV, 1653 *seqq.*

[6] On this agitation see *History of 'The Times'*, III, 22, 24, 28, 37; Cromer, *op. cit.* I, 402–4, 409–10, 427–8, 472–8, 522 *footnote*.

commitments seemed to confirm the Forward school's contention that only prolonged British occupation would secure the road to India. The Queen had impressed upon Harcourt (1882) "the absolute necessity...of...securing to ourselves such a position (short of annexation) in Egypt as to secure our Indian Dominions and to maintain our superiority in the East".[1]

To appease the anti-slavery movement General Gordon was sent to the Sudan (January 1884) to evacuate the Egyptian garrisons and to do whatever was possible by personal influence to secure the Egyptian frontier. When he was isolated at Khartoum, his relief became involved from April until August 1884 in the ministry's disputes over Egyptian policy. Already the diplomatic and financial disadvantages of the occupation of Egypt had become acute. The Cabinet was confronted with Egyptian budgetary deficits. Hostility of the Continental powers was reflected in the Franco-German *entente* and the Russian menace to the Indian North-West Frontier. Gladstone and Granville, against Hartington's opposition, persuaded the Cabinet (May 1884) to seek an international agreement under which Britain would evacuate Egypt in return for guarantees against subsequent occupation by the Continental Powers.[2] The advocates of early withdrawal in the Cabinet rejected Hartington's and Northbrook's proposed Egyptian loan, to be guaranteed by the Treasury, because it would prolong British occupation.[3] Chamberlain described the different policies urged by the three conflicting factions in the ministry (January 1885): his own was "Scuttle and repudiate" responsibility for the Egyptian debt; Hartington's and Northbrook's was "Pay and stay"; and Harcourt's was "Pay and scuttle".[4]

Gladstone, like the Little Englanders, suspected Hartington's proposal to send a relief expedition to Khartoum as another manœuvre to prolong the Egyptian occupation.[5] The Cabinet consequently would not agree to it until Gordon's personal danger became obvious enough to be detached from the wider question of Britain's future in Egypt. The Little Englander Radicals opposed the rescue expedition, though the ministry's policy was limited once more to the aim of "Rescue and Retire". Gladstone reassured the Commons that the Government had no intention of using the expedition to reoccupy the Sudan. The Parnellites were known to be negotiating with the

---

[1] Queen Victoria to Harcourt, 22 Sept. 1882, in Gardiner, *op. cit.* I, 460.
[2] Dilke, "Diary", 27 March, 18 July 1884, B.M. Add. MSS. 43936A.
[3] Harcourt, Cabinet Memorandum on Egypt, 16 Nov. 1884, in Gardiner, *op. cit.* I, App. II. See also Derby to Granville, 17 Jan. 1885, Granville Papers, P.R.O. 30–29/120.
[4] Lewis Harcourt's *Journal*, 22 Jan. 1885, in Gardiner, *op. cit.* I, 515. See also Dilke, "Memoir", 19 Nov. 1884, B.M. Add. MSS. 43930, pp. 311–12, and 4 Jan. 1885, B.M. Add. MSS. 43931, p. 17.
[5] Hartington to Granville, 16 April 1884, in Holland, *op. cit.* I, 445–6; Chamberlain to J. T. Bruce, 11 May 1884, in Garvin, *op. cit.* I, 516–17; and Fitzmaurice, *op. cit.* II, 388–405. See also Dilke, "Diary", 7–11 Feb. 1884, B.M. Add. MSS. 43935, and 27 March, 16, 25 July 1884, B.M. Add. MSS. 43936A.

Conservatives (November 1884); therefore, the ministerial majority depended more than ever on the support of both Little Englander and Forward wings of the Liberal party in the Commons.[1] When the Cabinet yielded to public indignation at Gordon's death (January 1885), and, urged by the Queen, Hartington, Selborne and North-brook,[2] authorised an advance on Khartoum to break the Mahdi, both Liberal wings revolted.

The Parliamentary debates of February 1885 upon the Opposition's censure of the Government's Sudan policy revealed the disruptive forces within the Liberal party, which its leaders for five years had striven to keep in balance by inaction, compromise or vacillation.[3] Conservative attacks upon the ministry's "betrayal of Gordon"[4] were surpassed by the crossfire of criticism within the Liberal party. John Morley and the Radical anti-expansionists moved an amendment criticising the Government for the advance to Khartoum and urging the earliest possible evacuation of Egypt. Morley summed up the recent Parliamentary history of imperial questions when he asked:

> What has been at the root of the debates...for the last five years? It has been that one side has constantly insisted upon pressing...forward to undertake...vast responsibilities beyond our political and military resources, and that the other side has not always had the courage to...say to the public plainly...that we have already been undertaking responsibilities long past the limits at which they can be effectually discharged.[5]

From their speeches Gladstone and Harcourt in the Commons[6] and Derby in the Lords[7] plainly sympathised with the Radicals. Although their amendment was lost, only one month after the sensation of Gordon's death, the Radicals with the Parnellites were still able to muster over a hundred votes against continuing the advance to Khartoum.

Liberals of the Forward school attacked the ministry from the opposite extreme. Goschen and Forster pointed out the absurdity of going to Khartoum to break the Mahdists and then retiring immediately without setting up a stable Sudan government. The ministry had decided "to go to Khartoum to please the Whigs; and ...they intended to retire from Khartoum to please the Radicals".[8]

[1] Harcourt's Memorandum in Gardiner, *op. cit.* I, 605; and Gladstone to Hartington, 21 Aug. 1884, in Holland, *op. cit.* I, 482.

[2] Holland, *op. cit.* I, 478; Queen Victoria to Ponsonby, 5 Feb. 1885, in Buckle, *op. cit.* 2nd ser. III, 598. See also Gardiner, *op. cit.* I, 518 *seqq.*

[3] Dilke noted in his "Diary", 30 June 1884, after a Sudan vote of censure, "Says Mr G. to me 'How splendid is the discipline of our Party. Not a man but voted against us'" (B.M. Add. MSS. 43936A).

[4] Lords, 26 Feb. 1885, *Hansard*, 3rd ser. CCXCIV, 1311 *seqq.*; Commons, 23 Feb. 1885, *ibid.* 1052 *seqq.*

[5] Commons, 23 Feb. 1885, *ibid.* 1078.   [6] *Ibid.* 1454 *seqq.*

[7] Lords, 20 Feb. 1885, *ibid.* 1389.

[8] Commons, 24 Feb. 1885, *ibid.* 1251. See also *ibid.* 1699.

Forster and Goschen demanded that the Government keep control of the Upper Nile by holding Berber, if not Khartoum.[1] They declared they would have supported the ministry if it had accepted Hartington's and Northbrook's prolonged occupation policy.[2] But they voted against the Government because Harcourt's policy of evacuation would prevail.

These revolts of Radicals on the one hand and the Liberal imperialists on the other, combined with the further defection of the Parnellites engineered by Churchill, almost brought down the Government. Its majority on the vote of censure fell to fourteen. Salisbury in the Lords insisted that Britain should administer the Sudan until a stable government was established and keep control of the road to India.[3] Hartington's ally at the Admiralty, Northbrook, openly endorsed Salisbury's opinions.[4]

The ministry managed to hold together four months longer. Its Egyptian dissensions had interacted with those regarding renewal of the Irish Coercion Act and the Redistribution of Seats Bill. With the Russian war scare (April 1885), there was urgent need to reinforce the Indian frontier against Russia. This gave the Consolidationists, Gladstone, Harcourt and Granville, the opportunity they sought to overcome the objections of Hartington, Selborne and Northbrook and to divert the Khartoum expedition to India, thus reaffirming the abandonment of the Sudan.[5]

When the Conservatives took office (June 1885–February 1886 and July 1886–August 1892) they did nothing to reconquer the Sudan, despite their criticisms of the evacuation when in Opposition. Salisbury was certain that the new Commons was no more eager than the old to vote supplies for the purpose. The Conservative ministry until 1888 was as anxious as the Liberal party to evacuate Egypt.[6] Salisbury, like Granville, reckoned the price of Egyptian occupation in terms of Continental hostility too great. He took up Granville's scheme of withdrawal in return for international guarantees for neutralisation of Egypt and for a British right to reoccupy Egypt in the event of anarchy or danger to the Canal. It was significant of Parliament's lack of territorial ambition in 1887 that Salisbury should have anticipated little serious opposition to a withdrawal from Egypt.[7] But the Powers upset the Anglo-Turkish Convention of 23 May 1887 which embodied these terms.[8] Only then did Conservative leaders accept the "inevitability" of prolonged occupation. At this point imperial policy began to pass from a defensive to a positive phase.

[1] *Ibid.* 1263. [2] *Ibid.* 1699.
[3] Lords, 26 Feb. 1885, *Hansard*, 3rd ser. CCXCIV, 1311–25.
[4] *Ibid.* 1343–4.
[5] Gardiner, *op. cit.* I, 518–19.
[6] Salisbury to Queen Victoria, 25 Dec. 1888, in Buckle, *op. cit.* 3rd ser. I, 459–60.
[7] Salisbury to Wolff, 4 May 1887, in Cecil, *op. cit.* IV, 45.
[8] *Vide infra*, chap. vii.

After 1888 the Egyptian question was to broaden into the issue of imperial control of the entire Nile Valley.[1]

The Liberal ministry's policy, which had led to the occupation of Egypt and to added responsibilities in South Africa, India and the Pacific, had been essentially defensive in design. Egypt had been occupied in over-anxiety to forestall French control, and held because of Sudan disasters and French refusal to agree to neutralisation. Elsewhere, the incentive to expansion had come chiefly from the colonies. Liberals had acquiesced reluctantly, and only on condition that colonial governments should bear the charges of extended dominions. Acquiescence had been encouraged also by nationalist feeling in the United Kingdom against Continental powers, which had strengthened the clamour of humanitarians, merchants and speculators for a Forward imperial policy. But their influence declined as international tension eased and Irish upheavals absorbed political attention. In 1887 it was observed in the Commons, without contradiction: "The Jingo fever appeared to be at the very lowest ebb, and the principle of non-intervention had received general support from both sides of the House."[2]

UNIONISM AND IMPERIALISM

Home Rule for Ireland was the determining issue in British politics from its adoption as the main plank in the Liberal platform (December 1885) until the defeat of Gladstone's second Home Rule Bill (September 1893). Its effects upon imperial policy were complex and indirect, but profound. Until the end of 1887, the Irish question, sharpened by the Parnellite "dictatorship" in the Commons,[3] confused party affiliations. The uncertainties of the political situation temporarily checked the trend towards a Forward policy which had emerged during the winter of 1884. "Torn in two by a controversy which almost threatens her existence," Salisbury told the Queen early in 1887, "[England] cannot...interfere with any decisive action abroad."[4]

The first Irish Home Rule Bill had split the Liberal party, ninety-three Liberals, led by Hartington and Chamberlain, having voted against it. Most of these dissidents by 1887 had formed an enduring Unionist alliance with the Conservatives. In dividing British leaders into two camps the Irish question proved to have united most of the

---

[1] Derby to Granville, Cabinet Memoranda, 28 Dec. 1884, in Granville Papers, P.R.O. 30–29/120. See also two contemporary observers who came to this conclusion: Lucas, C. P., "Introduction" to Lewis, *op. cit.* p. xxi; and Dilke, *op. cit.* II, 164–6.

[2] A. B. Winterbotham (Liberal Unionist), Commons, 3 Feb. 1887, *Hansard*, 3rd ser. cccx, 596.

[3] Parnellites held the balance of votes between Liberals and Conservatives from June 1885 to January 1886, and both Parties bartered for Irish support. See Gladstone to Hartington, 3 Sept. 1885, in Holland, *op. cit.* II, 79.

[4] Salisbury to Queen Victoria, 24 Jan. 1887, in Buckle, *op. cit.* 3rd ser. I, 262; similarly R. Churchill to Salisbury, 15 Sept. 1886, in Churchill, *op. cit.* II, 157.

Forward school of both parties against the Gladstonian Consolidationists. Whether by chance or some affinity of temperament or connection, the Liberals who became Unionists were those who had favoured a strong imperial policy in 1884–5. As well as Hartington and Chamberlain, they included Goschen, Forster, Northbrook and Selborne.[1] These Liberals of the Forward school henceforward were joined with its Conservative representatives in the Unionist alliance, and freed from their former frustrating association with the Gladstonians. The political influence of the Consolidationists, Gladstone, Harcourt and Morley, weakened by the Liberal schism, was to diminish still further with the rise of Rosebery and the Liberal imperialists to leadership of the Liberal Party in 1894.[2]

Tentatively at first, then with increasing confidence, the Unionists were to commit the British democracy to a course of imperial expansion. Nevertheless, the old Consolidationist tradition, expressive of Liberal convictions and persistent United Kingdom concern over the expense of Empire, endured to temper and check imperialism, and to regain supremacy in the twentieth century. The division remained at bottom the old one between the Cobdenite and Palmerstonian concepts of national expansion.

Salisbury himself, in retrospect, observed that it was Gladstone's fight for Irish Home Rule that had "awakened the slumbering genius of Imperialism".[3] Yet in 1886 there was little reason to believe that the Unionists who had defeated the Home Rulers at the July general election would be any more expansionist than their predecessors. Imperial questions played little part in the election, which was decided almost entirely upon the Home Rule issue. Unionist predilection for "twenty years' determined rule" in Ireland apparently had no necessary connection with a willingness to extend imperial rule. Even so, the two opposed attitudes of British leaders toward Ireland proved to correspond largely with the old and the new outlooks on the Empire.

Gladstonian Home Rulers, clinging to traditional ideas of Empire, conceived its future as a great league of autonomous British-settled dominions. They contended that imperial unity had been preserved only by concessions of responsible government to the great colonies. They insisted that Ireland be treated similarly to save the imperial unity of the British Isles.[4] The Unionist policy of coercion in Ireland, on the other hand, displayed a more authoritarian political attitude which seemed to appear also in their imperial outlook.[5] They tended to attach more importance to the maintenance of central imperial

---

[1] See Holland, *op. cit.* II, 59–63, 100–31.   [2] Gardiner, *op. cit.* II, 152–3.
[3] Churchill, *op. cit.* II, 116–17. See also Ensor, *loc. cit.* pp. 26–7.
[4] E.g. Commons, 31 Jan., 3, 13 Feb. 1893, *Hansard*, 4th ser. VIII, 110, 457, 1273–4; Gladstone to Queen Victoria, 13 Feb. 1882, in Buckle, *op. cit.* 2nd ser. III, 260–2; Fitzmaurice, *op. cit.* II, 22, 294–5; and Holland, *op. cit.* II, 140, footnote 1.
[5] Cecil, *op. cit.* III, 92; Commons, 14 Feb. 1893, *Hansard*, 4th ser. VIII, 1412, 1719–20; *History of 'The Times,'* III, 17.

authority. Similarly, the Unionists, free from Radical enthusiasm for introducing Western representative institutions among non-European peoples, insisted more strongly upon maintaining British rule and were more ready to extend it. Something of the spirit of Unionism was expressed by Arthur Balfour in 1893 during his attack on the second Home Rule Bill: "It has been by the concentration and not the dissipation of power that Empires have been built up."[1]

The affinity of Unionism with imperialism had material as well as ideological origins. As Gladstone and the press observed at the time, the "classes" as opposed to the "masses" had tended to rally to the Unionist cause. The Liberal Home Rulers' distaste for suppressing Irish disorder and upholding Irish property rights, Radical zeal for schemes of graduated income tax and universal suffrage, and Radical ministers' meddling with industrial undertakings and private property rights had alarmed landed and business interests alike. In the City many influential representatives of railway and canal interests, heavy industry and finance deserted the Liberal party with Hartington.[2] Thereafter, Unionist political strength was concentrated in the metropolis and urban industrial constituencies, while Liberal support centred in the Counties and in Scotland and Wales.[3] The Unionists, therefore, deferred the more to commercial opinion which began to shift in favour of imperial expansion, and by 1892 they had become the party most representative of British commercial and investment interests within the Empire.[4]

From the late 'eighties the movement for the acquisition of a new tropical Empire gained ground in British politics. A growing reaction against the colonial expansion of protectionist powers brought new support to the philanthropists and anti-slavers who, since the 'seventies, had urged Government to pacify and civilise the African interior.[5] The depression and unemployment of 1884–5 had been attributed widely to foreign competition and tariff discrimination in overseas markets. Fair trade agitation for tariff reciprocity and protection of British industry spread in the Midlands.[6] Evidence given to the Royal Commission of Inquiry into the causes of the depression expressed commercial and industrial associations' anxiety to secure new markets

---

[1] Commons, 31 Jan. 1893, *Hansard*, 4th ser. VIII, 107. See also "Disintegration" (unsigned, but attributed to Salisbury by Lady G. Cecil), *Quarterly Review*, CLVI (Oct. 1883), 562–3; and Grey, Earl, "Ireland and the Empire", *Nineteenth Century*, XIV (Nov. 1883), 739 *seqq.*

[2] See Armytage, W. H. G., "The Railway Rates question and the fall of the third Gladstone ministry", *E.H.R.* LXV (Jan. 1950), 18–51.

[3] Gladstone to Queen Victoria, 8 July 1886, in Buckle, *op. cit.* 3rd ser. I, 157; Ensor, *op. cit. Trans. R. Hist. Soc.* 4th ser. XXXI (1948), 17, 27; and Morley, *Life of Gladstone*, II, 422, 439.

[4] Thomas, J. A., *The House of Commons, 1832–1901*, pp. 20–2.

[5] Dilke and W. T. Stead, the editor of *The Pall Mall Gazette*, became the apostles of expansion to protect, pacify and civilise the "dark-skinned races of the world" during the 'eighties. See Whyte, F., *Life of W. T. Stead*, II, 324–5; and Bodelsen, *op. cit.* pp. 67 *seqq.*   [6] *Vide infra*, pp. 113–15.

and sources of raw materials.[1] Increasingly after 1884 protectionism seemed to be shutting out British trade and investment from regions open hitherto to all nations; and the acquisition of further imperial dominions began to seem the only assurance of United Kingdom prosperity and employment.[2] Reiterated in the press and by chambers of commerce, this idea began to be echoed by a few party leaders.

At the same time spectacular development of the Witwatersrand gold mines induced wild speculation in African mineral concessions,[3] and did something to dissipate the scepticism regarding commercial prospects in Africa which prevailed among British business men. Dilke expressed the more optimistic but still exceptional vision of Africa's future when in 1880 he described the Niger territories as the "New Indias of the next generation" and the central African highlands as potentially "Twentieth-century Australias".[4]

Thus self-interest and nationalism combined with altruism to stimulate an expansionist movement. The "Positive Policy", which had been the humanitarians' plan for civilising Africa since mid-century, now became more widely adopted as "the moral currency of imperialism". The years from the Anti-Slavery Society's Jubilee of 1883 until the International Anti-Slavery Conference at Brussels in 1890 saw a remarkable revival of religious and humanitarian interest in Africa; and the moral conception of an imperial civilising mission became as popular as it had been early in the century. Advocates of a new imperialism of tropical responsibility justified their demands in terms of employment for the worker, markets for the manufacturer, and civilisation and freedom for the African tribes. As Rhodes described it without a trace of cynicism, it was a philosophy of "philanthropy plus five per cent".

The expansionist movement was a direct revolt against the mid-Victorian imperial tradition and its idea of limited state function in the economic field. One section of the imperialist movement urged Government not only to carve out a new tropical empire directly dependent upon the United Kingdom, but also to develop communications, stimulate capital investment, guarantee loans, and improve native agriculture, in addition to the traditional task of trusteeship for native interests.[5] While British opinion continued to be faithful to free trade, its belief that trade depended upon rule began to revive. Advocates of state-promoted colonial development, however, did

[1] For an analysis of evidence submitted by business associations see Tyler, J. E., *The Struggle for Imperial Unity, 1868–95*, pp. 57 *seqq.* See also Berard, Victor, *British Imperialism and Commercial Supremacy*, pp. 56 *seqq.*
[2] *The Times*, 22 Aug. 1888, p. 8; Resolutions of Birmingham, Edinburgh and Glasgow Chambers of Commerce, 2 February 1893, in Lugard, Capt. F. D., *The Rise of our East African Empire*, pp. 379–80; and Bérard, *op. cit. passim.*
[3] *C.H.B.E.* viii, 781–4.　　　　　　　[4] Dilke, *op. cit.* ii, 163–4.
[5] For the growth and diversification of imperialist thought see Bodelsen, *op. cit.*, especially pp. 128–30, 205–6.

not achieve powerful political influence until Chamberlain went to the Colonial Office in 1895. Meanwhile their ideas gained currency among small but influential groups at Court,[1] in the City, chambers of commerce and manufacturers' associations and in the fashionable drawing-rooms of moralistic late-Victorian "Society".[2] The expansionists had secured the advocacy of *The Times* since 1884[3] and *The Pall Mall Gazette*.[4] Mid-Victorian imperial and economic beliefs, nevertheless, endured in the country. If the expansionists were aided by the nationalistic reaction to the rivalry of the Continental Powers, they were equally hampered by the economical spirit of Midlothian.[5]

The progress of the expansionist idea in the parties was illustrated by the gradual conversion of the two chief architects of the British African Empire, Salisbury and Chamberlain. Though of the Forward school before 1888 they could see no commercial need for expansion in Africa or for occupation of Egypt. Chamberlain and Dilke in 1885 had objected strongly to holding Egypt and the Sudan for the sake of bondholders, cotton or markets. Salisbury's correspondence frankly expressed his disdain for the "superficial philanthropy", blatant stock-jobbing and "roguery" of the expansionist "fanatics".[6] But by 1888 Salisbury, Rosebery and Chamberlain, becoming interested in Egyptian commercial development through railways and public works, were reconciled also to a prolonged occupation.[7] Salisbury's original acquiescence in African expansion was compelled more by the intensity of international rivalry and the pace of commercial penetration than by expansionist logic. He yielded to what he called "the dynamic force of adventure and colonisation" and to "a great civilising Christianising force".[8] He became convinced after 1888 that it must be regulated and controlled in order to avoid international conflict and oppression of indigenous populations.[9] Even Gladstone confessed that "natural causes", more than Salisbury's policy, were responsible for imperial expansion in Africa.[10]

During the depression of the early 'nineties, with its unemployment and industrial unrest, the imperialist leaders began to advocate

---

[1] When resident at Balmoral, Harcourt observed: "Of course the tone of the whole *entourage* here is of the most vehement jingoism" (Gardiner, *op. cit.* II, p. 198). Certainly the correspondence of Queen Victoria and the Royal Dukes indicates a consistent use of influence in favour of an imperialism of responsibility; e.g. Prince of Wales to Rosebery, 14 August 1892, in Crewe, *op. cit.* II, pp. 400–1.

[2] For an example of imperialism in the drawing-room see Gardiner, *op. cit.* II, 199.

[3] *History of 'The Times'*, *op. cit.* 159–61.

[4] The Gospel according to the Pall Mall Gazette", in Whyte, *op. cit.* II, 324–5.

[5] See Pope-Hennessy, Sir John, "The African Bubble", *Nineteenth Century*, XXVIII (July and Sept. 1890), pp. 1–4; 478 *seqq.*

[6] Salisbury to Baring, 22 Dec. 1888, in Cromer, *op. cit.* I, 387–8, footnote 1.

[7] See Chamberlain, J., "A Bill for weakening Great Britain," *Nineteenth Century*, XXXIII (April 1893), 545 *seqq.;* Crewe, *op. cit.* II, 399–400; Garvin, *op. cit.* II, 466; Gwynn and Tuckwell, *op. cit.* II, 255; Cecil, *op. cit.* IV, 252.

[8] Cecil, *op. cit.* IV, 336; cf. Crewe, *op. cit.* I, 315.

[9] Cecil, *op. cit.* IV, 228.

[10] Commons, 12 Feb. 1890; *Hansard*, 3rd ser. CCCXLI, 139.

expansion openly as a solution to the economic problem.[1] A new Empire now began to be thought of as a necessity as well as a philanthropic ideal. Resources of new territories brought under British political control would provide opportunity and security for state-encouraged loans and private investment; development of railways, minerals and agriculture would stimulate markets for British industry. Chamberlain in 1888 began to insist that exclusive United Kingdom control of the rich gold-bearing regions of South-Central Africa was vital to British commerce and industry.[2] Three years later Salisbury asserted that dominion overseas had become indispensable to British prosperity, employment and world power.[3] Both these imperial statesmen by 1895 had adopted the full programme of tropical imperialism. "It is [Government's] business in all these countries", Salisbury declared to the Lords, "to make smooth the paths for British commerce...for the application of British capital, at a time when...other outlets for the commercial energies of our race are being gradually closed."[4] Significantly, in reaching this conclusion he noted the mounting tariffs of the responsible government colonies and the Indian Empire as well as of Continental states.[5] In the same year Chamberlain went to the Colonial Office and began to intensify the drive for state-aided development of Britain's colonial estates.[6]

The conversion of these Unionist and Liberal leaders to tropical imperialism reflected a definite trend in English business, working class and religious opinion. The imperialist-humanitarian movement helped to justify to a public mostly still faithful to older Liberal beliefs the extension of direct and indirect state-aid to overseas trade and home industry. This humanitarian justification of the new tropical Empire created strong political pressures for higher standards of imperial trusteeship, which liberalised policy towards the dependent Empire for decades to come.

The rights of the Empire's non-European peoples to freedom from forced labour (except for public works), liberty of contract and equality before the law had long been established in the Crown dependencies. Colonial Office supervision of administrations aimed at securing sufficient land for subsistence to indigenous populations in the settled colonies and preserving customary forms of landholding and administration in tropical dependencies.[7] This minimum protection of non-European rights, the Colonial Office believed, was as essential

---

[1] Garvin, *op. cit.* II, 345, 448 *seqq.*, 465–7, 531–2; Commons, 12 March 1894, *Hansard*, 4th ser. XXII, 102; Garvin, *op. cit.* II, 466.
[2] Speech to London Chamber of Commerce, 14 May 1888, *ibid.* pp. 464–5
[3] Salisbury, Speech at Guildhall, Nov. 1891.
[4] Lords, 14 Feb. 1895, *Hansard*, 4th ser. XXX, 698–9.
[5] *Ibid.*
[6] Commons, 22 Aug. 1895, *Hansard*, 4th ser. XXXVI, 636, 640–2.
[7] See Commons, 24 July 1890, *Hansard*, 3rd ser. CCCXLVII, 751.

for the peace, economical administration and commercial development of dependencies as it was to forestall Parliamentary criticism.

Parliament rarely intervened directly in the Empire's dependent
administrations. But it exerted a strong negative influence, in that
government was conscious of its surveillance and careful to avoid
offending humanitarian and liberal consciences. Thus the imperial
power reserved authority in the Chartered Company territories and
in the Natal responsible-government constitution to enforce minimum
standards of native policy; but its exercise was largely ineffective
because of lack of imperial supervision and the strength of colonial
resentment against its use. Parliament, prodded by humanitarians,
also broadened the scope of imperial responsibility to include ending
domestic slavery in protectorates, suppressing the liquor traffic
throughout British native dependencies[1] and reducing, if not abolishing, the Indian opium export to China.[2] The idea of developing
dependencies by means of the bounty of Parliament, however, was
anathema,[3] although Chamberlain was powerful enough to sponsor
it after 1895. Imperial trusteeship consequently was protective
rather than progressive.

CONSOLIDATIONIST POLICY IN TROPICAL AFRICA, 1880-8

The crucial imperial question confronting the Salisbury Cabinet
of 1886–92 and the Liberal Ministries of 1892–5 was, as Harcourt
put it: "Are we to attempt the creation of another India in Africa?"[4]
Salisbury told a City audience (1889): "Africa is the subject which
occupies the Foreign Office more than any other."[5] The intensification of international political and commercial rivalry in tropical
Africa by the late 'eighties convinced him of the need to change from
a defensive policy of maintaining existing Empire interests to one of
extending imperial rule over further territory in order to reserve it
for future British development.[6] This transition was facilitated by
the progress of the expansionist movement, by the Conservative
Cabinet's deference to Salisbury's leadership in foreign affairs, and
by the Unionist alliance.

An expansionist policy, nevertheless, involved political dangers at
home. The mass of British opinion seemed indifferent or undecided
as between the old and new policies. It was a commonplace in
Westminster that the public was fickle, blowing hot and cold on

---

[1] Lords, 6 May 1889, *Hansard*, 3rd ser. cccxxxv, 1194 *seqq.*; Commons, 22 Aug. 1895, *Hansard*, 4th ser. xxxvi, 642.
[2] Commons, 29 April 1881, *Hansard*, 3rd ser. cclx, 1451 *seqq.*, and 24 May 1894, *Hansard*, 4th ser. xxxiv, 278 *seqq.*
[3] Cf. Colonial Office to Treasury, May 1883. C.O. 810/12, p. 2.
[4] Harcourt to Rosebery, 27 Sept. 1892, in Gardiner, *op. cit.* ii, 196.
[5] Cecil, *op. cit.* iv, 254.
[6] Dilke, *op. cit.* ii, 191.

imperial questions.[1] The ways of the newly-enfranchised voters were unpredictable. Whether the new democracy would approve the enlargement of the African Empire was uncertain. Salisbury observed (December 1888):

The misfortune—the root-difficulty—we have in dealing with [imperial] questions..,is that public opinion in its largest sense takes no note of them. Unless some startling question appealing to their humanity arises, the constituencies are quite indifferent. The result is that the Members of the House of Commons are each like a ship without an anchor. They drift as any chance current may drive them. Yet the combined resultant of their many drifting wills is omnipotent and without appeal.[2]

The practical politicians' question still remained. Would it be better for the party at the next elections to be attacked for squandering taxpayers' money on "jingoistic" native wars and burdensome dependencies, or for abandoning British interests in Africa to foreign rule?

Ministers throughout the 'eighties were wary of testing the issue.[3] They tried to keep the African hinterland open to British trade by international agreement and reservation of exclusive spheres of influence. But, step by step, the advance of protectionist powers and foreign enterprises forced British ministries from their non-interventionist resolutions. The autarkic aims of Continental imperialism made adequate diplomatic guarantees of free trade generally unattainable. Spheres of influence, with changes in international law, came to depend upon effective occupation and administration.[4] Only after the failure of diplomatic expedients did British ministries yield to events and extend the protection of the political Empire in Africa over the empire of trade and speculation.

On the West Coast of Africa, the Colonial Office held to a policy of minimum intervention until Chamberlain became Colonial Secretary. With the establishment of a German protectorate in the Cameroons and the French advance in the hinterlands of the British coastal dependencies, imperial protection of British trade interests in West Africa became a minor issue in British politics (1883–6). West African merchants and shipping interests in London, Liverpool and Manchester urged Kimberley and Derby to forestall foreign control of the inland sources of their trade by extending imperial rule and to guarantee loans for railway development.[5] "The question resolves

---

[1] E.g. Commons, 1 June 1894, *Hansard*, 4th ser. xxv, 188–9.
[2] Salisbury to E. Baring, 22 Dec. 1888, in Cromer, *op. cit.* 1, 387–8.
[3] See Forster, W. E. "Imperial Federation", *Nineteenth Century*, xvII (Feb. 1885), p. 215.
[4] See Lyall, Sir A., "Imperial Frontiers and Protectorates", *Nineteenth Century*, xxx (Aug. 1891), 312 *seqq.*
[5] Aberdare (National Africa Company) to Granville, 28 Feb. 1883, C.O. 806/203, pp. 8–10; John Holt to F.O., 22 Dec. 1882, *ibid.* p. 4; Memorial of Manchester Chamber of Commerce to Derby, 4 Dec. 1883, C.O. 806/212; and F. A. and A. Swanzy, to C.O., 20 Dec. 1883, *ibid.* pp. 108–9.

itself into one mainly of finance", a Colonial Office Memorandum of 1888 concluded.[1]

The Colonial and Foreign Offices throughout the period 1880–95 rejected most of the merchants' petitions.[2] Their objection to extending administrative responsibility was summed up in Kimberley's Minute (April 1882) upon a proposal for a protectorate in the Niger: "The coast is pestilential; the natives numerous and unmanageable. The result... would be almost certainly wars with the natives, heavy demands of the British taxpayer."[3] Derby informed the West African merchants (December 1883) that neither he nor the public wanted "to get mixed up in" the turbulent affairs of Ashanti.[4] Similarly, the Conservative Colonial Secretary, Sir Henry Holland, told the Commons that the Cabinet had no territorial ambitions in West Africa.[5] From 1881 until 1885 the National Africa Company's requests for a Royal Charter were refused.[6] The Colonial Office also refused to subsidise or guarantee loans to private enterprise.[7] Dispatches to imperial officials in West Africa warned continually against accepting formal responsibilities beyond existing frontiers.[8]

Imperial aid to West African enterprise beyond the frontiers was limited in principle to informal influence with the hinterland chiefs and negotiations with the powers.[9] Granville attempted to keep the Congo Basin open to British trade without the liability of administering it, first by the Anglo-Portuguese Treaty of February 1884, then through the Berlin Conference Act of 1885.[10] Fearing imminent French annexation he obtained international recognition of a British sphere of influence on the Lower Niger River.[11] But the Niger Act of Navigation, accompanying the recognition, imposed administrative responsibilities upon the United Kingdom. The Foreign Secretary acceded to the request of his good friend, Lord Aberdare, the chairman of the National Africa Company and persuaded the Liberal Cabinet (January 1885) that "the cheapest and most effective way

[1] C.O. Memorandum, "Proposals involving the cession of the Gambia to France" (A. W. Hemming), 18 Nov. 1888, C.O. 806/301, p. 12.

[2] Kimberley to Gladstone, 2 Jan. 1882, Granville Papers, P.R.O. 30–29/135. See also their views summed up in retrospect by Sir John Ferguson (Foreign Under-Secretary) in Commons, 24 July 1890, Hansard, 3rd ser. cccxlvii, 751.

[3] Kimberley, Minute, 6 April 1882, C.O. 806/203, p. 7.

[4] The Times, 13 Dec. 1883, report on Deputation of West African Merchants to Lord Derby.

[5] Commons, 6 Sept. 1887, Hansard, 3rd ser. cccxx, 1405.

[6] Wellesley, Dorothy, Sir George Goldie, Founder of Nigeria, p. 95.

[7] See C.O. 806/362 passim; Derby to Sir S. Rowe, 31 Dec. 1883, Parl. Pap. 1884, lvi [C. 4052], pp. 94–102; and The Times, 13 Dec. 1883.

[8] E.g. Kimberley to Sir S. Rowe, 23 Aug. 1881, Parl. Pap. 1881, lx [C. 4957], p. 9; Derby to F. F. Pinkett, 29 June 1883, Parl. Pap. 1883, xlvii [C. 3765], pp. 39–40.

[9] C.O. to London Chamber of Commerce, 28 May 1886, xlvii [C. 4906], p. 43. See also Derby to Rowe, 31 Dec. 1883, C.O. 806/212, pp. 112–13.

[10] Derby to Granville, 18 Oct. 1884, Granville Papers, P.R.O. 30–29/120.

[11] Kimberley to Granville, 12 Jan. 1883, Granville Papers, P.R.O. 30–29/135. See also C.O. Minutes by Derby, Sir R. Herbert, and Robert Meade, March–April 1883, C.O. 806/203, App. iii, pp. 11–12.

of meeting these responsibilities would be by the employment of the National Africa Company". He proposed "in order to strengthen their position...to grant them a Charter for which they have several times applied".[1] Even diplomatic means of maintaining commercial interests had led the imperial authorities into further commitments.

The National Africa Company's Charter[2] granted in July 1886 evoked little opposition in Parliament. Criticism came chiefly from other West African merchants who, until the Charter was revoked in 1899, objected to the Company's practical monopoly of Niger trade.[3] The sphere of influence involved no Treasury expenditure since the Company met the costs of administration out of its profits. Because imperial policy in West Africa remained defensive, the Colonial Office did not make full use of the Company for the purposes of expansion in this period. The Foreign Office under Granville, Salisbury and Rosebery gave priority to imperial interests elsewhere in Africa. They preferred, when the time came, to acquire tropical African "estates" along Rhodes's and Johnston's Cape-to-Cairo axis instead of executing George Goldie's conception of an imperial Sudan belt stretching from the West to the East Coast.[4]

British policy toward East Africa and Zambesia also remained defensive in purpose until 1888. The Liberals (1880) had refused the Sultan of Zanzibar's offer to place his territories under British protection.[5] Until the late 'eighties, the Foreign Office rejected all the expansionists' requests to extend imperial protection to the missions in Nyasa and Uganda and to the traders and concessionaires in Zambesia.[6] Since 1878 Foreign Ministers had refused to charter William Mackinnon's projected East Africa Company or to guarantee loans for its Tanga-Kilimanjaro railway scheme.[7] A large sphere of influence in East Africa was conceded to Germany by the Anglo-German Zanzibar Agreement of 1885 in return for Bismarck's support of British policy in Egypt.[8] During the negotiations Salisbury observed: "This matter of equality [of tariffs for British and German merchants] is the only point in which the whole negotiation really touches Englishmen."[9] Otherwise, British ministries were content to maintain free trade on the mainland indirectly through their influence with the Sultan of Zanzibar. Only the protests of the Cape Govern-

---

[1] F.O. to C.O., 6 Jan. 1885, in Granville Papers, P.R.O. 30-29/270, p. 15. See also Derby to Granville, 20 Oct. 1884, ibid. P.R.O. 30-29/120.

[2] Later called the Royal Niger Company.

[3] Wellesley, op. cit. pp. 37-8; Commons, 7 Sept. 1893, Hansard, 4th ser. XVII, 517.

[4] Wellesley, op. cit. pp. 22-4; See also Goldie's introduction to Vandeleur, S., Campaigning on the Upper Nile and Niger.

[5] Dilke, "Memoir", in Gwynn and Tuckwell, op. cit. I, 535.

[6] Knutsford to Robinson, 29 March 1888, C.O. 806/302, p. 15; C.O. to F.O., 24 Sept. 1888, ibid. p. 65.

[7] T. V. Lister to William Mackinnon, 2 Feb. 1885, in Granville Papers, P.R.O. 30-29/270, p. 12.

[8] Gwynn and Tuckwell, op. cit. I, 535-7, and ibid. II, 99-100.

[9] Salisbury to Malet, 24 Aug. 1885, in Cecil, op. cit. III, 230.

ment and South African opinion prevented Salisbury and Knutsford from recognising Portuguese claims to large territories north of the Zambezi in return for guarantees of free trade and navigation (1888).[1] At the same time Knutsford also rejected the Cape Government's request to extend the Bechuanaland Protectorate northward up to the Zambezi River,[2] and Salisbury again rebuffed the humanitarians' plea for government to aid the Nyasa missions.[3] He explained in the Lords: "It is not our duty to do it. We should be risking tremendous sacrifices for a very doubtful gain."[4]

EXPANSIONIST STRATEGY AND THE CHARTER POLICY, 1888–95

Nevertheless from 1888 onwards Salisbury concentrated upon reserving these territories to the Empire. The Foreign Office since 1884 had inclined to give priority to imperial interests in East Africa over those on the West Coast. An official Memorandum of that year declared that British vulnerability in Egypt made it dangerous to compete seriously with the Continental powers in West Africa. Therefore, the Foreign Office proposed "to confine ourselves to securing the utmost possible freedom of trade on that (West) Coast, yielding to others the territorial responsibilities...and seeking compensation on the East Coast...where the political future of the country is of real importance to Indian and Imperial interests".[5] Foreign expansion had not as yet become a serious threat in East Africa. The humanitarian crusade in the United Kingdom was concentrated against the East Coast slave trade, the Memorandum continued; the highlands were suitable for European colonisation; and the region was reputed to be rich in minerals. The settlement-colony ideal was still so strong that even anti-expansionists were not completely opposed to securing dependencies for colonisation.[6] As the anti-expansionist Radical, James Bryce, put it to the Commons in 1892, colonies of settlement grew naturally of themselves into imperial commercial assets, but native dependencies required large expenditure from public funds for pacification, administration and communications.

[1] F.O. to C.O., 20 June 1888, in C.O. 806/302, p. 37.
[2] Knutsford to Robinson, 29 March 1888, C.O. 806/302, p. 15.
[3] Commons, 21 Feb. 1889, Hansard, 3rd ser. cccxxxiii, 66, 98. See also Dilke, op. cit. ii, 176.
[4] Lords, 6 July 1888, Hansard, 3rd ser. cccxxviii, 550.
[5] "Memorandum on Policy at the Berlin West African Conference of 20 Oct. 1884", F.O. 84/1813. Dilke in his "Memoir" claims a part in shaping the policy, see Gwynn and Tuckwell, op. cit. i, 536.
[6] The only deliberate expansionist scheme produced by this Ministry was the Kilimanjaro plan advocated by Dilke, Chamberlain and Granville, but resisted by Gladstone. See Granville to Kirk, 5 Dec. 1884, and Granville Minute on Kirk to Granville, 23 Nov. 1884, F.O. 84/1679; and Dilke, "Memoir", 14 Dec. 1884, B.M. Add. MSS. 43930, pp. 348–9.

Development of native dependencies was necessarily artificial and the ultimate gain long in maturing and always doubtful, Bryce argued.[1] Thus London tended to evaluate unoccupied African territory by its proximity to the Suez-India lifeline, its mineral wealth and its suitability for colonisation.

Salisbury between 1888 and 1892 began to carry out the expansionist strategy of forestalling foreign advances towards the Nile Valley and the East and Central African highlands which had been suggested in the Foreign Office Memorandum of 1884. Generally supported by the Liberal imperialists headed by Rosebery, and the Liberal Unionists, Hartington and Chamberlain, whose group held the balance between the Parties in the Commons, the Conservative Prime Minister, Salisbury, determined upon a prolonged occupation of Egypt.[2] This decision was the key to his whole African strategy. He believed that the security of Egypt depended upon reserving Uganda and the entire Nile Valley to imperial control.[3] The Imperial East Africa Company was chartered (April 1888) to occupy Uganda and Salisbury hoped to aid its work by subsidising a Mombasa–Nyanza railway.[4] Plans to continue the Berber Railway eventually to Khartoum and reconquer the Sudan also followed upon the Egyptian decision. To further his scheme Salisbury took such diplomatic securities as he could obtain for imperial paramountcy in the Nile Valley and East Africa by the Heligoland-Zanzibar Convention (1890)[5] and the Anglo-French Agreement (1891).[6] The Conservative Cabinet acquiesced at the same time in Rhodes's, Gifford's and Johnston's plans for Zambesia[7] and chartered the British South Africa Company (1889) to secure Matabeleland and Mashonaland and the regions north of the Zambezi River, including Barotseland.[8] Rhodes and his associates had promised to bear the whole expense and responsibility of administration.

These decisions opened a new phase in African policy. For the first time the Foreign Office was carrying out a deliberate expansion according to a long-term conception of the Empire's strategic needs. Previous annexations by comparison had been haphazard expedients for the protection of existing interests, prompted mainly by the colonial governments. But if Salisbury departed from traditional anti-expansionist aims, his methods still conformed as far as possible to Consolidationist principles; and to forestall opposition in the

[1] Commons, 24 July 1890, Hansard, 3rd ser. CCCXLVII, 820–1.
[2] Lords, 12 Aug. 1889, Hansard, 3rd ser. CCCXXXIX, 1003–4.
[3] Cecil, op. cit. IV, 139–40, 252–3, 280–2.
[4] Ibid. pp. 282, 311. See also Sir Percy Anderson's Memorandum of Interview with Manchester Chamber of Commerce, 2 July 1885, F.O. 84/1740.
[5] Salisbury to Queen Victoria, 10 June 1890, in Cecil, op. cit. IV, 298.
[6] See below, chap. vii.
[7] Johnston, Sir H. H., The Story of My Life, pp. 221–2; "British Policy in Africa", The Times, 22 Aug. 1888; and Cecil, op. cit. IV, 242, 336.
[8] Johnston to Rhodes, 8 Oct. 1893, F.O. 2/55.

Commons and at the Treasury, he extended British rule in its most economical and tentative form.[1]

The use of chartered companies enabled the Conservative government to transfer the cost of pacifying and administering more African territories to the private enterprises which would profit most from their development.[2] Official recognition of the companies' land, mineral and trade concessions gave them legal ownership of the territories' major assets. In return the companies undertook to suppress the slave trade, respect "native" land and labour rights and relieve the imperial authorities of all financial and administrative responsibility. Thus the Government avoided going to the Treasury for grants-in-aid or to the Commons for legislative authorisation. Moreover, Cromer by 1888 had just managed to lift the Egyptian Government out of bankruptcy and the financial risks of a continued British occupation there had diminished.

Further in the direction of an imperialism of tropical responsibility Salisbury's ministry found it politically imprudent to go. It rejected the extreme imperialists' demands for formal annexations or protectorates in Egypt and Zanzibar;[3] and it refused to undertake immediately the reconquest of the Sudan. "The House of Commons would certainly decline to bear the cost",[4] Salisbury assured the Queen (December 1888). Except where private British enterprise or colonial or satellite governments would shoulder the additional burdens, the imperial authorities remained wary of expansion.

By these means the Conservative Cabinet managed to evade the Consolidationist resistance to tropical imperialism. Gladstonians could hardly object to the Charter policy which they themselves had employed for more limited purposes in Borneo and on the Niger. The second Gladstone ministry's record, as Harcourt confessed, was no advertisement for anti-expansionist principles.[5] Conservatives claimed credit for undertaking an imperial mission of civilisation and their ministers justified the chartered companies to Parliament as "three great associations...formed for the purpose of pushing forward the civilisation of Africa."[6] *The Times* welcomed them because they "ought to be able to draw into their nets most of what is worth having in Central Africa".[7]

Salisbury by 1890 was less worried by the possibility of Gladstonian attacks than by criticism from the extreme expansionists. Chamberlain advised his friend Dilke for his own good on re-entering politics as a

---

[1] Dilke, *op. cit.* I, 573–6.
[2] *Ibid.* II, 172.
[3] Cecil, *op. cit.* IV, 307.
[4] Salisbury to Queen Victoria, 25 Dec. 1888, in Buckle, *op. cit.* 3rd ser. I, 459.
[5] *Ibid.* p. 169.
[6] Salisbury, Speech in the Guildhall, 9 Nov. 1889. See also Baron H. de Worms, Commons, 26 Aug. 1889, *Hansard*, 3rd ser. CCCXL, 486.
[7] *The Times*, editorial, 15 Oct. 1889.

Radical to "be as Radical as you like, be Home Ruler if you must, but be a little Jingo if you can".[1]

Salisbury's plan for a state-aided Mombasa–Nyanza railway was the first of his expansionist schemes to run into opposition in the Commons. He supported the project not only as a means of enabling the East Africa Company to hold Uganda and the Nile head-waters, but as a blow against the East African slave trade.[2] Goschen at the Treasury objected to subsidising the railway and assured the Prime Minister that the Commons would reject such a proposal. The Gladstonians also protested.[3] Another of Salisbury's anti-slave schemes, the Tana–Nyanza railway, was rejected by Goschen in 1891.[4] Whatever the government, the Treasury remained the stronghold of Gladstonian economical principles, standing against the expansionist and anti-slavery aspirations of the Foreign Office. Chancellors of the Exchequer from Gladstone in 1880 to Harcourt in 1892–5 opposed expenditure on the acquisition of purely "native" dependencies. When Salisbury proposed the Uganda railway survey in the Commons, it was opposed on the ground that public money should not be spent to assist private enterprise such as the East Africa Company. The vote, supported by imperialists and humanitarians, passed by 211 to 113. But Salisbury dared not ask for the much larger subsidies required to build the railway.

Before Salisbury left office (August 1892) the other part of his plan for holding Uganda without Treasury expenditure had also broken down. The East Africa Company, a philanthropic-imperialist venture in commercial disguise instigated by the Foreign Office, had to withdraw from Uganda for lack of funds. The question whether the United Kingdom was willing to pay occupation and protectorate costs could no longer be evaded. Not only the railway scheme but the future of the whole Nile Valley was involved, according to the War Office, which feared that, if Britain withdrew from Uganda, France would move in and gain a base for expansion into Equatoria and, perhaps, into the Egyptian Sudan.[5]

The question of the future of Uganda thus became the centre of dispute from 1890 until 1895. Gladstonians and Little Englander Radicals insisted upon evacuating Egypt and consequently cared nothing for control of the Nile Valley or Uganda; while humanitarians[6] and imperialists, represented by Salisbury, Chamberlain and Rosebery, were determined to hold them for British commercial

---

[1] Chamberlain to Dilke, Jan. 1892, in Gwynn and Tuckwell, op. cit. II, 254.

[2] F.O. to Treasury, 20 Dec. 1890, Parl. Pap. 1892, LVI [C. 6560], pp. 1–2; Treasury to F.O., 10 Feb. 1891, ibid. pp. 3–4.

[3] Commons, 3 March 1892, Hansard, 4th ser. I, 1836, seqq.; and 4 March 1892, ibid. II, 91.

[4] Cecil, op. cit. IV, 313–14.

[5] Cabinet Memorandum by Sir P. Anderson, 7 Sept. 1892, F.O. 84/2258; Memorandum "Effect on Egypt of the withdrawal from Uganda", by Major F. R. Wingate (D.M.I.), 21 Aug. 1892, F.O. 84/2257.

[6] "Resolutions re British Protectorate in Uganda" (Oct.–Dec. 1892), F.O. 84/2192.

development and to eradicate the slave trade from the Sudan to the Great Lakes and the East Coast ports. The anti-expansionists, Gladstone, Harcourt and Morley, still feared that continued occupation of Egypt would cost Britain "another Crimean War". They objected to the occupation because, by forcing Britain to lean on German support, it was dragging her into the Continental alliance system;[1] it was provoking Franco-Russian moves against the Indian North-West Frontier and British interests in the Eastern Mediterranean, and thus driving up imperial defence expenditure. Anti-expansionists disdained the supposed commercial prospects of Uganda and the Nile Valley. "Cui bono?" Harcourt asked Gladstone, "Is it *trade*? There is no traffic. Is it *religion*? The Catholics and Protestants... are occupied in nothing but cutting each other's throats.... Is it *slavery*? There is no evidence that there is any slave trade question in this region."[2]

The Liberal victory at the election of July 1892, however, was no victory for the Consolidationists. Gladstone's fourth ministry, which included the anti-expansionists, Harcourt at the Treasury, Morley as Irish Secretary and Ripon[3] at the Colonial Office, also had Rosebery as Foreign Secretary. He was supported on imperial questions by the Unionists in Opposition. Gladstone's majority depended on the support of the Irish Nationalists. Until Gladstone's retirement in 1894, he and his fellow anti-expansionists blocked Rosebery's execution of Salisbury's African designs. They frustrated Rosebery's proposals to subsidise the Uganda railway and to undertake a Uganda protectorate.[4] Rhodes even offered the services of the British South Africa Company to occupy and administer Uganda to help Rosebery out of the deadlock.[5] While the Liberal Cabinet was preoccupied with the second Irish Home Rule Bill, it passed through a series of Egyptian and Uganda crises. Harcourt was able to withhold grants-in-aid of imperial expansion just as Goschen had done. The Cabinet at first decided to evacuate Uganda (November 1892) and to subsidise the Company for three months to facilitate this.[6] There followed vigorous demonstrations by anti-slavery and missionary societies and by chambers of commerce urging a Uganda protectorate and the railway subsidies;[7] and counter-demonstrations by the Little Englander

---

[1] Commons, 23 Feb. 1891, *Hansard*, 3rd ser. CCCL, 1425 *seqq.* and CCCLI, 297 *seqq.*; Harcourt to Gladstone, 8 Sept. 1891, in Gardiner, *op. cit.* II, 129; Lords, 9 Feb. 1892, *Hansard*, 4th ser. I, 23 *seqq.*; Commons, 1 May 1893, *ibid.* XI, 1634 *seqq.*

[2] Harcourt to Gladstone, 20 Sept. 1892, in Gardiner, *op. cit.* II, 192.

[3] Ripon to Gladstone, 10 Dec. 1892, Gladstone Papers, B.M. Add. MSS. 44287.

[4] Gladstone to Morley, 26 Sept. and 13 Dec. 1892, Gladstone Papers, B.M. Add. MSS. 44257. See also Gardiner, *op. cit.* chap. xi.

[5] Gardiner, *op. cit.* II, 199.

[6] Rosebery and Gladstone to Queen Victoria, 29 Sept. 1892, in Buckle, *op. cit.* 3rd ser. II, 159–61.

Commons, 15 March 1894, *Hansard*, 4th ser. XXII, 394–5; "Resolutions *re* British Protectorate in Uganda" (Oct.–Dec. 1892), F.O. 84/2192.

Radicals. The Government played for time and sent Sir Gerald Portal on a Commission of Inquiry to Uganda.[1]

Time was on the side of Rosebery. He, instead of Harcourt, succeeded the aged Gladstone (March 1894). It was characteristic of the relative unimportance of imperial issues in British politics that anti-imperialists like Morley should have supported Rosebery against the claims of the anti-expansionist leader as the more likely to win the next election for the Liberals.[2] Even as Prime Minister, Rosebery still felt too insecure to propose the Uganda railway subsidies to the Commons;[3] and although he insisted upon a Uganda Protectorate (April 1894), he told the Queen that "announcement of its retention was a bomb which would probably blow up the Cabinet".[4] In defending the creation of the Protectorate Grey, the Foreign Under-Secretary, was careful to explain that the Government undertook no responsibility for the Protectorate's commercial development.[5] With Unionist support the vote passed by 218 to 52. But it was not until the next year that Rosebery braved Harcourt's threats of resignation and the Cabinet agreed to propose capital guarantees for the Uganda railway to the Commons.[6]

The anti-expansionist ministers at the same time joined the Little Englander Radicals in attacking Rosebery's policy of holding Egypt and securing the Nile Valley against the French.[7] Gladstone, Dilke and Morley in 1891 had called upon Salisbury to fulfil the reiterated British pledges to evacuate Egypt. Harcourt protested to Gladstone against Foreign Office ambitions to annex "the whole country up to the Albert Lakes with a view to the reconquest of the Sudan via the Upper Nile".[8] The Consolidationists resisted Rosebery's proposal to strengthen British garrisons in Egypt after the Khedive had dismissed his ministers without Foreign Office permission.[9] Rosebery's attempt to persuade the Treasury to bear the cost of British occupation troops in Egypt was thwarted by Harcourt, who regarded it as the nearest step yet towards outright annexation.

Imperialist pressure to secure British supremacy in the Nile Valley increased as French expeditions advanced from the West. The London and Manchester Chambers of Commerce urged the Government to establish imperial control of the Nile from Uganda to Fashoda.[10] To forestall the French advance Rosebery made the

[1] Gladstone to Rosebery, 9 Dec. 1892, and Rosebery to Gladstone, 13 Dec. 1892, Gladstone Papers, B.M. Add. MSS. 44290.
[2] Morley, *Recollections*, II, 17; Morley to Harcourt (undated), *ibid.* pp. 14–15.
[3] Rosebery to Queen Victoria, 22 March 1894, in Buckle, *op. cit.* 3rd ser. II, 384–5.
[4] Rosebery to Queen Victoria, 7 April 1894, *ibid.* p. 389.
[5] Commons, 1 June 1894, *Hansard*, 4th ser. xxv, 188.
[6] Rosebery to Queen Victoria, 27 May 1895, in Buckle, *op. cit.* 3rd ser. II, 515–16.
[7] See Taylor, A. J. P., "Prelude to Fashoda", *E.H.R.* LXV (Jan. 1950), 52 *seqq.*
[8] Crewe, *op. cit.* II, 415–20.
[9] Commons, 30 May 1895, *Hansard*, 4th ser. xxxiv, 686 *seqq.*
[10] Langer, W. L., *The Diplomacy of Imperialism*, pp. 264, 267.

secret Anglo-Belgian Treaty (May 1894);[1] and Harcourt and the anti-expansionists again attacked Rosebery for thus provoking France.[2] The struggle for the Nile was to culminate at Fashoda.[3]

Meanwhile in South-Central, as in North-East Africa, the Salisbury government had inaugurated a policy of expansion by proxy towards the end of the 'eighties. Its motive for chartering the British South Africa Company (October 1889) arose out of the needs of the broader imperial strategy in South Africa. Imperialists though they were, Salisbury and Knutsford, like Rosebery and Ripon after them, still shaped their South African policy on the principle of "colonial expansion through Imperial aid".[4] They continued to aim at evading further direct territorial responsibility, transferring those already undertaken to the colonial governments, and thus working toward the eventual withdrawal of the imperial factor.

They were equally resolved, on the other hand, to frustrate the Transvaal-German challenge to British paramountcy in southern Africa. That challenge was taken ever more seriously in London. Kruger's encouragement of German commerce, Transvaal ambitions for territorial expansion, and Germany's sponsorship of Transvaal interests[5] appeared to threaten the imperial stake in the interior which had been raised by British investments in South African mining, railways and loans. It seemed to imperialists that the direction of South African trade as well as the allegiance of the future federation would depend upon the outcome of the rivalry between the Cape Colony and the South African Republic for the railway traffic of the Rand and the undeveloped resources of the northern interior.[6] The British interest was bound up with the fortunes of the Cape Colony as the German was identified with those of the Republic.

The imperial authorities' ability to decide the outcome remained marginal. They were hampered by South African resentment against direct Colonial Office intervention south of the Zambezi River and by the economically minded Treasury and Commons.[7] Prior British interests in Egypt and the need of German co-operation there necessitated tolerance of German support of the South African Republic. The solidarity of the Boers north and south of the Vaal River, evoked by Carnarvon's disastrous enforced confederation policy and the Transvaal War, warned against another attempt to coerce the Republic into a union with the Cape Colony. The Colonial Office was intent upon keeping the peace until the logic of inter-

---

[1] Hornik, M. P., "The Anglo-Belgian Agreement of 12 May 1894", *E.H.R.* LVII (April 1942), pp. 226 *seqq.*
[2] Gardiner, *op. cit.* II, 310–20; Crewe, *op. cit.* II, 502–4.
[3] See below, chap. xiii.
[4] Speech of Sir Hercules Robinson at Cape Town, 27 April 1889, C.O. 806/319, p. 4.
[5] Langer, *op. cit.* pp. 219–20.
[6] *C.H.B.E.* VIII, 539 *seqq.*   [7] Dilke, *op. cit.* I, 575–6.

dependence should persuade the South African governments to unite freely on their own initiative.[1] The South African problem facing the Colonial Secretaries, Knutsford and Ripon, thus became one of securing British paramountcy indirectly through the agency of the Cape Colony without embittering relations with the Republics.[2] More specifically the Colonial Office sought to block Transvaal expansion northward into Matabeleland and Mashonaland and did what it could to help to close the Republic's possible non-imperial railway routes to the east coast.[3]

This policy of indirect expansion through the Cape Government had broken down by 1888 in Bechuanaland, Mashonaland and Matabeleland. Knutsford's attempted transfer of the Bechuanaland administration from the Colonial Office to the Cape Government had been frustrated by Chamberlain and the humanitarian and extreme imperialist advocates of direct United Kingdom control.[4] The Cape Government proved as ineffective and unwilling an imperial agent for securing the territory across the Limpopo River from the Transvaalers and Germans as it had for Bechuanaland in 1884–5. Piqued by Colonial Office retention of the Protectorate, the Cape Legislature refused to finance the railway extension through Bechuanaland to hold the northern interior, which the High Commissioner, Sir Hercules Robinson, considered vital to British paramountcy.[5]

The secret of Rhodes's influence with Salisbury and Knutsford was that he offered to do through the British South Africa Company what the Conservative imperialists had desired but had failed to achieve through the Cape colonial government.[6] The Company would relieve the Colonial Office of the administration and charges of the Bechuanaland Protectorate; its associates would construct a Bechuanaland railway;[7] it would contain the South African Republic to the north and permit the imperial authorities to devolve the task of keeping order during this latest recurrence of the troublesome South African frontier problem.[8] Ultimately the Company promised to develop a rival Rand in the North which would counterbalance the Republic's newly-found wealth, and create from its private resources a strong British colony to help to secure the future confederation to the imperial connection. North of the Zambezi River the Company would hold native territories open to British development which

[1] Ripon to Rosebery, 4 Sept. 1894, in Wolf, *op. cit.* II, 225–6.
[2] Knutsford to Loch, 4 Nov. 1889, C.O. 806/321, p. 2; Ripon to Rosebery, 5 Sept. 1894, in Wolf, *op. cit.* II, 222–3.
[3] Knutsford to Loch, 4 Nov. 1889, C.O. 806/321, p. 2; Robinson to Knutsford, 17 Oct. 1888, C.O. 806/310, pp. 55–7.
[4] Garvin, *op. cit.* II, 464–6; Raphael, L. A. C., *The Cape to Cairo Dream*, pp. 111–15.
[5] Robinson to Knutsford, 7 Nov. 1888, *Parl. Pap.* 1890, LI [C. 5918], pp. 26–8.
[6] Dicey, E., "Mr Cecil Rhodes as Premier", *Nineteenth Century*, XXVIII (August 1890), 184.
[7] Raphael, *op. cit.* pp. 115 *seqq.*
[8] Knutsford to Loch, 28 June and 9 July 1891, C.O. 806/352, pp. 10, 18.

neither Goschen nor Parliament could be persuaded to support financially.[1] Knutsford and Salisbury hoped also to place the British missions on Lake Nyasa under the Company's protection.[2] Thus the expansionist power of private enterprise dwarfed that of an imperialist ministry.

In Parliament the British South Africa Company henceforward was attacked by Radical Little Englanders on the one hand, and on the other by the "South Africa Committee",[3] the missionary societies and other humanitarian and imperialist advocates of Crown colony rule. The efforts of the latter to reverse the traditional policy of withdrawal and minimum responsibility, and to substitute one of direct United Kingdom intervention and control in Bechuanaland, Swaziland and Natal as well as Zambesia, make up most of the history of the South African problem in British politics from the mid-'eighties onwards. Exeter Hall criticised the Government for shirking its responsibilities for the tribal populations and subjecting them to commercial rule. John Mackenzie prophesied that the South Africa Company would involve the Colonial Office in native wars.[4] The African Lakes Company and the Scottish missions agitated successfully against the transfer of Nyasa to the British South Africa Company (winter 1890).[5] But Goschen, the Chancellor of the Exchequer, refused to sanction grants-in-aid to enable the Foreign Office to administer as a protectorate what he regarded as a "white elephant" dependency acquired solely for philanthropic purposes. Rhodes saved the situation by promising to subsidise the Protectorate for four years.[6] Chamberlain criticised the Chartered policy as one which conferred a monopoly upon a few London and Cape Town capitalists and demanded that Zambesia be opened freely to all British enterprise.[7] He succeeded in thwarting Knutsford's projected transfer of the Bechuanaland Protectorate to the South Africa Company as he had done that of the Colony to the Cape Government.[8]

The Matabele War (1893–4) and the Jameson Raid (1895) revealed the dangers of Salisbury's apparently non-responsible method of expansion in southern Africa, as the East Africa Company's collapse had already done in Uganda. The South Africa High Commissioner, Sir Henry Loch, warned Knutsford that unless an imperial resident

[1] Dilke, op. cit. I, 573.

[2] Johnston to Rhodes, 8 Oct. 1893, enclosed in Johnston to F.O., 8 Oct. 1893, F.O. 2/55.

[3] See "The South African Question", a summary of press and other opinions in favour of direct imperial responsibility in South Africa, issued by the South Africa Committee, in Carnarvon Papers, P.R.O. 30–6/131.

[4] Aborigines Protection Society to C.O., 5 Feb. 1889, C.O. 806/310, p. 265.

[5] Johnston, op. cit. p. 239; Dilke, op. cit. II, 176.

[6] Johnston to Rhodes, 8 Oct. 1893, enclosed in Johnston to F.O., 8 Oct. 1893, F.O. 2/55, pp. 310–19; Commons, 7 Sept. 1893, Hansard, 4th ser. XVII, 512–13.

[7] The Economist, XLIX, 9 May 1891, pp. 591–2; Commons, 7 Sept. 1893, Hansard, 4th ser. XVII, 532–4.

[8] Cf. Gardiner, op. cit. II, 199–200.

commissioner was posted to Mashonaland to control the Company's dealings with Lobengula, a native war would be provoked which would jeopardise the security of the Bechuanaland Protectorate.[1] But Knutsford and his successor, Ripon, hampered by Treasury stringencies, could not provide the machinery for local supervision.[2]

With the outbreak of the Matabele War, Radical Little Englanders, humanitarians and advocates of direct Colonial Office administration joined in urging revocation of the Charter. Rumours of Company cattle-looting and atrocities stimulated "pro-native" sympathy in England. Henry Labouchere accused the Company of seizing Matabeleland to bolster its falling credit—a charge which Ripon inclined to believe.[3] The Conservative imperialist, Sir John Gorst, shrewdly expressed the objections to the Chartered policy. The Government, he observed, lacked sufficient control over the Companies to prevent them from quarrelling with the tribes, but the Companies had sufficient influence over Government to force it to come to their aid and save them from the penalties of their oppressive native policy. Precautionary measures in the Bechuanaland Protectorate in 1893–4 in support of the South Africa Company's forces had cost the Imperial Treasury £80,000. The policy of Chartered companies, Gorst warned, "seemed to be one of drifting into national responsibilities" which would lead to "some national disaster".[4]

But the humanitarian-imperialists failed to force the Liberal Government to revoke the Company's Charter—a step which would have saddled the Treasury with the administrative charges of territories whose main revenue-yielding assets were already owned privately by the Company.[5] As Ripon observed to Rosebery, there were both political and practical objections to multiplying grants-in-aid for the purposes of imperial development. Even Chamberlain, when he came into office and the Raid provided a supreme opportunity, could not overcome this financial obstacle to revoking the Charter.

The imperial authorities played an equally passive role in containing the South African Republic on the east and closing possible rail routes from Pretoria through Portuguese territory to Delagoa Bay, and through Swaziland and Tongaland to Kosi Bay.[6] British governments cautiously used their influence to further Rhodes's more responsible plans for manœuvring the Republic into a railway and customs union with the Cape Colony. But when Rosebery stressed

[1] Loch to Knutsford, 9 Dec. 1890 and 29 June 1891, C.O. 806/349, pp. 4, 119.
[2] Knutsford to Loch, 16 and 28 June 1891 and 8 July 1891, C.O. 806/352, pp. 8, 10, 17.
[3] Commons, 9 Nov. 1893, Hansard, 4th ser. xviii, 554; Ripon to Gladstone, 4 Nov. 1893, Gladstone Papers, B.M. Add. MSS. 44287.
[4] Commons, 8 Sept. 1893, Hansard, 4th ser. xvii, 678.
[5] Knutsford to Loch, 26 June 1891, C.O. 806/349, p. 43; Knutsford to Loch, 28 June 1891, C.O. 806/352, p. 10. Cf. Ripon to Gladstone, 27 Oct. 1893, Gladstone Papers, B.M. Add. MSS. 44287.
[6] C.H.B.E. viii, 522–4, 526 seqq.

the dangers of the Delagoa Bay railway passing from Portuguese into German hands, Lord Onslow, Secretary to the Board of Trade, replied that the British taxpayer could not be expected to purchase it.[1] Neither did British governments support financially Rhodes's bids for the railway. Germany objected to any extension of British control over the Portuguese East African Colonies;[2] and both Salisbury and Rosebery perhaps judged that German retaliation in Egypt was too high a price for shutting the Transvaalers in from the east coast.[3]

The Swazi question[4] in British politics centred upon the immorality of placing the Swazi population under Boer rule, rather than upon the problem of encircling the Republic on the east. The advocates of Crown colony rule could no more persuade ministers to undertake the administration of Swaziland than they could that of Mashonaland and Matabeleland.[5] In 1890 Knutsford offered to allow the Republic to build a railway to Kosi Bay and administer Swaziland if she would join the Cape customs union. But the Boers rejected the proposal.[6] Ripon eventually transferred the territory to Republican rule (December 1894). Fearing a Transvaal-German junction there, however, he sealed off Kosi Bay by taking Tongaland (May 1895).[7] The Colonial Office meanwhile ignored humanitarian objections and continued its withdrawal from direct responsibility, granting Natal responsible government with safeguards for native interests (1892), transferring to it the Zululand administration (1895), and preparing to transfer the Bechuanaland Protectorate to the Cape Government. There were few premonitions in London of the imminence of the Jameson Raid.[8]

PROBLEMS OF IMPERIAL UNITY

Immediate problems of frontier policy and the limitation of Empire tended to crowd longer-term questions of relations with the great colonies out of British politics. The day-to-day strife between the Consolidationists and the Forward school nevertheless manifested a deeper conflict between old liberal and new imperialist concepts of the Empire's future. To Gladstonians the United Kingdom's interests outside the Empire seemed far to outweigh those within it; and while they valued the great colonies they were resigned to their drift into

---

[1] Lords, 27 Feb. 1888, *Hansard*, 3rd ser. cccxxii, 1466 *seqq*.
[2] Langer, *op. cit.* pp. 219 *seqq.*; van der Poel, *op. cit.* pp. 61-2.
[3] Kimberley to Harcourt, 7 Dec. 1894, in Gardiner, *op. cit.* ii, 325; Cecil, *op. cit.* iv, 298.
[4] *C.H.B.E.* viii, 526-30.
[5] Ripon to Loch, 1 Dec. 1892, *Parl. Pap.* 1893-4, lxii [C. 7212], p. 140; Treasury to C.O., 19 Jan. 1893, *ibid.* p. 102; Aborigines Protection Society to C.O., 23 Oct. 1889, *Parl. Pap.* 1890, lii [C. 6200], p. 207; Commons, 4 May 1893, *Hansard*, 4th ser. xii, 131 *seqq.* and 6 Feb. 1895, *ibid.* xxx, 133 *seqq*.
[6] *C.H.B.E.* viii, 528.
[7] Wolf, *op. cit.* ii, 229-34.
[8] For the Uitlander question and the Raid *vide infra*, chap. x.

full national independence.[1] They looked to the Empire's future as a league of freely associated sovereign states.[2]

The imperialist reaction to foreign rivalry in the 'eighties, on the other hand, was characterised by a sense of the dependence of future British power, prestige and prosperity upon the Empire.[3] One expression of this reaction was the Forward school of frontier policy; the other, bound up with it in leadership and outlook, was the imperial federation movement. At the same time as imperialists like Salisbury, Carnarvon, Forster and Rosebery advocated extensions of imperial frontiers to meet foreign challenges, they sought to re-integrate relations with the great colonies in order to preserve central control of imperial defence and foreign policy. The Consolidationists, Gladstone, Harcourt, Morley and Ripon, in contrast, looked upon these efforts as unpractical, reactionary and even dangerous.[4]

The United Empire movement, nourished since the late 'sixties by the Royal Colonial Institute,[5] had made rapid progress both in the United Kingdom and the colonies by 1886.[6] Its maturity was marked by the foundation of the Imperial Federation League (November 1884),[7] headed by the Liberal imperialists W. E. Forster and Lord Rosebery, the Conservatives Carnarvon, Edward Stanhope, Holland and W. H. Smith, and such prominent colonial statesmen as Sir Charles Tupper and Sir Alexander Galt. The League's object of preserving and strengthening the unity of the Empire upon federal principles attracted far more sympathy in the Conservative than in the Liberal Party.[8] But the movement's impetus came from the growth of an imperial sentiment in several different quarters which expressed itself in divergent and even incompatible aspirations.

True federalists who proposed colonial representation in the Westminster Parliament and Cabinet were overruled by their political leaders who realised from the beginning that closer union was impracticable except through a concert between governments.[9] Proposals for an imperial customs union were deprecated also by the leading United Kingdom members of the League. Free-trader federationists like Sir George Baden-Powell, nevertheless, hoped for an imperial *Zollverein*; while the fair-traders Carnarvon, Dunraven

---

[1] E.g. Granville to Russell, 28 Aug. 1869, in Fitzmaurice, *op. cit.* II, 22. *Vide supra*, chap. ii.
[2] See for example Arnold-Foster, H. O., "The Liberal Idea and the Colonies", *Nineteenth Century*, XIV (Sept. 1883), 386–8.
[3] See Forster, W. E., "Imperial Federation", *Nineteenth Century*, XVII (Feb. 1885), 201 *seqq.*; Dilke, *op. cit.* I, 2 *seqq.*; and Seeley, *op. cit.* pp. 18–19.
[4] Wolf, *op. cit.* II, 209–11; Tyler, J. E., *The Struggle for Imperial Unity*, p. 137, footnote 1; and Harcourt ("Historicus"), Letter to *The Times*, 1 June 1876.
[5] Bodelsen, *op. cit.* pp. 94 *seqq.*; and Folsom, A., *The Royal Empire Society*, *passim*.
[6] Tyler, *op. cit.* p. 114.   [7] *Ibid.* chap. xi; and Bodelsen, *op. cit.* pp. 206–8.
[8] Dilke, *op. cit.* II, 478.
[9] Tyler, *op. cit.* pp. 110, 180; and Dilke, *op. cit.* II, 465–6.

and Harrowby advocated imperial preferential tariffs as the indispensable material foundation of imperial unity. The form of closer union most favoured in the United Kingdom was that of a *Kriegsverein*, in which the colonies as well as the United Kingdom would contribute to an imperial defence budget.

But the realities of colonial responsible government reduced all these aspirations to the problem Salisbury posed at the first Colonial Conference: "how far we must acquiesce in the conditions which that [geographical] separation causes, how far we can obliterate them by agreement and by organisation."[1] Even the federationists accepted the restrictions imposed upon the possibility of closer union by the colonial responsible governments' independent control of internal, tariff and defence policies. Conventionally the imperial authorities legislated for a great colony only in agreement with its government.[2] The imperial veto of colonial laws had fallen into disuse except when these laws were *ultra vires*, as in the case of Queensland assuming power to annex New Guinea.[3] Gladstone invoked this convention when urged by the humanitarians to veto the Cape Government's extension of the Disarmament Act to the Basutos (May 1880). He replied that he was powerless to intervene in matters within a responsible government's jurisdiction, except by "influence and advice".[4] Again, Knutsford refused to veto Australian laws against Chinese immigration (1888). "Can we suppose", Derby commented, "that that veto would be submitted to?....We are in the hands of the Colonists, and they must do in this matter as they please."[5] Similarly, the Liberal Colonial Secretary, Ripon, deferred to South African opinion and did not disallow the Natal Franchise Amendment Bill depriving Asiatics of the vote (1894). What was still constitutionally feasible had become politically impracticable.

The responsible-government colonies had also begun to claim a more formal share in imperial conduct of their external affairs. These demands arose from colonial suspicion that the United Kingdom was sacrificing colonial interests for a smile from Germany or to avoid a frown from France. At the Colonial Conference (1887) the Australasian[6] and Cape[7] Governments urged the imperial authorities to consult them more closely in dealings with foreign powers affecting

---

[1] Salisbury's Opening Address at Colonial Conference, *Parl. Pap.* 1887, LVI [C. 5091], I, p. 5.

[2] Todd, Alpheus, *Parliamentary Government in the British Colonies* (1880), p. 34; "Historicus" to *The Times*, 1 June 1876.

[3] Todd, *op. cit.* p. 429; Dilke, *op. cit.* II, 282-3. See also *C.H.B.E.* VII, pt. I, 417.

[4] Commons, 25 May 1880, *Hansard*, 3rd ser. CCLII, 456. See also Kimberley to Frere, 13, 20 May 1880, *Parl. Pap.* 1880, LI [C. 2569], pp. 46-7, 49-51; and *C.H.B.E.* VIII, 479-80.

[5] Lords, 8 June 1888, *Hansard*, 3rd ser. CCCXXVI, 1518.

[6] Granville to Loch, 26 May 1886, C.O. 808/67, p. 12; Strahan to F. A. Stanley, 5 Feb. 1886, *ibid.* pp. 4 *seqq.*

[7] Cape Colony Representatives to Holland, 1 April 1887, *Parl. Pap.* 1887, LVI [C. 5091], II, pp. 4-5.

their local interests.[1] The Australians desired to associate a colonial representative with the United Kingdom delegation to negotiate with the French on the New Hebrides and convict questions, and with Germany and the United States on the Samoan issue. Salisbury evaded these demands.[2] The New Zealanders requested also separate representation in negotiations of imperial commercial treaties[3]—a privilege which Canada already enjoyed. Dilke noted in 1890 that "the colonies have practically a supreme voice in making commercial treaties with foreign countries which concern themselves".[4]

If imperial statesmen watched the encroachment of the responsible governments upon imperial supremacy without enthusiasm, they accepted its inevitability. It was generally agreed that attempts to set constitutional bounds to the growth of colonial autonomy would disrupt rather than preserve the Empire. There could be no question of using force to prevent a responsible-government colony from leaving the Empire; their adherence was voluntary, depending upon loyalty to the Crown, goodwill and a reciprocity of mutual advantages.[5] They "already stand to us", Dilke observed, "in the virtual relation of friendly allied states speaking our tongue".[6] That imperial federation caused little dispute in British politics was due to the general recognition that in reality everything hung upon colonial initiative and consent.[7]

The question of closer union with the responsible-government colonies for the rest of the century turned upon two issues: the division of naval defence burdens and a common tariff policy.[8]

BRITISH IMPERIALISM

The verdict of Midlothian and the radical-democratic forces rising in British politics in 1880 seemed heralds of an era of imperial consolidation and rapid liberalisation of the established order. Instead they ushered in two decades of territorial expansion and conservative reaction. Irish anarchy and English radicalism united Conservatives in defence of property and order; and the challenges of the Continental powers to British commercial and colonial supremacy stimulated nationalism.

During the 'eighties, however, imperial aggrandisement had not yet become a popular appetite nor imperialism a mass emotion. The vitality of the old *laissez-faire* anti-expansionist tradition seemed

[1] Proceedings of Federal Council of Australasia (First Session) (May 1886), pp. 24 *seqq.*
[2] Dilke, *op. cit.* I, 437; Cecil, *op. cit.* IV, 33 *seqq.*
[3] *Parl. Pap.* 1887, LVI [C. 5091-I], pp. 475 *seqq.*
[4] Dilke, *op. cit.* I, 108. See also Kimberley Cabinet Note, 1 March 1882, Granville Papers, P.R.O. 30–29/135.
[5] Crewe, *op. cit.* I, 315–16; Fitzmaurice, *op. cit.* II, 23; Holland, *op. cit.* II, 245–6.
[6] Dilke, *op. cit.* I, 460.
[7] See for example Ripon to Gladstone, 2 Feb. 1893, in Wolf, *op. cit.* II, 210–11.
[8] Imperial Defence and Imperial Conferences are dealt with elsewhere in this volume.

unimpaired; imperial questions played little part in elections; and the inertia and indifference of the generality, if not the weight of British opinion, favoured the Consolidationists. In this decade, nevertheless, territorial acquisitions multiplied and an expansionist policy was adopted toward Africa, despite the anti-expansionist prejudice of Parliaments. The expansionist impetus arose, therefore, either outside British politics or behind closed doors, rather than from a spontaneous and irresistible imperialist outburst in the country.

There was indeed much that was fortuitous about the translation of that impetus into terms of politics and policy. Prior requirements of foreign policy and the tactical manœuvres of parties and faction on domestic issues were often the decisive though incidental factors in imperial policy-making. These, exaggerated by Liberal disunity, made sport of the Consolidationist concepts and resolutions of Gladstone's second ministry and produced deadlock and vacillation in his fourth. Spasmodically during the international crises of 1884–5, 1887–8 and 1893–5 nationalist feeling struck upon a colonial issue as the symbol of the wider clash of national interests, and, identifying prestige with territorial compensation, intervened in imperial policy. Again, it was the Irish question, not imperialism in general, which split the Liberal Party and brought most imperialists together in the Unionist alliance. Thus Irish Home Rule prepared the way for Salisbury towards the end of the 'eighties to steady the previous fluctuation of policy between the Consolidationist and Forward schools and to execute a more deliberate and purposeful expansion in the Nile Valley and in East and Central Africa.

On the other hand, there were slowly-growing expansionist pressures which a few powerful imperialist leaders by opportunism were able to translate into action:—the aspirations of colonial governments; the demands of private enterprise and philanthropists for imperial aid and protection against foreign rivals; and the private influence of the Court, the imperial Services, and sections of the old landed, and the new financial, aristocracy. Imperialism gained increasingly the advocacy of the press, of historians and philosophers. If in the 'eighties British imperialism was the product of chance and the devious opportunism of relatively few strong personalities, it became progressively during the next decade a popular nostrum for curing depression and unemployment, for easing national insecurity and ensuring future greatness.

Nevertheless the achievements and the impress of the older *laissez-faire* imperial tradition still checked and tempered the imperialist reaction. Protectionist tendencies were repulsed; attempts to strengthen the central imperial authority broke down because of United Kingdom loyalty to free trade; and the progress of the Empire continued unbroken towards that form of Commonwealth foreshadowed by the older Liberal ideal.

CHAPTER VI

IMPERIAL FINANCE, TRADE AND COMMUNICATIONS, 1870–1895

THE free-trade movement, said Gladstone, reached its height in 1860. A decade later, though Great Britain herself was even more definitely committed to this policy, the hope that she was leading the world along the new path was already shadowed and was destined to be completely disappointed in the quarter of a century that followed. Not that this influenced her own views of the policy most advantageous to herself in her circumstances, any more than her views influenced the young countries of the Empire to whom she had allowed freedom in economic no less than in political life. But it became a fact of increasing importance to her as a great industrial and trading state, that, while she followed a policy of free trade, the majority of foreign countries and her own great colonies did not. Advantages and disadvantages followed from this, as she rose in these years to occupy a unique position in the world as the leading exporter, shipper and banker among the nations. That Great Britain was rising to, and holding, this position determined her outlook on imperial economic policy.

Not less important were the great political changes taking place at the same time—particularly the formation of the German Empire with its increasing industrial activity, and the rapid growth of the United States—which gradually confronted her with two formidable competitors in the markets of the world; while the balance of international power shifted in a manner that raised for her new problems of defence, with all their financial and other consequences. None the less her geographical position, her industrial leadership, her far-extended possessions and her growing store of loanable capital gave her during this period a position of signal influence and importance. Peace was her prime interest, for it was the condition of her prosperity, and indeed, of the normal functioning of the external, commercial and financial activities on which her livelihood was coming more and more to depend. Peace and free trade with all parts of the world was her desire and also the prime motive directing her policy through these years.

The period is remarkable for the progress of invention and the application of science to the arts of life. Invention more than policy transformed the relations of states. Things were in the saddle and rode mankind. The means of communication were improved and multiplied, and there was a spreading of human enterprise over the world at a rate not known before. By the railway, the steamship and the electric telegraph, all economic movement was quickened—of men, of goods and of information. In the early 'eighties almost every place of importance in the world, not in the heart of China, could be reached by telegraph overland or undersea. The railways carried the bulky produce of the farm long distances at a small price and provided the cargoes for large ships.

Between 1870 and 1890, a series of inventions revolutionised the cost of transport and for many commodities made the world a single market. Cheap transport and expanding trade acted and reacted on each other. In addition, further stimulating trade, came the discovery of cold storage. With these developments, the agricultural industries were built up in new lands, and their capacity to feed the workers in European factories was immensely increased, while they themselves became growing markets for the manufactures of the Old World. The area of commerce was greatly enlarged and the economic relations of many parts of the world were put on a new footing. British agriculture declined in face of such competition, but British industry and trade continued to expand.

The development of the new lands called for capital. The change of our Company laws to admit of limited liability encouraged investment in oversea enterprises. To this too our fiscal system was highly favourable. Low taxation left in the hands of Companies and businesses a sufficient margin of profits and a strong inducement to extend their operations. As protective barriers were raised by colonies and other countries, British firms set up branches behind the barriers and joined in the expansion of other countries' industries and drew profits home. Financial policy alone would have been insufficient had it not been accompanied by the unflagging enterprise, both commercial and technical, characteristic of the period, and by the high reputation for quality which the inherited skills and integrity of our workmen ensured for our products. The profits of British trade and industry went increasingly to provide the railways, harbour works and cold storage establishments needed for the growing trades, to equip new towns with their public works, to finance ranches, mines and plantations, indifferently within and without the Empire—in America, Africa, Asia and Australia. So grew the immense body of British overseas investments which received its interest in the cargoes of food and raw materials pouring into the country. This was the new pattern of British economic life: food and raw material coming from abroad and paid for by the labour and skill that shaped the raw material into manufactured articles, by services of management and organisation, of transport and finance, and by the loan of capital. The outer parts of the Empire fitted into the general scheme, but all the world that she could reach was Britain's market and her source of supply.

The British Government itself did not attempt to plan, direct or even to influence the general course of this development. Its main principle was *laissez-faire*. The directing minds were the mercantile and industrial leaders and the bankers who financed them. The prevailing philosophy was that they would know what was best for themselves, that what they could make profitable would be right for them to do, and, subject to respect for the law, would be best for the nation as a whole. To finance the economic development of the Empire was quite outside the purview of mid-Victorian statesmen. Financial aid, financial guarantees, to a limited extent, might occasionally be given on philanthropic or political grounds, as Gladstone said in 1869—for "objects of broad imperial policy"; public opinion would support expenditure to suppress the slave trade. But, in general, economic leadership was regarded as outside the functions of government and as belonging essentially to private enterprise.

The exception, in India, for example, where government assumed a large measure of responsibility for the construction and operation of the railways, only showed the adaptability of the British imperial system to the necessity of circumstances and the extent to which the Government of India was always a matter *sui generis*.[1] Through the great Chartered Companies which appear again in British history in the 'eighties, the Government found a veiled means of bringing some State direction into oversea expansion and the economic development of other lands. But it was the multitude of small companies which did the main work of collecting the savings of individuals and risking them in enterprises all over the world, sometimes with profit and sometimes with loss.

The business of the Government was to open the way for British trade, to protect the merchants and their property overseas, but not to find for them profitable enterprises and direct them therein. In the dependencies, peace, order and security must be maintained under the British flag. That was the British tradition—the benefit it brought to harassed lands and peoples. And that way commerce was promoted, as the growth of great trading centres, like Singapore and Hong Kong, had convincingly shown. But economy was the order of the day, and dependent colonial governments must keep within their functions and not behave as merchants and adventurers. The sense of responsibility to the governed did not in the 'seventies include the economic development of their land in their interests and our own, nor placing on the British people the cost of extensive schemes of internal improvement in the dependencies. Earl Grey in 1853 had laid down the principle that "the surest test of the soundness of measures for the improvement of an uncivilised people, is that they should be self-supporting", and this principle still held good.[2] So the money that was going overseas was going for enterprises of

---

[1] A similar policy was adopted in West Africa from 1890 onwards.
[2] Earl Grey, *Colonial Policy of Lord John Russell's Administration*, II, 281.

profit, generally of immediate or near profit, in the opinion of the investor, not for schemes of welfare and development looking to a remote future, nor for defence and security.

The self-governing colonies did not in general follow the ideas of the mother country in regard to free trade or the functions of government. Except in foreign affairs their self-government covered the whole field of economic policy. It included the goal of national development, combining industrial with agricultural life, and full financial responsibility, save for external defence. As early as 1859 Canada had made clear that she intended to control her own fiscal policy. In 1876 Sir Wilfrid Laurier, speaking in the Dominion House of Commons on protection for Canadian industries, said "Protection is a matter of necessity for a young nation in order that it may attain the full development of its own resources. If I were in Great Britain I would avow free trade; but I am a Canadian...and I think that we require protection. I consider however that the present tariff affords sufficient protection."[1] The duties were at the rate of $17\frac{1}{2}$ per cent. In the general election of 1878 the Conservatives won on their programme of a National Policy for Canada and the following year the first tariff with high protective duties for Canadian manufactures was enacted.

Since Galt's tariff of 1859 there had been no remonstrance from the Colonial Office concerning Canadian tariffs, chiefly because there had been few changes that adversely affected British trade. The tariff of 1879 naturally excited comment in the British House of Commons and elsewhere, but the position was now definite, and Sir Michael Hicks Beach, the Colonial Secretary, made it clear that subject to treaty obligations the British Government held that the fiscal policy of Canada rested with the Dominion Parliament.[2] The last protests in Parliament were made in 1887 concerning an increase in the iron duties. But the matter had now passed into the region of sorrowful comment or friendly bargaining. No one any longer doubted that a self-governing colony controlled its own tariff.

The Australian colonies were aggrieved by the British treaty with the *Zollverein* (1865)[3] and their protest against it in 1871 produced "the first approach towards federal action" in Australia. They claimed the right to enter into arrangements with each other for the reciprocal admission of their respective products either duty free or on such terms as might be agreed upon, that no treaty made by the Imperial Government should restrict this right, and that imperial interference with intercolonial fiscal legislation should absolutely

---

[1] Porrett, E., *Sixty Years of Protection in Canada*, p. 286.
[2] *Ibid.* pp. 358–9.
[3] This treaty "made it impossible for colonial legislatures to favour British exporters by a policy of differential tariffs". Hancock, W. K., *Survey of British Commonwealth Affairs*, II, 77.

cease. The Home Government accepted this protest and in 1873 a Bill was passed to give effect to the wishes of the colonies. Lord Kimberley, the Colonial Secretary, thought "we should assume that the colonies knew their own business better than we knew it". Lord Carnarvon commented on the fallibility of modern prophecy, "which had predicted that free trade and the non-imposition of differential duties would be the chief features of colonial policy"; our Australian colonies, "with the most democratic form of government, utterly repudiated both doctrines".[1]

In the matter too of commercial relations with foreign states the self-governing colonies were passing out of their position of dependence. In the 'eighties the Home Government departed from its former practice and in most commercial treaties reserved to them and to India the right to adhere to the treaty, or not, as they pleased, and at times invited representatives of colonies to take part in the discussion in an advisory capacity.[2] In 1889, in answer to a question, the Under Secretary of State for the Colonies explained the position as follows: "It has been the practice for the Imperial Government alone to conclude treaties of commerce with foreign powers, but on special occasions the representatives of the colonies have been consulted or admitted to take part in the negotiations."[3] In 1893 the last restrictions were removed and Great Britain agreed to the general extension of the principle of preference. Lord Ripon, in a circular dispatch of June 1895,[4] explained the position that had been reached as regards the negotiation of commercial treaties for the colonies. The British representative, assisted when necessary by a representative of the colony concerned, would conduct the negotiations and any tariff concessions made to a foreign power should be extended to the United Kingdom and other parts of the Empire, and the terms obtained should not be to the disadvantage of any other part of the Empire. To this extent Great Britain upheld the economic unity of the Empire; for the rest the colony formed its own policy.

Thus the tariff policy of the Empire exhibited no unity. The mother country had a tariff for revenue; the policy of the Crown colonies was determined by her and followed the same principle, though they raised a larger proportion of their revenue by this means; India, too, had to fall into line. But in the self-governing colonies British example and influence counted for little. In newly-settled and sparsely-peopled countries the tariff is the simplest way of raising revenue and in most of them the old revenue tariffs had grown into protective tariffs, adjusted to what each country thought its own interest, and increasingly used for fostering infant industries. It was clear that the bonds of

---

[1] Cf. *C.H.B.E.* VII, 413; Page, W., *Commerce and Industry*, I, p. 291.
[2] Fuchs, C. J., *Trade Policy of Great Britain and her Colonies* (1908 ed.), p. 335.
[3] Page, *op. cit.* p. 310.
[4] Printed in Keith, A. B., *Speeches and Documents on British Colonial Policy*, II, 156–64.

the British Empire were not to be found in commercial policy. On the one hand, the former British protective system had not been shaped into an imperial *Zollverein*; British free-traders had rejected even so small a barrier to free trade as imperial preference. On the other hand, the colonies would not allow British regulation of their commercial policies; if they thought it their interest they would keep out British manufactures. In their view, not by serving Britain's economic interests, but by developing their own industries and making themselves strong, they best contributed to the power and greatness of the Empire. Canada, too, could feel that she had spent an immense sum on building the Canadian Pacific Railway, which was a great service to the Empire as a whole. Moreover, her trade policy was a good deal influenced by her geographical situation. American duties affected both the West Indies and Canada, and inclined them to special arrangements with the United States, while the isolated Australian colonies were more free to frame theirs according to their sense of their own needs. Diverse policies and interests meant that in all negotiations with other countries the Empire lacked unity and a single voice. While the United States had made itself into a mighty economic unity, as an economic unity the British Empire did not exist.

Nor was there an imperial financial policy. Britain determined and Britain bore the expenses of Empire. Of these the chief was defence. The recall of our troops from the colonies and the defeat of France in 1870–1 were expected to make possible considerable economies in both Army and Navy. But what did a world-wide Empire and a world-wide trade require for their defence? On this question different views were taken by the Prime Minister and his First Lord of the Admiralty, Mr Goschen. Gladstone asked for a reduction in the estimates (September 1871) and Goschen put the situation as the Admiralty saw it: "I do not think the public in any given direction is prepared to be content with less naval force. On the contrary demands are being made for more ships in every quarter. Take the case of the East African Slave Trade...the Committee were breast high for more ships notwithstanding my expenditure. It will be the same with the Polynesian Slave Trade, as it is called. More attention is being paid to that quarter than before, and in those vast regions, one or two ships do not go very far. On the American stations there may be some reduction possible...as regards our great fighting ships I think we may go very slowly." The estimates he continued, can only be reduced by building fewer ships, "and we can only afford to build fewer ships if we make up our minds to reduce our squadrons, and to undertake less duties in every part of the world.... The fact is half our expenditure is not for war service in the strict sense, but for keeping the police of the seas and protecting commerce during times of peace, and for carrying out our views as to

protecting semi-barbarous and barbarous men against kidnapping
and various forms of outrage. Philanthropy decidedly costs money."[1]
It was to be a recurring problem. The dissolution of 1874 was primarily due to difference of opinion between the Prime Minister and
at least two of his principal colleagues as to the provision to be made
for Army and Navy in the estimates of 1874–5. Nor was it confined
to Liberal governments. The same issue, the service estimates, brought
Lord Salisbury into conflict with Lord Randolph Churchill a decade
later. A far-flung empire has interests and risks in so many quarters
that it cannot foresee and define its dangers or afford to be caught in a
state of unpreparedness.

But though economy was the watchword of Gladstonian finance,
empire remained expensive. Before the Abyssinian War had been
paid for, the cost of the Red River expeditions had to be met (1870–1).
In 1873–4 our expenditure included a small sum for an Ashanti
War and a further sum (£105,000) for an expedition to help the
Sultan of Zanzibar suppress slavery and the slave trade in his
dominions—it was the year of Livingstone's death. The annexation
of Fiji in 1874 cost £40,000, including 18s. for repairing the club of
the late sovereign of the islands in order that it should be in a fit state
for presentation to the Queen. These small sums grew into larger ones
when more serious issues confronted the Disraeli administration. In
1875 £4 millions were secured by terminable annuities for the purchase of the Suez Canal shares, but this proved to be a profitable
investment, apart from its wider significance, economic and political.
On the occasion of the Prince of Wales's visit to India in 1875–6,
£60,000 was assigned for personal expenses. "A Prince of Wales",
wrote Disraeli, "must not move in India in a mesquin manner."
"The simplicity of arrangements which might suit a visit to our
fellow-subjects in the Colonies would not be appropriate in India
where visits must be arranged to ruling princes and presents exchanged."[2] In 1877 another Kaffir war (Transkei) began, which
was to cost £¾ million, and in April 1878 the same sum was expended
in bringing a contingent of Indian troops to Malta as an indication
to Russia of our reserves of military strength. This was only a part of
the expenditure on military preparations which the uncertain state of
Anglo-Russian relations involved. The Balkan question always excited
apprehension about the security of the Mediterranean route to India.
The year 1874 had opened with a surplus of £5½ millions; 1878 opened
with a deficit of the same amount. In the next two years troubles
multiplied in South Africa and India—in South Africa, the Zulu War,
two other small Kaffir wars and the occupation of the Transvaal; in
India, the Second Afghan War. Towards the latter, it was proposed
at first to make India a loan of £2 millions for seven years, free of

[1] Elliott, A. D., *Life of Lord Goschen*, I, 115–18.
[2] Buckle, G. E., *Life of Benjamin Disraeli*, v, 428.

interest; but before the war ended, it had cost £23½ millions, of which India paid about £18½ millions and Great Britain £5 millions. For the Zulu and Kaffir wars of 1878–9 a further £5½ millions had to be found, and, by 1880, Cyprus, acquired in the 1878 settlement, had become an expense. Thus the new Gladstone administration inherited unsolved problems and costly obligations for the protection and extension of imperial interests. Events in Egypt had led on to the Dual Control of Egyptian finance and then to war, and events in South Africa to war in the Transvaal. Meanwhile, the cost of the foreign and colonial services which fell on the British taxpayer had steadily mounted. Whether Liberal or Conservative Governments were in power, the protection of imperial interests had become an increasing financial burden.

With free trade and colonial self-government, and with the mother country controlling foreign policy, governing the dependencies and bearing the cost of imperial defence, the British Empire seemed in mid-Victorian days to have reached its natural goal. The relations established between the self-governing members left each free to adopt the policy best calculated in its own judgment to further its own well-being. There was no conception of the well-being of the whole save as the sum of the parts. Their economic relations, though influenced by political, racial and cultural connections within the Empire, were left to be governed by the same forces as governed economic relations with foreign states, following the natural order created by each pursuing its own interest. Imperial trade policy was merged in the general system of free trade. The volume and character of trade between the different members of the Empire were no longer important as indexes of the virtue of the system, for that rested on the assumption that each community was the best judge of its own interests and would direct its trade accordingly to the best of its ability. What would be important was whether all were prospering under the new order as well as they had under the old.

What had been realised was not of course Adam Smith's ideal. He wished perfect free trade within the bounds of the Empire at least, if it could not be achieved for the whole world—not the freedom of each part to follow its own commercial policy. And no less had he contemplated the political unity of the Empire, with its common Parliament, imperial revenue and system of defence—an equality of status, burden and opportunity. But, apart from other considerations, his idea of a vast internal market, ringed by a common customs union, was not attractive to the mother country when colonial trade was small, nor to the colonies when national feeling was born and diversity of development and conditions militated against unity of policy. Free trade had not meant to Great Britain that no customs duties should be levied. Such duties always provided a substantial part of her national revenue. But they were not an instrument of commercial policy and some were deliberately offset by corresponding excise duties.

There is thus no history of the economic development of the Empire as a whole, but only of each part, and of the manner in which each part was affected in its economic life by its membership of the Empire. But the nature of the general history was influenced by the absence of a common economic policy and conception of the economic unity of the whole. It is inconceivable that defence could have been so much left to the mother country, or political ties become so loose, or the colonies remained voiceless in foreign affairs for so long, if there had been a common economic policy and goal. On the other hand, the Empire might have been less acceptable to the world. The stronger it had become, the stronger it would have needed to be. Its free policy to some extent disarmed opposition, till it was carried to the point at which it invited attack. Free trade was in fact more than a commercial policy; it was part of a social philosophy, and a principle of political wisdom in foreign relations, intended to relieve us from the envy of less well situated nations, and constituting us guardians, as did also our naval power, of free and peaceful processes of oversea trade. Moreover, since we sought no exclusive positions, we had no desire for further annexations. The purchase of Elmina on the Gold Coast from the Dutch in 1872 was favoured in the House of Commons only because it would tend to check the slave trade. The possibility of its commercial development by the West African merchants had little influence on the debate; and, similarly, when the annexation of Fiji was discussed in 1873, Gladstone, confident in the virtue of tree trade, "could afford to say he did not feel the great pressure of the argument for securing guarantees for our commerce in the distant islands of the world".[1]

There could be no doubt of the progress made by our great colonies under this system, but what of the dependencies and of India? When it became clear that other countries intended to build up their industries, ought we to have looked after the industrial growth of the dependent parts of the Empire? It would have been difficult to give them protection and refuse it to manufacturers at home—for free-trade governments to practise abroad what they denied at home. Moreover, the British idea of Empire had been that the outer parts should send raw materials and take British manufactures, and we had not outgrown it. The dependent ones could be kept to this role, even when the others in turn rejected it. The relation with India was unique, for it rested with the British to initiate and guide the economic transition beginning in an ancient civilisation under the impact of Western ideas and arts, the scope and significance of which was only slowly revealing itself. In various ways principles

[1] Page, *op. cit.* pp. 282–4.

were adapted to circumstances but, on free trade, India always received the pure milk of the word, for no British Government dared surrender free trade to the detriment of our cotton industry. For this reason India's industrial progress was slower than it might have been.

The Crown colonies were not greatly considered in the imperial family. Occupied for a particular purpose and not much valued apart from it, they were left to shift as they could, to find their own place in the industrial economy of a changing world. They had the advantages of peace and order and non-interference, and from our point of view wanted little more. Why force Western energy and competition upon them? The administrators sent out were not the kind of men who would promote economic development, and there were as yet no specialised colonial services. Neither was there much investment in them. All was left to private individuals, who ventured money in colonial schemes if they thought them good. A railway might be built or a harbour deepened, and something provided as charity in a disaster. But the fact that Government did so little meant that the progress of these colonies lagged and in the vast Empire they drifted into a backwater.[1]

As for defence, free trade was a policy conceived in a world in which it was thought that Britain need not be involved in major wars. It could be argued that free trade strengthened her sea power and financial influence and promoted the growth of her wealth, all of which added to her security. That it ignored other vital aspects of the problem of defence in case of widespread war was hardly yet apparent. As for her bearing the whole cost of imperial defence, apart from the political argument that she controlled foreign policy and determined the issues of war and peace, there was the fact that she was richer than her colonies and had abundant capital that they lacked. It seemed not unreasonable that she should defend their trade and coasts. The relative stages of her development and theirs imposed that duty upon her, leaving them to offer such assistance as they could. The case was even stronger in favour of India, for she was poorer than the colonies and her commercial policy was subject to our control and generous to our trade. As expenditure increased and relative prosperity changed, the right distribution of the burden might become a different question.

Thus over a large part of the Empire economic relations, like political relations, were no longer determined by authority, but by tradition, habit and interest. Yet they were seen to be more than commercial. Attention was called to the colonies as a field for surplus population, for investment, for the employment of trained ability and

---

[1] Dilke, however, in 1889, wrote: "It is a mistake to suppose that our tropical Colonies are in a condition of decline. They hold a secondary place in our attention because of the immense development of Canadian and Australian interests; but they are on the whole fairly prosperous and progressive." *Problems of Greater Britain*, II, 222.

of shipping, and more and more were they valued as a cause of British power and influence in the world. And the trade advantages were not negligible, if not secured by legislative enactment. The greater mutual knowledge and confidence, existing contacts, the absence of a language difficulty, some common tastes, practices and institutions which the extension of British life and manners had spread —such factors increased commercial exchanges and created other economic relations. The lack of an imperial economic policy did nothing to promote a separatist movement. There were few bonds to chafe and strain against. Each took the advantages that the situation gave and the argument for the Empire shifted from material or at least from trade considerations to the defence of common interests, traditions and civilisation. The ties were to be looked for in the same hopes and purposes, in likeness of character, in the will to defend and preserve what all valued in the British achievement.

We may now consider how in fact the economic relations of the members of the Empire changed and developed in this period—the extent of the migration of men and of capital within the Empire, the improvement of means of communication, the place and importance of imperial trade within the general pattern of British trade, and the changing position of Great Britain and her consequent changing attitude to some of the economic problems of the Empire. During these years, though some single events, such as the opening of the Suez Canal, are of cardinal importance in imperial economic history, changes were gradual, and tendencies have more significance than events as an index and measure of the shifting attitude and emphasis in matters of imperial policy.

Emigration had diminished in volume since the middle years of the century, and though during the great depression there was a considerable outflow—in 1883 the number of emigrants exceeded 320,000—in the 'nineties the number declined again. The annual average for each quinquennium in this period was as follows:

1870–4	206,275	1885–9	251,151
1875–9	124,503	1890–4	203,302*
1880–4	262,441		

* 'British and foreign trade and Industry', Statistical Tables. *Parl. Pap.* 1903, xxxi [Cd. 1761], p. 402.

The emigrants went where employment and opportunity awaited them: not for the most part within the Empire. Adderley in his discussion of emigration in 1869 asked why the United States could get emigrants and British colonies were failing to do so. Britain had ended the transportation of criminals and the shipping of paupers overseas and he wished to see a free and natural movement of population between England and the colonies. Free and natural the movement had become, but there was little between England and the colonies. Some ill savour from the past still tainted emigration to the colonies, and the shorter distance and far larger range of opportunity weighted the scales in favour of the United States. He thought "our old system of local settlements and poor law, the stagnating effects of which are still uneradicated", was one obstacle to freer movement, and the common ignorance of the colonies another. "More knowledge about the colonies might be given in our primary schools, whose geography was till lately restricted to the Holy Land." He urged a more active policy. The Emigration Commissioners should "come out of their long hiding place in Park Street and be part of the Colonial Ministry, nothing being more essentially a part of the work of that Department than the superintendence, advertisement and agency of emigration"—the ghost of systematic colonisation lingered in the words. Assisted emigration, he recognised, was now out of fashion, but some assistance he thought desirable, separated, however, from poor rates. "There must be no smell of police or pauperism about it." Families should go out, and the most enterprising—not "shiploads of 'females' to follow a riddance of 'males'". The new policy should be inaugurated with a large vote of public money, followed by an annual vote of moderate amount and arrangements should be entered into with the colonies. The idea of emigration should not be deprecated lest emigrants be prejudiced in the eyes of the colonies. At the least the Government ought to remove all obstacles and to bring about the right conditions on each side for the natural flow of people.[1]

Adderley's sensible discussion of the matter reveals the discredit into which emigration had drifted and the indifference with which it was regarded in the heyday of *laissez-faire*. The work of the Colonial Land and Emigration Commissioners continued to diminish and in 1872 their remaining functions were transferred to the Board of Trade. By that time the colonies were beginning to establish their own emigration agencies in the mother country. For a time the Home Government took little, if any, interest in emigration, and the movement of men, like the movement of goods, was left to take its own course. As steam displaced sail, some old abuses in the emigrant trade disappeared, and emigrants travelled in comparative comfort. This had happened in the Atlantic traffic by 1870, and somewhat later in the Australasian.

The agricultural troubles and the great depression in industry and trade in the early 'eighties drew attention again to emigration as a remedy for unemployment. In 1880 Ireland was suffering from the failure of the potato harvest and the Irish Government set up Emigration Boards and gave grants-in-aid to assist the emigration of necessi-

[1] Adderley, Sir C. B., *Review of The Colonial Policy of Lord J. Russell's Administration*, pp. 405–16.

tous persons. In England the Government was disinclined to act, holding that private enterprise could do all that was required, that distress was local, and that no general action was called for. On a resolution that a judicious system of State-aided emigration to the colonies is both just and politic the House was counted out. However, in 1885 an Emigrants Information Bureau was set up in connection with the Colonial Office to advise intending emigrants on the choice of a destination.

That there was so little flow to the colonies was still chiefly due to the superior attractions—the expanding industries and free home-steads, of the United States. Canada and Australasia alone could compete, and not till late in the century were the western prairies of Canada coming under settlement and its Government active in filling them. Australia never attracted a large volume of immigration, except during the gold rushes and in the early 'eighties, when the country was prosperous and spending freely on railway building. The nature of Australian resources, chiefly pastoral, offered little opportunity to the man of small means, and between 1873 and 1890 the Australian colonies one by one gave up the policy of State assis-tance to immigrants. In the troubles of the early 'nineties emigration to Australia practically ceased. In South Africa, owing to the presence of a large native population, there was no demand for unskilled labour and this was true also of the dependencies. Each part of the Empire had its own special need and point of view, and in this as in other matters was forming its own policy. The colonies did not want Britain's unemployed and discouraged large emigration schemes. They wanted only good and suitable emigrants. To the British work-man State-aided emigration seemed a means of avoiding just reforms at home, while to the colonies it appeared likely to lower their standard of life.

In the decade 1886–95 the United States in most years took three-quarters of British emigrants; the number going to Canada increased and then declined a little, to Australia and New Zealand declined considerably—from 43,076 in 1886 to 10,567 in 1895; to South Africa, however, where new opportunities were opening, the numbers increased from 3897 in 1886 to 20,234 in 1895.[1]

As the self-governing colonies developed national feeling, they claimed the right to control immigration, and this the Home Govern-ment recognised; though, to avoid trouble with foreign states, the form and method of restriction were modified to meet its views. But the principle remained. No right of free movement within the Empire was inherent in a British subject; South Africa or British Columbia might claim to exclude the native of India, and Canada or Australia to refuse the undesirable Englishman, and the undesirable immigrant might include those without means or workmen under

---

[1] Page, *op. cit.* II, table 5, p. 31.

contract. This was the reverse side of the social and industrial legislation designed to raise the standard of life in Australia. The wheel
had come full circle. Once Great Britain had selected the classes of
her people whom she thought suitable to send to the colonies, now the
colonies selected the classes of Englishmen whom they thought suitable to receive. In England there was no longer, however, the same
pressure of expanding population. The birth-rate was on the decline.
In 1871–81 it had been 37·87 per thousand, and in 1891–1901 it had
fallen to 31·57. Industry and trade, too, had passed out of the doldrums
and difficulties of the 'eighties and early 'nineties and by 1895 there
was a steady improvement in general conditions.

While the main body of British emigrants came from the classes
known in Victorian days as the working classes, young agricultural
labourers and artisans from the towns, who were induced or obliged
to emigrate by industrial fluctuations or agricultural distress, there
was another kind of emigration of considerable importance. To the
educated and commercial classes the Empire, particularly India and
the dependencies, offered special opportunities of employment
abroad. Government services or the service of business houses and
companies—commercial, industrial, mining and navigational—and
the service of dependent states, attracted a growing number of young
men, some of whom remained to live abroad. Dispersed all over the
Empire, in its ports and towns, in commercial and mining centres,
were these groups, small and large, of British and other foreign
residents, many isolated on plantations and ranches or in forest and
bush. Most of them sent their children "home" to be educated and
to make their career in England: the division of families was a part of
the price of imperialism and widespread foreign trade. In the larger
communities of civil servants, traders and engineers was also a professional element of lawyers, doctors and clergymen. The Englishman abroad largely lived his own life, imported some of his own food
and drinks and clothing, maintained his own standards, and generally
mixed little and interested himself little in the social life of the people
around him. He was there for a political or economic purpose, and
in that he gave good value, but his leave and retirement and pension
he looked to spend at home. In many parts of the Empire, too, often
as pioneers, and seldom happily integrated in these close social groups,
were the representatives of the missionary societies. The opportunities
of employment which the dependent Empire and India offered to
our upper middle class, business and professional, were thus of
substantial economic importance and were regarded with growing
envy by Germany when she began to cherish ambitions for colonial
expansion. Of higher social status were the Governors of colonies,
usually recruited from the aristocracy, or eminent politicians or
distinguished soldiers, though occasionally a Governor had risen
from the ranks. Nor should we ignore the economic importance of

pioneers and adventurers of many sorts, "a legion that never was listed", *coureurs des bois* of the Victorian Empire, who all about the world had a part in "breaking the road for the rest".

The development of the tropical parts of the Empire stimulated other migrations of labour. Indians still went to the sugar plantations of Mauritius and the cinchona and tea plantations of Ceylon, the sugar, fruit and cocoa plantations of the West Indies and British Guiana, and since 1860, to the sub-tropical districts of Natal. The Chinese were flowing into Malaya and British North Borneo, and the sugar planters of Queensland were recruiting Polynesian labourers. In some of the colonies new and useful elements were thus added to the population, but in the European self-governing colonies social and political questions soon appeared. So the problem of Asiatic immigration arose in various forms in Natal, British Columbia and Australia.

Adam Smith said of the European colonies of his day that they owed little to Europe save as *magna virum mater*, but the British colonies in the Victorian age, and most other countries of the Empire, owed to Great Britain also that she provided a stream of capital for their development, which they could have got from no other source on the same terms at the time. The advantage was mutual, but it was of cardinal importance to the colonies at this stage of their growth. They were fortunate in their mother country—in her wealth, her temper and her financial experience, and the loan of her capital had more influence on their fortunes in this period than the coming of her emigrants. In this lending there was no financial imperialism, but mutual confidence and the hope of profit.

From about 1850 Great Britain had begun to invest heavily abroad. Her exports of goods and services generally paid for her imports and she had the interest on her capital for fresh investment. In the years 1873–8, with depression of trade and the rise of new industrial competitors, there was less demand for British goods, and in 1876–8 disastrous harvests, wars and other causes upset the balance of trade and checked oversea investment. With the 'eighties it was resumed, to rise to a peak of £80 millions in 1890. In this busy decade joint-stock issues and the underwriting of loans overseas went forward briskly. The acceptance of liability by the underwriting firms stimulated the process. In all this the house of Baring was prominent; it was one of their traditional activities. From 1881 for thirty years the fresh investment abroad almost equalled the yield of foreign investments, the total of which in 1885 Sir Robert Giffen estimated at £1,302 millions, and which was to reach £1698 millions in 1893 and nearly £4000 millions by 1914.

Overseas investments by no means exclusively followed the flag. "English capital", as Bagehot wrote, "is by far the most locomotive of all capitals.'' So far as enterprise was free, men, goods and money went to those who offered the most for their services. In the early 'seventies foreign loans, good, bad and indifferent, were greedily subscribed for without discrimination and without hesitation. A good deal was lost. In 1875 a Select Committee's enquiries made startling revelations as to the character of many of the loans and the gullibility of the public. From about this time, however, investors manifested an increasing tendency to lend to countries under the British flag. All the great colonies and India were building railways; in South Africa diamond and, later, gold mines were being exploited; in India and Ceylon were tea and coffee plantations, and in Malaya tin mines. New beginnings were being made to develop the tropics to serve the needs of the industrial West. Part of the capital was raised by the colonial governments, much went into private hands. Plantation and mining enterprises were financed by companies floated in England which were playing an increasing part in the development of the Empire.

In earlier days the colonies had been occasionally assisted by imperial guarantees in raising their loans. But by the 'seventies they had discovered that they had credit and could borrow for themselves on the London market, and, as they grew in population, developed their resources and showed the energy of their public life, their credit improved and large sums of money were borrowed by their Governments. In 1889 colonial government securities mainly held in the United Kingdom were put at £98 millions, and Indian government and railway securities at £196 millions.[1] Confederation strengthened the financial position of Canada. But Canadian loans were not as popular as those of some other colonies: the English investor was inclined to associate Canada with a troubled political history. Canadian loans floated between 1874 and 1878 were all 4 or 5 per cents and were only slowly taken up while contemporary Queensland loans were subscribed three times over. Later on, Canadian credit improved and the Canadian Pacific Railway was largely constructed by capital raised on the London market with a Government guarantee. In the later years of the century Canada was borrowing at 4, 3½ or even 3 per cent: more than three-fifths of her debt was in London.

The Australian colonies borrowed for railways and public works of various kinds—telegraph lines, roads, bridges, harbours and water supply, but the railways were by far the most important. Though their debt became considerable in proportion to their population, their credit on the London market greatly improved. Not until 1872 could New South Wales and Victoria borrow at under 5 per cent; in the late 'eighties both colonies floated a 3½ per cent loan above par.[2] In 1892 they were paying 4 per cent. It was fortunate

[1] Clapham, Sir J. H., *An Economic History of Modern Britain*, ii, 238.
[2] *Year Book of the Imperial Institute*, 1894, pp. 538–9.

for Australia that she could borrow in England, for, unlike Canada, she had no alternative market.

In the 'seventies all the Australian colonies followed New Zealand's lead in the issue of inscribed stock instead of debentures chargeable on a particular source of revenue, and Parliament in 1877 provided by a Colonial Stock Act for inscription and transfer in the United Kingdom. Colonial stocks were thus made familiar to the public and easily handled on the London stock market. Later the statutory grant to most of their issues of trustee status made them more marketable—a concession that proved of great practical service to the countries of the Empire.

It is interesting to observe the rate of growth and amount of their public debt as shown in the following table (in £ millions):[1]

	1870	1880	1890
India	108·1	160·3	192·6
Ceylon	0·7	1·3	2·5
Mauritius	1·1	0·8	0·7
Australia	28·3	59·3	143·4
New Zealand	7·8	28·5	38·8
Cape	1·1	11·3	23·7
Canada	21·4	31·4	58·7
West Indies	0·9	1·3	2·8
Natal	–	1·6	5·0
Totals	169·4	295·8	468·2

In 1870 the Indian Government had borrowed more than all the rest of the Empire put together and it remained the largest borrower till 1880, when the Australian colonies took its place. In the 'eighties an immense stream of capital was flowing into Australia. The banks, finance and trading companies and building societies were all borrowing as well as the colonial Governments, and more was supplied than could find employment through normal banking operations. After the financial crisis of 1893 British investment slowed down for a time.

The list of colonial securities showed few stocks issued in the Crown colonies. British Guiana, Fiji, Jamaica, Mauritius and Trinidad appear in it. Jamaica had a million 4 per cent inscribed stock standing at 109. Both Jamaica and Demarara had railway stocks. Except for Port Louis, whose 5 per cents stood at 99, the Corporation Bonds were all of towns in the self-governing colonies. The West African settlements, reluctantly held, struggled, with the aid of advances and loans, towards solvency. They were the Cinderellas of the Empire. In the early 'nineties there were signs of improvement, and the Gold Coast began to borrow for the construction of railways and harbours. Private enterprise was not attracted and had turned

[1] From the *Statistical Abstract for the Several Colonial and Other Possessions of the United Kingdom*.

away too from the West Indies to the new developments in Africa and Malaya. Colonial Stock Acts 1877–1900 did not apply to the Protectorates.

In the issue and management of their loans India and the colonies were now obtaining the services of the Bank of England. By 1870 the Bank was not merely lending to the India Council, but managing their debts. The Indian business, carried on from the beginning with the East India Company and now with the Secretary of State and the India Council, was always expanding, and from the late 'sixties the colonial business grew rapidly. In developing colonial business the Bank looked for a Treasury guarantee. In 1864 it had declined to lend New Zealand £500,000 or any part of it, but in 1866 it agreed to take New Zealand guaranteed bonds. In 1871 a financial concession was made to those Crown colonies which kept accounts with the Bank: they might be given short-term advances without depositing the additional security hitherto demanded. Further steps followed— in 1875 the Bank undertook the management of the New Zealand debt inscribed in the books of the Bank, and the next year the management of the public debt of Queensland. Thus "the era of colonial management", under which both sides were substantial gainers, had fairly opened. By 1890 the Bank was earning a substantial income from this source—over £21,000 from India, and nearly as much from the colonies, and, in addition, a windfall of £11,000 from a Queensland issue. So far had the Bank's functions developed in this respect that, when in 1885 the Government issued the English portion of the Egyptian loan of that year through the House of Rothschild instead of through the Bank, the Bank made a courteous protest. As it normally issued for India and the colonies, it felt almost a right to issue for this new sphere of British influence.[1]

The growing financial business with the colonies was reflected in the London banking world. By 1870 the old sixty or seventy London banks of all sorts had grown to more than 120, mainly by the arrival of some forty imperial and overseas companies.

The prevailing method of incorporation was now under the Companies Act. New banks like the National Bank of New Zealand and the Bank of Africa in the 'seventies sought limited liability by this means. Changes in the scope and technique of overseas banking business in general were making the restrictions of a charter irksome, and unless they had compensating advantages, the old banks found themselves outdistanced by newer institutions. The time had passed when a Royal Charter was necessary to attract capital to difficult enterprises and to ensure effective public scrutiny of a bank's affairs, while the supervisory arrangements involved trouble and responsibility for the government departments concerned, of which they wished to be relieved. Some of the old chartered banks were rein-

[1] Clapham, Sir J. H., *The Bank of England*, II, 301–2, 305, 316.

corporated under the Companies Act, and in 1890 the Government provided for the remodelling of the charters of the chartered banks in such a way as to relieve the Treasury from any responsibility for their management; the banks retained most of the advantages of their privileged status and were set free from most of its drawbacks. In spite of the difficulty of organising and controlling a series of branch banks from a centre thousands of miles away, and the difference between colonial and English banking problems, the imperial banks had done good work. At the same time, as national feeling grew, the colonies naturally wanted permanent banks of their own—native institutions, and not foreign institutions managed in London. One special difficulty of the overseas banks was the danger of pressure at one point reacting unfavourably on the whole concern, and the Australian crisis of 1893 had also illustrated the consequences of too close a financial integration between the mother country and the colonies. But the only considerable failure of an imperial bank in this period, that of the Oriental Banking Corporation in 1892, was due to a series of misfortunes and not to difficulties of organisation.

London was the centre of Empire banking and the Bank of England the only reserve bank of the Empire. Most of the Empire banks kept considerable sterling assets in London to enable them to draw gold if necessary. They wished also to attract English deposits and to make connections with foreign banks, few of which had offices in Empire cities. In 1886 there were twenty-eight colonial joint-stock banks with London offices, the Bank of New South Wales being the largest.[1] The British banks proper did not as yet seek business in the colonies. Australian and South African banking had its external communications in London, Canadian had a second, though less important, centre in New York.

Much of the capital that went abroad in this period was borrowed, as we have seen, for railway construction within the Empire. The length of railway line open in India and the colonies, which, in 1870, scarcely exceeded 8500 miles, had grown to 22,421 in 1880, and to 52,817 in 1895.[2] At the same time there had been a continuous increase in the mileage of telegraph line open and in the extension of shipping services. Thus was woven the network of communications by which the various parts of the Empire were bound together and along which their trade and intercourse were passing in the early 'nineties. A closer unity, material and cultural, was being achieved.

Some of the landmarks may be briefly noticed. In 1870 the direct and independent cable from England to Bombay, and the railway between Calcutta and Bombay were completed; in 1872 London and Adelaide were brought into telegraphic communication; in 1876 the Intercolonial Railway from Halifax to Quebec was opened and

---

[1] Clapham, *Economic History of Modern Britain*, II, 349, footnote 2.   [2] *Statistical Abstract*.

the cable between Sydney and Wellington was laid; in the early 'eighties an all-British route across the Atlantic, Canada and the Pacific was first mooted; in 1885 Canada was crossed by the Canadian Pacific Railway and in 1887 steamer traffic was active between Vancouver and Hong Kong; in 1889 the first trains ran from Adelaide through Melbourne and Sydney to Brisbane; in 1891 the railway was carried from Kimberley to Mafeking and the telegraph from Cape Town to Fort Salisbury.

The Colonial Conferences interested themselves in imperial communications. The Australasian and Pacific mail services, telegraphic communication with Australia and a proposal for an Imperial Penny Post were all discusseed at the Conference of 1887;[1] and at Ottawa, in 1894, resolutions were passed urging the establishment of a mail service between Great Britain and Australasia via Canada, and the connection of Canada and Australasia by a cable under British control. Defence of our possessions or of the trade routes, though not entirely ignored, was only a secondary motive in the improvement of means of communication in this period.

The most important single factor in the quickening and cheapening of transport between the various countries of the Empire was the increasing use of the Suez Canal. More and more it became the great highway of British traffic to India, Burma, Australasia and the Far East. In 1892-3 almost 70 per cent of India's total trade passed through the Canal—a decade earlier the proportion was 50 per cent. So great were its advantages that nearly 90 per cent of the trade that could use the Canal passed by that route. It shortened the voyage to India by 5600 miles; from London to Bombay the journey now took about 24 days and via rail to Brindisi a week less. Numerous lines of steamers, of which the chief was the Peninsular and Oriental, ran between the United Kingdom and the chief ports of India—Bombay, Karachi, Madras and Calcutta, calling at Gibraltar, Valetta and Aden, the main coaling stations on the route. Direct steam communication with Burma was opened in 1871-2 when three steamers from Glasgow arrived in Rangoon by way of the Canal. In 1889 another line opened a regular service between Liverpool and Rangoon, and by the end of the century practically the whole trade of Burma, export and import, was using the Canal.[2] Meanwhile, millions of money were spent in building ships suitable for its navigation, and British interest in its management and tolls grew increasingly and far exceeded that of all the world besides.

In November 1875 Britain purchased the Khedive's interest in the Canal and thus acquired two-fifths of the Company's shares and predominant influence in its management. Her object was to prevent

---

[1] Britain was slower than some other countries to reduce the postal rates to India and the colonies, but in 1890 a uniform colonial and Indian postage rate of 2½d. per half ounce was fixed.   [2] Furnivall, J. S., *Colonial Policy and Practice*, p. 79.

the French from holding them. The step was popular in England for the security it gave to great and growing interests: Egypt had become "the half-way station between Southampton and Bombay", as Cape Town had been. The purchase led on to active interference in Egyptian finance, and that to other consequences—the Dual Control, the occupation of Egypt and the Anglo-Egyptian conquest of the Sudan. Once the Canal had been cut and a vital imperial interest created, Britain was unlikely to draw back from the measures necessary for its protection.

The opening of the Canal tended to lessen our entrepôt trade in Oriental goods. The extension of Continental railways favoured direct dealings with the East by places in easy communication with Mediterranean ports, though shipping and financial facilities enabled Britain to hold some of her ground. Dealings in wool and other raw materials, for which London had been the world's market, tended inevitably to be diffused over many markets. "But the richness and variety of British demands for the finer products; the unrivalled specialisation, promptitude, and directness of action of her merchants and brokers; the ease and elasticity of her banking system; and the consequent preference for a bill on London over a bill on any other place, have tended to strengthen the re-export trade of London."[1]

Gibraltar, Valetta, Port Said and Aden were coaling stations and ports of call on the route. From 1892 fewer steamships coaled at Valetta, for many were being built with triple-expansion engines and a greater capacity for fuel for long voyages. At Gibraltar and Port Said, goods to and from Mediterranean and Black Sea ports could be trans-shipped, and, at Aden, goods to and from East Africa. Gibraltar, though not a mercantile town, was the entrepôt for a considerable trade between the United Kingdom and North Africa: in 1892 through railway and shipping communication with England was established.

All European and Northern Atlantic lines running to East Africa and the Far East, and most of those to Australia and New Zealand, made use of the Canal. On the Eastern route Colombo was an important coaling station and entrepôt; here the lines diverged either to the Far East or to Australia. Between 1874 and 1885 considerable works were carried out for the improvement of the harbour. Further east, Singapore was another great centre of sea communications. Over fifty lines of sea-going steamers—from the Far East, the Dutch possessions, Australia, India and Europe—touched at the port, which had exceptional advantages in the size and safety of its harbour. Hong Kong, like Colombo and Singapore, immensely increased its trade after the opening of the Canal. Its shipping cleared in 1892 exceeded that of Liverpool and almost equalled that of London. Favoured by its situation, and as a free port, it had become a great distributing centre for the trade of Southern China.

[1] Marshall, A., *Money, Credit and Commerce*, p. 126.

The Peninsular and Oriental and the Orient lines connected the United Kingdom and the Mediterranean countries with Australia. Steamers ran to Sydney in forty-two days, while the mails via Brindisi and Adelaide arrived in thirty-eight. Australia, as an exporter of food and raw materials to the industrial countries of Europe, depended on the development of ocean communications. It was a long distance from its market, but it had a large choice of routes. A new line, the Austral Canadian, just established in 1894, ran between Sydney and Vancouver, calling at Suva and Honolulu, and making the passage in twenty-one days, but at first found little business.

Trade between New Zealand and the United Kingdom had formerly gone through Melbourne and Sydney, but, as communications improved, most of the trade went direct. The first steamer lines followed the tracks of the sailing ships of the Shaw Savill Company and the New Zealand Shipping Company (established 1873), going out via the Cape and crossing the southern ocean to Wellington and other New Zealand ports. Homeward bound they ran with the westerlies to Cape Horn and then via Monte Video or Rio de Janeiro to Teneriffe. This was called the Blue Water route. Both Companies went into steam in 1883, and the following year the Shaw Savill Company's *Victory* steamed from London to Port Chalmers in fifty-six days, sighting land only once.[1] In 1893 the average time occupied was from forty to forty-five days. The Union Steamship Company, established 1875, ran a service to San Francisco and by that route the mails took from thirty-five to thirty-eight days.

The Fiji Islands were in regular steam communication with Sydney and New Zealand, and a sailing vessel, subsidised by the Imperial Government, visited Norfolk Island every three months.

Four leading lines of steamers—the Allan, Dominion, Furness and Beaver—ran between the United Kingdom and Canada, and when the Canadian Pacific Railway was completed, a western route to the East was opened. In September 1891 the mails from Yokohama were landed in London within twenty-one days—the average time by Suez was about forty.[2] The Canadian route to the East had become an important alternative to Suez—quicker for Japan, Shanghai, Hong Kong and New Zealand, and about the same for Sydney.

The Union Steamship and Castle Mail Packet Companies maintained a weekly service to the Cape of Good Hope and Natal, the journey to Cape Town taking from fifteen to twenty days. The Cape steamers called monthly at Ascension Island, important as a coaling station, and more frequently at St Helena; but St Helena, once a regular port of call for vessels in the eastern trade, had lost its commercial significance with the opening of the Red Sea route. Cable

---

[1] Lawson, W., *Pacific Steamers*, pp. 214–16.
[2] *Year Book of the Imperial Institute*, 1894, pp. 307 *seqq.*

communication between England and the Cape and Natal was by way of Zanzibar and Aden. Cape Town and Durban were coaling stations and, having connections with Australia and East Africa, still held an important position on ocean routes, though most of the Indian and Far Eastern trade went through the Suez Canal.

With West Africa communications were maintained by the Liverpool mail steamers of the African Steamship Company and the British and African Steam Navigation Company, which called at the Gambia, at Freetown, a coaling station and the only safe and convenient harbour for several hundred miles along the coast, the Gold Coast, where goods and passengers were landed in surf boats, and Lagos, which was about twenty-six days journey from Liverpool and had a safe harbour and good access to the interior by water. The Gambia also had regular communication, via Dakar, with Bordeaux; and the Gold Coast and Lagos with Hamburg. The West African settlements had no railways or internal telegraphs, but all were in cable communication with each other and with Europe. To the West Indies Royal Mail steamers ran fortnightly from Southampton; other lines ran from Liverpool and Glasgow. Bermuda, an important naval station situated midway between Halifax and the West Indies, was on none of the great Atlantic routes. Its trade was chiefly with New York and its mails went via New York; its telegraphic communication with England was via Halifax. Mauritius, for its external communications, was mainly dependent on the steamers of the Messageries Maritimes. The Castle Line had a service from Durban, and the British India Steam Navigation Company from Colombo. The Falkland Islands, occupied in 1833 for the protection of our interests in the whale fishery, had mail communication with Europe twelve times a year by the steamers of the German "Kosmos" Company which called on the voyage to and from Callao. The voyage between Stanley and London occupied four weeks. Cable communication was by way of Monte Video.

The steamship had steadily ousted the sailing vessel. By 1875 the steamer had a practical monopoly of mails, passengers and fine cargo on all routes except the Australasian.[1] Sailing vessels carried by far the largest proportion of goods traffic in the Indian and Australasian trade. Much of India's produce was cargo of lower grade—rice and jute, which could not afford to pay steamer freights and canal dues. The Suez route did not save nearly so much distance to Australia as to India, and the iron sailing ship still carried the southern wool. In 1891 there were seventy-seven sailing ships in Sydney alone loading wool for the London market.[2] Sailing vessels also carried coal to the Mediterranean, Indian, and Far Eastern bunker stations, and down to 1908 could compete in carriage of low-grade cargoes on long voyages;

[1] Fayle, C. E., *History of World's Shipping Industry*, p. 242.
[2] *Ibid.* p. 245.

it was the tramp steamers, not the liners, that were ousting them from this work. With changing routes of trade and the triumph of the steamship some places ceased to be ports of call, though others developed a new importance as coaling stations, for to feed our immense ocean traffic coal had now to be carried to all parts of the world, and a very large export of coal had grown up from this and other causes—in 1879, 11,703,000 tons, in 1895, 33,101,000.[1]

Between 1880 and 1895 Britain had a greater share of the traffic of the high seas than at any other time in her history.[2] The shipping that entered United Kingdom ports in 1875–7 had been two-thirds British in tonnage, in 1885–7 it was three-quarters. London was the great port, Liverpool, which came second, exceeded London as an exporter of British produce, for cotton goods were a quarter of British exports. The chief South African, South American and West Indian lines were based on Southampton.

By the early 'nineties some forty years had passed since the policy of Huskisson, Peel and Gladstone had freed the colonial trade and brought into being the general system of free trade which governed Britain's economic relations with the world, and it is possible to take a general view of trade relations within the Empire as they had taken shape in these conditions.[3]

Of Britain's total imports of merchandise in 1892, £423,793,882, British possessions supplied £97,766,304 or 23·07 per cent; of her total exports of £291,540,166 they received £81,211,541 or 27·82 per cent. The year was a low one for exports.

Her chief imports were food, raw materials for industries, and manufactured articles. Towards the last category the Empire contributed almost nothing, but, in some foodstuffs and raw materials, its supplies were of the greatest importance. Wheat came in from many countries, according to the various harvests; the United States and Russia were the chief sources, but Britain drew substantial amounts from India and Australia, and, though to a less degree, from Canada also. Bacon and hams, beef (fresh and salted), and preserved meat were imported chiefly from the United States, and butter and margarine chiefly from Denmark, Holland, France and Sweden, but of cheese imports Canada supplied nearly one-half, the United States most of the remainder. India, Ceylon and the British West Indies sent nearly one-third of Britain's coffee, and India and Ceylon between them about three-quarters of her tea. In preserved meat (other than salted) Australia was building up a trade, and of fresh mutton imported into Britain sent nearly one-half—the

---

[1] Page, *op. cit.* II, table 56.
[2] Clapham, *Economic History*, II, 212.
[3] For the particulars which follow, see *Year Book of the Imperial Institute*, 1894, and the annual *Statistical Abstract*.

Argentine about a quarter. Of rice imports, the great bulk came from India. Sugar, refined and unrefined, came almost entirely from foreign countries, though the West Indies, India and Mauritius sent a small part of the unrefined. Australia and British North America had begun to send apples. In wine and tobacco, Empire trade was unimportant.

As regards the raw materials of industry, the United States was the chief source of Britain's cotton supply, though Egypt sent a substantial amount. Indian cotton had fallen to an unimportant place and the efforts to find a fresh source of supply which the American Civil War had stimulated had died away. The hope of introducing cotton cultivation first attracted white planters to Fiji, but, with falling prices, cultivation declined, and Fiji's exports in 1892 were copra, sugar and fruit. India supplied almost all the import of dyes; indigo, the most important of them, reaching annually the value of £1,000,000. Of raw hides, dry, the Empire, particularly India, supplied two-thirds of the British demand; foreign countries almost all the wet. Practically the whole import of jute came from India. Most of the leather (undressed) came from the Empire—chiefly from India, though some from Australia, the United States supplying most of the remainder; the dressed leather was imported from various foreign countries. A small quantity of copper ore was obtained from British South Africa and Australasia, but the main part came from the United States and Spain; Australasia also sent to Britain more than a quarter of her supply of lead—pig and sheet—and more than half her silver ore, and a substantial part of her tin, though the bulk came from the Straits Settlements. Fish oil came from Norway and Newfoundland, palm oil from the West Coast of Africa, cocoanut oil from India and Ceylon. India supplied more than half of the seed cotton and flax or linseed. Raw silk came in a small quantity from India and Hong Kong. Of skins and furs, considerably more than one-half were obtained within the Empire—Australasia, British Africa, British North America and India all contributing. From Australasia came a substantial part of the tallow. Wood and timber were imported from many countries, most of it from Northern Europe—the Empire supply was about a quarter, chiefly from British North America. As for wool, "since 1850–60 the fine Saxon and Silesian merino wools had been finally replaced by those of Australia, New Zealand and South Africa".[1] Australasia was by a long way the chief source of supply; South Africa, which came second, sent as much as came from all foreign countries.

Turning now to British exports, of which the greater part consisted of articles manufactured or partly manufactured, we find the Empire (particularly Australasia and British South Africa) taking about four-fifths of the apparel and shoes; substantially more printed books

[1] Clapham, *Economic History*, II, 224.

(particularly Australasia) than all foreign countries; a very small part of the coal export (that part was taken by India, and places such as Gibraltar, Malta and Aden); about a quarter of the cotton twist and yarn (chiefly India), but of cotton manufactures nearly a half, with India again by far the chief buyer and the self-governing colonies taking little. The Empire took most of the haberdashery and millinery, the great self-governing colonies leading, nearly a half of the hardware and cutlery and, of the iron and steel exports, about one-third. Steam engines were going to many parts of the world (though not to the United States)—the Empire, particularly India, Australia and South Africa, took nearly one-third measured in value; other machinery was still more widely distributed, Empire countries taking about the same proportion. Australasia was the chief buyer of British paper, India came second, and foreign countries took rather less than one-third. Of pickles and confectionery, two-thirds were sold in the Empire; of salt manufactures two-fifths; of spirits five-sixths. Almost all the woollen and worsted yarn went to foreign countries, but of woollen and worsted manufactures the Empire took more than a quarter. Thus, from coal to the finest manufactures the Empire in greater or less degree absorbed the whole range of British produce.[1]

Colonial merchandise figured largely in the re-export trades. Coffee was re-exported to the Continent; jute to France, Germany and Holland; rice to the Spanish West Indies and Brazil; skins, furs and pelts to Germany and the United States; tea to Germany, Holland, the United States and British North America; tin to Germany, Holland and the United States; and wool to these last-named countries and France and Belgium. Of imports of wool (1880–4) more than half was re-exported: it was much the greatest single item in the re-export trade.

Britain's largest trade, imports and exports added together— excluding bullion and specie, was still with the United States of America; then, in order, came France, India, Germany, Australasia, Holland, Belgium, Russia, British North America, Sweden and Norway, Spain, China, British South Africa.

Thus the colonial trade fell into the general picture. We may now look at some of its special features. Trade with British possessions seemed less subject to fluctuation than trade with foreign countries, and in the years 1879–90 its proportion of our total trade, imports, exports and re-exports, showed a slight tendency to increase. The percentage calculated in five-year periods was as follows:[2]

Period	Percentage	Period	Percentage
1871–5	22·7	1886–90	25·8
1876–80	24·6	1891–5	25·2
1881–5	26·3		

[1] Clapham, *Economic History*, II, 229.   [2] Hancock, *op. cit.* p. 81 footnote.

The proportion was to remain at about a quarter down to the eve of the First World War. Clearly it was determined by some factors whose strength did not change much or rapidly.

There was truth in the saying that trade follows the flag, for even under free trade substantial advantages remained to the mother country. A part of British colonial trade has always consisted of articles of food and clothing of familiar use, which British emigrants preferred to have after the home fashion, and the same was true of exports for consumption by British residents in India and other tropical lands. The regular shipping connections and mail services with the colonies favoured the mother country. Also they raised their capital principally from her, and her merchants were more willing to supply their shopkeepers with goods on credit. Those in charge of their railways and other undertakings could place their orders more easily and with more knowledge in the home country. The British company under British management was dominant and gave a great advantage to the British exporter. Then there were the colonial and Indian government purchases through Crown agents resident in London. Some of these advantages were losing their force with time and changing circumstances. As new generations grew up, sentiment and custom were weakened, and, more important, the new countries developed their own industries and could produce many articles for which they had previously looked to the homeland. A mining community might want at first to import almost everything, but soon, by its side, arose industries to meet many of its wants. Thus, though colonial industrialisation was not in general a rapid process, the trade of a new country tended to be elastic and to change in character with changing needs and tastes as the land developed; Britain's demands for its raw material might change less, but she, too, under a free-trade policy, might find other more advantageous sources of supply. Moreover, a new country's demand for goods might be largely for capital expenditure, and such expenditure of necessity comes to an end and the demand ceases. Its capacity, too, to import depends largely on its credit, which, in turn, depends upon its resources and reputation for financial prudence. But the new countries were growing, and this offset the increasing competition of their own industries and of our industrial rivals. Except to the United States of America, our exports tended to expand in volume. But, since 1870, British trade fared better in Africa and Asia than in the United States or Germany, or in markets close to those competitors, and fared best in Empire countries for the reasons given.[1]

In 1896 Chamberlain instituted an enquiry into the progress of foreign competition in trade within the Empire. Apart from India, which still bought its manufactures primarily from Britain, the enquiry showed that foreign competition had substantially increased.

[1] See Marshall, *Money, Credit and Commerce*, pp. 123–6.

The increase in the competitive imports supplied by the foreigner was from 26 per cent in 1884 to 32 per cent in 1895.[1] Part of the increase was due to goods being bought direct from the producing country instead of through London, as, for example, Continental countries were buying their wool direct from Australia, and not in London, and so had to send goods back to Australia, thus increasing their Australian trade; or the colonial importer on his side had learned how to cut out the profit of the London middleman. But foreign countries were tending to increase their share of Empire trade as they too changed and developed a demand for colonial goods.

In trading with the British Empire the United States enjoyed some of the advantages which a common language and tradition gave to the mother country. But its export trade was as yet almost entirely in food and raw materials, while the United Kingdom chiefly exported manufactures. Owing to its proximity the United States was a powerful competitor in Canada and the West Indies, though it was Canadian tariffs more than American competition that restricted British imports. From 1876 to 1893, in every year but three, the volume of Canada's imports from the United States exceeded the volume of its imports from Britain—the latter were for the most part manufactured articles and tea, the former included foodstuffs, raw materials and coal as well as manufactures. On the other hand, Canada's exports, which consisted chiefly of the produce of her lumber industry and farms, e.g. lumber, cheese, wheat and other grains, and cattle, were sent more to the United Kingdom than to the United States. American tariffs affected Canadian trade and stimulated Canadian exports to England.

American competition was felt not only in the West Indies and Canada, as might be expected, but further afield too. American carriages and wagons found their way to the Cape, and American tools and light machines into Australia generally, and agricultural implements into Tasmania. German tools were imported into Victoria and, in New Zealand, American and German musical instruments had almost a monopoly. Though the best goods were said to be British, except for some American machines and tools, the colonist often found that the cheaper article would serve his purpose sufficiently, and everywhere there was some influx of cheap things. This was the door through which the Japanese manufacturer entered the competition for imperial trade, beginning in the Pacific markets, Australia and Hong Kong, and foreshadowing a future competition keener and far more extensive. Between 1885 and 1895 Japan's exports increased by 272 per cent.[2]

For the feeding of Britain the Canadian trade was of increasing importance. Although the United Kingdom still depended primarily

---

[1] See Clapham, *Economic History*, III, 38–40.   [2] Page, *op. cit.* I, 253.

on the United States for its bread, Western Canada was now coming under settlement, and the importance of Canada as a wheat-producing country was becoming apparent. Almost the entire export of cheese and butter was coming to the United Kingdom, and in the twenty years 1874–93 the value of cheese exported was nearly quadrupled. The first direct shipment of live cattle to England was made in 1874, and in 1891 the number exported exceeded 100,000, the value of this export to the United Kingdom exceeding that of any other except cheese. For British industry the most important raw material Canada provided was her lumber. Minerals were as yet unimportant; although Canada's mineral resources were becoming known, want of capital and means of communication still prevented their development.

Australia and New Zealand had as yet no large industries, and nearly a half of their whole trade was with the United Kingdom. Though not quite equal to the trade with British India, it was more than double that with British North America and not far below the trade with Germany and France. The Australasian colonies imported more than they exported, partly because their loans on the London market went out to them in the form of goods. The United Kingdom sent them chiefly manufactures—cottons and woollens, metals and machinery, apparel and leather, and took from them wool, first of all (wool in an average year was nearly 40 per cent of the whole body of their exports), mutton, silver (next to the United States and Mexico, Australia was the greatest silver-producing country), and most of their wheat. Except for such commodities as timber, tea, tobacco, jute and sugar, their imports were chiefly from the United Kingdom. London was still the central market for Australian wools, but the local sales in Melbourne, Sydney and Adelaide were increasing in importance. Between 1887 and 1892 some 40 to 50 per cent of the entire export was purchased locally. The seller gained a quicker market with less risk; the buyer got the wool to his factory six weeks earlier than if he waited for the London sales.

The price of wool had been falling with the improvements of transport and the introduction of refrigeration, which had given an increased value to the carcass. Cold storage and cheap transport united to promote the development of new and mutually advantageous trade. Refrigeration of food had been discussed in the 'sixties and experiments in the freezing of meat were made in New South Wales. In the late 'sixties Australian meat extract and tinned meat began to come into general consumption. But it was not until 2 February 1889 that the *Strathleven* brought a cargo of frozen Australian meat into London docks. The first shipment of frozen meat from New Zealand was made in 1882, and consisted of 450 tons of mutton, which arrived in good condition in London after a voyage of 98 days and was sold at 7½d. per lb. This experiment was made in a sailing ship, but soon most of the large steamers trading with New Zealand were fitted with a refrigerating chamber. By the middle 'eighties the trade was firmly established—in 1886 nearly 30,000 tons of frozen mutton, almost two-thirds of it from New Zealand, was landed at British ports. "Canterbury lamb" had a name in the London market. New South Wales did well with frozen mutton, though not as well as New Zealand, for the carcass of the Merino was lighter than the carcass of the New Zealand crossbred. The problem of temperature was more difficult for chilled meat, and experiments with chilled beef from Australia were not made till 1894 and did not at first succeed. Queensland led the way in exports of frozen and chilled beef, Tasmania in the export of fruit in cold storage, mainly apples, Victoria in the export of refrigerated butter. The first consignment of butter sent to London fetched sixteen pence a pound, and the export to England rose from 1,286,583 pounds in 1890 to 22,139,521 in 1894. "At the end of the nineteenth century it was easier to put Australian food on English tables in perfect preservation than it had been to put French or Irish produce there when Queen Victoria came to the throne."[1] Cheap food was poured into England —butter, cheese, mutton and beef. The pastoral industry was able to increase its output 50 per cent by the export of frozen meat. British industry gained too, for both Australia and America, which was now sending tinned fruits, used solely British tin plate.

In the markets of Cape Colony the United Kingdom had almost a monopoly, both of imports and exports. The Cape was as yet an agricultural colony with little industry. It bought our manufactures and sent us in return diamonds, wool, ostrich feathers, angora hair, skins, copper ore and the gold of the Transvaal. Almost all the shipping clearing its ports was British. Natal exported wool (much of it the produce of the Orange Free State), sugar and hides, chiefly to the United Kingdom, and gold from the Transvaal mines. It imported rice from India, and some manufactures from the United States, but most of its imports came from the United Kingdom.

The commercial prosperity of the whole of the West Coast of Africa was closely bound up with the trade in palm oil, palm kernels and other oil materials. The palm oil was either "hard" oil, used in the manufacture of candles, or "soft" oil for lubricating or soap-making. The best and purest oil came from Lagos and was wanted in the tin-plate manufacture of South Wales. Before the discovery of mineral oils, palm oil had fetched £52 a ton, but the price had fallen heavily and during 1891 the average price in England was £24 to £25. The bulk of the palm oil was sent to the United Kingdom, but large quantities went also to Marseilles, Rotterdam and Hamburg; in 1892 more than half our imports of palm oil came from Lagos.

---

[1] Shaun, E., *An Economic History of Australia*, p. 343. *See also* Clapham, *op. cit.* II, 90–1, III, 186–7.

Next to the palm and its products was the ground nut. Gambia was building up an export of ground nuts, for the most part to France, where the oil extracted was used in the manufacture of soap. The chief centre of the ground-nut crushing trade was Marseilles. An export trade in rubber from the Gold Coast and Sierra Leone was growing up, chiefly with the United Kingdom. At the time Brazil supplied nearly half of Britain's rubber, and the West Coast something like two-fifths of the remainder. The Gold Coast had also begun the cultivation of cocoa, but the dye-woods trade of West Africa had almost entirely disappeared. Gum and resin came from Senegal via France: no steps had been taken to develop this trade in the Gambia. In exchange for these raw materials a substantial quantity of cotton goods were imported, but in 1895 half the produce exported from West Africa was said to be purchased with spirits.[1] "The spirit trade", wrote Lord Lugard, "was a disastrous policy.... Not only was it a foreign manufacture, carried in foreign vessels...but since it supplied German vessels with outward cargoes, it enabled Germany to secure the practical monopoly of the homeward palm-kernel trade. ...The spirit trade was indeed synonymous with German influence in West Africa."[2]

Adderley in 1869 wished the British to withdraw from "these fatal shores" and questioned whether the settlements had done as much to promote as to disturb trade.[3] But within a few years the Ashanti War (1874) provoked a penetration into the interior of Africa and committed the conquerors to a task not purely economic.

Free to buy and sell where she chose, India was increasing her trade with foreign countries—partly because direct trade was taking the place of indirect; but Great Britain continued to supply the major part of her imports. The proportion in percentages of value was as follows:[4]

	United Kingdom	Other parts of British Empire	Foreign countries
Exports			
1870	54	20	26
1890	33	23	44
Imports			
1870	85	6	9
1890	70	15	15

Cotton goods made up the principal part of the imports from Britain; then machinery, railway plant, iron goods, woollens and coal. For iron and steel, Belgium and Germany were becoming

[1] Lugard, Sir F. D., *The Dual Mandate*, p. 598.
[2] *Ibid.* p. 601. [3] Adderley, *op. cit.* pp. 198, 218.
[4] Griffiths, P. J., *The British in India*, p. 194.

serious competitors; the United States and Russia sent the kerosene oil, and China raw silk; German beet sugar was coming in in large quantities in 1890–1, otherwise Mauritius supplied the sugar.

The Government of India encouraged local industry by buying in the markets of the country; of Government stores imported about 50 per cent was railway plant. A special feature of Indian imports was "the predominance of European luxuries for the consumption of the ruling classes, Native and European".[1] With cheap labour, raw material and a market at hand, India had advantages for the development of a cotton industry, and some measure of protection would no doubt have facilitated its establishment. But Lancashire needed the Indian market and strongly opposed any tariff advantage being given to the Indian manufacturer. During the Indian budget debates in the 'seventies vigorous protests were raised against the duties on the import of cotton goods as being directly contrary to the principles of free trade. India was not to be allowed to follow the example of the self-governing colonies, and in deference to England's free-trade views the duties were removed. And when in 1894 the Indian Government, faced with a serious deficit, decided to reimpose the old general duty of 5 per cent on all imports, the Secretary of State refused to sanction the duty on cotton goods, since the duty, though imposed for revenue, would have a slight protective effect. In this connection the defence of India's interests by the Viceroy's Council was the occasion of a constitutional pronouncement of no small significance.[2] The duty was subsequently restored, but with a corresponding excise to put Indian and Lancashire manufacturers on an equal footing. The number of Indian cotton mills, however, grew steadily from 20 in 1872 to 144 in 1894.

For her imports India paid in raw materials—jute, tea, cotton, wheat, oil seeds, hides and skins, dyes and coffee. Little more than half of the export trade was within the Empire. Britain took most of the cotton, chiefly for re-export; 90 per cent of Indian cotton was used on the Continent. Britain also took coffee, a large part of the indigo (though the demand for this was declining in face of the competition of artificial dyes), wheat (the export of which began in the 'seventies after the cutting of the Suez Canal made the export profitable), linseed, a great part of the jute and jute manufactures, and tea in large quantities. Within the Empire also, in Australia and the Straits, the Calcutta factories found an extensive market for gunny bags, which were 90 per cent of the exports of manufactured jute, for packing grain, sugar and wool. Of cotton manufactures, the yarn went to China and Japan, and piece goods to the East Coast of Africa, Ceylon and the Straits. Rice was sent to Egypt, Ceylon, the Straits and Mauritius; opium, chiefly to China, and a small quantity

[1] Marshall, A., *Money, Credit and Commerce*, p. 173.
[2] *Camb. Hist. of India*, VI, 233.

to the Straits. Australia wanted not only gunny bags, but also Indian tea.

A characteristic of Indian trade was the large excess of exports over imports, representing payments which India made in England for interest on loans, for pensions and other liabilities and services. The loans had built up the Indian railway system, and British investments had developed the tea and jute industries. The number of British officers drawing salaries or pensions was never large, nor was the payment for defence—for the British part of the Indian Army in particular—large in relation to the size and needs of the country. Other invisible imports were shipping and financial services. India paid her indebtedness to Britain partly through other countries, exporting to them much more than she received from them, and they doing the same with Britain.

The depreciation of silver caused insecurity in trade with silver-using countries and seriously affected British dealings with India. The Indian Government had to make its payments in London in gold and lost large sums each year on the falling exchange. Many circumstances affected the situation and the use and quantity of gold and silver, but by 1893, when a change of American policy threatened to flood the Indian market with the depreciating metal, the difficulties had become acute and in that year the Indian mints were closed to the free coinage of silver.

India had become a great trading nation, and the character of its trade illustrated its relation to Western industry. Like the new countries, it fed with raw materials and food the industrial life of the Western world. It was clearly destined to become an industrial nation, but in this direction its progress was slow owing to the disposition of the people to look to Government, the disinclination of the educated classes to take up technical occupations, the lack of enterprise of Indian financiers, and the rigidity with which Britain imposed her free-trade principles. As Western industrial methods were introduced and British investors taught India the joint-stock system, the practice of hoarding died down a little and less silver was imported in the 'eighties than in the 'sixties.

The exports of Ceylon were almost exclusively vegetable products—tea, coffee, cinchona, coconut oil, and cinnamon were the chief. The export of coffee reached its peak in 1877, but then rapidly declined owing to the spread of disease. Tea was supplanting coffee, and Indian and Ceylon teas were in 1892 rapidly capturing the English market. In 1888 for the first time their importation exceeded that from China—112·3 million lb. compared with 105·7. Four years later, it was 178 millions and China tea 75—a singularly rapid change of taste, probably due to the lower price. England took almost the whole of the Ceylon tea. Australia, though a large consumer of tea, still got the major part from China, though Indian and Ceylon teas were making rapid headway in 1889–92. England took also most of her coffee and almost all the cinchona bark. Of 106,401 cwt. of cinchona imported into the United Kingdom in 1892, 57,614 came from Ceylon. About 50 per cent of the cinnamon was shipped to the United Kingdom, the remainder to the Continent. The only important mineral export was plumbago or graphite. Half the output went to the United States and the remainder to Europe. The plumbago of Ceylon was of a singularly pure type and Ceylon was our chief source of supply. The United Kingdom, India, Australia, in that order, took most of Ceylon's exports; outside of the Empire the United States and Germany were the principal buyers.

From the United Kingdom Ceylon imported coal in large quantities, for Colombo was an important coaling station, cotton goods, metals, machinery and Government stores, and, for the rest, its imports came chiefly from British India and consisted of rice, specie, paddy, and cotton goods.

Singapore was an entrepôt where the mineral and vegetable products of the Malay Peninsula, the neighbouring Dutch colonies, Siam, Borneo, Labuan and Sarawak were brought for shipment to Europe, and whence the manufactured goods of Europe were distributed in return. The wealth of the Protected States at the time was chiefly in tin; rubber did not reach the plantation stage till the late 'nineties. Borneo was building up an export trade in tobacco; Labuan had been acquired for its coal.

The course of events in the West Indies had continued to illustrate what Lord Grey said: "How little of any true foundation of prosperity had been laid in the era of slavery and of protected monopoly."[1] The staple product of the West Indies had been cane sugar with its products, molasses and rum. The abolition of slavery and the ending of preferences were followed by the competition of the beet-sugar industry of Europe, encouraged as it was by bounties, and the West Indian industry had sunk into depression so deep that except in favourable conditions it seemed threatened with extinction. A Select Committee on the sugar industries appointed in 1879 (styled by one of its members a post-mortem inquest) reported that foreign bounties on the export of sugar had practically extinguished the loaf sugar refining trade in Britain and checked the development of sugar growing in the colonies. They recommended that bounties should be abolished by international agreement and that countervailing duties should be levied on bounty-fed sugar. These, it was argued, would not be inconsistent with free trade, as they offset an artificial advantage. Negotiations in 1881 produced no result, but the matter was revived in 1886, when a Royal Commission considered the depression of trade and industry. That the West Indies suffered there was no doubt. Imports of cane sugar from the British West Indies had

[1] Adderley, op. cit. p. 297.

fallen from 3,500,000 cwt. in 1872 to 2,000,000 cwt. in 1887. But further efforts to secure the removal of the bounties failed. English opinion was divided. Of the many who thought the foreign bounties injurious to England, some objected to countervailing duties even more, and extreme free traders regarded the bounties as a present from foreign taxpayers to British sugar consumers. From 1880 to 1895 the price of sugar fell continuously. The problem was not simply one of bounties, but of increasing competition, now that other countries had taken up the cultivation of sugar, and the remedy for the West Indies lay in improving their own industry and broadening the basis of their production. It was clear that the islands must look to other crops, and after 1886 miscellaneous exports began to form an increasing proportion of West Indian trade. Trinidad was developing its cocoa plantations and the cultivation of cocoa was introduced into Grenada and St Lucia. Arrowroot became an important product in St Vincent, cotton in Antigua, and, in Montserrat, limes. Jamaica had a variety of subsidiary products—tobacco, coffee and dyewoods, and after 1870 built up a considerable fruit trade with the United States.

While nearly half of the imports of the islands came from the United Kingdom, a larger part of their exports went to other countries and increasingly to the United States. The British took from them sugar (unrefined), rum, cocoa, dyewoods, coffee and spices, and sent them in return manufactures, particularly cottons, while the United States and Canada sent them food and timber. British exports did not decrease as much as imports, which in 1895 were only half their value in 1870, and probably West Indian exports to the United States paid for a portion of Britain's American imports in the roundabout of trade.

Barbados imported its foods from the United States, fish and timber from Canada, and manufactures from Britain, and exported its dry sugar to Britain, the muscovado to the United States, and molasses to Canada. Honduras sent its mahogany to Britain, its logwood to Britain and other countries, and bananas to the United States. Trinidad, owing to its situation and good communications, had a considerable trade with Venezuela; gold and other produce was brought to Trinidad for reshipment, and goods from Europe and elsewhere went to Trinidad for re-export to Venezuela.

Unlike the majority of the West Indian islands, the eastern sugar colony, Mauritius, had still a prosperous sugar industry. Interchange with India remained the chief feature of the island's trade. India provided a supply of labour for the plantations, bought most of the sugar, and exported to Mauritius coffee, rice and other grains. Trade with Australia was declining as Australia developed a sugar industry of its own. Great Britain took some of the sugar and sent in return coal and manufactured goods. Outside of the Empire, Mauritius traded chiefly with France, importing wine and some manufactures, as might be expected of an old French colony. Her economy remained of the old plantation type, primarily dependent on a single crop, raised for the foreign market—the other exports, rum, aloe, fibre and vanilla were relatively unimportant.

Under the treaty port system the British had built up a substantial interest in China and down to the Sino-Japanese war of 1894–5 their interests and influence exceeded those of any other Power. In 1890 there were 327 British firms and 3217 British residents in China.[1] Foreign economic enterprise was still primarily commercial and navigational; railway and industrial development had not yet begun. The British had a large share of the coasting trade, most of which was in the hands of two concerns, the China Navigation Co. (Butterfield & Swire), established in 1872, and the Indo-China Steam Navigation Co. (Jardine Matheson & Co.), established in 1881. Shanghai and Hong Kong were the chief centres of our economic activities, followed in importance by Tientsin, Hankow and Canton. China, which once accepted from the West only its silver, and then was forced to receive opium, had now become a general trader, importing British manufactures on a large scale and carrying on an extensive trade with other parts of the Empire also. In the 'seventies Lancashire cottons made up a third of its entire imports; machinery did not reach £100,000 till 1882.

The development of Hong Kong, inseparably associated with that of China, had proceeded apace. Most of the great merchant houses were Chinese and not European. Down to 1889 nearly half of British exports to China passed through Hong Kong, but from that time its importance as an entrepôt for the export trade decreased considerably; of imports most came direct from Chinese ports and only a small proportion through Hong Kong. For a long period British merchants bought much more from China and Hong Kong in most years than they sold there. Thus from 1874 the average annual value of exports was £8,432,000 and of imports £13,302,000. But from this time the value of British imports of tea and raw silk declined and exports came to exceed imports; in the years 1884–93, the annual value of imports fell to £7,415,000.[2]

There were a few industrial enterprises, banks and insurance companies, in Hong Kong and Shanghai, and, between 1874 and 1895, loans on a small scale had been made to the Chinese Government by the Hong Kong and Shanghai Banking Corporation[3]—most of them paid off—and the Customs administration had been established, but trade had been our main concern. China's relations with the West were on the threshold of change. The Sino-Japanese War opened the way to important economic developments. The inter-

---

[1] Gull, E. M., *British economic interests in the Far East*, p. 58.
[2] *Ibid.* pp. 51–2.   [3] *Ibid.* p. 74.

national loans began, inland waters were opened to foreign vessels, railway and mining concessions were made and foreigners acquired the right to establish industrial undertakings. British enterprise was embarked on the all-round development of the country, which had commenced, but was to lose its unique position as other Powers increased their interests.

Japan was not in this period so important a market as China for British goods, nor had Britain the same influence there. But, in 1870, her first foreign loan, for railway construction, £1,000,000 at 9 per cent, was floated in London. In Japan, as in China, trade was organised under a treaty port system—in Japan from 1854, but the system, including, as it did, commercial, navigational, residential and judicial rights, was no more popular in Japan than in China, and by a treaty of 1894, to take effect in five years, was brought to an end.

Such was the scope and nature of Britain's imperial trade, un-exampled in its magnitude and variety. A general view of its distribution between the various parts of the Empire and of the relative importance in the total overseas trade may be seen in the following tables :[1]

Exports of British Produce from U.K. to British Possessions

Percentage proportion of total exports

Annual average	British North America	British West Indies	Australia and New Zealand	India	Cape and Natal	Other British possessions	Total British possessions
1870–4	3·6	1·3	6·0	8·5	1·4	4·8	25·6
1875–9	3·5	1·5	9·1	11·3	2·5	5·2	33·1
1880–4	3·8	1·3	9·4	12·9	2·6	4·5	34·5
1884–9	3·4	1·2	10·2	13·7	2·4	4·1	35·0
1890–4	3·0	1·3	8·4	12·9	3·6	4·3	33·5

Imports into U.K. from British Possessions

Percentage proportion of total imports

Annual average	British North America	British West Indies	Australia and New Zealand	India	Cape and Natal	Other British possessions	Total British possessions
1870–4	3·0	1·8	4·7	8·7	1·0	2·8	22·0
1875–9	2·8	1·8	5·8	7·6	1·1	3·0	22·1
1880–4	2·8	1·4	6·5	8·7	1·4	2·7	23·5
1885–9	2·8	0·9	6·3	8·5	1·4	3·0	22·9
1890–4	3·2	0·6	7·3	7·1	1·4	3·3	22·9

[1] British and Foreign Trade and Industry, *Parl. Pap.* 1903, xxxi [Cd. 1761], Tables, pp. 402 *seqq.*

Widespread interest was awakened by the Colonial and Indian Exhibition of 1886, which had illustrated the wealth in natural products and the commercial and industrial activities of the overseas Empire. It was suggested that a permanent institution for this purpose should be founded as a national memorial of the Queen's Jubilee, and in May 1888 Her Majesty granted a charter of incorporation to the Imperial Institutes of the United Kingdom, the Colonies and India and the Isles of the British Seas. A site was chosen in South Kensington and buildings erected there for the collections and libraries.

Let us turn now to the changing position of the United Kingdom. During these years her wealth had continued to grow, her population to increase—from 31 millions in 1871 to 39 millions (estimated) in 1895—[1] and her standard of life to rise. She was still the economic centre of her Empire, the centre of wealth and power, and, in many ways, of example. But though, absolutely, prosperous and progressing, she was losing ground relatively. Compared with some other Powers, particularly the United States and Germany, she was not as strong as she had been in the middle of the century, and her share of the world's output was falling. Various influences were giving advantages to other countries, now that they had passed a certain stage of progress. They were no longer so much in need of her capital, nor as willing to take her manufactures. The industrial movement had become international. Britain still led, but not everywhere, nor so far ahead, nor was she moving so fast as others.

Moreover, she had become dependent on the outside world for food and employment—a dependence that steadily increased. In the 'seventies began the long decline of her agriculture. American wheat, pouring in with the expansion of American railways and cheap transport, struck agriculture a terrible blow. Gladstone, writing in 1880, described the American grain competition as "certainly a great fact and not one merely transitory". The area of arable land in Britain and the number of persons employed in farming fell continuously. To live, she depended on the importation of essential food and on her capacity to pay for it by the export of manufactures, services of various kinds, and coal. Other European countries which valued agriculture as a manner of life as well as an industry, or thought it essential to preserve it on military or political grounds, protected their farmers and landowners. In Britain political power was passing into the hands of the working classes and their sense of their interests had become of increasing account in economic policy. Firmly attached to free trade, they supported a policy of cheap food. Where Labour was most powerful in the colonies, as in Australia and New Zealand, it was inclining to protection to ensure

[1] Including Ireland: the population of Ireland was falling.

employment. Such countries were not importers of food, and work was what they wished to keep. The decline of her agriculture increased Britain's dependence on oversea supplies of food. If other peoples ceased to want her manufactures, she would become more and more at a disadvantage in purchasing the food and raw materials she needed. This was the danger of the future.

Ever since 1870 and earlier, Continental States were inclining to place security and stability before maximum income. Economic nationalism was returning. The scene on which Britain looked out in the 'eighties was not what Cobden had envisaged. France, Germany, the United States and her own colonies enjoyed her free market, but restricted their own according to their conception of their interests. To the new lands as they became industrialised, English competition was the principal danger. The founders of free trade misconceived the position. Britain's policy was successful for herself, since her industries were relatively mature. It would have been foolish for nations with immature industries to adopt her system pure and simple, and, like the older countries, they had not done so. The 'sixties had been a decade of falling tariffs and commercial treaties negotiated in a free-trade spirit. The following decade witnessed a change of heart, and by the early 'eighties the policy of the 'sixties was reversed and most of its work undone.

Still, it might be argued, Great Britain had followed the best policy for her own circumstances, and free trade had given her the maximum use of her opportunities. The wide extension of British interests, as Gladstone said in 1873, had given to trade and industry more firmness and solidity; Britain had established relations "with the wants of the whole human race",[1] and any particular failure was lost in the comprehensiveness of the relations in which she stood to all the world.[1] Nor was this falsified in the long depression which succeeded the spell of prosperity. The trade depression in the 'eighties was universal. The United Kingdom suffered severely—her great industries, iron and steel and shipping, were all affected. Between 1876 and 1885 her share in world trade fell from 23 to 19 per cent. The trade decline developed into a cyclical depression and was aggravated by the agricultural crisis. But Britain held her own in the smaller markets, and to a great extent also in distant markets, while her exports to her colonies, viewed over the years 1870–85, increased enormously (the case of imports was not so strong). Goschen, speaking in 1888, concluded that Britain's greatest hope was in her colonies, whose populations were growing fast.[2] This was true, with the qualification that the special stage of their development had stimulated their purchases from the mother country, particularly of

[1] At the Guildhall, 9 Nov. 1873; quoted in Buxton's *Finance and Politics*, II, 140, footnote.
[2] Goschen, G. J. G., Viscount, *Essays and Addresses*, pp. 231–4.

railway material, and her investment in their industries, and that this phase would pass.

The great depression had little influence on imperial policy. But in the circumstances the commercial relations of the Empire were under continuous discussion. The Fair Trade League, formed in 1881, the Report of the Royal Commission on the Depression of Trade and Industry in 1886, the Imperial Federation movement, and the Colonial Conference in 1887, all gave prominence to the matter, either as a means of meeting the depression of trade, or for the purpose of achieving a common fiscal policy or even a commercial union of the Empire. The proposals took various forms—the first was a *Zollverein*, with complete free trade within the Empire and a common tariff against foreign countries; the second, Hofmeyr's proposal, made at the Colonial Conference in 1887, that all members of the Empire should impose a supplementary duty of so much per cent on the already existing duties against foreign countries, the proceeds of which would go to imperial defence; the third, that Great Britain should give a tariff preference to the colonies on their exports to her, and they on her exports to them. But on none of these proposals did agreement seem possible. A customs union of the Empire was outside practical politics. It was impossible to go back on the fiscal freedom which the chief parts of the Empire enjoyed. Freedom was the animating principle of imperial relations and neither free trade nor protection could be imposed on those who did not choose it. To the colonial representatives in 1887 Lord Salisbury said:

I fear that we must for the present put in the distant and shadowy portion of our task, and not in the practical part of it, any hope of establishing a Customs Union among the various parts of the Empire. I do not think that in the nature of things it is impossible; I do not think that the mere fact that we are separated by the sea renders it impossible. In fact, the case of Ireland, which has a Customs Union with England, shows that it is not impossible. But the resolutions which were come to in respect of our fiscal policy 40 years ago set any such possibility entirely aside, and it cannot now be resumed until on one side or the other very different notions with regard to fiscal policy prevail from those which prevail at the present moment.[1]

The Fair Traders argued for retaliation and imperial preference, though in their plans the Empire took second place. They proposed that food imports from foreign countries should be taxed, but from British colonies and possessions admitted free, and that this taxation should be continued for a considerable time in order to give the colonies the opportunity to develop their production. Another of their proposals was that tea, coffee, fruit, tobacco, wine and spirits should be taxed to 10 per cent higher if imported from foreign countries than if imported from within the Empire. They argued that a profitable trade was growing with the colonies, but declining with

[1] Colonial Conference, 1907, Proceedings; *Parl. Pap.* 1907, LV [Cd. 3523], p. 229.

foreign countries, and they wished to transfer the great food-growing industries from protected countries to our own colonies. But in 1885 four-fifths of food imports came from foreign countries, and it did not seem practicable to legislate with a view to changing the source of supply. Lord Salisbury made it quite clear to his Fair-Trade followers that he was not in favour of reimposing a duty on corn.[1] In general, too, the colonial trade did not grow faster than trade with foreign countries. All overseas trade was intimately connected and influenced by the same general causes. In Britain's position, it was felt that a preference to colonial trade would not compensate her for the risk entailed of a larger loss of foreign trade. Moreover, at the time when the Fair Trade League was pressing for special terms for colonial trade, most English-speaking colonies, except New South Wales, were exhibiting protectionist tendencies quite as strong as those of the chief foreign countries. The Fair Trade movement failed to convince opinion at home that there was sufficient ground for modifying free trade by colonial preference. "Its strength lay less in its economics, though they were not negligible, than in its sense of a changing world and in its nationalism."[2] General opinion at the time was best summed up by one who, though then against the League, was later to revive its spirit. Speaking in the Devonshire Club on 9 April 1888, on his return from America after his mission concerning the fisheries, Chamberlain said:

Experience shows us that trade follows the flag, and even in commercial questions sentiment is a powerful influence on the question of profit and loss. A great part of our population is dependent at the present moment upon the interchange of commodities with our colonial fellow-subjects and it is the duty of every statesman to do all in his power to maintain and increase this commercial intercourse... we have to watch for opportunities to strengthen the ties between our colonies and ourselves....There is the question of commercial union and the question of union for defence....The difficulty in the case of commercial union is, no doubt, much greater. It is no use to expect that our colonies will abandon their custom duties as their chief and principal source of revenue. It is hardly to be hoped that the protected interests, fostered by their system, will willingly surrender the privileges which they now enjoy. All we can do is to wait until proposals are made to us; to consider those proposals, when they come, with fairness and impartiality; and to accept them if they do not involve the sacrifice of any important principle or of any interest vital to our population.[3]

The difference of economic policy between Britain and her colonies had wide imperial bearings and stood in the way of federal union. The Imperial Federation League could make no acceptable proposal. As John X. Merriman wrote to Goschen from Cape Town in February 1886: "The commercial and financial union of the Empire will be probably the rock upon which just now the Federation project

[1] Cecil, Lady Gwendolen, *Life of Robert, Marquis of Salisbury*, III, 267.
[2] Clapham, Sir J. H., *An Economic History of Modern Britain*, II, 251.
[3] Boyd, C. W. (ed.), *Mr Chamberlain's Speeches*, I, 322 *seqq*.

would split."[1] Economic policies could not be reconciled. Colonial opinion naturally favoured preference more than British. Most of the colonies did the greater part of their trade with Great Britain, and as most of them had already adopted protection, preference was a natural, simple and advantageous policy. Rhodes in 1891, in correspondence with Sir John Macdonald and Sir Henry Parkes, was trying to unite colonial opinion, believing that if the colonies were united in their views they would be able to obtain preference.[2] This was unlikely. In Britain the movement still lacked a leader. As yet imperial preference was not linked up with protection. Nor did British opinion show any sign of change during this period. When the matter was raised again at the Ottawa Conference in 1894, and a resolution passed in its favour, the Liberal government was not encouraging and Lord Ripon, in a Circular Dispatch, wrote that it would "react injuriously on every industry in the United Kingdom".

Though no change of policy was made, the discussions from the various points of view much increased the general knowledge and appreciation of the value of the colonial trade and its importance to all classes in the country. In his Guildhall speech in November 1891 the Prime Minister, Lord Salisbury, emphasised the point that the trade and prosperity of Britain depended on her far-extended possessions and that the working man no less than the rich man was concerned in it. Goschen had been much more emphatic: "The question of our colonies", he said in 1885, "is to a great extent a working man's question", for the working classes not only supplied most of the emigrants to the colonies but also found employment in the manufactures exported to them.[3] Critics of imperialism were apt to overlook this.

The conclusion that emerged from all these discussions was that the economic position of Britain was becoming too specialised, even perhaps too precarious, to admit of a change of policy, or to justify her taking any large risk in the general interest. By her leadership in the industrial revolution she had attained a unique and in some ways a dominant position in the economic activities of the Western world. That position was not built on a rock, but on the shifting foundations of international trade. Her chief exports were machinery, ships and rails, made from her coal and her iron, and textiles manufactured from imported cotton and wool. These industries gave her population half its employment and gave her supremacy in exports, and the profits of her exports produced her foreign investments. Her economy had come to rest on a few staple industries which were dependent on foreign markets, and her superiority in these industries was steadily disappearing. Britain had done much to create the

[1] Elliott, A. D., *Goschen*, ii, 26.
[2] Brown, B. H., *The Tariff Reform Movement in Great Britain, 1881–1895*.
[3] *Addresses*, p. 187.

pattern of world industry, but, from about 1875, a new industrial technology was emerging, changes in techniques, sources of power and materials, in which Britain had not the same advantages as she had enjoyed in the old.[1] Nor was she as well adapted to produce the newer kinds of goods. Her accumulated capital and experience in industry sometimes stood in the way of quick change to speedier processes, and trade conditions in the 'eighties did not encourage large capital expenditure on novelties. While rails were made of iron, that is, till the late 'seventies, Britain had almost a monopoly of the export trade. There was a rapid fall after 1877 with the extension of steel-making in the United States, Germany, France and Belgium. By 1896 Germany as well as the United States had passed her in steel production. In invention also she was losing her industrial leadership.

As for her share in international trade, from the 'seventies she had become conscious of her dependence on foreign markets, but hostile tariffs hit her exports of manufactured goods. From 1879 the tariffs of the chief continental countries, and then of the United States and even of some British colonies, were increasingly felt, and against them she had no remedy. As Disraeli said in a debate in the Lords in April 1879, "practically speaking, reciprocity, whatever its merits, is dead ...the opportunity, like the means, has been relinquished".[2] To Gladstone, putting duties on one's own imports to induce other countries to take them off one's exports meant "if a man strikes you on one cheek, you should smite yourself on the other also". Britain held her own for the time by increased exports of machinery, ships and coal—commodities which would diminish the export of other forms of her labour in the future. For a market for her cotton goods she relied increasingly on India, China and the Levant. She still retained a very large proportion of the world's carrying trade in spite of the increasing sale of ships. Her trade was in fact still growing, but the prospects were not good. By 1870 she could no longer pay for the imports she needed entirely by exports: already they were partly paid for by the income from her oversea investments and this tendency had increased as time went on. In 1888 Goschen in a Rectorial Address pointed out that supremacy had been attained owing to a "great start in industry and commerce". "We required greater efforts than formerly to hold our own. Mother wit and boldness in seizing great opportunities—the chief factors in our previous success—were no longer sufficient, if others were to be more strenuous, more painstaking, more widely informed."[3] But the problem was even more fundamental. An industrial State could be overtaken as other countries created industries—it was not easy, perhaps not possible, always to keep ahead of them, particularly if they were in a position by policy to re-inforce their natural advantages.

[1] Kahn, A. E., *Great Britain in the World Economy* (1946), p. 72.
[2] Buxton, *op. cit.* II, 268.   [3] *Life*, II, 253.

Financially Britain was still supreme—London had become the world's leading centre for the provision of both capital and short-term credit. Governments interfered very little, and monetary affairs were regulated by banks which had come to occupy a special position as central banks. The currencies of almost all countries stood in fixed and effective relationship to gold, either direct or through sterling, and the various money markets were closely responsive to one another. There was free movement of money, capital and trade. In the monetary affairs of the world London with its large accumulations exercised a "benevolent autocracy" and gave the world an economic unity which was to last in fact till the First World War.

The position of Britain in world affairs, strong in some ways, vulnerable in others, in danger of deteriorating, governed her attitude to imperial economic policy and made it difficult for her to contemplate any substantial change. Her sense of her own needs and interests had not changed. Free trade still seemed to her essential if she were to keep her position. Yet in 1895 she was the centre of a vastly different Empire from that of 1870 and in a very different world. Her problem was to adjust her policy to the changed circumstances. Was free trade right for her in the new competitive age? But where she was most conscious of the need to develop imperial policy was not in commercial relations but in the finance of defence.

Ever since 1870 it had been in the cost of defence that the British Budget continually reflected the existence of the British Empire. Gladstone spoke of the unequal arrangements under which we defended our colonies and they taxed our imports. In his first Budget speech in 1887 Goschen drew attention to "the proportions in which different parts and classes of the Empire contribute to imperial taxation, and the consideration whether these proportions are just",[1] and Harcourt's great reform of the death duties in 1894 was inspired by the prospect of a large increase in naval expenditure.[2] In the twenty years from 1875 to 1895, while population increased by 19 per cent, expenditure increased by 68 per cent, mainly owing to the Army and Navy estimates. That the colonies were not insensible to the problem was shown by Hofmeyr's proposal, and though this was not adopted, negotiations proceeded for sharing some part of the burden. It was on the finance of defence that the old Empire had broken down. The approach of the mother country to the colonies was made very differently a century later.

To many people free trade seemed to ignore vital aspects of the problem of defence—Britain's increasing dependence on foreign nations for her food supply as her population grew and her agriculture declined, and also for the supply of certain goods essential for the purpose of war. Carried logically through, free trade sacrificed military security in favour of maximum economic efficiency. Defence,

---

[1] Mallet, B., *British Budgets*, p. 8.   [2] *Ibid.* p. 100.

wrote Adam Smith, is "of much more importance than opulence"; but Britain seemed rather to be following the principle that opulence would be her best defence. Her accumulated wealth was to give her a marvellous power of endurance in the strain of war, and though her economic policy did not enable her to avoid war it contributed to her final victory when war came.

More striking than the growing appreciation of the importance of colonial trade was the changing attitude of the country on the question of further expansion of the Empire and on some aspects of colonial policy. These changing views were not the product of economic causes alone, but the balance of the economic argument shifted from the contraction to the expansion of the Empire. The free-trade policy had not influenced other countries to open their colonial trade equally to all nations, nor prevented them from seeking to acquire new colonies themselves. On the contrary, France, Italy and Germany were expanding, and were closing the door to British trade. The free trader had seen no advantage in possessing territories with which Britain could trade equally well without the responsibilities of government, and the mid-Victorian spirit of economy favoured the dropping of colonies to save expense. It was only when commercialists saw a danger of territories being closed to British goods by protectionist countries that free trade and expansion were brought into harmony in colonial policy. Britain must expand to preserve freedom of trade. If trade were circumscribed in one place, she must seek it in another, even at the price of extending her Empire. It was not the object to get exclusive commercial control, but to prevent others from assuming it. So, in the 'eighties and 'nineties, opinion was coming round to the view that in order to preserve overseas markets and to ensure for British industry increasing and reliable supplies of raw materials it would be necessary to accept further territorial expansion which had been unpopular for so long. In May 1895 Lord Salisbury summed up the situation: to hold our own we must open new markets for ourselves among the half civilised and uncivilised nations of the globe and "we must not be afraid if that effort, which is vital to our industries, should bring with it new responsibilities of Empire and government".[1]

Economic pressure thus combined with moral pressure to change British policy. As between the effort to preserve trade and the desire to suppress slavery it is difficult to give precedence. At the Berlin West African Conference in 1884, Lord Granville had instructed Sir Edward Malet to see that commercial interests were not the only subject of deliberations; while the opening of the Congo markets was to be desired, the welfare of the natives should not be neglected. Humanitarians, business men, overseas administrators, missionaries, consuls, were all coming, from different points of view, to the same

[1] Brown, B. H., op. cit. p. 83.

conclusion, that the extension of British power was necessary to achieve their several ends.

In the economic history of the Empire the opening of Africa and the Pacific Islands and the development of Malaya began a new phase. Here were not empty lands for settlement, nor ancient and civilised peoples, but a new problem—backward peoples and un-developed lands which would in time be profitable to Western industry. Her own needs and enterprise, and the activity of other nations, induced Britain to take a part: a part for which earlier actions had given her great advantages. The long peace, the spirit of adventure, the desire to suppress the slave trade, all assisted to bring public sympathy over to the side of new economic enterprise. We must not exaggerate the economic motive, strong though it was, for in Africa the economic advantages were less apparent then than since, and they were at first rather in trade than development. To Lord Salisbury, who played so great a part in negotiating the partition of Africa, the main object had been the peaceful conciliation of international rivalries. The question he repeatedly asked himself was: How far he was justified, for the rescue of these black populations, in placing fresh burdens of cost and responsibility upon the British people? In Uganda he felt hesitation to embark on the vast scheme of "pacification" to which a bankrupt Chartered company invited him. In Kenya he saw "a great work of civilisation", though without hope of economic reward. In Nyasaland, moved by his strong feeling against the slave trade, he agreed to act when Rhodes promised to find the money for the Nyasa force. Economic prospects were not the main motive in this African expansion and England did not seek to obtain all the territory she could.[1]

Chamberlain, pleading in the House of Commons in March 1893 for the retention of Uganda, combined the economic and moral appeal. But for the gigantic foreign trade created by expansion, forty millions of people could not live in these small islands. If the British closed the doors through which new trade must come, they ought to keep their population stationary. They were justified in pegging out claims for posterity. It was a duty, too, "to take our share in the work of civilisation in Africa". A railway to the coast would be necessary and the Government must guarantee the interest. The railway would be a good investment and to the advantage of the working classes and would take away the temptation to carry on the slave trade—in Africa, "largely a matter of porterage". We were spend-ing £200,000 a year for a squadron on the East Coast to stop the trade, when the railway would be far more fruitful of good results.[2] Chamberlain had not been attracted to Fair Trade, but he was becoming persuaded that Britain's future was bound up with her Empire and he wished to keep the door open to commercial arrange-

[1] Cecil, Lady Gwendolen, *op. cit.* vol. III.   [2] Boyd, *Mr Chamberlain's Speeches*, I, 341–53.

ments with the colonies, an imperial *Zollverein* if that could be; while in the dependencies he saw the neglected estates of the absentee landlord which would need Government assistance for their development. His ideas had influence and his opportunity was to come.

But if they were to expand the Empire, how could it be done most cheaply? The Chartered company appealed to the Colonial Office as a means of relieving the taxpayer. In spite of what Adam Smith had written about exclusive companies, the Government—and in this Liberal and Conservative Governments agreed—revived the long-abandoned device of sovereign commercial companies and put them in charge of the development of large territories in West, East and South Africa, and in Borneo. The Chartered company, it was hoped, would serve the ends of keeping out the foreigner, protecting the native and developing the resources of the country. It would take a larger view than the concession company and organise constructive activities. It would do the pioneer work, establish lines of communication—roads, railways and telegraph—and an administrative system, find out about climate and soil, and create potential markets for British goods. This would be an economy to the nation, and its position could be reviewed from time to time. The companies of course wished to make money, to have the right of taxation, to acquire land and minerals and monopolise trade, but they asked for public support for the sake not only of profit but also of philanthropy—they were opening the dark continent to the light of civilisation. Livingstone had associated these motives in the unforgettable appeal of his life to the British people. Thus the British East Africa Company, "telling its shareholders, before they subscribed at all, that any dividends would probably have to be 'taken in philanthropy', got the necessary money".[1] The companies were not to prove a success, economically or politically, nor could the Government protect the natives under this system as fully as public opinion desired; one by one they surrendered their rights, but they served their turn and bridged the time which public opinion took to accept the responsibilities of the new African dependencies.

A new colonial policy was thus in process of being formed. While Britain wished to keep markets open to her goods, and to develop the tropics by Western enterprise and so ensure a supply of their products for her industry and trade, a new consciousness of obligation to native peoples appears—a duty to promote their economic progress and welfare and a realisation that without economic improvement they could not make political progress. The idea of trusteeship included economic obligations and restraints: to take steps for the moral and material elevation of the native, encourage legitimate commerce and so regulate it as to mitigate its disruptive impact on native societies. From being unwilling to extend British administra-

---

[1] Argyll, Duke of, *Passages from the Past*, II, 576–7.

tion Britain was advancing to a much more responsible and expensive form of it. But the lands were poor and needed for the present to be ruled with regard to economy.

Such was the situation in which Great Britain was placed, or perhaps we should say the direction in which she was moving in the early 'nineties, and the kind of problem which the course of events was creating for her. Viewed as a whole, she could fairly feel that free trade had served her well—that she had grown richer, more active, more influential in the world, with a much increased population and a continuously rising standard of life. Her great colonies, too, had grown stronger and more populous; they were still united with her in loyalty to a common crown and tradition. In the great depression of trade her policy had served her as well as protection had served her neighbours. She suffered indeed from their tariffs and had no weapon with which to defend herself. She and her colonies had also suffered from their policy of bounties and subsidies to particular industries, and this had provided her with a difficult problem. Nor had she, by opening her own, and, where she could, her colonial, trade freely to other nations saved herself from their envy of her power, or discouraged them from emulating her, though she might fairly argue that their antagonism and determination to rival her would have been stronger if her policy had been an exclusive one. And her policy no longer satisfied her great self-governing colonies who had become dependent on an overseas market, in particular hers, and desired to secure and strengthen their place as against other competitors. In a system of tariff preferences they saw the best way of consolidating the Empire, and their proposals had opened up a possible future line of imperial development and organisation. But, in Britain, reviving trade and the new imperialism had awakened new hopes which for the time overshadowed questions of imperial preference and fiscal reform. So far as she could see, free trade still served her best. The difficulty was that no one could foresee the future —how far the policy of States, the international situation, with its rivalries entailing the possibilities of war, and also the progress of invention, might change the whole position. The nation was in much the same position as one of its enterprising middle class, who had made his way upwards by his wits and energy, accumulated a substantial fortune, incurred the liability of a growing family and faced the problem of maintaining it amid increasing competition and the rivalry of neighbours. Some disaster might sweep away his reserves and leave him with his liabilities and duties and less prospect of the same earnings in the future. Who could foresee for the country the circumstances that would swallow up its savings and reserves in wars in defence of freedom and existence, and deprive it of the fortunate position in which its earnings had been so great? This was the cataclysm against which no policy could provide.

It seems just, then, to say that as yet there was no reaction against free trade. All the great figures in our public life still defended it—confidently, even vehemently. They would no longer say, as John Bright said in 1879, that the protective system was "the last refuge of cowardice, idleness and greed", but scarcely an uncertain note had sounded. Other ideas were changing; individualism was ceasing to be the basic policy of the State; *laissez-faire* was giving place to organisation; increasing Parliamentary attention was given to trade and industry; and opinion on the value of colonies had moved on since 1870; but no statesman bearing the responsibility of government as yet proposed a departure from the policy with which so many historic names were associated and under which Britain had achieved so much of significance to herself and to the world.

CHAPTER VII

IMPERIAL DEFENCE, 1870–1897

FROM 1815 to 1870 British strategic policy, outside India, had been mainly concerned with "small wars" against non-European forces and with local defence problems. In the Crimean War (1854–6), though it had wide strategic implications, no attack was made on British colonial territory. After 1870 the Empire faced the increasing risk of a general war which might involve the conduct of large-scale offensive operations, supported by the man-power and the resources of the colonies. Meanwhile the term "colonial defence" was superseded by that of "imperial defence" as being more in accord with political developments. The use of the word "defence" suggested that British interests as a whole could be served by world peace and that British policy was non-aggressive, and reminded the self-governing colonies of the duty of providing for their own local defence. After the granting of the wide measures of self-government to Canada and to the Australasian and South African colonies, the garrisons of imperial troops hitherto stationed in these colonies had been largely withdrawn in conformity with the Gladstonian doctrine that "self government begets self-defence". No precise arrangements concerning defence, however, were made with these colonies, though there was a clearly accepted principle that the Home Government should provide for the external defence of the colonies. Disraeli drew attention to this omission in 1872.[1] Yet it is doubtful if more could have been done at that time, since, with the exception of Canada, the self-governing colonies lacked the necessary strength and status. Colonial militia forces for local defence were all that could then be hoped for, and these grew up largely haphazard, without any scheme of standardised weapons, training or organisation provided by the War Office.

In South Africa the policy of withdrawing the imperial forces, with the exception of one battalion for the defence of the naval station at Simon's Bay, proved unworkable, owing to the native danger. Despite the opening of the Suez Canal in 1869, the Home Government attached great importance to the Cape, not only as an alternative route to India, the Far East and Australasia, should the Mediterranean route become unusable in war, but also because of its value as a coaling station in the focal shipping area between the South Atlantic and the Indian Ocean.[2] When, in 1877, Disraeli decided to

---

[1] *C.H.B.E.* II, 679.

[2] The distance saved by the Suez Canal route from Plymouth to Bombay was 4,300 miles, to Singapore 3,300 miles and to Sydney 1,100 miles. See Donald Currie's correspondence with Lord Carnarvon, 1875–6, quoted in *Journal of the Royal United Services Institution*, no. XXI (1878), 233.

annex the Transvaal, he was faced by the kind of difficulty he had envisaged in 1872. In the war which immediately followed against the Galekas and Gaikas, John Molteno, first Premier of the Cape, and Sir Bartle Frere, Governor of the Cape and High Commissioner for Native Affairs in South Africa, each claimed an exclusive right to control the operations at a time when both imperial and colonial forces were stationed in South Africa.[1] In the more formidable Zulu War of 1879, Lord Chelmsford held undisputed command over some 18,000 white troops who, despite the disaster of Isandhlwana, were able to crush the massed charges of Zulus by volley fire from the breech-loading Martini rifle. These successes won against native forces, however, were completely reversed in the short but disastrous Anglo-Boer War of 1880–1. In the fighting at Laing's Nek and Majuba the Boers showed tactical superiority, not only in individual marksmanship, but also in the use of ground. The only other war in Africa at this time, in Ashanti (1873–4), provided valuable lessons in tropical fighting and in the handling of supplies.

Meanwhile the centre of imperial strategic interest had shifted back to the Mediterranean, largely through the repercussions of the Russo-Turkish War of 1877–8. Though the rapid transfer of Indian troops to Malta gave an impressive example of the advantages derived from the opening of the Suez Canal, it was clear that these advantages had been obtained at the price of the increased vulnerability of the Empire as regards the canal zone. The Second Afghan War of 1878–80, another outcome of Anglo-Russian rivalry, illustrates the central position occupied by India in matters of imperial defence. Not only was India permanently absorbing one third of the total peace-time strength of the British Army, but military training, equipment and professional thought were largely based on Indian experience and the needs of Indian service. Unfortunate as this may have been as regards the creation of a strategic reserve at home against the possibility of operations in Europe, the Indian Army, reorganised since the Mutiny, was gradually establishing a high standard of fighting efficiency, administrative flexibility and readiness to meet sudden emergencies.

The Russian war scare of 1878 also directed attention to the increasing speed and range of modern steamships, the *Britannic*'s time for the Queenstown–New York passage being now only seven and a half days. This development was alleged to have reduced Britain's margin of imperial security. France had reappeared as the hereditary enemy. Recovering from her defeat in 1870–1, she had renewed her colonial and economic initiative in Algeria, Tunis and Egypt, and was about to extend her activities to Somaliland, Madagascar, Siam and Indo-China. In addition, there was the new position of Italy to consider both in the Mediterranean and in

[1] See *C.H.B.E.* II, 834, for a somewhat similar situation in New Zealand, 1865–7.

the Red Sea. The broad picture of imperial strategy had thus changed considerably since 1870. Russia and France, singly or jointly, were now considered potential, if not probable, enemies.[1] Nor was the danger to British naval operating bases and coaling stations merely the negative danger of loss, though this in itself would have been serious enough in view of its crippling effect on the mobility of the strongest steam-propelled fleet in the world. A more positive danger lay in the possible capture and exploitation of these bases and stocks of coal by an enemy power.

In 1875 the Admiralty asked the War Office to investigate the whole problem, thus linking the idea of defence of maritime trade with defence of territory. A report made by Colonel Sir William Jervois on behalf of the Inspector-General of Fortifications suggested various measures of defence for Port Royal (Jamaica), Antigua, Ascension Island, Simon's Bay (Cape), Port Louis (Mauritius), Trincomalee (Ceylon), Singapore, Hong Kong, King George's Sound (Western Australia), Esquimalt, Falkland Islands.[2] Gibraltar, Malta, Bermuda and Halifax had a separate status as "imperial fortresses". Interdepartmental discussions followed, and as a result of the Russian war scare a Colonial Defence Committee was appointed in March 1878, consisting of Admiral Sir Alexander Milne (ex-First Sea Lord), Sir Henry Barkly (an ex-colonial Governor) and General J. L. A. Simmons (Inspector-General of Fortifications), to enquire into and report on the defences of certain colonial ports of strategic importance and especially "how to provide some early and temporary defence in case of any sudden outbreak of hostilities".[3] As a result of their reports in April 1879 and their further suggestions[4] a Royal Commission was appointed on 8 September, under the chairmanship of Lord Carnarvon, with broad terms of reference "to enquire into the defence of British possessions and commerce abroad".

The Commissioners made three reports (3 September 1881, 23 March and 22 July 1882), and so serious were the conclusions and the evidence on which they were based, that none of the reports was published. Important extracts were, however, later made available for the use of the first Colonial Conference in 1887. From these extracts it appears that the seaborne trade of the colonies as a whole was estimated at an annual value of £367,000,000, half being represented

---

[1] Better relations with the United States after the Treaty of Washington (1871) had reduced the number of potential enemies. *C.H.B.E.* II, 841.

[2] Memorandum by Colonel Sir W. F. D. Jervois with reference to the defenceless condition of our Coaling Stations and Naval Establishments abroad, 7 Jan. 1875. Carnarvon Papers, P.R.O. 30–6/122. Jervois is described in the *Dict. National Biography* (*1st Suppl.* III, 41) as "the confidential adviser of successive Secretaries of State for War on all questions of defence".

[3] *Parl. Pap.* 1887, LVI [C. 5091–I], p. 16. This committee, set up for a specific and temporary purpose, is not to be confused with the permanent interdepartmental Colonial Defence Committee set up in 1885 (see below, p. 235).

[4] C.O. 812/14–16.

by trade with the United Kingdom, the rest by trade with foreign countries and trade between colonies,[1] that Empire shipping had greatly increased in recent years especially in steam tonnage, and that of the total tonnage, sail and steam, the colonies owned 18 per cent.[2] The Commissioners regarded the old Cape route as important for Eastern and Far Eastern trade defence, in case of difficulties in the Mediterranean. The Cape Peninsula, they urged, should have defences sufficient for a naval and mercantile repair base; Simon's Bay should be developed for naval purposes and new guns installed in colonial shore defences generally.[3] The annual value of Empire ships and cargoes afloat was estimated at £900,000,000, of which £144,,000,000 was afloat at any given time; yet Hong Kong, Singapore, Ceylon and most of the Indian, Australian, North American and West Indian ports had no shore defence. Imperial cables were vulnerable. Owing to steam propulsion, close blockade of an enemy fleet in Europe was no longer possible. Single enemy raiders might obtain coal supplies from their own or allied or neutral ports, or from captured ports and ships lying in them, and from captured colliers at sea.[4] The Navy, they said, needed more defended coaling stations to enable it to fulfil its offensive role and to prevent large-scale invasions of British territory, and should not be concerned with the defence of a number of small and scattered ports, which ought to be defended mainly by garrisons raised locally, such defences being as light as was consistent with naval requirements.[5] The Admiralty should also make plans for using merchant ships as auxiliary cruisers in time of war by encouraging owners to observe standards of construction sufficient for naval gun-mounting. The Navy should be strengthened at once, since capacity to build warships quickly, though valuable "as a reserve power" in the course of a war, was of no account at its outbreak.[6] As to costs, the Commissioners stated that the Australian colonies "may reasonably be expected to take upon themselves some share of the defence—a burden hitherto exclusively borne by the Mother Country", and they recommended that the separate colonies should make proportionate monetary contributions towards the cost of the squadron maintained in Australian waters by the mother country for the benefit of the Empire as a whole. An analysis of defence expenditure for the year 1879 showed that, whereas the total naval and military expenditure of the United Kingdom was 15s.7½d. per head, New South Wales paid 2s. 4d. only, South Australia 1s. 9¾d., New Zealand 1s. 9d., Queensland and Tasmania less than 1s. and Western Australia nothing.[7] Reviewing coaling facilities on the main

---

[1] *Parl. Pap.* 1887, LVI [C. 5091–I], p. 312.
[2] *Ibid.* pp. 305–11. Even in 1869 one-eleventh of the steam tonnage of the Empire was colonial owned: see *Parl. Pap.* 1870, LXI (349).
[3] *Parl. Pap.* 1887, LVI [C. 5091–I], pp. 299–302, 304.
[4] *Ibid.* p. 313.   [5] *Ibid.* p. 314.
[6] *Ibid.* pp. 314–15.   [7] *Ibid.* pp. 327–8.

trade routes, including the China and Australian routes via Singapore, the Commissioners noted the need for a limited number of well-defended bases both for refitting and coaling, each an expensive item, as well as smaller coaling stations with minor defences, and added the accepted Admiralty doctrine that "not until the important coaling stations shall have been made secure can the strength of the British Navy be adequately exerted at sea".[1] Obsolete defences should be brought up to date. The colonies, they stated, should undertake the local defence of their own commercial ports as well as contributing towards "the protection of those naval stations upon which the security of their territory and trade so largely depends". Though acknowledging that the Australian colonies already recognised this in principle and were now taking practical measures for the local defence of their chief ports, the Commissioners stated that the colonies would have to take a bigger share as time went on, since colonial trade was increasing more rapidly than that of the United Kingdom.[2] The first and third reports of the Carnarvon Commission are of special importance because they lay down general principles of imperial defence conceived on a governmental basis and with full knowledge of the facts (an advantage not enjoyed by Sir John Colomb in 1867).[3]

The only immediate results of the Carnarvon reports were fresh proposals to fortify Aden, Trincomalee, Colombo, Singapore, Hong Kong, the Cape of Good Hope and Mauritius (Port Louis)—for which payment was to be made by a variety of means—and also Sierra Leone, St Helena, Jamaica (Port Royal) and St Lucia (Castries), it being understood, however, that, in the case of this second group, no local contributions could be afforded. The technical defence measures suggested—shore batteries and mines, designed to resist small-scale attacks only,[4] represented the principal reaction from the large-scale fortification mania of the early 'sixties.[5] Meanwhile the naval bombardment of Alexandria in 1882 (the technical lessons of which were wrongly interpreted at the time),[6] and the subsequent land operations of 20,000 British troops with Indian reinforcements under Sir Garnet Wolseley, had led to the British occupation of Egypt. This commitment was extended for a time to the Sudan and excited some fear lest part of the western shores of the Red Sea should fall under the control of unfriendly powers. The Egyptian operations of 1882 and the Sudan operations of 1884–5 showed the ease with which troops in the Nile Valley could be simultaneously reinforced by sea from the United Kingdom, India and Australia, provided such movements remained unchallenged by the sea forces of enemy or neutral states. This happy situation, however, might not continue,

---

[1] *Parl. Pap.* 1887, LVI [C. 5091–I], p. 337.   [2] *Ibid.* p. 338.
[3] *C.H.B.E.* II, 838–9.
[4] *Parl. Pap.* 1884, XLVIII [C. 4186], p. 687, and 1884–5, XLVI [C. 4226], p. 675.
[5] *C.H.B.E.* II, 826–7.   [6] See below, p. 250.

especially in view of the potential threat to the Suez Canal should the Russian Black Sea Fleet join with the French in the Mediterranean.

In April 1885, just before the resignation of the Gladstone ministry, the Hon. Robert Meade, Assistant Under-Secretary for the Colonies, had suggested the setting-up of a small standing committee composed of representatives of the three departments most closely concerned (Colonies, Admiralty and War) to deal with the demands reaching the Colonial Office from all quarters of the Empire for local shore defence against the *Ruriks*, a new class of Russian armoured cruiser. This proposal was merely one of office convenience: the establishment of a temporary clearing house for inter-departmental correspondence about the latest war scare. Nevertheless, it marked the beginning of something much more important. The original members of the committee, in addition to Meade, were Sir Andrew Clarke, Inspector-General of Fortifications (chairman), Colonel (later Lieut.-Gen.) Sir H. Geary, R.A., Assistant Director of Artillery at the War Office, and Captain T. S. Jackson, R.N., Chairman of the Admiralty Foreign Intelligence Committee.[1] In June Captain George Sydenham Clarke, R.E., the future Lord Sydenham, was appointed secretary. In November Colonel Lord William Seymour, Assistant Quartermaster-General, joined the committee as representative of the Duke of Cambridge. The committee, known as the Colonial Defence Committee, were instructed to consider various problems, mainly of harbour defences, and to recommend action. In October 1886 they drew up a memorandum for the guidance of colonial Governors on local defence matters. They also advised that every Governor should set up a "Standing Defence Committee" and send home an annual report on his defence scheme for criticism. This recommendation was adopted and worked well, though, to begin with, Gibraltar, Malta and Bermuda were excluded from the areas covered.[2] Thus appeared the first governmental body, having any kind of permanence, charged exclusively with handling matters of imperial defence. Even so the committee had only a lowly function and its influence was entirely due to the energy and ability of its original members and their secretary. In October 1885 a temporary special War Office committee was also appointed, with the Hon. G. C. Dawnay, Surveyor-General of the Ordnance, as chairman, to consider the distribution of troops with special reference to new defences constructed or projected for imperial coaling stations.[3]

Meanwhile, the earlier war scare of 1878 had led to the meeting at Sydney in 1881 of an Inter-Colonial Conference. The Conference resolved to make all possible efforts "to procure the efficient fortifica-

---

[1] Precursor of the Naval Intelligence Division, set up in 1887.
[2] *Parl. Pap.* 1887, LVI [C. 5091-I], pp. 17–20; Sydenham of Combe, Lord, *My Working Life* (1927), pp. 70–2.
[3] *Parl. Pap.* 1887, LVI [C. 5091-I], p. 18.

tions and land defence of the several ports in the Australian Colonies, at the cost of the several colonies interested", and also to ask for an increase in the Australian Squadron of the Royal Navy on the assumption that this and existing naval defence should still remain "at the exclusive charge of the Imperial Government".[1] South Australia, which desired that the squadron should be doubled, was alone in proposing that the colonies themselves should bear the cost of the increase. The Conference produced no reaction in London till after the three Reports of the Carnarvon Commission had been received, when Rear-Admiral George Tryon, on being appointed to command on the Australian Station, took out proposals drawn up by the Admiralty for strengthening the squadron, although by then it was more than five years after the original war scare of 1878. In fact by the time Tryon reached Australia and began his negotiations the next Russian war scare of 1885 had already matured.

The effect of the two war scares was to make the Australasian colonists extremely sensitive about the future of the island groups lying to their north and north-east. After the annexation of the Fijis by Great Britain in 1874, the Australians were anxious for the annexation of the New Hebrides. They were also anxious about German penetration in Eastern New Guinea, while New Zealand was anxious about the Germans in the Solomons. As in the case of the Fijis, the Imperial Government was unwilling to add to its commitments at its own expense, while the colonists wished to increase their security without charge to themselves. In 1883 Queensland hoisted the British flag in New Guinea. This strategic initiative was disowned by the Imperial Government, Gladstone assuring the colonists that Germany had no intention of taking possession. Yet next year Germany annexed a large part of New Guinea not already occupied by the Dutch. In 1886 Germany acquired a protectorate over all north-eastern New Guinea and Britain over the south-east known as Papua. Germany also obtained the Bismarck Archipelago with New Ireland, New Britain and Bougainville, while Britain obtained the southern Solomons. The lesson for the colonists was that strategical foresight was of no value without combined action on the part of all the colonies concerned, together with willingness to accept the financial and other obligations involved. Hence Admiral Tryon's mission had for its background far more than a merely technical question of extra warships for the Australian Station.

Tryon asserted that while all the colonies except Western Australia possessed coast defence units of some kind, these were mostly of low fighting efficiency. He told the Australian Premiers that whereas it had never been possible to prevent absolutely the escape of enemy warships by blockade, steam propulsion had made blockade even

[1] *Parl. Pap.* 1887, LVI [C. 5091–I], p. 213.

more difficult to enforce than in the past. By this, of course, he meant close blockade as practised under sail. Hence there was an increased danger of attacks by fast cruisers on colonial ports and on shipping in colonial waters. He then described the naval defence system as a whole, the chain of fortified bases and coaling stations on which the major fleets and more distant squadrons depended, and the need for defence measures at the terminal points and focal areas in Australian waters. These must be homogeneous and include some local, but sea-going, naval forces to deal with enemy raiders at sea and "to deny these waters as a cruising ground to our foes". Meanwhile shore defences could be used for dealing with coastal raids.[1] The Admiralty's view was that five cruisers and two torpedo-boats should be added to the Australian Squadron and that the colonies should pay for the maintenance of these extra ships in proportion to their population, since the defence afforded was for the benefit of all.[2] The replies of the colonies were considered unsatisfactory by the Colonial Office. The general assumption that Australia was vulnerable only to small raids and not to major attacks or invasions depended on "the great ironclad fleet maintained by the Imperial Government in European waters, using coaling stations and defended bases created and main-tained without charge to the Australian taxpayer". Australia's local defence obligations were thus reduced to a comparatively low cost, though her seaborne trade was worth £115,000,000 annually, of which only £58,000,000 was with the United Kingdom, the rest being inter-colonial and foreign.[3]

When the first Colonial Conference met in London in 1887, pro-posals for increasing the Australian Squadron were one of the main subjects for discussion. There was little disagreement as to the size or character of the naval force required, but only as to allotment of costs. Having once conceded the right of self-government the Imperial Government was in a delicate position. The withdrawal of the imperial garrisons had left the Royal Navy in fact and theory as the chief means of colonial defence both as regards territory and seaborne trade. Meanwhile under the pressure of industrial development and foreign competition, the cost of naval armaments was rising. The battleship *Devastation* cost £350,000 in 1871; in 1882, the *Colossus*, of the same tonnage, cost £646,000. The Imperial Government, therefore, claimed to be justified in asking the individual Australian colonies for monetary contributions on the grounds that their total trade and wealth per head were not only increasing very rapidly, but at a far greater speed than those of the United Kingdom. This, incidentally, made them more tempting prizes for enemy capture. Yet no Govern-

---

[1] *Parl. Pap.* 1887, LVI [C. 5091–I], pp. 217–21, 226–30. See also pp. 213–16 for the Colonial Office view of negotiations.
[2] *Ibid.* pp. 254–6 and [C. 5091] (main report), pp. 29–30.
[3] [C. 5091–I], pp. 256–8.

ment since 1815 had dared to think of levying an imperial defence contribution on any of the colonies even before they achieved self-government. Such a contribution could only be obtained by consent. As regards local and coast defences it was hoped that all the colonies might undertake the burden at any rate of fortifications, either by providing the garrisons or by paying for the materials. Naturally much depended on how the Imperial Government's case was put forward at the Conference, and here it was handicapped by lack oı technical means for providing a survey of the whole field. Admiral Tryon's original brief from the Admiralty had been excellent as far as it went, but it was never intended to give a complete picture. Moreover the Imperial Government was itself so vague on the subject, particularly as regards the respective roles of the Navy and Army, that it was unable to make itself sufficiently clear at the Conference. In consequence a magnificent opportunity was lost of giving the Conference an authoritative statement of the broad principles underlying the Imperial Government's strategic policy, and the means used to give them effect. Nevertheless, Lord Salisbury's opening statement was valuable and farsighted. He deprecated "the impression that the defence of the Colonies ought to be entirely a matter for the Imperial Government, because any danger that the colonies might run was exclusively the result of imperial action and policy".[1] Their distance from Europe was no longer a complete defence, and even if they were entirely free from the commitments of imperial policy, the colonies could no longer regard themselves as safe from attack. "The circumstances in which we live and the tendencies of human nature as we know it in all times of history teach that, where there is a liability to attack, and defencelessness, attack will come. The English colonies comprise some of the richest and most desirable portions of the earth's surface. The desire for foreign and colonial possessions is increasing among the nations of Europe. The power of concentrating military and naval force is increasing under the influence of scientific progress. Put all these things together and you will see that the Colonies have a real and genuine interest in the shield which their imperial connection throws over them, and that they have a ground for joining with us in making the defence of the Empire effective."[2] It was clear that the Imperial Government was more anxious to obtain a monetary contribution from the Australian colonies for the anticipated increased cost of the Australian Squadron than to initiate a general discussion on imperial defence as a whole. Edward Stanhope, Secretary of State for War, admitted that "It is only quite recently that we here in England have attempted to take a comprehensive view of our imperial duties in this respect [defence]. For a time we voted no doubt large sums for our Army and Navy; but it is only in recent years, stimulated, I am bound to say, largely by the

---

[1] *Parl. Pap.* 1887, LVI [C. 5091], p. 6.   [2] *Ibid.*

efforts of the colonies, that a comprehensive survey [the Carnarvon Reports] has been taken of all that we can accomplish, and of all that we ought to endeavour, towards making the Empire secure in time of difficulty."[1]

Twenty years earlier Sir John Colomb had laid down certain broad principles of imperial strategy, the value of which had received widespread public recognition.[2] Yet the Salisbury ministry's handling of the Conference showed nothing comparable in thought or exposition, and was clearly responsible for much of the parochialism apparently displayed by the colonial delegates. When, for instance, Lord George Hamilton claimed a free hand for the Admiralty in the strategic handling of the Australian Squadron, in answer to the delegates' claims that if they paid part of its cost they had the right to veto its removal from their local waters, he failed to explain why a free hand was necessary. Nor did he make any attempt to explain the broad distinction between local and general defence, and the strategical definition of the "floating trade in Australian waters". This phrase, though apparently intended to mean Australian territorial waters, may well have sounded like an attempt to saddle the Australian colonies with a more general defence obligation. The delegates were also left in doubt as to the efficiency of naval blockade under the new conditions of steam warfare, and naturally looked on the possibility of a large enemy force able to attack them by evading the main British battle fleets as a serious matter.[3] After prolonged and barren wranglings[4] an agreement was reached on the proposed increase of the Australian Squadron which provided for the addition of an auxiliary squadron of five fast cruisers and two torpedo gunboats for protecting "the floating trade in Australian waters". During peace two of the cruisers and one gunboat were to be in reserve. The Imperial Government was to pay the capital cost of commissioning the reserve ships in time of war, while the colonies were to pay the cost of general maintenance plus the interest on the capital cost at 5 per cent up to a limit of £35,000. The agreement was to last ten years.[5] The Imperial Government also proposed the fortification of King George's Sound and the Torres Strait, but not at its own expense. It nevertheless refused to regard these as special cases because they were not recommended as such by the Carnarvon Commission, and held that the colonies must pay a considerable share if they themselves really wanted the fortifications.[6]

---

[1] *Parl. Pap.* 1887, LVI [C. 5091], p. 277.   [2] *C.H.B.E.* II, 838–40.
[3] *Parl. Pap.* 1887, LVI [C. 5091], pp. 30–49, and [C. 5091–I], p. 221.
[4] [C.5091], pp. 298–310, 490–506.
[5] [C.5091], p.x and [C.5091–I], pp.260–2. See also Sydenham, *My Working Life*, pp.73–5.
[6] [C. 5091], pp. 245–69, 283–9, 422–6, 529–31 and [C. 5091–I], pp. 262–94. The Imperial Government offered some obsolete guns which were disdainfully refused. Stanhope's final statement (see pp. 529–31) shelving the whole question can scarcely be regarded as creditable to the Home Government.

The Canadians, though by far the largest colonial owners of shipping, claimed that their best service to the defence of the Empire lay in developing their internal resources, and particularly the Canadian Pacific Railway, which would enable imperial troops to be moved direct from Britain to the Pacific coast for the defence of Esquimalt. Canada's Militia already numbered 36,000 and behind it stood the Militia Reserve.[1] A Canadian proposal, made in 1880, that the Imperial Government should raise, pay, arm and clothe a Canadian reserve infantry force of seven battalions, had been rejected as impracticable.[2]

Jan Hofmeyr, for the Cape of Good Hope, advocated an imperial customs tariff on all foreign goods entering Empire ports, the proceeds to be used for imperial defence. The United Kingdom's foreign imports for 1885 were, he said, worth £280,000,000, and colonial imports of foreign goods were worth £66,000,000, making some £350,000,000 in all. A tariff of 2 per cent on this would provided an annual revenue of £7,000,000 for defence. His idea was to substitute a system of indirect taxation for what he saw might become a growing system of monetary subsidies, leading eventually to assertion by the colonists of "the principle of representation". His comment on the Conference as a whole was: "What have we arrived at? Simply this: that the Australian group of colonies will pay a certain amount annually to the support of a few ships in their own waters. But what has the rest of the Colonial Empire done towards the maintenance of the Imperial Navy? Nothing at all. The Cape has not agreed to do anything; Canada has not agreed to do anything; and none of the Colonies have agreed to do anything, for reasons which I think are weighty, and which the Conference will not overrule." But in thus stressing the unwillingness of the colonial delegates to bind themselves in any way to the spending of colonial funds for what were held to be extra-colonial purposes, he also pointed out that the British Navy was losing ground to the French and German navies as compared with its vast defensive commitments and their very limited ones.[3] Hofmeyr's proposal was supported by Natal and Victoria, but New South Wales considered it outside the terms of reference of the Conference, and it was consequently dropped.[4] The agreement reached on the strengthening of the Australian Squadron was embodied in the Imperial Defence Act of 1888, in which it was laid down that the ships, though under the Command of the Australian Station, should remain in Australian waters both in peace and war. New Zealand was normally to have two British warships, out of the general pool, stationed in her waters. The limits of the Australian station were defined so as to include New Guinea, New Britain, New Ireland, the Bismarck Archipelago and most of the

---

[1] *Parl. Pap.* 1887, LVI [C. 5091–I], pp. 271–7.
[2] W.O. 32/120/7696. [3] [C. 5091–I], pp. 464–5. [4] *Ibid.* p. 473.

Solomons.[1] The Act also authorised the expenditure of £2,600,000 on coast defences of which about half were to be for colonial ports and imperial coaling stations. The auxiliary squadron eventually reached Sydney on 5 September 1891.

The modest success achieved in defence arrangements at the first Colonial Conference was meanwhile being gravely offset by cumulative naval neglect which dated back, through the days of the second Disraeli ministry of 1874–80, to the policy of retrenchment announced by the first Gladstone ministry when taking office in 1868. From that year till 1884–5 the annual sum expended on new warship construction had remained at well under £2,000,000, except for a short-lived spurt during 1877–8, the years of the Russian war scare and the appointment of the Carnarvon Commission. Throughout the 'sixties and early 'seventies Britain's naval superiority over other countries, both absolute and relative, had remained unchallenged, but by the 'eighties the situation had changed considerably. The new French Navy was making rapid progress and threatening a new version of the traditional *guerre de course*, based on unrestricted sink-at-sight torpedo-boat warfare against British commerce, without any attempt to save crews or passengers or to salve ships and cargoes for prize-court investigation.[2] Russia, Italy and the United States were laying down modern warships. Colonial difficulties were arising with Germany in Africa and New Guinea, and Franco-German relations were much improved. Meanwhile, the British Navy, though still greatly superior to that of France, no longer had a "strategical sufficiency" to deal with the possible combination of France and Russia, supposing a third power, such as Italy, to be neutral but unfriendly. France and Russia, being less dependent on imports and shipping than Great Britain, could not be starved into submission, and having less overseas territory and shipping to defend, could in any future war devote their main naval effort to harrying British trade and attacking British home and overseas territory, either by bombardment or military invasion. The identification of France and Russia as still the most likely future enemies is confirmed by the Salisbury ministry's exchange of Heligoland for Zanzibar with Germany in 1890.

Unlike the Army, the Navy had not fought a real fleet action against a first-class naval power since the Basque Roads of 1809. By the late middle years of the nineteenth century a torpor had overcome the Service. The Board of Admiralty was still encumbered by the departmental duties thrust on it by the so-called reforms of Sir James Graham in 1832.[3] New guns and ammunition for the Navy were still included in the Army estimates, and the War Office had the

---

[1] *Parl. Pap.* 1888, III (Bill 346), p. 365; Statute 51 and 52 Vict. c. 32.

[2] This led to Admiral Tryon's proposal of May 1890 for State coverage of war risk insurances for merchant shipping, as a means of preventing panic and the cessation of wartime sailing. After years of abortive discussion the scheme was put into operation in 1914 immediately before the war (see p. 604 below).   [3] *C.H.B.E.* II, 810.

custody of the Navy's war stores. Gunnery was at a very low ebb and practice-firing was often a mere farce. Black powder was not replaced by smokeless till about 1900. Sights and range-finding equipment were very poor, and armour-piercing shells were not issued till 1902. Some ships were still armed with muzzle-loaders. In addition to lack of cruisers and destroyers, the main fleets were without such essential auxiliaries as colliers, ammunition, store, repair and hospital ships. Gibraltar lacked proper docks, defences, and reserves of coal and ammunition. The most important development in war organisation was the setting up about 1883 (ten years behind the Army) of a Foreign Intelligence Committee in the Admiralty which in 1887 blossomed into the Naval Intelligence Department (N.I.D.) and was given mobilisation and operations divisions.[1] It is difficult to exaggerate the early influence exerted by this Department on the policy of the Board.

Liaison was soon established between the Director (D.N.I.) and his opposite number at the War Office, the Director of Military Intelligence, and in 1892 an official conference was held between them on the possibility of combined operations in the Dardanelles.[2] Even so, there was still no naval staff college and no naval war staff at the Admiralty.

The full tide of naval revival, when at last it came, was of such force that it outlived the immediate era of the Triple Entente of 1904–7 with France and Russia, and, accepting the growth of the German Navy as a new challenge, continued unabated till 1914. It seems to have begun in September 1884 with a series of articles in the *Pall Mall Gazette*, entitled "The Truth about the Navy", by W. T. Stead. Press agitation followed and for the years 1885–6 and 1886–7 expenditure on naval construction rose to an average of £3,600,000. By 1887–8, however, this expenditure had dropped to under £3,000,000, the total estimates being £1,000,000 less than those for 1860–1, the year in which the *Warrior* was launched.[3] Nevertheless Lord Salisbury accepted Lord Randolph Churchill's resignation from the Exchequer when W. H. Smith refused to reduce the expenditure for the land defence of the ports and coaling stations recommended by the Carnarvon Commission.[4] The slump in naval construction had gone too far to enable the Admiralty to wait for foreign experiments and then follow with something better. Though Stead's earlier agitation had for the moment exhausted itself, his theme was soon developed on an exceptionally broad and influential basis. Brassey's *British Navy* (1882), another attempt to arouse interest, was followed

---

[1] See *Pall Mall Gazette*, 13 Oct. 1886, for Lord Charles Beresford's memo. on the need for organisation and preparation for war.

[2] Marder, A. J., *British Naval Policy, 1880–1905* (1940), pp. 111, 159–60. Quotes very important Admiralty material not available in other publications.

[3] *C.H.B.E.* II, 822.

[4] Churchill, W. S., *Lord Randolph Churchill* (1906), II, 235, also II, 227–31, 237–40, 315–16.

in 1886 by the first issue of the world-famed *Naval Annual*. Soon Sir John Colomb, G. J. Goschen, Sir Charles Dilke, Spenser Wilkinson, H. W. Wilson, J. R. Thursfield, Arnold White, Laird Clowes and Colonel George Sydenham Clarke were urging a big new naval construction programme. An influential school of professional writers and historians also appeared, including Admiral Philip Colomb, whose *Essays on Naval Defence* appeared from 1871 to 1889, J. K. Laughton, Julian Corbett, S. R. Gardiner, M. Oppenheim and J. R. Tanner. Their combined efforts, and particularly those of Corbett, gave a firm strategical and historical basis for the major theme simultaneously enunciated in the United States by the publication in 1890 of Captain A. T. Mahan's *Influence of Sea Power upon History*.

The turning-point in Government policy came with the appointment in 1888 of Admirals Dowell, Vesey Hamilton and Richards to investigate the lessons to be learnt from the recent naval manœuvres. They reported unanimously that the Navy was too weak to take the offensive by blockade against even a single enemy and at the same time carry out all the multifarious duties which would inevitably be thrust upon it in war. In the case of war against two Powers "the balance of maritime strength would be serious against England". "Without particularising her possible antagonist, there can be no doubt that were England involved in a maritime war, and were she to resume her natural rights as a Belligerent which appear to have been voluntarily laid aside by the Declaration of Paris in 1856,[1] complication with Neutral States would inevitably ensue, and her whole commercial position and the immense carrying trade by which it is sustained would be jeopardized at the outset were war forced upon her when her Navy was weak." Naval defeat would mean England's loss of India and her colonies. "No time should be lost in placing her Navy beyond comparison with that of any two powers. As there is nothing in our opinion to justify the belief that the days of ironclad battleships are over, we recommend a resumption and a steady continuance of ironclad building."[2] The danger of invasion, they stated, would be better met by increased naval expenditure than by costly shore defences. This Report was decisive, and resulted in the famous Naval Defence Act of 1889 which authorised the building of eight large and two small battleships, nine large and twenty-nine smaller cruisers, four gunboats and eighteen torpedo-gunboats at a cost of £21,500,000, spread over the next five years. All the ships were to be ready for sea by April 1894.[3] The general intention of the Act was to make the Navy superior, at least on paper, to the combined navies of any two European Powers. The precise strategical interpretation

---

[1] See *C.H.B.E.* ii, 870–2.

[2] *Parl. Pap.* 1889, L [C. 5632], pp. 29–31. This had been recognised by Lord Northbrook when he first took office as First Lord of the Admiralty in 1880; see his evidence before the Carnarvon Commission (5 July 1881), P.R.O. 30–6/52.

[3] 52 & 53 Vict. c. 8; *Parl. Pap.* 1889, v (Bill 186), p. 463.

of the so-called "two-power standard" gave rise to much subsequent dispute, especially in view of the Empire's long and vulnerable lines of sea trade and communication, its widely dispersed territories, the many tempting prizes it offered in the shape of ports, bases and coaling-stations, and the entanglements likely to arise with neutrals in time of war. Nevertheless, for some fifteen years the "two-power standard" provided a useful guide to Britain's naval needs.[1] The laying down *en bloc* of the eight large *Royal Sovereign* battleships under the Act, as a single homogeneous class, closed the transition or experimental period in British naval architecture begun by the launch of the *Warrior* in 1861, and established the standard form of battleship for all the leading navies.

In addition to the several new classes of "protected cruisers" (the equivalent of today's "light cruisers") laid down, the 'eighties and 'nineties witnessed important developments in the flotilla forces. Effective motive power for the torpedo gave ships mounting it a completely new tactical role. Instead of being confined to the attack and defence of trade, defence against invasion and fleet auxiliary work, the new torpedo boats could make direct attacks on the largest capital ships afloat. By 1895 the torpedo had an accurate range of 2000 yards. The first British torpedo boat, the *Lightning*, was built in 1877, and was followed by torpedo gunboats of the *Rattlesnake* class, intended for protecting capital ships against torpedo boat attack. These were superseded in 1893 by the first "torpedo-boat destroyer", H.M.S. *Havock*. Since, however, the destroyer could itself attack battleships as well as defend them against torpedo boats, it became necessary to give battleships anti-torpedo defences of their own. This "secondary armament" was of two types; quick-firing Hotchkiss and Nordenfelt guns for repelling surprise flotilla attacks at close range, and 6-inch guns for repelling torpedo craft in general at medium and longer ranges. Passive defence was also provided by extending the armour belt to the bow and stern, and by sub-dividing the whole of the underwater section into watertight compartments. Extensive armour plating below the waterline was impracticable because of the weight involved. Anti-torpedo nets could be used by ships at anchor. Competitive development in guns and torpedoes on the one hand, and ship design and armour on the other, had completely upset the old static relationship between attack and defence. Thus, no sooner had the big-gun armour-plated capital ships of the transition period reached a standardised form in the *Royal Sovereign* class, than their supremacy was challenged by the torpedo-firing surface flotilla, and subsequently by the submarine. At first described as the weapon of the weak, and useful only for coast defence, the submarine quickly acquired a capacity for comparatively long-range

---

[1] For the whole subject see Woodward, E. L., *Great Britain and the German Navy* (1935), pp. 455–73.

offensive action. By 1904 the Admiralty recognised that, owing to the submarine (and the mine), close blockade was no longer feasible, and that capital ships must have still greater underwater protection. Conversely, however, the submarine gave some increased protection against the invasion of Britain. With the torpedo came developments in the mine, also regarded as a weapon of the weak. Nevertheless the launch by Germany in 1906–7 of fast long-range minelayers constituted a new threat to British seaborne trade as well as to warships.

Meanwhile, the increasing importance of the Suez Canal led to proposals to develop Alexandria as a naval base. The main problem was how to prevent a Russian *coup de main* against Constantinople and the Straits, in the event of the two essentials of British strategy, namely Turkish co-operation and French neutrality, being absent or uncertain. Both Russia and France, moreover, appeared to regard the Naval Defence Act as a direct challenge, and by 1893 their combined naval estimates for new construction exceeded Britain's by a ratio of more than five to three. In the autumn the Russian Black Sea fleet visited Toulon and there were suggestions that a Russian squadron might be permanently in the Mediterranean. With Sir Frederick Richards as First Sea Lord it was certain that the Navy's case for further expansion would be strongly put, despite the fact that Gladstone was again in office and Sir William Harcourt Chancellor of the Exchequer. The Admiralty proposals for 1894–5, backed by the First Lord, Lord Spencer, envisaged a further five years' programme of expansion amounting to a second Naval Defence Act.[1] This eventually matured in the shape of the *Majestic* and *Canopus* class battleships and more cruisers and destroyers. The final acceptance of the estimates, however, created a major cabinet crisis and threatened the resignation of the Sea Lords *en bloc*. Lord Fisher's subsequent comment that "we got the ships and Gladstone went", is now known to be rather nearer the truth than Morley's evasive account.[2]

After the conclusion of the Franco-Russian alliance in 1894, Mediterranean strategy became even more important. It seemed possible that France might threaten invasion and so keep the British Army tied to Britain, thus preventing reinforcements being sent to India in case of a Russian attack. At the same time a new menace appeared in France's commerce-raiding armoured cruisers. In June 1895 the Rosebery ministry resigned on a vote of censure deploring the insufficiency of cordite ammunition supplies. The new Salisbury ministry was pledged to naval expansion, though such steps as it took amounted to little more than maintaining the numerical interpretation of the "two-power standard" and extending docking facilities at the Cape, Mauritius, Hong Kong and Gibraltar. Owing to the

---

[1] *Parl. Pap.* 1893–4, vi (Bill 450), p. 113.
[2] Morley, J., *Life of Gladstone* (1903), iii, 507–8, 563. In the index to this work, covering 71 double-column pages, the headings "Admiralty" and "Navy" do not appear. See also Marder, A. J., *British Naval Policy, 1880–1905* (1940), pp. 174–205.

continued importance of the Mediterranean, the self-governing colonies once more receded to the strategic periphery of the Empire, and when the second Colonial Conference met in 1897 imperial strategy as such received little attention. On the other hand the Admiralty was now looking to the East, partly because of the expansion of markets and seaborne trade in that area, and partly because of the political and strategic events arising out of the Sino-Japanese War of 1894–5. Joseph Chamberlain, the new Colonial Secretary, urged the colonial delegates to make further increases in their defence contributions, and an interesting proposal was made for exchange of visits between imperial and colonial military forces with a view to securing a more homogeneous system of organisation and training throughout the land forces of the Empire. The annual naval contributions from the colonies, amounting to £126,000, though appreciated by the Admiralty, meant very little in actual value. The Admiralty claimed that it must retain a free hand in the general disposition of all the sea forces of the Empire in time of war.[1] As a result of the Conference the Cape undertook to pay an annual and unconditional naval subsidy of £30,000 and Natal of £12,000, in addition to the existing colonial contributions.

The line of development followed by the Army was very different from that of the Navy. The Army had had continuous fighting experience unequalled by that of any contemporary army, though only in the Crimea (1854–6) had it met European troops in European territory. Hence Lord Wolseley, Lord Roberts, Sir Evelyn Wood, Sir George White, and Sir Redvers Buller, its leaders in the 'nineties, all of whom had been awarded the Victoria Cross, were specialists only in Asiatic and colonial warfare. Yet the British regular soldier of 1890, despite much that was antiquated in his arms, training, organisation and way of looking at war, was nevertheless a modern soldier. This was the indirect result of the withdrawal of the colonial garrisons which had enabled Lord Cardwell *in time of peace* to carry out his military reforms. By substituting the short-service system of seven years with the colours for the previous twenty-one, Cardwell had ended the strategic dispersal of the Army about the Empire in long-service and semi-penal exile.[2] With the short-service system came also the linking of the infantry battalions in pairs, which made possible a more reasonable balance between home and foreign service. One battalion in each pair now took its turn to serve abroad and received drafts from its linked battalion at home, an arrangement which mitigated the hardship of long service in India or the colonies by providing regular reliefs. Each battalion serving abroad

---

[1] *Parl. Pap.* 1897, LIX [C. 8596], pp. 7–17.

[2] On the other hand the Cardwell system caused great hardship to men who, being denied a full career in the Army, found themselves thrown on the labour market too old to adapt themselves satisfactorily to industry.

was also periodically relieved as a whole by the linked battalion from home.

The withdrawal of the imperial garrisons from the self-governing colonies was an essential condition of the reforms, since otherwise the balance between the infantry forces stationed at home and those abroad could not have been kept except by a very substantial increase in the total personnel of the Army. By 1890 service abroad was restricted mainly to India; Egypt, South Africa, Gibraltar, Malta and the Far East being minor commitments. The potential strength of the Home Army was also increased by the creation of the Army Reserve. Men who had completed their seven years with the colours under the new system were liable for the next five years to be recalled to the colours in case of war, and thus each home battalion could be brought up to strength. Yet it was hardly on these grounds that the withdrawal of the garrisons had been recommended to the taxpayers of the United Kingdom, but rather on grounds of finance and political expediency. Cardwell, also, in the teeth of very strong opposition, had abolished the purchase of first commissions and subsequent steps in promotion, the current prices of which had risen far above the heavy sums officially laid down. By an equally useful, though less obvious, reform, the Commander-in-Chief and his principal subordinates were brought into the same building as the Secretary of State for War, to whom they were made constitutionally responsible for the efficiency of the Army as a whole. In spite of these reforms the Home Army remained a mere residual pool, tied to the necessity of providing imperial reliefs, and unrelated to any kind of strategic plan. There was still no home-based striking force capable of operating as a whole in Europe or anywhere else. In practice, moreover, the balance between the infantry battalions at home and abroad eventually broke down owing to the demands of small wars, so that by 1897 it became necessary to raise six new battalions. A further cause of unbalance was the poor physique of many of the recruits which made them unsuitable for training service abroad.

The Militia, with an effective strength of about 100,000, though providing a very useful means of expanding the Regular Army, could not be termed a real army for home defence. It had no cavalry of its own, no army service corps, no field engineers, nor organised field artillery, and only a small medical staff corps. Agricultural labourers predominated in its ranks, while the new industrial towns were but poorly represented. More than one-third of the Militia artillery (garrison) and one-fifth of its infantry units were established in Ireland. In no sense did the Militia provide a good pattern for efficient citizen forces in the colonies. The Yeomanry, amounting to about 10,000 men, were an internal security force, local, not very efficient, and without transport. Nevertheless they had an important influence in the second South African War in connection with the "mounted infantry", a new development in cavalry warfare. The Volunteers with an effective strength of about 230,000 "contained a large amount of valuable raw material".[1] Their ranks included men of substance. The names of such units as the "Post Office Rifles", "Artists' Rifles", "Inns of Court" and "Central London Rangers", suggested a public-spirited urban intelligentsia. They were keen rifle shots, and included a valuable reservoir of specialised professional skill. But despite strong artillery and engineer establishments (including submarine miners, electrical and railway engineers), they had no regimental transport, no army service corps, and no organisation for war. There were no Volunteers in Ireland.

Meanwhile the low pay, bad food and extremely bad living conditions of the British regular soldier made it difficult to attract a good type of recruit, with the result that military efficiency suffered and the introduction of modern technical devices was delayed through lack of men capable of being trained to handle them. To increase the basic rates of pay was impossible without reducing the strength of the Army, owing to the unwillingness of either political party to see any substantial increase in the total estimates. When the colonies set about raising their own militia forces and, later on, their own regular forces, they invariably paid the same basic rates as those for comparable civilian work in the respective colonies and such rates were far higher than those paid for similar work in the United Kingdom.

Further army reforms were hampered by the peculiar position still occupied by the Duke of Cambridge, who, in addition to being the Queen's cousin, had a constitutional right of approaching the Crown direct in certain military matters.[2] Although the Secretary of State for War exercised nominal control over the Army, the Commander-in-Chief was still responsible for its entire efficiency, including personnel, training, discipline, organisation, weapons, ammunition supply, equipment, works and stores. Recent changes in War Office organisation had had the effect of still further increasing his power and responsibility.[3] Being strongly conservative in outlook, the Duke had tended since taking office in 1856 to preserve and enforce the formalistic side of the old Peninsular army, while allowing the well-organised operational staff system built up by Wellington through his development of the Quartermaster-General's Department to wither away. The Army had thus no trained and organised body of officers charged with the essential duties of providing the Cabinet with professional information and advice on military policy, studying and planning such operations as might be necessary, training troops in peace, and organising their employment in war. The modern Staff College,

---

[1] Dunlop, Col. J K., *The Development of the British Army, 1899–1914* (1938), p. 65.
[2] *Parl. Pap.* 1890, xix [C. 5979], p. xxiv; Esher, *Journals*, i, 269.
[3] *Parl. Pap.* 1888, lxvii [C. 5304].

founded in 1858 (largely through the Duke's support), produced a certain number of staff officers, trained mainly in military administration, supply, movement and engineering services, but there was no General Staff at the War Office. In these circumstances the whole development of the British Army was held back at the moment when so many important military changes were taking place elsewhere, particularly in Germany, the United States and Japan. Lack of training in the use of new weapons and modern tactics, and lack of interest in military education and scientific developments, thus did much to nullify the valuable opportunities created by Cardwell's reforms.[1] Except for Aldershot there was no large home military station, nor was there even any useful training provided for troops awaiting their turn for overseas service. A more fundamental defect was the lack of close ties with the industrial development of the United Kingdom, such as had been forced on the Navy by competitive developments in shipbuilding, marine engineering and ordnance in France, Russia, Italy and the United States. Admittedly the difference in function between the British Army and the armies of Europe was far greater than the difference in function between the leading navies of the world. Even so, the Army made little effort to relate its efficiency to Britain's industrial progress. In 1887 a Royal Commission under the chairmanship of Sir James Fitzjames Stephen, after an exhaustive examination of evidence, reported that there was "no definite responsibility" in the Ordnance Department. "The great defects of the existing system are three—First, It has no definite object. Secondly, It has no efficient head. And thirdly, It has no properly organised method of dealing with technical questions which arise as to the construction or purchase of warlike stores. In other words it requires more system, more publicity, more vigour in administration, and more special knowledge in Council."[2] Such action as was taken as a result of this report appears to have been mainly with an eye to "home defence".

Closely related both to the strategic and tactical problems facing the Navy and the Army was the problem of fortifications, especially in the colonies and naval stations. Writing in 1890, Major George Sydenham Clarke, R.E. (later Lord Sydenham), stated that, "In the works constructed within the past thirty years at our home ports and fortresses abroad, no sufficient indication of the results of the experience obtained in the Peninsula, the Crimea and the American Civil War can be traced. Some of these works might have been designed by clever cadets, quick to recognise the niceties of technical artifice; but unable, from sheer immaturity of thought and want of study, to grasp the broader aspects of the science in its relation to

---

[1] Part of the Duke's opposition to reform arose from his natural wish to prevent military patronage from becoming the perquisite of the political parties.
[2] *Parl. Pap.* 1887, xv [C. 5062], p. xxxvi.

war".[1] For coastal defence some standard of requirements was essential. "When Port Phillip [Melbourne], about 9,500 miles from Toulon, receives an armament more efficient than that of Malta at only 600 miles, it is evident that there is extremely little stability of judgment in such questions."[2] As regards ships *versus* forts, ironclads were by comparison infinitely worse off for bombarding coastal batteries on a low site than the old sailing ships of the line. Our success at Alexandria in 1882 had been overestimated owing to the incompetence of the Egyptians. Ironclads might be difficult to sink outright, but their lack of armour on the upperworks and at the extremities made them very vulnerable to modern 6-inch guns on shore, especially if they were mounted on a high site. No cruisers of any kind could stand up to the fire of coastal batteries.[3] All this showed the need for replanning our overseas defences. Considering how difficult our enemies would find it to move their warships against us in distant waters, it would be sufficient on many stations to mount guns only intended to repel cruiser attacks.[4]

Meanwhile some at least of the lessons of the American Civil War and the Franco-Prussian War had been taken to heart by the Army, as was shown by the creation in 1873 of an Intelligence Branch which later on was placed under the Quartermaster-General and transferred to the Adjutant-General's Department. In 1886 Lord Wolseley, then Adjutant-General, instructed its head, Major-General Henry Brackenbury, "to prepare a scheme for mobilisation of two Army Corps and the necessary lines of communication troops for war outside Great Britain and Ireland". Brackenbury's report showed that although there were enough infantry and cavalry, there were not enough medical, commissariat, transport, ordnance store or veterinary personnel even for one corps, and that nearly 8000 horses would have to be bought. As a result a Mobilization Department was formed under the Adjutant-General (A. G. 7) to produce the germ of a paper plan for a future expeditionary force. Even so, there was no General Staff. At this moment, however, Cabinet policy was following a retrograde line. The French invasion bogey had reappeared, and with it the usual assumption that the British fleet might be beaten in battle, blockaded by superior forces, or evaded by an armada of troop transports. To meet this threat yet another great system of forts was to be erected round London and the chief naval bases, reminiscent of the earlier fortification mania of the 'sixties. The general military policy lying behind the fortifications was

---

[1] Clarke, G. Sydenham (Lord Sydenham), *Fortification: Its Past Achievements, Recent Development, and Future Progress* (1890), pp. 81–2.
[2] *Ibid.* p. 217. [3] *Ibid.* chap. xv.
[4] *Ibid.* pp. 257–8. Similar ideas about the effect of the changing character of war on colonial defences had already been put forward by General Sir Andrew Clarke in a memo to Lord Hartington, 24 Nov. 1884 (W.O. 33/42, pp. 771–5). The virtue of Sydenham Clarke's book was that it gave information to the public.

explained in the "Stanhope Memorandum", dated 1 June 1891, but kept secret until its publication in 1901.[1] In it the functions of the British Army were officially defined as being to support the civil power in the United Kingdom, to garrison India, to garrison bases and coaling stations at home and abroad, to provide two Army Corps of Regular troops and one Corps of Regular and Militia troops, to organise the remaining auxiliary forces for the defence of London and the home mercantile ports, and, in case of necessity, to be able to send abroad two complete Army Corps, with a cavalry division and line-of-communication troops. But it was to be distinctly understood that the probability of the employment of an Army Corps in the field in any European War "is sufficiently improbable to make it the primary duty of the military authorities to organise our forces efficiently for the defence of this country". Although the memorandum claimed that "It has been considered in connection with the programme of the Admiralty and with knowledge of the assistance which the Navy is capable of rendering...", it would appear to be completely at variance with the spirit actuating the Naval Defence Act. No hint was given of the possible need for offensive action beyond the "sufficiently improbable" case mentioned. Nor was there any suggestion that the Army had an offensive part to play in helping the Navy to gain command of the sea, by reinforcing British bases abroad and by conducting combined operations against enemy bases and territory.

Meanwhile a serious preliminary effort had been made to reform the whole direction of imperial defence by the appointment in 1888 of a Royal Commission, with Lord Hartington as chairman and Major George Sydenham Clarke as Secretary, "to enquire into the Civil and Professional Administration of the Naval and Military Departments". The Commissioners did admirable work despite their somewhat limited outlook. Clarke wrote, "My general impressions were that few members or witnesses had ever made a study of administration or arrived at any principles, and that the two professional members [Admiral Richards and General Brackenbury] almost alone had any clear ideas on the subject. To the political members, the relating of the services to the Civil power and the maintenance of the fullest authority by the Minister for War seemed to be momentous."[2] Evidently the politicians were more concerned with establishing the power of the Secretary of State over the Commander-in-Chief, the Duke of Cambridge, than with fighting efficiency. "The evidence," continues Clarke, "some of which was most disturbing, has never been published. The general effect was to reveal an 'unsatisfactory and dangerous condition of affairs' which must have been apparent to every member of the Commission, but

[1] *Parl. Pap.* 1901, xxxix [Cd. 607], p. 255.
[2] Sydenham of Combe, Lord, *My Working Life* (1927), p. 100.

the remedies proposed were inadequate."[1] The Commissioners recommended the abolition of the office of Commander-in-Chief, and the establishment of a War Office Council under the presidency of the Secretary of State, with a Chief of Staff as first professional member.[2] This officer should be freed from all executive duties and charged with advising the Secretary of State on "general military policy", collecting information, preparing a scheme for the military defence of the Empire and "plans of action in certain contingencies". Owing to the diversity of our military problems we were more in need of a general staff than Continental countries. While the Admiralty administration appeared to the Commissioners to be almost a model system, at least as compared with the War Office, the complete lack of co-operation between the two departments was rightly deplored. "No combined plan of operation for the defence of the Empire in any contingency has ever been worked out by the two departments."[3] Yet the remedy, to "provide for very constant communication and consultation between two highly placed and responsible Naval and Military officers", in all matters of common interest, sounds too vague.[4] A more specific recommendation was for the formation of a "Naval and Military Council", to consist of the Service Ministers and their chief professional advisers under the presidency of the Prime Minister. This was clearly a demand for what eventually emerged as the Committee of Imperial Defence.[5] Henry Campbell-Bannerman, however, in a minority opinion, dissented very strongly from the proposal for a Chief of Staff. Unlike European states we had no need, he stated, for

planning possible operations in possible wars....In this country there is in truth no room for general military policy in this larger and more ambitious sense of the phrase....Indian Military policy will be settled in India itself and not in Pall Mall. In any of the smaller troubles into which we may be drawn by the interests of some of our dependencies, the plan of campaign must be governed by the particular circumstances, and would be left (I presume and hope) to be determined by the officer appointed to direct operations. As to the defence of these islands, and of our depots and coaling stations, although there may have been some slackness and delay in the past, we have reasons to believe that now, if full provision has not yet been made, complete schemes at least have been matured for protection against attacks which cannot vary greatly in character.[6]

Clarke commented: "This was good Liberal doctrine, but the absence of any defined policy lay at the root of most of the evils and of the waste at the War Office, where no one was charged with thinking out anything; a frequent resort to promiscuous and sometimes incapable committees had proved a futile substitute."[7]

---

[1] Sydenham, *op. cit.* p. 101.
[2] *Parl. Pap.* 1890, xix [C. 5979], pp. xix-xxix.
[3] *Ibid.* p. vi (para. 10).   [4] *Ibid.* p. viii (para. 19).
[5] *Ibid.* p. viii. (para. 20).   [6] *Ibid.* pp. xxix-xxxi.
[7] Sydenham, *op. cit.* p. 103.

The report of the Hartington Commission is rightly regarded as a landmark in the history of imperial defence, yet it provoked no immediate governmental reaction. When in 1895 the Duke of Cambridge, the great Aunt Sally of the political members of the Commission, resigned office, Campbell-Bannerman, then Secretary of State for War in the Gladstone ministry, announced that under the new arrangement the "main principles" recommended by the Hartington Commission would be followed.[1] Instead he produced a compromise scheme in which the only clear result was the triumph of the political element in the War Office but without any gain to the fighting efficiency of the Army. This scheme was later accepted by Lord Lansdowne on behalf of the new Conservative ministry. By it Lord Wolseley was appointed Commander-in-Chief, thus preserving that office in name, but with greatly restricted powers. The Adjutant-General, the Quartermaster-General, and the Inspectors-General of Fortifications and Ordnance were all made directly responsible to the Secretary of State, although technically the Commander-in-Chief was still the "principal adviser of the Secretary of State on all military questions and charged with the general supervision of the military Departments at the War Office". Actually Lord Wolseley had no personal authority except over the Departments of Mobilisation, Intelligence, and the Military Secretariat.[2] Yet all this time the "small wars" of the 'nineties were increasing the number of troops employed abroad at the expense of those at home, thus placing an almost unbearable strain on the Cardwell system. In these circumstances, the Salisbury ministry had no choice but to accept Lord Wolseley's advice and make provision for considerable additions to the strength of the Army in the estimates of 1897–8 and 1898–9. Lack of recruits was the real source of trouble rather than the need for more regiments, the home forces being nearly 20,000 short of their establishment on 1 January 1899. As an incentive to recruiting, therefore, the private soldier's pay was increased by a ration allowance of 3d. a day, making one shilling in all.

The "small wars" of the Empire during the 'eighties and 'nineties fell into three well-defined geographical groups: Egypt and the Sudan, tropical Africa, India and Burma. In all of these the Navy's unchallenged use of sea communications enabled expeditionary forces and reinforcements to be transported from the United Kingdom and other parts of the Empire to the various theatres of war with ease and efficiency. The North-West Frontier of India was the scene of almost continuous fighting. The Chitral operations in 1895 absorbed 15,000 men, and in 1897 a great series of tribal risings absorbed substantial forces, including a single operation by 30,000 men. The conquest of Upper Burma (1885–6) and the subsequent internal campaigns

---

[1] Parl. Pap. 1904, XL [Cd. 1789], pp. 133–4.
[2] Order in Council, Nov. 1895: Parl. Pap. 1896, LI (59), pp. 483, 487 (memo.).

which went on till 1898 against the Kachins, Chins and Lushais sometimes involved as many as 25,000 British and Indian troops. In tropical Africa operations of smaller scope were undertaken in Ashanti (1895–6), Gambia (1891–2), Sierra Leone (1899), East Africa, Zululand, Somaliland and Uganda (1897–1904). In several of these the Navy played an unobtrusive but influential part.

The reconquest of the Sudan (1898–9) by the British and Egyptian forces under Lord Kitchener, though involving fewer British troops than had been commanded by Wolseley in 1882, was more important internationally than any British military operations elsewhere during the period. It was preceded by various successful defensive operations in which the newly raised Egyptian Army acquired the morale and experience necessary for an offensive campaign. Tactically Omdurman taught the British soldier very little. By this time he was accustomed to face huge numerical odds in the shape of massed native attacks against which he used volley fire with his breech-loading Lee-Metford rifle, without having to consider the enemy's reply. Only in the first South African War (1881) had he encountered white marksmen using accurate fire from concealed positions. But the lessons of Majuba and Laing's Nek, though fully appreciated by the fighting troops, had been ignored at home. They were to be relearnt with pain and suddenness even before Wingate's force had finally destroyed the Khalifa's resistance in Kordofan (1899).

CHAPTER VIII

INTERNATIONAL RIVALRY, 1885–1895

I

IN 1885, while Great Britain's old rivalry with Russia was as deep as ever, all her old friendships had disappeared. Turkey had been alienated by the occupation of Egypt. France had become bitterly hostile on the same score. Germany was everywhere acting unfavourably to British interests; and something approaching an anti-British *entente* had been formed between Germany and France, using British difficulties in Egypt as its lever and colonial disputes as its field of operation. Austria had abandoned the hope of collaboration with Great Britain against Russia, enabling Bismarck to revive the Three Emperors' League. In the form of the Alliance of the Three Emperors, concluded in 1881 and revived in 1884, this had given Russia a free hand in Central Asia. Together with the encouragement Russia had derived from Great Britain's difficulties with France and Germany, it had converted Russia's latent hostility on the North-West Frontier into open antagonism and produced the Penjdeh crisis.[1]

For Lord Salisbury, returning to office in June 1885, appalled by "this abyss of isolation", the key to Great Britain's difficulties lay in her relations with Germany. Friction with Russia seemed unavoidable if Great Britain was to stand firm on the North-West Frontier and at the Straits. The alienation of France was axiomatic unless Great Britain surrendered in Egypt; and firmness was even more necessary in Egypt, "the Road to India",[2] than it was elsewhere. If he was to extricate the country from danger without some sacrifice on these three fronts, it could only be by recovering Germany's friendship. He aimed at this from the outset; and more than ever after July 1886, when he formed another government following a brief period of rule by Gladstone between February and July of that year. For in the interval a revolt in Eastern Roumelia in September 1885, and the reunion of that province with Bulgaria, had reopened the Eastern Question and, by offending Russia, had raised the possibility of a Russian march into the Balkans.

Circumstances in one way favoured Salisbury's efforts. As early as the autumn of 1885, because France and Russia had proved unwilling to press their quarrels with Great Britain, Bismarck had concluded that he must renounce his hostility towards her before he abandoned

---

[1] See above, chap. iv, pp. 122–6.
[2] Cecil, *Life of Salisbury*, III, 126–7; February 1885.

it at Salisbury's request.[1] By the autumn of 1886 the reopening of the Eastern Question had disrupted the Three Emperors' Alliance and forced Austria to look once more for British backing against Russia; and the beginnings of the Boulanger nationalist movement in France, by reopening that other major issue, the Franco-German frontier, had killed all prospects of Franco-German collaboration. Both developments emphasised the danger that France and Russia might draw together and made Bismarck even anxious for better relations with Great Britain. Another danger, occurring during the Franco-German war-scare of 1886 and having the same effect on Bismarck, was that Italy, discontented with the Triple Alliance, might draw towards France. On the other hand, Bismarck showed great skill and determination in his efforts to retain the control of European relationships which events were threatening to take from him. His aim in the Bulgarian crisis was to commit Great Britain to Austria; success in this would make it unnecessary for Germany to commit herself against Russia and leave her free to keep Russia away from France. His method of achieving it was to encourage Russia in the Balkans while urging Austria and Great Britain to resist her there. He similarly wanted to bind Great Britain to support Italian interests against France in the Mediterranean so that Germany could retain room for manœuvre in her relations with Italy and France.[2] Salisbury's problem, therefore, was not simply how to restore good relations with Germany, though that seemed necessary if Russia was to be restrained in the Balkans and Great Britain was to receive the support of the Triple Alliance in Egypt. It was how to do this without at the same time contributing to the return of those days in which, up to the autumn of 1885, Germany's domination of the relations between the Powers and Great Britain's dependence on Germany's favour had had such disturbing effects on the British freedom of action.

When the Bulgarian crisis came to a head at the end of 1886 Salisbury was forced, by Bismarck's ability and his own determination to defend British interests, to fall in with Germany's plans. Italy's demands for British as well as for German support in the Mediterranean had mounted with the crisis. To offset the danger of losing Italian support in Egypt, Salisbury accepted in February 1887 a loose understanding by which the two Powers would co-operate to uphold the *status quo* in the Mediterranean, the Adriatic, the Aegean and the Black Seas. Bismarck was then able to agree to assist Italy in certain circumstances in North Africa with the conviction that, in view of Great Britain's new commitment to Italy, the German promise would never

---

[1] Cecil, *op. cit.* III, 224–5, 257; Taylor, A. J. P., *Germany's First Bid for Colonies*, pp. 77, 82–4, 88–94; *Die Grosse Politik der Europäischen Kabinette*, IV, nos. 770, 779–83.
[2] Langer, W. L., *European Alliances and Alignments*, chaps. x and xi; Fuller, J. V., *Bismarck's Diplomacy at its Zenith*.

have to be fulfilled.[1] It was at Salisbury's invitation that Austria next joined the Anglo-Italian agreement by exchanging Notes with Great Britain which, though hardly less vague than those exchanged with Italy and containing no definite pledge, still promised her British diplomatic support; and he took this step, despite his suspicion of Bismarck's refusal to let Germany be involved, because he could see no other way of warding off the Russian danger to Constantinople and the Straits. With Germany refusing to promise support to Austria against Russia, with Austria reluctant to oppose Russia in those circumstances without British support, some members of the British Cabinet, who were also influenced by the wish for reconciliation with Russia in the interests of security in Central Asia and India, had wanted Great Britain to "depart from the traditional policy of resisting the designs of Russia in the Balkan peninsula".[2] Salisbury, however, feeling that "the loss of Constantinople would be the ruin of our party and a heavy blow to the country", was "anxious to delay by all means Russia's advance to that goal".[3] He justified the exchange of Notes with Austria by the statement that "England will fight...in case Russia should attack the Balkan states, and it is well that the Tsar should know it".[4] It was with the same object, that of bolstering up Austria and thus of deterring Russia, that in December 1887, after renewed rumours of impending Russian action against Bulgaria since the previous summer, he signed the so-called Second Mediterranean Agreement with Austria and Italy. This recapitulated the earlier Notes but contained additional and more specific clauses. These committed the three Powers to assist the Sultan in opposing Russian designs on Bulgaria, at the Straits and—Salisbury having insisted on this extension—in Asia Minor. The Powers also bound themselves to threaten him with naval action and the occupation of key points on Ottoman territory should he show signs of giving way to Russian pressure. Even more than in the spring, Salisbury felt he had no alternative but to accept these terms, though they were more binding than the earlier ones and amounted virtually to an alliance, on account of Great Britain's need for support in Egypt and at the Straits.[5]

But just as Bismarck wanted to regain control of European diplomacy, so Salisbury's object was to defend British interests without

---

[1] Albertini, L., *The Origins of the War of 1914*, I, 51–5; Pribram, A. F., *The Secret Treaties of Austria-Hungary*, I, 104 *seqq.*, II, 54–9, 67–79.

[2] Cecil, *op. cit.* III, 319–22; *Letters of Queen Victoria*, 3rd ser. I, 201 *seqq.*, 264 *seqq.*; Churchill, W. S., *Lord Randolph Churchill*, II, 155 *seqq.*

[3] Churchill, *op. cit.* II, 161.

[4] Cecil, *op. cit.* IV, 20–4. See also, for the first Mediterranean Agreement, Langer, *op. cit.* pp. 384–5, 397–8, 400–4; Medlicott, W. N., "The Mediterranean Agreements of 1887", *Slavonic Rev.* V (June 1926), 66–88; Penson, L. M., "Lord Salisbury's Foreign Policy", *Cambridge Hist. Jour.* V, no. 1 (1935), pp. 91 *seqq.*; *D.G.P.* IV, no. 918; Gooch and Temperley (eds.), *British Documents on the Origins of the War*, VIII, 3, 6.

[5] Cecil, *op. cit.* IV, 72–7; Langer, *op. cit.* pp. 432–41; Medlicott, *loc. cit.*; Pribram, *op. cit.* I, 124–33; *D.G.P.* IV, nos. 932–40; *B.D.* VIII, 12.

yielding to Germany the position that Bismarck sought. It was mainly for this reason that he limited as far as he could the obligations involved in the Mediterranean Agreements, keeping them secret and informal, and as vague as circumstances allowed, when the Triple Alliance Powers would have preferred a public, formal and binding alliance or military convention on each occasion. For the same reason he accepted the obligations, limited as they were, with great reluctance; and having accepted them, it was the fact that he had had no alternative, while Germany had been able to remain aloof, that weighed most heavily with him by emphasising the extent of Bismarck's commanding position. His suspicion of Bismarck's refusal to be involved, marked from the outset of the negotiations, steadily increased throughout 1887.[1] At the moment the first agreement was being signed, it was this suspicion that induced him to seek a way of escape from dependence on the Triple Alliance in Egypt. In the months during which the second agreement was being negotiated, the same suspicion led him to question for the first time the importance of defending the Straits.

Salisbury had already, in 1885, made an unsuccessful attempt to change the Egyptian problem from an international one to an Anglo-Turkish one by offering the Sultan a general assurance of Great Britain's intention to evacuate Egypt in due course in return for Turkey's recognition of the legality of the occupation while it lasted.[2] In February 1887, before the exchange of Notes with Italy, he decided to go further still. He sent Sir Henry Drummond-Wolff to Constantinople with a qualified offer to leave Egypt in five years' time if Turkey would recognise the legality of the British occupation meanwhile. The qualifications were important. Evacuation would only take place it there were no danger of anarchy or foreign invasion at the time; Great Britain would retain the right of re-entry at any time if anarchy threatened or the Egyptian Government failed to fulfil its obligations.[3] But his offer still involved a great concession; and his object in making it, as in the earlier attempt of 1885, was to sidestep all the Powers, especially Germany, by regularising Great Britain's status in Egypt in a direct settlement with the Sultan. The occupation of Egypt was a source of German pressure. His most recent experience of that pressure had been Bismarck's warning that Germany would not continue to restrain France and Russia, but would encourage them, if Great Britain did not accept the first Mediterranean Agreement.[4] "Egypt is a disastrous inheritance, for it enables the Chancellor to demand rather unreasonable terms as

---

[1] Cecil, *op. cit.* IV, 9, 26, 50–1, 69–71; *Letters of Queen Victoria*, 3rd ser. I, 268–72.
[2] Cecil, *op. cit.* III, 237; *Parl. Pap.* 1886, LXXIV [C. 4604], pp. 41–3.
[3] Cecil, IV, 38–40; *Parl. Pap.* 1887, XCII [C. 5050], pp. 538–45; Hornik, M. P., "The Mission of Sir Henry Drummond-Wolff to Constantinople, 1885–87", *E.H.R.* LV (Oct. 1940), 598–623; Drummond-Wolff, Sir H., *Rambling Recollections*.
[4] Langer, *op. cit.* p. 399; *D.G.P.* IV, nos. 883, 889.

the price, not of his assistance, but of his refusal to join in a coalition against us." "It is only Egypt that puts us in this difficulty for otherwise Bismarck's wrath would be of little moment to us. It is heartily to be wished that we were delivered from this inconvenient and somewhat humiliating relationship." This was the burden of all his correspondence during the Drummond-Wolff negotiations.[1]

It would have been unrealistic to expect France to accept the argument, on which Salisbury based those negotiations, that Turkey's independence extended to Egypt, where she was therefore free to make whatever arrangements she chose. If only because it was so hedged around with qualifications, he probably did not expect France to give her blessing to the arrangement; and this was still put to Turkey for signature after he had failed to secure French acceptance for it by offering to reduce the time-limit from five to three years. But if his object was not to pacify France, but to exchange the Triple Alliance's need of British support for the support of the Triple Alliance in a plan that would reduce Great Britain's dependence on the Triple Alliance, the mistake he made lay in not foreseeing that France would retaliate as forcibly as she did. Arguing, correctly, that the proposed convention would "establish a political condominium with Turkey and without Europe in place of a financial condominium with France under the control of Europe",[2] the French Government forced the Sultan, who had signed it in May 1887, to evade its ratification. France succeeded because she was supported by Russia. To the pressure of these two Powers, which culminated in their threat to occupy Syria and Armenia if he did not comply, the Sultan gave way, despite the support received by Great Britain in Constantinople from the Triple Alliance Powers.

This set-back, accompanied by so marked an example of Franco-Russian collaboration, was one of the circumstances that made for even closer relations between Great Britain and the Triple Alliance Powers in the second half of 1887. Together with events in the Balkans, it threw Salisbury into the second Mediterranean Agreement. But just as the first agreement had had the effect of making him resent more strongly than before the limits on British freedom of action that arose from the occupation of Egypt, so it is from the defeat of the Wolff Convention, in the period in which the second agreement was being prepared, that may be dated the beginnings of his readiness to consider withdrawal at the Straits. His chief anxiety in the second half of 1887 and in the early months of 1888, sustained at the time by Bismarck's support of Russia in Bulgaria and justified at least in part by what has subsequently been learned of Bismarck's aims in concluding the secret Reinsurance Treaty with Russia of June 1887,[3] was lest Bismarck, to keep France and Russia apart, would try

[1] Cecil, *op. cit.* IV, 40–6. [2] Freycinet, *La Question d'Égypte*, p. 319.
[3] Langer, *op. cit.* pp. 416–25; *D.G.P.* V, nos. 1034 *seqq.*, 1072, 1082 *seqq.*, 1092.

to involve Russia in a Balkan war against Austria and Great Britain or would buy off Russia with the offer of a free hand at Constantinople. It led him to question whether the British interest in the Straits was defensible or even worth preserving.[1] By the end of 1887, though he accepted the second agreement, his doubts had reached the point at which he could say that British interest "in the Turkish domination of their present Empire and"—this was the significant addition— "of the Straits is not on the same level as that of Austria and Italy.... Our interest is not as vital as theirs".[2]

It is noticeable that these doubts disappeared after the spring of 1888 and that Salisbury also gave up all thought of leaving Egypt on any conditions. The immediate reason for the change was that, so far as Great Britain was concerned, despite his reluctance to enter them, the Mediterranean Agreements had achieved their object. Though the Agreements had remained secret, the collaboration of Austria, Italy and Great Britain had become so obvious and close that Russia had abandoned in March 1888 the pressure in Bulgaria and against Turkey that she had kept up for two and a half years. More important still, Russia's withdrawal, while removing the immediate danger to Great Britain at the Straits and thus reducing one source of pressure on Salisbury that Bismarck had found most useful, had produced a set-back in Russo-German relations. These were made worse still by the accession of William II, with his anti-Russian views, in July 1888. At the same time, Franco-Russian relations were becoming closer. France had supported Russia in the last stages of the Bulgarian crisis; the first French loan to Russia was negotiated during 1888. Nor was it the only result of these developments that, by reducing Germany's commanding position, they enabled Salisbury to abandon the thought that some sacrifice of important British interests might be necessary if a dangerous degree of dependence on Germany was to be avoided. Whereas it was Salisbury who had had to plead for closer Anglo-German relations in 1885, Bismarck, whatever his motives, was asking for them by January 1889. Circumstances, which had been running so heavily in Germany's favour, had restored to Great Britain freedom of action to the extent that Salisbury was able to decide for or against an alliance with Germany on more even terms than those on which he had accepted the earlier alignment with the Triple Alliance Powers.

He declined Bismarck's alliance offer of January 1889. What Bismarck offered was an alliance against France, and Salisbury may well have thought that the equivalent of the French danger to Germany was not the French but the Russian danger to Great Britain. There is no reason to doubt, however, that he would still have

---

[1] Cecil, *op. cit.* IV, 50–1, 69–71, 83–4; *Letters of Queen Victoria*, 3rd ser. I, 268–70; Langer, *op. cit.* pp. 430–1; Penson, *loc. cit.* pp. 98–9; *D.G.P.* IV, nos. 907–8.
[2] Cecil, *op. cit.* IV, 78–9; 14 Dec. 1887.

refused if Bismarck had been willing to apply the arrangement against Russia as well as France. Certainly he made no effort to get the offer so extended.[1] The real ground for his refusal was his attachment to the principle of limited liability, his view that fixed associations with or against particular Powers, let alone alliances, were incompatible with British interests. Far from being prepared to tighten relations with the Triple Alliance beyond the Mediterranean Agreements, his aim was to reach a position in which even those agreements would be unnecessary. In particular, he preferred to try to widen Great Britain's freedom of action by improving her relations with France; and this despite the fact that good relations with France seemed further away than ever at the beginning of 1889 on account of his refusal to accept French terms in Egypt.

Relations with France had deteriorated over a wide area since 1882. In Burma and Indo-China, in Somaliland, Eritrea and West Africa, the two Powers were at odds over their expansion into new territory and the delimitation of new frontiers. French encroachments in Morocco disturbed Great Britain only less than Italy and Spain. In the New Hebrides, despite an understanding with Great Britain that neither Power would annex them, France had landed troops in 1886, and had since refused to budge. On the basis of an ancient right to land cod on British territory, she had raised a commercial dispute in Newfoundland to the level of an international incident. But all the bitterness of France in these disputes sprang from her disappointment over Egypt, and Salisbury, knowing this, and anxious to reduce the advantage given to Germany by the Mediterranean Agreements, refused to display bitterness in return. On the contrary, despite his considerable annoyance with the French after the destruction of the Drummond-Wolff convention, he had made every effort, subject to his refusal to give way in Egypt, to avoid a permanent estrangement. Beginning in the autumn of 1887, Great Britain and France had concluded several agreements—for the delimitation of their frontiers in Somaliland, the neutralisation of the Suez Canal, the French evacuation of the New Hebrides—in which he was accused at home of showing lamentable weakness.[2] He had not been deterred by this criticism. "I do not wish to depend on his [Bismarck's] good will," ran one of his comments on the second Mediterranean Agreement, "and shall therefore keep friends with France as far as we can do it without paying too dear for it."[3] "It is a matter of no common importance", he wrote in February 1888, "to avoid any unnecessary causes of conflict [with the French]."[4] These efforts were of no avail, however, against the effect on France of his firmness in Egypt. After 1888, while that firmness was strengthened by the

---

[1] Cecil, op. cit. IV, pp. 112–13; *Letters of Queen Victoria*, 3rd ser. I, 482 seqq.; *D.G.P.* IV, nos. 942–5.　　　　[2] Cecil, op. cit. IV, 49–51; Langer, op. cit. pp. 430–1.
[3] Cecil, op. cit. IV, 71.　　　　[4] Ibid. p. 95.

passing of the Balkan crisis and the greater willingness of Germany to co-operate with Great Britain, French animosity was increased by a recrudescence of Boulangism. Disputes between the two countries reached a new intensity, particularly over Newfoundland. In 1889 they produced in Great Britain the fear of a French invasion and led to the Naval Defence Act. Great Britain had as much cause as Germany to be disturbed by the drawing-together of Russia and France.

In these circumstances, when other changes had already convinced him that it could be preserved without undue risk, Salisbury, while rejecting Germany's proposal of an alliance, felt that the existing connection with the Triple Alliance Powers, though it must not be extended, must be preserved. The Mediterranean Agreements, moreover, which he had previously disliked, now came to suit his purpose closely, as they had earlier suited Bismarck's. While he no more trusted Germany than before and was no more willing than before to alienate France, they enabled him to rely on Germany and to check France by indirect means. "The alliance with Austria"—this was how he put the situation and described his policy in August 1888— "covers the only weak point in the English position. No foreign power (setting aside France for the moment) is in a position to threaten England's interests except Russia. . . . If Austria could be induced to view with equanimity the seizure of the Bosphorus by Russia, the English position would be very difficult, as England would have to defend the Bosphorus by herself; for Russia can always purchase the complicity of Italy and Germany by consenting to do what they like with France. But so long as Austria stands firm on this point, Germany, and consequently Italy, must go with her. . . ." In the same way, though "France is England's greatest enemy, that danger is dormant so long as the present strained relations exist between France and her two eastern neighbours".[1] In his determination to defend British interests without formal obligations to Germany or open conflict with France, it was in the enmity of Russia and Austria, of France and Germany, of Italy and France, rather than German reliability or French reasonableness, that he put his trust. The Mediterranean Agreements, on the other hand, though no more than a diplomatic safeguard against the danger that the other Powers would get on better terms, were still a necessary safeguard. For that danger, though not so imminent as it had seemed to be in 1885, would still be a serious danger if it ever materialised; and Salisbury still felt, as he had felt when adopting the first Mediterranean Agreement, that "if, in the present grouping of the nations . . . England were left out in isolation, it might well happen that the adversaries who are coming out against each other on the continent might treat the

---

[1] *Letters of Queen Victoria*, 3rd ser. 1, 436–8.

English Empire as divisible booty by which their differences might be adjusted...".[1]

From the autumn of 1889, however, his policy of close but informal relations with Germany, if not the Mediterranean Agreements as such, was threatened in two ways. The drawing-together of France and Russia had continued; and this was one threat. It had prompted Bismarck's proposal to Great Britain; because Salisbury had rejected the proposal, forcing Germany to consider alternative safeguards against the danger to herself, it was to be a disturbing element in Anglo-German relations after 1890. But even before that stage was reached the other threat to the existing relationship demanded Salisbury's attention. This was Anglo-German rivalry in Africa. The solution of that problem was to be dominated by the pattern of relationships between the Powers in Europe; better than anything else, it was to illustrate and justify Salisbury's satisfaction with the pattern as it existed after the spring of 1888 and it was because the struggle in Africa threatened that pattern, by disturbing the good relations between London and Berlin, that Salisbury was moved to solve it.

II

The Scramble for Africa had begun in the early 'eighties. Within ten years the entire continent, where it had not already been occupied in the eighteenth century and except for the Sudan and the Eastern Sahara, had been overrun. Already by the end of 1885 the south had been settled; in the west as far north as the Niger and in the east as far north as the Portuguese frontiers with Zanzibar, it presented no further problems to the Powers. Their rivalries were now confined to the east and centre of the continent and to the western bulge north of the Niger.

Great Britain had interests, if not a dominant position, in all these areas, but her possession of Egypt and of South Africa concentrated her attention on the east and centre. It was there, too, that the African rivalries of the Powers put the greatest strain on their relations in Europe. France was Great Britain's main rival in the western bulge. But friction between France and Great Britain already existed on the even more serious issue of Egypt; their rivalry in West Africa conformed to the existing pattern of relations between the Powers and did not threaten to distort it. In addition, it was kept within bounds by the fact that Germany was also established in West Africa and by the fact that Great Britain saw in France's activity in West Africa an opportunity to detach her from her Egyptian dreams and thus to reduce her hostility. Salisbury usually took the view that Great Britain should not oppose the French absorption of the hinter-

[1] *Letters of Queen Victoria*, 3rd ser. I, 271–2.

land in that area, but should rather encourage it.[1] It was largely for
this reason that, though incidents between British and French agents
on the spot inevitably continued, the joint commission of delimitation
established by the two Powers in February 1889 completed its work
rapidly and brought most Anglo-French friction in the area to a
close by fixing lasting frontiers for the British colonies of Gambia, the
Gold Coast and Sierra Leone. In East and Central Africa, however,
Great Britain's interests were less expendable on account of the
close connection between the destiny of those vast areas and the
existing British positions in Egypt and South Africa, each of which
bestrode a route to India. Great Britain's chief rival there among the
Great Powers—the competition with Portugal, though serious enough,
presented problems of a different order—was not France but Germany.
The struggle was not only more serious; after 1888 it also ran counter
to the friendly relationship established between Great Britain and
Germany in Europe.

It was in 1884, at a time when there was friction between the two
countries elsewhere and when Bismarck was striving for an anti-
British Franco-German *entente*,[2] that the added complications of
German trade and Bismarckian diplomacy had entered into the
already difficult situation in East and Central Africa. The authority
of the Sultan of Zanzibar over the East African mainland had been
dwindling for many years. In the 'eighties he still claimed sovereignty
over the land behind 6000 miles of the coast, down to the frontier of
Portuguese East Africa; but he could exert it only on the fringe of the
coast. In 1885, when the hinterland had become a no-man's-land
and when an Anglo-French agreement of 1862 dictated that it should
so remain, the two Powers having promised to respect the Sultan's
sovereignty, the German Karl Peters, with that haste and disregard
for rights and treaties which characterised the activities of most agents
in the scramble, whatever their nationality, had laid claim to 50,000
square miles of it and had received from Bismarck a charter for
his German East Africa Company. By the same year the Germans
had acquired control of most of the trade on the island of Zanzibar,
where Germany had appointed a consul in 1884. Rivalry between the
German East Africa Company and the recently formed British East
Africa Association had almost immediately provided Bismarck with
the occasion for a further dispute, on top of those in West Africa and
New Guinea, with the British Government.[3]

The quarrel had blown over when, coinciding with Gladstone's
succession by Salisbury, developments in Europe had forced Bismarck to work for closer relations with Great Britain. In October

[1] Cecil, *op. cit.* IV, 252–3.   [2] See above, pp. 121–2.
[3] Taylor, *op. cit.* pp. 85–6, 92. See also Townsend, M. E., *The Rise and Fall of Germany's
Colonial Empire, 1884–1918*; Hardy, G., *La Politique Coloniale et le Partage de la Terre au XIXe
et XXe Siècles*; Moon, P. T., *Imperialism and World Politics*.

and November 1886 Great Britain and Germany had reached an agreement by which, while the Sultan gave up his claim to illimitable empire on the mainland in return for the recognition of his authority over 6000 miles of the coast, to a depth of 10 miles, Germany and Great Britain had divided the rest of the hinterland between themselves. Great Britain had received a sphere to the north, Germany to the south, except that Germany retained a hold in the Witu area in the north. Both Powers had kept an influence in Zanzibar itself. France, brought into the negotiations on account of the agreement of 1862, had received a free hand in Madagascar in return for her acceptance of the new arrangement.[1]

Thereafter, on account of the situation in Europe, the German and British Governments had generally remained on good terms. But the German and British Companies had continued to disagree; and the rapid extension of the British and German spheres of influence into Central Africa had soon brought their friction to a head. While the British feared that German expansion inland from Witu would swallow Uganda and cut them off from the Nile sources, the Germans saw the threat of encirclement not only in British expansion westwards from East Africa into Uganda but also, after 1887, in Rhodes's advance to the north from Bechuanaland. Stanley's expedition from the Atlantic to Lakes Victoria and Tanganyika in search of Emin Pasha added to their anxiety.[2] Their own expansion was not confined to Uganda; they made steady progress to the south. By the end of 1889 competition between them and the British South Africa Company was intense. In the north, at the same time, the race for Uganda was intensified when Emin Pasha's withdrawal made Equatoria a no-man's-land which Karl Peters attempted to fill by declaring a German protectorate of the kingdom of Uganda in March 1890.[3]

The two home Governments were powerless to limit the activities of agents who were intent, on both sides, on establishing a favourable *de facto* position before a new settlement was negotiated. But Bismarck showed more anxiety than Salisbury to avoid the friction that these activities produced. As late as May 1887 he had still felt free to threaten Great Britain in Egypt in order to get his way in Zanzibar.[4] From then on, the steady deterioration of Germany's European situation forced him to give priority to improving his relations with Great Britain. "My map of Africa", he declared in December 1888, "lies in Europe. Here is Russia and here lies France; that is my map of Africa."[5] In January 1889 he mentioned in a Reichstag speech his "gravest apprehensions" about German colonial expansion and insisted that Germany should "ever proceed solely with and in

---

[1] Taylor, *op. cit.* pp. 94 *seqq.*; Cecil, *op. cit.* IV, 232–3; Langer, W. L., *The Diplomacy of Imperialism*, I, 112.
[2] Langer, *op. cit.* I. 112–15.   [3] *Ibid.* pp. 115–16.
[4] Cecil, *op. cit.* IV, 42–3, 100; Taylor, *op. cit.* pp. 95–6.
[5] Quoted in Langer, *European Alliances and Alignments*, p. 493.

agreement with...England". "The preservation of Anglo-German goodwill is, after all," he added, "the more important thing."[1] In the autumn of 1889, following his unsuccessful bid for an Anglo-German alliance, it was he who asked Salisbury for a settlement in Africa.[2]

Salisbury, little concerned for Africa up to 1887, had acquired a somewhat different outlook by the time this request was received. The last time he had referred to Egypt as a burden had been in April 1888.[3] By that date, public interest had grown, both in England and in Egypt, in the need to preserve the Nile Valley from the intrusion of foreign Powers, who might interfere with Egypt's water supply.[4] During 1888 and 1889, moreover, renewed attacks on Egypt's southern frontier by the dervishes were making the early evacuation of Egypt impossible at a time when Great Britain's improved diplomatic position was making it unnecessary for Salisbury to consider it. Under the combined effect of these developments, he had concluded not only that Great Britain should stay in Egypt, but also that she should undertake the reconquest of the Nile provinces. This undertaking would be deferred until Egypt's recovery enabled her to share the cost—and until opportunity offered; it was only after considerable hesitation that he would commit himself to the beginnings of a forward policy by consenting to a military expedition in the Tokar area in 1891. But the need to exclude other Powers from the Sudan until that time arrived had become the chief element in his African policy by 1889.[5] He no longer regarded East Africa as a pawn in the diplomatic game, to be used to get help from Bismarck in Turkey and Egypt, as he had done in 1885.[6] On the contrary, Germany had joined France, Italy and the Congo among what he regarded as Great Britain's rivals for the Nile; the most serious danger, indeed, was no longer from these other Powers but from the Germans to the south-east. Germany was the sole rival at Zanzibar itself, where he was now determined to end the system of multiple control to Great Britain's advantage.[7] And the Germans in East Africa also threatened another British interest in which Salisbury had recently become interested. From the summer of 1888, when northward expansion into Central Africa from Bechuanaland had become intensive, Salisbury, without having initiated it, had directly sponsored it. The plan was to bring as much as possible of southern Central Africa, in so far as it was not already effectively occupied by Portugal and

---

[1] Cecil, *op. cit.* IV, 125–6; *History of 'The Times'*, III, 142; Langer, *op. cit.* p. 493.
[2] Cecil, *op. cit.* IV, 248.
[3] *Ibid.* pp. 134–5.
[4] Langer, *The Diplomacy of Imperialism* I, 102–12.
[5] Cecil, *op. cit.* IV, 135–40; Lord Cromer, *Modern Egypt*, II, 76; Shibeika, M. el, *British Policy in the Soudan, 1882–1902* (1952).
[6] Cecil, *op. cit.* III, 230.
[7] *Ibid.* IV, 234–5, 286–8.

Germany, under British control.[1] Nor can the enthusiasm of others for this opportunity to establish a Cape-to-Cairo all-red route have escaped him entirely, if only because of the simultaneous increase of his own interest in the Sudan.

Two considerations weighed with Salisbury, therefore, when he considered Bismarck's African suggestion. On the one hand, and especially since he had already rejected Bismarck's offer of an alliance, he was anxious lest friction in Africa might endanger the close relations with Germany on which he, like Bismarck, set so much store. On the other hand, in his determination to secure Uganda and as much as possible of Central Africa, the extent of which may be judged from his resort to the methods of naval demonstration and ultimatum in the disputes with Portugal over her claims to Mashonaland, Nyasaland and the Zambezi basin in 1889 and 1890,[2] he saw no reason why he should not take advantage of Bismarck's marked concern for Great Britain's friendship by letting the race go on so long as it furthered his objectives in Africa without running too narrowly the risks of German hostility elsewhere. It was for this reason that as early as July 1887, while agreeing with Bismarck to discourage annexations behind their respective spheres of influence in East Africa, he had resisted Bismarck's wish for a more binding self-denying ordinance.[3] In the summer of 1889, for the same reason, he had refused Germany's request that the publication of the Charter of the British South Africa Company should be delayed until Germany had been consulted.[4] When Bismarck proposed a settlement in the following autumn he temporised again. He sent no reply till December. He then suggested that time was required to consider so difficult a situation, and that arbitration might eventually be the way out of the many difficulties.[5]

The German Government was not enthusiastic about this suggestion. Arbitration procedure had been followed in a dispute about the Witu islands in the previous summer; and not to Germany's advantage. But the suggestion was not rejected outright—so great was the German Government's anxiety for a settlement—and discussion of it had already begun in Berlin when, in the spring of 1890, Salisbury's attitude underwent a further change. It did so partly because, in the negotiations in Berlin, the possibility of an understanding favourable to Great Britain proved so great that the question of arbitration dropped into the background. No doubt the fall of Bismarck from power in March 1890, creating so much uncertainty for the future, also induced Salisbury to reconsider his attitude. But

[1] *Ibid.* pp. 239–44, 288–9; Langer, *op. cit.* I, 117–18; Johnson, H. H., *The History of the British Empire in Africa*, p. 120, and *British Central Africa*, p. 80.
[2] Cecil, *op. cit.* IV, chap. ix.
[3] *Ibid.* p. 238; Lovell, R. I., *The Struggle for South Africa*, pp. 254–5.
[4] Cecil, *op. cit.* IV, 244.
[5] *Ibid.* IV, 248; *D.G.P.* VIII, no. 1674.

more decisive still was the news of Peters's exploits in Uganda, which reached England at this time. This gave added reality to the German threat to the Nile sources and thus to the Sudan and Egypt. It faced Salisbury with the dangers of the East African situation, whereas he had previously concentrated on its possibilities. He who had been content to delay a settlement now became determined to reach one as soon as possible. He never referred to arbitration after April 1890; instead, in the middle of May, he presented the German ambassador with the outline of an Anglo-German Convention in which there was no question of competing claims to be adjusted.

What he offered was a bargain and a compromise. In the disputed territories north-west of Lake Nyasa and south-west of Lake Victoria he suggested partition. Germany would abandon some of the land she claimed on the principle of "hinterland", Great Britain some of the territory she claimed on the principle of "previous settlement". He demanded Germany's abandonment to Great Britain of her protectorate in the Witu area. In addition, he asked for Germany's recognition of an exclusive British protectorate in Zanzibar and in the island of Pemba. He threw out the offer of Heligoland to Germany in exchange for so many German concessions. The only other concession by him was that he undertook to persuade Zanzibar to sell to Germany the leasehold of her coastal strip. He knew that Heligoland, if anything, would turn the scales.[1]

The German Government protested that it could not accept any arrangement that cut off Germany's possessions in East Africa from the Congo Free State, which it one day hoped to purchase. It otherwise accepted the withdrawal of its claims and the reduction of its holdings in the disputed areas, confessing to its ambassador in London that "Heligoland at once becomes our chief consideration, by the side of which our East African interests merely come forward as matters of concession". Even on the question of an outlet to the Congo it ordered the ambassador to seek fresh instructions if Salisbury refused to yield and "if the conclusion of the agreement depends exclusively on this question".[2] Salisbury did not refuse. In so far as he was concerned for the all-red route, this was otherwise arranged for in talks with the King of the Belgians which led to the Mackinnon Treaty of 24 May 1890. By this the Congo was to grant the British East Africa Company a strip of land on some future suitable occasion, thus enabling it to preserve to some extent the continuity of north and south communication. But he was more interested in Uganda—in safeguarding the southern approaches to the Nile—and in the picture of British enterprise in Central Africa than in the Cape-to-Cairo scheme; and he was anxious to avoid further delay in reaching an agreement in view of Peters's exploits. And for all his deter-

---

[1] Cecil, *op. cit.* IV, 277–90; *D.G.P.* VIII, nos. 1676–8, 1684–8.
[2] *D.G.P.* VIII, nos. 1676–82.

mination to secure these things, he was interested in Europe as well as in Africa. To have insisted on the complete envelopment of German East Africa would have led, in his opinion, to a German sense of grievance, whereas one of his objects was to remove all occasion for quarrelling with Germany.[1]

It was from this point of view that he handled the British opposition to his proposals. The Mackinnon Treaty reduced the opposition of the British Companies in Africa.[2] But his offer to cede Heligoland, though it helped the German Government to override the objections of its own "colonists", met with even greater criticism in British circles than did the compromise partition in Africa. The German eagerness to receive it was based on strategic as well as on emotional grounds: work had begun on the Kiel Canal in 1887. The British objections to ceding it, advanced by the Queen and the Cabinet as well as by Salisbury's political opponents, were chiefly emotional, technical and constitutional, though there was some reluctance to abandon a naval asset.[3] Against those objections, Salisbury urged the great advantages to be gained in Africa in return: Great Britain was to receive not only the protectorate of Zanzibar and Pemba and the possession of the Witu area, but also the control of all territory, other than Abyssinia and Gallaland, between German East Africa and Khartoum, and a satisfactory settlement in the disputed area south of Lake Tanganyika. But he also argued that "any indefinite postponement of a settlement in Africa would render it very difficult to maintain terms of amity with Germany and would force us to change our system of alliances in Europe". "The alliance of France instead of Germany", he added, "must necessarily involve the early evacuation of Egypt under very unfavourable conditions."[4] It was this argument that turned the scales.

The agreement, published on 17 June, was signed in two parts on 24 June and 1 July 1890. The British and the German Governments had been moved to accept it by wider considerations than the issues at stake in Africa. The agreement, in its turn, had wide repercussions in its effect on the relations between the European Powers. It had a mixed reception in Germany and Great Britain. But nothing could conceal the satisfaction of the two Governments; and Austrian and Italian opinion echoed those sections of the German and British Press which welcomed the agreement as confirming the informal accession of Great Britain to the Triple Alliance. France and Russia, anxious in proportion to this enthusiasm, reached the same conclusion. France interpreted the Heligoland Treaty to mean that British naval support

[1] Cecil, op. cit. IV, 288–9, 294–6; Langer, op. cit. I, 119; Lovell, op. cit. pp. 265–7; Hornik, M. P., "The Anglo-Belgian Agreement of May 1894", E.H.R. LVII (1942), 229 seqq.
[2] Cecil, op. cit. IV, 285–6, 296.
[3] Ibid. pp. 290–3, 296, 299–300; Letters of Queen Victoria, 3rd ser. I, 610–15.
[4] Cecil, op. cit. IV, 298; Letters of Queen Victoria, 3rd ser. I, 613.

for the Triple Alliance had been guaranteed in the Mediterranean in return for German support in Egypt and Africa. In Russia it was regarded as further proof that Germany had embarked on an anti-Russian policy, for it had followed so soon on Bismarck's dismissal and had coincided with the decision of Bismarck's successors to abandon the Reinsurance Treaty with Russia which had replaced the Three Emperors' Alliance in 1887. Its publication thus advanced the cause of the Franco-Russian *entente*.[1]

III

The Heligoland-East African Treaty had coincided with the abandonment by Germany of her Reinsurance Treaty with Russia. It was itself followed by Germany's abandonment during 1890 of Bismarck's policy of supporting Russia in the Balkans in favour of a closer alignment with Austria; by the premature renewal of the Triple Alliance with Austria and Italy, due to expire in 1892, in May 1891; and by ostentatious German efforts to tighten relations with Great Britain. These signs convinced Russia that, however reluctantly, she must move into closer relations with France. The French fleet visited Cronstadt in July 1891; a vague and limited *entente* was concluded between the two Powers in the following month.[2]

What, above all, confirmed Russia's first suspicions was the belief that Great Britain had joined the Triple Alliance when it was renewed. This belief, widespread throughout Europe, was unfounded; but it was true that, at Italy's insistence, new clauses had been included in the Triple Alliance at its renewal which specified that Germany and Italy would seek a closer agreement with Great Britain for co-operation in North Africa.[3] Nor can it be doubted that, when Italian and German pressure was applied in London to this end in the summer of 1891, Salisbury had thought some gesture essential to preserve the Italian connection. He had emphasised, as usual, that an alliance was out of the question; public opinion would not accept one. But he had expressed his readiness to consider a revision of the first Mediterranean Agreement in the direction desired by Italy. And when he had received an Italo-German draft for an arrangement by which, in return for support in Egypt, Great Britain would at least uphold the *status quo* in North Africa, including Morocco, or even support Italy's ambitions there, he had been saved from carrying out his promise only by the fact

---

[1] Langer, W. L., *The Franco-Russian Alliance*, pp. 78–81; Lovell, *op. cit.* pp. 270–1; Meyendorff, *Correspondance diplomatique de M. de Staal*, II, 89; *Documents diplomatiques français*, 1ee sér.

[2] Langer, *op. cit. passim*; Pribram, *op. cit.* I, 156–62, II, 90–102; Albertini, *op. cit.* I, 65–72.

[3] Albertini, *op. cit.* I, 72–3.

that the negotiations had leaked out and led to embarrassing questions in the House of Commons. These questions, moreover, while they had provided Salisbury with an excuse to put an end to the project, had forced the British Government to reveal the existence of the first Mediterranean Agreement itself, and to declare that, though not bound to give Italy material support, it was "at one with Italy in desiring the maintenance of the *status quo* in the Mediterranean".[1] This revelation had more than offset the denial of a firm commitment, which had not been generally accepted at a time when rumours to the contrary appeared to be substantiated by the course of British policy, no less than by German and Italian statements, since the spring of 1890.

Salisbury had had good cause to work as actively, if not as noisily, as the Kaiser and the Italian Government for closer relations between Great Britain and the Triple Alliance in those months. He had still feared that Russia, in retaliation for her loss of face in Bulgaria, might move against Constantinople and the Bosphorus; and while the attitude that Germany would adopt in the Balkans had thus retained its old importance for Great Britain, Germany's apparent readiness to abandon Bismarck's policy in that area had encouraged him in his efforts to keep close to her.[2] Still more important had been his realisation that Egypt was the most convenient bridge for the co-operation of France and Russia, as it had been in 1887, and that Great Britain had as much reason as Germany to fear their drawing together. Here again, while France and Russia had continued to co-operate at Constantinople to frustrate British administration in Egypt, Germany had left him in no doubt of her readiness to support Great Britain against Franco-Russian pressure.[3] Egypt, moreover, the bridge between France and Russia, was also the connection between British interests at the Straits, in the Mediterranean, and in East Africa. If Salisbury had still been anxious, for all his doubts, to deny Russia the Straits, and more determined than ever to stay in Egypt, he had also been determined to retain the position he had recently established in East Africa. But France had at once protested against the Heligoland Treaty, arguing that the British protectorate in Zanzibar violated the Anglo-French agreement of 1862 and demanding the evacuation of Egypt or the abolition of the capitulations system in Tunisia in return for her acceptance of it.[4] Salisbury, who would not yield in Egypt or Zanzibar, had not been able to meet the French demand in Tunisia. Italy would have regarded concessions in Tunisia as an encouragement to France to annex that territory; it was still imperative to counter French attempts to secure

---

[1] Langer, *op. cit.* pp. 157 *seqq.*; Cecil, *op. cit.* IV, 378–82; *D.G.P.* VIII, nos. 1707–20.
[2] Langer, pp. 124, 127; *D.G.P.* IX, nos. 2073, 2082, 2086, 2087, 2095 *seqq.*
[3] Langer, p. 163; *D.G.P.* VIII, nos. 1775–80.
[4] Langer, p. 123; *D.G.P.* VIII, nos. 1601, 1691 *seqq.*

Italy's defection from Germany in Europe and Great Britain in Egypt. He had been glad, therefore, to agree with Germany that the two Powers would co-operate, if necessary, to resist the French demands; and, thus fortified, he had rejected them in August 1890, together with a Turkish proposal, inspired by France and Russia, for the evacuation of Egypt.[1] In the same month, under the pressure of Italy's efforts to mobilise Great Britain and Germany against French activity in Tunisia and Morocco, he had been forced to reassure her that Tripoli must not be allowed to fall to France. Crispi, at any rate, had interpreted this assurance as a promise of support in Tripoli; and Salisbury had then had to maintain his intimate collaboration with Germany for the further purpose of restraining Italy without offending her.[2]

That task had not been made easier by the existence of a separate dispute with Italy in which East Africa was directly at stake. Since 1889, Italy had agitated for expansion from Massowa and Eritrea northwards along the Red Sea and westwards towards Kassala, an important centre on a tributary of the Nile then held by the dervishes. Salisbury, unmoved by Italian expansion along the Red Sea, was determined to preserve the Nile and its tributaries against Italy, as he had preserved it against France in the Somaliland delimitation of 1888 and against Germany in the settlement of 1890. But it was in this direction that Italy was herself most interested. Since 1889, by the Treaty of Ucciali with Abyssinia, she had claimed a protectorate over that country, which had always regarded the Nile as its western frontier. Because of British dislike of this claim, and on account of Italy's insistence on her rights to Kassala, all negotiations in 1890 had been abortive. But in this matter, too, there had followed concessions to Italy and, for outside observers, the appearance of growing Anglo-Italian solidarity. In February 1891 a settlement had been reached in which, to safeguard Egypt's claim to Kassala and to keep the limits of Italy's sphere of influence a distance of a hundred miles from the nearest approach to the Nile, Salisbury had recognised the most extravagant Italian claims elsewhere, as well as Italy's freedom to occupy Kassala temporarily until Egypt was ready to take it over.[3]

If, up to the renewal of the Triple Alliance, Great Britain had thus been forced to manœuvre at all times in close step with Germany and Italy, the situation did not greatly alter after the middle of 1891. Tension in the Mediterranean declined; the possibility receded of a Russian advance to the Straits. After the French visit to Cronstadt, on the other hand, and in view of the knowledge that France and

---

[1] *D.G.P.* viii, nos. 1700, 1720, 1703, 1787, 1864.

[2] Langer, *op. cit.* pp. 122–9; Albertini, *op. cit.* i, 68–9; Cecil, *op. cit.* iv, 372–9; *D.G.P.* viii, nos. 1691 *seqq.*, 1700 *seqq.*, 1862–3, 1914 *seqq.*

[3] Cecil, *op. cit.* iv, 325–33; Langer, *Diplomacy of Imperialism*, i, 108–24; Ramm, A., "Great Britain and the Planting of Italian Power in the Red Sea, 1868–85", *E.H.R.* lix (May 1944), 211–36.

Russia were negotiating, the possibility that an *entente* between those Powers would involve the transfer of a Russian squadron to the Mediterranean could not be excluded; and the British Mediterranean fleet was at best equal to the French Mediterranean fleet and the Russian Black Sea squadron combined.[1] Throughout the winter of 1891-2 Salisbury was still anxious lest Russian warships might pass the Straits, even if Russia did not advance on Constantinople, lest Franco-Russian pressure would revive in Egypt and lest Italy, visited by the Russian Foreign Minister in October 1891, might yet be detached by the Franco-Russian combination.[2] And to these old fears was added another. In August 1891 Russia sent a force to the Pamirs, and expelled Captain Younghusband when he was sent to investigate her activities. Salisbury forced her to apologise for this step. But she increased the force in the summer of 1892, decided to try to establish her domination over the whole of the Pamirs and engaged in clashes with Afghan troops, renewing Anglo-Russian tension on the North-West Frontier at a time when, in another area adjacent to India, friction was mounting between France and Great Britain in Siam.[3]

In these circumstances, when Salisbury's Government was overthrown in August 1892, his policy was still what it had been since 1887. He described it in a memorandum he left for Lord Rosebery, his successor at the Foreign Office; his purpose was to emphasise the necessity of continuing it. "The key of the present situation in Europe", he wrote, "is our position towards Italy and, through Italy, to the Triple Alliance.... If England was to become more cold to Italy... or were to give any indication of likelihood that she would give even a moral preference to France in the event of a conflict, I think very serious risks to European peace would be run, as well as to the interests of this country." The risks he had in mind, as he went on to indicate, were not only the effects in Egypt and the Mediterranean of losing Italy's friendship. Such a departure from the present policy might also induce a reconciliation between Russia and the Central Powers and the revival of the Three Emperors' League, with all its consequences in south-east Europe and for the British position throughout the world.[4] Except that Italy had replaced Austria as the necessary link between Great Britain and the Triple Alliance, this was virtually a restatement of the views he expressed in August 1888. It was less likely now, however, than it had been in 1888, that this position would be maintained. The memorandum was careful to explain, that, though he had done his "best to show friendship to Italy" and

---

[1] Langer, *Franco-Russian Alliance*, pp. 194-5, 202-3.
[2] *Ibid.* pp. 172-5, 201-6, 211-7; *D.G.P.* VIII, nos. 1788 *seqq.*, IX, nos. 2109, 2111-17.
[3] Langer, *op. cit.* pp. 198-9, 203, 207-8, 267-8; Meyendorff, *Correspondance diplomatique de M. de Staal*, II, 157, 176, 209, 224; Sumner, B. H., *Tsardom and Imperialism in the Far East and Middle East, 1880-1914* (1942).
[4] Cecil, *op. cit.* IV, 404-5.

"agreed to consult with her. . .if the *status quo* should be threatened",
he had "always refused to give the assurance of material assistance".
Salisbury might have added that it was only with difficulty that he
had preserved this position, as laid down in the Mediterranean
Agreements. He might also have added that, despite his policy,
Germany had shown signs of reverting to her old friendship with
Russia. He had been gratified by Germany's break with Russia after
March 1890 and her anxiety to work closely with Great Britain. But
he had later found her unwilling to move far enough. In 1890 she had
dissuaded him from protesting against the passage of ships of the
Russian volunteer fleet; in the autumn of 1891, when he had protested
against this, she had refused to back him, though Austria and Italy
had been ready to do so.[1] Even more revealing had been his talks
during the Kaiser's first state visit to London in July 1891. The
German Foreign Minister had told him that Great Britain could
count on German support in the Balkans only if Great Britain took
the lead there. He had then discouraged Salisbury from taking
the lead by explaining that the German Government, whose chief
duty was to hold France in check, must show consideration to the
Tsar and respect the feeling of the German peoples, who had been
entirely converted to Bismarckian policy in the Near East.[2] The
equivalent of Germany's reluctance to side with Great Britain against
Russia—it would be misleading to claim that either caused the other
—had been Salisbury's anxiety not only to avoid giving specific obligations to the Triple Alliance Powers but also to avoid friction, as far as
possible, with France. His memorandum warned Rosebery not to
side with France. But he had been as careful as ever not to side
against her; and so much so that his relations with France had begun
to create another source of disharmony between Great Britain and the
Triple Alliance. When France protested against the Zanzibar protectorate he had tried to placate her, even while arranging for German
support against her demands in case of need. He had not granted
her demands; but in August 1890, in return for her acceptance of the
Heligoland-Zanzibar Treaty, an acceptance which Great Britain
could have done without, he had given her, instead, British recognition of a French protectorate in Madagascar and of the large addition
of the Algerian hinterland, as far south as Lake Chad and the frontiers
of the Nigeria Company, to her sphere of influence in Africa.[3] At the
same time, hindered by pressure from Italy and, sometimes, from his
own agents, and anxious lest Germany should take too vigorous a stand
on behalf of Italy, as Germany was anxious lest he should take too
vigorous a stand against Russia, he had done his utmost, if not to
leave France a free hand in Tunisia and Morocco, at least to avoid

[1] *D.G.P.* IX, nos. 2095 *seqq.*, 2113–16.
[2] Langer, *op. cit.* pp. 172–5; *D.G.P.* VIII, nos. 1724, 1727.
[3] Cecil, *op. cit.* IV, 317–22.

opposing her there.[1] The French Government, shirking an open breach with Great Britain if only because it was still uncertain of the *entente* with Russia, had co-operated with him to keep these issues quiet. French co-operation had made possible a more spectacular illustration of Salisbury's aim in the summer of 1891. After proclaiming once again, in a Mansion House speech, that Great Britain had not joined the Triple Alliance and knew nothing of its terms,[2] he had invited the French fleet to call at a British port on its way back from Cronstadt. When the fleet visited Portsmouth in September he had persuaded the Queen to review it. Salisbury's motives were as before. "Though in the present state of Europe", he had told the Queen, "our interests lie on the side of the Triple Alliance, it is most important to persuade the French, if we can, that England has no antipathy to France nor any partisanship against her."[3] His antipathy to a fixed alliance with either camp in Europe, his insistence that British action must depend on the issues and circumstances of the time, had only increased as Europe, with the drawing together of France and Russia, emphasised by the Cronstadt visit, had tended to become more divided. But the significance of the Portsmouth visit had not been missed in Europe, where it was regarded as a masterstroke, intended to show France that she could rely on Great Britain if Russia failed her, and thus to establish a balance controlled from London.[4] Least of all had the Central Powers ignored the visit and the other indications that freedom of action was Salisbury's aim; and least of all, among the Central Powers, could Germany afford to ignore them. Friction between Germany and Russia had become intense by the summer of 1892; relations between Germany and her allies were not untroubled. The resulting anxiety in Germany had combined with Salisbury's attitude to produce strained relations between London and Berlin as well, despite the mounting tension between Great Britain and Russia in Central Asia.[5]

It was thus easier for Salisbury to advocate continuity of policy than it would be for Rosebery to carry out his advice. To existing difficulties, moreover, must be added the fact that the change of government in Great Britain in August 1892 itself exerted a powerful influence in the same direction. Some European Governments feared, some hoped for, all anticipated a decisive change in British policy on account of Gladstone's past record and recent utterances. Was he not known to favour agreement with France? Had he not frequently declared that he would evacuate Egypt? The lengths he had gone to on earlier occasions to avoid friction with Russia on the

---

[1] Taylor, A. J. P., "British Policy in Morocco, 1886–1902", *E.H.R.* LXVI (July 1951), pp. 342–74.
[2] Langer, *op. cit.* p. 189; 29 July 1891.
[3] *Letters of Queen Victoria*, 3rd ser. II, 65.
[4] Langer, *op. cit.* p. 200.   [5] *Ibid.* pp. 235–43.

North-West Frontier! Was it likely that this enemy of the Turk would continue Salisbury's policy in the Balkans? Above all, he had criticised Italy's alliances and, as recently as 1889, announced that Great Britain ought not to support her in a conflict with France.[1] This, for the Triple Alliance Powers, was the immediate test. Not to prejudge the issue, they approached the new British Cabinet early in September for a clear statement of its attitude towards the Mediterranean Agreements and the additional informal assurances that Salisbury had given to Italy. Rosebery at the Foreign Office would have liked to maintain Salisbury's position. Convinced that "our great Empire has pulled us...by the coat-tails out of the European system...that our foreign policy has become a colonial policy", he yet realised that "we can never remove ourselves altogether from the European system";[2] and, like Salisbury, he thought the connection with the Central Powers should be as close as the withholding of definite commitments would allow. But definite commitments, which Salisbury had only narrowly evaded in 1891, were what the Triple Alliance now sought; and what Rosebery, short of splitting Gladstone's Cabinet, could not give. He went so far as to explain this difficulty to the German Ambassador, and to give him written confirmation of their talk for communication to the Italian Government. "My personal view", ran this document, "was that, in the event of France groundlessly attacking Italy, the interests of England as a Mediterranean and Indian Power would bring her naturally to the rescue of Italy...." But this "must be held to be nothing more... than my personal conviction..., and in any case I could not make an authoritative communication as from the British Cabinet...".[3]

As a result of this statement the Mediterranean Agreements were implicitly held by Italy and Austria to be still in force; and Italy was tolerably satisfied. But the British Foreign Office itself was uncertain whether or not the Agreements had been terminated; and for the German Government this further proof of British uncertainty was too much. Its efforts to commit Salisbury had been disappointed; but these had aimed at persuading Great Britain to go beyond the Mediterranean Agreements. They had been made on behalf of Italy; and the German Government had on the whole accepted as not unreasonable Salisbury's reluctance to fall in with them. Now, however, it was not certain that Great Britain would even go so far as to uphold the Mediterranean Agreements; and Germany had become anxious for herself. In August 1892 France had succeeded, after further negotiations, in strengthening her *entente* with Russia by the conclusion of a Franco-Russian military convention that could only

[1] Langer, *op. cit.* pp. 252–3, 286–7; Cecil, *op. cit.* iv, 391–5.
[2] Crewe, Lord, *Lord Rosebery*, i, 315; March 1892.
[3] Langer, *op. cit.* pp. 287–8; *D.G.P.* viii, nos. 1732–46; *British Documents on the Origins of the War*, ii, 78, viii, 4–6, 13; Gardiner, A. G., *Life of Harcourt*, ii, 245 *seqq.*, 252 *seqq.*

be directed against Germany. Germany knew little or nothing of the negotiations; what she knew was enough. After September 1892 she abandoned the attempt to rely wholly on the Triple Alliance and the connection with Great Britain and sought to re-establish the old connection with Russia.

Germany's change of attitude was not, however, the only or even the chief danger to Great Britain. It is true that it soon showed itself and proved embarrassing. Rosebery, feeling no less strongly than Salisbury that "while we hold Egypt both Constantinople and India are safe",[1] asked the Powers to approve an increase in the Egyptian Army. France refused to agree.[2] Germany, after giving her consent, withdrew it in December 1892 when she learned that British agents in Constantinople were opposing the award to a German syndicate of a railway concession to Konia, on the second stage of the Baghdad railway. Rosebery warned the German ambassador that such pressure would make it more difficult for him to advocate in the Cabinet a policy of close friendship with the Triple Alliance; but he had to submit to Germany in the railway dispute when the Khedive, by appointing an anti-British prime minister, precipitated a crisis and forced him to issue an ultimatum and increase the army of occupation in Egypt.[3] On the other hand, when France protested against this action it was the fact that Germany stood by Great Britain, Rosebery having given way in the matter of the railway, that made the protest ineffective. Germany had so far done no more than show that her relations with Great Britain were to be placed on a barter basis. She still had reason to adopt a lenient attitude to Great Britain even if she no longer intended to support Great Britain without a *quid pro quo*; for the Triple Alliance was also threatened by the Franco-Russian negotiations. In the further exchanges with Germany, moreover, Rosebery, instead of dwelling on the difficulty of pursuing a policy of collaboration with the Triple Alliance, admitted the impossibility, in his view, of pursuing any other. "What a position England would be in," he confessed to the German ambassador, "if the Triple Alliance were shattered and we were then to find ourselves alone in the face of the Franco-Russian Group."[4] The real danger to Great Britain arising from the Franco-Russian Alliance lay not so much in Germany's reaction to it as in the fact that Russia, reciprocating Germany's interest in improved Russo-German relations but unprepared to trust Germany to the extent of giving up the Russo-French *entente*, wanted Germany to abandon Great Britain, as Germany, while retaining her own connection with Great Britain, wanted Russia

---

[1] *Letters of Queen Victoria*, 3rd ser. II, 152, 211.

[2] Lord Cromer, *Abbas II*, chaps. ii and iii; Langer, *op. cit.* pp. 271–2.

[3] Langer, *op. cit.* pp. 272–3, 290–4; Cromer, *loc. cit.*; Crewe, *op. cit.* II, 415–22; Earle, E. M., *Turkey, the Great Powers and the Bagdad Railway*, chap. iii; *D.G.P.* VIII, nos. 1814–16, 1818, 1821–31; XIV, nos. 3961–7, 3969, 3972, 3974.

[4] *D.G.P.* VIII, no. 1823.

to give up France. Russia was also anxious that France should accept an anti-British rather than an anti-German emphasis for the Franco-Russian Convention which, though signed in August 1892, had still not been ratified. The great issue in 1893 was whether the German or the Russian purpose in seeking a *rapprochement* would prevail.[1]

If only because a Russo-German reconciliation was taking place at all, Great Britain would suffer in either case. But she would suffer more if Russia were successful. At this moment of uncertainty it was thus unfortunate for Great Britain that trouble broke out between herself and France in Siam, the last neutral buffer between the French in Indo-China and the British in Burma and India, and that the crisis was handled by a British Government but dimly aware of the wider issues at stake. In her advance in Indo-China the encroachment of France to the westward had led to friction with Siam. This came to a head in 1893. France invaded Siam, presented an ultimatum and, when this was rejected, announced a blockade of the country. This was a blow to Great Britain: 90 per cent of Siamese trade was in British hands. But a still more important British interest was the preservation of Siam as an independent buffer state between Burma and Indo-China, between, as Rosebery put it, "the French frontier and that of India, in order that a vast expenditure and danger may not be increased by the immediate proximity of a great military Power on our south-eastern flank".[2] However, France had accepted the principle of an independent and neutralised Siam in 1889; and for this reason, apart from Cabinet opposition to any other course, Rosebery's policy was to leave France free to settle her account with Siam so long as she continued to observe this principle and subject to the fact that Great Britain would not recognise France's claim to the left bank of the Mekong River in its upper reaches as her frontier with Siam. All the same, he was suspicious of French intentions, convinced that French pretensions would mount and British prestige suffer if France was wholly unopposed, and concerned for British trading interests and for India. These considerations had already induced him to send gunboats to Bangkok when it seemed clear that France would resort to force. When France announced the ultimatum and the blockade they led him, against his first intentions, to give diplomatic support to the Siamese and to sound out the Triple Alliance informally. With the German ambassador he went so far, indeed, as to suggest, as a friend and not as a minister, that a crisis might enable him to effect the Quadruple Alliance which Gladstone had so far vetoed.[3]

This was the situation when, on 30 July, France having already

---

[1] Langer, *op. cit.* pp. 258-65, 271-5, 281-5, 287-90, 300-15, 321-3.
[2] Crewe, *op. cit.* ii, 426.
[3] *Ibid.* pp. 426-7; *D.G.P.* viii, nos. 1749-51.

instituted the blockade earlier than the announced date, he learned that the French commander had ordered the British gunboats to leave Bangkok and stay outside the blockade area. He at once instructed the gunboats not to move, informed the French Government of his decision and then, through the Queen, asked the Kaiser, at Cowes, to send the German ambassador back to London for discussions. He evidently expected that France would reject his note. Nor is there much doubt that, the rest of the Cabinet being out of London, he would have accepted this challenge, which would have confirmed his suspicion of French designs. But the report from Bangkok, where the situation was highly confused, was cancelled later on 30 July; and news was received from Paris at the same time that France still adhered to the principle of a buffer state and had also accepted the British position with regard to the upper reaches of the Mekong.[1] Rosebery had never intended war in these circumstances. He had to withdraw as gracefully as possible the advances he had made to Germany. But he could not escape the consequences of the misunderstanding which had been created in Berlin and other capitals.

The Russian Government knew nothing of the report and counter-report from Bangkok or of the previous Anglo-French negotiations about Siam. The impression was unavoidable in St Petersburg that France had braved the risk of war with Great Britain to get her way in Siam. Within a week of the crisis Russia at last acceded to long-standing French requests by announcing that a Russian squadron would visit Toulon in the autumn and that some of the ships would remain permanently in the Mediterranean.[2] After negotiations in the autumn, the two Powers finally exchanged notes at the end of the year and the beginning of 1894 by which the military convention of August 1892, which the Tsar had hitherto hesitated to ratify, came into force and converted their *entente* of August 1891 into an alliance. The clauses of the convention were ostensibly anti-German. They pledged the two countries to mutual support in the event of an attack by Germany or Italy on France, or by Germany and Austria on Russia. They were to have the same duration as the Triple Alliance. But in its effects the ratification of the convention bore most heavily of all on the British position, whereas its origins had been primarily in the search for security against Germany. This was because, in view of the Russo-German *rapprochement*, it suited Russia, the dominant partner, to use it offensively against Great Britain and only defensively against Germany. At some sacrifice to France, Russia's intention was to use it to force Great Britain to yield in Central Asia and the Mediterranean, or at least to restrain her in Europe and the Far East, to which area Russia's interest was turning with the beginning, in 1892, of the Trans-Siberian Railway, by pressure in

---

[1] Langer, *op. cit.* pp. 326–30.   [2] *D.D.F.* 1ee sér. nos. 255, 264.

Central Asia and the Mediterranean. Meanwhile, she would rely on the alliance, but also on continued good relations with Germany, to deter the Triple Alliance from coming to Great Britain's assistance.[1]

France found it less difficult than before to make this double sacrifice—of risking a breach with Great Britain, of relaxing the anti-German implications of the alliance. Anxious, in any case, to convert the *entente* into an alliance in order to end her isolation in Europe, she had been angered when Rosebery had frustrated her attempt to appeal to Gladstone for an agreement in Egypt over the head of the Foreign Office, at the end of 1892; and more angered still when Gladstone himself had finally killed her hopes of an early evacuation of Egypt in May 1893 by announcing that no time limit could be set for the British occupation.[2] Even if her chief purpose was only to bring Great Britain to an Egyptian agreement by increased pressure, her determination to do this also contributed to the marked anti-British tendency assumed by the alliance. But more important still in producing this result were the conclusions drawn by the German Government from Great Britain's behaviour during the Siam crisis, from the Toulon visit, which took place in October 1893, and from her knowledge that the visit had been succeeded by Franco-Russian negotiations.

Knowing no more than the Russian Government of the details of the Siamese crisis, the German Government had first hoped, in view of Rosebery's approaches, that it would produce the offer of an alliance from Great Britain; and was then disappointed. Rosebery had never gone so far as to ask for German assistance.[3] It had also been convinced, notwithstanding Rosebery's efforts to explain his withdrawal, that a divided British Cabinet had succumbed to French threats.[4] It was next confronted with the Toulon visit and the subsequent Franco-Russian negotiations. In view of all these experiences it could not resist the temptation to draw closer to Russia and further away from Great Britain, both out of prudence where the Franco-Russian Alliance was concerned and in the belief that only the threat of isolation would now induce Great Britain to commit herself to the Triple Alliance. And this temptation was increased by the result of a further attempt by Austria and Italy to get a firm commitment out of Rosebery.

These two Powers were as much threatened as Great Britain by the improvement in Franco-Russian relations. But their efforts to persuade Great Britain to commit herself produced once again, after prolonged negotiations between November 1893 and June 1894, an inconclusive answer. Rosebery went so far as to agree to take over

---

[1] Langer, *op. cit.* pp. 332–6, 345–56, 392–400.
[2] *Ibid.* pp. 323–4; *D.G.P.* viii, nos. 1832 ff.; *D.D.F.*, 1ere sér. x, no. 37.
[3] Vagts, A., "William II and the Siam episode", *American Hist. Rev.* xlv (July 1940), 834 *seqq.*
[4] Langer, *op. cit.* pp. 326–7, 330–2; *D.G.P.* viii, nos. 1750–7.

the informal assurances given to Italy by Salisbury. The Cabinet, he said, "could not regard with indifference the defeat of Italy by France". But since the Cabinet was already deeply split by the battle over increases in the naval estimates which had followed the Toulon visit, and which led to Gladstone's resignation and his succession by Rosebery as Prime Minister in March 1894,[1] he dared not widen the breach by making these assurances official and definite. Against the danger that Austria, no less than Italy, might otherwise desert Great Britain for an alignment with France and Russia, he had similarly been unable to give more than a personal assurance that Great Britain would stand with the Triple Alliance in defence of the Straits. The Cabinet would be united in a crisis with Russia; but he could give no definite statement on a matter that lay in the future. Even this most qualified assurance had been made dependent in January 1894 on a promise from the Triple Alliance Powers that would have borne more heavily on Germany. When Germany alone among those Powers could influence France, Rosebery, recognising since the Toulon visit that Great Britain could no longer risk sending a fleet to the Straits in the face of combined Franco-Russian action, wanted a general understanding that Great Britain would continue to uphold the *status quo* at the Straits if she were assured that the Triple Alliance would deter France from taking sides with Russia on the issue.[2] Austria would have accepted his proposal. Germany would have none of it. If Great Britain was still prepared to defend the Straits, let her officially renew the Mediterranean Agreements. Before she herself would abandon her reconciliation with Russia and commit herself to Great Britain, as the Mediterranean Agreements had not committed her, she must insist, since the Franco-Russian alliance was an accomplished fact, that Great Britain should first bind herself to the Triple Alliance by official commitments that tied not only Rosebery but future British Governments. It would be argued that the British Parliamentary system forbade such an engagement. Germany could only reply that "we cannot subordinate our policy to the principles of English constitutional law".[3]

[1] Marder, A. J., *The Anatomy of British Sea Power. A History of British Naval Policy, 1880–1905.*

[2] Langer, *op. cit.* pp. 336–43, 357–81; Albertini, *op. cit.* I, 78–9; Temperley, H., and Penson, L. M., *The Foundations of British Foreign Policy* (1938), pp. 478–90, 487; Penson, L. M., "The New Course in British Foreign Policy, 1892–1902", *Trans. R. Hist. Soc.*, 4th ser. xxv (1943), 121–38; *Letters of Queen Victoria*, 3rd ser. II, 321, 329 *seqq.*; Morley, *Life of Gladstone*, III, 506 *seqq.*; Marder, *op. cit.* p. 221; D.G.P. VIII, nos. 2137–8, 2142–3, 2147–8.

[3] Langer, *op. cit.* pp. 352–3, 381–4, 387–91; Brandenburg, E., *From Bismarck to the World War* (1933 edn.).

IV

It was not only with those arguments, from requirements of security, that the German Government took up this position. If, unlike Bismarck, it wanted a tight association with Great Britain even more than it cared for good relations with Russia, its return to Bismarck's policy was made with another difference as well. Bismarck had been conservative and consolidatory in his aims. Expansionist aims now began to play an ever-increasing part in shaping Germany's policy. Her expansionist course was fatally encouraged by internal developments in Germany and by changes in the pattern of international relations as established in Bismarck's day. Inside Germany the pressure of expansionist forces, anxious for markets, determined that Germany should be treated as a world Power not inferior to Great Britain—for Great Britain was the major world Power—and little disposed to accept any haughtiness from Great Britain, had been growing since 1880, and growing fast since 1890. The beginnings of journalistic warfare between Germany and Great Britain on colonial issues may be traced to this second date. By the same date, Germany's existing colonies had acquired such a sentimental value for themselves that the surrender involved in the East African settlement had led within six months to the foundation of the Pan-German League. By 1892 the League had generated wide public interest in the colonial field.[1] Nor could the German Government itself avoid a new interest in extra-European affairs. The Franco-Russian alliance had achieved a new balance in Europe and was reducing old rivalries to a deadlock; combined with growing economic pressure in Europe, this was producing another intensive phase of extra-European expansion by the European Powers. The German Government, losing its old domination of international arrangements in Europe, was tempted to think that it would be unsafe to remain a mere spectator of the race beyond Europe. It also realised, after concluding that Great Britain would have to be forced to agree to those engagements in Europe which it was increasingly anxious to obtain from her, that the colonial field offered the obvious opportunities and the most effective scope for the application of pressure. The danger was that these two grounds for interest in the colonial field would prove incompatible; that Germany could not both serve the ambitions of her own imperialists and preserve the British connection; that she could not force Great Britain into engagements with the Triple Alliance and at the same time extract from Great Britain colonial concessions for herself.

Yet both these motives, as well as the more immediate object of diverting the Franco-Russian alliance from Germany's frontiers, underlay her policy after March 1894. In that month she granted

---

[1] *History of 'The Times'*, III, 140–6, 783–5; Taylor, *Germany's First Bid for Colonies*, pp. 6 *seqq.*

France freedom of action in the area to the west of the Sudan by agreeing to withdraw to the westward the eastern frontier of the Cameroons. She had herself received this area from Great Britain as recently as November 1893 in a delimitation agreement by which, while Germany renounced any interest in encroaching on the Nile Valley from the west by agreeing to place the eastern limit of the Cameroons at the Nile watershed, Great Britain, it was obvious enough, intended that the French should be excluded by the Germans from the Nile in that direction.[1] This set-back provoked the British Government into making the false move that provided the occasion for the threat by Germany of further Franco-German collaboration. Rosebery was as determined as Salisbury had been to exclude other Powers from the Sudan. His negotiation of the Anglo-Congolese Treaty of May 1894 was an attempt by Great Britain, thwarted by the Franco-German Cameroon Treaty of March 1894 in its aim of interposing the Germans between the Sudan and the French advance from the west, to use the Belgians to block the French. In return for the lease to the Congo Free State of the Bahr el Ghazal, the western gateway of the Sudan, where Germany had now given way to France, the Treaty also secured for Great Britain, in addition to the Congo's recognition of the British sphere of influence in the Nile Valley, the lease of a strip of Congo territory which would provide a connection between British South African possessions and Uganda. French indignation at these arrangements may easily be imagined. They furthered the British plan for an all-red route; they thwarted the French intention to cut the British line with a broad band of French territory running east and west across the continent. But French opposition had been expected. Unlike Germany and the Congo, France had never recognised the Upper Nile as a British sphere of influence. Neither Rosebery, now Prime Minister, nor the Foreign Office had been disposed to take trouble to avoid it. What chiefly caused indignation in London was the fact that Germany joined France in opposition.[2]

Perhaps Germany's opposition should also have been expected. Since concluding the Franco-German Cameroon Treaty in March, she had dropped hints in London that "advocacy of British interests must not be expected of us any longer".[3] There was a legal basis for her opposition in the fact that, together with Great Britain and France, she was a guarantor of the Congo's neutrality; and the lease of the Congo strip recalled the proposals which she had been loath to accept in 1890, and which Salisbury had not then pressed, for the insertion of Great Britain between the Congo and German East Africa. She

---

[1] Langer, *op. cit.* pp. 353, 384–6; Penson, *loc. cit.* p. 128; *D.G.P.* VIII, no. 2039.
[2] Langer, W. L., *The Diplomacy of Imperialism*, I, 130–6; Taylor, A. J. P., "Prelude to Fashoda", *E.H.R.* LXV (Jan. 1950), 52–80; Hornik, M. P., "The Anglo-Belgian Agreement of May 1894", *E.H.R.* LVII (1942), 227 *seqq.*
[3] Brandenburg, *op. cit.* p. 40.

did not exploit Rosebery's false move at once, however, only asking the Congo Government, when the Treaty was first published, for an assurance that the British strip would be not less than twenty kilometres from the German East African border. When she did exploit it after second thoughts, protesting against the lease of the Congo strip, she preserved an attitude to Great Britain that was as moderate as it was firm and legally sound; and this despite the pressure of German public indignation, which had surprised the German Government, and London's grudging reception of her first protests, which only increased the public excitement in Germany.[1] After first appearing to offer France an anti-British *entente*, moreover, she was careful to avoid subsequent French suggestions for collaboration against the British position in Africa, and especially in Egypt, the only basis on which an *entente* could rest.[2] Her purpose—and it is this which explains her attitude—was to put pressure on Great Britain, but not too much pressure; was not to alienate Great Britain, but to extract concessions from her. She would rather have been paid for withdrawing her opposition than be forced to insist on it. On the other hand, and this fact marks a further stage in the growing interest of even her Government in extra-European issues, the payment she sought was not only British acceptance of closer relations with the Triple Alliance but also, and perhaps to a greater extent, British support in Samoa, where she wished to replace the combined British, American and German suzerainty established in 1889 in favour of total German control.[3] In addition, it was the German public's interest in Africa as well as Great Britain's sharp reaction to Germany's protests which deepened the crisis beyond the German Government's intentions.

It was not Germany's opposition to the Treaty, however, which forced Great Britain to accept diplomatic defeat. Rosebery had to accept the suppression of the clause to which Germany had objected; his surrender to Germany may have strengthened the French position in the remaining stages of the dispute. But it was the French Government which compelled Leopold to renounce the Bahr el Ghazal and leave the way open to the Nile, and it was Leopold's withdrawal which ensured that the Congo State's recognition of the British sphere of influence in the Nile Valley was all that Great Britain was able to salvage from the Anglo-Congolese Treaty.[4] Rosebery's enforced withdrawal, being placed at Germany's door, was responsible, on the other hand, for a further deterioration in the relations between the two Powers. In the colonial field, by deepening Great Britain's

---

[1] *History of 'The Times'*, III, 149–53; Hornik, *loc. cit.* pp. 236–43.

[2] Taylor, *loc. cit.*; Brandenburg, *op. cit.* p. 44; *D.G.P.* VIII, nos. 2049, 2054, 2061, 2069; *D.D.F.*, 1er sér. XI, nos. 154, 157, 161, 172, 174–5, 223.

[3] Hornik, *loc. cit.* pp. 236 *seqq.*; Brandenburg, *op. cit.* pp. 40–1; *D.G.P.* VIII, nos. 2022–5, 2032–5, 2047, 2049, 2053, 2059, 2061, 2069.

[4] Langer, *op. cit.* I, 138–40; Taylor, *loc. cit.*

distrust of Germany,[1] it only reduced her disposition to yield to Germany's ambitions. This was one reason, those ambitions being in any case on the increase, why Germany kept up her pressure about Samoa and on African issues after the summer of 1894 and why the two Powers rapidly assumed the attitude of suspicious rivals on those questions. Unsatisfied in Samoa at the end of the Congo dispute, Germany was again repulsed by Great Britain when, in the autumn of 1894, she again requested British support for her wishes there as an earnest of British good-will.[2] When Great Britain sought Portuguese permission to land troops at Delagoa Bay against a local rebellion, Germany's interest in the future of the Portuguese colonies and the Transvaal and her suspicion of British intentions, both of which had been growing fast since 1891, led her to send warships to the area. Great Britain's attitude hardened still further as a result; determined to brook no interference at Delagoa Bay, she intimated to the German Government that it was a question involving the loyalty of the Cape and the security of a route to India on which she would not even "recoil from the spectre of war".[3]

These disputes did more than anything else to maintain and deepen the atmosphere of hostility in Anglo-German relations. They were the chief cause of Great Britain's growing lack of confidence in Germany. But colonial dissatisfaction and ambition were far from being the mainspring of Germany's behaviour in the colonial field, even if her behaviour in that field was what most disturbed Great Britain. "If confidence exists between the two Governments," *The Times* correspondent was told by Holstein in December 1894, "they will never quarrel over such [colonial] questions. They only acquire importance when other causes weaken confidence."[4] But for these other causes, colonial friction, though it would not have been avoided if only because of the force that colonial expansion had acquired as an influence on both British and German public opinion, could certainly have been contained. And chief among those other causes was the fact that German opposition to the Anglo-Congolese Treaty had helped to widen the gap between Great Britain and the Triple Alliance Powers in Europe that had already formed since the exchanges of the previous winter had shown the impossibility of further Anglo-Austrian collaboration against Russia.

V

Convinced at the outset that Germany's protest was due only to the desire to extract concessions in Samoa, Rosebery, instead of drawing closer to the Triple Alliance as Germany had hoped he would,

---

[1] *D.G.P.* VII, nos. 1765–7; IX, nos. 2157–9.   [2] Penson, *loc. cit.* pp. 126–7.
[3] *Ibid.* pp. 127–8; Brandenburg, *op. cit.* p. 45.
[4] *History of 'The Times'*, III, 154–6.

had dismissed it as bluster, to which the proper answer was counter-bluster. He had told the Austrian ambassador that, "if Germany is going to side...with France in this and other African questions, we must consider our general attitude in Europe, more particularly in the Mediterranean and the [Near] East"; and he had intended that this threat to withdraw such assurances as Great Britain had already given to Austria and Italy should "ricochet through Vienna to Berlin". He had quickly concluded that the German action was not as offensive as he had first thought, and had then confessed that the Congo bargain was "not important enough to England to cause a complete change in her policy".[1] But his subsequent withdrawal, and the humiliation it involved, still combined with other circumstances to launch him on what seemed to be a deliberate policy of reconciliation with France and Russia when the Anglo-Congolese dispute was over.

These other circumstances played a larger part than Rosebery's ill-temper in the approaches he made to the Dual Alliance Powers; and these approaches were less the result of a deliberate change of policy than they seemed. Given the frustration of the Anglo-Congolese Treaty, it was not surprising that Great Britain, beginning in the summer of 1894, should have attempted to negotiate with France a settlement of the Upper Nile problem by which France would recognise the British sphere of influence in return for concessions elsewhere in Africa. Having failed to interpose the Congo between the French and the Nile, as she had earlier failed to interpose the Germans, Great Britain was at last forced to step directly into the breach. She naturally tried the method of negotiation with France first; and France, ever hopeful of concessions in Egypt, was ready for negotiations.[2] While these negotiations were going on, Rosebery also abstained from antagonising the French in Morocco, to the despair of Italy. Here again, however, local circumstances had in any case made more and more for Anglo-French collaboration since 1892.[3] He also extended his approaches to Russia. But the first of these was forced on him by Japanese victories in the war between China and Japan that had broken out in Korea in the summer of 1894, which made him anxious to work with the other Far Eastern Power to maintain the *status quo* in China.[4] It was in the same Far Eastern context that Russia and Great Britain renewed in November 1894 the negotiations for a settlement of their dispute with regard to the Afghan and Pamir frontiers. Rosebery accepted a treaty, signed in March

---

[1] Crewe, *op. cit.* ii, 447–9; *Letters of Queen Victoria*, 3rd ser. ii, 404–5; Gardiner, A. G., *Life of Harcourt*, ii, 313 *seqq.*; Hornik, *loc. cit.* pp. 239–41.

[2] Taylor, A. J. P., *loc. cit.*; Hornik, *loc. cit.* pp. 241–2.

[3] Taylor, A. J. P., "British Policy in Morocco, 1886–1902", *E.H.R.* lxvi (1951), 342–74; *D.G.P.* viii, nos. 1958 *seqq.*

[4] Joseph, P., *Foreign Diplomacy in China, 1894–1900*; Langer, *op. cit.* pp. 167 *seqq.*; see also below pp. 289–92.

1895, which finally settled the Russo-Afghan frontier and in which most of Russia's frontier demands were conceded.[1] But European questions were not covered by the negotiations; and though the treaty was followed by a visit of the Prince of Wales to St Petersburg, where he worked for a widening of the frontier understanding into a general *rapprochement*, the visit was the outcome of the unexpected opportunity provided by the death of Alexander III.[2] External pressure and accidental circumstances, rather than any settled plan, similarly brought about the further collaboration of Great Britain with both the Dual Alliance Powers, France and Russia, in the matter of the Armenian atrocities. By the autumn of 1894 a succession of revolt, massacre and revolt in the Armenian districts of Turkey had produced in Great Britain a public outcry rivalling that earlier excitement over the Bulgarian horrors. Rosebery's government was forced by public opinion to make every effort short of single-handed military intervention—and even this was demanded by its radical supporters —to resume the old and wearisome efforts to impose restraint and reform upon the Porte. It was from anxiety to avoid the more serious course of single-handed action that Rosebery proposed that a British representative should be attached to a Turkish commission of enquiry. It was the Sultan, knowing that Russia shared his own interest in seeing the Armenian nationalist movement crushed, who retaliated with the proposal that Russia and France should also join the commission, they being the only other Powers maintaining consuls at Erzerum, and who thus brought into existence the so-called Armenian Triplice of Great Britain and the Dual Alliance.[3]

These approaches to France and Russia, though largely the product of circumstances, gave rise to rumours that Rosebery was attempting a revolution in British foreign policy. Nothing was further from his thoughts. It was chiefly because his policy was still to preserve the connection with the Triple Alliance against French and Russian designs on Egypt and the Straits, that he was led into giving substance to the rumours by deliberately exaggerating the scope of his efforts in public. It was for this reason that, in his Guildhall speech of November 1894, he made no secret of the British Government's interest in a *rapprochement* with Russia, but rather went out of his way to dwell on it; recalled the Anglo-French friendship of earlier days and looked to its renewal; and hinted at the isolation and encirclement of Germany.[4] He made much in public, too, and more than was justified by the facts, of the collaboration with France and Russia in Armenia. And here again, apart from the need to assuage British public opinion, his object, as he and Kimberley, his Foreign

[1] *C.H.B.E.* v, 426, 464.
[2] Lee, Sir Sidney, *Edward VII*, i, 689 *seqq.*; *History of 'The Times'*, iii, 189.
[3] Langer, *op. cit.* i, 147–64.
[4] *Ibid.* p. 146; Lovell, *The Struggle for South Africa*, p. 355.

Secretary, admitted to the Austrian ambassador, was to alarm Germany and make her more amenable.[1]

On the Austrian Government, on the German ambassador in London, these manœuvres had the desired effect. The ambassador feared an Anglo-Russian bargain involving British concessions to Russia at the Straits. The Austrian Government, though reassured by Rosebery's repeated denials of any intention to change his policy in this respect, blamed Germany's "systematic provocation" of Great Britain for creating this menace and for keeping it alive. It warned the German Government that, even though Rosebery still wanted to preserve the connection with the Triple Alliance, a growing section of influential British opinion had come to prefer good relations with all foreign Powers "but especially with Russia, France and America..., even at the cost of national self-esteem."[2] The effect on the German Government was more complicated, as was Germany's position compared with Austria's. Rosebery's approaches to the Dual Alliance Powers, and particularly his public comments on them, became an even more serious source of German complaint against Great Britain than the colonial question.[3] On this point there was unanimity in German Government circles, and no hesitation. Uncertainty and controversy, however, surrounded the question of what Germany's own course should be. Some, arguing deliberate enmity towards Germany as the source of Rosebery's conduct, or tempted to exploit Great Britain's many difficulties in pursuit of Germany's expanding interests, began to favour the conclusion of a Continental league of Germany, Russia and France at the expense of Great Britain's interests and by way of reinsurance with the Dual Alliance.[4] Others, though forced to conclude that British policy was too uncertain to permit close collaboration with Great Britain for the present, dreaded a policy that might make Germany too dependent on Russia, or were convinced that Great Britain could never grant the concessions that would alone make possible an Anglo-French or Anglo-Russian combination;[5] and were therefore reluctant to abandon for the future the old objective of binding Great Britain to the Triple Alliance by closer ties. Others again, including the Kaiser, who could not bring himself to take the final step in antagonising Great Britain or to impute deliberate hostility to Great Britain, but who fumed at Rosebery, finding his policy "a little difficult to understand",[6] took sometimes the one view and sometimes the other.

But if all was confusion in Germany, as all was drift about Rosebery's policy, and if Germany was inactive on this account through-

---

[1] Langer, op. cit. I, 146.   [2] Ibid. p. 146; Penson, loc. cit. pp. 129, 131-2 (Nov. 1894).
[3] See Chirol's report of Holstein's remarks of December 1894, History of 'The Times', III, 154-6.   [4] D.G.P. IX, chap. lxiv.
[5] The German Foreign Minister, Oct. 1894, cited by Brandenburg, op. cit. p. 70; D.G.P. IX, nos. 2161-8, 2201.   [6] Letters of Queen Victoria, 3rd ser. II, 535.

out the winter of 1894–5, Anglo-German relations had already deteriorated fast in the past year; and it was certain that they could not long remain suspended in the unsettled state they had reached.

VI

It was the situation in the Far East, now changing its character and beginning to bear directly on European relations for the first time, that ended Germany's inaction and showed British isolation, the logical outcome of recent developments, to be complete.

Unexpected Japanese victories in the Sino-Japanese war had brought Russia and Great Britain together in their anxiety to maintain the *status quo* in China. When German and American inaction had frustrated British and Chinese proposals for united intervention by all the Powers,[1] Great Britain, Russia and France had by the beginning of March 1895 reached an agreement by which they would insist on moderation and the maintenance of the integrity of Korea in any peace terms that Japan might impose on China. Germany was disturbed by this prospect of further collaboration between Russia and Great Britain. Behind her earlier refusal to join in any intervention schemes had lain the thought that the partition of China, now apparently begun by Japan, might provide herself with an opportunity for acquiring territory. The German Admiralty had begun to express an interest in acquiring a naval base in the Far East. Now, however, in order to prevent Japan from putting forward any demands which might encourage Anglo-Russian collaboration, and without informing the other Powers, Germany abandoned her earlier refusal to intervene and advised Japan to exercise restraint when the Japanese peace terms were announced in March.[2] With the same object, but also in the hope of diverting Russia and the Franco-Russian Alliance to the Far East—for some in Germany had already suspected in the Armenian Triplice a British effort to encourage Russian interest in the Balkans—and also out of anxiety lest the Dual Alliance should be strengthened if France alone supported Russia's policy, she took the next step. Having rejected earlier British proposals for joint intervention, she agreed to back Russia in making representations to Japan when Japan, ignoring Germany's earlier warning, persisted in April at Shimonoseki in forcing China to accept the independence of Korea and the cession to herself of Formosa and and the Liaotung peninsula.[3]

Germany's change of front was accompanied by an alteration of policy on the part of Great Britain. When Russia invited the Powers

[1] Langer, *op. cit.* I, 175–6; Brandenburg. *op. cit.* pp. 53–4.

[2] Langer, *op. cit.* I, 177; Brandenburg, *op. cit.* pp. 54–61; *D.G.P.* IX, nos. 2219–24, 2226, 2243 ff.

[3] Langer, *op. cit.* I, 182; *D.G.P.* IX, nos. 2232 ff., 2313, chap. lvii, especially no. 2735; Brandenburg, *op. cit.* pp. 65–7.

to intervene against the Shimonoseki settlement, using the argument that the Japanese annexations would be an obstacle to good relations between China and Japan and a constant menace to peace in the Far East, Great Britain, who had previously taken the lead in attempts to limit the Japanese peace-terms with similar arguments, refused, to Russia's disappointment and Germany's surprise, while France and Germany agreed. The British change of front had been preparing since the first Japanese military successes had begun to turn British public opinion away from China in the autumn of 1894. A movement for the revision of British policy in the Far East had grown while Rosebery was officially maintaining the old course. Even in April 1895 Rosebery and the Queen would have liked to adhere to this course and to join the representations of the other Powers. But they failed to carry the Cabinet, whose refusal to take action was based less on the feeling that Japan would prove a useful ally in blocking Russia in China, though that was beginning to exist, than on dislike of Rosebery's "imperialism" and distrust of the professed disinterestedness of the other Powers in intervening.[1]

This change in British policy contributed as much as the change in Germany's, to the widening of the breach between Germany and Great Britain that resulted from the Shimonoseki incident. It also showed, however, that the drift of British foreign policy, in so far as it had maintained consistent direction and was not simply the temporary result of haphazard and external developments, was nothing so obvious as a move away from the Triple Alliance and from the growing isolation which strained relations with the Triple Alliance had brought about since 1892. It was a drift away from all the European Powers into even greater isolation, not away from isolation in the direction of new combinations with other Powers to replace the earlier informal relationship with Germany and her allies. In the Shimonoseki incident Great Britain had not only parted company with Germany. She had also switched her policy away from collaboration with France and Russia in China. Nor was this the only case in which her efforts since the previous summer to work with the Dual Alliance Powers were breaking down or being abandoned. The Upper Nile negotiations with France had failed already: France would not recognise a British sphere of influence to which Great Britain refused to abandon her claim. The decision announced to the House of Commons on 28 March 1895, that the British Government would view "as an unfriendly act" the penetration of another Power into the Nile Valley, had given formal recognition to the beginning, in consequence, of a new and more intensive phase of Anglo-French rivalry in Africa.[2]

---

[1] Brandenburg, *op. cit.* p. 62; Langer, *op. cit.* I, 174–5, 185; *Letters of Queen Victoria*, 3rd ser. II, 496, 499, 507.

[2] *Hansard*, 4th ser. XXXII, 405–6; Taylor, A. J. P., "Prelude to Fashoda", *E.H.R.* LXV (1950), 52–80.

By that date, while nothing had come of the approaches to Russia for a general *rapprochement* the Armenian Triplice had shown itself to be less of a successful collaborative effort between the three Powers than some in Great Britain had expected and some in Germany had feared. Its sole result, produced in May 1895, was a modest and ineffective scheme of reform for Turkey's Armenian areas.[1]

Rosebery's efforts to work with France and Russia had failed because they had been limited. Even before she decided that her rivalry with Russia, carried over from older areas of struggle, should prevail in her policy in the Far East, Great Britain had shown herself unready for those sacrifices that were necessary elsewhere if new adjustments were to be reached. By the same token, as Rosebery had already made it plain at least to the Austrian Government, she was not yet ready consciously to abandon the old connections with the Triple Alliance. But Great Britain's relations with the Triple Alliance were not what they had been; and neither what they had been nor what they had become was what the German Government now wanted them to be. What was making British policy inadequate in the course it had taken since 1892, in its move away from the Triple Alliance without compensating sacrifice and adjustment in other directions, was the fact that, if the British Government was content with it, the German Government was not. It is true that, even after Shimonoseki, the German Government remained divided and uncertain as to what its own course should be. The fact that France as well as Germany had joined Russia, while Great Britain had abstained, brought nearer the temptation of a Continental league against Great Britain with Germany at its head, and some elements in Germany had not ceased to be interested in the possibility of expansion in China at the expense of rivalry with Great Britain. On the other hand, regret that the incident had widened the breach with Great Britain combined with the fear of becoming too dependent on the Dual Alliance to produce in other German circles the feeling that Germany had overreached herself, and the more so as other developments seemed to confirm that nothing would come of Great Britain's approaches to France and Russia. These circles pleaded for time in the difficult task of bringing London into the orbit of Berlin. Germany was still hesitating between these alternatives when Rosebery's government fell in June 1895.[2] If only because of the widespread belief that better things could be expected of Salisbury, she had, indeed, since April, been deliberately marking time. But even if the more moderate, more patient, more anglophil policy should prevail, Germany would still be dissatisfied, in a world dominated by alliances, with the British preference for good relations with all

---

[1] Langer, *op. cit.* I, 147, 162–4.
[2] Langer, *op. cit.* I, 185–9; Brandenburg, *op. cit.* pp. 68–71; *D.G.P.* IX, nos. 2276ff., 2313–18, 2343–58.

States and alliances withnone. Even if Salisbury, living up to her expectations, should prove willing to put an end to the drift and uncertainty in British policy over the past three years, it was still a question whether he would be willing to abandon this preference. And if he would not, the breach already formed between Great Britain and Germany might prove too wide to be bridged by other means.

CHAPTER IX

THE BRITISH EMPIRE AND THE
UNITED STATES OF AMERICA, 1870–1914

WHEN Sumner made his celebrated speech on the *Alabama* claims in the Senate of the United States on 13 April 1869,[1] the fortunes of the British Empire appeared to be at an exceptionally low ebb. Canadian protests against the suggested cession of their country raised little stir in London and were discussed by Edward Thornton, the British Minister at Washington, with Hamilton Fish, the new Secretary of State, quite unemotionally, although it was made clear that no British colony ever had been, or ever would be, surrendered against its will. Moreover, in that same spring the British Colonial Secretary, Lord Granville, flatly rejected a not unreasonable request from New Zealand that if, as it was rumoured, the colonial garrisons were to be withdrawn, the Imperial Government should at least guarantee a local loan for the continuance of the war against the Maoris.[2] Plans for the withdrawal of the troops, not only from New Zealand and Australia, but also from Canada, proceeded, and by January 1870 the *Times* correspondent in New Zealand was quoting part of the local press as saying that there too the only practicable solution might be looked for in America. It was with reason that Froude wrote in *Fraser's Magazine*: "While we are talking of dismembering our Empire, the Americans have made enormous sacrifices to preserve the unity of theirs. If we throw off the colonies, it is at least possible that they may apply for admittance into the American Union, and it is equally possible that the Americans may not refuse them."[3]

The year 1870, however, marked the slow but perceptible turning of the tide. In May, just before succeeding Clarendon at the Foreign Office, Granville pacified New Zealand by giving way about the loan,[4] and both he and Kimberley, his successor at the Colonial Office, publicly disclaimed any intention of dismembering the existing Empire.[5] In Canada the year was marked by the collapse of the first Riel rebellion,[6] in spite of Fish's questionable conduct in closing the

[1] *C.H.B.E.* II, 546–7.
[2] See above, chap. II.
[3] Schuyler, R. L., *The Fall of the Old Colonial System, 1770–1870*, pp. 264–5.
[4] Ramm, A. (ed.), *The Political Correspondence of Mr Gladstone and Lord Granville, 1868–1876* (Camden, 3rd ser. LXXXI, LXXXII; 1952), nos. 223, 235.
[5] Granville had already written privately to Russell to the same effect when the latter had protested to him against the withdrawal of the garrisons. Fitzmaurice, *Life of Granville*, II, 22.
[6] See *C.H.B.E.* VI, 471–2, 483, 532.

Sault Ste Marie Canal[1] to a Canadian Government store-ship, and the way was opened for the Red River Colony to enter the Dominion as Manitoba, instead of remaining an extension of Minnesota northwards, cutting off the rest of Canada from the Pacific.[2] In 1869 the territory remaining under the Hudson's Bay Company was secured by the Dominion. The British Government now supported the entrance of British Columbia into the Dominion, and this took place in 1871. The dream of an all-American Pacific coast-line, caused by Seward's purchase of Alaska from the Russians in 1867,[3] dissolved in the resentment felt by most Canadians against United States post-war nationalism of the Sumner brand, although two thousand miles of wilderness unbridged by rail still separated the new Province from her nearest neighbours.[4] And yet 1870 and 1871 are perhaps remembered less for the vast strides taken by Canadian federalism than for the sudden marked improvement, somewhat at Canadian expense, which took place in Anglo-American relations as a whole—culminating, as it did, in the Treaty of Washington, 8 May 1871, which has been held by some to be second only in importance for the United States to the Treaty of Versailles in 1783.[5]

Here too the roots go back perhaps to 1869, when the enigmatic John Rose, then Canadian Minister of Finance, first appeared at Washington and listened to suggestions, made by Fish himself,[6] for a joint commission to settle all outstanding issues with the British. But these conversations were both premature and unofficial, compared with those which Fish held with Thornton on the same subject in the following year,[7] and in any case all Fish's approaches would have failed if Her Majesty's Government had not in the meantime taken certain vitally important steps towards agreement on their own account. The first of these was the Naturalisation Convention of May 1870,[8] under which Great Britain surrendered that doctrine of "indefeasible nationality" which had grated on the United States since the beginning of the century and, through its use to justify impressments, had helped to bring about the War of 1812. The second was the new Foreign Enlistment Act of August 1870, which was not only based on the recommendations of the Neutrality Commission of 1868 for bringing up to date the antiquated Act of 1819, but even went beyond them in respect of warships built in Britain for a belligerent when she herself was not at war.[9] The third was Lord Tenterden's famous memorandum, laid before the Cabinet on 19 November 1870.

---

[1] This is the canal joining Lakes Huron and Superior, the natural difference of whose levels is as much as nineteen feet.

[2] Van Alstyne, R., *American Diplomacy in Action*, pp. 529–30; Brebner, J. B., *North Atlantic Triangle*, p. 178.   [3] *C.H.B.E.* II, 547.

[4] Brebner, *loc. cit.*   [5] Brebner, *op. cit.* p. 193.

[6] Nevins, Allan, *Hamilton Fish*, p. 433.   [7] Ramm, *op. cit.* nos. 336, 339.

[8] Gardiner, A. G., *Life of Harcourt*, I, 207.   [9] Gardiner, *loc. cit.*

Lord Tenterden was then only "a senior clerk in the Foreign Office, specialising in the American Department", but his memorandum was dynamic.[1] It explained the absolute necessity for a final, friendly settlement with the United States in view of the alarming implications for Great Britain of the *Alabama* precedent, should she herself become involved in the Franco-Prussian War.[2] It outlined a plan for obtaining that settlement, the early stages of which, so the Cabinet decided, should be entrusted to the unofficial ministrations of the newly-knighted Sir John Rose.[3] That not very popular Canadian politician was now the representative of an American financial house in London. Both at this time and throughout his subsequent career as Canadian Financial Commissioner in Britain, Rose, though loaded with honours and respectability, was perhaps not a wholly disinterested person,[4] but fortunately the private advantage of Messrs Levi P. Morton, Rose & Co. did in fact favour a peaceful settlement between Britain and America, and from January 1871, when Rose arrived in Washington, to the arbitration at Geneva in 1872, the unobtrusive influence of this firm in both countries certainly effected much towards that end.[5] To begin with, Rose secured the immediate consent of the United States Administration to the Tenterden plan, which was roughly that Great Britain should officially propose the setting-up of a joint commission to settle all outstanding questions about Canada, such as boundaries, fisheries, the navigation of lakes and rivers, the coasting-trade and the transit of goods in bond. The Americans were then to propose the reference to this body of the *Alabama* and other Civil War claims, and this reference would be accepted by the British Government.

By 8 March 1871 the Commissioners had in fact met, but Rose was now resident in England and therefore, as he himself recognised, no longer a suitable representative of Canada.[6] His place, therefore, was taken, somewhat reluctantly, by the Canadian Premier, Sir John Macdonald, who, though needlessly hampered by the Governor-General's betrayal to his British colleagues of all his confidential communications to the Canadian Cabinet, fought a brilliant rear-guard action for his country[7] and at the same time brought about the

[1] Baxter, J. P., "The British High Commissioners at Washington in 1871", *Mass. Hist. Soc. Proceedings*, LXV (1932–6), 334–57.

[2] I.e. the fear that if Great Britain were drawn into the war, commerce-destroyers might be fitted out for her opponent in the ports of a nominally neutral United States. This fear derived plausibility from the fact that, in 1866, in retaliation for Britain's part in the activities of the Confederate commerce-raiders, the House of Representatives had unanimously passed an amendment to the 1818 Neutrality Act which would have permitted Americans to sell ships to belligerents. The amendment, however, died in the Senate, cf. Brebner, *op. cit.* 166n.   [3] Ramm, *op. cit.* nos. 384, 386, 389, 442

[4] Long, M. H., "Sir John Rose and the Informal Beginnings of the Canadian High Commissionership", *Canadian Hist. Rev.* XII (1931) 23–43.

[5] Brebner, *op. cit.* pp. 189–90.

[6] Shippee, L. B., *Canadian-American Relations, 1849–1874*, p. 334.

[7] Ramm, *op. cit.* nos. 496–8, 514.

ultimate acceptance, however surly, of a settlement such as Rose could not have won.[1] It was a thankless role, for from this time forward, whenever Anglo-American *rapprochement* was desired, it was Canadian short-term interests which were ostentatiously sacrificed: Canada, it is true, may have gained in the long-run, but it was hard for Canadians to calculate these remoter and more indirect gains, while they were only too conscious of their immediate loss.[2]

The story of the Joint Commission's activities has been told more than once, but in most detail by the biographers of its leading members, Hamilton Fish and the Marquess of Ripon, then Earl de Grey and Lord President of the Council in Gladstone's Cabinet. Its main theme throughout is that the avowed object of the Commission was always subsidiary to its real object, and its main achievement not the much-praised Treaty of Washington but the arbitration of the Civil War claims, for which that treaty provided, at Geneva. When this fact is borne in mind it can be understood why the Commission almost immediately ran into difficulties over certain principles of international law put forward by the United States for the express purpose of covering the case of a neutral power guilty of fitting out commerce-destroyers in war-time. These principles were entirely unacceptable to the British Cabinet, which, however, after much heated argument, decided to give its Commissioners a free hand in attempting to amend them. The decision was well justified, for by this means the Americans were in fact persuaded to jettison the greater part of their original demands, so that the Rules as finally submitted went little beyond the new Foreign Enlistment Act of 1870, although in so far as they did go beyond it the British reluctantly agreed that their force should be retroactive.[3] The more concrete question of the actual American claims was also settled principally in favour of Great Britain—or so the British Commissioners believed— from the beginning. In a secret dispatch dated 8 March they wrote: "It was believed by the United States Government that they had also a good equitable claim for indirect or constructive losses. These latter, however, they did not prefer, and their not doing so must, they considered, be regarded as a great concession." On the other hand, in the agreed general Protocol there was only a vague reference to "an amicable settlement" of the American claims, which were left undefined, and this vagueness was to cause trouble later.[4]

In the meantime the Treaty of Washington was signed in May, and the Canadian questions either settled outright or referred to various special commissions or arbitrators, one of whom—for the

---

[1] Brebner, *op. cit.* p. 191; Pope, Sir J., *Memoirs of Sir John Macdonald*, II, 85–140.
[2] Brebner, *op. cit.* p. 245.
[3] For the whole of this passage, and for the two sets of Rules—before and after revision— see *Cambridge History of British Foreign Policy*, III, 66–9.
[4] Wolf, L., *Life of Ripon*, I, 255–6.

boundary through the Strait of Juan de Fuca[1]—was to be the German Emperor.[2] The United States refused to concede commercial reciprocity to Canada in return for free access to the inshore fisheries, which they had lost as a consequence of their termination (in 1866) of the 1854 reciprocity treaty with Canada; but they agreed to allow free admission of Canadian fish and fish oil and to refer to a special commission sitting at Halifax the assessment of the amount by which their retention of inshore fishing rights on the Canadian coasts exceeded in value all American privileges granted under the Treaty of Washington to Canadians in other respects. The assessment, when it came, proved a generous one,[3] and thus, in spite of the outcry over the "surrender" of the fisheries, they fulfilled in part what discerning Canadians realised to be their real function—that of a bargaining counter with the United States.[4] Finally an international Arbitration Tribunal was set up—to consist of single nominees of Great Britain, the United States, Italy, Brazil and Switzerland, who were to be guided by the three new principles of neutrality arrived at by the Joint Commission and laid down in Article VI of the Treaty; and also to assess damages, if it should be found that Great Britain had infringed them, even if she had done so at a time when the new rules did not exist.

When the arbitration opened at Geneva on 15 December 1871, the British press and public, and the greater part of the Cabinet, were deeply shocked to find that the indirect claims, originally put forward by Sumner but long thought to have been abandoned, were after all included.[5] The reason given was that two alternatives had originally been put to the Commission, namely, either the immediate payment of a gross sum by Great Britain, together with a waiver of the indirect claims by the United States, or else arbitration, leaving the United States a free hand, and that the British had deliberately preferred the second method of settlement. The British case, resting on their Commissioners' dispatch of 8 March 1871, was of course that the American waiver had applied to both alternatives alike, although there was enough doubt about this for Stafford Northcote, who had represented Her Majesty's Opposition on the Joint Commission, to admit to Lord Granville in a private letter of April 1872[6] the possibility of a genuine misunderstanding. In any case no reference could be made to the alleged American promise contained in the British

[1] Moore, J. B., *History and Digest of International Arbitrations to which the United States has been a Party* (Washington, 1898).
[2] *C.H.B.E.* II, 546.
[3] Owing to the equally generous British settlement of the *Alabama* and other Civil War claims, Skelton, O. D. *Life and Times of Sir A. T. Galt*, p. 513, cf. pp. 458, 460–1; Moore, *op. cit.* I, 703–53.
[4] Brebner, *op. cit.* p. 187.
[5] Ramm, *op. cit.* nos. 633, 640, 643. This last shows that Gladstone did not share the popular anger.
[6] Fitzmaurice, *op. cit.* II, 92; cf. Ramm, *op. cit.* no. 690.

secret document for fear of embarrassing the American Secretary of State in his difficult relations with the Senate, and for his part Hamilton Fish chose to take his stand upon the vague terms of the published Protocol. What were probably his exact motives—to resuscitate the indirect claims only to destroy them—were accurately guessed and analysed by Lord Blachford at the time, although Fish himself never seems to have put forward in so many words the plan, ultimately adopted by C. F. Adams and Bancroft Davis, of securing an adverse but extra-judicial opinion from the Tribunal,[1] so that the indirect claims would be finally ruled out of court and technically never come before that body at all.[2]

The main danger lay in the anger of the British Cabinet and the prolonged refusal to submit the British case, but the Marquess of Ripon (as he now was) and Lord Cairns, the Lord Chancellor, succeeded in delaying any final decision until it was learned that the Tribunal had refused to entertain the claims,[3] after which the British case was duly presented (on 27 June) and the arbitration proceeded. On 14 September 1872, the final award of 15,500,000 gold dollars was made to the United States, and although the British arbitrator, Sir Alexander Cockburn, who undoubtedly behaved very badly throughout the whole hearing, rejected a substantial part of it, the British Government did not contest the decision and payment was in fact made about a year later.[4] Their one reservation lay in a refusal to be bound in future by the Tribunal's construction of the words "due diligence" in the first rule of reference, while accepting it without prejudice for the time being, and in this refusal they were subsequently sustained by the Hague Conference of 1907, which substituted a different and unexceptionable form of wording.[5] The Americans for their part were well pleased, and President Grant's annual message of 2 December declared "no shadow on friendly relations with Great Britain" now existed. The one really profound dissentient—the one victim on the altar of Anglo-American friendship—was Canada. It was an unwelcome role from which, while it was by no means new to her, she would always find it very difficult to escape.

Compared with the Civil War claims the Fenians of this generation, who provided the only purely political problem of any importance between the United States and Canada, seem perhaps of minor interest, yet at least one British statesman of the 'eighties came to a belated sense of their significance. They had had their hey-day, as far as Canada was concerned, in the "invasions" of 1866 and 1870,

---

[1] Ramm, *op. cit.* no. 728.
[2] Fish, however, may have hinted at something of the sort to Granville after the Senate had adjourned early in June 1871. See Fitzmaurice, *op. cit.* II, 64, and cf. Wolf, L., *op. cit.* I, 258.   [3] Ramm, *op. cit.* nos. 696, 724.
[4] The whole story of the events leading up to the arbitration and the arbitration itself is told in Moore, *op. cit.* I, 495–682.
[5] For this reservation see *C.H.B.F.P.* III, 71.

when the open sympathy of American politicians with one eye on the Irish vote, and American failure to suppress the Brotherhood or try its leaders, had had a share in defeating annexationism. Coupled, on the other hand, with the lukewarmness of the British Government in supporting the Dominion's Anti-Fenian efforts, this American attitude had in fact done even more: it had helped to bring about the great outburst of Canadian nationalism which for over forty years would be intermittently directed almost as much against Great Britain as against the United States.[1] In 1881 it was the turn of the British Home Secretary, Sir William Harcourt, to see the red light, though he saw it in a different quarter: in and out of office during the next seven years he found it all-important to dissociate the Fenian editors, agitators and assassins from respectable Irish-Americans; to suppress the former mercilessly on their nefarious missions to the United Kingdom; to persuade American administrations too to play their part; and above all to prevent Englishmen from committing Chamberlain's error of using "bitter and insulting language" to a "great and influential section of the American people". By November 1888 he had hit upon, and publicly proclaimed, the doctrine that "while you have a hostile Ireland you can never really have a friendly America"—a theory which had much to commend it in its day, and indeed for many years to come, during which the powerful anti-British Irish vote would be of major concern to American politicians, at any rate of the Democratic Party.[2]

During the remainder of the century, however, the main interest in American relations with the Empire, Canada included, was less political than economic. It was an age in which British primacy in the export markets of the world, hitherto unquestioned, began first to stand still and then to disappear in face of American and, later, German competition, but the political implications of this "crossing of courses, and the lead of American energies",[3] were not worked out until the later 'nineties and the new century. In Britain there was a slow revival of interest in the Empire, at first federalist in tone, but quickening into a more flamboyant imperialism with the coming of the great Disraeli ministry of 1874.[4] This change of emphasis coincided with a long period of declining world prices, an approach in the United States towards an industrial self-sufficiency first foreshadowed in the 'fifties[5] and the final exploitation and disappearance of the American "frontier". In 1870 British investments abroad amounted to about £785 millions, three-fifths of which were in Government bonds (£160 millions in the United States and £105

---

[1] Stacey, C. P., "Fenianism and the Rise of National Feeling in Canada at the time of Confederation", *Canadian Hist. Rev.* xii (1931), 238–61.
[2] Gardiner, A. G., *op. cit.* i, 428–30, 438–9, 471, 482; ii, 60–1, 66.
[3] *Education of Henry Adams, sub anno* 1892.
[4] Foreshadowed in Disraeli's Crystal Palace speech of June, 1872.
[5] Nevins, *Ordeal of the Union*, ii, 243.

millions in the colonies). By 1885 overseas assets had grown to £1,280 millions, half of which were in the Empire as compared with a third in 1870. After the turn of the century foreign lending was resumed on a large scale, and in 1911 the nominal value of British investment overseas was about £3,500 millions; as in 1885, half of this total was in the Empire, Canada having taken the place of Australia and New Zealand as the main attraction. British holdings of securities in North and South America taken together were well over 50 per cent of total foreign investment in 1911 as compared with 40 per cent in 1885. The annual income derived from overseas assets increased from £50 millions in the early 'seventies to £180 millions in 1911–13.[1] The mid-'seventies saw a significant change in the character of British capital exports. Up to that time much of the lending had been to foreign Governments needing funds for military or strategic purposes; from the 'eighties onwards British investors concentrated on the undeveloped resources of the newer countries—Canada, Australia, the United States and Latin America. Each surge of foreign lending, accompanied by heavy emigration from Europe, helped to secure for Great Britain abundant supplies of food and raw materials which were indispensable to the growth of her industries and export trade.[2] These harmonious fluctuations in the movements of men and money were a feature of the economic development of the Atlantic community from the middle of the nineteenth century to the eve of the first World War;[3] but towards the end of the period, although Britain's strength as a creditor nation was as great as ever, there were signs that her industrial productivity was not keeping pace with that of the United States and Germany. The process of investment, inherently uneven in its course, suffered periodic setbacks. Thus in 1872 Costa Rica, San Domingo and Paraguay defaulted on their British loans, and in 1873 Bolivia, Uruguay and Guatemala suspended interest on theirs. There was nothing new in such suspensions and defaults, except that for the first time they produced developments of enduring importance, namely, the incorporation of foreign bond-holders in London into what eventually became a political pressure-group, and, secondly, the parliamentary investigation of 1875. The Council of Foreign Bond-holders has its significance in the age of Theodore Roosevelt and William H. Taft, while the Special Report of the parliamentary committee,[4] with its revelations of market-rigging

---

[1] The statistics of foreign investment used in this paragraph are based on Cairncross, A. K., *Home and Foreign Investment, 1870–1913* (Cambridge, 1953), chap. vi.

[2] On the whole subject of foreign investment in this period see Cairncross, *op. cit.* chaps. vi and vii; Hobson, C. K., *The Export of Capital* (1914); Feis, H., *Europe, the World's Banker, 1870–1914* (1930); Jenks, L. H., *The Migration of British Capital, to 1875* (1938); Rostow, W. W., *British Economy of the Nineteenth Century* (1948), chap. iii; Thomas, Brinley, *Migration and Economic Growth: a Study of Great Britain and the Atlantic Economy* (Cambridge, 1954), chap. vii.

[3] For a detailed analysis of this development see Thomas, B., *op. cit.* 83–189, 224–33.

[4] *Special Report on Loans to Foreign States*, and *Appendices: Parl. Pap.* 1875, xi (152), (367).

and other forms of fraudulent promotion, marks the point at which British foreign investment entered upon a new phase.

The gradual economic change in Anglo-American relations did not, however, affect the whole of the United States equally or simultaneously: thus for another twenty years the Middle West remained economically "colonial", in the sense that it continued to require capital in return for highly specialised, and mainly agricultural, exports. What happened was that the North Atlantic seaboard of the United States came to take the place of Britain as financier for the Middle West; New York gradually replaced London for this purpose, and such houses as that of J. P. Morgan inherited the role of Baring's.[1] By the end of the century such financing was entirely in American hands; industrial had overtaken agricultural production, even in the Middle West itself; and the United States as a whole was rapidly approaching that creditor status among nations which it finally achieved during the war of 1914–18.

In view of this increasingly self-sufficient economic background, it is not surprising to find that United States foreign policy during the last quarter of the nineteenth century was marked by "an inactive diplomacy" and a "high protective tariff".[2] Once the transition of the 'seventies and 'eighties had been completed—that is, if the passing of the frontier be given its traditional date of about 1890—the tariffs grew higher than ever, in order to protect the great home market in which so much native capital had now been sunk; but even this immense market could not long absorb the gigantic productive power of the United States. There followed, inevitably, the drive for exports starting in the 'nineties and, as its necessary concomitant, a much more active diplomacy.

Thus the 'seventies and 'eighties were in fact a seminal period— one in which the actual diplomatic events, while often appearing trivial, frequently reflect faint beginnings of untold importance for the future. This is perhaps most true of the steady expansion of American interests into the Pacific and the Caribbean, but it may be well for the moment to postpone considering the repercussion of these developments on British imperial policy, in order to trace the response made to the challenge of the United States by that *enfant terrible* of successive British cabinets, the young Dominion of Canada.

Unpopular as the Treaty of Washington was with the Canadians it maintained fairly stable relations for about a decade, but in its failure to come to grips with either fisheries or tariffs, or to provide any machinery for settling old scores, such as the Fenian question, or new problems such as the fur-seal industry, the treaty, to Canadian eyes at least, continued to stand self-condemned. Yet it was the

---

[1] Fish, C. R., *The United States and Great Britain* (Chicago, 1932), p. 53.
[2] Bellot, H. Hale, "Atlantic History", *History*, xxxi (1946), 56–63.

Americans who first attempted to amend it, mainly owing to an unexpected change in the habits of the mackerel.[1] From 1881–2 the mackerel shoals began to move further south, so that the sum of $5,500,000 which, by the decision of the Halifax tribunal rendered in 1877, the United States had been obliged to pay for the privilege of fishing in Canadian waters, was no longer worth their while. This fact, coupled with the indignation felt at what the United States considered the exorbitant assessment, moved Congress, in 1883, to direct the President to give notice of the termination of the fisheries clauses. They accordingly lapsed two years later, and the long-obsolete convention of 1818 automatically resumed its force. The main importance of the dispute lay in the fact that there were other fish in the sea besides mackerel and that the Canadians, having been alarmed in the meantime by the steady rise in general American tariffs, carefully enforced every letter of the 1818 fishery agreement[2] in the hope of blackmailing the United States over the tariff issue;[3] while the Americans for their part tried to use their tariffs to force the opening of the halibut and cod fisheries. Thus an ugly situation prevailed throughout 1886 and 1887, and it was in an attempt to remedy this that the Anglo-American Joint High Commission met in Washington from November 1887 to February 1888, and after much difficulty drew up the Bayard–Chamberlain Treaty.[4] This was rejected by the United States Senate in August, but a *modus vivendi* agreed upon by the Commission maintained substantial peace in the fishing grounds[5] until 1910 when the whole matter was settled by arbitration.[6]

Meanwhile the American tariff wall against the world in general and against Canada in particular rose steadily higher and higher. Its growth was, however, more especially associated with the Republican party, and so was partially delayed by the Democratic victory of 1884. It was not that the new President, Grover Cleveland, was really a free-trader, but he did at least prefer tariffs for revenue to tariffs for protection and indeed this was one of the reasons why he lost in 1888.[7] The triumph of the Republicans in that year led straight to what has been called the first really high and inclusive tariff measure of modern times in the McKinley Tariff of 1890, which was regarded in Canada as a deliberate reversal by the Harrison admini-

---

[1] Mowat, R. B., *Diplomatic Relations of Great Britain and the United States*, p. 233.

[2] Tansill, C. C., *Canadian–American Relations, 1875–1911*, pp. 26–7, 35–6, 41, 45, 46, 49, 54.

[3] *Ibid.* pp. 53–4, 57, 63.   [4] *Ibid.* pp. 52–77.

[5] *Ibid.* pp. 81–6. The fisheries dispute between 1885 and 1888 can be studied in detail in Tansill, C. C., *The Foreign Policy of Thomas F. Bayard* (New York, 1940), chaps. vi-x; and the whole question in the later nineteenth and early twentieth centuries in the same author's *Canadian–American Relations, 1875–1911* (New Haven and Toronto, 1943), chaps. i-iv.   [6] See below, pp. 694–5.

[7] The election of 1888 was particularly notable for its virulently anti-British tone. This found its most extreme expression in the dismissal of the British Minister, Sir Lionel Sackville-West, for alleged interference in American domestic affairs after he had tactlessly replied to the fraudulent "Murchison letter"; see Tansill, *Bayard*, chap. xi.

stration of Cleveland's more friendly approaches, and in fact as a declaration of commercial war.[1] There was, it is true, a "commercial unionist" party in the Dominion, of which the Englishman Goldwin Smith was perhaps the chief apostle—a party, that is to say, which demanded admission to the American *Zollverein* at almost any price —but it was smitten hip and thigh in the Canadian election of 1891, when Sir John Macdonald and the Conservatives were confirmed in power. Fortunately Canadian and American politics were out of phase in these years, for in 1892 the Republicans were again beaten and the second Cleveland Administration formed in 1893, with the result that the impending struggle to the death between Canadian fishery controls and American tariffs was once again postponed while other issues intervened—but it could not be postponed for ever.

All these were old problems, but they were much aggravated by a third, which, though new in the 'eighties, was to dominate British, Canadian and United States relations for nearly ten years. This was the growing extent of Canadian depredations on the valuable United States trade in seal-skins on the north-west Pacific coasts. The details of this controversy afford a fascinating study in the subtler ramifications of historical geography, natural science, commerce, international law and diplomacy, but perhaps it will be enough to say here that, while the American case was the sounder in common-sense and equity, it was defectively presented, especially by Blaine, and brilliantly attacked by the British, principally as counsel for the Canadians. Ultimately the matter was referred by treaty to an international arbitration tribunal of the type which had been so successful in settling the Civil War claims in 1872.[2] As the main habitat of the seals was in the Behring Sea, the resulting settlement came to be known as the Behring Sea Arbitration, held in Paris between March and August 1893. The arguments presented by both sides before the Tribunal were extremely legalistic, which may explain why the decision went on practically every point to Britain and her client Canada—the latter even being awarded substantial damages for the loss of ships seized by the Americans while engaged in "pelagic" sealing, that is, on the high seas. It is true that these decisions were sound from the lawyer's point of view, but the hard fact remains that no effective protection was given to the seals, with the result that by 1906 the American herd was on the verge of extinction[3] and was

---

[1] The Canadians tried to offset the adverse effects of the McKinley Tariff by endeavouring to persuade the United States to agree to some form of reciprocity with Canada. However, Secretary of State Blaine, although responsible for the inclusion of a provision for reciprocity with Latin America in the act of 1890, would have none of it, for he believed that reciprocity would delay that incorporation into the United States which he felt was Canada's ultimate destiny; Tansill, *Canadian–American Relations*, pp. 427, 434–5; Brebner, *op. cit.* p. 247.

[2] For the whole subject and especially the arbitration, see Moore, *op. cit.* 1, 755–961.

[3] American land-killings on the islands played a large part in depleting the herd. See Tansill, *Canadian–American Relations*, p. 364 (*sub anno* 1903).

saved only at the very last moment by the international convention of 1911, which substantially restored American methods of control.

The most important results of the picturesque controversy were, first, a considerable loss of faith in arbitration as a method of settling international disputes on the part of Americans in general, and of the young Theodore Roosevelt in particular[1]—a fact which was to be not without influence on American policy some ten years later. Secondly, it produced a still more alarming increase in the already existing tension between the United States and Canada—with Canada's protector, Britain, not excluded. It was in fact this hostility, already fed by Fenianism, the Atlantic fishery dispute and tariff questions—a hostility in which the main protagonist on the British side was not Britain herself but her unruly young Dominion—which helped to cause much of the sudden American resentment of the middle 'nineties against the whole British Empire.[2] This resentment, as powerful and real as it was unexpected by the British, found an unforeseen vent over the affairs of a much smaller British colony, Guiana, in what has gone down in history as the Venezuela "incident" of 1895.

As far as British Guiana and Venezuela were concerned, the story was an old one: it was effective intervention by the United States, frequently solicited by Venezuela but never before conceded, which was new. The matter in dispute was the frontier between the republic and the colony, which had been surveyed by Sir Robert Schomburgk for the British Government as far back as 1841. The "Schomburgk Line", about which the controversy turned from then onwards, had never been accepted by the Venezuelans, whose extreme claims would have included about half of British Guiana: the British on the other hand always postulated it as a basis of discussion, though they did not regard it as final. Compromises intermittently offered over a long period of years, first by one side then by the other, were invariably rejected, but the crisis in the quarrel was not reached until 1887. Early in that year Venezuela at last broke off diplomatic relations over a British refusal to go to arbitration—which, incidentally, resulted for the first time in an "earnest protest" against Britain from the United States. This protest, sent by Bayard, then Secretary of State, was however not delivered, although it was subsequently printed in *United States Foreign Relations, 1888* as if it had reached the British Government. But the truth was that Phelps, the American Minister in London, had refused to transmit it and Bayard had acquiesced. Neither action was on the official record, and the facts do not seem to have been known to Cleveland and Olney in 1895.[3]

[1] Mowat, *op. cit.* p. 257.
[2] Cf. Bailey, T. A., *A Diplomatic History of the American People* (New York, 2nd ed., 1942), pp. 477–9, for a summary of factors contributing to American hostility towards Britain.
[3] Mowat, *Life of Pauncefote*, p. 175; Tansill, *Bayard*, pp. 641–2.

The immediate effect of the rupture was to persuade the Venezuelans that their only hope lay in obtaining a more active intervention by the United States, and from this point their propaganda campaign was intensified. They industriously spread rumours, not without a basis of truth, that there was gold in the disputed region of Caratal over which the legislature of British Guiana was trying to assert jurisdiction: and they made much play with a decree issued by the Governor of British Guiana denying the validity of a recent Venezuelan railway grant on the ground that it crossed British territory. It was significant that the promoters of the railway were United States citizens, and it soon became clear that it was by enticing United States nationals into enterprises in the contested area that the Venezuelans hoped to win American support. Bayard, it appears, was not deceived: the British on the other hand were not wholly uninfluenced and made their first real concession in 1890, when they agreed to accept arbitration for all areas to the westward of the Schomburgk Line. This offer in turn was finally refused by 1893, and there followed a fresh Venezuelan appeal to Cleveland, then beginning his second Administration. The new campaign reached a climax in the second half of 1894 with the frenzied efforts of William L. Scruggs, who had been United States minister in Caracas under Harrison but had been relieved of his post when the Democrats came in.[1] Scruggs's nationwide publicity campaign had considerable effect in arousing United States opinion, mainly owing to a complex of factors such as the widespread irritation already mentioned against the British Empire and the rapid swing back to Republicanism shown by the Congressional elections of 1894. It was widely felt that Cleveland, on the record of his first Administration, was an ineffective, too pacific President, who did not care to assert the just claims of United States citizens. It is possible that Cleveland may have reacted somewhat to this feeling in what followed, though the direct influence of Scruggs upon him seems to have been slight and on the State Department non-existent. It may be that the temporary landing of British marines about this time, to protect British interests on the coast of Nicaragua —an action which recalled the old controversy about the Mosquito Protectorate—was really the deciding factor,[2] but it is probable that the simultaneous appearance of a new and far more aggressive Secretary of State in place of the pacific Gresham counted for even more.

When that grim Boston lawyer, Richard Olney, fresh from his triumph over the Pullman strikers, moved from the Attorney-Generalship to the State Department in June 1895 he was of course

[1] Perkins, Dexter, *The Monroe Doctrine, 1868–1907* (Baltimore, 1937), pp. 143 *et seq.* deal very fully with Scruggs and his activities.

[2] Blake, N. M., "Background of Cleveland's Venezuelan Policy", *American Hist. Rev.* XLVII (1941–2), 259–77.

aware that both President and Congress were theoretically committed to enforcing arbitration in the Venezuelan dispute,[1] but it was also patent that only the preliminary steps had been taken by his predecessor. It was his function not only to inject some life into an already settled policy but also to make Great Britain take the United States more seriously, and it may well have been at this stage that his immediate and vigorous study of the papers revealed to him the fact that the official British figures for the area of their colony had been given as only 76,000 square miles in 1885 but as 109,000 in 1887—entirely without explanation.[2] It was precisely this "grab", in supposedly auriferous territory, of which the Administration was determined to deprive Great Britain, and they now took steps to do so. The result was the famous Olney dispatch of 20 July 1895,[3] written it is true on Cleveland's instructions but going well beyond anything that Cleveland had originally envisaged. It informed Great Britain that her refusal of arbitration for the entire region in question was tantamount to an expansion of European territorial dominion in the New World in violation of the Monroe Doctrine; that the Doctrine, although not itself international law, represented the *fiat* of the United States "upon the subjects to which it confines its interposition"; and that its "infinite resources" and invulnerability "against any or all other powers" enabled it to make its invariable "wisdom and justice and equity" effective. Most unfortunate of all was the gratuitous statement that "three thousand miles of intervening ocean make any permanent political union between Europe and any American State unnatural and inexpedient"; while the final issue lay in the instruction to Bayard to take the grave diplomatic step of reading the Note aloud to Lord Salisbury.

Why the British did not take immediate offence at the Note is something of a mystery, but the fact remains that Salisbury merely expressed to Bayard verbally his surprise and regret at the tone of the communication—and then omitted to make any written reply for a period of four months. It is true that he was much concerned with other matters at this time, notably the Near Eastern Question, and that the Note required careful consideration by his legal and other advisers; it is also true that, while the good will of America was already urgently desired by at any rate some Englishmen,[4] it was still regarded with a certain Olympian detachment by Lord Salisbury, who was accustomed to pursue what he believed to be morally right at his own

[1] Cf. Cleveland's Message of 3 Dec. 1894 and the joint resolution of Congress in favour of enforcing arbitration, Feb. 1895.

[2] Smith, T. C., "Secretary Olney's Real Credit in the Venezuela Affair", *Mass. Hist. Soc. Proceedings*, LXV (1932–6), pp. 112–47. The figures are given inaccurately in this article.

[3] The best critical summary is in Perkins, Dexter, *op. cit.* 153–68.

[4] E.g. by Harcourt, now Leader of the Opposition, and the young Spring Rice. See a very significant letter on the subject from the latter, written in the spring of 1892. Gwynn, *Letters and Friendships of Sir Cecil Spring Rice*, I, 119–20.

time and in his own way, without overmuch consideration for those
who differed from him. The Behring Sea decision had just testified to
the essential rectitude of Britain, and the Prime Minister may have
felt that this gratuitous intervention of the United States in imperial
affairs was merely an attempt at tit for tat. There seems reason to
suppose that he consulted his Colonial Secretary, Chamberlain, who
may have had a share in drafting his reply—but all this does not
adequately explain the extreme slowness of his action, and there may
be something in the story that the dispatch was accidentally included
in the bag for Tokyo, and travelled to Japan and back before being
transmitted to its proper destination. Even then it was sent to the
United States through the mails instead of by cable, so that it arrived
too late to affect the annual message to Congress for 1895.

There were in fact two British Notes, both dated 26 November—
one dealing with the Monroe Doctrine in general on a level of a
"superior dogmatism, a patronising self-confidence",[1] and the other
with the current application of it. Olney's reference to the "unnatural and inexpedient" character of all non-American possessions
in the New World was rebuked with mention of the West Indies and
Canada, as well as of British Guiana, and there is no doubt that
imperial sentiment as a whole was strongly on Great Britain's side.
Cleveland on the other hand felt "mad clean through" at Salisbury's
answer, and since both Houses of the now Republican Congress
strongly agreed with him it is probable that the delay in the receipt
of the dispatch made little difference to the situation, beyond necessitating a Special Message to Congress dated 17 December 1895.

The Special Message was definitely war-like in tone. It made no
attempt to answer Salisbury's provocatively cool arguments, and
went even further than Olney in stubbornly and erroneously asserting
that the Monroe Doctrine did in fact constitute part of the accepted
law of nations. It recommended that Congress should make financial
provision, which was quickly forthcoming, for an American commission to survey and determine the true boundary on the spot, and
that if Great Britain would not accept such a boundary the United
States should thereafter resist any British attempt to infringe it "by
every means in its power". It was at this stage that the very able
British ambassador[2] at Washington, Sir Julian Pauncefote, became
seriously alarmed; that he had not warned his government long before
of the strength of American feeling may be attributed to the fact that
he was personally on very good terms with Olney and had comfortably thought that his original Note merely showed a certain "lack of
consideration".[3] The Special Message was another matter, but
although it undoubtedly expressed the mood of Congress and the

---

[1] Perkins, *op. cit.* p. 177.
[2] The British legation in Washington had been raised to the status of an embassy in 1893.
[3] Mowat, *Pauncefote*, 181.

people of the United States, the bank presidents and "financial bureaux", hitherto friendly to Cleveland, were extremely hostile to it from the start, and as the possibility of war approached something like a financial panic set in. Powerful religious interests too were generally opposed to war, and by Christmas Eve Pauncefote begun to feel slightly reassured.[1]

Meanwhile the irritation, if not the astonishment, which the British not unnaturally felt at the American attitude was even more rapidly evaporating. Salisbury had never lost his head, though he did not approve of the fact that various prominent Englishmen, including the Prince of Wales and the Duke of York, had thought it advisable to send vague but pacific answers through their secretaries to Joseph Pulitzer, the proprietor of the *New York World*, who had cabled them for their opinion on the crisis. On 3 January 1896, following the failure of the disastrous Jameson Raid into the South African Republic, came the Kaiser's Kruger telegram, which certainly did something to distract British attention from the still only half-realised danger of a breach with the United States; but the importance of this incident is often over-rated,[2] for Salisbury had almost certainly already changed his mind, and even Chamberlain himself was coming over to the Opposition Liberals' belief in moderation. Though Harcourt still regarded him with considerable mistrust, it was Chamberlain, according to his biographer,[3] who really initiated and worked out a plan in detail, even if Lord Playfair, that veteran Liberal, did "embody the suggestions in a memorandum of his own", which he submitted to ambassador Bayard on 12 January. Briefly, the plan was that the United States should call a conference of all countries having colonies in the New World, in order to discuss the application to them of the Monroe Doctrine in its latest guise. The specific instance of the Venezuela boundary might or might not be referred to such a conference, but it was suggested, almost as an after-thought, that, if it were, the Schomburgk Line should be abandoned and the traditional British principle, that actual settlement over a long period of years could be considered proof of title, adopted in its place—arbitration being limited to territory really in dispute.[4] Olney instantly rejected the first part of this memorandum when it was cabled to him by Bayard, but simultaneously and somewhat unexpectedly accepted the latter part of it as a possible basis for an arbitration convention. It was this acceptance which led to the final settlement.

Meanwhile other and more official measures were being taken towards the same general end. The first and most important of these

---

[1] Perkins, *op. cit.* pp. 196–9.   [2] Perkins, *op. cit.* pp. 217–18.
[3] Garvin, J. L., *Life of Chamberlain*, III, 161–2.
[4] As far as the "after-thought" is concerned, Mowat, *Pauncefote*, pp. 188–9, claims that Sir D. Chalmers, a retired chief-justice of British Guiana, had already made identical proposals in a private letter to the Foreign Office as early as 5 January.

was announced on 29 January in a speech made at Bristol by Sir Michael Hicks Beach, the Chancellor of the Exchequer, namely British willingness to assist the all-American boundary commission in its task. This was promptly reaffirmed by Balfour in the House of Commons, of which he was then Leader, and advance copies of the British papers to be presented to Parliament were thereupon supplied to the Government of the United States. On 11 February Salisbury himself made the strategic withdrawal which he had probably been contemplating for some weeks, when he professed in the House of Lords that, although he would continue to think that the invocation of the Monroe Doctrine had been totally unnecessary, he would welcome United States intervention, not only as perfectly natural in the circumstances but also as a guarantee that Venezuela would faithfully carry out in practice any award that might be made. On 3 March Pauncefote was accordingly empowered to enter upon negotiations for an arbitral convention with Olney and with the Venezuelan minister at Washington. The question was by no means settled yet, but there had been a decided *détente* which Salisbury was at least anxious to preserve: thus when the Venezuelans, who felt that they had been almost as summarily treated as the British,[1] tried to by-pass the United States and settle with Great Britain direct, Salisbury not only refused but, on Pauncefote's advice, did not even inform the United States of their approach.[2]

Nothing is more interesting in Salisbury's speech of 11 February than the reference to a possible guarantee by the United States of Venezuelan conduct in the future. Olney's stand had in fact amounted to the claim that if any American power had a quarrel with a non-American power which they could not settle freely between themselves the United States might intervene and impose its own solution; and this claim constituted a new and important corollary to the Monroe Doctrine.[3] Once he had been forced to concede it, Salisbury seems to have decided that there was no abiding half-way house to the assumption of the full police power by the United States[4] (the so-called Roosevelt corollary) and furthermore that it was in the British interest that there should be none. If the United States could be relied on to preserve the *uti possidetis* in the New World, together with the maintenance of order and financial integrity among the less stable Latin American republics, Britain might be free to withdraw her forces to deal with other and more pressing dangers in the remaining

[1] Young, G. B., "Intervention under the Monroe Doctrine: the 'Olney Corollary'": *Political Science Quarterly*, LVII (1942), 247–80.

[2] Mowat, *Pauncefote*, p. 202.

[3] Young, *loc. cit.*

[4] This idea was not new in 1896. Rippy, J. F., in *Pacific Hist. Rev.* IX (1940), pp. 267–79, lists two previous American and at least three British suggestions in the same sense, of which the earliest was made in 1860. He also finds a "negative implication" to the same effect in Salisbury's own dispatch of 26 Nov. 1895.

half of the world, for the "back-door to the British Empire" would have been secured. It is true that this military re-grouping did not take place before 1905 and that Salisbury himself can hardly have contemplated it, but it is clear that he had grasped the underlying essential that in such a policy the permanent good will of the United States, not on any terms but on the best terms Britain could win, would be absolutely necessary. To reverse Jefferson's dictum, the day might come when Great Britain would have to "marry herself to the American fleet and nation". As yet there was no American fleet worth the name, for in 1895 the United States possessed only one modern battleship, but it is significant that it was this very Congress of 1895–7 which made appropriations for three more, together with ten torpedo-boats, the remote beginning of the "two-ocean" navy which eventually became a reality with the construction of the Panama Canal. Salisbury himself would no doubt have been horrified at such implications, but the logic of events was irresistible, and the fact remains that it was in the winter of 1895–6 that British policy towards the United States began to make a decisive and far-reaching change.

At first it changed slowly, for Salisbury was prepared to move only step by step, fighting all the way, and Harcourt at least was convinced of the malign influence of Chamberlain. The hitch lay in the definitions of what constituted a "long-settled" area exempt from arbitration—a definition which was of vital importance to Great Britain as affording a possible precedent for the treatment of similar problems in South Africa and indeed throughout the whole Empire. The British Government's disingenuous policy at this stage was shown by their original suggestion of only ten years' settlement as the term, which of course would have confirmed all the expanded claims of 1886, but Olney was determined not to yield and held out for a sixty-year limit, going well behind the drawing of the Schomburgk Line.[1] The struggle went on throughout the summer with Pauncefote and Harcourt urging moderation upon Salisbury and Chamberlain, and Henry White being invoked by Harcourt to use such influence as he possessed with Olney.[2] A satisfactory "form of words" was found by 14 August in which to announce to the House of Commons the Government's decision to accept arbitration for "unsettled" areas, but the dispute about the definition of settlement dragged on, and it was not until November, long after Chamberlain, to Harcourt's great but unfounded alarm, had visited Olney in Washington, that a fifty-year compromise was finally agreed between the two Administrations. At last in January 1897 Opposition and Government formally exchanged congratulations on the settlement across the floor of the House of Commons.

[1] Smith, T. C., *loc. cit.*
[2] Gardiner, *Harcourt*, II, 402–3.

The scene in the House marked the real end of the Venezuelan incident, for by the time the Arbitral Tribunal actually met in Paris two years later the march of world events had driven the matter almost wholly out of mind. When the award was published in October 1899 it was found that the entire control of the Orinoco delta, together with a substantial area at the southern end of the Schomburgk Line, had been given to Venezuela, but the line itself had been followed at all points between the two, so that it has been possible for both British and American historians to claim a moral victory of little interest at the time to any but the inhabitants of the disputed regions. It is of more importance that the decision was peacefully accepted and that, when fresh trouble arose between Great Britain and Venezuela three years later, it was found that both British and United States views upon the subject were radically different from those of 1895.

There is another postscript which should be added to the story, namely the Anglo-American treaty of general arbitration which grew out of the Venezuela dispute, attained signature, but was defeated in the Senate of the United States. The prospects for such a treaty seemed good, for it had been approved in principle by Congress as early as 1890 and on more than one occasion by the House of Commons. Some insight into the movement of Salisbury's mind is also afforded by the fact that it was he who suggested through Pauncefote, in the spring of 1896, that the time was ripe for carrying the idea to a conclusion, although it is true that he insisted on the point of not permitting an umpire in territorial disputes. Since each country was to find three out of six arbiters, while for each decision five out of the six had to agree, this meant in practice that no award would be possible unless two arbiters voted against their own country.[1] Yet the Americans held similar views, as may be seen from their insistence on much the same procedure in the Alaskan boundary question of 1903: Olney was warmly in favour of a treaty on the suggested lines, and so was public opinion on both sides of the Atlantic. Its failure by only three votes in the Senate in May 1897, notwithstanding the support of President McKinley, must be accounted for by a non-party, cross-division vote made up of agrarians fearful of Wall Street, Anglophobes, silverites and, above all, senators simply jealous of their treaty-making power.[2] The result was that the United States, which had hitherto led the way in arbitration, began to lag behind during the ensuing decade, but this was not of sufficient importance to affect the increasing dependence on American

---

[1] Blake, N. M., "The Olney–Pauncefote Treaty of 1897", *American Hist. Rev.*, L (1944–5), 228–43.
[2] Nevins, *Henry White*, pp. 124–5, suggests one or two additional factors and mentions that Olney sent what was virtually an unofficial letter of apology, for White to circulate among his English friends. Through Balfour this was seen by the whole Cabinet.

friendship and co-operation felt during the same period by Great Britain.

Possibly "dependence" is as yet too strong a word, but the Venezuelan incident and its aftermath had at least lent sudden emphasis to certain facts about America which neither politicians nor business men throughout the Empire could afford any longer to ignore. For 1896 ushered in a long period of rising world-prices, following on twenty-three years of depression; and this in turn brought higher standards of living, mass-production and mass-immigration into both the United States and Canada.[1] American population was increasing by leaps and bounds, whereas that of Great Britain was practically standing still and in any case had long been out-distanced. By 1898 United States exports were regularly exceeding imports and increasing far more rapidly than those of Britain; thus American exports to the Empire alone had already reached £160,000,000, almost comparable with the £270,000,000 of 1912. Coal, iron and steel production were shooting far ahead of British and there seemed to be no limit to the rising flood of American economic power.[2] Everywhere British Chambers of Commerce were uneasily facing the prospects of keener competition: from Brazil[3] to China the desirability of some sort of collaboration with the American leviathan was becoming clearer and clearer. Even the Antipodes had felt the movement; thus, returning from Australia on 6 May 1898, Lord Brassey said there was no doubt that that community "would cordially welcome any understanding [sc. with the United States] which would mean common action in the larger affairs of the world".[4] Disraeli's warning, uttered over forty years before,[5] that the British must learn to take America seriously, was proving well-grounded and the emergence of the United States as a political world-power after her defeat of Spain in 1898 merely registered what was already an accomplished economic fact.

The enlightenment of British politicians on the subject had, however, certain other roots. It is true that the ex-business man, Chamberlain, was particularly well-informed in economic matters, but even Salisbury, who cared little for them, could and obviously did appreciate that there were other grounds for British friendship with America, such as the fact that the use of force in world affairs was not a British interest and that since 1815 at least, if not since 1794, the United States alone among the greater Powers had shown willingness to settle nearly all her differences without the use of force. Again the new phrase "splendid isolation", coined in January 1896 in the

---

[1] Brebner, op. cit. 225.
[2] Heindel, R. H., The American Impact on Great Britain, pp. 140, 164.
[3] The expansion of United States commercial interests in Latin America was convincingly demonstrated by the Pan-American Exposition of 1901. Perkins, Dexter, Hands Off! p. 195.
[4] Heindel, op. cit. p. 6.   [5] C.H.B.E. II, 542, 859.

Canadian House of Commons and promptly pirated by Chamberlain,[1] was from the first ironical in fact, if not always in intention, and there is no evidence that Salisbury took it seriously. It is true that he remained steadily opposed to all alliances such as those for which Chamberlain was pressing from 1898 to 1901, but this is not to say he cared nothing for the hostility of Europe and saw no importance in the German Navy Laws of 1898 and 1900. On the contrary, he was not only prepared to move cautiously but steadily closer to the United States as the rift with Europe widened, but he even went so far as to allow his last Foreign Secretary, Lansdowne, to resume that search for allies which was to result rather oddly, after Salisbury's own retirement, not in one of Chamberlain's strictly Anglo-Saxon embraces, but in the bizarre, if logical, agreement with Japan.

Even when the United States departed from its principles in 1898, and fought a war with Spain, Salisbury and the British public both remained unmoved. After all, the Americans were behaving quite well: thus at the outset they had unofficially hinted their intention "irrespective of Spain's attitude, to conform in practice to all the provisions of the Declaration of Paris", whereas Spain had haughtily reserved the right to use privateers.[2] Moreover, the American plea of intolerable provocation over Cuba, that "Crete of the Atlantic"[3], was generally accepted in Great Britain, though the foremost authority on this subject has suggested[4] that, although it may not be true to ascribe purely economic rather than altruistic motives to the United States,[5] yet the desire for colonies as adjuncts of that sea-power needed against the "yellow peril", and the attraction of what H. C. Lodge, writing to Roosevelt, called "the large policy that we both desire", played an equally important part. Be that as it may, the British press dutifully declared that the rule of Spain in Cuba was in fact "an outrage on humanity", and that Britons should support Americans because they were "their own flesh and blood".[6] If the second statement was by now only a half-truth, the first at least was what Americans wanted to hear, and both alike were infinitely preferable to the chorus of vituperation which arose from continental journalists. But the British went further than words, for when Germany, Austria, France, and perhaps even Russia, tried to mediate or even intervene, their proposals were extinguished, almost as in Canning's time, by dampers placed on them in London. Finally in August 1898 occurred

[1] Tarkow Naamani, I., "The Abandonment of 'Splendid Isolation' by Great Britain", *Canadian Hist. Rev.* xxvii (1946), 163–88.
[2] Mowat, *Pauncefote*, p. 209.   [3] Garvin, *Life of Chamberlain*, iii, 297.
[4] Pratt, J. W., "The 'Large Policy' of 1898", *Mississippi Valley Hist. Rev.* xix (1932–3), 219–42. Cf. the same author's *Expansionists of 1898*.
[5] The view that readiness for "financial imperialism" was the real cause of the war was formulated by Professor H. U. Faulkner, but has now been abandoned by him; see Faulkner, H. U., *American Economic History* (New York, 6th ed. 1949), p. 567.
[6] Cf. Chamberlain's speeches at Birmingham on 13 May, and in the House of Commons, 10 June, Garvin, J. L., *op. cit.* iii, 301–3.

the famous incident in Manila Bay, where Captain Chichester, R.N., moved the ships of his observing squadron between Dewey's ships, then engaged in the final bombardment on Manila, and the untactful German warships of von Diederichs. It is now known that the British commander merely wanted to get a better view of the bombardment, but Dewey was grateful to the British none the less—not for this particular movement, it is true, to which no one attached importance at the time, but for their moral support during the previous two months, when American strength had been temporarily inferior to the German. It was not long, however, before the legend of yet another demonstration that "blood is thicker than water"—this time furnished by the innocent British movement off Manila[1]—came to birth. No doubt the state of European international relations, German policy towards South Africa and the German naval programme had a good deal to do with all this British good will, but at the moment the Americans had no wish to look a gift horse in the mouth.

It was different when war was safely over, but even then the recoil was not marked. On the Philippines in particular the British attitude was at first most correct: it was merely said that Britain would prefer the United States to keep the islands but, since Germany was clearly angling for them, she would demand an option "in case of future sale". At the same time she refused an insidious Spanish offer of Manila, free of charge, made "to save it from the Americans". It is now known that if the United States had not annexed the Philippines there would have been Russian, as well as German, opposition to Great Britain acquiring them,[2] and indeed American annexation, though it caused McKinley prayer and self-questioning, was the only logical solution at that date. Mahan, then at the height of his influence, approved it on strategic grounds, and there were others in the United States who saw in Manila a wedge inside the Open Door and a possible entrepôt for the China trade. Once annexation was a *fait accompli* on the other hand, some annoyance was caused in the United States by a good deal of facile and gratuitous advice from Britain on the problem of governance—coupled with a rather tactless welcome to imperialism, of which Kipling's famous poem, *The White Man's Burden* (February 1899), was not more than a sample. The long struggle with the Filipino, Aguinaldo, did not ease matters; nor did British failure to recognise the very real achievement of Americans in the islands from the time when Taft took office in Manila.

But although the new amiability developed but slowly in the Far East it struck root and grew elsewhere, mainly owing to the judicious

[1] The coining of the original phrase has been attributed to Commodore Tattnall, U.S.N., who had helped the British off the Pei-ho in 1859. For the story of Manila Bay see the conclusive article by Bailey, T. A., "Dewey and the Germans at Manila Bay", *American Hist. Rev.* XLV (1939–40), 59–81.

[2] Eyre, J. K., "Russia and the American Acquisition of the Philippines", *Mississippi Valley Hist. Rev.* XXVIII (1941–2), 539–62.

pruning administered by the solitary figure of John Hay.[1] Both as ambassador in London (1897–8) and in his seven-year tenure of the State Department, this charming and highly cultivated man of letters turned diplomatist, this intimate of Henry Adams, Roosevelt and McKinley, never ceased to work for Anglo-American accord without failing to remain a good American. In his own country he was much misunderstood, and was indeed commonly accused at one time of concocting secret alliances with Britain, although he himself declared in June 1900 "all that I have ever done with England is to have wrung great concessions out of her without compensation". Probably the bitterness of his enemies was mainly caused by Hay's open dislike of and contempt for politicians; at the end of his life he spoke of years of "struggle with the unreason, the spite, the narrow-minded greed of some of our Senators", and words like these were not easily forgiven him. From the British point of view Hay's principal achievement was to disentangle, and to keep disentangled, the vital interests of the two countries without alienating either of them; to cut back a lush growth which threatened to run wild; and to free it from the encumbering weeds of sentiment. If at times he seemed less of a gardener than a surgeon, the healthy state of Anglo-American relations in the next ten years would justify his occasional severities, of which the harshest was perhaps his treatment of Canada and the most statesmanlike his handling of the Chinese question and the Isthmian Canal.

For Canada neither Hay nor, later, Roosevelt had much mercy: the old quarrels about fisheries, seals and tariffs still rankled and were complicated by the discovery of gold in the Klondike River in 1896, the opening of the whole Yukon region in 1897 and the boundary problems to which the new gold rush gave rise. From the first Hay's policy was to split the laboriously united Imperial front which had baffled the United States so far: when he was still ambassador in London he observed to Foster that the British "frankly avow their slavery to Canada and chafe under it", and from that moment it became the object of his diplomacy to set the British free. That in doing so he took the Canadian people another long stage towards independent nationhood does not seem to have occurred to him or his immediate colleagues and successors: it was enough that for Pauncefote's joint commission of 1898, to settle "twelve clear-cut subjects of dispute between the two countries", he succeeded in substituting a unilateral settlement forcibly imposed by an obedient Britain on Canadians.

The joint commission, on which both Canada and Newfoundland were represented, was obviously modelled on that of 1871, but it

---

[1] "Hay had no ally, abroad or at home, except Pauncefote, and Adams always maintained Pauncefote alone pulled him through". *Education of Henry Adams* (1919 ed.), p. 374.

enjoyed much less success. This was partly owing to the personal intransigence of the British commissioner, Lord Herschell, and the dislike felt for the American negotiator, Foster, by the Canadian representatives.[1] But more fundamental causes for the failure of the proposals for reciprocity between the two were to be found in the urgent and disproportionate importance of the Alaskan boundary question, coupled with British and Canadian unwisdom in trying to obtain concessions on this subject from the Americans in return for British concessions in the entirely separate matter of an Isthmian canal. It was in vain that Canada argued that she too was a Pacific power and therefore legitimately interested:[2] Hay would have none of it; the commission petered out, and negotiations over the two issues came to be concluded separately. An attempt made in April 1899 by Hay to secure a special boundary commission proved abortive, but a provisional boundary drawn by him without prejudice to any future settlement was accepted in October, for not only was the Yukon now in chaos but by this time the South African War had broken out, and the British were facing their Black Week in December. For the next two or three years Hay's diplomacy was immensely aided by Britain's commitments in South Africa and the genuine sympathy which he personally felt for her aims there—unlike most of his countrymen, and still more unlike the world at large. Thus in March 1900 he informed White it was "the feeling of most men of sense, that the fight of England in South Africa is the fight of civilisation and progress, and that all our interests are bound up in her success".[3] It was as much this friendly sympathy on Hay's part as the actual embarrassment and isolation in which Great Britain found herself in 1900 that enabled him to complete, with Pauncefote's help, the first of his two treaties for an all-American canal across the Isthmus of Panama.

The main obstacle in the way of a canal such as the United States desired was of course the Clayton-Bulwer Treaty of 1850,[4] the first and eighth clauses of which between them were designed to secure the *status quo* in the Caribbean, on the understanding that the development of any trans-isthmian routes whatever should be a matter for joint action by the two contracting parties and that the resultant canal, if any were constructed, should be neutralised and open to the world's traffic on equal terms. Although the exact force of the treaty was open to a certain amount of argument, successive Secretaries of State, of whom Blaine was the most conspicuous, had totally failed to

---

[1] Nevins, *Henry White*, p. 187. Foster, J. M. V., "Reciprocity and the Joint High Commission of 1898–9", *Annual Report of the Canadian Historical Association for 1939*, p. 93. This paper (pp. 87–98) challenges the accepted view that the United States was more to blame than Canada.

[2] Gelber, *Rise of Anglo-American Friendship*, pp. 42–3.

[3] Nevins, *White*, p. 151.

[4] *C.H.B.E.* II, 540–1, 850–1, 858–9.

explain it away or to induce the Foreign Office to accept a unilateral abrogation on the part of the Americans. None the less, it had never ceased to be proclaimed by the United States, ever since Evarts's famous Report and the resultant presidential Message of 1880, that "the policy of this country is a canal under American control". The great increase in American wealth and power in the 'nineties, the difficulty of concentrating Pacific units of the fleet in the Caribbean during the Spanish War,[1] and the new imperial commitments which that war produced: these factors between them made the canal a vital American interest by the end of 1898. Moreover, the new and friendlier attitude of Great Britain, followed by the outbreak of the South African War, which tied her hands in any event, seemed to indicate that the time was ripe. Hence it was that McKinley's annual Message of December re-opened the question, though in such ambiguous terms that Hay had to explain to Pauncefote that there was no intention of violating the Clayton-Bulwer Treaty, but merely of negotiating a revision of it so that a government canal could be dug through Nicaragua. Meanwhile Henry White, now again first secretary in London, was having preliminary conversations with Lord Salisbury, who agreed in principle to the construction of an American canal, provided that the tolls charged should remain equal for the ships of all nations. But because Pauncefote reported from Washington that the United States would not regard this concession as a *quid pro quo* in the affairs of the Canadian joint commission, then dwindling to its close, the first draft of the canal convention was left in cold storage by the British for the whole of 1899. The point in the mind of the Cabinet seems to have been that the construction of such a canal would double the effective strength of the United States Navy, and that it was inadvisable to permit this while so many possible Canadian *casus belli*, headed by Alaska, still existed.[2] In fact it was only the South African War, the Black Week and the threat of unilateral action by Congress over a Nicaraguan canal which made possible the revival of the defunct draft of January 1899 in February 1900.[3]

There is little doubt that Pauncefote's work on the Suez Canal Commission of 1885, done at a time when he was Permanent Under-Secretary at the Foreign Office, was of special value to him in negotiating this draft; indeed, the finished version bore a remarkable resemblance to the Suez Convention. Strictly speaking, it neither abrogated nor superseded the Clayton-Bulwer Treaty, but merely modified and supplemented it:[4] moreover, it contained non-fortification clauses which, together with Article III, inviting the adherence of other Powers, were certain to make it uncongenial to the Senate.

[1] Miner, D. C., *The Fight for the Panama Route* (New York, 1940), p. 82.
[2] Mowat, *Pauncefote*, p. 278.   [3] Miner, *op. cit.* pp. 93–6.
[4] Gelber, *op. cit.* p. 52.

The amendments introduced by that body were in fact so drastic and far-reaching that the British were compelled to reject them,[1] and the greater part of 1901 was taken up with the negotiation of a second treaty. Hay and Pauncefote were once more the principals and gave their names to the convention when completed, but by this time there were important new figures in the background, such as Lansdowne at the Foreign Office and Theodore Roosevelt, now President of the United States after the assassination of McKinley in September. Of these Lansdowne was favourable, while Roosevelt, who had opposed the first version, was at least not against a treaty in a revised form such as would enable the United States to "construct, maintain and control" a canal open to the commerce of all nations. In the end it was a revision in this sense which was signed on 18 November and ratified by both countries: repeal of the Clayton-Bulwer Treaty was made definite, third-party adherence left out, and a single sentence added which, when liberally interpreted, might be held to permit military defensive measures on the part of the United States.[2] It seemed as if Great Britain had conceded everything and gained nothing, yet the equality of tolls, on which Salisbury had always insisted, and the continuity of the treaty through any change of sovereignty in the Canal Zone were valuable considerations, while, as Gelber has pointed out,[3] from the moment it was proclaimed in February 1902 its mere existence forced the United States "to cover the rear of the British Empire against a foreign invader". By 1905 British naval stations in the West Indies, at Halifax, and at Esquimalt, British Columbia, were being dismantled and garrisons were being reduced to nominal strength in such key positions as Bermuda and Jamaica. It was already being openly admitted by United States naval experts that the scene of the next war would be the North Sea, and that the main danger was no longer a war with Britain but a war with Germany. Indeed, many of them insisted that the ultimate objective of the new German navy was America itself—a view which British diplomats naturally encouraged.[4]

During the years 1902 and 1903 while the Panamanian lobbyists worked frantically at Washington, while Hay vainly negotiated with Columbia and while the inspired revolution in Panama was planned and carried through—events fraught with infinite importance for the world-wars of the future—the new Anglo-American accord was tested in two very different fields, of which the more dangerous was the renewed controversy about Alaska.

Although the immediate cause of this dispute was, and remained, Canadian access to the Klondike through the Portland and Lynn

[1] Miner, *op. cit.* pp. 96–9, 105, 108.
[2] Miner, *op. cit.* pp. 117–18.   [3] *Op. cit.* p. 103.
[4] Vagts, A., "Hopes and Fears of an American-German War, 1870–1915", *Political Science Quarterly*, LV (1940), 53–76.

"canals" or inlets, there lay behind it a long historical argument going back to the British treaty of 1825 with Russia, whose rights the United States had acquired in 1867. The original treaty described the boundary as "the crests of the mountains running to the coast...at thirty miles distant from the ocean", and it was this line which Canada now insisted would intersect some of the bays, thus giving her ports of her own through which she could obtain convenient access to the gold-fields. The Americans on the other hand stood upon the treaty's reference to "a line parallel with the sinuosities of the coast", and argued that no viable state could consist of isolated headlands with no land connection between them. The provisional frontier drawn by Hay was naturally favourable to the United States, and it was therefore on the initiative of the new Liberal premier of Canada, Sir Wilfrid Laurier, and of the Governor-General, Lord Minto, that the negotiations were resumed in 1902. As a matter of fact Laurier had told White as early as June 1900 that he was sick of the whole question and saw no hope of Canada recovering what she had lost, but he would like arbitration in order to save appearances.[1] It was this feeling, in which Lansdowne concurred, which led to the signing of an arbitration treaty with the United States in January 1903, referring the matter to six impartial jurists, three to be appointed by each government, substantially on the lines of the lost arbitration treaty of 1897, but without the 5/6 majority rule. Unfortunately the ebullient Roosevelt was in no mood to be impartial on this question. Additional troops had been ordered to Alaska by the War Department as early as March 1902: the "impartial" jurists selected, after a half-hearted attempt to persuade justices of the Supreme Court to serve, were the Secretary of War himself and two virulent politicians: while finally the instructions given to them by the President included the hardly necessary phrase, "in the principle involved, there will, of course, be no compromise".[2] Not content with this, Roosevelt, Henry White and, perhaps, Hay set themselves to bring undue influence to bear through leading members of the British Cabinet on the solitary British commissioner, Lord Alverstone, in the hope that the Canadians would be left in a minority of two to four. In a famous letter to Judge Holmes, then in England, Roosevelt threatened "to run the boundary on my own hook" if a decision favourable to the United States was not speedily forthcoming; and it is clear that this letter was not meant to be strictly confidential. Hay wrote to White that he could not see "how a man of Lord Alverstone's ability and clearness of vision can avoid giving a verdict in our favor", and White set to work on Balfour, now Prime Minister, who as a result of his pressure had two interviews with Alverstone.[3] In the upshot it seems doubtful whether Alverstone could have acted

[1] Nevins, *White*, pp. 192–3.   [2] Pringle, H. F., *Theodore Roosevelt*, p. 292.
[3] Nevins, *White*, pp. 196–200.

judicially, though the point remains an open one;[1] but if he did it is certainly strange that whereas even the American arbiters had been impressed by the Canadian case and were prepared to make minor concessions, Alverstone not only rejected it but went out of his way to divide equally between the two countries four islands at the mouth of the Portland Canal, all of which were vital to Canada and concerning which he had heard no arguments at all.[2] This surrender was so indefensible that Allen Aylesworth and Sir Louis Jetté, the two Canadian arbiters, refused to sign the award—but this had little effect, for the bare majority decision was taken by both Great Britain and the United States as final. Both countries seemed perfectly satisfied, which was the more important in that before 1903 each had suspected the other of designs for naval bases in Alaska, and the new agreement represented another step towards amity, but Canada felt, not without cause, that she had again been sacrificed to power politics. Laurier immediately demanded a free hand for the Dominion in her foreign policy in future—that is, the treaty-making power—which he did not receive. Within ten years, Canada was to take her revenge on both her rivals, to their extreme astonishment: for nothing is more curious in this somewhat sordid story than the belief innocently held by Roosevelt that the United States in particular had acted with "a good-humoured courtesy in everything", not to mention "fairness and good will".[3] He was quite unconscious to the last of the effect of his policy upon Canadian sentiment, which he believed to be quite friendly to the United States, but the fact is that throughout the whole controversy he never really stopped to think deeply about Canada: for during these very months of 1902–3 what was preoccupying him chiefly, apart from the isthmian canal, was a revival of the Venezuelan question and the first clear indications, which went with it, of Germany's coming bid for world-power.

The new trouble in Venezuela, which gave Germany her opportunity, really began in 1899 with the appearance of what Roosevelt once called "that unspeakably villainous little monkey", president-dictator General Cipriano Castro. By repudiating his country's foreign debt, seizing property and threatening the persons of foreign nationals, Castro soon succeeded in quarrelling with every great Power, including the United States. Both Germany and Britain had substantial banking, railway and shipping interests in Venezuela: hence late in 1902 the British Government suggested to the Germans the idea of joint intervention. This was promptly accepted, and although a further British suggestion, that the United States be invited to participate, was rejected, it was finally agreed to notify the

---

[1] E.g. Pringle, *Roosevelt*, p. 292, thinks that his decision was based upon the evidence—Brebner, *op. cit.* p. 261—that it was political,

[2] Gelber, *op. cit.* p. 160.

[3] Bailey, T. A., "Theodore Roosevelt and the Alaska Boundary Settlement", *Canadian Hist. Rev.* xviii (1937), 123–30.

United States officially of the proposed Anglo-German action. When this was done on 13 November Hay raised no objection, while the President in his annual message seemed to bless the impending "policy" for Venezuela. The presentation and rejection of simultaneous British and German Notes early in December was followed by the withdrawal of both ministers and the seizure of Venezuelan gunboats by the British; but this was apparently as far as Lansdowne really wished to go.[1] The Germans, however, insisted on a joint blockade, and in January 1903 even proceeded to bombard Maracaibo, which aroused considerable resentment in America. Meanwhile Italy had joined the blockading Powers and Castro had appealed to the United States to enforce arbitration, as they had in 1895.

The attitude of President Roosevelt at this juncture constitutes a minor mystery. It is certain that at the beginning of December German truculence had created some annoyance in the United States and still more in Great Britain, where the Government's pro-German policy was surprisingly unpopular. Yet the Germans seem to have preceded Britain by a day or two in conditionally accepting the idea of arbitration, and the question therefore arises whether they did so under pressure from the President or of their own accord. In later years, but even before he had become a pronounced Germanophobe, Roosevelt himself was convinced that some time in the first half of December he had forced Germany to yield by what amounted to a threat of war.[2] Dexter Perkins was unable to find any contemporary evidence whatever for this statement in any national archive, and therefore categorically dismissed it,[3] but other recent historians are not so sure. Thus the President is said on good authority to have had two conversations of a strained character with the German ambassador, von Holleben, in the critical period of December 1902, and is definitely known to have made enquiries about the strength of the German squadron off Venezuela, at a time when actual arbitration was still not quite certain, in February 1903.[4] Moreover, there is the fact that early in 1902 the United States navy had planned most elaborate manoeuvres, based on Culebra Island, Puerto Rico, which had concentrated strong forces under Dewey in the Caribbean, and "these plans drawn up by the naval authorities and put into operation during...December...afforded the President every opportunity to act as later he said he did".[5] Again, in March 1903 Dewey told an American journalist that the winter manoeuvres "had been an object-lesson to the Kaiser more than to any other person",[6] while finally it

---

[1] Newton, *Lansdowne*, p. 255.
[2] Letter of August 1906 to Henry White (Nevins, *White*, pp. 215, 498-500). The more famous and explicit letter, however, is that of 21 Aug. 1916, to W. R. Thayer: Pringle, *Roosevelt*, pp. 285-6.
[3] *The Monroe Doctrine: 1867-1907*, pp. 377-8.   [4] Pringle, *op. cit.* pp. 287-8.
[5] Livermore, S. W., "Theodore Roosevelt, the American Navy and the Venezuelan Crisis of 1902-03", *American Hist. Rev.* LI (1945-6), 452-71.   [6] Pringle, *loc. cit.*

was from this point that Great Britain ceased to regard herself as a potential German ally in war against the United States and France— a fact of which Germany was well aware.[1] The incident indeed showed that, with the Alaska question still unsolved, the British were most anxious not to annoy the United States on any account, as was made abundantly clear by both Government and Opposition speakers in both Houses of Parliament during the winter of 1902–3.[2] None the less, even the British share in the blockade was not liquidated until February, and it was not until May 1903 that the protocols for referring the question to the new Hague Tribunal created in 1899 were at last signed by no less than ten Powers now declaring grievances against the Venezuelans, including the United States itself. The award of February 1904 called for the pledging of 30 per cent of the customs at La Guayra and Puerto Cabello to the creditor nations concerned—much as British investors had suggested two years earlier—and included a proviso for the installation of Belgian officials in case of a default. It is curious that the United States should have accepted this international solution of a purely American problem, for they never did so again and indeed 1904 is actually the year in which repeated British suggestions that the United States should assume the police power single-handed finally blossomed into the "Roosevelt Corollary" of 1904–5.

This Corollary, the detailed history of which belongs more to that of the Monroe Doctrine than to Anglo-American relations, may have had its American beginnings in the Platt Amendment,[3] reluctantly accepted by the Cubans at the third time of asking in June 1901, while McKinley was still alive, but it only reached full stature in Roosevelt's famous letter to Root three years later.[4] In its first practical application, to San Domingo, British interests were to some extent concerned, for the Council of Foreign Bondholders was intimately connected with the American San Domingo Improvement Co., which had taken over the financing of that disreputable republic's foreign debt from the international firm of Westendorp & Co., of Amsterdam, in March 1893. It was this company which now loudly demanded United States help and intervention and obtained it, but its British backers, while they warmly approved the Roosevelt Corollary in principle, in that by its means Dominican bonds, which had been worthless, were finally redeemed at 50 cents to the dollar, must have been sadly disappointed in its ultimate results, that is, as far

[1] Vagts, A., in *Political Science Quarterly*, LV (1940), 53–76.

[2] Perkins, *Hands Off!* p. 224.

[3] Originally an amendment to the army appropriation bill approved on 2 March 1901, and not abrogated in effect until 1934. For a summary see Bailey, T. A., *A Diplomatic History of the American People* (2nd edn.), pp. 548–9. The most material clause laid down that the United States was at liberty to intervene for the purpose of preserving order and maintaining Cuban independence.

[4] Pringle, *op. cit.* p. 294.

as any future investments were concerned. For not only was the San Domingo Improvement Co.'s award heavily discounted, but henceforward in several other Latin American countries United States syndicates with no foreign backing elbowed out the British companies which, in spite of frequent "first charges", that is, nominal priority in debt-collection, were not greatly helped. The effect of the Corollary, in short, was to usher in the age of "dollar diplomacy", and dollar diplomacy was "not strictly a program of benevolence toward Europe" in general or Great Britain in particular.[1]

With the coming of dollar diplomacy it becomes necessary to turn back to the slow development of Anglo-American relations in the other great field in which that diplomacy operated rather more benevolently, namely the Far East. Since, moreover, United States activities in China were to some extent conditioned by the acquisition of various stepping-stones across the Pacific,[2] this will also be a convenient moment to consider the preliminary clash of interests in Samoa and, in a less degree, Hawaii. The history of American trade with China goes well back into the eighteenth century, but it remains broadly true that the United States never attempted on its own account to lift the irritating restrictions imposed by the Chinese, as it did in the case of Japan, but was content to follow in the wake of Britain. By 1870 two British wars with China had created the treaty ports and effectively opened the market, but before this important development took place there had long been numerous American settlers in the Sandwich Islands, later known as Hawaii, since these were naturally a port of call for China traders. There was some initial competition with the French and British for the control of this group, but neither Power pressed its claim, and after Fish had secured a reciprocity convention with the native government in 1875 their ultimate annexation by the United States, already twice proposed, was only a matter of time. The contract labour question raised some further difficulties with British and even German interests, but these solved themselves without much trouble; in 1887 the United States obtained the right to the exclusive use of Pearl Harbour as a repair and coaling station; the last native queen was dethroned in January 1893 in favour of an American settlers' government, which deliberately gave un-neutral facilities to the United States in 1898 for operations against the Philippines; and annexation finally took place a few days before the Spanish War was over. The fact was that no Power seriously contested the United States' claim that, at any rate since the acquisition of California and still more if and when a trans-isthmian canal should be dug, the Islands had lain and would lie in an exclusively

[1] See the important articles by Rippy, J. F., in *Political Science Quarterly*, XLIX (1934), 195–206; *Hispanic American Hist. Rev.* XVII (1937), 419–57; and *Pacific Hist. Rev.* LX (1940), 267–79.
[2] Peffer, N., "The United States in the Far East", *Political Science Quarterly*, LIV (1939), 1–14.

American sphere of interest. As Blaine once remarked, they were on "the direct line of communication between the United States and Australasia", not to mention China, and constituted a sort of "Cuba of the Pacific".[1]

It was very different with Samoa, far away in the south, for here there was a very definite Australasian interest, together with much stronger competition on the part of Germany. American ambitions in this direction really dated from the completion of the Union Pacific railroad in 1869, after which William H. Webb, a New York ship-builder, had planned a government-subsidised service from San Francisco to Australia and New Zealand by way of Honolulu and Pago-Pago. This plan came to nothing, but it was through the recommendation of one of Webb's agents on the islands that a treaty granting the United States exclusive use of the harbour of Pago-Pago was secured in 1872. This, although not ratified by the Senate, was the starting point for further United States' approaches which issued in the less far-reaching, but more successful, treaty of 1878, whereby a United States naval base was established at Pago-Pago and United States good offices promised in any future dispute between Samoa and any other power. Meanwhile Sir Julius Vogel, the ambitious premier of New Zealand, chose to regard the Home Government's annexation of Fiji in 1874 as the first step towards a great Pacific empire in which Samoa was to play an important part. "The ultimate object which I have in view", said Vogel, "is the establishment of the Polynesian Islands as a Dominion, with New Zealand the centre of the Government, and the Dominion, like Canada, to be a British Dependency."[2]

Vogel's plans far outran the aims and intentions of the Imperial Government, but the appearance of a third competitor in Germany did at least lead to the obtaining of a British as well as a German treaty from the native government in 1879. Under this treaty Apia was made a joint neutral zone administered by the British and German consuls: the United States too was invited to adhere, but refused to do so, though it allowed the American consul to collaborate with the other two in most respects. By 1884 German interest in and exploitation of the group had become as great as that of Britain and the United States combined, and was making the Samoans so uneasy that they were almost ready to accept the proposals still being pressed by the persistent New Zealanders. Once again, however, the interests of the Empire as a whole conflicted with those of a particular Dominion, for 1884 was also the year of the first Berlin Conference on the Congo, in which, as it happened, the Imperial Government felt bound to support German claims not only in West Africa but also in the South Seas, in return for German sympathy and aid against France over

[1] Perkins, *The Monroe Doctrine: 1867–1907*, p. 278.
[2] Van Alstyne, *American Diplomacy in Action*, pp. 609–12: cf. Burdon, R. M., *The Life and Times of Sir Julius Vogel*, pp. 102 seqq.

the Egyptian question. This decision caused dismay in New Zealand, Samoa and the United States alike, and, whatever its merits on the larger issues, helped to bring about the state of civil war in Samoa so graphically described by Robert Louis Stevenson.[1] The war broke out in November 1885 with the deposition of the King, Laupepa, by the Germans: it was fought with more or less open American support on one side to balance German pressure on the other, and by the spring of 1889 had brought the two great Powers to the verge of war between themselves. During it British sympathies gravitated rapidly back to the American, or legitimist native, side; but it was perhaps neither this nor the famous hurricane of March 1889, which sank several of the rival warships in Apia Harbour, so much as Bismarck's evident reluctance to embark upon a naval struggle with America, that led to the tri-partite Berlin conference of April–June. This in turn produced a general declaratory act establishing equality of trading rights in the islands for all three Powers, together with a nominal return to native sovereignty. None the less, undue German influence continued, and in April 1894 New Zealand proposed annexation for the third time, offering to do the job herself, if need be, on behalf either of Great Britain alone or of all the treaty Powers. Sir Edward Grey, however, then Under Secretary of State for Foreign Affairs, thought that such a step would be incompatible with the recent Act of Berlin, and the Germans were of course very strongly opposed to it.[2]

The final crisis was precipitated by another outbreak of civil war among the native chiefs, leading to an Anglo-American bombardment of the town of Apia, in which German subjects and property suffered. In the three-power committee of investigation of April 1899, however, the Germans succeeded in dividing British from Americans; the terms offered to the former steadily deteriorated; and in the two conventions of November and December British interests in the islands were virtually eliminated and the group divided between the other two Powers. It is true that in return Britain received certain rights over the Tonga Islands and some of the Solomons from Germany, together with other minor compensation in West Africa, but the disappointment of New Zealand had been absolute and complete. In view of the South African War and the friction over Alaska, it is difficult to blame the Imperial Government, though it is possible that the African interests of Rhodes, who had had a very friendly interview with the Kaiser on that subject, may have had something to do with the decision,[3] and it is certain that another *quid pro quo* was offered in the German Emperor's visit to Windsor as a gesture of

---

[1] *A Footnote to History. Eight Years of Trouble in Samoa: Collected Works* (London, 1907), vol. xvi.

[2] Ellison, J. W. "The Partition of Samoa: a Study in Imperialism and Diplomacy", *Pacific Hist. Rev.* viii (1939), 259–88.   [3] Ellison, *loc. cit.*

disinterestedness in the face of European pro-Boer spirit.[1] Chamberlain at least was deeply distressed, and tried to find consolation in a prophecy to Salisbury that within fifty years both Germany and France would find themselves ousted from the Pacific by the forces of Australasia.[2] As far as Germany was concerned he wrote more truly than he knew, for it was not fifty, but fifteen, years later that a New Zealand expeditionary force seized the German islands in the Samoan group, and the Dominion has remained responsible for them ever since.

In spite of the sustained New Zealand interest, however, it is clear that all this jockeying for position in the Pacific was really much more vital to the United States than to the Empire as a whole. It was necessary for the Americans, not only to protect their long Pacific coast-line and the back-door to the Isthmus, but also to maintain their trans-Pacific trade-routes towards China and the Philippines, more particularly in relation to the rising power of Japan. In the Sino-Japanese War of 1894–5, during which Great Britain had twice offered mediation, the attitude of President Cleveland had, it is true, been singularly ineffective, although China was obviously being so much weakened that the possibility of her complete disintegration could no longer be ignored. Yet if that took place "the 'Open Door'—a fair field and no favour for all those who come to China to trade—" would be slammed for ever, and certainly America, and perhaps also Britain, would be left out in the cold. Of these two it was Britain which had by far the greater commercial interest and was therefore the more alive to the danger, but it was the British Chambers of Commerce, not the Government, which sent the author of the famous phrase just quoted, Lord Charles Beresford, out to China in 1898 to survey and report. Early in 1899 Beresford returned home by way of the United States, bringing with him the material for his book, *The Break-up of China*. He addressed American Chambers of Commerce in San Francisco, Chicago and New York, everywhere endeavouring to excite enthusiasm for the Open Door, but his general impression of America at this time was that the idea commanded no more than nominal support.[3] Before Beresford's departure the British Government had officially approached Hay's predecessor in the State Department, Sherman, on much the same lines, but had met with a rebuff, and a further approach in January 1899, this time to Hay, was no more successful owing to McKinley's conservatism. Hay's expert on China, W. W. Rockhill, who became the State Department's adviser on Far Eastern affairs in May, was hardly more co-operative at first.[4] But behind Rockhill stood, as an adviser,[5] the Englishman Alfred Hippisley, an ex-member of the Chinese Mari-

---

[1] Gelber, *op. cit.* p. 67.   [2] Garvin, *Chamberlain*, III, 335.
[3] Beresford, *Memoirs*, II, 458–60.
[4] Varg, P. A., *Open Door Diplomat: The Life of W. W. Rockhill*, Illinois Studies in the Social Sciences, XXXIII, no. 4 (Urbana, 1952), p. 31.
[5] Van Alstyne, *American Diplomacy in Action*, p. 309; cf. Varg, *op. cit.* pp. 29–31.

time Customs service, and it was on Hippisley's advice that the first cautious step was taken in the direction desired by the British when, in September 1899, Hay dispatched simultaneous and identical Notes to the Powers interested in China, asking them to guarantee the treaty ports and the Chinese tariff and maintain equality for all alike in the harbour-dues and railway-rates charged in their respective concessions. He also requested that each Power should use its influence to induce the other to accede to the terms of the Notes.[1] Although on 20 March 1900 Hay announced his satisfaction with the replies received from all six Powers, in fact they have done little but promise to observe some sort of common action.[2] The effect at best was merely to preserve the *status quo*, but at least it appeared that even if the United States would not openly co-operate with Britain in the Far East its policy was beginning to develop on what might prove to be roughly parallel lines.[3]

This independent struggle by both countries to preserve the Open Door against the rival theory of "spheres of influence"—a polite expression for partition—entered on a new and more anxious phase with the Boxer rising of 1900. In July this produced another circular from Hay, and on this occasion he did not hesitate to urge the Powers openly to "preserve Chinese territorial and administrative entity". But by this time the British Government, though it had joined the United States in refusing to consider itself at war with China, was definitely losing patience with the slowness of the American advance, and in October it took what proved to be the false step of signing an agreement with the Germans providing for the Open Door and the maintenance of the integrity of China. This virtually lapsed in 1901 when Germany refused to endorse British protests against Russian conduct in Manchuria early in the year; but the set-back to Britain did not last, for in 1902 came the announcement of the Anglo-Japanese Alliance and the simultaneous discovery that American policy was once more in tune with hers. In that year Hay, in short, did what Germany had just refused to do, when he published a memorandum denouncing the investment monopoly set up by Russia in Manchurian mines and railways.[4] Again the move was parallel to Anglo-Japanese policy rather than a part of it, but it met with a prompt response, for in April 1903 Lansdowne declared that he was ready to "follow the United States step by step up to any point that may be necessary for the protection of our common interests in China", and even the anti-British Lodge was recommending Hay to accept the offer. Hay refused, but asked to be kept in touch with the situation in the Far East, to which Lansdowne cordially consented. Moreover,

[1] Van Alstyne, *op. cit.* p. 309; see also Campbell, C. S., *Special Business Interests and the Open Door Policy* (New Haven, 1951), pp. 53–6.
[2] Varg, *op. cit.* pp. 33–5; Zabriskie, E. H., *American-Russian Rivalry in the Far East*, pp. 55–60.
[3] Peffer, *op. cit.* pp. 10–11.   [4] Van Alstyne, *op. cit.* pp. 315–16.

both Governments were not only pro-Japanese in the ensuing war with Russia but ready to permit their nationals, such as Jacob H. Schiff of New York, to act jointly in financing the Japanese war effort. The Germans did their best to wreck this intimacy by playing on the obvious American desire that the Japanese victory should not be too complete, and also on Roosevelt's temporary irritation with the British for refusing to bring pressure on their ally to make peace on easy terms. They also hinted broadly at an imaginary Anglo-Franco-Russian plan to partition China, but this intrigue failed completely and by early 1905 Great Britain and the United States were at last forming what was in effect a full and frank concert of power in the Far East.[1] It was the more unfortunate that Hay died at the end of June and his successor, Root, proved more interested in Canadian and Latin American than in European and Far Eastern problems.[2] True, while Roosevelt was still President some sort of accord persisted, for his momentary mistrust of British policy in this region of the world had been removed by the revision of the Anglo-Japanese Alliance after the Russian war had ended and by the reassuring Taft-Katsura conversations.[3] But between the end of 1905 and 1908 American policy in the Far East was already beginning to lose its grip and gradually to become estranged from that of Britain, mainly owing to the failure of both Root and Roosevelt to keep themselves properly informed of the growing complication and tension within the European balance of power, or to realise the inevitable repercussions in China and Japan of the mysterious moves and counter-moves which were taking place in Europe.[4] It is true that Roosevelt's intervention in the first Moroccan crisis of 1905–6, in which he was largely responsible for persuading France to consent to the calling of the Algeçiras Conference, was dictated by a wish to avoid possible complications in the Far East.[5] But even here American attempts to hold the balance evenly between the European Powers were marred by an incomplete grasp of the purely European situation,[6] in spite of the presence at Algeçiras of Roosevelt's best diplomat, Henry White, then ambassador to Italy: and again the very fact that Europe was regarded as a secondary, and the Far East as a primary, problem militated against the success of American diplomacy in either sphere. The Anglo-Russian understanding of 1907 brought about a radical change in world politics which the survivors of the Hay-Adams group, with their pronounced Russophobia, never really understood; especially when it was followed by a secret *rapprochement* between Russia and Japan. At the same time Britain had begun to sacrifice her interests in North China to the

---

[1] Gelber, *op. cit.* pp. 167–71, 180.
[2] Jessup, P. C., *Elihu Root* (New York, 1938), II, 3–4.
[3] Gelber, *op. cit.* pp. 231–2.   [4] Pringle, *Roosevelt*, p. 372.
[5] Gelber, *op. cit.* pp. 186–200.   [6] Pringle, *op. cit.* pp. 393–6.

Japanese alliance, so that on all sides "spheres of influence" were again gaining ground. Root's successor, Knox, was to prove wholly ignorant of the network of treaties now maintaining peace in Europe at China's expense and culminating in the Russo-Japanese pact of 1910, which put an end to the Open Door for ever in Manchuria:[1] while all that the United States had managed to obtain was the unsatisfactory Root-Takahira agreement of 1908, recognising the *status quo* in the Pacific and providing for consultations between the two Powers should that status ever be threatened.[2]

In his chosen sphere of the two Americas, on the other hand, Root did work of greater value. Although it was once thought that, in these his relatively early days, Root was a Rooseveltian imperialist and politician rather than the man of peace and great international jurist which he afterwards became,[3] it cannot be denied that he contributed materially towards the settlement of the Canadian question. The final boundary set up by the Root-Bryce treaty of April 1908 has remained final, while another treaty, dated January 1909, concerned with waterways, created a standing joint commission of six members which has steadily continued to do useful work. A similar standing commission ultimately solved the age-old problem of the fisheries,[4] while yet another treaty accorded mutual rights of territorial transit and entry for certain special purposes. So much had Canadian-American relations improved by 1911 that it was reasonable for Taft to think that once he had won Congress and the American lumber, news-print and agricultural interests to the idea of reciprocity,[5] so long demanded by Canadians, the almost equally ancient problem of the tariffs too was solved. But the Canadians still had bitter memories and a certain fear of Danaans bringing gifts, so that, much to the surprise of Taft and his Administration, their hard-won offer was rejected by the Dominion parliament.[6] Two years later Sir Robert Borden was heavily defeated in Canada, though he did not fall from power, over a proposal to contribute battleships to the imperial fleet, and thus the injury done to the Dominion over the Alaska boundary by Britain as well as by the United States was

[1] Pringle, *Taft*, pp. 687–90.

[2] Van Alstyne, *op. cit.* p. 326. Jessup, *op. cit.* II, 34–40.

[3] This view, which is set forth by Dexter Perkins in *The Monroe Doctrine: 1867–1907*, p. 429, is denied by P. C. Jessup, *op. cit.* I, 470.

[4] See Lansing, R., "The North Atlantic Coast Fisheries Arbitration", *American Journal of International Law*, V (1911), 1–31. Under the Anglo-American general arbitration convention of April 1908, the long-standing fisheries dispute between the United States on the one hand, and Canada and Newfoundland on the other, was submitted to the Permanent Court of Arbitration at The Hague in 1910. On this see Tansill, *Canadian-American Relations*, pp. 115–20, and Jessup, *op. cit.* II, 90–6.

[5] Taft, W. H., "Reciprocity with Canada", *Journal of Political Economy*, XIX (1911), 513–26—an address delivered in Chicago; Ellis, L. E., *Reciprocity, 1911* (New Haven, 1939).

[6] Another reason was that the British market, which had formerly absorbed only about the same amount of Canadian produce as the United States did, was now taking twice as much: Brebner, *op. cit.* p. 257.

finally repaid by the refusal of an important contribution to the Royal Navy upon the one hand and of reciprocity on the other.

In spite of such superficial bickerings, however, and the change of tone, not always for the better, which marked the end of the Roose-veltian period, the foundations laid during the diplomatic revolution of 1898–1906 remained secure. The Taft-Knox administration which followed is a difficult period to assess in the study of American rela-tions with the Empire. It is marked by an apparent rather than a real divergence of interests and foreign policies, accompanied by occasional minor friction, for example over the Panama Canal tolls. During it the British were becoming more and more obsessed with the German danger and had proportionately less time to spare to cultivate American susceptibilities, while the Americans for their part, refusing as they did to believe that the peace of the world was in jeopardy, became temporarily less interested in European and Asiatic questions and even more interested than usual in the commercial prosperity of the United States. Indeed the Open Door itself repre-sented to Americans that "unhappy marriage between idealism and commercialism"[1] which so often marks the policy of the State Department and, possibly as the result of the slow recovery of the United States from the financial crisis of 1907, but even more because of the change of administration and personalities, commercialism suddenly and rapidly advanced and idealism receded. One result was the great surge of irresponsible dollar diplomacy in Latin America, which undid most of Root's good work in those countries and would not be checked even when the idealists Wilson and Bryan came into power. Beyond leading to some rather unedifying com-petition with Great Britain and Germany in the sale of warships to South American republics,[2] to rising economic rivalry with both these Powers in Brazil, and to uneasy relations with Britain in the Argentine and, above all, Mexico, this development was of little immediate importance to the Old World; but the much less spectacular and more reluctant efforts of the dollar diplomatists in China were of greater international significance.

"The chief end of American policy in the Far East was to construct a balance of power",[3] and the means chosen by the Taft administration was to compel a group of New York bankers to assist the foreign financing of Chinese railways and other enter-prises. Mainly through the efforts of Willard Straight these bankers were in fact persuaded to subscribe to one international loan after another, none of which proved to be a financial success. On the other hand this continual transfusion of dollars did to some extent

[1] Pringle, *Taft*, p. 685.
[2] Livermore, S. W., "Battleship Diplomacy in South America, 1905–1925", *Journal of Modern History*, XVI (1944), 31–48.
[3] Van Alstyne, *op. cit.* pp. 322–3.

fulfil its intended function of preventing any one foreign Power establishing a stranglehold on China; further, it assisted her to preserve her political integrity and forestalled any general scramble for her territory and natural resources, such as had taken place in Africa. The policy was not only expensive, however, but still further handicapped by the outbreak of the Chinese revolution of 1910–11, and when Wilson became President the unfortunate bankers begged to be allowed to retire. Wilson recognised the new Chinese Republic but withdrew the financial support; however, the fact that he had to restore it in 1920 on much the same lines suggests that he may have been mistaken. To sum up, American relationship to China in the early twentieth century has been likened to that of Britain to Turkey in the nineteenth, with China the Sick Man of the Far East.[1]

The Far East was not the only sphere, however, in which the new Administration had to reach a quick decision: there was the irritating dispute with Britain over the Canal tolls, not to mention trouble with Mexico. The Panama Canal was now rapidly approaching completion and in August 1912 Taft had signed a regulatory Act, section 5 of which provided that "no tolls shall be levied upon vessels engaged in the coast-wise trade of the United States". This was in direct conflict with Article III of the Hay-Pauncefote Treaty, but Taft defended it on the ground that such trade was already strictly reserved to American shipping by the Merchant Marine Act of 1817 and "general usage", and that therefore no discrimination against any foreign vessel was involved. His original idea had been to subsidise the coasters by paying their tolls, as many countries did in the case of Suez, but this was rashly objected to by the British, who now found themselves confronted with a far more noxious proposal.[2] As a matter of fact Sir Edward Grey had no difficulty in pointing out that American oceanic shipping could easily transfer cargo to protected coasters and thus evade toll, but not unnaturally he took his main stand on the technical violation of the Treaty, his one concession being to offer arbitration, which was brusquely refused by both Congress and Administration. The fact was of course that free passage for American ships would presumably reduce freight-rates and thereby the cost of living, which was among the vital issues of the United States election in 1912. Wilson himself, as a presidential candidate, had begun by supporting tolls-exemption, and although after his election he seems to have been influenced in the contrary sense by the opinion of Professor J. H. Latané[3] and others, he had trouble with Bryan on the subject and did not ask Congress to repeal section 5 of the Taft Act until 5 March 1914, when he delivered his

---

[1] Van Alstyne, *op. cit.* pp. 333–5.
[2] Pringle, *Taft*, pp. 648–51.
[3] "The Panama Canal Act and the British Protest", *American Journal of International Law*, VII (1913), pp. 17–26.

famous Message on the Canal tolls to Congress in person.[1] Thanks to the unexpected help of Senators Root and Lodge repeal was finally achieved, but not until June 1914. By that time tolls-exemption had become the last serious cause of difference between Great Britain and the United States, and its removal just two months before the outbreak of war, which was itself quickly followed by the opening of the Canal, was therefore doubly fortunate.

In the Mexican imbroglio the Democrats inherited yet another unwelcome legacy from Taft. As far as the British were concerned, however, their relations with Mexico, as with other Latin American countries, during this period turned entirely on the encouragement of primary production for the British market by the use of British capital and engineering skill to improve transport facilities, carry out drainage operations, and install the necessary machinery for increasing natural yields, whether of fuel, food or raw materials; the sale of British manufactured goods to these countries in return for their increased production was of course also a consideration. Apart from minor boundary disputes, not only with Mexico but also with Guatemala and Brazil, and the perennial Falkland Islands question with the Argentine, Britain was not concerned with the political and constitutional problems which agitated the United States' relations with its neighbours. From 1863 at latest the historic British domination of Brazilian politics, which can be traced back through Anglo-Portuguese relations for over two centuries, had disappeared for good, although the British economic "empire" in that vast subcontinent persisted in the face of growing German and United States competition until 1914, and indeed revived spasmodically for a few years after the First World War.[2] The war, on the other hand, was fatal to the thirty-year-old British economic predominance in the Argentine, dating from the introduction of the *frigorifico* (refrigerator) about 1880 and assuming great proportions in the meat trade, and later in the wheat and linseed markets, especially in the ten years before the war. The disappearance of the United States beef export surplus led to the first inroad of the American Beef Trust into the Argentine in May 1907, followed by the significant saying of a New York banker, "South America is our nut and it is time we should crack it".[3] Thus United States firms, such as Swift and Co. and the National Packing Co., which finally established a stranglehold on the Argentine meat industry during the war years, were merely forerunners of a great drive seriously impairing, if by no means destroying, British commercial interests in South America.

In Mexico, on the other hand, increasing political tension with the United States served to postpone the absolute subordination of British

[1] Link, A. S., *Woodrow Wilson and the Progressive Era, 1910–17* (London, 1954), pp. 90–3.
[2] See Manchester, A. K., *British Pre-Eminence in Brazil, its Rise and Decline* (1933).
[3] Hanson, S. G., *Argentine Meat and the British Market* (1938), pp. 150 *et passim*.

economic interests, until the rise of Mexican nationalism in and after the war of 1914–18 imposed strict limits on Britain and the United States alike. Mexican development in fact owed much to Britain in the pre-war years: for example, the great drainage scheme for taking the surplus waters of the southern lakes out of the valley of Mexico was carried out in the generation before 1900 by a British firm, of which Sir Weetman Pearson was the head, and the construction of the Tehuantepec Railway, completed in 1906—the year in which heavy British participation in Mexican oil first began, was also British. Moreover, it is an ironic fact that the modern harbour of Vera Cruz, opened in 1902, was built by British enterprise; the United States, twelve years later, merely occupied it. The fact was that Mexican unrest, after the expulsion of the veteran dictator Diaz in May 1911, not only prejudiced the interests of the billion-dollar United States oil investment in the country—slightly older, and three times bigger, than that of Lord Cowdray and his associates—but proceeded in its complicated course to violate the constitutional doctrines of the resurgent Democratic Party north of the border. Wilson could and did stand up to the demands of the oil companies, but he was obsessed with the idea of discouraging dictatorships and carrying democratic forms of government ever southward, and this came to much the same thing in the end as Republican dollar diplomacy. The details hardly concern the history of Anglo-American relations, for by now the British were prepared to sacrifice most of their economic interests, if necessary, in order to retain United States goodwill:[1] Europe's dangers and difficulties, in short, were once more redounding to United States advantage, if indeed it was an advantage to be left free to pursue what the next generation, Republican and Democrat alike, was to concur in regarding as a policy that had been mistaken after all.

But if the Mexican trouble illustrates the whole gamut of Democratic idealism in conflict with the power politics from which it was never wholly able to free itself, there were other fields in which it could range undismayed. The cause of international peace was in fact very near to its heart, even if "the attempt to carry the gospel of Wilsonian democracy southward" simply landed it back in "the charted course of the Caribbean policy".[2] There were, for example, the traditions of American participation in The Hague Peace Conferences and the United States' record in international law and arbitration, both of them activities in which further co-operation would be welcomed, and indeed sought, by His Majesty's Government. At the first Hague Conference in 1899 the American record, it must be admitted, had been disappointing, for even the broad-minded Hay's instructions to his delegates had reserved everything

[1] Link, op. cit. pp. 119–20.   [2] Adler, S., "Bryan and Wilsonian Caribbean Penetration", Hispanic American Hist. Rev. xx (1940), 198–226.

worth discussing, and had been strongly reinforced by the extremely non-co-operative attitude of the delegates themselves. In the hands of men like Mahan and Andrew D. White, even the optional and innocuous Convention for the Pacific Settlement of Territorial Disputes had been subjected to the famous reservation that "nothing should be considered to require any abandonment of the traditional attitude of the United States towards questions purely American", and when this was received in dead silence, that is without formal objections, the occasion was saluted by at any rate some Americans as the first official European recognition of the Monroe Doctrine! It was not in short what the Americans had done at The Hague in 1899 so much as the fact that they were there at all which was in any way encouraging.

The Conference of 1907 on the other hand saw a considerable advance, and in some respects it was the British who now lagged behind. The presence of certain Latin American republics, on which the United States had insisted and for whose convenience the date of meeting had been specially deferred, was an event in itself, apart from the fact that it also led to a qualified acceptance of the Argentine's "Drago Doctrine".[1] There was general agreement between Britain and America on the disarmament problem, and the United States also accepted British and German proposals for the setting-up of an international Court of Prize, with the result that the American delegates were further instructed to attend the London Naval Conference of 1908–9. On the other hand the American reservation of 1899 was renewed in 1907 and there was at least one head-on clash between the Anglo-Saxon Powers; for when the United States delegation proposed the immunity from capture in time of war of all noncontraband private property belonging to neutrals, carried even in enemy vessels, on the high seas, and was supported by the Triple Alliance, the British drew back and "seemed all but single-handed to be holding out for the largest belligerent rights against the humane opinion which would limit them".[2] Lord Reay, one of the British delegates, was especially distressed at this passing of the *beau rôle* to Germany and America, and the Prime Minister, Campbell-Bannerman, went so far as to send his letter on the subject to the Foreign Office, but without effect; for the naval experts were obdurate. In the light of 1914–18 it was as well they were, both for Britain and America; but the United States did not welcome the defeat of a principle for which it had struggled intermittently for a century, and it returned to the charge in the ensuing naval conference by support-

[1] Perkins, *Hands Off!* pp. 247–8. The gist of this doctrine was that the use of force by foreign Powers in the collection of debts from Latin American States was not to be tolerated. Dr Louis Drago, Foreign Minister of the Argentine, had enunciated the doctrine during the blockade of Venezuela, 1902–3.
[2] Spender, J. A., *Life of Campbell-Bannerman*, II, 333.

ing, and all but ratifying, the Declaration of London. This Declaration, with its strict definition of contraband and rejection of "paper" blockades, would have ruled out most Allied action in the world-wars of the next generation, not to mention, *ex post facto*, the blockade of the South in the American Civil War as well.[1] Fortunately it had not been finally accepted by any Power when the United States formally invited its ratification on 6 August 1914. On that occasion the Central Powers agreed to it, but Great Britain consented only with such modifications as to destroy its original character and the negotiations fell through.[2]

It would appear then that, at any rate between 1899 and 1909, the United States had made a cautious advance towards supra-nationalism which compares favourably with that of any other nation. Yet if Britain reserved her maritime rights it is equally true that the United States reserved the Monroe Doctrine, and in fact between 1908 and 1914 the Americans frankly reverted to the wholly different conception of preserving not so much the peace of the world as their own peace by multiplying bi-lateral arbitration treaties between themselves and other Powers. It is odd that this development should be associated with the last years of the imperialist Roosevelt administration, and subsequently with men like Taft and Wilson, both of whom were to be champions of the multi-lateral Covenant of the League of Nations, and it may be that in each case it was less the policy of the Presidents than of their Secretaries of State. Root had started it with no less than twenty-five bi-lateral arbitration treaties concluded in 1908 and 1909, but even Knox had attempted similar treaties with France and Great Britain, which had broken down in 1911–12 on a point of technical differences with the Senate. Bryan went further than either, in both the nature of his treaties and the number he obtained: indeed, as Spring Rice wrote to Grey in August 1914, "Bryan, of course, regards the war as a background to his own peace treaties".[3] Their main differences from those of Root lay in points of procedure, especially in the so-called "cooling-off clause", and in their not excluding questions of vital interest and national honour. By October 1914 Bryan had obtained no less than thirty of them, eighteen of which had been ratified in a single batch by the Senate during August, whether owing to the impact of the war, the desire to escape from the summer heat of Washington, or the accidental absence of Senator Lodge, who considered such treaties "fatuous" and would certainly have opposed them.[4] But Bryan, for all his faith in them, did not regard his treaties as the only safeguard, for in January 1914 he had proposed, with Wilson's approval, the calling of a third Hague

---

[1] Van Alstyne, *op. cit.* p. 629.
[2] Notter, H., *The Origins of the Foreign Policy of Woodrow Wilson* (Baltimore, 1937), pp. 321–2.
[3] Gwynn, *op. cit.* II, 220.   [4] Perkins, *Hands Off!* p. 282.

Conference, to be attended by those Powers who had attended the last one and to meet in 1915.[1]

From the Treaty of Washington in 1871 to Bryan and his peace treaties is less than forty-five years, yet the changes within that period, not only in the relationship between the British Empire and the United States but in the internal economy of each, had been enormous. In 1870 the Empire sprawled inert around the globe, contriving to diffuse its force while at the same time neglecting its extremities. Though it had not an enemy in sight it was doubtful of the reasons for its own existence: in a sense it was its own worst enemy. Perhaps it is true that its salvation lay in that federation of Canada which had already taken place and, as Chamberlain was to say at Toronto in 1887, might yet be "the lamp lighting our path to the federation of the British Empire".[2] It was certainly significant that in the next few years not only such imperial aphorisms as "splendid isolation" were to be heard for the first time in the Dominion Parliament, but the more pregnant phrases of "Imperial Preference" and "Dominion Status" as well.[3] By the end of the nineteenth century the Empire was in fact becoming more and more decentralised under the lead given by Canada, at the very moment when the federated United States was becoming an imperialist republic.[4] The ideas of a decentralised British Empire and an Anglo-American *entente* were bound up together,[5] and they were more easily combined in that the effect of decentralisation was to make the Empire steadily more democratic. Anyone could see that the two great organisms were steadily converging, for just as the British aristocracy began to wilt under the impact of Lloyd George and the new radicalism, the United States began to exhibit "old, wealthy and highly developed societies" of an English type[6] alongside relatively simple agricultural or pastoral communities recalling the Dominions, not to mention native enclaves and even dependent peoples. The resemblance was concealed of course by the overwhelming concentration of one group in a single land mass and the dispersion of the other over the seven seas, but it was there. Social habits and cultural patterns too were becoming inextricably confused: to take only a few trivial examples, the multiple chain store reached England in the shape of Woolworth's in 1909, to be followed by the Rotary movement in 1911; while by 1914 the American cinema industry had captured the British market and Rudyard

---

[1] Notter, *op. cit.* p. 280.
[2] Garvin, *Chamberlain*, II, 334. Of course it is true to say that, despite the strong sense of Canadian nationalism, faith in the continued existence of the British Empire dates back, as far as Canada is concerned, to the concession of responsible government, and was for many years much stronger there than in the home country.
[3] Brebner, *op. cit.* pp. 256, 262.
[4] Dunning, W. A., *The British Empire and the United States*, pp. 343–55.
[5] Heindel, *op. cit.* p. 64.
[6] Dunning, *op. cit.* p. 355.

Kipling had become a best-seller in America.[1] One special consequence of imperial constitutional development has been the steady shifting of responsibility for imperial relations with America to the Dominion specially concerned on any given occasion. This process had not been carried far by 1914, except perhaps in Canada, which as usual led the way,[2] but it was capable of considerable extension and this in due course it received. It meant that Great Britain was no longer bound to bear the burden of Dominion differences with the United States, and that the United States for its part would now have to negotiate not with one British nation but with a group of nations.

Foreign policy is inevitably the crux of the whole question, especially when it is remembered that nine-tenths of American foreign policy—highly subject as it is to mass emotionalism—has usually been concerned with the British Empire and only one-tenth with other countries.[3] From 1898 the new imperialist United States assumed new responsibilities and incurred new liabilities, rivalries and dangers —and this at a moment when the British Empire, too, began to be threatened by third parties as it had never been for a century. Naturally the two empires, so increasingly similar in social and economic structure, grew closer together whether they wanted to or not: as McKinley said in 1901—and the Professor of Public Law at Princeton, Woodrow Wilson, had said it just before him—"isolation is no longer possible or desirable.... The period of exclusiveness is past".[4] But the diplomatic tempo of the two countries was not the same, and this caused difficulties, for, as R. M. Ferguson wrote to Spring Rice in January 1905, "they [the State Department] do not sufficiently realise that a proposal from our Foreign Office commits the more vulnerable empire to every consequence, whilst that of the most autocratic president commits his country to nothing".[5] Perhaps this is the real reason for that "essential conservatism of British foreign policy", which a recent American historian has noted[6]— "its concentration on the *status quo*, its deafness to the occasional importunities of British subjects abroad", whereas every President who has felt the urge to interpret or even anticipate dangerous swings of public opinion has been able to rely on his more speculative *ballons d'essai* being punctured by a conservative Senate. Naturally this can be a tragic process, perhaps more often than a salutary one, as the career of Wilson showed, and yet it is permissible to wonder whether executive boldness, ridden on the curb of the much-abused senatorial treaty-power, is really so inferior to the steady lucubrations of a Foreign Office directed by a Secretary of State with a mechanical

[1] The whole subject of the "impact" of the United States on Britain has been fully studied on these lines by Heindel, R. H., *op. cit.*
[2] Even there it was not settled until after the war of 1914–18.
[3] Mowat, *The American Entente*, pp. 5–6, quoting Klingberg.
[4] Notter, *op. cit.* p. 107.   [5] Gwynn, *op. cit.* I, 448.
[6] Van Alstyne, *op. cit.* p. 512.

majority in Parliament. The difficulty is to make the two methods work harmoniously together, and no doubt it is on this that we should concentrate rather than on assigning praise or blame to either system.

Increasingly decentralised, democratised—indeed beginning to be socialised—the Empire stood upon the brink of war in 1914, still powerful, still massive, with its immense financial reserves and overseas investments still intact, and wondered what the United States would do. There was no alliance, nor any question of an alliance, but there was previous common action over sixteen years, and a sense of slowly growing similarity of interest, which, if democracy should really be in danger, might flower into a common purpose. And in that event no one could deny that the British Empire would receive the greatest access to its strength which it had ever known.

CHAPTER X

CHANGING ATTITUDES AND WIDENING RESPONSIBILITIES, 1895–1914

THE two decades between the coming of Joseph Chamberlain to the Colonial Office and the entry of the British Commonwealth into a World War were scored deeply with contrasts. It is not hard to over-dramatise the contrast in time, however, and to represent the General Election of 1906 as a great divide bisecting these years into periods of Conservative-Unionist and Liberal-Radical rule: a flamboyant "jingo" imperialism strangely uncharacteristic of British "thinking on empire", followed by an almost guilty return to that more sober dedication to imperial responsibility which had bred both Wilberforce and Lord Durham. It is not difficult to over-simplify the issues and to forget that temperance, or education, divided men more clearly than did the colonies, or that Ireland remained a watershed of more fundamental importance than South Africa ever was.[1] The streams, however, co-existed and flowed to-gether: at the extremes the labels still attached to minorities, but beneath the noisy turbulent conflict there was a quiet (and steadier) undertow strong in tradition. The period of growing nationalism, foreign rivalries, Dominion sensitivities and Pan-Anglo-Saxonism had indeed a unity, not least in the loyalty of thinking men to deeply held convictions, which were tempered but superficially by discouragement or success. Within the frame the long-remembered threads of imperial history still dominated the new pattern, restlessly pulling and weaving themselves into a harmony.

The rise of this new and so-called "imperialist" temper in the last days of Victoria's reign was, indeed, as sudden as it proved to be short-lived.[2] In the passion for Greater Britain Little England was liable to be overlooked. Imperialism and social reform, though not necessarily a dichotomy, might appear so.[3] When men came to tire of the dubious arrogance and tawdry triumphs of an expensive "imperialism", they turned back to the regenerate liberalism which, almost despite the Liberal party, was at hand. In retrospect the half-

---

[1] Ensor, R. C. K., "Some political and economic interactions in later Victorian England", *Trans. R. Hist. Soc.*, 4th ser. XXXI (1949), 17–28.

[2] Some contemporaries contrasted the Jubilee of 1887, *royal* and still nation-wide, with that of 1897, *imperial* and already deeply compromised thereby in Radical circles. Koebner, R., "The concept of economic imperialism", *Econ. Hist. Rev.* II (1949), no. 1, pp. 10, 18, 20 *seqq.* See also Ensor, *England, 1870–1914*, p. 239; Wolf, L., *Marquess of Ripon*, II, 209; Hicks Beach, V., *Sir Michael Hicks Beach*, II, 127, 152; and Gardiner, A. G., *Sir William Harcourt*, II, 366.

[3] Masterman, C., in *The Heart of the Empire* (1901), pp. 3–4.

dozen "braggart years" came to be seen as a lapse from accepted standards of British imperial morality, a fever which could be explained away, perhaps too agreeably, as having been caught from Continental rivals. But the word itself could never thereafter recover its good name.

Conditions had long been making for such an outburst of self-congratulation. The foundations of Victorian society had been undermined. Cheap newspapers, manhood suffrage and bouts of depression made the old self-confidence more brazen. The German naval programme was to the shrewder observer a brisk warning that the *Pax Britannica* was no longer unchallenged. The identification of colonial possessions with British greatness and wealth prompted that "scramble for Africa" among her rivals which had drawn Britain into the vortex of Europe. There, in the network of alliances, she found herself isolated in a period when her position as an industrial and maritime power, even within the Queen's dominions, was being overhauled by foreign competitors who, while they copied British techniques, had no such designs upon her policy of free trade. The "scramble" had already made nonsense of Britain's "self-denying ordinance", her reluctance to assume administrative responsibility by the annexation of the "informal empire" which had been previously a sufficient guarantee of her commerce or strategy.[1] The zeal and emulation of new colonial competitors provided Britain with needful self-justification and may have satisfied the craving of many Britons, especially those herded in large industrial towns, for excitement and colour.

This sort of imperialism was a new phenomenon. An industrial imperialism had succeeded the mercantilist approach earlier in the century: now it was itself being replaced by a financial, "stock-jobbing", variety.[2] The sources of an imperial impulse had been—and of course continued to be—many: a devotion to justice and liberty, a desire for power, the necessity for maintaining law and order, a faith in British institutions, a greed for display; but commentators both then and since have remarked the speculative fever (nourished by the gold of the Rand and Kalgoorlie) which lay at the root of this phase of imperialism. For Britain in this sphere as exporter of capital remained supreme: she was still the banker, if no longer the workshop or the emporium, of the world.[3] All "imperialisms" have indeed been specifics; and so, in reaction, have been their "anti-imperialisms". This *fin de siècle* imperialism was itself a sharp, heady reaction against Little England and *laissez-faire*; its very extravagance was perhaps symptomatic of inner questionings. It was inflated by the new sensational Yellow Press and the popular music-hall, and through

[1] Cecil, Lady Gwendolen, *Lord Salisbury*, IV, 225. See also *Econ. Hist. Rev.* VI (1953), 1–15.

[2] Gardiner, *op. cit.* II, 389, 414, 514: Harcourt's speech, 8 May 1896, *Hansard*, 4th ser. XL, 886. See also "The New Jingoism" in *The Spectator*, LXXXI, 480.

[3] Langer, W. L., *The Diplomacy of Imperialism, 1890–1902*, I, 74.

these media caught the imagination, not only of Park Lane and the Stock Exchange, but also of the newly enfranchised artisans who seemed to prefer power and authority to liberty and principle.[1] In part, then, it was a repudiation of Gladstone, for long the keeper of the British conscience. Old idols were broken in a sudden conversion to this new religion of possession and race. Darwin's survival of the fittest was being elevated from a biological theory to a political precept.[2] In the search for justification, there was relief as well as hysterical pride in the crowing over the vanquished at Omdurman and Fashoda, and later in the unbridled vulgarity of "Mafficking". Not only Gladstonian morality but financial frugality (of which it was maybe an integral part) fell into temporary disrepute: the handsome surplus which Harcourt left to an embarrassed Hicks Beach was dissipated within four years.[3]

This reaction was more manifestly literary and emotional than political. In practice, policy devoted itself rather to development and consolidation than to expansion. The public might appear to have been converted for the moment to a "Forward" policy: substantially it would seem that it was only those who had previously been indifferent, or politically inarticulate, who had succumbed to this hysteria. Wales and Scotland (traditionally Liberal strongholds), and even industrial Yorkshire and Tyneside, remained more dourly unimpressed.[4] For the most part the ruling class was cynically indifferent to this mass religion. Governments, therefore, were still concerned with claims already "pegged out", and showed no noticeable alacrity to peg out new claims and thereby to assume further responsibilities. Lord Cromer's work in Egypt proved at once the spur and (perhaps) the model for further colonial development.[5] Chartered companies, previously providing inexpensive consolation for the Forwards, were now found inadequately equipped for the frontier problems which they created by dragging Britain into regions and interiors hitherto untapped. Private enterprise was now clamouring for Government backing for its imperial adventures.[6] A recrudescence of brutality throughout Europe, heightened by vicarious familiarity with savage warfare in Africa, did not fail to have some effect in blunting the sensitivity of a minority in Britain. The glorification of militarism may not have presented itself as absurd to a generation which had played no part in a major European war. In some the admiration of Prussianism, the policy of efficiency and "thorough", began to march

---

[1] Monypenny, W. F., in *The Empire and the Century* (1905), pp. 5–6.

[2] Gooch, G. P., in *The Heart of the Empire* (1901), p. 312.

[3] Gardiner, *op. cit.* II, 380–1, 450; Hicks Beach, *op. cit.* II, 65, 85, 111, 127, 152, 157.

[4] Ensor in *Trans. R. Hist. Soc.* vol. XXI. See *Northern Echo*, quoted Maccoby, S., *English Radicalism, 1886–1914*, p. 232.

[5] See Milner's book *England in Egypt* (1892) and, for the influence of Egypt on Chamberlain's imperialism, Garvin, J. L., *Joseph Chamberlain*, I, chap. xx–and II, pp. 447 *seqq.*

[6] Koebner, *loc. cit.* p. 17; Gardiner, *op. cit.* II, 199; Hicks Beach, *op. cit.* II, 76–85.

with a distrust in parliamentary institutions,[1] which had already revealed itself in the minds of those with frontier experience. Democracy began to be subjected to the subtle assaults of the cheap press which was finding it profitable to exploit a good hate; and the inflationists of empire strong in Fleet Street spread their net of publicity over the larger towns in the provinces.[2] In manufacturing centres the cry of Fair Trade, a return to Huskisson's reciprocity, claimed adherents. As Britain's foreign markets became threatened, her colonial customers, though still contributing but a fraction to her trade, became the more important.

The circumstances of the mid-century commerce had, of course, been exceptional, but to the generation of Cobden and Gladstone it had seemed the norm. Now it was Britain's monopoly which was being challenged, not her primacy; but where rivalry had been unknown or contemptible, this threat could be alarming. Traditional ideas—the economics of siege—of trade as a form of " cold war "—were reasserting themselves with a fervour which they had not known even in their defensive victory of 1783. This neo-Mercantilism (still seeking the elusive goal of imperial self-sufficiency) was to express itself in the Tariff Reform movement. It would declare itself in Chamberlain's notorious Glasgow speech of October 1903 in which he would apparently have consigned the self-governing colonies to a subordinate position in a centrally planned economy as producers of raw materials only: colonists would seem destined to remain a permanent peasantry under the flag. It might be seen in the revival of the merchant fleet as a "nursery of seamen" in Lloyd George's Merchant Shipping Acts.[3] But by 1886 it was already present in Froude's assumption that colonies must exist for the benefit, not so much of themselves, but of the mother country and the Empire at large.[4]

The issues, then, were clear enough in detail. In their multiplicity the divisions of opinion were not so clear. The leaders themselves were not divided from each other on coherent party lines. Nor was policy itself. To some degree Ireland had acted as a watershed: dividing "imperialists" who favoured coercion from their opponents; dislodging from the Liberals the whigs and gentry who were horrified at "moonlighting"; replacing a "Consolidationist" by a Forward as Liberal leader; and reuniting Chamberlain with his "ain folk", the businessmen and manufacturers now in a flaring awareness of socialism and from whom his own Radicalism had withdrawn him.[5] As a

[1] Gooch, loc. cit. pp. 312–30.

[2] Halévy, E., History of the English People, v (1895–1905), 8–12; Gardiner, op. cit. p. 477; Hamilton Fyfe, Northcliffe, passim; and Scott-James, R. A., The Influence of the Press (1913).

[3] Halévy, op. cit. v, 347; VI, pt. I, 14–16. See also Garvin, J. L., in The Empire and the Century, pp. 109–11.

[4] Froude, J. A., Oceana (1886), pp. 13, 392–6, ct. p. 391. See also Bodelsen, Studies in mid-Victorian Imperialism, pp. 198–205.

[5] Ensor's paper in Trans. R. Hist. Soc., 4th ser. XXXI; and his discussion of "The evolution of Joseph Chamberlain" in The Spectator, 3 July 1936.

result, in this period, the Conservative party became much more obviously a class party than it had been; and both the Disraelian version of Tory Democracy and Chamberlain's earlier Social Radicalism seemed likely to be submerged in the doctrine of "Forward" imperialism.[1] Chamberlain did indeed successfully co-ordinate romantic patriotism and economic argument; but, unlike Disraeli, he forgot, momentarily at least, that prestige was not enough; thereby his preoccupation with Empire helped create the opportunity for the Liberal-Radical triumph in 1906. For the moment, however, his personality seemed to dominate the ranks behind him. Even Lord Salisbury had been drawn against persistent conviction to countenance the Forward policy of those in his own party whom privately he still considered "fanatics", and old Toryism had been hitched reluctantly to Chamberlain's waggon with little sympathy for the aggressive spirit which it associated with him.[2] The party position therefore was still confused. Personalities and personal loyalties would appear to have bulked larger than principles in the divisions of opinion: Salisbury's suspicion of Chamberlain, Harcourt's of Rosebery; Morley's somewhat ascetic devotion to Gladstone; Balfour's studied ambiguity; the *religio Milneriana* of Jowett's young men, and Haldane's permeation of the Webbs.[3] None of them stood for peace at any price; each disliked the other's wars.[4]

Even if Chamberlain had not chosen the Colonial Office in 1895, imperial affairs would have been thrust into the forefront of foreign policy by way of the Nile.[5] The Foreign Office had acquired, particularly in East Africa, a considerable empire of its own and its African department negotiated with the Colonial Office as "with a foreign power".[6] At the Colonial Office, however, matters of urgency in the reform and reorganisation of business both in Downing Street and in the dependencies themselves demanded Chamberlain's energies, apart from his own passion for consolidation which would make the Empire strong, and development which would make the "neglected estates" profitable. But not least were the perennial problems of imperial policy. The restless dilemma of reconciling colonial autonomy with imperial unity had become the more poignant in a climate of emergent nationalism when (for Britain at least) some closer association for security within the dominions of the Crown seemed a preliminary to "touting for friendships"[7] outside the

---

[1] Bérard, V., *British Imperialism and Commercial Policy* (1905), p. 48.

[2] See Spender, J. A., *Campbell-Bannerman*, I, 209; Webb, Beatrice, *Our Partnership*, pp. 140–1, and Taylor, A. J. P., *Rumours of Wars*, pp. 156–7.

[3] Spender, *op. cit.* I, 344; Spender, J. A., and Asquith, C., *Lord Oxford and Asquith*, I, 113, 242; Gardiner, *op. cit.* II, 471; Cole, M., *Beatrice Webb*, p. 83.

[4] Spender, *op. cit.* I, 209 *seqq*. Even Morley would have been prepared to go to war with Turkey and many Radicals became "jingo" over Fashoda.

[5] Crewe, Lord, *Lord Rosebery*, I, 315.

[6] Taylor, A. J. P., "Prelude to Fashoda", *E.H.R.* LXV (Jan. 1950), 52–3,

[7] The phrase was Asquith's, quoted by Garvin, *op. cit.* III, 284.

charmed circle of Empire. The counter-demands of centralisation and devolution, the waywardness of divergent colonial evolution, the impulse for anglicisation and the tolerance of indigenous custom, the need (under a Treasury control which made, and was liable to unmake, policy) for strictest economy, the quality of administration at the centre and in the bush which, in the legacy of Dr Arnold, so often combined incorruptibility with insensitivity—these issues were ever present. So too, and pregnant of many doubts and heart-searchings, was the antithesis between the two central themes of nineteenth-century imperial history: the progressive realisation of self-government springing naturally from British institutions and favoured by distance, disdain and *laissez-faire*; and the developing sense of imperial mission for Christianity and civilisation under the paternal authoritarianism of Crown colony government. For long these two principles had been falsely isolated in colour-tight compartments, and had been thought of as being exclusively appropriate for either white-settled, or tropical non-European, colonies. In South Africa at the beginning of the new century, however, they came into signal opposition: and Liberals particularly, who by tradition were advocates of both these principles, had yet to learn that it was no longer possible to continue to have it both ways and that both nettles could not be grasped at once.[1] Generosity offered to the vanquished Boer would neutralise the cause of justice to the Bantu. In a meritorious act of liberality to the ex-Boer republics in 1906–7 they subordinated their own humanitarianism, or at most hoped that Providence would employ its reserve power to see that all would work out well in the end.

The current and eddies of opinion that made Britain's conception of empire were, indeed, many, complex and turbulent as they leapt the rapids of this period. Three main streams, however, may be observed, and each of them, the Gladstonian Free Traders, the "Radical Imperialists", the Socialists—gave to the broad flow of the twentieth-century inheritance of empire something that endured when much that was shoddy or merely temporary was overwhelmed. The Free Traders made a contribution pre-eminently political: the loose elastic form of Commonwealth consultation and the voluntary co-operative nature of full membership. The others demonstrated that political evolution in the self-governing Empire was not enough; the "Radical Imperialists" by quickening a sense of positive economic development in the dependent Empire, and the "Socialists" by preparing for replacement of an often complacent trusteeship by the more dynamic ideal of senior and junior partnership. There was,

[1] For example, the resolution of the National Liberal Federation, 27 Feb. 1901 (quoted by Spender, *op. cit.* I, 325), which demanded "equal rights for both white races, an honourable measure of self-government and a just and humane treatment for the natives". See Milner's comments on this dichotomy in *Milner Papers*, ed. C. Headlam, I, 177–81; II, 311–12.

moreover, one factor that could not be overlooked. The humanitarian conscience, deeply but unpredictably indoctrinated by a small devoted evangelical leadership, cut across party allegiance and drew strength as a political force from Free Traders, Imperialists and Socialists alike.

The Gladstonian Free Traders[1] were, of course, the heirs of the Manchester School, which had protested against that particular brand of empire which stood between British manufacturers and their command of the world's markets. Now they were on the defensive. Distrustful of Chamberlain and Milner, repelled by the Rand magnates and the squalid intrigues of the British South Africa Company, loathing provocative militarism and shamed by "grab and brag"[2] and by "filibustering expeditions in the mixed guise of commerce, religion, geography and imperialism under which names any and every atrocity is regarded as permissible",[3] it was not difficult, in the flood tide of imperialism, to represent them as merely negative in outlook. The creed of some may, indeed, have been sapped by an apathetic acquiescence in what seemed inevitable; but in self-justification they tumbled on principles which must be essential to any enduring empire and which had been a permanent inspiration in the thinking of many of their colleagues. They rejoiced in a continuing imperial association of free communities, cradled in a common faith in parliamentary institutions, as a step towards that world community which was their extension of Adam Smith's Great Commercial Republic. The Empire was not Chamberlain's invention: liberal enterprise had done much to create it. It provided homes for emigrants who could act as ambassadors for those accepted Manchester School principles of trade, peace, economy and non-intervention. Colonial independence still left secure the ties which mattered most. Imperial unity sprang from voluntary co-operation and mutual trust. It would elude any rigid pattern—political, economic or military—that did not allow for growth. The Gladstonians did not desire an exclusive league of Little Englands.[4] They were imperialists because they were internationalists: "sane", almost insular internationalists, indeed, who stood uncommitted by formal alliances, outside the cockpit of Europe, and acted therefore with benevolent impartiality as "the friendly policemen of a rather disorderly mob".[5] The policeman himself must be beyond reproach. Therefore they repudiated a ruthless land-grabbing imperialism not only because it was uneconomic in itself, but because it was isolating Britain from the goodwill of the Concert of Europe. Moreover, it was their cause, never more

[1] Gladstone, Morley, Harcourt, Campbell-Bannerman, Hicks Beach, Lloyd George, Courtney and Bryce belonged to this group.
[2] See Gardiner, op. cit. II, 311; and Labouchere, quoted Koebner, loc. cit. p. 13.
[3] Harcourt to Gladstone, 7 Jan. 1891, quoted Gardiner, op. cit. II, 94.
[4] Spender, op. cit. I, 96, 258, 303–5, 368; II, 215; Gardiner, op. cit. II, 386, 392, 414, 440–8, 496, 523, 597–8.　　　　　　　　　　　[5] Gardiner, op. cit. II, 329.

urgent than in the days after the Jameson Raid, to re-establish in the eyes of the world a respect for British standards of justice and fair-dealing.[1] So too it was Campbell-Bannerman's part, even in the heat of the battle, to remind the British conscience of its traditional regard for humanity and to keep alive the consciousness that post-war reconciliation of the Boers as fellow subjects in the Empire would be prejudiced by methods which would lay up "a fund of ineradicable personal hatred".[2] Ill-chosen means would only pervert even wise ends. It therefore behoved those who feared for Britain's good name to expose the mischief of appeals by Haldane to overlook inconvenient detail by "painting with a broad brush", or the plausibility of Asquith's recognition of "grim necessity", or the harshness of Chamberlain's excuse for "breaking" eggs and his invitation to contrast the great gain with the paltry price paid in blood.[3] In this appeal to the moral forces of empire the elder statesmen were aided not only by many Radicals and humanitarians but by a group of Young Liberals,[4] who strove to dedicate the party anew to the re-sponsibilities not only of the free but of the dependent Empire. Britain must endeavour by "strenuous and honest sympathy, justice and even magnanimity to obliterate our cruel conquests and justify our world-wide usurpation".[5] Thus fulfilling "almost the role of Providence",[6] she would speed the coming of that brotherhood of men of all races for which science, industry, free trade and demo-cracy were preparing. Although it was natural that these opinions should be championed by Liberal leaders, during the first decade of this period they were not exclusively to be found upon the opposition benches. The Chancellor of the Exchequer, Hicks Beach, resisted his Forward (and younger) colleagues, declaring himself devoid of all sympathy whatever "with the achievement of great ends by unjustifi-able means".[7] Moreover, in his stand against Tariff Reform, he proved himself a veritable paladin of Gladstonian principles. These men, heirs to Cobden and Goldwin Smith, provided in their several ways links with the later Wilson-Lenin concept of national "self-determination" and with post-war League of Nations idealism.

In opposition to them, those whom it might perhaps be permissible

---

[1] Gardiner, *op. cit.* II, 320, 370; and Spender, *op. cit.* p. 254.

[2] Spender, *op. cit.* I, 260, 275, 305, 333; II, 2, 401.

[3] Spender and Asquith, *op. cit.* I, 136–8; and *Mr Chamberlain's Speeches*, ed. Boyd, II, 4–5.

[4] Including G. P. Gooch, G. K. Chesterton, G. M. Trevelyan and the three authors of *Liberalism and Empire* (1900): F. Hirst, Gilbert Murray and J. L. Hammond.

[5] *Liberalism and Empire*, pp. xv–xvi, 120, 151–7, 163–5, 170–1.   [6] *Ibid.* p. 157.

[7] Hicks Beach, *op. cit.* II, 54. Hicks Beach detested the "jingo hurricane", opposed expansion, distrusted both Rhodes and Milner, and approved colonial nationalism and self-government. Under Disraeli he had regarded himself as an imperialist; but the temper of opinion had risen so much since that, as Gooch said (*loc. cit.* p. 331), even Seeley, with his scorn for the "bombastic school", would have been considered a Little Englander in the late 'nineties. Similarly the Marquess of Ripon, who had some claim to be con-sidered a "Radical Imperialist" earlier, found his creed insufficient to justify his patriotism in this period (Wolf, *op. cit.* I, 64; II, 209).

to describe as "Radical Imperialists" were a much more complex group.[1] The leadership was, of course, in the hands of a wayward triumvirate: Chamberlain, Rosebery and Milner. It could not be said that they thought alike either on personalities or on methods; but on the main goal—the rescue of the Empire from "salutary neglect" and its rehabilitation as a more powerful economic and military unit—they were united, and in this grand design they enjoyed the fitful support both of the young "Lib. Imps." (Asquith, Edward Grey and Haldane) and of the leaders of the Fabians.[2] They were sceptical of an Empire bound by sentiment alone and were impatient for practical results. The Empire, "the greatest business organisation in the world", must be developed efficiently: or colonial resources potentially valuable to a stronger self-contained British economy would be wasted.[3] Instinctively repelled by inefficiency and waste, and preferring leadership to democracy, they believed that immediate benefits would flow only from a British paternal administration, impeded as little as possible by "that mob at Westminster".[4] They had confidence in the British as "the greatest of governing races the world has ever seen", "predestined by our defects as well as our virtues to spread over the habitable globe".[5] In this genuine devotion to great ends, they were often careless of unjust means. Native land might be taken over to yield greater profit not only to Britain but to the native inhabitants themselves. Native labour might be forced (if need be) by economic sanction to find steady employment in the development of natural resources for all mankind.[6] But in their passion for uniformity with the British

---

[1] The phrase is taken from Chamberlain's correspondence with his ex-colleague, Morley (see Garvin, op. cit. I, 528-9). The group, thus aptly described in a way which recalls the Colonial Reformers earlier, were "Radicals" not only in the sense that many of them favoured social reforms at home, but that they sought by re-shaping and developing the Empire anew on a rational (even collectivist) plan to make it at once more useful and more efficient a unit: in Chamberlain's words, "to get the points right" so that it could provide the greatest equality of wealth, opportunity and security for the greatest number. They were "Imperialists" in the sense that their own preconception about the Empire took the prior place in moulding their policy at home.

[2] The group included at times Lord Curzon, Lord Selborne, C. J. Rhodes, L. S. Amery, Josiah Wedgwood, Alfred Harmsworth of The Daily Mail, E. T. Cook, later of the Liberal Daily News, Robert Blatchford of the Labour Clarion, W. T. Stead of the Review of Reviews, the Rev. Hugh Price Hughes, perhaps the most influential of the Wesleyan leaders; Acland, Buxton and Perks among the Liberals; Shaw, Wallas and the two Webbs among the Fabians; and later (briefly) H. G. Wells among the "Coefficients" (cf. Amery, My Political Life, I, 223-4).

[3] Garvin, op. cit. III, 181; Amery, J., Joseph Chamberlain [IV], 530.

[4] Milner Papers, II, 291. Curzon, Rosebery and Froude shared with Milner this antipathy towards parliamentary institutions.

[5] Chamberlain, J., Foreign and Colonial Speeches (1897), p. 89. See also his speech at Toronto in 1887, quoted Strauss, W. L., Joseph Chamberlain and the Theory of Imperialism, p. 60, and Lord Curzon in The Nineteenth Century and After (Jan. 1908), p. 153.

[6] See, for example, Amery, J., op. cit. IV, 73, 205; and Strauss, op. cit. p. 89. The Fabians, too, believed that aboriginal backwardness and inefficiency must not be permitted to obstruct the advance of international civilisation and development; Pease, E., History of the Fabian Society, p. 136.

model they were somewhat suspicious not only of indigenous aberration, but also of national deviation; like William Knox or the first Lord Hawkesbury they preferred order to freedom;[1] and like the younger Palmerston or Canning in their zeal for Greater Britain they cared little for international trends. In this they had emphasised the element of race in Dilke's (and Goldwin Smith's) much subtler moral association:[2] a factor further reinforced by a lunatic fringe with arguments from Darwin which rationalised British self-interest and which equated the strongest with the fittest, might with right, and the Elect with the big battalions.[3] But the leaders themselves did not despise intellect or sensibility, and were guiltless of that extravagance which, in the popular, semi-literate press, gave to the imperialism of the period its particular flavour. They found distasteful the boasts of the neo-Romantics, flag-wagging (as by the Laureate, Alfred Austin) in boisterous delirium at the triumphs of force, though they were not always innocent of making use of the popular chauvinism agitated by those powerful cheer leaders (like Harmsworth) who played on the fierce hunger for escape and colour.[4] Indeed, in most of these Radical Imperialists (including Kipling, although in his work it largely went unnoticed), there was a deep sense of responsibility. Instinct in their Radicalism was a distrust of the aims and methods of the capitalist groups: even the dreams of Rhodes, the use of money for the power and expansion of Britain, were deeply suspect by the majority who refused to admit such an excuse to place him above all law. The Imperialists of the Liberal League were not as tolerant of Rhodes's lapses as was their leader, Rosebery. They claimed to represent a "sane imperialism", assessing without bluster the increased value of empire in an age of *Realpolitik*. Although in the end they proved "too limp",[5] it was the presence of these "Lib. Imps." on the verge of a possible collectivist Toryism which encouraged the Webbs and Bernard Shaw, for a short period, to cherish hopes for a Fabian permeation of the Forward party. The Fabians desired to see the Empire as "a powerful and self-

[1] *C.H.B.E.* II, 187.

[2] Dilke, C., *Greater Britain* (1869), II, 157, 394; Smith, Goldwin, *The Empire* (1863), pp. 6, 123, and *Canada and the Canadian Question* (1891), p. 265.

[3] Alfred Austin, the poet laureate, in his poem on the Jameson Raid; Kidd, Benjamin, *Social Evolution* (1894) and Pearson, C. H., *National Life and Character* (1893) provide examples of this fanaticism, which Bérard called "the latest philosophy of history and almost the last dogma of religion".

[4] L. S. Amery quoted with approval Fisher's review of his *History of the South African War* as a book with a mission to preach imperialism: Amery, *My Political Life*, 1, 336. Chamberlain was prepared to use "jingo" agitation. He admitted that no *casus belli* existed in 1896, but added, "I do not think it wise to explain this from the housetops, and *I do not mind the noisy exaltation of the jingo party*, since it does not commit me and *may* put some pressure on the people in the Transvaal who are afraid of war. I should like to infuse a little more spirit into Sir H. Robinson and I wish he would shew his teeth to Kruger occasionally. But for all that I am not at all anxious for war—and do not believe it will come." Minute of 8 April 1896 to Fairfield: "Chamberlain Papers", quoted with permission of Miss E. Drus.   [5] Webb, *op. cit.* pp. 219, 227–8, 277.

conscious force" planned energetically for the exploitation of resources and united more closely as trustees for British standards in the common interests "not only of the whole British Commonwealth, but of the whole of civilised society".[1] They too were impatient of native rights which might obstruct progress: the bigger the unit, the greater its efficiency.[2] Chamberlain's diagnosis that all Uganda needed was "what Birmingham had got—an improvement scheme",[3] was naturally something that commended itself to Sidney Webb's municipal socialism. Chamberlain's influence seemed to them to be a restraint on what a resolution of the Society in December 1899 had called "the imperialism of capitalism and vainglorying nationalism", and his presence in the Government a guarantee that expansion would be accompanied by social reform.[4]

Two other groups, one newly articulate and the other traditional, deserve notice: the Socialists and the humanitarians. The representatives of Labour during the earlier part of this period formed a loose confederation of discontented groups, divided by personality but united in disapproval of *laissez-faire* as a social theory.[5] Socialism was not yet an accepted goal of the party, and the Socialist Democratic Federation was too pedantic for all but an exclusive handful of Marxists.[6] The great majority were just "disheartened Gladstonians".[7] Their new social radical creed owed as much to John Wesley and Robert Burns as to Karl Marx, and was indeed in much a rediscovery of earlier Liberal principles.[8] So the South African War, which saw the end of the wave of popular imperialism and threw Labour leaders together in association with pro-Boer Radicals, succeeded in giving them some semblance of unity in pacifism.[9] In retreat from the leadership of the Fabian imperialists Ramsay Macdonald and his fellow "Boer trekkers" were thrown into closer association with Keir Hardie and the I.L.P.[10] They did not dismiss lightly the British claim to be a chosen instrument for good,[11] but were suspicious of imperialism (a word reserved for policy towards the non-self-governing Empire) as a vicious form of capitalism in "its most predatory and militant phase", and a possible obstacle to social reform.[12] Some part of this hostile argument was enforced by

---

[1] *Ibid.* p. 228; and *Fabianism and Empire* (1900), drafted by Bernard Shaw, p. 32.
[2] Shaw, quoted Halévy, *op. cit.* v, 105.
[3] Chamberlain, *Foreign and Colonial Speeches*, p. 136.
[4] Pease, *op. cit.* p. 130; Webb, *op. cit.* pp. 74, 106, 131, 228.
[5] *Keir Hardie's Speeches and Writings*, ed. E. Hughes, pp. 14, 32, 59, 64, 94.
[6] Halévy, *op. cit.* v, 223–8, 245; Stewart, W., *J. Keir Hardie*, p. 213.
[7] Pelling, H., *The Origins of the Labour Party, 1880–1900*, p. 231.
[8] Cf. *Manchester Guardian*, 10 April 1901, "What most strikes a Liberal...is...how much of the proceedings is devoted to the advocacy of traditional Liberal principles".
[9] Keir Hardie wanted Morley as leader of the Labour Representation Committee in 1903: Stewart, *op. cit.* p. 161.
[10] Sacks, B., *J. Ramsay Macdonald*, p. 363; Elton, Lord, *J. R. Macdonald*, p. 92.
[11] Macdonald, J. R., *Labour and the Empire* (1907). See also Hansard, 4th ser. CLVIII, 364–8.
[12] Stewart, *op. cit.* p. 147; *Keir Hardie's Speeches and Writings*, p. 102.

J. A. Hobson's study of non-self-governing *Imperialism*, which was published in 1902. Such imperialism was "a depraved choice of national life imposed by self-seeking interests which appeal to the lusts of quantitative acquisitiveness and of forceful domination...: a deliberate renunciation of that cultivation of the higher qualities which for a nation as for an individual constitutes the ascendance of reason over brute impulse". Imperialism, he maintained, bred speculation and war. But the immediate liquidation of empire would be "a barbarous dereliction of a public duty on behalf of humanity and the civilisation of the world".[1] So Hobson evolved his solution, "A sane and legitimate imperialism" under international supervision for the benefit of all mankind: a principle which had a temporary set-back in King Leopold's Congo but received permanent recognition later in the Mandates system of the League of Nations. Following Hobson's lead,[2] Labour leaders gradually combined the application of Government promotion of colonial development under a "dual mandate" with the Durham gospel of devolution; and in the fullness of time they were to contribute to the transformation of the former principle to one of "partnership", and, by way of India, to take the gospel beyond the master in the creation of a multi-racial brotherhood. Tours of India in the first decade of the new century convinced Hardie and Macdonald of Britain's mission, and their criticisms were not unconstructive.[3] Macdonald defended the moral basis of empire; he pleaded for an "imperial standard" of behaviour to be established among those "free communities" in which he came to glory,[4] and which were in a very real sense (as Ruskin had seen) the creation of the working classes of Britain. In what was one of the last great periods of emigration Labour interest in the new Commonwealth naturally increased.[5] A pan-Saxon Trade Unionism was not least among the legacies of empire. Chamberlain, shrewd enough to see this affinity, sought unsuccessfully to attract the workers to Tariff Reform, not only by representing it as a condition of full employment, but by pointing to the protectionist creed of their emigrant brothers overseas.[6] The threat of taxes on imported foreign

---

[1] Hobson, J. A., *Imperialism*, 3rd ed., pp. 231, 368. See also the reply by Paish in *Journ. Roy. Stat. Soc.* (Sept. 1909 and Jan. 1911).

[2] For example, Macdonald in *Ethical World* (19 Nov. 1898), p. 12, and in *Labour and the Empire, passim*.

[3] Stewart, *op. cit.* pp. xxv, 250; *Keir Hardie's Speeches and Writings*, p. 128; Macdonald, J. R., *Awakening of India* (1910); Keir Hardie, *India, Impressions and Suggestions* (1909).

[4] Macdonald, *Labour and the Empire*, pp. 38, 109 and *Imperialism, its Meaning and its Tendency*, p. 5. See also Burns, J., in *Sixty Years of Empire* (1897).

[5] Lord Rosebery's address to the Trade Union Congress, 11 Sept. 1884. The Empire was too, for many Trade Unionists, a visible proof of responsibilities for conditions of labour at home evaded by governments. For Reports of the Emigrants' Information Office see *Parl. Pap.* 1896, LVIII [C. 7979], p. 175; [C. 8256], p. 183; 1897, LXI [C. 8360], p. 95; 1898, LIX [C. 8756], p. 85.

[6] Langer, *op. cit.* pp. 80–1; Strauss, *op. cit.* p. 84. (See *The Times*, 2 June 1892. Chamberlain said that the future of the working class depended on the maintenance and extension of the Empire.) See also Hancock, W. K., *Politics in Pitcairn*, pp. 65–93.

food (for agriculture was the only industry needing protection) was enough to throw the Labour party into a considered defence of Free Trade, in which, as in the Commonwealth, they saw preparation for a new international order based on co-operation between the working-class leaders.[1] But it was not all plain-sailing. They had become the professional under-dog party and were particularly concerned to get better conditions for labour overseas: cheap labour undercut British labour by unhealthy competition and discouraged British emigration. On the other hand, cheap native labour reduced the British cost of living and made wages go further.[2] As the Liberals might hesitate between self-government and trusteeship, so this was the Labour dilemma.

Finally, throughout this period, that watchdog of aboriginal rights, "Exeter Hall", continued to play its traditional role, "representing that continuity of moral policy which Great Britain could never afford to disregard".[3] But humanitarians deplored even more bitterly than had become customary since the unique enthusiasm of 1833 the general lack of support in all parties and in the public at large, who, it seemed to them, doubted the need to help the "unfit" to survive[4] and who, were emancipation still unachieved, lacked the enthusiasm to carry it through.[5] At times the Anti-Slavery and Aborigines Protection Societies (which were amalgamated in 1909) had the appearance of a tight "family compact" consisting of a few stray Radicals like Charles Dilke and E. D. Morel, and advanced Liberals like Herbert Samuel and Gilbert Murray, but backed in strength only by the Quaker clans. Humanitarians had always, and naturally, been somewhat impulsively selective, having curious blind spots and "pet" tribes; for their action depended upon the efficiency of missionary or official intelligence; and limited funds enforced concentration.[6] The zeal of some, as ever, could outrun knowledge; the unmodified lessons and expedients of British domestic philanthropy were not always necessarily appropriate as imperial exports to tropical conditions; and sometimes the effects of the protests of these devoted guardians proved in the long run harmful to the true interests of their

[1] Free trade was not enough without social reform, but it was a "necessary condition to greater equality of wealth", and preference was "a hindrance to international progress and peace" (Tsiang, *Labour and the Empire*, pp. 150–3). See also Burns, J., *Labour and Free Trade* (1903) and Macdonald, J. R., *The Zollverein and British Industry* (1903).

[2] Halévy, *op. cit.* v, 377–8; vi, 473. The position was further confused by fraternal relations with Dominion Trade Unionism in Australia and South Africa where labour leaders pursued an all-white policy. Stewart, *op. cit.* pp. 256–8.

[3] Crewe, *op. cit.* i, 405. Rosebery to the British and Foreign Anti-Slavery Society.

[4] Dilke remarked on the retrogression in the treatment of aborigines in *Sixty Years of Empire* (1897) pp. 97–8; and Gooch in *The Heart of the Empire* (1901), p. 328, wrote that it was very doubtful whether Governor Eyre would have been brought to book if he had hanged Gordon in 1901 instead of 1865.

[5] J. Macdonell in *Nineteenth Century* (Feb. 1901). See also *Anti-Slavery Reporter*, 1908, p. 35.

[6] Anti-Slavery Society Papers (deposited in Rhodes House Library, Oxford): Minute Book VI, nos. 632, 755.

wards—their opposition to Crown protection of tribal lands on the Gold Coast, for example. Nevertheless, they kept faith stubbornly, although they were now imperialists of a Forward pattern: "the philanthropic-missionary-civilising pretenders" whom Harcourt suspected.[1] Long since it had become clear that the choice was no longer (as a few like Dandeson Coates[2] had been tempted earlier in the century to believe) between British rule and pristine independence, but between British and foreign rule; and all were now agreed, if not on the sort of rule Britain should give, at least on the evident desirability of British expansion. This was the means of spreading British civilisation among less fortunate peoples as it was also the pre-condition for the suppression of slave raiding, the teaching of the Gospel, and the development of the resources God had bestowed on all.[3] The alliance of Christianity and legitimate commerce was now as evident in the advocacy of Mary Kingsley or E. D. Morel as it had been when Wilberforce and Fowell Buxton had first provided new industrial England with a creed of imperial duty which justified her wealth.[4] Trade was a civilising agency. Chartered companies, like the Royal Niger Company,[5] were, they believed, much better fitted to deal firmly with African slavery than the cumbrously tolerant Foreign Office, but they preferred direct Colonial Office control to both. At the elections of 1895 they had canvassed candidates against the continuance of slavery under Foreign Office protection in Zanzibar and Pemba. They fought against all kinds of forced labour;[6] and sponsored an abortive international Charter for African Labour and Welfare in 1897 and 1900. They protested against discriminating taxation in Sierra Leone in 1895-6, Fiji in 1903 and self-governing Natal in 1907. They resisted brutal duplicity against Lobengula in 1893 and flagrant injustice against Dinizulu in 1908. They called attention to the assault by Rhodes's Glen Grey Act upon Bantu tribal independence, and to im Thurn's attempts to individualise communal land holding in Fiji.[7] They opposed the dissolution of the special Aborigines Protection Board in the West Australian constitution and

---

[1] Gardiner, op. cit. II, 194. Dilke seems to have been an exception, for his imperialism concerned the settled colonies alone and he was opposed to further expansion in the tropics—Uganda, for example. Moreover, Fox Bourne, Secretary of the A.P.S., in a paper on "Natives under British rule" (Anti-Slavery Papers) remained clearly suspicious that the official claims to be spreading Christianity as justification for Government policy in West Africa were a mischievous pretence.

[2] C.H.B.E. VII, pt. II, 67-8.

[3] See Report of the A.P.S. 1896: "The negro races nearly always welcome British rule and cheerfully submit themselves to it when it is just."

[4] Kingsley, Mary, West African Studies (1889), pp. 291-9; Morel, E. D., Affairs of West Africa (1902), pp. 21-2.

[5] Anti-Slavery Reporter (1897), pp. 23, 48, 139; (1900) pp. 21-2.

[6] See Morel's anger at H. S. Grogan's plea for "a good sound system of compulsory labour": op. cit. pp. 178-9.

[7] See also Parl. Pap. 1907, LXXI [Cd. 3763], p. 1073: and Lord Stanmore (Sir A. Gordon) in Hansard, 4th ser. CLXXVIII, 473-83. Chamberlain had approved the preservation of the communal system: Parl. Pap. 1904, LIV [Cd. 2240], p. 439.

the insecurity of the African and coloured franchise in the South Africa Act.[1] They were also, of course, a motive force behind the Campbell-Bannerman protests against "methods of barbarism", and against "Chinese slavery" on the Rand, and behind Lloyd George's denunciation of the pride of Church and laity in bloodshed during the Boer War. In Frederick Lugard, Harry Johnston and Bishop Tucker they had notable allies in the field; and in Mary Kingsley and E. D. Morel critics of experience who, though not out of tune with Chamberlain's aims, were nevertheless ready to contrast with its high claims the meagre welfare and educational services of the Colonial Office and its fitful sense of trusteeship.[2] Perhaps their subtler success in this field was more important in the long run than the few impressive triumphs of agitation and rebellious conscience, of which the C.M.S. appeal and Captain Lugard's agitation for the retention of Uganda,[3] the A.P.S. organisation of Khama's visit to London,[4] and the Congo Reform Association proved them still capable.[5]

These diversities of view about the Empire were an outward manifestation of the social revolution which Britain was entering with quickening pace: adjustments in the relations between employer and employed would affect thinking about ruler and ruled. But in retrospect it is the body of agreement which strikes most forcibly. Men were divided on practical details of policy by shades of opinion or emphasis which cannot accurately be represented in the analysis of the main streams. Should Lord Salisbury be considered an "Imperialist" or a Gladstonian?[6] Why should Asquith be regarded as a Liberal Imperialist and not Campbell-Bannerman? In the group of Radical Imperialists there were those (like Milner and Chamberlain), whose imperialism was greater than their radicalism, those (like Dilke), whose radicalism was the stronger motive, and Lord Rosebery —a Whig rather than a Radical. Indeed, despite party wrangling, there was much common ground between, for example, Balfour, Asquith, Morley and Macdonald. In the years of reconciliation on

[1] These illustrations have been taken from the Minute Books of the Anti-Slavery and Aborigines Protection Societies among the Anti-Slavery Papers. It is interesting that the two Societies on amalgamation found it difficult to decide whether "constitutional and political matters like self-government" lay within their province: A.S.S. Minute Book VII, no. 1650.

[2] Kingsley, *op. cit.* pp. 303–4, 329, 358, 390–1. Morel, *op. cit.* XIII, 162–5, 178–9.

[3] Lugard, F. D., *The Rise of our East African Empire* (1893), II, 534–95. C.M.S. General Committee Minute Book, 11 Oct. 1892, and Oliver, R., *Missionary Factor in East Africa*, pp. 150–62.

[4] *Parl. Pap.* 1896, LIX [C. 7962]. Walker, E. A., *Lord de Villiers and his Times*, p. 263. The enthusiasts in philanthropic circles were successful in preserving British protection over the greater part of Bechuanaland and preventing the surrender of the territory to Rhodes.

[5] Morel, E. D., *The Congo Slave Trade, King Leopold's Rule in Africa*, and *Red Rubber*. Also Cocks, Seymour, *E. D. Morel*.

[6] Though he despised the "jingoes" (cf. Newton, Lord, *Lord Lansdowne*, pp. 156–7), he could speak the language not only of the Consolidationists, but also of the Forwards.

imperial matters, the noisy extremes of the days between the Jameson Raid and the Relief of Mafeking might be seen for what they were: an ostentatious deviation from a norm of sober responsibility towards colonial duty.

AN IMPERIAL ISSUE IN BRITISH POLITICS: SOUTH AFRICA

"Imperial policy", wrote Bernard Shaw in his Fabian apologia for Empire, "will mean South Africa."[1] Throughout this period, from the unbelievable folly of the Raid of 1895 to the singular spectacle of Afrikaner suppression of anti-British rebellion in 1914,[2] South Africa was the focus of empire in British politics, and its challenge was concentrated, severe and decisive. British opinion was thereby submitted to a multiple test: an ordeal which not only pricked the bubble of "jingo" imperialism (which had been largely inflated by South African gold), but left an enduring mark upon the character of the emergent Commonwealth.

The South African problems in 1895 were not new, but they were presented with an interdependence that made them sharper and more exacting. In the first place, most people, whether Afrikaner or British, had realised that there were compelling economic and geographical reasons for some closer political union between the two British colonies and the neighbouring Boer republics; but racial cleavage and ambition were all too strong at that time for the compromise which federal union required. In a period when external events had awakened in Britain a self-conscious, semi-revivalist belief in British methods, the metropolitan Government was brought into direct conflict with an Afrikaner nationalism no less fervent.[3] From its inception on the morrow of Majuba the Afrikaner Bond had advocated the total expulsion of the "English Usurper" from the whole of South Africa,[4] and, though under Hofmeyr it assumed a much less irreconcilable, more constitutional form within the Colony, most British South Africans declared themselves undeceived. Not the least difficulty in the problem, indeed, as it had been in Montreal in 1849,[5] was provided by the attitude of those with a vested interest in "loyalty", who expected to obtain, by invoking imperial arms or royal prerogative, those privileges which they were failing to acquire in the normal channels of constitutional politics. To them and to the jingoes in Britain Kruger's obscurantist despotism, bitterly resentful of the Uitlander within its gates, was a menace to a future British

---

[1] Shaw (ed.), *op. cit.* p. 22.
[2] What his biographer considered the "splendid justification" of Campbell-Bannerman's policy.
[3] On the dour conservatism of the Boer, observers as different as Olive Schreiner and James Bryce were agreed: see Schreiner, *Thoughts on S. Africa* (1923), p. 97, and Bryce, J., *Impressions of S. Africa* (1900), p. 473.
[4] *Milner Papers*, I, 45-6.　　　　　　　　　　[5] *C.H.B.E.* VI, 326.

South Africa[1] which had to be eliminated, first by firm diplomacy, or (if need be) by force. Even those who, like Cecil John Rhodes, conceived of an Anglo-Afrikaner nation were profoundly convinced of the need for Anglo-Saxon leadership. Although men of both races could learn to co-operate, they had no more doubt than Lord Durham that for the good and prosperity of all the stamp of that ultimate nationhood must be vigorously British. Some of Chamberlain's colleagues believed that the only possible predominance would come subtly by immigration and by industrialisation; but, deeply suspicious of the Rand magnates, they had little hope that the path followed in the fulfilment of time would be the same as that of a British Government.[2] Milner and Chamberlain, however, by taking careful provision, sought to secure South Africa in a more permanent British mould.

The presence of the Bantu and Coloured people, forming together more than four-fifths of the population, was a further complication of the plural society problem. Milner believed that he could have solved the "Dutch-English difficulty if it were not so horribly complicated by the native question",[3] for on this burning question nearly all Europeans in South Africa, Britons as well as Afrikaners, were united against the distant authority, even to the point of republican independence.[4] Furthermore, he affirmed to Asquith his anxiety both to improve Anglo-Boer relations and to protect the natives from oppression. "Object No. 2 is", he declared, "the principal obstacle to the attainmen of object No. 1 and always has been." He wanted to preserve the Bechuana and Basuto in their tribal lands from Rhodes and the Bond; he was scandalised by the ill-treatment of the Mashona and Matabele by Rhodes and the British South Africa Company. But imperial intervention would swing "Dutch" opinion on to the side of the Company. "You have therefore this singular situation that you might indeed unite the Dutch and English by protecting the black man, but you would unite them against yourself and your policy of protection." The desire to refrain from exacerbating an already explosive situation neutralised the position of Britain as the protector of native peoples even in Rhodesia where settlers were mainly British and the Charter could be revoked by the British Government. Moreover, the use of a supreme metropolitan authority against a properly constituted colonial government (as in the Cape or Natal) would evoke angry protests, not only in South Africa, but throughout the self-

[1] See Milner, quoted Garvin, *op. cit.* III, 370.
[2] Hicks Beach to Chamberlain: Minute of 29 Sept. 1899: "We can never govern from Downing Street any part of South Africa in which the whites are strong enough to defend themselves against the natives; so that equality of white races in the Transvaal would really secure all we can desire, viz. British predominance"—Chamberlain Papers.
[3] Milner to Asquith, 18 Nov. 1897: *Milner Papers*, I, 177–80.
[4] See Robinson to Chamberlain, 4 Nov. 1895: printed in Garvin, *op. cit.* III, 60.

governing Empire. In the estimation of men like Chamberlain and Rosebery it was vital for the cohesion of the Empire that Britain should uphold the common cause of the British settler in the form of Uitlander claims in face both of Afrikaner truculence and Bantu savagery.[1] There was moreover an international aspect of the South African problem which no British government could afford to ignore. The triumph of Afrikanerdom or of cosmopolitan finance (for only Rhodes and his associates wanted the British flag on the Rand)[2] would introduce an alien sphere of influence south of the Limpopo and thus weaken Britain's position throughout Africa and in the world. The German challenge in South Africa more particularly made strategy (as it had been from the first conquest) a matter of prime importance at the Cape.

The events of these two decades in South African history have been fully narrated elsewhere.[3] What alone seems necessary here is to consider briefly the main issues, sometimes in the light of recent revisions,[4] as they were seen from Britain and thereby to illustrate the conflict of ideas within the crucible from which a new concept of Empire was emerging.

The relentless duel between Rhodes and Kruger, the domestic expression of the South African political conflict, had reached a crisis and given Rhodes his opportunity. By closing the drifts on the Vaal in October 1895, Kruger had united against himself the Free State and colonists, while within the Transvaal his Government was being subjected to mounting criticism, not only from Uitlanders but from many Burghers.[5] Rhodes, on the other hand, seemed to have South Africa at his feet. The speed and ease of the defeat of the Matabele in the war of 1893 had inflated his confidence (and that of Jameson)[6] and had confirmed him in his respect for force. But circumstances now seemed to stress the need for haste and quick returns. Rhodes knew that his own time was short. He learned that Matabeleland was not to prove a second Rand.[7] He was alarmed by Kruger's success in calling Germany into the balance of South Africa against Britain. He conceived the plan of turning the Uitlander case (in which previously he had displayed no interest) to his own account; to take charge of it, to use his money deliberately to foment Uitlander discontent and his diplomacy to promote a rising. Swiftly and

---

[1] *Milner Papers*, I, 178.
[2] Even for Rhodes the matter of the flag was of secondary importance to the Rising. *Parl. Pap.* 1897, IX (311), Q. 290.
[3] *C.H.B.E.* VIII, 552–675.
[4] More particularly the revelations in the Chamberlain Papers published by Miss Ethel Drus in her articles in the *Bull. Inst. Hist. Research*, XXV (May 1952), 33–62, and the *English Hist. Rev.* LXVIII (Oct. 1953), 582–93; and those of the Bower Papers used by Miss Jean van der Poel in *The Jameson Raid* (1953).
[5] van der Poel, *op. cit.* p. 6. See also *C.H.B.E.* VIII, 558.
[6] Colvin, L., *The Life of Jameson*, I, 264.
[7] Hammond, J. H., *Autobiography*, pp. 289 *seqq.*

bloodlessly the Chartered Company police, in waiting on the border, would then enter to prevent the collapse of any interim revolutionary authority. The British Government would then intervene and, together with the President of the Orange Free State and Hofmeyr from the Cape, the High Commissioner would arbitrate and set up an autonomous government in the Transvaal united with the other governments in a customs and railway union which would be a step to a federated British South Africa. In Rhodes's hands "legitimate agitation was converted into a conspiracy".[1]

By 1895 the tension between the Uitlanders and the Transvaal Government had become so dangerous that a revolution, although not certain, seemed probable; and for Rhodes and his fellow conspirators the threat of such a revolt, though not necessarily the rising itself, was deemed more than sufficient. In the ostentatious plotting for "flotation" at Johannesburg much of the plan for a rising ceased to be a guilty secret. The question of the British flag divided the "shareholders", so that they themselves informed Jameson at Pitsani that his intervention was not required. But Jameson believed that he knew best: fortified by the reading of Macaulay's *Clive* and a purposely undated letter from Johannesburg appealing to his chivalry to save the women and children from the Boers, he led a British force from British Bechuanaland into the Transvaal on 29 December 1895 and ignominiously surrendered to the Boer commandos four days later. Rhodes's known disingenuousness[2] and Jameson's impatient confidence had made the conspiracy go off "at half cock". The fiasco of the Raid moreover had many lasting deleterious effects upon the South African problem, but perhaps most regrettable of all, it severed the Rhodes-Hofmeyr alliance and ruined, perhaps for ever, the hopes of white assimilation.[3] But it was not only Jameson's precipitate heroics that were guilty. Even if the rising had taken place first and British intervention could have been represented as a police action to restore order according to Rhodes's plan, the whole plot against the Transvaal would still have been an offence.[4] It is significant that Jameson believed, with some justification in those "jingo" years, that it was only his failure that was unforgivable. But in the condemnation he should not stand alone: those who plotted and those who desired the end such plotting sought to achieve were also guilty.

Chamberlain too, then, must share the censure. "So open"[5] was the preparation in Johannesburg, that there is of course no doubt

---

[1] *C.B.H.E.* VIII, 556–7.
[2] He had once advised another lieutenant of his to "take all you can get and ask me afterwards", Colvin, *op. cit.* I, 203. See Williams, Basil, *Cecil Rhodes*, pp. 151–5.
[3] van der Poel, *op. cit.* pp. 260–1.
[4] The Report of the Select Committee stated that nothing could justify the use of such a force in support of an insurrection in the Transvaal: *Parl. Pap.* 1897, IX (311), p. xvi.
[5] Bryce, *op. cit.* p. 425.

that he, like many others, believed a rising was imminent. More-over, he wanted that insurrection to take place, for it would provide opportunity for British intervention.[1] He had a real sympathy with Uitlander grievance: "no taxation without representation" was a well-tried appeal. He believed the discontent to be genuine; and certainly, even before the Edgar incident in 1898,[2] which gave it substantial working-class support, the agitation was not wholly, though it was predominantly, an artificial affair of capitalist manipu-lation. The interests of British emigrants on foreign soil, however, were officially a matter of foreign policy which could be served only by diplomacy. He made some display of refusing to "know too much".[3] The broad hints and guarded allusions of Rhodes's representatives sought to supply him with information which he refused to accept officially.[4] Recent evidence drives beyond the point of conjecture the suspicion that Chamberlain knew well enough not only of the rising, but also of the plan for armed intervention from outside: that is, he was not blind to the purpose of Jameson's force deployed upon the tactical strip of British Bechuanaland adjoining the Transvaal frontier. Earl Grey, a friend both of Chamberlain and of Rhodes and a Director of the British South Africa Company, had told him.[5] Of course, he had no complicity in the Raid as it took place in the end; even Rhodes was aghast at Jameson's action. But Chamberlain, somewhat cynically forecasting to himself the advantage to be gained and the action to be taken if (as seemed probable) the legally con-stituted government were overcome by Uitlander revolt, had put himself in the position of being accessory before the fact: abetting the plan to overthrow the Government of a State with which the Queen was at peace on the pretext of going to help. With remarkable dispatch he had made over the narrow "railway" strip of territory to the Company and had sanctioned the stationing of the Chartered Company's police at Pitsani out of Crown control.[6] That he knew the rising was being manipulated from outside was, despite Selborne's denial,[7] implicit in Chamberlain's instructions when he saw, in the crisis of the Cleveland ultimatum on the British Guiana boundary, that postponement was prudent: he took it for granted that a dis-creet word to Maguire, one of Rhodes's agents, would ensure that the rising would not take place. The insurrection should, if possible, be postponed for a year or two: if not, it should take place at once.[8] Maguire, however, more optimistic, believing that the movement was now beyond control of the capitalists, cabled Rhodes to "hurry" at the very moment when Rhodes himself was anxious to postpone

[1] Garvin, op. cit. III, 52–3.   [2] C.H.B.E. VIII, 588.
[3] Ibid. p. 83.   [4] Bull. Inst. Hist. Research, xxv (1952), 56.
[5] E.H.R. LXVIII (Oct. 1953), 584.   [6] Ibid. pp. 584–6.
[7] Bull. Inst. Hist. Research, xxv, 41.
[8] Garvin, op. cit. III, 70–3. See also the fuller version of Chamberlain's memo. (12 June 1896) printed in Bull. Inst. Hist. Research, xxv (1952), 46–51.

it because of lack of enthusiasm in Johannesburg and difficulties over the flag.[1] What Fairfield, the Assistant Under Secretary, and Maguire as intermediaries had failed to communicate to Rhodes was Chamberlain's intimation that Rhodes must decide for himself. In fact, influenced by these messages from London, Rhodes did not inform Jameson of the hitch at Johannesburg and confirmed that the rising would take place on the date originally fixed. As had been expected, that rising proved abortive and was finally abandoned. Then after some hesitancy Rhodes tried, as it proved somewhat ineffectively,[2] to halt Jameson. Broken by the knowledge that the invasion was afoot without his signal to move, he remained buoyed up by false hopes that audacity might yet succeed. Knowing his whole federation plan was in the balance and feeling a perverse loyalty to Jameson, he would not immediately repudiate the raiders. He gave them every chance to gain Johannesburg and prepared to blackmail Chamberlain into support. For, egged on by his reckless (and inebriated) moss-troopers, convinced of the omnipotence of the machine-gun, and armed with his sham humanitarian letter, Doctor Jim had decided to make his own "flotation".

It was Chamberlain's behaviour at this juncture which, in contrast to that of Rhodes, persuaded many of his critics of his ignorance of the plot.[3] Before it was known that the Raid would be a fiasco, Chamberlain acted promptly to recall Jameson. "If this succeeds, it will ruin me", he was reported as saying:[4] it is, despite Miss van der Poel, more than a confession of guilty conscience, for it is plain that he did *not* desire Jameson's premature Raid to succeed. While the yet unexposed Johannesburg "Appeal" was being used by the "jingoes" to make Jameson into a popular hero, Chamberlain denounced the Raid sternly both to the Company and to Kruger. When, however, news came of its ignominious end, Jameson became a reckless criminal and Chamberlain a champion of British honour.[5] Then almost immediately the Kaiser's telegram to Kruger restored Jameson to his pedestal. Anger at the Kaiser's intervention and the general desire, conscious and unconscious, that members of the Government and their representatives[6] should be shown to be free from all complicity or foreknowledge blunted the edge of British repudiation of the Raid. In the long run the shielding of Chamberlain and Chamberlain's condoning of Rhodes's "one gigantic mistake"[7] did far more harm than the Raid itself.[8]

---

[1] van der Poel, *op. cit.* pp. 72–4.   [2] *Ibid.* pp. 84, 86, 89 and 92.
[3] Gardiner, *op. cit.* II, 423.   [4] Garvin, *op. cit.* III, 89.
[5] *Ibid.* p. 92. See also *History of 'The Times'*, III, 211–12.
[6] There can no longer be any doubt that the High Commissioner, Sir Hercules Robinson, knew of the plot, though he detested the whole thing and remained "officially" ignorant: van der Poel, *op. cit.* p. 37.
[7] *Hansard*, 4th ser. LI, 1172. Beatrice Webb thought this defence sprang from a sense of "defiant loyalty", *op. cit.* p. 197.
[8] van der Poel, *op. cit.* p. 262.

That there must be an inquiry was obvious, but more than a year passed before the Committee was appointed. During that time Chamberlain had been able to narrow the crime by carefully distinguishing between the rising and the raid, to excuse the Pitsani force as innocently prudent and valuable "as a firebrigade",[1] and to ensure that the inquisition should not be very penetrating. "We have, I think," said Meade, the Permanent Under-Secretary, "made the china safe from our mad bull."[2] In a climate of blackmail and counterbluff Chamberlain threatened to cancel the Company's charter if the Government were implicated in their evidence, while Rhodes was ready to save the Charter by the sacrifice of his most formidable weapons, including "the missing cables":[3] the only doubt was whether his promise would withstand the heat and wounds of cross-examination. As it happened, Chamberlain himself had no wish to dissolve the Company, regarding it as the best and speediest instrument for developing Rhodesia.[4] This weakened his bluff. But his own position and that of the High Commissioner were secured as firmly as possible against incrimination in the sacrifice of official scapegoats (including Bower, the Imperial Secretary) who were prepared "to lie in state" convinced that the peace both of South Africa and of Europe would be involved in exposure.[5]

By their ineptitude and circumspection the Select Committee contributed to the conspiracy of silence. Although he kept his word, Rhodes, emboldened by public enthusiasm for his heroism against the Matabele, was unrepentant and contemptuous of the Committee.[6] Those who, like Harcourt and Campbell-Bannerman, sincerely desired justice to be done were hampered by a desire no less strong that, for Britain's future reputation, the verdict should exonerate the Colonial Office.[7] Again, though evidence would now appear to discount it, they had some cause to suspect that both Rosebery and Ripon were not guiltless of foreknowledge.[8] Moreover, both believed in Chamberlain's ignorance and considered it as sufficient victory that Rhodes and Jameson should in the final report be so decisively condemned for duplicity and breach of duty. As they expected, Chamberlain himself was cleared;[9] but, by then appearing to condone Rhodes's crime, Chamberlain torpedoed their plan for undoing

---

[1] *Hansard*, 4th ser. xxxvii, 282 *seqq.*, 362 *seqq.*   [2] van der Poel, *op. cit.* p. 199.

[3] Garvin, *op. cit.* iii, 113. On the suppression of the missing telegrams see *ibid.* p. 125 and van der Poel, *op. cit.* pp. 158, 187, 199.

[4] Chamberlain to Lord Grey, 13 Oct. 1896: quoted in *Bull. Inst. Hist. Research*, xxv, 55.

[5] van der Poel, *op. cit.* pp. 161–3, 194–5, 231.

[6] *Ibid.* p. 206. Some of his supporters, including Stead and Flora Shaw, tried to persuade him to deliver a monster "public confession" in the Albert Hall (Esher, *Journals and Letters*, i, 195 *seqq.*) See also van der Poel, *op. cit.* p. 206.

[7] Spender, *op. cit.* i, 195–7. Gardiner, *op. cit.* ii, 423–32.

[8] See E. Drus in *E.H.R.* lxvii, 590–3.

[9] See the general approval of his actions in *Hansard*, 4th ser. xxxvii, 304 and Report in *Parl. Pap.* 1897, ix (311), pp. xii–xvi.

the mischief of the Raid. Repeated efforts in Parliament revealed nothing but a suspicious dissatisfaction at the lax probing of the Committee.[1] Rhodes emerged less as culprit than as victor. In the condition of armed peace in South Africa the absence of vigorous censure was regarded by many[2] as an aggravation likely to lead to conflict.

That conflict was irrepressible, but it might still have been resolved without appeal to arms. The political fragments of Rhodes's federated South Africa had (temporarily at least) been scattered, but some *modus vivendi* might yet be found where economic pressures were so certainly postulating interdependence. Though the real issues lay deeper, the crux of the matter seemed to lie in Uitlander grievances. Unfortunately the problem of the powerful industrialist and speculator in the midst of conservative agrarian society required more sympathy than it was likely to get in that period.[3] Rhodes, "undaunted and unbroken...but also untaught",[4] was still capable of shipwrecking both his own dream and the permanent interest of Britain. Kruger, the more deeply distrustful of British policy since the Raid and seeing in the Uitlander franchise the betrayal of his own country to informal annexation by Britain, was now less ready to make concessions and was arming heavily. It was true that the Transvaal Government had shown considerable generosity towards the raiders; but Kruger had declined in the end to visit Britain in order to negotiate a new treaty in place of the London Convention of 1884.[5] For a time Chamberlain seemed prepared to wait for reforms, while both miners and magnates complained of increasing disabilities. A display of armed force, on the other hand, in March 1897, produced immediate results.[6] Chamberlain was thereby encouraged in his belief with Jameson that "Kruger would not look into the mouth of a cannon" to pursue that policy of bluff which in the opinion of his opponents led inevitably to war.[7] Although he underestimated the military strength of the Transvaal, Chamberlain nevertheless wanted to avoid war unless "upon the utmost and

[1] Debates took place in Oct. 1899, Jan. 1900 and March 1901.
[2] Even an "imperialist" like Asquith, see Spender and Asquith, *op. cit.* I, 129–31.
[3] Balfour pointed out with sympathy the difficulty of an "unparalleled" situation. The Boers might well describe a conversion of the franchise not as "electoral reform" but as a "transfer of nationality". "No doubt the Boers are engaged in fighting a hopeless cause. The S.A.R. may not last for ever, but it cannot for very long be a Boer Republic.... Were I a Boer brought up in Boer traditions, nothing but necessity would induce me to adopt a constitution which would turn my country into an English Republic or a system of education which would reduce my language to the *patois* of a small and helpless minority." Balfour's minute on Chamberlain's dispatch, 1 May 1899: "Chamberlain Papers."
[4] *Milner Papers*, I, 106.
[5] Correspondence in *Parl. Pap.* 1896, LIX [C. 7933], p. 51; [C. 8063], p. 8; 1897, LXII [C. 8423], pp. 15 *seqq.*
[6] *C.H.B.E.* VIII, 576.
[7] Spender and Asquith, *op. cit.* I, 132; Spender, *op. cit.* I, 231, 256.

clearest provocation".[1] Knowing that, despite "jingo" boasting, a war for the Uitlander franchise alone would not be tolerated by the Cabinet and would not long be popular with the public, he sought to build up pressure against the Transvaal until the cracks appeared from within. He was disappointed. Not only was Kruger re-elected as President in February 1898, but seven months later, in the Cape, Rhodes's Progressive party suffered defeat at the hands of the Moderates and the Bond. For those who, like Chamberlain and the new High Commissioner, Sir Alfred Milner, believed (as Lord Durham had in 1839) that friction could only finally be removed by the rule of a Government inspired by *British* ideals, a crisis had arrived. "The great game...for the mastery of South Africa" was afoot.[2]

Milner had clearly been entrusted with the mission of upholding the supremacy of Britain, if not her suzerainty, in South Africa; for on the value of Britain to the world he had never any doubt.[3] Since his appointment in April 1897 he had been studying the position and avoiding giving offence to the Transvaal.[4] Now he took alarm. Assuming war to be unavoidable, he became in effect the leader of the British party in the Cape and sought by accumulation of evidence to bring matters to a head.[5] Nor, egged on by the press, did he lack material for producing an "overwhelming" case for intervention.[6] The mutual suspicions of miners and capitalists on the Rand had been stressed by Kruger's attempt to appease the magnates, by the blunder of the Edgar incident and by the exposure of the Leyds-Lippert negotiations; but the failure of the Bloemfontein Conference had given their grievances a new unity.[7] Milner was not guiltless of creating that common front; for by breaking off the discussions precipitately he was largely (though excusably) responsible for their failure.[8] The second petition of the Uitlanders in May 1899 gave him, skilled ex-journalist as he was, opportunity to plead an impassioned case in his "helot" dispatch: the duty of Great Britain to secure redress for her defenceless subjects. It prompted Chamberlain to pledge Government protection for the Uitlanders, and to affirm British paramountcy.[9] After the deadlock at Bloemfontein the stirring

---

[1] *Milner Papers*, I, 227. Bower, however, thought he had evidence which suggested that Chamberlain was "stoking up for war" as early as 1896: Bower, G., *Reminiscences*, pp. 315 *seqq.*; van der Poel, *op. cit.* pp. 148, 160, 183.

[2] *Milner Papers*, I, 267; II, 37.

[3] Halpérin, V., *Lord Milner and the Empire*, p. 90.

[4] For example, even on the matter of the suzerainty preamble of the 1881 convention: see Chamberlain's dispatch, *Parl. Pap.* 1899, LXIV [C. 9507], p. 28, in which Milner had a reluctant but acquiescent hand in drafting: *Milner Papers*, I, 299–300.

[5] Garvin, *op. cit.* III, 392.

[6] Lord Harris denied, however, that the South African Republic represented "a crushing tyranny": 20 Nov. 1898, "Chamberlain Papers".

[7] *Parl. Pap.* 1899, LXIV [C. 9345], pp. 203 *seqq.*, 226; [C. 9404], pp. 14, 15. See also *C.H.B.E.* VIII, 588–93.

[8] Garvin, *op. cit.* III, 408 *seqq.* See also *Milner Papers*, I, 423.

[9] *Parl. Pap.* 1899, LXIV [C. 9415], pp. 14, 26.

appeal was passed on to the public, for whom it had clearly been penned. Throughout three months of crisis while Chamberlain insisted upon British participation in any Uitlander solution, and Milner, wary of evasions in Kruger's time-serving concessions, knew himself to be without the military force which Chamberlain's policy required,[1] the public was whipped up into such an *animus* that Kruger's ultimatum when it came, phrased in such a way that no British Government could honourably comply and dispatched only when the spring rains had begun to renew the veld grass, was greeted wildly as the chance "to revenge Majuba".

If Chamberlain's hand had been called, he had nevertheless by his skilful display of patience carried both Cabinet and public finally with him. Only a few months before, the time had been considered not yet ripe.[2] If Pretoria was deeply impressed by the mistaken belief that the swaggering of Fleet Street represented official British opinion, the British Government itself was still largely indifferent to the mob clamour. The Prime Minister had no enthusiasm for a fight on behalf of those whom he thoroughly despised; and both the Leader of the House and the Chancellor of the Exchequer were emphatic in their denial of Uitlander grievances as constituting anything like a *casus belli*. Britain had a right to ask for concessions; but, asked Balfour, "had redress of a like character... ever been forced upon one nation by another at the point of the bayonet?... It is a side which Sir Alfred Milner has somewhat ignored."[3] Hicks Beach, fresh from a successful call of characteristic "Rhodesian" bluff,[4] fought a persistent rearguard action against Milner's headstrong impatience and Chamberlain's increasing demands.[5] Milner himself summed up Chamberlain's difficulty well: "ultimatum has always", he cabled, "been great difficulty, as unless we widen issue, there is not sufficient cause for war, and if we do so, we are abused for shifting our ground and extending our demands."[6] Against his will and intention Lord Salisbury surrendered to Chamberlain's importunity in mid-September to make the break, not on the Uitlander franchise issue alone, but on the revision of the British claims to paramountcy and intervention under the Conventions of 1881 and 1884.[7]

[1] On Chamberlain's part in the want of military preparation, see Halévy, *op. cit.* v, 82, and Walker, E. A., *A History of South Africa*, p. 482.

[2] *Queen Victoria's Letters*, iii, 3: Journal, 18 June 1899. See also *Milner Papers*, i, 431. Over 53,000 signatures were secured to a National Memorial against war as late as October.

[3] Balfour's minute on 1 May dispatch: "Chamberlain Papers."

[4] Hicks Beach, *op. cit.* ii, 76–85. Rhodes had tried to get a Government guarantee but refused a loan.

[5] *Ibid.* ii, 102–5. Earlier, too, he had preached on the same need for patience: *Milner Papers*, i, 33.

[6] Milner's telegram, 29 Sept. 1899: "Chamberlain Papers" (a sentence not printed in *Milner Papers*, i, 552).

[7] *C.H.B.E.* viii, 594–8. See Salisbury's protest against Chamberlain's misuse of his words, 5 Sept. 1899, "Chamberlain Papers" (a part only is printed in Garvin, *op. cit.* iii, 440).

Milner, ever the "soul of directness",[1] found Government diplomacy too dilatory and "quite flabby"[2] and, here as later, having once sincerely made up his mind, was prepared to "damn the consequences". But Chamberlain was more shrewdly calculating: he could afford to wait until the right moment. Neither Harcourt in August 1898 nor Campbell-Bannerman in June 1899 was prepared to respond to Chamberlain's appeal for a "bi-partisan" approach and thereby to countenance his provocative diplomacy. They both cautioned Chamberlain against reliance on prejudiced misinformation from Cape Town or Park Lane and uttered warnings against the dangers of underestimating Kruger.[3] But Chamberlain no less than Milner saw that the stakes to be won were high: the chance of a British South African federation based upon Cape Colony instead of a Boer federation based upon the Transvaal. Nothing less than intervention could have saved Southern Africa for the British Crown.[4] While he too felt the Uitlanders were hardly worth the sacrifices demanded,[5] he believed that wider imperial and foreign issues were involved. He knew that other self-governing colonies were watching Britain critically on the vital matter of racial equality.[6] Moreover, he was convinced that the Boers were rushing headlong to their ruin. Though till the last he sought settlement by other means than arms, it was not suprising in these circumstances of facile confidence among Boers as well as British[7] that armed conflict should be the final arbiter.

When war came it released finally the full flood of "jingo" frenzy.[8] For the moment it restored to the Government a unity and popularity which the mounting disasters of the first campaigns as soon again dispelled; and for much longer it divided and disappointed the Liberals who by nature were "an unruly tribe", particularly in opposition.[9] On one point alone were they united: all denounced the bungling and bullying of the Secretary of State;[10] not all found blame for the seemingly more bellicose High Commissioner. Though he had some sympathy for both Chamberlain and Milner as old colleagues, Harcourt was constrained to hold them as "pattern jingoes", responsible for the war and for those undignified excesses which were a "negation of the British spirit".[11] His reasoned case, however, was too moderate for Henry Labouchere or Lloyd George.

---

[1] Lord Brand in *The Listener*, L, no. 1285 (1953), p. 631.
[2] *C.H.B.E.* VIII, 594.
[3] Gardiner, *op. cit.* II, 461–4, 499–500, 514; and Spender, *op. cit.* II, 234, 256.
[4] Garvin, *op. cit.* III, 458, 520.
[5] *Ibid.* p. 521. In a letter to Fairfield, 8 April 1896, Chamberlain had written that the Uitlander grievances did not provide a *casus belli*, "even if Kruger definitely refuses our invitations and declines to make any changes in his precious constitution", "Chamberlain Papers."
[6] Garvin, *op. cit.* III, p. 416.
[7] *Ibid.* pp. 468, 479–81. See also Chamberlain's letter to Fairfield quoted above.
[8] See, for example, Stewart, W., *op. cit.* p. 147, and Gooch, *loc. cit.* pp. 206–39.
[9] Spender, *op. cit.* I, 308, 315.   [10] Garvin, *op. cit.* III, 482.
[11] Gardiner, *op. cit.* II, 392, 461, 471, 498, 524, 597.

These pro-Boers saw the struggle in fairy tale terms similar to those of the "jingoes": of orphan children being threatened and enslaved by a monstrous giant. Campbell-Bannerman, to whom the "uneasy throne" of Liberal leadership had descended, believed that war had become inevitable and it must be prosecuted with energy and good faith. In the interest of the ultimate settlement the "equities" should not be lost sight of. The war of itself would settle nothing: neither Chamberlain nor Milner would seem to have the tolerance upon which racial harmony could alone be erected.[1] Boer and Briton would still have to build together some wider union. The English emigrant did not settle on the veld and the Afrikaner did not concern himself with business or industry. Though Asquith to his right and Labouchere to the left within his party advocated Boer independence, Campbell-Bannerman joined forces with Government spokesmen in urging the annexation of the Transvaal; but it was an annexation not like Lord Salisbury's, which would deprive the Republics of "every shred" of independent self-government, or like Chamberlain's, which demanded unconditional surrender and a period of "proving" under direct rule before the grant of responsible government, but one which, by generously granting those institutions, would secure the good will of new fellow subjects, just as that of French Canadians under Sir Wilfred Laurier would seem to have been won.[2] By masterly inactivity through prolonged hostilities which tried Liberals to the uttermost, Campbell-Bannerman remained nevertheless the link between the Radicals and the "Lib. Imps.".

The Liberal Imperialists, distrusting the extravagant war-fever,[3] remained (largely through Asquith) loyal to "C.-B." despite their personal attachment to the errant Rosebery and their faith in the infallible Milner.[4] The inefficiency of the War Office was naturally their chief target: a "free federated self-governing South African dominion" moulded by Milner was their goal.[5] Hopes of their collectivism and respect for their intellect and energy gave them Fabian support for a period, though at the expense of a Fabian schism which thrust Ramsay Macdonald over to the ranks of the Independent Labour Party in opposition to an obvious "capitalist war".[6] The general public, bewildered by disaster and angry with both Government and Opposition, made no nice distinction between shades of Liberal opinion. Nor did Chamberlain, organiser and only victor of the Khaki election of October 1900, determined as he was to

---

[1] Spender, *op. cit.* I, 260, 281 ff., 298, 323; II, 38, 87, 134, 401.
[2] *Ibid.* I, 250, *seqq.* 279–83.
[3] Trevelyan, G. M., *Grey of Fallodon*, p. 77.
[4] *Ibid.* pp. 76, 78–80; Spender, *op. cit.* I, 264, 300–2, 332; II, 16. Rosebery did not share their belief in Milner's infallibility.
[5] Spender and Asquith, *op. cit.* I, 140.
[6] Stewart, *op. cit.* p. 151: Webb, B., *op. cit.* pp. 109, 188, 219–20, 227. The peak of Fabian support was between June 1901 and May 1902. They admired Chamberlain and had links with his daughter (and with the *Daily Mail*), *ibid.* pp. 124, 196, 284.

"roast pro-Boer and anti-Boer Liberals together": "every seat won by the Liberals was a seat won by the Boers". But already the tide of public feeling had begun to turn.[1] The realisation that (despite electioneering assurances that the war was over) hostilities must be prolonged into dispiriting guerrilla warfare, and the effective appeal to humanitarian sentiment over the condition of the concentration camps, were combining to set the flood finally against "jingo" imperialism.

For himself Chamberlain had few regrets at the passing of a mood he had often found embarrassing, but the war had stimulated anew his dreams of imperial consolidation. The demonstration, in Britain's isolation, of a common interest and duty by the self-governing colonies and India had, it seemed to him, kindled British maternal pride and prompted her victory. Against the superciliousness of the War Office he had fought for colonial aid and it had been given, contingent after contingent, to an extent where it out-numbered the British Army at Waterloo. The Boer War was wildly popular in Australasia and volunteers exceeded requirements. But, although Chamberlain saw in the bonds of common bloodshed that *Kriegsverein* which would be the first step to a permanent closer political union, the difficulty experienced in getting the first Canadian detachment was symptomatic of a contrary impulse. Laurier had wanted to prove that Canada need not formally participate in a British war; but Chamberlain would not accept Canadian volunteers unless they were a demonstration of the support of the Canadian Government.[2] The proving of Dominion virtue and nationhood in war stressed that confident self-dependence which would effectively disappoint Chamberlain's hopes. It was an impulse for which Gladstonians like Campbell-Bannerman would have more sympathy.[3]

It was the question of the concentration camps which divided Campbell-Bannerman temporarily from the "Lib. Imps." and united him irrevocably with the pro-Boers. Asquith, Haldane and Grey were prepared to accept the camps and the scorched earth policy as military necessities: Campbell-Bannerman, though anxious to avoid criticism of the soldiers who carried out commands, was compelled to denounce "methods of barbarism" which were not only ruthless but impolitic.[4] In the presence of a horde of Bantu spectators the belligerents had fought stubbornly but not savagely.[5] But devastation would serve only to embitter and prolong the war; "military necessity" might be politically unwise. Following the lead

---

[1] The election failed to recover more than three seats; and for every eight votes cast for Chamberlain's policy, seven were given against it.

[2] Many French Canadians had a feeling of kinship with the Boers and Laurier's offer of contingents to Britain caused a split in his cabinet. See Garvin, *op. cit.* p. 532.

[3] Garvin, *op. cit.* III, 529, 544; Amery, *Joseph Chamberlain*, IV, 47.

[4] Spender and Asquith, *op. cit.* I, 138, 335–6.

[5] See Halévy, *op. cit.* V, 91–3.

of Emily Hobhouse, the national conscience must revolt against the appalling mortality in overcrowded camps. His courageous stand against inhumanity, as General Botha said later, made peace and union possible.[1] It gave the defeated Boers faith in Liberal promises and paved the way for those terms at Vereeniging which "brave men could accept without humiliation".[2] Kitchener's prophecy that a Liberal administration committed to granting self-government would soon be in power made the Boer leaders resolve to sign those terms, submitting to a treaty, but not to a dictated peace.[3]

Milner had opposed Kitchener's policy of farm-burning which, while of doubtful military value, was making his own task of re-construction more difficult; and with the aid of Anglo-Indian officials and ladies' committees, and with substantial grants from the British Treasury, he had been able to reduce mortality in the camps which were consequent upon that policy. But, even although his friends the "Lib. Imps.", following Rosebery's lead, were no longer prepared to hold out for unconditional surrender,[4] Milner still desired nothing less. The complete subjugation of the Boers was essential to his future policy, and he wrung his hands over Kitchener's generous concessions which he knew would hamper him.[5] He believed that he could unite the colonies by firm leadership, as Lord Sydenham united the two Canadas in 1840, and could stamp a permanent British character on the final settlement. So, under Chamberlain's displeasure, he desired the suspension of the Cape constitution as a means of buttressing his own authority with a Progressive majority.[6] So too he urged the need for British immigration and land settlement, not necessarily for the impossible end of swamping the Boer popula-tion, but for the communication of British initiative to administra-tive and agricultural methods.[7] In both he was disappointed. Chamberlain, realising the jealousy of Australia and Canada over any extinction of self-government, could not permit any tampering with the Cape constitution,[8] and British emigrants showed little disposition to settle in large numbers upon the land or to work for low wages with Africans in the mines. Milner had to face the period of reconstruction without either the authority or the population he required.

Long before the skirmishing was over, he had prepared, and recruited his "kindergarten",[9] for the post-war problems. These were such as called forth to the uttermost his talent for administration; for however tactless and forthright he was as a diplomat, Milner was

---

[1] Spender, *op. cit.* I, 351; II, 2, 40–1.   [2] Gooch, quoted Halpérin, *op. cit.* p. 122.
[3] Millin, S. G., *General Smuts*, I, 182–3.   [4] Spender, *op. cit.* I, 319; II, 11.
[5] *Milner Papers*, II, 211, 337.   [6] *Parl. Pap.* 1902, LXIX [Cd. 1162], p. 425.
[7] *Parl. Pap.* 1902, LXIX [Cd. 1163], pp. 37, 88, 126; 1903, XLV [C. 1551], p. 37.
[8] Amery, J., *op. cit.* IV, 114–15.
[9] Halpérin, *op. cit.* pp. 198–220. The group included Patrick Duncan, Basil Williams, Geoffrey Dawson, R. H. Brand, Philip Kerr, John Buchan and Lionel Curtis.

without doubt a great administrator. The unsuccessful exponent of a militant imperialism which so soon became old-fashioned, he was one of the chief architects of a pacific and constructive imperialism which held promise for the future. The work of decades, compressed into little more than three years, endured, withstanding the risk, and smoothing the course, of further concession by the Liberal government in 1906–7. The construction of "nation-building" railways and roads, repatriation and relief, education, and municipal government were pressed with imagination and vigour.[1] By land settlement, irrigation, drainage and afforestation he sought to save the burgher from dependence upon the middleman and South African economy from tyranny by the Rand. But he knew that the mines were, nevertheless, the key to prosperity, and labour in the mines was the crux of reconstruction. The wealth of the Rand must be the means of raising the standards of life and civilisation, and, by that "lift", of stimulating the economic life of the country towards a permanent organic union under the British Crown.[2] When European labour did not materialise and African labour melted away, Milner turned reluctantly, but firmly, with the support of miners and capitalists, towards the temporary experiment of Chinese indentured labour to save the Rand.[3] But he misjudged (as did Balfour) the temper of the electorate in Britain; and Campbell-Bannerman, with the "Lib. Imps." who were now re-united under his leadership[4] by a common opposition to Tariff Reform, was able again to rouse the humanitarian conscience, to stir up working-class resentment against the use of labour as a servile commodity and to rally Liberal protest in an overwhelming victory against Conservative policy in South Africa.

There was, of course, a characteristic myopia about the humanitarian outcry: just as it was West Indian, not East Indian, slavery which had prompted the enthusiasms of 1833, so it was "Chinese slavery" on the Rand, not African "slavery" at Kimberley, which now moved public opinion. Continuous protests about the condition of African employment had been largely disregarded;[5] but the "beastlike" segregation of the Chinese from the rest of the South African community and the abuse of their manhood as a mere tool to be worn out and cast off by the mine owners, struck the public imagination. Though there is little doubt that the Colonial Office had accepted it as an unwelcome necessity or that in fact it made no

[1] Halpérin, op. cit. pp. 124–53; Amery, L. S., My Political Life, I, 174 seqq.; Buchan, John, Memory-Hold-The-Door, pp. 103–15.
[2] Times History of the War in South Africa, VI, 19, 48–9, 169.
[3] Parl. Pap. 1904, XXXIX [Cd. 1896], pp. 29 seqq.
[4] Haldane alone among them abstained from the vote against Milner's policy on Chinese labour.
[5] Alert to watch "the capitalists' desire to exploit native labour after the war", objectors made protests in November 1900 (A.S.R. 1901, p. 112). The Chinese Labour Ordinance was denounced immediately for its "precipitate haste" and for its creation of a new race of "helots" (A.S.R. 1904, pp. 3–4, 86, 140).

small contribution to South African prosperity,[1] it is not surprising that it brought down nemesis upon the Balfour administration. The cry against "Chinese slavery" was not merely Liberal electioneering or misrepresentation.[2] Chamberlain,[3] the Trade Unions,[4] self-governing colonies in Australia, New Zealand and Cape Colony had all opposed the experiment. It was repugnant, they thought, to those standards of liberty, labour and humanity for which the Empire must stand. The moral conscience of the public, now returned to duty after the disillusionments of an imperialist war, revolted against the creation of a vicious tyranny. It was doubtful even in the Transvaal whether the majority of those about to be given representative government would now, on second thoughts, continue the policy.

The Balfour government had made a move towards those "representative institutions leading up to self-government" promised at Vereeniging. Both Milner and Chamberlain's successor, Alfred Lyttelton, had come independently to the conclusion that autocratic government must be tempered by a grant of representation: good government, supported by imperial loans and public works, could no more there than in the Canada of the 1840's stifle demands for self-government. But the constitution they proposed envisaged a preparatory stage to prevent power falling into the hands of an irreconcilable Afrikaner party. This concession, however skilfully designed to forestall reckless Liberal measures,[5] fell short of the full responsible government which the Boers and many British South Africans demanded. Moreover, the announcement of the Lyttelton constitution itself led to the formation of parties on linguistic lines. Finally, despite Lyttelton's suspicions that the Liberals would avoid their promises on the ending of Chinese labour by a rash grant of self-government, the fall of the Balfour government was followed forthwith by the fulfilment of both pledges: the annulment of the intermediate constitution and the stoppage of all further licences to import Chinese labourers.

Legal difficulties prevented the immediate dramatic repatriation of Chinese labourers already in the Transvaal as "C.-B." had wanted;[6] but General Botha, placed in power under the new constitution, secured in 1907 an imperial loan which freed him from dependence upon the Rand magnates and refused to re-enact the

---

[1] ' The Times' History of the War in South Africa, VI, 111–28; Halpérin, op. cit. p. 143.

[2] Contrast Ensor, R. C. K., England 1870–1914, pp. 376–7, with Amery, L. S., in the History of 'The Times', VI, 125. "C.-B." never pretended that Liberal administrations in the past had been clean-handed about indentured immigrant labour: see C.-B.'s protests, long before an election seemed likely, in Spender, op. cit. II, 144–6.

[3] Amery, J., Joseph Chamberlain, IV, 329–35. Asquith, Margot, Autobiography, II, 65, noted Milner's pleasure in contrasting Lyttelton's backing with Chamberlain's opposition.

[4] Milner Papers, II, 520–30. Spender, op. cit. II, 169. Parl. Pap. 1905, LV [Cd. 2400], [Cd. 2479], pp. 175, 623.

[5] Milner Papers, II, 521.   [6] Spender, op. cit. II, 228–32.

Labour Ordinance, so that the Chinese departed on the expiry of their contracts.[1] It was a vindication of Campbell-Bannerman's belief that security lay in trust, not in coercion.[2] Moreover, the Botha administration had obtained power with the aid of a considerable number of British votes: a proof that the pro-Boers had been right in believing that the Progressives did not exclusively represent British opinion in the new colony.[3]

The Empire had confused the Liberals for a time; but paradoxically it made a contribution finally to their reunion: defence of Free Trade and adherence to Home Rule had meant a return (hastened by the struggle over the Education and Licensing Acts) to regenerate Gladstonian liberalism under Campbell-Bannerman. Moreover, they had now acquired both the party organisation and financial backing on which they might win an election and realise a Liberal policy. The new Prime Minister had always believed that the public would demand a Liberalism that looked like Liberalism, not a hybrid like that of the "Lib. Imps." which aped Conservatism. He was proved right as far as domestic affairs were concerned.[4] It was Lord Rosebery in the end, and not Campbell-Bannerman, who was isolated. Everywhere the self-styled "Imperialists" had been marooned by the new tide of public opinion which had tired of excessive arrogance. In a period of evident prosperity Chamberlain had lost touch with the electorate and their demand for social, not tariff, reform. To prevent schism Balfour had belatedly accepted the principle of fairer competition for British trade; but his policy, the first step back to Huskisson's Reciprocity and Preference, was "Tariff Reform without conviction", and, full of "balfourian sophistry", was dismissed by Campbell-Bannerman, with fairly general approval, as a waste of time of the House. "Enough", he said, "of this foolery."[5]

The grant of responsible government to the Afrikaner and British population of the Transvaal, and—more boldly—to the almost wholly Afrikaner population of the Orange River Colony, was Campbell-Bannerman's act of faith. Like Grenville on the morrow of American independence, he was persuaded that for future good relations it was "true policy" to yield gracefully to demand rather than to have the gift forced from his hand.[6] He carried his Cabinet with him. Lord Selborne, Milner's successor, was instructed to work, not for British supremacy, but for racial harmony, in a South African union for which the period of responsible government was the penultimate step.[7]

---

[1] Parl. Pap. 1906, LXX [Cd. 2788], pp. 2–9.
[2] Spender, op. cit. II, 237.   [3] Halévy, op. cit. VI, 34.
[4] In the sphere of foreign policy of course the "Lib. Imps." triumphed over the Radicals and Gladstonians: witness the threatened schism in the Cabinet and the resignations of August 1914.
[5] Hansard, 12 March 1906, 4th ser. CLIII, 991–2.
[6] Grenville to Dorchester, 20 Oct. 1789 (Secret); see Kennedy, W. P. M., Statutes, Treaties and Documents of the Canadian Constitution, 2nd ed. p. 184.
[7] Spender, op. cit. II, 237–40.

The Labour leaders and the Fabians favoured this generosity, though some were already anxious about safeguards against forced labour.[1] The Conservatives opposed the measure strongly for other reasons, Balfour and Milner denouncing it as a "dangerous, audacious and reckless experiment" which was casting away the advantage of hard-earned victory; and it was somewhat fortunate for Campbell-Bannerman that he could use the prerogative instrument of Letters Patent to effect this change of policy, for it is clear that a statute could not have withstood the obstruction of the Lords. But the resolution of the Commons approving the Letters Patent some months later was unanimous; and in general the public and the newspapers (including the Unionist press) accepted the measure as wise and well-considered.[2] So indeed it was to prove so long as there were men like Botha and Smuts prepared to respond to the gesture.

Justice to Afrikaner and British aspirations in South Africa of course served, by removing imperial control, only to aggravate the difficulty of any solution to the native problem: this had been a factor in precipitating the South African War.[3] The public was taught that the Boers were ill-treating Africans and Coloureds with "actual brutality",[4] while it remained largely unaware of the abuse of the Matabele and Mashona by the Company in Rhodesia. Within Bechuanaland and Basutoland Milner had been able by his own authority to preserve the natives from the "tender mercies" of Rhodes and the Bond, but both he and Chamberlain had pressed ineffectually for reform in the Transvaal with damaging result to British prestige as a protector of native peoples.[5] Here, too, British victory in arms was no solution for a complex social problem which required a change of heart. British humanitarian hopes were frustrated by South African prejudice, British and Afrikaner. The Anti-Slavery and Aborigines Protection Societies had in November 1900 approached Chamberlain with their views on the treatment of the native races, asking for a comprehensive declaration of civil and legal equality between Europeans and non-Europeans, and for the abolition of all forced labour. Chamberlain was not alone in thinking that some form of forced labour by Africans in the mines was a necessary condition of prosperity not only for South Africa but for themselves.[6] Lord Milner believed that it was bad administration rather than injustice

---

[1] Dilke attacked the Government for accepting a political colour-bar.

[2] *Hansard*, 31 July 1906, 4th ser. CLXII, 611 *seqq.*; 17 Dec. 1906, CLXII, 939 *seqq.*, 1063 *seqq.* Spender, *op. cit.* II, 243 *seqq.*

[3] *Parl. Pap.* 1901, XLVIII [Cd. 714], p. 1. See also *Parl. Pap.* 1902, LXIX [Cd. 821], [Cd. 822], [C. 888], pp. 475, 481, 485. Chamberlain spoke of the need for the establishment of British supremacy as a method of securing justice for the Africans. *Hansard*, 5 Feb. 1900, 4th ser. LXXVIII, 590 *seqq.*

[4] See Minute Book VI, nos. 928–1038 *passim*: "Anti-Slavery Papers".

[5] *Milner Papers*, I, 177–82, 195.

[6] Amery, J., *op. cit.* IV, 73. Chamberlain had little sympathy with "Exeter Hallery" (Garvin, *op. cit.* III, 22) and was particularly dilatory in answering Anti-Slavery Society letters (A.S.S. Minute Book VI, no. 1038).

that had made the pass laws of the Transvaal oppressive, and considered that it would be unwise for an autocratic government to press on with a more liberal native policy, irrespective of South African sentiment. He was content to hope for a growing recognition by South Africans of their duty to the African peoples of the area.[1] "Equal rights for every civilised man south of the Zambesi", which Rhodes had recently and somewhat belatedly made a slogan, was, possibly even by design, an ambiguous one;[2] but at least it gave humanitarian opinion some hope that the barriers between colour might one day be broken down. That was their ultimate desire, the identification of European and African interests; but for the moment most of them preferred some temporary form of segregation under an imperial control which would progressively reduce the protecting walls until full assimilation could take place without prejudice or exploitation.

Kitchener's terms at Vereeniging had bound the Imperial Government not to enfranchise the Africans until after the introduction of self-government; but when that self-government was given, the Imperial Government had thereby forfeited its right to intervene. Lord Milner came bitterly to regret this concession to Boer prejudice as the greatest mistake he had ever made.[3] Meanwhile, though the prospect of federation made a common South African approach to the African problem essential,[4] the colonies continued to pursue different policies through different instruments. The Glen Grey Act had carried further into the Transkei the traditional Cape policy of "assimilation," but it was the Shepstone policy of "segregation" which was extended from Natal to neighbouring Zululand,[5] where, indeed, robbed of Shepstone's own original vision of it as a temporary means only, not an end, it contributed to a *laissez-faire* deterioration, which led to rebellion in 1906. For the Basuto and the Bechuana the Aborigines Protection Society had been successful in securing direct Colonial Office control. But, despite the Society's protests, in Rhodesia the Government had capitulated to the Company, and imperial control exercised through a Resident Commissioner in the partially elective Legislative Council (granted in 1898) could be uncertain at most.[6] What broad policy should, then, be followed in South Africa?

---

[1] *Milner Papers*, II, 307–13. Sir Hercules Robinson had protested against "amateur meddling of irresponsible and ill-advised persons in England which converts many a colonist from an Imperialist into a Republican". *C.H.B.E.* VIII, 533.

[2] Williams, B., *op. cit.* p. 211. One earlier version read "for every white man": Mitchell, L., *C. Rhodes*, II, 202.

[3] *Milner Papers*, II, 353.

[4] *Parl. Pap.* 1903, XLV [Cd. 1640], pp. 12 *seqq.*

[5] The conditions for the annexation of Zululand by Natal were laid down by Chamberlain, 4 May 1897: *Parl. Pap.* 1898, LX [C. 8782], p. 651.

[6] The similarities of the problem to that of the East India Company in 1784 were not overlooked: *Parl. Pap.* 1898, LX [C. 8732], pp. 1 *seqq.* The Resident Commission was, however, instrumental in the disallowance of a taxation measure, of 1902–3, which bore upon the Africans.

The Native Affairs Commission of 1903–5 gave some answer. It recommended individual land ownership in certain "native" areas only and communal representation of natives by Europeans. It found the Cape civilisation franchise "unwise". But it was primarily concerned with the African problem as one of labour and its more immediately acceptable recommendations sought to force more Africans to work for Europeans by levying rents on native lands and by preventing vagrancy and squatting.[1]

The Zulu rebellion against the poll tax and Gandhi's passive resistance campaign against Transvaal registration laws focused humanitarian attention in 1906 once more upon South Africa. In February of that year a motion declaring that any South African settlement should take account of imperial responsibility for "the protection of native races excluded from full political rights, the safeguarding of immigrants against servile conditions of labour and the guaranteeing of their lands and territories to the free tribes of Bechuanaland and Basutoland", had been accepted by the Government. Winston Churchill, as Under-Secretary, had pledged the Government to "advance the principle of equal rights for civilised men irrespective of colour", but he felt it necessary to point out that colonial self-government was a fundamental of Liberal policy.[2] The limits of imperial control were soon stressed in Natal; for, when the British Government intervened on behalf of Zulu leaders condemned to death by summary court-martial, the Natal Responsible Government resigned. Thereupon other Colonial Governments in Australia, New Zealand and the Cape protested at imperial interference with Natal self-government to such effect that the British Government drew back.[3] The executions started a severe and bloody rebellion, the aftermath of which, in the persecution of Dinizulu, the Zulu chief, caused pain and anxiety to the humanitarian conscience and to an uneasy Imperial Government for another three years.[4] Those who, like Ramsay Macdonald, believed in an "imperial standard" warned Natal to remember that she was not only responsible to herself but to the Empire of which she was a part; but the jealous insensitivity of the Australasian Dominions rendered such appeals vain.[5]

In dealing with the rebellion which its own local policy had inflamed, the Natal Government had had to call for assistance from the other South African colonies and even from the British Government. Such a self-government, which fell short of self-dependence, was unreal. The Selborne memorandum in January 1907 raised

[1] *Parl. Pap.* 1905, LV [Cd. 2399], pp. 69 *seqq.*
[2] *Hansard*, 28 Feb. 1906, 4th ser. CLII, 1216, 1243.
[3] *Parl. Pap.* 1906, LXXIX [Cd. 2905], pp. 3, 25–32; 1908, LXXII [Cd. 3889], pp. 5 *seqq.*, 47, 503 *seqq.* See Stuart, J., *History of the Zulu Rebellion*, pp. 151–3.
[4] *Parl. Pap.* 1908, LXXII [Cd. 4195], p. 659; 1909, LXI [Cd. 4585]. See Walker, E. A., *W. P. Schreiner*, pp. 277–303.
[5] *Hansard*, 4th ser. CLIV, 1646; CLV, 188, 245; CLVIII, 669–71; CXCIII, 1279–81.

anew the question of closer association in a specific form—federation; but now this federation could no longer be dictated (as Milner had hoped) by British supremacy. Events waited upon the defeat of Jameson's Progressives in the Cape. With the Moderates and the Bond in power at Cape Town, Botha and Smuts in the Transvaal and Fischer and Hertzog in the Orange River Colony, steps were taken towards union under Afrikaner auspices—the more speedily because the unwieldy Liberal phalanx at Westminster, on which their hopes were set, seemed to show signs of splitting.[1] A draft South Africa Act establishing, not a federation, but a union with limited power devolved on four provinces, was agreed on by a National Convention, and was sent for imperial enactment to Westminster at a moment when the attention of Parliament was absorbed by the struggle between the Government and the Lords over the Lloyd George budget. There, despite Schreiner's efforts to muster British opinion against the political colour bar,[2] it received its second reading in a thin, "practically empty" House of Commons, and was accepted as a solution agreed to by those who would have the task of working it and living under it.[3] Moreover, although made predominantly by Afrikaner politicians, it evidently followed the British unwritten practice of responsible Cabinet government.

One assumption of the Liberal government in granting responsibility to the former Boer republics in 1906–7 had been that this would remove that obstacle in the Treaty of Vereeniging to the extension of the native franchise into the Transvaal and Orange River Colony; and Selborne had pressed without success for some suffrage based upon a "civilisation qualification". The Government had been prepared to insist upon safeguards concerning any future transfer of the three High Commission Territories to the Union, but it was reluctant to dictate on an internal matter of such difficulty as the native franchise. The existing franchise, a matter of pride as well as habit in the Cape, would remain entrenched within the Act. In a hasty optimism Liberals both in Britain and in Cape Colony believed that their principles must of their own virtue spread in time and capture the citadels of conservatism north of the Orange.

The dominant note of the debates in Parliament was regret: disappointment at the freezing of the Coloured and African franchise to the Cape alone, at the alleged insecurity of the entrenchment of that franchise, and at the existence of a political colour bar against

[1] Walker, E. A., Lord de Villiers and his Times, p. 430. De Villiers' impression of friction within a federal system had been confirmed by his visit to Canada and had considerable effect on the final solution.

[2] See Walker, Schreiner, pp. 319–29. See also Anti-Slavery Reporter, 5th ser. I, no. 1 (1909), pp. 1–35, and A.S.S. Minute Book VII, nos. 1677, 1686, and A.P.S. Minute Book, 24 June 1909.

[3] Hansard, 5th ser. IX, 1000, 1017. One member declared however that he had rarely seen the House more aware of the momentous occasion or more earnestly interested (cols. 1014 seqq.).

non-European legislators. Often as Government and Opposition speakers rose in agreement to wish success to the great experiment of nation-building on which Parliament was setting its seal, the Prime Minister, H. H. Asquith, declared with evident truth that there was no difference of opinion in Parliament or country on these three provisions.[1] No member sought to justify the clauses; only two to excuse them. Conservative spokesmen were agreed with the Liberals in their dislike of the political colour bar, though naturally they were not loth to score a party point in showing that such discrimination was tolerated in the Transvaal and Orange River Colony constitutions granted in 1906–7, while a Liberal member pointed out that the "fortress" had been given away by the Conservative administration in the terms of Vereeniging. Nevertheless, Asquith expressed the sense of the House in declaring that it was an "invidious" principle, difficult to reconcile with fundamental British policy.[2] Yet, despite this, he urged the House earnestly to pass the Bill without amendment. It was either the measure as it stood or no Union at all. The Bill already embodied the limit of compromise. Interference from an Imperial Government would be resented not only in South Africa, but in other colonies too, and it would only cause deterioration in the attitude towards Africans. It would be less than useless to assert in an imperial statute an equality which white South African society would not tolerate. Benefits would accrue to the Africans from Union prosperity and South African native policy would be more comprehensive than that of any Boer republic. Asquith differed emphatically from Balfour in proclaiming his faith that Africans were capable of progress; but he reminded the House that especially in the subtle matter of race relations persuasion was better than force. The House had no right to shipwreck the future of this South African union; but he hoped that the display of Parliamentary misgiving would produce as "a gracious and spontaneous act" second thoughts on these unfortunate provisions.

His appeal failed, however, to silence Dilke and his Labour allies. The Government's warning at the Committee stage that no amendment could be accepted served to anger them further; but, in face of the gag, only one protest, that against the political colour bar, was pressed to a division and then one in four of the members present voted against the clause.[3] The minority, who were prepared to take their conscientious opposition so far, were convinced that the price of surrendering a British principle was too high for the Empire to pay.[4] The acceptance of civil rights for white men only was "a lowering of the flag of freedom", a denial of Christian brotherhood and a surrender of six and a quarter million wards to the arbitrary oligarchy of a mere million.[5] Dilke argued that the measure was not

---

[1] *Hansard*, 16 Aug. 1909, 5th ser. IX, 1012.   [2] *Ibid.* 19 Aug. 1909, 5th ser. IX, 1560.
[3] The voting was 55 to 155.   [4] *Hansard*, 5th ser. IX, 1566.   [5] *Ibid.* 1028–9.

sacrosanct: Chamberlain had obtained amendment of the Commonwealth of Australia Bill in 1900.[1] Moreover, the Prime Minister of New Zealand, with experience of the Maori franchise and Maori legislators, had protested against the exclusion of non-Europeans.[2] Must Dominion representations be respected only when they ran counter to British humanitarianism? Could Indian experience in associating non-Europeans so successfully with the administration of the Empire, so recently extended, too, with general good will by the Morley-Minto reforms,[3] be so lamentably disregarded? Ramsay Macdonald pleaded here again for a recognition of his "imperial standard";[4] but though Labour leaders found themselves nonplussed by the fact that fellow Trade Unionists in South Africa had welcomed discrimination in the Bill, Keir Hardie stoutly maintained his belief that no Afrikaner would surely be so foolish as to wreck the Union which all desired just over the small matter of justice to the natives:[5] a flagrant misunderstanding which Government speakers sought immediately to dispel. Hope, they said, must be cradled in liberty.[6] Within eighteen months of Campbell-Bannerman's death they were completing the statesman-like work he had begun: "that generosity which is the truest political wisdom". Despite disquieting quotations from the speeches of even moderate Afrikaner leaders, they must act in the expectation that such men would themselves display a similar statesmanship.[7]

Certain critics in the debates had expressed fear lest Rhodesia should enter the Union only to complicate by new demands the problem of cheap migrant labour. Rhodesia, had, indeed, been invited to send delegates to the National Convention, but it had not been contemplated that she would be an original member of the Union, for the dispute between the settlers and the Company over accumulated deficits and unalienated land had grown no less bitter with the achievement of an elective majority in 1908, and the British Government refused to intervene until the Charter expired in 1914. The responsibilities of the British Government as trustees for the native peoples had been, it was thought, sufficiently secured by the schedule of regulations in the Order in Council of 1898,[8] and the imperial authorities were not aware of the possible betrayal of their trust in handing over native policy to a handful of white settlers who, there as in Kenya, seemed to demand responsible government only in order to claim more land: indeed, even in 1923 when that respon-

---

[1] See Garvin, op. cit. III, 562–7.
[2] Hansard, 5th ser. IX, 989 (see also 4th ser. CXCVIII, 1974).
[3] See Morley, John, Recollections, II, 83, 213. Opposition by the King and many Lords had had to be overcome. See also Hansard, 5th ser. IX, 1038–9.
[4] Ibid. 1592–8, 1624.   [5] Ibid. 993–4.
[6] John Simon's speech was a warning from imperial history against granting "too little liberty". Ibid. 1590.
[7] Hansard, 5th ser. (Lords), II, 682, 753, 855; (Commons), IX, 951, 1533.
[8] Parl. Pap. 1899, LXIII [C. 9138], p. 157.

sibility was granted to Southern Rhodesia, supervision over "native" legislation was retained. But for many Rhodesians responsible government had become an end in itself. In men cut off from the Cape so long by the South African War, a new sense of independent destiny had grown up north of the Limpopo and, while it was recognised that the door was still open to incorporation into the new Union, colonial pride was hardening against it. At the elections of 1911 the elected members returned to the Legislative Council were unanimously opposed to Union.[1]

In that Union itself disunion persisted. Closer association had not banished hostility or prejudice. Racialism and provincialism were strong and cabinet solidarity was weak to the very verge of schism. Hertzog, preferring a "two stream" nationalism, broke with Botha's policy of closer Boer-British brotherhood. Land and labour problems almost overwhelmed the Government. Segregation was pushed further as the Union policy, but the Supreme Court blocked the application of the Natives Land Act to Cape Colony. A National Native Council organised a deputation to the King against the continual confiscation of African land. Those who sought redress still looked in bewilderment as a matter of habit to the Imperial Factor: expecting protection where now there was none.[2] But it was labour unrest, neither African, nor Indian, but European, which drew British attention once more to South African affairs and which provided Government spokesmen with a platform to instruct British critics of South African policy in the facts of Dominion autonomy. The deportation of ringleaders concerned in a general strike which had seen the use of imperial troops against rioters produced demands by Labour leaders for imperial intervention.[3] In their agitation, they were, moreover, backed by a sympathetic public opinion throughout the country. "Is there any meaning", asked Ramsay Macdonald, "in the expression *Civis Britannicus sum*? If not, then the Empire cannot stand in the place of honour." He was persuaded that the Empire stood for something "constitutionally magnificent". But, as Lewis Harcourt pointed out in reply, part of that magnificence was the renunciation of an Imperial Government's right to interfere even when the measures of Dominion Governments were repugnant to its views. Diversity in legislation and administration was a result of the liberal processes of devolution: a constant pride if also an occasional embarrassment. To meddle in battles which were exclusively the concern of Dominion citizens would "smash" the Empire. Tolerance and restraint alone could maintain continuing unity.[4]

It was South Africa's part in intra-imperial relations to burn the

---

[1] *Parl. Pap.* 1914, LX [Cd. 7264], p. 487.
[2] Even some of the British in Natal had acquiesced in union because they felt they could rely still on imperial protection.
[3] See resolution of Labour Party conference in *The Times*, 30 Jan. 1914.
[4] *Hansard*, 5th ser. LVIII, 353–78.

lessons of colonial self-government into British minds and to stress the need for diversity in any imperial association. In this way South African nationalism contributed substantially to the definition of the new Dominion status and to the emergence of a Commonwealth which, in a curious, semi-metaphysical way, combined with some abiding unity that national freedom on which both Briton and Afrikaner in the Union insisted. For Rhodes, no less than Hertzog, demanded that national sovereignty should be the paramount consideration, though he combined with a suspicion of the Imperial Factor a faith in the Empire itself.[1] The presence of South Africa as a daughter-in-law nation in family counsels was, like Canada's, a reminder that blood was not, despite Dilke or Kidd, the bond, any more than was white skin as her spokesmen would so often claim. Most of her electors were not only non-British, but even anti-British, to whom Vereeniging was no more than a truce. Harassed by new social, economic and political forces, "that unique conservatism"[2] hardened against alien dilution, maternal persuasion, or external criticism, as threats to its independence. Haunted by Voortrekker folklore that passed for history and (as had been the case with the Irish) proved stronger than political fact, they suspected treason in the slightest lapse—even Botha's silk stockings at Court in 1911. By 1915 Hertzog's Nationalists, denouncing Botha for flirting with Rand capitalism, the Trojan horse of British imperialism, were already the alternative Government of the Union. The unco-operative strength of Afrikaner sentiment deprived Britain of that social victory without which military and political success was valueless. Moreover, South African "perversity" was pre-eminently such as to conflict sharply with British liberal experience and humanitarian faith, and to rouse the itch to exhort to virtue. The pro-Boers, still claiming to have been right about the war, soon learnt that they were wrong about the Boers, who saw any concession to negrophile sentimentalism as racial suicide, an abdication of a bastion of white civilisation isolated at the end of a teeming black continent. Democratic principles of tolerance and equality were subjected to a rigorous test by racial and colour animosities. Rule was by a privileged caste of less than one fifth of the population; parties cohered round the nucleus of race, not of class or economic interest, and cabinet collective responsibility survived but precariously. The absence of internal compromise affected that co-operation which Botha claimed to value in the informal discussion and personal contact of Imperial Conferences.[3] South Africans often forgot that their national self-determination would affect that of others. As Lord Crewe said in 1911, no member

---

[1] For Jameson's claim for equality, for example, see Parl. Pap. 1907, LV [Cd. 3523], pp. 34–5.
[2] Schreiner, op. cit. p. 256.
[3] Parl. Pap. 1911, LIV [Cd. 5745], pp. 69, 193, 336.

of the family could live to herself alone.[1] South Africa overlooked her responsibility to the rest of the group: her policy did much, for example, to stimulate Indian nationalism;[2] for in intra-imperial relations her policy towards Indian fellow-subjects was causing embarrassment, as her policy towards Africans was destined to cause later on. Nevertheless, Britain learnt to refrain from chiding, though this might make her attitude appear sometimes like acquiescence. The force of events had led her to surrender absolutely a direct authority which had been without parallel. For many reasons she sought to retain the Union within the Empire: strategy, mineral wealth, loyalty to the Liberal dreams of 1906–7, and persistent faith in the subtle influence of common association upon particularism. South Africa's membership of the family stimulated demands for freedom and equality by her sister nations. She had been, through their contributions to the South African War, the proximate cause of bringing them on to the world stage and imbuing them with a wider sense of self-dependence. In the series of Colonial and Imperial Conferences[3] she had been largely instrumental both in encouraging, and then finally in dispelling, each of Chamberlain's hopes in turn—*Kriegsverein, Zollverein* and federal *Staatsverein.* It was his visit to South Africa which convinced him finally that political centralisation was impossible. Botha opposed a "meddlesome" central authority, and even consultation which might reduce freedom of action,[4] and by pleading against Dominion interference with British self-government in the matter of Tariff Reform, he set his seal on differentiation in imperial commercial policies. Only when national self-interest dictated would the family take shelter in the imperial ark. The faith of Botha and Smuts in the Commonwealth[5] sprang not from filial sentiment, but from proven utility. Imperial relations were the better for this infusion of realism and sound judgment.

The Emergence of Twentieth-century Issues in the Indigenous Colonial Empire

Within the dependent Empire and in the sub-continent of India the forces of growth latent within the system of Crown colony government were actively creating, by the concession of unofficial majorities and the representative principle, future candidates for self-government who would revolutionise the pattern of the British Commonwealth still more and reduce those of British (or European)

---

[1] *Ibid.* p. 399; [Cd. 5746], p. 277.

[2] See Hancock, W. K., *Survey of British Commonwealth Affairs,* I, 187–203.

[3] For the various contributions of Hofmeyr, Sprigg, Hime, Jameson and Botha at the Conferences see *C.H.B.E.* VIII, 737–49. See also *Round Table* (1911), pp. 84, 371, 515.

[4] Botha, realising that South African frontiers marched with those of several European Powers, did not, however, consider neutrality a possible policy.

[5] Millin, *op. cit.* II, 42–9.

stock to a small minority in the full counsels of a multi-racial fellow-ship. But British policy was not yet consciously pursuing that end. The vision of the final surrender of the British Raj in India, which had been clear to Sir Thomas Munro or Lord Macaulay earlier in the century, was now dimmed by routine administration and in need of revival by a nationalist Indian Congress party. Moreover, parlia-mentary government, even in the thinking of a Radical like Morley, was deemed inappropriate for non-European peoples. In his opinion, the recognition of the elective principle at the Centre and of un-official majorities in the Provinces in 1909 was emphatically not to be interpreted as a step towards a British constitution.[1] Nevertheless, as Macaulay had foreseen, British knowledge (and British political science) had created a demand for British institutions. Indian leaders quoted Locke, Durham and J. S. Mill just as French Canadians and Afrikaners had learnt to do. Despite the repudiation of parliamentary government as an export and of colonial self-government as a goal, the Indian Congress under Gokhale saw with satisfaction that India had been put on the same highway that had been pioneered by the United Kingdom and the "Dominions", and they were confident that, granted the subtle influence of English institutions, they also would arrive.

Elsewhere the extension of the representative principle to other plural societies had given rise similarly to communal (or corporate) election and nomination. The Indian practice of nominating repre-sentatives recommended by certain unofficial groups or communities was imitated. Unofficial opinion, whether of Chambers of Commerce in the Straits, of European settlers in the Convention of Associations in Kenya, or of embryonic African nationalists in the Aborigines Rights Protection Society on the Gold Coast, received some Govern-ment recognition. Unofficial majorities existed in Mauritius[2] and in Jamaica, and a reform in 1895 conceded to Jamaica what was in practice for a few years an elective majority. But modelled as it was on the curious and cumbersome constitution of British Guiana, the basic Jamaican constitution of 1885 did not provide a satisfactory solution to the problems of semi-representative government.[3] In 1899 legislative deadlocks occurred both in Jamaica and in Malta and were followed by a return to the security of an official majority.[4] The "working compromise" had failed: "it is in fact impossible", wrote Chamberlain to the Governor of Jamaica, "except where tact

---

[1] *Hansard*, 5th ser. III, 553; and Morley, J., *Indian Speeches*, pp. 35–6, 91.

[2] Financial troubles in Mauritius led to the appointment of a Royal Commission: *Parl. Pap.* 1910, XLII [Cd. 5185], p. 1.

[3] Wrong, H. H., *Government of the West Indies*, pp. 113–35.

[4] For the refusal of supplies by elected members over the language question in Malta, see *Parl. Pap.* 1899, LIX (287), p. 257; 1901, XLVI [Cd. 715], p. 97; 1903, XLIV [Cd. 1660], p. 613; 1904, LX [Cd. 2023], p. 251. Both Elgin and Crewe turned down firmly repeated requests for a return to an elective majority: *Parl. Pap.* 1910, LXVI [Cd. 5217], p. 515.

and good will and friendly feeling exist in an unusual degree, for the government of a country to be carried on where those who are responsible for it are in a permanent minority in the Legislature."[1] But, meanwhile, by way of nomination, it was becoming accepted that a white skin was not an indispensable qualification for legislators. An African had made his appearance on the Legislative Council of the Gold Coast—the pioneer African colony—in 1889, while the first specific provision for native nomination was made for Fiji in 1904[2] and for native election for Ceylon in 1910. It was in Ceylon in that year that Lord Crewe finally capitulated to a united front of Europeans and European-educated Sinhalese and Tamils and conceded what Chamberlain had previously been able to deny—a native elective representation.[3]

What claimed the vigour and imagination of British politicians interested in the Empire during this period, however, was not self-government, but the development of the resources of those neglected "estates" which other nations had learnt to envy and which the metropolitan power now found it inconvenient to overlook. Imperial development, the driving of furrows rather than the planting of flags, had become in this period a necessity as much as a duty. The Government, urged on not only by the yellow press, but by the Court, the City and the Chambers of Commerce, could no longer avoid responsibilities recently entrusted to Chartered Companies. By way of the sharp clash of international rivalries and the self-exhausting zeal of the Companies, there had been an extension of the protectorate system and "the Foreign Office empire". Indeed, it might seem that Foreign Office imperialism was different in character from that of the Colonial Office: that it was more expansionist, more inclined to think of colonies strategically as pawns to be seized promptly against the claims of foreign rivals. If this was so, the Foreign Office acted with evident reluctance; and while it might appear somewhat less careful than the more experienced Colonial Office of the traditions of British colonial behaviour, and though their reliance upon the Indian Army had no doubt some regrettable results in certain parts of East Africa,[4] the successive presence of Salisbury, Lansdowne and Edward Grey at the Foreign Office is sufficient ground for dismissing any charge of wanton annexation. Salisbury could, indeed, on occasions speak the language of Chamberlain on the imperial trust for British commerce and capital in future genera-

[1] *Parl. Pap.* 1900, LV [Cd. 125], p. 15. See also the Barbour Report, 1899, LIX [C. 9412], p. 1.

[2] In practice the Government nominated those elected by the Council of Chiefs, see im Thurn, "Fiji as a Crown Colony", *Quarterly Review* (Jan. 1912), p. 74; and Letters Patent (March 1904) in *C.O. List* (1905), p. 184.

[3] Ceylon Sess. Papers XXVI of 1903 and XXI of 1910; *Parl. Pap.* 1910, LXVI [Cd. 5098], p. 381; [Cd. 5427], p. 409; and Royal Instructions (Nov. 1910) in *C.O. List* (1910), pp. 142–3.

[4] Gregory, J. W., *Foundations of British East Africa* (1901), pp. 247, 260–1.

tions,[1] but he was strongly opposed to mere land-grabbing. Moreover, his one "latent idealism"[2]—like Palmerston's "benevolent crochet"—concerned the suppression of slave trading, and the opening up of Africa by railways was for him and others the modern equivalent of the old slave squadron and Fowell Buxton's "remedy for the illegitimate trade". The laxity and anomaly of Foreign Office rule was, however, subjected to a running barrage of criticism from the humanitarians,[3] and, realising gradually its ill-equipment for such responsibilities, the Foreign Office handed over its protectorates one by one to the Colonial Office[4] until by 1913, with the transfer of Zanzibar, it retained only the condominium of the Sudan. This administrative change did not immediately affect their protectorate status. British "protected persons" remained in law different from British subjects,[5] but many of the protectorates became identified closely with neighbouring colonies and in the course of time almost indistinguishable from them, possessing similar political rights and sharing in new schemes of economic development.

It was Chamberlain, of course, who gave colonial policy this direction. Trusteeship, he saw, had become too negative; imperial sins of commission were now few, but those of omission were still many. Yet, despite the inveterate hero-worshipping of Flora Shaw and the undoubted devotion of many governors who served under him, Chamberlain was not so much initiating new ventures as emphasising tendencies already in being; and some part of the results claimed by disciples for his policy was derived from decisions already taken (as in West Africa) or from enterprise already maturing (as in Malaya). By 1895 imperial development was an accepted policy: controversy centred not on ends, but on means. Alfred Lyttelton, Lord Elgin, Lord Crewe and Lewis Harcourt—Chamberlain's successors at the Office—carried forward that policy with no less zeal than he. Harcourt particularly, with his devotion to railway building and his encouragement of medical and scientific research, was undoubtedly "Joe's" heir: Elgin, the weak link in the succession, appeared the more negative only because of the contrasting dynamic personality of his Under-Secretary, Winston Churchill. Yet it was pre-eminently Chamberlain's policy, for he was the publicist who gave stimulus and imagination to the new trends. He persuaded the public to see that without imperial aid the West Indies would never be rehabilitated, nor could Africa be exploited wisely, for the benefit of their own peoples and for that of the greater world population outside.[6] Though policy might still fall short of these principles, later enshrined in Lugard's "dual mandate",[7] Chamberlain's empha-

---

[1] *Hansard*, 5th ser. xxx, 701. [2] Kennedy, A. L., *Lord Salisbury*, p. 227.
[3] E.g. *Hansard*, 5th ser. xci, 479. [4] Cf. Cecil, G., *op. cit.* iv, 302–3.
[5] See R. v. Earl Crewe, *ex parte* Sekgomé, 1910: L.J.R. 79 K.B. 874.
[6] *Hansard*, 5th ser. xxxvi, 641.
[7] Lugard, F. D., *The Dual Mandate in British Tropical Africa*, pp. 615–17.

tic enunciation of them was a contemporary approach to Hobson's "legitimate imperialism": the mutual benefit deriving both to guardians and wards from an honest stewardship. Although his phrases could later be given a sinister twist by the Empire Resources Development Committee in 1917,[1] he was himself sincere in believing that Britain's money and skill would enrich and illuminate African life, and that her defence of the Open Door would secure opportunities for the commerce of the civilised world.[2] Instinct of his own collectivism, his policy of imperial "slum clearance" could also commend itself to his Fabian allies and many Young Liberals. The tasks involved in this "imperialism" were more searching and arduous than those which won the plaudits of the press. Few in official circles saw imperialism in terms only of Omdurman or Fashoda; and many who were hostile to the fashionable enthusiasm paid just tribute to the talent and devotion demanded by this enlightened "administrative imperialism", contrasting the work of Johnston or Lugard with that of Rhodes and the "jobbers".[3]

Although a substantial portion of the dependent Empire was in 1895 not subject to Colonial Office control, Chamberlain was not wholly guiltless of the ambition to make that Office the centre of foreign, as of all imperial, policy. He brought vigour, acumen and a master's hand to his department.[4] The symbolism of his replacement of candles by electric light is well known; but perhaps his most valuable innovation was the provision of a policy-making secretariat which left to the sub-departments the routine work of "getting off the mails" and was thereby capable of that broad "philosophical view" which James Stephen so long before had seen to be so sorely needed. Moreover, he concentrated financial and commercial matters in the hands of the Crown Agents. He began the co-ordination of the Colonial Services on which the new imperial policy must rely. He combined the entrance examination for colonial servants with that for the rest of the home service; but he knew that advance in tropical medicine was a necessary preliminary to complete unification. Chamberlain played an important part in the establishment of Schools of Tropical Medicine in London and Liverpool: by their work on the mosquito Manson and Ross were able to make one-quarter of the world capable of white development.[5] He sought to secure in open competition a fairer share of imperial trade for Britain and the colonies. In a circular of 28 November 1895 he asked colonial governors to report on the displacement of British products by foreign manufactures and to send him specimens of foreign goods which sold well, for it was important that the Empire should be a

---

[1] Hancock, *op. cit.* II (pt. I), 107–10, 113 *seqq.*
[2] *Foreign and Colonial Speeches*, p. 141.　　　[3] See *The Spectator*, 2 Oct. 1897.
[4] See Parkinson, C., *The Colonial Office from Within*, chap. iii; Wilson, H., in *United Empire*, Feb. 1917; Garvin, *op. cit.* III, chap. i.
[5] Amery, J., *op. cit.* IV, chap. lxxxv. See also *Parl. Pap.* 1903, XLIV [Cd. 1598], p. 13.

profitable business concern.[1] He wanted to encourage the investment of British capital in colonial development. The Colonial Loans
Act of 1899 facilitated advances from the Treasury (on the model of
those to local authorities in Britain)[2] for the railways, irrigation
schemes and public works that "Joe Africanus" advocated.[3] The new
Colonial Stock Act of 1900 provided further this "Roman" programme by enabling colonies to borrow on favourable terms at the
Stock Exchange as trustee securities.[4] He was, however, thwarted
by Hicks Beach in his plan to earmark the dividends of the Suez
Canal shares for colonial development, and the cost of the South
African War curtailed many projects for West African railway construction.[5] He believed passionately in improved communications
as essentially an *imperial* responsibility, because they would be the
means of unlocking vast regions which, though potentially rich for
humanity as a whole, were hitherto unused, or misused, by a backward, "savage" minority. The aboriginal must not stand in the way
of the civilised. He must be dealt with justly: indeed, Britain's
correctness in this matter was all the more important when she
took the lead in exposing foreign crimes on the Congo or at Putumayo.[6] But to Chamberlain and his generation the paramountcy of
native interests appeared an absurd doctrine. Civilisation was itself
an acknowledged good, a trust for the whole world.[7] The First World
War, creating doubt, shaking conviction and exploding assumptions
of superior wisdom, lies between us and a full understanding of what
was a genuine and not wholly self-interested faith.

In the non-self-governing Empire these twenty years before the
outbreak of that War saw the establishment and consolidation of
British administration. From tropical Africa to Malaya and the
South Pacific, government became more effective; and already in
the process some of the issues of the twentieth-century Empire were
beginning to emerge: plural societies in Kenya and Malaya, nationalism in West Africa and Ceylon, *enosis* in Cyprus,[8] language difficulties in Malta, land and labour problems nearly everywhere,
conflicts between a new native *intelligentsia* and traditional authority,
or between that old order and the new, the costly methods of trial-
and-error in the economic sphere, the difficulties of long-term
planning in the yet untamed conditions of tropical agriculture.
The incidence and growth of some of these problems in the major
areas of the dependent Empire must now be briefly considered.

[1] *Parl. Pap.* 1897, LX [C. 8449], p. 1. See also *Parl. Pap.* 1913, LXVIII [Cd. 6771], p. 361.
[2] *Hansard*, 4th ser. LXI, 540; LXII, 742.
[3] 62 & 63 Vict. c. 36. See also *Parl. Pap.* 1901, XXXVII (94), p. 177.
[4] 63 & 64 Vict. c. 62.   [5] Garvin, *op. cit.* III, 175.
[6] E.g. Circular dispatch 15 Dec. 1913: *Parl. Pap.* 1913, LXXI [Cd. 7148], p. 693.
[7] See Huxley, E., *White Man's Country*, I, 79–84.
[8] *Parl. Pap.* 1900, LV [Cd. 227], p. 217; 1901, XLVI [Cd. 510], p. 15; 1908, LXXI
[Cd. 3996], p. 965.

East Africa

If it was Near East strategy which. by way of the Upper Nile, had drawn Britain into East Africa, it was missionary and anti-slavery agitation which kept her there.[1] The decision to remain had been taken by the outgoing Rosebery administration,[2] but it was the Salisbury government which undertook, with Liberal Imperialist support, the "clockwork" reconquest of the Sudan. Their motives were mixed: it would bring some comfort to the Italians in Abyssinia and some disquiet to the French in the western Sudan; it would avenge Gordon and put down slave-raiding fanatics; and it might perhaps, some said, also provide a distraction from Government embarrassment due to the Jameson Raid.[3] The annihilation of the Mahdi's hordes at Omdurman in September 1898 was the prelude to a prolonged crisis on the Upper Nile at Fashoda, where the British Government, with the backing of an almost unanimous country, refused to concede control to the French of an African empire which would extend southward to the Congo, westward to the Niger and eastward to the Red Sea and would cut off Britain from the territories of East Africa. The French challenge constituted what, as Sir Edward Grey had given warning in 1895, would be considered "an unfriendly act": but war was averted and agreement was reached in March 1899 which secured British influence on the Upper Nile.[4] Two months earlier an Anglo-Egyptian condominium had been established over the Sudan, and under Sir Reginald Wingate as Governor-General the foundations of a sound British administration were firmly laid.

The demise of the philanthropic Imperial British East Africa Company, on somewhat ungenerous terms arranged by the Rosebery government, left its successors with a legacy of vast territories and a high standard of conduct in that region which Sir John Kirk had once called "the America of India". The sultanate itself, after the bombardment of Zanzibar in support of the British nominee in 1896, gave the British Government little trouble save over the matter of its toleration of slave-ownership. In 1897, through Salisbury's intervention,[5] the Consul-General, Sir Arthur Hardinge, was able to obtain the abolition of the legal status of slavery, but there was no rush for freedom and in the teeth of humanitarian pressure, in Parliament and outside,[6] the Foreign Office was convinced by Hardinge's appeals to British "justice" on behalf of the Arabs that

[1] See Johnston Report in *Parl. Pap.* 1901, XLVIII [Cd. 671], p. 569.
[2] See *Hansard*, 4th ser. XXX, 693–705; XXXIV, 1086–142.
[3] Blunt, W., *My Diaries*, 10 April 1896.
[4] *Parl. Pap.* 1899, CXII [C. 9134], p. 957.
[5] *Parl. Pap.* 1897, LXII [C. 8394], p. 697; [C. 8433], p. 707.
[6] *Hansard*, 4th ser. XXXI, 644 *seqq.*; LIII, 293 *seqq.*; LXXXIV, 216 *seqq.*; XCVII, 1025 *seqq.* See also *Parl. Pap.* 1900, LVI [Cd. 96], p. 939.

it would be wise to permit emancipation to come about gradually. No decisive action, therefore, was taken until 1911 when opinion in Zanzibar itself had begun to change.[1]

It was as an anti-slavery measure that the construction of the expensive Uganda railway had been supported by many. The work of opening up the interior was carried forward from Mombasa to Kisumu by December 1901:[2] indeed, until its extension to Busoga in 1911, the line served the needs directly only of the British East Africa Protectorate (later called Kenya). Religious tension in Buganda had diminished considerably after the British assumption of the protectorate; but, as British administration extended its control, political unrest and confusion continued for several years until the final capture of Mwanga and Kabarega in April 1899.[3] The Government, running the gauntlet of searching criticism in Parliament over the costly mutiny of the Sudanese, sent Sir Harry Johnston in that same year as Special Commissioner to report on the condition and resources of the Uganda Protectorate and its prospects for self-supporting developments. In March 1900 Johnston concluded with the Regents of Buganda an agreement, which provided a model for others with Toro and Ankole: an elaborate system of indirect rule provided for the Kabaka and his Council to exercise government under the control of the British Government. The Commisioner reported favourably on the possibilities of rubber and coffee plantations under British supervision,[4] but it soon proved to be cotton grown by African smallholders which achieved the greatest success. By 1908, indeed, the view that Uganda would remain an African territory under the United Kingdom was receiving official acceptance. If "planting" was to be encouraged in Uganda, said the Governor, it should be concentrated in one suitable locality only. His tour had revealed a steady economic progress among the tribes despite the prevalence of sleeping sickness, and he remarked on the good will with which the extension of British influence had been accepted and the appreciation of peace and order which was wholly within the competence, legislative and executive, of a paternal Governor.[5] The comparative simplicity of the Uganda problem, moreover, had been facilitated by the transfer in 1902 of the lands in Naivasha and Kisumu, most suitable for European settlement, to the neighbouring B.E.A. Protectorate.

By contrast with Uganda the British East Africa Protectorate was showing signs of developing as "a white man's country"; for a

---

[1] Hollingsworth, L. W., *Zanzibar under the Foreign Office*, pp. 141–54. *Parl. Pap.* 1898, LX [C. 8858], p. 559; 1901, XLVIII [Cd. 593], p. 173.
[2] *Parl. Pap.* 1905, XLIV (166), p. 813.
[3] *Parl. Pap.* 1898, LX [C. 8718], [C. 9027], pp. 395, 525; 1899, LXIII [C. 9123], [C. 9232], pp. 477, 531.
[4] *Parl. Pap.* 1900, LVI [Cd. 256], p. 865; 1901, XLVIII [Cd. 671], p. 569.
[5] *Parl. Pap.* 1909, LIX [Cd. 4524], p. 245.

vociferous oligarchy of European settlers, in whom old-fashioned dreams of colonisation had been newly kindled, had assumed the exclusive importance of their own interests in this new land and were asserting, with impatience of Government red-tape, a theory of white domination. The railway had given to the territory a backbone; but "a backbone", argued Sir Charles Eliot, the Commissioner, in 1901 "is as useless without a body as a body is helpless without a backbone".[1] To repay the costs of construction and develop the country which Lugard, Johnston and others had deemed "admirably suited" for European colonisation, he advocated strongly the settlement of fertile spaces in the Rift Valley and the Mau Highlands with Europeans, who would grow crops and buy machines and thus convert the Protectorate into a stable British asset. He believed that he was dealing with a *tabula rasa*.[2] In his enthusiasm he dismissed the Africans as likely soon to be of "little interest". Believing the tribal system unworthy of preservation by any general organisation of reserves, he thought that it would presently die out together with the "brutal barbarism" which it represented.[3] Moreover, at home too, opinion was moving towards the encouragement of white settlement. Chamberlain's offer to the Zionists, so strongly opposed by the colonists already in Kenya, came to nothing,[4] but the end of the South African War brought settlers from not only Britain but South Africa and even Australasia. Those from the mother country, seeking refuge from the changing social structure of Britain, were uncommon emigrants: men of substance, the raw material Gibbon Wakefield had earlier sought in vain for his Australasian settlements. They came with capital to develop and supervise; but they came without their labourers. Neither pastoral Masai nor agricultural Kikuyu responded to their demands; so, holding the Government responsible for inviting them to settle there, they looked to the local officials to supply them with cheap labour, induced (if need be) by taxation, and pass laws. The Government, refusing to undertake recruitment itself, was ready to encourage Africans to work for the farmers, but soon discovered its terms for African employment too demanding of settler generosity. Angry scenes in 1908, and wild threats of armed revolt that were to be recurrent in Kenya's history, led to the temporary suspension of the nominated leaders of the Settler's Association, including Lord Delamere, from the Legislative Council.[5] Somewhat less exacting conditions, however, came to be adopted, with the result that in 1914 the Report and Evidence of the Native Labour Commission revived Parliamentary anxiety once more on the matter of compulsory labour in the Protectorate.[6]

[1] *Parl. Pap.* 1901, XLVIII [Cd. 769], pp. 379 *seqq.*
[2] Eliot, C., *The East Africa Protectorate*, p. 3.
[3] *Ibid.* pp. 304, 309–10.   Amery, J., *op. cit.* IV, chap. lxxxvii.
[5] Huxley, *op. cit.* I, 226–36.
[6] *Hansard*, 5th ser. LXII, 911; LXV, 1154, 1176.

The restriction of African land ownership was a measure urged by settlers as a means of securing African labour. The emptiness of the land was both a temptation and a delusion, for good land was limited and unclaimed land rare. Following legislation in 1902–3 which permitted Government alienation with less regard to African interests than the original Order-in-Council of 1898 had required, large blocks of unsurveyed land were granted to wealthy individuals and even to syndicates; indeed, the conflict of grants made in London with those in the Protectorate contributed in 1904 to Eliot's resignation. His successor, Sir Donald Stewart, who did not share his antipathy to reserves, negotiated in August 1904 a treaty with the nomadic Masai which opened the railway strip and the Rift Valley to European settlement and guaranteed two reserves to the Masai. Parliamentary opinion approved the extension of this reserve system to other tribes, emphasising the need to remove African apprehension by retaining trusteeship in Government hands,[1] and in 1908 Lord Crewe caused some consternation among the settlers by suggesting treaties with all tribes in Kenya to guarantee them in the absolute possession of their lands. However, both sides had failed to implement the terms of the Masai Treaty and, during the governorship of Sir Percy Girouard, settler envy of the Laikipia grazing grounds in the north of the Rift Valley sought to persuade the Imperial Government that the Masai desired to move into the single reserve in the south. Lewis Harcourt, having ordered an immediate halt to the move, required as a preliminary an agreed modification of the Treaty of 1904 and insisted on a further reserve in the west for the Masai.[2] His refusal to permit settlers who had been evicted from the south by the transfer to be compensated in Laikipia caused Girouard to resign.

Settler demands for easier alienation grew more articulate with their representation in the Legislative Council in 1906. Their Association, remodelled as a regular Convention in 1910, was capable of organising a spontaneous campaign of protest at will. Under Delamere they pressed for elective representation, and, confusing rent with taxation, cried out against "taxation without representation" under a Crown colony system. But Lewis Harcourt, who was prepared to sanction a loan of £3,900,000 for development in East Africa, stonewalled against the concession of the franchise to a small minority community in a colony where revenues came substantially from non-European sources—the only direct taxation until the termination of the imperial grant-in-aid in 1913 being the African hut tax of 1903. Moreover, another element complicated the racial problem. Because of the labour shortage, Indians had been brought

---

[1] *Hansard*, 4th ser. CLXXVIII, 682, 1156.
[2] *Parl. Pap.* 1911, LII [Cd. 5584], p. 705. See Sandford, G. R., *Administration and Political History of the Masai Reserve.*

to the Protectorate to build the railway and, since the Foreign Office had not insisted upon repatriation, many stayed to trade and to settle. Indeed, by 1905 they were already aspiring in the matter of land grants to claim equal rights with Europeans. Moreover, in reply to these Indian claims, though he acknowledged that in view of the limited area suitable for European colonisation some "reasonable discretion" was necessary as a matter of administrative convenience, Lord Elgin affirmed that legal discrimination against any of H.M.'s subjects was contrary to British policy:[1] a principle which, in the later crisis of 1921-2, when the British Government gave a three-dimensional proportion to the Indo-European struggle by affirming African paramountcy, was often to be quoted as an "Indian charter". But the Government at home was reluctant (as its predecessors half a century before had been towards squatters in New South Wales) to lock up land on long lease.[2] Large holdings had become concentrated in the hands of a few, and other emigrants with limited means were already loud in resentment of a moneyed monopoly. Before he left Kenya, Girouard was, however, able to announce an agreement which conceded the long leases demanded by the Convention, though new legislation was not ready until 1915.

West Africa

British West Africa was soon to become wholly, as in 1895 it was substantially, the province of the Colonial Office. The Foreign Office was naturally concerned with the rival claims of the French on the Upper Niger and of the Germans on the Upper Volta, but within five years these had been settled and the Colonial Office had accepted responsibility for the legacy. In an area where previously British policy had been notoriously vacillating there was now a firm determination to remain, and to press and to round off British territorial claims. Chamberlain was indeed less disposed to concession than was Salisbury. Chamberlain's unbending attitude over Borgu and his rapid organisation of the West African Frontier Force under Lugard caused the French to drop their claim of effective occupation and accept a new Convention which secured to Britain the western frontiers of Nigeria:[3] minor adjustments made in 1904 as part of the general settlement of Anglo-French colonial disputes (including that of the Newfoundland fisheries) were inspired by the new spirit of the *entente cordiale*.[4] But though regions might be recognised internationally as lying within the British sphere, British rule was not necessarily accepted by the inhabitants, nor effectively extended over them. The first task, then, was the assertion of that authority. For ten years

[1] *Parl. Pap.* 1908, LXXI [Cd. 4117], pp. 1039 *seqq.*, 19 March 1908.
[2] *Ibid.* 20 Aug. 1907.
[3] *Parl. Pap.* 1898, LX [C. 8854], p. 1. See also Garvin, *op. cit.* III, chap. lv.
[4] *Parl. Pap.* 1905, CIII [Cd. 2332], p. 241.

to come, policy from the Gambia to the Niger was devoted to pacification rather than development, though the railways that secured
peace would also stimulate prosperity.[1] In 1897 the Royal Niger
Company, under Sir George Goldie, undertook an expedition against
the slave-raiding Emirs of Nupé and Ilorin. But Sir John Kirk's
report on the attack of the men of Brass against the Company's
factory at Alassa underlined the inadequacies of the Company's dual
responsibility for commerce and administration. The Company had
acted within its rights, but in practice its virtual monopoly had caused
reasonable resentment among African traders.[2] With high praise
from humanitarians in Britain, Goldie had prohibited the liquor
traffic and had proclaimed the abolition of the legal status of slavery
within the territories of the Company; but he realised that his work
in countering French ambitions was accomplished and that direct
administrative responsibility must be surrendered to the Government. In July 1899 the Charter was revoked,[3] the Company receiving compensation from the Government for the new areas it bequeathed to the Protectorates of Northern and Southern Nigeria,
which were set up in January 1900 under the Colonial Office.
Meanwhile, the processes of subjugation had continued. In 1897 the
reign of appalling fetish worship in Benin was terminated by its
conquest,[4] as was that of the notorious oracle (the Long Juju) by the
defeat of the Aros five years later. In the Northern Protectorate Sir
Frederick Lugard as High Commissioner continued and completed
the conquest of the Fulani emirates, receiving the submission of the
Sultan of Sokoto and the Emir of Kano in 1903.[5] Thereafter, out-
breaks were isolated and sporadic only,[6] for Lugard employed the
Emirs as the channels of government, giving to the expedient of
"indirect rule" (which others had already used elsewhere) the status
of an orthodox philosophy. Under the guidance of a handful of British
Residents who caught something of Lugard's own enthusiasm and
devotion, the Emirs were given an interest in good, incorrupt government. British support was essential to their authority over the Hausa.
Their religion was respected. Their courts and customs were preserved
so long as they did not conflict with British ideas of justice and
humanity. Taxation, the very foundation of administration, was
carefully regulated on the basis of assessments made by the Residents with the aid of village councils.[7] The yield of revenue increased
manifold while the burden of taxation proportionally decreased with
honest stewardship. Girouard, who was a staunch disciple of Lugard's

[1] *Parl. Pap.* 1905, LVI [Cd. 2325], p. 361.
[2] *Parl. Pap.* 1896, LIX [C. 7977], p. 361.
[3] *Parl. Pap.* 1899, LXIII [C. 9372], p. 717; *Hansard*, 4th ser. LXXV, 370 *seqq.*
[4] *Parl. Pap.* 1899, LXIII [C. 9124], p. 367; [C. 9529], p. 395.
[5] *Parl. Pap.* 1903, XLV [Cd. 1433], p. 787.
[6] *Parl. Pap.* 1907, LVII [Cd. 3620], p. 173.
[7] *Parl. Pap.* 1907 LIV [Cd. 3309], p. 473.

and was later to introduce the main features of indirect rule into Kenya, carried the system further and gave particular attention to the construction of railways which would facilitate that unification of the two Protectorates towards which Government opinion was moving: the Southern Protectorate had already in 1906 been amalgamated with the Colony of Lagos. Lugard himself returned to effect that artificial and already quasi-federal union of North and South;[1] and in 1914, when the new Government of Nigeria was proclaimed, a great durbar at Kano afforded ample testimony to the popularity of Lugard's work in the North and encouraged him, as Governor-General, to attempt the application of the system to the South as well.[2]

On the Gold Coast, too, policy had displayed an unwonted decision which took the long-tolerated Ashanti kingdom by surprise, for Chamberlain was clearly prepared to force the pace. He refused to negotiate a new treaty and, in face of protests from Exeter Hall,[3] issued an ultimatum to King Prempeh, calling upon him to accept a British Resident. When the King proved obdurate, British forces entered Kumasi without bloodshed and installed a Resident, Prempeh himself being deposed and deported as security against the long-standing indemnity which he insisted that he could not pay. Suspicions of British sharp-practice in this matter remain,[4] but the Government was now determined to bring Ashanti under control. Tactless and somewhat offensive demands by Governor Hodgson in 1901 for the surrender of the Golden Stool of Kumasi (the symbol of sovereignty) provoked a rebellion, and Ashanti was formally annexed.[5] At the same time the whole of the Gold Coast was brought under a single authority—though there again without intrinsic unity—by the proclamation of a protectorate over the Northern Territories on the Upper Volta where British treaties with the tribes had been finally recognised by the Anglo-German Convention of 1899. Once more pacification was followed by a period of development in which railway construction (still imperfect) began to tap the important resources of the region: gold from Tarkwa and Ashanti, cattle from the North, and cocoa grown by African smallholders from Accra to Kumasi.

Farther along the coast on the banks of the Gambia and over the frontiers of the Colony of Sierra Leone British protection had been also considerably extended. With French co-operation, the protracted struggle on the Gambia of Marabouts and Soninkis, which came to a crisis in 1900, was terminated.[6] The extension of control over the Protectorate of Sierra Leone in 1896 and the imposition of a

---

[1] *Parl. Pap.* 1919, xxxvi [Cmd. 468]; *Hansard*, 5th ser. XL, 512.
[2] See Perham, M., *Native Administration in Nigeria*, pp. 201 *seqq.*
[3] See Garvin, *op. cit.* III, 21–2.
[4] Ward, W. E. F., *History of the Gold Coast*, pp. 298–303.
[5] *Parl. Pap.* 1901, XLVIII [Cd. 501], p. 443; 1902, LXVI [Cd. 938], p. 753.
[6] See Gray, J. M., *History of the Gambia*, pp. 469–74.

hut tax in that territory led to disorder which culminated in rebellion two years later. Whilst accepting the urgency of restoring the confidence and authority of the chiefs, Chamberlain dissociated himself from the Commissioner's criticism of the Governor's hasty and careless imprudence. Approving heartily of a tax which might induce the tribes to work more consistently, he instructed the Governor to apply the tax not only in the Protectorate but in the Colony itself[1]—a uniformity of treatment which, despite the wide divergence between their standards of civilisation, was crystallised in 1913 when the Legislative Council of the Colony (to which nominated unofficial members were added in that year) was given authority to legislate for Protectorate as well as Colony.

A matter of perennial importance and contemporary controversy was that concerned with the use of land: in turn giving rise to the question of the form of land tenure. If by developing her resources under the shelter of an extending British *Pax*, recompense would finally be made to Africa, was it better to adopt a plantation, or a co-operative smallholding, economy? Intelligent commercial opinion was divided. Lever Brothers were persuaded that the former (as in Malaya) was more efficient and economical, and in the long run better for native welfare and progress. The British Cotton Growing Association preferred the latter (as in Uganda) for the same reasons. With lasting memories of the West Indies and with present evidence of a stultifying, over-greedy frenzy in King Leopold's Congo, official humanitarian opinion threw its weight on the side of the smallholder and was successful in rejecting the plantation economy for British West Africa.[2] But on the secondary issue humanitarians found themselves divided. Granted that land in West Africa (if not in East Africa) should be guaranteed to Africans, was it better to retain control in the hands of tribal leaders or in the Crown? The Gold Coast and Northern Nigeria provided a sharp contrast in this matter. Amid African and humanitarian protests a Government attempt to defend Gold Coast tribes from concession hunters and from their own chiefs (who might be tempted by immediate profit to forgo their trust) by vesting all land in the Crown was renewed in 1897. It led to the formation of a Gold Coast Aborigines' Rights Protection Society, which, by the first of many unofficial African deputations to London, succeeded in obtaining from Chamberlain the withdrawal of the measure, and, encouraged by that success, began to claim a part, as representing African opinion, in advising the Governor.[3] In Northern Nigeria, on the contrary, Lugard had seen to it that this trust should be exercised by the Crown,

[1] *Parl. Pap.* 1899, LX [C. 9388], p. 1: also 1902, LXVI [Cd. 1907], p. 831.
[2] See Hancock, W. K., *Survey of British Commonwealth Affairs*, II, pt. 2, 173–200.
[3] See McPhee, A., *The Economic Revolution in British West Africa*, pp. 146–54. The compromise of 1900 also failed to vest sufficient authority in the Crown to safeguard the tribes.

but it was Girouard who, by the Lands and Native Rights Ordinance of 1910, provided the machinery—though not always satisfactory —to protect all lands, whether occupied or not, as African property.[1] In the South, however, the land law was more complex, and efforts to secure to the Crown all rights in land roused incipient nationalist sentiment against manœuvres which (it was claimed) were designed to deprive Africans of their communal patrimony. Here there were already signs, as on the Gold Coast in Casely Hayford's West African union movement,[2] of an impatient divergence of interest between the tribal leaders and the new intelligentsia. Yet on amalgamation in 1914 Lugard had secured that the Legislative Council at Lagos should confine its authority to the South, affirming that it was contrary to British colonial policy to subject the interests of a large native population to the will of any minority, whether of Europeans or of educated Africans.

West Indies

When in 1895 Chamberlain spoke so challengingly of "estates" for which, though British for centuries, the imperial landlord had done nothing,[3] he had some of the West Indies in mind, Dominica perhaps more especially.[4] Struggling long to overcome the mischievous legacy of over-concentration upon a single staple, amid the throes of a free-trade victory and the social revolution of emancipation, the Caribbean colonies had been hit recently by the increasingly severe competition of foreign, bounty-fed beet sugar which had dictated a fall in wages, a rise in unemployment and a cessation of investment. The poverty of the area in 1895 may, however, be too easily exaggerated. During the previous thirty years colonial governments had undertaken many social services without request for imperial aid: Sir David Barbour, indeed, noted with tolerant criticism the "laudable", but "over-sanguine", devotion of Jamaican governments to expensive welfare projects:[5] a foreshadowing of the concentration of mid-twentieth-century administrations on short-term welfare at the expense of long-term development. But the sugar crisis had brought those colonies dependent upon this single crop to the verge of disaster and ruin. If the Caribbean were not to become an imperial slum, action to deal with the distress was urgent. The outgoing Rosebery government had recognised the need for "exceptional" measures of relief in British Guiana and Barbados;[6] and now Chamberlain sought the root of the trouble. He appointed a Royal Commission under Sir Henry Norman including, in addition to Barbour, formerly Indian Financial

---

[1] *Parl. Pap.* 1910, XLIV [Cd. 5102], [Cd. 5103], pp. 271, 305. See McPhee, *op. cit.* pp. 180–2.

[2] Wight, M., *The Gold Coast Legislative Council*, pp. 26–7.

[3] *Hansard*, 4th ser. XXXVI, 641.   [4] *Hansard*, 4th ser. LXIII, 876.

[5] *Parl. Pap.* 1899, LIX [C. 9412], p. 167.

[6] *Parl. Pap.* 1897, LXI [C. 8359], p. 495.

Secretary, and Dr Morris of Kew Gardens, both Edward Grey from
the Opposition front bench and Sydney Olivier from the Fabians.
The report of the Commissioners confirmed Chamberlain in his
opinion that the sugar bounties were the cause of distress, but did not
agree with him (though their Chairman did) that the edifice of free
trade should be breached by British retaliation in countervailing
duties.[1] Without that sanction attempts in 1898 to obtain an international agreement against bounty warfare proved abortive. Under
threat of that sanction four years later the Powers concerned agreed
to a total abolition by the Brussels Convention.[2] Excessive competition in the bounty was spelling ruin on the continent of Europe; and
the adoption of countervailing duties by the Indian Government
under Curzon was an intimation that Britain meant business, even
at the sacrifice of her pure free-trade gospel.[3] In the interest of the
West Indies, Britain seemed prepared to forgo cheap sugar.[4] But
other considerations were involved. Chamberlain saw it as a contribution to imperial solidarity, a first lesson in demonstrating his
new creed of mutual economic advantage. By reason of the Convention and other measures, the condition of the West Indies began
to improve considerably, so that by 1911 the West Indies were
solvent and the Liberal government sufficiently confident to consider
withdrawing from the agreement.[5]

The Norman Commission had been unanimous on measures
which should be taken immediately not only to alleviate the present
distress, but to build more securely for future prosperity. Their
advocacy of closer settlement and diversification of crops had no
novelty; but their attitude towards peasant cultivation had a new
warmth and gave official approval to the work begun in Jamaica by
Sir Henry Blake.[6] The plantation economy, they affirmed, while
suited to certain crops, was not universal and could not claim
exclusive attention, to the detriment of majority interests. Barbour's
separate report on Jamaica finances carried their lessons further.
The compromise between representative and Crown colony government had proved unworkable, for power had been divorced from
responsibility. Where so much needed doing promptly, the solution
was not further devolution, but the subjugation of finance to an
efficient control. By 1898 Jamaica was practically bankrupt: the
railway, burdening her with an annual debt equal to one-sixth of

---

[1] *Parl. Pap.* 1898, L [C. 8655], p. 1.

[2] *Parl. Pap.* 1902, CIV [Cd. 940], p. 192. *Hansard,* 4th ser. CIV, 850; CXII, 290; CXV,
251; CXVI, 1314.

[3] Similarly a differential duty was placed on Malayan tin in 1903 to keep it within
the Empire.

[4] Seven-eighths of the sugar imported into the U.K. in 1896 was beet or bounty-paid:
Parl. Pap. 1898, L [C. 8656], p. 183.

[5] *Parl. Pap.* 1912–13, LX [Cd. 6282], p. 279. The Government had obtained modification
earlier in 1907: see Halévy, *op. cit.* VI, 18–19.

[6] See Lord Olivier, *Jamaica, the Blessed Island,* pp. 251–4.

the revenue, prevented other development schemes.[1] As a result of the Barbour report, the unofficial majority disappeared and the Colonial Office in effect took over the finances.[2] "It has been decided in regard to the West Indian question as a whole that where financial assistance is given to a colony by the imperial government the imperial government must have control over its finances."[3] Similarly, as a condition of imperial assistance, Antigua and Dominica lost the façade of fractional "representation"; and direct imperial control was considered, though not insisted upon, for British Guiana and Barbados.[4] In 1898 Chamberlain outlined what was "a five year plan for West Indian reconstruction":[5]— improving methods of cultivation as by the establishment of the Agricultural Department of the West Indies under Morris in Barbados; encouraging citrus and banana production by small co-operatives and initiating pilot schemes of peasant proprietorship in St Vincent and Dominica; and subsidising steamer services between Jamaica and British Guiana and negotiating with the Elder Dempster line for regular banana boats to Britain, now fitted with refrigeration plant.[6] This last scheme was an abortive imperial weapon against the American United Fruit Company; for, with United States influence growing in the Caribbean, Chamberlain feared lest the British West Indies should fall into some American *Zollverein*. Attempts to secure favourable terms for Caribbean trade with the United States failed,[7] and (as earlier in 1783) the West Indies looked to Canada, though now more as an export market than as a source for their imports. In 1898 and 1900 Canada, feeling "some imperial responsibility" with Britain in the Caribbean, had granted preference to the West Indies. The vast enlargement of the Canadian market since then led in 1912 to the establishment of reciprocity by the Liberal government in Britain as recognition of "the special relationship" of Canada and the West Indies.[8]

The years were not without their unrest. Disturbances in Trinidad in 1903 began ostensibly over a water works ordinance, but were to some degree stimulated by agitation for a representative constitution. Chamberlain was distressed that they should have revealed the want of that confidence between Government and community which was essential to the working of a Crown colony system, and that the heavy casualties inflicted by ill-disciplined police constituted an "outrage'

[1] *Parl. Pap.* 1899, LIX [C. 9177], p. 143.
[2] *Parl. Pap.* 1899, LIX [C. 9413], p. 219.
[3] *Parl. Pap.* 1900, LV [Cd. 125], p. 321.
[4] Lucas Memo.: C.O. 318/293. Barbados in fact received only a hurricane loan in 1898 and a proportion of the grant made in 1902 to tide over the sugar industry until the Brussels Convention came into force; but along with all West Indian estimates Barbadian finances were subjected to a strict scrutiny. Grants-in-aid totalled more than £1¼ million to the West Indies by 1910: *Parl. Pap.* 1910, XI [Cd. 5369], p. 159.
[5] *Hansard*, 4th ser. LIV, 1538; LXIII, 871.
[6] See Amery, J., *op. cit.* IV, 245–7.   [7] *Parl. Pap.* 1898, L [C. 8655], p. 1.
[8] *Par. Pap.* 1910, XI [Cd. 5369], p. 159.

which brought discredit on British colonial administration.[1] Two
years later rioting in British Guiana over wage demands drew from
Lord Elgin the warning that a governor should not intervene between
employer and labourer to prevent wage concessions.[2] In both these
colonies the demonstrations became involved in the resentment the
Africans felt against the East Indian immigrants: an antipathy
shared by the Europeans too, though they claimed that their reliability as workers made the Indians a "necessity".[3]

Malaya

Closer association in the British Caribbean had been a recommendation of the Norman Commission; but in that area British
policy was content, in Lyttelton's words, "to promote measures of
administration from which union might naturally spring" and was
indisposed to "coerce" the colonies into a federation.[4] In Malaya,
on the other hand, the Government had taken the initiative in
bringing those "Advised" States (which had accepted British Residents) under a more unified control, the so-called Federation of
1896: partly to share the revenues of the richer with the poorer States,
partly to strengthen British influence in South-East Asia against the
French in Siam, but primarily to bring more uniformity into a
complex and unwieldly régime. The work of the Residents, despite
the difficulties, had banished much of the tyranny and extortion from
the States. Roads and railways to open up the resources of the
mines had brought law and security and had given a value to new
lands and opportunities to new staples. But duplication and waste
dogged the several administrations. Though the Colonial Office had
suspected the proposal of "federation" at first,[5] in 1895 instructions
were issued to Frank Swettenham to obtain the consent of the Sultans
thereto: a legal fiction, because, of course, the Residents were the
effective rulers, and no trouble was taken to consult the State Councils. The loose union of nominally sovereign States which was thus
established had its central administration at Kuala Lumpur and a
Resident-General with executive control. Durbars of the Sultans
every four years provided an occasion for the demonstration of general
good will. With the development of the motor industry, rubber
challenged tin as the principal export;[6] and with the exposure of
atrocities on the Congo or at Putumayo the plantation system—it
might seem paradoxically—became favoured as a means of guaran-

---

[1] *Parl. Pap.* 1903, XLIV [Cd. 166], p. 613.
[2] *Parl. Pap.* 1906, LXXVII [Cd. 2822], [Cd. 3026], pp. 217, 343.
[3] See *Parl. Pap.* 1898, L [C. 8657], D. 397.
[4] *Hansard*, 4th ser. CXLVI, 694.
[5] *Pace* Swettenham (*British Malaya*, p. 272), federation does not appear to have been
primarily his suggestion (C.O. 273/197). See also *Parl. Pap.* 1896, LVIII [C. 8257], p. 303,
and *Parl. Pap.* 1897, LXVI [C. 8661], p. 209.
[6] See *Parl. Pap.* 1901, LXVI [Cd. 815], p. 863; 1907, LXXIII [Cd. 3741], p. 597; 1910,
LXVI [Cd. 5373], p. 779.

teeing humane supervision. The problem of cultivating rubber had been solved at Kew and there was no longer need to collect "wild" rubber in the jungle. Scarcity of labour remained the chief problem,[1] confused further by the rivalry of sugar and coffee planters for the limited amount of Indian labour and Government concern with the conditions of contract and passage.[2] By 1914, however, indentured labour, whether Chinese or Indian, was abolished and all labour and immigration became wholly free.

The durbars revealed a general satisfaction with the increasing prosperity. Only with the gentlest politeness did Sultans point out that both they and their Councils were being by-passed.[3] Even the presence of non-Malayan labourers was a subtle threat to the authority of the native rulers. That indeed was the direction, if not the intention, of policy; for in this period the tide within the F.M.S. was running strongly towards centralisation. Lack of identity of interest between the various Straits Settlements, and the Colonial Office's desire to retain control of the Native States, had prevented federation with the two colonies of Penang and Singapore, but in practice, since the F.M.S. had no legislature, the Straits Settlements Legislative Council made laws for the whole peninsula. In 1909, however, when Siam surrendered her suzerainty over Kedah, Kelantan, Trengganu and Perlis, these States passed under British protection, but (like Johore in 1914) remained unfederated, much to the irritation of the F.M.S. which had been saddled with Kedah debts by the transaction. The insistence of these Unfederated States upon their autonomy helped to focus attention upon the Rulers' loss of authority. At the same time the creation of a Federal Council finally "eviscerated" the States Councils. On paper the Agreement of 1909 left the Sultans' powers unimpaired, but it also gave unlimited legislative authority and complete control in the important sphere of finance to the new Council, an assembly in which the Sultans were ordinary members without veto or privilege. Herein lay the seeds of later discontents.

DOMINION NATIONALISM AND THE EMERGENT COMMONWEALTH

Apart from the exceptional grant to the ex-Boer republics, the twenty years before the outbreak of war saw no new devolution of responsible government, but rather the amplification of responsibility

[1] See *Parl. Pap.* 1899, LXI [C. 9524], p. 79, and Mills, L. A., *British Rule in Eastern Asia*, pp. 219–21.

[2] See Immigration Commission Report of 1896 (C.O. 273/235) and Chinese Immigration Bill of 1901 (C.O. 273/269, 270). The Bill restricted immigrants to British vessels to ensure regulation. *The Straits Times* hailed it with an article on the Navigation Acts as providing "a nursery of seamen"; but the C.O., fearing retaliation, demanded amended legislation.

[3] See *Parl. Pap.* 1898, LXI [C. 9108], p. 1, and 1904, LIV [Cd. 2243], p. 527.

already devolved: the invasion by those self-governing colonies, first styled "Dominions" in 1907, of the last of Durham's "imperial" subjects. In 1912 the Judicial Committee of the Privy Council had declared that, once self-government was granted, somewhere within the constitution must be found power to legislate in every internal matter.[1] Dominion sovereignty, of course, still had limitations. Disallowance and reservation were provided for; but the first should be employed, said Chamberlain, only to protect imperial interests as a whole and not in local matters of which the Imperial Government had divested itself absolutely,[2] and the second, used only on the advice of responsible ministers, had become no more than a convention for consultation and delay. Dominion legislation was subordinate to that of Westminster and subject to repugnancy under the Colonial Laws Validity Act.[3] It also lacked extra-territorial effect, but even in this the courts did not always insist strictly. Chamberlain set special value on the Judicial Committee as the tribunal of Empire and sought to establish an Imperial Court of Appeal,[4] but Australians had insisted on the restriction of appeals and South Africans on their right to abolish them and the Judicial Committee itself had disavowed any claim to be a regular court of criminal appeal. Moreover, in the field of external policy, Dominions had established their right to accept or withdraw from British commercial treaties, to have separate representation at international technical conferences, to wage their own tariff wars and to conclude their own reciprocal treaties: in 1907 Sir Edward Grey formally recognised the long-standing convention that Canadian negotiators knew their own needs best.[5] Even the tutelary supervision of a British covering signature, which gave the treaty international effect and preserved diplomatic unity, was avoided in 1911 by the reciprocal "agreement" Canada made with the United States. By 1914 the Dominions had obtained the right to be consulted, not only in matters relating to commerce or the Hague Conventions, but whereever time and the subject-matter permitted.[6] In practice consultation was often neglected: over the Japanese alliance, the partition of Samoa, the *entente cordiale*, and events leading to the First World War, for example. Sir Wilfred Laurier's Canada for her part did not demand consultation, feeling that thereby she would be committed to active participation: for, though Britain's declaration of war in 1914 meant that the whole Empire was at war, the degree to which Dominions would co-operate with men and materials was

[1] A. G. for Ontario *v.* A. G. for Canada: L.J.R. 81 P.C.C. 212.
[2] *Parl. Pap.* 1899, LIX [C. 9137], p. 301. See also *Parl. Pap.* 1901, XLVI (362), p. 7.
[3] See Wheare, K. C., *The Statute of Westminster and Dominion Status*, pp. 62–99.
[4] *Parl. Pap.* 1902, LXVI [Cd. 846], p. 621. See also his speech, 1897, LIX [C. 8596], p. 631.
[5] See Keith, A. B. (ed.), *Selected Speeches and Documents in British Colonial Policy*, II, 165–6.
[6] *Ibid.* II, 182–9.

already theirs to decide. In international law, however, they had yet no personality. The major responsibility in foreign affairs was still legally and effectively that of the British Government, and Asquith had declared emphatically in 1911 that it could not be shared.[1]

A sense of Dominion nationalism was developing rapidly in tune with the times: Jebb's *Studies in Colonial Nationalism* (1905) maintained, contrary to Seeley, that a common British nationality was obsolete, and that the Dominions were already distinct nations with their own policies and prejudices. Canadian nationalism was stimulated by a period of unexampled prosperity which brought over three million immigrants to the new factories and the empty prairies. In 1905 Alberta and Saskatchewan were admitted to that federation which, itself a recognition of unity in diversity, conditioned the Canadian contribution to the new Commonwealth. Canada was an experiment in compromise—geographical, racial, industrial—held together by the threat of internal disunity and fear of the United States.[2] She was well equipped to supply those lessons in reconciliation which South Africa lacked and the Empire needed. Canada's enforced sacrifice on the altar of Anglo-American understanding at the Joint High Commission of 1898 and over the Alaskan Boundary awards of 1900–3 promoted bitter anger against Britain and the United States[3] until, with the improving relations over boundary waters and fisheries, in a standing International Commission and at The Hague, Canada learnt prudently that, since she could not afford to let them disagree, she must become the "golden hinge" in Anglo-American relations. She was no more prepared to be absorbed into Pan-American union based on the States than into a centralised Empire based upon Britain. Canadian insistence on autonomy, economic and political, was no more Sir Wilfrid Laurier's invention than it had been Sir John Macdonald's: the circumstances having changed, it needed asserting now, not against Cobden, but against Chamberlain. Nor was Sir Robert Borden less jealous of the principle, though, unlike Laurier, he was prepared to assume some responsibility for imperial foreign policy as a partner. But it was Laurier who was the chief spokesman for Canadian nationalism in these twenty years: he alone of all the Prime Ministers was present at every one of the Conferences. He did not lack admiration for Britain, but it was the Britain of Burke and Gladstone which claimed his approval. But he had confidence that the new century belonged to Canada: "a nation perfectly independent", at liberty to give or

[1] *Ibid.* II, 302; *Parl. Pap.* 1911, LIV [Cd. 5741], p. 17.
[2] The break of Bourassa and the Quebec isolationists with Laurier was a contemporary proof of this: see Skelton, O., *Life and Letters of Sir W. Laurier*, II, 104–14.
[3] See *C.H.B.E.* VI, 561, 728; Glazebrook, G. P., *Canadian External Relations*, pp. 256–64; and Brebner, J. B., *North Atlantic Triangle*, pp. 256–62. Newfoundland felt similarly sacrificed: see *Parl. Pap.* 1906, CXXXVII [Cd. 3262], p. 389; 1908, LXXII [Cd. 3765], pp. 1, 21, 61, 90 *seqq.*

refuse aid as she judged right in the "plenitude" of her colonial sovereignty under the British Crown.[1] It was natural that he and Botha should have found so much in common.

Temperamentally different, though awakening already to new responsibilities, was the more homogeneous nationalism, radical and strongly racial, of the Australasian democracies. In their Pacific isolation they were more aware of dependence on Britain than was Canada, sheltering behind the Monroe Doctrine and the growing United States navy. But despite the exuberant, and sometimes embarrassing, imperialism of Richard Seddon, Alfred Deakin and Joseph Ward, British policy caused defiant resentment and stimulated national divergence. Seddon protested vigorously to Chamberlain against the Convention with Germany and the United States whereby, in return for concessions elsewhere in the Solomons and West Africa, Britain retired from Samoa. Deakin complained bitterly to Elgin that Australia had not been consulted over the New Hebrides Convention of 1906 and received in return a lecture on the effects of Australian tariffs on island prosperity.[2] The annexation of the Gilbert and Ellice Islands in 1896, the assumption of a British protectorate over Tonga in 1900, and the assignment of the Cook Islands to New Zealand in 1901 and of Papua to Australia in 1906 did something to appease those who still wanted to see the South Seas a British lake. Further differences occurred with the British Government over protection, and over Australian shipping legislation which conflicted with new British navigation laws,[3] and the "white Australian" policy[4] which embarrassed the Indian Government. In 1900 the Commonwealth of Australia Act had established a federation of the former colonies on a loose centrifugal pattern agreed by the Australians themselves.[5] Although Chamberlain had insisted, against the wish of their delegates, on minor concessions, the Australian High Court had emerged with the initiative in the matter of constitutional appeals.[6] The fact that immigration was a State matter frustrated the development of a positive Commonwealth policy which in opposition to Kanakas, Asians and Italians earned a reputation for a prejudiced exclusiveness. State loyalties remained strong even to the point of claiming separate representation at Colonial Conferences.[7] Western Australia had finally joined the

[1] See Dawson, R. M., *Development of Dominion Status*, pp. 135–6; Skelton, *op. cit.* II, pp. 70–86, 321–8, 332; *C.H.B.E.* VI, 704–37.
[2] *Parl. Pap.* 1907, LVI [Cd. 3288], p. 649.
[3] *Parl. Pap.* 1905, LIV [Cd. 2483], p. 5; 1906, LXXVII [Cd. 3023], p. 149.
[4] *Parl. Pap.* 1902, LXVI [Cd. 1258], p. 825; 1903, XLIV [Cd. 1554], p. 103; *Hansard*, 4th ser. CXII, 1081; and Chamberlain's speech in Keith, *op. cit.* II, 227–9. The Commonwealth Parliament also addressed the King against British policy in Ireland and in favour of Home Rule: *Parl. Pap.* 1906, LXXVII [Cd. 2821], p. 217.
[5] 63 & 64 Vict. c. 12. See *Hansard*, 4th ser. LXXXV, 579.
[6] *Parl. Pap.* 1900, LV [Cd. 124], p. 1.
[7] *Parl. Pap.* 1903, XLIV [Cd. 1587], p. 71; 1907, LIV [Cd. 3340], p. 739.

federation, but New Zealand had not. The movement for federation with Fiji was strong in New Zealand during the first few years of the century, but, in face of a sturdy championship of Fijian independence by its Governor, it came to nothing. Meanwhile, in a period of prosperity, the impetus of Seddon's state socialism did not diminish. Factory legislation, old age pensions, the beginnings of a health service were provided. The requirement of compulsory arbitration provoked, and survived, the challenge of a revolutionary trade unionism. Letters home from these Pacific democracies where citizens trained in arms, and women had won political rights with men, helped to nourish in what Ward habitually called "the Old Land" that pride in Empire (and in being British) which was one manifestation of the new emancipation of the labourers in Britain.[1]

In desiring to shepherd these colonies into a permanent union organised efficiently for prosperity, stability and security, Chamberlain overlooked these national divergences. His zeal for Greater Britain was conditioned inevitably by his devotion to *British* interests. At the root of his imperialism he was a Little Englander. Britain could retain her supremacy and ensure world order only by drawing together that Empire from which Free Trade had caused her to secede. Colonial isolation had been dissolved by improved communications: imperial reunion could be assured by similar means— an all-red Pacific cable, for example.[2] The Imperial Federation League had taught people to evaluate anew the principle of association. Want of success and support for more formal bonds had caused the League to suspend operations in Britain,[3] but enthusiasts looked for champions and evangelists among Dominion statesmen: Laurier in 1897, Seddon in 1902, Deakin in 1907 and Ward in 1911.[4] Each time, however, the strength of Dominion nationalism disappointed them. In his adroit and disarming way it was Laurier's role to refuse all of Chamberlain's nostrums.[5] When Chamberlain had gone, the threat to Dominion independence came not so much (as Laurier supposed) from "lionising duchesses" in London society,[6] but from expatriate Britons in the South Pacific, and it was warded off by the mother country and the daughter-in-law nations. In the assertion of British and colonial self-determination Chamberlain's dreams of more union—federal, commercial, defensive—faded.

A federal *Staatsverein* remained the main goal of those who favoured closer association because it would imply the others; but in whatever form a central Council was proposed—by Chamberlain with tact in 1897 and with vigour in 1902, by Lyttelton's dispatch of 1905, or

---

[1] See *C.H.B.E.* VII, pt. I, pp. 493–545; pt. II, pp. 201–23. On the quality of Australian nationalism see Hancock, W. K., *Politics in Pitcairn*, pp. 51–64.

[2] See Garvin, *op. cit.* III, 173–5.

[3] The calling of a Conference in 1887 and the appointment of colonial judges to the J.C.P.C. were its two achievements.   [4] See Skelton, *op. cit.* p. 342.

[5] Dafoe, J. W., *Laurier*, pp. 64 *seqq.*   [6] *Ibid.* p. 57.

by Ward in 1911—it was effectively repudiated or entirely ignored. Even Lyttelton's Secretariat and Harcourt's Standing Committee of High Commissioners commended themselves to none but the Australasian Dominions.[1] Laurier, who had flirted mischievously with the idea of colonial representation at Westminster,[2] spoke clearly for the others in 1897 when he affirmed Canada's satisfaction with the existing relationship. The imperial connection rested, as Campbell-Bannerman said ten years later, on freedom and independence. Regular conferences proposed by Seddon in 1902 were the highest common factor of agreement; and, in reply to Lyttelton's proposals, the Prime Ministers decided in 1907 on four-yearly *Imperial* Conferences of *Dominions* as the limit of change desired. The unequivocal repudiation of Ward's confused scheme by all his fellow-premiers in 1911 was a final blow at imperial federation, despite "Kindergarten" enthusiasm in the "Round Table" group. Flexibility and informality in discussion were vindicated. Dominions were aspiring even to equality; Australia and Canada suggested that the next Conference should be held in a Dominion capital.

Similarly, Dominion economic nationalism and British loyalty to free trade extinguished hopes of some commercial union under central control.[3] Laurier's unconditional preference in 1897 had been the bait: with Liberal Imperialist support Chamberlain was ready to represent Free-trade-within-the-Empire as an extension of Cobdenism, and even to forfeit considerable trade under Belgian and German treaties as an earnest of his hopes of an increasing imperial commerce. His advocacy in 1897 was, however, tempered with a cautious realisation of the difficulties involved in erecting an imperial customs union. Britain's imposition of a corn duty during the South African War provided the pretext, and Chamberlain's more enthusiastic concept of a "self-sustaining" *Zollverein* the alarm, for urgent demands by the colonies for British reciprocity.[4] Though Chamberlain had ruled this out of consideration and could not accept the resolution unamended, the Conference of 1902 convinced him that closer union lay only by way of Tariff Reform: a subversion of free trade which won him the support of many protectionists for reasons unconnected with Empire, and forfeited that of the Liberal Imperialists and many Conservatives who believed that Britain could not survive upon a mere fraction of imperial trade alone. Since 1897 other colonies, following Canada's lead, had given preferences to Britain

[1] *Parl. Pap.* 1897, LIX [C. 8596], p. 631; 1902, LXVI [Cd. 1299], p. 451; 1906, LXXVII [Cd. 2784], p. 53; 1907, LIV [Cd. 3337], p. 727; 1907, LV [Cd. 3404], [Cd. 3406], [Cd. 3523], pp. 1, 29, 61; 1911, LIV [Cd. 5741], [Cd. 5745], [Cd. 5746], pp. 17, 103, 547.
[2] Dafoe, *op. cit.* p. 62. Still hoping for a federal Council, Chamberlain spoke against a motion for colonial representation in Westminster: *Hansard*, 4th ser. LXXX, 1131.
[3] See Hancock, *op. cit.* II, pt. 1, 72–110; Halévy, *op. cit.* V, 285–355; VI, 3–118; Garvin, *op. cit.* III, 185–95; Amery, J., *op. cit.* IV, 289–533.
[4] *Parl. Pap.* 1897, LIX [C. 8596], p. 631; 1902, LXVI [Cd. 1299], p. 451; *Hansard*, 4th ser. CVIII, 43; CIX, 1029; CXXIV, 723; CXXXV, 254; CXXXVIII, 890; CXXXIX, 284.

and to each other;[1] but the Liberal landslide of 1906 doomed immediate hopes of Tariff Reform in Britain. At the Conference next year Dominion Prime Ministers were reminded by Asquith that Britain's foreign trade alone enabled her to shoulder the burdens of imperial defence and were warned by Churchill that a dearer food policy dictated by them would undoubtedly create a new anti-imperialism. They were "a family, not a syndicate"..."better employed in making roads than building walls". Already Canada was showing more interest in reciprocity with the United States and, with Botha's support, Laurier opposed Dominion interference in British self-government. The principle of freedom of action as most likely to promote greater imperial trade was accepted and was reaffirmed in 1911.[2] But facts were stronger than aspirations, and in the gradual retreat from the "Great Commercial Republic" centripetal tendencies were given some recognition by the appointment in 1912 of a Royal Commission, which, though underestimating national diversity, produced a realistic analysis of the meagre chances of imperial self-sufficiency.[3]

If the Dominions displayed interest primarily in preference, it was in defence that most British statesmen felt the need for closer union,[4] seeking (as had their predecessors a century before from an autonomous Ireland) some sharing of the burden under which "the weary Titan" stumbled. When Chamberlain pleaded for some community of sacrifice, he wanted colonial defence contributions. Seeing that these would leave control under the British Admiralty, the Dominions resented "taxation without representation" and called instead for some British sacrifice of free trade. At first small contributions had been offered—even by a Moderate-Bond ministry at the Cape. But the Australasian colonies had made them under conditions which kept a British squadron based in the South Seas; and with Admiral Fisher's concentration of the British Navy in the North Sea and with the Dreadnought scare of 1909, Australia claimed the right to her own navy, proving that such an ambition was not, as Chamberlain had supposed of Laurier's refusal of a contribution in 1902, a personal French-Canadian eccentricity.[5] Although Haldane managed to obtain an Imperial General Staff and some standardisation in case Dominions might wish to assist Britain in an emergency, the Imperial Defence Conference of 1909 would have nothing to do with local imperial reserves (which Seddon had suggested in 1902), and

---

[1] See *Parl. Pap.* 1905, LIII [Cd. 2326], p. 441. Seddon had made reciprocal agreements with Australia and there was Milner's South African *Zollverein* in 1906.

[2] *Parl. Pap.* 1907, LV [Cd. 3406], pp. 29 *seqq.*; 1911, LIV [Cd. 5741], pp. 17 *seqq.*

[3] *Parl. Pap.* 1912–13, XVI [Cd. 6515], [Cd. 6516], [Cd. 6517], pp. 91, 95, 393; 1914, XVII, [Cd. 7170], [Cd. 7171], [Cd. 7172], [Cd. 7173], pp. 101, 361, 731; XVIII [Cd. 7210], [Cd. 7351], pp. 137, 213.

[4] *Hansard*, 4th ser. LXXXVI, 435; LXXXVII, 831; XCIV, 636; CXLII, 805. See also *Parl. Pap.* 1903, XLIV [Cd. 1597], p. 1.

[5] Amery, J., *op. cit.* IV, pp. 422–5; Skelton, *op. cit.* II, 296–9.

recognised national particularism in defence.[1] Three years later, the Senate's treatment of Borden's Naval Service Bill finally disappointed hopes of renewed Canadian co-operation.[2] New Zealand alone continued to contribute to the British Navy until the outbreak of war, realising, nevertheless (as Ward had pointed out in 1911),[3] that her loyalty in this matter of imperial tribute put her to some disadvantage in deciding for herself her degree of "active participation" when war was declared.

The new pattern of Empire emerged not from zeal for order and centralisation, but gradually from that "better understanding and closer sympathy" with Dominion nationalism which Chamberlain came to urge "as the highest object of statesmanship in the new century" in a speech which proved his political farewell. Only under the immediate dynamic of total war or world slump (as in the Imperial War Cabinet or at the Ottawa Conference) or in dawning realisation in the mid-century of the impossibility of complete sovereign independence in a shrinking world was Dominion particularism prepared to make concession to the "associate principle" in an undemanding fellowship: Grey's confidential "facts-of-life" talk on British foreign policy in 1911 had already given observers a glimpse of unexampled solidarity. His confidence had bred confidence. Devolution led to strength in a new comradeship. Instead of federal union there was the Imperial Conference—without formality or authority; instead of *Zollverein* or *Kriegsverein* there was a growing sense of mutual need soon to prove itself in a war which saw the collapse of many empires and the birth of many new states, less stable than those in Laurier's "galaxy of free nations" round the British Crown whose style and title now gave special recognition to its "Dominions overseas".[4] An *entente* rather than an alliance, it combined, as Asquith had said in 1911, "local autonomy—absolute, unfettered, complete—with loyalty to a common head, co-operation, spontaneous and unforced, for common interests and purposes, and...a common trusteeship" for all fellow-subjects.[5] They were "units in a greater unity", aspiring no longer to separation but to equality. The British Prime Minister presiding at their Conferences, *primus inter pares*, symbolised their emancipation from the Secretary of State for the Colonies.[6] The war which called all these young nations to arms strengthened their claim to sovereignty: they were, said Resolution IX of the Imperial

---

[1] *Parl. Pap.* 1909, LI [Cd. 4475], p. 627; LIX [Cd. 4948], p. 335. Australia and New Zealand had adopted conscription.

[2] *Parl. Pap.* 1912–13, LIII [Cd. 6513], p. 445; LX [Cd. 6560], pp. 513, 637.

[3] Keith, *op. cit.* II, 250, 255–6, 258.

[4] *Parl. Pap.* 1901, XLVI [Cd. 708], p. 1. Chamberlain had suggested "Greater Britain beyond the seas". Canada wanted separate Kingships by name: Australia "British Realms beyond the seas". "British Dominions beyond the seas" was chosen.

[5] Keith, *op. cit.* II, 242–3.

[6] Contrast the photograph of the 1897 Conference: Chamberlain sitting, the colonial premiers standing: see Skelton, *op. cit.* II, 64.

War Conference, "autonomous nations of an Imperial Commonwealth" claiming an "adequate voice" in foreign policy, and consultation in all matters of "common concern".[1] The mood was gone which had given heart to the Federalists. No longer was it sufficient for the self-governing colonies to be present at family reunions: they now desired their opinions to be heard and to be respected.

In adjusting itself to contain these new nations the Second British Empire jettisoned many assumptions which were outdated and proprieties that were no longer proper: the supremacy of the British Parliament as sole amending body and of British legislation as supreme law, common subjecthood, the doctrine of repugnancy, diplomatic unity, allegiance to an undivided Crown, Britain's right to declare war on behalf of the whole group. To mark these changes begun within this period, a good Saxon word was rescued from mid-Victorian notoriety by men as different as Lord Rosebery, Bernard Shaw and Lionel Curtis and was given notable publicity by General Smuts. In the shaping of this "Commonwealth" many men and many opinions had had a hand: Radicals, Unionists, Gladstonians, Socialists, Imperialists and nationalists. Chamberlain and Laurier, Botha and Campbell-Bannerman, Dilke and Seddon, they fashioned a compromise: a characteristic solution which united freedom and association, and embraced both Nationalism and imperialism. Together they managed to secure that union of free peoples under a single monarch which Madison, Franklin and others had conceived,[2] and to achieve by evolution and mutual respect what Washington had gained, and lost, by revolution and force of arms. In the last resort the strongest bonds of union were those which stemmed from a common stock of ideas.

[1] Keith, *op. cit.* II, 376.
[2] See Kennedy, W. P. M., *Essays in Constitutional Law*, pp. 19–20.

CHAPTER XI

THE DEVELOPMENT OF THE IMPERIAL
CONFERENCE, 1887–1914

THE first of what became a regular series of Colonial or, after 1907, Imperial Conferences was held at the Colonial Office in London between 4 April and 9 May 1887 in connection with the Golden Jubilee of Queen Victoria. It had, however, much more than a merely ceremonial significance. If it had not been for a recent and considerable increase of interest in the idea of imperial unity, it is doubtful if such a Conference would have played any part in these celebrations. Appropriately, therefore, the Imperial Federation League, which since 1884 had been actively propagating the idea of imperial unity, played a leading part in bringing about this first official conference between representatives of Great Britain and the colonies.

Encouraged by the success of an unofficial Conference held earlier in the year at the time of the Indian and Colonial Exhibition, the Council of this League sent a deputation to Lord Salisbury, the Prime Minister, on 11 August 1886. It asked the Government either to call a conference or to appoint a Royal Commission to consider practical means to improve imperial defence, promote commercial intercourse within the Empire "and all other means for securing the closer federation or union of all parts of the Empire". Salisbury's response, though guarded so far as anything beyond defence and communications was concerned, was on the whole sympathetic, and the dispatch summoning the first Colonial Conference was sent from the Colonial Office on 25 November.[1]

It would hardly be correct, however, to ascribe the sole credit for this official action to the League. The idea of holding such a conference was, in any case, not new in 1886; indeed, in one form or another, it had been under discussion for some time. Nor is this surprising in view of the interest, prevalent since the early 'seventies, in various imperial questions and especially in imperial unity. Salisbury's emphasis on defence when he received the League's deputation is also significant, especially as it was soon to be repeated in the Colonial Conference itself. Throughout the 'eighties, indeed, defence questions had become increasingly urgent. It was a period when British power at sea, not seriously challenged for decades, was being forced to adjust itself to important changes in naval construction and armament which, apart from more serious considerations,

---

[1] For the part played by the League, see Tyler, J. E., *The Struggle for Imperial Unity, 1868–1895*, pp. 112–14.

seemed sure to increase the cost of the Royal Navy to the British
tax-payer. Already, when he was Prime Minister, Disraeli had been
anxious to restore "military relations with our Colonies" and a Royal
Commission on Imperial Defence had actually been set up in 1879.[1]

Thus the happy occasion of a Royal Jubilee, the initiative of the
Imperial Federation League and the manifest importance to various
parts of the Empire of defence questions, all combined to make the
first Colonial Conference a possibility in 1887.

Though sometimes described in the press as an "Imperial Conference", it was officially designated "Colonial", apparently because
it did not include any representatives of the Empire of India.[2] Even
so, in comparison with later meetings, the representation on this
first occasion was remarkably wide. It was not confined, as the
deputation from the Imperial Federation League had suggested, to
the United Kingdom and the self-governing colonies. It also included
representatives of the Crown colonies as well as a large number of
public men associated, either officially or otherwise, with imperial
affairs. Nor were the self-governing colonies represented in all cases
by their premiers or even by members of the government of the day.
Indeed, in summoning the Conference as Colonial Secretary, Edward
Stanhope had called for as wide a representation as possible since, in
his view, it was not "material" that the colonies should have equal
or proportionate representation in what would necessarily be a
purely consultative body.[3] At the opening ceremony (4 April) there
were present 11 members of the United Kingdom Government,
25 representatives of self-governing colonies (including W. Australia
which attained to self-government in 1890 and Natal, which attained
to it in 1893), 33 representatives of 23 Crown colonies and 54 other representatives, e.g. former colonial Governors-General and Governors,
the Chairman of the Royal Colonial Institute and M.P.'s.

The British Government, therefore, did not conceive of the Conference as one between itself and the self-governing colonies only.
It was rather designed to enable the suzerain power to assess the views
of as wide a colonial circle as possible on certain subjects, notably
defence or communications, and, if possible, to obtain some help from
the colonies in bearing the burdens involved. It is true that Sir Henry
Holland, who succeeded Stanhope at the Colonial Office after the latter
had issued the original invitation, asked the colonies to submit subjects
for discussion. But the British Government nevertheless kept a firm
hand on the proceedings. It ruled out altogether the discussion of
political federation, obviously deprecated any colonial intrusion into
the field of foreign relations, and was evidently not anxious to enter

[1] Tyler, *op. cit.* pp. 15, 24–5 for this Royal Commission. Bodelsen, C. A., *Studies in Mid-Victorian Imperialism* mentions early proposals to bring the Colonies into consultation. See particularly the section headed "A Council of Advice", pp. 142–4.

[2] *Parl. Pap.* 1887, LVI [C. 5091], pp. 371.

[3] *Ibid.* p. viii.

deeply, if at all, into the discussion of inter-imperial trade which actually took place on the initiative of Queensland and the Cape.

In fact, the Conference devoted half its working time to defence, the subject on which the British Government laid most emphasis. Even so, there was, in addition, the important discussion of inter-imperial trade policy, and colonial views on British foreign policy—so far at least as some colonies were concerned—were expressed and, indeed, forcibly expressed. As was no doubt inevitable, whatever the wishes of the United Kingdom might be, the Conference tended from the first to take control of its own agenda and procedure and to develop an initiative in these matters which it never lost.

Moreover, though the official composition of the Conference was very wide, the dominant part on the colonial side was played throughout by the self-governing colonies. In this sense, too, the Conference really began as it was to continue and no future Conference had, even formally, the large and amorphous composition of the first.

Nor was it only in this connection that the Conference established precedents. Salisbury, as Prime Minister, attended only the formal inaugural session of the Conference; the Colonial Secretary, Holland, actually presided over the day-to-day deliberations and not until 1907 did a British Prime Minister again play even this limited part in the proceedings. In 1887 Salisbury once more attended for the discussion of the activities of foreign Powers in the Pacific Islands; but it was as Foreign Secretary, just as in future Conferences British Cabinet Ministers were similarly to attend when matters affecting their own departments arose. The Conference of 1911 was the first in which the British Prime Minister (in this case Asquith) acted as Chairman and by virtue of his office as first minister of the Crown.

Similarly, as regards publicity, certain principles were adopted in 1887 which, if criticised from time to time by members of successive Conferences, were to become customary. Reporters, said Holland, would be present only when Salisbury formally opened the Conference. At later sessions business would either be confidential, or such as it would be desirable to discuss "informally and without the restraint which would be imposed by immediate publication of proceedings". But he undertook to supply the press and the colonial Governments with brief and authentic notes of subjects which had been under consideration.[1] When the Conference was over, a full official report was presented to Parliament. This was a *verbatim* account of what had passed, except the discussions relative to the Pacific Islands and some matters of minor significance. This, too, was done in the case of later Conferences with the exception of those of 1897 and 1902 when the full reports were never made public. Generally speaking, throughout the whole of this period, the Conference felt that it could work more effectively in private, especially on subjects which aroused strong party

[1] *Parl. Pap.* 1887, LVI [C. 5091], Papers, p. 1.

feeling either in Britain or the colonies. As Asquith remarked in the Conference of 1911, it was not "in the nature of a public meeting".[1]

The character of the Conference was also involved in the question of resolutions. The adoption of formal resolutions was not favoured by Holland in 1887.[2] This may have been due to fears lest resolutions on controversial questions such as imperial federation or, more particularly, imperial preference, might embarrass the home Government or some other participating Government. Nor had formal resolutions necessarily any essential part to play in a conference designed primarily for an exchange of views. The colonial attitude could be tested without them, as it was on this occasion, for example, on the question of preferential trade. If resolutions on such a subject were adopted, they could have greater force than that of mere recommendations only if the Conference itself became something more than a meeting of the representatives of autonomous governments simply exchanging views. Nevertheless, the Conferences were always to discuss and adopt resolutions, however "informal", and with regard to their own constitution and procedure these could have binding force.

The main achievement of this first Colonial Conference might appear, in retrospect, to have been the agreement by the Australian colonies to pay an annual subsidy towards the cost of a naval squadron in Australian waters. The insistence of the British Government on defence was to this extent rewarded. If, however, there had been any hopes of using this or a similar conference simply as a means to enable the British Government to extract such "subsidies" from an obedient assembly of colonial representatives, they must soon have been qualified by the reaction of public opinion in the Australian colonies themselves. There is, in fact, little evidence that such hopes were ever widely entertained and not the least important achievement of the Conference was the educative influence which it had in this respect. Few people can have heard Alfred Deakin, for example, on the subject of the South Pacific without wondering whether such a conception of imperial relations was not at least obsolescent.

It may be that Deakin's presence at the first Conference was for this reason of particular importance. In the words of his biographer, he was "the embodiment of that spirit of 'colonial nationalism' which, though its existence had hardly begun to be suspected by British statesmen, was already subtly transforming the whole character of Imperial relations".[3] No doubt the sooner this "transformation" was appreciated by all concerned with the problem of imperial unity the better, and Deakin's vigorous language must have helped considerably in this respect.

[1] *Parl. Pap.* 1911, LIV [Cd. 5745], p. 31.
[2] E.g. in the discussion of publicity on the first day of the Conference, [C. 5091], p. 2.
[3] Murdoch, *Alfred Deakin*, p. 99.

Even so, others besides Deakin realised the great significance which might attach to the present occasion and, especially, its promise for the future. When, at the closing session, Sir Samuel Griffith, Premier of Queensland, spoke of the Conference as having "the rudimentary elements of a Parliament" and dwelt on its possible development into a "legislative...or at any rate a consultative body", he may neither have been using carefully chosen language nor expressing the views of the majority. But without doubt he reflected their views when he assumed that this Conference would be followed by others which would become a recognised part of the constitutional machinery of the Empire. The composition, procedure, and indeed the entire character of future Conferences, were certain to be influenced by the experience gained in 1887.

Nor did it escape notice at the time that, by holding periodic conferences of this sort, the very problems which had recently aroused interest in imperial unity might be solved. This had the greater importance as the doubtful, if not positively unfavourable, attitude of much colonial opinion towards the idea of federal union was becoming apparent. It may be recalled, too, that the British Government had expressly excluded political federation from the agenda of the Conference, ostensibly because there had been no expression of colonial opinion in its favour and to discuss it might therefore jeopardise "the ultimate attainment of a more developed system of united action".[1] Whatever the motives of the British Government, the exclusion of political federation helped to emphasise the Conference as an end in itself instead of as a means to another, for example federal, end. Here, in any case, had been an occasion for joint deliberation on matters of common interest and of suggestions for common action. This was not only important from the point of view of the Conference as a continuing institution, but was to have an important bearing on the argument for and against imperial federation if only because it suggested a possible alternative to formal federation.[2]

There was general agreement that another Conference should be held at some future date and that it would be wise, therefore, to consider any weaknesses which the first had revealed in its actual working. Throughout the whole of this period, indeed, the Conference was concerned with such questions as the preparation of agenda or the best way in which to follow up the work done at one Conference before the meeting of the next. The question of a "link" between the Conferences was particularly important. As will be seen, it was not simply one of a technical or "business" character; it had also an obvious bearing on the question whether the Conferences were to be isolated occurrences or something quite different, the regular "sessions" of a permanent institution.

It was not until 1897 that a second Colonial Conference, fully

[1] [C. 5091], p. viii.   [2] Tyler, *op. cit.* chap. xvi.

comparable in character and purpose with the first, took place. A subsidiary Conference, however, met at Ottawa in 1894 (28 June– 4 July) at the invitation of the Canadian Government. This was "subsidiary", not so much because it met outside the capital of the Empire, but because of the occasion of its meeting. It was the result of informal resolutions at the Conference of 1887 on the Pacific Cable project, one of the subjects then discussed. In this way it anticipated the practice of holding subsidiary conferences of this type which was formally adopted as an element in the conference system in 1907.[1]

These, however, were early days and more than one speaker at Ottawa recalled the Conference of 1887 and the hopes then expressed that it would be the first of a series. Was this not perhaps the second? Such precedents as were offered by 1887, for example in the matter of publicity,[2] were followed and the earlier practice and experience frequently cited. Indeed, de Villiers, of the Cape, actually saw in the place of meeting and the scope of the Conference, precedents which might some day be followed when weightier matters such as defence or even imperial federation were discussed.[3] But on this point his colleagues were not unanimous. Foster, of Canada, described the meeting as a "Colonial" rather than an "Imperial" Conference on the grounds that it was primarily concerned with colonial interests and would have to express colonial wishes to the only Power (i.e. Great Britain) which could gratify them.[4] Moreover, the Earl of Jersey, who represented the British Government at Ottawa, undoubtedly occupied a special position which lent point to Foster's remarks. He was instructed not to express any views on behalf of Her Majesty's Government, but simply to listen and to report on matters of fact. The Government would reserve its views until it had the report of the proceedings and the resolutions adopted.[5] And it was Bowell of Canada, not Jersey, who actually took the chair.

In addition to Jersey, there were at Ottawa representatives of all the self-governing colonies except Newfoundland, which was not apparently invited, and Western Australia and Natal, which did not send representatives owing to pressure of state business. The govern- ment of Fiji, invited to send a representative because of Fiji's geo- graphical situation in connection with the cable, also declined for the same reason. Membership was thus restricted to the United Kingdom and all but one of the self-governing colonies. Equally important was the fact that, with two exceptions, the colonial repre- sentation was confined to ministers or members of a legislature; the exceptions being Sandford Fleming,[6] who had special knowledge of the cable project, and A. Lee Smith, the representative of New

---

[1] See below, p. 429.   [2] *Parl. Pap.* 1894, LVI [C. 7553], p. 61 and cf. pp. 257–8.
[3] *Ibid.* pp. 42–3.   [4] *Ibid.* p. 210.   [5] *Ibid.* p. 372.
[6] *Ibid.* pp. 375–6.

Zealand chosen, as he said, purely as a "commercial man".[1] But Fleming, it was explained, would merely open the discussion; he was not to propose any resolution since he was not in a position to "pledge any government".

So far as resolutions were concerned, the Conference of 1894 having an object at once precise and more limited than its predecessor, no one seems to have doubted that questions should be put to the vote. As Thompson of Canada pointed out, resolutions need not be carried unanimously. This raised the question of voting-power and it was decided that each colony should have one vote. But there was no question, if only because of Jersey's instructions, of any resolution, unanimous or otherwise, being binding. The matter was, nevertheless, important. Must such a Conference confine itself to resolutions of such a general or "neutral" nature as would enable all to approve, or could it, by a majority vote, make more precise and vigorous recommendations even though they would bind no one? These were questions which the Conference, as it developed, had frequently to consider since its own character and powers were involved.

Actually the adoption on this occasion of the principle of "one colony, one vote" did establish a precedent.[2] But whether this and the acceptance of majority voting was to be the first step towards agreement by participating Governments to be bound by majority decisions, or an early sign of an equality of status really incompatible with any submission to majority voting, only the future could show. Either development was still possible.

Another question, which was to lose none of its importance as time passed, was raised by Wrixon of Victoria when the Conference was coming to an end. He suggested that someone should concern himself with carrying on technical, practical business, "to keep the thing from expiring before the next conference", and a resolution was adopted asking Canada to attend to this. The assumption that there would be further Conferences is itself interesting, and though Wrixon, with the cable project in mind, was thinking of a highly technical matter, he had raised again the question of continuity of business or a "link" between the Conferences which would surely be essential if they were to become something more than merely sporadic occurrences.[3]

For various reasons, then, apart from its date (it met half way, as it were, between the first two Conferences and in connection with no great imperial festival) it is impossible to dismiss the meeting at Ottawa as being, if subsidiary, unimportant. Its resolutions in favour of preferential trade showed that Colonial Governments

---

[1] *Parl. Pap.* 1894, LVI [C. 7553], p. 45.
[2] On the question of resolutions see [C. 7553], p. 212.
[3] *Ibid.* pp. 170, 252.

welcomed a further official opportunity to express their views on an important subject which affected them all. It is undoubtedly important, too, as being essentially a meeting of representatives of the United Kingdom and the self-governing colonies only, and this was to be true of all future Conferences.

The second "main" Conference met at the Colonial Office in London in 1897, there being five sittings in all, held every three or four days. It was the first of two over which Joseph Chamberlain presided as Colonial Secretary and which as a result felt the impact of his powerful personality and distinctive views on imperial questions.[1] As to these, though the means which he favoured varied from time to time, the end, a firmer union of the Empire so that it might play a more effective part in British and world politics, did not. In particular he can be seen, in 1897 and 1902, attempting to persuade the Colonial Conferences to take positive steps towards an ultimate political federation of the Empire. On both occasions he failed. But his failure was not unimportant. It left the Conference much more firmly established in its own right as being in fact (apart from the Crown) the main institutional expression of imperial unity.

As a federalist, or for that matter as one dissatisfied with the degree to which imperial unity had already been organised, Chamberlain did not stand alone at home, or in the colonies or, indeed, in these Conferences. But he had able opponents. If the Conference of 1897 is important as the first over which Chamberlain presided, it seems, in retrospect, no less so as the first at which the chief representative of Canada was Sir Wilfrid Laurier. In 1897, either Laurier's views on the Conference and on imperial unity in general had not fully developed or, newly in office, he hesitated in the Queen's Jubilee year to give them free expression.[2] But there is no evidence that at this time he had the least sympathy with Chamberlain's federalist views, and later he was certainly the strongest opponent of federalism in the Conferences and as such was to influence profoundly their character and functions. This was especially so after the advent of a Liberal government to power in Britain in 1905, so that, having helped to resist Chamberlain in the Conferences of 1897 and 1902, he survived the latter's disappearance from the Conference to play a much more positive part in those of 1907 and 1911.

The Diamond Jubilee in 1897 provided a convenient opportunity to hold a Colonial Conference since the Premiers of all the self-

[1] See Garvin, *Life of Joseph Chamberlain*, iii, chap. liv.
[2] For Laurier and the 1897 Conference, see Skelton's *Life and Letters*, ii, chap. xi. On one occasion (the date is not given by his biographer) Laurier said that there "was little serious discussion in the Colonial Conference of 1897, which was a mere curtain-raiser. The debates were academic; we did not come to sufficiently close quarters to bring out the cleavage of opinions" (Skelton, *op. cit.* ii, 299, n. 1). This was apparently an opinion expressed by Laurier in later years when he was reflecting on the Conferences as a whole, but it may help to explain why Laurier did not give more vigorous expression to his views in 1897.

governing colonies had been invited to take part in the celebrations. In addition to Laurier, the Prime Ministers of New South Wales, Victoria, New Zealand, Queensland, Cape Colony, South Australia, Newfoundland, Tasmania, Western Australia and Natal attended the Conference. But though, as in 1887, the Conference was closely associated with a royal occasion, it is impossible to believe that Chamberlain, given the nature of his views and the sense of urgency which moved him, would not have found an opportunity to hold such a Conference at some time during his tenure of the Colonial Office. Nevertheless, the Jubilee helped to fix not only the date of the 1897 Conference but its composition, and it was confined to Chamberlain and the Premiers of the self-governing colonies.[1] Thus it conformed to what was to be the fixed pattern; after 1887 the Crown colony representatives and the distinguished public men do not make a formal appearance.

Although a full report of the proceedings was compiled, the Conference deliberated in private and the full report was never actually published.[2] On this occasion, unlike 1887, Salisbury, who was again in office as Prime Minister of the United Kingdom, did not take part even in a formal inaugural session. Chamberlain opened the Conference and also presided over its deliberations. Addressing the Conference for the first time, he disclaimed any desire on the part of the British Government to press its own views. On the contrary, it was anxious to hear what the colonies had to say on such big questions as political relations, defence and commerce, and these subjects did in fact engage most of the Conference's attention. Chamberlain, however, clearly indicated which of these subjects seemed to him to be of the greatest importance. It was undoubtedly the first, or what he also called "closer relations". He wanted to see a "great Council of the Empire" established and had in mind the "Federal council" which, he insisted, must be the "ultimate ideal".[3]

Chamberlain's hope that the Conference would make some advance in the direction he had indicated was not, however, realised. His proposals were fully discussed (in contrast to what was to be the case in 1902), but the conclusion to which the Conference came must have disappointed him. A resolution was adopted to the effect that "the present political relations between the United Kingdom and the self-governing Colonies" were "generally satisfactory under the existing condition of things". This opinion, it is true, was not shared

---

[1] Garvin, *op. cit.* III, p. 187, describes Chamberlain as "attended" by Selborne, his Parliamentary Under-Secretary. The First Lord of the Admiralty and the First Sea Lord attended the fifth and last meeting owing to some misapprehensions concerning the views of the British Government on the agreement with the Australian colonies (*Parl. Pap.* 1897, LIX [C. 8596], p. 15), and, in discussing imperial defence, the Conference had the expert advice of Capt. Nathan, Secretary of the Colonial Defence Committee (*ibid.* p. 18).

[2] Garvin used the confidential report.

[3] See Garvin, *op. cit.* III, pp. 187–9, for an account of Chamberlain's opening speech, and pp. 189–92 for the discussions. Cf. *Parl. Pap.* 1897, LIX [C. 8485], pp. 4–5.

by all the colonial Premiers since both Seddon of New Zealand and Braddon of Tasmania dissented. But the majority of them evidently either felt that the time had not yet come to take the positive steps which Chamberlain had suggested, or suspected his proposals in any case as likely to encroach on colonial self-government. In these circumstances the resolution cannot be regarded simply as a broad statement without much precise meaning designed to smooth over differences of opinion. If only by implication, it was a rejection by the only "Imperial Council" which as yet existed of Chamberlain's federal proposal.

On the other hand, in another resolution, all agreed that it was desirable to hold "periodical conferences of representatives of the Colonies and Great Britain for the discussion of matters of common interest".[1] Chamberlain admittedly described this proposal as the "beginning of a Federal Conference", though to do this was surely to subject the meaning of the word "federal" to a considerable degree of strain. The resolution seems more susceptible of another and quite different interpretation. Immediately after the Conference of 1887 it had been possible to see in the "method of Conference" a feasible alternative to the federal solution of the important problems of political relations, defence and trade which the whole question of imperial relations involved.[2] It might now be argued that the Conference itself had not only rejected the federal solution but had adopted, as it were formally, the alternative. Certainly, if it had ever in fact been a case of "federate or disintegrate", it now seemed questionable if this was still true. Was there not a third possibility compatible with both the colonies' scrupulous regard for their own autonomy and their anxiety nevertheless not to leave the Empire? Indeed, more than ever before, the problem of imperial unity had become one of reconciling precisely these two things.

Actually five, and not three, years were to elapse before another Colonial Conference was held. It was not until the South African War was over and the coronation of King Edward VII due to take place that Chamberlain summoned the Conference which met at the Colonial Office between 30 June and 11 August 1902.

Much had happened to affect the Conference since 1897. One obvious change was the establishment of the Commonwealth of Australia so that, from 1902, a single Government represented Australia instead of six as hitherto, although it was to be some time before the several State Governments in that country were entirely reconciled to their loss of separate representation.[3] Other changes, if less obvious, were no less important. This was a "post-war" Conference and the nature

---

[1] For these resolutions and the dissentients see *Parl. Pap.* 1897, LIX [C. 8596], p. 15. Garvin, *op. cit.* III, 192, writes that "the general feeling" favoured triennial meetings.

[2] See above, p. 411.

[3] For their views on the subject as late as 1906–7, see *Parl. Pap.* 1907, LV [Cd. 3524], pp. 11 *seqq.*

of the war had raised doubts among important sections of opinion, not only in Britain, but throughout the Empire. In this sense the atmosphere in which the Conference of 1902 met was certainly different from that prevailing in 1897, at a time of Jubilee and in the still tranquil evening of a great reign. Yet, if this kind of post-war reaction was apparent, so, nevertheless, was another. As Chamberlain was to say when inaugurating the Conference, "very great anticipations" had been aroused by the material support recently offered by the colonies to the mother country in the South African War.[1] He was perhaps thinking mainly of the high hopes which the Government of the United Kingdom certainly entertained that the colonies might be persuaded at this Conference to accept a greater share of the burden of defence. But no doubt he also felt that experience of the crisis through which the Empire had just passed and the wave of imperial sentiment which, despite all criticism and misgivings, it had undoubtedly aroused, made the moment psychologically favourable for a renewal of the effort he had already made in 1897.

However, not only Chamberlain, but Laurier also, was present in 1902. By this time the Canadian Premier had been in power for some years and was apparently less hesitant than in 1897 to express his views on the larger questions of imperial politics. While sacrificing none of his convictions, he probably hoped to follow a moderate course calculated to win sufficient approval from both the nations in his own country to prevent a serious clash between them on these delicate issues. He made his position clear before the Conference opened. When summoning the Conference Chamberlain proposed subjects for discussion and asked the colonies to suggest others. Laurier had none to offer; but he expressed the opinion that no useful result could be expected from a discussion of either political relations or defence. His Government, he said, was chiefly interested in the preference which, on its own initiative, it had now been offering since 1897. In particular he expressed his anxiety not to involve Canada in that "vortex of militarism" which was, in his view, "the curse and blight of Europe". It may be observed that he was to express exactly the same anxiety on the eve of the Conference of 1907 and it always seems to have had a powerful influence on his attitude towards relations with Britain.[2] Indeed, Laurier's general attitude on the imperial relationship was so different from Chamberlain's that the latter came to the conclusion in 1902 that what Laurier really wanted was an independent Canada.[3]

The Conference of 1902, following the pattern of 1897, was restricted to the self-governing colonies. The Premiers present were

---

[1] *Parl. Pap.* 1902, LXVI [Cd. 1299], p. 9.
[2] For Laurier's attitude both before and during the Conference of 1902, see Skelton, *op. cit.* II, 292–300.
[3] See his letter to Austen Chamberlain in Amery, J., *Life of Joseph Chamberlain*, IV, 435.

Laurier (Canada), Barton (Australia), Seddon (New Zealand), Sprigg (Cape Colony), Hime (Natal) and Bond[1] (Newfoundland). On this occasion, however, others besides the Premiers attended, Laurier being accompanied by no less than four colleagues[2] and Barton by one.[3] In addition, from the United Kingdom Government, Selborne, First Lord of the Admiralty, Brodrick, Secretary for War, and Gerald Balfour, President of the Board of Trade, were present at the discussion of questions affecting their special departments.

The inclusion of additional colonial ministers was apparently by courtesy only. When discussing the status of such ministers on the first day of the 1907 Conference, Lord Elgin referred to their position in 1902.[4] He said it had been "distinctly ruled" on that occasion that the Conference was a conference between Prime Ministers and the Secretary of State. One of the colonial representatives had objected to the admission of additional ministers and Chamberlain had ruled that, since the Conference was not unanimous, they could not be admitted. By "admitted", Elgin presumably meant "regarded as having full membership", since in 1902 the additional ministers certainly addressed the Conference.[5]

The objections to which Elgin referred had been raised by Seddon of New Zealand, who had no colleagues with him.[6] He must have feared that this innovation would give colonies nearer Great Britain than New Zealand an undue weight in the deliberations. But more numerous representation need not confer any greater voting-power; "one colony, one vote" could still be the rule. Even so, despite the manifest advantages of having additional ministers present who were particularly qualified to deal with certain subjects, their admission was still causing more discussion than might have been expected in 1907.[7]

If the presence of these additional colonial ministers shows that the Conference was still, in 1902, in process of evolution so far as its composition was concerned, the character it was assuming was already apparent. As we see it in this year, the Colonial Conference was, in effect, confined to the autonomous Governments of the Empire and the Government of the United Kingdom. It could not be so formally and completely, however, until the chief representative of the latter was the Prime Minister and not the Colonial Secretary.

---

[1] Amery (op. cit. IV, 420) writes that Bond was "only there by courtesy, as he was himself almost painfully aware".

[2] Fielding (Finance), Paterson (Customs), F. Borden (Defence) and Mulock (Postmaster-General).

[3] Forrest (Defence).

[4] Parl. Pap. 1907, LV [Cd. 3523], pp. 15, 16.

[5] See Amery, op. cit. IV, 441–3 for an example.

[6] Amery, op. cit. IV, 418. At the 1907 Conference, Ward stressed the great distance of New Zealand and the inconvenience which would arise if several ministers were away at a Conference at the same time.

[7] See below, p. 426.

So long as the Colonial Secretary was the chief British representative and presiding officer the Conference would still appear to be, as Elgin described it,[1] a conference between the colonial Premiers and the Colonial Secretary. And this, as Campbell-Bannerman was to point out in 1907,[2] was not the same thing. However, in 1902, as in 1897, the Conference was not even formally inaugurated by the Prime Minister; it was Chamberlain who summoned it and presided over all the sessions. Of these there were ten in all and the work of the Conference was held up for a fortnight while Chamberlain recovered from the effects of an accident.

When calling the Conference, he had again taken the opportunity to emphasise political relations, commercial relations and defence as the most desirable subjects for discussion, though he had also asked the colonies for suggestions and even for the text of resolutions. New Zealand responded with resolutions, the most important of which dealt with defence and a proposal that a Colonial Conference should meet every three years. Australia, Cape Colony and Natal also made suggestions without submitting formal resolutions. Canada, too, did not put forward resolutions, though Laurier pointed out before the Conference opened that preference was the subject in which his Government was mainly interested.[3]

It was once again agreed to hold the discussions in private, apparently at the instance of the Australian Premier. The so-called "naval tribute" had aroused strong feelings in Australia and day-by-day reports of a debate on imperial defence could easily give rise to misunderstanding in a distant part of the Empire. It was no doubt natural that a colonial representative should prefer to explain his conduct at the Conference on such controversial issues without prior misunderstanding and after his return from London. Certainly Barton, on his way to the Conference of 1902, wrote to Chamberlain from Rome and raised the question of publicity. He stressed the delicate stage which some of the subjects to be discussed had reached and suggested that, if the proceedings of the Conference were to be reported and eventually published, representatives of the self-governing colonies might be unable to address Chamberlain with the absolute frankness necessary to explain why they held certain views. And so, just as in 1897, although a *verbatim* report of most of the proceedings was made, only a short summary was actually published when the Conference was over.[4] Even this unpublished report did not include two of the ten meetings. At one of these, apparently, defence was discussed and at the other the decision not to publish the full minutes was taken.[5]

The agreement to hold the discussions in private did not of course mean that any Prime Minister was understood to bind himself by the

[1] See above, p. 417.   [2] See below, p. 425.
[3] Amery, *op. cit.* IV, 418.   [4] *Parl. Pap.* 1902, LXVI [Cd. 1299].
[5] On the full minutes, see Amery, *op. cit.* IV, 417–18.

terms of any resolution which he might support. No such powers or intentions were ever ascribed either to this Conference, or to any of the others held before 1914. Indeed, when defining the nature and scope of the Conference of 1902, Chamberlain did so in such a way as to suggest that it was still regarded by the British Government in much the same light as that of 1887, i.e. as an excellent means of testing the views of the "great self-governing Colonies" on what he called "the policy of the Empire".[1] Apparently the "policy of the Empire" was still something decided by the Government of the United Kingdom, though that Government might, as it was now doing, consult colonial opinion. It was, in fact, the transformation of the Conference into something which, ultimately at least, should have policy-making powers that Chamberlain was still seeking to bring about in 1902.

However, he had no greater success in 1902 than in 1897; in fact he may be said to have suffered a greater rebuff. Outlining the business of the Conference when it opened he spoke of the political federation of the Empire as being "within the limits of possibility", though admitting that the demand for it must come from the colonies. In his view, there could be no objection to colonial representation in either or both Houses of Parliament. But he would prefer a "real Council of the Empire", originally, perhaps, merely advisory, but eventually possessing "executive functions and perhaps also legislative powers". Such a council would have as its principal concern imperial defence and commercial relations, the subjects which were to engage the "special attention" of the present Conference.

When the Conference actually discussed the questions of defence and trade, the strength of colonial nationalism and the consequent suspicion of anything that seemed likely to endanger colonial autonomy were immediately apparent.[2] The colonies were already thinking in terms of local defence forces of their own over the disposal of which they would have complete control. Thus the War Office scheme for an imperial reserve in the colonies was rejected and, apart from a slight increase in the amount of naval contributions, British hopes of spreading the burden of imperial defence were disappointed. Similarly, in the trade discussions, it was once more reciprocal preference, a system compatible with the colonies' complete control over their own fiscal policies, which found favour—a fact which had a profound influence on Chamberlain's own future actions. But the most important feature of this Conference was undoubtedly the fact that Chamberlain's idea of a "Council of Empire" was never even debated. In 1897 there had been a long discussion of the similar proposal which he had made. This time it

---

[1] *Parl. Pap.* 1902, LXVI [Cd. 1299], p. 1. There are lengthy extracts from Chamberlain's opening speech in Amery's account of this Conference, *op. cit.* IV, 420–5, 436–7.
[2] Amery, *op. cit.* VI, 422 *seqq.*

was ignored. The colonial premiers apparently saw little point even in debating a plan designed to set up a body which, if it were to have the executive and "even legislative" powers of which Chamberlain had spoken, must surely be superior to their own local Parliaments.

This does not mean that the imperial tie was something which they wished to cut. Rather they were thinking of it in new terms which, destined to become familiar enough in later years, were strange and even startling. They were well expressed in a speech by Barton,[1] one of the premiers in question, when he described the Empire as a "brotherhood of nations". With this conception the colonial premiers evidently felt that Chamberlain's federal council was incompatible. They turned instead to the Conference itself to make definite provision for its own continued existence and in terms more precise than those used in 1897. A resolution was adopted whereby a Colonial Conference should meet in future at intervals not exceeding four years.[2] In this way the assembly of Colonial Conferences was made much less casual or dependent on the occurrence of a royal occasion such as a Jubilee or Coronation. It was now established, so to say, in its own right.

Since Chamberlain twice failed to convince a Colonial Conference of the wisdom of his proposals, it might seem that he was over-optimistic in putting them forward. Yet the Council plan was not abandoned by the British Government when Chamberlain left office in 1903. Evidently it was not a purely personal policy of the retiring Colonial Secretary and its recurrence, or something comparable to it, was to be the main reason why the Conference of 1907 devoted so much time to the question of its own constitution and, for this reason, became possibly the most important of all the Conferences held before the outbreak of the First World War.

Until 1907 all the main Conferences were held when a Conservative or Unionist government was in power in the United Kingdom. The Conference of 1907, being held after the general election of 1906, took place under the auspices of a Liberal administration and the party was still in office when the last of this series met in 1911. The development of the Conference could not fail to be affected by this important change on the British political scene.

It was not that the movement for imperial unity, of which these Conferences were one result, had ever been exclusively associated with the Conservative party. Liberals as eminent as W. E. Forster and Lord Rosebery had presided over the affairs of the Imperial Federation League and men who avowed themselves "Liberal

---

[1] Amery, *op. cit.* iv, 422.

[2] [Cd. 1299], p. ix. On p. vi is the resolution on the subject submitted by the New Zealand Government. This suggested triennial conferences and also spoke of the "relations of the Mother Country and His Majesty's *Dominions* over the seas". The word "Dominions" was embodied in the resolution adopted by the Conference. On the use of the word in 1907, see below, p. 428.

Imperialists" were a small, though able and active group in the Liberal Governments after 1905. Nevertheless, there persisted in the mass of the Liberal Party an important tradition or point of view, which, if not actively "anti-imperialist", did not regard the question of imperial unity with the same sense of urgency, or, still less, with the same hopes as, for example, Chamberlain. Moreover, the latter's Tariff Reform campaign had recently enmeshed imperial with British politics in a way unknown, certainly, for at least sixty years, and the Liberal victory of 1906 was due in large part to the fact that this "tariff reform" was an attack on Free Trade. Chamberlain, indeed, had not only split the Conservative and Unionist parties on the issues of Protection, but had in the process profoundly influenced British opinion on imperial questions. He had, for instance, given the impression that the only sort of closer union which appealed to the colonies was one based on Preference. Moreover, it was undeniable that some colonial representatives at every Colonial Conference so far held had spoken in favour of a preferential tariff system. Accordingly, after 1906, the Liberal party was not only enabled by its very Liberalism to make the famous grant of self-government to the former Boer Republics, but was the less disposed to resist what might seem to be centrifugal tendencies in the Empire, since the alternative seemed to involve the abandonment of Free Trade. In consequence the influences emanating from the new British Government, though not necessarily less vigorous than in the time of Chamberlain, were quite different.

Though Chamberlain left the Colonial Office in 1903, the Balfour government remained in power until December 1905, and certain proposals made by Chamberlain's successor, Lyttelton, proved to be of considerable importance. By the terms of the 1902 resolution, another Conference was due to meet in 1906 and, on 20 April 1905, Lyttelton addressed a circular dispatch on the subject to the self-governing colonies. Briefly, he proposed the transformation of the Colonial Conference into an "Imperial Council" and, in addition, the creation of an associated and permanent "Commission". Comparable proposals had already been made by a private group (which, incidentally, included prominent members of the Liberal party) and some discussion had followed.[1] The question of the Conference's own future was to this extent attracting attention before it met in 1907.

In his dispatch,[2] Lyttelton spoke of the Conference as having, since 1887, "assumed a more definite shape and acquired a more continuous status". The resolution of 1902, he continued, which provided for meetings at fixed intervals, had removed it from any dependence

---

[1] For an account of this, see Jebb, R., *Imperial Conference*, II, 8–10. Sir Frederick Pollock was a leading figure in a discussion which also included R. B. Haldane.

[2] Printed in *Parl. Pap.* 1906, LXXVII [Cd. 2785].

on "important Imperial celebrations". So had come into existence, "by a natural process", "an Imperial Council" for the discussion of matters which concerned alike the United Kingdom and the self-governing colonies. Accordingly, the British Government thought it might be well to discard the title "Colonial Conference", which imperfectly expressed the facts, and in future to speak of these meetings as meetings of an "Imperial Council". No change of composition was intended. In addition to this "permanent body of the Imperial Council" there might be set up in London a permanent Commission whose members could be nominated proportionately by His Majesty's Government and the Colonial Governments. This Commission would make for continuity since, in the nature of things, colonial representatives could only spend a short time in London at meetings of the "Imperial Council". It might profitably deal with questions of a civil character affecting the whole Empire as the Committee of Imperial Defence now dealt with defence. It could, for instance, provide the information which the Governments would need before taking any action and it might act either by reference from the Imperial Council when that was in session, or from the British or a Colonial Government. Its secretary could also be the secretary of the Imperial Council when the latter was in session.

These proposals were comparable, at least in spirit, with those put forward earlier by Chamberlain. They cannot be called federalist, though they might well have led in that direction. But they undoubtedly sought to strengthen such organised unity as the Empire already possessed and were designed to increase in practical ways the efficiency of the existing Conference as an integrating force.

At the end of November 1905, owing to local political circumstances in Australia and New Zealand, it was necessary to postpone the meeting of the next Conference from 1906 until 1907. When it eventually met at the Colonial Office (15 April–9 May 1907) the change from Conservative to Liberal government in Britain had occurred and it was Lyttelton's successor, the Earl of Elgin, who took the chair. At the opening meeting (in addition to Elgin) the Prime Ministers of Canada (Laurier), Australia (Deakin), New Zealand (Ward), Cape Colony (Jameson), Natal (Moor) and the Transvaal (Botha), were present, as well as three other colonial ministers, F. W. Borden (Canada), Lyne (Australia) and Smartt (Cape Colony). Campbell-Bannerman, Prime Minister of the United Kingdom, who attended this first meeting, was accompanied by his colleagues Morley, Haldane, Tweedmouth, Burns and Lloyd George; while described as "also present", though apparently in a separate category, were Mr Winston Churchill (Parliamentary Under-Secretary for the Colonies), Sir F. Hopwood, Permanent Under-Secretary for the Colonies, the Assistant Under-Secretary for the Colonies, Sir J. L. Mackay, "on behalf of the India Office", and the private secretaries to Elgin and the colonial representatives. Bond, the Prime Minister of Newfoundland, did not arrive in time for the earlier part of the Conference and, in his inaugural speech, Campbell-Bannerman explained that the Prime Minister of the Orange River Colony was not present because the Constitution of that colony had not been brought into effect in time.[1]

Before the Conference met, the Colonial Governments, with two exceptions, had shown themselves generally favourable to Lyttelton's proposals. The two exceptions were Newfoundland and Canada. The former's objections were based on the colony's small size and poverty and consequent inability to undertake obligations which might result from the establishment of the proposed Council. Much more importance naturally attached to the objections of Canada, which had been stated formally and at some length. The Canadian Government considered that any changes in the title or status of the Conference should originate with the Conference itself. It was wise to allow political institutions to develop "as it were of their own accord". To change the name of the Colonial Conference in the way proposed "would be interpreted as marking a step distinctly in advance of the position hitherto attained in the discussion of the relations between the Mother Country and the Colonies". As it understood the phrase, "a Conference is a more or less unconventional gathering for informal discussion of public questions...possessing no faculty or power of binding action". Such had been the Conferences of 1887, 1897 and 1902. The term Council, on the other hand, indicated "a more formal assembly, possessing an advisory or deliberative character" and, in conjunction with the word "Imperial", suggested a permanent institution "which, endowed with a continuous life, might eventually come to be regarded as an encroachment upon the full measure of autonomous legislative and administrative power now enjoyed by the self-governing Colonies". While not advocating any such change at the moment, the Canadian Government would prefer the title "Imperial Conference". With regard to the proposed Commission, it also believed that, though this might "greatly facilitate the work of the Conference as well as enhance its importance", it might again, conceivably, interfere with the working of responsible government. Nevertheless, Canada's spokesmen at the Conference would gladly take part in a general discussion of the whole matter.[2]

In contrast, the Australian Government, now headed by Alfred Deakin who had been present at the Conference of 1887 and was also present at that of 1907,[3] showed a great and, on the whole,

---

[1] *Parl. Pap.* 1907, LV [Cd. 3523], p. 4.
[2] [Cd. 2785], p. 14. Statement by "the Committee of the Honourable Privy Council (of Canada)".
[3] For an account of Deakin at the 1907 Conference, see Murdoch, *Deakin*, chap. xv.

favourable interest in the Lyttelton plan. Invited like the other governments to propose subjects for discussion, the Australian put forward no less than fourteen resolutions. These showed a general agreement with the plan, actually used the term "Imperial Council" and urged the value of such a permanent secretariat as had been proposed.[1] Indeed, in the Conference itself, Deakin was to be the most persistent advocate of such proposals, as Laurier was to be their most determined critic. Neither, however, stood alone. Deakin had a large measure of support from Jameson, as Laurier had from Botha.

By this time Laurier's views on the Conference and on imperial unity in general were, of course, well-known. His nationalism, if no less ardent, was quite different in both derivation and spirit from Deakin's. On the eve of the Conference of 1907 there had even been doubts whether he would attend, and it was only after the question had been raised by the Opposition in the Canadian House of Commons that these doubts were dispelled. However, in this debate, Laurier said again that Preference was the question which mainly interested Canada and he evidently believed that, in view of the result of the recent general election in Britain, little could be expected from the Conference in this connection. He condemned the proposal for an Imperial Council and repeated his determination not to be drawn into the "vortex of European militarism". He spoke of the "deplorable condition of merely armed peace in Europe", in which, he seems to have felt, discussion of imperial defence was all too likely to involve Canada. His nationalism, unlike Deakin's, had thus a certain "isolationist" flavour, and Laurier entered the Conference of 1907 in no frame of mind to welcome any schemes, whether of imperial defence or not, calculated to reduce the degree of his country's North American isolation.[2]

He had also, it seems, a strong suspicion of the "imperialist campaign" (the phrase is his own) to which, he believed, colonial representatives at these Conferences were always subjected. "We were looked upon", he once said, "not so much as individual men but abstractedly as Colonial statesmen to be impressed and hobbled." In 1897 and 1902 he thought Chamberlain's personal influence had been in this respect strongest; "but in 1907 and after, Society pressure was the chief force". He thus implied that, after the change of government in 1905, this social pressure was called in by way of compensation for the decline of "imperialist" influence in the Government itself. He certainly thought it formidable; it was, he said, "hard to stand up against the flattery of a duchess", weak

---

[1] The text of the Australian and New Zealand resolutions on the Imperial Council is in *Parl. Pap.* 1907, LV [Cd. 3404], pp. 12 *seqq.* For a general statement of Deakin's views on the subject, see *Parl. Pap.* 1907, LV [Cd. 3523], pp. 26–30.

[2] Jebb, *Imperial Conference*, II, 50–3.

men's heads were turned in an evening, and there were few who could resist for long. Indeed, he told Deakin in 1907 that this was one of the reasons why they could not agree to a parliament or council in London. They could talk "cabinet to cabinet", but could not send Canadians or Australians as permanent residents to London, "to debate and act on their own discretion".[1]

Deakin's reply on this occasion is, unfortunately, not available; but it is very doubtful if he was ever so fearful of the perils of London Society as his Canadian colleague. He had not found it at all tempting in 1887, and if the offer of a knighthood was one of the dangers in question he had certainly survived it successfully then, at the age of thirty.[2] Laurier, on the other hand, became "Sir Wilfrid" in 1897.[3] It seems probable that Deakin, when in London, derived much more personal satisfaction from his meetings with George Meredith and other leading figures in the literary and artistic world than from any high social occasion. As for the "imperialist campaign", it did not alarm him. Deakin's object in 1907, as it had been in 1887, was to make "imperialism" really up-to-date, to mould it to what he considered a great purpose, not to defeat or to destroy it.

The views of the British Government in 1907 on the plan put forward by its predecessor emerged during the debates in the Conference. They were, however, foreshadowed by Campbell-Bannerman when he followed the example of Salisbury twenty years earlier and formally opened the proceedings.[4] Some of the colonial ministers had suggested that he should do this precisely in order to show that the United Kingdom, in the person of its Prime Minister, was taking part in the same way as the Colonies. Judging by what he said, Campbell-Bannerman was quite willing to give them this satisfaction. The Conference, he argued, was not a conference between the colonial Premiers and the Colonial Secretary, but between the Premiers and the members of the Government under the presidency of the Secretary of State for the Colonies, "which was a very different matter". It was also the first of the Conferences not identified with any great ceremonial occasion. He then referred to the "more or less ambitious" schemes to provide, during the intervals between Conferences, the "definite communications" which were necessary. Something, he felt, might be done to maintain the impetus given by the Conference to the consideration and settlement of questions discussed, without running counter to the spirit of freedom and independence which was the essence of the British connection. Subsidiary conferences might be useful for this purpose.

---

[1] Skelton, *op. cit.* II, 299, note 1.   [2] Murdoch, *op. cit.* p. 103.
[3] Though, in 1902, he apparently declined a peerage. Amery, *Life of Chamberlain*, IV, 419, footnote.
[4] His speech is printed in [Cd. 3523], pp. 4–6.

Laurier and Deakin also discussed the Conference in general terms when the British Prime Minister had spoken. Laurier saw it as one between "government and governments", these latter being the Governments of what he preferred to call, not "colonies", but "self-governing dependencies". Deakin described the Conference as one between "governments and governments" with due recognition of the "seniority and scope of those governments"; by his two plurals possibly suggesting an equality of status though not, in view of his parenthesis, of power. He welcomed the presence of the Prime Minister of the United Kingdom, hoping to see him present in future as the titular if not actual president, so that the nature of the Conference as Campbell-Bannerman had described it might be made clear.[1]

When the Conference began work, it considered once more the questions of publicity and the position of ministers who were not prime ministers.[2] Deakin was very anxious to secure daily publication of reports of the proceedings in order to impress the importance of the occasion on the public, and possibly also to let the Conference feel the pressure of opinion outside. Laurier was opposed to this, favouring the customary plan of privacy at the time and a full public report later. Elgin, too, opposed Deakin, and while summaries were given from time to time to the Press, the publication of a full record had to await the end of the proceedings. As to the other ministers, the Canadian Government had pointed out the convenience to the Premiers of having the assistance of colleagues with special knowledge or qualifications when certain subjects were under discussion. In 1902 such ministers had only been received by courtesy and in face of some objections. The Canadian Government felt that they should participate of right and the rule of "one colony, one vote" need not thereby be affected.

Elgin preferred to leave this question to the Conference, especially as it was, in any case, to discuss its own constitution; and in the official report of the first day's proceedings only Elgin and the colonial Premiers are actually described as "members". Eventually, although objection was raised to the presence of Sir Richard Solomon alongside Botha because he was an agent-general and not a member of Government, the other ministers attended. The "absolute rule" at the Conference of 1902 which confined membership of the Conference to Premiers was abandoned. The arrangement was that the other ministers were to come into the room and be entitled to "sit at the table", but that they were there to assist the Premier and that it depended on the subject under discussion which of any number of ministers in attendance should take part in that discussion. It was

[1] The speeches of Laurier and Deakin are in [Cd. 3523], pp. 6–10.
[2] The questions of membership and procedure were discussed on the first day of the Conference, *ibid.* pp. 14–23.

an "honourable understanding" that "not more than one minister from each colony should assist his Premier at one and the same meeting".[1]

Other questions of procedure were decided. Thus the Conference agreed that specialised but relatively small subjects (e.g. Stamp Charges on Colonial Bonds; Double Income Tax) might be better handled by meetings at the Treasury of those best qualified to discuss them. As to the resolutions which were to be considered, Elgin referred to the earlier practice of discussing a subject, not "under the strict presentation of a resolution such as you would have in a House of Parliament" but generally, and keeping in view any resolutions which had been submitted. Then an attempt might be made to "adjust such representation of the discussion, or expression...of the views of the Conference as may be recorded in our proceedings".[2] His object, no doubt, was to secure as wide a measure of agreement as possible; indeed, the nature of the Conference as one between autonomous governments made this desirable if not, perhaps, inevitable. But it also meant that "general agreement" could take the form of the "pious affirmations" of which Smartt of Cape Colony actually complained at this Conference. It was also possible that "one colony" might in a sense enjoy more than "one vote" if a majority felt inclined to defer to a minority in the interests of general agreement. And this could be the case even when the Conference was dealing with its own constitution, and so when its resolutions had a binding effect, which they certainly lacked in any other connection.

The most important resolution adopted by the Conference of 1907 was a "constitutional" resolution of this sort and was itself in the nature of a compromise. It read as follows:

That it will be to the advantage of the Empire if a Conference, to be called the Imperial Conference, is held every four years, at which questions of common interest may be discussed and considered as between His Majesty's Government and his Governments of the self-governing Dominions beyond the seas. The Prime Minister of the United Kingdom will be *ex-officio* President, and the Prime Ministers of the self-governing Dominions *ex-officio* members of the Conference. The Secretary of State for the Colonies will be an *ex-officio* member of the Conference and will take the chair in the absence of the President. He will arrange for such Imperial Conferences after communication with the Prime Ministers of the respective Dominions. Such other Ministers as the respective Governments may appoint will also be members of the Conference, it being understood that, except by special permission of the Conference, each discussion will be conducted by not more than two representatives from each Government, and that each Government will have only one vote.

[1] See the statement by Elgin in reply to Lyne of Australia, who was apparently dissatisfied by his position in the Conference, [Cd. 3523], pp. 50–2, and *ibid*. pp. 15–18, for the discussion of the subject on the first day. On the question of the actual number of "other ministers" attending from any one colony, see *ibid*. pp. 55–6.
[2] [Cd. 3523], pp. 24–5.

With regard to the Commission or Secretariat, the resolution read:

That it is desirable to establish a system by which the several Governments represented shall be kept informed during the periods between the Conferences in regard to matters which have been or may be subjects for discussion, by means of a permanent secretarial staff, charged under the direction of the Secretary of State for the Colonies, with the duty of obtaining information for the use of the Conference, of attending to its resolutions, and of conducting correspondence on matters relating to its affairs,

and on subsidiary Conferences:

That upon matters of importance requiring consultation between two or more Governments which cannot be conveniently postponed until the next Conference, or involving subjects of a minor character or such as call for detailed consideration, subsidiary Conferences should be held between representatives of the Governments concerned specially chosen for the purpose.[1]

The new name of the Conference was thus in the compromise form suggested by the Canadian Government before the Conference met; if it is "Imperial", it is still a "Conference" and not a "Council". The provision for quadrennial Conferences was also a compromise; Laurier would have preferred a longer interval[2] and Deakin a shorter.[3] The Prime Minister of the United Kingdom was now to be the President *ex-officio*, as was appropriate for a Conference defined in this resolution as one of "Government and Governments". It is not, in Deakin's phrase, one of "Governments and Governments"; but if Deakin had, in fact, sought in those words to express equality of status, he could derive some satisfaction from the substitution of "Dominions" for "Colonies" as an official designation, since the former was clearly intended to imply a status superior to that of "Colony". Certainly the Conference is no longer, even in theory, one between the "Secretary of State for the Colonies and the Prime Ministers of the self-governing Colonies", as it had described itself in one of its resolutions in 1902.

The use of the term Dominion in the resolution of 1907 caused considerable discussion. Deakin on 17 April spoke of "the Dominions represented here". Ward, anxious to reorganise the Colonial Office in order to separate the Self-governing from the Crown colonies, deprecated the use of the word "colony" in connection with the former, preferring for those not already Dominions or Commonwealth the phrase "States of the Empire". In a draft resolution put before the Conference by Elgin the phrase "H.M. Dominions over the seas" was used. Mr Churchill on one occasion suggested "H.M. Dominions overseas". Laurier was doubtful about "Dominions overseas" since Trinidad, for example, was one of

---

[1] These resolutions and others adopted by the Conference are printed in [Cd. 3523], pp. v–x.
[2] *Ibid*. p. 56. He said that he had suggested six years in 1902.
[3] *Ibid*. p. 56.

H.M.'s Dominions overseas; he wanted to include the phrase "self-governing", but to drop "colonies". He would have liked "States", but there were "States" in the Commonwealth of Australia. On 20 April Jameson suggested the "H.M. Government and His Governments..." of the first paragraph of the resolution. Laurier still had doubts since they were all "H.M.'s Governments" and would have preferred to specify "the Government of the United Kingdom".

The second part of the resolution sought to provide a link between the periodic sessions of what could now reasonably be regarded as a permanent institution; the need for such a link had been felt since the series began. The lengthy debate on this Secretariat was unfortunately confused by a failure to distinguish clearly between business arrangements (e.g. the date or the agenda of Conferences) and the political problem of making more effective provision than a four-yearly Conference for effective consultation on matters of common interest. But it is apparent that not only Laurier, but also Elgin, was reluctant to set up anything in the nature of a political body, external, as it were, to all the Governments, lest, in Elgin's own words, it might be "a danger to the autonomy of us all".[1] Nevertheless, a Secretariat was established and its duties defined, if only in general terms. But it was placed, despite the strong criticism of Deakin and others, under the Colonial Secretary, not the Prime Minister. However, the Australian Premier at least succeeded in restricting the scope of the Colonial Office in matters concerning the Dominions, since the new Secretariat made necessary a "Dominions Division" of that Office.

If these decisions were based on compromise, there was sufficient time before the outbreak of war in 1914 to show that, though by no means perfect, they could work. If Federalism had been rejected, an alternative had been adopted which made co-operation between these autonomous "Dominions" and the United Kingdom possible. Indeed, this can be seen already in the Conference of 1907 in connection with defence, when the Dominions showed their willingness to organise their respective forces with a view to possible, though not automatic, co-operation with those of the United Kingdom in case of war.

This particular decision, in itself of great and, to some observers, even alarming importance, raised a variety of problems especially of a technical nature. Under the terms of the resolution of 1907 these were referred to a subsidiary Conference on defence held in 1909. It was attended by representatives of the Governments of the United Kingdom and the Dominions and self-governing colonies whose official duties were concerned with defence and by "experts" from both the United Kingdom and the Empire such as the Chief of the

[1] [Cd. 3523], p. 37.

Imperial General Staff. They included three colonial Premiers, Ward (New Zealand), Merriman (Cape), Fischer (Orange River Colony); and Asquith, who had now succeeded Campbell-Bannerman as Prime Minister of the United Kingdom, took the chair at the first meeting in his capacity of President of the Imperial Conference, the Colonial Secretary later acting as his deputy.[1]

The meetings were private, but, later, Asquith reported in general terms on the Conference's work to the House of Commons. He described it as purely consultative; the resolutions, so far as the Dominion members were concerned, being *ad referendum* and of no binding force unless and until submitted to the various Parliaments. The detailed work on military matters, he said, had been submitted to a sub-conference of the military experts, presided over by Sir William Nicholson, acting for the first time as Chief of the recently formed Imperial General Staff. Its conclusions had then been approved by the main Conference and by the Committee of Imperial Defence which sat for the purpose under the Prime Minister's own presidency.[2]

From the purely strategic or technical points of view this way of handling wide-ranging questions of defence was no doubt open to criticism. But the fact that this subsidiary Conference met and did its work at least demonstrated that the principle of co-operation embodied in the resolution of 1907 need not be a matter merely of cautious phrases or subtle theories.

The Imperial Conference of 1911, which met at the Foreign Office and not, like its predecessors, at the Colonial Office, was the first over which, by the terms of the 1907 resolution, the Prime Minister of the United Kingdom presided.[3] His deputy was the Colonial Secretary, Harcourt; though on one interesting occasion (16 June) Laurier took the chair as *doyen* of the Prime Ministers present.[4] This Conference was also the first to include, in the person of Louis Botha, a prime minister from the newly-constituted Union of South Africa.

The arrangements made for publicity were the same as in 1907, Ward pleading in vain for the admission of the Press except when confidential matters were under discussion.[5] There were, however, some changes in procedure. Ministers other than Prime Ministers were now given greater freedom to take part in the discussion. Fisher (Australia) asked if these ministers were to speak after the Prime Minister or after the other Prime Ministers had spoken.

[1] Relevant correspondence and papers are printed in *Parl. Pap.* 1909, LIX [Cd. 4948].

[2] For the Dominions' representatives sitting on the Committee of Imperial Defence on this occasion, see below, p. 435.

[3] The term "president" was adopted instead of "chairman" in the resolution of 1907 and is used in the Minutes of Proceedings of the 1911 Conference. *Parl. Pap.* 1911, LIV [Cd. 5745].

[4] *Ibid.* p. 382. He is described, where necessary, in the minutes as "chairman", not as 'president'.

[5] *Ibid.* pp. 28–32.

Laurier suggested that they should speak when the spirit moved them and Asquith agreed that a "very free discussion" was desirable, and, in fact, the other ministers frequently intervened in the debates.[1] In addition, Asquith made certain proposals concerning defence questions. Referring to the "precedent created in 1909", he suggested that these "should be discussed in the Committee of Imperial Defence with the assistance of the advice of its expert members, at meetings at which the Dominions would be represented by the Prime Ministers and the ministers directly concerned in naval and military defence". He also said that at the first of these meetings, which, like the rest, would be confidential, Sir Edward Grey, the Foreign Secretary, would attend and speak on the international situation so far as it affected the Empire as a whole.[2]

The Committee of Imperial Defence, with its elasticity of composition, its consultative[3] character and its secrecy, was thus being made to play a useful and important part in relation to the Conference. The convenience of discussing such questions where the experts were immediately available was obvious and, in view of Asquith's remarks on the Subsidiary Conference of 1909, did not make more binding any decisions which might be reached. This course made it easier, however, to avoid the publicity to which the main proceedings of the Conference were destined.

As regards other subjects which were technical and of limited range, it was agreed that, being first "mooted", as Laurier put it, in the main Conference, they could properly be handed over to committees of the Conference. Such were "Board of Trade" subjects (e.g. Labour Exchanges) or "Treasury matters" (e.g. Double Income Tax). One such committee, on arbitration awards, met under the chairmanship of Rufus Isaacs, Attorney-General of the United Kingdom.

If, by this time, the Conference was beginning to find certain practices and methods of procedure customary and even traditional, it was, nevertheless, confronted in 1911 by a suggestion which would have superseded the constitutional resolution of 1907 and, in fact, the Conference itself. This was Sir Joseph Ward's proposal of an Imperial Council of Defence.[4]

Ward already had considerable experience of the Conference, having been present in 1907 and 1909, and had strong views on the importance of effective imperial unity which, in his view, was now more necessary than ever. Separatism seemed especially to have shown itself in matters of defence, in, for example, Canada's intention to have its own navy which should only participate in an "imperial war" if Canada thought fit. Ward pointed out that the United

---

[1] [Cd. 5745], pp. 35–6.   [2] *Ibid.* p. 23.
[3] Asquith, H. H., *Genesis of the War*, p. 113.
[4] Debated on the first and second days of the Conference, [Cd. 5745], pp. 36–75.

Kingdom could, in fact, commit the whole Empire to war and seems to have feared lest, in such circumstances, Canada would be faced with the dilemma of either participating in such an "imperial war" or leaving the Empire. But it is also quite clear that he did not wish simply to fetter the Dominions to British policy. On the contrary he was looking for means to give the Dominions an effective share in the making of a really imperial policy. Surely, he said, they were entitled to "some voice—proportioned it may be, to their size and contribution—in such a vital question as peace or war". He was thus going to the roots of a question which Deakin had raised as long ago as 1887 and which the Conference was in any case to discuss in view of Australia's criticism of the recent Declaration of London[1] and the resolution on the subject which Fisher was to move.[2]

Ward's plan was both elaborate (indeed, in some respects, it was not very clear) and, in essence, federal, a word which he himself did not hesitate to use. The Empire, he said, had now reached a stage of development which rendered it expedient "that there should be an Imperial Council of State, with Representatives from all the constituent self-governing parts of the Empire, in theory and fact advisory to the Imperial Government on all questions affecting the interests of His Majesty's Dominions overseas". Though he used here the word "Council", Ward really had in mind the representation of the United Kingdom and the Dominions, on a proportionate population basis, in an "Imperial Parliament of Defence" for the purpose of determining peace or war, contributions to imperial defence, foreign policy (so far as it affected the Empire) and "such other Imperial matters as may by agreement be transferred to such Parliament". He also envisaged a Senate of twelve members and an Executive of fifteen "entirely responsible to the Parliamentary body".[3] Ward, in reply to Asquith, said he regarded the terms "Imperial Council of State", "Imperial Parliament of Defence" and "Defence Council" as synonymous. Later, when Laurier insisted that "Council" and "Parliament" were different, Ward chose "Parliament of Defence".

His proposals did not commend themselves to the Conference. Since the opposition of any one Prime Minister would no doubt have served in any case to defeat such fundamental plans, too much should not be made of the "lone hand" which Ward played on this occasion. Indeed, his object may well have been to influence opinion rather than carry a scheme which he does not seem to have thought out completely in all its implications. Ward certainly sought to give the Dominions the greater share in the determination of policy which to some (though not all) Dominion representatives seemed desirable. But he sought it in a way which by this time had little hope

---

[1] See chap. xv below.
[2] Text in [Cd. 5745], p. 5. It was discussed on 1 June.
[3] *Ibid.* pp. 47, 55–6.

of being adopted. Whatever opinions had been expressed by individual members, the Conference as such had consistently opposed federalism. It was not likely to change its mind so soon after the resolution of 1907, especially as it was really being asked to agree to its own destruction. The Conference could surely have found no place alongside the Parliament and responsible Executive which Ward proposed.

Botha, in proposing rejection of the plan, spoke of the "policy of decentralisation which has made the Empire" and, at the same time, showed clearly what he regarded as the most desirable form of "Imperial Council". The Imperial Conferences, he said, were admittedly held in order to knit the various parts of the Empire together. But they were not primarily an opportunity to pass resolutions which would subsequently be carried into effect throughout the Empire. They had no such intention. Nevertheless, they had great value in bringing together periodically the various Governments, enabling them to discuss matters of common interest without in any way binding themselves. The discussion was the main point.[1]

When inaugurating the Conference, Asquith, in anticipation of Ward's resolution, had stressed the value of elasticity and flexibility in imperial organisation. Later, when the Conference was actually discussing Ward's proposals, he condemned them as impairing, if not altogether destroying, the authority of the Government of the United Kingdom in foreign policy.[2] Foreign policy was now in the hands of the Imperial Government subject to its responsibility to the Imperial Parliament, and this authority could not be shared. Laurier dismissed the plan in very few words[3] and Fisher was also opposed, though less completely. At least, he urged the value of some means, possibly an advisory council, with which the Government of the United Kingdom might keep in touch, especially at times of crisis.[4]

Ward's resolution was accordingly withdrawn. The Conference, however, had other opportunities to examine the question of prior consultation in matters of high policy. One was the discussion of a connecting link between a Conference and its successors. In this connection Harcourt put forward certain proposals on behalf of the British Government.[5] It was, he said, prepared to set up a Standing Committee of the Imperial Conference, to consist of the Secretary of State, the Parliamentary Under-Secretary and the Permanent Under-Secretary (for the "Dominions", if the Colonial Office were so divided), to whom should be joined the High Commissioners of all the Dominions or any representatives in their place whom the Dominions might prefer. This Committee might meet at intervals

[1] [Cd. 5745], pp. 69–70.
[2] Ibid. p. 71.
[3] Ibid. pp. 67–8.
[4] Ibid. p. 69.
[5] Ibid. pp. 76 seqq.

under the presidency of the Secretary of State to do the sort of work which the Secretariat was already doing. It would be purely advisory and not executive, "advisory of the Secretary of State and informative of...all Dominions constituting the Conference".

Harcourt emphasised that these proposals for a "continued subsidiary Conference on Conference matters" were designed to meet what were thought to be the wishes of the Dominions, not to supply any need felt by the British Government. But, with the exception of Ward and Fisher, the members of the Conference did not show much disposition to welcome his proposal. Ward favoured a committee of the sort acting as a connecting-link between Conference and Conference. Fisher, with the Declaration of London constantly in mind, also saw a use for such a committee. He was anxious, he said, both to preserve the "present autonomous powers of the oversea Dominions" and to provide effective means whereby the United Kingdom could learn the views of Dominion Governments especially in matters of foreign policy.[1] He strongly expressed the same views on another occasion devoted specifically to the Declaration of London.

Laurier, for his part, handled the question of prior consultation with great caution, apparently afraid that consultation meant commitment. He was willing to come to Conferences and discuss certain questions which, however, he described as "eminently in the domain of the United Kingdom". But these questions, though discussed, must nevertheless remain where they were. If they did not, the Dominions might be automatically undertaking to participate in war. This Canada could not entertain; she did not feel bound to participate in every war. Thus, in the specific matter of the Declaration of London, it was better, Laurier believed, to leave negotiations concerning the way in which a possible war might be waged to be carried on by what he described as the "chief partner of the family".[2]

The Conference did not, in fact, set up any body in close association with itself which, in addition to other functions, might have made possible some consultation with the Dominions on foreign policy. But a degree of consultation was not necessarily incompatible with that unimpaired authority of the British Government of which Asquith had spoken. Grey, having heard Fisher complain that the Australian Government had asked in vain to be consulted about the Declaration of London, agreed that there were some questions of foreign policy on which such consultation would be both desirable and useful.[3] When the Dominion Premiers and defence ministers sat

---

[1] [Cd. 5745], p. 87.   [2] *Ibid.* pp. 116–18.
[3] He was speaking about the Declaration of London and prior consultation before another Hague Conference, but gave the impression that other matters might be brought within the scope of such consultation. *Ibid.* pp. 115–16.

on the Committee of Imperial Defence and Grey gave a general survey of British policy, he actually described the occasion as a "consultation".[1] Whether this was a correct description of the proceedings or not, his speech was certainly followed by a discussion, mainly of the proposed prolongation of the Anglo-Japanese Alliance which "the Committee, including the Dominion delegates, unanimously approved".[2]

Grey directly related his statement of policy to the creation of separate "Fleets and Forces" in the Dominions, just as Ward had argued that these made an "Imperial Parliament of Defence" a necessity. Indeed, it was impossible for anyone to regard imperial defence and its specific problems as existing independently, as it were, of the relations of Britain and the rest of the Empire with foreign Powers. "Defence", after all, was conditioned by "Policy". In addition, as Asquith said in 1909, since the main problem of imperial defence was "a single one, common to every part of the Empire", a "homogeneous organisation for imperial defence and a single direction was necessary".[3] There was thus a need for both a "homogeneous" policy and a "homogeneous" organisation and in 1911 Asquith seems to have been hoping to find both when he brought the Dominion representatives into the Committee of Imperial Defence. They were present at three meetings[4] and it was at the first of these that Grey expounded British policy. Moreover, the practice of Dominion representation was continued after 1911 even though the Imperial Conference was not actually in session; Borden, who succeeded Laurier as Prime Minister of Canada in 1911, and other Dominion statesmen coming to London to sit on the Committee.[5]

Grey's speech was undoubtedly an important innovation. It may be contrasted with the great reluctance of Lord Salisbury in 1887 to allow any colonial "intrusion", as he saw it, into the field of British foreign policy. The difference was due partly, no doubt, to the greater uncertainties of the world situation in 1911. But it was also due to the greater appreciation by the British Government of the nature and strength of that "colonial nationalism" of which Deakin had been the outspoken representative in the first Colonial Conference. To this, successive Conferences, by enabling colonial statesmen as diverse in their ideas as Deakin, Laurier, Seddon, Botha or Ward, to discuss the fundamentals of the imperial relationship, had notably contributed.

When he wrote in later years[6] of the entry of the Dominions into

[1] Gooch, G. P., and Temperley, H. W. V., *British Documents on the Origins of the War*, VI, 781 *seqq.*
[2] Asquith, *The Genesis of the War*, p. 128.
[3] Meeting of the Committee of Imperial Defence which the Dominion representatives at the Subsidiary Defence Conference of 1909 attended on 19 Aug. 1909. Asquith, *op. cit.* pp. 119–20.
[4] Asquith, *op. cit.* pp. 121 *seqq.*
[5] Asquith, *op. cit.* p. 138.
[6] In *The Genesis of the War*, published in 1923.

the Committee of Imperial Defence, Asquith made the comment that "these meetings were the fore-runners of the Imperial War Cabinet".[1] Certainly if Dominion Governments were now collaborating to some extent in the making of British policy they were doing so not in the Imperial Conference, but elsewhere. As Grey pointed out, the nature of the subjects involved made the confidential atmosphere of the Committee essential. Even so, the method of holding a "secret session" of the Conference could have been adopted, and this part of the proceedings omitted from the published record. There was more than a difference of venue involved, and Asquith's reference to the Imperial War Cabinet may be a reminder that a "Cabinet" is not merely a "conference". If there had been time for the practice adopted in 1911 to develop in a period of peace, the position of the Imperial Conference might have been considerably affected. Certainly, when in the war years an Imperial War Cabinet came into existence side by side with an Imperial War Conference, there was no doubt which was the more important.

The final meeting of the Conference of 1911 provided the usual opportunity for general reflections on the Conference itself and its place in the imperial system. Fisher made the interesting suggestion that the next session of the Conference might be held in one of the Dominions;[2] Laurier approved,[3] but both Botha[4] and Ward[5] doubted if it would be practical. They pointed out the obvious advantages of meeting in the capital-city of the Empire where all British ministers were available and Asquith also wondered if the Conference could meet outside London without risk to its efficiency.[6]

Thus, by 1914, the Imperial Conference had become an institution, with a recognised composition, regular sessions and customary methods of procedure. To some extent undoubtedly it owed its inception to an accident, to the occasion of a Sovereign's Jubilee. But even the first Conference of 1887 was of more than ceremonial importance. It was an attempt to give positive and effective expression to imperial unity amid the uncertainties of a rapidly changing world. During the years which followed 1887 this attempt continued. But if there was a large measure of agreement about the end to be sought, men differed widely as to means. Indeed, it is possible to follow this controversy over means in these Conferences, as well as, if not better than, elsewhere. All the Conferences after 1887 until 1914 were, in varying degree, affected by the conflict between the advocates and opponents of federalism. And though the conflict was proceeding as late as 1911, the anti-federalists evidently won a very important victory in 1907.

---

[1] Asquith, *op. cit.* p. 138.
[2] *Parl. Pap.* 1911, LIV [Cd. 5745], pp. 432–3.
[3] *Ibid.* p. 433.
[4] *Ibid.*
[5] *Ibid.*
[6] *Ibid.* pp. 434–5.

In this connection it is impossible to overlook the importance of personalities and those accidents of political fortune which explain why one British or colonial statesman was present at a particular Conference and not another. During these years Laurier, for instance, was in office long enough to gain more experience of the Conferences than any other statesman, either British or colonial. In retrospect, it seems especially important that in 1907 he, as spokesman of the senior Dominion, found a Liberal Government in office in the United Kingdom and a Government whose recent policy in South Africa enabled Botha to join him in possibly the most important of all these Conferences and to reinforce his resistance to Deakin. Indeed, with the Conferences of 1907 and 1911 in mind, it may even be permissible to speak of the triumph of a "Laurier-Botha-Asquith" conception of Empire.

On the other hand, the degree of imperial co-operation which was attained through these Conferences before 1914 may well have been the maximum which could be secured in assemblies representing the different points of view of a number of democratic, national Governments. However these Governments might differ, all were agreed on the question of preserving, not to say enlarging, their autonomy. Before the potentialities latent in their co-operation were either revealed or developed, a totally new situation arose as a result of the First World War. But it is doubtful whether, after 1918, there was ever much likelihood of any change in the direction of federalism. The entry of the Dominions into the "vortex of European militarism" was to strengthen the anti-federal forces already at work; and the Conference itself, which was to survive the War, was destined again on occasions quite as important as that of 1907 to be the effective instrument of these forces.

CHAPTER XII

IMPERIAL FINANCE, TRADE AND COMMUNICATIONS, 1895–1914

IN 1895, forty years had elapsed since Britain had fought any war on the European continent. During that period, as we have seen, she had become increasingly dependent on overseas sources of supply not only to feed her rapidly increasing population, but to maintain her industrial and commercial supremacy. Domestic agriculture had been sacrificed in the interests of industry and commerce, and a merchant marine totalling more than half the tonnage of the world was busily carrying from abroad the food supplies and raw materials to support the vast labour force in factory and workshop. On the whole it had been an era of unique economic progress, and with few exceptions the British people were ready to acknowledge their debt to an almost sacrosanct economic system that had enabled the country to enjoy the world's abundance at the least cost. The manufacturer paid bottom prices for his raw materials and machinery; the shipowner for his ships and stores, and the wage earner for the bread, sugar, tea and a variety of other articles that satisfied his basic needs. It was generally acknowledged that free trade had given to the United Kingdom its industrial superiority over other nations.

None the less, there had been a continuous retreat from pure "Cobdenism" since the 'sixties. Free trade had not conquered the world, and in the new age of competitive imperialism many of its erstwhile advocates were willing to admit that its advantages had been "bought with a price"; as Great Britain lost in self-sufficiency, she had become increasingly vulnerable. How would Adam Smith have regarded a state of affairs wherein the British people had to import more than three-quarters of their bread, and almost half of this amount from a country with which Britain had quite recently seemed to be on the verge of war? So mused Sir William Ashley at the turn of the century. Modern circumstances, he went on, were so much more complex than those of the time of Cromwell, "that the maxim 'defence is more important than opulence' may not be as easy for us to observe as it was for the Long Parliament. Yet it would be extravagant optimism to maintain that it can be safely forgotten."[1]

Originally, free-trade advocates had argued on the principle that each country should produce the goods for which it was best adapted; but the newly-industrialised countries had revealed a

[1] Ashley, W. J., *The Tariff Problem* (4th ed. 1920), p. 37.

tendency towards "identity of employment". Acquired aptitudes fostered by Government were becoming as important as natural aptitudes.[1] Moreover, they were learning the advantages of tariffs as weapons of national defence. While anxious to secure the largest possible benefits from the British imperial free trade area, they were using a variety of protectionist devices to exclude British goods from their markets. Attempts to meet this problem by arranging commercial treaties had broken down chiefly through Britain's lack of any instrument of bargaining. Even the colonies had begun to chafe under the one-sided restrictions and to ask, as did Canada in 1891, for full freedom to negotiate commercial treaties with foreign Powers outside the imperial treaty system. In a world where competitors were building up their customs tariffs, introducing export taxes, applying bounties and subsidies without consultation or even prior notification, the free-trade system seemed, in the view of a growing number of its critics, inadequate and conceivably hazardous.

Although British commercial and financial supremacy at the end of the nineteenth century was still a fact, the contest for leadership was becoming more exacting. Already there was public controversy over the relative progress of American and German trade—the adaptability of the Americans and the aggressiveness of the Germans in comparison with the conservatism and lethargy of the British. The tide of industrial advance seemed to be slowly receding; even those unprepared to acknowledge the ebb were despondent. Looking backward to *fin de siècle*, Sir John Clapham[2] recalled the apprehension of contemporaries who read with foreboding the Kipling warning of 1897:

> Lo, all our pomp of yesterday
> Is one with Nineveh and Tyre.

But the "power and glory" had not yet waned; the Diamond Jubilee celebrations of 1897 were in no way pretentious. Only the year before, Lord Rosebery had told an Edinburgh audience that within twelve years 2,600,000 square miles had been added to the Empire, chiefly in Africa. Yet the vague feeling persisted that something was going wrong. Published tables and digests of trade values and tonnages, even when their worst implications were qualified or annulled by the evidence of more optimistic statisticians, induced certain unpleasant reflections. For one thing, it was clear that the British export trade in terms of tonnage had increased, but not in comparison with imports. Moreover, although exports had grown in bulk if not in value, the gains over the last twenty years had not kept pace with those of other countries. Official enquiries bore witness to the fact that foreign manufactured goods were invading

---

[1] Drage, Geoffrey, *The Imperial Organisation of Trade* (1911), p. 319.
[2] Clapham, Sir J. H., *An Economic History of Modern Britain*, III, 34.

British colonial markets, while British manufactured goods were meeting increasingly formidable competition in traditional foreign markets. Other nations were encroaching upon the prosperity of "the world's commercial centre", and economists were reluctantly coming to the conclusion that the balance of commercial, like the balance of political power, was beginning to shift in a world whose markets were no longer constantly expandable.

Anxiety concerning the export trade was mainly responsible for the Government's comprehensive survey of 1896 to determine the extent to which foreign goods were displacing British in colonial markets.[1] In order to obtain the most precise information, the questionnaire sent to the governors of all the colonies in the Empire included a long list of commodities about which exact information was required. Replies were to deal with prices, freight-rates, subsidies, terms of credit, as well as matters of pattern and packing. If possible, actual specimens of competing foreign goods were to be returned. When the results were finally examined, it appeared that in 1884, of the total imports into the colonies, excluding India, at least 25·8 per cent had been foreign, and by the end of 1894 this percentage had increased to 31·5.[2] In many instances, usually because of lower prices, foreigners had gained 50 per cent of the total trade, and in a few cases they were ousting the Briton altogether. In the Far East, Japan was emerging as a potentially dangerous competitor and was beginning to test the Australian and Hong Kong markets with cotton goods, clothes-brushes, undershirts and a vast array of cheap substitutes. In 1884 Japanese imports into the Straits Settlements totalled 59,000 dollars; in 1894 they had reached 3,662,000 dollars.[3] With low labour-costs her trade seemed bound to expand.

There was no disputing the fact that within the markets of the Empire British trade was losing ground. Between 1881 and 1900 British possessions had increased their purchases by 17 per cent; yet British exports to those same colonies had revealed an actual decrease of 1 per cent.[4] During the same period, the proportion to total imports of imports *from* the United Kingdom had fallen, in the case of India, from 77 to 65 per cent; of Canada, from 49 to 24 per cent; of Australia, from 73 to 61 per cent, and of South Africa, from 83 to 65 per cent. Similarly, while colonial imports *into* the United Kingdom had increased from slightly over £91 millions in 1893 to some £94 millions in 1897, the proportion to the value of total imports had gradually decreased. In 1897 it was estimated at 20·8 per cent,

---

[1] *Trade of the British Empire and Foreign Competition. Dispatch from Mr Chamberlain to the Governors of the Colonies and the High Commissioner for Cyprus and the Replies thereto: Parl. Pap.* 1897, LX [C. 8449].
[2] *Ibid.* p. 3. [3] *Ibid.* p. 277.
[4] Day, Clive, *History of Commerce* (1917), p. 381.

the lowest percentage since 1860.[1] In other words, the trade between the mother country and her colonies was not increasing at the same rate as the total trade of Great Britain.

But the colonial trade was hardly the main cause of disquiet. Apart from India, which ordinarily received about 40 per cent of British exports to the Empire,[2] the United Kingdom was bound to do a great deal more business with foreign countries than with the Dominions, whose total population at the end of the century numbered about 11 millions, or with the heavily populated but as yet undeveloped colonies in the tropics. In 1901 British overseas trade amounted to some £800 millions, of which about £592 millions was carried on with foreign countries, and a little over £200 millions with British possessions.[3] Recently, however, the United States and Germany had begun to compete aggressively in world markets. Both had fought successful wars for unity, and in both the progress of industrial revolutions had been marked by a diminishing dependence on sales of raw materials abroad and on imports of foreign capital. Indeed, not only were both nations extending their manufactured exports, they were beginning the large-scale export of capital. To foreign observers, it seemed possible to predict "with an almost mathematical certainty" the day when they would overtake Great Britain in the race for commercial supremacy.[4]

Cotton goods were by far the most important of British exports; of the total output of the industry, more than 80 per cent was exported. Liverpool was still the largest cotton market in the world, but it was no longer the only important supplier for the Continent of Europe, and statistical curves of export revealed an alarming slackening of progress, "approaching something like stagnation".[5] Coal and iron and steel stood next in export value, and production of the latter was regarded as vital to the country's economic health and security. By the beginning of the 'nineties, however, the United States had taken first place as an exporter of iron and steel; by the turn of the century, the total production of Germany (which stood in

---

[1] Ireland, Alleyne, *Tropical Colonisation* (1899), p. 97.

[2] Flux, A. W., "British Trade and German Competition", *Economic Jour.* VII (1897), 40–1.

[3] British Overseas Trade in 1901:

Imports	£ millions	Exports	£ millions
From foreign countries	416·9	To foreign countries	175·8
From British possessions	105·4	To British possessions	104·6
	522·3		280·4

Ashley, *op. cit.* p. 140.

[4] Halévy, E., *A History of the English People, Epilogue (1895–1905) Book I: Imperialism* (1929 ed.), p. 13. Export statistics for 1894 show: United Kingdom £216,000,000; United States £181,100,000; Germany £148,100,000; France £123,100,000. In 1892 American exports had reached the figure of £211,600,000 as against £277,000,000, the sum of British exports. See also *Memoranda, Statistical Tables and Charts prepared in the Board of Trade with reference to various matters bearing on British and Foreign Trade and Industrial Conditions*, 1903, pp. 5 *seqq.*   [5] Ashley, *op. cit.* p. 61.

second place) and the United Kingdom was only slightly more than the total production of the United States. In 1899 American exports to Britain of iron and steel manufactures had risen within a decade from £500,000 to nearly £4,000,000 and there was every reason to believe that American metallurgical skill and organisation would expand sales a great deal further.[1] The British markets were not protected by tariffs or other economic safeguards, and British firms were facing, not simply duties on their exports of 10 to 30 per cent or more *ad valorem*, but great foreign trusts and cartels, buttressed by government subsidies and high tariffs.

A less disturbing cause for disquiet was the decline in merchant shipping. Britain was losing her almost monopolistic hold on the carrying trade of the world. Not only Germany but France, Japan and the United States were anxious to foster merchant shipping, either by subsidies, direct or indirect, or, in the case of the United States, by confining their coastal trade to their own nationals. Britain's commercial marine was still far greater than that of any other country, but Germany in particular was expanding her direct shipping services not only to foreign countries but to British colonies throughout the Empire. German ships were diverting Australian wool to Hamburg and Antwerp: German ships were carrying plant for South African mines, while Americans and Japanese as well as Germans and French were disputing the trade of China. More than that, trusts like the North Atlantic Shipping Combine were taking shape; in 1901 Pierpont Morgan's U.S. Steel Corporation acquired a majority of the shares of the Leyland Shipping Company. In the following year it was to gain control of all the best Atlantic shipping, except the Cunard and Allan lines. "The supremacy of the mercantile marine", warned the *Annual Register* of 1902, "had slipped from us while we had slept."[2] In part these developments reflected the accumulation of American capital seeking investment; partly they were a recognition of the importance of a large mercantile marine to the growth of sea power, which the writings of Admiral Mahan had vividly emphasised. There was small comfort in the consideration that the apparently slow growth of the British shipping industry (on a percentage basis) could be attributed to the enormous tonnage of British shipping already in existence.[3] The significant consideration for the future was the foreign *rate* of progress, which did exceed that of the United Kingdom.

A limit seemed to have been reached to the development of European markets, as well as to the territorial extension of the Empire; the emancipated foreigner was now beginning to carry his own manufactures in his own ships, and the relative decline of the British mercantile marine was hardly likely to be checked. Where then

---

[1] Clapham, *op. cit.* III, 44.   [2] (Published 1903), p. 134.
[3] Flux, *loc. cit.*; *Economic Jour.* VII (1897), 43.

could new markets and new incentives be found, if British industry and commerce were not to lose still further ground? To the devotees of a new school of imperialism the answer seemed to lie in the closer economic union of the existing Empire. The United Kingdom as a single economic unit was losing ground, but could not the consolidation of the Empire—the substitution of Empire for nation—help to offset the waning supremacy of the mother country? Especially within the white colonies, where a great increase in wealth and population was probable, Britain might restore and extend the markets upon which importunate foreign competitors were fast encroaching.

In practice, however, the new imperialists were facing two separate problems, the threatened loss of British industrial and trading supremacy, and the need for closer integration of the Empire; and it is difficult to be certain at all times whether the main object of the promoters of imperial unity was to rehabilitate British commercial supremacy or whether a reform of the commercial policy of Great Britain was urged, as Cecil Rhodes urged it, to provide solid support for imperial unity. In 1842 Cobden had had no doubts that free trade would "gradually and imperceptibly loose the bands which unite our colonies to us". A half century later Rhodes had written: "The whole thing lies in the question, can we invent some tie with our Mother Country that will prevent separation? It must be a practical one, for future generations will not be born in England. The curse is that English politicians cannot see the future. They think they will always be the manufacturing mart of the world."

It is probably nearer the truth as well as safer to say that motives were inextricably mixed; that by the end of the nineteenth century any new imperial policy could not be divorced from a new commercial policy, and that a reform of imperial commercial policy, while it might not entirely serve the interests of the British consumer, would confer benefits in terms of the greater political, and therefore defensive, strength of the Empire. If the far-flung group of British colonies and dependencies could be bound together as a commercial whole, Britain was assured a safe market for her manufactures in the fast-developing regions of the earth, and the colonies in turn a protected market for their raw materials in Britain. Such in essence was the idea that gradually matured in the mind of Joseph Chamberlain, who entered the Colonial Office in 1895 determined to subordinate the "annals of a kingdom" to the "history of an Empire".

Chamberlain's attitude to the Irish question would suggest that his predominant motive was political, namely, the unity of the Empire; and his earlier ambition to link this objective with social reform may have been strengthened by the success of Bismarck's mixed programme for combining social and industrial welfare with Protection and imperial expansion. Whether or not commercial objectives were always subordinate to this larger aim, he saw clearly, like Rhodes, that sentiment and blood would not provide a permanent bond of union; the political ties had been unravelling for half a century. He believed, moreover, that centrifugal forces were slowly shifting the economic centre of gravity from Britain to the overseas Empire. "We are old and laden with honours, our future cannot rival the greatness of our past. But the Empire is young and in the Empire we may find a future greater than anything upon which we look back." Heretofore the colonies had been considered as individual units, the problems of each being dealt with separately according to needs and the circumstances of the day. Chamberlain would merge the interest of Great Britain in the interest of the Empire. The object of the new imperialism would be not to aggrandise the United Kingdom at the expense of the colonies; for the first time in its history the Empire and its development should be considered as a whole.

Such a solution implied, of course, a change in the fiscal system of Britain, involving conceivably a close commercial relationship of the *Zollverein* type, or a preferential tariff system that would encourage intra-imperial trade and at the same time prevent foreign rivals from dumping cheap surplus goods in imperial markets. To Chamberlain some such innovation appealed not only as the answer to the menacing advances of Britain's rivals, but as a buttress of the imperial unity he was to seek so resolutely. Commerce could be the practical tie that would prevent growing separation and consequent weakness. Admittedly, no one could be certain that an imperial tariff system would effect the salvation of British world trade, even if it were generally acceptable. The resources of the tropical dependencies had been barely touched, and their commercial potentialities were still uncertain. The self-governing colonies were becoming infected with economic nationalism; indeed, some of them were aping the financial system of the foreigner, and trying to turn themselves into little economic fortresses.[1] Nevertheless, if Great Britain could no longer rely entirely on free trade to keep her former trading supremacy, tariff defences offered at least a fighting chance.[2] To the new imperialists, they might mean not only "good politics", but "good economics".

Before the South African War, however, it was too soon to contemplate such a thing as a British tariff, and in the beginning Chamberlain confined himself to "talking Empire"—an Empire re-organised for trade and defence, moving in its own way, as J. L. Garvin put it, "not at all towards rigid centralisation of any sort, but towards some elastic kind of *Zollverein* and *Kriegsverein*".[3] Conditions made an exact replica of the German *Zollverein* obviously out of the question.

[1] See Bérard, V., *L'Angleterre et l'impérialisme* (Paris, 1900), pp. 244-6.
[2] Ashley, W. J., *The Tariff Problem* (4th ed. 1920), p. 263.
[3] *Life of Joseph Chamberlain*, III, 28.

The British colonies were widely scattered, and they were racially mixed. Yet the lesson of German experience remained; out of a series of commercial conventions had grown German political unity. A British *Zollverein* could be formed "on the terms of absolute free trade as between the mother country and the Colonies", the latter being left free to make their own tariffs against foreign competition, and the United Kingdom imposing duties upon certain goods that competed with colonial products.[1] A modest break with unconditional free trade could be justified in terms of Britain's precarious industrial leadership, for after all, whatever might be said of their present position, the colonies were "more likely to develop and increase prosperity and population than any of the foreign States with which we have relations".[2] "The establishment of commercial union throughout the Empire", Chamberlain told the Congress of Chambers of Commerce of the Empire in June, 1896, "would not only be the first step, but the main step, the decisive step towards the realisation of the most inspiring idea that has ever entered into the minds of the British statesmen."[3] Given a form of commercial union based on the imposition of small duties on various foreign raw materials and foods, political centralisation might follow as a matter of course.

Unhappily for Chamberlain's plans most British people, either by conviction or tradition, were "free-traders", and in 1896 there was not the slightest chance of any reversion to protection, even under the banner of "free trade within the Empire". The substitution of Empire for nation as the basis of national faith required changes still unacceptable not only to the Opposition but to influential elements within his own party. For this reason, Chamberlain was careful to insist in the beginning that the "grand conception" meant no radical deviation from the principles of free trade. In theory, he was himself, he declared, a convinced free-trader,[4] quite ready to accept the Cobdenite doctrine that in a world of free trade every nation would become more prosperous. Yet "I have not such a pedantic admiration for it that, if sufficient advantage were offered to me, I would not consider a deviation from the strict doctrine". In a world which had refused to follow Cobden's lead, he pleaded for open-minded consideration of the new problem.

But would the self-governing colonies provide the "sufficient advantage"? Since the middle of the century, economic conditions within the Empire had changed radically. With the granting of

[1] "Report of a Conference between the Right Hon. Joseph Chamberlain and the Premiers of the Self-governing Colonies of the Empire at the Colonial Office, in June and July 1897": *C.O. Confidential Print* (copy in P.R.O., C.O. 885/6 no. 111).
[2] To Canada Club, 25 March 1896; quoted Jebb, R., *The Imperial Conference*, i, 308.
[3] Boyd, C. W., *Mr Chamberlain's Speeches*, p. 368.
[4] See Report of Conference of 1897, *doc. cit.* p. 84.

self-government, anything like a common fiscal policy for the Empire was out of the question. Differences of revenue requirements, differences of attitude and practice made the adoption among the varying colonies of a common policy almost impossible of achievement. Canada certainly was unwilling to contemplate anything like a central customs authority, which suggested a diminution of national sovereignty. At bottom, the question of an imperial tariff system was bound to turn on constitutional as well as economic issues. Indeed, the desire for political autonomy asserted itself in a growing unwillingness to open domestic markets wide to British manufactures. Behind newly-erected tariff barriers local manufacturing industries had developed, and even the Liberal prime minister of Canada, Sir Wilfrid Laurier, who took office in 1896, had learned the political wisdom of his predecessor's "national policy" and was already dexterously extricating himself from the meshes of free trade. Imperial preference in the form of differential duties favouring the mother country and Empire were one thing, but the "grand conception"— an enclosed domain of Empire with no internal tariff barriers, fenced against the outside world—that was a different matter. Few self-governing colonies were likely to risk the sacrifice of national revenue and pride for the benefit of the Empire as a whole. Nothing would be more detrimental to the existence of the British Empire, Laurier was to tell the Imperial Conference of 1907,

than to force upon any part of it, even for the general good, a system which would be detrimental locally, or might be believed to be detrimental locally. For my part, I would have no hesitation at all in resenting any attempt made to force upon the Canadian people anything which the Canadian people would not believe in even for the broad idea of doing good to the whole Empire. I think the best way of serving the whole is, by allowing every part to serve and recognise its own immediate interests. So far as, and as long as, the interests of the British Empire depend upon this and recognise this principle—that every one of those communities which are allowed the privilege of administering their own affairs by their own parliaments—the best way is to leave to each parliament to decide for itself, and for the people whom it represents, what is best for that community.[1]

The idea of imperial preference had been mooted as early as 1887. At the Colonial Conference of that year the question of preferential treatment in United Kingdom markets had been briefly discussed. In 1894 at the Ottawa Conference a resolution had been submitted in favour of reciprocity between colonies and mother country, and recommending inter-colonial reciprocity should the United Kingdom be unable to participate. But the first definite step in the direction of preferential trade within the Empire was taken by Canada in 1897. The new Canadian tariff was in form at least one of general reciprocity; it had to be, since tariff discriminations were barred by the

[1] Minutes of Proceedings of the Colonial Conference: *Parl. Pap.* 1907, LV [Cd. 3523], pp. 411–12.

British treaties that conferred on foreign countries rights of equal treatment. In practice, however, it was a British preferential tariff, providing for a reduction of one eighth, to be increased a year later to one-fourth, on imports from *any* country that admitted the products of Canada on terms equally favourable. It was expected that Great Britain and New South Wales would be the only countries that could so qualify.[1]

While members of the British Government may have had fears as to the legal validity of the new Canadian regulation, there could be no doubt about its popular appeal in Britain, and the Colonial Secretary must have been stimulated by its public reception. "For the first time in my experience," wrote the London correspondent of the *New York Times*, "England and the English are regarding Canadians and the Dominion with affectionate enthusiasm....The spirit of preference for the Mother Country appeals to the imagination here. This change will make Mr Laurier, when he comes here in June, far and away the most conspicuous and popular of all the visiting premiers of the Empire."[2]

When the Colonial Conference met in June, 1897, it was soon clear that the general opinion of the Conference was opposed to any project of a *Zollverein* or comprehensive free-trade area within the Empire. Mr Chamberlain himself admitted in his opening speech that "it would be a matter of the greatest complication and difficulty to arrive at any conclusion which would unite us commercially in the same sense in which the *Zollverein* united the empire of Germany".[3] On the other hand, there was no opposition to Laurier's resolution "that the Premiers of the self-governing Colonies unanimously and earnestly recommend the denunciation at the earliest convenient time of any treaties which now hamper the commercial relations between Great Britain and her Colonies".[4] They were, said Laurier, a serious impediment to colonial development, and he urged the strongest possible expression of Conference approval in order to strengthen the hands of the United Kingdom.[5]

The immediate abrogation of all treaties impeding imperial preference was bound to involve the British Government in a certain amount of diplomatic embarrassment with the possibility of active retaliation, and Chamberlain urged the wisdom of a general pledge of preferential advantage. "As it is...we have only one offer before us, the offer of Canada, and of course it will be argued by some people, at any rate, that it is not worth our while to denounce the Belgian and German treaties merely for the purpose of receiving what advantage it would be to us from Canada."[6] In the end,

[1] Skelton, O. D., *Life and Letters of Sir Wilfrid Laurier*, II, 56.
[2] *Ibid.* II, 57.
[3] Report of the Conference of 1897, *doc. cit.* p. 6.
[4] *Ibid.* pp. 36–7.   [5] *Ibid.* p. 34.   [6] *Ibid.* p. 82.

although there was some feeling that the colonies could hardly be expected to grant preferences without calling upon Britain to reciprocate, "in the hope of improving the trade relations between the mother country and the Colonies" the colonial Premiers undertook to confer with their colleagues overseas to see whether such a result could "be properly secured by a preference given by the Colonies to the products of the United Kingdom".[1]

Not until the Conference had ended did the British Government announce its decision and prepare the way for the general adoption of the Canadian system of preference. As things stood, Belgium and Germany were entitled to the Canadian minimum tariff. If the Canadian offer were to be fully exploited, denunciation would have to come, and Lord Salisbury, as from 28 July 1897, gave the required one year's notice to end the treaties. Until the end of the year, the Canadian Government applied the minimum tariff on goods from Belgium, Germany and other most-favoured nations; but in the following year repealed the reciprocity tariff and established as from 1 August 1898 an unambiguous British preference of 25 per cent (subsequently raised in 1900 to 33⅓ per cent) on products of the United Kingdom and certain of the low-tariff colonies. The consequence was a Canadian tariff war between Canada and Germany which lasted until 1910.

The Canadian concession obviously pointed the way to reciprocity with the Empire. Yet any reversal of the commercial policy of Cobden and Peel postulated a revolution in national thinking; it meant tempting the British nation from its abiding faith in a world market and teaching it to trust in distant colonial sources for the raw materials on which both population and industry depended. Until he began his final crusade Chamberlain probably under-estimated the domestic obstacles in his path. Speeches on the development of the Empire were exciting and harmless; the cry of "dearer living for the working classes" had not yet been raised; nor the furious charge of "increased costs of production". He had not yet tested the stubbornness of the "free trade" faith, nourished as it was by a multitude of financial and social prejudices. The consolidation of the Empire appealed in a shallow way to national pride, but the nation was afraid of trade laws and navigation laws. The mere mention of preferential duties suggested a cramping of the free flow of British goods at the expense of the British consumer.

None the less, it was evident after 1897 that "Free Trade lay under a threat".[2] The disciples of Cobden were on the defensive; politicians and pamphleteers were assailing their doctrines more assiduously than had been the case for half a century. Furthermore, the South African War had created currents of sentiment in the self-governing colonies,

---

[1] Report of the Conference of 1897, *doc. cit.* pp. 87–8.
[2] Spender, J. A., *Life of Sir Henry Campbell-Bannerman*, II, 93.

which seemed to run stronger than ever in imperial channels. In January 1901 Australia became a federal Commonwealth and along with Canada and New Zealand she furnished contingents of troops for service in South Africa. Such loyal assistance might in itself predispose British public opinion in favour of fiscal alterations that benefited colonial allies. Finally, the vast expenditure in war was gradually forcing the Government to consider new methods of collecting revenue.

Early in 1902 Hicks Beach, the Chancellor of the Exchequer, innocently introduced in his budget a shilling a quarter tax on corn and flour in an effort to raise some two and a half million pounds to meet the war expenditure. Scarcely conscious of the subtleties involved in the imperial relationship, and assuming they were doing no more than broadening the domestic basis of taxation, the Treasury had provided Chamberlain with the grand opportunity for offering a preference to the Dominions and most of the Crown colonies without detriment to the exchequer. "Although there is no rebate on Colonial corn, such as there ought to be", said the *National Review*, "the slow-moving mother-country is gradually working towards a position in which she will be able to enter into preferential trade relations with the daughter nations."[1] To establish, for example, reciprocity with Canada, and thereby obtain a promised increase in preference,[2] the British Government had merely to remit the existing corn duty on colonial produce at the next budget, and, if revenue were a trifle short, compensate for the colonial remission by slightly increasing the duty on foreign produce. Such was apparently the expectation of Sir Wilfrid Laurier, who could not conceive that Mr Chamberlain would invite the colonial representatives to discuss that subject at the forthcoming Imperial Conference "unless the British Government had something to propose". In Laurier's view, a step had been taken which at long last made possible a British preference for Canadian goods.[3]

Confronted by this challenge from the Dominions, the Colonial Secretary found himself in a most awkward position when the Conference opened.[4] His Government had accepted with gratitude a Canadian preference, raised in 1900 to $33\frac{1}{3}$ per cent, and yet, less than five years later, had imposed a duty on food and raw materials

---

[1] *National Rev.* xxxix (May 1902), p. 364.
[2] See *Mr Chamberlain's Speeches*, ed. C. W. Boyd, ii (1914), 136.
[3] *The Times*, 14 May 1902.
[4] Apart from a skeleton report issued in October 1902, the full proceedings of the Conference, like those of 1897, were never published. Mr Chamberlain's latest biographer, Julian Amery, has seen no evidence to suggest that Chamberlain himself was responsible (*Life of Chamberlain*, iv, 417), and in the course of the 1907 Conference Sir Wilfrid Laurier remarked that he could see no reason why the report of 1902 could not be made public. The full proceedings are now available in the Public Record Office; see "Conference between the Secretary of State for the Colonies and the Premiers of Self-Governing Colonies", *C.O. Confidential Print* (copy in P.R.O., C.O. 885/8 no. 144).

from which none of the Dominions was exempt. The moral injustice of this situation was not lost on a well-briefed Canadian delegation who, unmindful perhaps of their completely negative stand on the matter of contributions to imperial defence, demanded that "Canadian food products should be exempted in the United Kingdom from the duties recently imposed".[1] Following a merciless indictment of Board of Trade statistics the Canadian representatives made it clear that if the principle of preferential trade were not acceptable to the colonies generally, or to the mother country, then Canada would feel free to take such action "as might be deemed necessary in the presence of such conditions".[2] By comparison the official conference resolution was mild; it did little more than repeat the recommendations of 1897, respectfully urging upon His Majesty's Government "the expediency of granting in the United Kingdom preferential treatment to the products and manufactures of the colonies, either by exemption from or reduction of duties now or hereafter imposed".[3]

For Chamberlain, action was now imperative, and despite the bitter opposition of the new Chancellor of the Exchequer, C. T. Ritchie, he won the provisional consent of the Cabinet to the maintenance of the corn duty, and its eventual preferential remission in favour of the British Empire.[4] In November he sailed for South Africa, only to learn shortly before his return three months later that the corn duty had been repealed. It is too much to say that the Colonial Secretary had been betrayed; no final decision had been taken in 1902, and no promises had been made to the Canadian Government.[5] That Chamberlain reluctantly acquiesced was almost certainly owing to his recognition of Balfour's political difficulties in the face of strenuous free-trade opposition to imperial reciprocity. Moreover, since he had obviously failed to convert the Cabinet, retention of the corn duty was hardly compatible with the refusal of any form of reciprocal preference to the Empire.[6]

Whatever the circumstances, the initiative had now passed into the hands of the free-traders. All through the late winter and spring of 1903 Chamberlain fought a defensive battle behind the scenes, until on 15 May at Birmingham, rejecting all compromise, he cleared his conscience by declaring that food taxes, preferences and the power of tariff retaliation against foreigners were essential to the

---

[1] *Papers relating to a Conference between the Secretary of State for the Colonies and the Prime Ministers of Self-Governing Colonies: June–August, 1902: Parl. Pap.* 1902, LXVI [Cd. 1299], p. 37. See also Appendix IX, pp. 118–30: Canadian Memorandum respecting the operation of the Preferential Tariff.

[2] *Doc. cit.* pp. 37–8; see also Minutes of Proceedings (C.O. 885/8 no. 144), *doc. cit.* pp. 50–60.

[3] *Ibid.* p. 36.

[4] See Amery, J., *Life of Chamberlain*, IV, 523–8.

[5] *Ibid.* p. 526.

[6] See in this connection, Jebb, *op. cit.* I, 363–4; Denison, G., *The Struggle for Imperial Unity*, pp. 334, 356–7; Spender, *Campbell-Bannerman*, II, 94–5.

consolidation and maintenance of the Empire.[1] On 16 September he resigned from the Cabinet to lead his crusade unhampered by official disciplines and loyalties. The result was the split in the Unionist party and its collapse in the general election of 1906.

When the fifth Colonial Conference assembled in London in April 1907 it was known in advance that the new Liberal government would block any proposals for economic correlation based on mutual preferential tariffs, which the Australasian Dominions were certain to propose. Still a burning issue in domestic politics, preferential tariffs were equally combustible material in the Conference chamber, and for several days in May Asquith, Lloyd George and Churchill were clearly on the defensive before the assaults of Deakin, Smartt, Jameson and Sir William Lyne.[2] Even if the price of corn in Britain were not raised, both the Dominions and India, it was argued, would benefit from large-scale production for an assured market. "The question that is coming home to Australia", declared Deakin, is:

can the Commonwealth without preference in the British markets retain even its present trade? And the answer undoubtedly is that without fresh efforts and a new policy it cannot....If we are to expand our markets, and to place ourselves beyond the reach of foreign aggression, preferential treatment must be obtained... Upon the enormous gains to the Empire as a whole from the settlement, population, and development of its immense territories, it is unnecessay to dwell. There are no such opportunities elsewhere and there is urgent need of their immediate utilisation. We are and shall continue to be far your best customers.[3]

But no armoury of statistics could weaken the immovable defences of the British Cabinet or exorcise what Jameson called "the fetish of free trade".[4] In an angry exchange with Deakin, the Chancellor of the Exchequer, Asquith, replied:

I do not like these questions of terminology which are apt to generate heat, but never light. We may be an absolute set of lunatics, wandering in twilight and darkness—fiscal twilight—and the time may come when we shall have a rude awakening. We may think, on the other hand, that Free Trade within the Empire will be recognised as an idea which all the various communities of the Empire ought to aid in constructing. But, I am pointing out, so long as the British people have taken Free Trade as the basis of their fiscal system, that is to say, so long as they impose duties for revenue and for revenue only, by seeking to introduce this element of a penal duty directed against foreign produce, the Imperial motive being to benefit your own Colonies and Dependencies, you are introducing something into the system which is absolutely alien to it, which cannot be reconciled with it, and which will sooner or later, and even at once, develop an antagonism which in the course of time must lead either to the exclusion of the new element or to the complete abrogation of the old system. There is no compromise possible between the two.[5]

[1] *Mr Chamberlain's Speeches*, ed. C. W. Boyd (1914), II, 136; his specific proposals were contained in a speech delivered in Glasgow, 6 Oct. 1903, *ibid.* II, 158–9.
[2] *Minutes of Proceedings of the Colonial Conference, 1907: Parl. Pap.* 1907, LV [Cd. 3523], pp. 228–440 *passim*.
[3] *Ibid.* p. 249.   [4] *Ibid.* p. 317.
[5] *Ibid.* pp. 317–18.

The various colonies had used their fiscal independence, charged the Chancellor, "to build up tariff walls, not only against foreign countries, but against the Mother Country also".[1] In short, they were excluding British manufacturers from their own markets.

Dr Jameson fired the last shot, in what had become clearly a hopeless engagement, when he proposed:

> That while affirming the resolution of 1902 this Conference is of opinion that as the British Government through the South African Customs Union—which comprises Basutoland and the Bechuanaland Protectorate—do at present allow a preference against foreign countries to the United Kingdom, Canada, Australia, New Zealand, and all other British Possessions granting reciprocity, His Majesty's Government should now take into consideration the possibility of granting a like preference to all portions of the Empire on the present dutiable articles in the British tariff.[2]

The main Australian motion was supported by Natal, New Zealand and Newfoundland. General Botha abstained, and Sir Wilfrid Laurier had discreetly withdrawn to keep another engagement. The Canadian Prime Minister, as Chamberlain once sadly remarked, was "not a man with whom to go out tiger shooting".[3]

The delegates must have known what the result would be, although probably few had guessed how decisive would be the rejoinder. The Jameson resolution, said Mr Asquith, raised the question whether foreign countries and colonies should receive different treatment, "and that we conceive we are not able to do".[4] The British Prime Minister had given the expected *coup de grâce* to the Chamberlain design. That the defeat was final was made even more obvious by the reluctance of General Botha and Sir Wilfrid Laurier to take any steps that might imply interference with Britain's domestic affairs; they cautiously refused to set a precedent that might conceivably be used one day to limit the exercise of dominion autonomy.

Laurier's wariness was, however, more than a matter of national sensitivity. In Canada a racial self-consciousness also affected traditional concepts of colonial status. Suspicion and fear of the English-speaking majority produced in the minority a determination to maintain their identity against Anglo-Saxon pressures and temptations. The French-Canadian Prime Minister believed in, and sought to develop, a comprehensive Canadianism; yet he could not ignore the prejudices and aspirations of a province on whose votes he leaned heavily for political support; moreover, he shared the instinctive French-Canadian antipathy to any form of imperial consolidation. But in opposing Chamberlain's plans he naturally represented his obduracy as wholly a product of *Canadian* nationalism. In the

[1] *Parl. Pap.* 1907, LV [Cd.3523], p. 306.   [2] *Ibid.* p. 439.
[3] Buchan, J., *Life of Lord Minto*, p. 166. For an analysis of Laurier's earlier tactics, see Colvin, J. A., "Laurier and the Imperial Problem 1896–1906", Ph.D. Thesis, University of London, 1954.
[4] [Cd. 3523], p. 439.

Australasian Dominions, especially in New Zealand, this defensive attitude was less developed, and its expression less strident. The Australian desire for a preferential trade agreement with the mother country was not, as Sir William Lyne put it, "absolutely a commercial desire"; it was also an "instinctive feeling", and there was more sorrow than anger in the comment of Deakin on Great Britain's "strange Imperial doctrine", which afforded "another illustration of the precept that where the treasure is there will the heart be also".[1]

The resolutions of the 1902 Conference were re-affirmed by all the delegates with the exception of the British representatives, who were unable to accept the recommendations in so far as they implied "that it was necessary or expedient to alter the fiscal system of the United Kingdom".[2] In the picturesque language of Churchill, the Government had:

banged the door upon Imperial taxation of food. Yes, they had banged it, barred it, and bolted it. It was a good stout door of British oak, and the largest Liberal, Radical and Labour majority ever seen in the House of Commons had their backs firmly against it.... They would not concede one inch, they would not give one farthing preference on a single peppercorn.[3]

None the less, neither international nor domestic issues prevented imperial trade from being a principal object of attention at the Imperial Conference of 1911. Outwardly the Conference was notable for the vigorous though confused efforts of Sir Joseph Ward of New Zealand to secure the adoption of some form of parliamentary federation for the Empire; but the really decisive discussions concerned the expanding powers of the Dominions in the field of foreign policy as related to commercial affairs. No serious attempt was made to resurrect reciprocal preferences; indeed, it was agreed that any recommendations should take account of the existing fiscal policies of the Dominions and of the mother country.

Early in the course of the Conference, Sir Wilfrid Laurier had given notice of a resolution to the effect:

that His Majesty's Government be requested to open negotiations with the several Foreign Governments having treaties which apply to the Overseas Dominions with a view to securing liberty for any of those Dominions which may so desire to withdraw from the operation of the Treaty without impairing the Treaty in respect of the rest of the Empire.[4]

It was a far call to the days when Lord Salisbury's government, in the interests of imperial co-operation, had denounced the German and the Belgian treaties. In 1897 Laurier had attacked them on the

[1] [Cd. 3523], p. 248.   [2] Ibid. p. vii.
[3] Morning Post (and The Times), 20 May 1907.
[4] Minutes of Proceedings of the Imperial Conference, 1911: Parl. Pap. 1911, LIV [Cd. 5745], p. 333; also, Précis of the Proceedings: ibid. 1911, LIV [Cd. 5741], p. 31.

ground that they barred the way to British preferential treatment. In 1911 he was urging the abolition of all agreements that barred or impeded commercial negotiations with any country. As far as Canada was concerned, he wanted a free hand to negotiate with the United States, and he found ready support in the Australian desire to secure removal of the treaty obstacles which stood in the way of an Australian preference to British goods carried in British ships.

To most people who had not followed the bewildering advances in Dominion status since Lord Ripon wrote his challenging dispatch in 1895, the resolution suggested new perils for the Empire; certainly local autonomy seemed to be in process of demolishing the remaining framework of union. The implementation of the resolution meant the release of any dominion, that so desired, from any of the most-favoured-nation treaties between the United Kingdom and foreign states. Denunciation of the existing most-favoured-nation treaties, according to *The Times*, "even if followed by their resumption on terms allowing Canada or any other Dominion to stand out when it so desired, could only have the gravest results, since it would destroy for good and all the principle of commercial unity within the Empire...."[1]

But commercial unity had already been destroyed; the passing of the resolution unanimously (with the insertion of the word "commercial" before "treaties") sealed the principle of equality in commercial negotiation by self-governing dominions. As Sir Edward Grey explained to the Conference, there had been a constant evolution in practice since 1896. Without exception, for fifteen years, every new treaty allowed the Dominions the option of adhering or withdrawing, but the old treaties—some of them going back to Oliver Cromwell and Charles II—had remained as before. Now that the Dominions had developed separate fiscal systems of their own, the imperial commercial system had to be brought into line with "the modern state of things which now exists".[2]

It was clear, as Harcourt, the Colonial Secretary, remarked, that the governing note of the Conference had not been "Imperial concentration", but "Imperial co-operation". It was also clear that national autonomy and imperial collaboration would not always go hand in hand. Sir Wilfrid Laurier had shown more than once that he had no wish to sacrifice Canada's increasing freedom of action in the interests of a common policy that spelled centralisation; centralisation in the commercial field was no more attractive to him than centralisation in the parliamentary field. The commercial relations between the different parts of the Empire were, he once declared, the results of "haphazard" development, and Sir Wilfrid more than any

---

[1] 7 June 1911.
[2] *Minutes of Proceedings of the Imperial Conference, 1911: Parl. Pap.* 1911, LIV [Cd. 5745], p. 336.

other imperial ststesman of his time was responsible for encouraging this "haphazard" growth. On the other hand, his opposition to Australasian resolutions urging greater co-operation "in commercial relations and matters of mutual interest" was not aimed solely at diverting Conference discussions to less provocative topics. He was on safe ground when he pointed out that any proper organisation of commercial intercourse within the Empire would be difficult without fuller information on economic conditions in the Dominions. His resolution, which had the blessing of Harcourt and the full support of the Conference, was to lead in the following year to the appointment of a Royal Commission representing all the Dominions, including Newfoundland, "with a view to investigating and reporting upon the natural resources of each part of the Empire represented at this Conference,...the trade of each part with the others and with the outside world, the food and raw material requirements of each, and the sources thereof available. To what extent, if any, the trade between each of the different parts has been affected by existing legislation in each, either beneficially or otherwise."[1]

Already, however, the chain of Imperial Conferences and less formal meetings had paved the way for the establishment of services and organisations, whose object lay in furthering knowledge of the Empire's resources and commercial potentialities. In 1905 the "Advisory Committee on Commercial Intelligence" first appointed by the Board of Trade five years previously, added to its membership four representatives of the Dominions, three of whom were High Commissioners. Among the committee's tasks was that of advising the Board of Trade on matters relating to foreign tariffs, the use of commercial commissions abroad, and generally "obtaining and diffusing information for the benefit of British trade".[2] In 1908 the Board of Trade took another step forward with the appointment of four trade commissioners to reside, respectively, in Canada, Australia, South Africa and New Zealand. Their principal duties were to secure and further trading opportunities with the Dominion concerned, and to maintain a constant flow of information on such commercial matters as, for example, alterations in customs duties. The trade commissioners also maintained liaison with chambers of commerce, whose general congresses developed an increasingly imperial flavour. The first congress had met in London in 1886 under the auspices of the London Chamber. In 1903 it met in Montreal, and in 1909 in Sydney. Such non-official meetings undoubtedly contributed to strengthen the feeling of a world-wide community of interests.

Finally, the Imperial Institute, constituted by royal charter in

---

[1] See *Final Report of the Royal Commission on the Natural Resources, Trade and Legislation of Certain Portions of His Majesty's Dominions: Parl. Pap.* 1917–18, x [Cd. 8462].

[2] Ashley, W. J. (ed.), *British Dominions, their Present Commercial and Industrial Condition* (1911), p. xi.

1888, had become in a sense the Empire's scientific research bureau of economic resources. Transferred to the Board of Trade in 1902, it functioned after 1907 under the authority of the Colonial Office. Until the Dominions, a generation later, had reached a stage of maturity when they could take responsibility for their own surveys, the Board of Governors of the Imperial Institute (including representatives of the various Dominions, whose governments contributed to the expense of the undertaking) aimed "to provide for the scientific and technical investigation of raw materials, more particularly those produced within the Empire, with a view to their commercial utilisation, and to supply information respecting the production, commercial employment, and value of such materials".

There were, however, a number of stubborn obstacles in the field of imperial co-operation, which seemed to defy the arts of the statesman and the wisdom of the lawyer. There was no uniform naturalisation law for the Empire, nor a uniform patent, trade mark or copyright law. To secure an invention for the whole Empire, it was necessary to take out at least twenty-eight patents; to protect a trade mark throughout the Empire required between thirty and forty registrations; the law of copyright contained anomalies which implied, at least, injustice to both author and publisher. At the Colonial Conference of 1907 it was resolved "that His Majesty's Government, after full consultation with the Dominions, should endeavour to provide such uniformity as may be practicable in the laws for the granting and protection of trade marks and patents".[1] A similar resolution recommended greater uniformity in Company Laws of the Empire.[2] Copyright was discussed, but owing to objections from Sir Wilfrid Laurier no resolution was passed.[3] During the Conference of 1911 further discussions took place, supported by bulky memoranda from the Board of Trade.[4] Once again it was resolved "that it is in the best interests of the Empire that there should be more uniformity throughout its centres and dependencies in the law of copyrights, patents, trade marks, companies".[5] Obviously the Dominions were agreed in principle, but without previous detailed exploration it was absurd for an Imperial Conference to attempt a settlement of such technical subjects, especially where there was so much divergence of legislation and when nationalism tended to confuse clear thinking on imperial projects that called for uniformity. The Dominions Royal Commission of 1912 took up the investigation, but accomplished little beyond outlining the diversities, which in themselves suggested that imperial uniformity either in patent law, trade marks, company law or currency was not an immediate prospect.[6]

[1] Minutes of Proceedings: Parl. Pap. 1907, LV [Cd. 3523], p. 488.
[2] Ibid. p. 491.   [3] Ibid. pp. 489–90.
[4] Papers Laid Before the Conference: Parl. Pap. 1911, LIV [Cd. 5746–I], pp. 140–204
[5] Minutes of Proceedings: Parl. Pap. 1911, LIV [Cd. 5745], p. 162.
[6] Parl. Pap. 1917–18, x [Cd. 8462]; pp. 154–8.

As a wholesale business partnership of world-wide connections the British Empire experienced its most creative phase during the "Chamberlain era". Improvements in communications alone transformed its economic pattern, while advances in medical, chemical and entomological science cleansed some of its worst physical blemishes. The discovery in 1897 of the association between the mosquito and malaria represented the beginnings not only of a new era of tropical medicine, but a revolution in tropical labour conditions. For the first time in history, tropical areas had become important fields of industrial enterprise. The older colonies had long shared the services of the engineer, the industrialist and the financier; now similar agencies were at work in Africa, where the most important developments of the whole period were taking place. West Africa was soon in the forefront as a laboratory of economic experiment, and even stagnant backwaters like East Africa, or bankrupt areas like the West Indies, were to respond to the mechanical and capitalistic impulses of the new age. Cocoa, ground nuts, sisal, cotton, coffee, sugar, palm oil and minerals were to flow with increasing abundance from the agricultural perimeter to the industrial and financial centre of Empire. At the same time the expansion of banking and joint-stock investment techniques increased the flow of capital for overseas railways and public works and encouraged large-scale specialisation in Canadian wheat, Australian wool, African cotton or Malayan tin.

For the more mature colonies it was increasingly advantageous to have connection with the central money market of the world; it meant not only rapid but cheap development. It has been estimated that the comparatively low rates at which they borrowed meant an average saving to them of £10,000,000 a year.[1] Moreover, under the Colonial Stocks Act of 1901, their government stocks were included in the precious list of British trusteeship securities. From London's point of view, productive colonial territories provided investments in which the risks were regarded as somewhat lower than in most foreign areas, partly because certain political controls were retained by the Home Government, and partly because the capital was expended largely by British agents or engineers under British laws.[2]

The financial crises of the 'nineties in Argentina, Australia and the United States temporarily slowed down the rate of overseas investment, but even during the period of general depression British capital continued to flow to Canada, South America, India, Australia and to various parts of Africa. The development of new countries demanded heavy expenditure on railways, mines, irrigation, drainage and general construction work. Railways were by far the most attractive investment, but British capital was also in demand for manufacturing

---

[1] Sir Edward Speyer in *The Times*, 25 May 1911.
[2] Royal Institute of International Affairs, *The Problem of International Investment*, Report by a Study Group of Members (1937), p. 113.

and business enterprises, cotton and textiles, iron and steel works, paper mills, breweries, power plants, oil refineries, shipping, insurance and telegraphs. Following the South African War there was a lull; but after 1903 the totals of oversea investments climbed again. Britain was in fact starting her "last and greatest campaign of capital export".[1] Despite political tensions, national and international, the export of capital reached in 1907 a total of £140 millions. By the end of that year it was calculated that British investments in colonial and foreign lands in terms of publicly issued securities alone amounted to £2,700 millions.[2] During the following two years there was some decline, but the amount exported always exceeded £100 millions a year.[3]

The most striking feature of imperial economic history after 1895 was the relentless search for food and raw materials; and because British capital sought out agricultural lands a heavy concentration of investments within the Empire was inevitable. Out of the £1000 millions of new capital invested between 1907 and 1913 inclusive nearly £500 millions went to the Empire, including India.[4] Since mechanical transport alone could render undeveloped lands accessible, the greater part of these enormous sums was devoted to railway construction. The total British investment in oversea railways in 1913 was estimated at £1531 millions, or just over 40 per cent of all British holdings of overseas securities. Of this amount Empire railway securities accounted for £447·2 millions (including India's £140·8), or about 25 per cent of the total.[5]

With the exception of the United States, Britain sent more capital to Canada than to any other country. Practically the whole of the money used to build two new railway systems, each about 3000 miles in length, was furnished by the British investor. At the end of 1910 the amount of capital publicly invested in Canada amounted to £373 millions, at least £40 millions being expended each year in loans on mortgage, land purchase and such like investments.[6] The United States was only beginning to exploit the Canadian field, although it was estimated that American investments in Canada had increased from $100 millions in 1900 to some $350 millions by 1911.[7] Australia and New Zealand together received about as much British capital as

[1] Clapham, op. cit. III, 43.

[2] Paish, G., "The export of capital and the cost of living", The Statist, Supplement (14 Feb. 1914), p. iv.

[3] Hobson, C. K., The Export of Capital (1914), p. 159.

[4] See statistical table, Paish, loc. cit. p. v.

[5] The Problem of International Investment, pp. 122-3.

[6] Paish, G., "Great Britain's capital investments in individual colonial and foreign countries", Journ. R. Statist. Soc. LXXIV (Jan. 1911), p. 176. Paish estimated the total British public capital investment in Canada as of December 1913 at £514,870,000 (The Statist, Supplement, 14 Feb. 1914).

[7] Viner, Jacob, Canada's Balance of International Indebtedness, 1900–1913, pp. 129, 134. Viner estimated that American investments in Canada from 1900 to 1913 amounted to approximately $630 millions.

Canada—£301,500,000 and £78, 500,000 respectively. Most of the money was borrowed for railways, which were built by Government, in contrast to Canada which left the task to private enterprise. British investments in South Africa before 1910 reached £351 millions, of which £125 millions represented capital invested in mining companies. All told, in the Dominions of Canada, South Africa and Australasia, with a total white population in 1910 of about 14 million people, Great Britain had invested over £1100 millions sterling.[1]

In India the amount of capital invested from Great Britain by 1910 was about £365 millions, again the larger portion being used for the building of railways. The burden of interest was low—some 3·87 per cent for railways—and the effects of this expenditure upon the development of natural resources and the reduction of famines was immense. Sir George Paish was inclined to think that the improvement in the condition of the people resulting from railway construction was "one of the most potent factors in maintaining loyalty of the vast populations of India to the British Empire".[2]

Although the British Empire was not becoming the commercial organism for which Chamberlain hoped, the network of trade relations continued to grow in breadth and intricacy. Canada was negotiating tariff agreements with Australia, New Zealand, the South African colonies and the West Indies; Australia and New Zealand were similarly engaged with South Africa; proposals for a reciprocity treaty between Australia and New Zealand on foodstuffs and timber were under consideration.

The application of preferential duties between one Dominion and another was not always, however, the result of reciprocity arrangements. As a general rule, preferential treatment was not accorded by special arrangement, and the same situation applied to the grant of preferences on United Kingdom produce entering the Dominions.[3] In Australia preference was granted by means of a reduction in the ordinary rate of duty, whereas in New Zealand more or less the same result was obtained by a surtax on certain classes of foreign manufactured goods. In Canada, as a consequence of the Fielding revisions of 1907, there were (excluding the surtax) three tariffs: a British preferential tariff, an intermediate tariff and the general tariff. This carefully graded schedule made provision for the extension of preference throughout the whole Empire. Not only self-governing colonies were included, but India and Ceylon, the Straits Settlements and the West Indies. Moreover, the preferential tariff could be

---

[1] Paish, "Great Britain's Capital Investments", *loc. cit.* p. 179.
[2] *Ibid.* p. 178.
[3] For the amounts of rebate on United Kingdom goods entering Canada, Australia, New Zealand and South Africa between 1910 and 1913, see table included in *Final Report of the Royal Commission on the Natural Resources*, etc.: *Parl. Pap.* 1917–18, x [Cd. 8462], p. 14.

extended to any British colony or possession by order-in-council without recourse to Parliament. To many optimistic tariff reformers a great system of inter-colonial commercial treaties seemed to be taking shape. Already, on the basis of a preferential tariff, Canada was exchanging food and timber for West Indian sugar; Indian jute bags were being traded for Australian wheat, or West African cocoa and palm kernels; the South African colonies had begun to build trading connections not only with the Dominions but with Kenya, Nigeria and the great inland empire of Rhodesia. Any doubts as to the validity or expediency of preferential agreements between parts of the British Empire were extinguished in 1910, when a Royal Commission appointed to inquire into the trade relations between Canada and the West Indies laid it down as "a settled principle" that such arrangements were to be considered "matters of a domestic character which cannot be regarded as discriminatory by any foreign power".[1]

Whatever the shape of these colonial tariff discriminations, they were not intended to confine trade within the Empire. Increasing quantities of Australian wool went to Japan and the United States, along with Canadian lumber and pulp. Indian hides and rice, Nigerian palm oil, Malayan wolfram, Canadian nickel, Australian zinc and silver-lead, went to Germany; Malayan tin and rubber to the United States. Moreover, the Empire was not self-sufficient; the mother country especially relied on the outside world for petroleum and raw cotton, meat and even sugar. On the other hand, most of the staples could be obtained within the Empire—wheat, cotton, wool, cocoa, timber, rubber, tin and the other vital metals.[2] In 1901 only about one-fifth of Britain's imported wheat requirements came from British possessions. By 1913 the total had risen to nearly one-half.[3]

---

[1] *Parl. Pap.* 1910, xi [Cd. 5369], p. 49.

[2] Board of Trade estimates of colonial production and export are contained in *Statistical Abstract for the several British Self-Governing Colonies, Possessions, and Protectorates in each year from 1900 to 1914*, no. 52: *Parl. Pap.* 1916, xxxii [Cd. 8329]; preceding numbers cover the period after 1895, e.g. no. 47: *Parl. Pap.* 1910, cvi [Cd. 5420]. A new *Statistical Abstract for the British Empire*, no. 1, *Parl. Pap.* 1905, xciv [Cd. 2395], which covered successive periods from 1889, was issued to meet the growing demand for statistical information on the trade, shipping and production of the Empire as a whole. The last number of this series, the eleventh, covering the period 1899-1913, was published in 1916: *Parl. Pap.* 1914-16, lxxvii [Cd. 7827].

[3] *Final Report of the Royal Commission on the Natural Resources, Trade, etc. of His Majesty's Dominions: Parl. Pap.* 1917-18, x [Cd. 8462], p. 185. The production of wheat in the Empire during five years (1909-13) averaged about 705 million bushels a year:

	Million bushels
United Kingdom	59·6
India	356·6
Canada	184·6
Australia	90·5
New Zealand	6·9
South Africa	5·0
Cyprus	2·0
	705·2

Between 1901 and 1911 the wheat area in Australasia had grown by nearly 50 per cent, although the supply was liable to severe fluctuation owing to drought. In Canada the peopling of the western plains, the introduction of new machinery and hardier seeds, produced a world granary within the same decade. For the years 1910-14 the average annual production of the Dominion was 196 million bushels, and the average export of wheat and flour nearly 97 million.[1] Food grain continued to be India's most important export article. In 1904 India sent more wheat to Britain than did any other country, and in 1905 more than any other except Argentina. During those two years she provided one-fifth of the total United Kingdom import.[2] The other importing countries of the Empire—South Africa, Newfoundland, the West Indies and West Africa—obtained the bulk of their imports from imperial sources.

After wheat, raw cotton was the most valuable of all British imports. But the growth of cotton manufacturing in Europe, the United States, and more recently in Japan, tended to advance more rapidly than the world production of fibre; American sources seemed to be showing signs of exhaustion, and the United States had been Britain's principal support. During the first years of the twentieth century Lancashire's looms had required on an average about 2000 million pounds of raw cotton, of which some 1500 million had come from the United States, 400 million from Egypt and 100 million from British India and other parts of the Empire.[3] The fact that some three-quarters of the supply came from American sources, which might be subject to "cornering" operations, was embarrassing to British manufacturers; the only safe solution in the opinion of the experts seemed to be, first, that of improving the supply from India and Egypt; secondly, expediting cultivation in British colonial areas previously unexploited, such as Uganda, Nyasaland, Rhodesia and especially the Sudan; finally, reviving cultivation in areas reduced through American competition, such as Cyprus, the west coast of Africa, Fiji, Queensland and the West Indies.

In contrast to cotton, the imports of wool were almost entirely obtained from British sources. The estimated consumption in the United Kingdom during the period 1909-13 averaged 566 million pounds, of which imported wool amounted to 471 million. Australia provided nearly one-half the United Kingdom import, of which about 80 per cent was re-exported. Between 1902 and 1907 the price of wool went up steadily, and Australian pastures and flocks grew in correspondence. After Australia, which produced the best quality merino, came New Zealand and, in order of importance, the South African colonies, India and the Falkland Islands. In keeping with centuries-old tradition,

---

[1] [Cd. 8462], p. 18. [2] Clapham, *op. cit.* III, 48.
[3] Grice, J. W., *The Resources of the Empire* (1917), p. 13; see also "Products of the Empire: Cotton", *United Empire*, IV (April, 1913), pp. 311-18.

Britain still produced her own native wool, of which some 95 million pounds were retained for home consumption out of a total clip of about 136 million.[1] A large part of the surplus was exported to the United States.

Of the imports of tea, coffee and raw cocoa, the British Empire provided roughly 90, 15 and 50 per cent respectively. The tea supplies were almost entirely derived from India and Ceylon, although the plant was cultivated to a slight extent in Natal and Nyasaland. As in Ceylon, coffee production in India had declined rapidly in the latter part of the nineteenth century, but tea planting had made enormous advances. Between 1885 and 1900 the area of planting had expanded 85 per cent, and production had increased by 167 per cent.[2] The English thirst for tea had been the salvation of Ceylon, after fungus had ruined coffee, and canker disease and foreign competition smitten quinine. Despite the fall in prices and competition with the China product (which had failed to win popular regard), tea became before 1914 the basis of the country's economy. The export from Ceylon in 1910–11 was 183,905,153 pounds, of which more than 108,000,000 went to the United Kingdom.[3] Only a small proportion of coffee was produced for export within the Empire; it was grown chiefly in India, the West Indies and British Guiana. Plantations had been started in Nyasaland, East Africa and Uganda, but the prospects remained uncertain. For raw cocoa, Britain relied mainly on West Africa, the West Indies and Ceylon. Starting in 1890, the Gold Coast was rapidly becoming the leading cocoa area of the world.[4]

In Rangoon, Burma possessed the rice capital of South-East Asia. Extensive irrigation developments followed the opening of the Mandalay canal in 1902, and another in the Shwebo district in 1906; during the period 1909–10 to 1913–14 the annual average export of rice was 1,814,000 tons.[5] German mills shared with British the labour of polishing and re-exporting the final product; thence rice "followed the coolie round the world". Annual imports in Trinidad, Barbados and Jamaica exceeded 18,000 tons, with corresponding quantities of Indian jute for packaging.[6]

Timber and wood imports came mainly from foreign sources in northern Europe. The British Empire supply came chiefly from Canada and Newfoundland, and amounted only to some 16 per cent. Of mechanical pulp, imports from the Empire amounted to 91,000 tons or 11 per cent of the United Kingdom consumption.[7] Most of

---

[1] *Parl. Pap.* 1917–18, x [Cd. 8462], pp. 186–7.   [2] Knowles, *op. cit.* p. 389.
[3] Willis, J. C., *Agriculture in the Tropics* (3rd ed. 1922), p. 60.
[4] Export figures for quinquennial periods 1892–1936 are contained in Hancock, W. K., *Survey of British Commonwealth Affairs*, ii, pt. ii (1942), p. 209; production figures for West Africa, p. 338.
[5] Scott, Sir George, *Burma, A Handbook of Practical Commercial and Political Information* (rev. ed. 1921), pp. 256–62, 290.
[6] *Department of Overseas Trade, Commissioners, Report for the West Indies, 1922*, p. 16.
[7] *Parl. Pap.* 1917–18, x [Cd. 8462], p. 186.

the Canadian supply went to the United States; that of Newfoundland, to Britain. On the whole, the timber trade which had dominated the history of early nineteenth-century Canada played but a small part in the development of the rest of the Empire.[1] Although British Guiana, Malaya, Southern Nigeria and India possessed considerable resources of hardwoods, mahogany from Honduras and teak from Burma were the only important commercial timbers supplied by tropical colonies. The annexation of Upper Burma in 1886 had added extensive forest areas, of which some 4,438 square miles had been reserved by 1896. In 1913–14 exports of teak from Rangoon amounted to 42,406 tons, valued at £406,200, and from Moulmein, 6122 tons, valued at £65,300.[2]

Gold was still the most valuable of the precious metals, and by far the most important source was the Witwatersrand in the Transvaal. By 1904 the gold output of the Rand had returned to the pre-war level; by 1908 it had nearly doubled. Stimulated by the work of reconstruction and renewal, South African markets had expanded, and the increasing gold supply made purchase and borrowing a simple matter.[3] In 1912 the Rand yielded its record output—some £38,700,000—40 per cent of the world's output. Elsewhere, Australia produced £9,800,000, Rhodesia £2,700,000, the Gold Coast £1,000,000, India £2,200,000, Canada £3,100,000, British Guiana slightly over half a million, and British Borneo about a quarter of a million. Of the world total gold production before the war (1914–18), the British Empire contributed nearly two-thirds.[4]

Australia produced nearly all the zinc and about 85 per cent of the silver-lead obtained throughout the Empire. For some years before 1914, however, almost the entire output of zinc concentrates (about 500,000 tons annually) had been sold under contract to smelters in Germany and Belgium. The zinc smelting capacity of the Empire was far below consumption.[5] In 1912, from a total output of silver and silver-lead concentrates valued at £1,074,153 those same countries took £900,630; only £19,835 worth was exported to the United Kingdom. Germany in particular had acquired an almost dominant influence over many of the metal industries of the Empire, and during the last few years before the outbreak of war there was much public discussion on the need for safeguarding imperial resources.

From Burma, Malaya and Australia the annual average output of tungsten ores (wolfram and scheelite) during the period 1909–13 was approximately 1200, 700 and 1100 tons respectively. Yet only a

---

[1] See "Forestry Report", in *Record of Proceedings and Documents, Imperial Economic Conference, 1923: Parl. Pap.* 1924, x [Cmd. 2009], p. 546.
[2] Gull, E. M., *British Economic Interests in the Far East* (1943), p. 94.
[3] Clapham, *op. cit.* III, 48.
[4] Grice, *Resources of the Empire*, pp. 32–3.
[5] [Cd. 8462], pp. 182–3.

fraction of this supply went to the mother country. By purchasing and treating low-grade ores which British firms would not touch, Germany acquired control of most of the best tungsten. Her net imports averaged 3690 tons a year, and more than half of this came from Empire sources. Before the outbreak of war in 1914 practically the whole supply of tungsten for the manufacture of British high-speed steels came from Germany.[1] Of nickel and nickel ores, Canada furnished the bulk of the world's supply; ores mined in 1913 represented about 22,000 tons. The deposits were largely controlled by American capital and, owing chiefly to the absence of refining facilities, the larger part of the ore mined was smelted in the United States.[2] The annual production of tin in the Empire was about 81,500 tons, or 65 per cent of the world's output; the United Kingdom production from the smelting of Empire ores was approximately 2500 tons.[3] Altogether, foreign countries were dependent on the Empire, especially Malaya, for nearly 60 per cent of their total requirements of tin. Malayan mines had been worked throughout the nineteenth century by Chinese, but only with the growth of the tinplate industry in the 'seventies and 'eighties did the industry begin to expand, supported by new roads and railways and Chinese labour. This demand was strengthened after 1900 with the rapid growth of the canning industry, ship-building and railways. Within ten years Singapore possessed the largest tin-smelting works in the world.

In 1900 the world rubber supply was about 53,000 tons, of which plantation rubber accounted for four tons.[4] But by 1902–3, plantation rubber had overtaken wild rubber production, and after 1907 Amazon exports steadily declined as Malayan plantations expanded with the development of the rubber-tired bicycle and automobile, and the demands that followed the extension of electricity as a source of light and power. Rubber planting in the Federated Malay States began in 1895, based on plants raised at Kew from Brazilian seedlings.[5] By 1900 there was still no export; in 1905 it was 104 tons; by 1913 it had risen to nearly 2400 tons. By the end of the

---

[1] [Cd. 8462], p. 182.
[2] *Ibid.* p. 178.
[3] *Ibid.* p. 181. The world production of tin in 1913 was 127,000 tons (the average was about 118,000 tons for the previous five years):

	Tons
Malaya	64,600
United Kingdom from native ores	5,200
United Kingdom from imported ores	14,000
Australia	4,800
Nigeria	4,500
Germany	11,300
Dutch East Indies	17,100
China	5,800

[4] Knowles, *op. cit.* p. 482.
[5] Masefield, G. B., *A Short History of Agriculture in the British Colonies* (1950), p. 53.

First World War almost half the rubber of the world was coming from Malaya.[1]

To the world supply of petroleum in 1913, amounting to some 50 million tons (of which the United States provided about 32 million), the British Empire contributed barely a million and a quarter. Of this, the larger proportion came from the fields of Upper Burma, 300,000 tons from Scotland, only 50,000 from Canada and an insignificant amount from Sarawak where the first well was sunk in 1910. In 1898 the annual production of Burmese crude oil was less than 100,000 tons; by 1913, thanks to the initiative of the Burmah Oil Company, it had reached more than 900,000.[2]

During this period, responsibility for the economic progress of most of the tropical areas had been assumed by the State, which had become a landowner and commercial manager on the grand scale. The tropical colonies still required the energies and talents of explorers, merchants and private capitalists, but these pioneers of colonisation no longer directed policy; the colonial administrator had become the driving force in all projects for economic development. In Africa, the West Indies and Malaya, the British Government arranged for loans and grants-in-aid to build public works such as roads, railways and irrigation reservoirs, or for the encouragement of scientific agriculture, the study of tropical medicine and the war against insect pests. By 1914 the three colonies of Nigeria, Gold Coast and Sierra Leone had borrowed £10,421,000. "One of the things I am proudest of in West Africa", remarked a former Governor of Southern Nigeria, "is that I found Nigeria with hardly any debt, and I left it with a debt of five millions."[3] In 1899 the Royal Niger Company was bought out for £865,000; between 1901 and 1918 Nigeria received grants-in-aid totalling £4,261,000.[4] During the same period, Uganda received £2,648,000 and East Africa (Kenya), before it became self-supporting in 1912, £2,843,383.[5] The Uganda railway was built at a cost of £5,500,000, and on this expenditure no interest was charged. Partly owing to the discovery of new gold deposits, British investments in West Africa totalled by 1910 over £29 millions, of which about £12 millions went into mining, and £8 millions for government loans, chiefly for railways. At the same time, some £22 millions of British capital found its way to the Straits Settlements and the Federated Malay States, of which over £10

---

[1] Knowles, *op. cit.* pp. 482–3.

[2] See Grice, *op. cit.* p. 26; also the same author's "The Oil Resources of the Empire", *United Empire*, IV (Sept. 1913), pp. 745–53; Holland, Sir Thomas, "Trend of Mineral Development in India", *Jour. R. Soc. Arts*, LIX (12 May 1911), p. 642; Scott, Sir George, *op. cit.* pp. 244–6.

[3] Quoted in McPhee, A., *The Economic Revolution in West Africa* (1926), p. 213.

[4] *Report by Sir F. D. Lugard on the Amalgamation of Northern and Southern Nigeria, and Administration, 1912–1919: Parl. Pap.* 1919, XXXVI [Cmd. 468], pp. 47–8.

[5] Knowles, *op. cit.* pp. 97–8.

millions went into rubber plantations, and £8 millions for Government loans.[1]

With the transfer of authority from Company to Crown, economic exploitation became more dependent on Government loans than on joint-stock development. In the Crown colonies especially, the predominance of the "official trader" was assured. Practically all Government requirements were handled by Crown Agents of the Colonial Office, who were responsible not merely for the issue of loans to some forty-four colonies and protectorates, but for most of the business connected with the projection of public works such as railways, harbours, drainage and water schemes, and the purchase of the necessary British stores for such undertakings.[2] The office of Crown Agent was self-supporting; no part of the cost was voted by Parliament, although its accounts were audited by the Comptroller and Auditor-General. The Treasury was still loth to free itself from nineteenth-century traditions of "penny-pinching"; on the other hand, a great deal more colonial revenue was available than had been hitherto. For one thing, the rule of law was gradually establishing itself in regions where Lugard had found "populations numbered in millions, seething with internal strife...."[3] Pacification meant reductions in military expenditure, and hence a greater proportion of revenue could be spent on railways and other public works.

Like the Romans, the British had always laid tremendous stress on communications; and perhaps the genius of British colonial method lay as much in engineering skill as in administration. Roads, rails, steamships, cables, bridges, harbours, docks and waterworks opened up isolated tribal areas to the men and machines of western civilisation. Only with the laying down of railways and roads did the colonies make any substantial fiscal or commercial progress. And because private capital could not undertake all the risks, most of the railways in the tropics were built and worked by the State. Even in India a guarantee of interest had been necessary to attract capital; in Africa, where labour was scarce, populations scattered and large areas of wilderness unexplored and unsurveyed, Government initiative was inevitable. The financial history of Ceylon, Malaya and Jamaica bears out this rule of the jungle.

Just as the building of the Canadian Pacific Railway represented a turning-point in Canadian development, so were the Sudan, Uganda and Nigerian railways epoch-making achievements in African history. The battle of Omdurman in 1898 opened the Sudan to rails, which followed steadily on Kitchener's heels in the direction of Khartoum.

[1] Paish, "Great Britain's Capital Investments", *loc. cit.* p. 179; see Table of investments, p. 180.
[2] *Dispatch from the Secretary of State for the Colonies relating to the Commercial Business of the Crown Agents for the Colonies: Parl. Pap.* 1904, LIX [Cd. 1944], p. 6–8; see also *Papers explanatory of the Functions of the Crown Agents for the Colonies: Parl. Pap.* 1881, XLIV [C. 3075].
[3] *The Dual Mandate.* p. 607.

Only slowly did nomadic herding in the Sudan give way to economies based on cultivation of the land; as in Northern Nigeria, cattle meant prestige. But the cotton industry did take root, and by the end of the First World War the annual production was 12,000 bales;[1] by 1924 this figure was almost quadrupled. The Uganda line had been started in Mombasa in 1895 and had been carried by Indian labour over two mountain chains to its destination at Lake Victoria. The first train reached Lake Victoria at the end of 1901. In 1903 two steamers were put on the Lake, thus linking the railway with the country further inland.[2]

The commercial importance of East Africa had originally been based on the slave trade of the coast, and afterwards on the cloves of nearby Zanzibar, and the native coconut. The Uganda railway, along with a feeder road system, brought prosperity to the interior. Within three years the average monthly tonnage of the line doubled, from 1200 tons up and down, to 2400. The Uganda cotton trade grew from 54 bales in 1904 to 20,000 in 1911; by 1914 the cotton export alone was valued at a million pounds.[3] In 1903, under Government auspices, settlers began to move into the Highlands, but the immigration was hardly more than a trickle until 1908. At no time prior to 1914 did the white population number more than two thousand. The new immigrants tried various crops such as flax, wheat, sisal, hemp and coffee, but apart from cotton the chief exports in the first few years were simple products of the country like ivory, rubber, hides, ground-nuts, wax and chillies.[4] Only slowly—and never in the case of cotton—did there emerge in East Africa a plantation economy based on capital and skill, and the same was true of Nyasaland, where small-scale coffee and cotton production was supplemented by tobacco and tea. Although the British Government contributed, apart from transport, little to the development of the country, the colony of Kenya was soon paying its way; in 1913 the annual grant-in-aid was withdrawn; by 1914, trade through the principal port of Mombasa was worth nearly £5 millions sterling, and the harbour had become inadequate to deal with the shipping.[5]

In West Africa, George Goldie, who had created the Niger Company in 1886, had already launched his drive for pacification and exploitation, based on steam and mechanical transport to replace porterage, money and credit to oust "slave currency", and the development of export trade to stimulate commercial crops. Before the Company lost its Charter in 1900, the Mohammedan Emirs of Nupe and Ilorin had been conquered, the West African Frontier Force had

[1] *Report to the Board of Trade of the Cotton Growing Committee, 1920: Parl. Pap.* 1920, xvi [Cmd. 523], p. 26.
[2] Eliot, Sir Charles, "The progress and problems of the East Africa Protectorate", *Jour. R. Colonial Institute*, xxxvii (1905–6), p. 85.
[3] Knowles, *op. cit.* p. 505.   [4] Eliot, *op. cit.* p. 95.   [5] Knowles, *op. cit.* p. 505.

been formed, the hinterland of Sierra Leone finally demarcated, and the last Ashanti campaign was nearing its finish. In consequence, trade had begun to spread from the coastal and river entrepôts deep into the interior. The reduction in ocean freights, partly the result of competition between rival shipping companies, now enabled the trader to face the exhausting and costly journey to inland markets without risk of loss of profit.[1] The great era of West African commercial expansion had begun; steamships, shortly to be reinforced by railways, carried increasing quantities of ground-nuts from Gambia, cocoa and minerals from the Gold Coast, and the traditional palm oil and kernels from Sierra Leone and Nigeria. Hides, tin, kola-nuts and cotton followed. Between 1884 and 1894 the tonnage of British shipping to West Africa had doubled; ten years later it was doubled again.[2]

As in East Africa, railways were the final answer to the fast-disappearing slave-raider. By 1911 the Mohammedan city of Kano in Northern Nigeria was linked with Lagos on the sea, and the way prepared for an expanding production of cotton and ground-nuts. Nigeria exported 1,179 tons of ground-nuts in 1910, 2,518 in 1911, and in 1912, one year after the railway reached Kano, 19,288 tons.[3] Cotton growing was similarly a by-product of railway construction. Cotton had made its hazardous start before the American Civil War; but with the turn of the century the threat of American scarcities forced further consideration of African sources. The British Cotton Growing Association, formed in 1902, took the lead in planting, buying and ginning; in the end, they "left production to the natives, experiment to the Department of Agriculture and purchase to European firms". Eleven bales of Nigerian cotton marked for export in 1914 grew to 7000 by 1921. Cocoa proved to be a poor European plantation venture, and cultivation remained in African hands. The rise of the cocoa industry on the Gold Coast had its origin in the 'nineties but not until the 1920's, with the development of motor roads and motor transport, did it reach phenomenal heights. The seeds brought from Fernando Po to the Gold Coast in 1879 produced an export cargo worth £4 in 1891; by the end of the First World War the export was valued at £8 millions. For the period 1907–11, the Gold Coast exported on an annual average 20,934 tons; Nigeria, 2,375; for the period 1912–16, the annual average was 58,306 and 6,002 tons respectively.[4] The Gold Coast had become the leading cocoa-

---

[1] McPhee, *op. cit.* p. 71.
[2] Tonnage of British Ships visiting West Africa:

1894	2,269,000
1904	4,674,000
1914	5,360,000

See Page, W. (ed.), *Commerce and Industry: an Historical Review of the Economic Conditions of the British Empire from 1815 to 1914*, II, 168, for the amount and value of West Africa's chief exports in 1911; see also Hancock, *op. cit.* II, pt. II, 170–1.

[3] McPhee, *op. cit.* pp. 38–9.   [4] Hancock, *op. cit.* II, pt. II, 209.

producing area in the world. Meanwhile, rich deposits of alluvial tin were discovered on the Bauchi Plateau of Nigeria, and a light railway was constructed to reach the source. In 1909 coal was found at Enugu, and subsequent mining operations produced, after 1915, sufficient fuel to meet the demands of the Nigerian railways as well as power stations as far away as Lagos.[1] Moreover, a policy of deep-water harbours had been inaugurated, aimed at bringing the whole coast into dependable relationship with outside markets.

In the palm oil trade primitive native methods of extraction still meant poor quality and enormous wastage—probably 50 per cent of the oil was lost in processing. None the less, the export grew steadily from 55,000 tons in 1900 to 120,000 twenty-five years later, and of palm kernels, from 110,000 to 250,000 tons.[2] In 1913 the export value of West African vegetable oils and oil-producing substances from all the European colonies amounted to about £10 millions sterling. Of this total, exports from British possessions amounted to some £7½ millions, representing a trebling of the trade for the decade prior to 1913. Half the total exports from West Africa consisted of palm kernels, amounting in 1913 to over £5 millions sterling; of this total four-fifths came from British colonies.[3]

The great advance came in 1910 when the urgent world demand for vegetable oils and oil seed increased the pressure on the Home Government for more extensive and more efficient exploitation under plantation management. The British Government preferred, however, to lend its support to the rapidly expanding peasant production. Lever Brothers had failed to win their claims for plantation extension in 1907; subsequent attempts were equally unsuccessful.[4] "The soap-boilers of the world", declared the Colonial Secretary, Harcourt, in 1913, "are tumbling over one another to acquire the raw material of their industry. But I am the officially constituted protector of the natives in our own colonies, and it is my duty to see that they are not, as far as I can prevent it, unduly damaged by this foreign competition."[5] The final decision to bar the "planters' frontier" was not taken until after the First World War; meanwhile, the British Government, in rejecting the less wasteful plantation system, had tacitly admitted its responsibility to support the peasant economy by providing transport facilities, drainage and irrigation schemes, increased port facilities, scientific and health instruction, and social services generally. The United Kingdom, by repudiating private monopolies, had confirmed its adoption of a new conception of colonial respon-

---

[1] *Report by the Hon. W. G. A. Ormsby-Gore on his Visit to West Africa: Parl. Pap.* 1926, VII [Cmd. 2744], p. 127.

[2] *Ibid.* p. 101.

[3] *Report of the Committee on Edible and Oil-producing Nuts and Seeds: with a dispatch from the Secretary of State for the Colonies: Parl. Pap.* 1916, IV [Cd. 8247], p. 5.

[4] See Hancock, *op. cit.* II, pt. II, 190–4.

[5] 31 July 1913: *Hansard*, 5th ser. LVI, 786.

sibility that embraced moral as well as economic, universal as well as national or imperial, considerations. Lord Lugard expressed it when he outlined the design of a *Dual Mandate*.

The assumption of a policy of trusteeship for native peoples was a new feature of British economic imperialism; economic guardianship, as well as political education according to the Durham text of self-government, was now to accompany the exploitation of the world's backward dependencies. Colonial policy would, of course, still be directed to the advantage of the imperial power, but self-interest, in the age that opened after the South African War, involved the material welfare of millions of coloured peoples whose particular interests had now to be justified in the court of public opinion. Hitherto, British governments had been content to justify efficient and benevolent rule in terms of law and order; British theories of colonial government had been simply a reflection of their own domestic political ideas, and at the end of the nineteenth century the strength of *laissez-faire* principles had diminished but little. "Les Anglais", wrote Jules Cambon, "ont de la méthode mais pas de système." Hitherto, either the Colonial Office or the Treasury had refused the money to deal effectively with colonial and social problems; Parliament had refused to vote the sums demanded by enlightened colonial Governors, and colonial revenues had been completely inadequate to meet the need. The new doctrine meant spending money sometimes with no immediate prospect of a return. In the twentieth century, the British people were to gain "that balm of conscience" which in the future was to reconcile them to so many attacks on their purse.

In 1897 the doctrine of trusteeship had first found official expression in the recommendations of a Royal Commission appointed to enquire into the condition and prospects of the British West Indies; the pledge contained therein was repeated in a further report of 1910: "We have placed the labouring population where it is, and created for it the conditions, moral and material, under which it exists, and we cannot divest ourselves of responsibility for its future."[1] Much had been done in previous years to modernise the sugar industry of the West Indies. In some islands improved machinery and techniques had helped to lower the price of sugar by more than half.[2] Nevertheless, the position of the colonies at the end of the nineteenth century seemed hopeless; in the face of competition from beet sugar countries, whose produce after 1880 was heavily subsidised by export bounties, the possibility of relieving chronic depres-

[1] *Report of the Royal Commission on Trade Relations between Canada and the West Indies, September 1910: Parl. Pap.* 1910, XI [Cd. 5369], p. 49.
[2] Masefield, *op. cit.* pp. 48–9; see also Beachey, R. W., *The British West India Sugar Industry in the late 19th century.* Oxford, 1957.

sion seemed remote. The Commissioners of 1897 saw no solution unless Continental nations abolished the bounty system, a renunciation, which they reluctantly confessed, was not likely in the immediate future; doctrinaire free-traders in the Government would scarcely consider tariff retaliation in the interests of humanity. Meanwhile, the sugar industry stood in danger of a "great reduction", which in some colonies was equivalent to extinction.[1] Less than one-tenth of Britain's sugar now came from her own islands.

Unable to agree on any departure from "the settled policy of the United Kingdom", namely countervailing duties, the Commissioners had no alternative but to recommend active Government assistance on a long-term basis. They suggested improved and subsidised steam communications between the Islands, as well as to market areas such as Great Britain and Canada, the establishment of a peasant proprietary, encouragement of minor agricultural industries and provision for the scientific teaching of agriculture.[2] As the lesser evil, these recommendations were adopted. In 1898 Parliament voted £161,500 for the relief of the West Indies; about two-thirds of this sum was used at once to balance some of the Island budgets; the remainder, with subsequent generous additions, laid the foundations of the first great colonial development scheme.

In 1898 Canada had extended her preferential tariff to include the West Indies, without demanding (until 1909) any concessions in return.[3] The effect of the preference was not immediately realised, because the American markets remained the most convenient, the largest and the most accessible.[4] In 1902, however, the adoption of the Brussels Convention led to the abolition of bounties on beet sugar, and as a consequence its admission into the United States without the countervailing duty previously imposed. As a result, West Indian sugar lost its best market, and sought therefore to take full advantage of the Canadian preference, which had been indirectly enhanced by the imposition of a surtax on German beet sugar. The change in the course of trade was soon evident. In 1897 importations from the West Indies did not exceed 11,000 tons; in 1903 they reached 50,000 tons; in 1909 they had reached a total of 133,000 tons valued at £756,206 which represented about 60 per cent of the total production of the British sugar colonies.[5]

Meanwhile Parliament, on the initiative of Chamberlain, had arranged for the setting up of an Imperial Department of Agriculture, with an initial annual expenditure of £17,400 a year. Barbados was made the headquarters of the organisation, whose ultimate objective was adequate insurance against colonial bankruptcy.

[1] *Report of the West Indian Royal Commission: Parl. Pap.* 1898, L [C. 8655], p. 69.
[2] *Report* [C. 8655], pp. 67 and 70.
[3] See *Report on Trade Relations* [Cd. 5369].
[4] *Ibid.* p. 6.   [5] *Ibid.* p. 4.

The results were soon forthcoming. Experimentation in the field produced varieties of cane yielding from 19 to 25 per cent more sugar, and during the period prior to 1914 sugar remained the dominant industry in British Guiana, Barbados, St Lucia, Antigua and St Kitts. On the other hand, the policy of encouraging alternative industries had shown impressive results. There were substantial increases in the production of cocoa in Trinidad, Grenada and Jamaica and of asphalt in Trinidad; Sea Island cotton was introduced into St Vincent, Barbados and the Leeward Islands, the cultivation of limes accelerated in Dominica, and rice crops not only produced in, but exported from, British Guiana. Although dangerously subject to hurricanes and "Panama disease", the banana had become the salvation of Jamaica; in a good year she produced approximately a third of the total world output. All told, by 1910, while the export value of sugar and sugar products had slightly declined, that of cocoa, fruit, cotton, tobacco, rice, coconuts and rubber had more than trebled.[1]

Over an area some 800 miles from north to south and 1000 miles from east to west, the Department of Agriculture extended its beneficent sway. Its responsibilities included experiments not only in cane and plant culture, but also in the improved breeding of cattle, horses and small stock, the restoration of soil fertility, the extension of bee-keeping, the destruction of insect and fungoid pests as well as the work of education in field cultivation and marketing. Botanical gardens grew into large research stations; mycologists and entomologists were employed for the first time. In 1906 the services of the mycologist were lent to Trinidad to investigate the diseases of coconuts and cacao; the entomologist was required by British Guiana in 1908 to investigate the ravages of the moth-borer in sugar-cane.[2] Many of the lessons learned in Ceylon about coffee-leaf disease and cacao canker were applied in the West Indies.

Throughout British possessions in the tropics the study of scientific agriculture expanded under the stimulus of West Indian success. Similar agricultural departments were set up in India, Ceylon, the Federated Malay States, Nigeria, the Gold Coast, British East Africa and Egypt. Kew, which had become after 1900 the centre of botanical economy for the whole Empire, contributed in knowledge and personnel to these colonial developments. In 1913 a research committee founded in 1909 to deal with insect pests of the Empire was absorbed by a larger co-ordinating body, the Imperial Bureau of Entomology. The latter years of the nineteenth century had witnessed the opening of great colonial wildernesses; the twentieth was to

---

[1] Morris, Sir Daniel, "The Imperial Development of Agriculture in the West Indies", *United Empire*, II (1911), p. 78; see also *Report of the Royal Commission, 1910: Parl. Pap.* 1910, XI [Cd. 5369], pp. 5–14; and *Report by the Hon. E. F. L. Wood on his Visit to the West Indies and British Guiana, 1921–22: Parl. Pap.* 1922, XVI [Cmd. 1679], pp. 38–42.

[2] Morris, *op. cit.* pp. 74–5.

witness intensive scientific efforts to understand this tropical environment and subdue its worst perils.

During this time, science continued to annihilate distance. Commercial strength depended not only on penetrating vast hinterlands with railways, but on spanning oceans by means of submarine cables, wireless and steamships. Faster and progressively cheaper facilities for communication brought colonies and mother country into closer correspondence. What penny postage did for the United Kingdom after 1840, sixpence-a-word cables might accomplish for the whole Empire. "Cable communication", ran the report of a Dominions Royal Commission in 1914, "tends to quicken the pulse of nationality and forms an effective supplement to the broader, though slower, interchange of thought and sentiment by means of postal communication. It reinforces the feeling of joint life in a manner not possible by correspondence when two months or more are required for a reply to any letter."[1] The initial work of girdling the Empire had been undertaken by private companies whose administration was not always free from foreign intrusion, and who were naturally reluctant to jeopardise their finances by any drastic reduction of rates. Private enterprise had undertaken two lines to South Africa, the last completed in 1889. Between 1899 and 1901, because strategical considerations outweighed commercial, a third line nearly 7000 miles in length was laid direct from England via Madeira, St Vincent, Ascension and St Helena to the Cape barely in time to meet the exigencies of war in South Africa. Aided by a subsidy, a tributary line was laid from Ascension to Sierra Leone, providing a further connection with the West African colonies. Strategic needs were similarly predominant in the establishment of a direct line between South Africa and Australia. It was an expensive business involving operating stations at Mauritius, Rodrigues, Cocos and Perth, but the Admiralty were insistent. By 1901 the connection was completed from Durban to Perth, and thence in 1902 to Adelaide, at a total cost of about £1,750,000.[2]

Like the five British North Atlantic lines, the Australian extension was built without subsidy under private management. Already, however, there was talk of State ownership. The claims of colonial Governments to work as partners in the field of submarine telegraphy had been discussed at the Ottawa Conference in 1894, and the British Government had taken belated and unsuccessful steps to secure Neckar Island in the Hawaiian group as a link in a Pacific cable, whose 8000 miles should be laid under the joint auspices of the

[1] *Second Interim Report of the Royal Commission on the Natural Resources, Trade and Legislation of Certain Portions of His Majesty's Dominions: Parl. Pap.* 1914, xviii [Cd. 7210], p. 40.
[2] *Reports of the Interdepartmental Committee on Cable Communications: Parl. Pap.* 1902, xi [Cd. 1056], Appx. F, p. 59.

British, New Zealand, Australian and Canadian Governments. But private companies, such as the Eastern Telegraph and Eastern Extension Telegraph Companies, which were already competing effectively in various parts of the world with American, French and German enterprises, had no wish to see the State added to the list of rivals, and for a time their opposition was successful in shelving the scheme. The advent of Chamberlain, however, gave new life to the Pacific project. A Royal Commission, including representatives of the Treasury, the Colonial Office and the Colonial Governments concerned, examined the whole problem in 1896, and reported favourably. Despite further efforts to forestall public control, the Pacific Cable Bill passed through its final stages and became law in August 1901. Under its terms, a submarine cable was to be constructed from Vancouver Island, by way of Fanning and Fiji Islands, to Norfolk Island, and thence, by means of two branches, to New Zealand and Queensland. The capital required for construction— some £2,000,000—along with annual subsidies was to be provided as follows: the United Kingdom, five-eighteenths, Australia, six-eighteenths, Canada, five-eighteenths, New Zealand, two-eighteenths. The cable was to be the joint property of the Governments concerned, and its management was vested in a Pacific Cable Board established in 1901 as a kind of federal executive.[1] Laying operations were begun in the spring of 1902 and completed with incredible speed; the new Pacific cable was open for public traffic before the end of the year. Unfortunately, the first section between Vancouver and Fanning Island was too long for the most efficient transmission speed; (indeed, this section, touching depths of three and a half miles, was the longest unbroken line yet laid, being 284 nautical miles longer than the French Atlantic cable from Brest to Cape Cod).[2] Despite this disadvantage, the effects of closer connections between Canada and Australasia were immediately apparent. Instead of nearly a day, a message across the Pacific now took less than an hour.

A through State-controlled service now existed from Australasia to Vancouver Island, and thence by means of a leased telegraph wire to Montreal. To complete imperial control as far as the United Kingdom it only remained to secure, by lease or other means, one of the seventeen cables crossing the Atlantic, as well as the land line to Montreal.[3] At the Imperial Conference in 1911 both New Zealand and Australian representatives moved resolutions in support of such an "all-red route", but, owing to the reluctance of the British Government to undertake further heavy expense, they were withdrawn. Instead the Conference accepted as an alternative: "That,

---

[1] Bright, C., *Imperial Telegraphic Communication* (1911), pp. 77-9.
[2] *Ibid.* pp. 81-2.
[3] *Final Report of the Royal Commission on Natural Resources, etc.: Parl. Pap.* 1917-18, x [Cd. 8462], p. 138.

in the event of considerable reductions in the Atlantic cable rates not being effected in the near future, it is desirable that the laying of a State-owned cable between the United Kingdom and Canada be considered by a subsidiary Conference."[1]

Meanwhile, wireless telegraphy had begun to revolutionise inter-imperial systems of communication. On 12 December 1901 Marconi's signals from Poldhu in Cornwall were picked up by means of a kite-aerial on Signal Hill, St John's, Newfoundland. By 1911 transmission was slow, but it was becoming more reliable, and it was cheap. The British Government favoured an imperial net-work, partly for commercial reasons, partly for strategic. Wireless stations, which could be put in protected places, were as useful to the Admiralty as to the Stock Exchange; although providing speedier, more certain and more secret means of communication, cables could be cut in time of war. In 1909 an Australasian conference held in Melbourne discussed plans for a system of regional stations; in 1911 Sir Joseph Ward proposed to extend the scheme as far as practicable throughout the Empire, "with the ultimate object of establishing a chain of British State-owned wireless stations, which, in emergency, will enable the Empire to be to a great extent independent of submarine cables".[2] The Imperial Conference of 1911 was unwilling to entertain detailed suggestions as to ways and means, but unanimously endorsed the Ward proposal on grounds of social, commercial and defensive need.[3] By the time of the outbreak of war in 1914, wireless supplemented cable in a chain of stations that embraced the Empire.

It is in the nature of trade that it should seek the most direct and profitable channels. Manufacturer and merchant, colonial planter and rancher were alike concerned with obtaining cheap and punctual ocean transport for their produce. As long as freights were cheaper and means of communication better organised within the Empire than outside it, trade could be tempted to follow the line of least resistance through imperial channels into imperial markets rather than into those of foreign states sometimes more conveniently situated. Supported by abundant coal supplies, a dense and growing population to serve as home market for foodstuffs and raw materials, and with plenty of capital available for investment in shipping, the British mercantile marine seemed in no danger of shrinking, despite the encroachments of competitors on certain valuable preserves. Between 1890–1 and 1902–3 the world's steam tonnage had increased from 13 millions to 26 millions. Although the British proportion of this total had fallen from 63·4 per cent to 52·8, while the German

---

[1] *Minutes of Proceedings of the Imperial Conference, 1911*: Parl. Pap. 1911, LIV [Cd. 5745], pp. 291, 305.
[2] *Ibid.* p. 307.
[3] *Ibid.* p. 315; see also, *International Radiotelegraph Convention signed at London, July 5th, 1912*: Parl. Pap. 1913, LXXXI [Cd. 6873].

proportion had risen from 7·2 to 10·2 per cent, the more significant consideration was that British steam tonnage had increased from 8¼ millions to 13½ millions, a net gain of 5¼ million tons, while German tonnage had increased from 928,000 to 2,600,000, a gain of less than 1,700,000 tons. In other words, for every additional German ton, Britain had added three.[1]

These advances in cheap and efficient carriage depended in the last resort on the use of larger vessels of deeper draught, and consequently on the existence of harbours and docks adequate to receive such vessels. The dominant feature of ship-building at the beginning of the twentieth century was the steady increase in the size of vessels, with resulting gains in cargo space. But the larger, longer ship could not be driven economically at relatively high speeds without proportionate increase of draught, and this had necessitated the progressive deepening of coastal harbours and of such waterways as the Suez. It called for a constant correlation of effort between the harbour and canal engineer and the naval architect. In 1906 the Suez Canal allowed a maximum draught of 26 feet 3 inches; increased in 1908 to 28 feet, it was increased slightly in 1914, and future plans provided for 33 feet. At the same time, selected harbours were deepened or improved along the routes from the United Kingdom to Australia via the Cape of Good Hope, to Australia via Nova Scotia, Jamaica and the Panama Canal, and from British Columbia to New Zealand and Australia. Including such ports as Halifax, Quebec, Auckland or Sydney, where nature had scoured good approach channels as well as harbours, the important imperial ports provided by 1914 minimum depths averaging some 32 feet at the quays.[2]

British shipowners and naval architects had helped to withstand the challenge of intense competition by progressive improvements in imperial shipping facilities. The chief danger to British supremacy lay, however, in the determination of various foreign governments to increase their share of the carrying trade by means of subsidies. Indeed, economists like Sir Robert Giffen were willing to urge a partial restoration of the Navigation Acts, with the exclusion of foreign subsidised shipping from the coasting trade of the United Kingdom. The Parliamentary Committee on Steamship Subsidies which reported in 1902 admitted that foreign subsidies had favoured the transfer from British to Continental ports of some branches of foreign and colonial trade; competition had become more strenuous; notwithstanding, they were convinced that British steam shipping could hold its own without the introduction of any subsidy system. They opposed the reservation of the coastwise trade of the Empire as likely to lead to an increase in the cost of raw and semi-manufactured

[1] See "Minutes of evidence" in *Report from the Select Committee on Steamship Subsidies: Parl. Pap.* 1902, ix (385), p. 171.
[2] See [Cd. 8462], pp. 112–15.

materials through the encouragement of British monopolies which would raise rather than lower freights.[1] Moreover, it was hardly likely that all the colonies would agree to a general limitation of this sort. Conflicting evidence made it clear that what might appeal to Australia might not be satisfactory to Canada. Hence, the Committee reported against the grant of subsidies except in a few special cases.

Hitherto, apart from postal subventions granted to mail lines, only a small number of fast liners received aids to cover certain specific costs of construction and maintenance which enabled them in emergency to serve as armed merchant cruisers. Since, however, the majority of the great liners complied with Admiralty requirements irrespective of subsidy, this subvention gradually fell away. By 1914 the only ships receiving any form of subsidy from the British Government were the Cunard's *Mauretania* and *Lusitania*, and the West Indian fruit ships of Messrs Elder and Fyffe.[2]

The Committee did, however, insist that Board of Trade safety regulations should be applied to foreign ships using ports in the United Kingdom. Ever since the appointment of a Royal Commission on unseaworthy ships in 1874—the fruit of Samuel Plimsoll's agitation—shipowners had complained that the resulting legislation had placed them at a serious disadvantage in competition with the foreigner, whose industry was not cramped by strict humanitarian rules. These complaints were accepted, and met by the Merchant Shipping Act of 1906 which not only swept away many obsolete regulations but applied the greater part of British safety regulations to foreign ships using British ports throughout the Empire. At the same time, the creation of the Merchant Shipping Advisory Committee, on which shipowners, seamen and ship-builders were represented, provided a permanent liaison between the Board of Trade and the shipping industry.[3]

But such regulation of the carrying trade in British waters could little affect the rising tide of foreign competition. By 1914 British tonnage, including ships registered in the Dominions and colonies, had diminished to 45·2 per cent of the world's steam tonnage. (For Great Britain alone, the percentage was 41·6.) Nevertheless, British and Empire tonnage still carried half the total volume of world sea-borne trade, 92 per cent of intra-imperial trade, 63 per cent of the trade between the Empire and foreign countries and 30 per cent of the trade between countries outside the Empire.[1] Germany stood in second place with about a quarter of the total British steam tonnage, but two and a half times that of any other country apart

---

[1] See *Report of Select Committee on Steamship Subsidies: Parl. Pap.* 1902, IX (385), pp. 87 and 155.
[2] Fayle, C. E., *A Short History of the World's Shipping Industry* (1933), p. 274.
[3] *Ibid.* p. 285.

from the United States, which enjoyed third place by virtue of an extensive Great Lakes and coastal shipping.[1]

If an expanding shipping industry was a necessary condition of imperial prosperity, an expanding British population overseas seemed equally important. In the imperial sense, the two were indissolubly linked. The Dominions could only achieve their fullest development with adequate man-power; and progress in this direction could be partly measured in terms of imperial trade statistics. Trade between the United Kingdom and the Dominions represented a predominant part in the economy of the latter, and a substantial part of the total trade of the mother country. There were, therefore, apart from sentimental justifications, good economic reasons for strengthening the kinship ties of Empire by encouraging emigration from the British Isles to overseas colonies. One British resident in Australia, so it was said, consumed as much British produce as ten similar emigrants settled in the United States.[2] Moreover, there was the strategic consideration. In terms of the common defence of the Empire, the need for sufficient and homogeneous populations in the Dominions was obvious;[3] without an effective emigration policy there was no guarantee that these territories would remain in the control of the British race.

At the beginning of the twentieth century, the balance of population in terms of strategic and economic strength seemed to be turning against Great Britain as compared with her rivals, Germany and the United States. The German population was increasing twice, and the American three times as fast as the British. In ten or fifteen years it was predicted that the German Empire would have a total of over seventy millions, and the United States about one hundred millions.[4] British expansion at home was limited "at the outside", it was assumed, to forty-eight millions. Hence the question of directing emigration within the Empire became one of considerable, if not pressing, importance, and sentiment in the new era of imperial migrations played possibly as substantial a part in determining the direction of the flow as economic considerations. In propagating interest in the Dominions as homes of settlement the Emigrants' Information Office, as well as organisations like the Colonial Institute and various charitable associations, did much to nourish the idea of Greater Britain.

In the decade prior to 1900 only 28 per cent of emigrants from the

---

[1] Fayle, *op. cit.* p. 274.

[2] Murray, K. B., "Mr Chamberlain and Colonial Commerce", *Economic Journal*, VII (1897), p. 27.

[3] Cf. *Report of the Oversea Settlement Board, May 1938: Parl. Pap.* 1937–38, XIV [Cmd. 5766], p. 5.

[4] Garvin, J. L., "The maintenance of Empire: a study of the economic basis of political power", *The Empire and the Century* (1905), p. 73.

British Isles had stayed within the Empire; but between 1901 and 1912 the number remaining within the Empire increased to 63 per cent of the total, and in 1913 it was 78 per cent.[1] Unhappily before 1912 the returns of passenger movements at British ports did not distinguish permanent immigrants from temporary arrivals and departures. The returns therefore probably under-estimated the outflow, since the method of computation was to subtract from total departures the arrivals in the British Isles from non-European countries, and to take the difference as representing the net emigration from the mother country.[2] In any event, the numbers emigrating overseas during the last decade of the nineteenth century could have been little more than a trickle, averaging probably less than 55,000 a year; in one year, 1894, it was under 38,000. Excluding the unknown Irish total, the figure for Britain must have been inconsiderable.[3] During the ten years 1900–1910, the total emigration from the United Kingdom to other parts of the Empire was 1,297,217 or an annual average of approximately 130,000.[4] The surge began with the year 1907, when United Kingdom emigration reached 235,000, of whom 218,000 went to the United States and Canada.[5] The movement reached its peak between 1910 and 1913 when 1,217,710 British subjects left the United Kingdom for one or other of the Dominions or colonies, an average of approximately 394,000 a year. With the coming of the war, this movement naturally came to a standstill.

The increase during these latter years was almost entirely from England and Scotland, for the Irish source had begun to dry up on nationalist grounds, and there was a growing hostility to emigration on the part of the Roman Catholic Church and the Sinn Fein movement. From 1905 to 1914 British emigration to Canada exceeded that to the United States with the exception of the year 1909; during the years 1911–13 it was more than two-and-a-half times that to the United States. Emigration to Australia had been restricted at the end of the nineteenth century owing to the opposition of Labour and the depressing effects of drought. Australians had no wish to provide "a destitute[s'] asylum for any nation".[6] But national policy soon veered around. "White Australia" became a slogan; Government assistance which had been discontinued was renewed, and from 1905 there was a steady increase of British immigrants.[7] In 1904 New Zealand also reverted to a discriminating policy of assisted immigra-

---

[1] Final Report of the Royal Commission on Natural Resources, etc.: Parl. Pap. 1917–18, x [Cd. 5745], p. 85.
[2] Ibid. p. 83.
[3] Ibid. p. 85; also Clapham, op. cit. III, p. 40.
[4] Report to the Secretary of State for Dominion Affairs of the Inter-Departmental Committee on Migration Policy: Parl. Pap. 1933–34, x [Cmd. 4689], p. 6.
[5] Johnson, S. C., Emigration from the United Kingdom to North America (1913), p. 347.
[6] Report of Colonial Conference of 1897, doc. cit. p. 15.
[7] Carrothers, W. A., Emigration from the British Isles (1929), pp. 246–7.

tion. In South Africa the war had interrupted the steady flow of British immigrants, but within two years after the peace it was temporarily resumed as a result of an artificial prosperity that was partly encouraged by various re-settlement schemes. The subsequent depression lasted until the time of the Union, and only in 1910 was there any addition to population by immigration.[1] Thenceforward until 1914 the increases were slight.

During this period it was the settled policy of the British Government not to vote State money for emigration. It was assumed that voluntary emigration was as much as Great Britain could afford, and that Parliamentary assistance would merely interfere with the work of the voluntary societies. Admittedly, in the past there had been various small Government schemes of assisted emigration and settlement (such as the New Zealand Colonisation Company) but, until 1919, large-scale movements from the United Kingdom took place without financial support from the State. The Government merely tried to provide more or less accurate information for the benefit of the emigrant, while the voluntary society often eased his path by providing the passage money in whole or in part, or by putting him in touch with societies or persons overseas. Under the provisions of the Unemployed Workmen Act of 1905, Boards of Guardians and Distress Committees spent substantial amounts; those not eligible for such aid were assisted by some forty charitable associations, such as the Salvation Army, the Church Army, the Charity Organisation Society or Dr Barnardo's agency. "The process was in fact a process of what may be called infiltration by individuals into the life of developed or developing communities overseas, as, where, and when there were actual openings for newcomers."[2]

During the course of the Imperial Conference of 1907, a resolution was adopted on the initiative of the Australians stressing the desirability of encouraging British emigrants to proceed to "British Colonies rather than to foreign countries".[3] A similarly innocuous resolution was accepted by the Imperial Conference in 1911, with the additional recommendation that such encouragement should "be continued on the present lines and that full co-operation be accorded to any Dominion desiring immigrants". In view of the new and growing tide of voluntary migration, a change in present policy was felt to be necessary.[4] Australia's enthusiasm for a "plan" was not equally shared by the other Dominions, who showed reluctance to co-operate in any scheme that might mean the dumping of unskilled and even undesirable emigrants. All of them, however, as the

[1] *South African Year Book*, no. 2, 1918 (1919), p. 182; and *ibid.* no. 3, 1919 (1920), p. 176.
[2] *Report of Inter-Departmental Committee on Migration Policy: Parl. Pap.* 1933–34, x [Cmd. 4689].
[3] *Minutes of Proceedings of the Colonial Conference, 1907: Parl. Pap.* 1907, LV [Cd. 3523], p. 155.
[4] *Minutes of the Proceedings of the Conference: Parl. Pap.* 1911, LIV [Cd. 5745], pp. 198–205.

instinct of nationhood became more fully developed, tended to favour racial homogeneity, which meant in essence the exclusion of coloured or so-called unassimilable races.

Although the "White Australia" policy was born in the days of the Gold Rush, the principle of exclusion was not officially accepted until the Intercolonial Conference of 1896. As such, it affected all non-European peoples, Chinese, Kanakas, Japanese or Indians, and threatened to complicate the problem of British imperial relationships, especially with India. In the following year, thanks to pressure from Joseph Chamberlain, the situation was relieved by the adoption of the so-called Natal dictation test, which spared Japanese as well as Indian feelings.[1] After federation in 1901, the first Commonwealth Parliament welded the State policies into a national system, whose basic provisions were embodied in the Commonwealth Immigration Restriction Act. This act became the foundation of Australia's racial and social policy. "The principle of White Australia", wrote an Australian historian, "is now almost sacrosanct; any questioning of it, even as applied to the remote tropical North, occasions an outcry, and even academic research workers feel that the subject is surrounded by a tacit censorship."[2] In Canada, there were climatic obstacles to large-scale Asiatic immigration, although some thousands of Chinese and Japanese entered British Columbia despite restrictions imposed in 1908 and 1913. The problem of Indian immigration was effectively met in 1910 by the rule of continuous voyage, since no shipping line had direct connections between India and Canada. In South Africa, under the General Immigrants Regulation Act of 1913, Asiatic immigration into the Union was stopped, although a gentleman's agreement between Smuts and Gandhi protected the trading rights of Indians already domiciled. In 1914 there were approximately 140,000 Indians in the country, chiefly in the Transvaal and Natal.

The problem of Asiatic immigration was an Empire problem which continued to bristle with difficulties. Because it concerned the prestige and the status of India, it affected the whole fabric of imperial unity, and it became involved in the long run with the question of British trusteeship in Africa. Under the system of indentured labour the vast populations of India and China were still being tapped by railway and steamship, and during the latter years of the nineteenth century the flow increased rather than lagged. The rapid rise in the export of most plantation products indicated the success of the scheme. Chinese had long before peopled and changed the character of Malaya; in East Africa Indians built the railways and were becoming the mainstay of retail trade. In Mauritius Indian im-

---

[1] See "Report of Colonial Conference of 1897", *doc. cit.* pp. 9–10.
[2] Roberts, S. H., "History of the Contacts between the Orient and Australia" in *Australia and the Far East* (Sydney, 1935), p. 13.

migration had changed an African colony into an Asiatic; by 1910 immigrant Indians and their descendants formed 72 per cent of the population.[1] In British Guiana Indians helped to resuscitate the sugar industry and introduced rice culture.[2] By 1910 the colony was exporting some seven million lb. annually. In Fiji the Indians had created the sugar industry after 1879, and continued to keep it alive. Trinidad benefited from both Indian and Chinese settlers; Jamaica received, and kept, but few.

In the nineteenth century, the indentured labour system had been a frequent object of official enquiry, sometimes on the initiative of the Indian Government. In 1910 the Sanderson Committee rejected renewed charges that the system was a veiled form of slavery.[3] Despite frequent abuses, indenture, since the 'nineties at least, meant medical care, sanitary housing and a guaranteed minimum daily wage. After the period of indenture—in 1914 normally five years, with five years' additional residence in the colony—the immigrant was entitled to free or assisted passage home, or the right to settle in the colony as a private citizen, acquiring land, as many of them did, or engaging in various business occupations. On the whole, the immigrant gained by the transfer, and there is little reason to doubt that the tropical colonies profited immeasurably, although at the cost of increasing racial diversity.

In the three years before 1914 there was little evidence of any serious decline in Britain's productive capacity; official and unofficial statistical tables show general agreement on the matter of British leadership in world commerce. The falling-off which had caused so much doubt and anxiety at the end of the nineteenth century had been followed by a marked recovery—a steady rise in the value of the export as well as the import trade. On the other hand, much of this progress had been simply the sharing in a general revival of world trade, and critics were able to demonstrate that British commercial advances had not been equal to those of her principal foreign competitors. In the years before 1913 the United States was rapidly reducing Britain's lead as an exporting country, while Germany's ambitious programme was threatening to make her a rival for second place.[4] Obviously, Britain retained her tenuous supremacy simply by reason of her import and carrying trade.

---

[1] *Report of the Committee on Emigration from India to the Crown Colonies and Protectorates: Parl. Pap.* 1910, xxvii [Cd. 5192], p. 42; also pp. 43–51.

[2] See Dwarka Nath, *A History of Indians in British Guiana* (1950), pp. 161–5.

[3] [Cd. 5192], *doc. cit.*

[4] See *Historical Statistics of the United States* (U.S. Department of Commerce, 1949), p. 246; also Clapham, *op. cit.* pp. 46–7; cf. Hobson's less reliable estimate, *op. cit.* p. 166. After deducting re-exports, there was between 1905 and 1913 a more rapid rise in the value (and volume) of British exports than of net imports. In this connection see Imlah, A. H., "The terms of trade of the United Kingdom, 1798–1913", *Jour. Economic History*, x, no. 2 [Nov. 1900), pp. 181–2.

Evidence for a reliable comparison of industrial conditions within the major competing countries was lacking. At the same time, if the test of national efficiency in production was successful competition in major markets, there were grounds for pessimism; and subsequent investigations have served to justify contemporary fears. Had contemporaries been masters of all the facts, observed Sir John Clapham, "they might have been confirmed in a common opinion that Britain, though as fully occupied with work in 1910–13 as any country can hope to be, was yet not so stirring industrially as America or Germany, nor so stirring as she herself had once been...."[1]

In absolute terms, British trade with the Empire had increased since the beginning of the twentieth century, just as total trade had increased; but relatively it had decreased. Foreign countries had increased their proportion of the Empire's trade almost everywhere. Comparing the percentage of British exports to a dependency with its total imports, Professor Clive Day came to the conclusion that by 1909 the United Kingdom had its place in only one of its colonial markets, Mauritius, a purchaser of little significance.[2] Later estimates based on a greater fund of statistical material hardly warrant so dismal a view,[3] and the same holds true of the findings of the Dominions Royal Commission appointed in 1912[4] (in consequence of a resolution passed by the Imperial Conference of 1911) to report among other things upon the trade of the self-governing dominions "with the United Kingdom, each other, and the rest of the world". This report confirmed the widespread assumption that while the share of the United Kingdom in the Dominions' export trade (with the exception of Canada) had been increasing, its share in the import trade had been decreasing. In 1913 exports from the Dominions to the mother country exceeded imports therefrom by £52 millions, whilst imports from foreign countries exceeded exports thereto by £61 millions.[5]

In 1913, 38 per cent of the imports into the five self-governing Dominions (including Newfoundland) came from the United Kingdom; of the exports, 59 per cent went to the mother country. Of the total imports into the United Kingdom in the same year, the Dominions contributed 17 per cent, while of the total exports of British and Irish produce and manufactures, they received 15·8 per cent.[6] An

---

[1] Clapham, op. cit. p. 7.   [2] Op. cit. p. 585.

[3] Cf. Schlote, Werner, British Overseas Trade from 1700 to the 1930's (Oxford, 1952), p. 162, table 20b.

[4] Doc. cit. [Cd. 8462].

[5] Ibid. p. 16. See the somewhat more favourable interpretations of Schlote, op. cit. pp. 164–74. It should be noted that imports were valued after, and exports before, shipping and insurance charges were paid. Actually, an excess of imports was natural and even desirable, partly because failure to accept some excess of imports would almost certainly at this stage have had a harmful effect on capital investments in Empire and foreign countries.

[6] Final Report of Royal Commission on Dominions: Parl. Pap. 1917–18, x [Cd. 8462], see tables, pp. 12–13.

analysis of trade returns reveals, however, how much imperial trade depended on the foreigner. The Dominions now purchased almost as large a quantity of manufactured goods from foreign states as from the United Kingdom, and their sales of raw materials to foreign countries were probably larger than to the mother country.[1] To a considerable extent Canada was responsible for this change in the imperial balance. In the fiscal year 1913–14 she bought goods from the United States to the value of £89 millions; Canadian exports across the border amounted to £42 millions.[2] Contiguity with the United States undoubtedly made the Canadian position exceptional. Despite the obstacle of high tariffs, nature encouraged a certain gearing of the two economies across a frontier of continental extent, and the same tendency was to be noted in the new relationship between India and Japan.

For some four or five years before the First World War, Britain had ceased to dominate the market for Indian produce. She was taking only a quarter of the total Indian exports, whereas in 1880 she had taken almost 40 per cent.[3] Although most of India's imports still came from the United Kingdom—cotton manufactures, iron and steel, machinery, harbour equipment and railway plant—Germany up to 1914 had steadily improved her position in the second place, and Japan was following closely. Japan was adding to her industrial epuipment and, like Germany and the United States, adopting protective tariffs to safeguard and stimulate existing manufactures. She had the advantage of lying closer to the Indian market, possessed vast quantities of cheap labour, and she had demonstrated a facility for imitating most European goods that gained entry to Indian and other eastern markets. Great Britain had supplied the machinery to establish Japan as a dangerous competitor; now the colonies and India were feeding the machines. India was sending raw cotton, Malaya, rubber and tin, Australia, wool and Canada, timber and pulp.[4]

In China, the Empire as a whole still held a substantial margin of supremacy. Estimates of Chinese imports are bound to be uncertain, but there is evidence to indicate that Japan by 1913 had won a share of more than 20 per cent; the United States proportion was probably over 6 per cent. Excluding the mother country, India led the imperial field in exports to as well as imports from China; the share of Australia and Canada was small. China's exports were chiefly tea, raw silk, hemp, hides, soya beans and bristles, and of these her exports to Japan and the United States were greater than to Britain. Indeed, in 1900 and 1913 her exports to Japan were greater than to the whole British Empire, including Great Britain and

[1] *Ibid.* see tables, p. 16.   [2] *Ibid.*
[3] Hewins, *op. cit.* p. 256; Knowles, *op. cit.* p. 461.
[4] Gull, E. M., *British Economic Interests in the Far East* (1943), p. 87.

excluding Hong Kong. Of the total trade of China, however, including exports, imports and the entrepôt trade of Hong Kong, the Empire's share was by far the largest.[1] So long as the "Door" remained open, Britain might reasonably count on continued commercial expansion. British capital had built the railways that opened up the Yangtse valley to trade and "influence". Inland steam navigation was gradually linking the coastal treaty ports with vast territories whose latent resources were still incalculable. The colony of Hong Kong remained the chief centre of trading activity, although its importance as entrepôt for British export trade had declined since 1889.[2] The bulk of British exports encouraged by various "concessions" entered China through Shanghai, Tientsin and Canton, accelerated by Chinese tariffs which guaranteed most-favoured-nation treatment, and which could only be changed after consultation with all the treaty Powers.[3]

In the history of imperial commercial relations during the decade before 1914 two features are outstanding: one was the refusal of the United Kingdom to adopt any form of Imperial preference despite the relative contraction of export trade and the expanding markets in the Dominions and colonies; the other was the gradual separation of the self-governing Dominions from the imperial treaty system, and the development on the part of these Dominions of a more positive and independent control of commercial relations with foreign countries based on protective tariffs. In Australia and New Zealand the Preferentialist was really a Protectionist; the method of granting preference was simply, as has been mentioned, that of allowing slightly lower duties than those imposed on foreign countries. New Zealand, moreover, was prepared to make reciprocal treaties with countries outside the Empire. Both South Africa and Canada offered substantial preferences on the great majority of imports, preferences which, in the case of Canada, were almost entirely responsible for successful British competition against the dominant United States. But even the Canadian preference to the United Kingdom was being watered down by the growth of a Canadian free list open to all countries, and by the introduction in 1907 of an intermediate tariff, applicable to all foreign countries which were prepared to give fair terms to Canadian trade. Indeed, it was already evident that the Dominions were prepared to negotiate treaty arrangements with foreign States even at the expense of the mother country.

It was the Franco-Canadian convention of 1910 that first emphasized the consequences of Dominion nationalism in the commercial

---

[1] *Ibid.* pp. 55–6.

[2] See statistics of the United Kingdom's Customs and Excise Dept., quoted Gull, *op. cit.* p. 52. The average annual value of U.K. imports from China (1904–13) was £4,011,000, from Hong Kong £580,000. Of exports the total to China was £11,131,000, to Hong Kong £3,594,000.   [3] *Ibid.* pp. 101, 103.

sphere. With full plenipotentiary powers, and armed with the new bargaining schedule, the Canadian Minister of Finance negotiated a treaty, which was finally ratified in 1910, giving to France intermediate rates on some ninety-eight items of her tariff, and less than intermediate rates on twelve more. In the same year, a similar but less extensive agreement was made with Italy, while the benefits of the intermediate tariff were opened to Belgium and the Netherlands in view of the lowness of their general rates. As a consequence the British preference on a number of competing articles was practically extinguished. In the same years an agreement was reached whereby the Canadian surtax was suspended, leaving German products to be admitted under the general—not the intermediate—tariff, while Germany conceded her conventional or minimum rates on some twenty-five of Canada's most important dutiable articles. Under the new doctrine of commercial autonomy, the self-governing Dominions, like the mother country, were functioning in international commercial relations as independent States, concerned in the first place with their own material needs and advantages and not with the interests of the Empire.

In India, too, the growth of nationalism was influencing fiscal policy by encouraging the movement towards large-scale industry. In 1905 the newly organised Indian Industrial Conference started its campaign for progressive industrialisation; capitalists were asked to lend money, and educated Indians to learn industrial management. In the years before 1914, cotton and jute mills almost doubled in number;[1] in 1907 the great Tata organisation was formed, and it began to operate in 1912. Emotional impulses as well as industrial advances barred for the future any restrictive tariff policy that might favour Lancashire. On the contrary, Indian nationalists were pressing hard for high protective tariffs to overcome the handicaps of competition with more industrialised competitors. *Swadeshi* took shape as a movement designed to make India self-supporting through the boycott of foreign goods, and the safeguarding of Indian raw materials for India's own factories. History would record, wrote Romesh Chunder Dutt, "how the people of India, in the commencement of the twentieth century, effected their own industrial salvation. Without any control over our own tariff or financial arrangements, ...we have determined, simply by giving preference to our home manufactures, to revive the industrial activity of this vast country and to improve the condition of our industrial population".[2]

Obviously, Britain's commercial position was less secure than in the days when Chamberlain had carried out his exhaustive survey.

---

[1] See *Statistical Abstract for British India: Parl. Pap.* 1924, xxv [Cmd. 2033], pp. 615, 625, 630-1, 636-7; *Statistical Abstract for British India: Parl. Pap.* 1914, xcvii [Cd. 7078], p. 263; also Anstey, Vera, *The Economic Development of India* (1929), chap. xi, *passim*.
[2] Lethbridge, R., *India and Imperial Preference* (1907), pp. 27-8.

In the Dominions nationalism was expressing itself, not simply in political language, but in the form of intermediate tariffs and other like concessions to the foreigner. In imperial markets generally Germany and the United States were pressing their advantages regardless of the follies of Kaiser or Congress. In the Far East the cloud of Japanese competition had grown since the 'nineties far larger than a man's hand. Yet the threatened end of British commercial supremacy probably caused less anxiety in 1914 than in 1895. Generally speaking, Empire had lost its later-Victorian halo; except to an attentive few, domestic problems were as customarily far more absorbing. Even the Tariff Reformers had little conception of the actual position of the self-governing Dominions and the effects of national self-determination on the future of imperial trade. As a matter of fact, there were extremely urgent domestic problems to be solved in the last years before the First World War, and problems of imperial economics were bound to appear of less public consequence than the Lloyd George budget, or the powers of the House of Lords, or Irish Home Rule. Moreover, the threat of a European war that might challenge the security of the whole Empire tended to make defence the most important of imperial questions.

Yet in spite of political and financial anxieties Britain's "economic pulse" remained strong. The year 1913 had been "one of the most, if not the most, prosperous periods ever experienced by the British people".[1] The sum total of investments in colonial and foreign countries had reached the neighbourhood of £4,000 millions, and of this staggering total nearly one-half had been supplied to the overseas colonies,[2] whose prosperity was still dependent on exports of food and raw or partly manufactured materials. Moreover, British exports and the services of merchant marine, insurance companies and other overseas agencies combined with British foreign investments had produced, when all accounts were cleared, the amazing balance of nearly £224 millions in her favour.[3]

Chamberlain had failed to realise his dreams of an imperial *Zollverein*, but the British Empire in 1914 was still functioning as a world emporium of primary and industrial products dominated by a highly specialised and superbly organised headquarters in the United Kingdom.

[1] *The Statist*, LXXIX (Jan.-Mar. 1914), p. 73.

[2] Paish, G., "The export of capital and the cost of living", *The Statist*, Supplement, (14 Feb. 1914), p. vi. Paish uses this as an overall figure to include privately placed capital. See also Imlah, A. H., "British balance of payments and export of capital, 1816–1913", *Economic Hist. Rev.* 2nd ser. IV, no. 2 (1952), pp. 232–3, and Feis, Herbert, *Europe: the World's Banker, 1870–1914* (New Haven, 1930), pp. 23–4. Feis's amendments raise the values slightly, and estimate investment within the Empire at 47 per cent, of which 73 per cent was placed in the self-governing Dominions.

[3] Imlah, "British balance of payments and export of capital", *loc. cit.* p. 239.

Parts of the Empire to which Great Britain supplied Capital during the years 1907–1913

	1907 £	1908 £	1909 £	1910 £	1911 £	1912 £	1913 £	Total, seven years £
Canada and Newfoundland	7,601,550	31,309,558	37,687,464	33,039,566	36,793,419	37,400,488	66,255,540	250,087,585
Other American	100,000	124,144	567,100	2,167,000	263,958	30,000	186,600	3,438,802
New South Wales	432,000	1,766,908	4,730,559	829,000	375,000	5,778,000	4,757,500	18,668,967
New Zealand	252,000	645,717	849,135	5,258,717	176,742	1,969,405	3,658,900	12,810,616
Queensland	266,000	—	1,990,000	75,000	2,064,000	2,490,485	2,216,500	9,101,985
South Australia	—	—	117,600	897,294	100,000	50,000	970,000	2,134,894
Tasmania	21,500	247,000	295,500	6,249	—	277,750	251,000	1,099,249
Victoria	252,144	135,500	1,663,000	5,000	109,206	12,549	2,056,900	4,234,299
West Australia	1,090,000	1,047,833	1,618,925	2,884,686	757,343	2,866,678	3,460,000	13,725,546
Other Australasian	—	50,000	750,000	224,485	60,000	—	1,936,000	3,020,485
British West Africa	50,500	3,382,992	1,899,003	2,490,906	5,568,352	1,166,262	1,073,412	15,631,427
Rhodesia	61,850	1,526,323	2,422,050	6,686,176	1,339,697	1,158,421	175,000	13,369,517
Transvaal	332,100	2,487,435	8,858,093	2,767,828	3,503,003	4,008,368	1,284,630	23,241,457
Other African	5,285,213	3,833,854	1,161,150	1,005,312	1,997,661	220,005	5,138,450	18,641,645
India and Ceylon	7,260,387	13,469,787	15,884,581	14,675,503	5,278,488	4,391,320	3,752,909	64,712,975
Straits Settlements	5,278,000	233,502	3,092,513	9,246,237	2,186,598	1,972,638	1,136,070	23,135,538
British N. Borneo	208,000	164,000	1,159,126	848,948	198,927	490,000	Nil	3,069,021
Unenumerated	—	171,000	250,000	300,000	160,000	125,000	400,000	1,406,000
Total, India and Colonies	28,481,244	60,595,553	84,995,799	83,407,907	60,932,394	64,407,369	98,709,661	481,529,927

Miles of Railway in Countries which chiefly supply Great Britain with Food

	Estimated 1915 miles	Partly estimated 1913 miles	1912 miles	1910 miles	1905 miles	1900 miles	1895 miles	1890 miles	1880 miles	1870 miles	1860 miles	1850 miles
United States	266,000	260,800	257,729	249,992	225,196	194,334	184,628	166,654	93,262	52,922	30,626	9,021
Canada	36,000	29,000	26,727	24,731	20,487	17,657	15,977	13,256	6,891	2,671	2,065	66
India	36,000	34,300	33,484	32,099	28,295	24,633	19,531	16,345	9,300	4,775	839	—
Argentina	24,000	22,500	21,000	17,381	12,233	10,412	8,832	5,434	1,536	637	58	—
Australia and New Zealand	23,000	22,200	21,527	20,222	17,313	15,531	13,782	11,480	4,919	999	215	—
Total	385,000	368,800	360,467	344,425	303,514	262,567	242,750	213,169	115,908	61,950	33,803	9,087
Russia	53,000	50,700	49,733	47,815	41,503	35,623	21,948	18,059	14,026	7,198	988	310
Total, including Russia	438,000	419,500	410,200	392,240	345,017	298,190	264,698	231,228	129,934	69,148	34,791	9,397

BRITISH FOREIGN POLICY AND COLONIAL QUESTIONS, 1895–1904

I

WHEN Lord Salisbury returned to office in 1895 the international situation was similar to that which he had inherited ten years earlier. Great Britain was still at loggerheads with France and Russia on colonial and strategic issues throughout the world. While British relations with Austria and Italy were cool again, as a result of Rosebery's disowning of the Mediterranean Agreements, Germany both maintained an alliance with those Powers and was friendly with Russia; and in 1894 as in 1884–5, she had shown herself both able and willing to threaten Great Britain with a Franco-German accommodation as well. Her interest in colonial questions was also reviving and Anglo-German relations were once more becoming strained in Africa as a result. The isolation of Great Britain from the other Great Powers was again the underlying problem for those in charge of her foreign policy.

In the years after 1885 Salisbury had met this problem by accepting closer relations with Germany and her allies. After 1895 the course he took was altogether different; he embarked on a persistent search for reconciliation with France and Russia. This policy was in many ways a logical continuation of changes that had taken place not only under Gladstone and Rosebery between 1892 and 1895 but also during his own earlier administration up to 1892; even then he had been reluctant to accept French and Russian hostility as inevitable, and anxious to avoid dependence on Germany. It was interrupted on occasions after 1895 when opposition to the Dual Alliance was necessary in the defence of British interests as Salisbury saw them. But there was still a marked change of emphasis in British policy from that date. A determination to reach, and if necessary to make sacrifices for, an accommodation with France and Russia replaced the uneasiness that had underlain his own policy up to 1892; a sense of purpose overtook the tendency to drift that had characterised policy under Rosebery.

The change was due in the last resort to the fact that in 1895 British isolation was more complete, British freedom of action more restricted, than ten or even five years earlier. The formation of the Dual Alliance had altered the conditions of Anglo-German collaboration in a direction which Salisbury was certain to dislike. Germany had her own needs as a result of the alliance of France and Russia;

to have drawn closer to her as before, and as she expected him to do again, would have meant paying a higher price than he, with his distrust of Germany, apart from the traditional British dislike of advance commitments and Continental obligations, was willing to accept. But the Dual Alliance had also increased the effectiveness of French and Russian opposition to British interests to such a point that some adjustment of policy had become essential if those interests were to be preserved. If closer relations with Germany were ruled out, the only possible policy was to try to give Great Britain greater freedom of manœuvre by reducing French and Russian hostility.

It was with these considerations already in mind that Salisbury faced his first problem. When he took office the makings of another crisis over the Eastern Question had already appeared. Massacres in Armenia and proposals for intervention in Turkey to put a stop to them had kept the Powers on edge for the past year. In 1885 he had met a Near Eastern crisis by joining Austria and by trying to enlist Germany's support against Russia in defence of Turkey's integrity. If he now set out to solve this problem in collaboration with Russia at Turkey's expense, it was, in the first place, because Russia's agreement was essential for a solution. Rosebery's experience had already shown that, while nothing but intervention by the Powers could convert the Sultan's promises into effective action to end the massacres, Russia, backed by Germany and France, was opposed to intervention. At the same time, the effect of the Armenian massacres on British public opinion had been such that Rosebery's failure to win over the other Powers to intervention, and his refusal to intervene alone, had been among the causes of his downfall. If Salisbury was not to lose office on the same issue it seemed that he must succeed where Rosebery had failed. These were the immediate reasons why he suggested to the German ambassador in July 1895 that the Powers would best control the Sultan and end the massacres by establishing spheres of influence in Turkey, whose dissolution was in any case inevitable, against the day when partition could no longer be delayed.[1]

Russia's sphere would include the Straits and Constantinople, though there would be restriction of some sort on her control of the area. The Western Balkans would fall to Austria, Albania and Tripoli or Morocco to Italy, Morocco or Syria to France. Mesopotamia and Egypt would be recognised as the British Sphere. Turkey would be left with little more than Anatolia.[2] Nor is it difficult to see how Salisbury's immediate difficulties would have been solved if this suggestion had been adopted. Further massacres would have been more easily avoided if the Powers, instead of continuing to rely on the

[1] The German records assume that Salisbury proposed immediate partition, and his own are not available [1950]. The Germans probably assumed more than he intended. See his attitude in 1895–6 and his proposals of January 1898, below, pp. 501–9.
[2] Langer, W. L., *The Diplomacy of Imperialism*, pp. 196–8, 209; Brandenburg, E., *From Bismarck to the World War*, pp. 72–9; *Die Grosse Politik*, x, nos. 2369–72, 2381, 2396.

ineffective Concert of Europe, had become responsible for order in their own spheres. Even if the massacres had been renewed, the basis of any future British agitation for isolated action against them would have been destroyed. Rosebery, indeed, had sought a similar solution of the Armenian problem in December 1894, when he had suggested to Russia, without success, that she should occupy the Armenian areas and that France should be compensated in Syria and Great Britain by the recognition of her special position in Egypt.[1]

There was, however, an important difference between Salisbury's plan and his predecessor's. This was not the fact that he put it to Germany whereas Rosebery had approached Russia; in this he was only recognising Germany's decisive role as both the leader of the Triple Alliance and the friend of Russia. A more significant advance on Rosebery's plan, and the chief feature of Salisbury's, was his readiness to yield Constantinople and the Straits to Russia. It was none the less significant for the restrictions he would have placed on Russia's control or because he had been contemplating such a step since 1887.[2] In view of the reasons he had advanced for it on these earlier occasions, it must be supposed that when he finally offered to take it in 1895 he thought of it not only as a way out of immediate difficulties but also as a move towards escape from dependence on Germany by means of a reconciliation with Russia.

If this was among his objectives to begin with, it assumed increased importance because the German Government, ignorant of his domestic difficulties, in any case suspected some such aim behind the proposal; assumed, indeed, that his object was more Machiavellian than it was. Knowing that Austria would dislike a division of the Balkans with Russia and Italy, it concluded that he was out to disrupt the Triple Alliance and to set the Triple and Dual Alliances against each other for Great Britain's advantage. It therefore rejected his proposal out of hand in an interview which the Kaiser gave him at Cowes in August. The Kaiser, moreover, so offended him in some way—we do not know exactly what took place—that, though the German Government immediately changed its mind and asked for further discussions, he refused to reopen the subject.[3] During the remainder of 1895 an increased distrust of Germany thus joined his long-standing lack of faith in Turkey's ability to reform herself, his indignation at Turkish incompetence, his concern for British interests and the pressure of British public opinion, among the chief influences on his Armenian policy; and this only added to Germany's distrust of him. He first approached Russia and France with similar proposals, but with an

---

[1] *Turkey*, no. 1 (1896): *Parl. Pap.* 1896, xcv [C. 7923], nos. 89, 91–2, 94, 110.
[2] See above, chap. viii, pp. 259 *seqq.*
[3] Langer, *op. cit.* pp. 197–201; Sontag, R. J., "The Cowes Interview and the Kruger Telegram", *Polit. Science Quart.* xl (1925), 217–47; *Letters of Queen Victoria*, 3rd ser. ii, 544–8; *History of 'The Times'*, iii, 813–14; *D.G.P.* x, nos. 2373–88, 2392–6; xii, nos. 2194, 2930, 2932.

equal lack of success.[1] Next, when the expected renewal of the massacres in September was followed by Russian preparations in the Black Sea, which led him to fear a Russian descent on the Straits, he tried to persuade Austria and Italy to join in a naval demonstration to prevent such a move. He had been prepared to let Russia have the Straits by arrangement, and in return for a *quid pro quo* in Egypt, in the hope that the Sultan would then be curbed or the British demand for isolated intervention could be side-stepped. He was not yet prepared to countenance unilateral action by Russia; and so little so that, in addition to his efforts with Austria and Italy, he brought before the Cabinet in November a proposal to send the Mediterranean fleet up the Dardanelles. But the collaboration of Austria and Italy, which would otherwise have been forthcoming, was prevented by Germany's pressure on her allies, who were warned not to commit themselves to Great Britain until Great Britain had committed herself to them; and his other proposal was rejected by the Cabinet on account of the Admiralty's reluctance to risk the fleet's being caught between the naval forces of the Dual Alliance.[2]

When the Anglo-Russian crisis passed in January 1896, with nothing done by either side, it had thus shown that, while an accommodation with Russia was still out of the question, opposition to Russia in the Near East was no longer possible without definite commitments to the Triple Alliance. But it had also driven Great Britain and Germany further apart by seeming to confirm both Germany's suspicion that Salisbury was trying to set the Dual and Triple Alliances against each other and Salisbury's distrust of Germany. She had resorted to threats of collaboration with France and Russia if British backing for Austria were not forthcoming; he concluded that she had been trying to use the crisis as an opportunity to revive and extend the Mediterranean Agreements of 1887, by which Great Britain was committed to Germany's allies without Germany being committed to them or to Great Britain against Russia.[3] Rather than return to these arrangements he now chose to abandon Great Britain's traditional policy of barring Russia at the Straits. When Austria asked him in February 1896 for an undertaking that Great Britain would join her in opposing a Russian advance if the crisis were renewed, he not only refused to give such a pledge of material support in advance, which he would have refused in any case but, by going further than Rosebery had done along this road, he made it plain that he would not even renew the more informal second Mediterranean Agreement for the maintenance of Turkish integrity.[4]

---

[1] Langer, *op. cit.* pp. 201–2; *D.G.P.* x, nos. 2381, 2387, 2392.
[2] Langer, *op. cit.* pp. 205–8; Marder, A. J., *British Naval Policy, 1880–1905*, pp. 210–26 241–51; *D.G.P.* x, nos. 2497, 2538, 2542.
[3] *D.G.P.* x, no. 2572; xi, nos. 2579, 2759.
[4] Gooch, G. P. and Temperley, H. W. V. (eds.), *British Documents on the Origins of the War*, viii, 4–5, 13.

The events of the next twelve months, almost exactly repeating those of 1895, only completed this major change of British policy. When the Armenian massacres broke out again in August 1896 Salisbury made another fruitless attempt to persuade Russia and France to agree to intervene, and even to depose the Sultan, in exchange for concessions at the Straits, where he offered freedom of passage to the warships of all nations, and in Syria.[1] It was fruitless because, among other things, Russia, her interest in the Far East on the increase, saw greater security in the Near East if the Straits were kept closed. When this attempt had failed, though isolated intervention was demanded in Great Britain with more fervour than ever, he fell back, by the end of September, on the unworkable Concert of the Powers. The Concert spent the next twelve months in failing to end the troubles in Armenia or to prevent their spread to Macedonia and Crete;[2] but it was in an attempt to show that there was no alternative to collaboration with the other Powers that he publicly declared in January 1897 that "in 1853...we put all our money on the wrong horse".[3] He adopted this course despite the fact that the fear of a Russian seizure of Constantinople had revived, and was not to pass away till the Spring of 1897. He did so partly because investigations set on foot in October 1896 had quickly confirmed that Great Britain could not oppose such a step without taking unjustifiable risks.[4] This was one reason why, in January 1897, when Austria renewed her request for a British guarantee of support against a Russian advance, his reply was the same as in the previous February.[5] On the earlier occasion he had given as his reason for refusing to renew the Second Mediterranean Agreement the fact that British opinion was so aroused against the Sultan that it would no longer "sanction a war to defend the Ottoman Empire no matter who the Power attacking it might be". He now added the excuse that the Sultan no longer wanted British support against Russia and the fact that, as Turkey had fortified the Dardanelles while leaving the Bosphorus undefended, it had become more difficult than formerly to force a way to Constantinople with the British fleet. No doubt these considerations had helped to shape his policy. But the chief reasons for his attitude, the main lessons of the Armenian crisis in Salisbury's mind, were otherwise.

They were the increased difficulty of opposing Russia, since the formation of the Dual Alliance, without the certainty of German support; the unreliability of Germany, in view of her closer relations

---

[1] *D.G.P.* x, no. 2918; *Letters of Queen Victoria*, 3rd ser. II, 82–6.

[2] Langer, *op. cit.* pp. 331–5.

[3] Medlicott, W. N., "Lord Salisbury and Turkey", *History*, XII (Oct. 1927), 244–7.

[4] Marder, *op. cit.* pp. 266–72; Langer, *op. cit.* pp. 335–49.

[5] Gooch and Temperley (eds.), *B.D.* IX, pt. I, pp. 775–6; Marder, *op. cit.* pp. 272–3; Penson, L. M., "The Principles and Methods of Lord Salisbury's Foreign Policy", *Cambridge Hist. Jour.* v, no. 1 (1935), pp. 100–1.

with Russia, in a war between Russia and the Mediterranean Powers; and the fact that the only way to reduce that unreliability would have been to increase Great Britain's ties with, and thus her dependence on, the Triple Alliance. He had begun by trying to cut through these difficulties by means of an accommodation with Russia. When that had proved impossible, rather than accept the consequences on relations with Germany of continued opposition to Russia, he had preferred to withdraw.

II

There had meanwhile been a clash between Great Britain and Germany in South Africa which, though less important than the Armenian crisis for its effect on Salisbury's foreign policy, had thrown more light on Germany's.

The threat of German intervention in South Africa, where Bismarck's reconciliation with Great Britain in 1885 had given London a free hand, had raised its head again since 1893. In more than one diplomatic quarrel in the next two years, while Great Britain had complained that Germany was encouraging Boer intransigence and had warned Germany that she could not allow Delagoa Bay to fall to another major Power, Germany had frustrated Rhodes's attempt to buy Delagoa Bay from Portugal, had pointed to "the large German interests involved both on the coast and in the Transvaal" and had announced her determination to uphold the independence of the Boers to the extent that this had been recognised in the Anglo-Boer Convention of 1884.[1] By October 1895, so soon after Salisbury's return to office and at a time when all the elements had formed of a serious struggle between Great Britain and the Boers, South Africa, as the British ambassador told the German Foreign Minister, had become "the black spot" in Anglo-German relations.[2]

One reason for Germany's change of front in South Africa after 1893 was that, wanting Great Britain to join the Triple Alliance, she had become more and more convinced that Great Britain must be forced to join it. By the autumn of 1895, despite Salisbury's return, from which so much had been hoped, and largely as a result of his Armenian policy, from which so many deductions had been drawn, she felt this more strongly than ever; and rivalry with Great Britain in South Africa, like Germany's policy of supporting Russia in the Armenian crisis, was regarded as a means of exercising the necessary pressure. Thus the Kaiser, in his outburst on hearing of the British ambassador's remark, implied that Great Britain could only escape isolation and avoid this rivalry by coming out "either for or against

---

[1] See above, chap. viii, pp. 263–70; *C.H.B.E.* viii, 524–30; Lovell, R. I., *The Struggle for South Africa*, pp. 324 *seqq.*; Brandenburg, *op. cit.* pp. 45 *seqq.*; Garvin, J. L., *Life of Joseph Chamberlain*, iii, 64 *seqq.*; *B.D.* i, 323–4; iii, 408; *D.G.P.* xi, no. 2577.
[2] *D.G.P.* xi, nos. 2578–84.

the Triple Alliance", and that she could come out for it only by giving advance and signed guarantees.[1] But this was not the only motive behind Germany's growing opposition to Great Britain in Africa as is sometimes claimed, even if it was the more important. German commercial interests in the Transvaal, already considerable when Bismarck had signed a trade treaty with the Boers in 1885, had grown rapidly with the discovery of the Rand gold-fields, the development of the Transvaal railways and the determination of the Boers to escape absorption by Rhodes. German colonialists looked to the day when the Boer States and Portuguese East Africa would fall to Germany; and even in Government circles the Kaiser and others already harboured designs on Delagoa Bay as a naval base and toyed with the prospect of a German protectorate over the Transvaal.[2] By all these interests, as by German public opinion as a whole, the gradual encroachment of British power on the Boers was regarded as aggression; on all these grounds, Germany's interest in the continued independence of the Boers as against Great Britain was a feature to be reckoned with. Even if Germany underestimated the importance Great Britain attached to South Africa, despite recent warnings to the contrary, it is still significant that a memorandum by Holstein, finished at the end of December 1895, omitted South Africa from the list of vital British interests that Germany should not challenge. Holstein advocated a temporary alliance with France and Russia. Since the aim should be not to alienate Great Britain for ever, but only to force her to recognise her need for Germany's friendship, India, Egypt and Persia should be excluded from the field of Germany's collaboration with those Powers. But, while Russia might get Korea and France the Congo as their reward, Germany should demand in return their help in maintaining the *status quo* in South Africa against British expansion.[3]

At the end of 1895, indeed, Germany's determination to uphold the *status quo*, in her own interests and on behalf of the Boers, overshadowed and compromised her diplomatic objective. It did so the more decisively because of the sudden and high-handed way in which the *status quo* was threatened by the Jameson Raid.[4] This jolted the German Government into making a stand at the risk of war with Great Britain, despite its anxiety to drive Great Britain into the Triple Alliance. It would have found it difficult to avoid a declaration of war if Jameson had succeeded; it had warned Great Britain so often, and once again as late as 28 December, the day before the

[1] *D.G.P.* xi, no. 2579.

[2] Lovell, *op. cit.* pp. 345–7; Langer, *op. cit.* pp. 235–6, 247; van der Poel, J., *The Jameson Raid*, p. 136; Townsend, M. E., *The Rise and Fall of Germany's Colonial Empire*, pp. 106 *seqq.*; *History of* The Times, iii, 145–6, 177.

[3] *D.G.P.* xi, no. 2640.

[4] *C.H.B.E.* viii, chap. xxi (*b*); van der Poel, *op. cit., passim*; Walker, E. A., "The Jameson Raid", *Cambridge Hist. Jour.* vi, no. 3 (1940), pp. 283–306.

raid,[1] of its determination to insist on the *status quo*. So great was this determination that war with Great Britain was only narrowly avoided before it was learned that Jameson had failed. If Portugal had not delayed her reply to Germany's request of December 13 for permission to send men to the Transvaal from her ships in Delagoa Bay, the men would have made the passage and a British ultimatum must have followed. On the same day Germany instructed her ambassador in London to ask for his passports if the British Government did not disapprove of Jameson's action; on 2 January 1896, before she knew of Jameson's failure, though Salisbury had already expressed his disapproval, she protested in a second note to London that she was "unwilling to accept any alteration in the position of the South African Republic". This note would also have brought war dangerously near if the news of Jameson's failure had not reached Berlin in time to allow it to be cancelled before delivery.[2]

Even after Jameson had failed, Germany was not content until she had registered another protest. On 3 January, in an open telegram, the Kaiser congratulated the Boer President on having maintained the "independence" of the Transvaal "without appealing to the help of friendly Powers". The chief responsibility for the dispatch of the Kruger telegram may safely be attributed to the Kaiser.[3] But the German Government as a whole approved of its dispatch and made no attempt to offset its inevitable effect on the British Government; and this was because, though differing from the Kaiser in not wanting to risk war with Great Britain once the threat to the *status quo* had passed, it was anxious, once the raid had failed, to return to its plan of forcing Great Britain into the Triple Alliance. It was for this reason that, in the week following the raid, it took care to inform Salisbury that only Jameson's failure had spared him the receipt of a sharp note. For the same reason it brought still greater pressure to bear indirectly through *The Times*' correspondent in Berlin, who was told that the Kruger telegram had been a deliberate act of state and warned that Germany would form a continental league against Great Britain if she continued to threaten the Boers and if her policy elsewhere continued to be unsatisfactory; and it encouraged Kruger to appeal to the Powers for a conference to determine the international status of the Transvaal by amending the disputed Convention of 1884.[4] Nor would Germany have stopped there in her exploitation of the situation had she not discovered that, if she went further, it would be not only in the face of a British Government that was prepared to take up any challenge, but also without support from the other European Powers.

[1] *D.G.P.* xi, nos. 2585–8.
[2] *Ibid.* nos. 2588–91, 2599–604.
[3] *Ibid.* nos. 2605–6; Langer, *op. cit.* pp. 234–8; Lovell, *op. cit.* pp. 368–70.
[4] *D.G.P.* xi, nos. 2607, 2609, 2621; *History of 'The Times'*, iii, 261–3, 267–71.

The Jameson Raid had not only prompted Germany to jeopardise her chances of gaining a closer British connection for the sake of German interests. It had provoked her into a hasty and unprepared attempt to implement the plan for limited collaboration with the Dual Alliance. France and Russia, approached on 1 and 2 January on the lines suggested in Holstein's memorandum, were not prepared to work with Germany "to limit the insatiable appetite of England" in areas of secondary importance to themselves.[1] Germany's allies were also reluctant to follow her. Italy, in difficulties in Abyssinia, needed British help;[2] Austria was still hoping for British guarantees against Russia in the Balkans;[3] both blamed Germany for the rift between Great Britain and the Triple Alliance and feared any widening of it.[4] The evident firmness of the British Government completed Germany's embarrassment. On 7 January, though undertaking to respect the *status quo* in South Africa and compensate the Transvaal for the raid, it made it known that it would refuse a conference; on 8 January it announced the commissioning of a flying squadron "ready to go anywhere and do anything as the necessities of Empire may require".[5] Germany had no alternative but to retreat. By 11 January, after the Kaiser had apologised in strange terms to the Queen, the German Government had decided to advise the Boers not to press their demand for a conference and not to raise the awkward question of sovereignty.[6]

The wave of patriotic fury which had swept Great Britain after the dispatch of the telegram had meanwhile equalled the German public's indignation at the news of the Jameson Raid;[7] and the increased mutual distrust of the two countries was to have serious consequences in the future. But it was to continue undiminished, and to have these consequences, because the South African crisis had little effect on the policy of either Government. On 11 January, making one of her motives in the crisis doubly clear, Germany accompanied one more warning to Salisbury of the dangers of isolation with the offer of a secret Anglo-German alliance. He refused on the old ground that "isolation is much less a danger than the danger of being dragged into wars that do not concern us".[8] Official relations remained as before. The main reason for this was the fact that the

---

[1] Langer, *op. cit.* pp. 233, 247–8; Hargreaves, J. D., "Entente Manquée: Anglo-French Relations, 1895–6", *Cambridge Hist. Jour.* XI, no. 1 (1953), pp. 78–9; *The Kaiser's Letters to the Tsar*, pp. 29, 30; *D.G.P.* XI, nos. 2618, 2622–5, 2641, 2651, 2735; *Documents diplomatiques français*, 1ere sér. XII, nos. 254–5, 257, 262.

[2] See below, pp. 501–2.   [3] See above, p. 493.

[4] Langer, *op. cit.* p. 248; Pribram, A. E., *The Secret Treaties of Austro-Hungary*, II, 105–10; *D.G.P.* XI, nos. 2642, 2649, 2656.

[5] Marder, *op. cit.* pp. 275–6; van der Poel, *Jameson Raid*, pp. 139–40.

[6] Langer, *op. cit.* pp. 249–50; *Letters of Queen Victoria*, 3rd ser. III, 17–18; van der Poel, *op. cit.* pp. 136–7; Sontag, *loc. cit.* pp. 258 *seqq.*; *D.G.P.* XI, nos. 2613–33.

[7] Langer, *op. cit.* pp. 252–3; Marder, *op. cit.* p. 258.

[8] Langer, *op. cit.* p. 250; *Letters of Queen Victoria*, 3rd ser. III, 20–2.

fundamental source of conflict in Anglo-German relations was that while Germany, on account of the formation of the Dual Alliance, was anxious to tighten Great Britain's connection with the Triple Alliance for reasons of security, Salisbury was determined, on account of the same development, to reduce the connection he had previously maintained with Germany and her allies. But if Germany learned no lessons from her misuse of threats, except that it was galling to be weak at sea and that her threats must be moderated until she was less weak; if she failed, even when Salisbury's refusal to be deflected was followed in the next month, as a result of the Armenian crisis, by his denunciation of the second Mediterranean Agreement, to see that pressure was not the way to bridge the great gap between the two countries, this was for another reason as well. It was because she had two motives in demanding a closer British connection just as she had had two motives for intervening in South Africa. It was because she was jealous of the British position in the world; anxious for Great Britain's subordination as well as for British friendship in the new situation created by the Dual Alliance. The major divergence of Germany and Great Britain on the question of the Dual Alliance contained within itself the separate but growing problem of Anglo-German rivalry in a wider field.

III

Salisbury was made to suspect this all the more by the fact that, after the South African crisis and his first refusal of Austria's request for a guarantee against Russia, he was forced to return to collaboration with the Triple Alliance by the need to safeguard British interests in the Sudan and Egypt.

His immediate object in outlining his Turkish proposals to Germany in July 1895, and in approaching the Dual Alliance with similar proposals in the following month, had been to get Russian collaboration against the Sultan. But another reason for making those moves had been his wish to get Russian and French acceptance of Great Britain's special position in Egypt. He—and Rosebery too —had long wanted this because it would have made Great Britain a free agent in relation to Germany.[1] It would also have made Great Britain a freer agent in the government of Egypt; and the Anglo-Russian crisis of the next few months, by confirming Great Britain's inability to defend the Straits, emphasised that this was important too. In November 1895 the Cabinet Defence Committee, warned that Great Britain would be powerless in the event of a Russian descent on Constantinople, was also advised that "by taking Egypt absolutely we could secure what we have so long sought to maintain by keeping Russia outside Constantinople"—naval supremacy in the

---

[1] See above, chap. viii, pp. 257–63.

Eastern Mediterranean.[1] In addition there was a close connection between the desirability of freedom of action in Egypt and Salisbury's plans for the Sudan. He had been intent on the eventual reconquest of the Sudan since 1889.[2] One of his first acts on returning to office in 1895 had been to get Parliament to vote the necessary money for building the Uganda railway, which would make possible an advance into the Sudan from the south.[3]

On all these grounds Egypt, which had provided him with an additional motive for seeking reconciliation with the Dual Alliance in the first place, provided him with a reason for continuing his efforts in this direction despite their failure in the Armenian question. Throughout the Anglo-Russian crisis over the Straits in the last months of 1895 he continued negotiations with France that had begun in September. In January 1896 he brought them to a conclusion involving concessions in Burma and Siam which Rosebery and the Opposition regarded as inspired by an excessive anxiety to please the French. He made them in the belief that it "is important in the present state of things to settle as many questions with France as possible".[4] But agreement with France on Egypt, though he hoped for it, was more difficult to reach than a settlement in South-East Asia. The subject was raised at the end of the Siam negotiations[5] and again in February 1896 in talks with the French ambassador;[6] but the result only showed that its discussion would be premature.

One reason for this was that, though some members of the French Government would have been glad to recognise the British occupation of Egypt in return for concessions to French *amour-propre* and public opinion, they had been unable to withstand either Russia's insistence on no compromise with Great Britain or the great increase of colonialist pressure in Paris that had followed the breakdown of the Nile Valley negotiations during Rosebery's administration. Grey's statements in the House of Commons at the end of those negotiations in March 1895 had not only warned France against expansion into the Sudan; they had claimed the whole of the Nile Valley for Great Britain and Egypt whereas Great Britain had previously claimed only the area as far south as Khartoum and as far north as Fashoda.[7] Against so public a challenge the French Government had been forced to retaliate. It had decided on a bold advance to the Nile which would force Great Britain to negotiate an Egyptian settlement on more equal terms by threatening Egypt's water supply. By the

---

[1] Marder, *op. cit.* pp. 246-9; see also pp. 271, 578.
[2] See above, chap. viii, pp. 266-70.
[3] Langer, *op. cit.* pp. 121-4, 268, 537-8.
[4] See below, p. 500; J. D. Hargreaves, *loc. cit.* pp. 69-75.
[5] Hargreaves, *loc. cit.* p. 78; *D.D.F.* 1ere sér. xii, nos. 295, 403, 439.
[6] Hargreaves, *loc. cit.* pp. 82-3; Lord Zetland, *Lord Cromer*, pp. 265-8; *D.D.F.*, 1ere sér. xii, no. 306.
[7] Langer, *op. cit.* pp. 262-7.

end of November 1895 it had sanctioned the Marchand mission; in February 1896 the mission was finally given its instructions after much hesitation and because it had emerged by then that Salisbury would not go back on Grey's position.[1] This was the second obstacle to an Egyptian settlement. The importance Salisbury attached to Egypt and the Sudan ruled out concessions in that region, though he was prepared to make them elsewhere.

For the same reason, Egypt complicated Salisbury's general policy. In the Turkish question, failing to reach agreement with the Dual Alliance, he chose retreat from the Straits rather than dependence on Germany. In Egypt he did not intend to retreat. He would do what he could to avoid a break with France by postponing action in the Sudan; he preferred to wait in any case till Egypt could help to finance the reconquest and till the Uganda railway was ready. But after February 1896, when it became obvious that France intended some stroke with the Marchand mission, even his wish to delay action for fear of friction with France began to give way to the feeling that action might be necessary to forestall her, despite the fact that such action would deepen the gulf between Great Britain and the Dual Alliance and involve Great Britain in concessions to the Triple Alliance.

It was the need to make concessions to the Triple Alliance, indeed, which forced his hand. While there was no need for urgent action on Marchand's account, Italy's difficulties in Abyssinia made some decision imperative. Undeclared war between Italy and Abyssinia, who had denounced the treaty of Ucciali,[2] had broken out at the end of 1894. Throughout 1895, Italy, backed by Germany, had been asking for British help; in particular, she had demanded permission to occupy the port of Zeila in British Somaliland, the obvious base for an attack on Harrar and the Abyssinian rear. Salisbury, to the annoyance of Germany and Italy, had steadily refused to yield this without French agreement, which was withheld, because of his wish to improve relations with France and because Great Britain was bound by the Anglo-French treaty of 1888 to maintain the neutrality of Zeila and the independence of Harrar.[3] He was still refusing when, on 2–3 March 1896, Europe learned of Italy's disastrous defeat by the Abyssinians at Adowa. Adowa might open the way for a French advance to the Nile from the east. It was, moreover, a serious blow for the Triple Alliance, increasing the danger that Italy would desert it for collaboration with France if she were not helped; and

---

[1] Hargreaves, *loc. cit.* pp. 66, 75–6; Langer, *op. cit.* pp. 268–9; Taylor, A. J. P., "Prelude to Fashoda", *E.H.R.* LXV (Jan. 1950), pp. 52–80, and "Les Premières Années de l'Alliance [Franco]-Russe", *Revue Historique*, CCIV (July–Sept. 1950), pp. 62–76; *D.D.F.* 1ere sér. XII, nos. 142, 152–3, 180, 197, 219–20.

[2] See above, chap. viii, p. 272–6.

[3] Langer, *op. cit.* pp. 276–80; Hargreaves, *loc. cit.* pp. 77–8; *History of 'The Times'*, III, 253–4; *D.G.P.* VIII, nos. 1999–2012; X, nos. 2369–72; XI, nos. 2621, 2748–61; *D.D.F.* 1ere sér. XII, nos. 240, 242, 245.

this might also embarrass Great Britain. At the same time, Italian and German dissatisfaction at Great Britain's attitude about Zeila, and Austria's dissatisfaction at Salisbury's recent rejection of her request for a guarantee against Russia, suggested the need to work for some kind of reinsurance with the Triple Alliance against the possibility that Great Britain and France would one day be in conflict on the Nile.[1] It was partly on these grounds that Salisbury changed his mind and offered to help Italy.

He did not change his mind at once, however, or give way on the Zeila issue. On receiving the news of Adowa, the Kaiser called on the British Embassy in person to express the hope that "England would join the Triple Alliance or at least come to the assistance of the Italians"; Salisbury's first reply was that he still could not see his way to help Italy.[2] When the Cabinet did agree to help Italy ten days later, it decided to do so by an advance from Egypt to Dongola in the Sudan, where the dervishes might take advantage of Italy's set-back and where French designs were beginning to cause anxiety; and the decision was due more to the wish to safeguard the Sudan for Great Britain than to the need to give help to Italy.[3] "It was inspired", wrote Salisbury to Cromer, "specially by a desire to help the Italians at Kassala and prevent the dervishes from winning a conspicuous success that might have far-reaching results. In addition, we desired to kill two birds with one stone, and to use the same military effort to plant the foot of Egypt further up the Nile. For this reason we preferred it to any movement from Suakim or in the direction of Kassala, because there would be no ulterior profit in these movements."[4] Unlike these other movements, however, the advance to Dongola, completed in September 1896, can hardly have been expected to help the Italians or affect the military situation in Abyssinia, except indirectly: Dongola was five hundred miles from Kassala.

Although the move was thus, above all else, what France was in any case bound to assume it to be, the first major step in the reconquest of the Sudan and a blow at French designs on the Nile, Salisbury was reluctant to accept, and made efforts to avoid, its consequences on British relations with the Dual Alliance. Approaching France, as a member of Egypt's International Debt Commission, for her agreement to the financing of the Dongola expedition from the reserve of the Egyptian debt, he went so far as to promise that the expedition would not alter the political status of Egypt or Great Britain's intention eventually to evacuate the country. But his efforts were to no avail. France withheld her approval only after

[1] Langer, op. cit. pp. 281–2; Pribram, op. cit. II, 105 seqq.
[2] Langer, op. cit. pp. 282–3; D.G.P. XI, nos. 2770–6.
[3] Hargreaves, loc. cit. pp. 84–5; Shibeika, M. el, British Policy in the Soudan, chap. XII.
[4] Langer, op. cit. p. 286; Zetland, op. cit. p. 273; Lord Cromer, Modern Egypt, II, chap. 32.

much hesitation and under Russian pressure.[1] But she did withhold it; and Russia did more than support her on the Debt Commission. After the middle of 1896, both because of her growing dependence on traffic through the Straits and the Canal, in view of her increasing foreign trade and her increasing strategic interest in the Far East, for which the trans-Siberian railway was inadequate, and from the wish to strengthen the French Alliance, Russia added to Great Britain's embarrassment by demanding the implementation of the Suez Convention of 1888.[2] By replacing the existing dependence of the Powers on a British guarantee of free passage in the Canal by international control of the Canal, this would have undermined Great Britain's position in Egypt. The Dongola expedition thus led to increased hostility to Great Britain on the part of the Dual Alliance.

Increased British dependence on the Triple Alliance followed from that. German support on the International Debt Commission was given to Great Britain, though French and Russian opposition still forced Great Britain to finance the expedition herself in the end.[3] It was Germany's support, and not Salisbury's offers of concessions to Russia at the Straits and in the Suez Canal in October and November 1896,[4] that enabled him to evade the Russian and French demands for the implementation of the Suez Convention.[5] But it was partly to avoid dependence on Germany that Salisbury had hesitated to move into the Sudan without an agreement with France; and dislike of that dependence, reinforced by his experiences in the Armenian and South African crises as well as by the need to return to it, was one reason why he continued to look for reconciliation with the Dual Alliance after the middle of 1896. "The Germans seem greatly to preoccupy the Marquis," noted Hanotaux in March 1897, when Salisbury took the unusual step of calling on the Quai d'Orsay to discuss the possibility of an Anglo-French treaty of arbitration. "'There is the dark cloud', he said to me."[6]

IV

There was yet another reason, in addition to his distrust of Germany, why Salisbury continued these efforts, despite their failure in the Armenian question and the set-back necessitated by his concern for British interests in Egypt and the Sudan. In China after the

[1] Langer, op. cit. pp. 288–9; Hargreaves, loc. cit. pp. 86–92; D.D.F. 1ere sér. xii, nos. 324–5, 329, 331–4, 341–7, 349–55, 365; D.G.P. xi, nos. 2697–2708, 2712–22.

[2] Langer, op. cit. pp. 290–2; Meyendorff, A., Corresp. diplomatique de M. de Staal, ii, 315–18; D.D.F. 1ere sér. xii, nos. 355–6,[1] 358, 360–1, 367, 386, 442; Taylor, A. J. P., The Struggle for Mastery in Europe, p. 358.

[3] Langer, op. cit. pp. 288–9.

[4] Ibid. pp. 292–3; Meyendorff, op. cit. ii, 321–2; Letters of Queen Victoria, 3rd ser. iii, 68–75; B.D. i, no. 380.

[5] D.G.P. xi, nos. 2728–46.

[6] Kennedy, A. L., Salisbury, pp. 280–2.

middle of 1896, as in Turkey since the middle of 1895, he saw in an accommodation with Russia the only hope of safeguarding British interests in China in a period of rapid change.

The rivalries and ambitions of the European Powers in China had recently been intensified, first by the formation of the Dual Alliance, for France had designs in the south-east and Russia in the north, and then by China's defeat in the Sino-Japanese War of 1894–5. As soon as the war had ended, France had forced China to grant concessions to French firms, including the first for the building of a foreign railway in China, in the provinces of Yunnan, Kuangsi and Kuangtung.[1] If Russia's plans in the north had been slower to mature it was only because they had aimed at even greater inroads into Chinese sovereignty. The Times' report of October 1895, to the effect that she had acquired the right to take the Trans-Siberian railway across Manchuria and to anchor ships at Port Arthur, had been premature; but it had only announced what all the world expected and what Russia had acquired by September 1896.[2] By this time Russia had also reached an agreement with Japan by which the two Powers had set up virtually a joint protectorate over nominally independent Korea.[3] It had also to be feared that there were plans for connecting the Russian advance from the north with the Indo-Pacific empire that France was building in the south, for cutting across the great commercial interests of Great Britain in the Yangtse Valley, for ousting Great Britain from China in due course.[4] Beside these developments, the growing interest of Germany in China was as yet unimportant; but it was known that one of her interests before joining France and Russia against Japan at Shimonoseki had been the wish to acquire a Far Eastern naval base and that she had since been surveying possible sites.[5] Since 1895, moreover, she had made successful efforts to increase her share in the China trade, already second only to the British, and had concentrated on the Yangtse Valley, thus challenging Great Britain's virtual monopoly in that area.[6]

Great Britain, possessing the largest Asiatic interests to begin with, was the Power most threatened by these developments; was, indeed, the only Power with anything to lose as a result. Her policy had previously been to maintain the independence of China and the principle of "the open door" in Chinese trade. This had best suited

[1] Langer, op. cit. p. 394; Joseph, P., Foreign Diplomacy in China, 1894–1900 (1928), chap. vii; D.D.F. 1ere sér. XII, nos. 15, 48.
[2] History of 'The Times', III, 198–9; Langer, op. cit. pp. 400–4; Dallin, D. J., The Rise of Russia in Asia, pp. 51–2.
[3] Langer, op. cit. pp. 404–7; Dallin, op. cit. pp. 47–8.
[4] Langer, op. cit. pp. 410–11; Morse, H. B., The International Relations of the Chinese Empire (1918), III, 373.
[5] See above, chap. viii, p. 289–91; Brandenburg, op. cit. pp. 56–7; Langer, op. cit. pp. 448–50.
[6] Kawai, K., "Anglo-German Rivalry in the Yangtse Basin, 1885–1902", Pacific Hist. Rev. VIII (1939), pp. 413–14.

the lead she held in the commerce of the world and the hold she had established since the 1850's on the markets of the Yangtse Valley. Shimonoseki had shown her, however, that China's independence was unlikely to survive if China were left to her own devices; and since 1895 she had hardly known where to turn to preserve her interests. Some, like Curzon, had advocated a more forceful policy, by which she would have taken the lead in the reform of China and insisted on her maintenance as a buffer state, if necessary under British dominion.[1] This solution had already been out of the question when first suggested. It would have been opposed by the Dual Alliance, which was nowhere so effective or so certain of German backing as in the Far East; it would have been beyond Great Britain's strength if only because she had already assumed so many similar responsibilities elsewhere. Another solution, which had also had its advocates among those who were convinced that China was about to be partitioned,[2] would have been to abandon the Open Door and join in the race for spheres of influence. But this policy would also have involved friction with the Dual Alliance; and it would have meant the exclusion of British trade from such areas as the other Powers were able to absorb. Reluctant to adopt it, unable to adopt the suggestion of the Curzon school, the British Government had fallen back under Salisbury on the difficult if not impossible task of attempting to reconcile the expansion of the European Powers with the maintenance of the Open Door by means of agreements with France and Russia.

Salisbury had refused to share the indignation of the British public at *The Times*' report of October 1895, or to protest against concessions to Russia in Port Arthur so long as other nations were not excluded from the port.[3] "In Asia," he had declared in his Guildhall speech of November 1895, deprecating unnecessary alarm, "there is room for us all."[4] Balfour and Chamberlain in other speeches and in talks with the Russian ambassador had adopted the same attitude in February 1896, and had as good as invited Russia to take a Chinese port.[5] Meanwhile, in January 1896, Salisbury had concluded a settlement with France, after failing to block her demand for concessions in China in June 1895.[6] In return for concessions in Tunis and on the Lower Niger and for the abandonment of the principle of a buffer state on the Upper Mekong, on which Rosebery had insisted in the dispute about the borders of Burma and Indo-China since 1893, he had secured an agreement by which the two Powers would share whatever concessions had been or might be granted to them in Yun-

[1] Curzon, G. N., *Problems of the Far East*; *History of 'The Times'*, III, 186–7.
[2] Langer, *op. cit.* p. 461; *History of 'The Times'*, III, 358.
[3] *D.G.P.* x, nos. 2393, 2493.
[4] Langer, *op. cit.* p. 400.
[5] *Ibid.* pp. 252–3, 400; Meyendorff, A., *Corresp. diplomatique de M. de Staal*, II, 309.
[6] Langer, *op. cit.* pp. 394–5.

nan, where French influence was predominant, and Szechuan, where Great Britain was more favourably placed.[1] His aim had been to accept the fact of expansion by Russia and France, to approve of it even, in the hope that they would agree not to exclude British trade from the areas where they acquired concessions. Nor had he adopted this policy only because it seemed the best possible in the interests of British trade. He had known that he could not oppose the Dual Alliance in China and hope to gain its collaboration elsewhere, as, from distrust of Germany, from anxiety to end the Armenian massacres, from the wish to get France to give way in Egypt and on the Nile, he had been hoping to gain it since 1895.

Yet this policy suffered from fundamental weaknesses. The Open Door was eminently suitable for Great Britain; for Russia and France, who could not compete with Great Britain or Germany in the open market, it involved serious disadvantages. Great Britain's anxiety to maintain it, moreover, and her inability to enforce it, offered France and Russia a standing invitation to use their opportunities in China to force Great Britain to retreat elsewhere. All hope of French collaboration in China was accordingly killed by the Dongola expedition. By the beginning of 1897 the race between Great Britain and France for concessions in South China had been resumed and the British Government had been forced, in this area at least, to contemplate the seizure of spheres of influence in competition with France instead of maintaining the Open Door in agreement with her.[2] Yet failure in the south only increased Salisbury's determination to persevere with Russia in the north. Since the breach with France, moreover, he had other reasons for attaching more importance than ever to reconciliation with Russia. Whereas, from opposition to Russia at the Straits, he had previously attached priority to the conciliation of France, he had now abandoned the Straits; and knowing that he might soon be at war with France over the Sudan and that he could not afford to be at loggerheads with Russia in China and France in Africa simultaneously, he preferred to reserve his strength for the African issue.[3] "It is easier to lament than to repair", he wrote in August 1896, reflecting on the interlocking problems facing him at the Straits, in Egypt, China and Europe. "It may not be possible for Russia and England to return to their old relations. But it is an object to be wished for and approached as opportunity offers.... It is the best chance of an equilibrium of Europe...."[4] It was on these grounds that, in his Guildhall speech of 9 November 1896, he declared that it was "a superstition of an

[1] See above, pp. 504-5; *C.H.B.F.P.* III, 196-200; Langer, *op. cit.* pp. 250-1; Hargreaves, *loc. cit.* pp. 69-75; *D.D.F.* 1ere sér. XII, nos. 141, 144, 151, 160, 177.

[2] Langer, *op. cit.* p. 395; McCordock, R. S., *British Far Eastern Policy, 1894-1900*, pp. 152 *seqq.*; Morse, *op. cit.* II, 286 ff.

[3] See below, p. 512.   [4] *B.D.* VI, p. 780.

antiquated diplomacy that there is any necessary antagonism between Russia and Great Britain".[1]

Russia's policy, like Salisbury's, though for different reasons, was to keep north China immune from a scramble by the Powers; she hoped eventually to establish a virtual protectorate over it all by means of control over Peking. For this reason Salisbury's hopes of a settlement with Russia were not put to the test in this area till November 1897. When they were, it was action by Germany and not by Russia that brought the situation to a head. Germany's seizure of the Shantung harbour of Kiao-chau in that month forced Russia to follow suit.[2] But the Russian occupation of Port Arthur and Talienwan, like the German move into Kiao-chau, again caused a storm of indignation and fear in Great Britain and again dashed Salisbury's hopes. Throughout the crisis that followed, the British Government tried to exchange its acceptance of Russia's occupation of the ports for Russia's agreement not to close them to the trade of others.[3] Such a bargain in China was part of a general settlement, covering Egypt and Turkey, where conditions still remained unsettled, as well as China, which Salisbury offered to the Russian Government during the crisis, in the middle of January 1898. What he proposed, as in the summer of 1895, was not a partition of territory "but only a partition of preponderance". "We contemplate", he wrote, "no infraction of existing rights. We could not admit the violation of any existing treaties or impair the integrity of the present empires of China or Turkey. These two considerations are vital." He suggested, nevertheless, that, since Russia and Great Britain were both interested in China and Turkey, neither of which could stand on its own feet, it might be "possible to arrange that where our counsels differ the Power least interested should give way to the other". In Turkey Great Britain would give way at the Straits and down the Euphrates as far as Baghdad if Russia would do so along the Euphrates beyond Baghdad, in Arabia, and in Egypt and the Sudan (Turkish Africa). A similar division might be drawn in China along the line of the Hwang-ho Valley, British influence preponderating to the south, Russia's to the north, where Great Britain "would go far to further Russia's commercial objects... if we could regard her as willing to work with us". The result might be "a cordial and closer understanding" between the two Powers instead of the existing situation in which they were "neutralising each other's efforts much more frequently than the real antagonisms of their interests would justify".[4]

[1] Langer, op. cit. p. 335.
[2] Langer, op. cit. pp. 445–80; Dallin, op. cit. pp. 54–6.
[3] Meyendorff, op. cit. II, 355–8, 370; China, no. 1 (1898): Parl. Pap. 1898, cv [C. 8814], nos. 48, 61, 63, 67, 72, 76, 123. Langer, op. cit. pp. 464–7; Joseph, op. cit. pp. 234 seqq.; Hicks Beach, Victoria, Life of Sir Michael Hicks Beach, II, pp. 58–9; Letters of Queen Victoria, 3rd ser. III, 237–8; B.D. I, nos. 23 seqq.
[4] B.D. I, 5–15; China, no. 1 (1898), pp. 21–33.

Unfortunately this diagnosis of the situation, accurate so far as it referred to Great Britain, bore no relation to the facts of Russia's international position. Russia's policy in China, as elsewhere, was backed by France and Germany; even with Austria, after Salisbury's rejection of Austria's suggestions, she had been able to reach in May 1897 an understanding for the maintenance of the *status quo* in the Balkans which left her a free hand in the Far East.[1] She had also bought off Japan by agreeing to withdraw from Korea. Though she was disturbed and angered by the German move and, to check Germany, might have accepted a proposal to divide China with Great Britain into exclusive spheres of influence, she evaded Salisbury's effort to induce her to respect the Open Door, to give up, as Chamberlain later put it, "the idea of political predominance and military occupation in China";[2] and she was no more inclined than before to accept a compromise settlement in the Near East. In the subsequent negotiations Salisbury's proposal, impracticable or at least premature for these reasons, was ignored. Russia gave equivocal verbal assurances that she would respect the rights of other Powers in the ports; it was always obvious that she would not do so.[3] On 27 March 1898 she finally obtained the lease of them. All that the British Government would do was to reserve its freedom "to take what steps they think best to protect their own interests and diminish the evil consequences they anticipate",[4] to move the fleet to the Gulf of Pechili[5] and to follow the German lead, as Russia had done, by taking a lease of the Chinese harbour of Wei-hai-wei.[6]

Many members of the Cabinet were loath to accept the diplomatic defeat involved in the conclusion that Port Arthur was not worth a war. Salisbury could point out that Great Britain's total isolation left her no alternative: Russia, he admitted, had "behaved abominably", but "in six months time we shall be on the verge of war with France: I can't afford to quarrel with Russia now".[7] He could justify his policy as being based on a correct assessment of British interests. British interests in China, unlike the British position at the Straits, were not, in his view, expendable; unlike the British position in Egypt and the Sudan, they were not, however, to be upheld entirely at all costs. There was room and time for manœuvre. In north China they were small compared with those in the Yangtse Valley and the south-west, where a different policy might have been

[1] Langer, *op. cit.* pp. 373–5; Pribram, *op. cit.* I, 185–95.
[2] Langer, *op. cit.* p. 470; Birmingham speech of May 1898.
[3] Langer, *op. cit.* pp. 462–3, 468–70, 474; *China*, no. 1 (1898): *Parl. Pap.* 1898, cv [C. 8814], nos. 54 *seqq.*
[4] *B.D.* I, nos. 41; Meyendorff, *op. cit.* II, 375–7.
[5] *China*, no. 1: *Parl. Pap.* 1900, cv [Cd. 93], nos. 129, 138.
[6] Langer, *op. cit.* pp. 473–4; Lord Ronaldshay, *Life of Lord Curzon*, I, 278–9; Marder, *op. cit.* pp. 309–10; Garvin, *op. cit.* III, 248–9; *B.D.* I, nos. 28, 30, 39 *seqq.*; *China*, no. 1 (1898): [C. 8814], nos. 90–1, 138; [Cd. 93], nos. 125, 144.
[7] Kennedy, *op. cit.* pp. 275–6.

justified. These were the considerations that weighed with him in the Port Arthur crisis, that had shaped his China policy since 1895. They explained why he was reluctant to take Wei-hai-wei, a move which implied the final abandonment of the attempt to maintain China as a buffer state under "the Open-Door" principle.[1] In the last resort he adopted this line, as he had changed his policy in Turkey, because, as his policy in Egypt had shown, no other course was possible without drawing closer to Germany. But in his determination to avoid this he had now met a serious set-back in China without having reaped any positive success elsewhere. He thus found that he had no choice but to give way to pressure in the Cabinet and the country for the seizure of Wei-hai-wei by way of consolation; and some of his colleagues, reluctant to accept the result in China despite this consolation, and fearful of other disasters to come, were at last convinced that the Foreign Secretary must also be overridden in his policy as a whole.

V

Chamberlain, who had favoured an understanding with Russia after the German seizure of Kiao-chau, had already approached the United States, Japan and Germany after the Russian seizure of Port Arthur and Talienwan. The United States had evaded his suggestion that all Chinese ports should be treaty ports and Russia driven out of Port Arthur if she refused to agree.[2] Japan, preferring another settlement with Russia that gave her a free hand in Korea, had ignored his proposal for an Anglo-Japanese Alliance.[3] Private discussions which he had begun with the German Counsellor, von Eckardstein, had then given way to more serious exchanges. At the end of March 1898, in Salisbury's absence abroad, admitting to the German ambassador that Great Britain could no longer remain isolated in the face of the Dual Alliance, he offered an Anglo-German Alliance and asked Germany to state her terms. In further talks, to counter Germany's suspicion that his aim was to use her against Russia in China and her argument that a British alliance might be binding only on the minister who signed it, he explained that his object was not to deprive Russia of what she had already gained, only to regulate the future of those Chinese areas that had not yet been absorbed by the Powers, and he undertook to get Parliament to ratify an alliance.[4]

These assurances carried no weight. Germany's objections arose

[1] Garvin, op. cit. III, 249.

[2] Langer, op. cit. p. 472; Garvin, op. cit. III, 251; Dennis, A. L. P., Adventures in American Diplomacy, 1896–1906, pp. 170–1.

[3] Garvin, op. cit. III, 248–9; Ronaldshay, op. cit. I, 278–9; Langer, op. cit. pp. 472–3; Dallin, op. cit. pp. 49–50.

[4] Langer, op. cit. pp. 494–7; Garvin, op. cit. III, 259–60, 263; D.G.P. XIV (i), nos. 3782–4, 3789.

from serious divergences between the outlook and interests of Great Britain and Germany which Chamberlain, with his narrow experience at the Colonial Office and his absorption in the Far East and with trade, did not wholly appreciate and which could not be so easily bridged as he imagined. Germany, despite her growing extra-European interests, was a Continental Power. Her main consideration being the security of her frontiers, her chief aim was to divert the other European Powers from the Continent. Because she could not be certain of achieving this, or achieve it for ever, she also wanted reinsurance within Europe; and since 1890, and especially since the formation of the Dual Alliance, she had hoped that Great Britain could be weaned from her old dislike of alliances. But apart from the fact that her growing extra-European interests clashed with her wish for a British connection, her two aims were incompatible: an Anglo-German alliance would have forced Russia and France back to the Continent and faced Germany with the danger of a war with the Dual Alliance. Great Britain, on the other hand, her chief requirements being to safeguard her world position, had an interest in the balance of power in Europe and no interest in German hegemony there. In its consequences beyond Europe this, indeed, might prove more dangerous than the Dual Alliance. She had therefore been increasingly anxious since 1890 to avoid the European commitments to Germany and her allies on which Germany, in any alliance, was bound to insist. And by the time the situation in China had nevertheless induced Chamberlain to offer an alliance, Great Britain's previous attitude and her many difficulties with the Dual Alliance, Germany's improved relations with Russia and her recognition of the incompatibility of the two aims she had previously pursued, had all fused together to modify Germany's attitude as well. Her aim had become to revive Bismarck's system of agreements between Great Britain and Germany's Triple Alliance partners which did not commit Germany against Russia. When Chamberlain, anxious above all for help in China, proved as uninterested in the revival of the Mediterranean Agreements as Germany was in a direct alliance, she decided that she could afford to delay "until, on the one hand, German interests are jeopardised by Russia, and, on the other hand, England has come to realise that she cannot count on the support of Russia and France". Because reconciliation between Great Britain and the Dual Alliance was judged impossible and because Chamberlain had confessed that Great Britain wanted support, Germany felt she could accept a British alliance only when she needed one and only on her own terms.[1]

[1] Langer, *op. cit.* pp. 501–3; Garvin, *op. cit.* III, 273–4, 276–7; Morrow, I. F. D., "The Foreign Policy of Bülow", *Cambridge Hist. Jour.* IV, no. 1 (1932), pp. 70–2; *D.G.P.* XIV (i), nos. 3778, 3782–5, 3788–90, 3793–4, 3798–802.

It was this attitude on Germany's part which frustrated both Chamberlain's efforts in the Spring of 1898 and another suggestion he made in the following August. Realising that he could not expect unpaid German support against Russia, he then offered a defensive alliance by which each Power would help the other if it were attacked on two fronts. The Kaiser thought well of this suggestion: one of his comments on the earlier proposals had been that Chamberlain ought to show himself willing to extend the suggested alliance to Europe. But Bülow won the day with the argument that, by remaining independent of both Great Britain and Russia, "Your Majesty can be *arbiter mundi*".[1] On the other hand, even if Germany had been more forthcoming—and it is not easy to see why she should have been—Chamberlain's efforts would probably still have come to nothing. His proposals were made with the knowledge of his Cabinet colleagues;[2] it is another question how far they shared his views or would have gone along with him if Germany had responded. Balfour, like Salisbury, who returned at the end of April, was less confident than Chamberlain that Parliamentary approval for an alliance could be obtained.[3] Salisbury, apart from doubting its practicability, was convinced that an alliance with Germany was unnecessary and unwise. On 4 May, having made it clear to the German ambassador that the talks with Chamberlain should stop now that he had returned to the Foreign Office,[4] he publicly stated this opinion in the Albert Hall. "We know we shall maintain", he said, "against all comers that which we possess, and we know, in spite of the jargon about isolation, that we are amply competent to do it." A week later, though Chamberlain in the interval, in a speech at Birmingham, had denounced isolationism and advocated an alliance with Germany and the United States, he told the House of Lords that "our policy has not changed: we shall cultivate...the friendship of all the Powers with whom we come into contact".[5] But more revealing than any of Salisbury's remarks is the obstinacy with which he persisted in his efforts to reach an accommodation with France and Russia, despite the failure of his earlier attempts, when the chances of success seemed more remote than ever. It is this which provides the best evidence of his determination to resist Chamberlain's influence.

In the issues left outstanding after the Anglo-French negotiations of 1895–6, issues in which no progress had been made since the British advance to Dongola and the French annexation of Madagascar by way of retaliation in May 1896, the two years after the

---

[1] Langer, *op. cit.* pp. 527–8; Garvin, *op. cit.* III, 290 *seqq.*; *D.G.P.* XIV (i), nos. 3804–5, 3865, 3867; *B.D.* I, nos. 87, 122.

[2] Langer, *op. cit.* pp. 492–4, 503; Garvin, *op. cit.* III, 256 *seqq.*

[3] Garvin, *op. cit.* III, 278–80; *D.G.P.* XIV (i), nos. 3786, 3788, 3796.

[4] Garvin, *loc. cit.*; *Letters of Queen Victoria*, 3rd ser. III, p. 263; *D.G.P.* XIV (i), nos. 3797–801.

[5] Langer, *op. cit.* pp. 504–9; Garvin, *op. cit.* III, 282 *seqq.*

spring of 1898 were the period of greatest strain. In West Africa, where a commission appointed in 1896 to delimit French and British frontiers had failed in its work, local disputes produced an international crisis in February 1898.[1] In China, where Anglo-French relations had further deteriorated since the Port Arthur crisis, the race for concessions between the two countries was intense throughout 1898.[2] Mutual intransigence in these widely separated areas was the result of continued French discontent and continued British firmness on the central question of Egypt and the Nile; and the race for the Nile itself entered the final stage in the same year. The British advance to Khartoum began in the spring; Marchand reached Fashoda in September; and the outcome was a still more serious crisis in which war threatened for several months.[3] Russia was meanwhile penetrating into Manchuria, and Great Britain and Russia were involved in disputes about the control of the railways between Manchuria and Peking. More serious still for Great Britain was the growth of Russian influence at Peking; and she was threatened in the Yangtse Valley itself when, in the summer of 1898, Russia and France jointly secured the concession for the Peking-Hankow railway.[4] In 1899 the threat of Russian expansion and the dangers of Franco-Russian collaboration spread to Persia. The Indian Government resorted to strong measures to thwart a French attempt to lease a depot at Muscat in February;[5] Russian infiltration into Persia was uninterrupted from then on and caused ever increasing alarm.[6] And these dangers to British interests, in Africa, in the Far East and on the Indian frontier, were emphasised by the visit of the French Foreign Minister, Delcassé, to St Petersburg in August 1899, which publicised the strengthening of the Dual Alliance and the continued hostility of its members towards Great Britain.[7] At the outbreak of the South African War in October 1899 it seemed as if the threat from the Dual Alliance had never been greater and that all chance of reconciliation with France and Russia had disappeared.

These difficulties with the Dual Alliance could have been reduced if Salisbury had been prepared to retreat on major questions. But he continued to draw a firm line around those interests, particularly the Sudan, on which Great Britain must not give way. In the race for the Nile he never wavered from the argument that no Power other than Great Britain "has any claim to occupy any part of the Sudan". This was stressed in the instructions given to Kitchener before the advance to Khartoum, as it had been in reply to every French approach

[1] Hargreaves, loc. cit. pp. 76–7, 81–2, 92; Langer, op. cit. pp. 550–1.
[2] Langer, op. cit. pp. 475–6, 486–7.
[3] Ibid. chap. xvi.
[4] Ibid. pp. 584, 679–80; Joseph, op. cit. p. 337; B.D. I, no. 55.
[5] Langer, op. cit. pp. 642–3; Ronaldshay, op. cit. II, 45 seqq.; B.D. I, nos. 255–60.
[6] Langer, op. cit. pp. 752–3; B.D. IV, nos. 319–21.
[7] See below, pp. 530–2; Renouvin, loc. cit. pp. 301–3.

before the advance began;[1] on it he based his handling of the crisis that broke out when Marchand and Kitchener met at Fashoda. Brushing aside the legal arguments, which were as strong on the French as on the British side, he took his stand from the outset on the declaration that "by the military events of last week all the territories which were subject to the Khalifa passed by right of conquest to the British and Egyptian Governments".[2] In refusing to negotiate with France till Marchand had withdrawn, he needed none of the encouragement so freely given by the Press and the public, the Opposition and his own colleagues. On the contrary it was due more to his own preparations than to anything else that British opinion was unanimous and faced the crisis without a panic; that Russia and Germany refused to help France; that France, with force on Kitchener's side and herself unready to redress the local balance by general war, capitulated unconditionally for the first time in the dispute that had begun in 1882 by agreeing to withdraw Marchand on 2 November 1898.[3] A sense of timing always characterised Salisbury's foreign policy, as did the careful arrangement of British interests in a considered order of priority; and they never yielded a more marked success than in the Fashoda crisis.

Nor did Salisbury neglect British interests in China, though they ranked lower in his estimate than the achievement of monopoly on the Nile. His policy was still to try to maintain the Open Door in the spheres of influence of other Powers while accepting the establishment of such spheres so far as concessions were concerned and attempting to develop the Yangtse Valley as an exclusive British sphere from that point of view. It still proved impossible fully to succeed in either of these aims. But this does not hide the persistence he showed or the progress that was made. Great Britain did not come out second best in the race for Chinese concessions in 1898: she received nine compared with three by France, three by Russia and two by Germany. More important still, her victory at Fashoda, which restored her prestige after the Port Arthur crisis, as Salisbury's handling of the South African incident had compensated for his helplessness in the Armenian question, induced Russia, after months of wrangling, to accept a settlement in North China in April 1899. While Great Britain reciprocated north of the Great Wall, effectively recognising Russia's control of Manchuria, Russia abandoned her claims to the province of Chihli (or Pechili), south of the Wall, and recognised the Yangtse Valley as an exclusive British sphere for railway concessions. She still refused to go further and accept the British wish for equality of trade in all spheres, even when, in Hay's Open Door Note of

---

[1] Langer, *op. cit.* pp. 550–1; *Letters of Queen Victoria*, 3rd ser. III, 260.
[2] Kennedy, *op. cit.* pp. 288–91; *B.D.* I, no. 189.
[3] Giffen, M. B., *Fashoda, passim*; Riker, T. W., "A Survey of British Policy in the Fashoda Crisis", *Political Science Quarterly*, XLIV (March 1929), pp. 54–78; Langer, *op. cit.* pp. 552–63; *B.D.* I, nos. 182, 190–1, 196, 221 *seqq.*

September 1899, the United States at last espoused this principle for which Great Britain had struggled for so long. Russia's evasion made the Note inapplicable; Anglo-Russian friction in China was far from being at an end. But the new agreement was never violated until it was brought to an end in 1904; and France, Germany and Italy accepted Hay's Note. Great Britain, apart from losing no ground in China, had thus greatly improved her diplomatic position in China by the autumn of 1899.[1]

But if Salisbury had refused to give way on these issues, he had also remained as ready as ever to make concessions to the Dual Alliance when they could be made and as determined as ever to avoid provocation when they could not. Like the agreement with Russia in China, the settlement reached in the West African dispute with France in June 1898 was essentially a compromise. In the settlement of the Fashoda crisis in March 1899, though France was cut off from the Nile, Great Britain accepted boundaries which enabled France to satisfy her ambition of uniting her territories in north, west and central Africa into a homogeneous whole. Other members of his Government had been impatient with his attitude, as may be judged from the views and actions of Curzon in India on the Persian situation,[2] as well as of Chamberlain in the West African dispute,[3] and of Chamberlain and Balfour on the question of Morocco.[4] Chamberlain's group, in view of Salisbury's moderation in the West African quarrel, had feared in advance of the Fashoda crisis that he would not be firm on the Nile.[5] They had also been discontented with his flexible China policy, the keynote of which had been struck in his speech of May 1898. If this had announced his confidence in Great Britain's ability to defend her interests, it had also declared that, "on the other hand, we shall not be jealous if desolation and sterility are removed by the aggrandisement of a rival in regions in which our arms cannot extend".[6] Their views he had regarded as unnecessarily belligerent because, despite the difficulties, despite his own refusal to give way on major questions, he still hoped for an accommodation with the Dual Alliance in the end. He still hoped for this because of his aversion from the alternative of seeking refuge with Germany, which was again advocated by Chamberlain in public in December 1898[7] and in secret in November 1899.[8]

When the South African War broke out the struggle between Salisbury and the advocates of this second course was still undecided.

[1] Langer, *op. cit.* pp. 487–8, 680–3, 686–8; McCordock, *op. cit.* chap. iv and pp. 277–88, 291 *seqq.*; Joseph, *op. cit.* chaps. xii–xiv, xvii–xviii; Dallin, *op. cit.* pp. 59–60; Kent, P. H., *Railway Development in China*, pp. 55 *seqq.*; Dennis, *op. cit.* chap. viii.
[2] *B.D.* I, nos. 255–60; IV, nos. 319–21.
[3] Langer, *op. cit.* pp. 550–1, 555; Garvin, *op. cit.* III, chap. lv; *B.D.* I, chap. iv, pt. I.
[4] See below, pp. 531–2.
[5] Langer, *op. cit.* pp. 561 *seqq.*; Garvin, *op. cit.* III, 228–31.
[6] Langer, *op. cit.* pp. 504–5.   [7] *Ibid.* p. 570.
[8] See below, pp. 518–19.

On the one hand, his success in the issues he had chosen to defend suggested that his confidence had not been wholly misplaced in Great Britain's ability to defend her interests without German help. It had still not been accompanied, on the other hand, by any sign that a reconciliation with France and Russia could be realised, and it could be argued that it had destroyed all possibility of reconciliation. The question in the autumn of 1899 was whether Salisbury's policy would stand the test of the South African War or whether, since the Dual Alliance seemed as hostile as ever, this new embarrassment would force him to accept Chamberlain's solution.

But Salisbury had already acquired one major advantage in the struggle. Relations with Germany in the past eighteen months had made it more doubtful than before whether Chamberlain, any more than Salisbury, would accept German terms for an alliance, even if Germany were ready to offer terms. And they had made it more than doubtful whether Germany wanted an alliance.

Anglo-German relations had been closer in 1898-9 than they had been for several years. They had not become less embittered. The chief reason for this was that, while Great Britain had resented enforced concessions, Germany's rejection of Chamberlain's approaches in 1898 had been made with an eye to success in enforcing them. Bülow cannot be blamed for rejecting Chamberlain's approaches. In urging, however, that Germany should remain independent of both Great Britain and Russia, in arguing that she should abandon the idea of a Continental league to put pressure on Great Britain with which she had toyed since 1894, he had done so on the ground that she would thereby increase her chances of extracting colonial concessions from Great Britain pending Germany's decision to accept a British alliance on Germany's terms; and his interest in making the most of the situation was tactless and unwise.

The first product of this policy was the Anglo-German Agreement of August 1898 on the subject of Portugal's African colonies. Hearing that Great Britain was hoping to secure, in return for a loan to Portugal, some form of control at Delagoa Bay and in Portuguese East Africa, where arms were passing to the Boers, Germany protested and demanded a share of the spoils; and she accompanied her demand with the familiar threat of collaboration with France against independent British action at Delagoa Bay. The British Government had no choice but to succumb to pressure and sign an agreement with Germany. The Agreement was innocuous in itself: the two Powers agreed to make equal and simultaneous loans to Portugal, if Portugal approached either for help. It contained, however, a second convention and a secret note by which, if Portugal defaulted on her loans and it became impossible for her to maintain her colonies, they would oppose the intervention of a third Power and would each avoid making claims in the sphere of influence of the other. Germany's sphere was defined as the northern half of Portuguese East Africa and central Angola, Great Britain's as the southern half of East Africa and northern and southern Angola.[1]

By signing the secret clauses Great Britain made certain of detaching Germany from her previous interest in Delagoa Bay and from the Boer cause at a time when a conflict with the Boers was imminent; and she forestalled any surprise German move into other African territory in which she was interested. Only by avoiding their implementation, however, could she avoid a breach of faith with Portugal, to whom she was bound by ancient treaties, and a large expansion of German territory in Africa; and this is what Salisbury tried to do. While Germany expected him to help her bring about Portugal's financial collapse, he was soon helping Portugal and protecting her from German threats. In October 1898, when Portugal, suspecting the existence of secret clauses in the Anglo-German Agreement, refused a loan, Germany's resort to pressure in Lisbon brought forth a British protest. In May 1899, when Germany decided on a naval demonstration off the Portuguese coast, British ships appeared off Lisbon to prevent it. And when the South African War was about to begin, Portugal having refused to stop the passage of arms to the Transvaal unless Great Britain guaranteed her colonies, Salisbury accepted in October 1899 a secret Anglo-Portuguese declaration. Great Britain reaffirmed her obligation to maintain Portugal's integrity under the old treaties in return for a Portuguese promise not to let arms into Lourenço Marques and not to declare herself neutral in the South African War and thus prevent British ships from coaling in Lourenço Marques.[2] Salisbury's policy, culminating in this declaration, was not legally incompatible with the Anglo-German treaty. But it was contrary to the spirit of the earlier Agreement as Germany had been allowed to understand it; and it was no consolation to Germany, as it is no defence of Salisbury, to reflect that Great Britain had been forced into the treaty by Germany's insistence and forced out of it by Portugal's. She should have disowned it; her position was too precarious to enable her to do so.

On this same account Great Britain's hand was soon forced again by German insistence in the question of Samoa. Germany had wanted a partition of the Samoan Islands ever since three-Power Government by Great Britain, the United States and herself had been set up there in 1899. Great Britain, from regard for Australasian opinion and reluctance to yield to Germany, had always refused to consider

---

[1] Langer, *op. cit.* pp. 519–32; Garvin, *op. cit.* III, 309 *seqq.*; Dubois, P., "The Anglo-German Treaty of August 30, 1898", *Revue d'Histoire de la Guerre Mondiale*, XVII (1939), 232–46; *B.D.* I, chap. ii; *D.G.P.* XIV (i), chap. xcii.

[2] Dubois, *loc. cit.*; Bixler, *op. cit.* pp. 135 *seqq.*; Temperley, H., "British Secret Diplomacy from Canning to Grey", *Cambridge Hist. Jour.* VI, no. 1 (1935), pp. 17–20; *B.D.* I, nos. 94 *seqq.*; III, no. 8; VIII, p. 49, footnote; *D.G.P.* XIV (i), nos. 3873 *seqq.*; Langer, *op. cit.* pp. 624–6.

it. The suggestion, accompanied by the threat that Germany would secure her interests by other means if it were refused, was made again in August 1898, and again rejected, at a time when the British Government was already disturbed by the possible consequences in the Pacific of the outbreak of the Spanish-American War in April 1898. Wanting no Spanish territory itself, it was anxious to prevent the other European Powers from getting any; it helped to persuade the United States Government to take the Philippines in order to thwart German designs on them, just as, in 1897, it had already resisted German proposals for a protest against the projected American annexation of Hawaii.[1] In the winter of 1898–9, far from reconsidering the rejection of Germany's Samoan proposals, Salisbury, according to the Permanent Under-Secretary at the Foreign Office at the time, "did his best to rouse the opposition of the United States" to them; and Rhodes in March 1899 found Chamberlain as opposed to them as Salisbury. In the following summer, however, the approach of the South African War made capitulation to increasing German pressure inescapable. In June, when even Salisbury had granted that circumstances made it "desirable that the world should believe in an understanding between Germany and England",[2] the Kaiser refused an invitation to visit England until the Samoan dispute had been settled. Negotiations were therefore resumed and the invitation renewed; and Germany at last got her way in a treaty signed early in November. She received western Samoa, the United States took the eastern half; Great Britain, withdrawing altogether, was granted Tonga and the Johnson Islands and territory in West Africa in compensation.[3]

The settlement was welcomed in Germany, but the German public was told that a larger navy would be needed to maintain Germany's expanding world position. It was regretted in Great Britain, as in Australia and New Zealand.[4] And this uneasy conclusion reflected the deterioration of Anglo-German relations in the previous eighteen months. Great Britain's difficulties with the Dual Alliance and Salisbury's considerable success in meeting them had both contributed to this result. Great Britain's difficulties had tempted Germany to be ruthless in the application of pressure. Determined to make the most of her opportunities, she had not hesitated to resort to threatening "other combinations" if Great Britain did not give way; noting the contrast between Great Britain's readiness to make concessions to the

[1] Halévy, E., *History of the English People, 1896–1905*, pp. 44–5, 57; Langer, *op. cit.* pp. 517–19.

[2] Langer, *op. cit.* pp. 569–70; *Letters of Queen Victoria*, 3rd ser. III, 312, 321–5.

[3] Ellison, J. W., "The Partition of Samoa", *Pacific Hist. Rev.* VIII (1939), pp. 259–88; Brandenburg, *op. cit.* pp. 103 *seqq.*; Garvin, *op. cit.* III, 329 *seqq.*; Langer, *op. cit.* pp. 619–24; *Letters of Queen Victoria*, 3rd ser. III, 357–9, 375–9, 416, 424; *D.G.P.* XIV, nos. 4028, 4045–7, 4049 *seqq.*, 4072, 4074–6, 4079, 4081; *B.D.* I, nos. 127 *seqq.*, 133 *seqq.*, 141, 146 *seqq.*, 154.

[4] *C.H.B.E.* VII, pt. II, 210–12.

Dual Alliance and her disposition to haggle over Germany's demands, she had found in the negotiations fresh proof that an expansionist policy was hampered by the lack of a powerful navy.[1] The German attitude had strengthened Great Britain's long-standing distrust of Germany and her feeling that the German Government was using her difficulties to make demands where it had no right to interfere. Together with her successes, especially at Fashoda, which had released her from the need for the support of the Triple Alliance in Egypt, it had encouraged her to add to Germany's resentment by withstanding German demands even when her difficulties forced her temporarily to appear to fall in with them. Even Chamberlain had shared the growing dislike of German methods, despite his anxiety for a German alliance. "We pay blackmail to Germany," he had written during the Portuguese negotiations, "to induce her not to interfere where she has no right of interference." In the Samoan negotiations, when he was less ready to pay it, he had complained to Salisbury that "the policy of the German Government has always been one of undisguised blackmail".[2] What Chamberlain felt, all felt; it was in these months that it first became widely accepted in British Government circles that Germany, as Crowe was soon to argue, would always be "the professional blackmailer".[3]

If, therefore, there seemed to be a greater need than ever for an arrangement with Germany at the beginning of the South African War, there was less disposition in Great Britain to seek one. The wish to do so still persisted in some quarters on account of the danger from the Dual Alliance during the early months of the War. But it was further weakened when Chamberlain and Balfour made another approach to Germany during the Kaiser's visit to Windsor in November 1899. They again made it clear that, in their view, British isolation could not continue and that they preferred an alliance with Germany to any other solution. Because Salisbury, absent from the talks because his wife had just died, was still opposed to an alliance, they offered a looser, but still a general, arrangement by which Germany would have received British financial help in the development of the Baghdad railway and, in a division of Morocco into spheres of influence, parts of the Atlantic coast of Morocco. But the Germans were still uninterested, as in the spring of 1898 and for the same reasons, in a general understanding. The discussions came to nothing. More than that, their outcome only increased the mutual irritation produced by the earlier negotiations. Chamberlain's speech at Leicester at the end of the talks, advocating "a new Triple Alliance between the Teutonic race and the two great branches of the Anglo-Saxon race", was a piece of imprudence: though Bülow had encouraged him, he had not encouraged him to go so far. Bülow's

---

[1] See, especially, *D.G.P.* xiv, nos. 4074, 4076.
[2] Garvin, *op. cit.* iii, 315, 334.   [3] *B.D.* iii, 416, 419.

speech in the Reichstag in December 1899, after Chamberlain's speech had aroused widespread protest in Germany, was equally unfortunate. It pointedly ignored Chamberlain's remarks, and its chief object was to get Reichstag approval for the second Navy Bill. This, unlike, the first of 1898, which had been of an unambitious character considering the vast developments of Germany's colonial and commercial interests, was inspired by Tirpitz's theory that the German fleet must be so powerful that not even Great Britain could attack Germany without serious risk. It was to double the establishment so recently set up by the earlier Act and to create for the first time a high-seas battle fleet.[1]

Germany still showed herself consistently favourable to the British cause in the South African War, refusing to encourage the Boers, vetoing Russian and French suggestions for European intervention on their behalf.[2] But there were special reasons for this attitude. French and Russian preparedness to co-operate with Germany was qualified and far from being certain.[3] Tirpitz's fleet was not yet built. "I am not in a position to go beyond the strictest neutrality", wrote the Kaiser, "...In twenty years time when the Fleet is ready I can use another language."[4] Meanwhile it was advisable not only not to offend Great Britain but also to preserve her good will. Together with her achievement in the Samoan dispute, the outbreak of the war had encouraged Germany to expect that further concessions would be forthcoming from Great Britain even if a general settlement were refused by Germany. It was for this reason that, far from making any secret of her good offices, she drew attention to them, and that, though she had abandoned all serious thought of collaboration with the Dual Alliance, she continued to threaten this if rewards were not forthcoming or her interests appeared to be disregarded.[5] And, because she remained more interested in forcing concessions than in reaching a general settlement, she cancelled out the good effects on Great Britain that her neutrality might have reaped.

It was in China that Germany chiefly sought to make capital and most freely used her threats. The outbreak of the South African War was quickly followed by the Boxer rising of the spring of 1900 and the siege of the European legations at Peking.[6] When Russia suggested in August 1900, after the legations had been relieved, that the Powers should withdraw their troops, Germany, who had taken the lead in organising a common programme against the risings, suspected, like

[1] Langer, op. cit. pp. 654, 656–60; Garvin, op. cit. III, 496 seqq., 511 seqq.; Bülow, Memoirs, I, 369 seqq.; Asquith, H. H., Genesis of the War, pp. 21–5; D.G.P. xv, nos. 4396 seqq.
[2] Langer, op. cit. pp. 619, 662–7, 669–71.
[3] Taylor, A. J. P., The Struggle for Mastery in Europe, pp. 387–8.
[4] Woodward, E. L., Great Britain and the German Navy, p. 27.
[5] Ibid. pp. 654–6, 661–2; Garvin, op. cit. III, 492 seqq.; Bixler, op. cit. pp. 152 seqq.; B.D. I, nos. 304, 306; D.G.P. xv, nos. 4404, 4411, 4425, 4429, 4456; Lee, Sir Sidney, Edward VII, I, 769.
[6] Langer, op. cit. pp. 683–4, 692–4; McCordock, op. cit. pp. 336 seqq.

Great Britain and Japan, that Russia's object was to consolidate her occupation of Manchuria by placating the Chinese Government.[1] But Germany's immediate object was to use Great Britain's suspicion of Russia and her difficulties in South Africa to secure the neutralisation of the Yangtse Valley and prevent its establishment as an exclusive British sphere. She had already refused to recognise the Yangtse Valley as an exclusive British sphere for railway concessions in the spring of 1898, though gaining British recognition of similar German claims in Shantung in payment for her own acceptance of the British lease of Wei-hai-wei. In August 1899 she began to suggest that Great Britain must choose between claiming a monopoly of the Yangtse Valley, in which case she would have to defend it on her own against Russia and France, or accepting an Anglo-German partnership to safeguard it as an area of free trade.[2] While British public opinion, like the Japanese Government, concentrated on the Russian danger, the British Government attached more importance to the threat from Germany. Manchuria, where, in any case, its aim was not to deny Russia's special position but only to reserve the Open Door, was less important than the Yangtse Valley. And though its aim in the Yangtse Valley was not to destroy the Open Door but to safeguard its own special position in the matter of concessions against the infiltration of German firms, it still disliked the German suggestions, which implied that, while Germany should remain free to establish a monopoly in Shantung and Russia should remain free to establish a monopoly in Manchuria, Germany and Great Britain should become jointly responsible for preventing the establishment of a British monopoly in the Yangtse Valley. It seemed imperative, on the other hand, to guard against the danger that Germany would join Russia in a scramble for territory in China while Britain was engaged in South Africa; and it was for this reason that the British Government accepted the negotiations which, on the basis of Germany's proposals and under German pressure, produced the Anglo-German Convention of October 1900. The two Powers agreed that "the open door should be applied in all Chinese territory" so far as they could "exercise influence"; undertook "to direct their policy towards maintaining undiminished the territorial condition of the Chinese Empire"; and, "in case of another Power making use of complications in China to obtain...territorial advantages", reserved their right "to come to a preliminary understanding as to the eventual steps to be taken for the preservation of their own interests".

This Convention was widely regarded at the time as a futile

---

[1] Langer, op. cit. pp. 695–9; Dallin, op. cit. pp. 63–5.

[2] Kawai, loc. cit. pp. 413–22; Joseph, op. cit. chap. xiv; D.G.P. xiv (i), nos. 3760–1, 3763, 3769, 3772, 3774–5; xvi, nos. 4533, 4590, 4701, 4707, 4712; B.D. ii, nos. 8; China, no. 1 (1899): Parl. Pap. 1899, cix [C. 9131], pp. 4–6, 82–3, 91, 192, 209–11, 214–15; China, no. 1 (1900): Parl. Pap. 1900, cv [Cd. 93], pp. 14–18, 118–21, 175–80.

British attempt to enlist German support against Russia in Manchuria; it has usually been so regarded since.[1] Germany was certainly able to explain its publication to Russia as being directed solely against British interests in the Yangtse Valley; and Russia, when asked to subscribe to its principle, could interpret it as being restricted to maintaining the Open Door in the German and British spheres of influence. But Great Britain had known that Germany, throughout the negotiations, had refused to include Manchuria in its scope. She had signed it, despite the exclusion of Manchuria, because Salisbury's chief object had been to guard against the danger of a German move, as when making the agreement about the Portuguese colonies, while at the same time evading Germany's demand for a share in the Yangtse concessions. He succeeded in both aims. The Convention contained Germany's agreement to maintain the Open Door in Shantung. Germany in return forestalled a supposed British attempt to destroy the Open Door in the Yangtse Valley; but Salisbury had never intended to bring that to an end, only to preserve the area, as he did preserve it, by making the Convention so vague as to be inapplicable, as an exclusive British sphere from the point of view of concessions.[2]

Thus, if one development during the first year of the South African War was ever-growing British distrust of Germany, another was the slow discovery that Great Britain could still hold her own against German pressure, if she was not even freer to resist it, since her withdrawal from the Straits and her success in placing her occupation of Egypt and the Sudan on a military basis. Apart from thwarting Germany in the China Convention, Salisbury had still been able to avoid the execution of the Anglo-German Portuguese treaty of 1898. At the same time, nothing had come of the much-discussed anti-British Continental league of Germany and the Dual Alliance; and the dreaded contingencies of a Franco-Russian frontal attack or major diversion, while Great Britain was engaged in South Africa, had not materialised. Salisbury had always calculated that France and Russia would be unlikely to conclude an arrangement with Germany which, by strengthening her, would ultimately weaken themselves. He had not embarked on the South African War before concluding that France, after Fashoda and on account of the Dreyfus case, and Russia, because of financial distress, were themselves unlikely to go beyond modest exploitations of Great Britain's distraction.[3] Even more than Fashoda, the first year of the War, by confirming the accuracy of these calculations, was a vindication of his policy which few could overlook. France had taken the opportunity, it is true, to

[1] Penson, L. M., "The New Course in British Foreign Policy", *Trans. R. Hist. Soc.* xxv (1943), pp. 138 *seqq.*; Taylor *op. cit.* p. 392–3.

[2] Kawai, *loc. cit.* pp. 422–4; Langer, *op. cit.* pp. 700–3; *B.D.* ii, nos. 1, 8, 12, 17, 20–1, 34, 38; *D.G.P.* xvi, nos. 4617, 4721, 4732, 4744–7, 4766.

[3] Langer, *op. cit.* p. 618; *D.G.P.* xv, no. 4374.

expand into Morocco,[1] and Russia to increase her influence in Afghanistan and Persia[2] as well as in Manchuria. But there had been less inclination in Great Britain than before the War to criticise Salisbury's refusal to make an issue out of what he regarded as minor questions, both because much worse had been expected of the Dual Alliance and because much better had been expected of Germany.

Nor was this fact, that the Cabinet, on all these grounds, was less divided about the merits of his policy than at any time since the Port Arthur crisis, the only development that had taken place in Salisbury's favour when, towards the end of 1900, he retired from the Foreign Office. Changes had also begun in the relations between the Powers which, if not the result of his policy, were at least a reward for his patience and a further justification of the course he had pursued. The so-called interpenetration of the European alliance system, which had been so dangerous and inhibiting to Great Britain because the two Alliances had not been opposed to each other, and especially in the shape of the Russo-German *entente* since 1893, was in some respects coming to an end by 1900. Distrust between Russia and Germany had first revealed itself in Germany's dislike of the Tsar's peace move of August 1898, which had led to the Hague Disarmament Conference of May 1899, and in Russia's suspicion of Germany's obstructive behaviour during the Conference.[3] The danger of a clash between Russian and German interests in the Near East, brought into existence by Germany's growing interest in the Baghdad railway scheme since the end of 1898, had first emerged in a quarrel at the end of 1899. Germany, ignoring Russia's protests at her infiltration into Turkey and even Russia's threat to reach an agreement with Great Britain against it, had refused to give Russia an assurance that she would receive Constantinople and the Straits in the event of Turkey's collapse; Russia had decided to oppose the grant of all future concessions to Germany in Turkey.[4] Nor had Germany, herself unable to suppress a growing dislike of Russian activity in Manchuria after the Boxer rising, concluded the China Convention of 1900 with Great Britain without adding to Russia's distrust.[5] The danger that Germany would clash with both of them in the Far East, brought into existence by her organisation of a sphere of influence in Shantung, between the Russian and the British spheres, since 1897, could not always be avoided. And if Russia had thus become more disposed to strengthen the Dual Alliance

---

[1] Langer, *op. cit.* p. 667; *B.D.* II, nos. 304, 307.

[2] Langer, *op. cit.* pp. 667–9; *B.D.* II, nos. 376–7.

[3] Langer, *op. cit.* pp. 591, 600–1; Albertini, L., *The Origins of the War of 1914*, I, 107–9; *D.G.P.* XIII, nos. 3540–8; XV, nos. 4217, 4222, 4258–60, 4262.

[4] Langer, *op. cit.* pp. 629–42; Earle, E. M., *Turkey, the Great Powers and the Bagdad Railway, passim*; *D.G.P.* XIV, nos. 3982, 4015–25.

[5] Dallin, *op. cit.* pp. 65–6.

against Germany, her chances had declined of reviving against Great Britain the Alliance, which had reached a low ebb as an anti-British force during the Fashoda crisis.

Since 1896 France and Italy had been seeking additional re-assurance in a *rapprochement*; they concluded in December 1900 an agreement that gave France a free hand in Morocco in return for a free hand for Italy in Tripoli.[1] Italy's wish for friendship with Great Britain combined with France's wish for friendship with Italy to weaken Russia's chances of reviving the Dual Alliance as an anti-British weapon.[2] When the Dual Alliance had been strengthened during Delcassé's visit to St Petersburg in 1899, Great Britain had naturally feared that it had been strengthened against herself.[3] But the main reason for the visit had been Franco-Russian fear of the disintegration of Austria-Hungary, which had been in the throes of a constitutional crisis since 1896; and the main result had been to commit France more closely, if still inconclusively, to Russia in the Balkans. The Dual Alliance was further extended, and this time, admittedly, against Great Britain, in the summer of 1900 in negotiations in which the French and Russian Chiefs of Staff arranged for the first time, if only provisionally, to support each other in a war against Great Britain. But it was never again to regain the efficiency against British interests that it had possessed while it had been informal in this respect.[4] And if one reason for this was the rift between Russia and Germany and another the *rapprochement* between Italy and France, a third was the fact that France herself, though unable to abandon the Dual Alliance, had become since the Fashoda crisis more anxious than ever before for reconciliation with Great Britain.[5]

It must be supposed that Salisbury was aware, if incompletely, of these changes, which foreshadowed so closely the future development of international relations and conformed so closely to the objectives of his policy since 1895. In the spring of 1899 he had told the German ambassador that the day of alliances was over, that international relations were becoming a matter of agreements between States with common, or at least not contradictory, interests.[6] Others in England may also have begun to realise that his persistence was being rewarded; and there was certainly less confidence in 1900 than in 1898 in the merits as well as in the feasibility of the alternative policy of alliance with Germany. But if, when he left the Foreign Office, his Cabinet was less divided than before, it was still not united.

---

[1] Langer, *op. cit.* pp. 295–6, 592–6, 736–7; Albertini, *op. cit.* i, pp. 104–7; Anderson, E. N., *The First Moroccan Crisis*, chap. ii; *D.D.F.* 2me sér. ii, nos. 1, 17, 59, 88.

[2] Langer, *op. cit.* p. 294; Glanville, J. L., *Italy's Relations with England, 1896–1905, passim.*

[3] See above, p. 512.

[4] Langer, *op. cit.* pp. 576–7, 596–9; Albertini, *op. cit.* i, 110–11; Renouvin, *loc. cit.* pp. 301–4; *D.D.F.* 2me sér. iii, 601–14.

[5] Langer, *op. cit.* pp. 576–7; see below, pp. 531–3.

[6] *Ibid.* p. 592; *D.G.P.* xiv, no. 4044.

If his policy was beginning to be justified, it had not yet achieved any concrete results. The hostility of the Dual Alliance, though not more dangerous than before, was still not less; and since the possibility of reconciliation with France and Russia seemed as remote as ever, the temptation to reach a settlement with Germany, though Germany was more than ever distrusted, still persisted in some quarters. In another crisis, occurring before these changes in the relations between the Powers had been consolidated, it would rise again to the surface before being laid aside.

VI

The Manchurian crisis came to a head when Russia, in order to regularise her occupation of North China, presented an agreement for China's signature in February 1901. In February and March the Japanese Government, which had already approached Great Britain in January with suggestions for collaboration against Russia, asked the British Government to join it in advising China not to sign and in opposing Russia if she persisted. The British Government would still have preferred to reach an accommodation with Russia which recognised her special position in Manchuria while restricting her control there; but Russia's behaviour made this impossible. In these circumstances it was afraid that, if it refused Japan's request, Japan would reach an agreement with Russia which would make the British position in the Far East untenable; and it hoped that by supporting Japan it would still keep Russia in check. To accept the request, on the other hand, in view of the recent Franco-Russian negotiations and Japan's evident determination to fight Russia if she could find support against France, might be to risk war with the Dual Alliance while Great Britain was still occupied with the Boers. Lansdowne, who had succeeded Salisbury at the Foreign Office, decided to try to neutralise France before reaching a decision in Japan's favour, and to do so by enlisting Germany's support. Late in February and again early in March he asked the German Government whether it would join Great Britain in a declaration to France that the two Powers would stay neutral in a Russo-Japanese quarrel if France would also do so. He referred to the Anglo-German China Convention of 1900 when making this suggestion. The German Government refused to consider it; and in a speech on 15 March Bülow emphasised that the Convention had been limited to the Yangtse Valley and was "in no sense concerned with Manchuria".[1]

This speech caused public consternation in Great Britain, where the Convention had never been properly understand by the public. With less justification than the public, British ministers supported the charge of German bad faith. But their chief ground for doing so was

[1] Langer, *op. cit.* pp. 711–25; *B.D.* II, nos. 32–5, 42, 45, 47, 50–6; III, pp. 412–13, 426 *seqq.*; *D.G.P.* XVI, nos. 4765, 4781, 4819–32.

not the fact that they had forgotten that Germany had excluded Manchuria from the outset. Bülow, himself made anxious by the changing situation, had previously seemed to be moving towards Japan and Great Britain. He had known that Great Britain was reluctant to commit herself to Japan without being joined by Germany; he had wanted her to do so. He had begun to think that Germany's interests were at last being "jeopardised by Russia" and that it might now be wise to accept the general agreement with Great Britain he had hitherto refused. If he could persuade Great Britain to join Japan without joining her himself, Russia might, of course, be kept in order without the need for Germany to oppose her; but if it became necessary to take precautions because Russia continued to be threatening, Great Britain might also be more ready to renew her alliance offer to Germany and to accept Germany's terms if she were already committed to Japan.[1] In February, therefore, he had joined Japan and Great Britain in urging China to reject an agreement with Russia, and had hinted to those Powers that Germany was not committed to Russia and would remain neutral if they clashed with her. Beyond neutrality, however, he dared not go when requested to do so: the Far East was not worth a war with France and Russia.[2] The contrast between Bülow's earlier behaviour and his speech of 15 March finally convinced the British Government not so much that Germany would never allow herself to be involved against Russia, for it had always been doubtful whether she would do so, as that her object was to get the British Government to tie itself to Japan and quarrel with Russia in order to bring it into Berlin's orbit on Berlin's terms. It was for this reason that the speech put an end to all serious possibility of Anglo-German co-operation.[3]

It is true that Lansdowne again asked Eckardstein on 18 March, in spite of Bülow's speech, whether Germany would help to hold France in check in the event of a Russo-Japanese conflict. This talk, moreover, gave rise to more prolonged Anglo-German alliance negotiations than any that had previously taken place. But these negotiations, if they show that Germany was at last ready to accept an alliance, though still only on her own terms, also show that the British Government had already concluded that its policy must be conducted independently of Germany. They would not have taken place if Eckardstein had not misled both Lansdowne and his own Government into thinking that the other was prepared to offer "a long-term defensive alliance". Despite this misunderstanding, Chamberlain took no part in them. The opening of the Manchurian crisis had led him in January 1901 to repeat his offer of a German

---

[1] Langer, *op. cit.* p. 739; *D.G.P.* XVII, nos. 4981, 4983, 4993, 5174; Bülow, *Memoirs*, I, 301.

[2] Langer, *op. cit.* pp. 719–21; *D.G.P.* XVI, nos. 4810–17; XVII, nos. 4988–91.

[3] Langer, *op. cit.* pp. 771–2; Kennedy, *op. cit.* pp. 334–6.

alliance; he had received from Bülow an encouraging reply.[1] But he had been finally disillusioned by Bülow's subsequent behaviour. The same disillusionment accounted for Lansdowne's view, at the beginning of the negotiations, that "when each side comes, if it ever does, to formulate its terms, we shall break down"; and Lansdowne's scepticism was not reduced when he learned from the German ambassador in May what Eckardstein had conceded since March— that Germany would consider no arrangement in which her Triple Alliance partners were not included.

Lansdowne still had two drafts prepared in the Foreign Office on this basis. The arrangement they outlined was that if Germany, Austria or Italy were attacked by France and Russia, or Italy by France and Spain, Great Britain would go to their assistance; and that, if Great Britain were attacked by two Powers, the Triple Alliance would come to her rescue. It was these drafts that provoked Salisbury's intervention. Salisbury in a memorandum of 29 May doubted whether the bargain, even if practicable in the state of German and British public opinion, would be to Great Britain's advantage; and he again opposed an alliance as unnecessary. Great Britain had never yet suffered from her isolation: "it would hardly be wise to incur novel and most onerous obligations in order to guard against a danger in whose existence we have no historical reason for believing."[2] It is questionable, however, whether Salisbury's views did more than confirm Lansdowne in the opinion that, rather than reply to Germany, he should await the official German offer which he had been led to expect but which never came. And if Salisbury's memorandum put an end to the negotiations, it was chiefly because the most pro-German members of the Cabinet now had grave doubts, not only about Germany's reliability, but also about the wisdom of accepting her terms.

These doubts were quickly reinforced. In the summer and autumn of 1901, while Germany retained her own suspicions of the effects of a British alliance on her relations with Russia and held to her view that Great Britain must make the approaches and accept German terms, the circulation in Germany of stories of British atrocities in South Africa provoked Chamberlain to make a public complaint that further embittered relations. The renewed bitterness led the British Press to advocate more seriously than ever before a *rapprochement* with France and Russia.[3] And such a *rapprochement* seemed more feasible than ever before. It was in these months that it became generally realised in Government circles that the South African War would end without the threatening diversions by other Powers that

---

[1] Langer, *op. cit.* pp. 717, 741; *D.G.P.* xvii, nos. 4979–85.

[2] Langer, *op. cit.* pp. 728–42; *B.D.* ii, nos. 77, 79, 81, 85–7, 89; *D.G.P.* xvii, nos. 4994, 4996–7, 5001, 5003 *seqq.*; Lord Newton, *Lord Lansdowne*, pp. 215 *seqq.*

[3] Langer, *op. cit.* pp. 774–6; *History of 'The Times'*, iii, 323, 335–43, 346–7.

had long been feared; that the danger of a Continental league against Great Britain had passed away; that Great Britain, having regained her balancing position between the Dual and Triple Alliances, could have the support of the other in the event of a war with either, and could have it without concluding formal alliances in advance; that it was Germany, not Great Britain, who was losing the freedom to choose her friends.[1] These were positive grounds, to reinforce the negative obstacles of reluctance by Germany and distrust of Germany, for abandoning all wish for a German alliance. It was on them that the British Government at last became united behind Salisbury's opinion that an alliance with Germany, apart from being unattainable and unwelcome, was unnecessary.

In November 1901, though arguing against Salisbury that "we may push too far the argument that, because we have survived in the past in spite of our isolation, we need have no misgivings in the future", Lansdowne agreed that the difficulties in the way of an alliance with Germany were "virtually insuperable". It was he who first took up the threads with Germany that had been dropped in May; but all he was prepared to offer the German ambassador in December 1901 was "a declaration of common policy, of a desire to maintain close diplomatic relations", similar to the Mediterranean Agreements of 1887 and straying beyond them only in the direction of an understanding for the maintenance of freedom of traffic in the Persian Gulf,[2] where Russian activity had begun to cause anxiety.[3] Great Britain, he added, could not risk "involving herself and her great colonies in disputes which do not concern her" by joining the Triple Alliance. The ambassador refused the offer: for Germany it was "all or nothing". Nor had Lansdowne expected any other reply. His only reason for renewing the discussions of the previous spring and for making this last approach was the fear that Germany, in view of the earlier confusion, would otherwise accuse him of breaking off the negotiations "in a discourteous and unfriendly manner"; and he was particularly anxious on this score because he had meanwhile almost completed the negotiation of an alliance with Japan of which Germany must soon learn and by which "we have virtually admitted that we do not wish to continue to stand alone".[4]

VII

The Manchurian crisis had not waited on the Anglo-German exchanges; and, though the Anglo-Japanese negotiations had been long drawn out, what had held them up had not been Great Britain's

---

[1] Langer, *op. cit.* pp. 771–2; Brandenburg, *op. cit.* pp. 176–81; *B.D.* II, no. 91; *History of 'The Times'*, III, 347–8.

[2] Langer, *op. cit.* pp. 772–3; *B.D.*, II, nos. 92–4; *D.G.P.* XVII, no. 5030.

[3] See below, p. 528.   [4] *B.D.* II, nos. 92–3.

hope of committing Germany with her, which had been abandoned by April 1901, but the fact that the Cabinet would still have preferred an arrangement with Russia to an alliance with Japan. In April Lansdowne had informed Russia that he was still ready to recognise her special position in Manchuria.[1] Another approach had been made to her in the summer of 1901, when Russia had withdrawn her proposed treaty with China, though keeping her troops in Manchuria, and when her activity in Persia, including the establishment of consulates on the Persian Gulf, had joined her occupation of Manchuria as another source of British anxiety. But this had also come to nothing, if only because Russia's demand for a Gulf port was unacceptable. "I agree, and have long agreed," wrote Salisbury in September, "in the expediency of a closer friendship with Russia...But the possibility...is constantly becoming more questionable...I wish it were otherwise; but wishing is no good." "We would have been glad", was Lansdowne's comment later on, "to make other arrangements, but we always found Russia's door closed."[2] On these grounds the British Government had already begun to accept the desirability of a Japanese alliance in principle in July; at the end of that month Lansdowne, resuming the talks with the Japanese minister on his own initiative, had told him that he would be ready to discuss an alliance at any time.[3]

By October he had become anxious to conclude one because Japan had then hesitated between the alternatives of a settlement with Russia and an alliance with Great Britain, so that a Japanese alliance had come to seem the only way of averting a Russo-Japanese understanding.[4] After the middle of October there had been further delay because Japan had still professed to be undecided, in order to get British acceptance of her terms, and because the British Government had tried, though unsuccessfully, to get the best possible terms in these adverse circumstances. In particular, it would have liked to extend the alliance to India, when Japan wanted to restrict it to the Far East, and to draft it so as to prevent the absorption of Korea by any Power, whereas Japan's aim was to obtain freedom of action in Korea. Salisbury, Lansdowne and Chamberlain had all disliked Japan's conditions; they finally accepted them because of Japan's continued negotiations in St Petersburg and Paris.[5]

The Anglo-Japanese Alliance, signed on 30 January 1902, was limited to the Far East: its purpose was to uphold the integrity of

[1] B.D. II, no. 99.
[2] Langer, op. cit. pp. 753–9; Russell, op. cit. pp. 282–3; Newton, op. cit. pp. 215 seqq.; B.D. II, no. 131; D.D.F. 2me sér., I, no. 243; II, no. 81.
[3] Langer, op. cit. pp. 748–51; The Secret Memoirs of Count Hayashi, pp. 126–32; B.D. II, nos. 102–3.
[4] Langer, op. cit. pp. 747–8; Hayashi, op. cit. pp. 119–32.
[5] Langer, op. cit. pp. 759–61; Hayashi, op. cit. pp. 133–67; Newton, op. cit. p. 222; B.D. II, nos. 105, 107–10.

China and Korea and to maintain the Open Door in those areas. But it also gave Japan a free hand in Korea; for in the clauses by which each Power undertook to remain neutral if the other was at war with a third for this purpose, and to join the other if it was at war with two Powers, Japan evaded any obligation to consult Great Britain in advance of taking action.[1] In a separate note attached to the treaty Great Britain made a third concession by accepting Japan's demand for a pledge that each of the Powers would maintain a Far Eastern fleet at least equal to that of any third Power. On this account, instead of making possible an immediate redistribution of the British Navy, the Alliance made it difficult for Great Britain to increase the Home Fleet at the expense of the China squadron.[2] In signing the Alliance she thus did more than abandon her insistence on isolation, on those "musty formulas and old-fashioned superstitions" against which Lansdowne appealed when defending it in the House of Lords.[3] As a result of Russian intransigence in the Far East, which had become more disturbing during her trial in South Africa, and of her alienation from all the Great Powers in Europe, which Japan had been able to exploit, she gave up these things on apparently unfavourable terms.

But if, from one point of view, the Alliance was disadvantageous, its acceptance a recognition of the failure of Salisbury's policy of co-operation without alliances, from another it was a sign that Great Britain's freedom of manœuvre, which Salisbury had always sought to recover, was being regained. In the summer of 1901 she had decided both that she could accept an alliance with Japan and that she could do without an alliance with Germany; and the two decisions had been interconnected. The decision to dispense with Germany had resulted from a growing confidence in her world position; the same growth of confidence had enabled her to conclude that she could accept an alliance with Japan without German collaboration and without the fear that dreaded commitments to Germany or the other European Powers must necessarily follow. Though technically it marked the end of the British policy of isolation, the Alliance in fact testified to Great Britain's growing ability to maintain that policy at its important point, where it involved aloofness from the balance of power in Europe. And if it was to some extent the outcome of a new sense of freedom, its conclusion added to British freedom of action by its immediate and longer-term effects.

Japan had retained freedom of action in Korea; but had agreed not to enter into separate agreements with other Powers without consulting Great Britain. The publication of the Alliance, together

---

[1] Langer, *op. cit.* pp. 761–71, 776–8; Hayashi, *op. cit.* pp. 139–95; Newton, *op. cit.* pp. 228 *seqq.*; *B.D.* II, nos. 112–13, 125 *seqq.*

[2] Langer, *op. cit.* p. 772; Marder, *op. cit.* pp. 427–31.

[3] Langer, *op. cit.* p. 779; Temperley, *loc. cit.* pp. 21–2; *Hansard*, 4th ser. CII, 1174 *seqq.*

with the declared opposition of the United States to concessions to Russia in Manchuria in February 1902,[1] forced Russia in April 1902 to agree conditionally to withdraw from Manchuria within eighteen months.[2] Whereas a Russo-Japanese settlement in North China would have diverted Russia against the British line of defence in Persia and on the North-West Frontier, the Anglo-Japanese Alliance also relieved the pressure on this line. Great Britain was at once able to announce, in January 1902, that she would not concede to Russia a port on the Persian Gulf or economic and political privileges in Southern Persia;[3] within twelve months the Government of India felt able to propose an expedition to Tibet to put an end to a boundary dispute that had vexed it for a decade and to Russian infiltration that had begun in 1901.[4] If the Alliance did not make possible an immediate redistribution of British naval forces, it raised the Anglo-Japanese fleet to unquestioned superiority over the combined squadrons of Russia, France and Germany and thus put an end to the dangerous situation in which, since 1895, Great Britain had found it increasingly difficult to maintain equality even with the Far Eastern squadrons of the Dual Alliance.[5] And the change in the Far Eastern balance, of which this was one illustration, was soon to have wider repercussions. By embarrassing France it was to complete the slow process by which, especially since Fashoda, she had been concluding that she must seek a reconciliation with Great Britain. By isolating Russia in the Far East it was to pave the way to her eventual acceptance of a Russo-British accommodation.

VIII

If only because a settled policy was more than ordinarily difficult to pursue in the shifting state of relations between the Powers after the beginning of 1902, the British Government did not assume that the Japanese Alliance, though it had been rendered unavoidable by Great Britain's failure to come to terms with the Dual Alliance, had made reconciliation with France and Russia impossible or undesirable. But neither did it assume that the Japanese Alliance, of which Germany was informed in advance, implied the estrangement of Great Britain and Germany; while the Alliance itself and the improvement in Great Britain's position made it less willing to make sacrifices, less anxious to take the initiative, to bring about reconciliation with the Dual Alliance. What was needed, then, if Great Britain and the Dual Alliance were to come to terms, was a change of heart in France

---

[1] Langer, *op. cit.* pp. 780–1.
[2] *Ibid.* pp. 781–2; Dallin, *op. cit.* p. 74.
[3] Langer, *op. cit.* pp. 758–9; *B.D.* IV, no. 321 a; *Hansard*, 4th ser. CI, 574 *seqq.*, 599 *seqq.*, 609 *seqq.*, 615 *seqq.*
[4] *History of 'The Times'*, III, 396; Dallin, *op. cit.* p. 43.
[5] Marder, *op. cit.* pp. 238–40, 302–9, 429.

and Russia. Partly because of the Japanese Alliance, though it was
not an intended result of that move, in France, though not in Russia,
such a change took place at once.

Up to the beginning of 1902, Delcassé, the Foreign Minister who
brought the change about, had been an advocate of the tightening of
the Dual Alliance; except that he was opposed to further annexations
in Indo-China, he was as determined as any of his predecessors on
French colonial expansion. In April 1901, during another visit to
Russia, he had approved the protocol drawn up by the Chiefs of
Staff in the previous summer for joint action if war was imposed on
the Dual Alliance by Great Britain alone or by Great Britain aided
by the Triple Alliance; as late as December 1901 the Quai d'Orsay
had been considering a naval accord to supplement this military
arrangement.[1] During the Fashoda crisis, on the other hand, he had
shown signs of wanting a reconciliation with Great Britain; and it is
probable that, in subsequently extending the Dual Alliance against
her, he had still wanted this but, being aware that Anglo-German
and Anglo-Japanese negotiations were taking place, had feared the
worst and felt obliged to take precautions against it. In any case,
when the Anglo-Japanese Alliance brought nearer the danger of a
Russo-Japanese clash in the Far East and pointed to the possibility
that France and Great Britain might be involved on opposite sides,
he was in an embarrassing position. Russia wanted to retaliate with
a declaration by herself and France, and if possible Germany, that
they would concert measures to safeguard their interests: Delcassé
was anxious to avoid such a step. Because he dared not desert Russia,
he agreed in March 1902 to an announcement that Russia and France
reserved their right to take counsel together in the event of any threat
to their positions in China. But this was no more than a demonstration. Russia, whose suggestion had been rejected by Germany, was
still left with no alternative but to promise to withdraw from Manchuria.[2] And while the change in the Far Eastern balance was thus
causing Delcassé alarm, the more so in view of the new commitments
to Russia and because of France's decline as a naval Power, which
was making her increasingly reluctant to contemplate fleet actions
against Great Britain,[3] another element in Delcassé's policy was
similarly turning him towards a settlement with Great Britain.

Cut off from the Nile since the retreat from Fashoda, the French
Government had become intent on the absorption of Morocco.
In June 1901 Delcassé had even approached Germany with the
suggestion of co-operation there. This had come to nothing.[4] But he
had also continued negotiations with Italy since the Franco-Italian

---

[1] Langer, *op. cit.* pp. 761–2; Halévy, *op. cit.* p. 400; *D.D.F.* 2me sér. I, nos. 310, 399,
435, 447, 500; III, appendix, pp. 601 *seqq.*; Renouvin, *loc. cit.* pp. 303–4.
[2] Langer, *op. cit.* pp. 780–1; *D.D.F.* 2me sér. II, nos. 97, 103, 110, 117, 129, 138, 145;
D.G.P. xviii, no. 5050.
[3] Marder, *op. cit.* pp. 468–72, 486.   [4] *D.G.P.* xviii (ii), no. 5871.

agreement of December 1900 and, in an exchange of letters in June 1902 which also contained a more precise Morocco-Tripoli agreement, he made France freer to move in Morocco by at last detaching Italy from her obligation in the Triple Alliance to help Germany in a Franco-German war.[1] Italy's agreement to give France freedom of action in Morocco, however, like that of Spain, with whom negotiations were also taking place, though less successfully,[2] was unimportant beside the probable opposition of Great Britain to any French move. It was with this problem in mind, as well as under the influence of the Anglo-Japanese Alliance, that in August 1902, after tentative soundings in London since the previous February, Delcassé submitted to Lansdowne proposals for the partition of Morocco between France and Spain in such terms as to suggest that, in return for British agreement, he would accept a general settlement of colonial disputes on the basis of a Morocco-Egypt bargain.[3] Salisbury had just resigned the premiership when this offer, a reward for all his patience, was received.

If the British Government did not take up the offer at once, it was not because it was not interested in the possibility of reconciliation which French willingness to make concessions, and especially in Egypt, seemed to open up. It was divided, however, about one of the difficulties that stood in the way of an immediate bargain and hesitant about another. Great Britain had the largest share of Moroccan trade; among her trading interests and among the British colony in Morocco there was considerable opposition to French designs on Morocco.[4] Some members of the Government shared this attitude: for this reason Lansdowne assured Moroccan interests in October 1902 that France would not be given a free hand there and in November 1902 Balfour, the new Prime Minister, warned France in his Guildhall speech that her Moroccan policy involved a danger to peace.[5] But the Foreign Office had already abandoned the idea of a Moroccan settlement with Germany, which Chamberlain had pressed and Germany had rejected more than once since 1899, in the summer of 1901, together with the wish for a German alliance. The suggestion had been made to Germany for the last time, and again rejected, in July 1901.[6] In the same summer Lansdowne had also rejected an offer from the Sultan of Morocco which would have given Great Britain a virtual monopoly of the country.[7] A bargain with France

---

[1] Albertini, *op. cit.* I, 106–7, 127–32; Anderson, *op. cit.* chaps. ii and iii: *D.D.F.* 2me sér. II, nos. 168, 235, 329, 340 and pp. 695–9.

[2] Langer, *op. cit.* p. 737; *D.D.F.* 2me sér. no. 483.

[3] Halévy, *op. cit.* pp. 404–5; Manger, J. B., "Notes sur la Crise Marocaine de 1905", *Revue d'Histoire de la Guerre Mondiale*, XII (1934), pp. 315–16; *D.D.F.* 2me sér. II, 437; *B.D.* II, 264.

[4] Halévy, *op. cit.* pp. 402–3; *History of 'The Times'*, III, 349–50, 409–13, 825, 828–9.

[5] Halévy, *op. cit.* pp. 405–6; *B.D.* II, no. 328.

[6] Langer, *op. cit.* pp. 736–42; Manger, *loc. cit.* pp. 313–15; *D.G.P.* XVII, nos. 5177, 5185.

[7] Kennedy, A. L., *Old Diplomacy and New* (1922), pp. 116–17.

was the only remaining solution; and Lansdowne was sufficiently worried by the dangers of isolation and sufficiently pleased with French willingness to share Morocco with Spain, which would enable him to avoid the establishment of France opposite Gibraltar, to continue to exchange views with the French ambassador after Cambon had approached him with Delcassé's proposal.[1] The Foreign Office itself, however, shared the general hesitation about a second problem. Just as France, though turning to Great Britain, was unable to desert Russia, so the British Government, though it had decided against an alliance with Germany, still wanted Germany's friendship, and was not yet ready to widen the breach with her by negotiating with France. Like large elements of the country, moreover, some of its members could oppose both closer relations with Germany and the grant of concessions to France because they still adhered to the principle of isolation in relation to the European Powers. Lansdowne told Cambon that there were grave dangers in the proposals to divide Morocco between France and Spain because Germany and Italy were also interested in the country; as late as the end of 1902 he repeated to him his anxiety that Germany should not be excluded.[2] Such, indeed, was his anxiety to keep Anglo-German relations friendly that he did more than merely mark time with France. He and Balfour persuaded the Cabinet in the autumn of 1902 to collaborate with Germany in a blockade of Venezuela with the object of getting compensation for the seizure of British and German ships and the non-payment of debts to British and German nationals. During 1902 and as late as the spring of 1903 they wanted to meet a German request for a loan for the development of the Baghdad railway, for which Germany had at last received the concession from Turkey.

Towards the end of 1902, however, it became impossible to ignore the fact that this policy had become highly unpopular. An outburst of suspicion greeted the Kaiser's private visit to Sandringham in November.[3] When the Venezuelan blockade was announced at the beginning of December there was more public indignation.[4] The British press sharply objected to the proposed railway loan as being in the interests of German imperialism; and in April 1903 Chamberlain, who had publicly washed his hands of Anglo-German collaboration and announced his support for the policy of splendid isolation in January 1902,[5] used the opposition to it of the public and of financial circles to persuade Balfour and Lansdowne to go back in the Cabinet

---

[1] Manger, *loc. cit.* pp. 315–16; *D.D.F.* 2me sér. II, 437; *B.D.* II, 264.
[2] Manger, *loc. cit.* pp. 315–16; *D.D.F.* 2me sér. II, 437, 682–6; *B.D.* II, 264, 274. Cambon failed to report Lansdowne's doubts to Delcassé on either of these occasions.
[3] Halévy, *op. cit.* pp. 131–2, 405–6.
[4] *C.H.B.F.P.* III, 294–7; Halévy, *op. cit.* pp. 133–4, 400; Marder, *op. cit.* pp. 465–6; Manger, *loc. cit.* pp. 317–18.
[5] Langer, *op. cit.* p. 775.

on their decision to meet the German request.[1] And if the public distrust of Germany was at last exerting an influence on policy, it was because it was more and more being shared by Government circles.

Official resentment had been aroused by Germany's refusal throughout 1902 to evacuate the troops she had sent to Shanghai during the Boxer rising. Her attempt to connect the evacuation with a promise by China that no Power would be granted special privileges in the Yangtse Valley, though frustrated by Great Britain, evoked in December 1902 a sharp protest from London to Berlin.[2] But the decisive factor in the growth of official distrust of Germany was the growth of the German Navy. A source of public concern by the end of 1901, underlying the public hostility to Germany during 1902, this became a serious anxiety in Government circles for the first time in the winter of 1902-3. Not since 1897 had it been ignored by the Government altogether; not till 1905 was it to become an obsession. But by the beginning of 1903, the year in which Parliament sanctioned the establishment of the North Sea Fleet, centred on a new base at Rosyth, the Government had come to regard the Germany Navy as the greatest potential menace. It had replaced the Russian and French fleets in that role, whereas only its alliance value in association with France and Russia had previously caused concern; and whereas concern had previously been intermittent, it now became a continuous force. Nor was the anxiety less serious because it derived more strength from distrust of Germany's aims than from the size of the German Navy as such.[3]

This new anxiety, more than anything else, accounted for the process by which, commencing with a speech by Lansdowne in December 1902 in which he argued that France and Great Britain should negotiate over Morocco, the British Government settled its differences over Morocco, braved the opposition in the country to making concessions there to France, overcame its hesitation on the score of offending Germany, and negotiated the Anglo-French *entente*. Widespread revolts in Morocco itself in December 1902, which threatened the complete destruction of the crumbling power of the Sultan, did not cause this process, but were only the occasion for it to begin. The approach of the Russo-Japanese War during 1903 only hastened the process. By threatening to involve Great Britain and France against each other, by threatening to neutralise Russia in Europe and thus upset the balance of power in Europe to Germany's advantage, this weakened the bargaining position on each side. But

---

[1] Halévy, *op. cit.* pp. 407-8; Earle, *op. cit.* p. 182; *B.D.* II, 174-97; *D.G.P.* XVII, 369-463; Manger, *loc. cit.* pp. 312-13.

[2] Kawai, *loc. cit.* pp. 424-32; *D.G.P.* XVI, nos. 4942-6, 4948-55, 4958-9, 4962, 4964, 4966; *D.D.F.* 2me sér. II, nos. 364-6, 368, 379, 422, 427, 432, 479; *B.D.* II, nos. 151, 155-6, 167, 170.

[3] Marder, *op. cit.* pp. 288-307, 452-64; Langer, *op. cit.* pp. 425-7, 441-2.

since it weakened the French more than the British bargaining position, it was not this that put an end to Great Britain's hesitation. Nor can it be true, as is sometimes argued, that Lansdowne had merely waited till Salisbury resigned the premiership, expecting him to oppose a settlement with France as firmly as he had opposed an alliance with Germany.[1] Apart from the fact that the Prime Minister had resigned before the receipt of Delcassé's proposal, and well before the decision to negotiate, the *entente* was a logical culmination of Salisbury's policy since 1893. In ending the feud with France, in falling short of an alliance, in freeing Great Britain in Egypt at the expense of concessions elsewhere, especially in Morocco, in reducing her dependence on Germany, it conformed in detail to the objects and methods of his diplomacy and might almost have been his work. What made it possible was the fact that, while Great Britain's anxiety about Germany ended her reluctance to treat with France, French anxiety in the Far East induced France to accept Great Britain's terms. Not all the details of the negotiations are yet known, if they ever will be: rumours of them got about but they were conducted in great secrecy and on an informal level, King Edward VII playing a large part for Great Britain, Delcassé negotiating without the knowledge of the Quai d'Orsay for fear of the anti-British feeling in Paris. The *entente cordiale* is normally dated from King Edward's visit to Paris in May 1903, which began the conversion of French public opinion. But the visit was itself the outcome of a general understanding already reached by the two Governments; it still remained to settle the details of an agreement covering the many colonial disputes that had arisen over twenty years. This had still not been concluded when, with the outbreak of the Russo-Japanese War in February 1904, the negotiations, as Landsowne wrote to Lord Cromer in March, "after sticking in all sorts of ignoble ruts, suddenly began to travel with the speed of an express train" towards the Anglo-French Agreements of 8 April. But there had been from the beginning a steady determination on both sides to see the negotiations through to the end, whatever the difficulties; and the effect of the outbreak of the Russo-Japanese War, as, earlier, of its approach, was only to hasten a settlement that would sooner or later have been reached.[2]

By the terms of these Agreements Great Britain's view prevailed in the Newfoundland fisheries dispute: France lost the right to dry fish on "the French shore". By way of compensation France received a port on the navigable part of the Gambia, the Los Islands off the Ivory Coast, and an important frontier rectification between the Niger and Lake Chad; and Great Britain also recognised her right to

[1] Kennedy, *Lord Salisbury*, pp. 334–6.
[2] Halévy, *op. cit.* pp. 406–9; Albertini, *op. cit.* 1, 146–7; Manger, *loc. cit.* pp. 318–19; *B.D.* II, nos. 283 *seqq.*; Zetland, *Lord Cromer*, p. 281.

establish a customs tariff in Madagascar. The two Powers determined their respective spheres of influence in Siam and set up a condominium in the New Hebrides. But the most important part of the settlement concerned Egypt and Morocco. Both Powers disclaimed any intention of altering the political status of either country. Subject to the maintenance of "the open door" in trade, to the safeguarding of Spanish interests and to the non-fortification of the northern coast, Great Britain recognised the French right to establish themselves in Morocco, to preserve order and to bring about reforms there, as the British had already done in Egypt. Subject to Great Britain's undertaking to accept the stipulations of the treaty of 1898 guaranteeing free passage of the Suez Canal, France recognised the existing British position in Egypt, promising not to obstruct British action there by demanding evacuation or in any other way and agreeing to the abolition of her veto on the free disposition of the funds in the *Caisse de la Dette*. Each Power promised the other diplomatic support in securing the execution of these provisions. These public provisions were extended in a secret convention, to be published only after seven years, which envisaged the annexation of Morocco by France and of Egypt by Great Britain, and which stipulated that if either Power judged such action to be necessary the other would still provide diplomatic support. In this eventuality in Morocco, the country would be divided into a French and a Spanish zone, Spain receiving the northern coast.[1]

In the Agreements as a whole Great Britain thus received all she contended for: immediate French recognition of her position in Egypt and, in Morocco, French agreement not to fortify the coast opposite Gibraltar and not to end "the open door". But the secret clauses were probably the result of French initiative. Lansdowne, though not opposed to them, insisted that some part of the Agreements must be communicated to Parliament whereas France would have been content with a wholly secret arrangement. These clauses, moreover, were chiefly for France's benefit: Great Britain had no intention of annexing Egypt, but French designs on Morocco were well developed and the execution of the secret provisions in Morocco was almost immediately advanced by a Franco-Spanish Agreement of October 1904 which determined the zones of influence.[2] In this respect, at least, the British Government's attitude had thus changed considerably in the months since its reception of Delcassé's first proposal, even if it was France who made most of the concessions. And if it now took up a position for France and against Germany in Morocco for the future, this was because the Agreements, like the achievement of Anglo-French friendship which had preceded them, though concerned exclusively with colonial questions, had been negotiated with

---

[1] Albertini, *op. cit.* I, 147–8; Halévy, *op. cit.* pp. 410 *seqq.*; Brandenburg, *op. cit.* p. 184.
[2] Temperley, *loc. cit.* pp. 23–4; Marder, *op. cit.* pp. 473–4.

an eye on the German problem. Although it had sought no more than a settlement of colonial differences, the British Government had been aware that this would have its effect on the relations between the Powers; and it had realised that one of the first effects would be to enable attention to be concentrated on the emergence of the naval rival in the North Sea.[1]

The British Government had changed its attitude in Morocco the more readily, on the other hand, because it had also felt that the Agreements would assist with the German problem while themselves limited in terms of the commitments they involved. What had especially commended them had been the thought that, though undeniably a pacific move, they would still restrain Germany, and that, far from being an alliance, they would increase British freedom of action.[2] Few realised that France was not likely always to remain content with a limited arrangement, fewer still that Germany, even less content to be thwarted, would use every conceivable device to destroy the pact that had brought about a new balance of power in Europe and, in conjunction with the Anglo-Japanese Alliance, in the world.

[1] Marder, *op. cit.* pp. 475, 479–81.   [2] Halévy, *op. cit.* p. 412.

CHAPTER XIV

GREAT BRITAIN AND THE POWERS, 1904–1914

I

GERMANY had not at first been disturbed by the Anglo-Japanese Alliance; it had been what she wanted. Confident that, by emphasising the divergence between Russia and Great Britain, it had made a British *rapprochement* with the Dual Alliance even more impossible, she had come back to the belief that she could afford to wait until her growing military and naval strength forced Great Britain, as it surely would, to ask again for a German alliance and to accept German terms.[1] But she had soon begun to realise that the Alliance had strengthened Great Britain at the point where, in some British circles, German support had been considered indispensable; and her uneasiness was increased by her knowledge of the Franco-Italian Agreement of June 1902,[2] by the drawing together of France and Great Britain during 1903 and by the publication of the Anglo-French Agreements of 1904.[3]

These shifts in the balance of power to her disadvantage, which produced in France and Great Britain much comment on Germany's isolation,[4] produced in Germany both widespread despair and divided counsels as to the means by which isolation might be avoided. The German Government remained united in the determination to force its way back to the predominant position that events were taking from it. It was unanimous, and not far wrong, in its reading of the situation: the chief danger was that, if Germany did not detach France from Great Britain, Great Britain and France might use their new friendship to produce an accommodation between Russia and Great Britain as well. It became divided as to how this aim should be achieved and this danger diverted; and the rocks on which it split were Russia's inability to risk the loss of France and the difficulty of detaching France from the Anglo-French *entente* when, far from wishing to be detached, she made no secret of her hope of bringing Russia into it. One possible but, as events were to prove, impracticable method was a Russo-German alliance which would either destroy the Dual Alliance or use it to draw France from Great

---

[1] Langer, *The Diplomacy of Imperialism*, p. 780; Newton, *Lord Lansdowne*, p. 247; *Die Grosse Politik*, XVII, no. 5043; Gooch and Temperley (eds.), *British Documents on the Origins of the War*, II, nos. 118, 120, 126–8.

[2] See above, p. 532; Albertini, *The Origins of the War of 1914*, I, 119–27; D.G.P. XVIII (ii), nos. 5711–15.

[3] Albertini, *op. cit.* I, 149–51; D.G.P. xx (i), nos. 6378–9; *Documents Diplomatiques Français*, 2me sér. VI, nos. 44, 77, 83, 122.

[4] *History of 'The Times'*, III, 392–3; Marder, *British Naval Policy, 1880–1905*, pp. 479–81.

Britain. This would also have enabled Germany to recover her lead in the disintegrating Triple Alliance; for, apart from Italy's negotiations with France, Austria-Hungary had been collaborating with Russia since 1902 to maintain the *status quo* in the Balkans against the effects of revolution in Macedonia.[1] During 1903 and in the early part of 1904 the Kaiser, Bülow and Holstein all joined in a bid for a Russian alliance and, if possible, for a fusion of the Dual and Triple Alliances under German control, for a continental bloc "well able", as the Kaiser put it, "to hold all unruly neighbours in order and to impose peace, even by force, if there should be a Power hare-brained enough to wish to disturb it (i.e. England, from any agreement with whom France must be detached)".[2] In October 1904 the Kaiser offered Russia an alliance with this object in view.[3]

The Kaiser had only been encouraged in this direction by the outbreak of the Russo-Japanese War, by the Dogger Bank Incident, in which Russian warships fired on British trawlers, by Russia's dislike of the British expedition to Tibet and by the conclusion of a secret Austro-Russian treaty of October 1904,[4] of which Germany was informed. This guaranteed Austria against Italy and Russia against Great Britain in the Balkans, but it still further reduced the efficiency of the Triple Alliance and Germany's leadership in it.[5] Bülow and Holstein, on the other hand, were frightened away from an alliance with Russia by other considerations, Great Britain's warning that she would intervene on behalf of Japan if Germany supported Russia —if she committed, for example, such unneutral acts as the refuelling of the Russian fleet—and the publication of the Anglo-French Agreement. These developments of the spring of 1904 made them, after the middle of the year, fear too great a dependence on Russia, shirk a final break with Great Britain and doubt whether Russia's agency would be enough to draw France away from Great Britain;[6] and they led them to propound an alternative scheme for destroying the Anglo-French *entente*.

This was vetoed by the Kaiser until the end of 1904. But when the Russo-German alliance negotiations broke down in December, the Tsar refusing at the last moment to sign a treaty till France had seen it, the Kaiser refusing to let France be consulted in advance,[7] his advisers were able to persuade him to adopt the scheme. Their pretext lay in Delcassé's omission to reach an understanding with Germany about French penetration in Morocco, despite his care to do so with Great Britain, Italy and Spain, and despite the fact that the

---

[1] Albertini, *op. cit.* I, 132 *seqq.*
[2] *The Kaiser's Letters to the Tsar*, pp. 190–4; *D.G.P.* xix (ii), note to no. 6226. See also *D.G.P.* xx (i), no. 6484.
[3] *The Kaiser's Letters to the Tsar*, p. 129.
[4] *History of 'The Times'*, III, 395–400, 404–6.   [5] Albertini, *op. cit.* I, 136–8, 307.
[6] *D.G.P.* xix (i), nos. 5944, 5961; xix (ii), no. 6157.
[7] *Ibid.* nos. 6124, 6126, 6146.

Madrid Convention of 1880 had declared Morocco to be an international question. They felt they could legitimately argue that Germany could not afford to be ignored, as Delcassé had ignored her, if only for reasons of prestige. But they had previously intimated to France that Germany was uninterested in Moroccan developments;[1] and if they had had no ulterior motive they could have submitted this complaint to the French Government. They did not do this because their object was to challenge France in Morocco in such a way as to show her, on the one hand, that the Anglo-French *entente* could not be relied on and, on the other hand, that she needed German collaboration in Morocco, as Great Britain had hitherto needed it in Egypt. Their chief argument for adopting the plan they followed was that the Russian negotiations had failed and that the Dual and Triple Alliances were not likely to be amalgamated so long as Germany lacked a source of direct pressure on France sufficient to bring about a reorientation of French foreign policy. It was for this reason that the Kaiser, though still reluctant, landed at Tangier at the end of March 1905; that, in theatrical circumstances and beyond all possibility of retreat, he then declared his determination to uphold Morocco's independence; and that his speech was followed by the German demand for an international conference to safeguard this.[2]

If the Kaiser's ambition to achieve a continental *bloc*, by means of a Russian alliance with Germany and Russian pressure on France, had proved a mirage, and was soon to fail again at a second attempt, the weakness of the Bülow-Holstein scheme which produced the first Moroccan crisis was that it rested on over-subtleties and sophisms. Though the chief aim was to destroy the Anglo-French *entente* by force, it was hoped that the demand for a conference in the name and interests of Europe would hide the element of German ruthlessness and make unnecessary any direct complaint against the *entente* such as might only serve to strengthen it. Though the other aim was to persuade France to trust Germany and seek her collaboration, and though this was hardly consistent with challenging her in Morocco, it was hoped that this inconsistency could be avoided by representing Delcassé as the only stumbling block to good Franco-German relations. The first danger was that, if France refused to be intimidated by the demand for a conference, the ultimate resort could only be the threat of war on France—a curious way of defending the interests of Europe and a strange preliminary to the offer of Franco-German

---

[1] *D.D.F.* 2me sér. III, 24; IV, no. 368.

[2] Williamson, H. T., *Germany and Morocco, 1905, passim*; Anderson, E. N., *The First Morocco Crisis*; Sontag, R. J., "German Foreign Policy, 1904–6", *American Hist. Rev.* XXXIII (1928), pp. 278–88; Manger, J. B., "Notes sur la Crise Marocaine de 1905", *Revue d'Histoire de la Guerre Mondiale*, XII (1934), pp. 321–4; Muret, P., "La Politique personnelle de Rouvier et la Chute de Delcassé", *Revue d'Histoire de la Guerre Mondiale*, XVII (1939), pp. 225–6; Halévy, *op. cit.* pp. 419–20; Albertini, *op. cit.* I, 151–4; *The Kaiser's Letters to the Tsar*, pp. 100, 133–7, 151–2; *D.G.P.* XIX (i), nos. 6118–19, 6131; XX (i), no. 6521; XX (ii), nos. 6635–6, 6640, 6645.

friendship. The second was that, if Germany threatened war in order to avoid diplomatic defeat, she might find it necessary to implement the threat, not against France alone, but against France supported by Great Britain; the third that, if she shrank from that prospect, her diplomatic defeat would be even more complete.

Each of these dangers materialised. Delcassé refused to be intimidated; the demand for a conference had to be accompanied by the implied threat of attack on France if it were not accepted unconditionally. This, indeed, proved effective in securing the overthrow of Delcassé. If only because Russia had recently been prostrated by her defeats in the war with Japan and because even British military support would have proved of no avail against a German invasion, the French Government refused to follow him in a policy which was based on the conviction that Germany was bluffing and that, since he could at least rely on British diplomatic support, he could call her bluff. Delcassé finally resigned on 6 June. But that was the limit of Germany's success. The Kaiser at once returned to his efforts to bring France over to Germany by means of an alliance with Russia, and was reluctant to keep up the pressure on France. Bülow, losing confidence in the outcome of the crisis, dropped the threat of war and began to compromise with France in order to get her agreement to a conference. Holstein alone continued to regard the Moroccan crisis as the sole means of recovering diplomatic supremacy and therefore as an issue on which war was preferable to defeat. And the chief reason why Bülow wavered and why Germany lost the initiative was that general war and withdrawal had become the only alternatives. France continued to resist the unconditional German demand for a conference, whereas Bülow had hoped that, after the fall of Delcassé, thinking that she had either to desert the British connection or abandon her interests in Morocco, she would give way and turn to collaboration with Germany.[1]

France was able to resist because the British Government supported her. It was the fact of British support for France that forced Germany, because she shrank from general war, to beat a retreat. Bülow and Holstein had believed that Great Britain and the United States would support the German stand for the internationalisation of the Moroccan question and the integrity of Morocco; at least that they might find it impossible to oppose a position that was legally so irresistible. But the British Government realised from the beginning that the issue at stake was not so much a Franco-German quarrel over Morocco as an Anglo-German conflict to decide on which side France

---

[1] Sontag, *loc. cit.* pp. 288–93; Muret, *loc. cit.* pp. 221–30, 305–31, 338–52; Manger, *loc. cit.* pp. 324–30, 335–9; Anderson, *op. cit.* pp. 178 *seqq.*, 206, 217–19; Hall, L. J., "A Partnership in Peacemaking, Theodore Roosevelt and Wilhelm II", *Pacific Hist. Rev.* xiii (1944), pp. 393–4, 396–8; *D.G.P.* xx (ii), nos. 6557, 6561, 6563–4, 6591, 6594, 6597–9, 6601–2, 6604–11, 6617, 6619, 6623–4, 6636–50, 6652–3, 6655, 6671; *D.D.F.* 2me sér. vi, nos. 261–2, 265, 296, 301, 307, 312, 314, 381, 402; viii, pp. 556–7.

would be ranged. It acted accordingly. In the first stage of the crisis, fearing that the fall of Delcassé in the French domestic struggle would lead to a French capitulation to Germany and the destruction of the *entente*, it applied pressure to persuade Delcassé to withdraw his first resignation of 19 April and resisted American suggestions that Germany's demand for a conference should be accepted. The German stand on internationalisation and "the open door" made it difficult to offer Delcassé more formal support; but Great Britain tried to solve this problem by assuming that Germany was out to seize a Moroccan port. On 22 April Lansdowne offered to join France in presenting strong opposition to such a move and begged the French Government to afford him a full opportunity of conferring on the steps that might be taken against it. Delcassé replied, however, that he had received no hint of a German demand for a port; and the essential question, both for him in his struggle in the French Cabinet and for the British Government in its diplomatic battle with Germany, was whether British support would be given in the event of a German attack on France, and not merely against German intervention in Morocco.[1]

How far Lansdowne went in this direction in the second stage, between the middle of May, when the question was put to him, and the fall of Delcassé, is still debated. Probably it always will be: the situation was so confused, his language was so vague and, on account of the fall of Delcassé, his undertakings were never put to the test. They were not put to the test, and Delcassé fell, because the essential question for the French Cabinet, which had to face the grim fact of German military superiority, was not whether British help would be provided but whether it would avail against a German invasion of France. It was on this question that the battle between Delcassé and his colleagues was fought. But it was fought by contestants who all believed that Lansdowne had not only promised support in the event of German aggression in the present crisis, but had also offered a general defensive alliance. Lansdowne subsequently denied both the promise of armed support and the offer of an alliance. But too much credence has perhaps been placed on what he said after Delcassé's resignation, when France had shown herself unwilling to accept an alliance, about what he had done before the resignation in his anxiety to prevent it; and Delcassé was probably right in assuming that, because the crisis was fundamentally an Anglo-German struggle, Great Britain would at least have given armed support in this instance if Germany had attacked.[2]

---

[1] *D.G.P.* xx (ii), nos. 6601, 6604.

[2] Muret, *loc. cit.* pp. 307-13, 331-52; Manger, *loc. cit.* pp. 330-3; Hall, *loc. cit.* pp. 396-9; Halévy, *op. cit.* pp. 423-6; Albertini, *op. cit.* i, 155-8; Anderson, *op. cit.* pp. 228 *seqq.*; Seton-Watson, R. W., *Great Britain and Europe*, p. 603; *B.D.* iii, nos. 90, 93-5, 97, 98 and pp. 67-8, 97, 103; *D.D.F.* 2me sér. vi, nos. 351, 353, 390, 443, 445, 465, 470, 480, 491, and pp. 601-4; *D.G.P.* xx (ii), nos. 6645, 6647, 6648, 6649, 6673, 6680, 6858 and p. 636.

This is, indeed, the only conclusion to be drawn from Great Britain's attitude in the third stage of the crisis, after Delcassé's fall. Though the discussion of an Anglo-French alliance was no longer relevant, her close and continued support of the French case, against American as well as German pressure, not to speak of her pressure on the French Government, was what chiefly influenced the French Government in its continued evasion of Germany's unconditional demand for a conference; and it was the firmness of the Anglo-French combination which transformed American pressure on France to accept Germany's demands into American pressure on Germany to accept a compromise. In this period, moreover, Lansdowne not only made an offer of support to France; he did what he had not considered doing before Delcassé's fall. He warned Germany on 28 June that if she unleashed war on France he could not tell whether British public opinion might not force the British Government to go to France's assistance.[1] In this period, too, at the end of June and the beginning of July 1905, the first naval and military conversations took place between France and Great Britain. They were informal; there is no evidence that they were authorised by Lansdowne. But it is impossible to believe that he was unaware of them and difficult to believe that they were inconsistent with his policy. Their inception is another indication of the extent to which the Government contemplated joint resistance with France to a German move.[2]

It was Lansdowne's warning of 28 June, coming on top of the recent change of front by the United States Government, that finally led Bülow to reduce his pressure on France and accept what amounted to capitulation. On 8 July he finally received, it is true, French acceptance of an international conference on Morocco. Preferring compromise to war in these circumstances, however, he accepted a compromise formula for the summoning of a conference which had first been suggested by Theodore Roosevelt and which was expanded to France's advantage in Anglo-French discussions before being submitted to Germany. Lansdowne approved it before it was so submitted. It stated that the conference should not discuss Moroccan questions in which the honour of any Power or previous agreements between the Powers were involved. By accepting it, the German Government gave assurance in advance that it would respect both the special interests of France in Morocco and the Anglo-French and

---

[1] Lansdowne's account of this interview with the German ambassador does not mention this threat. But Grey subsequently stated both to the French and the German ambassador that Lansdowne had uttered it, thus bearing out the German ambassador's record of the talk in *D.G.P.* xx (ii), pp. 635–7. Cf. *B.D.* iii, pp. 180 and 209; *D.G.P.* xxi (i), no. 6923. See also Manger, *loc. cit.* pp. 333–8; Hall, *loc. cit.* pp. 402–5; Gooch, *Before the War*, i, 59 *seqq.*; *B.D.* iii, 89–90, 96–7, 103; *D.G.P.* xx (ii), nos. 6697, 6707, 6746, 6856.

[2] Marder, *op. cit.* pp. 501–3; Fay, S. B., *The Origins of the World War*, i, 198; Temperley, H., "British Secret Diplomacy from Canning to Grey", *Cambridge Hist. Jour.* vi, no. 1 (1938), pp. 25–6; *B.D.* iii, pp. 87, 169, 171.

Franco-Spanish agreements already made.[1] France now refused, moreover, to repeat the offer of an *entente* with Germany which she had previously made on 9 June in the attempt to avoid a conference.[2] Nor does it give the full extent of Germany's defeat to state that the Anglo-French *entente* had thus been saved and the United States brought into line with it; that Great Britain had won in the struggle for the alignment of France. Germany had not only won a Pyrrhic victory in order to get a conference. She had won, at this great expense, a battle on the one issue in the crisis which, used originally as her pretext, she had never had at heart. She was too deeply committed to abandon her demand for a conference; and she was constrained to negotiate one although she did not want one except on her own terms and although its assembly might well involve yet another diplomatic defeat.

Even before the conference agenda was drawn up in September 1905, Germany knew that France would be supported by Russia, her ally, and by Great Britain and Spain. "The coalition is here in fact!" wrote the Kaiser in November, "King Edward has managed in good shape." "England has, in effect, made an offer of armed support to France", he added in December.[3] Even if she failed to notice the full extent of the *rapprochement* that took place between the United States and the Anglo-French *entente* in the second half of 1905, she knew before the end of the year that she could not rely on American support.[4] At the beginning of 1906, on the eve of the Conference, she learned from Italy, what she had already assumed, that Franco-Italian agreements had been made concerning Morocco. The blow was not softened by Italy's assurance that they were not hostile to Germany.[5]

When the Conference met at Algeçiras on 16 January 1906, apart from the fact that its scope had been restricted in advance to France's advantage, Germany's isolation was thus virtually complete, whereas she had originally expected to have her two allies and Russia and possibly the United States on her side. All the European Powers stood behind France except Austria; Austria counselled Germany to retreat and made it clear that she would not go the whole way with her ally. The American delegates had been instructed to support France's legitimate interests and to avoid "even apparent antagonism to the Anglo-French *entente*". Still, Germany proved unyielding to begin with, opposing a French mandate for the maintenance of order in Morocco on the grounds that it would endanger the principle of

---

[1] Manger, *loc. cit.* pp. 338–40; Hall, *loc. cit.* pp. 400, 404–5; *D.G.P.* xx (ii), nos. 6743, 6836; *B.D.* iii, 110–11, 115–16, 155; Gooch, *op. cit.* pp. 258–60; Brandenburg, *From Bismarck to the World War*, pp. 226–8.

[2] Hall, *loc. cit.* pp. 402, 404–5; *D.G.P.* xx (ii), nos. 6700, 6836.

[3] Bülow, *Memoirs*, ii, 215–16; *D.G.P.* xix (ii), no. 6255.

[4] Hall, *loc. cit.* pp. 407–9.

[5] Albertini, *op. cit.* i, 162–5; *D.G.P.* xxi (i), nos. 6912, 6921, 6925, 6928.

equal economic opportunity for all. But after 12 March, again against the protests of Holstein, who claimed that retreat would mean the end of German hegemony, Bülow ordered another retreat for fear that, unless concessions were made, the outcome would be war at a time when Germany's chances were, in the Kaiser's words, "as unfavourable as they could be". There followed a gradual and progressive acceptance of the French demands by the German delegates. They did not make a total surrender. In the general text of the Conference, signed on 7 April, though France won for herself and Spain the mandate for the Moroccan police, Germany safeguarded the principle that the Moroccan question was the concern of all the Powers. This gave her a stronger international standing in Morocco than she had previously possessed and enabled her to keep the question open, to make use of it again in subsequent crises. But it was an insignificant achievement beside her diplomatic defeat. Her real aims in the Moroccan crisis had been frustrated. The extent of her defeat could not be disguised by success at the Conference because her real aims had been generally understood.[1]

While it completed Germany's discomfiture, the Algeçiras Conference also completed that transformation of the Anglo-French *entente* that had begun in the previous summer. The original agreements had been received unwillingly in some French quarters; after the Conference the *entente* was universally regarded with enthusiasm as the salvation of France. On the eve of the Conference the French Government, which had been loath to accept British support in the previous summer, asked the new British Government—Grey had replaced Lansdowne at the Foreign Office at the turn of the year— whether it would provide France with armed support if the conference failed and Germany resorted to war. Grey felt at least as strongly as Lansdowne that it was "a matter of interest as well as a point of honour" to preserve the *entente*; he himself feared the possibility of a German attack.[2] He had already told the German ambassador that the Liberal Government was as resolved as its predecessor to support France at the Conference; had reminded him of Lansdowne's warning that, if war broke out over Morocco, public opinion might force Great Britain to go to the help of France; and had repeated the warning.[3] He was more cautious on 10 and 11 January in reply to the French ambassador's enquiry: no British Government, he said, could pledge itself to intervention in advance. But Cambon agreed that such a formal pledge was unnecessary, and Grey gave it as his personal opinion that in the event of a German attack Great Britain would support France. He also confirmed and somewhat extended

[1] Sontag, *loc. cit.* pp. 295 *seqq.*; Hall, *loc. cit.* pp. 408–9; Albertini, *op. cit.* I, 168–75; *D.G.P.* xxi (i), nos. 6995 *seqq.*; *B.D.* III, nos. 342, 345, 349, 352–3; Bülow, *Memoirs*, II, 199–202; Nevins, A., *Henry White*, pp. 267–8.
[2] Maurice, Sir F., *Haldane* (1938), I, 172–3; Grey, *Twenty-Five Years*, I, 104.
[3] *B.D.* III, no. 229; *D.G.P.* xxi (i), no. 6923.

the position adopted by Lansdowne after the fall of Delcassé by agreeing with Cambon that talks should continue between the British Admiralty and War Office and the French naval and military attachés regarding the action to be taken if the two countries found themselves in alliance in a war. Though they were now to take place "in a proper manner, that is with the cognizance of the official heads of the Admiralty and War Office", the talks remained informal; in authorising them Grey specified that they must be "solely provisional and non-committal"; their authorisation did not receive the formal approval of the Cabinet, though this was a departure from the practice of constitutional government, because of the over-riding need to avoid a split between the radical and Liberal Imperialist wings in the Cabinet.[1] But they were authorised and, as Grey later admitted, their authorisation had "given an expectation of support" —and not only in Morocco.[2]

Grey realised this equally clearly at the time, but did not see how it could be avoided. By the end of 1905 it had become the firm conviction of the inner group of the British Government, if not of the new Government as a whole, of Grey no less than of Lansdowne, that in the event of a war between the Powers which might advance the German domination of Europe—and what war might not?—Great Britain must intervene against Germany.

"If there is a war between France and Germany", wrote Grey in a secret memorandum of 20 February 1906, "it will be very difficult for us to keep out of it.... [If we do] the French will never forgive us.... The United States would despise us. Russia would not think it worth while to make a friendly arrangement with us about Asia, Japan would prepare to re-insure herself elsewhere, we should be left without a friend and without the power of making a friend, and Germany would take some pleasure...in exploiting the whole situation to her advantage....The more I review the situation the more it appears to me that we cannot [keep out] without losing our good name and our friends and wrecking our position in the world."

That these risks could not be accepted was never doubted by Grey in the years that followed, years in which he was endlessly preoccupied with the European balance of power. His memorandum, it is true, went on to say that "the prospect of a European war and of our being involved in it is horrible". The determination to do all in Great Britain's power to prevent it, both on this ground and for fear of divisions in the Liberal Cabinet, was to be the other plank in his policy. The means to that end on which he was in future to rely were also laid down in the memorandum of February 1906; and the first of these was to refuse to believe that "Germany has made up her mind

[1] *B.D.* III, nos. 210, 219, and pp. 174, 186 and 203; *D.D.F.* 2me sér. VIII, no. 385; IX (i), no. 106; Trevelyan, G. M., *Grey of Fallodon*, pp. 133–40; Temperley, *loc. cit.* pp. 26–7; Tyler, J. E., "Campbell-Bannerman and the Liberal Imperialists, 1906–8", *History*, XXIII (1938), pp. 257–8; Grey, *Twenty-Five Years*, I, 133–6 and chap. vi.

[2] Grey, *Twenty-Five Years*, I, 95.

that she wants war and intends to have it anyhow", and thus to be prepared to humour her whenever possible. But the other was to try to contain Germany by adding a *rapprochement* with Russia to the Anglo-French *entente*. "An *entente* between Russia, France and ourselves would be absolutely secure. If it is necessary to check Germany, it could then be done."[1]

II

In his search for an agreement with Russia, as in his attitude to France, Grey only continued the policy of the previous Government in more favourable circumstances. Salisbury had wanted such an agreement since 1895; the clash of British and Russian interests had produced, instead, the Anglo-Japanese Alliance. An indirect outcome of the Alliance had been the Russo-Japanese War; but Russia, neglecting her promise to evacuate Manchuria and giving her Far Eastern policy over to extremists, had had only her own obtuseness to blame for that.[2] The British Government had not regarded the Alliance as ending its effort to reach an accommodation with Russia, let alone as a means of mobilising Japan against her.[3] The war had made the prospects of Russo-British friendship even more remote; but it had also preserved Great Britain's interest in an accommodation with Russia by increasing the prospects of an alliance between Russia and Germany. During 1904 and 1905, while relations had become closer between Germany and Russia, what was regarded by both sides as a struggle for the alignment of Russia, similar to the contemporary struggle for the alignment of France, had grown up between Germany and Great Britain.

The Kaiser, making his second bid for a Russian alliance at Björko in the Baltic in July 1905, when he had offered the Tsar a draft treaty which the Tsar had agreed to sign, had cherished high hopes that it would "block the way to the whole world's becoming John Bull's private property".[4] In his mind and in Bülow's it had become the answer, not only to the consequences in Europe of the Anglo-French *entente*, but also to British efforts to form an Anglo-French-Russian-Japanese quadruple alliance for the partition of China and the exclusion of Germany from the Far East as well as from Morocco.[5] This had not been the intention of the British Government,[6] but its anxiety at the progress of the Russo-German negotiations had been

---

[1] *B.D.* III, no. 299.
[2] Dallin, *op. cit.* pp. 45–7, 68–9, 70–6; Taylor, A. J. P., *The Struggle for Mastery in Europe*, pp. 417–19.
[3] Langer, *op. cit.* pp. 779–81, 783–4.
[4] Albertini, *op. cit.* I, 159–61; Sontag, *loc. cit.* pp. 292–4; Brandenburg, *op. cit.* pp. 233–43; *The Kaiser's Letters to the Tsar*, pp. 178–9, 190–4; *D.G.P.* XIX (ii), nos. 6220, 6226, 6247–8, 6254–5; XX (ii), nos. 6644, 6646, 6650, 6652–4.
[5] Hall, *loc. cit.* pp. 391–2, 395–7, 399–402; *D.G.P.* XX (i), no. 6302; XX (ii), nos. 6851, 6856; XXI, no. 6897.
[6] Hall, *loc. cit.* pp. 391–4.

none the less for that. It had feared that a Russo-German alliance, even if it did not destroy the Anglo-French *entente*, would go far to neutralise it. With the growth of the German Navy, moreover, it had become less willing than ever to be involved against Russia in Asia as, even without an alliance, German encouragement of Russia might force it to be. "If we are at war with Russia," wrote a British observer in the summer of 1904, "Germany would either take Russia's side or exact very hard terms from us for her neutrality. The German Fleet has really revolutionised politics."[1] It was on these grounds that in April 1904, despite the outbreak of the Russo-Japanese War, Edward VII had suggested to the Russian minister at Copenhagen that the Anglo-French *entente* might be completed by a similar arrangement between Russia and Great Britain. Later in the year and in 1905, as British suspicions of Russo-German negotiations had been confirmed, British distrust of Germany and British anxiety for a settlement with Russia had increased.[2] Not British efforts, however, but Russia's total defeat by Japan, which was only a matter of time after the battle of Tsushima in May 1905, and Russia's distrust of Germany, had ended the struggle to Germany's disadvantage before the end of the year.[3] Up to Russia's disowning of the treaty of Björko in October 1905 nothing had come of Edward VII's approach. Far from being able to counter Germany's efforts, the British Government had feared Russian ambitions and had had to stand by Japan, if not to fight for her, so long as the war lasted. At the end of April 1904 it had warned Russia that an attempt to send a fleet through the Dardanelles would not be tolerated.[4] When President Roosevelt became mediator between Russia and Japan in June 1905 it had ignored his appeals that it should use its influence to moderate Japanese demands.[5] And before the Russo-Japanese peace treaty was signed it had renewed in August 1905 the Anglo-Japanese Alliance for ten years in a form that was more anti-Russian than the original treaty of 1902. The clause committing the two Powers to co-operate in defence of their rights and interests had been extended to cover India as well as the Far East. The *casus foederis* had been extended to cover an attack on either by a single Power instead of being limited to an attack by two Powers. The first extension had aimed at deterring Russia from an attack on India, where she might be diverted after her defeat in China; the object of the second had been to destroy Russia's hope of revenge in a single-handed war with

[1] Gwynn, S., *Letters and Friendships of Spring-Rice*, I, 422–3; Marder, *op. cit.* pp. 475–6.
[2] Albertini, *op. cit.* I, 187; Halévy, *op. cit.* p. 415; Sir Sidney Lee, *Edward VII*, II, 283–9; *History of 'The Times'*, III, 390–1, 395–9; Hales, O. J., *Germany and the Diplomatic Revolution, 1904–6* (1931), pp. 56–7; Langer, W. L., "Russia, The Straits Question and the European Powers, 1904–8", *E.H.R.* XLIV (Jan. 1929), 59 *seqq.*
[3] Albertini, *op. cit.* I, 159–61; *D.G.P.* XIX (ii), nos. 6247, 6254.
[4] Marder, *op. cit.* pp. 436–7.
[5] Hall, *loc. cit.* pp. 401, 406; Newton, *op. cit.* p. 322.

Japan after the revival of her fleet. The new *casus foederis*, it had been hoped, would deny Russia all incentive to rebuild her fleet, for she could not hope to attack Great Britain and Japan combined; and it "might conceivably lead to a definite abandonment of her aspirations as a sea-power".[1] Yet the very closeness of the Anglo-Japanese relations, and particularly the publication of the new Alliance, had emphasised the finality of Russia's Far Eastern defeat. And if this had destroyed the possibility of a Russo-German alliance, so it had contributed to the possibility of a Russo-British *rapprochement*.

Great Britain had long sought a *rapprochement*, supposing acceptable terms could be found. Neither British hostility to Russia during the Russo-Japanese War nor British readiness to renew the Japanese Alliance, and thus to ignore the Dual Alliance and cut across the Anglo-French *entente*, could hide from other Governments that the German problem had become Great Britain's chief concern and that she was more ready than ever to make some sacrifice in her competition with Germany for Russia's friendship. It was because Russia at last began to respond that a better tone had become noticeable between Russia and Great Britain by the autumn of 1905 and that, following Russia's repudiation of the treaty of Björko, talks had begun between the Russian Government and the British ambassador in St Petersburg at the end of the year, before Grey succeeded Lansdowne.[2]

No progress was made in these talks before the Algeçiras Conference. But the Conference, at which Russia and Great Britain were agreed in supporting France, brought the two Powers still closer together; and in May 1906, Grey being as interested as his predecessor, further conversations began in St Petersburg. They lasted for fifteen months. The arrangement they produced in August 1907 was limited to Asia. It included an agreement by which the two Powers pledged themselves to respect the integrity and independence of Persia, but also agreed to divide that country into a Russian zone of influence, adjacent to the Caucasus, in the north, a British zone of influence in the south-east, where Persia bordered on India, and an intermediate neutral zone in which they were to enjoy equal opportunities; an agreement relating to Afghanistan, which Russia recognised as a British zone of influence; and an agreement on Tibet which recognised its territorial integrity and independence under the suzerainty of China.[3]

There had been many difficulties to overcome; agreement had been uncertain till the last moment. Not all the facts are yet known; but it may safely be conjectured that the two obvious difficulties, the

---

[1] Marder, *op. cit.* pp. 441–54.
[2] Albertini, *op. cit.* I, 187.
[3] Churchill, R. P., *The Anglo-Russian Convention of 1907, passim*; Albertini, *op. cit.* I, 188–9; *B.D.* IV, pp. 618–20.

reluctance of Great Britain's Liberal government to engage in power politics and deal with Tsarist Russia, and of Russia to abandon her freedom of action in Persia and on the North-West Frontier, had been separately surmounted by the two Governments under the pressure of circumstances before the talks began. Russia's acceptance of a compromise had already been forced on her by her defeat by Japan and by the revision of the Anglo-Japanese Alliance. An understanding with Great Britain had become the condition of her freedom from subservience to Germany.[1] For Great Britain as for Russia there was little choice, though the convention was no more popular in London than in St Petersburg. The dominance of the German problem, the necessity of facing it, had become so great by 1906 that, though Campbell-Bannerman, the head of the new British Government, like some other members of his Cabinet, was an unrepentant Gladstonian, opposed to foreign commitments, Grey did not have to put pressure on him to get his agreement to the negotiations. The Prime Minister and his followers might console themselves with the argument that the new agreement, like the French *entente*, was merely a good-will settlement. But, like Grey and unlike some of his own followers, he also knew that the only alternative was to return to isolation in circumstances far more hazardous than those in which it had been abandoned, and that this was unacceptable.[2]

It is also probable, however, that, of the difficulties that still remained when the negotiations began, disagreement in detail about the agreements actually signed had proved far less important than conflict about the bearing of the new arrangement on the relations between the Powers. Grey and the Prime Minister realised that, as well as being unavoidable, it would have such a bearing; but they were determined to limit the involvement of Great Britain in Continental politics as far as possible. The issue in the Russian negotiations which raised this difficulty was the question of Russia's aspirations to free passage of the Straits, for which the Russian Government sought a promise of British support. To have given this would not have been difficult from the point of view of Great Britain's material interests. British government departments had concluded as long ago as 1895 that Russian control of this area would not be strategically important so long as Great Britain held Egypt;[3] again in 1903 the Defence Committee had decided that, although Russia would obtain advantages from the possession of Constantinople and the opening of the Straits to herself but not to other Powers, this would not fundamentally alter the strategic situation in the Mediterranean.[4] As long ago as 1895–6, moreover, the British Government had recognised, though without admitting it to the other Powers and least of all to

---

[1] *B.D.* IV, no. 243; Nicholson, H., *Sir Arthur Nicholson, First Lord Carnock*, p. 235.
[2] Tyler, *loc. cit.* pp. 254 *seqq.*   [3] See above, p. 492.
[4] Manger, *loc. cit.* pp. 311–12.

Russia, and though continuing to hope that the Straits could be open to all Powers, that a Russian seizure of this area could no longer be opposed by force.[1] Grey did not entirely refuse to accept the Russian requirements during the negotiations. The question was seriously discussed; he appears to have assured Russia that Great Britain would not oppose her claims. But to agree not to oppose Russia was one thing, and to agree to support her was another; and he would not commit Great Britain to support Russia on an issue which was likely to lead to dispute between Russia and the Central Powers.[2]

As a result of Grey's stand on this point, the Anglo-Russian convention of 1907, like the Anglo-French *entente*, was ostensibly only a settlement of differences in extra-European and what might be called colonial questions. But neither Grey's stand nor the care taken by the Russian Government to inform Germany of the agreement could conceal or reduce the effect it was bound to have, and was intended to have, on the European balance of power. The wheel had come full circle since 1895. The alignment of Germany and the Dual Alliance, based on German, French and Russian hostility to Great Britain beyond Europe, had been replaced by the alignment of the Dual Alliance and Great Britain, based on the fear of a German domination of Europe and of the use to which it might be put throughout the world. British isolation had been replaced as the chief feature in international relations by the encirclement of Germany, not, indeed, in the sense that she would now be attacked, but at least to the extent that a counterpoise to her strength and a limit to her freedom of action had at last been established.

III

That Germany would not be attacked was implicit in the loose and limited nature of the new Triple Entente, as also in the dualism which characterised the policies of Russia, France and Great Britain after 1907. All three made greater efforts than before to seek better relations with Germany; these efforts were not inconsistent with the arrangement existing between them. Each did so partly from the general wish for freedom of action, partly from the knowledge that the others were doing so, partly from the fear of war. In this process even the Dual Alliance, shaken already by Russia's defeat in the Russo-Japanese War and deprived of much of its function by the Anglo-French entente, was further weakened. In the Bosnian crisis of 1909 France, completing her return to the original interpretation of the Alliance by which Russian influence in the Balkans was not an interest she was bound to defend, refused Russia support.[3] In

---

[1] See above, p. 493; *ibid.* pp. 311–12; Albertini, *op. cit.* I, 227; Grey, *op. cit.* I, 155 *seqq.*, 179.

[2] *B.D.* IV, nos. 257, 268.

[3] Renouvin, *loc. cit.* pp. 305–7; *B.D.* V, no. 368.

February 1909, at the height of the same crisis, she reached a settlement with Germany by which, while Germany recognised French political preponderance in Morocco, France undertook to respect Morocco's integrity and guaranteed equality of economic opportunity for Germany.[1] During the Agadir crisis in 1911 Russia repeated to France the counsel she had herself received in 1909, advising France against obstinacy towards Germany and doubting whether French vital interests were at stake in Morocco.[2] And if the Dual Alliance was weakened, the even greater looseness of Great Britain's relations with Russia and France kept the Triple Entente in a state closely bordering on sterility.

In the case of Russia and Great Britain, the limited nature of the entente was emphasised by their continuing rivalry in the colonial field. This was also an additional motive for their wish for good relations with Germany. Even Persia, despite the 1907 convention, remained a source of Anglo-Russian friction as a result of Russia's continued effort to expand there. In the Far East, where Russia similarly found it impossible to control her ambitions, Anglo-Russian relations also remained strained and uneasy. The main development after 1907 was a Russo-Japanese Alliance for the exploitation of the whole of north China, directed against those "Trading Powers", Great Britain, Germany and the United States, who still sought to maintain China's independence.[3] In both areas Russia was tempted to play off Germany against Great Britain—in Persia to the extent of concluding the Potsdam Agreement of August 1911, in which she withdrew her opposition to Germany's Baghdad Railway project in return for German recognition of her predominance in the northern half of the country[4]—and Russia's activities heightened British reluctance to work with Russia in Europe. But that reluctance would have existed in any case, and on more serious grounds, as may be judged from British relations with France. With France, Great Britain had no important conflict of material interests, in the colonial field or elsewhere, after the 1904 Agreements. Unlike Russia, France was not hated by British radicals. After 1906 the leading members of the British Government, at least, never doubted that she must be supported if she were attacked. But they were equally emphatic that France must not be supported in any provocative action, that she must not even be allowed to count on support if attacked, and that the intention to support her if attacked did not rule out the need to improve Anglo-German relations. For these reasons, and because

---

[1] D.G.P. xxiv, nos. 8490–2.

[2] Renouvin, loc. cit. pp. 305–7; Marchand, R. (ed.), Un Livre Noir, Diplomatie d'avant-guerre d'après les documents des archives russes, I, 132–4; II, 419; D.D.F, 3me sér. I, no. 383; II, nos. 3, 90.

[3] Dallin, op. cit. pp. 87–112.

[4] Albertini, op. cit. I, 367–8; D.G.P. xxvII (ii), nos. 10155, 10158–9, 10167, 10169, 10174, 10218, 10224.

France was herself anxious to avoid being drawn into Anglo-German quarrels, relations between the two Powers remained distant until after the Agadir crisis, each being as anxious to work with Germany as it was ready to suspect the other for doing so. And when Anglo-French relations in Europe remained so distant, it is not surprising that Anglo-Russian relations were even more so; that Great Britain's attitude to Russia in the Bosnian crisis, for example, was even more unhelpful than that of France.[1]

In these circumstances, relations between the European Powers being at least as flexible and uncertain as before, Germany could have found scope enough for reasonable requirements of security or ambition in the resources of normal diplomacy, despite the diplomatic revolution that had taken place between 1903 and 1907, had she been able and willing to bend to circumstances. Had she been so able and willing, the diplomatic revolution might, indeed, have been reversed; for the Triple Entente might well have lost its *raison d'être*, so restricted and defensive was it in character. Instead, she used the years from 1907 to 1911 to offend all the Triple Entente Powers; and, if the Triple Entente was at least maintained in those years, losing nothing, however, of its defensive nature, that was almost wholly due to the policy she pursued. The diplomatic revolution had come about because she had allowed her predominance to threaten the interests of too many Powers, and of Powers as much at variance as Russia and Great Britain. After 1907, as before, her interests still cut across those of all the other Powers. Friends could only be won, as, before, they could only have been retained, by sacrifices in some parts of her programme, and if, as she naturally concluded, her security was menaced as well as her predominance undermined, her security could be safeguarded only by the same method of limited liability. Whatever may be said for her refusal to make sacrifices up to 1907 in her determination to pursue the forward policies her strength made possible, her subsequent refusal to take account of the security needs of others as well as of herself, her continued inability to distinguish between the demands of security and the comforts of hegemony, were no less disastrous for herself and the world because they can be explained and understood. It was this which distinguished her policy from that of the other Powers. Great Britain and France, Japan and Russia, faced, as they had each been faced, with the problem of security or the decline of position, had cut their losses, negotiated bargains, accepted compromises, made adjustments by 1907; and they remained ready to do so after that date. They did not do so easily or without reluctance; but they did so, prepared to shift as circumstances required. Germany was no more ready to do so after 1907 than she had been before. It was this attitude on her part,

[1] *B.D.* v, nos. 277, 279, 289, 294, 299, 302, 311, 314, 335, 358, 363–4, 371–2, 377, 381, 387, 409, 567, 572–3, 578, 581, 585, 593.

moreover, which was chiefly responsible for the growth of tension between the major Powers between 1907 and 1912; and it was that tension which, in conjunction with the Eastern Question, produced the situation that led to the War. The disintegration of Turkey and Austria-Hungary made it unlikely that the Eastern Question would be solved by peaceful means. Germany's attitude in the previous five years was what made it impossible to localise the trouble when it arose.

She first refused to accept compromise in her naval rivalry with Great Britain. The British Liberal Government was well qualified to bring about a settlement of this problem, so great was its anxiety to reduce armaments expenditure in the interests of social reform. Its frequent attempts to do so had failed beyond serious hope of recovery as early as the second Hague Peace Conference of 1907, partly because the British Government had introduced in 1906 the "Dreadnought" class of battleship, but chiefly because Germany was unyielding in her determination not to be outdone by this step which made all existing battleships obsolete. In 1906 she amended the second Navy Act of 1900, which had introduced naval rivalry with Great Britain as a major element in her policy; in 1908 she introduced the third Act, which converted all the cruisers of the previous programmes into Dreadnought battleships, because, as the Kaiser said, she "had no desire for a good relation with England at the expense of the increase of the German Navy". After the middle of 1908 Bülow began to realise the folly of believing that "our future lies on the water"; in 1909 he went from office and Tirpitz remained.[1] His successor, Bethmann-Hollweg, made continuous efforts until 1912 to barter a limited naval agreement for a British pledge of neutrality in Europe.[2] But the problem was insoluble on these lines when Great Britain believed that, if she lost naval preponderance or gave such a pledge in order to retain it, she must surrender to Germany in colonial questions and the European balance of power, and when, in Germany, more influential men than Bethmann-Hollweg insisted not so much on a British pledge as on Germany's right to build as she chose.[3]

That right need not be questioned; but neither need Germany's lack of good sense. Nothing in British politics had been so striking in the previous twenty years as the virtual unanimity of both parties in the State on the importance of naval supremacy. And if it be argued that it was precisely Germany's purpose to bring pressure to bear on Great Britain where it would be felt most keenly, one answer is that she should have learned that pressure did not pay, another that this possible justification of German naval increase, if it had given

---

[1] Tyler, loc. cit. pp. 254 seqq.; Woodward, E. L., Great Britain and the German Navy, pp. 123 seqq.

[2] Albertini, op. cit. I, pp. 184–6, 321–4; D.G.P. XXIII (i), nos. 7731–46, 7771, 7779, 7781, 7783, 7788, 7809; XXIV, nos. 8217, 8219; XXV (ii), no. 8820; XXVIII, nos. 10247, 10306.

[3] B.D. VI, nos. 169, 174, 186–7, 190–1, 193, 195.

some point to the original "risk theory", had been rendered out of date by 1906. After 1905, as a result of the elimination of Russia's naval power in the Russo-Japanese War, and because Great Britain, when renewing the Japanese Alliance, escaped the original pledge to maintain a strong China squadron and, leaving her Far Eastern interests in Japan's keeping, concentrated her margin at home, the British Government had no difficulty in maintaining the old "Two-Power" standard plus a good margin, based on the naval strengths of France, Russia and Germany. Since war with France and Russia became increasingly unlikely after the same date, by 1912 the new standard could itself be replaced by that of 60 per cent superiority in battleships over Germany.[1] Great Britain was not immune from naval scares like that of 1909;[2] her naval rivalry with Germany involved her in expense and in sacrifices resulting from the reduction of her naval strength elsewhere. But her naval position in relation to Germany was sufficiently assured after 1906 to make it certain that German competition would be a blunt and ineffective tool, only infuriating to the victim, harmful only to the user. Yet pride and false dignity, and the predisposition to be jealous of Great Britain and to challenge her, sustained it in Germany, as well as "the risk theory", as they had to inspire it from the outset; and when all but Tirpitz and the Kaiser had recognised its unwisdom, and all but Tirpitz had become uncertain as to why Germany wanted a High Seas Fleet and for what purpose she would use it, none would move to stop it.

While maintaining her naval policy at the expense of British hostility—and from the British point of view it was this, rather than the earlier breakdown of the Anglo-German negotiations or the formation of new friendships by Great Britain, that caused the long-term estrangement of the two Powers—Germany proceeded, carelessly and unnecessarily, to affront Russia. She was not responsible for the outbreak of the Bosnian crisis of 1908–9; it arose from the breakdown of a bargain between Russia and Austria by which Russia's consent to Austria's annexation of Bosnia and Hercegovina would have been exchanged for Austria's support for the opening of the Straits to Russian warships.[3] But when Austria destroyed Austro-Russian collaboration by annexing the provinces prematurely, the German Government not only assured Austria of its support, even if she went so far as to attack Serbia, which Austria had not the will-power, if she had the wish, to do; it also allowed the German and Austrian Chiefs of Staff to transform the defensive and conditional Austro-German Alliance of 1879 into an offensive military convention guaranteeing in advance a German attack on France if France and Russia should retaliate against an Austrian attack on Serbia. With this step the European alliance systems, hitherto defensive,

[1] Marder, *op. cit.* pp. 441–52, 509–14; Woodward, *op. cit.* pp. 460–73.
[2] Albertini, *op. cit.* I, 323.   [3] *Ibid.* pp. 190 *seqq.*

ceased to be an influence for peace and became a danger to it; and the foundations were laid for "the blank cheque" which Germany gave to Austria in 1914, when Germany's earlier attitude had encouraged Austria to undertake adventures which she had not the strength to accomplish and might not otherwise have begun. More than this, the German Government, after refusing a conference of the Powers to regularise the annexation and meet Russia's susceptibilities, and after encouraging Austria to do the same when she might otherwise have given way, forced Russia to accept the annexation without even the formality of a limited conference. By issuing a threatening note that amounted to an ultimatum, and by doing so when the crisis was beginning to recede, it needlessly wounded Russia's self-respect. If the growth of Serbian irredentism, as a result of the annexation, increased the chances of endless trouble in the Balkans, Russia's determination not to yield again was to be as important as Germany's encouragement of Austria in making it impossible for the trouble to be localised.[1]

Germany next acted with the same irresponsibility against France in Morocco. In the spring of 1911, as the Sultan was failing to keep order and because she wanted to replace his authority with her own, France ordered troops to Fez, the capital. Germany's behaviour was at first above reproach. She had treaty rights and commercial interests in Morocco; since 1909 France had procrastinated in executing her agreement of that year to give Germany economic equality.[2] After the French action at Fez the German Foreign Minister, Kiderlen-Wächter, warned France several times that it might endanger the Algeciras settlement and that he wanted to avoid a dispute in Morocco, and these warnings were ignored. But if Germany had grounds for complaint there was no justification for her unfortunate and sensational decision, reached in May and carried out on 1 July, to send the gun-boat Panther to Agadir. Agadir was a closed Moroccan port; the Panther was sent ostensibly to defend German firms, though none existed there, in fact with the intention of wiping out Germany's earlier failure in Morocco and of getting colonial compensation elsewhere. Her arrival was followed by the demand for practically the whole of the French Congo in return for the abandonment of Morocco to France. "We must have the whole of the French Congo", wrote Kiderlen to the Kaiser, who had again proved reluctant to make an issue of Morocco. "It is the last chance of getting something substantial in Africa without a fight."

But though she backed her demand with the familiar threats, Germany failed to get it granted. She had no intention of carrying out the threats at the risk of war; they were therefore shown to be

---

[1] Albertini, op. cit. I, pp. 228–88, 302–3; Schmitt, B. E., The Annexation of Bosnia, passim.; D.G.P. xxvi (i), nos. 8820, 8939, 8992, 9006, 9026, 9033, 9061, 9064–5, 9072–3, 9079; xxvi(ii), nos. 9187–8, 9392, 9451, 9454, 9460–1.   [2] See above, p. 552.

empty when France proved obstinate and Great Britain intervened. A financial panic in Berlin completed Germany's retreat. In the settlement of October 1911 the paucity of her territorial gain in the French Congo was in sharp contrast to the vigour of her challenge, and so much less advantageous to her than her recognition of the French protectorate over Morocco was to France that the German Colonial Secretary resigned. In return, moreover, for "275,000 square miles of primeval forest" she had set the nerves of Europe on edge again when they were just recovering from the Bosnian alarm; had weakened her prestige when one of her objects had been to enhance it; and had put such life into the Triple Entente as it had never previously possessed. For the two chief consequences of the Agadir crisis were the advent to power of Poincaré in France in an outburst of French nationalism and the confirmation of Great Britain's worst fears as to Germany's intentions.[1]

The German move to Agadir did not have these effects at once. France's first reaction was not to turn to Great Britain but to offer Germany compensations and even to contemplate a discussion with her of all outstanding matters, except Alsace-Lorraine, which would lead to a settlement like that of 1903–4 with Great Britain. She also agreed to Germany's demand for compensation in the Congo after the dispatch of the *Panther*; and not until 18 July 1911, alarmed by German threats and the request for the whole of the Congo, did she inform Great Britain of Germany's demands and ask her whether she would stand by her in a war. The British reply was cautious and reserved in its turn. If Grey felt that he must not oppose French action in setting aside the Algeçiras Act, he was convinced that he must not go to war to help France to do so. "If we go to war," he wrote in the early stages of the crisis, "it must be in defence of British interests. An attempt by Germany to humiliate France might affect British interests so seriously that we should have to resist it; but there is no case for that at present." He therefore replied to France that a breakdown of the Franco-German Congo negotiations would leave her with no alternative but to return to the *status quo* in Morocco or to buy off Germany with compensation there.[2] After the middle of July, however, Agadir had become an Anglo-German crisis more than anything else; and though many in France still feared that this development would endanger a settlement with Germany, and though Grey continued to advise France to make reasonable concessions to Germany, British support of France was assured.

[1] Barlow, I., *The Agadir Crisis*; Gooch, G. P., "Kiderlen-Wächter", *Cambridge Hist. Jour.* v (1936), 185 *seqq.*; Brandenburg, *op. cit.* pp. 370–85; Albertini, *op. cit.* I, 327–33; *D.G.P.* xxix, nos. 10523, 10526–7, 10538–9, 10542, 10545, 10549, 10572, 10576, 10598, 10600, 10607–8, 10613, 10675, 10677–9, 10734, 10770, 10772–6.

[2] Gooch, *loc. cit.* pp. 186–9; Albertini, *op. cit.* I, 329–32; *D.G.P.* xxix, nos. 10572, 10576, 10588, 10598, 10600, 10607, 10675, 10677–9, 10685; *B.D.* vii, nos. 347, 392, 397, 405.

Grey had told Germany as early as 4 July that Great Britain would recognise no arrangement reached with France without consultation with herself.[1] His statement had not called for a reply, but some reassurance should have been given by Germany. Her failure to give this, her ominous silence, had played into the hands of those who, unlike Grey, felt certain from the beginning that it was her intention to settle at Agadir and threaten Great Britain from this new naval base. It had also worried those, including Grey, who, without suspecting Germany of Moroccan aims, were not prepared to see her achieve a diplomatic victory by bullying methods; and so much so that on 19 July, having heard nothing from Germany but having learned from Paris of the extent of her demands, he feared a war and asked the Prime Minister for "authority to impress on Germany... that we must become a party to the discussions and send ships to Morocco". The warning was given not by Grey but by Lloyd George, widely considered to be the leader of the pro-German and pacifist school in the Cabinet. It was given in a public speech, with the approval of Asquith and Grey, on 21 July. "If a situation were forced upon us", Lloyd George had declared, "in which peace could only be preserved...by allowing Great Britain to be treated where her interests were vitally affected as if she were of no account in the Cabinet of nations..., peace at that price would be a humiliation intolerable for a great country like ours to bear." This speech aroused Germany's indignation, but it also contributed to her retreat. She did not retreat at once; she first threatened to maintain the Act of Algeciras by force of arms if a satisfactory settlement were not reached with France. Other factors intervened before she did give way. But in the mind of the German Government and public, as also in the calculations of other Powers, Great Britain had forced Germany to accept diplomatic defeat under the threat of war, as Germany had forced Russia to do in 1909.[2]

IV

War had been in the air since the Bosnian crisis; after Agadir Europe began to prepare for it in earnest. Even in this last phase of pre-war diplomacy it would be easy to exaggerate the extent to which the Powers willingly accepted alignment into two camps. The Triple Alliance was renewed prematurely in 1912; but Italy's desertion of it was by then complete.[3] As between Germany and Austria it retained its new offensive character and Germany made no firm or successful stand against her growing dependence on Austria; but during 1912–13 she at least feared that Austria would face her with a *fait accompli*

---

[1] *B.D.* VII, no. 356.
[2] Albertini, *op. cit.* I, 330 *seqq.*; *D.G.P.* XXIX, nos. 10617, 10625–6; *B.D.* VII, nos. 395, 412.
[3] Albertini, *op. cit.* I, 426–32.

involving her in a general war.[1] France under Poincaré, remembering Russia's recent attitude, responded to the increased tension by adding a naval Convention to the Dual Alliance, by issuing a loan to complete Russia's mobilisation schemes, by making concessions to Russia's pressure for an integration of the Alliance that would ensure French support in the Balkans. But it remained uncertain at the time, and it is still debated, whether these concessions amounted to a promise of support not only, as originally, in the event of German or Austro-German initiative in an attack on Russia but also if Germany attacked Russia after a Russian attack on Austria; or whether Poincaré avoided such a "Balkanisation" of the Alliance and preserved the original *casus foederis* to which France had returned after 1905.[2] This debate may perhaps be dismissed as academic if it is remembered that France went to war in 1914 not because of the Dual Alliance, but because she was attacked. There is no evidence, in any case, of any willingness on Russia's part to attack Austria and run the certain risk of war with Germany as well. And if the policies of the European Powers thus remained hesitant and uncertain, since all saw the abyss, Great Britain's became no more decisive after Agadir than it had been before.[3]

Although the outstanding result of the Agadir crisis had been to increase Great Britain's suspicion of Germany, she renewed her efforts for an agreement with Germany in 1912 and 1913, and even lowered her terms. Until 1911 she had insisted that a reduction of the German Navy must precede a political agreement. Now she offered a political agreement if the German Navy were not further increased;[4] and was prepared, in addition, to make concessions on the Baghdad railway project, undertaking not to impede its construction or prevent the participation of British capital,[5] and to resurrect and revise in Germany's favour the Anglo-German Agreement of 1898 on the subject of Portugal's colonies.[6] The naval negotiations, begun by Haldane's mission to Berlin in February 1912, soon broke down. Germany not only refused to reduce or slow down the naval programmes already approved, but was unwilling to abandon entirely an additional programme, the *Novelle* of 1911, announced to the Reichstag at the time of Haldane's arrival. In return for minor alterations to it she demanded a pledge of neutrality, which was more definite than the political formula the British Government was

[1] *Ibid.* pp. 379–82, 388, 397–402.
[2] *Ibid.* pp. 369–74, 404–16; Renouvin, *loc. cit.* pp. 307–10; *D.D.F.* 3me sér. IV, no. 469; Marchand (ed.), *Un Livre Noir*, I, 342, 345–6, 362–8.
[3] Albertini, *op. cit.* I, 341–63.
[4] *B.D.* VI, no. 444.
[5] *B.D.* x (ii), chaps. xci–xciv; Chapman, M. K., *Great Britain and the Bagdad Railway*, 1888–1914.
[6] See above, p. 515; Dubois, P., "Anglo-German Negotiations concerning Portugal's Colonies, 1912–14", *Revue d'histoire de la Guerre Mondiale*, XVII (1939), pp. 353–68; *B.D.* x (ii), chap. xcv; Grey, *op. cit.* I, 167.

prepared to offer.[1] But despite this breakdown, negotiations on the Baghdad railway and the Portuguese colonies, which for Great Britain had been conditional on a naval agreement when they began, went on until the outbreak of war.

At the same time, though the Agadir crisis and Haldane's failure had driven her closer still to France and Russia, Great Britain not only made them anxious by continuing to negotiate with Germany,[2] but continued to refuse them an advance pledge of support, as she had refused Germany an advance pledge of neutrality. The Anglo-French military talks, especially, became closer after Haldane's failure. In September 1912 they resulted in a naval redisposition by which the main British forces were concentrated in home waters and the French forces in the Atlantic were sent to the Mediterranean;[3] and Grey, under pressure to do so since the previous spring from the French and from his own officials, went so far in November 1912, in an exchange of letters with the French ambassador, as to agree that "if either Government had grave reason to expect an unprovoked attack by a third Power, or something that threatened the general peace, it should immediately consult with the other whether both Governments should act together...."[4] This encouraged the view in France, where great importance was attached to the promise of consultation, and even in Great Britain, that a positive commitment had been undertaken; the new naval dispositions and these letters had certainly created an obligation of honour no less binding than a formal pledge. Yet the letters as such, far from being a definite pledge of support for France, stated that such a pledge had not been given; for they were the outcome of a British Cabinet crisis as much as of French pressure.

The secret clauses of the 1904 Agreement had been published in November 1911. This fact, together with the need for Cabinet approval for the naval agreement, had forced Grey to reveal to many members of the Cabinet for the first time the existence of the secret naval and military conversations with France since 1905; and this had led to the demand that "it should be put in writing that the talks were non-committal".[5] Grey's letter to Cambon was finally drafted in the Cabinet and, before saying anything else, it declared that the talks "are not and ought not to be regarded as an engagement that commits either Government to action in a contingency that has not arisen and may never arise. The disposition, for example, of the

[1] Albertini, op. cit. I, 334–8; Grey, op. cit. II, 75–7; Woodward, op. cit. chap. xviii; D.G.P. xxxi, nos. 11347–8, 11350, 11353, 11361–2, 11370–1, 11373, 11379, 11381–2, 11387, 11399, 11441; B.D. VI, nos. 537, 544, 556, 569, 571.

[2] D.D.F. 3me sér. II, no. 329; III, no. 404.

[3] Albertini, op. cit. I, 374.

[4] B.D. VI, nos. 564, 580; x (ii), nos. 385, 410; D.D.F. 3me sér. II, nos. 105, 119, 266, 319; IV, nos. 301, 534.

[5] Albertini, op. cit. I, 405–6; Grey, op. cit. I, 96–9; Temperley, loc. cit. pp. 24–5.

French and British Fleets...is not based on any engagement to co-operate in war." On the assumption that it had not limited Great Britain's freedom of action, it was not communicated to Parliament till August 1914.

On the same assumption, when under French pressure and "for the purpose of keeping Russia in good disposition" Grey, though refusing to consider Russia's wish for an alliance between the Triple Entente Powers, agreed to consider a naval convention with Russia in April 1914, he asked that she should first be shown the Grey-Cambon correspondence in order to avoid giving her illusions.[1] And as late as June 1914, since this had been his sole concession to Russia and since there had been no further definition of Anglo-French relations since the letters of 1912, he felt able to declare in the House of Commons that there were "no unpublished agreements which would restrict or hamper the freedom of the Government or of Parliament to decide whether or not Great Britain should participate in a war".[2]

Grey's policy of keeping contact with Germany and of retaining as indeterminate a character as possible for the Triple Entente, like the hesitations of the other Powers, mattered little, however, beside the political facts that all the Powers were arming, that Europe was fast dividing into two groups, and that Great Britain, unable to remain aloof, had no choice as to the side on which she stood. Up to the Agadir crisis, though even then the danger from Germany had induced her to recognise that she must support France if France was attacked and to show more tolerance than she would otherwise have done towards continued Russian activities in Persia, and more tolerance than Germany and the United States towards continued Russian expansion in China, the continued existence of the Triple Entente had been uncertain and its relationships undefined. Its obvious weakness, indeed, had been one of the factors contributing to Germany's unfortunate policy during those years. Germany's decision to send the ultimatum to Russia in the Bosnian crisis had been prompted less by fear of the consequences of the Anglo-Russian Convention than by the opportunity to destroy it which seemed to be offered by the obvious lack of common policy between the Entente Powers.[3] In the Agadir crisis, if Kiderlen-Wächter had been more interested in colonial concessions than Bülow had been in the first Moroccan crisis, and less interested in destroying the Dual Alliance and the Anglo-French Entente than Bülow had been in 1905 or in the Bosnian crisis, that had again been because Russia and Great Britain were already trying to get on good terms with Germany, because

[1] Albertini, *op. cit.* I, 573–4; Grey, *op. cit.* I, 284–5; Gooch, G. P., *Before the War*, pp. 356–9.
[2] Grey, *op. cit.* I, 341–2; II, 46, 295.
[3] *D.G.P.* XXVI (i), no. 9074; XXVI (ii), no. 9372.

Anglo-German relations were bad and because the Triple Entente seemed so weak that Germany could believe that France was isolated. But after Agadir the Triple Entente, though it remained indefinite, was never in danger and could not be ignored. And there was little doubt left that Great Britain would be on that side in a conflict, so strongly had all her earlier suspicions been confirmed that Germany was seeking domination. None of her efforts to continue working with Germany and to avoid a pledge to France and Russia were efforts to avoid that alignment, should a conflict take place, however unwelcome it might be. They were efforts to avoid a conflict. Grey's aim between Agadir and the outbreak of war, his objective throughout the Balkan wars and the Serajevo crisis, was to show all the Powers that the Triple Alliance and Triple Entente could co-exist in peace. In particular it was to make certain, as he said in July 1914, that "no hostile or aggressive policy would be pursued against Germany and her allies by France, Russia and ourselves, jointly or separately."[1] As this and other remarks indicate, he did not doubt that Great Britain's place was with the Triple Entente should peace break down.

Grey's efforts to avoid a conflict were also of no avail against that chain of crises in south-eastern Europe, beginning with the Italian attack on Turkey in September 1911 and passing rapidly to the formation of the Balkan League in the spring of 1912 and the outbreak of the Balkan wars in October 1912, which were made more difficult to control by the tension which already existed between the Great Powers, and which became interlocked with that wider problem to bring about a general war. "These great armies," he wrote in June 1914, reflecting on this situation, "these alliances and counter-alliances, had come into being independently of us and of British policy. We could not influence them."[2] Certainly his policy had not had much effect against events, and least of all did it do so against impetuousness and irresponsibility in the final crisis. He had based it from the beginning on the determination to contain Germany without encouraging her opponents, and on the hope that she would be reasonable when contained. After the Agadir crisis, and to the end, for all the changes of emphasis that the Agadir crisis had brought about, he continued to base it on the same principles. After the Serajevo murder, when Germany showed him once again that she would not be reasonable, it left him, quite apart from Germany's invasion of Belgium, with no alternative but to recommend war against her. It will long be debated whether, in all the circumstances, a different policy would have had a different result.

[1] *B.D.* xi, no. 303.　　　　[2] Grey, *op. cit.* ii, 114–16.

CHAPTER XV

IMPERIAL DEFENCE, 1897–1914

1897–1905

ON 1 August 1899 there were just under 10,000 British troops in South Africa, but by the time fighting against the Boers began in late October they had been increased to 27,000 by reinforcements from India, Gibraltar, Malta, Mauritius and the United Kingdom. Meanwhile, at home, 25,000 "first class Army Reservists" had been called up, and within a few weeks the Field Force of three divisions for overseas service, totalling 47,000 men, had been embarked, though it did not achieve the technical status of mobilisation till it reached South Africa. Much of the reservists' strength was absorbed at the start in replacing regular troops who were unfit, too young, or insufficiently trained for overseas service. When early reverses had given a better appreciation of the formidable task ahead, the mobilisation and dispatch of three more regular divisions began, inclusive of men of the main Army Reserve. By the end of February 1900 all these divisions had embarked, as well as a division of which the infantry were entirely Militia or Volunteers, including the specially raised City Imperial Volunteers. Large contingents of Imperial Yeomanry were also organised and sent out during the course of the war. About 37,000 regular troops remained at home for the time being, mostly immature boys, in addition to about the same number of reservists who were unfit for service overseas.

According to the Esher Report, "the mobilisation scheme was so well advanced that the equipping and transport to the ports of embarkation of successive units was smoothly carried out".[1] The sea transport arrangements made by the Admiralty were also rapid and efficient.[2] All this reflected the greatest credit on the new Mobilisation Department of the War Office. When, however, it came to the further expansion of the South Africa force, apart from the mere replacing of casualties, and to the employment of the Militia, Volunteers and Imperial Yeomanry contingents, serious defects in preparation and organisation became apparent and were still further emphasised in South Africa itself. These were due to the inefficiency of the land transport and supply services (reports on earlier Bechuanaland and Egyptian experiences having been ignored) and to the medical services having been organised only on a peace footing. In addition, the Army lacked general training and experience of

[1] *Parl. Pap.* 1904, VIII [Cd. 1968–I], p. 22.
[2] *Parl. Pap.* 1904, XL [Cd. 1789], pp. 125–7.

staff work in the field, while many of its officers lacked a proper sense of responsibility. Evidence given before the Elgin Commission showed that the Navy had quite a different sense of responsibility due to a "totally different training from early youth".[1] "The whole system", says the Elgin Report, "as it stood at that date was tested by the war in South Africa."[2] How was it that 90,000 Boer colonists, of whom very few were professional soldiers, were able to inflict severe defeats on a first-class professional army, highly experienced in colonial war, and then hold out against an overwhelming superiority in numbers and resources for another two years and a half? Only the obvious military inefficiency of the Boers prevented them winning the war outright in the first few weeks. In the words of the Esher Report, "The Report of the Elgin War Commission revealed a condition of affairs which outraged public feeling throughout the Empire".[3]

As far back as 22 February 1896, Lord Wolseley, the Commander-in-Chief, had advised that reinforcements should be sent to the Cape.[4] In the following July, in answer to an inquiry from Lord Lansdowne, he had urged that reinforcements should be sent to Natal also. In April 1897 he recorded in his diary that he had urged reinforcements both for the Cape and Natal, the troops to be sent out in small numbers so as not to attract attention or appear provocative. "But the Cabinet", he wrote, "won't face the cost." In April 1898, and again in August 1899, he warned Lord Lansdowne of the serious situation likely to arise in case of war in South Africa. Local unpreparedness, he pointed out, was merely an incentive to Kruger. "Let us not lead others into temptation should be a daily prayer on the lips of every British Cabinet Minister."[5]

As far back as 11 June 1896, the Director of Military Intelligence, General Sir John Ardagh, had envisaged the possibility and the resultant dangers of a surprise Boer offensive. He possessed detailed information about the character of the Boer forces and knew almost the exact number of guns they possessed, and all this information was passed on to the Cabinet by Wolseley. But the War Office, lacking a General Staff, had prepared neither intelligence reports nor instructions for the officers chosen by the Government for the chief commands. It had not defined the scope of the operations envisaged, nor prepared a "precise and careful definition of the object in view".[6] Though the failure to send out early reinforcements was clearly due to political reasons, the Elgin Commissioners accepted Lord Lans-

[1] *Journals and Letters of Reginald Viscount Esher* (1934), I, pp. 389–90: letter to the King, 17 March 1903.
[2] *Parl. Pap.* 1904, XL [Cd. 1789], p. 4.
[3] *Parl. Pap.* 1904, VIII [Cd. 2002–II], p. 1.
[4] *Parl. Pap.* 1904, XL [Cd. 1789], p. 15.
[5] Maurice, Sir F., and Arthur, Sir G., *Life of Wolseley* (1924), pp. 310, 313–17.
[6] *Parl. Pap.* 1904, XL [Cd. 1789], p. 23.

downe's claim that the forces and stores actually in South Africa when war began were as large as his military advisers had recommended, thus implying that Lord Wolseley was also in some measure to blame.[1]

In less than a year from the start of the war the Government had admitted the need for a general inquiry into army matters. This eventually took the form of the Royal Commission under the chairmanship of Lord Elgin, with Lord Esher and five others as members. The Commission began work in August 1902, its terms of reference being "to inquire into the military preparations for the War in South Africa, and into the supply of men, ammunition, equipment and transport by sea and land in connection with the campaign, up to the occupation of Pretoria [June 1900]." The witnesses examined included all the leading soldiers and politicians concerned. The Report[2] itself is drastic enough, but Lord Esher's private journals and his letters to the King on the evidence and demeanour of the witnesses suggest that the impressions actually received by the Commissioners were even more disturbing. Lord Esher considered that the responsibility for neglect of preliminary preparations and financial outlay was "a deliberate political act, for which the Cabinet as a whole, and the Cabinet only, can be held responsible". The soldiers, however, had failed to estimate the military capacity of the Boers. The late Commander-in-Chief, Lord Wolseley, appeared mainly to blame for this, but his constitutional relations vis-à-vis his War Office colleagues, and the failure of the Cabinet to consult him personally, had made his position intolerably difficult. Lord Wolseley, Lord Kitchener, Lord Roberts, Sir Evelyn Wood and Sir Redvers Buller had all described their varying difficulties of liaison with the politicians and with the civil branches of the War Office. Sir John Ardagh had described how the Finance Branch of the War Office had "scoffed" at the idea of having maps of the frontiers of the Empire printed, and had never even referred it to the Treasury.[3]

Two main conclusions emerged from Lord Esher's private comments; the need for an Army Board or Council, involving the abolition of the office of Commander-in-Chief in its existing form, and, more important still, the reconstitution of the Defence Committee of the Cabinet, so as to include Service members. But in writing to the King he was by no means hopeful about these reforms. "Lord Esher is strongly of the opinion that if the Report of the Hartington Commission had been seriously considered by the Government, and had been acted upon, thousands of lives, and an expenditure of a hundred

---

[1] Ibid. p. 30.

[2] Report of the Commissioners appointed to inquire into Military Preparations and Other Matter connected with the South African War, 9 July 1903; Parl. Pap. 1904, XL [Cd. 1789], Report; 1904, XL [Cd. 1790], Minutes of Evidence, I; 1904, XLI [Cd. 1791], Minutes of Evidence, II; 1904, XLII [Cd. 1792], Appendices to Evidence.

[3] Esher Journals, I, 355–69, 378, 394–6, 417–19.

millions, would have been saved. But Your Majesty well knows that Royal Commissions are, as a rule, the expedient employed by politicians to relegate awkward and difficult questions to the official pigeon hole."[1] This implied indictment of Salisbury, Gladstone, Rosebery and their chief colleagues supports the view that the leaders of both parties had shown more zeal for securing a political victory over the Duke of Cambridge than for promoting the fighting efficiency of the Army.

The Elgin Commissioners had been appointed to hold an inquiry and "to report their opinion on the evidence", but not to offer advice. As a result of Lord Esher's initiative, however, they did both. The published report noted Lord Wolseley's unsatisfactory position after the compromise made about the status of the Commander-in-Chief, and the untruth of Campbell-Bannerman's claim that the "main principles" recommended by the Hartington Commission had been adopted. It also noted with approval the tentative reconstitution in the winter months of 1902–3 of the Defence Committee of the Cabinet. This Committee had been set up by Lord Salisbury in 1895, perhaps as a salve to conscience for ignoring the recommendations of the Hartington Commission. Though apparently intended to provide some means of co-ordinating the conflicting policies of the Admiralty and the War Office (a subject of great importance in the view of the Hartington Commission), it seems to have concerned itself mainly with adjusting the Service estimates before they came before the full Cabinet, and with settling the conflicting financial claims of the Navy and Army. It was now to deal with "the larger questions of policy". The Elgin Report recommended that the Secretary of State's formal War Office Council, originally constituted by Cardwell and now meeting once a week and keeping minutes, should be put on a more regular and official basis.[2]

Before noting the failure to do anything towards systematising the experiences of the war, by such means as handbooks, the Report stated:

no military system will be satisfactory which does not contain powers of expansion outside the limit of the Regular Forces of the Crown, whatever that limit may be. If the war teaches anything it is this, that throughout the Empire, the United Kingdom, its colonies and dependencies, there is a reserve of military strength which, for many reasons, we cannot and do not wish to convert into a large standing army, but to which we may be glad to turn again in an hour of need as we did in 1899....We regret to say that we are not satisfied that enough is being done to place matters on a better footing in the event of another emergency.[3]

[1] *Esher Journals*, I, 418–19 (11 July 1903).
[2] *Parl. Pap.* 1904, XL [Cd. 1789], pp. 133–6, 138, 142. The Elgin Commissioners also noted that the Dawkins Committee on War Office Organisation (with G. S. Clarke as a member) had recommended a "War Office Board on a permanent basis". *Parl. Pap.* 1901, XL [Cd. 580], para. 131.
[3] *Parl. Pap.* 1904, XL [Cd. 1789], p. 89.

In addition to these unanimous recommendations, Lord Esher wanted a reorganisation of the War Office Council, the decentralisation of War Office business, and the abolition of the office of Commander-in-Chief.[1] Lord Esher, Sir George Taubman-Goldie and two others were in favour of "National Military Education".[2] Lord Esher had meanwhile been privately urging the immediate setting up of a committee empowered to make specific recommendations for the reform of the War Office. His recommendation was accepted by the Cabinet, together with the still more important demand that whatever the committee recommended should be immediately put in hand. On 7 November 1903 the setting up of the War Office (Reconstitution) Committee by the Prime Minister, A. J. Balfour, "with the King's approval", was publicly announced. Although Campbell-Bannerman considered this method of appointment to be "without' any precedent, and...an infringement... of the decent conduct of public affairs", others considered that the method was warranted by the seriousness of the subject. The members were Lord Esher (chairman), Admiral Sir John Fisher (Commander-in-Chief, Portsmouth), and Colonel Sir George Sydenham Clarke (later Governor of Victoria). Major (later Lieut.-General) Sir Gerald Ellison was appointed as Secretary and played a considerable part in the actual drafting of the Reports.[3] "The dauntless three" called no formal evidence but worked by interviews. They had their first report ready on 11 January 1904 and followed it up with two more on 26 February and 9 March.[4]

The Esher Report, Part I, opens with the criticism that: "The scientific study of Imperial resources, the co-ordination of the ever-varying facts upon which Imperial rule rests, the calculation of forces required, the broad plans necessary to sustain the burden of Empire, have, until quite recently, found no place in our system of government."[5] War Office reform would be useless by itself, "unless associated with provision for obtaining for the use of the Cabinet all the information required for shaping national policy in war and for determining the necessary preparations in peace. The evidence taken by the Elgin Royal Commission proves that the Cabinet had in 1899 no adequate means of obtaining reasoned opinion on which to base a war policy."[6] The Report, therefore, recommended the setting up of a Department for the Defence Committee under the Prime Minister. It also recommended the setting up of a War Office Army Council consisting of the Secretary of State, a First Military Member (responsible for military policy and operations), Military Members responsible for personnel, supply and armament, a Civil Member

[1] Ibid. pp. 144-6.   [2] Ibid. pp. 147-50.
[3] Amery, L. S., My Political Life (1953), i, 193-4.
[4] Report of The War Office (Reconstitution) Committee, pts. I-III: Parl. Pap. 1904, viii [Cd. 1932], [Cd. 1968] and [Cd. 2002].
[5] [Cd. 1932], p. 1.   [6] Ibid. p. 3.

and a Finance Secretary.[1] Although Part I (11 January 1904) was only published on 1 February, the Army Council was set up on 6 February, by Letters Patent.[2] This involved the abolition of the office of Commander-in-Chief, which had been held since Lord Wolseley's resignation in 1901 by Lord Roberts. On 4 May 1904 the new Committee of Imperial Defence under the Prime Minister was also set up.

The Esher Report, Part II, dealt with the need for a modern staff system:

> While, therefore, the Great Powers of Europe were seeking to perfect their General Staffs, the arrangements at the War Office provided only for the collection of intelligence (since 1873), and for the preparation of plans for mobilisation (since 1886), the branches concerned being passed from one high official to another in accordance with the views which prevailed at the moment....Not only, however, was there no trained General Staff but some of the most important duties of such a staff were not assigned to any body of officers. At this time "drill and military training", combined with such incongruous subjects as cooking, school of music, and sergeants' messes were dealt with by a small section under two officers.[3]

Detailed plans for a Staff were laid down, while Part III of the Report gave in still fuller detail a plan for the allocation of staff duties. A little over a year later the General Staff came into being, its final form being worked out by General Ellison (Secretary of the Esher Committee). Though carefully related to recent Continental developments, it embodied the old Wellingtonian system of an operational staff under the Quartermaster-General. This system had been abandoned and forgotten in England but had been preserved in the Indian Army. Lord Roberts had brought it up to date and had strongly advocated its adoption prior to his retirement.[4]

Thus within two years of taking up their task the Esher Committee had seen all their demands accepted and acted upon. Each demand was of a radical nature and required intense activity behind the scenes on the part of Lord Esher to secure the necessary action.[5] The creation of the Army Council had an important effect on the constitutional development of the Dominions, since it led to the immediate creation of the Canadian Militia Council, and the Aust-

---

[1] [Cd. 1932], pp. 4, 8–9. It is significant that on 30 Dec. 1903 Esher wrote to Balfour that the "Three" would "demand" a Defence Committee under the Prime Minister and a War Office Council: *Esher, op. cit.* I, pp. 34–5. In addition to Cardwell's War Office Council, Wolseley's "Adjutant-General's Meetings" had been converted in 1895 into an unofficial Army Board, and re-organised as such in 1899. The placing of the Command and Staff under the control of the Secretary of State, unlike the system adopted in Germany, was considered the most suitable method of relating them to Cabinet control.

[2] Appreciation in *Monthly Review* (March 1904), pp. 26–36.

[3] *Parl. Pap.* 1904, VIII [Cd. 1968], p. 22.

[4] James, D., *Lord Roberts* (1954), pp. 404–8. The term "General Staff" for the Operations Branch was only substituted at the last minute.

[5] Clarke considered, though apparently without sufficient justification, that the War Office reforms were hampered by the preconceived ideas of the Secretary of State, H. O. Arnold-Forster. Sydenham, *My Working Life* (1927), p. 176.

ralian and New Zealand Defence Councils. These councils ended the friction hitherto caused by the appointment of a United Kingdom officer as local Commander-in-Chief, and provided a better means of imperial liaison.

The only major change in the imperial situation facing the Colonial Conference of 1902, apart from the South African War, was the federation of the Australian colonies a year earlier. This had resulted in the new Commonwealth Government taking over the various flotilla and coast defence units (now mostly obsolete) owned by the States. Meanwhile the United Kingdom's normal defence expenditure, especially naval, was being forced up by competition with other Powers.[1] Yet for the year 1900 the total trade of the Dominions equalled one-third of the total trade of the United Kingdom, while a quarter of the Dominions' trade had no direct connection with the United Kingdom. Less than one-half of India's and Australia's and New Zealand's trade was with the United Kingdom, yet the United Kingdom paid more than seven-eighths of the cost of the naval forces in Eastern waters. Of Canada's seaborne trade less than half was with the United Kingdom, yet Canada paid nothing towards naval defence.[2]

The limitations, the awkwardness, and the possible dangers of the naval subsidies policy were becoming obvious. The problem was how to give the Dominions and self-governing colonies an active interest in naval defence without endangering the imperial basis on which the Royal Navy was maintained, and destroying the Admiralty's system of centralised strategical control. The creation of efficient Dominion Navies, administered by Dominion Governments, seemed to mean the creation of a series of vested interests in strategical dispersion and local defence, the "Balkanising" of Britannia.[3] As Admiral Sir Lewis Beaumont, commanding on the Australian Station, 1900–2, observed, the raising of local naval forces was wasteful and inefficient, but "the future may see the creation of an Australian Navy".[4] Meanwhile the Commonwealth Government had asked Captain William Creswell, R.N., Naval Commandant of Queensland, to report on Australia's naval needs. Taking a middle view he advocated the gradual building up of an Australian-manned "reserve Squadron to the Imperial Fleet in these waters". At the Colonial Conference, however, the Commonwealth Government proposed the further strengthening of the Australian squadron, both in quality and quantity, the extra cost of maintenance to be met in the same proportions as before, by the United Kingdom and the Commonwealth, with the shares of the individual States reckoned on a population basis.[5] The proposal was accompanied by the statement

[1] *Parl. Pap.* 1902, LXVI [Cd. 1299], pp. 4–5.
[2] [Cd. 1299], pp. 55–6. [3] *Ibid.* p. 15.
[4] *Ibid.* pp. 10–11. [5] See chap. vii above.

that "our aim and object should be to make the Royal Navy the Empire's Navy, supported by the whole self-governing portions of the Empire, and not solely by the people of the British Isles as is practically the case at the present time". Since the Commonwealth could not raise a navy of her own, fit "to meet on equal terms the powerful cruisers and highly trained crews which would certainly be used against us", it was suggested that Dominion personnel might be used to man H.M. ships.[1] This last proposal was accepted by the Admiralty. Australians and New Zealanders were to provide the ratings for one or two of the ships in the Australian squadron, these ships, under "R.N." officers, being sent on exchange visits to other stations,[2] a plan in line with the developments anticipated under the terms of the Colonial Naval Defence Act of 1865.[3] Nevertheless the whole system of contributions was clearly in need of revision. The expedient originally devised to suit the conditions of a group of individual colonies was unsuitable for the Australian Commonwealth. This was one of the reasons why the Dominion Government of Canada had consistently refused to make naval monetary contributions. For the Imperial Government the future would be uncertain if a Dominion, having acquired a navy and a stake in imperial naval strategy, insisted on remaining strategically inactive or even neutral in a large-scale naval war. The Conference finally agreed that the annual naval subsidies hitherto paid by the separate Australian colonies and by colonies which did not form part of a Dominion should be extended and increased. The Commonwealth Government of Australia was to pay £200,000 a year for an "improved" Australian squadron and an Australian branch of the Royal Naval Reserve. New Zealand was to pay £40,000 for the same benefits. The Cape and Natal raised their unconditional contributions towards general naval maintenance from £30,000 to £50,000 and from £12,000 to £35,000 respectively. Newfoundland was to pay £3,000, plus a capital sum of £1800 for starting and maintaining a branch of the R.N. Reserve. The limits of the Australasian, East Indian and China stations were freshly defined.[4] Canada still made no naval contribution, but nevertheless contemplated raising a local naval force.[5]

By far the most important document placed before the Conference was an Admiralty memorandum stating that the function of the Royal Navy in war was to obtain command of the sea and to exercise control over sea communications for the purpose of trade and military expeditions. Foreign battlefleets were growing and there were dangers in a wide dispersion of imperial naval forces. The importance of strategical concentration in war pointed to the need

---

[1] [Cd. 1299], pp. 9–14.
[2] *Ibid.* p. 16.
[3] *C.H.B.E.* II, 835–6.
[4] [Cd. 1299], pp. 24–7.
[5] *Ibid.* p. 18.

for a single imperial navy under centralised control. Then came the significant sentence.

In the foregoing remarks the word *defence* does not appear. It is omitted advisedly, because the primary object of the British Navy is not to defend anything, but to attack the fleets of the enemy, and, by defeating them, to afford protection to British Dominions, supplies and commerce. This is the ultimate aim. To use the word *defence* would be misleading, because the word carries with it the idea of a thing to be defended, which would divert attention to local defence instead of fixing it on the force from which attack is to be expected. The traditional role of the Royal Navy is not to act on the defensive, but to prepare to attack the force which threatens—in other word to assume the offensive.[1]

It must have been with considerable surprise that, after this clear and vigorous exposition, the delegates heard the Secretary of State for War say that some 190,000 troops were kept at home ready "for the defence of London and of strategic positions which might be threatened in case of invasion. But large as these preparations may sound, they are certainly not deemed too large by our military advisers, in view of the possibility of our at any time losing the command of the sea."[2] He added, however, that a field army of 120,000 could be sent overseas "to any part of the British Empire which may be threatened". But how could a field army be sent overseas if command of the sea were lost? How, moreover, could the United Kingdom feed its home army and civil population if command of the sea were lost?

The other outstanding event of the Conference was New Zealand's proposal for the creation in each Dominion of an "Imperial Reserve Force", drawn from the Dominion militia, specially trained, and under an obligation to serve overseas as "a part of the Army Reserve of the Imperial Force". This proposal, though accepted by the Cape and Natal, was doomed by the opposition of Australia and Canada, the latter objecting that it would be derogatory to the principles of self-government.[3] The proposal, however, produced some valuable information and views about the militia resources and organisation of the Empire prepared by the Colonial Defence Committee. Owing to the War, South Africa still remained an uncertain factor as regards Militia. Canada had a so-called "Active Militia" of 38,000 and might be asked to set aside 3,000 men for the Imperial Reserve. New Zealand, with only 17,000 volunteers, might contribute 4500, while Australia, with a total of 27,000 militia and volunteers, might contribute 9000. The Committee had suggested a combined field force for the separate Australian colonies as far back as May 1890, and schemes for this had been drawn up in 1894 and again in 1896. Yet, despite federation, nothing had been done, though Australia recognised the need for a field force capable of serving abroad in addition

---

[1] [Cd. 1299], pp. 54-5.
[2] *Ibid.* p. 28.   [3] *Ibid.* pp. 30-2, 73-4.

to the permanent militia artillery for harbour defence and the other militia and volunteers. An Australian Military Defence Conference was also proposed. With regard to militia pay, as envisaged in White-hall and Sydney respectively, it was noted that the minimum civilian wage paid by New South Wales for government contract work was seven shillings a day.[1]

It was clear from the course taken by the Conference that, despite the excellent work done by the Colonial Defence Committee, no real progress could be made in imperial defence until the fundamental divergencies of outlook between the Admiralty and the War Office had been reconciled. What was the Army for? To fight in Europe? Apparently not; for in the Army Estimates debate of 7 March 1904 St John Brodrick stated that "India is our only possible place of contact with a great European Army." Even this was a serious com-mitment, implying large-scale operations in difficult country at a distance of over 6000 miles from home. In shipping and supply services it might well be more costly than diversionary raids in Europe in support of a main strategy of naval blockade. Bound up with the question of organisation and first-line strength was that of expan-sion for overseas service and for defence against invasion, involving the whole organisation and constitutional status of the Auxiliary Forces. To many influential critics it seemed as if conscription was the only solution.[2] Opposed to this view, and indeed to any increase in military expenditure, stood the Navy League and the "blue water" school, scouting invasion dangers as an aberration of the "blue funk school". According to Sir Winston Churchill, then one of their leaders, "either we have command of the sea or we have not. If we have it we require fewer soldiers. If we have it not we want more ships."

An attempt to resolve this central problem came from an unexpected quarter. On 23 April 1903 a Royal Commission was appointed, under the chairmanship of the Duke of Norfolk and including a number of militia colonels, to inquire into the general state of the Militia and Volunteers and to recommend changes necessary to put them "in a condition of military efficiency and at an adequate strength". With great, though inconvenient, perspicuity the Com-missioners invited the Admiralty to allow the Director of Naval Intelligence to attend as a witness and to answer questions as to the Navy's capacity to prevent invasion, the limit of numbers likely to be landed if invasion was not preventable, and how long it would take to establish command of the sea in a war with one or two Continental Powers. In other words the Commissioners wanted to know whether their units were to be expected to face trained troops from Europe, and if so in what numbers. This meant real business at last, since

---

[1] [Cd. 1299], pp. 58–71.
[2] *Journal of the Royal United Service Institution* (1902), pp. 570–656.

without being clear on first principles it was impossible to recommend how the auxiliary forces should be organised. The Admiralty and the embryo Committee of Imperial Defence, however, succeeded in stifling the inquisitiveness of the Commissioners, who, not to be baulked, recommended in their Report (29 May 1904), "that it is the duty of every citizen of military age and sound physique to be trained for national defence, and to take part in it should emergency arise".[1] The Cabinet's reply was that it was not in favour of conscription, which on the basis of an annual intake of 380,000 men would cost nearly £26,000,000.[2] Such was the type of problem confronting the newly constituted Committee of Imperial Defence.

This Committee had a double parentage. Much of its business had been previously handled by the Colonial Defence Committee, which, owing to the wide interpretation given to its duties by its original members, and notably by its secretary, Sir George Sydenham Clarke, had quickly become a very influential body and had provided a number of important "appreciations" for the first Colonial Conference of 1887. Nevertheless, its lowly origin, restricted initiative and lack of ministerial representation meant that it could never, in its original form, have had a sustained influence on high policy. The more readily acknowledged parent of the Committee of Imperial Defence was, therefore, the Defence Committee of the Cabinet. From the standpoint of imperial defence this committee, in its existing form, was of little value. It had no regular meetings and kept no minutes. Sir John Colomb once described it as a "pious political imposture". In November 1902, on the insistence of the First Lord of the Admiralty and the Secretary of State for War, it had been reconstituted on a broader basis, so as "to survey as a whole the strategical military needs of the Empire", but without a secretariat or a departmental organisation of its own. From this time onwards the Prime Minister, A. J. Balfour, attended regularly, and after November 1903 became Chairman. The permanent nucleus of membership, as announced by Balfour on 5 March 1903, was the Lord President, the Prime Minister, the Secretary of State for War, the First Lord of the Admiralty and the First Sea Lord, the Commander-in-Chief, and the Directors of Naval and Military Intelligence. Other persons, ministerial or otherwise, might be called in for consultation, notably the Chancellor of the Exchequer and the Secretary of State for India. A year later it was still in this makeshift state when the Esher Report, Part I, was received.

By a Treasury Minute of 4 May 1904 the Committee of Imperial Defence "was formally brought into existence". The Prime Minister was to be Chairman, and the only permanent member. "In practice

[1] *Parl. Pap.* 1804, xxx [Cd. 2061], pp. 3–5, 15–16, 36–7, 49; see also *Monthly Review* (June 1904), pp. 29–39, and (July 1904), pp. 36–49.
[2] *Parl. Pap.* 1904, LI [Cd. 1909].

Mr Balfour and his successors summoned regularly those Cabinet Ministers and Staff Officers of both Services who were especially concerned with the larger questions of defence, other Cabinet Ministers, officials and experts being invited *ad hoc* according to the particular business before the Committee. In this way the number of people associated with the Committee and its sub-committees in the course of a year came to number hundreds."[1] The Committee remained advisory and consultative, as regards the Cabinets of both the United Kingdom and the Dominions.[2] It had no executive authority of any kind. But its permanent secretariat, with Sir George Sydenham Clarke at the head, preserved the dual influence of the superseded Colonial Defence Committee and Lord Esher's "dauntless three". Its earliest tasks were to hammer out "the great first principles governing our imperial defence in such matters as reliance on sea-power; the respective rôles of the Navy and Army; home defence; the Defence of India; Coast Defence, etc." The prestige and comprehensiveness of the new Committee, the regular attendance of Balfour at every one of its first sixty meetings, and the sterling work of Sir George Clarke ensured its success. At the start the Committee lacked Dominion representatives.[3] Apparently it was not until the Imperial Defence Conference of 1909 that a complete group of Dominion ministers took part in a meeting. Thereafter, single ministers attended when visiting Britain. Naturally the professional side of the attendance and committee work was facilitated by the creation of the Imperial General Staff, but the political side remained weak, and not till 1912 did Sir Robert Borden give the Canadian High Commissioner authority to attend meetings of the Committee of Imperial Defence when required.[4]

On 11 May 1905 the Prime Minister gave the House of Commons a review of imperial strategy directly inspired by Lord Esher, and reflecting the achievements of the Committee in its first year. Henceforward "Empire Defence" was to be regarded as a whole, and the Navy and Army's roles as inter-dependent. Concentration "at the centre of the Empire" was to be the basis of general strategy. Despite a fresh scare, a surprise invasion of Britain now seemed impossible, since 70,000 men at least would be required for it, involving an armada of 210,000 gross tons of seagoing merchant shipping, the preliminary assembling of which could not happen unobserved. For purposes of illustration only France was treated as the possible invader, no mention being made of Germany. In the view of the Government and the Committee, the defence of India, involving the possible dispatch of eight divisions from the United Kingdom, was still the most important military task of the Empire. Behind the

---

[1] Hankey, Lord, *Diplomacy by Conference* (1946), p. 85.

[2] *Hansard*, 4th ser. CXXXIX, 617–19.

[3] *Parl. Pap.* 1907, LV [Cd. 3524], pp. 15–17, gives the constitution of the C.I.D. in 1907 and proposals for Dominion representation on it.

[4] This caused a mild stir in London, see *Westminster Gazette*, leading article, 9 Dec. 1912.

scenes, however, Admiral Sir Charles Ottley, the new Director of Naval Intelligence, was pointing out that existing plans for combined operations were inadequate and in any case were for colonial warfare only. No plans existed for enabling the Navy to land and supply a substantial military force in Europe.[1]

Meanwhile the South African War and its political aftermath had tended to obscure the significance of contemporary naval developments, though it was largely as a result of naval striking power held discreetly in reserve that the operations in South Africa had remained free from armed interruption by third parties. So far, British naval expansion had been based on the possibility of war with France and Russia and the consequent supreme strategic importance of the Mediterranean, Suez Canal and N.W. India areas. In 1897, however, two new factors had appeared: the rise of the German Navy and the extension of international rivalry to the Far East, consequent on Japan's defeat of China (1894–5) and the abrogation of the treaty of Shimonoseki. The rise of the German Navy was at first interpreted in England chiefly as an anti-French and anti-Russian move. Only a few Englishmen, such as Arnold White and H. W. Wilson, scenting its connection with the Kruger telegram (1896), were prepared to speak outright of Germany's "ultimate intention of measuring herself with England".[2] In the Navy Estimates for 1898–9 the German Navy was taken into account for the first time as regards future British construction. By 1895 Admiral Beaumont, then Director of Naval Intelligence, thought that Germany might attempt to invade England via Belgium.[3] In the Far East Germany in 1897 obtained a site for a naval base at Tsingtau, France following her at Kwangchow-wan in 1898, Russia at Port Arthur the same year, and Britain at Wei-hai-wei in 1899. Britain had three battleships and ten cruisers in the China Seas and arrangements were ready for reinforcing the Australian, East Indies and Pacific stations. Japan was laying down a very formidable fleet to counter the even larger fleet which Russia intended to base at Port Arthur. War with the Transvaal seemed at the time almost inevitable and there was a recrudescence of the frequent trouble about Spanish military works threatening Gibraltar. Then came the Anglo-French crisis over the Fashoda incident in the Sudan (1898), which necessitated precautionary measures in view of a possible war with France involving combined operations against French colonies. In the view of Admiral Beaumont, the French gave way "solely because they recognised their maritime inferiority, as they themselves publicly admitted".[4]

In 1898 the Empire was faced by four strategical problems in the Sudan, South Africa, the Far East, and on the North-West Frontier

---

[1] Marder, A. J., *British Naval Policy, 1880–1905* (1940), pp. 506–7.
[2] *Ibid.* p. 290.   [3] *Ibid.* p. 299.   [4] *Ibid.* p. 568.

of India, where the Chitral operations involved the use of as many as 30,000 British and Indian troops in a single force. Counterbalancing these difficulties was the improvement in relations with the United States arising out of the Spanish-American War of 1898, and with it the guarantee of support for the Open Door policy in China. By this time, too, the United States Navy was equal on paper with the German Navy as the third strongest in the world, while the French Navy only just maintained its position as second to that of Britain.

Towards the end of 1899 a new German Navy Law was announced and Admiral von Tirpitz's memorandum set out the famous "risk theory" of German naval strategy. Germany, according to the memorandum, must have a navy strong enough to make Britain unwilling to risk heavy losses in order to defeat it—losses which would weaken Britain in relation to third parties. By 1906, Germany would probably be the second naval power in the world. Inside Germany the invasion of Britain was publicly discussed as a strategical possibility, with the result that there were popular demands in Britain for the creation of an east coast naval base in addition to Chatham. On 14 September 1901, Admiral Custance, the new Director of Naval Intelligence, drew the Admiralty's attention to the danger of the German Fleet in the North Sea, but it was not till the next year that his masters became convinced of the truth.[1] Two facts decided them: the short radius of action and the cramped quarters for the crews of the new German battleships. The danger now seemed to be that Russia might use the occasion of the South African War to invade India and Egypt, while the French fleet kept the remainder of the British Regular Army tied to the United Kingdom by threat of invasion, and meanwhile cut British communications with India by means of forces based on Diego-Suarez. In October 1900 the Channel Fleet had actually been sent to Gibraltar owing to the possibility of a strategical concentration of the French Mediterranean and the Russian Black Sea fleets taking place in the Levant. With the end of the South African War the situation improved. By 1902 better relations with Italy as regards Tripoli and Malta restored an earlier friendship that had been less cordial since the Franco-Italian *rapprochement* following the Fashoda crisis.

In the Far East another awkward corner had been turned as a result of the relief of the Pekin legations and the defeat of the Boxer rebels by an international force of Japanese, German, Russian, French, British, Indian, United States, Austrian and Italian troops, amounting at the end to nearly 70,000. From a strictly naval point of view it was hoped that the Anglo-Japanese Alliance, signed on 30 January 1902, would afford some relief in fleet distribution. In this, however, the Admiralty were disappointed, since by a secret arrangement each signatory was to maintain a fleet in the Far East equal to that of any

[1] Marder, *op. cit.* pp. 463–4.

other Power. When, however, the Alliance was renewed on 12 August 1905, the situation had been greatly changed by the Japanese victory over the Russians. Although the new Alliance was extended to include special interests in East Asia and India, Britain refused any longer to be secretly pledged to maintain battleships in the Far East, the Cabinet apparently thinking it necessary to interpret the "two-power standard" in such a manner as to ensure a "strategical sufficiency" against Germany in the event of war with France and Russia combined.[1] In no case was war contemplated against the United States or Japan. This retreat from the Far East, though highly propitious to the cause of Anglo-American good will, tended to leave the China Seas and the East Indies at the mercy of Japan and to reduce British power there to a mere façade.

By the end of 1902 the British Cabinet had decided to sanction the development of an east coast base at Rosyth, on the Firth of Forth, though no construction work was done there till 1905. In June 1903 the duties of the Home Fleet[2] were still defined in terms of possible war with France and Russia, Germany not even being mentioned. As late as the summer of 1904 Prince Louis of Battenberg, Director of Naval Intelligence, was writing two separate memoranda, one discussing plans for a war with Germany, and the other on fleet distribution to counter the naval dispositions of a possibly hostile France.[3] Meanwhile the relative strength of the French fleet was steadily declining, the task of attempting to outbuild Britain being seen to be neither economically possible nor any longer desirable; Britain, moreover, was now more anxious to accommodate France in the Mediterranean, since, should France intervene on Russia's side against Japan, Britain would be bound by treaty to support Japan and so weaken herself in home waters. By the summer of 1905 Naval Intelligence was considering the possibilities of British naval intervention in support of France, if she were attacked by Germany. Admiral Sir Arthur Wilson pointed out that in an Anglo-German war blockade would be sufficient, but with France as an ally and vulnerable to land invasion combined operations would be needed "on the largest possible scale". "It is only by putting forth the whole military strength of the Empire that we can hope to succeed."[4]

1905–1914

The year 1905 marks the end of the transition period of imperial strategy which had begun in 1897–8. Russia was greatly weakened, as a result of sea and land disasters in the Far East, while, in Japan,

---

[1] *Ibid.* pp. 509–10. See also Admiral Mahan's article, "Considerations Governing the Disposition of Navies", *National Review* (1902), pp. 701–19.

[2] This fleet represented the Reserve Squadron (henceforward always kept fully manned) when actually at sea. The main force in home waters was the Channel Fleet.

[3] Marder, A. J., *op. cit.* pp. 479–81, 495–6. [4] *Ibid.* p. 505.

a new ally had been discovered capable of balancing her possible recuperation. France, no longer a serious naval rival and weakened strategically by the defeat of Russia, was steadily extending her *entente* with Britain against the increasing menace of Germany. In view of the size of France's North African and colonial territories, with their many well-placed harbours, this "diplomatic revolution" was of immense strategical significance. Good relations with the United States and improved relations with Italy still further ensured the strategical position in the Far East, the Mediterranean, and the Red Sea. Owing to the relative decline of the French Navy, the United States Navy was now the second strongest in the world. Germany thus became the Empire's chief naval rival.

On Trafalgar Day 1904 Admiral Sir John Fisher had become First Sea Lord and begun his great programme of naval reforms; accelerating various inevitable changes, then maturing slowly, and making other radical changes *de novo*, all in the space of five years. In principle Fisher should have had the support of most progressive elements in the Navy, at least for the majority of his reforms. But his violent and spectacular methods, his grandiloquence and megalomania, and above all his dictatorial and vindictive attitude towards critics, alienated many of the best brains in the Service and cut deep rifts in its traditional fraternity. Fisher's volcanic methods were the price paid by the Navy (and only just in time) for years of internal torpor and political neglect, unrelieved either by a political Cardwell or a Service Wolseley. Considerable progress, however, had been made since 1901; the Mediterranean Fleet had been strengthened, and provision made for fleet auxiliaries; armour-piercing shells, telescopic sights and gyroscopes were being issued, while the scheme of 1894–5 for developing the west side of Gibraltar at a cost of five millions had at last been carried out.

Fisher's new policy was so framed as to achieve efficiency with economy, thus pleasing his political masters. All gunboats were withdrawn from foreign and colonial stations, except from West Africa and the Chinese rivers, and all battleships from the China, Australian, and East Indies squadrons, which were to consist henceforth of cruisers. Better relations with the United States enabled the Pacific and South Atlantic squadrons to be abolished. Better relations with the United States and France also enabled the old West Indian and North American squadron to be abolished. For this a "particular service" cruiser squadron was substituted, based on Devonport, which was to visit the West Indies annually, and be available to reinforce either the Channel or Mediterranean Fleets in case of war. Thus ended Britain's traditional command of the Caribbean. The United States superseded her there quite naturally after the Spanish War of 1898, and by 1903 showed a determination to dominate the Caribbean with a view to constructing the Panama Canal. These naval withdrawals, comparable to Cardwell's withdrawal of the imperial garrisons, made it possible for the Admiralty to strike off the effective list 113 sloops, gunboats, slow cruisers, and old battleships, together with a number of auxiliaries. The Admiralty was also able to close the dockyards at Halifax, Esquimalt, Jamaica, Ascension Island and Trincomalee,[1] and to carry out economies and major reorganisations in the Royal Dockyards at home. Out of these substantial monetary savings in warships, personnel, and dockyard expenditure, Fisher was able to finance various reforms necesary for war efficiency, including the new "particular service" cruiser squadron. The new Home Fleet became the Channel Fleet and was considerably strengthened. The original Channel Fleet, the first-line home defence force, became the Atlantic Fleet. Following a new strategic conception, it was based on Gibraltar, from whence it could reinforce either the Mediterranean or Channel Fleets. The base for the Mediterranean Fleet was now Malta. In accordance with the changes already made in 1901–4, ships kept in reserve at home and manned chiefly by officers and specialised ratings were given additional officers and ratings so as to make them into a new Reserve Fleet capable of immediately reinforcing the main fleets in case of war. The extra men for these "nucleus crews" were found from the crews of the ships brought home from distant stations and now laid up or scrapped. The smaller number of warships on foreign and colonial stations enabled all seagoing commissions to be reduced to two years. This reform not only increased efficiency by avoiding constant small changes in personnel but greatly mitigated the previous hardship of long spells abroad with only very short leave spells between. It was a reform comparable to Cardwell's short-service system and the linked battalions.[2]

Fisher's most controversial action was the building of the *Dreadnought* battleship and the *Invincible* battle cruiser. His assumption was that future naval battles would be fought at long range, because of the increased speed now possible, which gave choice of range and action, the premium thereby placed on superior skill in gunnery, and the increased range of *accurate* torpedo fire.[3] Hitherto accurate long-range fire had been prevented by smoke and inefficient instruments, but this was being remedied by smokeless powder and better sights and range-finders. By 1904 ranges of 10,000 yards and over were considered possible, given accurate observation of fire from a control position aloft. But since at long ranges observation could only be obtained by salvoes, a uniform armament of eight or more heavy

[1] Canada undertook to garrison Halifax and Esquimalt, while in 1910–11 she also took over the dockyards themselves subject to certain rights of use by the Admiralty.
[2] *Brassey's Naval Annual* (1905), pp. 40–57, 433–7, 455–69, gives the official statements and statistics with comment.
[3] *Ibid.* p. 169, where Admiral Sir Cyprian Bridge drew similar conclusions from the course of the Russo-Japanese War, then still in progress.

guns was required. This implied a sudden jump in the number of big guns mounted, the existing standard for all navies in the world being four or less, and it was realised in the *Dreadnought* with her ten 12-inch guns. Her high speed of 21 knots was obtained by turbine engines used for the first time in a battleship, both coal and oil being carried until a constant oil supply for the Navy was assured. Better armour and a more effective system of watertight compartments gave increased underwater protection, though her 17,900 tonnage represented an increase of only 1,500 tons on the next biggest battleship afloat, the Japanese *Kashima*. No limit had been laid down for her size beyond ability to use the docks at Portsmouth, Devonport, Gibraltar and Malta. The most remarkable fact about the *Dreadnought's* construction was its speed, since she went to sea for trials one year and a day after being laid down on 2 October 1905. At one stroke Fisher had anticipated the building of the all-big-gun battleship and caused Britain to take the lead therein. The *Dreadnought* was followed by the battle cruiser *Invincible*. Having a speed of 25 knots, and thinner armour than the *Dreadnought*, but with a main armament of eight 12-inch guns, she was faster than any cruiser or armed merchant cruiser afloat, and yet was strong enough to keep touch with an enemy battle fleet.[1] The *Dreadnought* was an experimental ship and no new battleship could be laid down till she had finished her trials, hence the need for speed in building

According to Fisher's critics it was utterly wrong for the British Navy to take the lead in rendering obsolete the existing type of battleship in which we then held a world-wide preponderance. We should have waited for other countries to make the change and then have followed with something better.[2] Politically also it was unsound, since naval competition was automatically accelerated and the impression given that Britain was seeking world domination. To this Fisher could reply that the building of the all-big-gun type, projected by the Italian designer Cuniberti in 1903, was not only inevitable but actually imminent, and that the industrial conditions under which Britain could afford to let other navies make experiments and then build quicker in reply no longer held good, at least as regards Germany.[3] Meanwhile all other navies held up construction for a year and a half to see British results. Reports, moreover, on the Russo-Japanese War confirmed the wisdom of the *Dreadnought's* design. The fact that Germany would be forced to widen and deepen the Kiel Canal locks, before they could be used by her own future *Dreadnought* types, apparently formed no part of the British

[1] For the importance of speed and coal endurance see *The Times*, 21 Aug. 1903, p. 10, Special Correspondent's account of the naval manœuvres; cf. Official report, *Parl. Pap.* 1904, LIII [Cd. 1824].   [2] Sydenham, Lord, *My Working Life* (1927), pp. 208–9.
[3] See *Nineteenth Century* (Feb. 1907), pp. 195–208: "Recent Attacks on the Admiralty", by Julian S. Corbett, for an extremely well-informed and trenchant defence of Fisher's policy as a whole.

Admiralty's calculations. By 1905, therefore, naval affairs were in a highly satisfactory state. The general principles on which the Royal Navy should act in war had been laid down at the Colonial Conference of 1902. The particular enemy of the future had been clearly designated, and the necessary measures in construction and strategic distribution were already well advanced.

Speaking on the Army estimates of 1904, H. O. Arnold-Forster admitted that the Army "in its present form is not suited to the requirements of the country or adapted for War".[1] Nevertheless considerable progress had been made in army reorganisation since the resignation of Lord Lansdowne in 1900. Under St John Brodrick the Army had been re-armed and re-dressed, and the Artillery greatly strengthened. England, Scotland and Wales had been divided into six decentralised command areas, with an Army Corps, or the nucleus of one, in each. A new training area had been established on Salisbury Plain. Here and at Aldershot the first two Corps were stationed. Yeomanry, Militia and Volunteers were to be used to complete the wartime establishment of the remaining Corps. Arnold-Forster had been responsible for completing these reforms and also for providing reserves of artillery and machine guns, ammunition, clothing and general stores, as recommended by the Mowatt Committee in 1900.[2] He also prepared plans which would have ended the Cardwell system. There was to be a General Service Army, serving nine years with the colours and three with the reserve, and a short-service Home Service Army, only to be sent abroad in case of a large-scale war.

When the Campbell-Bannerman ministry took office in December 1905 "the friends of the Committee of Imperial Defence felt some misgivings, as the new Prime Minister was known to feel doubts as to its usefulness". Richard Burdon Haldane, the new Secretary of State for War, "begged its life", however, and the Prime Minister, "after he had served on the Committee a few years,...was satisfied that it was a useful, and indeed an invaluable addition to our constitutional machinery".[3] Under Campbell-Bannerman's direction permanent sub-committees were set up to deal with Overseas Defence and Home Ports Defence. Here, however, a new difficulty appeared. Despite its zeal and efficiency the Committee was not and was never intended to be anything more than consultative and advisory. When the question arose of deciding whether the British Army should be prepared to fight on the Continent of Europe and, if so, how, Cabinet direction, though essential, was not forthcoming. Until 1907, moreover, the General Staff had no official liaison with, and still less any authority over, the land forces of the Dominions. Luckily the new

---

[1] *Parl. Pap.* 1904, LI [Cd. 1907].
[2] *Parl. Pap.* 1904, LI [Cd. 1908]. This gives a subsequent summary of the recommendations. The report itself was secret.
[3] Hankey, Lord, *Diplomacy by Conference* (1946), p. 87. See also *Esher Journals*, II, 114–15.

Secretary of State was prepared to take the initiative in answering part at least of this all-important question. Haldane combined cautious modesty in approaching army matters with an enthusiasm for his task unusual in a Liberal minister of the period. In the House of Commons he described his task as a "fascinating one. . . . The men one comes across, the new school of army officers—entitled to the appellation of men of science, just as much as engineers or chemists— were to me a revelation." Unlike his immediate predecessors in office, Haldane was able to work from first principles. For what object did the British Army exist, and how could that object be best attained? Having asked himself these two questions, he found that the answer to the first was not "for home defence" or "mainly for the defence of India," but rather to fight in Europe in support of France and possibly Belgium in a war with Germany. Here, admittedly, he had the great advantage of taking office when the German danger was becoming obvious. He also had the advantage of going to work with an Army Council and an embryo General Staff already in existence. Very wisely he chose as his personal Military Secretary General Ellison (previously Secretary to the Esher Commission). He was thus able to proceed straight towards answering his second question by the creation of the future British Expeditionary Force, without having to set up a new War Office organisation.

Out of the existing Regular Army, Army Reserve, Yeomanry, Militia and Volunteers, lacking clearly defined functions and a proper relationship as regards drafts and expansion, Haldane proposed to create two armies; the Expeditionary Force to fight in Europe and the Territorial Force for home defence. The Expeditionary Force was to be formed out of that part of the Regular Army which was stationed at home. In this respect there was to be no change in the Cardwell system. Unlike the reorganised forces proposed by both Brodrick and Arnold-Forster, the Expeditionary Force was to be specifically organised and trained to fight in Europe as a complete and tactically balanced force.[1] It was not to consist merely of a pool of regular troops stationed in Britain and available for general service overseas. It was to be of the finest quality, highly mobile (according to existing methods and standard of transport), and to be capable of proceeding overseas, fully mobilised and ready for battle, in the hitherto unheard of limit of fifteen days.[2] It was to

---

[1] *Parl. Pap.* 1906, LXVII [Cd. 2993].

[2] This last point was of great importance. "In the days when British troops were employed many weeks' sail from the Home Country, when vessels were small and at the mercy of bad weather or indifferent engines, when ports of disembarkation were cramped or scattered, then there was at least some excuse for being content with a system which shipped individual units, and grouped them into larger bodies in the overseas theatre of war, forming Highland Brigades, Irish Brigades or Light Divisions as the case might be. A casual arrangement like this would not do for the new conception for the employment of British troops." Dunlop, J. K., *Development of the British Army, 1899–1914* (1938), pp. 244–5.

consist of six "great divisions", each of twelve infantry battalions, supported by a total of 66 batteries of field artillery and adequate complements of Royal Engineers, together with five cavalry brigades, divisional cavalry and various Army Troops, including the new Air Corps (later the Royal Flying Corps). Of the 150,000 or more men required, only 50,000 would be permanently serving with the colours, 70,000 being Army reservists. The Yeomanry would supply 3000 men for the cavalry, and the Militia would supply men for the artillery ammunition column, while the Engineers and the various "services", including the Army Service Corps, the Medical, Veterinary and Ordnance Corps, would be made up to strength by the inclusion of some 27,000 men engaged to serve on a "non-regular" basis. Spare guns, harness, transport, small arms, equipment and stores, sufficient to bring the whole force up to strength, were to be kept ready for instant issue.

In planning the force Haldane had nothing like a free hand, for the ministry had taken office on the understanding that it would reduce army expenditure. Consequently he began by disbanding two Guards and eight Line battalions of infantry, and one out of the eleven native regiments used for colonial purposes. He also abolished the garrison of St Helena, reduced the garrisons of Gibraltar, Malta and Ceylon and made the defence of Halifax and Esquimalt an exclusively Canadian concern, this last measure being in conformity with Lord Fisher's naval policy. Thus Haldane's first army estimates, of 1906–7, showed a reduction of £17,000 on those of the previous year; valuable troops being sacrificed to obtain a minimum military efficiency.[1]

Although Haldane's remodelling of the Regular Army was revolutionary, his creation of the new Territorial Force for home defence attracted even more public attention. Many local, sectional, and feudal interests were concerned and his reforms cut away much of the root relationship between land tenure and national defence. Long, complicated and acrimonious discussions took place with the interests concerned, and carefully drafted legislation was necessary. A beginning was made with the Territorial and Reserve Forces Act of 1907.[2] The auxiliary forces as they then existed came to an end, and out of a mass of units lacking fighting efficiency a real Home Army was created. The Militia was disbanded, and a large part of its personnel (including many regiments taken over *en bloc*) were formed into Special Reserve Battalions, to act as reinforcements for the immediate war needs of the regular infantry of the line. By the end of 1908 they numbered 67,740 out of an establishment of 80,300. The Yeomanry and the Volunteers were also abolished as such, and reconstituted as the Territorial Force for Home Defence, existing units being again transferred as far as possible *en bloc*, with the help of County Associa-

[1] *Parl. Pap.* 1906, LXVI [Cd. 2694].
[2] *Parl. Pap.* 1907, XLIX [Cd. 3366], Memo. by Sec. of State for War.

tions. The purpose of this force was two-fold: "to compel any hostile power which may attempt invasion, to send a force so large that its transports could not evade our own fleet and flotillas; and to free the Regular Army from the necessity of remaining in these Islands." The Territorial Force as planned was to consist of 204 infantry battalions (including 10 cyclist battalions) out of which 14 divisions could easily be formed; 56 cavalry regiments (drawn from the reconstituted Yeomanry), and various corps troops. The field, howitzer and garrison artillery of the Volunteers were also taken over, and with the addition of new horse artillery gave the Territorial Force a substantial artillery establishment. The Engineers were to number 14,000. Great care was also taken to build up a strong Territorial Medical Corps totalling 15,000. By the beginning of 1910 the Territorials numbered over 276,000, but this strength (88·5 per cent of the total establishment) was not fully maintained. In case of war the Territorial Force was to be embodied and receive six months' training. As regards subsequent service abroad, Haldane could only say that as a force they not only would be "enormously more efficient" than the existing Yeomanry and Volunteers, but that they would be ready, finding themselves in their units, to say, "We wish to go abroad and take our part in the theatre of war, to fight in the interests of the nation and for the defence of the Empire." Nevertheless, the creation of the Force was a great achievement and provided a new standard of excellence for the militia forces of the Dominions.

The fourth Colonial Conference of 1907 produced important developments in the co-ordination of the land forces of the Empire. New Zealand, advocate of an imperial military striking force at the Conference of 1902, was now a Dominion. There were thus three Governments capable of giving more effective expression to the principle that, while the general defence of the Empire was guaranteed by the Royal Navy, local defence was an obligation contingent on the acquisition of colonial self-government. Since, however, local defence included the land defence of naval bases, the Royal Navy was directly interested. An illustration of this was Canada's acceptance in 1905 of the whole responsibility for the land defences of Halifax and Esquimalt, Britain having hitherto supplied the troops at Canada's expense. A Canadian Militia Council had been established in 1904, modelled on the new Army Council of the United Kingdom, with the Minister of Militia and Defence as President. By Laurier's Militia Bill all Canadian males aged 18 to 60 became liable for militia service in time of national emergency. The Venezuelan crisis (1895) and the South African War (1899–1902) had hastened the process of Militia regeneration dating from the establishment of the Royal Military College at Kingston in 1876. Yet as late as 1898 the Canadian Militia had been officially described as "a collection of military units without cohesion, without staff" and without administrative departments, a description equally true of the United Kingdom Militia at the same date.

In Australia a Council of Defence had been established by the Commonwealth Government to take over control of the various State Militias. By the Defence Act of 1903, amended in 1904, compulsory militia service could be imposed in time of war. In 1907 proposals were made for the compulsory military training of all males while at schools and colleges from the ages of 12 to 21, and their compulsory enrolment in a National Guard which would gradually absorb the existing militia and volunteers. By the Defence Act of 1909 something of the same principle was adopted, to be further amended in 1910 as a result of Lord Kitchener's visit.

New Zealand, on becoming a Dominion in 1907, also set up a Council of Defence. By the Defence Act of 1909, amended in 1910, she established compulsory military training as well as liability for militia service in case of emergency from the ages of 17 to 55. New Zealand's military organisation, however, was at first more rudimentary than those of Canada and Australia. Pending union, South Africa could make no corporate effort, but by the Defence Acts (1903-6) Natal established compulsory military training. In view of the danger that these various military organisations might develop on divergent lines, the General Staff laid before the Conference a memorandum on the "Possibility of assimilating war organisation throughout the Empire",[1] and Haldane secured the acceptance of a resolution placing the General Staff on an imperial footing. It was in future to be "selected from the forces of the Empire as a whole", by a system of interchanges, and to be charged with collecting and circulating information, and with preparing defence schemes on a common principle. Such help as it might give in training by means of officers seconded from the War Office to Dominion military headquarters would be purely advisory.[2]

It was clear by the time the Conference met that Australia would be content with nothing less than an Australian Navy. In 1905 the Premier, Alfred Deakin, had informed the Colonial Office that he wished to change the scheme agreed to in 1902, on the grounds that Australia's contribution appeared inadequate in London and unsatisfactory in Australia, and that the identification of the Commonwealth with the ships was not sufficiently clear. He proposed instead that Australia should pay the cost of establishing a steamship line, capable of conversion to armed merchant cruisers in war. The Admiralty

---

[1] *Parl. Pap.* 1907, LV [Cd. 3524]: papers laid before the Conference (pp. 22-7). These also included memos. on the constitution of the Committee of Imperial Defence (pp. 15-17), the General Staff's view of imperial defence (pp. 18-21), patterns and reserves of arms and equipment, and the desirability of ordering Dominion war stores through the War Office (pp. 30-7).

[2] *Parl. Pap.* 1907, LVI [Cd. 3404], pp. 19-24, summary of discussion; 1907, LV [Cd. 3523], pp. v-vi, resolutions, pp. 94-128, minutes.

disliked this scheme, while the Committee of Imperial Defence informed Australia in May 1906 that, although the Royal Navy guaranteed Australia's general defence, it might be necessary in case of war to withdraw the Australian squadron from local waters, thus laying Australia open to raids by enemy cruisers. For this reason Australia should be prepared to provide land defences for her chief ports. The Committee did not favour a local navy as "a purely defensive line", especially as regards destroyers; such warships being designed for attack as well as for defence.[1] This correspondence was followed in September 1906 by a conference at Melbourne of six Australian naval officers commanding the various State flotillas recently taken over by the Commonwealth, under the chairmanship of Captain Creswell, appointed in 1904 to the new office of Director of the Commonwealth Naval Forces. At this conference the Admiralty view was strongly contested, and the demand made for a Commonwealth force to keep the "sea frontier", the force to consist of three ocean-going destroyers, sixteen coastal destroyers, and four torpedo boats, at a construction cost of £2,250,000 spread over five years.[2] It was as a result of this conference that the Commonwealth Government had given advance notice to the Colonial Conference of its resolution to reconsider the agreement of 1902. New Zealand, however, having only a small population to draw on, was content to continue the contribution system, but tabled a motion in favour of increased contributions. When the Colonial Conference eventually met in London the naval discussions were comparatively unproductive. No decision was reached on the Australian and New Zealand resolutions. Lord Tweedmouth sought only to secure freedom for the Admiralty as regards strategical distribution, advising the Dominions and Colonies to build or buy submarine flotillas for their own local defence and, where possible, provide local docking facilities large enough for dreadnoughts.[3] At the same time it was made clear to the Conference that the United Kingdom was still bearing a huge and disproportionate financial burden in respect of imperial defence. For naval purposes, Canada and the Transvaal spent nothing and contributed nothing.[4]

On returning to Australia, Alfred Deakin proposed that instead of a direct subsidy to the Royal Navy, Australia should supply 1000 seamen at an estimated annual cost of £100,000, to serve in two cruisers of the Royal Navy to be permanently stationed in Australian waters, and in addition should pay £69,000 annually to help to maintain the cruisers. Australia would devote the remainder of the total annual sum contributed under the 1902 agreement to maintaining a flotilla,

Australian owned and controlled. Apart from this Australia would spend £300,000 on coast defences during 1907. To this the Admiralty replied that it could not guarantee to keep cruisers permanently on the Australian station both in war and peace, and that any local flotilla raised by the Commonwealth should be under the complete operational control of the Commander-in Chief (Royal Navy) on the station.[1] In 1908 Australia put forward a further scheme for a squadron consisting of six destroyers, nine submarines and two depot ships, to be manned by R.N. personnel recruited in Australia. The initial cost was calculated at £1,277,400 and the annual cost at £350,000, all to be defrayed by Australia. This squadron should be under Commonwealth control while in Australian waters under peace conditions, but under Admiralty control in war or when cruising outside Australian waters for peacetime training.[2] This scheme raised the old difficulty of how to keep the naval personnel of a small self-contained force efficient, without continuous redistribution and progressive promotion as in the Royal Navy. Nevertheless the offer was too good to be refused outright, quite apart from the political feelings behind it; so that the Admiralty could only give a qualified refusal based on the need for absolute strategical control at all times and the need for exchange and efficency of personnel.[3] Meanwhile New Zealand, realizing the importance of the Admiralty having a completely free hand, offered to increase her annual contribution from £40,000 to £100,000 unconditionally.[4] Next year, 1909, concern about the international naval situation, expressed in the Imperial Parliament, led to the spontaneous offer by New Zealand of the cost of a dreadnought (£1,700,000 or more), or of two, if necessary. The Federated Malay States offered the cost of a dreadnought, as also did Victoria and New South Wales, should the Commonwealth Government itself fail to act.[5] When the Commonwealth offer came it amounted to little more than a less precise repetition of the last scheme for an Australian squadron. The Colonial Secretary in a telegram to all the Dominions quoted a resolution passed in the Canadian House of Commons that Canada should assume "her proper share of the responsibility and financial burden incident to the suitable protection of her exposed coastline and great sea ports". Meanwhile Alfred Deakin's return to power in Australia led to the expected offer of the cost of a dreadnought.[6] In view, however, of the clearly expressed opinions of Canada and Australia in favour of Dominion naval forces, it seemed opportune to call a special Imperial Defence Conference.

This Conference duly met in London in July and August 1909. A Pacific Fleet was projected, to be made up of three separate

[1] *Parl. Pap.* 1908, LXXI [Cd. 4325], pp. 2–4.   [2] *Ibid.* pp. 36–9, 47–56.
[3] *Ibid.* pp. 49–56.   [4] *Ibid.* p. 41.
[5] *Parl. Pap.* 1909, LIX [Cd. 4948], pp. 1–3.   [6] *Ibid.* p. 13.

squadrons known as the East Indies, Australia and China squadrons, each consisting of one battle cruiser, three light cruisers, six destroyers, and three submarines; each squadron to cost £3,695,000. Australia undertook to maintain the whole of her squadron and to provide most of the construction cost of the battle cruiser. New Zealand would pay the whole cost of the battle cruiser for the China squadron and £100,000 a year towards the squadron's maintenance. These were notable advances, the principle of a real Australian Navy being accepted without prejudice to Admiralty control or to the establishment of tactically balanced sea-going forces. Canada, with two seaboards to cover, contemplated a force of light cruisers and destroyers, costing a little over three millions, in addition to maintaining the dockyards at Halifax and Esquimalt.[1] The South African Colonies were represented at the Conference, but could still take no action pending the establishment of the Union.

The immediate results of the Conference were that in 1910 Canada passed a Naval Service Act, bought two old cruisers from the Admiralty and invited tenders for the construction of four light cruisers and six destroyers during the next nine years. But when the Laurier ministry fell in 1911, the succeeding Borden ministry cancelled the tenders. In 1910 Australia passed a Naval Defence Act giving the Commonwealth Government wide powers, and in the same year the battle cruisers *Australia* and *New Zealand* and two of the light cruisers for the new Australian squadron were laid down in Britain. Legislation both in Canada and Australia ensured that Dominion warships and personnel should remain under the peacetime control of their respective Governments while in home waters, but should be transferred to Admiralty control in war and during peacetime service outside Dominion waters.

The Conference also produced valuable military results. Following the suggestions made at the Colonial Conference of 1907, General Sir W. G. Nicholson, Chief of the General Staff, drew up a memorandum showing that imperial defence implied "offensive action", with the General Staff acting as an "entity throughout the Empire" for the preparation and conduct of war. For this the Staff must have a central division in Britain, under a single recognised head, and local divisions in the Dominions concerned with local defence and the maintenance of a common system of training. Nevertheless, the Chief of an Imperial General Staff could only have advisory powers in relation to the local divisions which would be under their own respective Governments.[2] When, therefore, the 1909 Conference met, the way was already well prepared for the metamorphosis of the General into the Imperial General Staff. Nicholson's memorandum

---

[1] *Parl. Pap.* 1909, LIX [Cd. 4948].

[2] *Parl. Pap.* 1909, LI [Cd. 4475], pp. 7–14. The change of title from C.G.S. was made by an Order in Council of 22 Nov. 1909.

advocating standardisation of organisation, weapons and transport arrangements was accepted so as to make it possible to combine the various Dominion forces "rapidly into one homogeneous Imperial Army" in case of emergency. But, as before, the control of each Dominion over its own forces was to remain undisturbed.[1] Detailed plans were accepted for standardisation of staff training, the setting up of Dominion Staff Colleges, and the education and interchanges of Staff Officers. The principle was also laid down that imperial defence now consisted of three elements: sea power, local defence and mutual support. Britain's respective contributions to these were the Royal Navy, the Territorial Force and the Expeditionary Force.[2] Further progress was made in the development of the Dominion land forces, and the influence of the Imperial General Staff was extended as a result of General Sir John French's visit to Canada in 1910. Similar results were obtained as a result of Lord Kitchener's visit to Australia and New Zealand in 1909–10, each Dominion agreeing to adopt schemes for compulsory military training. Previous to this Lord Kitchener had reorganised the Indian Army, with a view to increasing its war efficiency and to help still further to reduce the burden on the British Army, already lightened by improved relations with Russia.[3] In South Africa a Territorial Army was created in place of the old commando military system.

Some idea of the work done by the Committee of Imperial Defence at this time can be gathered from the reports of its various sub-committees set up to study the military requirements of the Empire as affected by India (report of 1907); Europe (1908–9); Egypt, Southern Persia and the Persian Gulf, with special reference to the Baghdad Railway (1909); the Suez Canal and Hong Kong; neutral and enemy shipping in war; trading with the enemy; wartime national insurance of ships and cargoes; cables (British and enemy); counter-espionage (all of 1909).[4] Standing sub-committees were also set up to deal with overseas Defence, Home Ports Defence, Co-ordination, and Air. These studies of particular problems represent the second phase in the Committee's development, the first having been solely concerned with establishing general principles. The reports dealing with military requirements of the Empire all contained an identical and disquieting theme; the inadequacy of the United Kingdom's existing military man-power for the imperial tasks envisaged, a theme closely connected with the recommendations already made by the Elgin and Norfolk Commissions for compulsory military training in peace. The most persistent advocate of conscription was Lord Roberts, now in retirement though a member of the

---

[1] *Parl. Pap.* 1909, LIX [Cd. 4948], pp. 19, 29–30.
[2] *Ibid.* pp. 36–52.
[3] The failure of the Indian Supply and Medical Services in the Mesopotamian operations, 1914–15, casts doubt on the value of these measures.
[4] Asquith, H. H., *Genesis of the War* (1923), pp. 116–17.

Committee of Imperial Defence,[1] assisted by Colonel Charles a'Court
Repington, sometime military correspondent of *The Times*. Their
case was at least arguable in view of the huge imperial commitments
shouldered by a regular army of less than 250,000 men actually
serving with the colours. Nor had the Franco-Russian Alliance
(1894) and the Anglo-Russian *entente* (1907) eased the total burden,
since in place of possible Russian invasions of India and Egypt, there
were now probable German invasions of France and Belgium involving war on a continental scale, with the further possibility of a
German attempt to invade Egypt with the help of Turkey.[2] Unfortunately, Lord Roberts and the "National Service League" (founded
1901) failed to base their case on broad imperial needs, as Lord
Roberts himself had begun by doing. Instead they chose to demand
conscription as a defence against the invasion of Britain, thinking, no
doubt rightly, that this was their best means of rousing popular
interest.[3] The result was that they antagonised the Navy, whose
cardinal doctrine was that, granted sufficient means, they could make
invasion even less possible than it had been in the days of sail. Hence
the "blue water" school rejected the warnings of the "bolt from the
blue" school, Lord Fisher in particular thinking, and with good
reason, that the agitation was being made use of in some quarters to
discredit his policy as First Sea Lord and to divert public money from
the Navy to the Army.

In the Navy's view the more enemy troops committed to an
invasion the easier the task of intercepting them. For an invasion
to succeed, the Navy must be defeated in a major fleet action, which
would mean the blockade of Britain and complete defeat all round,
regardless of how many men were mobilised for "home defence".
During the winter of 1907–8 the invasion question was investigated
before a special and highly influential sub-committee of the Committee of Imperial Defence.[4] On 22 October 1908 following, the
Committee of Imperial Defence confirmed the sub-committee's
report by stating that invasion was impossible provided naval supremacy was assured, though naturally complete defeat must result if
that supremacy were lost. Home defence should be on a scale
sufficient to compel an intending invader to make the attempt in
force and not merely to repel raids, thus exposing the armada of

[1] James, D., *Lord Roberts* (1954), pp. 411–63, based on Roberts's official and private
correspondence.
[2] Military Correspondent of *The Times*, *Foundations of Reform* (1908 reprinted), chap.
viii, "Teuton and Turk", pp. 111–27.
[3] *Ibid.* chaps. i–v. Repington also acted as intermediary in the early stages of the Anglo-
French Military Conversations, 1905–6.
[4] The Admiralty's case was based on a memorandum prepared by Julian Corbett
showing the advantages enjoyed by the British Navy under conditions of modern naval
warfare. The memorandum was strongly approved by Haldane. (Correspondence of
Lord Fisher, Admiral Sir Edmund Slade and Sir Julian Corbett.) See also *The Times*,
2 Dec. 1908, for a good subsequent statement of Repington's view, and James, D., *Lord
Roberts* (1954), pp. 430–2.

transports and their escort to naval interception. For that reason the home defence force should number 70,000.[1] If a war on the frontiers of India necessitated 100,000 troops being sent there from Britain as reinforcements during the first year, there must be sufficient regular and other troops left behind to deal with 70,000 invaders. Assuming that the Territorial Force was immediately embodied, there should be enough regular and trained troops available in six months to make certain that no invasion would be attempted with less than 70,000 men.[2] These findings were eventually made known by the Prime Minister, H. H. Asquith, in 1909. Nevertheless, the imperial aspects of the man-power problem were not disposed of so easily. To the majority of politicians and to the Liberal party especially, naval and military expenditure was always something to be "scrutinised with a jealous eye" and if possible to be reduced, while conscription itself was anathema.[3] Nevertheless, it should have been clear to both the Cabinet and the National Service League that in case of war many thousands of valuable lives were likely to be sacrificed unnecessarily as a result of the inadequate training of hastily improvised formations. In 1912 the Imperial General Staff investigated the possibilities of conscription, but concluded that to attempt such far-reaching changes "during a period of unrest on the Continent" might prove too strong a temptation "to a foreign General Staff to make an early end of what it might insist on interpreting as preparation for aggression on our part...to be risked".[4] This was reasonable enough; but there seems less justification for the Cabinet's rejecting General Sir Ian Hamilton's scheme for preliminary legislation and the registration and allotment of man-power so as to provide for an orderly system of call-up, taking account of the civil employment involved and the equipment and training facilities available. The Cabinet, moreover, gave no public warning of danger nor of the enormous call on military and industrial man-power which war on a Continental scale must inevitably involve. Nor did the Imperial General Staff seize such chances as offered to present their own views to the public.[5] Equally serious was the failure of the Cabinet to authorise any investigation of the calls on heavy industry and munitions in case of war.

[1] The figure of 70,000 first put forward by Roberts himself is important since it provided at least some hypothetical standard by which the needs of home defence could be gauged. See Roberts's correspondence with Churchill, James, *op. cit.* pp. 451–6. See also Amery, L. S., *My Political Life* (1953), i, 214–18.
[2] Asquith, H. H., *Genesis of the War* (1923), pp. 114–16.
[3] *Ibid.* pp. 106–7 where, after defining the Liberal attitude to defence expenditure, Asquith states (p. 139) that the conscription issue "would have split the Cabinet, split the House of Commons, split both political parties, and split the whole nation". It must not be imagined, however, that this attitude was peculiar to the Liberals; see, Churchill, W. S., *Lord Randolph Churchill* (1906), ii, 429, for an interesting calculation as to the 7,500 man-hours of work lost per man in countries having conscription in the year 1890.
[4] Haldane, Lord, *Before the War* (1920), p. 174.
[5] Robertson, Sir W., *Soldiers and Statesmen* (1926), i, 39–40.

The Balfour Cabinet as part of its general *entente* policy had given some consideration to the possibility of land operations in support of both France and Belgium. When the Campbell-Bannerman ministry took office they found that the French Government's estimate of the danger from Germany was more serious than they themselves had supposed. The Prime Minister agreed, therefore, that the unofficial military inter-Staff conversations and exchanges of information which had already begun might be continued on an official basis, with both France and Belgium, provided that the Cabinet was in no way committed to military action, still less to any particular plan. The fact that a man with Campbell-Bannerman's record should be thus converted to accepting "dangerous necessities justified by the evilness of the times" shows the extent to which nineteenth-century principles were giving way before the pressure of new forces. Even so it was deemed fit that at first not more than five or six members of the Administration should know that the military conversations were taking place. Nor did the Cabinet as a whole learn the truth officially till 1912. Herein lay the seeds of a serious misunderstanding should an emergency suddenly arise. To what extent the Dominion Governments were eventually informed is uncertain.[1] More remarkable still was the decision of the Prime Minister and Sir Edward Grey, the Foreign Secretary, the two Ministers most immediately concerned, to dissociate themselves from all knowledge of the technical results of the inter-Staff conversations. The same policy was later followed by Asquith. In a famous statement Grey wrote: "The military experts then conversed. What they settled I never knew—the position being that the Government was quite free but that the military people knew what to do, if the word was given."[2] And again, as to preparatory Anglo-French action in the face of German danger: "If these measures involved action, the plans of the general staffs would be taken into consideration, and the Governments would then decide what effect should be given to them."[3] The degree of fastidious detachment here portrayed goes far to explain Continental impressions of British perfidy. Not only were the Prime Minister and the Foreign Secretary content to remain officially ignorant of the nature of the plan made by their constitutional military advisers, but they deliberately accepted the serious risk of Britain being forced in a sudden emergency to accept a plan unsuitable from a political standpoint when it was too late to prepare a substitute. In fact it is difficult to see how a technical military plan once made could avoid hardening into a fixed military commitment. A too heavy responsibility was thus placed on the embryo General Staff. Much also

[1] Borden, H. (ed.), *Robert Laird Borden: his Memoirs* (1938), i, 358, provides negative evidence so far as his 1912 visit to England is concerned.
[2] Grey to Asquith, 16 April 1911, Grey, *Twenty-five Years* (1925), p. 94.
[3] *Ibid.* p. 97.

depended on close co-operation between the War Office and the Admiralty which it was the plain duty of the Cabinet to enforce.

Meanwhile Haldane proceeded with his work of organising the Expeditionary Force, thereby making it daily a more valuable asset in the eyes of the French General Staff. To begin with, the inter-Staff conversations centred round the place or places of disembarkation of the Force, and its subsequent employment. No strict alignment with the French Army was envisaged, it being assumed that Belgian neutrality would be violated by Germany and that Belgium would resist. The Admiralty's decision to close the Channel in war, however, ruled out Antwerp for disembarkation, and also combined operations along the Belgian coast. This restricted the Expeditionary Force to the main French orbit and whetted the French appetite for bringing it under their own command.

The year 1909 brought to a head the growing divergence between Admiralty and War Office policy, Lord Fisher being strongly against tying the Expeditionary Force to the main French Armies to the prejudice of combined operations in which we should enjoy the traditional advantages of flexibility arising from sea power. Here was a clear case for intervention by the Cabinet, especially as much tentative planning, accompanied by some acrimonious wrangling, was taking place in the Committee of Imperial Defence, which meanwhile remained as before a purely consultative and advisory body.[1]

In August 1910 General Sir Henry Wilson was appointed Director of Military Operations of the Imperial General Staff and a new impetus was given to British war preparations. Wilson was sceptical about sea power and paid little heed to the cumulative strength of the Empire and its strategic resources in the event of a long war.

His vision was focused upon a single point and in the light of his own conversations, he saw that point so clearly that he saw no other.... War was coming in France. The French Army was the substitute for the army which we ought to have, but could not get.... So far as any single individual was able to do so, he committed us definitely to the military support of France on the great day of test. Not only did he commit us to France, but also, to a great extent, to their methods of conducting battle, holding that, as they would be the predominating partner in a Franco-British effort in the field, it was better we should conform to their ways than they should conform to ours, or, that we should adhere too closely to insular views of our own, inspired as they were for the most part by our experiences of colonial and savage warfare.[2]

Broadly speaking Wilson's plan was to make the Expeditionary Force a left-flank appendage of the French Army. The endorsement given to Wilson's plan by the Imperial General Staff itself may have been partly due to its lack of corporate experience in taking a wide view of Britain's imperial strategic needs.

On 23 August 1911 a famous meeting of the Committee of Imperial

[1] Fisher to Esher, 15 May 1909: Fisher, Lord, *Memories* (1919), p. 189.
[2] Montgomery-Cuninghame, Sir Thomas, *Dusty Measure* (1939), pp. 53-5.

Defence was held at which Wilson forecast with complete accuracy, based on personal observation, the German invasion of Belgium and France, and the lines of advance the Germans would take. He then explained his own policy and plans with such clarity and eloquence that he entirely convinced the members of the Cabinet present as to the desirability of aligning the Expeditionary Force with the French. Admiral Sir Arthur Wilson, Fisher's successor as First Sea Lord, then explained the Admiralty view. But to the consternation of the ministers he proved unconvincing and inarticulate in presenting the case for *close* blockade together with combined operations on the German coast, and in his refusal to guarantee the safe passage of the Expeditionary Force. Nevertheless, his insistence on the need for strategical freedom so as to reap the maximum value of sea power in the use of the Expeditionary Force reflected traditional experience. The ministers, however, having made no effort *as a body* to familiarise themselves with the subject-matter of the discussion, were incapable of exercising independent judgment, and, confused by the Admiral's secretive obscurantism, accepted the clearer and more eloquent presentation of the soldier. Indeed, so inefficient did the Admiralty's war organisation appear to be, that Haldane insisted on the creation of a Naval War Staff as a condition of his continuance at the War Office; hence the subsequent appointment of Mr Winston Churchill as First Lord. Meanwhile the uncertain attitude now adopted by the Belgian Government towards Anglo-French help in the defence of their neutrality still further strengthened the case for abandoning all idea of combined operations round Antwerp. When at last the Cabinet as a whole became fully informed of the situation a split developed, some members, including Morley, Crewe, Harcourt and McKenna, complaining, not that Sir Henry Wilson's strategy was wrong, but that it was leading Britain into a by no means inevitable war as an ally of France. Opposition in the Cabinet was reinforced by the naval agreement with France of 1912 and the subsequent exchange of the Grey-Cambon letters. Although the peace party succeeded in preventing the letters from being binding, their own participation committed them to acceptance of the military conversations and the strategic implications involved. The whole Cabinet thus gave an implicit benediction to Sir Henry Wilson's plans, though without promising to perform them. By August 1914 detailed schedules for embarking and disembarking the Expeditionary Force, together with train time-tables both in England and France, had been carefully worked out. Either the Force must fight as Sir Henry Wilson wished or else Britain must remain militarily inactive.[1] It was in this manner that Britain abandoned her traditional strategy and became committed to a "continental" war.

[1] The whole subject is exhaustively dealt with in Tyler, J. E., *The British Army and the Continent* (1938).

The fifth Colonial Conference met in 1911, and since, with the inclusion of South Africa, four separate Dominions were now represented, it took the name of the Imperial Conference. Imperial defence as such was not discussed in the main Conference, though recent debates in the Australian and New Zealand Parliaments had shown a marked feeling of uneasiness at the world situation, and the desire for exercising a greater and more direct influence on imperial foreign policy. Sir Joseph Ward, the New Zealand Premier, proposed the setting up of an "Imperial Parliament of Defence" having consultative and revisionary powers with regard to imperial foreign policy and defence. With this he coupled a scheme for a single Imperial Navy financed on a general *per capita* basis. His proposal failed mainly because of Asquith's uncompromising refusal to allow any derogation from the Imperial Government's sole right to frame foreign policy. It was also opposed by Sir Wilfrid Laurier, the Canadian Premier, on his familiar isolationist grounds.[1] In the end, New Zealand's claim that Dominion High Commissioners should be invited to attend the Committee of Imperial Defence when matters affecting the Dominions were discussed was conceded, an acknowledgement of the Committee's imperial status.[2] Australia strongly criticised the failure to consult the Dominions about the recently negotiated Declaration of London. South Africa proposed that in future Dominion money contributions for naval defence should be counted as part of their expenditure on local naval defence and defence of bases.

A separate strategical conference was held by the Committee of Imperial Defence, fitted in between the sessions of the main Conference. Here Sir Edward Grey pointed out that, since Britain's foreign policy was based on naval power, the creation of separate Dominion navies would make a common foreign policy for the Empire more necessary than ever. He revealed that the two-power standard (meaning two European Powers) had now been virtually abandoned in favour of a sixty per cent superiority over Germany alone, without regard either to Austria or Italy. Reginald McKenna, the First Lord, stated that the Admiralty still favoured a single Imperial Navy, partly for reasons of control and partly to facilitate efficiency through continuous interchanges of ships and personnel.[3] Battleships could only be built in Britain, and all naval building could be done faster in Britain than in the Dominions. Nevertheless, the principle of establishing separate navies in Australia and Canada under the financial and administrative control of their respective governments was fully conceded. In the formal agreement, however, the two new

[1] *Parl. Pap.* 1911, LIV [Cd. 5745], pp. 36, 46–75.
[2] *Parl. Pap.* 1911, LIV [Cd. 5513], pp. 6–7.
[3] Asquith, H. H., *Genesis of the War* (1923), pp. 122–34; Gooch & Temperley (eds.), *British Documents on the Origins of the War*, VI, 781–90.

forces were to be known as the Royal Canadian and Royal Australian Navies, and their training and discipline were to be identical with that of the Royal Navy. In peace they would remain under Dominion control while inside Dominion waters; outside these waters they would come under Admiralty control. In war they would come entirely under Admiralty control if and when placed at the Admiralty's disposal by the Dominion Government.[1] Apart from strategical considerations, the agreement determined the position under international law of Dominion warships and personnel serving outside their own waters in peace. These waters were now re-defined. Canada's Atlantic station included everything north of lat. 30° N. and west of long. 40° W., and her Pacific station everything north of lat. 30° N. and east of long. 180°, thus including waters adjacent to the United States Atlantic and Pacific coasts, and the coasts of Alaska and of north-eastern Siberia. The Australian station was to include eastern Papua, the Louisiade Archipelago, Norfolk Island, Lord Howe Island and all waters southwards to the Antarctic Circle between long. 95° E. and 160° E.[2] A Commonwealth Naval Board was set up in April 1911, under powers conferred by the Australian Naval Defence Act of 1910, its functions being analogous to those of the Board of Admiralty. Admiral Creswell became First Naval Member (the equivalent of First Sea Lord).

On the land side the Imperial General Staff arrangements were stated to be working well, sections having been set up in Australia, New Zealand and Canada.[3] Haldane explained that the British Army was both voluntary and professional because of its overseas commitments. "It is very different from any other army in the world, and in some respect different from any other army which has ever existed in the time of history."[4] Hence the special function of the Imperial General Staff "to relieve us from the necessity of asking you to subject your local troops to any manner of control or centralised command in order to attain unity". There were now 77,000 British troops in India, 38,000 in Egypt, Africa and the Mediterranean garrisons, and 167,000 at home ear-marked for the Expeditionary Force. In addition, there were some 20,000 extra troops, thus giving a total of about 300,000 regular troops available for long-term service with overseas obligations.

In July 1912 Sir Robert Borden, accompanied by other Canadian ministers, arrived in London for a special conference with the Committee of Imperial Defence, arising out of the unsatisfactory progress of the Royal Canadian Navy. They learnt that the German fleet was designed for large-scale offensive action in the North Sea and North Atlantic "against the strongest naval Power", that Power being forced

[1] *Parl. Pap.* 1911, LIV [Cd. 5746–2], pp. 1–3.
[2] *Ibid.* Map.   [3] *Ibid.* pp. 3–6, 10.
[4] Asquith, H. H., *Genesis of the War* (1923), p. 131.

to keep its fleet partially dispersed for various imperial purposes. Moreover, German submarines were being built with a wide range of offensive action and not merely for coast defence. Hitherto there had been two safety signals: annual winter demobilisation and the stationing of Germany's big ships in the Baltic. With the new German Navy Law and the deepening of the Kiel Canal, to be completed in two years time (1914), both these signals would disappear.[1] Moreover, Austria-Hungary, the ally of the German Empire, was unofficially building dreadnoughts, thus creating the possibility of a strategical deficiency for Britain. Hence a naval gesture by Canada, even in general terms, would be extremely welcome, since, apart from its great moral effect, it would enable the Cabinet to avoid defining Britain's naval strength in comparison with that of Germany and Austria combined in terms which were too precise.[2] On 23 July, Mr Churchill told the House of Commons that Germany now had nearly four-fifths of her navy in full commission. To meet this there would be an increase in the striking power of British ships of all classes, and twenty-one capital ships would be laid down during the next five years instead of seventeen. He also hinted at the Austrian building programme and the new reason for giving attention to the Mediterranean where the British fleet would be strengthened.[3] Guarded mention was made of the Borden talks.

After his return to Canada, Borden consulted the Admiralty about a Canadian naval contribution and asked for a statement of Britain's naval needs. He received a memorandum stating that:

Naval supremacy is of two kinds; general and local. General supremacy consists in the power to defeat in battle and drive from the sea the strongest hostile navy or combination of hostile navies wherever they may be found. Local superiority consists in the power to send in good time to, or maintain permanently in, some distant theatre forces adequate to defeat the enemy or hold him in check until the main decision has been obtained in the decisive theatre.

Great Britain had hitherto protected the Empire by her general naval supremacy. Canada's seaborne trade had increased considerably, both in the Atlantic and Pacific, and, for the protection of this trade, "Canada is dependent, and has always depended upon the Imperial Navy, without corresponding contribution or cost". Britain's power to aid the Empire would be diminished by the growth of the German and other modern navies.

Whatever may be the decision of Canada at the present serious juncture, Great Britain will not in any circumstances fail in her duty to the overseas Dominions of the Crown. She has before now successfully made head alone and unaided against the most formidable combinations and the greatest military Powers: and she has

---

[1] *Ibid.* pp. 78–80.
[2] Tucker, G., "Naval Policy of Sir Robert Borden", *Canadian Hist. Rev.* (March 1947), pp. 1–30.
[3] *Hansard*, 5th ser. XLI, 835–946 and 1198–308.

not lost her capacity, even if left wholly unsupported, of being able by a wise policy and strenuous exertions to watch over and preserve the vital interests of the Empire.... But the aid which Canada could give at the present time is not to be measured only in ships and money. Any action on the part of Canada to increase the power and mobility of the Imperial Navy, and thus widen the margin of our common safety, would be recognised everywhere as a most significant witness of the united strength of the Empire.... The Prime Minister of the Dominion having enquired in what form any immediate aid that Canada might give would be most effective, we have no hesitation in answering after a prolonged consideration of all the circumstances, that it is desirable that such aid should include the provision of a number of the largest and strongest ships of war which science can build or money supply.[1]

On receiving this formidable hortation, in which Churchill's hand is clearly seen, Borden began to prepare his plans, first for an immediate "ship-money" gift to Britain and, second, for a future Canadian Navy to be built locally. The immediate cost of building ships in Canada was prohibitive and it would have taken four years to set up the necessary dockyard plant. When, therefore, in December 1912 Borden introduced his Naval Aid Bill in the Canadian House of Commons, it was for the sum of $35,000,000 to pay for three dreadnoughts to be built in Britain. The bill was strongly opposed by Laurier's Liberal isolationists who denied the danger, disliked paying so-called "tribute" money to Britain, and wanted merely a local defence navy, locally built. Laurier himself favoured reserving Canada's right to remain neutral in a British war. Meanwhile Mr Churchill was outlining in the British House of Commons a scheme for an "Imperial Squadron", based on Gibraltar, to fulfil a special imperial function, and consisting of the three Canadian dreadnoughts, together with H.M.S. *New Zealand* and the projected H.M.S. *Malaya*. Then the Bill, having duly passed the Canadian Lower House, was rejected by the Senate in May 1913, a severe blow to the Admiralty, which was noted carefully in Berlin.[2]

The huge increases in naval strength necessary to maintain a strategical superiority over the rapidly growing German Navy, subsequent to the launch of the *Dreadnought*, led to Cabinet crises over the estimates for 1909 and 1914, the latter being aggravated by Canada's abrupt naval retreat.[3] Liberal critics of the Cabinet concentrated their efforts mainly on expense, the fear of appearing provocative, and the pacific intentions of the non-liberal regimes in Germany and Austria-Hungary. All through the period 1905–14 continuous political attention was given to naval expenditure, while public interest was kept alive by news of increases in the German Navy and of the various diplomatic attempts by Britain to avoid a

---

[1] *Parl. Pap.* 1912–13, LIII [Cd. 6513].
[2] By August 1914 the Royal Canadian Navy consisted of the two old cruisers, in very poor condition, and a total personnel of under 400.
[3] See McKenna, S., *Reginald McKenna, 1863–1943* (1948), pp. 70–83, for the 1909 crisis.

policy of competitive building.[1] The developments in battleship design immediately following the *Dreadnought* were mainly in the direction of an increase in tonnage, horse-power and secondary armament, but with no increase of speed and little difference in armour-plating. In 1911–12 came the completion of the four *Orions* of 22,500 tons, mounting ten 13·5 inch guns, Lord Fisher's final achievement prior to his first retirement. Comparable German ships still mounted 12-inch guns. In 1913 there followed the four *King George V's* and by August 1914 two of the new *Iron Dukes* had actually joined the fleet. All these ships mounted ten 13·5 inch guns and were in effect improved *Orions*, the *Iron Dukes* also having a speed of 22·5 knots in place of 21. But, behind these and already nearing completion, there was, in addition to two more *Iron Dukes*, the name ship of the new "Fast Division", the famous *Queen Elizabeth* mounting eight 15-inch guns and having a speed of 25 knots. The "Fast Division" was the personal achievement of Churchill, the recently appointed First Lord.[2] Yet, although the German Navy was outmatched, it had the advantage of being built entirely for North Sea and North Atlantic service, while the British ships had to be built for service in all parts of the world. In addition the British Navy had to make provisions for "the bolt from the blue". "For our system to work," wrote Corbett, "the main concentration must not only be overwhelming but instantaneous."[3] To make this certain, trade routes and distant stations and even the northern isles of Britain had to be left exposed. No such naval problems had ever confronted Britain before.

It was the backwardness of the Navy's operational plans for fighting Germany that had led to the appointment of Mr Churchill as First Lord. Hitherto the Admiralty had possessed no Naval War Staff analogous in function to the Imperial General Staff at the War Office. Lord Fisher had disliked the idea.[4] Churchill succeeded in creating one, though its usefulness was impaired at the start by the conservatism of the Board, and by the opposition of the Treasury to all preparations involving extra expenditure. Even before the war began, however, its plans for *distant* blockade, war mobilisation, and the transport of the Expeditionary Force were accepted and acted on, and under stress of war many of its earlier proposals received recognition.[5]

The decision to build a "Fast Division" of battleships led to a further decision of the highest international importance, the con-

[1] Exhaustively dealt with in Woodward, E. L., *Great Britain and the German Navy* (1935).

[2] Churchill, W. S., *World Crisis*, I (1923), pp. 121–7.

[3] Corbett, Sir Julian, *Naval Operations*, I (1920), p. 10.

[4] "A Naval Staff at the Admiralty is a very excellent organisation for cutting out and arranging foreign newspaper cuttings." Bacon, Sir R., *Life of Lord Fisher*, II, 137–8.

[5] Churchill, W. S., *World Crisis*, I, 507–11. The traditional prestige and pre-eminence of the Board of Admiralty naturally placed the Naval War Staff in a different position from that of the Imperial General Staff *vis-à-vis* the newly-created Army Council.

version of the entire British Navy of the future from coal to oil fuel. This was the result of the setting up in 1912 of the Royal Commission on Oil Supplies, under the chairmanship of Lord Fisher (then in retirement), and the subsequent signing of the Anglo-Persian Oil Convention. Apart from the need for a tanker fleet to bring the oil from the Persian Gulf, for huge oil storage facilities in all naval bases at home and abroad, and for the provision of fleet oilers for refuelling at sea, the oil-burning policy meant a radical departure from processes of engineering and economics fundamentally associated with Britain's nineteenth-century supremacy in trade and shipping.

Amongst the many false impressions that prevailed, when after the lapse of a century we found ourselves involved in a great war, [wrote Corbett] not the least erroneous is the belief that we were not prepared for it. Whether the scale on which we prepared was as large as the signs of the times called for, whether we did right to cling to our long-tried system of a small Army and a large Navy, are questions that will be long debated; but, given the scale which we deliberately chose to adopt, there is no doubt that the machinery for setting our forces in action had reached an ordered completeness in detail that has no parallel in history.[1]

The first sentence of Corbett's judgment has often been quoted, the second very seldom. "Scale" is the conditioning word. Within the limits of its size, function and constituents the Committee of Imperial Defence achieved something near perfection. At Haldane's instigation a standing sub-committee for "the co-ordination of Departmental Action on the outbreak of war" was set up in January 1911, to deal with trading with the enemy, intelligence, censorship, control of wireless and cables censorship, control of aliens, harbour traffic and treatment of enemy merchantmen in port. A "War Book", compiled for the use of the government departments mainly concerned, tabulated necessary action in chronological form under three heads: peace-time preparations and precautions, action on the secret announcement of a period of "strained relations" and action on the outbreak of war. "Action" included financial and administrative measures, quite apart from those directly concerned with naval and military mobilisation, harbour traffic, signal services, intelligence and the protection of harbours, railways, reservoirs and vulnerable points. The Dominions had no direct representation on the "Co-ordination" Sub-committee, though they were kept informed about the results of its investigations, in so far as they were concerned with like problems. In the case of the colonies similar preparations were made to those listed in the "War Book". It is beyond the scope of this chapter to deal with the collateral preparations which were made in the Dominions. Important and most valuable instructions were issued to British diplomatic and consular representatives outside the Empire.

Apart from what Lord Hankey describes as "some very important

[1] Corbett, Sir Julian, *Official History of the Great War; Naval Operations*, I (1920), 18–19.

lacunae" in the work of the Committee of Imperial Defence, namely lack of arrangements for expansion of the Army, the control of man-power and the control of industry,[1] the chief defect of the Committee was that it was still not sufficiently imperial. Between 1912 and August 1914 a number of Dominion statesmen attended meetings while on visits to Britain, but apart from official Conferences these attendances were largely fortuitous. Nor did the authority given to the Canadian High Commissioner by the Canadian Government to attend the Committee in any way imply the acceptance by his Government of the measures recommended. The other Dominions had no permanent representatives. Only in the case of the Imperial General Staff was there a close association of imperial thought and action, based on a common doctrine of war.[2] On a broad view it seems difficult to suggest what the Imperial Government could have done to make the Committee more representative under the existing conditions of imperial relationships. As regards local defence by land the Dominions had been better than their word, having in effect prepared the way for wartime military expansion by means of absolute or conditional conscription acts. Whether they had forces immediately capable of taking the field abroad was another matter, as also was the question of whether local politics would allow their respective schemes to be put into effect as a whole when the time came for action.

"In every respect the Expeditionary Force of 1914 was incom-parably the best trained, best organised, and best equipped British Army which ever went forth to war."[3] This highly authoritative expression of opinion by the Official Historian requires some qualifica-tion. Plans were complete in every detail for rendering the Force immediately mobile, and dispatching it to France in such a manner that it could take the field immediately on landing without having to reorganise in the manner of the old time colonial expeditions sent out in troopers. For three months' fighting in a war of movement the Force was perfect of its kind. For a long war and a static war, on a Continental scale, it was desperately weak, and in this respect had a weakening effect on the armies of the Dominions whose organisation reflected its own. There were less than 200 machine guns for the whole Force, though the School of Musketry had recommended six per battalion in 1909. The reason was the expense. Despite the lessons of the South African War, there were only twenty-four of the new long-recoil 60-pounder guns for the whole Force. To meet a modern European army of Continental strength, the British fire-power was of very light weight. Despite brilliant experimental work by the Royal

---

[1] *Diplomacy by Conference* (1946), p. 90.

[2] Codified in *Field Service Regulations*, Part I, Operations, and Part II, Organisation and Administration (1909).

[3] Edmonds, J. E. (ed.), *Official History of the War: Military Operations in France and Belgium*, I, 10.

Engineers and the Army Service Corps, developments in mechanical haulage and transport, including caterpillar traction (invented as far back as 1909), had been stifled by the ban on petrol for military vehicles which was only lifted in 1912. Though Britain was the leading industrial country, the guns and transport of the British Army were mainly horse-drawn. Behind the Expeditionary Force stood the Special Reserve, ready to form the necessary drafts, and behind this again the Territorial Force, consisting of fourteen divisions, fully equipped with guns and rifles, and with its full complement of army services. But the total artillery ammuntion reserve for all purposes was "considerably less than a million rounds".[1] Nor had any extensive plans been worked out for harnessing British industry to the task of producing guns, small arms, ammunition, equipment and military vehicles, rapidly and on an increasing scale. Consequently, when the demand for guns and ammunition came, involving industrial man-power on a very large scale, it was seriously complicated by the equally sharp and extensive demand for military man-power in the field, a dual contingency which the Cabinet had never seriously considered. "We then had to face the fact that, whereas our foreign policy had gradually assumed a Continental character, our military preparations had remained insular and almost parochial."[2]

In order to have a real army and yet avoid disrupting the Liberal Cabinet, Haldane and his successor, Colonel Seely, had been forced to put all their goods in the shop window. Political timidity, the fetish of economy in military expenditure, failure to foresee position warfare, and in general a non-industrial outlook on land warfare, were responsible for making the Army of the "world's workshop" almost impotent for want of ammunition after less than six months' fighting. Yet even this army was by Continental standards "contemptible" in numbers.

The quantitative limitations of Britain's technical preparation for war are equally illustrated in the case of the Royal Flying Corps. Manned largely by brilliant experimenters, the R.F.C. had four squadrons ready for active service by August 1914.[3] The Royal Naval Air Services had thirty-nine aeroplanes, fifty-two seaplanes and seven airships. This was all the air strength allowed for the greatest Navy in the world. It was Churchill who foresaw that, with the Royal Flying Corps engulfed in a Continental war, it would be the duty of the Royal Naval Air Service to protect Britain against air attack (in addition to serving the fleet), and that this could best be done by a large-scale bombing of German air bases.

[1] Robertson, Sir W., *Soldiers and Statesmen* (1926), 1, 41–2. Sydenham, Lord, *My Working Life* (1927), pp. 195–6.
[2] Robertson, *op. cit.* p. 45.
[3] Raleigh, Walter, *Official History of the War: The War in the Air*, 1 (1922), 259.

Naval preparations were more satisfactory, national industry and national service having gone hand in hand. But here again the demands for shipbuilding, ship repairs, marine engineering, guns, torpedoes, mines, shells and general naval equipment were to add to the pressure on industrial man-power and material already over-strained by the commitments of a Continental war. The British Navy had a substantial numerical advantage over the German Navy in all categories of new surface warships, thus enabling the "Grand Fleet" for the long-range strategical blockade of Germany, conducted from Scottish waters, to be formed out of the newest and most powerful ships with a smaller force to block the Straits of Dover. The importance of the pre-war decision to establish this blockade can scarcely be exaggerated. Since British and German peacetime trade routes made use of the same focal waters, i.e. the Channel and North Sea, the British fleet, which denied Germany the use of all but part of the North Sea, could automatically cover British and Allied trade against naval interference, except from submarines or independent surface raiders. Similarly, the Grand Fleet could guarantee the passage and subsequent reinforcement and supply of the Expedition-ary Force, while automatically denying Germany the use of the North Sea for landing troops in France. In the Mediterranean a stronger British fleet was established than might have seemed necessary, partly because of uncertainty about the French Navy arising from the absence of any definite alliance, and partly because of uncertainty about Italy.

In Eastern waters the Admiralty automatically assumed opera-tional control of all Dominion warships. The scheme for a Pacific Fleet, laid down at the Imperial Defence Conference of 1909, had, however, been modified, none of the three squadrons, China, Australian and East Indies, being fully up to strength in modern sea-going warships. Nor had it been possible, in view of the German menace, to carry out a still more ambitious scheme for the Royal Australian Navy recommended by Admiral Sir Reginald Henderson in 1911. Meanwhile slow progress with the 1909 scheme led to a protest early in 1914 from the Australian Government. An even stronger protest came from New Zealand, where, under the powers of the Naval Defence Act passed in 1913, a New Zealand "Division" was being organised as part of what was now to be known as the Eastern Fleet. So far the Division consisted of three semi-obsolete protected cruisers and a sloop. New Zealand now offered to increase her annual contribution to £150,000 in return for two new light cruisers in her waters. In default of receiving them she threatened to withdraw her contribution altogether and start building a navy of her own in British dockyards. To this the Admiralty could only plead the German danger and the security resulting from the Anglo-Japanese Alliance. Nevertheless, the British Navy was weak on distant stations for guarding focal trade areas, particularly off north-east Brazil. The good will of the United States was of course a very important asset, but the anticipated opening of the Panama Canal was about to create a new international waterway usable by belligerent warships. It was, therefore, of great importance that two days before war was declared the Cabinet cut through a long tangle of abortive negotiations between various commercial interests, and guaranteed the re-insurance of British merchant shipping against war risks, provided Admiralty instructions were followed as to routes. Otherwise British seaborne trade might have come to a dead stop in view of the threat of German surface raiders.[1]

There are two possible views of Britain's pre-war preparations: the first, that, taking into account the absence of a great war for a hundred years and the concentration of the Government on social and political reforms, they fulfilled more than reasonable and minimum aims;[2] the second, that the Empire sustained huge and possibly irreparable losses for lack of political courage in making more comprehensive preparations and through an obstinate refusal to devote a greater proportion of what were then easily gained revenues for this purpose. In the Dominions there was undoubtedly some backwardness in acknowledging the full strategical implications of self-government, a backwardness, it is to be noted, varying more with geographical position than with political maturity. By August 1914 the Royal Australian Navy, though only a small force, had a strategical value for the Empire well worth the early rebuffs suffered by its sponsors. Yet it was in terms of military man-power that the Dominions were to make their most timely and effective contributions in the approaching war, since, unlike the wars of the eighteenth century, the Great War of 1914–18 tended rather to suck British Empire man-power inwards than to disperse it in colonial operations. In this the Dominions proved better than their word, the convoys of Canadian and ANZAC troops which left home ports in the autumn of 1914 being followed by a steady stream whose numbers, as well as fighting efficiency and fine physique, were to be a significant factor in the defeat of the Central Powers in the major theatres of land operations. Whether the Imperial Government could have made better strategic arrangements with the Dominions before the War began is a matter that can only be discussed in terms of their political relationships, to which all other matters, however important, had to remain subordinate.

[1] Forty-seven point nine per cent of the world's steam tonnage was British in 1914, Germany's share being 11·9. British shipping carried 52 per cent of the world's seaborne trade.

[2] Hankey, Lord, *Government Control in War* (1945), pp. 22–31.

CHAPTER XVI

THE EMPIRE AT WAR, 1914–1918

THE NAVY AND THE GATHERING OF THE ARMIES

THE British entered the First World War better prepared for the event than they have been at the beginning of any other war in their long history. This is not to say that the stresses and strains of 1917 and 1918 had been, or could have been, anticipated, but that the armed forces stood ready, in 1914, to carry out such tasks as were then assigned to them. The Grand Fleet, the Expeditionary Force for Flanders, the Territorial Forces at home and in the Dominions, all were ready in August 1914 and all stood to arms. In sharp contrast, the civilians in all parts of the Empire were taken by surprise. From 23 July, the day of the Austrian ultimatum to Serbia, the diplomatic crisis developed so rapidly that there was no time for the promised consultation with the Dominions; nor did they ask for it.

In Australia Parliament was dissolved and a general election in progress in August 1914. "Whatever happens," said Mr (later Sir) Joseph Cook, the Premier, on 31 July, "Australia is part of the Empire. When the Empire is at war, so is Australia at war." Mr A. Fisher, the Leader of the Opposition, who won the election and succeeded Mr Cook as Premier in September, was no less emphatic. On 3 August, the day before war was declared, Mr Cook placed the Australian Navy unconditionally at the disposal of the Imperial Government and made an offer, which was instantly accepted, to provide an expeditionary force of 20,000 men. In New Zealand Mr W. Massey, the Premier, made an offer on 2 August to dispatch a contingent of 8000 men, with confidence that both parties in Parliament, then in session, would support him.

Similarly in Canada, the fact of war was at first accepted by all parties. The mobilisation plans were put into operation by Order-in-Council and, after an inquiry had been made of the Imperial Government, an expeditionary force of one division was offered. In Canada, as in the other Dominions, it was assumed that the forces sent overseas would be composed of volunteers, of whom a sufficient number appeared before August was out. A foretaste of later Canadian munificence was a gift of one million bags of flour from the Canadian to the British Government. All these steps were taken before Parliament met at Ottawa on 18 August. The speech from the throne announcing the policy of the Conservative Government was approved by Laurier on behalf of the Liberal opposition. This generous mood of unity was extended even to the Irish party in the British House of

Commons where John Redmond supported Asquith. Even in India, official and non-official members of the Legislative Council vied with one another (8 September 1914) in expressing their loyal enthusiasm. The Princes overwhelmed the Government with their offers of service; the nationalist opposition was silent; and the Council proceeded to provide financial and military aid to the war effort on a scale that the British Government would not have dared to demand. Only in South Africa was there a discordant note in the chorus of devotion to a cause which elsewhere was almost universally held to be justified. There only was there talk, among certain sections of the European population, of abstention from an "imperialist" war begun without prior consultation.

When the Regular Army went to Flanders there went with it the cream of the General Staff, the officers who had prepared the plans for the Committee of Imperial Defence. In their place appeared the massive figure of Lord Kitchener, a professional soldier, as Secretary of State for War in a Liberal Cabinet. For nearly two years he reigned at the War Office, keeping all secrets under his own cap, holding all the reins in his hand, decentralising as little as possible. On his third day, 7 August 1914, he astonished the nation and the General Staff by appealing for a national army of volunteers who were to enlist "for three years or the duration of the war". Kitchener's achievement, under-rated by his critics in later years, was to create five new divisions by withdrawing detachments of troops from India and the colonies, to bring to Europe more than eleven divisions from the Dominions, to raise the new army of thirty divisions which bore his name, and to convert the British people from their age-long habit of dependence upon professional troops for their defence. His greatest error, perhaps, was to build his new army on an improvised foundation instead of using the existing foundation of the Territorial Army. Nevertheless, he was able at the same time to increase the strength of the Territorial Army from fourteen to twenty-eight divisions. All this was done while he supervised a great campaign in France, and five or six secondary campaigns in all parts of the world. He consulted no one; he imposed his conception of the long war and the national effort upon his Cabinet colleagues, upon his fellow-soldiers, and—not least—upon the Dominions, by sheer force of character. Mr W. M. Hughes (Premier of Australia, 1915–23) has declared that, during the first three years of the war, the Dominions were never consulted about a military plan.[1]

The concentration of the Grand Fleet at Scapa, to protect commerce, to blockade Germany, and to guard the narrow seas while the Expeditionary Force crossed to France, held the attention of the Admiralty during August 1914. The main body of troops was

[1] Hughes, W. M., *The Splendid Adventure*, p. 72.

established in France by the 19th and, on the 28th, the Navy was able to demonstrate its aggressive spirit by a daring raid into the Heligoland Bight. In the Mediterranean, though the German squadron was not brought to action, it had taken refuge in the Dardanelles by 10 August, and no longer threatened the sea-routes through the Suez Canal. Ocean-going submarines had not yet appeared to menace British shipping, so that the only danger came from five fast merchant ships which the Germans had armed as commerce-raiders, and from eight cruisers which constituted their foreign squadrons. The five armed merchant ships were hunted down and dispatched without alteration in British strategic plans; the eight cruisers,[1] especially the German China squadron, were powerful enough to cause a major diversion. As early as 6 August the Cabinet was obliged to issue instructions, from which, in Mr Churchill's words, they would have "averted their minds, a month earlier, with horror and disgust", for dispatching six separate expeditions to seize the German colonies in every part of the world which these ships might use as their base or refuge.

For two generations the British Empire, considered strategically, had been a system of coaling-stations and cable-stations, which at all costs must be preserved; the German naval power was obliged to depend upon coal from neutral ports, and upon communication by wireless telegraphy from a few powerful transmitting stations recently erected in the German colonies. The strategic necessity to baffle the German commerce-raiders, by silencing their communications, was intensified as Kitchener's plans for expanding the Armies called for greater convoys of troops from India and the Dominions.

The six colonial operations were authorised and set on foot by a sub-committee of the Cabinet quaintly known as the "Offensive Sub-Committee": against Togoland, already threatened by an enterprising British officer from the Gold Coast; against the Cameroons, which was to be invaded from Nigeria with co-operation from French Africa; against German East Africa (Tanganyika), an operation at first commended to the Indian Government; against German South-West Africa, which was commended to the Union Government; against German New Guinea and against German Samoa, which Australia and New Zealand respectively undertook. The Governments of the two Pacific Dominions enthusiastically agreed to divert a small part of their promised contingents to these preliminary tasks.

Von Spee, the commander of the German Pacific squadron, dispatched the *Emden* on a raid against shipping in the Indian Ocean, and the *Nürnberg* to disrupt the Pacific cable, while his three larger units vanished among the Caroline and Marshall Islands, then under German rule. There was but one allied ship in the Pacific, H.M.A.S.

---

[1] *Scharnhorst, Gneisenau, Emden, Nürnberg, Leipzig* on the China station; *Dresden, Karlsruhe* in the West Indies: *Königsberg* in East African waters.

Australia, capable of both overhauling and out-fighting Von Spee's ships, the *Scharnhorst* and *Gneisenau,* and her movements must be nicely timed. She took station at Noumez, in French New Caledonia, in company with a French warship. The New Zealand Government having agreed on 6 August to occupy Samoa, their expedition of 1400 men in two transports set sail on the 15th, made rendezvous with H.M.A.S. *Australia,* and reached Apia on 29 August. There was no opposition and the British flag was hoisted on the following day. Leaving this little garrison in Samoa, the *Australia* picked up an Australian convoy for New Guinea. On 11 September about two battalions of Australian volunteers, led by marines, landed at Kokopo (Herbertshöhe), the German administrative capital near Rabaul in the island of New Britain. The opposition was confined to a little sniping in the bush, ending with the German capitulation on the 17th.

By this time the main convoys were forming in Australian and New Zealand ports, anxiously awaiting their escorts. But, while the *Australia* lay off Rabaul, on 14 September, the *Scharnhorst* and *Gneisenau* steamed into the roadstead of Apia, to find it garrisoned by New Zealand troops. Von Spee suspiciously turned away and next appeared at Papeete, in French Tahiti, which he bombarded on the 22nd. Wireless intercepts, picked up in Fiji and New Zealand, located the German ships far to the east in October. On 1 November they destroyed Admiral Cradock's squadron of weaker ships at Coronel off the Chilean coast. Meanwhile the strategic situation had been changed by the adherence of Japan to the alliance. Though nothing in the Anglo-Japanese treaty required it, the Japanese Government, remembering the diplomatic hostility of Germany in 1905, sent an ultimatum demanding the surrender of the German concession at Tsing-tau in precisely the same terms as the Germans had used in demanding the Japanese withdrawal from Port Arthur nine years earlier. Tsing-tau was strongly fortified and held by good German troops who put up a stout resistance. A formal siege, in which a detachment of British-Indian regular troops from Wei-hai-wei took part, lasted from 27 August to 7 November 1914 when Tsing-tau surrendered. The Japanese also agreed to provide a battle cruiser and a light cruiser for operations in Australian seas. These were accordingly used during October to escort the New Zealand convoy of ten ships to King George's Sound in Western Australia, where it joined the main Australian convoy of twenty-eight ships.

The crossing of the Indian Ocean by this great fleet was made the occasion of a sweep by several British, Australian, and Japanese cruisers to find the *Emden* which had done no small damage to commerce in the Bay of Bengal, even throwing some shells into Madras on 22 September. She was located and destroyed by H.M.A.S. *Sydney* on 8 November 1914 at the Cocos Islands, where she had attacked the cable station. Since Von Spee had gone off to the South American

Coast and had picked up there the three outstanding German cruisers, only the *Königsberg* showed the German flag in eastern seas. She was found on 30 October, hiding in the Rufiji River, in German East Africa, and was blockaded there until measures could be taken for her destruction. The long arms of the Royal Navy also reached out and closed upon Von Spee's squadron, which in its turn was annihilated by superior forces in the running fight from the Falkland Islands, 8 December 1914. H.M.A.S. *Australia* took part in the search but had not the good fortune to be present at the fight. The outer seas were now secure for British commerce and British troop movements.

During the same period a convoy of thirty-one ships had brought the 1st Canadian Division from Quebec to Plymouth, picking up on their way ships with volunteeers from Newfoundland and one with a regular regiment from Bermuda. Two divisions of British regulars and three of Indian troops had been brought from India to the Mediterranean, three divisions of British Territorials had gone to India to replace them, and there had been many minor moves.

These large and complex naval operations were accomplished so swiftly, without loss, because of the world-wide British system of cable communications. Only at two points, Fanning Island and Cocos Island, and in each case only for a few hours, did the German warships disrupt the system. On the other hand, German intelligence in the Pacific was based upon five wireless stations, at Apia (Samoa), Rabaul (New Guinea), Yap (Caroline Islands), Angaur (Pelew Islands), and Nauru. The New Zealanders occupied Apia on 29 August; the Australians Rabaul on 11 September, Nauru on 6 November. It caused some heart-searchings in Australia when the Japanese also advanced into the German islands, occupying Yap on 7 October and Angaur a few days later. The British Government had assured the Australian Government in August that the Japanese had no intention of seizing German islands in the Pacific, and a force was being organised in Australia to take them over. On 3 December 1914 the Secretary of State urged the Australian Government to accept a change of policy. "We consider it most convenient, for strategic reasons, to allow them (the Japanese) to remain in occupation for the present, leaving whole question of future to be settled at the end of the war. We should be glad therefore if the Australian expedition would confine itself to occupation of German islands south of the equator." To this the Australian Government loyally but reluctantly agreed.

THE TURKISH WAR

All these widely dispersed operations, though they were to have a lasting effect upon the progress of the war, seemed but small matters compared with the bitter campaign in France and Flanders. After the first shock at the Battle of the Frontiers, in which the British action at Mons (23 August 1914) was one incident, the retreat, the counter-check and then the recoil of the German armies from the Marne (6–9 September), tactics on the Western Front assumed a form unexpected by either the French or the German General Staff. At that stage of mechanical invention, the power of the defensive proved immensely superior to that of the offensive. It was to be a gunner's, not a bayonet-man's war. The armies dig in, confronting one another, extending their flanks until, by mid-November, static warfare prevailed along a continuous line from the Swiss frontier to the Belgian coast. Deadlock induced thought, with the result that two schools of strategists emerged: the Western-Front men, mostly professional soldiers trained in the Staff Colleges, whose tradition demanded maintenance of the aim towards a single objective, with concentration of force at the decisive point; and the Eastern-Front men who felt that there must be some way round the immovable obstacle of the entrenched lines. On the enemy side the Eastern-Front offered brilliant hopes. The veteran Hindenburg, with his Staff Officer, Ludendorff, had saved East Prussia from Russian invaders at the Battle of Tannenberg. For them 1915 was to provide a succession of victories in Poland. For the Eastern-Front men in France and Britain the centre of interest lay in the Balkans. When Venizelos, then Prime Minister of Greece, had offered to join the alliance in August, he had been discouraged by Sir Edward Grey on the grounds that such a move would antagonise Turkey; but Turkey was inexorably drawing towards the enemy's camp. Grey made a last vain bid for Turkish neutrality by offering, what British Governments had so often promised, to guarantee the integrity of the Turkish Empire. Germany bid higher, by offering the Young Turks the two warships, *Goeben* and *Breslau*, which had taken refuge in the Dardanelles. Since these ships were strong enough to give the Turks supremacy over Russia in the Black Sea, they tipped the scale. During October the Turks committed acts of war against Russian shipping and sea ports, whereupon war was declared by Great Britain on Turkey, 5 November 1914.

Already the worsening relations between Great Britain and Turkey had led to intrigue and conspiracy. The building of the Hejaz railway from Damascus, through Amman, to Medina, in 1908, had marked an endeavour by the Turks to affirm their suzerainty over the Arab lands and over the liberty-loving Arab tribesmen. Already Arabs and even Syrians had begun to regard the British as potential liberators. Some confidential approaches had been made by Arab leaders, early in 1914, to Lord Kitchener, then Consul-General in Egypt, but without inducing him to commit Great Britain to the Arab cause.[1] These activities had the effect, rather, of inciting the

[1] Gooch and Temperley (eds.), *British Documents on the Origins of the War*, x, 824–38.

British to strengthen their treaty relations with the Sultanates of Southern Arabia, and thus to tighten their grip upon the Suez Canal.

Palace influence in Egypt played off Turkey against Britain. The Khedive, Abbas Hilmi, having been worsted in a bout of intrigue by the formidable Kitchener, was cooling himself, in August 1914, by a visit to his nominal suzerain, the Sultan, at Constantinople. Kitchener too, was on leave in London, and neither he nor the Khedive was destined to return to Egypt. After considering the alternative of direct annexation, the British Government decided to transfer Egypt, in name as in fact, from Turkish to British protection. The Protectorate was proclaimed, amid scenes of tranquillity, on 18 December 1914. At the same time the Khedive was deposed *in absentia*; his uncle was proclaimed Sultan of Egypt, a title that, seven years later was changed to King. The Egyptians were assured that the British Army and Navy would defend them, without expecting them to take a direct part in offensive operations. Egypt thus became, almost by accident, the base for the strategic reserve of the British Empire, and provided scope for the plans of the Eastern Front men.

First blows in the Turkish war were struck by an Indian Brigade sent to reinforce the garrison of Aden; they drove off a concentration of Turkish troops in November 1914. About the same time the Bikanir Camel Corps was also in action against restive tribesmen east of the Suez Canal. When, in February 1915, the Turks were ready to launch a probing attack against the Canal defences, it was easily driven off, since Australians and New Zealanders as well as Indian troops were by that time in position. Their convoy, arriving at Suez at the onset of the Turkish war, had disembarked in Egypt. In addition to the Indian detachments (and another sent to East Africa which will be mentioned later) the Indian Army had become involved in operations at the head of the Persian Gulf, which were to prove a deepening drain on British and Indian man-power throughout the war.

As early as 26 September the India Office in Whitehall had made an appreciation of "the role of India in a Turkish war", asserting India's historic interest in the affairs of the Persian Gulf. It was the India Office, rather than the Admiralty, that insisted upon the necessity of securing Anglo-Persian oil. On 23 October the Indian Army landed a brigade on Bahrein, an island under British protection, merely to show the flag in India's historic sphere of influence. When war broke out with Turkey a few days later, these troops were ordered to take possession of the refineries at Abadan, in Turkish territory, and then of Basra, the Turkish seaport which was the outlet of the Persian oilfields. As will happen in such cases, the brigade became a division, the division an army corps, when the tactical situation demanded deeper penetration in order to cover the pipeline from the Persian frontier. The plans were made, rather loosely, between the India Office and the Commander-in-Chief at Simla, without much reference to War Office or Admiralty; the troops and their supplies came from India. In March 1915 Sir John Nixon was sent from Simla, where optimism prevailed, to enlarge the scope of the campaign. He was to occupy the *vilayet* of Basra and to make plans for occupying the *vilayet* of Baghdad, three hundred miles upstream. In April he beat off a Turkish attack at Shaiba and began his preparations for a general advance.

While the Indian Government undertook this private war, the British Government had fallen into a Tragedy of Errors over the Dardanelles. It began with a survey of the situation presented to the Cabinet by Lieut.-Col. M. P. A. (now Lord) Hankey in December. The two most ingenious brains in the Cabinet, those of Mr Lloyd George and Mr Churchill, were not slow to react. Mr Lloyd George convinced his colleagues that the pressure on the Russians should be relieved by opening a second front, and this could best be done by inducing Greece to join the Allies. Meanwhile, Mr Churchill took council with Admiral Sir S. H. Carden, commanding the Mediterranean Fleet, about the practicability of forcing the Dardanelles. On 13 January 1915 the plan to achieve this purpose by naval means alone was somewhat coolly approved by the War Council of the Cabinet. The long, confused and bitter dispute over the ensuing failures turned upon the personalities of the two old warriors, Lord Fisher (aged 74), the First Sea Lord, and Lord Kitchener (aged 65), the Secretary of State for War. Fisher had already proposed a grand combined operation, for which Kitchener could not or would not find the troops. Thus rebuffed, Fisher was an increasingly reluctant colleague, though he did not record his disapproval of the decision taken by the War Council on 13 January. Kitchener, sceptical at first and ready with an alternative plan for a landing elsewhere, gradually came round and, at last, produced the troops which he had said were not available. Mr Churchill urged his professional adviser, Lord Fisher, to employ the *Queen Elizabeth*, the first ship armed with 15-inch guns, then actually in the Mediterranean for her trials. He urged Lord Kitchener to employ the 29th Division, British regular troops collected from overseas garrisons, and reputed the best division in the army. They were not, at first, conceived as an assault force but as a following-up force to exploit the naval success. On 26 February Kitchener informed General Sir W. Birdwood that the Australians and New Zealanders under his command would also be available for this task. He sent Birdwood as his personal observer with the naval squadron to the Dardanelles.

The naval bombardment of the Turkish forts guarding the Narrows began on 19 February 1915. First results seemed favourable and had an immediate diplomatic effect. M. Venizelos, the Greek Prime Minister, who previously had not committed himself further than to allow the Allies to use the Island of Lemnos as a base, now immediately offered to mobilise the Greek Army for a march on Constantinople. To the consternation of the British Government this proposal was vetoed by the Russians, on the 3 March, for political reasons. The British, it seemed, must either call the Dardanelles operation off—and there was still time to do so—or they must send an army of their own. A second bombardment of the forts had already begun and made good progress during the first week of March. Even in spite of Lord Fisher's misgivings this was no moment for retreat, especially since Lord Kitchener was at last committed to military support, and the 29th Division on its way to Egypt. At the third bombardment, on 18 March, three old battleships (two British and one French) were sunk by floating mines, while H.M.S. *Inflexible*, a new battle-cruiser, was severely damaged, in the presence of Sir Ian Hamilton, whom Kitchener had appointed to command the troops. On the following day, acting on their own responsibility, Hamilton and the Admiral (Sir J. M. de Robeck, who had replaced Carden) stopped the naval action and decided for a combined operation. Kitchener loyally supported the men on the spot, and the Cabinet merely acquiesced. It does not appear that they ever formally minuted their approval of the Gallipoli landings. Only after the war was it known that on 19 March the Turks had hardly a shot left in their locker.

Hamilton's army was not trained nor equipped for beach-landings, nor were the transports of the 29th Division loaded in readiness for an assault. A further delay of five weeks was necessary—was indeed too short—for the mounting of an assault on a defended beach. In those five weeks a German General, Liman von Sanders, took command of the Turkish forces and converted into wired and entrenched fortresses the scrub-covered hills of the Gallipoli Peninsula. Thirty thousand lives were lost in vain attempts to regain observation posts which had been used freely by landing-parties from the warships during the first naval bombardment.

At first light on 25 April 1915, the 29th Division began to land on five beaches near Cape Helles, in the face of heavy machine-gun fire. Of the 9000 men put ashore on the first day 3000 were killed or wounded. On the western face of the Peninsula, outside the Straits, the 1st Australian Division, supported by a New Zealand brigade, was carried by the tide past its objective and went ashore at Ari Burnu (afterwards known as Anzac Cove). Since this landing was begun before dawn, about 20,000 men got ashore without heavy losses though with some confusion. But the commander of the Turkish defensive sector was an officer of middle rank, named Mustapha Kemal, who took charge of operations in the very front, with great skill and resolution. A fierce soldier's battle developed, in which the "Anzacs" for ever established their reputation as individual fighters. So confused and precarious was the situation that night, that Birdwood, on the advice of his brigadiers, proposed to re-embark, but was firmly told by Hamilton to "dig in and stick it out". The Australians did so. By 8 May the two beach-heads were secure but static, with three British divisions and one French division at Helles, two Australian and New Zealand divisions at Anzac. A deadlock, as in France, had been achieved at a cost of 20,000 casualties. Worst of all, German submarines were reported in the Mediterranean, whereupon Lord Fisher withdrew the *Queen Elizabeth* and, washing his hands of the whole operation, suddenly resigned.

Evident weakness in the war organisation, and in particular the shortage of munitions, brought about a Cabinet crisis in London, instigated by Northcliffe's newspapers. A coalition Government was formed in May under Mr Asquith, with the dynamic David Lloyd George as Minister of Munitions (after 9 June). Mr Churchill left the Admiralty, but Kitchener rode out the storm at the War Office, with some loss of prestige. After weeks of political delays the new Cabinet, working through a new War Council, the Dardanelles Committee, decided to press on with the ill-fated campaign. Meanwhile, repeated attempts by the British to advance from Helles were checked in the three battles of Krithia. The Turks were in a position to bring up their reinforcements far more rapidly than the British.

A threefold operation to break out of the beach-heads was launched on 6 August. The British troops in Helles were again committed to costly holding attacks, which preceded a general assault from Anzac by Australian and some British troops. The Australian battle for the Lone Pine position was perhaps the occasion of the most ferocious fighting of the whole campaign. While the Anzac troops bore the brunt, it was a platoon of Gurkhas that topped the hill and saw the tranquil waters of the Strait beneath them on 8 August. The third, and what was to have been the decisive, stroke failed because of the inexperience of the troops and the lethargy of their commanders. Two new army divisions were put ashore at Suvla Bay on the morning of 7 August. Though the landing was unopposed, they lost time regrouping on the beach instead of pushing inland. Again it was Kemal who organised the defence, stopped the advance when it at last began, and sealed off the new beach-head. On the 9th and 10th he recaptured the vital hill-crests that dominated Anzac. Fighting continued for a fortnight, then lapsed again into static warfare.

The entrance of Italy into the war (23 May 1915), on the side of Britain and France, encouraged Mr Lloyd George, whose star was rising in the new administration, to revive his old project for a Balkan campaign. Proposing that troops should be diverted from the Dardanelles to Salonica, he won support from a party in the French Government. To this proposal the British General Staff raised the strongest objections; it was another diversion and one likely to make heavy demands on shipping. However, the politicians prevailed and ordered four more divisions, with a large French army, to the Mediterranean—too late. In October 1915 the German General Mackensen overran Serbia, with assistance from the Bulgarians, and invaded Greece. The Salonica force was thrown on the defensive and remained so for three years, growing as such armies do. Confronting the Bulgarian Army of 16 divisions and a handful of Germans, there were eventually 670,000 allied soldiers in Macedonia, more than a third of them British, immobilised and consuming ship-borne supplies.

Gratitude for Kitchener's immense services could hardly outweigh the evidence of military failure in the Mediterranean. A Western Front officer, General Sir C. C. Monro, was sent to report on Gallipoli in October. "He came, he saw, he capitulated"; recommending immediate evacuation. In November, Kitchener went to Gallipoli to confirm Monro's observations and, after some fluctuation of opinion that revealed his ageing temper, he concurred. Nature intervened, on 26 November, by sending a blizzard that washed down the ravines and flooded the beaches, drowning 280 soldiers and sending 16,000 to hospital with frost bite and exposure. The campaign died of exhaustion. On 12 December, orders were given for a secret withdrawal which was skilfully conducted by General Birdwood, from Anzac and Suvla on 19 December, from Helles on 8 January 1916, without loss of life. In the campaign 400,000 troops had been employed, with no material effect except that of containing 300,000 Turks. The total of casualties in the invading armies reached the number of 120,000, of whom about 18,000 British, 8000 Australians and 2600 New Zealanders lost their lives.[1] The heroes of the campaign were the British 29th Division and the redoubtable Anzacs, whose valour astonished the world. Morally they could claim a triumph and, to this day, Anzac Day (25 April) is their national day of remembrance.[2]

The evacuation of Gallipoli and the fiasco at Salonica followed hard upon the fruitless battles of Champagne and Loos fought by the French and British armies in France. There, too, the deadlock clamped down again. Sir John French was replaced as British Commander-

---

[1] All figures given here, unless otherwise noted, are taken from *Statistics of the Military Effort of the British Empire in the Great War* (War Office, 1922). Other figures are quoted elsewhere, especially in the apologies of politicians and commanders. There is great variation in the method of compiling military statistics, for example in the phasing of campaigns in time and space, in distinguishing combatants from non-combatants, in the time-lag between the occurrence and the registration of casualties, in the rigour with which slight wounds are recorded, and in the laxity with which consequential deaths are admitted. See Edmonds, J. E. (ed.), *Military Operations, France and Belgium, 1916*, I, 496, commenting on Churchill's *World Crisis*, III, 52.

[2] On the same day, 25 April 1915, an Australian submarine, A.E. 1, made its way through the Dardanelles to operate in the Sea of Marmora, the first of such exploits to be successfully accomplished.

in-Chief in France by Sir Douglas Haig in December 1915, and Sir William Robertson, a rigorous professional soldier, was recalled from France to become Chief of the Imperial General Staff. Though loyal to Kitchener he made an end of Kitchener's autocracy in the War Office. It was his task to disentangle confusion in the Mediterranean, where the Salonica force was thrown on the defensive, where twelve exhausted divisions from Gallipoli were re-organising in Egypt, and where the military planners urged a larger commitment in Mesopotamia.

On 23 October the Cabinet gave a qualified approval to General Nixon's proposed campaign. They did not give him an order but permitted him to proceed with the qualifying condition, "if he is satisfied", and agreed to send him from France the two Indian divisions, since they had not adapted themselves to the distressing campaign in Flanders. Nixon selected for the advance the 6th Division, under Sir Charles Townshend, who had distinguished himself as a young officer by defending Chitral (1895) on the North-West Frontier. Townshend accepted the task with misgivings. His force proved insufficient and, after a check at Ctesiphon, he fell back on Kut-el-Amara, where, by 8 December, he was closely invested. At this stage Sir William Robertson arrived at the War Office. He warned General Aylmer (Nixon's successor) to expect no further reinforcements beyond the two promised divisions, and to be content with relieving the garrison of Kut. Later he relented and sent one more British division from Egypt.

In February 1916 the War Office took charge of the Mesopotamian operations, though transport and supply must still be based on India. Three attempts to relieve Kut were made, in January, March and April; and all were brought to a halt at the Sanna-i-Yat position, another triumph for the defensive in battle. A deeper humiliation followed; negotiations were begun to induce the Turkish commander to raise the siege, in return for an indemnity (or bribe) of £2 millions. When this was haughtily refused, General Townshend was instructed to capitulate. Of the 3000 British and 6000 Indian troops who surrendered, on 29 April 1916, half died in captivity.

The whole unhappy story was investigated by a Royal Commission, with Lord George Hamilton in the Chair. The Mesopotamia Report (issued on 26 June 1917) distributed its censures lavishly on General Nixon, on the Indian Government, on the Secretary of State (Mr Austen Chamberlain), and on the War Cabinet itself. Divided counsels, and responsibilities shared between Simla and Whitehall, explained everything. The Indian Army organisation had proved unable to administer—what it was not designed to administer—a war overseas on the grand scale. Medical arrangements had quite collapsed and at no time was transport adequate to the demands made upon it.

Robertson took over entire charge of the administration in July 1916. A new Commander-in-Chief, Sir Stanley Maude, was appointed by the War Office to reorganise the system in Mesopotamia, with strict instructions not to attempt rash exploits. In December he convinced the War Office that he could safely advance. By an "imperceptible offensive", conducted with deliberation and economy, he made his way forward, entering Baghdad on 12 March 1917, the first spectacular triumph of the Eastern war. Nixon had done his best with three river-steamers; Maude eventually used two hundred.

British prestige had fallen so low in the East, after Gallipoli and Kut, that Turkish attempts to raise a *jehad* against the British had some slight success. Between December 1915 and April 1916, a little campaign had to be fought against the Sheikh of the Senussi in the Western Desert. A composite force of Indians, British and New Zealanders, which began the operation, was reinforced for the decisive blow by a brigade of South African infantry. Far to the southwest, in the remotest province of the Sudan, another campaign was launched in April against the Sultan of Darfur, by Sudanese troops of the Egyptian Army. With the defeat of these two potentates, the *jehad* died away. These ripples were taken as evidence of a tidal wave which was expected to break upon the defences of the Suez Canal. A very able German General, Kress von Kressenstein, had succeeded in bringing a striking force of Turks across the desert from Palestine, though not in sufficient strength to threaten the great army assembled in Egypt. He outmanœuvred and defeated a brigade of English yeomanry in a cavalry action at Katya and was then decisively checked by British, Australian and New Zealand mounted troops at the neat little action of Romani, August 1916. As a result of these operations it was resolved to push forward the defences of the Canal to the frontiers of Palestine which could be held by fewer troops. While the Australian and New Zealand mounted men went forward to take part in the Palestine campaign, the Anzac infantry, now consisting of one New Zealand and two Australian divisions, were transferred to France.

The Western-Front men were again in the ascendant, both at the Allied headquarters and at the headquarters of the Central Powers. The Allies stood on the defensive in Greece, in the Egyptian Desert, in Mesopotamia, in Poland. The Germans held all South-Eastern Europe except Greece, the whole strategic axis from Berlin to Baghdad, in a secure grip.

Before turning to the great battles which were fought on the Western Front, it will be convenient to summarise the four colonial campaigns in Africa.

FOUR COLONIAL CAMPAIGNS IN AFRICA

Since General Sir C. Dobell, the commander of the troops in West Africa, was in London in August 1914, he was able to advise the "Offensive Sub-committee" of the Cabinet upon operations against the German colonies. The objective of these operations was not territory nor even prestige, but the silencing of the four wireless transmitting stations by which the German Admiralty controlled its ships at sea.

German Togoland, the nearest to Europe, was a comparatively simple matter. Even before the Cabinet issued an order, Captain F. C. Bryant of the Gold Coast Regiment had sent an officer to Lomé the capital, demanding its surrender (6 August 1914). After an attempt to negotiate, on the grounds that the Congo treaties constituted Central Africa a neutral zone, the Germans fell back to Kamina, the wireless station, which they prepared to defend. Five days later, Bryant invaded Togoland with a battalion of African troops, in co-operation with a small French column from Dahomey. It appears that Bryant's men were the first British soldiers on any front to open fire during the First World War, in a sharp skirmish on 12 August. After a fortnight's resistance, the Germans demolished the wireless station and capitulated (26 August 1914).

The great territory of the Cameroons, more than twice as extensive as the British Isles, was a more difficult proposition, requiring naval support and a prolonged campaign which the world has forgotten. Unlike the other colonial Powers, the British did not raise large native armies in time of peace. The whole strength of the British West African forces did not exceed five effective battalions in 1914, and almost all were needed to invade the Cameroons. French and British probing attacks at several points made it clear that the Germans would resist. Accordingly a combined operation under General Dobell against Duala, the capital and the wireless station, was launched on 26 September 1914. After naval bombardment, Duala surrendered and the German troops withdrew inland, fighting a series of rearguard actions. Between December 1914 and March 1915 converging movements, in support of General Dobell's advance, were made by a column under Colonel F. H. E. Cunliffe, which came up the Benue River from Nigeria, and by a French column working northward from the Congo. By June 1915, when the wet season imposed a lull, Colonel Cunliffe had made contact with the French, near Ngaundere in the heart of the colony. The advance by all three forces was renewed in October. The main German stronghold at Nyaunde was captured on 1 January 1916, whereupon the remaining Germans fled over the border into Spanish territory, and were interned. The whole campaign had been concluded at the cost of about 60 British and 850 British-African soldiers killed. The French employed a force of similar strength and suffered about as many casualties. On 1 April 1916 Togoland and the Cameroons were taken under Allied administration and divided by agreement into French and British zones which, four years later, were converted into Mandated Areas by the League of Nations. The whole operation was a pleasing example of military co-operation between allies. In the course of the campaign the British West African forces had been expanded until their strength reached 25,000 men. When the Cameroons was annexed, a Nigerian battery and four infantry battalions were dispatched to the East African front.

The conquest of German South-West Africa is bound up with the story of the rebellion in the Union, which is fully described in the South African volume of this series.[1] Here it will be sufficient to allude to the military dispositions and movements. When in London, in 1911, General Botha had given his generous word—or so Mr Lloyd George asserted[2]—to march into German South-West Africa with 40,000 horsemen, if Germany should make war on Britain. This was not a binding commitment on the Union of South Africa. More to the point was the agreed staff plan for withdrawing the British regular troops, when the Empire mobilised. Since the South African War (1899–1902), the British garrison had been gradually reduced to 7000 men, and since Union in 1910 they were at the disposal, if not actually under the command, of the Union Government. So recently as July 1913 some of them had been used by Botha to suppress the Johannesburg riots. Before 1914 was out they were withdrawn to Europe with his approval (excepting a detachment of British gunners who manned the batteries of the Cape Peninsula until March 1916). Botha was thus physically obliged to defend his own frontiers and morally obliged to accede to the request made by the British Government, in August 1914, for action against German South-West Africa. He was asked to co-operate with the Royal Navy by occupying the seaports of Lüderitzbucht and Swakopmund, and to destroy the wireless station, 200 miles inland at Windhoek.

In September Botha dispatched a small force, by sea, to occupy the undefended German port of Lüderitzbucht. At the same time he began to concentrate troops on the land frontier, but the commander at Upington, one of the advanced bases, was Colonel S. G. Maritz, an extreme Afrikaner nationalist, who had lived in the German colony and had held a commission in the German colonial forces. After some weeks of diffused unrest, an "armed protest" against war with Germany, Maritz threw off his allegiance to go into open rebellion (9 October 1914). Worse still, the Commandant-General of the South African Defence Force, General C. F. Beyers, resigned his commission to join the rebels. Botha was obliged to postpone his external war while he dispatched columns of loyalist Afrikaner

---

[1] C.H.B.E. VIII, chap. xxvii.   [2] War Memoirs, IV, 1729.

troops against Maritz, who was soon hustled over the German frontier; against Beyers, who was defeated near Rustenberg; and against the redoubtable guerrilla leader, Christian De Wet, who was driven out of the Orange Free State into the Kalahari Desert. By the beginning of February 1915, Maritz was a fugitive in Portuguese territory, Beyers was dead—drowned while swimming a flooded river—De Wet was a prisoner.

Meanwhile the Germans had withdrawn from their other sea-port, Swakopmund, to concentrate upon the defence of Windhoek. In January South African forces occupied Swakopmund from the sea, and in February Botha took charge of the campaign. He himself led the advance from the northern sea-port, Swakopmund, and, after overcoming administrative rather than tactical difficulties, reached Windhoek on 18 May 1915. Simultaneously Smuts directed the advance of the three columns from Lüderitzbucht and from the frontier to the central railway. The German Governor capitulated with 3300 German soldiers on 9 July. Of the 40,000 South Africans who took part in the campaign, 269 were killed and 263 wounded. Smuts had already returned to administrative duties at Pretoria; Botha returned in July to fight an election campaign, in which he was bitterly reproached by the South African nationalists. Already the British Government were urging him to undertake an East African campaign, and this he deputed to Smuts.

The campaign in German South-West Africa had been a white man's war, in which neither party employed African natives as combatants. In East Africa, it was tropical campaigning in which both parties employed large numbers of *askaris* under white officers. This, the only successful strategic diversion made in a German colony, almost the only heroic exploit in German colonial history, was the work of Von Lettow-Vörbeck, the talented German commander. Starting with 250 German soldiers and 2500 *askaris*, he recruited white settlers and natives until his force reached 3600 whites and 11,000 natives, with whom he kept the field throughout the war. The Allies deployed more than 100,000 men against him, at a cost of over £70 millions and over 7000 lives (1000 British, 2000 white South African, 4000 Native African).

A conventional frontier divided the vast wild territory of East Africa into the British and German colonies, now known respectively as Kenya and Tanganyika. It was served by three railways running inland from Dar-es-Salaam, Tanga and Mombasa towards the Great Lakes. Of these the third, the Uganda railway, lay in British territory. Until the arrival of an Indian infantry brigade, in September 1914, this line was guarded only by a few detached companies of the King's African Rifles, against whom Lettow-Vörbeck acted aggressively. The first round was, however, fought at sea by the *Königsberg*, which sank the light cruiser *Pegasus* at Zanzibar on 30 September.

That concluded her exploits and, a month later, she was blockaded in her hiding-place, up the Rufiji River, where she was destroyed in July 1915 by monitors dispatched from England. Her crew joined the German army in the bush, with ten of the ship's guns. The German wireless station at Dar-es-Salaam was destroyed by naval bombardment.

A concerted attack by two Indian brigades with naval support was made upon the German port of Tanga, on 4 November 1914, and was repulsed with a loss of 800 casualties. Thereafter the British stood on the defensive in East Africa for more than a year, leaving Lettow-Vörbeck in full control of Tanga, of its railway up to Moshi near Mount Kilimanjaro, and of an angle of British territory at Taveta.

In February 1916 General Smuts arrived at Mombasa at the head of a South African force which built up to two strong infantry brigades, five mounted regiments, five batteries, and two battalions of Cape Coloured troops. The three battalions of the King's African Rifles were expanded to make twenty-one. With British, Indian and African units General Smuts's composite force amounted to about three divisions. He could also count upon support, far inland, from a Belgian column operating from the north of Lake Tanganyika, and from a Rhodesian column (under General E. Northey) which invaded the German colony through Nyasaland.

Smuts decided to operate on a broad front, southwards from the Uganda railway, avoiding the fever-stricken coastal plain. First manœuvring the Germans out of Taveta, he sent his subordinate, General J. van Deventer, to seize Moshi, threatening their northern flank. In April 1916 Smuts began his general advance, again sending Deventer in a wide sweeping movement far to the west. Lettow-Vörbeck first manœuvred to hold off Deventer, but was obliged to turn and face Smuts who marched due South in June, through 300 miles of wild country, for Morogoro, the German administrative capital, on the southern railway line. By this movement Smuts forced the Germans to abandon the whole of their northern territory, including Tanga. Deventer and Smuts converged upon Morogoro in August, thus gaining control of all the developed areas of the colony. By September, after six months of hard marching and severe bush-fighting, both railways, both sea ports and the coastline were under Smuts's control, while the Belgians and General Northey had cleared the western half of the colony. But Lettow-Vörbeck was at large, with a reduced, but organised and disciplined, force.

When, in January 1917, Smuts was recalled to attend the Imperial Conference, it was left to his successor, Major-General Sir R. Hoskins, to reconstitute an army which the indefatigable Smuts had driven desperately hard. Most of the South African troops were then withdrawn. Deventer, with about 30,000 men, remained to pursue Lettow-Vörbeck into the south-western corner of the colony. In

November 1917 the Germans crossed the Rovuma River into Portuguese territory, and there eluded Deventer, Northey, the Belgians and the Portuguese until the final armistice.

THE WESTERN FRONT, 1915–1917

An Allied conference at Paris, in November 1915, took a step that was long overdue by preparing a concerted plan for the following year's campaign. The Western Front was to be the main theatre for a combined offensive. The French High Command still predominated in Allied counsels, by virtue of directing the most powerful group of armies.

The seven British divisions that had stopped the gap at Ypres, in October 1914, conspicuous as they were in valour and efficiency, formed but a small component of the Allied front, when ranged beside fifty French divisions. This British component was formed of regular troops and their first reinforcements were regular divisions of the Indian Army. In February 1915, formations of British Territorials began to cross to France, and with them went the 1st Canadian Division, after a winter spent on Salisbury Plain. The first Canadian unit to go into action was Princess Patricia's Canadian Light Infantry, which was attached to a British division at Festubert, in the last week of February. In April the Canadian division took over a sector of the front, on the southern face of the acute salient covering Ypres.

For some weeks reports had been coming to the High Command that the Germans intended to use poisonous gases as a weapon, in defiance of their obligations under the Geneva Convention. These warnings were ignored, and it came as a surprise to the French colonial troops who held the northern face of the salient when clouds of chlorine gas were discharged against them, on 22 April 1915, from cylinders in the German trenches. The unfortunate Africans fled, leaving a four-mile gap to the left of the Canadians, who stood their ground, throwing back a defensive flank as did the Belgian army on the other side of the gap. Luckily the German General Staff was as half-hearted in using its new invention as the British General Staff was to be, eighteen months later, over the use of tanks. Having secured their tactical gains, the Germans made no effort to exploit their success. Two days later, when a further discharge of gas was made against the Canadian flank, it caused no panic. The men from the Dominion fought stoutly, covering their mouths, until the gas-cloud passed away, with improvised pads of cotton moistened with urine. Many Canadians were asphyxiated, and more were killed or wounded in the hasty counter-attack launched on 25 April (the day of the Gallipoli landing). When several attempts to restore the original front had manifestly failed, the British front was withdrawn to a better line, though still covering Ypres which the allies were unwilling to abandon. In this shallower salient, held for little tactical advantage but chiefly on a point of honour, the British armies provided a target for the German guns, almost until the end of the war. Canadian blood was shed as lavishly there as Australian blood at Gallipoli.

The Second Battle of Ypres was one of several, in the spring of 1915, which revealed the weakness of the British armies in respect of munitions. The establishment of heavy guns, and the supply of shells for the field guns, proved woefully inadequate to the demands of modern war. The new armies were beginning to arrive in France, ready to do all that men could do with rifle and bayonet; but rifle and bayonet could not destroy the thickets of barbed wire that protected the German trenches. In May the British launched attacks at Festubert, in September at Loos, and were checked with heavy losses, their attacks in each case being subsidiary to greater French attacks which met a like fate. The prospect for 1916, however, looked brighter. There was general confidence in Sir Douglas Haig, the new British Commander-in-Chief, a better understanding with the French, a larger army in the field, a growing supply of guns and munitions.

In January 1916 the British armies in France numbered over a million men. They were formed into five cavalry divisions (two of them Indian) and thirty-eight infantry divisions (two of them Canadian). By June, the date selected for the general offensive, nineteen more infantry divisions had been brought to France, including the 3rd Division from Canada, and two Australian divisions and one New Zealand division from Egypt, making a grand total of sixty-two divisions, and an aggregate strength of 1,400,000 men, disposed on a battle-front of eighty miles. The number of heavy batteries was increased from 36 to 191 in eighteen months; the strength of the Royal Flying Corps from 12 squadrons of 12 aircraft each, at the Battle of Loos, to 27 squadrons with an establishment of 18 aircraft each, in June 1916. The principles of air warfare were first established in that period with the differentiation of aircraft types for tactical bombing, interception, photographic reconnaissance and artillery observation. Though Kitchener's Army had taken the field, its creator did not live to see that day in 1918 when, for the first and last time in history, the British Army was the most powerful in the world. As the last of his divisions was actually crossing to France, a few days after the Battle of Jutland (31 May 1916), the old Field-Marshal was lost at sea while on a mission to Russia. Though Jellicoe did not win a decisive victory at Jutland he made it plain that the Royal Navy could still hold the ring. It was for the Allied armies to fight the decisive battles.

The war had entered a new phase, when greater masses of troops were assembled for battle than ever before or since, when only massed artillery could clear a path for the advance of infantry. While the locomotive and the automobile followed in the rear of the armies, horses, mules and men were the only carriers for cross-country work. Aircraft could observe but could not yet disperse the crowded camps and horse-lines outside artillery range. Weapons, at that stage in the progress of warlike invention, were more mechanised than vehicles: radio had not yet solved the problem of inter-communication on the battlefield; the tanks were too late and too few. Sluggish, unwieldy armies, equipped with terrible striking power, fought a series of heavy-weight contests in 1916 and 1917, bloodier and more dogged fights than any in human history, without reaching a decision. In these contests the troops from the Dominions were distinguished for their stubborn courage.

The senior officers of the Dominion troops were, at first, British regular officers, who were gradually replaced as Dominion officers gained the necessary experience. When the arrival in France of a second Canadian division, in May 1915, justified the formation of a Canadian Corps, the two divisional commands, under a British corps commander, were given to Canadian officers, Generals (Sir) A. Currie and Sir R. Turner. A third division came into action in January, and a fourth in August 1916, thus completing the normal corps establishment. The Canadian authorities devoted themselves to maintaining the strength of this corps, rather than to creating a larger establishment which they might be unable to maintain. General Currie, a professional officer of the Canadian Militia, succeeded Sir Julian Byng in Command of the Canadian Corps when Byng was promoted Army Commander in August 1917.

The Australian forces passed through a similar process. General Birdwood brought the 1st Anzac Corps to France in March 1916. Two more Australian divisions, numbered the 4th and 5th, had already been formed in Egypt and came to France three months later. A 2nd Anzac Corps, under General Sir A. Godley, included the 5th Australian Division and the New Zealand Division. The last of the Australian divisions, numbered as 3rd, was trained in England by General (Sir) J. Monash, an Australian civil engineer, who had distinguished himself as a brigadier at Gallipoli. He brought out the 3rd Division to join the 1st Anzac Corps late in 1916. A year later the five Australian divisions were drawn together as an Australian Corps and, when Birdwood became an Army Commander in May 1918, Monash succeeded him, the only civilian to reach the grade of Corps Commander in any of the British armies. New Zealand maintained one strong infantry division in France from April 1916 until the armistice, under command of Sir Andrew Russell, a British regular officer whose home was in New Zealand.

In addition to the ten infantry divisions from the three Dominions, and the two Indian cavalry divisions, numerous other units overseas served in the French campaign. The Canadian Cavalry Brigade, forming part of the 3rd British Cavalry Division, was fortunate in seeing mounted action several times—even on the Western Front. Canada also provided forestry companies and railway construction companies in great numbers. As early as November 1915, the South African Government decided to send to Europe two heavy batteries, and an infantry brigade under Brig.-Gen. H. T. Lukin. Having been first diverted to Egypt where they took part in the Senussi campaign (at a cost of 261 lives), they joined the 9th Scottish Division in France in April 1916. No formation of troops had a better reputation, and few endured heavier losses. Their thirty months in France cost them 4648 casualties. Newfoundland sent an infantry battalion which served in Gallipoli and France with the celebrated 29th Division. Bermuda sent a detachment which served with the 1st Lincolnshire Regiment, Rhodesia a detachment which served with the King's Royal Rifles. British volunteers from South America served together as a group in King Edward's Horse, and men from overseas were to be found by thousands serving in British regiments, many of them in unrecorded groups.[1] Late in the war the neglected, loyal man-power of the Caribbean colonies was tapped and six battalions of the new Royal West Indies Regiment[2] were raised for service in France, Italy, Palestine, and Mesopotamia.

Many individuals from the Dominions also served in the Royal Flying Corps (R.A.F. after May 1918), 12,000 from Canada alone. At least two leading " aces ", W. A. Bishop and W. G. Barker, were Canadian pilots serving in British squadrons. Australia preferred to create its own Air Service and sent Australian squadrons as con-tingents to the Royal Flying Corps, while Canada built up an organisation for flying training, the precursor of the Empire training scheme of the Second World War.

Before the Allied offensive could get under way, the early pre-parations were spoiled by a German offensive towards Verdun, in February 1916. The Germans hoped to compel the French to use up their munitions and reserves, and so to bleed France to death, by a series of assaults, "with limited objective", launched successively against positions softened by artillery bombardment. France was not defeated, but was indeed bled white, with the consequence that Marshal Joffre delegated an ever-growing share of the forthcoming Allied offensive to the British.

The Battle of the Somme opened on 1 July 1916, after a week's bombardment, with a frontal assault by eighteen British and five French divisions, against twelve German divisions strongly entrenched astride the river. The concentration was intense and the casualty-

---

[1] Volunteer units from Ceylon, Hong Kong and the Straits Settlements served in Gallipoli and Palestine.

[2] The two regular battalions of the historic West India Regiment served respectively in the Cameroons and in East Africa.

rate unparalleled. On a front of twenty miles, 57,000 British soldiers were killed, wounded or missing after a single day's fighting, the cruellest slaughter in the history of the British Army. Only one unit from the Dominions, the Newfoundland Regiment, took part, and was, in a military sense, annihilated, losing all its officers and 700 men. On the right, the French sector, where surprise was effected, the first objectives were taken; in the centre there was some measure of success; on the left there was complete and bloody failure. Sir Douglas Haig decided to continue the battle by a series of partial attacks deepening the breach he had made and extending it northwards. The French took little further part, but every division of the British Army successively was thrown into the struggle, was withdrawn when exhausted, and was revived only to be thrown into the battle again. A second climax was achieved late in July when, for a moment, a break-through seemed possible. In this phase the 1st Anzac Corps, among others, was brought south from a quiet sector, while the 2nd Anzacs remained to stage a costly diversion at Fromelles. The 1st Anzacs lost 20,000 men in taking Pozières and the furious close fighting with bomb and bayonet that ensued. In the same phase of the battle the South African Brigade made a mark in history by the defence of Delville Wood against German counter-attacks. Again the German front was stabilised until a new series of attacks culminated in the general assault on 15 September, the day when a few tanks were experimentally, and rather imprudently, sent into action. In that phase the Canadian Corps was placed on the main axis of advance at Courcelette; it, too, lost 20,000 men in the ensuing fighting. The 2nd Anzac Corps, led by the New Zealanders, made an advance, on 15 September, from High Wood to Flers. But there was no break-through—merely an occupation of bitterly contested ground:

> ...a plot
> Which is not tomb enough and continent
> To hide the slain.

The battle dragged on for two more months of rainy weather before dying away in mud and misery.

Misgiving over the unending casualties and limited successes of the Somme battle had contributed to a political crisis in London. After the Eastern war, it seemed that the Western war also had miscarried, and the naval outlook grew worse as the U-boats struck harder month by month. It was dissatisfaction with the conduct of the naval war that precipitated the fall of Mr Asquith's Coalition and its replacement by a new Coalition Government under Mr Lloyd George, in December 1916.

There is no doubt that the direction of the whole war effort was far more firmly handled by Mr Lloyd George than by his predecessor. The creation of a small executive committee of the Cabinet in place of consultative committees that had served Mr Asquith was in itself a long step towards victory. On the other hand Mr Lloyd George's relations with the General Staff were far from happy. An unrepentant Eastern-Front man, he conducted a vendetta with Haig and Robertson, mistrusting their appreciations and grudging the supplies of men whom they poured into the battles in France and Flanders. Yet, for all his energy and authority, Lloyd George was never strong enough to overrule them. His constant aim was to create a Supreme Allied Command which could take a broad view of the war and restrict the demands of the Western-Front generals; his error was to suppose that he could safely repose more confidence upon a French general than upon General Haig.

A second time, plans were prepared for a joint French and British offensive and, on this occasion, the brilliant and persuasive General Nivelle, one of the heroes of Verdun, was stepped over the heads of many seniors, as Supreme Commander, with powers never enjoyed by Marshal Joffre. While insisting on his responsibility to the British Government and not to the French Headquarters, Haig concurred as a loyal colleague with Nivelle's proposals, though they did not square with his own judgment. At the critical moment the Germans again spoiled the plan, by a sudden withdrawal to a much shorter prepared line of defence which they called the Siegfried position, but which the British nicknamed the Hindenburg Line after the new German Commander-in-Chief.

Among the formations that relished the unwonted interval of open fighting, during the German withdrawal, was the Canadian Cavalry Brigade, led by General J. E. B. Seely. Australian divisions were also among those that took part in the advance, running their heads, in April, into a sharp encounter at Bullecourt.

Though the withdrawal to the Hindenburg Line robbed Nivelle's plan of half its meaning, the armies were now committed to it. On 9 April 1917, the British holding attack was delivered near Arras and followed, a week later, by the main French attack, seventy miles away, in Champagne. The Battle of Arras, in its early stages an outstanding success, was fought by Allenby's Third Army with three British Corps, and Horne's First Army with the Canadian Corps. The most spectacular feat was the capture of the dominating Vimy Ridge by the Canadians. Throughout April the offensive was urged on against increasing resistance; for the complementary French operation was a gigantic failure, so dreadful a defeat that the French Army never quite recovered from it.

The breakdown of the French plan enabled Haig to switch his effort further north where he had long been considering schemes to clear the Flanders Coast. A preliminary measure, to secure his right flank before breaking into the coastal plain, was the seizure of the Messines Ridge by the most perfect "set-piece" operation of the war.

Nine divisions took part in the assault, on 7 June 1917, after a preparation which included the explosion of nineteen mines beneath the German trenches. The attackers carried and held the ridge with losses that were light by the standard of those bloody campaigns, a mere thousand in each division. The 2nd Anzac Corps (with the 3rd Australian and New Zealand Divisions leading) was on the right of the line.

The main assault, the Third Battle of Ypres, could not be launched earlier than 31 July. It was rainy weather, and bombardment soon reduced the artificial drainage of Flanders to a sea of mud deep enough to drown wounded stragglers. Neither tanks nor guns could make progress off the roads. Though conducted with greater tactical skill than the suicidal mass attacks on the Somme in the previous year, the successive advances at Third Ypres made shorter bounds, and exhausted the troops no less painfully. As the weather worsened, hopes of victory receded until all thought of breaking through to the coast had faded. In the third phase of the battle, when the autumn rains had set in, the two Anzac Corps fought side by side. Later the Canadian Corps relieved the Australians, and earned the barren honour of reaching the ill-starred village of Passchendaele, the tactical objective, late in October. In this battle of attrition, the attackers were the most worn down. The British soldier, while not losing courage, lost confidence in his commanders who refused to break off this hopeless enterprise. The disillusionment of the post-war generation, the unreasoning pacifism of the nineteen-thirties, and the strategy of the Second World War were to a large extent derived from memories of the carnage at Passchendaele. It was not then known, and it has not yet been generally accepted as a justification, that Haig maintained the struggle out of loyalty to his French allies.

At the year's end, a new note was sounded by General Byng's breach of the German lines at Cambrai, a success achieved by the proper use of tanks. It was entirely a victory for troops from the British Isles, and somewhat disheartening for them to learn that there were no reserves left either to exploit the victory or to check the violent German counter-attack.

War Policy and Organisation

Russia, France and Italy were dwindling assets to the Allies throughout 1917, while the first entry of the U.S.A. into European affairs was an unpredictable new factor. The Russian armies, driven back and defeated in 1915, had made a good recovery in 1916 and then collapsed in the First Revolution of March 1917, just when in France the Germans were withdrawing to the Hindenburg Line. During the summer, the social democratic parties in Russia, professing their antagonism to Imperial Germany, tried to keep their armies in being. The Second Revolution, of November 1917, came when the fortunes of the Western Allies were very low, after the French mutinies, after Passchendaele, and after a new and decisive defeat of the Italian armies at Caporetto. The reserves which ought to have been used at Cambrai were diverted, perforce, to prop up Italy against collapse.

Lenin and Trotsky, no less hostile to Western capitalism than to German militarism, deemed it wise to come to terms with the Germans who were enabled to transfer assault-troops from the Eastern Front to the West. While Trotsky was but the leader of a faction, in uncertain control of Moscow, St Petersburg (Leningrad) and not much else, three-quarters of Russian territory was, if under any organised rule, under one or other of the Russian groups that remained faithful to their allies. No other course was wise or just than for French, British and Americans to send them military assistance. In any case, Russia, in the 1918 campaign, was a liability.

The French collapse was a nearer, more obvious peril. For a moment, in May 1917, France seemed to be going the way of Russia, but she was saved by Clemenceau and Pétain (a solid cautious commander who had succeeded Nivelle), to play a valiant part in the last campaign of the war. At the time the malady of France was quite unknown to the British public. Only those with private sources of information heard of the defeats and mutinies, which were excluded by the censorship from the newspapers.

The summer of 1917, marked by defeats in France and by the gradual failure of the Russian war-effort, saw also the worst of the German submarine war against British shipping. If the naval campaigns do not fill many pages in this chapter it is not because their importance is undervalued but because, after the first few months, they form a single process in which the distinctive parts and the distinctive interests of the Dominions cannot be emphasised. The effort of the Royal Navy was concentrated upon the single task of destroying or immobilising the German Navy, wherever, or in whatever form it might appear. After Jellicoe's strategic victory at Jutland, the German High Seas Fleet accepted defeat and never again played an effective part in the war. Their leaders reverted to the alternative policy of submarine warfare, which brought the United States of America into the war and so tipped the scale in favour of the Allies. Earlier attacks on American shipping had somewhat slackened in 1916, so that there was little likelihood of a change in American policy until after the presidential election of November in that year. Once safely re-elected, President Wilson was able to devote his attention to reconciling the pacific American peoples to the prospect of a World War. His opportunity came in February 1917, when the Germans announced a policy of unrestricted submarine warfare.

All ships approaching the British Isles, whatever their nationality, were to be sunk at sight. Wilson withdrew his ambassador from Berlin and, in April, Congress declared war on Germany after American ships had been attacked. This was an end to the traditional isolation of America, a fulfilment of Canning's prophecy that the New World must redress the balance of the Old, a diplomatic revolution no less remarkable than the death and resurrection of Russia; but a political, not a strategic reversal, since little military help could be expected from unarmed America for at least a year after the Declaration of War.

Meanwhile that very month, April 1917, brought the sharpest crisis. Since January the rate of sinkings had doubled, reaching the high figure, in April, of 373 allied ships, aggregating 800,000 tons. At that rate England would have been starved out by November. On the other hand counter-measures, especially the convoy system, were coming into use with the result that when November came the monthly rate of sinkings had fallen to what it was in January. In the last year of the war the relief afforded by the U.S. Navy was immense, but the actual destruction of the U-boats (175 out of 199 destroyed) was accomplished by the British Navy.

Since the war in its last year was conducted by the Western Allies upon sounder principles than in the first three years, it will be convenient, at this stage, to recapitulate the process by which these principles were evolved. The Committee of Imperial Defence had done its work before the war and vanished in November 1914, leaving behind it files, minutes and a permanent secretary, Sir Maurice Hankey, who reappeared in all its successive transformations and survived to carry over its traditions into the Second World War. On 5 August 1914, Mr Asquith had summoned a Council of War, including at its first meeting the two old Field-marshals, Roberts and Kitchener; but not including representatives of the General Staff, whose function was not clearly understood. In November he instituted a new War Council of eight members to make recommendations to the Cabinet. Its weaknesses became so evident at the time of the Dardanelles expedition that it was severely censured by the Royal Commission, under Lord Cromer, which reported on the campaign. The diverse struggles of soldiers, sailors and politicians to urge on, or to cut short, the Gallipoli adventure stifled the War Council, which never met after 14 March. Two months later, 28 May 1915, one of the first acts of the new Coalition Government was to set up the Dardanelles Committee, a standing committee of eleven members of the Cabinet, with authority to supervise the war in the Mediterranean. Though they did somewhat better, they still lacked executive powers, merely making resolutions for approval or rejection by the twenty-three members of the full cabinet, which was not provided with the secret information. Thus knowledge was divorced from power.

When the decision was taken to leave the Gallipoli Peninsula, the committee was reorganised with a wider scope and a more definite function. Throughout 1916 it was known as the War Committee, a great improvement on its predecessors, in particular because it made proper use of the military and naval staffs. As with the Committee of Imperial Defence, so with the War Committee, Opposition leaders, and officers with special qualifications, were sometimes called in to conference and, according to Lord Hankey,[1] the Premiers of Canada, Australia and New Zealand attended individually when on visits to England.

In its turn the War Committee was found wanting, chiefly because of the disunity of Mr Asquith's Coalition Cabinet. Mr Lloyd George's Coalition was formed, in December 1916, specifically in order to set up a small executive free from departmental business, with final responsibility for war policy. The inner group of five members (Lloyd George, Bonar Law, Curzon, Milner and Arthur Henderson) had access to secret information together with the power to use it.

Mr Asquith had never fully appreciated the new status of the Dominions, and never took their Governments into his entire confidence. To be sure, several statesmen from the Dominions had attended meetings of the Committee of Imperial Defence since 1909, but to discuss what concerned them only. It was, however, a long step forward when Sir R. Borden was invited, as a Privy Councillor, to attend a routine meeting of the British Cabinet, when on a visit to England (14 July 1915). When Mr Asquith pressed him to send more Canadians to France, he riposted by demanding first that the British war effort should be better co-ordinated. Next year Mr W. M. Hughes, the new Premier of Australia, was in England; he too was invited to sit in at a Cabinet meeting on 9 March 1916. A dynamic Welshman, a Labour leader and an Imperialist, Mr Hughes made a great hit in London. He was invited, with Sir George Foster, the High Commissioner for Canada, to attend the Allied Economic Conference in Paris in June 1916. When accepting, he insisted that he was a plenipotentiary entitled to vote for Australian interests, not a junior member of the British delegation. However, when the test came, Britain, Canada and Australia were in agreement and voted solid.

Mr Lloyd George regarded the new nations with a sympathetic eye. He at once invited the Premiers of the Dominions to London for a meeting that was two years overdue. This was to be "a series of special meetings of the War Cabinet", not a session of the "ordinary Imperial Conference". The Premiers met on 20 March 1917 and on fourteen occasions during the following six weeks for these special meetings, while during the same period a session was held of the

---

[1] *Government Control in War*, p. 45, but not confirmed in the published memoirs of Mr W. M. Hughes or Sir R. Borden.

"ordinary Imperial Conference", which lesser lights attended as well as these great luminaries. The formal membership of the Imperial War Cabinet is given by Mr Lloyd George as fourteen persons: the five members of the War Cabinet, with the addition of Mr Balfour (First Lord), Mr Walter Long (Colonial Secretary), Mr Austen Chamberlain (Secretary for India), Sir R. Borden and Sir G. Perley[1] (Canada), Mr W. F. Massey and Sir Joseph Ward (New Zealand), General Smuts (South Africa) and Sir E. P. Morris (Newfoundland). Though their proceedings were confidential, it does not appear that this body attempted to formulate war policy, nor could they usefully do so for they were an assembly of delegates with ill-defined powers. Their most useful function seems to have been the exchange of information and the discussion of war-aims and post-war problems. When they met for a second session in the summer of 1918 they were much concerned with the preliminaries for a Peace Settlement.

During those years Imperial Federation was being canvassed by some influential persons who supposed that the Imperial War Cabinet was the rudiment of a Federal Council. In the Dominions the actual tendency was in the opposite direction, and the pronouncements of Sir R. Borden and General Smuts, in London, pointed rather to Dominion Status as it was to be recognised, some year's later, by the Statute of Westminster (1931). Less contentious subjects were discussed by the Imperial Conference with its wider membership. It was notable that, in addition to the Secretary of State for India, three representatives of the Indian Government (two of them, the Maharajah of Bikaner and Sir S. P. Sinha, natives of India) were summoned to the Conference. It will be remembered that the Montagu-Chelmsford Report was published between the Conferences of 1917 and 1918. Equally notable was the complete absence of any Australian representative in 1917. Mr Hughes was fighting a furious general election and dared not leave Australia.

General Smuts now stepped into the place of Mr Hughes as the interpreter of the new Commonwealth to the British people and to the world. So pre-eminent was he at the conference that Mr Lloyd George invited him to remain in London, in May 1917, as a permanent member of the War Cabinet. Though in no sense a plenipotentiary of the Dominions, or even of South Africa, he stood for their prestige in the eyes of the British people and their leaders. As an independent member of the War Cabinet, General Smuts undertook an astonishing variety of special tasks and missions: an abortive negotiation to detach Austria-Hungary from its German allies; a reorganisation of the air defences of London and, consequently, a

[1] Sir R. Borden appointed Sir G. Perley Resident Minister in London, with Cabinet rank and the task of administering the Canadian Forces overseas. Sir Sam Hughes, Canadian Minister of Defence since 1911, resigned as a protest against this diminution of his authority.

first plan for the establishment of the R.A.F. as a separate service; a plan for renewing the offensive against the Turks by a campaign in Palestine; and several others that lie outside the scope of this history. The chief command in Egypt and Palestine was first offered to General Smuts and, only when he refused, to Sir Edmund Allenby, who had won Mr Lloyd George's confidence by his conduct of the Battle of Arras.

Mr Lloyd George's policy was coloured by his mistrust of the Western-Front generals. He repeatedly urged the claims of diversionary operations in Italy, Macedonia or Palestine, and was met, time after time, by General Robertson's assertions that no troops could be safely withdrawn from France, or that transport for them was not available. The scanty shipping, said Robertson, would be better employed in bringing Americans to France. Mr Lloyd George next set himself to form a Supreme Allied Council at Versailles, a plan which led to long negotiations in the winter of 1917–18.

Man-power was the vital problem early in 1918, and the dwindling strength of the British divisions in France made the problem, from day to day, more urgent. Since the Russian collapse, the German strength on the Western Front was steadily increasing, from 129 divisions in March 1917 to 177 in January 1918, a figure that exceeded the Allied strength of 173 divisions. No more than twelve American divisions could be trained and shipped from the U.S.A. before midsummer, whereas it was expected that thirty more German divisions would be brought from Russia to France.

In Great Britain the age-long Liberal tradition had been cast away by the National Service Act of January 1916, which led to the rigid enforcement of conscription in May of that year. The mere threat of conscription in Ireland had a deplorable effect and was a contributory cause of the Easter Week Rebellion in Dublin. In the Dominions, too, conscription was a contentious issue. Though public opinion in every Dominion was accustomed to national service for home defence, conscription for service overseas was another matter. In New Zealand alone was a full measure of conscription enacted, soon after the British set the example, but with the proviso that drafts for foreign service should be selected by ballot from suitable age-groups. In quality and quantity, the New Zealand Division maintained its standards until the end of the war. "No division in France", wrote Haig, "built up for itself a finer reputation." In South Africa the question did not arise since the national defence forces were mobilised for service on their own frontier. The expeditions to East Africa and Europe were manned by volunteers.

A strong and earnest opposition to conscription for the European war arose in Australia among the industrial workers. Although there were seditious elements among the objectors, for the most part the

Australian workers approved the Allied cause; they were proud, as well they might be, of the exploits of their voluntary army; and yet they boggled at the proposal to send conscripts 10,000 miles away to fight under a supreme command which they could not control. After Turkey and France, might not the Australians next be sent to fight in Russia, or in Ireland? A powerful voice against conscription was that of Dr D. Mannix, the Roman Catholic Archbishop of Melbourne, an Irishman with a traditional grievance against England and a large following among Irish-Australians in the State of Victoria. The issue was put to a referendum in September 1916, with the result that conscription was rejected by a majority in the proportion of about eleven to ten. Of the Australian soldiers in France 72,000 voted for, and 59,000 against, conscription. A reconstruction of the Government followed, still under Mr Hughes, and he later tried another referendum with a similar result. The recruitment of volunteers for the Australian forces overseas, of course, produced a diminishing return. Nevertheless the five Australian divisions in France undertook, with dwindling numbers, tasks as exacting and extensive as neighbouring divisions at full strength; and often outstripped their neighbours.

In Canada, Sir Robert Borden introduced a Bill in 1917 for a modest measure of conscription which was vehemently opposed by the veteran Liberal, Sir Wilfrid Laurier. The Bill was fought on racial lines. It was estimated that, of 400,000 Canadian soldiers overseas, more than half were British-born immigrants, and less than 30,000 were French-Canadians. Again, this did not imply sedition among the French-speaking section, or antipathy to Allied war-aims, but a conviction that the war affected Canada only indirectly and did not justify conscription. The Act was passed, but very loosely administered. Exemptions were so numerous in the predominantly French Province of Quebec that few conscripts were enrolled. Passive resistance was frequent and active rioting against the enforcement of the Act occurred in some instances.

It will hardly be necessary to mention that conscription for military service was unheard-of in India and the Crown colonies, though in Egypt, and in East and West Africa, some compulsion was used, according to the custom of those countries, in the enlistment of men for labour corps.

THE LAST CAMPAIGNS

When the campaign of 1918 opened in the West, the initiative, as in the two previous years, was seized by the Germans, and in this instance inevitably. On 21 March 1918 Ludendorff, who exercised the chief command in the name of the old Marshal Hindenburg, launched the first of his five great assaults against the British Third and Fifth Armies, which had recently taken over a widely extended

front, astride the Somme. This was no battle of attrition, fought
for a succession of limited objectives like those of 1916 and 1917,
but a decisive stroke, such as the British might have delivered at
Cambrai, four months earlier, if reserves had been available. Tactically Ludendorff won great advantages, striking the heaviest blow
ever struck at any British army. Strategically, he failed to reach any
one of his objectives. Though the Fifth Army was driven back forty
miles with crippling losses, the gap was plugged by divisions brought
from other sectors, and Ludendorff's attempt to swing northwards
against the open flank broke upon the rock-like defence of the Third
Army, which included the Canadian Corps. It was here that
Mr Churchill found the 9th Division, "like an iron peg hammered
into the frozen ground", and observed the South African Brigade,
"serene as the Spartans of Leonidas on the eve of Thermopylae".
Among many feats done by troops drawn into the battle, the seizure
of the Moreuil Ridge, by mounted action of the Canadian Cavalry
Brigade, was selected by Marshal Foch as a turning-point in the
battle. The deepest German penetration was to Villers Bretonneux,
within sight of the towers of Amiens, where the enemy were resolutely
stopped by the 3rd Australian Division.

When the outlook was at its worst, Pétain had threatened to
abandon further co-operation with the British in order to concentrate
on the defence of Paris. Since Haig was equally determined to
defend the Channel ports a deadlock was reached. At the Doullens
Conference (26 March 1918), convened by Lord Milner to solve the
problem of a united command, it was at Haig's request that Foch
was appointed to co-ordinate the action of the Allied armies. The
appointment came in time to parry Ludendorff's second stroke, a
diversion against the narrow British sector in Artois where there was
no space to absorb the shock by yielding ground. In the Artois
battles of April 1918 the painful gains of previous years were lost.
On 11 April the outlook was so black that the taciturn, unemotional
Haig was moved to issue his one personal message to his armies:
"We are fighting with our backs to the wall." Among those who
were in the line to respond to it were the New Zealand Division and,
again, the South African Brigade. It was the Germans who called
the battle off, having failed to break through.

After an uneasy pause of a month Ludendorff moved again. His
last three blows, between 27 May and 15 July, were struck at the
French and met with an equally heroic resistance. Only the first of
them, a drive forward from the Aisne to the Marne, bringing Paris,
as in 1914, within sound of the guns, came near to victory. Again the
gap was stopped, partly by a British corps which had been transferred, for a rest, to this supposedly quiet sector, and partly by a
division from the U.S.A. which counter-attacked fiercely, on 4 June,
at Château Thierry, the first of many such divisions, and an assurance

that the man-power problem was solved. This was however, tactically, but a tiny incident in a great French battle which was triumphantly concluded by General Mangin's counter-attack on 18 July.

Ludendorff was stopped but not defeated. It was Haig, not the politicians nor the planning staffs, who determined upon final victory in 1918, and Haig's armies that fought the decisive battles. During the last hundred days of the war, more than half of the German fighting forces were arrayed against Haig's sixty-two divisions. On Haig's front two-fifths of the 390,000 prisoners were counted.

The general counter-offensive began with the Battle of Amiens on 8 August 1918, which Ludendorff called the "Black Day" of the German Army. The attack was delivered, without previous bombardment, by troops of the Fourth Army—the Canadian Corps, the Australian Corps and the 3rd British Corps, preceded by 500 tanks (manned by soldiers from the British Isles). A French army operated on the right of the Canadians. The Germans were pushed back into the waste of the Somme battlefield, and thereafter were not allowed to rest. By Haig's judgment, and rather ,against Foch's, the battle was switched north into the area of the British Third Army. At the end of August the Germans on this front were driven from their old line, the trenches of 1914 to 1916, by the Battle of Bapaume, in which Canadians, New Zealanders and British troops played their part. On the right the Australians forced the enemy from the banks of the Somme by the audacious capture of Mont St Quentin, a commanding hill.

The co-ordinated offensive resolved itself into three main assaults; on the right by French and Americans through the Argonne towards the Meuse; on the left by Belgians and British in Flanders; and in the centre by the British Armies against the Hindenburg Line. The whole war saw no fiercer fighting, no more skilful leadership, than the struggle for the series of natural and artificial obstacles which were forced in the central battle between 26 September and 5 October. Eighteen British divisions as well as Canadians, Australians, New Zealanders and two American divisions shared the task. The last day of the war saw the Canadians at Mons. Long before the battle for the Hindenburg Line was over, Ludendorff was making overtures for peace.

DESTRUCTION OF THE TURKISH EMPIRE

When, in the spring of 1917, events in Russia changed the character of the war, the British were standing on the defensive in the Middle East. General Sir A. Murray, having brought his armies across the desert, was checked and held on the Palestine border, after two hard battles in February and March at Gaza; General Maude in Mesopotamia had occupied the *vilayet* of Baghdad, with strict instructions not to run risks or increase his commitments. Each of these campaigns was an offensive-defensive, and each was limited by problems of supply. Murray had constructed a broad-gauge railway across the desert and had brought Nile water through a pipeline to the Holy Land; Maude had established a flotilla of two hundred steam-boats on the Tigris.

The capture of Baghdad left the British with an open flank to the north-east, a political vacuum into which the Germans were infiltrating by diplomatic methods and by secret service. It was soon known that a great counter-stroke against the British in the Middle East was being prepared under the code-name of "Yilderim" (lightning), which made it the more urgent to close the gap. As early as May 1916 a Cossack patrol from the Caucasus had made contact with the British in Mesopotamia and it was hoped that a Russian advance would bring their armies to the Euphrates, on the British right flank. It never came and, by April 1917, the War Office was beginning to realise that it never would come.

With the permission of the Persian authorities the Indian Government raised an irregular force, the South Persia Rifles, and threw a cordon across the British Zone in Persia with the object of excluding German and Turkish agents. As Russian influence waned in the north with the progress of the Revolution, so British intervention was enlarged. By June 1918, the War Cabinet was urging General Sir W. R. Marshall (who had succeeded to the command on Maude's death in November 1917) to extend his activities and so "to induce the Persian Government to subserve British interests".[1] In July General L. C. Dunsterville's column reached Baku on the Black Sea. Mosul on the upper Tigris was not occupied by Marshall until November. This diplomatic and military infiltration was intended to guard the approaches to India. Though under the military direction of the War Office the campaign in Mesopotamia, in its later stages, and the operations in Persia were carried out by the Indian Army. Occupied territory on the Tigris was directly administered by officials from India under Sir Percy Cox, the chief political officer; on the whole they tended to treat the inhabitants as a conquered rather than as a liberated nation. Among the desert chiefs they favoured Ibn Saud as their most likely ally against the Turks.

Five hundred miles away, on the western side of Arabia Deserta, the British administration in Egypt saw the political problems in another light. Two corps of Turkish regular troops still garrisoned the Hejaz railway, in the midst of Arab tribes who were in a mood to rise against them. The negotiations for British support to an Arab revolt, which had been prudently damped down by Kitchener in 1914, were resumed under the stress of war by his successor, Sir Henry

[1] Edmonds, J. E. (ed.), *Official History...Military Operations, Mesopotamia*, IV, 187.

MacMahon. The first of the pledges to the Arabs, which have had such far-reaching consequences, was given to Hussein, the Grand Sherif, on 24 October 1915. MacMahon undertook, with the approval of the Foreign Office, to support an Arab revolt with the object of establishing a free Arab state or states in Syria, Mesopotamia and Arabia; excepting the *vilayets* of Basra and Baghdad, those parts of coastal Syria where the population was not predominantly Arab, and those areas where we were obliged in honour to respect French interests. The MacMahon pledge was given without consulting the Indian Government and, as it proved, against their wishes. It was believed in India, and rightly, that Indian Moslems would take offence at Hussein's pretentions.

During the winter of 1915–16, when Egypt was packed with troops, and Cairo seething with intrigue, a special intelligence section, the Arab Bureau, was set up to provide information about the Arab world. Dr D. G. Hogarth assembled a team of experts, scholars, archaeologists and explorers, whose knowledge of the Near East gave them an influence far wider than their nominal duties. T. E. Lawrence began his career of military adventure in the Arab Bureau, having qualified for the post of expert on the Turkish Army by his researches and travels in the Near East as a young Oxford man.

Since the French Government was not a party to the MacMahon pledges it was necessary to reconcile them with our obligations to the French. This was done by the secret convention known as the Sykes-Picot Treaty of April 1916, to which the Russian Imperial Government adhered. No casuistry can wholly adjust the pledges given secretly to the Arabs in October with the pledges given secretly to the French in the following April. It was then agreed to partition the whole Arab area into a French and a British "zone of influence" The British at Baghdad and Basra, the French in a large part of Syria, were to set up protectorates. Worst of all, the terms of the Sykes-Picot Treaty were not communicated to the Arab leaders, then on the point of breaking out in rebellion.

It showed great courage on the part of Hussein and his sons to let loose the revolt in the Hejaz on 5 June 1916, at a time when the fall of Kut had again lowered British prestige. Though Hussein quickly got control of Mecca and its port of Jedda, whereby he could receive help from the Royal Navy, his sons were soundly defeated at Medina by the Turkish troops who continued to hold the line of the railway. Hussein demanded military help, with the High Commissioner's approval; but the General Staff stoutly resisted this new diversion of effort.

At this point the masterful members of the Arab Bureau took charge of the situation. The part played by T. E. Lawrence in the revolt has been variously estimated. He was but one, and by no means the senior, of the group of British and French liaison officers who acted as technical advisers to Hussein and his sons. Lawrence made three specific contributions to the Arab revolt: first, he devised a new technique of guerrilla operations which has been an inspiration to all succeeding partisans; secondly, he extended the scope of the revolt from the *bedouin* of Arabia Deserta to the *fellaheen* of Trans-Jordan and Syria; thirdly he chose a figure-head, Hussein's third son the Emir Feisal, and imposed him upon Levantine magnates and British officials alike, as the proper leader for a national movement. In this Lawrence was justified, for Feisal, alone among the Arabs, was educated in the west, though desert-bred; and his status in the Hejaz would enable the revolt to be nourished by the Royal Navy through the Red Sea ports. The rival prince, Ibn Saud, who held his court far inland, could not be made an instrument for the liberation of Palestine and Syria. In January 1917 the Arabs, with their British advisers, began to clear the Hejaz coast. Their base was established at Akaba in June, just when Allenby arrived to take command in Palestine.

The winter campaign which led to the fall of Jerusalem, on 11 December 1917, was a masterpiece. Allenby restored to the art of war the factors of mobility and surprise which had vanished from the Western Front. This was the more remarkable since his opponent was no less a man than General Falkenhayn, formerly Chief of the German General Staff, who had been sent east to conduct the mysterious "Yilderim" operation. First compelled by Allenby's measures to shift his ground and stand on the defensive, Falkenhayn was out-generalled and out-fought, not least by Allenby's bold use of massed cavalry, among whom were the two divisions of Australians and New Zealanders under Sir H. Chauvel. Brilliant as were their exploits, these troops did not co-operate easily with the Arab guerrillas, and an unfavourable version of the Arab achievement is to be found in the Australian Official History. The cavalry raids across the Jordan towards Es Salt and Amman, in the spring of 1918, were repulsed with heavy loss, largely because the Arabs failed to play their part.

The fall of Jerusalem had supplied Mr Lloyd George with an argument in favour of his own policy. It was a tonic to the British people at the end of a gloomy year, and it renewed the prospect of winning the war in the East. (The campaign had been preceded by Mr Balfour's pledge to the Zionists, October 1917, that the British would support the establishment in Palestine of a "National Home" for the Jews.) But all hopes for next year's campaign were dashed by the news from France of the German break-through, which obliged Allenby to send most of his British infantry to France in exchange for Indian cavalry. His final stroke was accordingly delayed until September 1918, when the Turkish Empire was nearing exhaustion.

Allenby's crowning victory at Megiddo, another triumph for secrecy and surprise, was the last great cavalry action in history.

The mounted men poured through a breach in the depleted Turkish line, near the coast, to ride round the western flank of the Turks into Damascus, on 1 October 1918. Though Allenby's army had defeated two Turkish armies, it was the studied policy of Lawrence and his friends to emphasise the other aspect. With Allenby's help, Trans-Jordan, Syria, and even Damascus had, in fact, been liberated by their own people in the name of the Emir Feisal. The Arabs could thus demand fulfilment of the MacMahon pledges.

When the Turkish war ended on 30 October 1918, British arms were supreme almost throughout Islam, along a wide front from Stamboul to Singapore. In the Sudan, in Egypt, on the Bosphorus, where the Royal Navy now lay at anchor; in Syria, Palestine, Mesopotamia and Arabia; in Persia, India, Malaya, British or British-Indian troops protected the tranquillity of Moslem peoples, and in most of these lands by consent of their own leaders. The weakness of Russia, then in utter confusion, meant that Britain had no powerful rival on the mainland of Asia. This was perhaps the most astonishing consequence of the war; the disposal of this mighty sphere of influence was to prove the most intractable problem for post-war diplomacy.

Yet the destruction of the Turkish Empire was but a small part of the British effort, a sideshow to the drama in the main theatre of war. There, the British wielded more powerful instruments of war than any other belligerent. In the air their supremacy was unquestioned, either in relation to the strength of enemies or allies. At sea the Royal Navy, no longer attempting to maintain a two-power standard, was about equivalent to the Navy of the U.S.A. in strength, and far superior to it in war experience. On land the British Army, after all its sacrifices, was still the most effective striking force in the world. Never in her long history had Great Britain disposed of such powerful forces as in November 1918. But the troops had one desire only, to unarm now that the long day's task was done. A prearranged plan of demobilisation moved too slowly for their patience. A wave of unrest, better described as a tendency to strike than as mutiny, was soothed only when Mr Churchill was sent to the War Office, in January 1919. So rapidly did he work that the five million soldiers had shrunk to one million by June. Conscription was discontinued immediately after the Armistice and at the end of twelve months Mr Churchill was hard put to it to find a single British infantry division for a sudden contingency.

A SUMMARY OF THE BRITISH WAR EFFORT

The Royal Navy in 1918 was almost twice as strong as it had been four years earlier, in spite of the loss of 16 capital ships and 238 other combatant vessels during the war. At Scapa the Grand Fleet included 38 British battleships and 9 battle-cruisers, as well as an American squadron. The total strength[1] of the British armies in the field, on 1 November 1918, was 5,336,943, of whom 3,226,879 were in the theatres of war, 1,603,384 were in the United Kingdom, and 482,269 in India. Their transport depended upon an establishment of 500,000 horses and 200,000 mules. The fighting formations on the various fronts were disposed as follows:

Divisions...	British Cav.	British Inf.	Dominion Cav.	Dominion Inf.	Indian Cav.	Indian Inf.	Total
France	3	51	—	10	—	—	64
Italy	—	3	—	—	—	—	3
Palestine	—	1	2	—	2	6	11
Salonica	—	4	—	—	—	—	4
Mesopotamia	—	1	—	—	1	4	6
India	—	3	—	—	—	3	6[2]
E. Africa	—	—	—	—	—	—	2[3]
U.K.	1	4	—	—	—	—	5
	4	67	2	10	3	13	101

In addition, small forces, including some Canadians, were co-operating with Russian forces against the Bolsheviks and their German allies. Before they were withdrawn, in September and October 1919, their strength was about 11,000 combatants at Archangel and about 5000 at Murmansk. In South Russia, British military missions, not British combatant troops, remained with the White Russians until 1920.

The total loss to the British Empire in soldiers killed, missing, or died of wounds has been estimated at 908,371, to which must be added 32,208 seamen of the Royal Navy and 14,661 of the Merchant Service. 1413 civilians lost their lives in air raids, and about 150 in naval raids, upon the United Kingdom.

To compare the relative effort of Britain and the Dominions is a difficult task because of the nomadic habits of the British race. Numerous young men from the Dominions and Colonies served in British units, and conversely, numerous temporary visitors from the United Kingdom served in the armies of the Dominions. The War Office estimated that 6,704,416 men, 22·11 per cent of the adult male population of the British Isles, were recruited, and that 704,803 were killed or died of wounds. Canada recruited 628,964 soldiers, of whom 458,218 served overseas and 56,639 lost their lives. The overseas force was estimated as 13·48 per cent of Canadian male citizens,

[1] See above, p. 615, footnote 1.
[2] Including three Indian divisions on N.W. Frontier.
[3] A mixed force of British, South African and Native troops equivalent to about two divisions.

excluding those born outside the British Empire. Australia recruited 412,953 soldiers and sent overseas 331,814, that is 13·43 per cent of the male white population; 59,330 lost their lives. New Zealand recruited 128,525 soldiers of whom 112,223, that is 19·35 per cent of the white male population, served overseas, and 16,711 lost their lives. South African figures are more difficult to summarise since her war was fought from bases in her own territory. It appears that of 136,070 whites who were recruited 76,184, that is 11·12 per cent of the male white population, served in Egypt, East Africa or France, and 7121 lost their lives either in those campaigns or in German South-West Africa. In addition to the 2000 Newfoundlanders who served in the Royal Navy, 6173 enlisted as soldiers and 1204 were killed or died of wounds. The number of deaths in the smaller colonial detachments is given as 507.

India's war effort is on another footing. During the war 1,440,437 volunteers passed through the ranks of the Indian Army, and of these 62,056 lost their lives in action. Two Indian cavalry divisions and ten infantry divisions served overseas. Three divisions, equipped for active service, guarded the North-West Frontier throughout the war. The tribes were, however, quiescent and Afghanistan, so long as Habibulla was Amir, remained a friendly State.

About 34,000 combatant troops were raised in British East Africa and about 25,000 in British West Africa. The losses in battle were about 2000 and 850 respectively. From various colonies over 30,000 transport drivers were recruited. In addition, very large numbers of colonial natives (and of other Asiatics) were recruited, from time to time, for service in non-combatant labour units. In November 1918, 82,000 Egyptians, 20,000 Indians, 8000 West Indians, 1200 Cape Coloured, 1000 Mauritians, even 100 Fijians were serving in these units outside their own countries. An even larger contingent was provided by 92,000 Chinese labourers.

The financial contributions to the war effort are not easily distinguished from current items in the accounts of each State in the Commonwealth. A simple factor is the series of free gifts to the British Treasury[1] offered by British dependencies great and small, according to their means, ranging from the imperial largess of £100 millions, a full-year's revenue, presented by the Indian Government, to the equally generous sum of £200 sent by the poverty-stricken Galla tribe from British East Africa. Canada, Australia and New Zealand "bore the whole cost of their own Armies, and South Africa the whole cost of the South-West African campaign, and a large part of the cost of maintaining its forces in East Africa. The larger part of the current cost of the Indian expeditionary forces was borne by the British exchequer."[2]

[1] For contributions from colonies, see *Parl. Pap.* 1918, xvii [Cd. 9183], *et al.*
[2] *Report of the War Cabinet for 1917: Parl. Pap.* 1918, xiv [Cd. 9005].

In financing their own war effort the great Dominions hastened their own economic development. As always in wartime, primary producers flourished and, while direct taxation was doubled in several communities, it did not keep pace with farmers' profits. Prices of raw materials were stabilised by national supply and munition boards which, in each Dominion from 1915 onwards, began to experiment in bulk purchase.

While borrowings were, by pre-war standards, gigantic they did not impair the strength of the young communities, as was proved by the buoyancy of revenues and the high proportion of money raised locally. No small part of the capital outlay was expended on public works and industrial enterprises that would be valuable after the war. The national debt of Canada rose from about £67 millions in 1914 to about £317 millions in 1919. The figures are complicated by exchange transactions between Great Britain and Canada, from which it appears that Canada borrowed, on balance, about £48 millions in London and the rest locally or in New York. During the same period the debt of the Australian Commonwealth was increased from £19 millions to £325 millions, of which increase about £114 millions were borrowed in London, the rest in Australia. The total cost of the war to Australia was estimated at £311 millions, paid for as to 15 per cent from revenue, as to 85 per cent from loans.[1] There were also large increases in the public debts of individual Australian States. New Zealand, already heavily indebted in 1914, raised war loans to the amount of £80 millions and found two-thirds of the money locally. South Africa enjoyed a boom period throughout the war. The output of gold was maintained, farmers received high prices for their produce, and much private capital from abroad was invested in the new secondary industries. A windfall was the diversion of traffic, and accordingly of shipping profits, from the Suez Canal to the Cape route. It was estimated that the war and the rebellion cost the Union Government £38 millions, of which only £6 millions were borrowed.

As was proper, the accumulated wealth of the Mother Country was poured out more copiously for expenditure that was entirely unproductive. Though the British national debt rose from £660 millions to £8000 millions, the City of London carried the load and remained the financial capital of the world.

Before the war, the Powers of Europe had been all unconscious of the new nations appearing within the circle of the British Commonwealth. They could hardly now ignore the scale of the effort made by the four great Dominions, nor could there be any doubt that Sir R. Borden, Mr Hughes, Mr Massey and General Botha were the responsible heads of truly national administrations. If Belgium and Portugal ranked as sovereign Powers, equally with France and Britain,

[1] See *C.H.B.E.* VII, pt. I, 589. Another estimate made by W. M. Hughes at Versailles is discussed below.

how could that status be denied to Canada and Australia? Their prowess in war proclaimed their maturity; the character of their leaders established their right to appear at the post-war conferences, though their precise constitutional status remained uncertain.

Not less remarkable was the changed character of the British-Indian Empire. After the first loyal outburst in 1914, had come the news of disaster in Mesopotamia which induced a more critical mood. Not only in Ireland but also in India did doubts arise about the purity of British war aims. If it was a war for the rights of oppressed nationalities, had not Irishmen and Indians a claim to register? The Congress Party began in 1916 to demand "Home Rule for India". Though Mr Lloyd George nominated Indian representatives to the Imperial Conference, and initiated the Montagu-Chelmsford Policy in 1917, these were but palliatives. The reaction of Asia against Western domination was now a flowing tide.

CHAPTER XVII

THE EMPIRE AND THE PEACE TREATIES,
1918–1921

WHEN, on 14 December 1916, Lloyd George, upon his accession to the Prime Ministership, called an Imperial War Cabinet into existence, it became an accepted fact that the Dominions would be consulted about the making of peace. For the invitation to the Prime Ministers spoke of discussions not only upon "urgent questions affecting the prosecution of the war" but also upon "the possible conditions on which, in agreement with our allies, we could assent to its termination and the problems which will then immediately arise".[1] Such discussions indeed were held at the sessions of the Imperial War Cabinet in 1917 and 1918, and were attended by representatives not only of the Dominions but also of India. Within six weeks of the conclusion of the meetings in August 1918, however, the collapse of the Central Powers made it necessary for the members of the Imperial War Cabinet to be summoned once more to London, "in order to be in close touch, as members of the Imperial War Cabinet, with the whole situation, and to take part in the discussions between the Allies as to the peace settlement itself".[2] The summons was prompt and urgent, but events in Europe were so swift and ships were so slow that it was inevitable that the effective response of the Dominions should be delayed. When the Imperial War Cabinet began its consideration of the peace settlement on 20 November 1918, Australia and Canada alone were represented by Prime Ministers. Mr W. M. Hughes, the Prime Minister of Australia, had decided to stay on in London for some weeks after the conclusion of the meetings of the Imperial War Cabinet in August 1918 in the hope that victory might soon be achieved.[3] The Canadian Minister, Sir Robert Borden, had sailed from New York on 11 November and had arrived in London on 17 November. South Africa was represented by General Smuts, who was a member of the British War Cabinet and had been in England since April 1917, but it was not until 18 December that the Prime Minister of South Africa, General Botha, could attend a meeting. The representatives of India, the Maharaja of Bikaner and Sir S. P. Sinha, attended on the same day, but the Prime Minister of New Zealand, Mr W. F. Massey, did not arrive until January 1919.

In practice, therefore, it was not possible for all the Dominions to

---

[1] *War Cabinet Report, 1917: Parl. Pap.* 1918, xiv [Cd. 9005], p. 6. See also Lloyd George, D., *The Truth about the Peace Treaties*, i, 52, 60, 94.
[2] *War Cabinet Report, 1918: Parl. Pap.* 1919, xxx [Cmd. 325], pp. 9–11.
[3] Hughes, W. M., *The Splendid Adventure*, p. 88.

be represented in all the consultations that occurred from 20 November onwards. Moreover, it is important to recall that the conditions upon which the armistice with Germany was granted, and which were to have a bearing upon the subsequent terms of peace, had been negotiated with little, if any, consultation of the Dominions. The Supreme War Council of the Allies had met on 29 October in Paris and had discussed, in a series of meetings, whether they should agree to an armistice with Germany on the terms proposed by President Wilson. Lloyd George and Balfour were the British representatives, but although small States like Belgium and Serbia were represented, the Dominions were neither represented nor consulted. Hughes of Australia protested on 7 November, in a speech in London to the Australasian Club, at this procedure, more particularly because he had remained in London himself in order to be available for just such consultations. He believed that the armistice terms prevented Australia from obtaining full reparations from Germany.[1] The British Government defended its action by pointing out that speed had been necessary and that nothing had been done by the British representatives at the meeting of the Supreme War Council which was inconsistent with the general conclusions already reached by the Imperial War Cabinet.[2] Hughes's protest evoked no public support from any other Dominion Government, but the problem to which he had drawn attention was already being discussed by them in private. Was the participation of the Dominions in the making of the peace to be confined to discussions with the United Kingdom's representatives in the Imperial War Cabinet on matters of general principle, while the actual conduct of negotiations would be carried on solely by the United Kingdom's representatives? Or were the Dominions to be directly represented in the negotiations?

This question had been raised with Lloyd George by Sir Robert Borden in a letter dated 29 October 1918,[3] after he had received his summons[4] to come to Europe for discussions preparatory to the Peace Conference. He said that Canada expected to be represented at the Peace Conference. Lloyd George replied that he realised the importance of the question, but he thought it better not to try to discuss it by correspondence and to defer it until Borden had reached London.[4] Accordingly, as soon as he arrived in London, Borden discussed the question with Lloyd George and Bonar Law. He soon realised that the problem of representation was not a matter for determination by the British nations alone; it raised questions upon which foreign Powers had the last word.

---

[1] *C.H.B.E.* vii, pt. i, 541.
[2] It would seem from Hughes's account in *The Splendid Adventure* that he was given several opportunities in meetings of the Imperial War Cabinet to express his views at this tage. See pp. 90–3.
[3] See Borden, H. (ed.), *Robert Laird Borden: His Memoirs*, ii, 891.
[4] *Canada, Sessional Papers*, Special Session, 1919 no. 41 J, p. 1 (19 Oct. 1918).

An indication of the views of France was given on 15 November 1918, in a document dealing with the organisation of the proposed Peace Conference. France was opposed to any separate representation of the Dominions and compared their status with that of States in the American Union.[1] Although this position was modified slightly in a second version of the document, delivered on 21 November, which admitted that Britain's promises to the Dominions must be respected, it was emphasised that any representation for the Dominions must form part of the total British representation.[2] Lloyd George in his discussions with Borden consequently assumed that France and other foreign countries would object to any separate representation of the Dominions, and that the most they could be expected to tolerate was some Dominion representation on the British delegation. Accordingly, in the discussions that followed Borden's arrival in London, it was proposed that he should form one of the proposed British delegation of five—the others being Lloyd George, Balfour, Bonar Law and Barnes—and should be regarded as the special representative of the Dominions. But as Borden realised and as Hughes quickly confirmed, this arrangement would not satisfy all the other Dominions.[3]

The matter was taken a stage further at the meetings in London on 2 and 3 December[4] of the representatives of Great Britain, France and Italy—usually called the London Conference—when it was decided that there should be an inter-Allied Conference of the great Allied and Associated Powers, namely, France, Great Britain, Italy, Japan and the United States of America, at which each would be represented by a delegation of five. It was understood that the Dominions and India would have one representative on the British delegation of five. In addition it was agreed that representatives of the British Dominions and India were to attend as additional members of the British delegation when questions directly affecting them were under consideration. This gave the Dominions an advantage over the smaller Allied Powers, for it was decided at the same Conference that the smaller Allied Powers should have no right of representation at all the meetings of the Inter-Allied Conference, but that each of them should have the right to be represented only when questions concerning them were being discussed.[5] This arrangement

[1] Miller, D. H., *My Diary at the Conference of Paris*, I, 6; II, Doc. 5, pp. 21–2. Referred to in Marston, F. S., *The Peace Conference of 1919*, pp. 35–8.
[2] Miller, D. H., *op. cit.* II, Docs. 4, 13, 14, espec. pp. 13, 81, 84.
[3] Borden, H., *op. cit.* II, 866, 871–2.
[4] Lloyd George gives the date, December 1: *The Truth about the Peace Treaties*, I, 136. Borden was uneasy that such discussions should take place without Canadian representation. Borden, H., *op. cit.* II, 874.
[5] Lloyd George, *op. cit.* I, 205–6. Borden appeared to think that the London Conference had accepted separate representation for the Dominions: *Canadian Constitutional Studies*, p. 117; Borden, H., *op. cit.* II, 892. But as he states later, *ibid.* pp. 894–5, it was not till the last day of the year that separate representation was accepted by the Imperial War Cabinet.

meant the Dominions were not only being given all the rights of the smaller Allied Powers of being represented when their interests were concerned, but also, through their one representative on the British delegation of five, they would have an opportunity, denied to the smaller Powers, of participating in all the important discussions of the Great Powers. Lloyd George pointed out these advantages[1] when certain French proposals[2] for the organisation of the Conference were discussed "at the last meeting of the Imperial War Cabinet in the year 1918",[3] but he failed to convert the Dominion Prime Ministers to them. There were at least two objections. In the first place the Dominions were being denied separate representation which it was proposed none the less to accord to other small States, like Belgium or Portugal or even to a neutral like Sweden, whose contribution to the war had been much less than that of the Dominions. Hughes asserted that "the Dominions were entitled to representation equal to that accorded to neutrals. Australia had put and kept more men in the field than Belgium, and deserved as much representation at the Conference."[4] The second objection was urged particularly by the Canadian Prime Minister. If the Dominions were to be heard only when their interests were affected, Canada, which in Borden's words, "had no special material interest in the war, and no claims to additional territory", would seldom if ever be heard. Such an arrangement "would be regarded as little better than a mockery". Borden therefore urged that "the delegation representing the British Empire should be in part selected from a panel, upon which each Prime Minister from the Dominions should have a place, and that one or more of these Prime Ministers should be called from time to time, as occasion might require, to sit in the delegation representing the whole Empire at the Conference".[5] It will be seen that the Dominions were asking for the best of both worlds. They wanted separate representation, as small States, and claimed three representatives each—the number which had been suggested for the small States in the French proposals. They wanted also to obtain the advantage of membership in a Great Power. However, the Imperial War Cabinet supported these proposals, though Lloyd George expressed misgivings at the possible ill-effects of asking for so much.[6]

[1] Lloyd George, op. cit. 1, 206.
[2] Probably some elaboration of the Pichon Note of 13 Dec. 1918, reproduced in Miller, D. Hunter, My Diary at the Conference of Paris, II, Doc. 69. See Marston, F. S., The Peace Conference of 1919, p. 51.
[3] Lloyd George, op. cit. 1, 204. Actually the meeting appears to have been held on 2 Jan. 1919. Borden's Memorandum upon the meeting bears that date: Canada, Sessional Papers, 1919, Special Session, no. 41 J.
[4] Ibid. p. 205. Hughes, in his agitation for separate representation for the Dominions, was going further than his own Cabinet thought wise. They had cabled to him that they could not support such a position. Australian Commonwealth Debates, 1 Oct. 1920, XCIV, 5817.
[5] Ibid. pp. 206–7. See also Borden's Memorandum to the Canadian Cabinet, 2 Jan. 1919. Canada, Sessional Papers, 1919, Special Session, no 41 J.   [6] Ibid. p. 208.

It was necessary now to get these proposals accepted by the other Great Powers. No objection was expected or encountered to the plan for a panel of delegates from which the British Empire's representation would be chosen; but separate representation on an equal footing with Belgium and other smaller Allied States aroused some opposition. The matter was discussed in the sessions of the five Great Powers, held in Paris in January 1919 before the plenary session of the Conference opened. On 12 January there had been a preliminary skirmish when Lloyd George made the proposal that each of the Dominions and India should have two representatives—the figure now intended for Belgium—and Newfoundland one.[1] Clemenceau showed some friendliness; President Wilson and Lansing, the American Secretary of State, had been critical. Wilson apparently was not opposed to the idea of separate representation, but he felt that, with two representatives for each of the five Dominions and India and five for the British Empire, the total British representation was too large and would be impossible to justify to the American people.[2] After some discussion, in the course of which it was proposed that the Dominions and India should have one representative each,[3] Lloyd George undertook to consult the representatives of the Dominions further. When the gist of these discussions was reported to Borden he called the other Dominion ministers together—Botha and Smuts of South Africa, and Hughes and Cook of Australia—and they agreed to insist on representation equal to that of the other small Powers.[4] However, when they met Lloyd George and heard his account of the situation, they felt obliged reluctantly to acquiesce in a proposal of one representative for each Dominion.[5] But the outcome was better than expected. When the five Great Powers met on the afternoon of 13 January Lloyd George appears to have maintained his bid of two representatives each for Canada, Australia, South Africa, New Zealand and India, and one for Newfoundland. After discussion he accepted an amendment by President Wilson that Canada, Australia, South Africa and India should have two representatives each, New Zealand one, and that Newfoundland should not be given separate representation.[6]

This was a very satisfactory result. But its effect was marred by the news later in the week that, because Brazil was to be accorded three representatives, the representation of Belgium and Serbia had been increased from two to three. Lloyd George protested, but he could not prevent the decision, nor were the Dominions consulted about it. The whole principle of equality between the Dominions and Belgium and the other smaller Powers had thus been overthrown. Borden

[1] *Ibid.* p. 216.
[2] *Ibid.*
[3] Borden, H., *op. cit.* II, 895, 899.
[4] Borden, H., *op. cit.* II, 899.
[5] *Ibid.*
[6] Lloyd George, *op. cit.* I, 216.

protested strongly and even discussed with his colleague Sifton the proposal that they should go home.[1] On 18 January, however, the first plenary session of the Conference was held and rules of representation were adopted. The United States, the British Empire—not, be it noted, Great Britain—France, Italy and Japan, as "the belligerent forces with general interests" were to be entitled to five representatives each and to attend all sessions and commissions of the Conference. In the list of "belligerent powers with special interests", entitled to attend sessions at which questions concerning them were discussed, came Belgium, Brazil and Serbia with three delegates each; China, Greece, the Hedjaz, Poland, Portugal, Roumania, Siam and Czechoslovakia with two each; Cuba, Guatemala, Hayti, Honduras, Liberia, Nicaragua, Panama, Bolivia, Ecuador, Peru, Uruguay with one each; and the British Dominions and India with the representation already agreed upon. The list illustrates the sort of company which the Dominions, by their efforts and by the support of Great Britain, were thought fit to keep in the society of States. Finally, the panel system could be adopted by any State, and it was explicitly added that the representatives of the Dominions (including Newfoundland)[2] and of India could be included in the representation of the British Empire by means of the panel system. In spite of Belgium's greater numerical representation, this arrangement of double status which the Dominions achieved gave them in practice fuller representation in the affairs of the Conference.[3] As Borden wrote: "The Dominions secured a peculiarly effective position."[4]

If double representation had its advantages, it had disadvantages also. Had the Dominions been content with separate representation as small Powers, even with a numerical inferiority to Belgium, they could have claimed that their separate existence as States had been acknowledged. "Great Britain" or "the United Kingdom", not "the British Empire", would, in that case, have appeared in the list as one of the five Great Powers. But when the Dominions claimed also to be considered as part of that Great Power it was necessary for "the British Empire" to be listed as one of the Great Powers. The status of the Dominions became thereby ambiguous, and, although the advantages of ambiguity were exploited to the full during the course of the negotiations, its disadvantages become prominent when the questions of signature and ratification of the peace treaties came up.[5]

The second plenary session of the Conference met on 25 January 1919, and the Dominions were, of course, separately represented, while the Canadian Minister for Justice, C. J. Doherty, occupied the

---

[1] Borden, H., *op. cit.* II, 902–3.
[2] In fact the Prime Minister of Newfoundland attended the first plenary session of the Conference as a member of the British Empire delegation.
[3] See the testimony of Hughes, for example, in his *The Splendid Adventure*, p. 237.
[4] Borden, H., *op. cit.* II, 893.   [5] See below, pp. 662–6.

Dominion seat on the British Empire delegation. It was proposed that five commissions should be set up, each of which would be responsible for one of the following topics: the League of Nations, reparations, labour, international transit, and responsibility for offences against the laws of war. The five Great Powers had decided that these Commissions should consist of fifteen members each, and that each Great Power should be represented by two members (except on the Reparations Commission, when they were to have three), while the smaller Powers should choose five representatives. This aroused some strong protests from the smaller Powers. Borden, who had been uneasy at the way in which, during the week that had elapsed between the first and second plenary sessions of the Conference, the affairs of the Conference seemed to have slipped into the hands of a few leading statesmen so that the Dominions could hardly expect a chance of influencing decisions,[1] now supported the smaller Powers in their protests.[2] In the result, they did in fact gain some increase of representation on three of the Commissions.

It is interesting to notice, however, that the Dominions themselves did not gain their representation upon the Commissions as a result of this move. They did not attend the meeting at which the smaller Powers chose their representatives. Instead, they obtained representation through their membership of the British Empire panel which was entitled, as a Great Power, to nominate two delegates. As a result of this process Hughes of Australia sat on the Commission on Reparations and was its vice-chairman; Massey, Prime Minister of New Zealand, sat on the Commission dealing with responsibility for offences against the laws of war; Sifton and Sir George Foster of Canada sat on the International Transit Commission and on the Economic Commission respectively, and each was vice-chairman; and Smuts of South Africa sat on the League of Nations Commission. When, later on, committees came to be set up to deal with particular problems, representation from the Dominions was similarly secured. Borden sat on the committee to deal with Greece and Albania, Sir Joseph Cook of Australia sat on the committee dealing with Czechoslovakia,[3] and General Botha of South Africa on that dealing with Poland. Smuts was dispatched upon an important mission to Budapest to make contact with the revolutionary Bela Kun, and to Prague where Masaryk's new state of Czechoslovakia was being organised.[4]

The Dominions' gain from their membership of the British Empire panel was not confined to representation upon commissions and committees. As negotiations proceeded at Paris the real centre of

---

[1] Borden, H., *op. cit.* II, 903.　　　　[2] *Ibid.* pp. 904–5.
[3] His attitude, says Harold Nicolson, who was one of his official advisers, was one of "benevolent boredom": Nicolson, H., *Peacemaking*, 1919, pp. 272 *seqq.*
[4] There is an account of the journey in Nicolson, *op. cit.* pp. 292 *seqq.*

power moved from the Council of Ten (a meeting of two delegates from each of the five Great Powers) to the Council of Four—Clemenceau, Lloyd George, Orlando and President Wilson—so that not only were the smaller Powers excluded, but also four-fifths of the representatives of the Great Powers. The Dominions were thus, formally, unrepresented at the most vital discussions. But in practice they were fully consulted, as members of the British Empire delegation, at all stages in the discussion of the delegation's policy, the principles and practice of the Imperial War Cabinet being carried on in Paris in the delegation.[1] Indeed, towards the close of the Conference, when Lloyd George was obliged to be in London, Borden held the chairmanship of the delegation[2] and, on several occasions took Balfour's place on the Council of Five.[3]

What part did the Dominions play in the making of the Treaties? Their interests were varied. Australia, New Zealand and South Africa had taken part in military expeditions to conquer German territory which adjoined or was adjacent to their homelands. They were concerned that no such threat to their security should be permitted to occur again. Canada had felt no such threat and had no territorial conquests to claim. All the Dominions might be said to feel a general interest in the making of a just and durable peace, but their capacity and opportunity to make a contribution to that end was limited and varied indeed according to the quality of their representatives. On these wider issues South Africa, through General Smuts—not, be it noted, its Prime Minister—undoubtedly made the greatest contribution.

The framing of the Covenant of the League of Nations may first be considered. All the Dominions had some say in the discussions on this subject in the Imperial War Cabinet in London;[4] the Canadian delegation, for example, had prepared some memoranda on the scope and organisation of the League and the Canadian Minister for Justice, Doherty, had been working on a draft, which, to his indignation, was never to be discussed.[5] None of them, however, was so influential as Smuts[6] who in his pamphlet, dated 10 December 1918, and entitled *The League of Nations—A Practical Suggestion*, immediately took a first place in the discussion of the project. Smuts also influenced discussions in the Imperial War Cabinet by a memorandum he produced at Mr Lloyd George's invitation.[7] Smuts went

[1] Borden, R. L., *Canada in the Commonwealth*, p. 101; Hughes, W. M., *The Splendid Adventure*, pp. 105–6.
[2] Borden, H., *op. cit.* II, pp. 935–41.
[3] Borden, R. L. *op. cit.*, II, p. 101. The Council of Five was a council of the foreign ministers of the five Great Powers.
[4] See, for example, Lloyd George, *op. cit.* I, 628–35.
[5] Glazebrook, G. P. de T., *Canada at the Paris Peace Conference* (1942), pp. 60–61.
[6] See Millin, S. G., *General Smuts*, II, chaps. 8, 18, 19 *passim*.
[7] It is summarised in Lloyd George, *op. cit.*, I, 620–28; Borden was impressed by it. See Borden, H., *op. cit.* II, 883.

further in his proposals than had any responsible statesman hitherto. "Europe is being liquidated", he wrote, "and the League of Nations must be the heir to this great estate. The peoples left behind by the decomposition of Russia, Austria, and Turkey, are mostly untrained politically; many of them are either incapable of or deficient in power of self-government; they are mostly destitute and will require much nursing towards economic and political independence." The League of Nations should be made "the reversionary in the broadest sense of these Empires". As a compromise he was prepared to agree that "partly to conciliate the Great Powers and partly in view of the administrative inexperience of the League at the beginning...suitable Powers may be appointed to act as mandatories of the League in the more backward peoples and areas", but these mandatories would act "subject to the authority and control of the League, which I mean to be real and effective", and he hoped that it would "prove to be only a temporary expedient". The League itself he saw as "a permanent conference between the Governments of the constituent states for the purpose of joint international action in certain defined respects". It was to consist of a General Conference and of a Council or Executive Committee on which the Great Powers would have only a bare majority and in which the three or more Powers would have a veto. There was to be a permanent secretariat and courts of conciliation and arbitration. But Smuts went further—he advocated the abolition of conscription, the nationalisation and inspection of armament factories, and compulsory arbitration for justiciable disputes.

In many ways Smuts expressed in his pamphlet the leading ideas upon the relations between peoples which the development of the British Empire had brought to light. In one passage he expresses this aspect very well.

The vital principles are: the principle of nationality involving the ideas of political freedom and equality; the principle of autonomy, which is the principle of nationality extended to peoples not yet capable of complete independent statehood; the principle of political decentralisation, which will prevent the powerful nationality from swallowing the weak autonomy as has so often happened in the now defunct European empires; and finally an institution like the League of Nations which will give stability to that decentralisation and thereby guarantee the weak against the strong.[1]

Smuts's contribution was, in some sense, a contribution of the experience of the British Empire.

The representatives of the British Empire on the Commission on the League of Nations at Paris were Smuts and Lord Robert Cecil, himself an author of an influential proposal on the British side. Smuts was therefore able to exercise considerable influence on the

---

[1] See Millin, S. G., *op. cit.* II, Appendix A, for a summary of the ideas and words of Smuts which occur in the League Covenant.

framing of the Covenant. Moreover, the draft upon which the Commission worked—the Hurst-Miller draft as it was called from the names of the British and American legal advisers who drew it up—was greatly influenced by Smuts's proposals. It had a mixed ancestry, but President Wilson, who of course had a large share in framing it, and who presented it to the Commission, testified to the modifications he had made in his own ideas as a result of studying Smuts's plan.[1] Smuts's influence was enhanced also by the fact that he and Cecil worked closely together and each understood and appreciated the other's ideas, while both co-operated closely and successfully with President Wilson,[2] the chairman of the Commission. They sat, in fact, quite near him in the proceedings of the Commission—on his left was Colonel House and next to House were Cecil and Smuts—and it has been asserted with authority that "the harmony between the American and British delegates, on which the making of the Covenant largely depended, was distinctly favoured by the fact that they could consult together without leaving their places".[3]

The story of the making of the Covenant cannot be re-told here.[4] It is possible only to select certain topics which the Dominions considered affected their interests. First of all it is necessary to consider how the Dominions and India achieved membership of the League. Their actual admission to membership of the League, and therewith of the Assembly, appears to have been accomplished with little difficulty in the Commission. Once their membership of the Peace Conference itself had been accepted, the rest followed fairly easily. It is true that the wording of the Hurst-Miller draft, which provided that members of the League should be represented by an ambassador or minister, might be held to exclude the Dominions which at that time had no separate diplomatic representation.[5] On the other hand Miller had contemplated that the Dominions would be members[6] and at the second meeting of the Commission the wording was altered to allow of diplomatic or other representatives.[7] At this meeting also some discussion of the position of the Dominions arose, and Cecil asked that it should be held over for a future occasion.[8] In fact the subject was never brought up again and discussions proceeded on the assumption that the Dominions were to be members. India was included among the members at the third meeting of

---

[1] Baker, R. S., *Woodrow Wilson and World Settlement*, I, 225-8; III, Doc. 11.
[2] Smuts had a high respect for Wilson; he thought him a greater statesman than Lincoln. Millin, *op. cit.* II, chap. 18.
[3] Butler, J. R. M., in *History of the Peace Conference of Paris*, VI, 435.
[4] See Miller, D. Hunter, *The Drafting of the Covenant* (2 vols. New York, 1928); Zimmern, Sir Alfred, *The League of Nations and the Rule of Law*.
[5] See Miller, D. Hunter, *The Drafting of the Covenant*, II, Doc. 19, and Baker, S, *op. cit.* III, Document 16, p. 145.
[6] See his draft of 26 Jan. 1919, prepared for a meeting with Cecil next day. Miller, D. Hunter, *My Diary at the Conference of Paris*, IV, 171.
[7] Miller, *The Drafting of the Covenant*, II, 257.   [8] *Ibid.*

the Commission.[1] It is interesting to notice that this granting of "six votes to the British Empire" passed easily through the Commission and that it was not until later on, when the American Senate began its consideration of the Treaty, that strong objections to Dominion membership came to be expressed.

Though admission to membership of the League and of the Assembly was easily obtained, difficulty was experienced over the question whether the Dominions and India should be eligible for membership of the Council. As first envisaged by Cecil the Council was to consist of Great Powers only, and this proposal found its way into the Hurst-Miller draft. Accordingly, before the Commission met, the Dominions had agreed, after discussions in the British Empire delegation, that their representation on the Council must be achieved through membership, on the panel system, of the British Empire delegation. But Smuts—and President Wilson had followed him on this point in his draft—had advocated that the small Powers should be represented, though with one less place than the Great Powers.[2] Thus, when the Commission turned its attention to the question, and the small Powers immediately asked for representation, they secured it with little difficulty. It was decided that the five Great Powers would be permanent members of the Council, four other *States*, members of the League, should be added as temporary members.[3] But were the Dominions "States"? Miller thought not. He wrote: "It was the intention of the Commission to exclude the Dominions and Colonies from such representation. The subject was not, so far as I recall, specifically discussed, but the representation of the smaller States was debated at great length, and was always debated, so far as I remember, as the representation of States."[4] The Dominions do not appear to have gathered at once that they were excluded from the Council and it was not until 21 April that, at a meeting of the British Empire delegation, Sifton of Canada raised the question. Cecil stated that he thought no such exclusion had been intended, and in the ensuing week he undertook negotiations with the American delegation which resulted in the adoption of an amended wording whereby the Council should consist of "representatives of the Principal Allied and Associated Powers together with representatives of four other *members* of the League".[5] The Canadians were still uneasy and were not finally appeased until Clemenceau, Wilson and Lloyd George signed a memorandum on 6 May formally concurring in the opinion that "the representatives of the self-governing Dominions of the British Empire may be selected or named as members of the Council".[6]

[1] *Ibid.* p. 261. [2] *Ibid.* I, 137. [3] *Ibid.* I, 227.
[4] *Ibid.* I, 480. [5] *Ibid.* pp. 477–83, 487–93. My italics.
[6] Though Borden took the lead in this (see Glazebrook, G. P. de T., *Canada and the Paris Peace Conference*, pp. 63–67), the concession he obtained applied to all the Dominions. The memorandum is printed in *Canada, Sessional Papers*, 1919, Special Session, no. 41 J, p. 19.

Though the Dominions were all anxious to become members of the League, they were not all equally enthusiastic about the obligations which they might be called upon to assume under the Covenant. Article 10 in particular excited anxieties among the Canadian delegates. In the draft before the Commission it read:

The High Contracting Parties undertake to respect and preserve as against external aggression the territorial integrity and existing political independence of all states members of the League. In case of any such aggression or in case of any threat or danger of such aggression the Executive Council shall advise upon the means by which this obligation shall be fulfilled.

Borden, in a memorandum[1] which later received the full support of the Canadian Cabinet and which was circulated to the other members of the British Empire delegation and to President Wilson, held that by this article the signatories would declare: "(a) that all existing territorial delimitations are just and expedient, (b) that they will continue indefinitely to be just and expedient, (c) that the Signatories will be responsible therefor." This was a pledge, he thought, to underwrite the *status quo*, and he felt that it was committing Canada too far. Yet, in spite of all his efforts, no change was made in the substance of the article. Anything less would have failed to satisfy France, and both Wilson and Cecil felt unable to weaken its terms. The Canadians therefore acquiesced at the time; and they defended the article as best they could against criticisms in Canada which they had anticipated.[2] But, later on, at the first meeting of the League Assembly, Canada was to attempt to delete the article from the Covenant.

One topic which aroused the concern of the Dominions and of Great Britain was the disposal of the former German Colonies, the greater part of which had been conquered and occupied by their troops. The Union had occupied German South-West Africa;[3] a mixed force, including British and South African troops, for most of the time under the command of Smuts, had occupied German East Africa (now Tanganyika) after a long and hard campaign;[4] New Zealand had occupied German Samoa,[5] and Australia German New Guinea. They had all declared that, whatever might happen to these territories, they were not to be returned to Germany. Canada supported this view, but insisted at the same time that any action which might be taken on the disposal of the colonies must take

---

[1] Borden, H., *op. cit.* II, 90, 920. It is printed in Miller, *The Drafting of the Covenant*, I, 354. Doherty also wrote a memorandum criticising the article. It is printed in Glazebrook, G. P. de T., *Canada and the Peace Conference*, Appendix C.

[2] Glazebrook, *op. cit.* pp. 67–71.   [3] *C.H.B.E.* vol. VIII.

[4] *C.H.B.E.* VIII, 723–8.

[5] 29 Aug. 1914. *C.H.B.E.* VII, pt. II, 229; Corbett, Sir J. (ed.), *Naval Operations*, I, 137–40. German Samoa was Western Samoa; Eastern Samoa was in the hands of the United States.

account of American susceptibilities.[1] As discussions proceeded, Smuts's idea of mandates, which he had originally proposed for the peoples of the Russian, Austrian and Turkish empires, came to be proposed as a solution for the problem of the disposal of the colonies of the German Empire—a twist of Smuts's original idea which he did not approve, at any rate so far as the territory of German South-West Africa was concerned. The Dominions indeed, while not wholly opposed to the mandatory principle, did not wish it to be applied to the territories they had conquered. Borden supported this view and said that,

so far as the colonies conquered by South Africa, Australia, and New Zealand were concerned, he would be prepared to support their retention on one consideration, and one only, and that was that their acquisition was necessary for the future security of the Empire. As regards the remaining conquered territories, he was in favour of entrusting their control and dominion to whichever state was appointed as mandatory for that purpose by the League of Nations, on the lines suggested in General Smuts's paper.

Lloyd George records that the Imperial War Cabinet accepted unanimously the doctrine of the mandate in respect of enemy possessions, except in South-West Africa and the islands conquered by Australia and New Zealand,[2] and he notes that Smuts urged that Britain herself should undertake a mandate for German East Africa.[3]

The British Empire, therefore, entered the discussions pledged to the annexation of certain former German colonies, and to the application of the mandatory principle to the rest. At the meeting of the Supreme Council of the Allies on 24 January 1919, Smuts put forward the claim of the Union of South Africa to annex German South-West Africa.[4] He was supported by Hughes, who claimed New Guinea for Australia, and Massey, who claimed Western Samoa for New Zealand. Borden supported their claims.[5] Wilson was opposed to annexation,[6] and it became essential for some compromise to be found by which the mandate principle could be fully adopted for all the German colonies. In discussions in the British Empire delegation a compromise was worked out, by which there were to be three classes of mandates, A, B and C, the last of which was to consist of territories so backward that they should be governed as integral portions of the territory of the mandatory Power. It was intended that the colonies claimed by Australia, New Zealand and South Africa should be placed in this class C. The compromise[7] was proposed and

---

[1] Borden's remarks on this subject in the Imperial War Cabinet are quoted in Lloyd George, D., *The Truth about the Peace Treaties*, I, 117. See also Borden, H., *op. cit.* II, 884, 889–90.
[2] Lloyd George, *op. cit.* I, 123.   [3] *Ibid.* I, 119–20.
[4] An account of the meeting is in Lloyd George, *op. cit.* I, chap. 10.
[5] Lloyd George, *op. cit.* I, 523.
[6] He had made this clear to Lloyd George at their first interview in London. Lloyd George, *op. cit.* I, 191.
[7] It is printed in Lloyd George, *op. cit.* I, 538–41.

drafted by Smuts and supported by Lloyd George and Borden. Hughes resisted it strongly and there were some heated scenes in the British Empire delegation.[1] But it was adopted and on 30 January the Supreme Council approved it after a hard discussion in which Hughes and Wilson had some spirited encounters and in which General Botha's conciliatory speech did much, according to Lloyd George, to win the assent of President Wilson.[2] It was destined to appear as Article 22 of the Covenant of the League of Nations. In the outcome Australia received the mandate for the German possessions in the Pacific south of the Equator—those to the north were granted to Japan under a C class mandate also—German Samoa passed to New Zealand, and German South-West Africa to South Africa. Nauru, a valuable source of phosphates, was granted to the British Empire,[3] but in practice it was proposed that the United Kingdom, Australia and New Zealand should operate the mandate jointly, each Government in turn appointing the Administrator, with Australia making the first appointment. It may be noticed that the United Kingdom itself obtained no C class mandates. It accepted German East Africa (except for the north-western portions, Ruanda and Urundi, which were alloted to Belgium as a C class mandate) and a portion of the Cameroons and of Togoland in West Africa— the larger portion in each case going to France—as B class mandates, binding itself thereby "to secure equal opportunities for the trade and commerce of other members of the League" in these mandated territories. To the United Kingdom also were allotted the mandates for certain territories of the former Turkish empire—which alone of the empires to which Smuts had originally applied his mandate system was treated in this way—and these, namely for Palestine and Iraq, were intended to be held as A class mandates. This class of mandate was designed to apply to communities which had reached a stage of development when their existence as independent nations could be provisionally recognised, subject to the rendering of administrative advice and assistance by the mandatory until such time as they were able to stand alone. Iraq's independence was indeed soon recognised by the United Kingdom, but Palestine remained under the mandate until 1949.

Though the Dominions and the United Kingdom reached a substantial measure of agreement in dealing with the former German colonies, and indeed on most issues before the Conference, the subject of reparations provided a sharp division. Hughes of Australia had been chairman of a British committee, set up by Lloyd George, to

[1] Borden, H., op. cit. II, 906.
[2] Lloyd George, op. cit. I, 542–6. Borden confirms this. Borden H., op. cit. II, 905, 907.
[3] There had been a dispute between Australia and New Zealand about who should have it, and in the end it was agreed to share the mandate (and the phosphates) jointly. See Massey's statement in the New Zealand Parliament, 2 Sept. 1919, N.Z. Hansard, p. 52. C.H.B.E. VII, pt. II, 222.

determine Germany's capacity to pay[1]—a committee upon which Foster, the Canadian Finance Minister, also sat. Hughes was also vice-chairman of the Peace Conference Commission on Reparations and came out vigorously for exacting from Germany the whole cost of the war. In the case of his own country, for example, he claimed that the whole of Australia's war costs, estimated at £364,000,000, together with a sum of £100,000,000 representing the capitalised value of pensions, repatriation, and the losses of civilians, should be repaid by Germany and that, as a step towards the recovery of these sums, all German private property in the mandated territories should be expropriated. This claim brought Hughes directly into conflict with the American delegation and raised an argument about the meaning of the terms upon which the armistice had been signed with Germany. One of Wilson's Fourteen Points had stipulated that invaded territories should be restored; but, when the Allies had accepted the Fourteen Points as a basis for the armistice, they had stipulated "that compensation will be made by Germany for all damage done to the civilian population of the Allies and their property by the aggression of Germany, by land, by sea and by the air". The view of the United States delegation was that this meant that the Allies could claim reparation for German acts against civilians which were contrary to international law, such as the sinking of merchant ships without warning, the invasion of Belgium contrary to treaty obligations, the deportation of civilians, or attacks on undefended towns. The United Kingdom rejected this view and a battle of legal opinions ensued. Smuts supported the American view; Borden, expressing the Canadian anxiety that no breach should occur between the British Empire and the United States, also inclined in the same direction. Hughes, and Massey of New Zealand, strongly opposed. In the end the problem was referred to the Council of Four, and there the American view prevailed. But a final problem had still to be disposed of. Could injured soldiers' pensions, widows' and children's pensions, and separation allowances be included justifiably in a claim for compensation for damage to the civilian population? If they could, then the Dominions and the United Kingdom would receive some substantial reparation; if not, their actual claim would be small.[2] The American delegation itself was divided on this matter, but Smuts, surprisingly, came out strongly, in a memorandum on 31 March 1919, in favour of the view that such pensions and allowances were chargeable to reparations. His advocacy impressed President Wilson,[3] and his view prevailed, though there was much controversy about whether it was consistent with Smuts's earlier position on the reparations question.[4]

---

[1] Lloyd George, op. cit. 1, 458–61, 475–83.
[2] This argument weighed with Lloyd George. See Truth about the Peace Treaties, 1, 491.
[3] Lloyd George, op. cit. 1, 496; Millin, op. cit. 11, 219–20.
[4] Millin, op. cit. 11, chaps. 23, 24.

On one other question there was a divergence between Australia and South Africa—the matter of war crimes. Hughes advocated the bringing to trial of all those who had treated Allied soldiers cruelly; Botha, on the other hand, thought that wholesale trials were wrong and that selected ringleaders only should be brought to trial. It was Hughes's view which prevailed in the Conference.

Why did this divergence develop between the representatives of the Dominions? It has been suggested that the fact that South Africa had a considerable number of German people among its population made Smuts and Botha cautious of action which might alienate them. Perhaps, too, they had recollections of the advantages of a peace without reparations such as that which Britain had made with the Boer Republics at the beginning of the century. Canada was influenced largely by her desire to keep in step so far as possible with the United States. Australia and New Zealand, on the other hand, had suffered great dislocation of trade and shipping in the war, and had obtained little territory of value in return. Perhaps, too, the pugnacious temperament of Mr Hughes explained a good deal.

In contrast to these differences over reparations and war criminals, all the Dominions were united in refusing to accept the proposal of Japan that, in effect, unrestricted Asiatic immigration should be permitted into their territories.[1] In this view they were at variance with Indian opinion, of course, and the United Kingdom was placed in a difficult position. But the United States was at one with the Dominions on this issue.

A word should be said about the share of the Dominions in the work of the Conference on labour questions. At the first plenary session of the Conference a Commission on Labour was set up "to inquire into the conditions of employment from the international aspect", "to consider the international means necessary to secure common action on matters affecting conditions of employment", and "to recommend the form of a permanent agency to continue such inquiry in co-operation with and under the direction of the League of Nations". The Dominions were not represented on this Commission, either among the smaller Powers or on the British Empire delegation, but they were kept in close touch with its proceedings through the meetings of the delegation and in particular from the fact that the most influential member of the Commission was Mr George Barnes, one of the plenipotentiaries of the United Kingdom. The Commission worked on a British draft, moreover, which had been discussed in a full meeting of the British Empire delegation on 31 January 1919, and in the preparation of which Sir Robert Garran, the Australian Solicitor-General, had had a share. This British draft provided that the Dominions should become separate members of the General

---

[1] But see Borden, H., *op. cit.* II, 926–8. Borden attempted to find a tactful formula to express the views of Canada. Hughes dispensed with tact.

Conference which it envisaged; but it intended that any representation which they might achieve upon the council or governing body of the organisation should be obtained through membership of the British Empire delegation. It would appear that the Dominions acquiesced in this proposal on 31 January.[1]

However, when, as the Conference proceeded, the Dominions' rights in regard to the League of Nations came to be asserted and recognised more fully, it was natural that their position in the proposed International Labour Organisation also should be affected. The Commission's report was discussed in some detail in the British Empire delegation and it was agreed that the model of the Covenant of the League of Nations should be followed in providing for the Dominions' membership. A plenary session of the Conference accepted this view and authorised its drafting committee "to make such amendments as may be necessary to have the Convention conform to the Covenant of the League of Nations in the character of its membership and in the method of adherence". But did this mean that the Dominions were to be eligible on the same terms as other states for membership both of the governing body of the Organisation as well as of the General Conference?[2] The American labour expert, H. M. Robinson, firmly maintained that membership of the General Conference alone had been conceded, and Borden found it impossible to convert him.[3] It was only after strong appeals to President Wilson himself by Borden, supported by Lloyd George, that Wilson decided to overrule his advisers and to agree that the Dominions and India should have as full membership in the International Labour Organisation as in the League of Nations.[4] It would seem, on the whole, that the Dominions had to encounter greater resistance to their claim to be eligible for membership of the Governing Body of the I.L.O. than of the Council of the League.

When the whole draft of the Treaty of Versailles had been completed, it was handed to the German delegates on 7 May 1919, and their comments in writing were invited within fifteen days. In the interval the members of the British Empire delegation discussed the settlement, and when on 30 May the German replies were received, a full meeting of the delegation was called for the next day to discuss the draft treaty and the German suggestions for its modification. Borden had already returned to Canada, but before leaving he had expressed the view to Bonar Law and Sir Edward Carson that the treaty was too severe.[5] In long discussions lasting the best part of two days, all the Dominions inclined to this view.[6] Smuts maintained strongly that the German case was sound and that the treaty should

---

[1] Shotwell, James T. (ed.), *The Origins of the International Labour Organisation.*
[2] There is a collection of material on this subject in Borden, H., *op. cit.* II, 944–61.
[3] Borden, H., *op. cit.* II, 945–6, 950.   [4] *Ibid.* II, 952.
[5] *Ibid.* II, 965.   [6] Lloyd George, *op. cit.* I, 688–720.

be recast, to bring it into conformity with the Fourteen Points.[1]
The representatives of the other Dominions did not go so far as this;
but, in answer to a direct question by Lloyd George, each member
said that he was in favour of some concessions. Lloyd George was
authorised to attempt, at the meeting of the Supreme Council, to
obtain the revision of certain boundaries on the Eastern frontiers of
Germany, of reparations, and of the arrangements for the army of
occupation. Moreover, he was urged to try to obtain "some sort of
promise regarding the League of Nations which would give the
Germans the hope of coming in if it was found that they were making
a real effort to fulfil their obligations".[2] The whole discussion was
conducted with moderation and Lloyd George paid tribute to the
spirit of mercy and justice which was shown for the fallen enemy.
The delegation was unanimous in asserting that the settlement as a
whole was too severe and, indeed, in authorising Lloyd George to say
that, if necessary, the British Empire would refuse to send its army into
Germany or use its navy to blockade Germany, in order to enforce
such a peace,[3] but it is clear that its members differed in emphasis.
General Botha's moderation was the product of experience. He also
had had to make peace, he said. "Lord Milner would remember
that it was exactly seventeen years on that very day that Peace was
signed in South Africa. On that occasion it was moderation which
had saved South Africa for the British Empire, and he hoped on this
occasion that it would be moderation which would save the world."[4]
But when Massey of New Zealand followed Botha, he expressed the
hope, while agreeing to the proposed modification, that "there was
no question of going back on the decisions reached in regard to the
German colonies" or "on the proposals relating to those guilty of
atrocities".[5] Botha and Smuts would not have dissented from this
view about colonies; but they took a wider, a longer and a more
lenient view of the provisions of the treaty than did the representatives
of Australia and New Zealand. In the outcome Lloyd George secured
some concessions from Wilson and Clemenceau which went some way
to meet the objections of the British Empire delegation. On 10 June
the delegation approved his proposed amendments and they were
embodied in the reply sent to the German delegates.[6]

It was natural that the Dominions, having taken part individually
in the negotiation of the treaties at Paris, should expect to sign them
and ratify them individually. Borden took the lead in this as he had
in the matter of negotiation. On 5 February 1919, in the early weeks

[1] Millin, op. cit. II, chaps. 25, 26: "As the document stands at present", he said,
"I cannot vote for it and I doubt if I can sign it", p. 237.
[2] Lloyd George, op. cit. I, 714, 718–20.
[3] Ibid. I, 719.   [4] Ibid. pp. 713–14.
[5] Ibid. p. 714.
[6] Ibid. pp. 720–8. Smuts still felt uneasy and was with difficulty finally persuaded to
sign the treaty. Millin, op. cit. II, chap. 29.

of the Conference, he sounded Lloyd George on the question and suggested that plenipotentiaries from the Dominions should sign the treaty. Lloyd George raised no objections.[1] Later on that day, Borden called together the other Dominion Prime Ministers and obtained their approval of his proposals and of a series of propositions which he placed before them.[2] On 12 March 1919 a memorandum was drawn up embodying these in more detail (the proposals and propositions which Borden had placed before his colleagues on 5 February). It laid down that "all the treaties and conventions resulting from the Peace Conference should be so drafted as to enable the Dominions to become Parties and Signatories thereto". To this end, while the treaties should be made in the name of the King, the plenipotentiaries whom he would authorise to sign on his behalf should be grouped under the name of the part of the Empire for which they would respectively sign. "Under the general heading 'The British Empire' the sub-headings 'The United Kingdom', 'The Dominion of Canada', 'The Commonwealth of Australia', 'The Union of South Africa', etc., would be used as headings to distinguish the various plenipotentiaries."[3] The Dominion Prime Ministers proposed that "it should be made an instruction to the British member of the Drafting Commission of the Peace Conference that all treaties should be drawn according to the above proposal".[4]

These proposals raised some difficulties. The Dominions had enjoyed during the conduct of negotiations the advantages of a double status. They were either individual small Powers or parts of a Great Power, the British Empire, as it suited their interests. But when the question of signature and ratification of the treaties came up, they were proposing to throw off the guise of parts of a Great Power, the British Empire, and stand forth to the world as sovereign, individual States, associated with a Great Power—the United Kingdom. They were asking not only the United Kingdom but also the society of States to recognise that the King was not the head, in international law and relations, of one State only—the British Empire—but of at least five—the United Kingdom, Canada, Australia, New Zealand and South Africa—and of six, if India were included. This was not completely new doctrine within the Empire itself. The Imperial War Conference of 1917 had accepted the principle, as the Dominion Prime Ministers said in the memorandum of 12 March 1919, that "the organisation of the Empire is to be based upon equality of nationhood". But if not completely new doctrine, it was recent doctrine, and neither British constitutional law nor international law had yet caught up with it. It was not surprising,

---

[1] Sir Robert Borden's diary (unpublished); quoted in Glazebrook, G. P. de T., *Canada at the Peace Conference*, p. 108.

[2] Borden's unpublished papers; quoted in Glazebrook, *ibid.* p. 109. See also Borden, H., *op. cit.* II, 909.

[3] *Canada, Sessional Papers*, 1919, Special Session, no. 41 J.   [4] *Ibid.*

therefore, that although, according to Borden, the proposals in the memorandum were accepted in principle by the British Empire delegation and the Conference,[1] the treaty was drawn up on more old-fashioned lines. Under the name of the King came the names of five plenipotentiaries, equipped with full powers to sign but restricted in no way by any territorial designation; these five plenipotentiaries were in fact chosen from the United Kingdom. There followed sub-headings: "For Canada", "For Australia" etc., with the names of the plenipotentiaries appointed to sign for them. Shortly stated, what happened was that Sir Robert Borden's scheme was adopted except in so far as the United Kingdom was concerned, and it was this exception, of course, which wrecked his whole scheme. Since the signatures of the plenipotentiaries from the United Kingdom were subject to no territorial restriction, it could be argued that they bound the whole Empire, and that the signatures of the Canadian, Australian and other plenipotentiaries were superfluous, in the strict letter of the law. At the same time these Dominion signatures had a political significance. They testified to the fact that the Dominions had individually assented to the peace treaties. Had they refused to sign, it is certain that the plenipotentiaries from the United Kingdom would not have signed the treaty without ensuring that some qualifying clause had been inserted in the treaty stipulating that it did not apply to the Dominions concerned. This is the great significance of the Dominions' individual signature of the treaty. Their right individually to decide whether or not they would accede to the treaty was conceded by Great Britain, though the forms of the law did not yet explicitly acknowledge this.

Even on legal grounds, however, there was a case for saying that the Dominions' signatures were something more than a superfluous underlining of the United Kingdom's action. It could be argued that the signatures of the five plenipotentiaries from the United Kingdom must be read subject to the signatures on behalf of each Dominion and India which followed, and that these subsequent signatures narrowed the scope of the United Kingdom signatures. On the whole this argument is less convincing. The Canadian delegates at the Peace Conference certainly did not accept it. Sifton wrote to Borden[2] when he saw the form in which the treaty had been drawn up: "On constitutional grounds, of course, it is absurd as it practically includes the Dominions twice, precluding, if my interpretation is correct, any necessity for signature on the part of Canada at all." And Borden himself was to write later that the Dominions had "the doubtful advantage" of a double signature.[3]

---

[1] Borden, Sir R., *Canada in the Commonwealth*, p. 103.

[2] Borden Papers, Sifton to Borden, 12 May 1919, quoted in Glazebrook, *op. cit.* p. 111.

[3] *Canada in the Commonwealth*, p. 103. The whole controversy is well analysed and discussed in Noel Baker, P. J., *The Present Juridical Status of the British Dominions in International Law*, pp. 67–83.

Some further controversies arose over ratification. On 4 July, a week after the signature of the Treaty of Versailles, the Secretary of State for the Colonies, Milner, telegraphed to the Canadian Government that "it is hoped German treaty may be ratified by three of the Principal Allied and Associated Powers and by Germany before end of July".[1] The Treaty had stipulated that, on ratification by Germany and by three of the principal Allied Powers, it would come into effect for those Powers. Milner clearly regarded the British Empire (not the United Kingdom) as one of the principal Allied Powers and he contemplated one ratification by the King on behalf of the whole Empire. At the same time he realised that the Empire, though one Power, was a composite Power, and that the consent of the Dominions severally to ratification was a political, though not a legal, necessity. Some difference of opinion arose, however, about the procedure which should be followed before consent to ratification was given. In the United Kingdom it was thought proper for the King to ratify on the advice of ministers; parliamentary approval might be sought later. But in Canada and in certain of the other Dominions, it was considered essential that parliamentary approval should precede any executive action. Accordingly it was agreed that in each Dominion a resolution of approval would be carried through each parliament; then an Order in Council would be passed in each Dominion requesting the King to ratify the treaty on behalf of the Dominion concerned; and finally Acts would be passed to give force of law in the Dominion to any parts of the treaty for which that was necessary. Needless to say this process was not completed by the end of July; indeed it was prolonged for some months and ratification was not completed until 10 January 1920.

It should be emphasised that in all these actions by the Dominions in regard to signature and ratification of the treaties the last word, as a matter of law, rested with the United Kingdom ministers. Though Canada, for example, passed an Order in Council requesting the King to issue full powers to the Canadian representatives to sign the treaties and, later, requesting the King to ratify the treaties "for and on behalf of Canada", the actual documents issued were issued under the authority of the Secretary of State for Foreign Affairs. As the law stood that was necessary. The Canadian and other Dominion Orders in Council, like the signatures on the peace treaties, were therefore, in strict law, superfluous; though here again they had great political, and indeed constitutional, significance. They represented the Dominions' right of separate self-determination in foreign affairs. And the law would one day be obliged to catch up with this political and constitutional situation.

Thus the Dominions stood, in 1919, signatories of the peace treaties and members of the new League of Nations upon which such high

[1] *Canada, Sessional Papers*, 1919, Special Session, no. 41 J.

hopes were set. They had entered the League with that same ambiguous double status which they had enjoyed at the Peace Conference. They were individually members of the Assembly and individually eligible for membership of the Council, while at the same time, through their membership of the British Empire, they might secure additional representation on the Assembly or permanent representation on the Council. They were not yet sure, nor was the society of States yet sure, whether they were or were to become a collection of independent, though associated, States, or one complex State. In the meantime this future uncertainty and present ambiguity were well expressed by the printer of the Covenant of the League, who, in setting up the list of original members, adopted this form:

> United States of America
> Belgium
> Bolivia
> Brazil
> British Empire
>   Canada
>   Australia
>   South Africa
>   New Zealand
>   India.

That was the most accurate statement possible in 1919 of the status of the Dominions in the League of Nations and in the world.

CHAPTER XVIII

INTERNATIONAL LAW AND
COLONIAL QUESTIONS, 1870–1914

IN the history of international law the period 1870–1914 is in some ways more significant than any other period of comparable length. During this period international society seemed to have a pronounced degree not only of well-being but also of stability. Yet, in essence, the mutual relations of civilised States continued to be those of primitive communities. Although nearly two generations had elapsed without a major war in Europe, a profound observer was able to write in 1908 "the spectre of war has become terrible";[1] that the "irresponsibility of international action" had become the transcending phenomenon of the time;[2] and that "to bring that action under some responsibility is the object of a great cry which goes up from modern Europe, a cry based on no new spiritual vision, but wrung from suffering and fear".[3] In some ways the period from 1870 to 1914 produced a conscious effort on the part of the leading States to live up to that responsibility. But the attempt was rudimentary. It was directed towards mitigating the evils of war, not towards eliminating it or providing effective procedures for its avoidance.

Yet even in that field important, though hesitating, developments took place. International arbitration emerged from the realm of mere theory. Some significant arbitrations were conducted; steps were taken in the direction of setting up permanent agencies for that purpose; the first treaties of obligatory arbitration were concluded. In this and other spheres Great Britain, partly in collaboration with the United States, assumed a position of leadership. The adherent of the economic interpretation of history may urge that, as the British Empire at that juncture reached the zenith of its territorial expansion and of corresponding political and strategic power, its interests became identified with the requirements of international stability and order, of which an effective international law was an essential condition. Be that as it may, the fact remains that in this period some of the salient features of British foreign policy constituted a distinctive contribution to a progressive development of international law. That contribution included those parts of international law which are concerned with the protection of the dignity and the freedom of human personality, such as the prohibition of the slave trade

---

[1] Westlake, *Collected Papers on Public International Law*, ed. Oppenheim (1914), p. 532.
[2] *Ibid.* [3] *Ibid.*

(a constant theme of British international action in the nineteenth century), the limitation of slavery and forced labour, and the protection of minorities. With regard to the law based on the principle of asylum and non-extradition of political offenders, Great Britain continued the liberal policy of the preceding period. In the same category must be included British policy concerning recognition of Governments: a practice which, by insisting on the subsequent legitimation of revolutionary changes through constitutionally expressed popular approval, tended to encourage political freedom and the ideals of democracy. In the matter of acquisition of territory the British contribution was of distinct usefulness in mitigating the rigours of annexation and in devising territorial adjustments such as condominia and leases which, in falling short of the drastic expedient of outright cession, assisted in solving the recurrent problems of the most potent source of international friction. Great Britain was actively associated in surmounting, through the decisions of the Berlin Conference of 1884-5, some of the difficulties resulting from the unregulated scramble for colonial acquisitions in Africa. She took a prominent and, in some cases, a leading part in the formulation of rules of war on land and at sea. The nature and extent of her contributions in these various fields will be surveyed in this chapter. It may be added that in the internal sphere English courts continued, with one exception, the tradition of the most enduring contribution of the common law to the law of nations—the tradition of the incorporation of international law as part of the law of England. In the case of the *Franconia*,[1] some of the judges of the Court of Crown Cases Reserved held that even if, according to international law, English courts were entitled to exercise jurisdiction over an alien in respect of an offence committed in British territorial waters, they could not, according to English law, exercise such jurisdiction unless there were a clear rule of English law, statutory or other, conferring that power upon them. This aspect of the decision gave rise to some trenchant criticism. Sir Henry Maine came near to suggesting that by that decision Great Britain placed herself outside the orbit of civilised countries.[2] A subsequent Act of Parliament—the Territorial Waters Jurisdiction Act, 1870—laid down that British courts had—and always had had—jurisdiction over territorial waters. Apart from the *Franconia* case, there was no interruption of the "even and accustomed" flow of "the majestic stream of common law, united with international law".[3]

[1] *Reg.* v. *Keyn* (1876), 2 Ex. Div. 63.
[2] *International Law* (Whewell Lectures, 1887; 2nd ed. 1894), p. 38.
[3] Judge Moore in the case of the *Lotus* (*Permanent Court of International Justice*, ser. A, no. 10, p. 75).

I

The period under review opened with two events of significant, though of unequal, importance for international law. The first was the Protocol of 17 January 1871, between Austria, Great Britain, France, Germany, Italy, Russia and Turkey—all signatories of the Treaty of Paris of 1856—affirming the binding force of treaties. The second was the Treaty of Washington of 8 May 1871, between Great Britain and the United States, referring to arbitration what has since become known as the Alabama controversy. The Protocol of January 1871 was adopted at a Conference convened in London on the initiative of Great Britain, who was the first to protest against the unilateral Russian denunciation of the provisions of the Treaty of Paris relating to the Black Sea. On 31 October 1870 Prince Gortchakof, relying on the preoccupation of the signatories of the Treaty of Paris with the events of the Franco-Prussian war,[1] informed the signatory Powers that Russia no longer considered herself bound by the obligations of the Treaty of Paris in so far as they limited her sovereign rights in the Black Sea. Great Britain protested. In his dispatch of 10 November 1870, to Sir A. Buchanan, the British ambassador at Moscow, Earl Granville instructed the ambassador to voice the strongest objection on the part of Great Britain to the Russian method inasmuch as it amounted not to a request by a signatory State for the reconsideration of the Treaty but to an announcement that "she has freed herself, or holds herself to have been freed, from any stipulations of the Treaty of which she disapproved". It was quite evident, the Foreign Minister said, that "the effect of such doctrine, and of any proceeding which, with or without avowal, is founded upon it, is to bring the entire authority and efficacy of Treaties under the discretionary control of each one of the Powers who may have signed them; the result of which would be the entire destruction of Treaties in their essence."[2]

The London Conference did not undo the results of the Russian denunciation. It abrogated previous treaties in so far as they referred to the neutralisation of the Black Sea and the limitations imposed upon men-of-war in it. But the acceptance of the Protocol affirming the binding force of treaties disapproved by obvious implication of the Russian action and saved as much from the wreckage as circumstances permitted. The Declaration was in the following terms: "C'est un principe essentiel du droit des gens qu'aucune Puissance ne peut se délier des engagements d'un traité, ni en modifier les stipulations, qu'à

---

[1] See Headlam-Morley, *Studies in Diplomatic History* (1930), pp. 232, 233, for a graphic description of the situation.

[2] *Parl. Pap.* 1871, LXXII [245], p. 78. See also, for Prince Gortchakof's explanation given to Sir A. Buchanan, *ibid.* p. 16. And see, for the statements by other Powers, *Fontes Juris Gentium, Digest of the Diplomatic Correspondence of the European States, 1856–1871,* ed. Makarov and Schmitz, 1 (1932), 758–68.

la suite de l'assentiment des parties contractantes, au moyen d'une entente amicale."[1] The Declaration is occasionally referred to as a typical example of the euphemistic insincerity and ineffectiveness of diplomatic language; this is to underestimate its importance. In comparison with what was to follow, this was a law-abiding age. In fact, apart from the annexation by Austria-Hungary, in 1908, of Bosnia and Hercegovina in violation of the Treaty of Berlin, there is no instance in this period of a major violation of a treaty by a Great Power—though it is difficult to assess to what extent, if any, this was the result of the solemn affirmation, in the Declaration of 1871, of the sanctity of international compacts.

The second event—one of considerably greater importance for international law—was the conclusion of the Treaty of Washington providing for arbitration of the claims of the United States in the matter of the *Alabama* and other vessels. That Treaty (of which it is convenient to give an account in another part of this chapter)[2] is also a milestone in the history of Anglo-American relations. The same double significance is true, within a more limited compass, of the British Naturalisation Act of 1870 in so far as it bears upon the right of expatriation. This Act abandoned the traditional doctrine of the common law according to which the subject cannot at will renounce his allegiance. As a corollary of that doctrine Great Britain, prior to the Act of 1870, continued to claim the allegiance of British subjects naturalised in a foreign country, and the impressment into the British Navy of British subjects naturalised in the United States was one of the contributory causes of the Anglo-American War of 1812. After the American Civil War the growth of the Fenian movement brought the controversy to a head once more. When naturalised American citizens of British origin were arrested in Ireland while engaged there in revolutionary activities, Great Britain, who regarded them as British subjects, denied the right of the United States to afford them diplomatic protection. On 27 July 1868 the Congress of the United States declared "the right of expatriation" to be an "inherent right of all people" and instructed the Government to adopt, when necessary, any requisite measures, short of war, for the protection abroad of naturalised American citizens. In the same year a Royal Commission was appointed to enquire, in this connection, into "the legal position of natural-born subjects, who may depart from and reside beyond the realm in Foreign Countries" and "the legal position of persons, being aliens, entering into or resident within the realm and becoming naturalised as subjects of the Crown".[3] The main point covered by these studiously general terms of reference was the question

---

[1] See Martens, *Nouveau Recueil Général des Traités*, xviii, 278.
[2] See below, p. 689.
[3] For an account of the work of the Commission see Jones, J. Mervyn, *British Nationality Law and Practice* (1947), pp. 76–88.

of the right of expatriation. The Commission came to the conclusion that the common law doctrine of the "indelibility" of allegiance was "neither reasonable nor convenient" and that it conflicted with the "freedom of action which is now recognised as the most conducive to the general good as well as to the individual happiness and prosperity". The Commission recommended the abandonment of the common law doctrine on the subject. A Convention, on the lines of the recommendation of the Commission, was concluded in 1870 between the United States and Great Britain.[1] One of the objects of the Naturalisation Act was to give effect to that recommendation. The result was not only the removal of an irritating source of friction between the two countries: it also signified the acceptance, as part of international law, of a view more congenial to the humanitarian and liberal tradition of British foreign policy in matters involving the dignity and freedom of the individual. Both are incompatible with a legal doctrine which transforms the State into a prison and allegiance into an unwilling relationship of bondage.

The humanitarian tradition of the past was continued with vigour in the granting of asylum to political refugees and others. A constitutional lawyer, writing in 1890,[2] summarised the legal position on the subject in the sense that the Executive had no constitutional power to refuse admission to any person. Although, in 1905, such power was granted on the ground of "undesirability", political and religious refugees were expressly exempted.[3] In 1871 asylum was granted to the French Communards; in 1885 to the Comte de Paris, the claimant to the French throne; in 1889 to General Boulanger, accused in France of high treason. Belgium had previously declined to admit the Communards, and had expelled General Boulanger. In 1906 the Home Secretary made an order laying down that, in cases where it was uncertain whether persons claiming admission were political refugees, such persons should be given the benefit of the doubt if they came from politically-disturbed countries.[4] Moreover, no onerous restrictions were placed upon the political activities of the refugees thus admitted. In *Rex* v. *Antonelli and Barberi*,[5] the Court declined to hold that publications directed against foreign governments constituted criminal libel. Phillimore, J., delivering judgment in this case, said: "Seditious libels are such as tend to disturb the government of this country, and in my opinion a document published here, which was calculated to disturb the government of some foreign country, is not a seditious libel, nor punishable as libel at all.... To hold otherwise... would make our great statesmen guilty of seditious

---

[1] See *Parl. Pap.* 1870, LXIX [C. 192], p. 471, and 1871, LXX [C. 345], p. 59, for the supplementary Convention of 23 Feb. 1871. See also for previous correspondence with the United States on the subject *Parl. Pap.* 1868–9, LXIII [4144], p. 735.
[2] Craies in *Law Quarterly Review*, VI (1890), 39.
[4] 5 Edw. VII, c. 13, I (3).   [3] *Hansard*, 4th ser. CXLV, 743.
[5] (1905) 70 J.P. 4.

libel, and those persons also who espoused the cause of Italian liberty." Although the Aliens Restriction Act of 1914[1] expressly conferred upon the Home Secretary the discretionary power to refuse admission or to authorise expulsion, such power was limited to the time of war; it was only in 1919 that it was extended to peace time.[2]

II

It was during the period under review that international law clearly emerged from the stage of being merely a law between States, and began to be concerned also with the individual. This important development began in the movements to protect three main classes of persons: the native races of colonial territories, minority peoples in the new national States of the old world, and finally the labouring classes in the countries of western Europe and the United States.

Efforts to ameliorate the lot of native peoples and in particular to eradicate slavery and the traffic in slaves continued throughout the latter part of the nineteenth century.[3] Some progress had already been made towards giving practical effect to the sentiment expressed at Vienna in 1815 that the slave trade was "repugnant to the principles of humanity and to the universal laws of morality".[4] It was clearly impracticable, however, to control the slave trade unless warships were given rights of visit and search over vessels suspected of carrying slaves; and such a right they did not possess under customary international law.[5] Accordingly the right could only be secured by treaty. Great Britain had succeeded in negotiating a number of such treaties with several of the principal European Powers,[6] but bilateral treaties were of little avail, so long as flags remained under which the slave-traders could enjoy immunity from visit and search. Efforts to conclude more general treaties had been only partially successful owing to the distrust in some quarters of a measure which might have the incidental result of increasing the powers of the British Navy. A different but closely related problem was how far a warship might lawfully grant asylum to a fugitive slave. In July 1875 the British Admiralty issued a circular instruction to officers of the Royal Navy allowing that a captain might receive fugitive slaves on board his warship, but adding the proviso that, if the ship entered a port of the country from which a slave had escaped, he must be handed over on a properly-authorised demand from the local authorities. This circular, which appeared to

---

[1] 4 and 5 Geo. V, c. 12.   [2] 9 and 10 Geo. V, c. 92.
[3] See Coupland, R., *The British Anti-Slavery Movement.* 2nd edn. (1939).
[4] Annex XV of the Vienna Final Act.
[5] See the judgment of Lord Stowell in the case of *Le Louis* (1817), 2 Dods., 210; and the American decision in *The Antelope* (1825), 10 Wheaton, 66.
[6] See *C.H.B.E.* II, 854.

be a reversal of former British policy, aroused a storm of protest in the country and in parliament. On 4 November 1875 "Historicus"[1] wrote a letter to *The Times* in which he argued that foreign jurisdiction could not run on board a British warship even in foreign waters, that the captain could do no other than administer English law on board the vessel, that as English law did not recognise slavery the slave once on board was a free man, and that therefore he could not thereafter lawfully be handed over as a slave.[2] In the following year a strong Royal Commission made an exhaustive inquiry into the law involved. Its report[3] showed that there was room for differences of opinion, and that while certain principles were undoubtedly accepted the limits of their application could not always be precisely stated. A revised Admiralty circular of 1876 attempted a compromise between the requirements of law and humanity, and went some way towards meeting the demands of a liberal public opinion.

It was clear, however, that the trade could not be satisfactorily dealt with except by means of a multilateral convention, and the British Government continued to work towards this end. The question was raised and discussed at the Berlin Conference of 1885; but the only result was a vague clause in the Final Act condemning slave trading in general terms and an undertaking by the signatory Powers to use "the means at their disposal" for putting an end to it. Effective action was at last taken, however, at the Brussels Conference convened in 1890 by the King of the Belgians at the suggestion of the British Government. The Brussels Act[4] provided systematic measures for the suppression of slave trading in the Indian Ocean, the Red Sea and the Persian Gulf, including a limited reciprocal right of visit and search in certain zones, the reception of fugitive slaves aboard government vessels, and the establishment of an International Maritime Office at Zanzibar.[5]

The fight against slavery, however, was only part of the movement to secure the welfare of native peoples. This period of active colonial expansion also raised anew the old question of the duties of colonial Powers towards the native peoples of occupied territories. The basic rule of international law was that a State might do as it pleased in

[1] Sir William Vernon Harcourt, afterwards first Whewell Professor of International Law in the University of Cambridge. See Gardiner, A. G., *Life of Harcourt* (1923), I, 296 *seqq.*

[2] *Somersett* v. *Steward* (1772), Lofft. I.

[3] *Report of the Royal Commission on Fugitive Slaves: Parl. Pap.* 1876, xxviii [C.1516–I].

[4] Ratified by Great Britain, Germany, Austria-Hungary, Belgium, Denmark, Spain, the Independent State of the Congo, the United States of America, France, Italy, Holland, Persia, Portugal, Russia, Sweden-Norway, Turkey, and Zanzibar. France ratified but with reservations to the articles dealing with reciprocal rights of visit and search and detention of suspected vessels.

[5] For an important controversy between Great Britain and France over rights of visit and search see the award of the Permanent Court of Arbitration in the case of *The Muscat Dhows* (1905): Scott, *Hague Court Reports*, I (1916), pp. 1–95. See also Westlake in *Law Quarterly Rev.* xxiii (1907), 83–7, and in *Collected Papers*, pp. 523–30.

its own territory, subject of course to the somewhat vague requirements of natural law: requirements which had from time to time
received authoritative expression,[1] but were necessarily lacking in
precision and sanction. The latter part of the nineteenth century,
however, saw the beginnings of more effective protection of native
peoples by means of treaty obligations. The primary objective of the
Berlin West African Conference of 1884–5 was to ensure that all the
interested Powers should have a say in the development of the Congo
Basin;[2] but several delegates took the occasion to speak of the need of
positive measures for the welfare of the natives, and the Berlin Act
provided not only for the freedom of navigation and commerce for
all nations in the regions of the Congo and Niger Basins, but also, by
Article 6, the Powers exercising rights in the Congo Basin undertook
to suppress slavery and the slave trade and to care for the improvement of the moral and material conditions of the natives and to
guarantee "freedom of conscience and religious toleration". The
Brussels Act of 1890 too, though mainly concerned, as we have seen,
with the suppression of the slave trade, contained promises of positive
measures for the improvement of the natives' lot.

The question of the legal nature of these treaty obligations was
subsequently raised in an acrimonious dispute between Great Britain
and the Independent State of the Congo.[3] The Free State of the
Congo was under the personal dominion of Leopold II, and united
with Belgium only by a personal union. It became apparent from the
reports of British missionaries and traders that a monopolistic system
of exploitation had been set up by which, with almost insignificant
exceptions, the entire natural wealth of the land was claimed as the
private property of the State or its concessionaires; this being accompanied, moreover, by taxation in the form of compulsory labour, in
practice hardly distinguishable from slavery. Against this state of
affairs the British Government, acting for the most part alone, carried
on a protracted but ultimately successful campaign, the British
Government itself being driven by an informed and insistent public
opinion instructed by influential organisations such as the "Aborigines Protection Society". A most effective diplomatic weapon was
found in the legal argument that this policy of the Congo Government was a clear breach of the provisions of the Berlin Act, both those
which safeguarded the rights of the natives and those which required
freedom of commerce. The legal argument of the right of intervention
arising from the treaty obligation of the Congo Government was
from the outset made the gravamen of the campaign; as appears
from the wording of Mr Herbert Samuel's (as he then was) motion

---

[1] See, e.g., the precedents collected in Lindley, M. F., *The Acquisition and Government of
Backward Territory in International Law* (1926), chap. xxxvi.

[2] See *C.H.B.F.P.* III, 208 *et seq.*

[3] See *C.H.B.F.P.* III, 366–73, 424–9.

in the House of Commons on 20 May 1903, which was accepted by the Prime Minister and carried without a division:

That the Government of the Congo Free State having at its inception guaranteed to the Powers that its native subjects should be governed with humanity, and that no trading monopoly or privilege should be permitted within its dominions; this House requests the Government to confer with the other Powers, signatories of the Berlin Act, by virtue of which the Congo Free State exists, in order that measures may be adopted to abate the evils.

Lord Lansdowne, indeed, suggested that the question whether the acts complained of were permissible under the Berlin Act might be referred to the newly-created court at The Hague; but this suggestion met with no response from the Government of the Congo, or for that matter from the other parties to the Berlin Act. The sheer weight of the evidence eventually compelled the Congo Government to submit to a Commission of Inquiry which reported in 1905, and in the following year Leopold signed decrees which purported to give effect to the Commission's recommendations. The decrees were accompanied, however, by a provocative declaration denying the legal right of any other Government to interfere in the government of the Congo, which Leopold apparently regarded as a matter purely personal to himself. Moreover, it immediately became apparent that the scandalous situation in the Congo was still continuing, and it seemed unlikely to be effectively remedied until the Congo State was rescued from the personal rule of the King and annexed to the Belgian State. The British Government was now no longer acting alone; the United States Minister in Brussels supported his British colleague, and in November 1908, as a result of joint pressure, the Congo was annexed to Belgium. At once, therefore, the British Government was possessed of yet another legal weapon in the form of recognition; though France and Germany immediately recognised the annexation, Great Britain refused recognition in the absence of actual guarantees of reformed government. In fact, recognition of the annexation was not given until 1913, when the British Government was finally satisfied that the abuses had ended. This humane campaign of the British Government, acting for the most part in isolation, marks therefore an important step in the gradual transition of the natives' rights, and indeed ultimately of human rights in general, from the sphere of the sovereign discretion of each separate government to the higher plane of general international law.

In many ways the most significant of the trends towards the international protection of the individual was the movement for protection of labour. The suppression of slavery had necessarily raised the problem of the protection of labour in general; for the line between slavery and the compulsory recruitment of underpaid labour was difficult both to draw and to maintain. A beginning had already been made with bilateral conventions protecting particular classes of native labour in the colonies; e.g. the 1860 convention between Great Britain and France regulating recruitment of natives of Bengal to work in French colonies, and a convention of the same year between Great Britain and China concerning Chinese labour in British colonies. The latter part of the nineteenth century, however, saw the beginnings of international action to protect labour in the principal European countries themselves; a movement which, though initially concerned with domestic labour, was to lead to general standards by which conditions in colonial as well as in metropolitan territories would be judged. The idea was not new; indeed, a British cotton manufacturer, Robert Owen, had presented a memorandum on the subject to the delegates at Aix-la-Chapelle in 1818. It was not, however, until after the turn of the century that the spread of industrialisation and increased competition, together with popular agitation for betterment of the lot of the workers, gradually created a realisation that the problem was international and not merely domestic. In England, far and away the most industrialised country, the battle for domestic labour legislation had already been fought and won under the influence of men like Robert Owen and Richard Oastler;[1] but the British Government, like almost all others at this time, was at first suspicious of what it tended to regard as foreign interference in a domestic matter. It was the Swiss Government that supplied an initiative which resulted in the Berlin Conference of 1890. However, the Conference did not attempt to do more than offer recommendations in general terms. In particular, the British delegation made it quite clear that they must oppose regulation by international convention, which "could not take the place of legislation peculiar to each country". For a time, the leadership of the movement then passed to private enterprise in the shape of the *International Association for Labour Legislation*, founded by a group of scholars at Paris in 1900. This unofficial but influential association carried out necessary preparatory studies of particular problems, and in 1905 the way was open for the Swiss Government to call a further technical conference at Berne to consider two questions: the employment of women at night, and the use of white phosphorus in the manufacture of matches. This purely technical conference of 1905 was successful, and was followed by a diplomatic conference in 1906, which actually drafted the appropriate conventions for ratification by States. Between the first and second Berne conferences the British Government informed the Swiss Government of its willingness to enter into a convention, subject to adherence by all countries "whose competition in the industries affected was likely to be serious". It also took the opportunity to point out the importance of adequate means of enforcement, and suggested that execution of the conventions should

[1] See Clapham, Sir J. H., *An Economic History of Modern Britain: the Early Railway Age*, chap. xiv.

be supervised by an international commission, any differences arising between parties being settled by arbitration. In addition, the memorandum pointed to the need for providing proper procedures for settling such matters as the agenda of future conferences, procedures and so forth. These British proposals were pressed very hard at the 1906 conference by the first British delegate, Mr Herbert Samuel. Opposition by the Central Powers and Belgium prevented for the moment the general acceptance of the British proposals, even in a modified form, but their importance for the subsequent development of the international regulation of labour should be emphasised. Moreover, the acceptance in 1906 of the general principle of regulation by multilateral convention was a great step forward. Although the British Government had at first been shy of international regulation in what appeared to be a domestic matter, it was clear by the end of our period that Great Britain was henceforth to take a leading part in the working out of adequate organisation and techniques, and to make a substantial contribution to the movement, which reached a new and decisive stage in 1919 in the establishment of the International Labour Organisation.

III

What has been described as the liberal tradition of British foreign policy in this period manifested itself also in the consistent British practice in the recognition of Governments. The principle of legitimacy was definitely abandoned. On the other hand, there was no inclination to adopt the easy and automatic test of recognising any *de facto* authority for the mere reason that it is in power and enjoys the obedience, however unwilling and resentful, of the bulk of the population. What was required—and always insisted upon—was that the government *de facto* either should be freely-chosen or, after having come to power by revolutionary means, should be confirmed by a free expression of popular approval. That principle had already been formulated, with some clarity, in 1852 after the *coup d'état* of Louis Napoleon. On that occasion Lord Malmesbury stated in the House of Lords on 6 December 1852: "It has been our usual policy...to acknowledge the constitutional doctrine that the people of every country have the right to choose their own sovereign without any foreign interference, and that a sovereign having been freely chosen by them, that sovereign, or ruler, or whatever he may be called, being *de facto* the ruler of that country, should be recognised by the sovereign of this."[1] In the period under review the principle of popular consent as a requirement of recognition received the imprimatur of a consistent and reasoned practice. When M. Thiers visited England in September 1870 and urged the recognition of the

[1] *Hansard*, Lords, 2nd ser. CXXIII, 971.

Government of the new French Republic he was informed by Lord Granville that it would be "contrary to precedent to do so at present" and that the new Government had no legal sanction so long as it had not been confirmed by a freely-elected constitutional Assembly.[1] In a dispatch of 1 October 1870 to the British ambassador in Paris Earl Granville said that he had "pointed out to him (M. Thiers) that the Government, though administering *de facto* the affairs of France, itself recognised that the voice of France speaking in a Constituent Assembly could alone determine the form and the character of the Government to whom the destinies of France should be finally committed".[2] In a further communication the Foreign Secretary insisted that,

the first element of recognition was still wanting and that, as the Government of National Defence itself admitted that it does not possess that stability which a formal vote of the Constituent Assembly alone could bestow upon it, it would be premature for Her Majesty's Government to recognise, as the national Government of France, a Government which is only administering the affairs of the country pending its decision as to the form of government under which it may ultimately elect to live.[3]

It was not until February 1871 that these conditions of recognition were deemed to have been fulfilled.

An identical practice was followed in connection with the recognition of the successive revolutionary governments in Spain in 1869 and 1874.[4] Again, after the establishment of the revolutionary government in Portugal in 1910, the British representative in Lisbon was instructed to inform the local authorities that "as soon as Portugal shall, by a formal vote of a constituent assembly, or in some other unambiguous manner, have determined the form and character of the future government of the country, His Majesty's Government will be prepared to advise the King to recognise it, and will be happy to enter into official relations with it when established in accordance with popular vote".[5]

The insistence on popular approval of the revolutionary régime as a condition of recognition continued to be a prominent feature of the British practice until the period following the end of the First World War. In that period the establishment of dictatorships in a number of States led Great Britain—and other countries—to base their policy of recognition on the purely factual test of control.

---

[1] *B.F.S.P.* LXI, 751.   [2] *Parl. Pap.* 1871, LXXI [C. 244], p. 111; *B.F.S.P.* LXIV, 802.
[3] *Parl. Pap.* 1871, LXXI [C. 266], p. 258; *B.S.F.P.* LXI, 995.
[4] *Hansard*, Lords, 3rd ser. CCXXII, 1382. See also Smith, *Great Britain and the Law of Nations*, I (1932), pp. 198–205.
[5] As quoted in Lauterpacht, *Recognition in International Law* (1947), p. 122. When, during and after the Second World War, the right of man to government by consent became inevitably part of those human rights and fundamental freedoms the enthronement of which had been declared to be one of the major purposes of the war, the practice of recognition showed a pronounced tendency to revert to standards more closely in keeping with British notions of the rule of law and of the rights of man.

IV

The colonial expansion of the Great Powers in Africa and the Far East had important results in the clarification and elaboration of the law concerning the acquisition and government of territory. Two main tendencies can be distinguished: first, an increasing strictness in the conditions required for the acquisition of full territorial sovereignty by the traditional mode of occupation; and secondly, elaboration of the law by new concepts sanctioning the acquisition of an authority or interest falling short of territorial sovereignty.

"International law," said the arbitrator in a modern case, "the structure of which is not based on any super-State organisation, cannot be presumed to reduce a right such as territorial sovereignty, with which almost all international relations are bound up, to the category of an abstract right, without concrete manifestations."[1] Ever since the eighteenth century there had been an increasing tendency to insist on the actual display of authority over territory as a condition of the acquisition of the corresponding right of sovereignty over it. In the latter part of the nineteenth century Great Britain's influence was strongly asserted in this direction both in international conferences and in her attitude towards territorial claims as, for example, in her argument in the Delagoa Bay Arbitration of 1875;[2] in 1876 by protests over Spanish activities short of actual settlement in the Sulu Archipelago; in 1885 by the recognition of Spanish sovereignty over those parts of the Sulu Archipelago which had been effectively occupied; and in 1877 in an intimation to Portugal that effective occupation and the exercise *de facto* of jurisdictional powers were essential conditions for the acquisition of territories in Central Africa and that the British Government could not recognise Portuguese sovereignty over territories "not occupied by her in sufficient strength to enable her to maintain order, protect foreigners, and control the natives".[3] Nor was she alone in this attitude, for it was generally realised, at any rate amongst the more important Powers, that a mere paper claim could not be regarded as creating dominion without the risk of divorcing sovereignty and responsibility.

This general opinion of statesmen and jurists was formally stated in the Final Act of the Berlin Africa Conference of 1885.[4] Article 34 provided that future takings of possession of any territory on the coasts of the African Continent, or the establishment of protectorates

---

[1] Judge Huber in *The Island of Palmas Arbitration* (1928), *Annual Digest*, 1927–28, Case no. 68 (at p. 105).

[2] See Hall, W. E., *A Treatise of International Law*, 8th ed. (1924), para. 33.

[3] All these precedents are discussed in Lindley, *The Acquisition and Government of Backward Territory in International Law* (1926), chap. xix.

[4] The Final Act was signed by Austria-Hungary, Belgium, Denmark, France, Germany, Great Britain, Italy, the Netherlands, Norway, Portugal, Russia, Spain, Sweden, Turkey and the United States.

there, should be accompanied by a notification addressed to every other signatory Power, to enable them, if need be, to make good any claims of their own. Article 35, which referred only to annexations and not to protectorates, recognised the obligation of the parties to ensure "in the regions occupied by them on the coasts of the African Continent" the establishment of authority "sufficient to protect existing rights and, as the case may be, freedom of trade and of transit under the conditions agreed upon". The usefulness of the notification required by Article 34 is manifest, but in contrast with Article 35 there is no doubt that Article 34 went further than existing customary law required; nor has notification even since the Act become a requirement of general law. The position was accurately stated by the British representative that notification was "rather an act of courtesy than a rule of law".

On the other hand, Article 35, in requiring a claim to sovereignty to be supported by the exercise of *de facto* authority, probably went no further than existing law required. For this reason the British representative at the Conference had at one point suggested that the Article might be expressed to cover the whole of Africa and not merely the coasts. Although this suggestion was not accepted, it was clear at the Conference and afterwards that in the British view the Declaration had done no more than emphasise in particular respects already established rules of international law. Thus when, in 1887, Portugal laid claim to a region in Central Africa lying between her existing possessions of Angola and Mozambique, and argued that effective occupation was not a requirement in central as opposed to coastal Africa, Lord Salisbury asserted that the Berlin Act "did not in any way affect the well-established principles of international law in regard to the occupation of lands in the interior", and that "no paper annexation of territory can pretend to any validity as a bar to the enterprise of other nations".[1]

In the original draft of Article 35, the requirement of effective authority was declared to apply to the establishment of protectorates as well as to the acquiring of sovereignty by occupation. The reference to protectorates, however, was struck out on the insistence of the British Government.[2] This was logical enough if "protectorate" were used in the proper sense of a treaty relationship between two States. In the uncivilised regions of Africa, however, there was no "State" with which such a treaty relationship could exist, and the so-called "colonial protectorates" with which the Conference was in fact concerned were no more than steps towards the acquisition of sovereignty over the territories in question. The term "colonial protectorate" had, as Westlake said, "the double advantage of

---

[1] *Parl. Pap.* 1884–5, LV [C. 4361], p. 10.
[2] For the political background of the British attitude see Crowe, Sybil E., *The Berlin West African Conference, 1884–1885* (1942), pp. 179 *et seq.*

giving a flavour of international law to a position intended to exclude other States before such exclusion could be placed on the ground of duly acquired sovereignty, and at the same time of allowing that position to be abandoned with less discredit than attaches to the abandonment of sovereignty...".[1] The pretence that such colonial protectorates were analogous to orthodox protectorates, where the protecting Power derives its authority by cession from the protected State, was to say the least disingenuous; for while it must be conceded that the colonial protectorate differed from annexation, this distinction, as Westlake pointed out, "even while it lasts, is attenuated by the circumstance that a colonial protectorate is intended by the State assuming it to exclude the action of other powers as completely as it would be excluded by annexation, since otherwise the protectorate would not have the desired effect of earmarking the country for the future enjoyment of the assuming State".[2] It is significant that the British Government, in spite of the attitude adopted at the Conference, seems shortly afterwards to have been prepared to read into the Final Act an implied provision not unlike the express provision that it had so strenuously opposed. Thus in the African Order in Council, 1892,[3] it was recited that "by the General Act of the Conference of Berlin signed in 1885, the several Powers who were parties thereto declared, with respect to occupations in Africa by any of the Signatory Powers, that the establishment of authority in protected territories was an obligation resting upon the respective Protecting Powers".

The increasing strictness in the conditions for acquiring full sovereignty encouraged Powers to experiment with new legal devices, usually based on analogies of municipal law, by which they could support claims to the acquisition of an authority which, while falling short of full sovereignty, might nevertheless be sufficient for their immediate aims. There was an obvious advantage in giving these lesser claims the appearance of perfect legal rights rather than the appearance of inchoate attempts at annexation. One important method frequently employed, both in Africa and the Far East, was the "lease"[4] of territory. There is, of course, no reason why one State should not lease to another the beneficial enjoyment of land for a period of years, following strictly the analogous institution of municipal law.[5] The so-called "political leases", however, are quite different, in that what is leased includes not only territory but also political authority within the leased territory. In this way Great Britain as well as Italy and Germany acquired grants of territory

[1] Westlake, *International Law*, Part I, *Peace* (1904), p. 120.
[2] *Ibid.* p. 123.   [3] 84 S.P. 290.
[4] See Westlake, *op. cit.* pp. 133–4; Lindley, *op. cit.* chap. xxv.
[5] For examples see Lauterpacht, *Private Law Sources and Analogies of International Law* (1927), p. 183.

from the Sultan of Zanzibar;[1] the leases were in the first instance for fifty years, but the British interest was in 1891 converted into one in perpetuity in consideration for an annual payment of rent to the Sultan and was transferred to the Crown in 1895. Several Powers acquired important territorial interests in China by lease. In 1898 Great Britain was granted a lease of Wei-hai-wei "for so long a period as Port Arthur shall remain in the occupation of Russia", and there was no stipulation for compensation to China.[2] Other leases of Chinese territory, e.g. Port Arthur to Russia, Kaulmang to Great Britain, Kiauchau to Germany, Kwangchauwan to France, were made for a period of years.[3]

Such "leases" come near to being cessions; and clearly they were often intended to be virtual cessions disguised so as to appear less offensive to the susceptibilities of the lessor State. At the same time they were not cessions in law, for the use of the lease analogy must be given some legal meaning, which could only be that the arrangement must be interpreted as leaving at any rate the ultimate or residuary sovereignty vested in the lessor. Thus, at the Washington Conference in 1921 the Chinese delegate was able to say concerning the Chinese leases:

> While the measure and extent of control by the lessee powers over these leased territories varied in different cases, the leases themselves were all limited to a fixed period of years. Expressly or impliedly they were not transferable to a third power without the consent of China. Though the exercise of administrative rights over the territories leased was relinquished by China to the lessee power during the period of the lease, the sovereignty of China over them had been reserved in all cases. The leases were all creatures of compact, different from cessions both in fact and in law.[4]

Another private-law analogy pressed into service at this time was "condominium", by which two Powers might conjointly enjoy the sovereignty over a territory. The most notable example was the Agreement of 19 January 1899, between Great Britain and the Khedive of Egypt, whereby the Sudan became subject to a condominium of Great Britain and Egypt; expressed as a regularising of the situation created by the fact that the reconquest of the Sudan had been a joint enterprise of the two Powers. In practice of course,

[1] Grants were made by the Sultan to the British East Africa Company in May 1887, October 1888 and March 1890.

[2] Wei-hai-wei was returned to China under the Washington Agreements of 1922.

[3] A curious example of the use of the term "lease" is in the Anglo-Congolese Agreement of 1894. Great Britain and the Congo State granted leases of African territory to each other for "so long as the Congo territories as an independent state or as a Belgian colony remain under the sovereignty of His (Belgian) Majesty and His Majesty's successors". In this agreement, it is to be noted, Great Britain was purporting to grant a lease of territory she had never in fact occupied, nor was there in this agreement any stipulation for a rent. The arrangement was rescinded by the Treaty of London, 1906.

[4] Cited by Lauterpacht, *op. cit.* p. 186; where also there is a full discussion of this question on pp. 181–90.

Great Britain was, to say the least, the major partner in the exercise of the joint sovereignty, more especially as Egypt was at the time subject in fact to her authority. In 1882 Egypt had been occupied by the British. At this stage the occupation was intended to be of a temporary character, with the sole purpose of restoring order and financial stability in the country; but it tended of course to become permanent by reason of its very success, and the position of the British in Egypt was recognised by France in the Agreement of 1904 and later by other Powers; although it was not until 1914, after the outbreak of war with Turkey, that Egypt was formally declared a British Protectorate. Nevertheless, despite the inequality of the partnership in the government of the Sudan, the term "condominium" can only be interpreted as having legal results in conformity with the analogous institution of private law and is by no means to be re-garded as a mere formula covering a unilateral assumption of power; and the significance of the term has of course become more apparent as Egypt has progressed towards independence.[1]

Another method of acquiring authority without prejudice, as it were, to the ultimate disposal of sovereignty, was to enter into a treaty granting the right to occupy and administer the territory. By an Anglo-Turkish Convention of 1878, expressed to have "the object of securing for the future the territories in Asia of His Imperial Majesty the Sultan", the Sultan agreed "to assign the Island of Cyprus to be occupied and administered by England".[2] It was further provided in an Annex that England would pay the Porte "whatever is the present excess of revenue over expenditure in the Island", and also that "if Russia restores to Turkey Kars and the other conquests made by her in Armenia during the last war, the Island of Cyprus will be evacuated by England". It was made clear that the authority transferred in this arrangement included full legislative power, and indeed third States recognised this to the extent of foregoing their capitulatory rights in the Island. The natives of the Island were not, however, regarded as British protected persons and there remained in the Sultan a part of the external sovereignty which was, as Westlake said,[3] not quite a *nudum jus*, but was insignifi-cant. On the outbreak of war with Turkey in 1914, the island was formally annexed by Great Britain. A somewhat similar arrangement in the Treaty of Berlin, 1878, and in a convention of the following year, gave rights of occupation and administration in the Turkish provinces of Bosnia and Hercegovina to Austria-Hungary.[4]

---

[1] The Treaty of Alliance of 1936 between Great Britain and Egypt reserves the question of the Sudan, and according to the Annex to Article 11, the participation of the Sudan in international conventions is effected by joint action of Great Britain and Egypt.

[2] For the political background of the Cyprus Convention, see Headlam-Morley, *Studies in Diplomatic History* (1930), chap. vii.

[3] *International Law*, Part 1, *Peace* (1904), p. 138.

[4] This is discussed in detail in Westlake, *op. cit.* pp. 135-7.

It will be apparent that all these new institutions of public law were from one point of view mere devices of diplomacy; they offered a means of acquiring sufficient power where downright annexation was thought to be politically inexpedient, and quite often they were employed as preparations for annexation. Nevertheless, it is important to remember that in law they were not equivalent to annexation. When a legal term of art is used which clearly means in law the transfer of something less than sovereignty, it cannot be argued by any proper canon of interpretation that sovereignty is transferred. A lease necessarily implied the existence of some reversionary interest in the lessor; a grant of the right to occupy and administer carried the implication that some remnant of sovereignty remained in the former sovereign; and even a colonial protectorate was at least an admission that full sovereignty had not yet been formally acquired.[1] In short, the significance of these institutions lay in the fact that each of them carried with it a specific legal connotation which excluded the possibility of their being interpreted as mere euphemisms for annexation. In the development of international law, these admittedly subtle legal distinctions are important in that they mark the beginning of that shyness of annexation which, coupled with the marked development in international responsibilities towards native peoples, culminated in 1919 in the mandates and trusteeship system of the League of Nations and, later, of the United Nations.

In connection with acquisition of territorial sovereignty reference may be made to developments in the law of State succession following upon territorial changes. When a State ceases to exist by absorption into another State, whether by cession or conquest, the difficult question arises how far the absorbing State succeeds to the obligations as well as to the rights and territory of the former State. When, in 1886, Great Britain annexed Upper Burma, she recognised the existing financial obligations while refusing to admit any legal obligation to do so. Much the same attitude was adopted when in 1900 Great Britain annexed the two Boer Republics.[2] A Commission was appointed under the chairmanship of the Hon. A. Lyttelton to examine the maintenance of concessions granted by the former Transvaal Republic. Their report maintained that "it is clear that a state which has annexed another is not legally bound by any contracts made by the state which has ceased to exist, and that no court of law has jurisdiction to enforce such contracts if the annexing state refuse to recognise them".[3] It seems, however, as

---

[1] See R. v. Crewe [1910], 2 K.B. 576, where L.J. Vaughan-Williams said that Bechuanaland was "under His Majesty's dominion in the sense of power and authority, but is not under his dominion in the sense of territorial dominion".

[2] The Orange Free State was annexed by proclamation on 24 May 1900, and the South African Republic by proclamation on 1 Sept. 1900. The proclamations were premature, for the surrender of the Dutch forces was not received till 31 May 1902.

[3] Parl. Pap. 1901, xxxv [Cd. 623], p. 7.

Westlake suggested,[1] that the Commissioners were using the term "legal" in a very narrow sense to mean only such rights as were enforceable in the municipal court.[2] The absence of a remedy in the municipal court does not dispose of the question of succession in international law, and indeed the Commissioners go on to admit that "the modern usage of nations has tended in the direction of the acknowledgement of such contracts". After this somewhat unpromising introduction, however, they examined the several concessions on their merits, recommending the recognition of some and rejection of others, though all the while regarding this process as a matter of ethics rather than of law. Yet, although the Commissioners were unduly influenced by "the baneful effects of Austin's definition of law",[3] their report was valuable in making practical distinctions between different classes of cases, and provided material for the later elaboration of what are now generally acknowledged to be rules of law. Even then it was significant that the British Government paid compensation in most cases involving foreign creditors whose claims were supported by their governments.[4]

However, in *West Rand Central Gold Mining Company* v. *The King*,[5] the High Court rejected a claim by the underwriters to recover from the British Government the value of gold commandeered by President Kruger on the eve of the South African War, and committed themselves to the view that there was no principle of international law by which, after annexation of conquered territory, the conquering State becomes liable, in the absence of express stipulation to the contrary, to discharge the financial liabilities incurred by the conquered State before the outbreak of the war. In this case, however, the plaintiff was in fact a British company, and the decision could not therefore give rise to an international claim. It is doubtful whether this dictum would even at that time have been accepted by an international court. On the other hand it is generally agreed that there is no State succession to obligations arising from tort, and an Anglo-American Claims Commission held that the British Government was not liable in international law for a denial of justice suffered by an American citizen in the courts of the former South African Republic.[6]

Before leaving the question of territory, mention must also be made of the Suez and Panama canals. These canals were of such strategic

---

[1] *International Law, Peace* (1904), p. 82. See also Westlake in *Law Quarterly Rev.* XVII (1901), 392, and XXI (1905), 335.
[2] Following *Cook* v. *Sprigg* [1899], A.C. 576.
[3] Westlake, *op. cit.*
[4] See Feilchenfeld, *Public Debts and State Succession* (1931), pp. 380 *et seq.*
[5] L.R. (1905), 2 K.B. 39.
[6] "The claim of Robert E. Brown", *American Jour. International Law*, XIX (1925), 193–206.

and commercial importance that they could hardly be left as internal waters of the States through which they passed. Particular legal régimes were therefore devised to govern their use.[1] The Suez Canal was opened in 1869 and, although proposals for the "neutralisation" of the canal had been made even before work on it was begun, it was not till some years afterwards that the legal problem was solved. In 1875 Great Britain had acquired a controlling interest in the canal shares and two years later made it plain to a general meeting of shareholders that "an attempt to blockade or otherwise interfere with the canal or its approaches would be regarded by His Majesty's Government as a menace to India and a grave injury to the commerce of the world". There was moreover general acceptance among the Powers of the principle that the canal ought to be removed from the theatre of war. Great Britain was at first chary of this principle being put in the form of a general treaty; and indeed the first warlike operation in the canal zone was Sir Garnet Wolseley's landing at Ismailia in 1882 and his successful expedition against an insurgent Egyptian government, leading to the British occupation of Egypt. As this operation was undertaken in order to protect the canal the other Powers did not complain. However, with Egypt now occupied by a strong Power it had clearly become appropriate that the general understanding about the canal should be given legal form in the shape of a general treaty, and Lord Granville proposed this in a circular of 1883.[2] A conference met at Paris in 1885 and the Suez Canal Convention was signed in 1888, by which the canal was to be "open, in war as well as in peace, to ships of war and merchant ships of all flags; and is never to be blockaded". Owing to the transitory state of affairs in Egypt the British Government only became a party to the treaty subject to a substantial reservation which, however, was removed after the Anglo-French understanding of 1904.

An even more important role was played by Great Britain in the creation of the legal régime of the Panama Canal; which indeed still depends principally upon the terms of a bilateral treaty between Great Britain and the United States. As early as 1850, when the idea of an inter-ocean canal was first mooted, the Clayton-Bulwer Treaty between the two Powers had provided for the free navigation and "neutralisation" of the proposed canal in terms that prevented either Power from independently making or owning the canal. After the failure in 1888 of the de Lesseps scheme, the United States Government again became interested in the project, but found the 1850 treaty a

---

[1] See Westlake, *International Law*, Part I, *Peace*, p. 321, and the entire chap. xv which has a valuable account of the legal history of the Suez Canal.

[2] The opinion of writers on international law had already hardened in favour of a special legal régime for the Canal. In 1875 Sir Travers Twiss had advocated the "neutralisation" of the Canal in an article in *Revue de Droit International et de Législation Comparée*, VII, 682, and the Institute of International Law had voted in favour of a general treaty in 1879, see *Annuaire*, III and IV (i), p. 349.

serious embarrassment, more especially as the strategic importance of such a canal was very evident and American opinion had begun to harden in favour of an all-American canal. Lord Salisbury, however, readily agreed to a modification of Great Britain's rights under the 1850 Treaty, and to the surrender of her right to participate in the construction of a canal. By the Hay-Pauncefote Treaty of 18 November 1901, all obstacles to the construction of a canal by the United States and to the exclusive regulation and management of the proposed canal by her were removed. Provision was again made, however, for the so-called "neutralisation" of the canal in terms substantially following those of the Suez Canal Convention: it was to be open to the vessels of commerce and of war of all nations on terms of entire equality: it was never to be blockaded, and no act of war or hostility was to be committed within it.

The Hay-Varilla Treaty of 1903 between the United States and the newly created Republic of Panama gave the United States a lease in perpetuity of the required territorial rights, and the Panama Canal was opened on 14 August 1914. In the meantime, however, a dispute had arisen between Great Britain and the United States over the interpretation of the Hay-Pauncefote Treaty. By Article 3 of that Treaty, the canal was to be free and open to the vessels of commerce and of war of "all nations", and on "terms of entire equality": but in 1912 Congress passed a bill, section 5 of which authorised the President to prescribe the tolls to be charged, but provided that no tolls should be charged upon vessels engaged in the coastwise trade of the United States. The British Government had already protested against this provision as being contrary to the Hay-Pauncefote Treaty, arguing that "all nations" must include the United States. The United States replied that their coastwise trade was in any case limited to United States vessels by municipal law and that the 1912 Act, therefore, was not introducing any new discrimination. Although, however, the United States' arguments showed that the proposed exemption of her coastwise shipping from tolls was not unreasonable, they did not touch the charge that the exemption was in plain contravention of her treaty obligations, and on this point the British Government quietly but firmly insisted, while offering nevertheless to have the legal question submitted to the Hague Court. This the United States Government refused to do. The controversy was not settled until Taft went out of office and Wilson came in. Wilson's advisers had no doubt that the British objection was well founded and Wilson settled the matter in a statesmanlike way by waiving the American claims.

V

Probably the most important British contribution to international law in the period under review was in the field of international arbitration. It falls under three heads: the first, and most important, is the actual submission to arbitral settlement of territorial and other disputes; the second is the contribution made by Great Britain to the development of international organs of arbitral settlement; the third lies in the British participation in the movement to bring about a wider measure of obligatory settlement of disputes.

Settlement of Disputes by Arbitration

In the first—and most significant—of these three spheres the British contribution was effected in close co-operation and partnership with the United States. The history of international arbitration in the nineteenth century—and in particular in the last quarter of the nineteenth century—is to a large extent the history of the arbitral settlement of disputes between Great Britain and the United States. In a very real sense the Jay Treaty of 1794 between these two States had marked the beginning of modern arbitration. That Treaty submitted to arbitral settlement, through mixed commissions adjudicating on the basis of law, not only troublesome boundary disputes affecting vast stretches of territory: the commissions were also given jurisdiction to decide upon claims arising out of alleged violations of neutral rights as the result of the conduct of maritime war by Great Britain, and of breaches of obligations of neutrality by the United States in the course of the war with France. These were questions which, to use the modern terminology, affected the "vital interests" and "honour" of the parties. However, notwithstanding delays, disagreements and occasional bitterness of argument, the commissions proved equal to their task. They paved the way for a series of similar commissions under the Treaties of 1814 (the Treaty of Ghent), of 1822, of 1842 and of 1854, and of 1863.[1] The cumulative result of their experience was the imposing series of five great arbitrations between the United States and Great Britain in the last thirty years of the nineteenth century and in the first decade of the twentieth: The *Alabama* arbitration of 1871 and 1872; the Behring Sea Arbitration of 1893; the British Guiana Arbitration of 1897 (for although the parties to these proceedings were Great Britain and Venezuela, this was, in many ways, a British-American arbitration); the Alaskan Boundary Arbitration of 1903 (although the parties were the United States and Canada, this was essentially a British-American arbitra-

[1] The work of these commissions is surveyed in Moore, J. B., *History and Digest of the Arbitrations to which the United States has been a Party* (6 vols., 1898), referred to in this chapter as *Digest*; Moore, J. B., *International Adjudications, Ancient and Modern* (6 vols., 1929–33); Lapradelle et Politis, *Recueil des Arbitrages internationaux*, vol. I, 1798–1858 (1905) and vol. II, 1858–72 (1924).

tion); and the North Atlantic Fisheries Arbitration of 1910. These arbitrations were the first to reveal on a large scale the potentialities of international judicial settlement. They were preceded by an exchange of written pleadings—cases, counter cases, replies, arguments and counter-arguments, rejoinders and sur-rejoinders—occupying bulky volumes. They were argued with zest and acumen in oral proceedings lasting weeks, if not months. They would not have been possible had they not been conducted between two nations bound by the tradition of the common law, speaking the same language and animated by the same respect for the peaceful solution of international disputes.

The *Alabama* arbitration was the greatest and, in many ways, the most significant of those arbitrations. Its origins and circumstances are recounted elsewhere in these volumes, and the observations which follow are—as with the four other arbitrations mentioned above—limited to a survey of their contribution to the general development of international law and of the judicial settlement of international disputes. The *Alabama* arbitration was the first example of the arbitral settlement of an international issue which one of the parties regarded as affecting its national honour and which it had therefore originally declined to submit to arbitration. While for the United States reparation for the wrong inflicted upon them as the result of alleged violations of neutrality on the part of Great Britain became a question of national dignity, Great Britain, on the other hand, deemed it inconsistent with her honour to submit to a foreign judgment on the questions whether her Government observed duties of neutrality in good faith and whether the Law Officers properly interpreted the neutrality laws.[1] Earl Russell was emphatic on that point when in 1865 the United States asked for an impartial determination of the controversy: "It appears to Her Majesty's Government that neither of these questions could be put to a foreign government with any regard to the dignity and character of the British Crown and the British nation.... Her Majesty's Government are the sole guardians of their own honour."[2] Neither was the national dignity of the United States fully appeased by the Convention of 1869 which provided for the settlement of the American claims. The Senate refused to ratify the Convention for the reason that its conclusion was not accompanied by a suitable expression of regret for the events which led to the American claims. That satisfaction was given in a declaration made by the British negotiators of the Treaty of 8 May 1871 which submitted the *Alabama* claims to an

[1] *Parl. Pap.* 1864, LXII [3241], pp. 1 *et seq.*, 109 *et seq.*, and *Parl. Pap.* 1868–9, LXIII [4144], pp. 735 *et seq.* See also on this, and other, aspects of the controversy Lapradelle et Politis, *op. cit.* II, 902–83; Bernard, *A Historical Account of the Neutrality of Great Britain during the American Civil War* (1870), pp. 385 *et seq.*; Cushing, *The Treaty of Washington* (1879); Nevins, A., *Hamilton Fish* (1936), pp. 296–301, 423–48, 481–90. Cf. chap. ix above.
[2] Moore, *Digest*, p. 496.

international tribunal. In that declaration the British representatives expressed "in a friendly spirit the regret felt by Her Majesty's Government for the escape, under whatever circumstances, of the *Alabama* and other vessels from British ports, and for the depredations committed by those vessels". The American Commissioners, it was stated, "accepted this expression of regret as very satisfactory to them and as a token of kindness, and said that they felt sure that it would be so received by their Government".[1] The principal provision of Article 6, which defined in advance much of the law to be applied by the arbitrators, was as follows:

A neutral Government is bound:
First, to use due diligence to prevent the fitting out, arming, or equipping, within its jurisdiction, of any vessel which it has reasonable ground to believe is intended to cruise or to carry on war against a Power with which it is at peace; and also to use like diligence to prevent the departure from its jurisdiction of any vessel intended to cruise or carry on war as above, such vessel having been specially adapted, in whole or in part, within such jurisdiction, to warlike use.

Great Britain, while agreeing that the Tribunal should decide according to the rules laid down in that Article, declined, in an express statement made in that Article, to agree that it was part of international law at the time when the claims arose. The two parties agreed nevertheless, in the same Article, "to observe these rules as between themselves in the future, and to bring them to the knowledge of other maritime Powers, and to invite them to accede to them".[2]

The fact of this submission of a grave issue to arbitration, and the circumstances surrounding it, were even more important for the future of international arbitration than the legal questions involved in the arbitration and decided by the Tribunal which met in Geneva on 15 December 1871 and which, after various adjournments, gave its award on 14 October 1872.[3] Nevertheless, the legal matters decided by the Tribunal were in themselves important. In its answer to the question of what constitutes the "due diligence" required from a neutral in the discharge of the obligation defined in Article 6 of the Arbitration Treaty the Tribunal held that: "The due diligence ...ought to be exercised by neutral Governments in exact proportion to the risk to which either of the belligerents may be exposed from a failure to fulfil the obligations of neutrality on their part."[4] The findings of the Tribunal on the subject, although subjected to much criticism, did not differ materially from the formulation sub-

---

[1] Moore, *Digest*, p. 544. See also *Parl. Pap.* 1871, LXX [C. 346], and [C. 386], p. 45 for the text of the Treaty of 8 May 1871.
[2] See *Correspondence with the Government of the United States respecting the communication to other Governments of the Rules of the Treaty of Washington*: *Parl. Pap.* 1874, LXXV [C. 1012].
[3] See *Papers relating to the Proceedings of the Tribunal of Arbitration at Geneva*, Part I. *Protocols, Correspondence, etc.*: *Parl. Pap.* 1873, LXXIV [C. 688].
[4] *Award of the Tribunal, and the Reasons of Sir Alexander Cockburn for dissenting from the Award*: *Parl. Pap.* 1873, LXXIV [C. 689].

sequently adopted in Article 25 of the Hague Convention no. XIII of 1907 defining neutral duties in maritime warfare. In any case the voluminous discussions before the Tribunal made a substantial contribution to the elucidation of that intricate branch of international law.[1]

In one respect the contribution of the Tribunal to international law was purely negative, namely, on the right of States to indirect damages for injuries sustained by them. The Tribunal, in an interlocutory decision announced on 19 June 1872, held that its members had arrived "individually and collectively" at the view that indirect losses "do not constitute, upon the principles of international law applicable to such cases, good foundation for award of compensation or computation of damages between nations".[2] The rule thus enunciated is contrary to general principles of law and has been consistently disregarded by international practice. The explanation lies in the character of the claims advanced by the United States. These included damages for losses suffered by the transfer of the American commercial fleet to the British flag (a device adopted in order to protect American vessels from depredation by insurgent ships equipped in British ports), the enhanced payments of insurance, the prolongation of the war and the suppression of the rebellion; and moreover these claims were advanced subsequent to the signature of the arbitration agreement. They became the subject-matter of an emphatic repudiation in the Queen's Speech and of an indignant and heated debate in Parliament. If not disposed of by the Tribunal, they would have rendered the continuation of its work, with the participation of the British arbitrator, impossible.[3] In disposing of them in a summary way, the Tribunal performed what was in fact a political function. But this very fact showed, indirectly, the significance of the *Alabama* arbitration. It is probably not an exaggeration to say that, if the Jay Treaty marks the beginning of modern arbitration, the proceedings and the award in the case of the *Alabama* revealed the full political potentialities of judicial settlement among States and the inaccuracy of the widely adopted view that international arbitration is necessarily confined to minor issues and that it must stop short of questions that matter. It is in that vital respect that the influence of the British-American contribution to the cause of international arbitration has been beneficent and lasting.

The same considerations apply to the British Guiana arbitration of 1897 between Great Britain and Venezuela. In law the United

---

[1] See *Cases, Counter Cases and Arguments presented by Great Britain: Parl. Pap.* 1872, LXIX [C. 469], [C. 476], [C. 505], [C. 506], [C. 506–VII], [C. 531], [C. 545], [C. 548], [C. 566], [C. 570], [C. 571].

[2] For this aspect of the award see Lauterpacht, *Private Law Sources and the Analogies of International Law* (1927), pp. 219–21.

[3] *Correspondence respecting Claims for Indirect Losses put forward in the Case presented by the United States Government: Parl. Pap.* 1872, LXIX [C. 545], pp. 653 *et seq.*

States was not a party to the dispute, but it was so in fact. It insisted on the arbitration and brought it about by intervention based on the unilateral assertion of the Monroe Doctrine and by what some considered to be a threat of war. The President proposed to the Senate the appointment of an American Commission charged with the task of investigating the dispute between Great Britain and Venezuela and of submitting a report to be acted upon by the United States. Citizens of the United States played a prominent part in the composition of the Arbitration Tribunal and in the oral proceedings before it. It was this complexion of the arbitration which, once more, imparted to it the character of a controversy affecting the honour of the parties. John Westlake, who did not easily yield to excesses of national pride, wrote in *The Times* on 6 June 1896 that the message of the President of the United States, in which the intervention by the United States was asserted in a manner both drastic and peremptory, "had first to be met in this country by an assertion of our own dignity and independence".[1] But after having said that, Westlake made practical suggestions which were, in effect, accepted by Great Britain and the United States and formed the substance of the crucial provision of Article 4 of the Arbitration Treaty of Washington of February 1897. That Article provided: "Adverse holding or prescription during a period of fifty years shall make a good title. The arbitrators may deem exclusive political control of a district, as well as actual settlement thereof, sufficient to constitute adverse holding or to make title by prescription." The effect of that provision was to circumscribe at the outset the powers of the Tribunal and to remove the possibility of long peaceful possession being challenged before the Tribunal. This precaution did not prevent lengthy and able argument by British and American lawyers before the Tribunal on the meaning of prescription in private and in international law. In this matter, as well as on the general question of occupation and discovery as original title to territorial sovereignty, the proceedings of the Tribunal contributed to a clarification of a difficult branch of international law. Thus there was no hesitation in resorting to the technicalities of the common law doctrine of estoppel with regard to a substantial aspect of the case before the Tribunal.[2]

---

[1] The letter is also printed in *The Collected Papers of John Westlake on Public International Law*, ed. L. Oppenheim (1914), pp. 414–16.

[2] See *British Guiana Boundary Arbitration with the United States of Venezuela: Case, Counter Case and Argument, with Appendices and Maps* (9 vols., printed at the Foreign Office, London, 1898); *Venezuela-British Guiana Boundary Arbitration: the Case of the United States of Venezuela* (3 vols.), *the Counter Case* (3 vols.) *and Argument* (2 vols.), printed in New York, 1898; *British Guiana-Venezuela Boundary Arbitration (Oral Argument*, 11 vols., Paris, 1899). See also Cleveland, *The Venezuelan Guiana Boundary Controversy*, 1913; and Moore, *Digest*, vi, 966; see also *Parl. Pap.* 1896, xcvii [C. 7972], [C. 8012], [C. 8016], [C. 8194], [C. 8195], pp. 1–988 for the correspondence preceding the arbitration; and *Parl. Pap.* 1899, cxi, [C. 9336], [C. 9337], [C. 9338], [C. 9499], [C. 9500], [C. 9501], pp. 217 *et seq.* for the British and Venezuelan written pleadings and for the Venezuelan *Argument*; and *Parl. Pap.* 1899, cxii [C. 9533], for the Award of the Tribunal.

The antecedents of the Alaskan Boundary arbitration were less dramatic than those of the British Guiana case, but the arbitration did not materialise without much initial difficulty. There was a tendency in the United States to regard the Canadian claim as frivolous. Thus, T. W. Balch, who had the cause of international arbitration much at heart, wrote: "There is no more reason for the United States to allow their right to the possession of this unbroken Alaskan lisière to be referred to the decision of foreign judges, than would be the case if the British Empire advanced a claim to sovereignty over the coast of the Carolinas or the port of New York and proposed that this demand should be referred to the judgment of subjects of third Powers."[1] The submission of the dispute to arbitration was not secured, therefore, without resort to a precautionary device which caused the Tribunal to resemble, in some respects, a body of political negotiators rather than a court adjudicating upon the basis of law. The United States originally rejected the proposal to arbitrate the dispute. It was agreed eventually to submit the matter for a decision of "six impartial jurists of repute", three to be appointed by each party. The impartial jurists chosen by the United States were said by the President of the United States to be "men who had already committed themselves on the general proposition".[2] A decision by a tribunal thus constituted was made possible by Lord Alverstone voting in favour of the American contention. However, the written and oral proceedings before the arbitrators were strictly in the nature of legal proceedings concerned largely with the interpretation of the treaty of 1825 between Great Britain and Russia (to whose rights the United States succeeded as the result of the purchase of Alaska in 1867). The proceedings abounded in much learned argument not only on interpretation of treaties but also on the place, in international law, of prescription and estoppel and the authority of Roman law and common law rules of evidence.[3]

The Behring Sea Arbitration, decided in 1893 by an imposing tribunal sitting in Paris, was concerned with a jurisdictional issue closely related to the freedom of the high seas: an issue upon which maritime States feel strongly.[4] The main question put to the Tribunal was: "Has the United States any right, and, if so, what right, of protection of property in the fur seals frequenting the islands of the United States in Behring Sea where such seals are found outside the ordinary three-mile limit?" The United States based its claim to

---

[1] See *The Alaskan Frontier* (1903), p. 178; see also, *Correspondence respecting the Alaska Boundary: Parl. Pap.* 1904, cxi [Cd. 1877].

[2] See *Selections from the Correspondence of Theodore Roosevelt and Henry Cabot Lodge*, ii, 67.

[3] The printed *Cases, Counter Cases, and Arguments* of both parties, as well as the oral proceedings are printed in *Proceedings of the Alaska Boundary Tribunal, U.S.A.* 58th Cong. 2nd Sess. Sen. Doc. no. 162 (7 vols., 1904).

[4] For the prolonged and occasionally bitter correspondence preceding the arbitration see *B.F.S.P.* LXXXII (1889–90), pp. 202–91 and LXXXIII (1890–91), pp. 306–55.

exercise jurisdiction over foreign vessels engaged in fur seal fishing in the Behring Sea on purely legal, though unorthodox, grounds. The seals, having been born and reared on islands belonging to the United States and having retained throughout the *animus revertendi* to these islands, were the property of the United States; the continued existence of the species depended upon the care and protection by the United States. This part of the argument was conducted with much reliance on the rules of Roman law and common law on the subject of animals *ferae naturae*. The United States also appealed, not unnaturally in the circumstances, to the law of nature. The Tribunal, however, considered the principle of the freedom of the seas to be paramount and gave its award accordingly. At the same time—and here lies the principal significance of the Behring Sea Arbitration— the Tribunal availed itself of what constituted an entirely novel feature of arbitral procedure, namely, of the power conferred upon it to propose recommendations. Article 7 of the Arbitration Agreement of 29 February 1892 laid down that, should the answer of the Tribunal leave the subject in such a position that the concurrence of Great Britain was legally necessary for the establishment of regulations for the proper protection and preservation of the fur seals, the arbitrators shall, in addition to the award, determine which concurrent regulations are necessary outside the jurisdictional limits prescribed by international law.[1] The Tribunal availed itself of that authorisation and framed detailed regulations which were subsequently accepted by the parties.[2] Thus the ingenuity and the good will of the statesmen of the two countries enriched international practice by a useful expedient amounting to a conferment of legislative authority upon an international tribunal in cases when the situation demands the adjustment of the law to the exigencies of the situation. An expedient of this nature is of special usefulness in the international sphere where there is no legislature having the power to adapt the law to the changing conditions of society.[3]

That innovation was repeated, in a somewhat different form, in the Arbitration Agreement of 27 January 1909 between Great Britain and the United States which provided for the settlement of the serious dispute which arose between the two States concerning the North Atlantic Fisheries. The Agreement provided that, after making the award, the Tribunal should recommend, for consideration by the parties and in accordance with the principles of the award, rules and

---

[1] *Parl. Pap.* 1892, xcvi [C. 6639].

[2] The regulations of the Tribunal which prescribed the periods and methods of seal-fishing were fully incorporated in the Schedule to the Behring Sea Award Act, 1894 (57 Vic., c. 2; Hertslet, *Treaties*, xix, 925).

[3] See *Parl. Pap.* 1893–4, cx [C. 6918], [C. 6919], [C. 6920], [C. 6921] for the British *Case, Counter Case and Argument* and for the *Case, Counter Case and Argument* of the United States. See *ibid.* cxi [C. 6949], [C. 6950], [C. 6951], [C. 7161], pp. 955 *et seq.* for the Papers relating to the Proceedings of the Tribunal, and [C. 7107], p. 1065 for the award.

procedures for the settlement of future disputes concerning the exercise of the rights of fishery. The award of the Tribunal was in favour of Great Britain. It declined to accept the contention of the United States that the Treaty of 1818 which created certain fishery rights in favour of the United States was in the nature of an international servitude necessitating prior consent of the United States to any legislative regulation of the subject by Great Britain and Canada. But the recommendations proposed by the Tribunal and accepted by the parties[1] came very near to making such consent necessary. In addition, the award and the proceedings, which were conducted under the aegis of the Permanent Court of Arbitration in the great forensic tradition of the previous Anglo-American arbitrations, threw much light on such questions as the doctrine of international servitudes and the extent and measurement of bays. The importance of that particular arbitration in the relations of the two States may well be gauged by the following passage which because of its general significance may be quoted here in full, from the opening remarks in the oral argument by Senator Root before the Tribunal:

It is not alone a controversy that, through lapse of time, has acquired historic interest, that, through the participation of many of the ablest and most honoured statesmen of two great nations through nearly a century, has acquired that sanctity which the sentiment of a nation gives to the assertion of its rights, but it is a controversy which involves substantial and, in some respects, vital interests to portions of the people of each nation....

When two great nations, bound to protect the interests of their citizens, however humble, find themselves differing in their views of rights which are substantial, find themselves differing so radically that each conceives itself to have a right which it cannot abandon without humiliation, and cannot maintain without force, a situation arises of the gravest importance and the first dignity.[2]

Reference may also be made in this connection to the Convention of 1910 between the two countries in which they set up the British-American Claims Tribunal for the settlement of a variety of claims arising from events prior to the annexation of the South African Republics.[3] The Tribunal gave awards in a large number of cases and had not concluded its work by the time the First World War broke out.

While arbitrations with the United States constituted the bulk of active British participation in the arbitral settlement of disputes, a number of interesting arbitrations also took place in that period between Great Britain and other States. These included the *Savarkar* case arbitration with France, decided on 24 February 1911 by a Tribunal of the Permanent Court of Arbitration: an interesting case

---

[1] See Agreement of 20 July 1912 between the United States and Great Britain (Hertslet's *Treaties*, xxvii, 1095).

[2] *Argument of the Honorable Elihu Root on behalf of the United States*, ed. J. B. Scott (Boston, 1912), pp. 1, 2.

[3] *Parl. Pap.* 1912–13, cxxii [Cd. 6201].

in which France claimed, unsuccessfully, that Great Britain was bound to surrender to France an Indian political prisoner who, while being conveyed in a British ship to India, escaped from that ship in Marseilles and whom the French police, apparently in ignorance of the law of extradition, handed over to the authorities of the British ship;[1] the Delagoa Railway arbitration decided in 1900, between Great Britain and the United States on the one hand and Portugal on the other;[2] the arbitration with Brazil in 1904 concerning British Guiana;[3] and the arbitration with Germany in 1911 concerning the Walfisch Bay territory.[4] The well-known Dogger Bank incident with Russia which, according to some, brought the two countries to the brink of war[5] was settled as the result of the findings of a Commission of Enquiry set up in accordance with the provisions of the Hague Convention for the Pacific Settlement of International Disputes.

Contribution of Great Britain towards the Development of International Organs of Arbitral Settlement

The experience of a century of arbitration by sporadic tribunals made feasible the consideration, at the end of the century, of permanent organs of international arbitration. To that development Great Britain, once more in partnership with the United States, made a major contribution. As early as 1825 James Mill, in one of his essays published in a supplement to the *Encyclopaedia Britannica* and entitled the "Law of Nations", had discussed such subjects as "The Constitution of an International Code and an International Tribunal; How an International Tribunal should be constructed; Form of Procedure before an International Tribunal". John Stuart Mill's *Essay on Representative Government* included a section on a Federal Supreme Court. However, it was at the First Hague Conference of 1899 that an opportunity was given to Great Britain to make a distinct contribution in this field.

In the matter of arbitration the first Hague Conference was confronted with two distinct problems. The first was the formulation and acceptance of obligations of compulsory arbitration, and in that sphere the achievements of the Conference were purely nominal.[6] The second was the creation of a permanent international arbitral tribunal. Proposals submitted to that end were opposed by some States not only because the very notion of a judge over sovereign States seemed to be incompatible with the sovereignty of States; they were also opposed on the ground that the mere existence of an

---

[1] See *Treaty Series*, no. 25 (1910) [Cd. 5394] for the Arbitration Agreement.
[2] *Sentence Finale du Tribunal Arbitral du Délagoa* (1900).
[3] For the arbitration agreement see *Parl. Pap.* 1902, cxxx [Cd. 916]; and *Parl. Pap.* 1904, cx [Cd. 2166] for the award of the King of Italy.
[4] See *Parl. Pap.* 1911, lii [Cd. 5857], for the award of the arbitrator.
[5] See for the Correspondence on the subject, *Parl. Pap.* 1905, ciii [Cd. 2350], [Cd. 2382].
[6] See below, p. 697.

international tribunal, even if not endowed with obligatory jurisdiction, might be dangerous as implying an indirect pressure to submit disputes to it. It was for this reason that the Russian proposals on the subject rejected in effect the idea of an international tribunal.[1] According to these proposals the Conference was to designate five Powers which, when so requested by the parties to a dispute, should each name a judge either from among its own nationals or others. The proposal of the United States was to establish an international tribunal composed of members appointed by the highest court of justice of each State; a supplementary convention between the parties was to determine whether in any particular case all the members of the tribunal or several of them were to sit. The British project, which was a compromise between the Russian and the American plans, was accepted as the basis of the work of the Conference and eventually adopted, in substance, by the Conference. According to that plan each of the signatory Powers was to designate an equal number of arbitrators to be entered upon a general list as members of the Court. From this list parties to a dispute could select members to form a tribunal in any particular case. This was the Permanent Court of Arbitration as established by the first Hague Conference[2] in the Convention for the Pacific Settlement of International Disputes. It was neither a court nor permanent. It was a panel of arbitrators. However, with the help of a permanent bureau and a code of procedure framed by the Conference and embodied in the Convention, it provided the necessary facilities for the arbitration of a number of important disputes.[3] After the First World War it was overshadowed—and, in effect, replaced—by the Permanent Court of International Justice set up by the League of Nations.

Contributions of Great Britain to Compulsory Arbitration

While the proposals of the United States for an international arbitral tribunal were more ambitious than those put forward by Great Britain, the latter took the leading part in the movement for obligatory arbitration. No substantial progress was made in this respect, however, by either of the Hague Peace Conferences. Article 16 of the Convention I of 1899 for the Pacific Settlement of International Disputes amounted, when stripped of the niceties of diplomatic language, to a rejection of obligatory arbitration. It provided that "in questions of a legal nature, and especially in the interpretation or application of international conventions, arbitration is recognised by the signatory Powers as the most effective, and at the same time,

[1] For the text of the Russian, American and British proposals see Carnegie Endowment for International Peace, *Reports to the Hague Conference of* 1899 *and* 1907, ed. J. B. Scott (1917), pp. 101, 110 and 108 respectively.

[2] *Parl. Pap.* 1902, cxxx [Cd. 798].

[3] For a collection of the awards rendered by the various Arbitrators of the Permanent Court of Arbitration see *The Hague Court Reports*, ed. J. B. Scott (1916); 2nd ser. (1932).

the most equitable, means of settling disputes which diplomacy has failed to settle". The Second Hague Conference emphasised in effect the purely nominal character of this provision (which became Article 39) by adding to it the following sentence: "Consequently, it would be desirable that, in disputes about the above mentioned questions, the contracting Powers, if the case arise, have recourse to arbitration, in so far as circumstances permit." The efforts to accept the principle of obligatory arbitration with regard to specified categories of disputes failed owing to determined opposition in which Germany took the most vocal, though not the exclusive, part. Great Britain's affirmative attitude to the proposals found eloquent expression in Sir Edward Fry's reply to Baron Marschall von Bieberstein's outspoken repudiation of any system of obligatory arbitration worthy of that name.[1] In view of this the efforts of successive British Governments were directed towards securing compulsory arbitration by way of bilateral treaties. In 1903 Great Britain concluded with France what was the first treaty of obligatory arbitration. The crucial Article 1 of the Treaty provided as follows:

Differences which may arise of a legal nature, or relating to the interpretation of treaties existing between the two contracting parties, and which it may not have been possible to settle by diplomacy, shall be referred to a Permanent Court of Arbitration established at The Hague by the Convention of 29 July 1899, provided, nevertheless, that they do not affect the vital interests, the independence, or the honour of the two contracting States, and do not concern the interests of third Parties.[2]

Before the outbreak of the First World War Great Britain had concluded sixteen treaties of that type. At the same time British efforts were directed towards securing obligatory arbitration with the United States. These efforts were not successful. While the United States, together with Great Britain, could justly claim to have participated in a greater number of international arbitrations than any other country, it exhibited, through its Senate, a conspicuous reluctance to enter into commitments of obligatory arbitration for the future. American governments and statesmen viewed with favour—and with fervour—the conclusion of such treaties. But these, once signed by the Executive, were subsequently amended by the Senate in such a way as to deprive them of their obligatory character. Following upon the Arbitration Treaty with France the United States signed identical agreements with Great Britain and other countries. In February 1904 the Senate amended these agreements by substituting in each case the word "treaty" for "agreement", in such a way that in each dispute as it arose, the advice and consent of two-thirds of the

[1] See *Parl. Pap.* 1908, cxxiv [Cd. 4081], p. 368. See also Higgins, Pearce, *The Hague Peace Conference* (1909), pp. 82–4, and Hull, W. I., in *American Journal of International Law*, II (1908), 740.
[2] Hertslet, *Treaties*, xxiii, 492; *Parl. Pap.* 1904, cx [Cd. 1837].

Senate would have been required for its submission to arbitration. As this would have divested the treaties of their obligatory character, the Executive did not proceed with the matter.[1] Previously the Olney-Pauncefote Treaty, signed on 11 January 1897 and warmly recommended to the Senate in a special message by President Cleveland, had failed to secure the concurrence of the Senate.[2] This was also the fate of the Treaty concluded between the two States on 4 August 1908.[3] The last of these attempts—the Knox Arbitration Treaties—was made in 1911.[4] But these efforts, while not successful in relation to the United States, were not without indirect influence upon the movement for obligatory arbitration in general.[5]

VI

Parallel with the developments in the sphere of international arbitration, various efforts were made to codify the laws of war. Before 1870 these efforts were limited to the humanitarian aspects of the regulation of warfare. The Geneva Red Cross Conventions of 1864 and 1868, and the Declaration of St Petersburg of 1868, have been mentioned elsewhere in these volumes.[6] After 1870, however, efforts began to be directed towards the improvement and codification of the laws governing the conduct of war. In 1874 the Czar Alexander II of Russia convened a conference at Brussels to consider a "project for an international code, with the object of determining the laws and usages of warfare". The British Government seems to have viewed the conference with some suspicion, as it was feared that the question of maritime capture might be reopened. The Foreign Secretary accordingly required and got an assurance from the other Governments that there was no intention of discussing the right to capture private property at sea, before consenting to send a British delegate. Even so the British Government made it clear that the British delegate would not have plenipotentiary powers and that his function would be merely to observe and report the proceedings, Her Majesty's Government retaining entire liberty of action, and that the British delegate would not be free to discuss "general principles of international law not already universally recognised and accepted". Perhaps, as Maine said,[7] the Conference was held too soon after the Franco-Prussian War, and the suspicion with which the British Government viewed the proceedings at Brussels is no doubt readily

---

[1] *Parl. Pap.* 1904, cx [Cd. 1837], pp. 103, 104.
[2] For details see Moore, *A Digest of International Law*, VII, 74–88.
[3] Hertslet, *Treaties*, xxv, 203.   [4] See Taft, *The Presidency* (1916), pp. 102–4.
[5] An arbitration treaty of more limited compass, safeguarding the powers of the Senate, was concluded and duly ratified in 1908: *Parl. Pap.* 1908, cxxv [Cd. 4179]; see *Parl. Pap.* 1914, ci [Cd. 7357] for a renewal of that Treaty.
[6] *C.H.B.E.* II, 881.
[7] *Whewell Lectures on International Law* of 1877 (1915), p. 128.

understandable when viewed against the contemporary political background. The nature of that suspicion is very clearly revealed by a passage in a dispatch of Lord Derby to the British Ambassador at St Petersburg, in which he announces his refusal to enter into any arrangement which would facilitate aggressive wars and "paralyse the patriotic resistance of an invaded people".[1] However, in spite of the unfavourable atmosphere, the delegates did manage to draw up a Declaration of fifty-six articles covering some of the more important questions of the laws and customs of war on land.[2] The Declaration, however, could only be signed by the delegates as a record of the proceedings of the Conference, even though in form of a draft convention, and without pledging their Governments. It was never ratified. The so-called Brussels Rules, however, were later to provide a useful basis of discussion at the 1899 conference at The Hague.

When the Czar Nicholas II called the first Hague Conference of 1899 to discuss the "maintenance of universal peace and a possible reduction of the excessive armaments", Her Majesty's Government this time at once accepted the invitation, pledged co-operation, and sent a strong delegation to The Hague under Sir Julian Pauncefote. The disarmament proposals failed, in large measure owing to the technical difficulty of the subject, and on this matter the Conference had to be content with a resolution that the restriction of military budgets was extremely desirable. The Conference settled down, therefore, to efforts first to provide means for the pacific settlement of disputes, as described above, and secondly to codify the laws and customs of war. Differences of opinion amongst military and naval experts made it impossible to do more than to attempt a partial codification of existing rules. The United States delegation, following traditional American policy, tried to press for the immunity of private property from capture at sea; but the British delegates, following their explicit instructions, refused to enter upon a discussion of the subject.[3] There was a sufficient area of agreement, however, to enable the drawing up of a Convention on the adaptation of the principles of the Geneva Convention to maritime war (based in part on the Additional Articles of 1868). It was reasonable to expect that some headway could be made also with the work on the laws and customs of war on land, for the subject had already been studied *in extenso*: Francis Lieber's code of the rules of land warfare had been prepared for the United States Government as early as 1863, and the American example had been followed in several European countries;

---

[1] Cited in Woolsey, T. D., *Introduction to the Study of International Law*, 6th ed. (1888), p. 237.

[2] There is a useful summary of the proceedings of the Conference in the Report of the British Delegate, Sir A. Horsford, to Lord Derby, which is reprinted as Appendix II to Lorimer's *Institutes of the Law of Nations* (1884), II, 337–402.

[3] See letter from Sir Julian Pauncefote to the Marquess of Salisbury of 28 June 1899: *Parl. Pap.* 1899, cx [C. 9534], p. 108.

there were the Brussels Rules of 1874; and the Institute of International Law meeting in Oxford in 1880 had prepared the so-called "Oxford Manual". In 1883 the British War Office had allowed Lord Thring to add a chapter on the customs of war to the *Manual of Military Law* (though it was labelled as having "no official authority", and it was not until 1904 that T. E. Holland was permitted to write an official manual). This expectation was fulfilled and a convention was signed containing the agreed rules of warfare in an Annex (the so-called Hague Regulations), the parties undertaking to issue instructions to their land forces in conformity with these regulations. The Convention was not reached, however, without difficulty. In particular there was an important difference of opinion over the vital question of the qualifications of belligerent forces and the position of the levy *en masse*. This difficulty had already appeared at Brussels in 1874. Germany and the other Continental Powers naturally wished to restrict privileges of the Convention—such as the status of prisoner of war—as nearly as possible to professional armies. This had some historical justification, for the effective application of rules governing the conduct of war had first become a practicable proposition with the advent of disciplined professional armies. Smaller Powers, however, which had perforce to depend for their defence upon the improvised organisation of local militia, naturally tended to regard the proposed rules as a threat to their security and as putting a premium upon prepared aggression; there were also lively memories of the severe treatment of "franc-tireurs" by the Germans in 1870. In this the smaller Powers were strongly supported by the British military delegate, who proposed an additional article that "nothing in this chapter be considered as tending to diminish or suppress the right which belongs to the population of an invaded country to patriotically oppose the most energetic resistance to their invaders, by every legitimate means".[1] In the result a compromise was reached partly by modification of the offending articles and partly by a formula in the preamble stating that it had not been possible to agree on provisions embracing all circumstances that might occur in practice.[2] It was not, however, until after the Russian delegate, M. de Martens, had pleaded with the Conference and had pointed out the possible disastrous effect of yet another failure to agree following the failure at Brussels in 1874, that the Convention was signed; yet it was apparent that the agreed Regulations, useful as they were, in some measure obscured or avoided fundamental disagreements.

[1] For the report of the British military delegate, Sir John Ardagh, on this part of the discussion, see *Parl. Pap.* 1899, cx [C. 9534], pp. 160–3.

[2] Westlake's comment is pertinent: "...since it applies only to cases not included in the Regulations, it does not profess to relax those Regulations as operative in the cases which they include; and [one] may wonder how it produced the assuaging effect which it is recorded to have produced." See *International Law*, II (1907), p. 62.

Although the initiative in calling together the second Hague Conference of 1907 came originally from the United States, it was actually summoned by the Czar Nicholas II at his own desire. It was proposed by Russia that the Conference should seek to secure improvements in the working of the Hague Court and to draw up conventions on the rules of land and sea warfare and the rights and duties of neutrals at sea, "leaving untouched, however, those questions which might affect the limitation of military or naval forces".[1] The British Foreign Secretary replied that the British Government wished to see disarmament included in the agenda of the Conference.[2] Despite German opposition the question of disarmament was in fact raised by Sir Edward Fry at the Conference, with the support of the United States, France and Spain; the matter, however, was disposed of by a reaffirmation of the 1899 resolution, and thereafter the Conference concentrated on the pacific settlement of disputes and the rules of warfare and neutrality.

After four months' work the participating States were able, in the Final Act of the Conference, to record the conclusion of thirteen conventions.[3] Three of these were revisions of the corresponding Conventions of 1899. The others covered between them a much wider field than it had been found practicable to attempt at the earlier Conference. It is not possible within the limits of this chapter to discuss the work in any detail, and it must suffice briefly to indicate the British participation in those parts of the discussion in which she was chiefly concerned; mainly of course questions of maritime law. Discussions on neutrality laid bare the old disagreements about the test of enemy character. The Anglo-American "domicile" school opposed the Continental "nationality" school, and this particular point had to be avoided in the Conventions. Serious disagreement was revealed over the position of enemy merchantmen found in port at the outbreak of war. The majority wished them to be allowed time to depart, but the British insisted on the rules laid down in their Prize Courts[4] that such vessels were liable to seizure and condemnation; in the end the Convention avoided the difficulty by the use of the formula "it is desirable" that such vessels should be allowed time

---

[1] Count Benckendorff to Sir Edward Grey, 3 April 1906, see *Parl. Pap.* 1908, cxxiv [Cd. 3857], p. 2.   [2] *Ibid.*

[3] Conventions are:—I. The pacific settlement of international disputes; II. The limitation of the employment of force for the recovery of contract debts; III. The opening of hostilities; IV. The laws and customs of war on land; V. The rights and duties of neutral powers and persons in case of war on land; VI. The status of enemy merchant-ships at the outbreak of hostilities; VII. The conversion of merchant-ships into warships; VIII. The laying of automatic submarine contact mines; IX. Bombardment by naval forces in time of war; X. The adaptation to maritime war of the principles of the Geneva Convention; XI. Certain restrictions with regard to the exercise of the right of capture in naval war; XII. The creation of an International Prize Court; XIII. The rights and duties of neutral Powers in naval war.

[4] E.g. by Lord Mansfield in *Lindo* v. *Rodney* (1781), 2 Doug. 612, and by Lord Stowell in the *Boedus Lust* (1803), 5 G. Rob. 245.

to depart. The British attitude was much condemned at the time, but experience since then has shown that it was clearly right. On the other hand, the British delegation was bitterly opposed to the legalising of the use of submarine contact mines in the maintenance of blockades. "We declare without hesitation," said Satow, "that the right of the neutral to security of navigation on the high seas ought to come before the transitory right of the belligerent to employ those seas as the scene of the operation of war." The use of mines, however, was defended by Germany on grounds of military necessity, and the Conference was able to agree only upon unsatisfactory provisions forbidding certain types of mines, in view of which Great Britain felt it necessary to enter the caveat that "it is not permissible to presume the legitimacy of an action, for the mere reason that this Convention has not prohibited it". The question of the conversion at sea of merchantmen into warships had been brought to a head by the incident in 1904, during the Russo-Japanese War, when the Russian vessels *Petersburg* and *Smolensk* sailed through the Bosphorus and Dardanelles and the Suez Canal under a commercial flag, then hoisted a naval flag at sea and stopped and captured neutral merchantmen. A British proposal to forbid such conversion at sea was whittled down to an innocuous provision to prevent the evasion of the 1856 rule abolishing privateering. It was found possible to agree upon a convention limiting the bombardment of coastal towns and villages in time of war; a practice which had already been condemned as contrary to the modern rules of international law by Professor Holland in letters to *The Times*.

More important general issues arose concerning the whole question of maritime capture and commercial blockade. As always, the United States proposed the adoption of the principle of the immunity of private property from capture at sea, except when contraband or bound for a blockaded port; a proposal which, as an American observer has said, had "long been a favourite doctrine, though never the practice of the United States",[1] but one to which Great Britain as the leading maritime Power was traditionally opposed.[2] The British argued the case for commercial blockade as a weapon at once powerful and less cruel than military operations on land. Nevertheless the British attitude was conciliatory, and it was indicated that His Majesty's Government would be prepared to consider sacrificing even this vital weapon if it could prove a means of bringing about a measure of general disarmament; for one of the grounds on which Germany was demanding a large navy was that it was required to defend merchant shipping in time of war. Although the Americans were able to organise an impressive majority for a test vote on a side

[1] See Scott, *The Hague Peace Conference, 1899 and 1907*, 1, 699.
[2] Others were France, Russia, Japan, Spain, Portugal, Mexico, Argentina and Colombia.

issue, the opposition was too important, and the matter was shelved by the adoption of a non-committal *vœu*.

It was Great Britain herself, however, that startled the Conference by a revolutionary proposal for the abolition of contraband. The proposal was in the following terms: "In order to lessen the difficulties suffered by neutrals in case of war, the Government of His Britannic Majesty is ready to abandon the principle of contraband in case of war between Powers signatory of a convention to this end. The right of visit shall only be exercised to establish the neutral character of the merchant vessel." At first sight it seems barely credible that within seven years of a war, in which the British were to be compelled rapidly to extend the contraband lists until they covered almost every conceivable commodity, the British Government could have proposed the total abolition of this vital technique of naval warfare. The British argument makes curious reading to-day: it seeks to show that, by reason of scientific advances in the warlike use of materials, the difficulty of searching modern merchant vessels on the high seas and the complicated voyages with calls at many neutral ports possible for steam vessels, the law of contraband was in danger of becoming so extended that "the prohibition to be useful must be stretched to the point of rendering the Declaration of Paris a dead-letter". These, of course, are precisely the reasons which shortly afterwards did indeed cause the growth of contraband out of all proportion in the two World Wars. To that extent the British case was founded on a correct appreciation of the situation. It was true that the law of contraband must in the near future be either enormously extended or entirely abolished; what is astonishing is that it could have been supposed that Great Britain could afford to press for the latter alternative on the ground that the first would "inflict upon neutral commerce a trouble disproportionate to the legitimate interest of the belligerent".[1]

The fact of the matter was that Great Britain had ceased for the moment to be a Power which approached these questions exclusively from the standpoint of a potential belligerent. Already in 1887 Sir Henry Maine pointed to the tendency to establish new classes of contraband as constituting a source of "unexampled danger" to Great Britain. He predicted that in any future war of larger dimensions coal and provisions would be included as contraband at the very outbreak of the hostilities, and he went so far as to counsel early adherence by this country to the principle of immunity of private property at sea advocated by the United States.[2] Professor Westlake also, giving evidence in 1905 before the Royal Commission on the supply of food and raw materials in times of war, considered the

---

[1] It is instructive to compare this argument with the decisions in the leading cases of the First World War, *The Stigstad* [1919], A.C. 279, and *The Leonora* [1919], A.C. 974.
[2] *International Law* (2nd ed. 1894), p. 121.

immunity of private property at sea to be a practical proposal. He was generally of the opinion that the attitude of Great Britain, as a country vitally dependent on supplies from overseas, should be directed rather towards what he described as neutral rights than belligerent rights.[1] He clearly envisaged the practicability—and desirability—of abolishing contraband: a view from which his Oxford colleague, Professor T. E. Holland, dissented.[2]

The deliberations of the Royal Commission, moreover, were clearly influenced by the revealing experience of the Russo-Japanese War, on the outbreak of which Russia had declared both coal and provisions to be absolute contraband. Great Britain protested vigorously. In a statement made to a deputation representative of British shipping interests Mr Balfour, the Prime Minister, laid it down as being "in absolute conformity with the law of nations" that, while coal carried to a belligerent for the purpose of aiding him in his warlike operations was undoubtedly contraband and while the same applied to foodstuffs carried to a beleaguered fortress or to an army in the field, coal, foodstuffs and cotton could not lawfully be declared to constitute absolute contraband (i.e., contraband irrespective of their destination). Russia partially complied with the British protest by agreeing to treat foodstuffs as conditional contraband. Even so, it appeared that the concession was rendered largely illusory by the insistence of Russian prize courts on the owners proving that the captured cargo might not come into the hands of the enemy forces: an almost impossible task.[3]

It is not after all surprising, therefore, that the proposal to abolish contraband altogether should have gathered sufficient momentum to be put forward officially by Great Britain at the second Hague Conference. Twenty-five States rallied in favour of the British proposal; only five opposed. Yet some of the support was clearly half-hearted. For when Great Britain proposed that the States in favour of abolition of contraband should conclude as between themselves a convention to that effect, no favourable response was forthcoming. For the rest the Conference found itself fatally attracted towards the traditional but hitherto insoluble problem of drawing up agreed lists of contraband, so that, in the end, nothing came of this extraordinary proposal.

In many ways the most ambitious of the proposals actually adopted by the Conference was that for the setting up of an international court of prize. This was not on the original agenda, but both the British and the German delegations came to the Conference armed with draft schemes. The German scheme was for a tribunal of five

[1] *Report of the Commission: Parl. Pap.* 1905, xxxix [Cd. 2643], [Cd. 2644], p. 241; and xl [Cd. 2645].
[2] *Ibid.* p. 236.
[3] Smith and Sibley, *International Law as Interpreted during the Russo-Japanese War* (1907), p. 216.

45

members (two admirals and three members of the Permanent Court of Arbitration) would be set up *ad hoc* at the outbreak of hostilities, to hear appeals, which might be brought even by individual litigants, from national prize courts. The British scheme was for a permanent tribunal of judges nominated by signatories whose mercantile tonnage exceeded 800,000 tons; this was to be a court of appeal from national tribunals, but competent only in matters affecting a neutral, and on the motion of the neutral State concerned. The Convention XII was reached largely by way of compromise. There was to be a permanent court at The Hague, with competence to hear appeals by neutral states or individuals and in certain cases by belligerents, and consisting of fifteen judges, eight permanently representing the Great Powers of Europe, the rest representing minor States on a rota system. The proposed constitution of the court aroused bitter opposition from many of the smaller States led by Brazil, in spite of the argument of Sir Eyre Crowe, the British representative, that the scheme based on combination of political power and mercantile tonnage meant that the privileged States were those who were making the most real sacrifice in assenting to the setting up of a court, and that the smaller Powers had much to gain and little to lose by the success of the scheme.

However, the principal difficulty was to decide what law the proposed court should apply; for clearly the projected court might have to decide precisely those questions of maritime rights on which the Conference had been able only to register a fundamental cleavage of opinion. Article 7 of the Convention provided that the Court should give its decisions, in the first instance, on the basis of treaties applicable between the States concerned. In the absence of such treaties the Court was to apply generally recognised rules of international law. Where that source failed, judgment was to be given "in accordance with the general principles of justice and equity". This elastic formulation of the sources of law to be applied by an international court would have been bound to cause misgivings even if its jurisdiction were confined to administering the law of peace. The clause conferring upon the Tribunal the power to decide in accordance with "justice and equity" was to be found occasionally in treaties creating *ad hoc* arbitration tribunals. It found no place in such general instruments of compulsory arbitral settlement as existed at the time. (In the Statute of the Permanent Court of International Justice set up in 1920 the Court was given the power to decide *ex aequo et bono* only if the parties expressly agreed thereto.) Here it was proposed to confer wide powers of judicial discretion, under the name of "justice and equity", in the most controversial and elastic branch of international law. It was therefore clear from the outset that, unless this part of the law of sea warfare could be codified with some approximation to precision, the prospects of the Convention being ratified by a considerable number of States were indeed tenuous. It was agreed therefore that ratification of Convention XII should be delayed until a further conference had agreed upon a codification of prize law.

The necessary initiative came from Great Britain. On 27 February 1908 the British Government proposed that a Conference should be held "with the object of arriving at an agreement as to what are the generally recognised principles of international law within the meaning of paragraph 2 of Article 7 of the Convention, as to those matters wherein the practice of nations has varied, and of then formulating the rules which, in the absence of special treaty provisions applicable to a particular case, the Court should observe in dealing with appeals brought before it for decision".[1] The British Government referred to the impression created at the second Hague Conference "that the establishment of an international Prize Court would not meet with general acceptance so long as vagueness and uncertainty exists as to the principles which the court, in dealings with appeals brought before it, would apply to questions of far-reaching importance affecting naval policy and practice". The invitation to attend the Conference, to be held in London, was extended to a limited number of States only, namely, Austria-Hungary, France, Germany, Italy, Japan, Russia, Spain, Holland and the United States of America. The work of the Conference, which sat between 4 December 1908 and 26 February 1909, resulted in a *Déclaration relative au droit de guerre maritime*, commonly referred to as the Declaration of London.

There were three main topics on which a reconciliation of the divergent views proved to be unattainable: the essentially British doctrine of the Rule of War of 1756[2] according to which a vessel loses her neutral character if she engages in trade which the opposing belligerent, before the war, reserved for his own trade; the question whether the test of the enemy character of cargoes should be the domicile or the nationality of the owner; and the conversion of merchantmen into men-of-war on the high seas. Outside these topics, however, the Declaration provided a comprehensive scheme of laws for six major questions of the law of prize: wartime blockades, contraband, unneutral service, destruction of enemy prizes, transfers to the neutral flag, and the right of convoy. Of these, the vital questions were of course blockade and contraband. The chapter on blockade represented almost entirely the British view. It is true that Great Britain abandoned her claim to capture blockade runners at any distance from the blockaded coast. On the other hand the former Continental view, which the Armed Neutralities of 1780 and 1800 had attempted to enforce, that a lawful blockade could only be

---

[1] *Parl. Pap.* 1909, LIV [Cd. 4554]; see also Gooch and Temperley (eds.), *British Documents*, VIII, 306 *seqq.*
[2] *C.H.B.E.* I, 551.

maintained by stationary vessels was rejected; and so also was the requirement of a special notification to the captured vessel of the existence of the blockade. The problem of contraband was more obdurate. The difficult question of the limits of the doctrine of continuous voyage was apparently solved by permitting its application to absolute contraband and rejecting it for conditional contraband; however, this and indeed almost every other matter concerning contraband depended in the long run on the solution of the persistent problem concerning the lists of contraband. The Declaration boldly attempted a solution by agreed lists. That provision, the crux of the Declaration, requires some explanation.

The Declaration adopted an elaborate distinction between goods placed on the "free list", which could not in any circumstances be declared to constitute contraband; secondly, absolute contraband, *viz.* goods which were always contraband provided they had enemy destination; and—most important of all—goods within the category of "conditional contraband". These last included the vital category of foodstuffs. With regard to conditional contraband, Article 33 of the Declaration seemed to adopt the traditional British principle as enunciated by the Prime Minister during the Russo-Japanese War. It laid down that conditional contraband is liable to seizure and condemnation only if it is actually destined for the armed forces or the government departments of the enemy State. But Article 34 added certain presumptions of enemy destination which critics in Great Britain considered to be of devastating comprehensiveness: for example, the destination required in Article 33 to be presumed to exist where goods were consigned to a merchant in the enemy's country who, "as a matter of common knowledge", supplies the enemy with goods of that kind. The Article thus formulated lent itself to the construction that it covered the furnishing of provisions to the enemy population in general. The official Report, which accompanied the Declaration and which the Conference treated as authoritative, attempted to allay that apprehension by explaining that the intention of Article 34 in this connection was to cover the case of a merchant notoriously furnishing provisions to the enemy government. The second presumption, equally disquieting, established by that Article was that goods were to be treated as contraband if they were consigned to a place serving "as a base for the armed forces of the enemy". The critics of the Declaration pointed out that this might include any port in the United Kingdom. The General Report explained that the intention was to refer to a base either of operations or of victualling (*ravitaillement*)—a form of words which indicated a necessary connection between a commercial port and the military or naval operations.

Thus one of the most vital aspects of the code of maritime law was made to hang on the slender thread of the controversy as to the authority of the General Report of the Conference. The Report was drafted by M. Renault, a jurist of acknowledged distinction. It received the endorsement of the Conference as a whole. But it was not ostensibly an integral part of the Declaration. It was extremely unlikely that any international tribunal acting in good faith would have disregarded it as a legitimate instrument of interpretation. But the fact remained that a vital aspect of the Declaration—there were others[1]—now hinged on the uncertain results of discussion, familiar to lawyers but disconcerting to the layman, on the place of the so-called *travaux préparatoires* in the interpretation of treaties.[2] It is perhaps not surprising that Professor Westlake, the most distinguished British international lawyer of the time, who was otherwise an emphatic advocate of the Declaration, eventually suggested that, unless the Powers represented at the London Conference met again and formally declared the General Report to be an official and authoritative commentary binding upon the judicial, military and administrative authorities of the Contracting Parties, it would be preferable not to ratify the Declaration of London.[3] There was the further relevant fact that, in addition to the questions which the Declaration clearly left unsolved, the solution of some others was so elastic and nominal as to leave a wide field to the exercise of judicial discretion by the application of not only generally recognised principles of international law but also those of justice and equity. These considerations determined the fate of the Declaration when the question of its ratification came before the House of Lords. Before the House of Commons the Government expressed itself strongly in favour of ratification. Mr McKenna, the First Lord of the Admiralty, said:

In this matter of international law, under the practice of the Admiralty, the expert adviser is the Director of Naval Intelligence who is always an admiral of distinction and whose office is one of the most important of the Admiralty outside the Board. I know for certain the opinion of four Directors of Naval Intelligence upon this point, and I believe I know the opinion of a fifth, and they are unanimously in favour of the Declaration of London.[4]

The House, with diminishing majorities, approved the Bill before it. The House of Lords rejected it.

Thus came to an unsuccessful conclusion the most ambitious attempt ever undertaken to codify a substantial branch of international law. In this effort Great Britain took a leading part. Even after the rejection of the Declaration by the House of Lords the British Government did not altogether jettison its principles. When the First World War broke out in 1914, the Government, through an Order in Council, declared their intention to act on its principles.

[1] See McNair, *The Law of Treaties* (1938), p. 264.
[2] See *ibid.* chap. xxv.
[3] Letter to *The Times* newspaper, 1 March 1911; also printed in *The Collected Papers of John Westlake on Public International Law* (1914), p. 670.
[4] House of Commons, 28 June 1911: *Hansard*, 5th ser. xxvii, 546.

The Courts, with some hesitation, applied it for a while. But the realities of total war soon cut short the span of its precarious life. On 7 July 1916 the Declaration was formally abandoned. However, this fact in no way detracts from the historic significance of the Declaration. Much of that significance is of a negative character. While the effort to put the Declaration on the international statute book revealed the laudable determination to introduce an element of order and legality into the relations both between the belligerents themselves and between belligerents and neutrals, it is probable that, even more than in the case of war on land, the very basis of the codifying and legislative effort of the Declaration of London was artificial and unreal. That basis was the assumption that the conduct of modern war can be effectively regulated by reference to a workable distinction between the belligerent State and its nationals, between the military effort of the State engaged in a struggle for survival and the normal pursuit of its economic life. To demonstrate the falseness of that assumption it is sufficient to compare the lists of articles of contraband as formulated by the Declaration of London and those which finally emerged at the end of the First World War. Indeed, in contrast with the changes, during this period, in the law of peace—where the foundations were laid of new developments in international law which were to become of increasing importance— the efforts made in the field of the laws and customs of war were in large measure an attempt to codify rules which had already served their purpose and which were shown to be outmoded as soon as they were put to the test of a total war.

CHAPTER XIX

THE COLONIAL OFFICE

I

ON 17 March 1801 Lord Hobart was gazetted Secretary of State for War and the Colonies.[1] This is the birth-day of the Colonial Office. Responsibility for colonial affairs was then transferred from the Home Office, where it had rested since 1782, to the War Department, where it nominally remained for half a century. The reasons for this redistribution of functions, for which there was no public demand, are unknown. Perhaps the strategic aspect of the colonies seemed pre-eminent; perhaps the prospect of prolonged peace and the union with Ireland indicated that the Home Secretary would henceforth have more to do than the Secretary of State for War; perhaps a fairer division of the patronage was at the bottom of it. Be the reasons what they may, the consequences were unhappy. When hostilities broke out again in 1803 the Secretary of State's energies were consumed in the war effort. The colonies were neglected and Governors' dispatches went unanswered.[2]

So matters remained until 1806 when William Windham became Secretary of State. He appointed a military Under-Secretary and so to some extent freed the existing Under-Secretary for colonial work. In 1812 there was a further improvement. Lord Bathurst became Secretary of State and Henry Goulburn Under-Secretary and from that time military operations ceased to monopolise the attention of the department. Various explanations for this development suggest themselves. Both the Prime Minister and the Foreign Secretary had preceded Bathurst as War Minister, and their experience probably eased Bathurst's responsibilities; the chronic madness of the King may have relieved the Secretary of State of some tiresome work as the interpreter of the Cabinet to the Sovereign on military matters. The chief reason, however, for the change of direction was the personal interest that Bathurst, and still more Goulburn, took in colonial affairs.

Thus it came about that, when the war ended, the Colonial Office, as it was beginning to be called, survived as a colonial and not as a military department. Its value, however, in the post-war world of retrenchment and reaction was at first but grudgingly acknowledged.

---

[1] Secretaries of State were appointed by letters patent until 1867 (Office Minutes, 1866–8, no. 21 A).

[2] Thanks are due to Mr Murray Young for suggesting some improvements in this section.

On 3 April 1816 Tierney moved in the House of Commons the abolition of the third Secretaryship. He reminded the House that the post had been created for a War Minister in 1794; it had therefore been necessitated by war alone; the colonies had had nothing to do with its creation and now that the war was over there was no need to keep it. He admitted that our colonial responsibilities had been enlarged, but thought that they could be adequately handled by the Home Secretary, if he were to be given an extra Under-Secretary and a staff of trained clerks. If this would not do, the colonial business might be divided upon a geographical basis between the Home Office and the Board of Control. Tierney and his supporters were strongly if not very imaginatively combated by the Government, and the motion was decisively lost; nor did it meet a better fate when it was reintroduced the next year.

The Tierney motions mark the nadir of Colonial Office prestige. Other forces were at work to counteract the faction and ignorance that induced ninety-nine M.P.'s to vote for the first of them. It was in the very year 1816 that Parliament forced upon the Office the first steps towards emancipation: West Indian governments were compelled to register their slaves. Three years later, in debates upon Australia, Parliament taught the Office another lesson—that the constitutional issues underlying possession of overseas territories of settlement must be submitted to Parliamentary scrutiny. Thus almost from the outset the two Houses began to play the part which was theirs until quite recent times—the part of an ignorant, fretful but well-intentioned critic. In such an atmosphere the Office breathed with difficulty; its prestige was low, its ministers puny, its staff exiguous; yet it continued to breathe.

In 1812 the establishment of the Office consisted of the Secretary of State, the two Under-Secretaries (one Parliamentary and one military), a private secretary, a chief clerk, twelve clerks, a précis writer and some interpreters. There were also seven "additional" or "extra" clerks. This establishment was partly military and was reduced as soon as the war was over. In 1816 the military Under-Secretary went, and the twelve ordinary clerks were cut to eight. The actual strength was approximately the same in 1821, but in that year a scientific remoulding of the establishment, which can be paralleled in other departments, began. The clerks were then graded into three classes for the first time. Next year the establishment was systematically regulated by an Order in Council, certain allowances, long enjoyed by Secretaries of State's clerks, were consolidated, and salaries were put upon a scale. Provision was also made for the accumulation of a superannuation fund and under this two clerks were retired, presumably for incompetence, in 1824. A further Order in Council of 5 July 1825 authorised the appointment of a permanent Under-Secretary, and R. W. Hay came from the Admiralty to fill the post. For all practical purposes we may look upon him as the first permanent Colonial Under-Secretary.[1]

Before the reforms of 1821-5 the clerks of the Office were the humble servants of their ministers. They did not seek to give, and perhaps were unfit to offer, advice. They were gradually eliminated and replaced by young men of better attainments. The best remembered of those new recruits was (Sir) Henry Taylor who came in 1824 and remained for 52 years. T. H. Villiers, Lord Clarendon's brother, was his contemporary, but he was soon enticed into politics and his talents lost to the Office. Ministers were quick to profit by the abilities of such men; during his first few months Taylor drafted a Cabinet paper and prepared a brief for Canning—remarkable accomplishments in those days for a callow clerk. There is only one other contemporary official who deserves commemoration—(Sir) James Stephen. His father of the same name, a champion of the slaves, had been a kind of unpaid adviser of the department in the early years of the century. He seems to have lost his influence about the time of Waterloo, but the son, who from 1813 was retained by the department as Counsel, perpetuated his father's outlook. Through his hands passed an ever-growing body of colonial legislation, the bulk of which had become so great by 1824 that he was obliged to give up his private practice and devote the whole of his time to the State. From August 1825 his services, and the cost of them, were shared between the Colonial Office and the Board of Trade. His unobtrusive work as an examiner of laws gave a direction to policy and established his reputation as a colonial expert.

The fragmentation of responsibility for colonial administration that had been a feature of eighteenth-century government continued in Bathurst's day. The Treasury, Customs, Post Office and Board of Ordnance were still represented by their own officials in many, if not most, of the colonies. The Treasury still controlled the expenditure of moneys raised by colonial assemblies or appropriated colonial revenues arising in colonies without legislatures. The Colonial Office now began, however, to insist that other departments should act according to its advice. Thus the Ordnance officers were required to comply with local law in preference to their own service rules, and the Customs officers to subject themselves to the wishes of the local governments. It was the Colonial Office that took the lead in establishing an efficient system of colonial audit, through the agency of the statutory Commissioners for Colonial Audit, set up in 1814. The ensuing instructions, first issued in 1816, were a co-operative

[1] The reductions of 1815 are deduced from *The Imperial Calendar*. Hay dated the classification of clerks from Jan. 1824: *Hist. Studies, Australia and N.Z.*, II, 147. The memorial upon which the Order in Council of 28 March 1822 (P.C. 2/204, ff. 88–92, 103) was grounded had pointed out that classification could not be effected at once. See also Order in Council of 31 Jan. 1824 (retirement of clerks): P.C. 2/205, ff. 288–9; 5 July 1825 (appointment of P.U.S.): P.C. 2/206, ff. 270–1.

effort, as were the parallel regulations of 1820 requiring Governors to draw up annual estimates on which colonial budgets could be based. Indeed the latter instructions, contrary to the original intention, were actually drafted in the Colonial Office and issued in the Secretary of State's name.

Financial reform was thus effected by a system of dyarchy, the Colonial Office taking political responsibility and the Treasury operating the controls in detail. Though it was ultimately to prove noxious, the system probably suited the primitive conditions of the time. Effective control could hardly have been exercised by the diminutive Colonial Office, devoid of any financial experience. Where, however, there seemed no advantage in a division of responsibility the Colonial Office proved no friend of dyarchy. The Board of Trade, which had been revived in 1786 as the Government's main colonial adviser, was not allowed to maintain that position but was forced to restrict itself to advice upon commercial relations with the colonies. Though it long continued the formal scrutiny of colonial laws, it did so with decreasing regard to their political content. It was the Counsel of the Colonial Office who was now the effective scrutineer.

The concentration of colonial business into the Secretary of State's hands was hampered by the rival claims of ministers to colonial appointments. During the eighteenth century colonial offices had been a valuable and much abused source of Government patronage, and inter-departmental disputes about the right of nomination consumed the time of ministers and generated ill-feeling between them. Bathurst united with Henry Goulburn to reform the misapplication of the patronage of his own Office; but the rights of ministers other than the Colonial Secretary could not be easily restricted and their continued exercise long remained a source of imperial weakness.

Such were some of the domestic counterparts of a crop of administrative improvements in the colonies adorning the latter years of Bathurst's rule. When that minister resigned in 1827, after a longer term than any other Colonial Secretary has enjoyed, he could look back upon his years of office with some satisfaction. The Office had taken root; it had a recognised function in the scheme of government; it had a name;[1] the importance of its work was recognised by the improved quality of its novitiate. Bathurst, however, is not a hero. The revival of interest in colonial affairs which dates from 1812 is associated rather with Goulburn than with his chief, while Wilmot Horton, Goulburn's successor, was the main influence in remoulding the Office machinery. Though Bathurst's geniality, good nature and considerateness were remembered by his officials, his

[1] Cornewall Lewis said that it had been called "the Colonial Department" since 1815: *Hist. Studies Australia and N.Z.*, 1, 178. *The Imperial Calendar* for 1817 calls it "Secretary of State's Office, Colony and War Department", for 1818 "Secretary of State's Office, Colonial Department". The *Calendar* for 1819 adds "for conducting all matters relative to the Colonies".

talents were mediocre, his industry and enthusiasm fitful, and his policy unimaginative. He reformed his department, or allowed it to be reformed, less out of conviction than in response to the clamours of a noisy if enlightened "pressure-group", whose conscience was troubled by the fetters of the slave.

II

The second period in the history of the Office extends from the first appointment of a permanent Under-Secretary in 1825 to the creation of a fourth Secretaryship of State in 1854. In it the standing of the Colonial Secretaryship remained relatively low. Prime Ministers at this time seldom took interest in colonial questions. Even Peel and Russell were not exceptional in this, though they set a higher value on the post than did their predecessors. Peel urged Stanley to prefer it to the Home Secretaryship and extolled colonial business when making Gladstone Colonial Under-Secretary.[1] Russell, by appointing Lord Grey, showed the value he placed upon enterprise and *expertise*. Other Prime Ministers, however, filled the office with second-rate politicians or whisked away good ones after terms of short duration.

The status of a political office is apt to be measured by the estimate formed of it in Parliament, and the parliamentary business of the Colonial Office was then comparatively light. Goderich told Huskisson in the 'twenties that "the House of Commons detail business" was not such as would demand a "perpetual sitting up all night upon detail points".[2] In the early 'forties Stanley declared that colonial affairs seldom came on, and, when they did, were discussed before a bored and ignorant audience.[3] Stephen remarked upon the domestic predilections of M.P.'s. It is indeed the case that Select Committees upon colonial questions were sometimes convened.[4] This, however, but serves to illustrate the fitful and fractious interest that the House of Commons displayed in colonial affairs. These were only debated in a critical spirit and the Colonial Secretary was not encouraged to explain his policy as a whole.

Though Parliamentary business may have been light, administrative business was increasingly burdensome. Labouchere, who was Parliamentary Under-Secretary from 1835 to 1839, described his work as "very severe" throughout the year and actually found that he had less to do in 1850 as President of the Board of Trade. Lord Grey noticed that work had increased since his days as Under-Secretary.[5] "You judged well in your choice of an office," said Lady Holland to

---

[1] Peel's words to Gladstone will be found in Brit. Mus. Add. MS. 44819, ff. 9–10.
[2] Melville (ed.), *Huskisson Papers*, pp. 225–6.
[3] Parker, C. S., *Sir Robert Peel...*, III, 155.
[4] Grey was too busy to attend them himself: *Parl. Pap.* 1850, xv (611), Q. 1468.
[5] *Ibid.* Q. 785 (Labouchere), Q. 1459 (Grey).

Russell in 1840, "unless it half kills you from fatigue."[1] Thus the Colonial Secretaryship was an unattractive office, full of labour and difficulty and unrewarded by parliamentary triumphs.

An ample and efficient staff and well-designed methods of business will sometimes palliate the consequences of indifferent ministers. The Colonial Office at this time lacked these advantages. The establishment, as settled by the Order in Council of August 1825, consisted, besides its parliamentary chiefs, of a Permanent Under-Secretary, a Chief Clerk, seventeen clerks divided into four classes, the Counsel, a Librarian and his assistant, a Registrar and his assistant, a private secretary to the Secretary of State, a Précis Writer, two officekeepers, two porters and a housekeeper. This is a total of thirty-one. At the beginning of 1833 the number of permanent officials actually in post (excluding the Counsel and officekeepers and the like) was twenty-five. In 1849 it was twenty-three. Thus Grey was broadly justified in stating in 1850 that the staff was then "very nearly about the same" as in 1830.[2] These figures do not, however, take into account those clerks who were not upon the establishment. Shortage of staff was partly met during this period by recruiting "supernumerary" clerks. These officers, condemned to extinction in 1846 but reprieved, were in 1850 welded into the establishment in the humble capacity of copyists, so that by 1853 the total number of "superior" officers and clerks of every kind had reached forty-six. The staff was also covertly expanded by another device. In 1840 the Land Board (to be described later) was established as a sub-department, and to it was diverted much detailed work that would otherwise have fallen to the department itself.

It would be tedious to follow the numerous small changes that occurred—not always in an upward direction—in the strength and remuneration of the staff during this period. One feature, however, must be noted: the efforts made, ultimately with success, to increase the number of officials at the top. The fewness of these officials was a leading defect in the structure of the Office and was responsible for depriving the hierarchy of the necessary leisure for planning. Taylor would have welcomed six Permanent Under-Secretaries. Nothing on this scale was of course achieved, but in 1834 an Assistant Under-Secretaryship was created for the first time. This was done for the express benefit of Stephen, who thus realised an ambition that he had cherished since 1827. The title, however, was purely honorific and lapsed when Stephen replaced Hay as Permanent Under-Secretary in 1836. The post was not revived until 1846 when Stephen was on the point of collapse and retirement.[3] The main function of the

---

[1] Walpole, S., *Life of...Russell*, 1, 338.
[2] *Parl. Pap.* 1850, xv (611), Q. 1461.
[3] A second Assistant Under-Secretaryship was created in 1847 to tide things over during Stephen's enforced absence; but it did not survive his final departure: *Parl. Pap.* 1847–8, XLII (42).

occupant of this post was to be the revision of colonial legislation which had fallen previously upon the Permanent Under-Secretary himself. In order to win Treasury consent it was combined with a post at the Land Board. From 1840 the number of higher officials was further augmented by reviving the offices of Chief Clerk and Précis Writer, both of which had been abolished in 1833.

It is characteristic of Stephen that, though he frequently complained of the insufficiency of his subordinates, no radical alteration of the establishment was proposed in his time. Such an alteration was put forward to the Treasury shortly after his departure, but was overtaken by events of wider import. The Budget of 1848 precipitated an economy campaign, one consequence of which was the reform of the public service. After a Select Committee had considered the general state of administration, local enquiries into the conduct of each Office were set on foot, under the able superintendence of (Sir) Charles Trevelyan and (Sir) Stafford Northcote. These enquiries are best known because they generated the idea of a unified and graded civil service recruited by examination. The adoption of their reports, however, marks a turning-point in the history of each individual department they surveyed.

The Colonial Office was tackled early. Trevelyan himself, Gibson Craig and Herman Merivale (Stephen's successor) conducted the inquiry. Appointed on 21 November 1848, they reported on 15 December 1849. They found the permanent staff to consist of an Under-Secretary, an Assistant Under-Secretary, a Précis Writer, twenty-three clerks in four classes, two Librarians and a Registrar. They proposed to retain the first three top posts; to create "as a permanent prospective arrangement" a single class of clerks to be employed in helping the higher ranks in the execution of "intellectual duties"; and below them to form a class of copyists, into which "supernumeraries" would be amalgamated, to perform "mechanical" work under a Superintendent of Copyists.[1] The essence of this programme was gradation of work and a twofold grouping of the clerks who performed it. It was in no way peculiar to the Colonial Office, but harmonised with principles already adopted in the Treasury and gradually extended throughout the public service. It was approved by the Colonial Secretary with but little alteration, and put into effect by Treasury minute of 3 May 1850.

Before 1855 the public departments were (with rare exceptions) recruited by patronage. In this the Colonial Office was no different from the majority except that it secured better men on the whole. The normal method of entry was by probationary clerkship. The two junior probationers originally received no salary, but this had been altered by 1848. The probationary period was supposed to last one year only, but probationers were not admitted into the class of

[1] Stephen had urged gradation in 1832: C.O. 537/22. Minute of 30 March.

assistant junior clerks until a vacancy occurred and meanwhile could enjoy no increments. Grey disliked this system of waiting very much and it ceased no doubt in 1850 when "supernumeraries" were amalgamated into the establishment. The fusion, however, did not wholly dispense with probation, which lasted until 1855; though in the eight preceding years no clerk failed to survive the ordeal.

It was one of the worst features of the unreformed civil service that men were admitted very young and at exiguous salaries into departments where they rose very slowly and rarely to the top. It was partly because the opportunities offered to a clerk to improve his prospects were so limited that promotion was so largely effected by a rigid seniority. In the case of the Colonial Office the Order in Council of 1822 had laid it down that vacancies in clerkships could only be filled from the class immediately below. When in October 1839 this limitation was removed, an agitation amongst the clerks prejudicially affected seems nearly to have resulted in a restoration of the *status quo*. Such incidents must have made ministers cautious about varying the routine of promotion. The Commissioners of 1848 said that it had been found very difficult to apply the alternative criterion of merit even when filling up the first-class clerkships, and that in the case of the other classes appointment by seniority had become habitual. There had been exceptions, and Grey had made it a rule to require the Permanent Under-Secretary to report what member of the class below that in which the vacancy had occurred was the most deserving. Indeed, Grey went so far as to declare that he would make seniority "absolutely subordinate to superior aptitude".[1] At the same time, however, it was plain that he was unwilling to frustrate reasonable expectations and, since the duties of the junior clerks were largely mechanical, a merit test was not easy to apply.

Though Grey wished to encourage efficient clerks, he was not prepared to guarantee their succession to the highest posts. As a matter of principle he welcomed outside experience. In particular he was convinced that the Permanent and Assistant Under-Secretaries must be lawyers. Since lawyers were not normally to be had from among the clerks, the only way to fill these posts was to bring in men, and quite young ones, from private practice at the bar. He imported new blood in other ways. (Sir) T. W. Clinton Murdoch, who left for the Land Board in 1847, was replaced by W. Strachey, a "very distinguised" servant of the East India Company who had recently been engaged upon an inquiry in Ceylon. Thus the Office acquired some valuable experience of the Indian sub-continent, though at the expense of disappointing the hopes of men bred up in Downing Street. It was one of the aims of the reforming Commissioners to obviate disappointments like these by staffing departments with men of such quality that they could rise to positions of the highest trust.

[1] *Parl. Pap.* 1847–8, xviii (543), 2, Q. 6866–8.

From at least 1825 the Office was divided into a general and four geographical departments—the North American, the West Indian, the Eastern, and the African and Mediterranean. Thus was established that system of grouping by territorial propinquity which, though greatly modified, has endured in the Colonial Office, though not in the Commonwealth Relations Office, to this day. Colonies of varying constitution and racial origin were handled together and there was little machinery for dealing with special subjects. In 1843, on a reorganisation, a fifth geographical department, the Miscellaneous, was proposed and perhaps for a short time added. At the same time some attempt seems to have been made to place the general department under the Chief Clerk, whose office, an ancient one, had been revived in 1840. The structure of 1843 (Chief Clerk's department, four or five geographical divisions, the library and the registry) cannot have endured, for six years later there were but five departments in all, four of them geographical. In 1849, however, the general department was still in the charge of the Chief Clerk, who dealt with general and establishment questions, accounting, the drafting of formal instruments, and what remained of the military business of the Secretary of State for War. He also supervised the Office papers, the statistical returns and the library. Each of the geographical departments was from 1840 under a senior clerk, and under him was normally a clerk of each class until in 1850 the four classes were fused into two.

The official relations between the Secretary of State and his Under-Secretaries, and between the Under-Secretaries themselves, had as yet by no means reached their modern form. At the outset the Parliamentary and Permanent Under-Secretaries were of co-ordinate authority and divided the Empire between them on geographical lines. To the end Hay had little to do with the West Indies, while Stephen at times was prepared to leave matters to his Parliamentary colleague, confessing his incapacity or unwillingness to advise. This distribution of work was partly due to shortage of staff, which prevented the Permanent Under-Secretary, through sheer weight of business, from seeing every paper on its way to the Secretary of State. The creation of an Assistant Under-Secretary in 1834 was intended to remedy this acknowledged defect, but, as has been seen, the post did not last. When it was revived in 1847 Stephen was broken and on the eve of departure. But his successors profited. Grey gave orders that business was henceforth to be divided between the two most senior officials. A block of lesser subjects was assigned to the Assistant Under-Secretary, who was to minute upon them direct to the Parliamentary Under-Secretary. This gave the Permanent Under-Secretary his chance to deal with every great one. Moreover, all drafts were to pass through the Permanent Under-Secretary. The division between the two officials may not have lasted long, though, to judge from a memorandum drawn up by Carnarvon in 1858, something very like the modern relationship between the Permanent and Parliamentary Under-Secretaries had by then been established.

Stephen's relations with successive Secretaries of State varied with the personalities concerned. Lord Glenelg and Lord Normandy were under his close supervision. Stanley kept much business from him. This was indeed partly due to mutual dislike and ended when Stanley left. But however close the harmony, Stephen was not the man to claim as of right the position of universal adviser. This is partly attributable to his modesty, which sometimes even reflected itself in deference to his juniors, but still more to the temper of the times. The idea that even very senior officials were no more than clerks to their ministers died hard. It was accepted doctrine in the 'twenties that ministers should draft their own dispatches. Palmerston did so till the end. He disliked Permanent Under-Secretaries, and so did Peel and Graham. This attitude helps to explain the attacks which Charles Buller and others launched on Stephen. The antagonists not only disliked his personality and believed his influence to be baneful; they thought his powers unconstitutional. Nor were such views confined to politicians. They were shared, for example, by Taylor. In an outburst to Lord Howick (later Lord Grey) in 1833 he complained that he had been employed "not in the business of a clerk, but in that of a statesman". To him it was no matter for self-congratulation that "in ninety-nine cases out of a hundred the consideration which has been given to a subject by the Secretary of State" had "consisted in reading the draft submitted to him", and that the minister's decision had "consisted in adopting it".[1] In consequence of this doctrine most papers rose to ministerial level, though by the end of the period the Secretary of State expected that all "ordinary business" would reach him in such a form that he could dispose of it by adding his initials. This resulted in congestion amongst the highest officials and boredom among their juniors.

Nor were these disadvantages offset by the method of acting on papers. Originally many papers were first examined by the Permanent Under-Secretary himself, who doled them out or worked upon them according to the degree of difficulty. Stephen effected some improvement by elaborating the system of minuting and by demanding précis of long papers. By 1849 it was the usual thing for papers to go first to the heads of departments. They rose, however, from that level with nothing on them but proposals for action, and then had to return to the same or a lower level for drafts to be prepared. The papers then rose again with the drafts. This was not expeditious, and in Grey's time it had become necessary to maintain fortnightly lists of arrears. Yet it remained the system in the Office for close on a century.

---

[1] *Autobiography*, I, 139–40. For Palmerston's attitude to Permanent Under-Secretaries see *Queen Victoria's Letters*, 1st ser. (1908 ed.), I, 106; for Peel's see B.M. Add. MS. 44819, f. 105; for Graham's see *Parl. Pap.* 1850, xv (1850), Q. 2880.

Stephen's achievement in perfecting this part of the Office machinery has been exaggerated. It may have been wise in his own interests to stop the semi-official correspondence that had previously been maintained between Governors and Under-Secretaries. The fuller and more careful minutes that begin about 1836 were certainly an aid to clear thought, and were perhaps indispensable when ministers spent much time in their country houses. Short minutes, semi-official letters and abundant devolution are all, however, aids to swift action and by enforcing a more formal system Stephen decelerated the machine and so brought some discredit upon his department.[1]

In other ways, too, he showed himself less conscious of the needs of administration than one might have expected of so great a man. Throughout his time there was no central registry. A Registrar with an assistant had been appointed in 1825, but did not survive after 1833. For fifteen years thereafter registration was divided between various functionaries. This arrangement was described in 1835 as "replete with inconvenience",[2] but, despite several abortive attempts, was not finally amended until 1849–50. The library was also neglected. Since at least 1839 the Librarian's chief duty had been the custody and indexing of old Office papers. From about 1832 he had also had to prepare the growing volume of parliamentary returns, a duty which was later devolved upon a Clerk of the Parliamentary Papers. The existence of these miscellaneous functions militated against the accumulation of books, though numerous maps, "serving in place of pictures when drawn down", hung in rollers upon the Office walls.[3] No less valuable than the maps were reports and statistical tables. These had originated in 1822, when there begins the long series of "Blue Books" purporting to give for each colony "a species of comprehensive budget". Badly compiled as they were at first, their quality slowly improved. From at least 1837 each Governor was also required to send home a report "exhibiting generally the past and present state of the Colony and its prospects in every political branch".[4] Finally, under comprehensive regulations first issued in 1837, Governors were instructed to forward legislative Acts and proceedings, official lists, gazettes and useful books and pamphlets.

In Stephen's oft-quoted opinion (voiced in 1853) most of the men in the department in his time "possessed only in a low degree, and some of them in a degree almost incredibly low, either the talents or the habits of men of business, or the zeal or the knowledge required for the effective performance of their appropriate functions". He

---

[1] Hall (*Colonial Office*, p. 19) dates the system of full minuting from 1836, the year of Stephen's assumption of the Permanent Under-Secretaryship. This is over-precise. Minutes of a kind will be found several years earlier.
[2] C.O. 537/22. Stephen to P. Smith, 21 Sept.
[3] Merivale, H. C., *Bar, Stage and Platform*, p. 2.
[4] Cf. *C.H.B.E.* II, 301 footnote.

went on to divide the staff into three classes: a small one at the top of which he would speak only in terms of the highest praise; an intermediate one of "meritorious Public Servants"; and the most numerous third class of whose "official characters" he was reluctant to speak at all.[1] Stephen's standards must always have been exacting and his impressions may have been dimmed after six years of Cambridge society. What little we yet know of the performances of the clerks at this time does not quite bear the judgment out, though of course only the more capable have left a mark. Thus good opinions have been formed of Gordon Gairdner, a clerk in the Australian department in the 'thirties, and of E. T. Harrison, a member of the West Indian department. Of greater distinction were Murdoch—"one of the very best men", to quote Taylor[2]—and (Sir) T. Frederick Elliot. Their abilities have impressed modern students of their minutes no less than their contemporaries. Both served for a period in Canada. Elliot was but a stripling when he entered the Office and so belied Stephen's opinion that good men only came in at a mature age. James Spedding and (Cardinal) H. E. Manning, however, figures of equal or greater brilliance, were lost after a few years' stay.

For half a century (Sir) Henry Taylor claimed, if he did not always occupy, a seat in the West Indian department. He was a man of unusual talents and varied tastes, who by judiciously exercising the former rose quickly to a point where he could, spasmodically at least, comfortably indulge the latter. His ambition was small. He rejected two Governorships, the succession to Stephen, and other offers. His interest in current events was restricted. He did not seek to widen his departmental experience, nor did he take kindly to any form of official drudgery. Yet he had many gifts that are looked for in good officials: a genuine interest in the higher forms of administration; a reflective yet practical mind; a judgment sound and temperate. Though he was less religious than Stephen, his principles were elevated. His desire to improve the Negro's lot was strong, and he was prepared to force his views, not always with becoming modesty or always with success, upon unwilling or pusillanimous ministers.

His zeal was based upon an *expertise* then rare in public servants. On first entering he saw that there was a big job to be done and few to do it. He worked with energy, amassed great knowledge and early gained a wide repute outside his own department. But once the battle for emancipation was won his interest appears to have flagged. A dispute about his pay in 1833 led him to vow that thenceforth he would sacrifice less of his leisure to the public. He was unfaithful to this resolve, his conscience leading him to resume heavy burdens in times of stress. But, such crises past, he would relapse into the good

---

[1] Quoted in *Hist. Studies Australia and N.Z.* II, 144–5.
[2] *Autobiography*, I, 239.

life of cultured ease—writing plays and verses, corresponding with the Lake poets or travelling abroad.

Of R. W. Hay, first Permanent Under-Secretary in the Office, not much is known. He had been a private secretary in the Admiralty. In the Colonial Office he specialised in the African and Mediterranean dependencies. He was a Conservative, said Taylor, who lived much with Conservative politicians. Taylor disliked him and gave him the worst possible character that a higher civil servant can earn: the inclination to rush at a decision, "which was right or wrong as might happen".[1] In 1836 Glenelg, apparently with reluctance, replaced him by Stephen.

The frequent attacks made upon Stephen by his contemporaries have led historians to examine his contribution to colonial policy with care. In consequence we have a picture of the man more detailed than that of any of his successors. It is very favourable to the sitter. Of the imputations of despotism, dilatoriness, disloyalty to Governors, lack of sympathy with colonial ambitions and a tendency to subordinate national interests to the caprices of the missionaries, he has been successfully cleared. He is shown, on the contrary, to have been a man of liberal and humane sentiments; incorruptible; reluctant to weaken the prestige of Governors; the protector of the colonies in inter-departmental strife at home. Above all he will be remembered as the architect of West Indian emancipation and the originator of *laissez-faire* in dealing with colonial Governments. In both these respects he founded traditions which are still at work in the Colonial and Commonwealth Relations Offices—that the welfare of native peoples is paramount and that the autonomy of Commonwealth countries is to be continuously championed. His extreme reluctance to veto colonial legislation, at a time when it would have still been politically practicable to do so, is the strongest testimony to the reality of his conviction that the second of these principles was sound. Perhaps too we may detect in him the originator of another tradition: a tendency to avoid all forms of political dogmatism. Yet Stephen had his own philosophy. Looking ahead he foresaw, without regret, the time when the colonies of settlement would become our partners. This being so, he held it best to allow them to work out their own salvation. Thus he would not dwell upon their shortcomings, but preferred that they should learn wisdom by experience.

To Stephen's keen mind and immense industry there are many tributes. Taylor thought him "one of the largest intellects of his day and generation".[2] He would sit over his papers when others had long discarded thoughts of business, thereby depriving himself of the services of a private secretary, since there was no colleague "who did not shrink from the severe duty of remaining with me every day of the year until $\frac{1}{2}$ past 6 o'clock, or 7 in the evening".[3] Unfortunately,

---

[1] *Ibid.* I, 118.   [2] *Ibid.* II, 300.   [3] Office Minutes, 1836–59, no. 11.

however, these sterling qualities were not balanced by the gift for making personal contacts, and the external relations of the Office suffered in consequence. His asceticism was perhaps the main irritant to some; his almost morbid shyness (which took the not uncommon form of excessive loquacity) to others. The range of his sympathies was limited both by his intellectuality and his Puritanism. He was apt to attribute to men of high virtue but indifferent understanding an importance which they did not possess. He could not understand rabid forms of enthusiasm, and where, as in Gibbon Wakefield's case, he thought that a zealot also lacked good faith, he hardened his heart and chose to make him his enemy. In this case perhaps some small measure of compromise would have been the lesser evil even by the most exacting moral standard. The head of a great Office should be *persona grata* with what has been called its "special public",[1] and by that test Stephen must be accounted a failure.

Another of Stephen's virtues was carried to excess; he engrossed too much work. "I almost think", said Taylor "he preferred...not to be much helped."[2] In consequence improvement in the quality of clerks and a better distribution of their functions were delayed, while the Permanent Under-Secretary continued to overload his own shoulders until they gave way. His interest probably lay more in policy itself than in the machinery for putting it into effect.

What were the administrative gifts of the ministers who flitted in and out of Downing Street in these thirty years? Huskisson's short but promising reign (August 1827–May 1828) was followed by that of Sir George Murray. Hay thought Murray's intellect meagre and believed him to be incapable of using his subordinates profitably. In fact he declared that he had never known "any public officer so totally inefficient".[3] Ellenborough's first impressions, however, were quite different. Other ministers had notable faults of temper. Stanley's flashy intellect rendered him particularly ill-suited to an office pre-eminently requiring patience and cool judgment. He was notable for alienating his officials, invoking their opinions sparingly and flaunting his preference for outside advice. Although this aloofness was partly due to differences purely political, it is hard to condone it.[4] Thomas Spring Rice (later Lord Monteagle), who deferred to Taylor, restored relations. The timid but conscientious Glenelg has commonly been held up as the classic case of a Colonial Secretary who was dominated by his officials; Stephen, said Taylor, "virtually ruled the Colonial Empire" during his term of office. Recent research, however, suggests that this is an exaggeration and that in his dealings

[1] Dale, H. E., *Higher Civil Service*, p. 181.
[2] *Autobiography*, I, 233. [3] Greville, *Journal*, II, 11.
[4] Taylor told Gladstone that he thought Stanley "surrounded by parasites and flatterers and that whenever he came into contact with a man that could cope with him at all in point of talent, he got rid of him": B.M. Add. MSS. 44819, ff. 14–15.

with Stephen Glenelg often displayed the stubbornness of the weak.[1] Normanby is also credited with having "resigned himself into the hands of King Stephen".[2] Russell must have provided a contrast, but one of which the officials nevertheless wholly approved. In a short term he won a high reputation. Taylor liked his "way of doing business".[3] Stephen found him an "admirable" chief, of most statesmanlike qualities; Charles Greville said that "all his subordinates admit that colonial affairs were never so well administered".[4] Though not the best administrator, Lord Grey was perhaps the most enterprising of all the ministers in his period—hard-working, public-spirited, with an independent if sometimes rather ill-guided judgment. He was agreeably solicitous of the well-being of Governors and other colonial officials and he had a knowledge of colonial affairs, partly gained as Parliamentary Under-Secretary, with which few Secretaries of State of any generation could have competed. The views he expressed before two Select Committees about office management are often sound, and were delivered with a conviction suggesting they were largely his own.

Thrice during this period proposals were made to bring outside experience to the aid of the small and not wholly efficient group of public servants in Whitehall. Only one of these came to anything. In April 1848 Grey successfully proposed, on Stephen's initiative, that the Board of Trade's consultative functions in colonial questions should be revived. Stephen and Sir Edward Ryan (a Railway Commissioner) were sworn of the Privy Council for the purpose and were to attend meetings of a new Committee for Trade and Plantations with the President of the Board and the Colonial Secretary. Questions of high policy were to be debated by this assembly, interested persons were to have the right to appear before it, and its decisions were to be embodied in Orders in Council. The Committee met to deliberate upon Australian constitutional problems in 1849 and issued a report which formed the basis of the Australian Government Act of 1850. But it was used sparingly thereafter and soon fell out of use entirely.

The sub-department called the Land and Emigration Board was to prove a more useful piece of machinery. Set up in 1840 upon the amalgamation of two earlier Commissions, the Board consisted at first of three salaried Commissioners. In 1841 one of these was replaced by the Secretary of the Board of Trade, who served in this capacity without pay. He was in turn superseded in 1846 by (Sir) Frederic Rogers, who at first combined the office with an Assistant Under-Secretaryship in the Colonial Office, but he transferred to the

[1] Taylor, *Autobiography*, I, 233.
[2] New, *Lord Durham*, p. 558. The words are Wakefield's.
[3] *Autobiography*, I, 265.
[4] Walpole, *Life of Russell*, I, 338, quoting Greville's *Journal*.

Board completely next year. In the Board's premises in Park Street a proportion of the Colonial Office migration correspondence was disposed of. Here too some high officials, later to move to Downing Street, were nurtured. In 1846 the Board acquired as a special function the task of examining non-commercial colonial legislation. This heavy labour was mainly carried out by the two junior Commissioners, both lawyers. It is curious that the Office should have preferred to entrust this important duty to an ancillary department, but Grey was averse to unification, though the Commissioners of 1848 proposed it.[1]

The legal business of the Office was distributed in other ways. After 1848 the practice began of sending Colonial Office Bills to be drafted by the Counsel to the Home Office.[2] Furthermore, all Acts sent home by colonies with representative legislatures still had to be formally reported upon by the Board of Trade, who advised the Queen in Council whether they should be confirmed by Order. The Board's formal responsibility was universal, but in practice only commercial Acts (which eluded the Land Board) were considered. Such measures were numerous, and work fell behind. To cope with the pressure the Board appointed (Sir) Stafford Northcote as legal assistant in 1841, but apparently without immediate effect. Nor was the Board of Trade the sole referee. Many commercial Acts affected the Treasury as well, and had to be examined by the two departments successively—a delaying factor which the disharmony that sometimes prevailed between the two Boards accentuated.

All commentators on colonial affairs in the nineteenth century have drawn dismayed attention to the deplorable relations that then existed between the Colonial Office and the Treasury. Full responsibility for colonial expenditure was first assumed by the Treasury in 1831, when (in Stephen's words) the practice formerly prevailing of frequently appropriating public money in the colonies "by a mere Order from the Secretary of State" was terminated and it was agreed that the Treasury should always be consulted. It was realised that this would involve more correspondence, and measures were contrived to avoid the delays that were expected to ensue. By 1840, however, these measures had lapsed in part and grave delays were occurring. The Colonial Office tried in that year and in 1842 to remedy the defects and was constantly sending in long lists of arrears; but with little effect.[3]

The Treasury records have never been examined to establish the causes of these delays; until this has been done it is unjust to conclude,

---

[1] The history of the Board will be found in Hitchens, F. H., *Colonial Land and Emigration Commissioners* (Philadelphia, 1931).

[2] *Parl. Pap.* 1847–8, xviii (543), QQ. 2927–61, 4133–61.

[3] For the arrangements of 1831 see C.O. 168/15, ff. 269, 298 and C.O. 323/213 from Treasury, 29 July. For the position in 1842 see C.O. 323/226 (minutes at end of Treasury sub-section). The Colonial Audit Board sat last on 5 April 1832: A.O. 6/140, f. 784.

as has commonly been done, that the Treasury were invariably to blame. The public service was then too small and too poorly staffed to handle all its commitments, of which the largest share fell to the Treasury. Moreover, the Colonial Office failed to work out an effective system of departmental liaison. Thus in 1843 a complex correspondence arose over some New Brunswick customs regulations. Stephen complained that the authorities involved were "all writing to each other on the subject", while "no one hand grasps and weaves together all the scattered threads of this intricate series of letters".[1] It might have been expected that Stephen would have done the grasping and weaving; as indeed he could have done by the simple expedient of oral discussion.

In this generation the grip of other departments of State upon colonial administration began slowly to slacken, while the Colonial Office gathered the reins of government into its own hands or surrendered them to the colonies. The departments, however, were tenacious of their patronage. Appeals to the Treasury and Post Office to renounce colonial appointments went unheeded. It was only when, in 1847, the mother country ceased to levy import duties in British North America that customs appointments were perforce abandoned there; and though the Post Office seems to have lost much patronage in or about 1850, it continued to exercise it in the West Indies until 1860. This is the more to be regretted since in the matter of patronage the Colonial Office itself set a good example to others. In 1844 it made a substantial renunciation and thenceforth a growing number of vacancies in the lesser offices was filled on the advice of Governors and by colonists.

The old system of colonial agencies passed away in this period. In the early 'twenties there were separate agents in London both for Canada and the West Indies and for the "new" colonies. Normally natives of the British Isles, they often held public and even political office as well as their agencies. Some were Colonial Office clerks. The business they did was commercial and financial, and in doing it they were obliged to conform to the Secretary of State's direction.[2] They were apt to be unprofitable servants and demands for better qualified officers grew, until in 1833 nine separate agencies were consolidated as the "Joint Agents for the Crown Colonies" under two Colonial Office officials. The West Indian colonies retained their separate agents for a while, though as such colonies receded from responsible government they were forced to use the new body. Other colonies, on the forward constitutional path, contracted out as soon as they secured responsible government.

In the generation now under review more care was taken in choosing Governors, and those chosen were better supported. The

---

[1] *Journ. Mod. Hist.* I, 48 and *Canadian Hist. Rev.* v, 38–40.
[2] There were also popular agents, e.g. Roebuck for the French Canadian Assembly.

Colonial Administrative Service, as we now call it, was too primitive to provide many candidates, though three Governors in post in 1850 have been reckoned "professionals".[1] The Indian Civil Service, Parliament, and above all the Army, made their contributions. Politicians were still sometimes chosen to reward them for their services to the government in power or because their views on colonial policy were known to coincide with those of the Secretary of State. On the other hand, Lord Grey sent (Sir) Henry Barkly (a member of the Opposition) to British Guiana on account of his presumed acceptability to local opinion. In the late 'forties some advance was made towards separating the civil from the military command in those colonies that were virtually garrisions—Gibraltar, Malta, the Ionian Islands and Mauritius. Fox Maule (later Lord Panmure) thought that the Colonial Office would be more likely to trust Governors if it were free to select them. He held that the steps that had been taken had been beneficial.[2]

In form all appointments were made by the Secretary of State. The choice of a Governor, however, was and is an act of high policy into which the whole Government, or at least the Prime Minister, needs must enter; Peel and Russell said that the Colonial Secretary was bound to consult the Prime Minister before selecting a Governor. Our concern here is rather with the treatment of the Governor once he had been appointed. One of the most important functions of the Colonial Office is to ensure that a new Governor goes out fully "briefed" upon the colony in which he is to serve. We do not know how effectively this was done. When Lord Belmore went to Jamaica in 1828 he complained to Greville that he had received no instructions, other than formal ones, and had not had a chance to speak to anyone in authority about conditions in the colony nor upon Government policy in relation to them.[3] It is pleasant to contrast with this the picture of a dinner party at Greville's house in 1839. C. E. Poulett Thompson (later Lord Sydenham and Toronto) was on the point of departure for Canada. Stephen and Taylor were also present as guests. "We talked", said Henry Reeve, "of Canada and other Colonies with all our might."[4] Once in post Governors were supported, and, as better men were chosen and appointments grew less political, recalls became rarer. In this respect Stanley and Grey have a good record, though with the advance of self-government it became politically easier for the Colonial Office to acquiesce in acts of the Governor, which, though to some extent at variance with imperial policy, conformed to the wishes of local legislatures. Good men were left increasingly free to follow their own courses and Stephen was averse from any heavy-handed treatment. The Office

---

[1] Hall, *Colonial Office*, p. 89.
[2] *Parl. Pap.* 1850, x (662), QQ. 1411–4.
[3] Greville, *Journal*, I, 227.
[4] *Memoirs of...Henry Reeve*, I, 91–2.

was perhaps less careful to see that its own acts were agreeable to Governors, but to seek concurrence was hard in days before the telegraph.

III

In the history of the Colonial Office a third phase begins with the creation of a fourth Secretaryship of State and the removal of all military business from the Colonial Secretary's hands. The appointment of a fourth Secretary had been an ambition of Russell's during his premiership. Though the matter was dropped, the outbreak of the Crimean War forced its revival and very naturally it fell to Russell to take the lead. In a Cabinet paper circulated in May 1854 he argued successfully that the present was not the time "for heaping upon one man the conduct of an arduous war in addition to an office which in itself is one of the most laborious in the service of the State."[1] The Queen's scruples were overridden. Newcastle, the then Secretary of State, was given his choice between War and the Colonies and took the former as "the harder task".[2] The Colonial Office machine was little affected by the change. The military work had been largely formal, and the higher officials had not been troubled with it. But for ministers it must always have been something of a burden. Grey at least was convinced that the union of the two functions was an unhappy one and that the colonial business was so heavy that it was impossible to superintend the land forces as well.

The Colonial Secretaryship still did not rank very high. Though men of natural ability like Edward (later Lord) Cardwell and Lord Granville, or of experience like Lord Stanley and Lord Carnarvon, were occasionally chosen, they were not left with the seals for long. Sir William Molesworth, an acknowledged expert, died after a few months' service (1855). Newcastle stayed five years—a longer spell than any of his predecessors except Bathurst—but was of lowly stature. On the other hand, the office was not unpopular, and W. E. Forster, who became Under-Secretary without having made any previous study of colonial questions, found the work "intensely interesting".[3]

The strength and character of the establishment changed little in this period. One Permanent and one Assistant Under-Secretary and the Précis Writer constituted, as before, the official hierarchy. To them a Legal Adviser was added in 1866 to deal with the revision of colonial laws. Rogers had brought this work with him from the Land Board, and by so doing had modified the functions of that body. Below these four were the established clerks, nineteen of them in 1844 and twenty-two in 1860. In the financial year 1866–7 they had

[1] Walpole, *Life of Russell*, ii, 218; Gooch, *Later Correspondence of...Russell*, ii, 165. The fourth Secretary had originally been intended to deal with Ireland.
[2] Martineau, *Life of...Newcastle*, p. 132.
[3] Reid, *Life of...Forster*, i, 391.

risen to twenty-six and were divided once again into four classes, with a Chief Clerk and a Clerk for the Parliamentary Papers. Extra temporary clerks were occasionally engaged, but their employment was not favoured. Below the clerks were the copyists, paid at piece-rates and fluctuating in numbers with the pressure of business.

Since December 1855 clerks had been recruited by limited competition. The Secretary of State kept a list of candidates, the first six of whom were notified upon a vacancy. This was believed to be a larger number of candidates than competed in other Offices. An examination, which included papers on "Colonial law and constitution", was conducted in two stages, of which the first was a preliminary "knock-out". This system of limited competition was peculiar to the Colonial Office and was probably Merivale's invention. After a five years' trial he held that it had proved its worth. The Office, he thought, was more secure than it had been before from the introduction of men "of any great incapacity".[1] Nor had his earlier fears that such a system might attract clerks without the needful moral qualities been justified. It is instructive to compare this cautious judgment with that of (Sir) William Baillie Hamilton, who entered the Office in 1864 when there were still several "out-and-out non-competitors" in it. He thought that the latter were "somehow men of greater personality, more suited for command", than the average head of a department in his own day, who was apt to lack the gift of dealing tactfully with overseas officials and ministers.[2]

The number of departments or divisions in the Office, which in 1849 had been five, rose to eight in 1869. There were still four geographical divisions, but the general division had branched out into the Chief Clerk's division, the Parliamentary division, the library and the registry. The first of these superintended an accounts branch set up under the Exchequer and Audit Act of 1866. To the Chief Clerkship itself an allowance was attached, which the Treasury, worsted for once, failed to abolish when a vacancy occurred in 1859. In 1860 the Permanent and Assistant Under-Secretaries shared responsibility for the divisions, each taking two geographical divisions and a number of special subjects. Thus the Permanent Under-Secretary was still not pre-eminent, which suggests that Grey's scheme of 1847 had been abandoned. In 1868, however, it was decided to divide the work between the Permanent Under-Secretary and his two chief assistants on a functional instead of a geographical basis, and henceforth no paper destined for ministers eluded the permanent head.

The ministers and the officials with whom they worked have united to praise the character and abilities of the two Permanent Under-Secretaries of these middle years. Herman Merivale, a barrister, had

---

[1] *Parl. Pap.* 1860, ix (440), Q. 3935.
[2] *Nineteenth Century*, LXV (1909), 607–8.

been for the ten years preceding his succession to Stephen part-time Professor of Political Economy at Oxford, where his *Lectures on Colonisation and the Colonies* had won him some fame. He was not doing very well at the bar, and this fact is said to have induced him to accept less remunerative but steadier employment. Clear-thinking, hardworking, sound in judgment, he was universally respected. Lord Lytton (a man of erratic temperament) thought him one of the most remarkable men he had met. "The leading characteristic of his mind is massiveness, and it is the massiveness of gold."[1] Carnarvon praised the way in which he had guided the affairs of the Office "steadily and safely".[2] Deeply interested in colonial questions, he moved to the India Office in 1859 with regret. A Liberal in politics, he gave discriminating support to the Wakefield theory of colonisation and advocated free trade and colonial self-government.

Thanks to his delightful memoirs (Sir) Frederic Rogers (later Lord Blachford), who became Permanent Under-Secretary in May 1860, is better known to us. While he was still mainly occupied at the Land Board his advice was increasingly drawn upon by Colonial Secretaries. In 1857 he served as a West Indies Incumbered Estates Commissioner. In 1858–9 he went to Paris to discuss coolie labour with the French Government. He therefore brought to the desk that had been Stephen's a variety of experience that even Stephen never possessed. As a personality he is very attractive, religious, though without Stephen's austerity, affectionate, kindly to his subordinates, modest, generous-minded. Though the sharp tone of many of his minutes and dispatches at times gave offence, his judgment and decisiveness as a man of business have been acclaimed by friends like Cardinal Newman and colleagues like Taylor. Nor were ministers behind-hand in their praise. Cardwell called him the "motive power" in the Office. Gladstone expostulated with him over his intention to retire in 1871, "having made for yourself such a position as you have". Granville, when Foreign Secretary, tried to induce him to migrate to the Foreign Office. He is believed to have been the first civil servant to be raised to the peerage.[3]

As is well known, Rogers believed in the inevitability of imperial disintegration and strove only to preserve the best possible relations until the process was complete.[4] He thus adopted Stephen's views on disallowance, eschewed direction from Whitehall, and was disinclined to mediate in inter-colonial disputes, or to offer gratuitous advice in colonial domestic matters. He espoused these non-interventionist principles, however, rather from the almost cynical conviction that good advice would be wasted than from robust belief in

[1] Grant Duff, *Notes from a Diary, 1873–81*, II, 336.
[2] Hardinge, *Life of…Carnarvon*, I, 113.
[3] *Complete Peerage*, II, 179 footnote.
[4] *C.H.B.E.* II, 699.

the merits of any form of colonial civilisation. He was impatient at the unreasonableness of colonial Governments, contemptuous of the passions of Australian democracy. Australian economic prosperity, however, he greatly desired, and preferred that the populations of settlements should be dense rather than diffuse, castigating the occupation of colonial lands by those who were unwilling to exploit them. In native questions he believed in the efficacy of British rule, and championed the Maori against New Zealand settlers.[1]

Other senior officials besides the Permanent Under-Secretaries were still being imported into the Office at a mature age. F. R. J. Sandford (later Lord Sandford), of the Education Department, joined the staff in 1868 as an Under-Secretary, (Sir) Henry Holland in 1867 as Legal Adviser. Rogers liked them both, particularly Holland. Promising young clerks recruited by the new examination were coming on too—R. P. Ebden and Edward Fairfield among them. The older clerks in between were a mixed bunch. In 1859 Taylor represented that his health had broken down. The Office, reluctant to part with his wisdom, licensed him to do his work at home. So for eleven years he sat in his study at Sheen writing minutes that were "monuments of erudition"[2] upon papers sent down to him in pouches, and travelling to London only at some moment of crisis or to meet a newly-appointed Governor.

Officials were now concerned with all the affairs of the department. Merivale spent "half his time...in teaching his various chiefs their elements".[3] Rogers used to "lecture" Carnarvon almost in the tone of an old college tutor.[4] Yet the form of Higinbotham's well-remembered reference to Rogers,[5] and the tone of faint surprise with which Rogers himself records the many instances when his advice was accepted, remind us that the partnership was novel.

Nor had ministers by any means abdicated in favour of their officials. They still took a personal interest in the *minutiae* of administration, and most papers rose to their level. For Carnarvon, while still an Under-Secretary, this was a matter of principle. It was he and not Merivale who decided what papers should reach Lytton. But he never over-ruled Merivale, and when there was a difference left it to Lytton to adjudicate. Carnarvon had come in under Stanley, then enjoying his third term as Colonial Secretary, and perhaps had learnt from him the doctrine that ministers must be effective; for to the last Stanley was determined to dominate the Office. Lytton, like Stanley, was industrious, but he was inexact and unmethodical, and a crisis agitated him. "Half mad about his

[1] Marindin, *Letters of Lord Blachford*, p. 223.
[2] *Nineteenth Century*, LXV (1909), 600.
[3] Merivale, H. C., *Bar, Stage and Platform*, p. 14.
[4] Marindin, *Letters of Lord Blachford*, pp. 263–4.
[5] The colonies had "been really governed during the whole of the last fifteen years by a person named Rogers". *C.H.B.E.* II, 696.

responsibilities" he would rise in the middle of the night to write dispatches.[1] He must have been troublesome to handle. Rogers liked Newcastle, who was very ready to accept his guidance. The Duke was reputed to have a good grasp of detail. He never shirked a responsibility once assumed, but was hesitant and dilatory. Cardwell was one minister whom Rogers could not manage; his "fidgets" were a "great torment". He was acutely preoccupied with Parliamentary reactions and, though this made him "enormously safe", Rogers felt that it prevented him from persisting in right courses.[2] Carnarvon, when he took the seals, became at once Rogers's friend. In the pursuit of policy he seemed unusually disinterested; he did not fuss, but was apt to be too much attracted by showy schemes. The Duke of Buckingham, "rough, hearty and full of work",[3] was not a man of any mark, and the preoccupation with detail which his business career had given him seemed to Rogers to spoil him as a minister. Perhaps the most noteworthy Colonial Secretary of this period in point of ability, and certainly the minister who would appeal most to an official, was Granville. He trusted his subordinates if he judged them to be capable. On the other hand, he kept a firm control and did not shrink from effective action in "Ministerial, as distinct from departmental policy".[4]

There is not a little evidence that in the 'fifties and early 'sixties pressure at all levels was less acute than it had been in the preceding generation.[5] The public at home was out of sympathy with forward policies. Nor was the pace of events yet greatly quickened by telegraphy. As late as 1864 the only ocean cable in existence serving Colonial Office needs was the line to North America opened in 1858. The Eastern colonies, Australia and the West Indies were not reached until 1871. In these circumstances official effort was controlled by the arrival and departure of slow-moving mails. By 1868 pressure began to increase again. New rules were circulated for keeping track of arrears. In the copying department there was a steady growth of work. In 1870 Rogers tried to reduce delays by simplifying procedure.

Between the days of Grey and Granville the Colonial Office succeeded in gathering into its own hands the loose ends of colonial administration. The Post Office relinquished its patronage in 1860. In 1861 the ancient system of referring all colonial legislation to the Board of Trade was quietly dropped. Commercial legislation continued to be referred, though Cardwell, shortly after becoming Secretary of State, argued (unsuccessfully as it turned out) that this

---

[1] Godley, Letters...to...Adderley, pp. 284–5.
[2] Marindin, Letters of Lord Blachford, pp. 226, 252, 263.
[3] Pemberton, Childe, Life of Lord Norton, p. 206.
[4] Fitzmaurice, Life of...Earl Granville, II, 500.
[5] In the 'sixties the juniors sometimes played fives in Number Eleven during office hours: Nineteenth Century, LXV (1909), 602.

was unnecessary, and that his department ought to be able to form its own conclusions on economic questions.[1]

In 1868 Buckingham proposed the termination of Treasury control over Crown colony expenditure. The suggestion was renewed by Granville next year and was agreed to by the Treasury on 28 February 1870. The old system had grown anomalous. As the result of historical accident Treasury control prevailed in some colonies but not in others of comparable status. The justification for control had originally been that surplus colonial revenue ought to fall into the Imperial Exchequer, but this theory was no longer valid and, that being so, the grounds for practical control were destroyed. The Colonial Office were convinced that Treasury officials were too unfamiliar with colonial conditions to exercise any effective supervision, and that in those circumstances they tended to concentrate upon points of detail. This caused endless delay, which naturally bred irritation in the colonies. But it also resulted in colonial money that was ripe for investment lying idle, while the Treasury, without any means of doing so adequately, pondered upon the best means of laying it out. The Treasury evidently disliked the system as much as the Colonial Office, for they made no difficulty about abolishing it. They stipulated, however, that control should continue in the case of grant-aided or insolvent colonies. The audit of colonial accounts by the Imperial Government had been discontinued in some colonies in 1865 and was finally ended by the Exchequer and Audit Act whereby the old Audit Office, in which colonial audit had for long been carried out, was in 1867 abolished. It was ultimately arranged that in the case of grant-aided colonies audit should be effected in the Treasury at United Kingdom expense, and in the case of other Crown colonies by the local governments at their own expense.[2]

A measure of concentration of a different sort took place in 1867 when responsibility for our settlements in Malaya was transferred from the India Office. This had been first proposed in 1858. All parties—the Colonial and India Offices, and the Governor General of India in Council—favoured the transfer in principle. Problems, however, cropped up over the departmental responsibility for any deficit in local revenues and over the cost of local defence. The War Office was drawn in, and, at an unduly late date, the Treasury, and a correspondence, displaying all the worst features of diplomacy without conference, ensued. The difficulties, genuine but not intractable, were not threshed out orally and at one stage negotiations had to be suspended for over a year. This incident reflects discredit on the Treasury, who presented a front of lofty inflexibility towards a proposal which was obviously in imperial interests. The Colonial

---

[1] *Parl. Pap.* 1864, VII (493), Q. 1968, 2043–51, 2344, 2711, 3411.
[2] C.O. 323/302 from Treasury, 28 Feb.; *Parl. Pap.* 1911, XLV (36), p. 80–3.

Office, however, cannot be excused for failing to recognise the full implications of the proposal at the outset.

In this period Colonial Secretaries were for the first time required to cultivate personal relations with prominent colonists. Canadian ministers from 1857 and Australians from 1866 onwards began to make the long journey across the oceans to deal direct with London. The earlier Canadian visits did not achieve much; the later ones successfully begot Confederation. Carnarvon, who was Under-Secretary or Secretary of State during most of them, put the visits to imaginative use. He would not allow the delegates to confine themselves to business but had them to stay with him at Highclere. The result was that they commonly returned home contented. Visits were not entirely in one direction; Newcastle went to Canada with the Prince of Wales in 1860. He was the first Colonial Secretary to go overseas while in office and, unfortunately, the last for some time to come.[1]

A little development, which had its importance in the realm both of Colonial publicity and of practical administration, occurred in this period; in 1862 the *Colonial Office List* made its first appearance. Compiled with ministerial sanction from official records and edited by two colonial clerks, but published as a private venture, the first number took the form of a volume of 154 pages. Official lists, historical and geographical descriptions and biographies are features still characteristic of the latest, much expanded, volumes.[2]

In 1858 Stanley decided that the Agents General for the Crown Colonies must be reconstituted as a joint body, and that the Agents must cease to specialise individually in the affairs of particular colonies. (Sir) Penrose G. Julyan was brought in as Crown Agent. He had not, like his predecessors, served in the Colonial Office, but the practice of recruiting agents from Downing Street was not abandoned. In 1863 the Agents were given complete control of their staff and responsibility for their actions, subject to the general superintendence of the Colonial Office.

In this period the Office took some important steps towards professionalising the Colonial Service. It has been reckoned[3] that of thirty-three Governors in post in 1865 eleven were in the most exact sense "professionals". In 1871 the proportion was roughly the same.[4] Newcastle claimed that in his first administration he had done much to establish the principle, initiated by Grey, that Governors should not be cast off after a single tour. He kept a list of Governors awaiting re-employment and new men not on it had small chance of attractive employment. The Governors' Pensions Act of 1865 naturally

---

[1] Stanley had visited Canada in youth (Hardinge, *Life of...Carnavon*, I, 12).
[2] The compilers appear to have been granted an allowance in the financial year 1869-70: *Parl. Pap.* 1870, XLVIII (145-II), p. 83.
[3] Hall, *Colonial Office*, p. 89.   [4] *Ibid.* p. 92.

fortified the tendency to build up the community of Governors into a service. "Professionals", however, enjoyed no monopoly. The higher posts tended to go increasingly to men of high political or social standing. The Army continued to serve as a breeding-ground, though with growing opposition from the Office. E. J. Eyre, whom Taylor proposed for Jamaica, was an explorer. (Sir) Francis Hincks, who went to the Windwards in 1855, and thence in 1861 to British Guiana, was a Canadian politician. For the latter appointment Molesworth, who made it, took great credit as a progressive move in the direction of mixing up the several elements of the Empire and of using colonial talent. From many gubernatorial posts, however, colonists were barred; the Queen disapproved, as Grey had done, of appointing them to serve in their homelands.

Not much is known of the way in which the Office handled the Governors after appointment. Hincks was at once asked to see Taylor and established relations with him of lasting profit. New-castle sent Sir George Grey, while still at the Cape, a set of papers on New Zealand affairs designed to make him *au fait* with developments there since the termination of his last Governorship. Cardwell arranged for Frederick Seymour, before his departure for British Columbia in 1863, to discuss the constitutional problems of that colony with Sir Edmund Head, a former Governor.[1] Taylor broke his rustication to come and bid farewell to Sir John Grant on his departure for Jamaica. These were creditable acts. But Lord Monck complained that he could get no information out of the Office about the pay of his staff or the location of his residence.[2]

IV

In the eventful period between Sir Robert Herbert's appointment as Permanent Under-Secretary in 1871 and the creation of a Dominions Department in 1907, ministerial ability reached its highest level. Several Secretaries of State possessed before appoint-ment, or rapidly acquired, a store of expert information. Sir Henry Holland (later Lord Knutsford), who had served in the Office as an official, and Joseph Chamberlain, are examples of the former; Lord Ripon of the latter. Yet it was only gradually and under the pressure of the looming crises in Africa, that the Office gained repute. In 1876 Carnarvon was deemed able to take charge of the India Office as well as his own during the absence of the Secretary of State for India. Disraeli tried to transfer Hicks Beach to the India Office very shortly after he had gone to Downing Street, and Salisbury uprooted Edward Stanhope after only five months of office, and was only prevented by the Queen's intervention from appointing the senile

---

[1] Reid, *Life of W. E. Forster*, p. 391.
[2] Godley, *Letters...to C. B. Adderley*, p. 305.

Earl of Iddesleigh in 1887. The Prince of Wales thought it a "come down" for Granville to move from the Foreign Office in 1886 and wondered that he had not preferred the Presidency of the Council. Some thought Chamberlain "diminished" by accepting a department "that counted as second rate".[1] Chamberlain's career dis pelled for a time the belief that the Office was unimportant and, when he went, Balfour was at pains to find a qualified successor. He chose Alfred Lyttelton, who knew both South Africa and Newfoundland.[2] But Campbell-Bannerman's appointment of Elgin, that "weak and unimaginative administrator",[3] shows that even after Chamberlain's time Prime Ministers could make strange appointments.

A period has now been reached where materials are sufficient for the continuous study of the Secretary of State's relations with the Prime Minister and the Cabinet. Unfortunately, this attractive subject lies off the path, and only a few generalisations can be permitted. As might be expected, relations varied greatly with personalities and circumstances. Thus Kimberley deferred much to Gladstone, and Gladstone to the Cabinet. Carnarvon, on the other hand, was given by Disraeli disastrous latitude. Sir Michael Hicks Beach at first found it hard to stimulate Cabinet discussions on South Africa. The South African crisis of 1879 seems, however, to have raised colonial issues to Cabinet level and kept them there. In Gladstone's second administration they were a constant topic and provoked many debates in the Cabinet in which the Colonial Secretary was sometimes overruled. In Gladstone's third government, it seems to have been hard to get Cabinets on any subject, and Ripon complained that he had to bear an immoderate responsibility.[4] Chamberlain, on the other hand, was all too ready to commit Prime Minister and Cabinet in advance. Probably no other Colonial Secretary has been quite such an autocrat. In general, colonial affairs grew in importance in the Cabinet's eyes during this period; Cabinet Committees on colonial subjects began to make their appearance.[5] But what caused this elevation was rather their international and military consequences than their inherent interest or significance.

Nothing has yet been said of the relations between the Colonial Office and the Sovereign during the long years of Victoria's reign. In very early days Melbourne, *more avunculi*, himself reported upon colonial as upon all other affairs. Thereafter the Colonial Secretary

[1] Garvin, *Life of...Chamberlain*, III, 8, 10, 102.
[2] Balfour tried unsuccessfully to get Milner: *Milner Papers*, II, 472 *et seq.*
[3] Jebb, *Imperial Conference*, II, 25.
[4] B.M. Add. MSS. 41224, ff. 41-4.
[5] The first known colonial Cabinet Committee (on West Africa) was formed during Gladstone's second Government: Gwynn and Tuckwell, *Life of Dilke*, I, 535. There was a Committee on Swazi affairs in 1894: Wolf, *Life of...Ripon*, II, 224.

or his staff normally bore the burden. Colonial questions that were debated in Cabinet or in Parliament were of course reported by the Prime Minister, and there are several recorded instances of such reports from Gladstone during his second administration. Otherwise the Prime Minister was mainly drawn in when the Queen disliked something that the Secretary of State had done.

It does not seem that the Queen took much interest in colonial questions in the first forty years of her reign; her references to them are few. In 1847, however, Grey was aware of the need to submit certain classes of papers to the sovereign. In 1855 the Queen asked to receive colonial dispatches more often. In 1867 she complained very properly that the arrival of the Governor of Canada and the Canadian delegation to discuss confederation had not been reported. She made two somewhat similar complaints in the same year and the next. The third complaint was coupled with the request that she should see the drafts of all important dispatches before they were sent. The rules that the Office formed to give effect to this request evidently did not satisfy. The Queen continued to complain to Prime Ministers of both parties of lack of information, but to the credit of the Office not often. Indeed, the Office was sometimes at pains to win her advance approval of its courses, and always strove to keep her posted on South African affairs, in which, as Lord Knutsford noted in 1889, she was much interested.[1] Once she thanked Chamberlain for keeping her so well informed[2] and she evidently appreciated the oral reports that he made to her upon South Africa both before and after the outbreak of war.

No keen observer, especially Queen Victoria, could fail in curiosity about the unfolding of the South African *imbroglio* in the last thirty years of the century. It was perhaps fortunate for a busy and not over-staffed Office that her interest in other colonial questions was restricted. Perhaps her imagination would not readily have grasped the more complicated problems of Empire. Upon the nomination of Governors, however, she maintained a steady and on the whole a beneficent influence. She had early insisted that candidates must be men of standing and she asked that names might be submitted to her before soundings were taken, to ensure that she was satisfied on this point. She objected to colonists, and as time went on she supported colonial demands for noblemen and peers of the Blood Royal. Lord Lorne's appointment to Canada in 1878 obviously pleased her greatly and she would have liked him to be replaced by some other member of her family. She tried to prevent the reappointment of Sir Hercules Robinson (later Lord Rosmead) to South Africa in 1895, because she believed him to be too old; when she failed, she worked for his removal.

---

[1] *Queen Victoria's Letters*, 3rd ser. I, 533.
[2] *Ibid.* III, 42.

Edward VII was perhaps somewhat more interested in imperial questions than his mother. He insisted, as she had done, on prior consultation in matters of moment; both Alfred Lyttelton and Lord Elgin were censured for failing to arrange it. The King contested certain Government decisions, but is not known to have withheld consent in any matter of importance.

As one of his last acts Rogers prepared the reorganisation of his department. Its chief features were the consolidation of some small branches into a proper general department, and an improvement in the prospects of the higher ranks of established clerks. These reforms were proposed to the Treasury in 1869 and gradually achieved over the next seven or eight years. They had the immediate result of increasing the total emoluments and reducing the numbers of the men in what was soon to be called the "Higher Division". Between 1871 and 1877, several old clerks were retired, until numbers had been cut from twenty-six to eighteen. The subsections into which the Division was broken up were reduced from five to four, and thence to three—principal clerks, and senior and junior clerks; it was claimed that the lengthening of the salary scales thus effected would benefit the clerks in times of slow promotion.

This was the last occasion on which purely departmental reforms could be effected; for in 1870 there began a series of general measures for regulating the recruitment and promotion of the public service to which the Colonial Office, like other departments, was forced to adjust itself. Thus, it had been laid down in 1870 that, with the exception of the Foreign and Home Offices, clerks could only be admitted to established posts after passing one of two open examinations. This virtually brought patronage to an end and divided the service into two broad classes, without any means of transfer from the lower to the higher. Various difficulties arose which were to some extent eased by the creation in 1876 of a "Lower Division" common to the whole Service. Promotion from lower to higher division was then rendered possible, though it was still hard.

The Colonial Office disliked these innovations. It already had a well-devised examination of its own and specially high rates of pay, and justified both by the peculiar difficulty of its work. Any measures of uniformity seemed likely to result in levelling down the high standard it sought to maintain. It was, of course, forced after 1876 to recruit both types of clerk by open competition, but it pleaded before the Ridley Commission on the Civil Service (1888) for a special test for a few Offices of exceptional standing like itself. Nor would it admit the practical possibility of promotions into the Higher Division from below. The lower division resented this exclusion and complained generally of the limits imposed upon its chances of promotion. To this the hierarchy rejoined that there existed a number of "staff" clerkships—a book-keeper, a librarian and the like—which were often but not necessarily filled from the lower ranks; if such posts could be guaranteed to the lower-division clerks, grievances about inadequate promotion would be met.

The Colonial Office members of the lower division took a lead in ventilating these grievances, which were not peculiar to the Colonial Office, before the Ridley Commission. Their claim was partly met in 1890 by splitting the division into two grades and reserving some supervisory posts for men of the division. In so far as this was a surrender to service co-ordination, it must have been repugnant to the Colonial Office. On the other hand, no encouragement, unless a moral one, was given to the idea of promotion from lower to higher division.

In the preceding period the Office staff had been roughly divisible into two classes, performing "superior" and "mechanical" tasks respectively. In the present one the division was threefold: the higher (in 1890 renamed first) division, representing the old establishment revitalised by the fruits of a universal examination; the lower (in 1890 renamed second) division, recruited under a variety of systems but eventually grouped into two classes of Assistant Clerks; and the copyists. (Sir) Robert Meade, an Under-Secretary, spoke proudly of the first class in evidence before the Ridley Commission. He thought that the system which had brought in such men was better than any that had preceded it.[1] To Sydney (later Lord) Olivier, who came out top in the 1882 examination, it was plain that there was a difference in calibre between the old type of clerk and the new.[2] The first two candidates to enter by the new door rose to be Under-Secretaries. Chamberlain secured that the salary scales, already favourable in comparison with those elsewhere prevailing, should actually equal those of Treasury clerks, and this was no doubt a leading cause for the popularity of the Office at the turn of the century, Civil Service candidates commonly preferring it to any other department, except perhaps the Treasury.[3] Apart from material inducements the Office must have won a good name in the Universities on other grounds; for it was one in which men were allowed from the outset to undertake difficult work and from which they might occasionally go on overseas tours.

The establishment changes of 1869–70 had included the elevation of the Legal Adviser to Assistant Under-Secretary rank; the abolition of the post of Précis Writer, whose occupant had become a kind of financial adviser; and the provision of a salary for an assistant private secretary to the Secretary of State. Despite initial Treasury objections a plurality of Assistant Under-Secretaries was henceforth maintained. A third post was created in 1874, and from then until

---

[1] *Parl. Pap.* 1888, xxvii [C. 5545], Q. 12338.
[2] Lady Olivier, *Sydney Olivier*, pp. 31–4.
[3] *Empire Review*, i (1901), 284; Earle, *Turn over the Page*, p. 82.

1897 two of the three incumbents were always barristers. In consequence no doubt of Treasury pressure, one of the legal Assistant Under-Secretaries was laicised in 1897 and a Legal Assistant appointed to work under the surviving legal Assistant Under-Secretary. A second Legal Assistant was added in 1898. A fourth Assistant Under-Secretary's post was included in the 1899–1900 estimates. By 1888 the Treasury had won the battle over the chief clerkship. This was now purely honorific.

In these years the private secretaries came into their own. The office of Principal Private Secretary (as it would now be called) had originally been bestowed upon some inexperienced but promising young ministerial protégé. In early days such an arrangement may have worked well enough, for the duties were mechanical. From 1882, however, principal private secretaries were usually established clerks, though Ripon, Chamberlain and Lyttelton to some extent reverted to the old practice. In 1866–7 there were three assistant secretaries (with special salaries) for the under-secretaries and, by a rather informal arrangement, the Secretary of State had had one too for a while.[1] The four posts as such were abolished in 1872 and the duties assigned to four second-class clerks. In 1881–2 three of them were re-established with the understanding that they should be filled by second-class clerks who should share in the general work of the Office. From well before 1887, when Holland defended the system in Parliament,[2] it had been the custom to attach unpaid secretaries to the private office. Chamberlain carried this to considerable lengths. Between 1896 and 1903 there were never fewer than four private secretaries, and usually there were five. In 1900 there were six, including a Parliamentary private secretary, a figure who then made his first appearance in the Office. This phalanx of secretaries were largely engaged in exercising the Secretary of State's patronage, which the expansion of the tropical Empire had enlarged. There was no appointments branch at the time; so, at the turn of the century, as no doubt long before, the assistant private secretaries could any day be found entering the names of candidates in large registers, interviewing them, or considering their promotion.[3] The system was rendered somewhat more expert in Chamberlain's time when a regular system of reporting on Colonial Service officers began.

The influence of the lower (or second) division, whose numbers in the late 'eighties broadly speaking balanced those of the higher (or first), bore little proportion to its strength. In its superiors' eyes its work was lowly. There is no sign, however, that its members were other than a worthy band, drudging faithfully on low salaries eked

---

[1] Even in 1839 an allowance was provided for a private secretary to the Permanent Under-Secretary, but no such officer was then actually in post: Office Minutes, 1836–59, no. 11.

[2] *Hansard*, 3rd ser. cccxvii, 1163–4.

[3] A patronage register existed in 1870: Office Minutes, 1869–74, vol. 4, no. 56.

out by spare-time earnings, and anxious to rise in their own Office rather than in one which might take a less rigid view of their eligibility for promotion.

Recruitment to the old class of copyists was stopped in 1871. Its members were gradually absorbed into the lower division or sought their fortunes elsewhere. The need for them slackened off in 1872 when the Office gave up the practice of entering copies of outgoing communications in books and relied solely upon the drafts which had long been preserved with the in-letters. Male "writers" were, however, still employed in the late 'eighties, paid at piece rates. In 1888 the Registrar looked after them, but by 1898 there was a separate superintendent. Typewriting machines came in 1893 and by 1901 all copying was done by "lady type-writers". The Office was slow to employ shorthand writers, but there was one on the staff by the end of the century.

By 1873 the number of geographical departments was reduced to two, which must have been unbearable. By 1875 the number had risen by one.[1] By 1880 there were again four, as there had been in earlier times. Three of these—the West Indian (much favoured as a training-ground for juniors owing to the variety of its work),[2] the Eastern and the African and Mediterranean—still bore their ancient names though they did not deal with the same groups of colonies. The fourth, the North American and Australian department, formed in 1871, had been united. This interesting union concentrated all the "constitutional governments" (except those in South Africa) under one control. It was thus the precursor of the Dominions department and the Commonwealth Relations Office.
precursor of the Dominions department and the Commonwealth Relations Office. An intermediate stage had been reached in 1871 when all Crown colony work was excluded from the American department.

In 1880 there began a process which, besides its wider implications, affected the grouping of colonies in departments: the first Protectorate was handed over to Colonial Office management. Cyprus had been administered by the Foreign Office since 1878, but Dilke urged his department to abandon it.[3] It was added to the African and Mediterranean department. Though British Africa was still relatively small, the old African department, from the 'eighties the most important in the Office, had been split into a South African and a West African section. By 1900 the latter had been further divided, no doubt in order to accommodate the Nigerian Protectorates which the Foreign Office discarded in that year. By 1902 the Nigerian

---

[1] The number of departments and the distribution of work among them may be deduced, not perhaps with perfect accuracy, from successive editions of the *Colonial Office List*.

[2] Lady Olivier, *Sydney Olivier*, p. 227.

[3] Gwynn and Tuckwell, *Life of Dilke*, I, 325. For official opposition see the minute by (Sir P.) Currie of 4 May in C.O. 67/14.

group of territories was being managed by one section, and the Gold Coast, Sierra Leone, Malta and Gibraltar by the other. In 1905 it had become necessary to divide the South African department, one section dealing with the territories that now make up the Union, together with Basutoland, and one with various other southern territories including Nyasaland, which had been handed over in 1904, and the Rhodesias. For practical purposes this division was in being in 1903. A little branch to deal with the West African Frontier Force is now first named in the *Colonial Office List*. Uganda, the East African Protectorates and Somaliland came in in 1905. By next year an East African department had been formed to deal with them. The geographical departments were normally under the charge of a principal clerk with three subordinates. Lower Division clerks were not assigned to these departments, though apparently certain copyists were occasionally borrowed for "special duty".

A proper General department had been created *eo nomine* in 1870 to deal with general (including defence) questions, most of the establishment work and emigration. Its head also took charge of the Copying department, Library and Registry, which formed separate branches. The remainder of the establishment business and responsibility for the Parliamentary clerk were ultimately transferred to the General department as well. Financial work, which was at first left with the chief clerk, was also brought under the General department in the end. The Financial department, to give it the name that it had acquired by 1874, enjoyed a partial autonomy; it was under a first-class clerk, the financial clerk, whereas the other branches were under clerks of lower rank. A principal clerk was in charge of the whole and he, as the financial clerk's superior, was in effect the Secretary of State's financial adviser. The Emigration department which existed from 1878 to 1896 was apparently comparable in status to the Financial department. In 1895 the General department was re-entitled the General and Financial department, and the old Financial department (called the Accounts department by 1897) lost all first-division staff. In 1906 the title Chief Clerk's department was adopted for the General and Financial department.

The Library had lost its titular librarian, and, after a period of unsatisfactory experiments, had in 1880 been given a whole-time staff of its own. The collection of books had been augmented in 1873 when the old Board of Trade library was shared out. By 1888 the library, to which public access was allowed, was reckoned to have reached a point of high efficiency. Its staff dispatched Parliamentary Papers overseas and looked after the records, which had begun to assume gigantic proportions. The files created between 1873 and 1900 were estimated to weigh forty tons and by 1905 a special branch had been created to weed them.

In 1888 there was still a single central registry for non-confidential papers, which opened, circulated and housed them. Secret papers were kept apart and guarded in the geographical departments by higher division clerks. In 1896 a sub-registry for the North American, Australian and West African departments had been formed. By 1900 there were three and by 1904 four such sub-registries. At the turn of the century the registries had won a reputation for swift production. Finally, there was a printing branch which prepared, indexed and kept Parliamentary and Confidential prints.

The department's prestige at the end of the century was due in part to the efforts of (Sir) Robert Herbert, its Permanent Under-Secretary for twenty-two years (1871–92). Herbert, who was Carnarvon's cousin, had had a remarkable career. He had been Colonial Secretary and later Premier of Queensland. On returning home, he went to the Board of Trade and, in 1870, moved to Downing Street as an Assistant Under-Secretary. On promotion next year to the highest rank, he brought with him a training in statesmanship which his three predecessors had not had.

Herbert was a man of great tact, charm, culture and kindliness; industrious and imperturbable; patient and conciliatory; a graceful writer; persuasive to his chiefs, considerate to his subordinates, trusted by colonial ministers. Sir M. E. Grant Duff called him "the ideal colleague", "the perfect permanent official", "a man in whose geography the hill Difficulty does not exist".[1] Olivier, a more reliable judge, said he was "exceedingly brilliant and capable."[2] Three special characteristics have been noticed. He was the first expansionist Under-Secretary.[3] Secondly, he was a continuous advocate of South African federation, and it was probably due to his influence that that policy was pressed to achievement by successive governments of different complexions. Thirdly, he was for his age unusually interested in the economic welfare of the Crown colonies. A true appreciation of Herbert must await the close scrutiny of some thousands of his Office minutes, his only literary monument.[4]

(Sir) Robert Meade, who followed Herbert, was the first Permanent Under-Secretary in the Office who may be regarded as a professional civil servant, and the first non-lawyer since Hay. After service in the Foreign Office and abroad he entered the Colonial Office as Granville's private secretary in 1868. With the warm support of Rogers,[5] Kimberley made him Assistant Under-Secretary in 1871. He specialized chiefly in African questions, and his advice and skill were much valued by the British ambassador in Berlin at the

---

[1] Grant Duff, *Notes from a Diary, 1873–81*, II, 337.
[2] Lady Olivier, *Sydney Olivier*, p. 32.
[3] He was, however, opposed to the annexation of Fiji: *Trans. R. Hist. Soc.* 4th ser. XXXII, p. 96.
[4] Inquiries conducted by the author among Herbert's surviving relatives have failed to trace any private papers.
[5] B.M. Add. MSS. 44224. Kimberley to Gladstone, 14 March 1871.

time of the African Conference of 1884–85.[1] He was keenly interested in imperial defence, and on becoming Permanent Under-Secretary promoted the work of the Colonial Defence Committee. A Liberal Free-Trader and friend of Granville, he could never have been popular with nor very happy under Chamberlain. One senses too that Chamberlain, while appreciating his charm and tact, felt that he was too easy-going. Yet there are no evidences of friction.

Meade's successor was Sir Edward Wingfield, the legal Assistant Under-Secretary since 1878, capable, hard-working, shrewd and self-sacrificing. He succumbed to overwork (as Meade nearly did) and had to retire prematurely in 1900. Herbert came back for a few months to fill the breach. Then Sir Montagu Ommaney, a former private secretary to Carnarvon, came in his place.[2] Since 1877 he had been a Crown Agent and won a reputation for great financial ability, business acumen, equanimity and kindliness.

In this brilliant generation many of the subordinate officials are as worthy of notice as the Permanent Under-Secretaries. Some of them, who in due time rose to be heads of the Office or Governors, will be mentioned in their place. Space can here be spared only for that charming, popular, human, slightly flippant, slightly dissipated personality Edward Fairfield, of whom Sir Harry Johnston has left an engaging portrait (thinly disguised) in his novel *The Gay-Dombeys*.[3] Fairfield began his official career in the West Indian department under Taylor, who admired his abilities. There and elsewhere he devoted his energies to colonial prison reform and left behind him several caricatures to illustrate his activities. He became a first-class Clerk in 1880 after only eight years' service and in Olivier's opinion he was then and for long "the only really able and statesmanlike" man in that class.[4] He was almost unique among his colleagues in taking an interest in Africa. In 1892 he became the Assistant Under-Secretary in charge of the African departments, and acquired an enthusiasm for those parts of the continent then under the Colonial Office. On South Africa he became an acknowledged expert and Chamberlain paid a high tribute to his knowledge in Parliament. His "habit of charging a very remarkable memory with all details rendered a constant personal reference inevitable and constituted an onerous charge upon his time".[5] The result was that like others of his generation he was over-driven, collapsed under the strain of the preliminaries to the War and died in the spring of 1897. Fairfield was known to be a Radical who believed in the policy towards South Africa represented by the Pretoria Convention of 1881. He was regarded as a strong opponent of Rhodes, though he was a close

[1] For his reputation as an African expert see G.D. 29/120, Derby to Granville, 16 Oct. 1884.
[2] The post was offered to Milner: Garvin, *Life of...Chamberlain*, III, 143.
[3] For the identification see Johnston, Sir H. H., *The Story of My Life*, p. 151.
[4] Lady Olivier, *Sydney Olivier*, p. 32.   [5] *The Times*, 29 April 1897, 10d.

friend of Rhodes's lawyer, Hawksley. At the time of the Select Committee on the Jameson Raid he was allowed to negotiate with Hawksley on his own account to a degree that is surprising, and was posthumously charged by the Opposition with playing politics. Chamberlain, however, defended him as a man "absolutely honourable, absolutely truthful"[1] and there is at present no reason to doubt the accuracy of that judgment.

No official of this period has depicted his ministers as Taylor or Rogers did. There are, however, impressions to be gleaned. Carnarvon had the reputation of being alert, prompt, punctual and hardworking. His confidence was given slowly, but, once given, was not withdrawn. He inspired his staff by treating them as a family and they responded with devotion. Kimberley was immensely painstaking and liked dealing with important papers at first hand.[2] Hicks Beach, "an overbearing and forcibly-spoken man",[3] cannot have been a favourite. Derby was incurably dilatory, but as much from principle as through constitutional incapacity. Stanhope's statesmanship and originality were unlike anything to which the Office had formerly been accustomed. Meade thought Granville a man of fine judgment and an excellent administrator because he trusted his reliable subordinates "while holding all the threads in his hands".[4] One might have expected that Chamberlain's commanding personality would have made him unpopular. But this was apparently not so. Like Granville, he had the gift of delegation, and he inspired devotion in his subordinates by his loyalty and patience and by his generous acknowledgment of assistance. He was kindly and hospitable and is even said to have won "enthusiastic support" for his policy among the staff. He was outstandingly industrious. His forceful intervention in the daily working of the Office was admired in that age of hero-worship, and the business spirit and promptness which he injected into a rather slow-moving department were remembered by the public in later years. Lyttelton's "charm and versatile ability" were recalled by more than one official. He treated the staff as his friends, and gave them his confidence and credit for their achievements. While Chamberlain was The Master, Lyttelton was the Captain of an Eleven. His judgment, courage, high principle and intense interest in his work were found equally impressive. Qualified witnesses spoke far less enthusiastically of Elgin, who found the work beyond him. He had to lean heavily upon his officials, and

[1] Garvin, Life of . . . Chamberlain, III, 73.
[2] Office Minutes, 1869–74, vol. 5, no. 72.
[3] Lady Olivier, Sydney Olivier, p. 33.
[4] Fitzmaurice, Life of . . . Granville, II, 500. Contrast this with Kimberley's opinion (Journal, pp. 75–7, 79) that he was slipshod, "nonchalant and yielding", and too lazy to master the details of a subject. Granville called Meade by his nickname (Letters from the Berlin Embassy, p. 367). Perhaps the official was too intimate with his master, and too much of the same type, to make him a reliable witness.

his relations with (Sir) Winston Churchill, his Under-Secretary, are known to have been inharmonious.

Notwithstanding the progressive extension of self-government, the business of the Office by day and night[1] was growing yearly throughout this period. An estimate based on the number of papers handled shows it to have doubled in the twenty years following 1868. No respite could be foreseen at that time, and certainly none was vouchsafed. There were various ways of meeting the situation: an increase in staff; longer hours; a broadening of responsibility. Herbert, who experienced the pressure in his earliest days, was for a time debarred by the new establishment scheme from the first expedient. He therefore strove to lay a heavier burden on each clerk. There was indeed no nominal increase in hours, which in 1873 and even in 1888 were but six, as they had been in 1850. The early 'eighties were still an age of spacious holidays and there was a good deal of leisure in high places. Nevertheless the word went out that each man was to do the work of a man and a half, and ultimately of two men. These measures were not without effect. Extra burdens were borne cheerfully: papers were taken home; clerks came in on Sundays. The staff stood up well to the Jameson Raid (1895–6) and were thanked by the Prince of Wales in person for their efforts. They could not, however, keep pace. In 1896 work fell into arrear and never recovered. By 1903 minuting had become sketchy and drafting accordingly difficult. Heads of departments were dealing with more than 5000 papers a year. The establishment was by no means commensurately increased. The work had quadrupled in the forty years from 1873, but the cost of doing it had only doubled. Despite the arguments afforded by new Protectorates and the South African War, the numbers of the first division were but thirty-three in 1900.

Herbert also tried to get work disposed of at a lower level. The contraction in the higher division demanded that principal clerks should exercise more responsibility and that clerks of all grades should minute and draft. Instructions to this end had only a limited success. Some of the older principal clerks, timid, procrastinating and unimaginative creatures, were still apt in 1888 to load their seniors with papers. In 1880 every dispatch reached the Permanent Under-Secretary, and about three-quarters of the correspondence the Secretary of State himself.[2] Kimberley considered, if only perfunctorily, some very trifling cases. By the end of the century such ministerial surveillance had ceased to be possible; Chamberlain is said to have refused to pass or sign routine dispatches.[3] This was looked upon as an innovation, though in fact as early as 1869 Granville had sanctioned the substitution of an Under-Secretary's signature

---

[1] Provision for two resident clerks was first made in the estimates for 1876: *Parl. Pap.* 1875, XLIX (100), p. 84.
[2] *Empire Review*, 1 (1901), 281.   [3] Office Minutes, 1869–74, vol. 4, no. 41.

in such cases. Under-Secretaries, however, still signed domestic correspondence, and few papers failed to reach one of them. Lower down the Office it was the same. In the early 'eighties brilliant higher-division clerks still filled in routine forms, drew up mail schedules and watched messengers pack bags. Lower-division clerks were even more humbly employed. None was assigned to the geographical divisions. In the General department, where they abounded, they seldom minuted and only did elementary drafting. They claimed before the Ridley Commission that they were fit to do better work, but, with an inconsistency that must have ruined their case, also alleged that some of the work they did was of higher-division standard. The hierarchy would not listen to such arguments and the lower division toiled on as hewers of wood and drawers of water.

To us it seems that man-power was being wasted and high officials being overworked. Contemporary Governors also thought that the affairs of the Crown colonies were too meticulously scrutinised in London. At the same time, however, they complained that clerks were invested with too much power and refused requests without ministerial authority. This, it was thought, resulted in a needless repetition of requests which had to be dealt with by hard-pressed officials at the top. The existence of this gubernatorial attitude must have strengthened the determination to restrict devolution.

In 1870 the Office's telegraph bill amounted to £800. By 1880–1 it had more than trebled and by 1900–1 (notwithstanding the introduction of the economy code) had multiplied more than twelve times. The extension of imperial communications, to which these figures are an index, was in itself a potent influence in magnifying the work of the Office. In 1875 there was still no cable to South Africa—then the most important destination—and the mail took two months. Carnarvon complained that he had to provide in dispatches for very varied contingencies. By 1878 there was a mixed cable-mail route which took only sixteen days. But it remained difficult to keep South African affairs under control until, in March 1879, a direct link from London to Cape Town was established. The link with Australia was also improved, but tardily. An all-British cable to connect Canada and Australia was first proposed in the 'seventies, but was not achieved until December 1902, when messages which had formerly taken a day got through in an hour. Ocean cables serve every class of the community, but benefit governments before all. If the network is inadequate, as it certainly was in the last quarter of the century, administration suffers. It is hard to believe that the Colonial Office was as prompt and forceful in improving the system as circumstances demanded.

Another development which marked off the age of Victorian imperialism from the age of colonial *laissez-faire* was the erection and occupation of a new block of buildings for the Office. Number 14, from which the Empire was formerly governed, had blocked the west end of Downing Street. It had overflowed into a house towards the north. The buildings were damp and insecure. The basements, in which the copyists worked, had to be pumped out daily and fires had to be kept burning to prevent the records packed below ground to stabilise the building, from becoming irretrievably sodden. The walls were not sound-proof. By the 'sixties ominous sounds and vibrations were constantly heard and felt, and supported the belief that the whole pile would some day crash. In 1839 the Surveyor of Works had given the houses only another twenty to thirty years of life. A Select Committee had at that time recommended that both the Foreign and the Colonial Office should be furnished with a new home. These views were endorsed by the Commissioners of 1849. Eventually building was begun on the area between Downing Street and what is now King Charles Street. On 17 January 1876 Carnarvon, after fighting the War Office for possession, was able to move into the north-east corner of the block. On the eve of his departure the staff were occupying odd rooms in Nos. 10, 11, 12 and 13 Downing Street as well as their original office.

The new Office, on Palmerston's insistence designed by Sir Gilbert Scott in Renaissance instead of Gothic style[1] and equipped with such amenities as a spacious library and a lift, evidently pleased its first occupants. The result is not happy by modern standards. Though the Secretary of State's room is, as Carnarvon said, "simply vast" and other rooms on the same floor are majestic enough, many of the smaller rooms are poky and dark and look out upon a gloomy well. Since some of these were meant only for storage it is unreasonable to blame the architect. Chamberlain had electric light installed and improved the furnishings.

In 1878 the Land Board, whose office had been moved to Downing Street in 1876, came to an end with the retirement of the last Commissioner. Such work as remained was divided between the Agents General, the Crown Agents and the Colonial Office, and for eight years a small corner of the last housed the United Kingdom Government's sole emigration agency. In 1886 an Emigrants' Information Office was established under the actual management of a Colonial Office clerk aided by a specially recruited staff. The work of this Office, which published circulars and handbooks, grew steadily. By 1906 the Board of Trade Labour Department and the Local Government Board were represented upon its managing Committee, and its staff then numbered half a score.

The "Agents General for Crown Colonies", renamed "Crown

---

[1] The façade is adorned with figures depicting different parts of the Empire and nine former Secretaries of State. Kimberley chose the ministerial subjects (Office Minutes 1869–74, vol. 5, no. 52).

Agents for the Colonies",[1] continued during this period to represent the interests of some of the self-governing communities. Between 1878 and 1880 steps were taken to shift as much as possible of this work to the shoulders of Agents appointed by the self-governing colonies themselves, and it may be reckoned that from 1881 the Crown Agents were specialists in Crown colony work alone. Their previous connection with the Treasury was severed and they became almost a sub-department of the Colonial Office, whose premises they advantageously shared between 1875 and 1903.[2] The Crown Agents themselves were appointed by the Colonial Secretary, but chose their own staff. Their work grew even between 1881 and 1888, but still more after Chamberlain had embarked upon an active policy of colonial public works. The Colonial Office found them useful guides on various commercial and financial issues.

In 1901 Chamberlain asked Governors whether they were satisfied with the Crown Agents. He got the impression that they were. Some Governors, however, entertained private doubts, and a public inquiry had eventually to be conducted in 1909 which exculpated the Agents from vague charges of excessive autonomy. The Exchequer and Audit Act of 1866 had excluded colonial accounts from the purview of the Comptroller and Auditor-General. In 1889 at the request of the Colonial Secretary the Exchequer and Audit Office volunteered to audit some of them, and a Colonial Audit Branch, staffed at colonial government expense, was established. In 1906 it audited the accounts of seventeen dependencies. The arrangements were not entirely happy and in 1907 the Branch was amalgamated with the parent Audit Office. The system was finally refashioned in 1910, when a separate authority, responsible to the Colonial Secretary, was set up to give general instructions to local audit staff.

Meade told the Ridley Commission in 1888 that there was no friction between his department and the Treasury.[3] This can only have been true in a formal sense. Despite the settlement of 1871, champions of the Colonial Office find no difficulty in convicting the Treasury of inordinate delays, of interfering in the domestic arrangements of the Colonial Office, of writing offensive letters, of refusing to sanction trivial items of expenditure, of wrecking projects almost perfected at an advanced stage, and even of downright incompetence.[4] Great undertakings, on which the Colonial Office had set its heart, fared no better than small ones, and Chamberlain himself fought

[1] Called since 1954 The Crown Agents for Oversea Governments and Administrations.
[2] A branch Crown Agents Office had been established at 1 Tokenhouse Buildings, E.C., in 1886. Their Downing Street Office was moved to 4 Whitehall Gardens at Michaelmas 1903 (*Colonial Office List*, 1887, 1903).
[3] *Parl. Pap.* 1888, xxvii [C. 5545], Q. 12378.
[4] In 1873 Kimberley ('Journal', p. 97) said that formerly the Treasury "did its work efficiently, however unpleasantly....Now the work is ill done, or not done at all". He instanced the failure of the Treasury to consult the Colonial Office before making a new contract for carrying mail to the Cape.

several fierce and not always victorious battles for his pet schemes, especially in the field of communications.

At the end of the century there was a rise in expenditure, previously unparalleled. The taxpayer was more than usually unwilling to meet it, particularly where his sacrifices would have been for the benefit of territories to whose welfare he was commonly indifferent. Rigid parsimony in the Treasury was therefore hard to avoid. What is less excusable is the spirit in which control was administered. "There have been many times within my recollection", wrote Hamilton in 1909, "when I have shared a deep and general feeling of indignation and resentment, not only at the manner in which the representatives of the Colonial Office have been treated, but at the tone in which the Treasury letters have been worded." It was suspected, too, that these letters had been written by junior officials without ministerial approval, and their occasional withdrawal at Colonial Office request supports the view. At the same time, as Hamilton confessed, the Colonial Office was not always vigorous in pressing its case.[1] Certainly it ought to have indulged in more preparatory discussion, and little effort to interest the Treasury in colonial questions can be detected.

It was during this period that for the first time in history the Foreign Office found itself playing an important role in colonial affairs. The desire of Canada and other self-governing colonies to negotiate autonomously with foreign powers, and the cession, acquisition and assumption of protection over new territories, formed the major points of contact. The two sets of officials who were apt to meet at international conferences must have got to know one another well, and the respective ministers developed the practice of frequent semi-official intercourse. But the Colonial Office was not always a forceful champion of colonial interests and, over the Franco-Canadian treaty of 1882, showed itself distinctly less imaginative than the Foreign Office.

With the War Office, too, the Colonial Office had been forced by events into unprecedentedly intimate touch. In Ripon's time semi-official correspondence over the Governorships of Malta and Gibraltar (War Office appointments) and the seconding of military officers for service in the colonies was constant and fruitful.[2] And there were more important occasions for collaboration. A unified system of imperial defence had not seriously been examined before Disraeli's second administration (1874–1880). Carnarvon, keenly interested from the start, had put forward a scheme to his chief as early as 1874. In the crisis year of 1878 a Colonial Defence Committee was formed, consisting of representatives of the Colonial Office and the defence departments. Next year a Royal Commission on Imperial Defence

---

[1] *Nineteenth Century*, LXV (1909), 610–11.
[2] Ripon's semi-official correspondence with the War Office is in B.M. Add. MS. 41224.

was established, with Carnarvon, now out of politics, as its chairman. The Commission's report (never published) has been said to mark "a new departure in our national history".[1] The Colonial Defence Committee continued long in being. Its early history seems to have been unhappy and in 1892 it was apparently threatened with extinction.[2]

The staff neither of the War Office nor of the Horse Guards, who then divided between them the control of the land forces, showed sufficient understanding of colonial aspirations and susceptibilities when making appointments, nor of Colonial terrain when planning strategy.[3] Sir John Ardagh, Director of Military Intelligence 1896–1901, was an honourable exception. Little supported by the rest of his department, and starved of assistance, he managed to get on to such terms with the Colonial Office as to enable him to see, and to submit, by and through private channels, valuable intelligence material. The Colonial Office, often timid or torpid in its dealings with soldiers, responded to this initiative and sought Ardagh's advice on the equipment and constitution of local defence forces.

The less formal relations which the Office had begun to maintain with other departments were carried a stage further by the formation of inter-departmental committees on which it had a seat. In 1901 attendance upon such committees was already a heavy burden. Some were *ad hoc* bodies. The early years of the present century also saw the beginnings of the existing system of standing advisory committees, composed of a mixture of officials and experts. The impetus given by Chamberlain to the study of tropical diseases resulted in 1904 in the establishment of an advisory committee to administer a Tropical Diseases Research Fund. It was followed in 1905 by a Colonial Survey Committee, to accumulate accurate information about various territories, mainly tropical, under United Kingdom control.

Critics argued at this time that officials visited the colonies all too rarely and were ignorant of local conditions in consequence. It could not of course be said that such visits were unknown. In 1877 a man had been sent out to report on Transvaal finances. In 1888 Meade could enumerate some seven visits paid by various officials to Crown colonies alone.[4] It was felt, however, that there were not enough of such visits and that in those cases where they were tried the experience gained was largely wasted when the official returned. A system of exchanges, with which Chamberlain seems to have toyed, was advocated after his resignation, and regular periods of secondment were also recommended. Neither appears to have been adopted at this time, though in 1903 the establishment was based on the supposition that two first-division clerks would always be absent in the

[1] Monypenny and Buckle, *Life of Disraeli*, VI, 550.
[2] B.M. Add. MSS. 41224 ff. 19, 20.
[3] Sir William Butler was appointed to the South African command without the knowledge, and to the dismay of Chamberlain. Garvin, *Life of...Chamberlain*, II, 384, 452.
[4] *Parl. Pap.* 1888, xxvii [C. 5545], Q. 12359.

colonies. Perhaps the Office felt that short tours and exchanges were unnecessary in view of the growing custom of filling higher colonial posts on a permanent basis with officials from Whitehall. In 1873 Kimberley sent a first-class clerk to Ceylon. Next year Carnarvon, on nominating another clerk to a Governorship, remarked that it was "of advantage when some at least of our Governors are men who have been well trained in this Office, and are familiar with its traditions and practice".[1] Between 1890 and 1907 Sydney Olivier had three spells in the West Indies, ending with the Governorship of Jamaica. (Sir) Augustus Hemming and (Sir) John Anderson were both clerks before they became Governors. In like manner, by sending out (Sir) George Fiddes and J. F. Perry to Cape Town, the Office did not fail to contribute towards the building of the "new" South Africa at the turn of the century. But the just claims of "professional" members of the Colonial Services prevented this type of appointment from being common.

Colonial ministers, especially Canadians, naturally now paid frequent visits to London and groups of Premiers came for the Jubilees. The evidence suggests that the visits were successful and some of the credit for it is due to the Office. Carnarvon continued to entertain at Highclere even after he had left office, and Chamberlain and Lyttelton extended hospitality.

The visits of colonial statesmen, apart from their main purpose, had been welcomed by the Office as a means of gaining rapid and authoritative opinions upon particular colonial questions. But the coincidence of visits and crises was fortuitous and the Office must on balance have been glad when the first High Commissioner (for Canada) was appointed in 1880. Sir Alexander Galt, and his two successors, Sir Charles Tupper and Lord Strathcona and Mount Royal, were men of distinction in Canadian life who understood the ways of government. The two former had held Cabinet rank in their own country. This doubtless helped to give prestige to the High Commissionership and to enable its occupant to lead the corps of colonial quasi-diplomats in its dealings with the United Kingdom Government.

Naturally enough the Colonial Secretaries were the High Commissioners' main point of contact, but from the first they dealt with officials in the department and were not denied access to other ministers and even to the Prime Minister himself. On some of these occasions at least the Office seems to have played singularly little part beyond putting the negotiators into touch. This was sometimes so even where the situation was delicate. Both sides no doubt had yet to learn the advantages of "commendation" by the weaker to the stronger.

Between 1871 and 1901 "professional" Governors of Crown

[1] Office Minutes, 1869–74, vol 5, no. 92.

colonies appear to have outnumbered every other type. But even in Crown colonies non-professional appointments were made and in the self-governing colonies and for Governor-Generalships they were the rule. The Governors-General were drawn from a high social stratum. In 1878 Hicks Beach suggested to Disraeli that Lord Lorne (afterwards Duke of Argyll), the Queen's son-in-law, should succeed Lord Dufferin at Rideau Hall. The idea went down well and a connection between Governorships and the Royal Family was thus established. When his term in Canada ended Lorne made it known that he would like to go on to New South Wales. But later he dropped the idea[1] and when in 1899 he was suggested as the first Governor-General of Australia the Queen objected. In 1888 Queensland advanced the suggestion that Governorships should only be filled after the advice of local governments had been taken. Other self-governing colonies were invited to give their views, but Canada was opposed to the idea and it was not formally adopted. Thenceforth, however, the Australian colonies were in practice normally consulted, and this led to their putting forward their own recommendations. In 1898 Chamberlain reported that it was becoming hard to find men to fill Governorships. This was due to the demands of the colonies themselves for men "of high rank and remarkable distinction" coupled with a disinclination to pay salaries attractive to such persons. The Colonial Secretary contemplated inviting the Governments concerned to improve the emoluments. No doubt the Australian colonies were the chief applicants for highly placed Governors and in their case the difficulty was removed when, upon confederation, the Governors of States necessarily lost prestige to the Governor-General. Chamberlain accordingly felt that those colonies would have to forgo their previous aversion to Governors who had served in Crown colonies.

The High Commissionership in South Africa was one of the most difficult posts to fill. It has been seen that the Queen disliked the re-appointment of Sir Hercules Robinson in 1895 and tried to get him removed. When he returned to England there was an interval of six months during which a successor was sought. It was Selborne, the Parliamentary Under-Secretary, who eventually suggested Milner (believed at the time to be Rhodes's candidate) after Salisbury had failed to persuade Chamberlain to accept Sir Harry Johnston.

In this era of high imperialism the Office took some steps to educate public opinion in colonial affairs. In the nineteenth century official information was imparted mainly through papers called for in Parliament. Though this system had its merits, it did not supply that steady flow of semi-popular material that political instruction demands. Thus the public was occasionally subjected, as after Isandhlwana, to rude shocks. Carnarvon, who had a stronger publicity sense than most politicians of his time and studied the

[1] G.D. 29/120. Derby to Granville, 18 Aug. 1884 and 15 Jan. 1885.

colonial press, perceived that all was not well. He is credited on one occasion with sitting up all night to ensure that a reliable text of one of his speeches should reach South Africa. Ripon began the practice of cabling the texts of Parliamentary statements to colonial destinations[1] and Chamberlain and Sir Winston Churchill followed this lead. "Before controversy became too rancorous" Chamberlain was also in the habit of receiving journalists of all parties.[2] Flora Shaw (later Lady Lugard), the chief correspondent of *The Times* in South Africa, was a constant associate of his. Visual publicity was catered for by a Visual Instruction Committee set up in 1902 to give the peoples of the Empire, especially schoolchildren, a picture of imperial geography, social life and economic possibilities. To provide more solid reading the Office tried, though without much success, to improve the quality of colonial Annual Reports.

V

The latest age opens with a notable change: the separation of what we must now begin to call "Dominions" work from the management of the dependent Empire. At the Imperial Conference of 1907 the Australian and New Zealand Prime Ministers had urged this separation. While not alleging that the old Colonial Office had failed in its duty, they pointed out (through Deakin's mouth) that "the whole tendency of the whole department, and of its officers, is to become imbued, both consciously and unconsciously, with principles of government properly applicable to the great countries with which they are dealing,...but which are very foreign, and in some cases almost antagonistic, to the principles on which the affairs of self-governing Colonies are conducted".[3] Elgin supported the proposed separation during the Conference and, soon after its close, informed Dominion Governments that a "Dominions Division" was in being. The division dealt with Canada, Australia, New Zealand and Newfoundland (the four Dominions of those days), the four self-governing South African colonies, and, because of their proximity to autonomous communities, with the South African High Commission territories (Basutoland, the Bechuanaland Protectorate and Swaziland), the Western Pacific High Commission territories and Fiji.

A permanent secretariat to collect information for the Conference and generally to attend to its affairs was another outcome of the meetings of 1907. It was formed within the Dominions department on 1 December 1907. (Sir) Hartmann Just, an Assistant Under-Secretary, was made permanent secretary of the Conference and was given two assistant secretaries. These officers carried on their ordinary

[1] *Hansard*, 4th ser. CLXIX, 686.
[2] Garvin, *Life of...Chamberlain*, III, 15.
[3] Quoted in Fiddes, *Dominions and Colonial Offices*, p. 246.

duties in addition to serving the secretariat. The arrangement was condemned by Conservatives as hampering the growth of an "Imperial Council",[1] and they later argued that the commingling of Conference and ordinary business must result in neglect of the former. The Government, however, would not admit that extra staff or a finer demarcation of function was required, and asserted that the Dominions were satisfied with what had been contrived. It has been claimed[2] that the business of the next (1911) Conference, the first to be called "Imperial", was more carefully arranged than ever before, but it is doubtful whether the secretariat could have been very valuable.

Since at least the end of the last century the argument had been heard that responsibility for Dominion affairs should be entirely removed from the Colonial Secretary's hands.[3] The project was much in Deakin's mind before and during the Colonial Conference of 1907, and Lord Crewe when in office is said to have favoured it.[4] Dr A. A. Lynch, an Irish Nationalist member and a native of Australia, asked in Parliament in 1910 for a Dominions Secretary of State,[5] and J. E. B. Seely (later Lord Mottestone), speaking on the 1911 Colonial Office estimates, gave it some attention. He remarked that the practical alternatives were to give Dominion affairs to a sinecure minister or to the Prime Minister himself. The former suggestion would not suit the Dominions and the latter would not suit the Prime Minister.[6] Consideration at the forthcoming Imperial Conference was promised, and proposals were in fact then brought forward by New Zealand and South Africa. L. V. Harcourt would have been reluctantly willing to accept a Secretary of State for Imperial Affairs, though not under that title. Canada, ever conservative over questions of imperial organisation, did not, however, want a change, and the Conference framed no resolution on the point. The First World War stopped these constitutional debates for a time. In 1916 and 1917, however, suggestions for a change in title or a division of the Office were again heard in Parliament. The Government turned them all down. No doubt it could safely do so, for public interest in them was eclipsed by broader issues of imperial consultation.

On the outbreak of war in 1914 the United Kingdom had refrained from intervening in Dominion policy. It felt equally debarred from consultation, and by the end of 1916 nothing had been achieved beyond securing for Borden and Hughes, when in London, temporary seats in the Cabinet. The exclusion of the Colonial Secretary from the

[1] Hewins, *Apologia of an Imperialist*, I, 208, 211.
[2] *Oxford Survey of the British Empire, General*, p. 6.
[3] See an article in *Fortnightly Review*, new ser. LXVIII (1900), pp. 25–7, by Beckles Willson who advocated a Secretary of State for each self-governing colony!
[4] *Hansard*, 5th ser. XVIII, 998.   [5] *Ibid.* 22–3.
[6] *Ibid.* 966–7, 971.

small War Cabinet formed by Lloyd George in December 1916 did not improve matters. Walter Long protested, alleging that the Dominions would resent it. Lloyd George's response was to tell Long that the Dominions ought to be brought more into consultation and to that end should be invited to a discussion. Events moved rapidly thereafter—so much so that Long gave Professor W. A. S. Hewins the impression that the Cabinet were "jumped" into constituting an "Imperial War Executive" without prior consultation with the Colonial Office or the Dominions.[1] Though this is hardly fair to Lloyd George, there is little doubt that Long was, in this all-important question, dragged behind his ebullient chief and took little part himself in framing the agenda for the ensuing meetings. Though Long sat in the new Imperial War Cabinet and presided over the Imperial War Conference, it was Lloyd George and (Sir) Maurice (later Lord) Hankey who were the heroes of those remarkable experiments. From their successful inception a decline in the prestige of the Office on the Dominions side may be dated, which the system of direct communication between Prime Ministers (begun in 1918) may have helped to promote.[2]

Towards the end of the war and immediately after its close the Dominions division seems to have been very short of staff and to have dissipated a proportion of its energies upon matters of secondary importance—"donkey work" for the Dominions, as a former private secretary called it.[3] In economic policy, however, it made a valuable contribution. Public interest in imperial economic solidarity was, of course, much older than the War. It had been fostered by Tariff Reformers and in 1912 the step had been taken of appointing a Royal Commission to survey the economic resources of the Dominions and the requirements of both the Dominions and the United Kingdom in primary products. Tariff policy was excluded from the Commission's purview. An expert has said that the Commission was appointed "not before it was time",[4] perhaps implying that if the Colonial Office had been up to the mark it would have long before collected the information for itself. The Commission's evidence and the factual material which the Tariff Commission had been assembling must have been of great value to the Imperial War Conference which, from its inception in 1917, largely concerned itself with the increase and employment of the Empire's food supply and natural resources. The 1917 Conference, having passed a resolution in favour of Imperial Preference, left its residual problems in the hands of a United Kingdom Cabinet Committee on Trade Relations of the United Kingdom within the Empire. The Colonial Secretary presided, and, with the

---

[1] Hewins, *Apologia of an Imperialist*, II, 102.

[2] Borden rubbed in the consequences of this new system by telegraphing direct to Lloyd George as soon as he was back in Canada: *Memoirs*, II, 855.

[3] *Hansard*, 5th ser. CLXVII, 1426–7. The speaker was Lord Sandon.

[4] Howarth, (Sir) Rupert, *Oxford Survey of the British Empire, General*, p. 342.

enthusiastic aid of Professor Hewins, the staff of the Colonial Office and the War Trade Committee, put together a notable series of reports on Empire resources. The 1918 Conference took some important decisions upon the future availability of economic supplies in the light of these reports. But, for reasons which were no doubt partly political, these resolutions were overlooked after the Armistice and, when Hewins was dropped from the Administration, the chief motive force was lost. It is, however, noteworthy that economic preparation for the coming peace was largely centred upon the Colonial Office. A vigorous promotion of imperial trade implied some organisation at home to deal with traders' daily needs. In 1917 the Department of Overseas Trade was established with this object, and by 1921 had seventy-seven "Trade Commissioners and Correspondents" in the Empire overseas. It is perhaps indicative of the impaired prestige of the Colonial Office that it obtained no voice in the Department's affairs, which from the start had been controlled by the Foreign Office and Board of Trade.

After the war the Colonial Office acquired on its Dominions side two new responsibilities. In December 1922 the Irish Free State was created with Dominion status. This brought Southern Irish affairs technically within the purview of the Colonial Office. The Chief Secretary's Office was abolished in September 1922 and the Irish Office thereupon became jointly responsible to the Colonial and Home Offices, until in April 1924 it was abolished in its turn and the surviving work absorbed by the Dominions division. In 1917 an Empire Settlement Committee had been established. This was succeeded by a Government Emigration Committee in 1919, subsequently renamed the Oversea Settlement Committee, under the chairmanship of the Colonial Secretary, and the vice-chairmanship of an Assistant Under-Secretary. An Oversea Settlement Office was set up to serve it, which absorbed the Emigrants' Information Office and handled migration questions as a sub-department of the Dominions division.

From 1919 there had been some Parliamentary agitation to take Dominion affairs from the Colonial Office. Sometimes the Prime Minister, sometimes the Lord President, was designated as the ideal person to handle them. Blank refusals were returned by the Government. From June 1920 critics varied their tactics and asked for a change in the minister's title. These suggestions were at first also rejected, but from February 1921 met with promises of consideration and, after November 1922, with surmises that, if the Dominions required a change, they would lay a resolution before the Imperial Conference. The Labour government of 1924 was no more favourable than its predecessors. On the next change of administration *The Times*, dwelling upon the importance of the burdens of the Office, urged L. S. Amery to part with the largest share of his responsibilities, and declared that the time was over-ripe for the frank recognition that his department was not the proper channel for Dominions *liaison*.[1] A statement of 11 June 1925[2] showed that the plunge had at last been taken and in Committee of Supply on 27 June the reasons for severance were expounded.[3] The new burdens that had been laid upon both sides of the Office were emphasised. Ireland and Empire settlement pressed upon the Dominions division; while to the Crown colonies division there had recently been added Zanzibar (1913), the ex-enemy colonial territories immediately after the war, and Northern Rhodesia (1924). By the separation, as Amery pointed out a little later,[4] both sides of the Office should profit. The Government was as much opposed as any of their predecessors to putting Dominion affairs under the Prime Minister, and the only course seemed to be to create, by executive action, a new department.[5] This came into being on 1 July and was welcomed by the Opposition at Westminster, and the Prime Ministers of Australia and New Zealand.[6] Others, Hewins and Berriedale Keith among them, were less enthusiastic.[7] Though it is hard to follow their objections, it must be admitted that the change had little immediate effect. The Dominions and Colonial Secretaryships of State, to the regret of *The Times*,[8] continued to be held by Amery, thus to some extent frustrating the arguments for separation; and many services, notably the important establishment branch, remained common to the two departments, which continued to share the same building. In fact the change amounted to little more than the creation of additional Parliamentary and Permanent Under-Secretaryships.

Was there any substance in the argument that the old Colonial Office was ill-equipped to deal with Dominion affairs? In 1902 Chamberlain had set a good example by visiting South Africa. Had he stayed in office he would have visited all the Dominions. The experience of Milner, Secretary of State from 1919 to 1921, needs no bush. Bonar Law was bred in Canada, and the Duke of Devonshire had been her Governor-General. Visits by officials were favoured by the Office before the First World War and their resumption was from time to time asked for. But except for (Sir) George Fiddes, who had been a member of Milner's South African staff for years, no official had spent any length of time in a Dominion, and with the

---

[1] *The Times*, 11 Nov. 1924, 15*b* and *c*.   [2] *Hansard*, 5th ser. CLXXXIV, 2239–40.
[3] *Ibid.* CLXXXVII, 66–70.
[4] *The Times*, 12 June 1925, 5*f*, and 23 June, 18*d*.
[5] It was evidently believed at first that legislation would be necessary: *The Times*, 12 May 1925, 16*g*.
[6] *Hansard*, 5th ser. CLXXXVII, 92, 103; *The Times*, 13 June, 14*b*. The President of Toronto University gave an informal Canadian blessing: *ibid.* 16 June, 11*e*.
[7] Keith, *Responsible Government in the Dominions* (1928 ed.), II, 915; Hewins, *Apologia of an Imperialist*, II, 299.
[8] 1 July, 17*b* and *c*.

more distant territories the Office may well have been out of touch. The Agent-General for New South Wales declared in 1918 that the staff of the Dominions department ought to have "served their apprenticeship" in the Dominions, and recommended the never popular system of exchange.[1]

The augmentation of the corps of High Commissioners, however, helped to draw closer the contacts hitherto largely maintained by Governors-General and Governors. To the Canadian High Commissioner there had been added in 1905 a High Commissioner for New Zealand, replacing an Agent-General. Australia (1910), South Africa (1911), Newfoundland (1921) and Southern Rhodesia (1925) had subsequently appointed High Commissioners, and the Agents-General for the Australian States remained. F. S. Malan, however, had to admit in 1911 that the South African High Commissioner was little more than a commercial agent.[2] Harcourt had begun the practice of seeing the High Commissioners regularly every month, and they sometimes called upon him as often as once a week. By 1913 the Australian High Commissioner is said to have won the leadership.[3] If this was so, the Office, which had had something of a Canadian and South African bias, should have benefited.

The evolution of a technique for dealing with the autonomous communities within the Empire should have aroused the interest of every politician who held the seals. Colonial Secretaries of the twentieth century must nevertheless have felt that the most fascinating parts of their work lay with the dependencies. Here there were three main problems to be faced: the development of tropical regions along the lines laid down by Chamberlain; the provision of staff to manage them; and the administration of the new mandated territories in the Middle East.

After the war was over the Middle East was in turmoil. Two Arab kings, the recipients of subsidies from different departments in London, were at war; in the winter of 1920 a revolt in Iraq had had to be put down at great cost. The multiplicity of authorities dealing with these territories was in part to blame for this situation. Palestine and western Arabia were the concern of the Foreign Office; Mesopotamia and central Arabia of the India Office. The Government was urged to form a unified department to deal with this wide area and so end the conflict between authorities "hitherto engaged in promoting rival policies".[4] T. E. Lawrence, attributing the crisis to mismanagement by Curzon, expostulated with Lloyd George, and the Prime Minister, unwilling to move Curzon, decided to transfer the whole area to the Colonial Office and put the Office under a vigorous

[1] *The Times*, 21 June 1918, 3*c*; *Empire Review*, XXXII (1918), 224.
[2] *Parl. Pap.* 1911, LIV [Cd. 5745], p. 92.
[3] Tupper, *Supplement to the Life of...Sir Charles Tupper*, p. 112. The first U.K. High Commissioner (to Canada) was appointed in 1927.
[4] *Hansard*, 5th ser. CXXXVI, 1289–90. The words are the present Lord Harlech's.

minister. Accordingly (Sir) Winston Churchill moved to the Colonial Office early in 1921 and, by March, had established a Middle East division to deal with Palestine, Iraq and Arabia, staffed with "half a dozen very able men" from outside. Lawrence was made Political Adviser and, during his stay of under eighteen months, worked admirably with his chief and colleagues, while Sir Winston Churchill threw himself into the work with great energy.[1] The connection of the Middle East with the Colonial Office, though not a long one, was vital while it lasted. In the later nineteenth century it seemed the path of wisdom to deprive the Foreign Office of administrative functions; in the twentieth to deprive the Colonial Office of quasi-diplomatic ones. By a strange reversal the former lost a portion of its diplomatic work to the Colonial Office at the very moment when the latter was discarding its secular responsibility for the new Empire democracies. Thus Colonial Office attention was deflected from the more primitive dependencies as effectively as though Dominion affairs had remained.

The Crown Colonies division achieved much during this period. It had no easy task. Problems were wide in scope and technical in nature. They defied the frontiers of geographical departments, yet could not be brought within the narrow bounds of the General department. They were accordingly tackled by means of committees and bureaux, temporary and permanent. Of these the more permanent bodies are the more interesting and more peculiar to colonial administration. The Imperial Institute, whose management was transferred in 1907 from the Board of Trade, must first be named. As early as 1898 Colonial Office clerks had been advised to draw upon its stores of knowledge. In 1909 Crewe established the Advisory Medical and Sanitary Committee for Tropical Africa and the Tropical Entomological Research Committee. The former became the Colonial Advisory Medical Council. The latter was absorbed in 1913 into the Imperial Bureau (later Institute) of Entomology. A Colonial Veterinary Committee sprang up in 1907. A Sleeping Sickness Bureau (renamed the Tropical Diseases Bureau after 1912) was in existence by 1909. In pursuance of a resolution of the Imperial War Conference, an Imperial Bureau of Mycology was established in 1920. An outcome of somewhat similar wartime initiative was the Colonial Research Committee which was formed in 1919 to promote scientific and economic research in the colonies. In 1922 the functions of the Medical and Sanitary Committee were extended to the dependencies outside Africa. A "Discovery" Committee was set up in 1923. All these committees expressed the Chamberlain policy of exploiting the resources of the dependencies by means of scientific study and of improving the health of their human, animal and plant

---

[1] It appears to have been the original intention to transfer responsibility for the Aden Protectorate at this same time: *Hansard*, 5th ser. CXLIV. This, however, was not done until 1937.

populations. But at the same time some interesting experiments took place in other directions. West and East African Currency Boards were established in 1912 and 1920 respectively; while expert guidance in less material matters was provided by an Advisory Committee on Native Education in Africa which came into being in 1923.[1]

These committees were variously constituted. Some at least of them were mainly staffed by outside experts, official or academic. Some were chiefly concerned to advise on policy; others to administer a Treasury grant; while the chief function of the bureaux was to collect and distribute information. All were in greater or less degree connected with the Office, which frequently provided the chairman, the secretary, or some of the more powerful committee men.

The best advisory committee is ill adapted to supply daily guidance. For that purpose a body of full-time technical advisers is needed. As we know, the Office had had a Legal Adviser almost from its outset, and in 1897 Chamberlain had appointed (Sir) Patrick Manson, the authority on tropical diseases, his Medical Adviser. The Inspectors-General of the African regiments, when at home, acted as military advisers. Otherwise there were no advisers until the First World War had ended. Then in 1921 Sir James (later Lord) Stevenson, a financial expert, was made Commercial Adviser. Five years later a full-time Medical Advisership was created and the corps of advisers began gradually to swell. The existence of experts in all major colonies and the fear that the creation of complementary posts at the centre would look like interference, deterred the Office, despite Parliamentary advocacy, from moving forward rapidly on these lines.

The total establishment of the Colonial Office, including all ranks, was 125 in 1909, 187 in 1919 and 431 in 1925. The last figure included temporary staff retained for liquidating Irish business and the officers of the Oversea Settlement department. The Middle East and other mandated territories also help to account for the great increase over 1919. The 1909 figure seems small by contrast, but was not so by the standards of the previous century. The increase, which had occurred in the past fifteen years or so, was largely in the second division, which in 1909 numbered more than fifty; though observers still thought the first division was over-weighted.[2] In 1909 this division consisted of the Permanent and four Assistant Under-Secretaries (one a Legal Adviser), a chief clerk, thirty-two clerks in three classes and four private secretaries. In 1911 the Permanent Under-Secretaryship was still in the Colonial Secretary's gift. By

---

[1] The list is not complete. Cf. the list in Vernon and Mansergh's *Advisory Bodies*, pp. 498 *seqq.*, which purports to give all C.O. committees created 1919–39. Some Committees there mentioned do not occur above and *vice versa*. See also Dearle, *Dictionary of Official War-time* [1914–18] *Organisations*, pp. 74–8.

[2] Parkinson, *Colonial Office from Within*, p. 24; *Parl. Pap.* 1912–13, xv [Cd. 6535], p. 24; QQ. 5730, 5733, 5790.

1920 it had become a Government appointment. In 1911 three Assistant Under-Secretaryships (two of them legal) were abolished in pursuance of the old aim of putting more work upon the heads of departments. One of these posts, however, was revived in 1916, and the other in 1921 upon the creation of the Middle East division. The ancient office of chief clerk was abolished in 1917. In 1919 common salary scales were adopted throughout the service, and in 1920 the ranks of the Administrative class (the old first division) were renamed Assistant Secretary, Principal and Assistant Principal. Thus passed away the last vestiges of Colonial Office exclusiveness.

With insignificant exceptions appointment by patronage had gone by 1907. Administrative officers were recruited by the Class I Examination and the higher posts were usually filled by promotion from within. Two Permanent Under-Secretaries, however—Sir Francis Hopwood (later Lord Southborough) and Sir James Masterton Smith—came in from other departments. It was also still the practice to appoint private secretaries from time to time, who were not Colonial Office clerks. Thus (Sir) Lionel Earle followed Crewe to the Office in 1908 and stayed on after his departure: post-war examples can also be cited. In 1910, in an attempt to put recruitment to the Colonial Office upon a better footing, an additional assistant private secretary was appointed. He was mainly concerned with this patronage, and eventually created a proper Appointments Branch for the Colonial Services.

The quality of Administrative officers remained high. Sir John Anderson declared that there had been "no failures" in the first division.[1] Long paid a tribute to his staff, and in 1916 a private member took the unusual step of publicly praising the foresight of two officers of the department.[2] Perhaps in some ways the calibre was a shade too high, for it began to breed an arrogance and "brusquerie" which did not go down well with the public.

The second-division clerks continued to suffer from a sense of frustration. They laid their grievances before the MacDonnell Commission in 1912. Anderson said there had been no promotions from their class to the first division within living memory, but he was satisfied that this was solely due to a lack of merit. The hierarchy was still opposed to much devolution or regrading. Registration, posting letters, collecting and marking off papers were the appointed tasks of the division and they did them very well. Work of higher grade they might do less efficiently and so discredit themselves. War helped to dissolve this somewhat rigid attitude and in 1916 a clerk (H. T. Allen) was promoted from the second division into the first. A colleague followed him in 1919 and thenceforth such promotions, though never common, were not abnormal.

---

[1] *Parl. Pap.* 1912–13, xv [Cd. 6535], QQ. 5612, 5632, 5833.
[2] Long, *Memories*, p. 236; *Hansard*, 5th ser. LXXXV, 624–5.

Doubtless more devolution was required. In 1909 still too much of the work of juniors in the first division was routine. Those who thought that better grading would reduce the number of administrative officers were clearly in the right. Nor were men lacking upon whom much of this work could have been cast. As in the 'eighties, there were several higher-grade clerical posts. Only to the Accountant and the Librarian, however, was any real measure of discretion extended. Anderson thought that the existence of these posts, to which second-division clerks could hope to aspire, furnished that division with a sufficient incentive, and in a material sense he may have been right. By 1912 copying was in the hands of a staff of sixteen female typists, four of them shorthand writers. There were also four "supplementary clerks", a legacy from the Royal Niger Company, and a number of boy clerks, later abolished as a grade on the recommendation of the MacDonnell Commission.

The distribution of work in the Crown Colonies division, known from 1919 as the Colonies and Protectorates division, was not greatly affected by the changes of 1907. In 1908 the Mediterranean is found in the East African department. It was transferred next year to the West African—renamed the Gold Coast and Mediterranean department in 1918. A separate Niger department had been formed in the latter year, to be known from 1918 as the Nigeria department. In 1920 the Eastern department was divided into a Far Eastern and a Ceylon and Mauritius department and a Tanganyika and Somaliland department created. Such the structure remained until 1925. As is apparent, the departments were still almost wholly geographical—a distribution of work which was favourably commented upon by a departmental committee in 1927.[1]

Registration underwent no radical change before 1925. In 1907, however, as was to be expected, the Registry was split into two, and the Colonial Registry further divided into two and sometimes three branches. These two main sub-registries existed until 1917 when a military one was added. This had disappeared in 1925. A separate Middle East Sub-Registry first appears in 1921 and separate Telegraph and Dispatch sections in 1924.

The widening employment of the telegraph continued to revolutionise the conduct of imperial affairs. In 1902 the average daily number of telegrams received was 12·7; in 1904 it had dropped to 7·8; in 1914 it was 18·2, in 1918 32·2 and in 1922 19·7. Telegrams dispatched, which had numbered 2536 in 1907, had risen to 17,237 in 1915.[2] The wartime increase in words by cable was partly accounted for by the system begun by Long of dispatching to the Dominions a weekly appreciation of events. These circular telegrams subsequently became an outstanding feature of Commonwealth consultation.

---

[1] C.O. Confidential Print, Misc. no. 382, p. 7.
[2] *Hansard*, 5th ser. CLXIII, 1643–4.

During the early years of the twentieth century the work of the Office had much increased. Returning in 1911 after seven years overseas, Anderson noted a great change. The union of South Africa had barely affected the total quantity of work; for any reduction it may have achieved was offset by the keener interest now taken in the dependencies. The war must have been a painful burden, and peace brought no relief. The later Lord Elibank, then Gideon Murray, a former Colonial Service officer with experience in Downing Street, complained in Parliament in July 1919 that the department was understaffed and over-worked, and evoked a "Hear, hear" from Amery. He asked for more expenditure on staff (a desire gratified next year) and a system of regular discussions among officials.[1]

Not much that is significant has yet appeared about the personalities of ministers and officials who passed through the Office in this exciting period. Seeley thought Crewe "a man of outstanding quality of heart and brain".[2] Earle found Harcourt always ready to stand up for his department and careful to make the acquaintance of overseas visitors.[3] Bonar Law was one of the few members of Asquith's Coalition Cabinet who impressed W. M. Hughes as a realist.[4] Long was a conspicuously good administrator and a tireless correspondent.[5] He was fortunate in finding in Hewins, his Parliamentary Under-Secretary, a harmonious and energetic ally. (Sir) Winston Churchill, who had made his mark as Parliamentary Under-Secretary in Campbell-Bannerman's Cabinet, is remembered for vigorous onslaughts upon the Irish problem and the Middle East. The Duke of Devonshire's "high qualities", "kindliness" and "flashes of dry and ironical humour" were the admiration of his private secretary,[6] who equally found J. H. Thomas "a capital master and companion".[7]

The Office was fortunate in its Permanent Under-Secretaries. Sir Francis Hopwood (later Lord Southborough) came to it from the Board of Trade versed in Empire affairs. He was one of those figures, encountered from time to time in the public service, whose tact, restraint and presidential gifts mark them out for any task of special delicacy and he soon passed on to such work at the Admiralty. He was succeeded by Sir John Anderson whose whole career had been spent in the Office, until in 1904 he had gone to Singapore as Governor. "He was a lovable man", said one who worked under him.[8] He left for Ceylon in 1916, and Sir George Fiddes took his place. "That great civil servant", as Long called him,[9] had had a career of outstanding brilliance. His work first in the South African department and then

[1] *Hansard*, 5th ser. cxviii, 2210.
[2] Seeley, *Adventure*, p. 131.   [3] Earle, *Turn Over the Page*, p. 86.
[4] Lord Addison, *Four and a Half Years*, i, 183.
[5] Petrie, *Walter Long...*, p. 209.   [6] Marsh, *A Number of People*, p. 400.
[7] *Ibid.* p. 401.   [8] *Ibid.* p. 123.
[9] *Memories*, p. 236.

at the Cape had established his reputation. On returning to England, he had specialised in the Crown colonies and developed a peculiar aptitude for finance and currency questions. Intolerant of slowness or slacking, he sometimes appeared to his subordinates rather impatient, but on rising to the highest rank he seemed to lose some of his fierceness without any of his force. He was replaced by Masterton Smith, an outsider of varied experience. He has been described, perhaps with exaggeration, as "a miracle of efficiency".[1] He drove himself too hard, and, like several of his predecessors, broke down through overwork in 1924.

No account of the Colonial Office staff in this period could omit mention of (Sir) Charles P. Lucas who entered the Office in 1877 and rose to be an Assistant Under-Secretary. He was known to be an "Imperialist" of the Chamberlain school and shared that statesman's interest in Tariff Reform. He warmly welcomed Chamberlain's appointment and admired his successor. It has been suggested that these sympathies became publicly known and put him out of favour with Liberal governments, so that he was passed over when Ommaney left in 1907 and again in 1911. But a "certain modest shyness" that never left him may have been the real cause.[2] He retired prematurely in 1911, and, supported by an All Souls fellowship, devoted himself to writing about the Empire. He was long responsible for Dominion affairs, and was the first head of the Dominions division. His attractive personality had won him many friendships in the Dominions on his not infrequent visits. He was the editor and part author of a comprehensive set of handbooks called *The Historical Geography of the British Empire*—the *vade mecum* of all Imperialists of his day.

In the first twenty-five years of the present century, efforts, incomparably greater than any that had gone before, were made to provide the Colonial Service with an able and well qualified staff. These efforts drew attention again to a long-felt need: a closer personal contact in both directions between the Office and the dependencies. Previously this contact had been effected only by bringing permanently into the Office exalted colonial personages or sending to the colonies, as Governors, officials at the top of the Office. A few hasty visits, both by ministers and officials, had indeed been paid. Anderson said in 1912 they could well have been commoner.[3] No doubt they would have been but for the troublous times. At best, however, they could give but a superficial insight into conditions, and critics clamoured for a system of exchanges. The idea was not popular. A few "beachcombers", as officers seconded from the colonies came affectionately to be called, could have been found at work in White-

---

[1] Marsh, *op. cit.* p. 242.
[2] *The Times*, 8 May, 1931 (obituary).
[3] *Parl. Pap.* 1912–13, xv [Cd. 6535], Q. 5685.

hall shortly before and during the war, but suggestions made in 1921 and 1922 for a regular system of interchange were ignored or parried.

During this period some striking developments took place in the field of publicity. In the first decade of the century the Opposition usually made the colonial estimates debate an occasion for sallies. When notice was given of the directions from which attacks would come it was possible to prepare and present some general picture of colonial affairs by way of answer. The possibilities of this technique were, however, limited, and in 1912 Harcourt adopted the imaginative course of delivering a sweeping *tour d'horizon* which he hoped would spike the critics' guns and prevent attention from being concentrated upon shortcomings. His survey, arranged topically, was confined to the Crown colonies. The speech met with a mixed reception, but on the whole may be reckoned a success. The experiment was repeated the next year, resumed in 1919 and normally imitated afterwards.

Efforts to provide literary information of the kind that members of Parliament had on these occasions demanded were made from time to time. Committees sat in 1910 and 1917 to review the quality of colonial Annual and Administration Reports and statistical abstracts. Their recommendations for a more attractive presentation seem, however, to have been ineffective. From 1909 to 1914 severely factual surveys of the work of the Dominions division were issued as Command Papers. A more interesting enterprise was the foundation of the *Colonial Office Journal* in 1907. Edited by officials, with ministerial approval, it was intended as a review of literature about the colonies and as a forum for the discussion of administrative but not of political questions. Originally concerned with the Dominions and with Downing Street, it came at length to confine itself to the dependencies. In 1913 it changed its name to the *Colonial Journal*, and it died in 1920.

During the war the Office, long opposed to any kind of governmental aid to the press, started to cable out the texts of important speeches and later to subsidise a news-service. The subsidy, then shared between several Empire governments, was still in being in 1920, by which time the Office had a part-time press officer to scrutinise the cables.

VI

The historian of a church or a party, a factory or an academy, may hope, when his work is done, to be able to delineate the character of his subject. The British Civil Service, or a branch of it, is more elusive. The Civil Service is but a vehicle for achieving the ever-changing aims of a succession of ministers. Inferentially the Colonial Office is the repository not of a single tradition of imperial policy, but of a variety of traditions.

Nevertheless, one who has worked in the Office—or for that matter in any other department of State—will soon perceive that his conduct is swayed by a body of custom—a local adaptation of something that pervades the whole Service—which displays the "mind" of the Office. The Treasury "mind", the Colonial Office "mind" are real, if intangible, entities, which all officials will recognise either with affection, resignation or animosity. It is this "mind", so hard to capture in dead files or to record by exact historical method, that the definitive history of the Colonial Office must some day portray. Meanwhile any generalisation must perforce be provisional and perhaps naïve.

During the Victorian age the Colonial Office was never without extremely able men, and their number waxed as time advanced. They were actuated by the highest principles; they were tireless and, in an academic sense, their knowledge of the colonies was immense. What, then, was wrong with the Office? Briefly, it lacked inspiration. By word of mouth, by well-phrased literature, it could have painted the colonies in all their exciting variety and fired the public to demand bigger votes and ampler staff. It never did. In the nineteenth century ministers did not rise in the Commons to extol the virtues of colonial society. The House waited until 1912 for a general appraisement of progress in the dependencies. No efforts were made to improve the quality of colonial Annual Reports until Ripon's time, and then they failed.

In short the Colonial Office staff was too intellectual to be imaginative. Moreover, it was imprisoned in its environment. The culture of London seemed so polished that it was hard to treat with perfect seriousness the aspirations of Toronto or Auckland, Lagos or Belize. To the men of Whitehall the civilisation of the colonies, whether newly contrived by expatriated Britons or the child of the primordial jungle, was not merely different from their own, it was inferior to it. Colonial peoples were like children and were to be treated with all the kindness and severity of the Victorian parent. By the end of the First World War many events had occurred, both in the Office and outside, to make a change in that outlook inevitable. How far that change had actually taken place by 1925 will only be determined upon the "opening" of the files.

BIBLIOGRAPHY

Part I. Collections of Manuscripts in Public and Private Archives, and Official Papers and Publications

1. Public Record Office.
2. Other Collections.
3. Select List of Parliamentary Papers.
4. Select List of Parliamentary Debates.

Part II. Other Works

1. General Bibliography
   (a) Bibliographies and Guides.
   (b) Periodicals.
   (c) Collected Historical Records.
   (d) General Histories and Descriptive Works.
   (e) Biographies.

2. Special Bibliographies
   A. Colonial Policy and Administration in General, 1870–1921 (chapters I, II, V, X and XI).
   B. The Opening of Tropical Africa, 1870–1914 (chapters III, IV, etc.).
   C. Imperial Finance, Trade and Communications, 1870–1914 (chapters VI and XII).
   D. International Relations and Colonial Affairs, 1869–1914 (chapters IV, VIII, XIII and XIV).
   E. The British Empire and the United States of America, 1870–1914 (chapter IX).
   F. Imperial Defence, 1870–1914 (chapters VII and XV).
   G. The Empire at War, 1914–18 (chapter XVI).
   H. The British Empire and the Peace Treaties, 1918–19 (chapter XVII).
   I. International Law and Colonial Questions, 1870–1914 (chapter XVIII).
   J. The Colonial Office (chapter XIX).

A note, added for the second impression, is printed after page 908.

BIBLIOGRAPHY

Compiled by A. Taylor Milne

For the history of individual countries of the Commonwealth reference should be made to the bibliographies in vols. IV–VIII. Attention here is confined to general matters of imperial policy and administration during the period under review (1870–1921). Similar material for earlier periods is described in vols. I and II of the History.

PART I

COLLECTIONS OF MANUSCRIPTS IN PUBLIC AND PRIVATE ARCHIVES, AND OFFICIAL PAPERS AND PUBLICATIONS

I. PUBLIC RECORD OFFICE

(a) COLONIAL OFFICE

The emergence of a separate department of state concerned with colonial affairs is noted in the Bibliography of *C.H.B.E.* vol. II, p. 885, and its development is described in chapter XIX of the present volume (above, pp. 711–68). From 1870 until 1925 the Secretary of State for the Colonies was responsible for relations with the self-governing Dominions, as well as for the administration of the non-self-governing territories. Within the Colonial Office the two aspects of its work gradually became separated and this practical separation was formally recognised in 1907 by the division of the Office into three sections—one responsible for Dominions Affairs, another for the Crown Colonies, the third a General Division. Until 1925, however, all these divisions continued to operate under a single head, with a common establishment and common services, housed in the building in Downing Street erected for the Colonial Office. In 1925 the Dominions Office took over all business relating to the self-governing Dominions, the Irish Free State, Southern Rhodesia and the High Commission territories of Basutoland, Bechuanaland and Swaziland, together with all work relating to the Imperial Conference.

SECRETARIES OF STATE FOR THE COLONIES, 1870–1921

1870, July 6.	John Wodehouse, 1st Earl of Kimberley.
1874, February 21.	Henry H. M. Herbert, 9th Earl of Carnarvon.
1878, February 4.	Sir Michael Hicks Beach (later Earl St Aldwyn).
1880, April 28.	Earl of Kimberley.
1882, December 11.	Edward H. Stanley, 24th Earl of Derby.
1885, June 24.	Frederick A. Stanley, cr. Lord Stanley, 1886 (later 25th Earl of Derby).
1886, February 6.	Granville George Leveson-Gower, 5th Earl Granville.
August 3.	Edward Stanhope.
1887, January 14.	Sir Henry T. Holland, 1st Lord Knutsford, 1888 (later 1st Viscount Knutsford).
1892, August 17.	George F. S. Robinson, 1st Marquess of Ripon.
1895, June 28.	Joseph Chamberlain.
1903, October 9.	Alfred Lyttelton.

1905, December 11.   Victor A. Bruce, 2nd Lord Elgin.
1908, April 16.   Robert O. A. Crewe-Milnes, 1st Earl of Crewe (later Marquess of Crewe).
1910, November 7.   Lewis Harcourt (later Viscount Harcourt).
1915, May 27.   Andrew Bonar Law.
1916, December 11.   Walter H. Long (later Viscount Long).
1919, January.   Alfred Milner, 1st Viscount Milner.
1921, February 14.   Winston L. S. Churchill (later Sir Winston Churchill).

PERMANENT UNDER-SECRETARIES OF STATE FOR THE COLONIES, 1870–1921

1859–71.   Sir Frederic Rogers (later Lord Blachford).
1871–92.   Sir Robert W. Herbert.
1892–97.   Sir Robert Henry Meade.
1897–1900.   Sir Edward Wingfield.
1900–07.   Sir Montagu Ommaney.
1907–11.   Sir Francis Hopwood (later Lord Southborough).
1911–16.   Sir John Anderson.
1916–21.   Sir George V. Fiddes.

The records of the Colonial Office preserved at the Public Record Office are now, with few exceptions, open to public inspection to the end of the year 1902. No permits are required for the inspection of later printed gazettes, colonial and dominion sessional papers and similar papers issued in Commonwealth countries. M. S. Giuseppi's *Guide to the Manuscripts preserved in the Public Record Office* (2 vols. 1923–4) will continue to be useful for indicating relevant classes of documents until the printed *Lists and Indexes* of Colonial Office, Foreign Office, Admiralty, Board of Trade and other records are more up-to-date. The current printed *List of Colonial Office Records in the Public Record Office* (P.R.O. Lists and Indexes, No. XXXVI, 1911) notes only original correspondence to 1837, together with sessional papers of the colonies and other printed material to 1899. A comprehensive *List of Colonial Office Records* has been issued in typescript form (10 foolscap vols. P.R.O. 1950), with two *Supplementary lists* (P.R.O. 1954). There are also at the Public Record Office type-script lists of *Colonial Office Registers* (P.R.O. 1948) and of *Colonial Office Confidential Print* (P.R.O. 1947).

Most of the classes of documents noted in *C.H.B.E.* vol. II, pp. 887–94, continue through the period covered by the present volume. Many of the papers noted below are not yet open to public inspection but are included for convenience of future reference. Classes to be found for most colonies are as follows: (1) Original correspondence with the Secretary of State (in-letters, reports and enclosures); (2) Entry-books of out-letters, commissions, warrants, etc.; (3) Registers of original correspondence; (4) Registers of out-letters; (5) Colonial Acts; (6) Sessional papers, consisting of minutes and journals of Colonial Councils and Assemblies, the earlier ones in manuscript; (7) Government Gazettes of colonies; (8) Miscellanea, com-prising colonial newspapers (often the only surviving copies), blue books of statistics, shipping and other returns. Other classes relating to the colonies as a whole and to the dependant Empire are included, also a few series not available when the lists were drawn up for previous volumes.

AFRICA, BRITISH CENTRAL, AND NYASALAND PROTECTORATE

C.O. 525. Original Correspondence. 1904–39. 183 volumes.
C.O. 625. Acts. 1901–36. 4 volumes.
C.O. 626. Sessional Papers, 1907–40. 21 volumes.
C.O. 541. Government Gazettes. 1894–1939. 14 volumes.
C.O. 452. Miscellanea. 1897–1939. 44 volumes.

Africa, East (Kenya)

C.O. 533. Original Correspondence. 1903–39. 515 volumes.
C.O. 628. (Ind. 17849, 18432–3, 18758–61, 19091, 19099.) Register of Correspondence. 1904–26. 17 volumes.
C.O. 629. (Ind. 17850, 18434, 18788–90, 19100–?.) Register of Out-Letters, 1924–26. 9 volumes.
C.O. 630. Acts. 1901–40. 14 volumes.
C.O. 542. Government Gazettes. 1908–40. 38 volumes.
C.O. 544. Sessional Papers. 1903–40. 58 volumes.
C.O. 543. Miscellanea, 1901–39. 30 volumes.

Africa, East, and Uganda Protectorate

C.O. 519. Original Correspondence. 1904–5. 1 volume.
C.O. 457. Government Gazettes. 1899–1907. 7 volumes.

Africa, West

C.O. 554. Original Correspondence. 1911–39. 122 volumes.
C.O. 537. Original Correspondence. Supplementary. 1884–1909. 16 volumes.
C.O. 555. (Ind. 18762–3, 19123–7.) Register of Correspondence. 1911–26. 7 volumes.
C.O. 694. Vol. 9 (Ind. 15631). Register of Secret Correspondence, 1889–98. 1 volume.

Africa, West: Niger and West Africa Frontier Force

C.O. 445. Original Correspondence. 1898–1926. 69 volumes.
C.O. 581. (Ind. 15640.) Register of Correspondence. 1898–9. 1 volume.
C.O. 582. (Ind. 15641.) Register of Out-Letters. 1898–9. 1 volume.
C.O. 641. (Ind. 17865–7, 18437, 18812–4, 19126–30.) Register of Correspondence. 1900–26. 12 volumes.
C.O. 642. (Ind. 17868–70, 18438, 18815–7, 19131–3.) Register of Out-Letters. 1900–26. 10 volumes.
C.O. 694. Vol. 9 (Ind. 15631.) Register of Secret Correspondence. 1889–98. 1 volume.

Antigua and Montserrat

See also under Montserrat

C.O. 7. Original Correspondence. 1702–1872. 144 volumes. Registers for 1850–72 are included under Leeward Islands.
C.O. 393. Entry Books of Correspondence. 1816–72. 15 volumes.
C.O. 8. Acts. 1668–1936 (Antigua). 38 volumes.
C.O. 9. Sessional Papers (Antigua). 1704–1940. 71 volumes.
C.O. 10. Miscellanea. 1666–1887. 71 volumes.

Bahamas

C.O. 23. Original Correspondence. 1696–1939. 320 volumes.
C.O. 333. (Ind. 12909–18, 15381–2, 18369, 18833, 19138–40.) Register of Correspondence. 1850–1926. 17 volumes.
C.O. 24. Entry Books of Out-Letters. 1717–1872. 34 volumes.
C.O. 508. (Ind. 12919–21, 15596–7, 18412, 18834, 19141–2.) Register of Out-Letters. 1872–1926. 9 volumes.

C.O. 25. Acts. 1729–1938. 36 volumes.
C.O. 26. Sessional Papers. 1721–1939. 130 volumes.
C.O. 564. Government Gazettes. 1894–1940. 11 volumes.
C.O. 27. Miscellanea. 1721–1938. 136 volumes.

BARBADOS

C.O. 28. Original Correspondence. 1689–1873, 1886–1939. 323 volumes and bundles. From 1874–85 under WINDWARD ISLANDS.
C.O. 565. (Ind. 15633–5, 17812, 18835–6, 19143–4.) Register of Correspondence. 1886–1926. 8 volumes.
C.O. 29. Entry Books of Out-Letters, etc. 1627–1872. 41 volumes.
C.O. 501. (Ind. 12922–4, 15586–7, 18837, 19145–6.) Register of Out-Letters. 1872–1926. 8 volumes.
C.O. 30. Acts. 1643–1939. 48 volumes.
C.O. 31. Sessional Papers. 1660–1939. 130 volumes.
C.O. 32. Government Gazettes. 1871–1928. 99 volumes.
C.O. 33. Miscellanea. 1678–1941. 150 volumes.

BERMUDA

C.O. 37. Original Correspondence. 1689–1939. 289 volumes.
C.O. 334. (Ind. 12925–30, 15383–4, 17725, 18838–9, 19147–8.) Register of Correspondence. 1850–1926. 13 volumes.
C.O. 38. Entry Books of Out-Letters. 1615–1872. 38 volumes.
C.O. 499. (Ind. 12931–3, 15584, 18840, 19149.) Register of Out-Letters. 1872–1926. 6 volumes.
C.O. 39. Acts. 1690–1936. 43 volumes.
C.O. 40. Sessional Papers. 1687–1940. 116 volumes.
C.O. 647. Government Gazettes. 1902–40. 9 volumes.
C.O. 41. Miscellanea. 1715–1940. 140 volumes.

BORNEO, BRITISH NORTH

C.O. 531. Original Correspondence. 1907–39. 29 volumes.
C.O. 777. (Ind. 19150, 19152.) Register of Correspondence. 1915–26. 2 volumes.
C.O. 778. (Ind. 19151.) Register of Out-Letters. 1915–26. 1 volume.
C.O. 648. Sessional Papers. 1908–40. 22 volumes.
C.O. 855. Herald and Official Gazette. 1883–1940. 54 volumes.
C.O. 824. Brunei. Sessional Papers. 1906–40. 2 volumes.

CEYLON

C.O. 54. Original Correspondence. 1798–1939. 971 volumes.
C.O. 337. (Ind. 12967–81, 15393–6, 17730–1, 18373, 18853–5, 19158–61.) Register of Correspondence. 1849–1926. 29 volumes.
C.O. 55. Entry Books of Out-Letters. 1794–1872. 121 volumes.
C.O. 488. (Ind. 12982–6, 15561–4, 17783, 18404, 18856–7, 19162–5.) Register of Out-Letters. 1872–1926. 17 volumes.
C.O. 56. Acts. 1835–1939. 21 volumes.
C.O. 57. Sessional Papers. 1831–1941. 264 volumes.
C.O. 58. Government Gazettes. 1813–1940. 288 volumes.
C.O. 59. Miscellanea. 1795–1939. 154 volumes.

CYPRUS

C.O. 67. Original Correspondence. 1878–1939. 305 volumes.
C.O. 512. (Ind. 12990–2, 15599–601, 17792, 18413, 18871, 19179–81.) Register of Correspondence. 1878–1926. 12 volumes.

C.O. 516. (Ind. 12993–4, 15606–8, 19182–3.) Register of Out-Letters. 1878–1926. 7 volumes.
C.O. 68. Acts. 1878–1939. 9 volumes.
C.O. 69. Sessional Papers. 1878–1939. 45 volumes.
C.O. 70. Government Gazettes. 1878–1938. 25 volumes.
C.O. 456. Miscellanea. 1880 1940. 69 volumes.

DOMINICA

C.O. 71. Original Correspondence. 1730–1872. 144 volumes. After 1872 included with LEEWARD ISLANDS.
C.O. 72. Entry Books. 1770–1872. 18 volumes. After 1872, see LEEWARD ISLANDS.
C.O. 73. Acts. 1768–1939. 25 volumes.
C.O. 74. Sessional Papers. 1767–1939. 46 volumes.
C.O. 75. Government Gazettes. 1865–1940. 20 volumes.
C.O. 76. Miscellanea. 1765–1887. 77 volumes.

FALKLAND ISLANDS

C.O. 78. Original Correspondence. 1831–1939. 212 volumes.
C.O. 537. Original Correspondence. Supplementary. 1872–98. 1 volume.
C.O. 399. Entry Books. 1832–70. 7 volumes.
C.O. 339. (Ind. 12995–8, 15397–8, 17732, 18911–2, 19211–3.) Register of Correspondence. 1849–1926. 12 volumes.
C.O. 79. Acts. 1846–1931. 4 volumes.
C.O. 80. Sessional Papers. 1845–1939. 13 volumes.
C.O. 458. Government Gazettes. 1891–1939. 18 volumes.
C.O. 81. Miscellanea. 1846–1940. 95 volumes.

FIJI

C.O. 83. Original Correspondence. 1860–1939. 230 volumes.
C.O. 537. Original Correspondence. Supplementary. Vol. 115. 1874–97. 1 volume.
C.O. 419. (Ind. 13002–5, 15505–6, 18395, 18914–5, 19216–8.) Register of Correspondence. 1860–98, 1900–26. 12 volumes.
C.O. 400. Entry Books of Out-Letters. 1859–62. 1 volume.
C.O. 515. (Ind. 13006–8, 15605, 17793, 18484, 18916, 19291–20.) Register of Out-Letters. 1874–1928. 9 volumes.
C.O. 84. Acts. 1875–1939. 11 volumes.
C.O. 85. Sessional Papers. 1875–1940. 30 volumes.
C.O. 86. Government Gazettes. 1874–1939. 30 volumes.
C.O. 459. Miscellanea. 1876–1940. 66 volumes.

GAMBIA

C.O. 87. Original Correspondence. 1828–1939. 249 volumes.
C.O. 341. (Ind. 13009–15, 15402–3, 17735, 18917–8, 19221–2.) Register of Correspondence. 1849–1907. 14 volumes.
C.O. 401. Entry Books. 1827–72. 16 volumes.
C.O. 481. (Ind. 13016–7, 15534–5, 17775, 18919, 19223–4.) Register of Out-Letters. 1872–1926. 8 vols.
C.O. 88. Acts. 1843–1939. 9 volumes.
C.O. 89. Sessional Papers. 1843–1940. 24 volumes.
C.O. 460. Government Gazettes. 1883–1940. 21 volumes.
C.O. 90. Miscellanea. 1822–1940. 114 volumes.

GIBRALTAR

C.O. 91. Original Correspondence. 1705–1939. 511 volumes.

C.O. 537. Vols. 30, 31 and 116. Original Correspondence. Supplementary. 1873–98. 3 volumes.

C.O. 342. (Ind. 13018–28, 15404–6, 17736, 18920–1, 19225–7.) Register of Correspondence. 1850–1907. 15 volumes.

C.O. 92. Entry Books. 1803–72. 33 volumes.

C.O. 517. (Ind. 13029–30, 15609–12, 19228–9.) Register of Out-Letters. 1872–97. 5 volumes.

C.O. 93. Acts. 1832–1939. 8 volumes.

C.O. 832. Sessional Papers. 1909–40. 7 volumes.

C.O. 94. Government Gazettes. 1839–1940. 150 volumes.

C.O. 95. Miscellanea. 1704–1940. 123 volumes.

GOLD COAST

C.O. 96. Original Correspondence. 1753–6 and 1843–1939. 762 volumes.

C.O. 343. (Ind. 13031–40, 15407–13, 17737–8, 18376–8, 18922–4, 19230–4.) Register of Correspondence. 1849–1926. 30 volumes.

C.O. 402. Entry Books. 1843–72. 13 volumes.

C.O. 482. (Ind. 13041–6, 15536–42, 17776–7, 18402, 18925–6, 19235–8.) Register of Out-Letters. 1872–1926. 26 volumes.

C.O. 97. Acts. 1852–1939. 12 volumes.

C.O. 98. Sessional Papers. 1829–1939. 77 volumes.

C.O. 99. Government Gazettes. 1872–1940. 67 volumes.

C.O. 100. Miscellanea. 1845–1940. 90 volumes.

GRENADA

C.O. 101. Original Correspondence. 1747–1873. 135 volumes. After 1873 see WINDWARD ISLANDS.

C.O. 714. Vol. 70. (Ind. 18530.) Alphabetical Index to Correspondence, 1815–70.

C.O. 102. Entry Books. 1763–1872. 25 volumes.

C.O. 504. (Ind. 13047–9.) Register of Out-Letters, 1872–82. 3 volumes.

C.O. 103. Acts. 1766–1936. 27 volumes.

C.O. 104. Sessional Papers. 1766–1939. 53 volumes.

C.O. 105. Government Gazettes. 1834–1940. 39 volumes.

C.O. 106. Miscellanea. 1764–1938. 132 volumes.

GRIQUALAND WEST
(After 1880 under CAPE COLONY)

C.O. 107. Original Correspondence. 1875–80. 9 volumes.

C.O. 344. (Ind. 13050.) Register of Correspondence. 1875–80. 1 volume.

C.O. 522. Vol. 1. (Ind. 13051.) Register of Out-Letters. 1876–80. 1 volume.

C.O. 108. Sessional Papers. 1873–80. 3 volumes.

C.O. 109. Government Gazettes. 1876–80. 1 volume.

C.O. 461. Miscellanea. 1873. 1 volume.

GUIANA, BRITISH

C.O. 111. Original Correspondence. 1781–1939. 757 volumes.

C.O. 537. Vols. 2–4. Original Correspondence. Supplementary. 1872–98. 3 volumes.

C.O. 345. (Ind. 13052–63, 15414–7, 17739, 18379, 18927–8, 19239–41.) Register of Correspondence. 1850–1926. 23 volumes.

C.O. 112. Entry Books. 1801–72. 42 volumes.
C.O. 502. Vols. 1–6. (Ind. 13064–6, 15588–90, 17789, 18929, 19242–3.) Register of Out-Letters. 1872–1926. 10 volumes.
C.O. 113. Acts. 1837–1939. 21 volumes.
C.O. 114. Sessional Papers. 1805–1940. 233 volumes.
C.O. 115. Government Gazettes. 1838–1940. 171 volumes.
C.O. 116. Miscellanea. 1686–1940. 309 volumes.

HELIGOLAND

C.O. 118. Original Correspondence. 1807–94. 62 volumes.
C.O. 537. Vol. 17. Supplementary Correspondence, 1890–4. 1 volume.
C.O. 346. (Ind. 13067–72.) Register of Correspondence. 1850–1910. 6 volumes.
C.O. 119. Entry Books. 1807–77. 7 volumes.
C.O. 347. (Ind. 13073–4.) Register of Out-Letters. 1874–90. 2 volumes.
C.O. 120. Acts. 1883–9. 1 volume.
C.O. 121. Sessional Papers. 1881–90. 1 volume.
C.O. 122. Miscellanea. 1834–90. 36 volumes.

HONDURAS, BRITISH

C.O. 123. Original Correspondence. 1744–1939. 377 volumes.
C.O. 537. Vol. 1. Original Correspondence. Supplementary. 1872–98. 1 volume.
C.O. 348. (Ind. 13075–83, 15418–20, 17740, 18930, 19244–6.) Register of Correspondence. 1855–1926. 17 volumes.
C.O. 124. Entry Books. 1630–1872. 15 volumes.
C.O. 503. (Ind. 13084–6, 15591–2, 17790, 18931, 19247–8.) Register of Out-Letters. 1872–1926. 9 volumes.
C.O. 125. Acts. 1855–1937. 14 volumes.
C.O. 126. Sessional Papers. 1848–1940. 39 volumes.
C.O. 127. Government Gazettes. 1861–1940. 35 volumes.
C.O. 128. Miscellanea. 1807–1940. 114 volumes.

HONG KONG

C.O. 129. Original Correspondence. 1841–1939. 582 volumes.
C.O. 537. Vols. 33–7. Original Correspondence. Supplementary. 1873–1907. 5 volumes.
C.O. 349. (Ind. 13087–97, 15421–3, 17741–2, 18380, 18932–4, 19249–52.) Register of Correspondence. 1849–1926. 24 volumes.
C.O. 403. Entry Books. 1843–72. 21 volumes.
C.O. 489. (Ind. 13098–101, 15565–7, 18405–6, 18935–6, 19253–5.) Register of Out-Letters. 1872–1926. 15 volumes.
C.O. 130. Acts. 1844–1939. 13 volumes.
C.O. 131. Sessional Papers. 1844–1939. 104 volumes.
C.O. 132. Government Gazettes. 1846–1940. 86 volumes.
C.O. 133. Miscellanea. 1844–1938. 109 volumes.

IONIAN ISLANDS

C.O. 136. Original Correspondence. Entry Books, etc. 1802–73. 1432 volumes and bundles. Including local records of Residents.
C.O. 537. Vol. 18. Original Correspondence, Supplementary. 1875–1910. 1 volume.
C.O. 350. (Ind. 13102–6, 15424.) Register of Correspondence. 1849–1910. 6 volumes.

JAMAICA

C.O. 137. Original Correspondence. 1689–1939. 839 volumes.
C.O. 537. Vol. 5. Original Correspondence. Supplementary. 1873–98. 1 volume.
C.O. 351. (Ind. 13107–20, 15425–28, 17743, 18381, 18937–8, 19039, 19276–8.) Register of Correspondence. 1850–1926. 26 volumes.
C.O. 714. Vol. 89. (Ind. 18553.) Index to Correspondence. 1815–70.
C.O. 138. Entry Books. 1661–1872. 83 volumes.
C.O. 494. (Ind. 13121–4, 15577–80, 18410, 18939, 19279–80.) Register of Out-Letters. 1872–99. 12 volumes.
C.O. 139. Acts. 1662–1939. 118 volumes.
C.O. 140. Sessional Papers 1661–1940. 296 volumes.
C.O. 141. Government Gazettes. 1794–1940. 103 volumes.
C.O. 142. Miscellanea. 1658–1940. 154 volumes.

LABUAN

C.O. 144. Original Correspondence. 1844–1906. 81 volumes.
C.O. 532. (Ind. 13125–9, 15429, 18940.) Register of Correspondence. 1849–1914. 7 volumes.
C.O. 404. Entry Books. 1847–72. 5 volumes.
C.O. 487. (Ind. 13130, 15560, 18941.) Register of Out-Letters. 1873–1914. 4 volumes.
C.O. 145. Acts. 1849–1906. 3 volumes.
C.O. 434. Sessional Papers. 1849–89. 1 volume.
C.O. 573. Government Gazettes. 1890–1906. 1 volume.
C.O. 146. Miscellanea. 1848–1906. 59 volumes.

LAGOS

C.O. 147. Original Correspondence. 1861–1906. 179 volumes.
C.O. 421. (Ind. 13132–5, 15507–11, 17768.) Register of Correspondence. 1861–1906. 10 volumes.
C.O. 420. Entry Books. 1861–72. 5 volumes.
C.O. 483. (Ind. 13136–7, 15543–6, 177778–9.) Register of Out-Letters. 1872–83, 1886–1906. 8 volumes. [Register for 1884–5 under GOLD COAST.]
C.O. 148. Acts. 1862–1905. 3 volumes.
C.O. 149. Sessional Papers. 1872–1906. 7 volumes.
C.O. 150. Government Gazettes. 1881–1906. 12 volumes.
C.O. 151. Miscellanea. 1862–1905. 43 volumes.

LEEWARD ISLANDS

C.O. 152. Original Correspondence 1689–1815, 1872–1939. 481 volumes. During the period 1813–72 see under ANTIGUA, NEVIS, ST CHRISTOPHER and VIRGIN ISLANDS.
C.O. 537. Vol. 5. Original Correspondence. Supplementary. 1873–98.
C.O. 354. (Ind. 13138–51, 15431–3, 17744–5, 18382, 18942, 19281–3.) Register of Correspondence. 1850–1926. 24 volumes. For 1850–72 this Register covers Antigua and the other islands.
C.O. 507. (Ind. 13152–5, 13593–5, 17791, 18943, 19284–5.) Register of Out-Letters. 1872–1926. 11 volumes.
C.O. 154. Acts. 1644–1936. 14 volumes.
C.O. 155. Sessional Papers. 1680–1940. 21 volumes.
C.O. 156. Government Gazettes. 1872–1940. 29 volumes.
C.O. 157. Miscellanea. 1683–1940. 54 volumes.

MALAY STATES, FEDERATED

C.O. 717. Original Correspondence. 1920–39. 140 volumes.
C.O. 786. (Ind. 19307–9.) Register of Correspondence. 1918–26. 10 volumes.
C.O. 787. (Ind. 193349–52.) Register of Out-Letters. 1918–26. 3 volumes.
C.O. 828. Acts. 1925–33. 2 volumes.
C.O. 576. Sessional Papers. 1896–1940. 70 volumes.
C.O. 574. Government Gazettes. 1909–40. 85 volumes.
C.O. 575. Miscellanea. 1896–1939. 29 volumes.

MALTA

C.O. 158. Original Correspondence. 1801–1939. 523 volumes.
C.O. 537. Vols. 6–8, 38, 117. Original Correspondence. Supplementary. 1870–1902, 1914, 1836–73. 5 volumes.
C.O. 355. (Ind. 13156–65, 15435–6, 18383, 18944–5, 19294–7.) Register of Correspondence. 1850–1910. 15 volumes.
C.O. 159. Entry Books. 1799–1872. 32 volumes.
C.O. 518. (Ind. 13166–8, 15613–5, 18946, 19298–9.) Register of Out-Letters, 1872–97. 5 volumes.
C.O. 714. Vol. 94. Alphabetical Index to Correspondence, 1815–70.
C.O. 160. Acts. 1834–1939. 11 volumes.
C.O. 161. Sessional Papers. 1835–1940. 124 volumes.
C.O. 162. Government Gazettes. 1818–1940. 82 volumes.
C.O. 163. Miscellanea. 1816–1938. 156 volumes.

MAURITIUS AND SEYCHELLES

C.O. 167. Original Correspondence. 1778–1939. 909 volumes.
C.O. 537. Vol. 39. Original Correspondence. Supplementary. 1871–98. 1 volume.
C.O. 356. (Ind. 13169–84, 15437–40, 17746.) Register of Correspondence. 1850–1903. 21 volumes.
C.O. 654. (Ind. 17877, 18947–8, 19300–3.) Register of Correspondence. 1904–26. 7 volumes.
C.O. 168. Entry Books. 1810–72. 63 volumes.
C.O. 490. (13185–8, 15568–71, 17785, 18949, 19304–6.) Register of Out-Letters. 1873–1926. 13 volumes.
C.O. 694. Vol. 6. Register of Secret Correspondence. 1889–98.
C.O. 169. Acts. 1833–1939. 37 volumes.
C.O. 170. Sessional Papers. 1825–1939. 340 volumes.
C.O. 171. Government Gazettes. 1823–1940. 108 volumes.
C.O. 172. Miscellanea. 1810–1940. 167 volumes.

MONTSERRAT

C.O. 175. Original Correspondence. 1726–87 and 1853–72. 21 volumes. See also ANTIGUA and LEEWARD ISLANDS.
C.O. 381. Vol. 3. Entry Book. 1850–71. 1 volume.
C.O. 176. Acts. 1668–1937. 19 volumes.
C.O. 177. Sessional Papers. 1704–1940. 36 volumes.
C.O. 178 Miscellanea. 1829–87. 57 volumes.

NEGRI SEMBILAN, SUNGEI UJONG AND JELEBU

C.O. 435. Sessional Papers. 1888–1929. 4 volumes.
C.O. 463. Government Gazettes. 1896–1909. 9 volumes.
C.O. 474. Sungei Ujong. Sessional Papers. 1883–93. 1 volume.
C.O. 475. Sungei Ujong. Government Gazettes. 1893. 1 volume.

NEVIS

C.O. 184. Original Correspondence. 1703–1807 and 1854–72. 20 volumes. After 1872 see under LEEWARD ISLANDS
C.O. 185. Acts. 1664–1882. 15 volumes.
C.O. 186. Sessional Papers. 1721–1882. 22 volumes.
C.O. 187. Miscellanea. 1704–1882. 56 volumes.

NEW GUINEA, BRITISH (PAPUA)

C.O. 422. Original Correspondence. 1884–1900. 15 volumes.
C.O. 578. (Ind. 15637–8.) Register of Correspondence. 1884–1900. 2 volumes.
C.O. 579. (Ind. 15639.) Register of Out-Letters. 1884–1900. 1 volume.
C.O. 200. Acts. 1888–1906. 2 volumes.
C.O. 436. Sessional Papers. 1888–1924.
C.O. 453. Government Gazettes. 1888–1921. 4 volumes.
C.O. 667. New Guinea (former German Territory). Government Gazettes. 1914–25. 2 volumes.

NIGER COAST PROTECTORATE

C.O. 444. Original Correspondence. 1899. 4 volumes.
C.O. 464. Miscellanea. 1896–1900. 4 volumes.

NIGERIA

C.O. 583. Original Correspondence. 1912–39. 244 volumes.
C.O. 763. (Ind. 18967–72, 19313–9.) Register of Correspondence. 1912–26. 13 volumes.
C.O. 764. (Ind. 18973–6, 19321–4.) Register of Out-Letters. 1912–26. 8 volumes.
C.O. 656. Acts. 1914–39. 9 volumes.
C.O. 657. Sessional Papers. 1910–40. 51 volumes.
C.O. 658. Government Gazettes. 1914–40. 44 volumes.
C.O. 659. Customs and Trade Journal. 1911–16. 3 volumes.
C.O. 741. Railway. 1912–22. 2 volumes.
C.O. 660. Miscellanea. 1913–40. 31 volumes.

NIGERIA, NORTHERN

C.O. 446. Original Correspondence. 1898–1913. 114 volumes.
C.O. 584. (Ind. 15642, 17819–21, 18418–9, 18977.) Register of Correspondence. 1898–1913. 7 volumes.
C.O. 585. (Ind. 15643, 17822–4, 18420, 18978.) Register of Out-Letters. 1898–1913. 6 volumes.
C.O. 587. Proclamations. 1900–13. 3 volumes.
C.O. 586. Government Gazettes. 1900–13. 4 volumes.
C.O. 465. Miscellanea. 1900–13. 14 volumes.

NIGERIA, SOUTHERN

C.O. 520. Original Correspondence. 1900–13. 131 volumes.
C.O. 589. (Ind. 15644, 17825–7, 18421–3, 18979.) Register of Correspondence. 1899–1913. 8 volumes.
C.O. 590. (Ind. 15645, 17828–9, 18424–5, 18980.) Register of Out-Letters. 1899–1913. 6 volumes.
C.O. 588. Acts and Proclamations. 1900–13. 4 volumes.
C.O. 591. Government Gazettes. 1900–13. 12 volumes.
C.O. 592. Sessional Papers. 1906–13. 16 volumes.
C.O. 473. Miscellanea. 1900–13. 14 volumes.

Pacific, Western

C.O. 225. Original Correspondence. 1878–1939. 321 volumes.

C.O. 537. Vol. 136. Original Correspondence. Supplementary. 1876–97.

C.O. 492. (Ind. 13248, 15573–5, 17786, 18408, 18981–3, 19339–41.) Register of Correspondence. 1878–93. 12 volumes.

C.O. 493. (Ind. 13249, 15576, 17787, 18409, 18984–5, 19342.) Register of Out-Letters. 1879–1926.

C.O. 665. King's Regulations. 1879–1934. 2 volumes.

C.O. 692. Government Gazettes. 1914–40. 6 volumes.

Pahang

C.O. 437. Sessional Papers. 1888–1924. 3 volumes.

C.O· 466. Government Gazettes. 1897–1909. 6 volumes.

Perak

C.O. 438. Sessional Papers. 1888–1924. 4 volumes.

C.O. 467. Government Gazettes. 1888–1909. 2 volumes.

St Christopher

C.O. 239. Original Correspondence. 1702–1872. 126 volumes. After 1872 see under Leeward Islands.

C.O. 407. Entry Books. 1816–72. 15 volumes.

C.O. 240. Acts. 1701–1936. 27 volumes.

C.O. 241. Sessional Papers. 1704–1939. 56 volumes.

C.O. 242. Government Gazettes. 1879–1939. 11 volumes.

C.O. 243. Miscellanea. 1704–1887. 75 volumes.

St Helena

C.O. 247. Original Correspondence. 1805–1939. 235 volumes.

C.O. 537. Vols. 41–2. Original Correspondence. Supplementary. 1877–98.

C.O. 366. (Ind. 13262–7, 15456–7, 18388, 19367–8.) Register of Correspondence. 1849–1936. 12 volumes.

C.O. 248. Entry Books. 1815–72. 18 volumes.

C.O. 491. (Ind. 13268, 15572, 18407, 19369–70.) Register of Out-Letters. 1872–88. 5 volumes.

C.O. 249. Acts. 1837–1911. 5 volumes.

C.O. 250. Sessional Papers. 1836–1939. 10 volumes.

C.O. 251. Government Gazettes. 1845–1932. 4 volumes.

C.O. 252. Miscellanea. 1836–1939. 104 volumes.

St Lucia

C.O. 253. Original Correspondence. 1709–1873. 150 volumes. After 1873 see Windward Islands.

C.O. 367. (Ind. 13269–73.) Register of Correspondence. 1850–81. 5 volumes.

C.O. 254. Entry Books. 1794–1872. 19 volumes.

C.O. 505. (Ind. 13274–6.) Register of Out-Letters. 1872–82. 3 volumes.

C.O. 255. Acts. 1818–1935. 17 volumes.

C.O. 256. Sessional Papers. 1820–1939. 40 volumes.

C.O. 257. Government Gazettes. 1857–1940. 59 volumes.

C.O. 258. Miscellanea. 1722–1940. 136 volumes.

ST VINCENT

C.O. 260. Original Correspondence. 1668–1873. 118 volumes. From 1873 see under WINDWARD ISLANDS.

C.O. 714. Vol. 142. (Ind. 18606.) Alphabetical Index to Correspondence. 1816–70.

C.O. 261. Entry Books. 1776–1872. 24 volumes.

C.O. 506. (Ind. 13277–9.) Register of Out-Letters. 1872–82. 3 volumes.

C.O 262. Acts. 1768–1936. 30 volumes.

C.O. 263. Sessional Papers. 1769–1939. 51 volumes.

C.O. 264. Government Gazettes. 1831–1940. 37 volumes.

C.O. 265. Miscellanea. 1763–1940. 120 volumes.

SARAWAK

C.O. 802. Sessional Papers. 1900–24. 1 volume.

C.O. 604. Government Gazettes. 1903–40. 25 volumes.

SELANGOR

C.O. 439. Sessional Papers. 1888–1924. 3 volumes.

C.O. 469. Government Gazettes. 1890–1909. 19 volumes.

SEYCHELLES

(See also under MAURITIUS)

C.O. 530. Original Correspondence. 1904–39. 85 volumes.

C.O. 712. (Ind. 18607, 19004, 19371–2.) Register of Correspondence. 1904–26. 4 volumes.

C.O. 768. (Ind. 19005, 19373.) Register of Out-Letters. 1904–26. 2 volumes.

C.O. 266. Acts. 1889–1939. 5 volumes.

C.O. 440. Sessional Papers. 1889–1939. 16 volumes.

C.O. 470. Government Gazettes. 1889–1939. 23 volumes.

C.O. 471. Miscellanea. 1899–1939. 41 volumes.

SIERRA LEONE

C.O. 267. Original Correspondence. 1691–1939. 673 volumes and bundles.

C.O. 368. Vols. 1–16. (Ind. 13280–91, 15459–62, 17751–2, 18389, 19006–7, 19374–6.) Register of Correspondence. 1849–1926. 24 volumes.

C.O. 268. Entry Books. 1672–1872. 57 volumes.

C.O. 484. Vols. 1–7. (Ind. 13292–4, 15547–50, 17780, 18403, 19008, 19377–9.) Register of Out-Letters. 1872–1926. 13 volumes.

C.O. 269. Acts. 1801–1939. 12 volumes.

C.O. 270. Sessional Papers. 1776–1940. 76 volumes.

C.O. 271. Government Gazettes. 1817–1940. 48 volumes.

C.O. 272. Miscellanea. 1819–1940. 117 volumes.

C.O. 672. Board of Education. 1889–1900. 1 volume.

SOMALILAND

C.O. 535. Original Correspondence. 1905–39. 134 volumes.

C.O. 713. (Ind. 18613, 19009, 19380–2.) Register of Correspondence. 1905–26. 5 volumes.

C.O. 769. (Ind. 19010, 19383.) Register of Out-Letters. 1905–26. 2 volumes.

C.O. 673. Acts. 1900–36. 3 volumes.

C.O. 830. Sessional Papers. 1925–35. 2 volumes.

C.O. 607. Miscellanea. 1901–38. 38 volumes.

STRAITS SETTLEMENTS

C.O. 273. Original Correspondence. 1838–1939. 659 volumes.

C.O. 537. Vols. 45–8. Original Correspondence. Supplementary. 1873–98. 4 volumes.

C.O 426. (Ind. 13295–302, 15514–8, 17769–71, 18997 8, 19011–5, 19384–8.) Register of Correspondence. 1867–1926. 28 volumes.

C.O. 425. Entry Books. 1867–73. 8 volumes.

C.O. 486. (Ind. 13303–5, 15555–9, 17781–2, 19016–8, 19389–92.) Register of Out-Letters. 1873–1936. 17 volumes.

C.O. 274. Acts. 1867–1940. 23 volumes.

C.O. 275. Sessional Papers. 1855–1940. 155 volumes.

C.O. 276. Government Gazettes. 1867–1940. 158 volumes.

C.O. 277. Miscellanea. 1867–1939. 91 volumes.

TOBAGO

C.O. 285. Original Correspondence. 1700–1873. 91 volumes. After 1873 see under WINDWARD ISLANDS.

C.O. 286. Entry Books. 1793–1872. 11 volumes.

C.O. 498. (Ind. 13318–20.) Register of Out-Letters. 1872–82. 3 volumes.

C.O. 287. Acts. 1768–1898. 15 volumes.

C.O. 288. Sessional Papers. 1768–1898. 30 volumes.

C.O. 289. Government Gazettes. 1872–98. 7 volumes.

C.O. 290. Miscellanea. 1766–1893. 73 volumes. For Blue Books after 1889 see under TRINIDAD.

TONGA

C.O. 861. Sessional Papers. 1914–39. 1 volume.

C.O. 676. Government Gazettes. 1905–27. 3 volumes.

TRINIDAD

C.O. 295. Original Correspondence. 1783–1939. 616 volumes.

C.O. 537. Vol. 9. Original Correspondence. Supplementary. 1872–98. 1 volume.

C.O. 372. (Ind. 13226–35, 15468–70, 17753–4, 19020–1, 19395–7.) Register of Correspondence. 1850–1926. 20 volumes.

C.O. 296. Entry Books. 1797–1872. 31 volumes.

C.O. 497. (Ind. 13336–9, 15581–3, 18411, 19022, 19398 9.) Register of Out-Letters. 1872–1926. 11 volumes.

C.O. 297. Acts. 1832–1940. 31 volumes.

C.O. 298. Sessional Papers. 1803–1940. 182 volumes.

C.O. 299. Government Gazettes. 1833–1940. 125 volumes.

C.O. 300. Miscellanea. 1804–1940. 152 volumes.

TURKS AND CAICOS ISLANDS

C.O. 301. Original Correspondence. 1848–82. 66 volumes.

C.O 495. (Ind. 13340.) Register of Correspondence. 1868–82. 1 volume.

C.O. 409. Entry Books. 1849–72. 5 volumes.

C.O. 496. (Ind. 13341–2.) Register of Out-Letters. 1872–81. 2 volumes.

C.O. 302. Acts. 1849–1916. 8 volumes.

C.O. 303. Sessional Papers. 1849–1939. 9 volumes.

C.O. 681. Government Gazettes. 1907–34. 5 volumes.

C.O. 304. Miscellanea. 1852–1940. 88 volumes.

UGANDA PROTECTORATE
(See also under AFRICA, EAST)

C.O. 536. Original Correspondence. 1905–39. 204 volumes.

C.O. 682. (Ind. 17900, 18444, 19023–4, 19400–3.) Register of Correspondence. 1905–26. 9 volumes.

C.O. 683. (Ind. 17901, 19025, 19404–6.) Register of Out-Letters. 1905–26. 5 volumes.

C.O. 684. Acts. 1901–39. 4 volumes.

C.O. 685. Sessional Papers. 1907–40. 26 volumes.

C.O. 612. Government Gazettes. 1908–39. 18 volumes.

C.O. 613. Miscellanea. 1901–40. 40 volumes.

C.O. 614. Railway. Construction. 1895–1904. 14 volumes.

C.O. 615. (Ind. 15648–54.) Railway. Register of Correspondence. 1895–1905. 7 volumes.

VIRGIN ISLANDS

C.O. 314. Original Correspondence. 1711–1872. 24 volumes. After 1872 see under LEEWARD ISLANDS.

C.O. 315. Acts. 1774–1926. 11 volumes.

C.O. 316. Sessional Papers. 1773–1931. 12 volumes.

C.O. 317. Miscellanea. 1784–1896. 67 volumes.

WEI HAI WEI

C.O. 521. Original Correspondence. 1898–1931. 32 volumes.

C.O. 770. (Ind. 19026, 19407–8.) Register of Correspondence. 1902–26. 3 volumes.

C.O. 771. (Ind. 19027, 19409–11.) Register of Out-Letters. 1907–26. 4 volumes.

C.O. 841. Acts. 1903–30. 1 volume.

C.O. 744. Government Gazettes. 1908–30. 3 volumes.

WEST INDIES

C.O. 318. Original Correspondence. 1624–1939. 437 volumes and bundles.

C.O. 537. Vol. 5. Original Correspondence. Supplementary. 1873–98.

C.O. 375. (Ind. 13358–60, 15475, 17755, 19028–9, 19412–5.) Register of Correspondence. 1849–1926. 14 volumes.

C.O. 319. Entry Books. 1699–1872. 56 volumes.

C.O. 509. (Ind. 13361, 19030–1, 19416–7.) Register of Out-Letters. 1872–1926. 5 volumes.

C.O. 441. West Indies Incumbered Estates Commission. 1857–92. Journals and Entry Books. 25 boxes.

WINDWARD ISLANDS

C.O. 321. Original Correspondence. 1874–1939. 391 volumes.

C.O. 376. (Ind. 13362–76, 15476–8, 17756, 19032–6, 19418–20.) Register of Correspondence. 1850–1907. 19 volumes.

C.O. 377. (Ind. 13377, 15479–81, 17757, 19034, 19421–2.) Register of Out-Letters. 1883–1926. 8 volumes.

ZANZIBAR

C.O. 618. Original Correspondence. 1913–1939. 75 volumes.

C.O. 772. (Ind. 19035, 19423–4.) Register of Correspondence. 1913–26. 3 volumes.

C.O. 805. (Ind. 19425–6.) Register of Out-Letters. 1913–26. 2 volumes.

C.O. 688. Sessional Papers. 1909–39. 18 volumes.
C.O. 689. Government Gazettes. 1913–40. 34 volumes.
C.O. 690. Miscellanea. 1913–40. 28 volumes.

EMIGRATION

C.O. 384. Original Correspondence. 1817–96. 199 volumes.
C.O. 385. Entry Books of Out-Letters. 1814–71. 30 volumes.
C.O. 428. (Ind. 13378–88, 15519–21.) Register of Correspondence. 1850–96. 14 volumes.
C.O. 485. (Ind. 13389–93, 15551–4.) Register of Out-Letters. 1872–1903.
C.O. 386. Land and Emigration Commission. 1833–94. 193 volumes.

COLONIES (GENERAL)

C.O. 323. Original Correspondence. 1689–1939. 1714 volumes.
C.O. 537. Original Correspondence. Supplementary. 1759–1929. 156 volumes.
C.O. 432. (Ind. 12873–4.) Register of Miscellaneous Correspondence. 1860–70. 2 volumes.
C.O. 324. Entry Books of Commissions, Warrants, Instructions, etc. Series I. 1662–1872. 175 volumes.
C.O. 381. Entry Books. Series II. 1740–1872. 93 volumes.
C.O. 378. (Ind. 12855–65, 15482–5, 17758–9, 18391–2, 18858–63, 19166–74.) Register of Correspondence. 1852–1926. 34 volumes.
C.O. 379. (Ind. 12866–70.) Register of Correspondence. Indexes. 1871–83. 5 volumes.
C.O. 854. Circular Despatches. 1808–1900.

REGISTERS AND INDEXES

Until 1849 all correspondence was registered in the series C.O. 329. From 1849 correspondence has been recorded in the Daily Registers and the various other registers noted below, also in the several registers described under the individual colonies. All these now have numbers at the Public Record Office in the general series of Indexes ("Ind.").

C.O. 382. (Ind. 10625–37, 10686–98, 15361–73, 15490–504, 17762–7, 18988–99, 19353–62.) Correspondence. Daily Registers. 1849–1929. 82 volumes.
C.O. 383. Acts. Registers. 1781–1892. 93 volumes. These refer to the volumes of Colonial Acts.
C.O. 570. (Ind. 15636, 18764.) Secret Entry Books and Register of Out-Letters. 2 volumes.
C.O. 562. (Ind. 20319.) Record of non-registered and filed letters, 1909–12.
C.O. 652. (Ind. 17876, 18869–70, 20319.) Register of Unregistered Correspondence. 1886–1927. 4 volumes.
C.O. 694. Register of Secret Correspondence.
C.O. 714. (Ind. 18451–6, 18459–504, 18511–7, 18519–606, 18608–12, 18614–31.) Alphabetical Indexes to Correspondence. 1795–1879. 170 volumes.

COLONIAL OFFICE ACCOUNTS BRANCH

C.O. 431. Original Correspondence from Colonial Governors, Treasury and other Departments, and from individuals on financial matters. 1868–1925. 152 volumes.
C.O. 621. Entry Books and Registers of Out-Letters. 1868–1919. 19 volumes.
C.O. 622. (Ind. 17830–43, 18428–9, 18745, 19082.) Register of Correspondence. 1868–1921. 18 volumes.
C.O. 701. Miscellaeea. 1794–1903. 26 volumes.

COLONIAL STATISTICAL TABLES

C.O. 442. 1833–1912. 63 volumes. Board of Trade returns on foreign and colonial trade.

PATRONAGE

C.O. 429. Original Correspondence relating to applications for appointments, etc. 1861–70 and 1881–1919. 131 volumes.

C.O. 430. (Ind. 13394, 15522–8, 17772–3, 18399, 18986–7.) Register of Correspondence. 1867–70, 1881–1918. 13 volumes.

DOMINIONS (WAR OF 1914–18)

C.O. 616. Original Correspondence. 1914–18. 82 volumes.

CONFIDENTIAL PRINT

Since 1943 copies of its own series of *Confidential Print* have been transferred from the Colonial Office to the Public Record Office. These were prepared largely for departmental or interdepartmental use and include material, such as Cabinet memoranda and correspondence with other departments, not to be found in Colonial Office manuscripts. The series so far available are valuable both for supplementing and interpreting the original documents.

C.O. 806. Africa. 1642–1899. 365 nos.
C.O. 807. America, North. 1677–1891. 84 nos.
C.O. 808. Australia. 1873–94. 95 nos.
C.O. 809. Eastern. 1872–96. 44 nos.
C.O. 810. Mediterranean. 1879–91. 37 nos.
C.O. 811. West Indies. 1787–1893. 44 nos.
C.O. 812. Miscellaneous. 1870–1902. 150 nos.
C.O. 601. (Ind. 15376, 15646–7.) Catalogues of Confidential Print. 1852–1915. 3 volumes.

(b) FOREIGN OFFICE

The printed *List of Foreign Office Records to 1878* (P.R.O. Lists and Indexes, No. LII, 1929), is supplemented by typed lists on the open shelves at the Public Record Office: *List of Foreign Office Records 1879–85* (2 vols. 1930), *List of Foreign Office Records after 1885* (4 vols. 1948) and two volumes of *Addenda*. F.O. 566 contains Registers of General Correspondence, 1817–1900 (553 vols.). F.O. 605 contains microfilms of these and of Indexes of Registers of Correspondence General. There are many classes of papers in the period 1870–1921 which have a direct bearing on the subjects covered in the present volume. Several of the series of F.O. *Confidential Print* are also highly relevant. Specific references are given in the "Special Bibliographies" below; of prime importance are the following series:

GENERAL CORRESPONDENCE

ABYSSINIA. F.O. 1. Original Correspondence [with agents, ambassadors, consuls, etc.]. 1808–1905. 56 volumes.

AFRICA. F.O. 2. General. Including papers relating to trade, expeditions, etc. 1825–1905. 983 volumes. Vols. 50–56 are drafts and despatches on Niger Coast Oil Rivers Protectorate, 1893; 57–59, Imperial British East Africa Company; 60–61, Portal Mission to Uganda, 1893, etc.

AFRICA. F.O. 367. Correspondence. General. New series. 1906–13. 361 volumes.

AMERICA, CENTRAL AND GUATEMALA. F.O. 15. Correspondence. General. 1824–1905. 367 volumes. Including boundary disputes.

AMERICA, UNITED STATES OF. Correspondence. General. Series II. F.O. 5. 1793–1905. 2625 volumes.

BORNEO. F.O. 12. Correspondence. 1842–1905. 130 volumes.

CHINA. F.O. 17. Correspondence, including Shanghai, etc. 1815–1905. 1786 volumes.

PACIFIC ISLANDS. F.O. 58. Correspondence: Hawaii, New Guinea, Samoa, Tonga, etc. 1822–1905. 345 volumes.

SIAM. F.O. 69. Correspondence. 1849–1905. 276 volumes.

TURKEY. F.O. 78. Correspondence. 1780–1905. 5490 volumes. Vol. 1156 is "Suez Canal, etc."

VENEZUELA. F.O. 80. Correspondence. 1835–1903. 498 volumes.

ZANZIBAR. F.O. 107. Correspondence: Agents, consuls, slave trade, etc. 1893–1905. 131 volumes.

GREAT BRITAIN AND GENERAL. F.O. 83. Correspondence, with Colonial Office and other government departments, proceedings of international congresses and so on. 1745–1930. 2480 volumes.

SLAVE TRADE. F.O. 84. Correspondence, with foreign powers, with the Colonial Office and its agents, with Slave Trade Commissions, etc. 1816–92. 2276 volumes.

MISCELLANEA. SERIES II. F.O. 96. Draft despatches, minutes, etc., including slave trade material, special missions and commissions. 1816–1929. 216 bundles and volumes.

SUPPLEMENT TO GENERAL CORRESPONDENCE. F.O. 97. Correspondence and papers supplementing the General series, arranged under countries. 1781–1905. 621 volumes. Vol. 411 is "Suez Canal", vols. 430–2 "Slave Trade".

EMBASSY AND CONSULAR ARCHIVES

AMERICA, UNITED STATES OF. F.O. 115. Correspondence. 1791–1929. 3392 volumes. F.O. 117. Registers. (Ind. 13399–412, 17626–37, 20925–38.) 1823–1929. 40 volumes. F.O. 281–5 are New York consulate archives.

EGYPT. F.O. 141. Correspondence. 1815–1909. 424 volumes. F.O. 142. Letter Books, 1805–73. 38 volumes. F.O. 143. Registers. (Ind. 13514–22, 17910–30.) 1839–1909.

CHINA. F.O. 228. Correspondence: treaty ports, etc. 1834–1939. 4371 volumes. F.O. 230. Letter Books. 1834–1917. 185 volumes. F.O. 231 contains Registers. F.O. 232. Indexes.

GUATEMALA. F.O. 252. Correspondence. 1825–1925. 615 volumes. F.O. 253. Letter books. 1829–74. 6 volumes. F.O. 255. Registers.

TURKEY. F.O. 329. Vols. 10, 11. Correspondence re Cyprus. 1865–76. F.O. 230. Letter Books. 1844–1917. 113 volumes. F.O. 231. Registers, 1841–78. 4 vols. F.O. 232. Indexes. 1843–1928. 13 volumes.

ARCHIVES OF COMMISSIONS

AMERICA: FISHERIES. F.O. 301. Registers, minute books and correspondence of Halifax Commission, 1873–6, and Washington Commission, 1887–8. 9 bundles and volumes.

AMERICA: NORTHWEST BOUNDARY. F.O. 302. Regular correspondence, letter books, plans, etc. 1872–6. 29 bundles and volumes.

BRITISH AND AMERICAN CLAIMS, 1871. F.O. 305. Papers, accounts, correspondence and awards under the Treaty of Washington, 1871. 1871–5. 98 bundles and volumes.

MISCELLANEOUS. F.O. 317. Vol. 2. Washington Commission, 1871. Register of correspondence. Vol. 3. Minutes of Commission to revise instructions to British Naval Officers engaged in the suppression of the slave trade, 1881–2.

GIFTS AND DEPOSITS

The numerous private and family papers of former Foreign Secretaries, Under-Secretaries, Ambassadors and other persons connected with the Foreign Office, which have been presented to, or deposited in, the Public Record Office, are now placed in one class: P.R.O. 30. This includes the following series:

P.R.O. 30/6. Carnarvon Papers. 1866–86. 131 nos.
P.R.O. 30/22. Russell Papers. 1804–1910. 118 nos.
P.R.O. 30/29. Granville Papers. 1604–1909. 429 nos.
P.R.O. 30/30. Milner Papers. 1918 only. 3 nos.
P.R.O. 30/48. Cardwell Papers. 1834–1911. 54 nos.

The papers of Edmund, Lord Hammond, are classified under F.O. 391 (1831–85). 28 nos.

F.O. CONFIDENTIAL PRINT

Among the series now available at the Public Record Office are the following:

F.O. 403. Africa and Slave Trade. 84 nos.
F.O. 405. China. 104 nos.
F.O. 407. Egypt and the Sudan. 66 nos.
F.O. 414. America, North. 59 nos.
F.O. 420. America, South and Central. 69 nos.
F.O. 422. Siam and South East Asia. 40 nos.
F.O. 423. Suez Canal. 42 nos.
F.O. 426. Inter-Imperial Relations. 10 nos.
F.O. 435. Anglo-Egyptian Treaty Negotiations. 2 nos.
F.O. 436. Far Eastern Affairs. 32 nos.
F.O. 461. America. 12 nos.
F.O. 462. United States of America. 3 nos.
F.O. 468. British Commonwealth. 10 nos.
F.O. 548. Settlements of Questions between the United States, Canada and Newfoundland, 1908–15. 7 nos.

(c) WAR OFFICE

The office of Secretary-at-War was abolished in 1863, leaving control of the Army in the hands of the Secretary of State for War and of the Commander-in-Chief. An Order in Council of 4 June 1870 declared the latter to be completely subordinate to the Secretary. The office of Commander-in-Chief was abolished in 1904. Records of the War Office are open to public inspection to the end of the year 1902, but subjects of colonial interest cannot always be traced as late as that date from the *Alphabetical Guide to...War Office Records in the Public Record Office* (P.R.O. *Lists and Indexes*, No. LIII, 1931). The series containing most relevant material are as follows:

W.O. 1. Correspondence. In-Letters. From 1732.
W.O. 2. Indexes of Correspondence.
W.O. 3. Out-Letters. Commander-in-Chief. From 1765.
W.O. 6. Out-Letters. Secretary of State. From 1793.
W.O. 7. Out-Letters. Departmental. From 1795.
W.O. 33. Reports and Miscellaneous Papers. Includes much material on campaigns, such as those in Egypt and the Sudan from 1876 onwards.
W.O. 112. Army Estimates. 1876–88.
W.O. 123. Army Circulars, Memoranda and Orders, 1886–1907.

(d) ADMIRALTY

The classes containing most material on imperial and international affairs are the following:

SECRETARY'S DEPARTMENT. ADM. 1, In-Letters. 1680–1902. 7643 volumes. Includes "Letters relating to the Colonies", "Admirals Despatches", West African Stations, Cape of Good Hope Station, East India Station, etc. ADM. 2, Out-Letters. ADM. 3, Minutes. ADM. 7, Miscellanea. ADM. 12, Indexes and Compilations, Series III, 1886–1902. 237 volumes. ADM. 13, Supplementary Collection of Papers (1803–1902), 250 volumes. ADM. 50, Admirals' Journals (1702–1911), 413 volumes. ADM. 51, Captains' logs. ADM. 52, Masters' Logs. ADM. 53, Ships' Logs.
NAVY BOARD. ADM. 106. In-Letters, Out-Letters. Minutes.

(e) TREASURY

For a description of Treasury records see Giuseppi, M.S., *Guide to the Public Records*, vol. II, pp. 142–52. Those of particular significance for imperial affairs are:

T. 1. Treasury Board. In-Letters and Papers. 1557–1920. 12,625 nos.
T. 2. (Ind. 17710–21, 18010–13, 18642–5, 23273–329.) Registers of Papers.
T. 7. Out-Letters. Colonial Affairs. 1849–1920. 44 volumes.
T. 12. Out-Letters. Foreign Office. 1857–1920. 47 volumes.
T. 23. Out-Letters. Treasurers Abroad. 1856–1913. 7 volumes.
T. 24. Out-Letters. War Departments. 1855–1920. 63 volumes.
T. 27. Out-Letters. General. Letter Books, Miscellaneous. New Series. 1857–1920. Including correspondence with the Emigration Commission.
T. 28. Out-Letters. Various. 1763–1888. 113 volumes. Including letters to Colonial Secretary, Foreign Secretary, Consuls and Ministers abroad, War Office, India Office.
T. 39. Treasury Chest. Accounts of Foreign and Colonial Stations. 1846–78.
T. 63. Maps and Plans. Series II. 1838–82. 38 parcels, including material on colonies and dependencies.
T. 64. Various, including Colonies, 1680–1867. Shipping and trade returns, correspondence, etc.

(f) BOARD OF TRADE

The Board of Trade in its present form dates from 1786, when a permanent committee was instituted by an Order in Council. A comprehensive library of trade returns, statistical yearbooks and similar material is maintained at the Commonwealth Statistics Library, Board of Trade, Lacon House, Theobald's Road, London. A duplicated list of *Public Records—Board of Trade Registered Papers* (1846–85) is available in a few libraries; otherwise the typed lists in the search rooms o. the Public Record Office must be used. There are many references to colonial matters in the papers of the Commercial Department (to 1873) and the Commercial and Statistical Department (from 1873). B.T. 11 had Correspondence and Papers of the Department, B.T. 12 Out-Letters, 1864–1900. The Exchequer and Audit Department has much relevant material, especially in A.O. 16. Miscellanea, 1568–1910 (including documents not yet open to public inspection).

(g) CUSTOM HOUSE

For inter-imperial trade the records of Customs and Excise are indispensable sources in this period; for instance C. 10, Ledgers of Exports of Foreign and Colonial Merchandize—arranged under countries; C. 11, similar ledgers—arranged under articles, 1809–99. They have so far hardly been examined.

2. OTHER COLLECTIONS

(a) BRITISH MUSEUM, DEPARTMENT OF MANUSCRIPTS

The most recent published lists and indexes of manuscripts added to the collections in the British Museum are the *Catalogue of the Additions to the Manuscripts*, 1921–25 (British Museum, 1950) and *Catalogue of the Additions to the Manuscripts. The Gladstone Papers* (Add. MSS. 44085–835) (B.M. 1953). The more important later additions have been noted in the *British Museum Quarterly* or the *Bulletin of the Institute of Historical Research*, vols. III– (1926–).

In addition to the Gladstone Papers, the following collections are relevant:

Campbell-Bannerman Papers, Add. MSS. 41206–52.
Correspondence and Papers of John Bright, Add. MSS. 43383–92.
Confidential Political Diaries, Memoir and Correspondence of Sir Charles Dilke, Add. MSS. 43922–64.
Letters to Lord Kilbracken, Add. MSS. 44900–02.
Correspondence and Papers of Herbert Viscount Gladstone, Add. MSS. 45985–46118 and 46474–86.
Papers of Baron Welby on imperial defence (1888–91), Egerton MS. 3291.
The Khartoum and other papers of General C. G. Gordon are also in the Department of Manuscripts.

The Map Room of the British Museum has the finest collection of official maps prepared in Commonwealth countries: those issued by the Directorate of Colonial Surveys and by individual colonial Survey Departments. Manuscript maps are kept in the Department of Manuscripts or the Oriental Department.

(b) OTHER BRITISH COLLECTIONS

Few documents of the period since 1870 have been recorded so far in the *Reports of the Royal Commission on Historical Manuscripts*. The work of the Commission has been considerably extended since the setting up of the National Register of Archives at the Public Record Office, London. The duplicated reports of the Register and its annual *Bulletin* are a mine of information on the whereabouts of private and semi-public collections of manuscripts.

The Bodleian Library and Rhodes House at Oxford are rich in documents relating to modern British history in all its aspects. The annual *Report(s) of the Curators* of the Bodleian note the principal additions to the Department of Western Manuscripts and to Rhodes House. It should be noted that microfilm or photostat copies of historical material in other collections are also being acquired on a considerable scale by Rhodes House. Among original manuscripts there are many of the British Anti-Slavery Society; the Molteno Papers, 1837–85; the Cawston Papers relating to the British South Africa Company, 1888–1911; the Portal Papers relating to Cairo, Zanzibar and Uganda, 1885–95; the Diaries of E. J. H. Russell relating to the British East Africa Company, 1895–1900; the papers of Sir John Kirk; papers of the Royal Niger Company, 1884–1930, including Lugard correspondence; the reports of the British North Borneo Company from 1882 to 1914, with accompanying correspondence; the great collection of Melitensia presented by Sir Hannibal Scicluna. The Lugard Papers are to be deposited at the Bodleian Library shortly; the papers of Asquith (Lord Oxford) are there at present. The papers of the 3rd Marquess of Salisbury are deposited at Christ Church, and most of the Milner Papers are at New College, Oxford.

Among manuscripts in Cambridge University Library are the Zanzibar collection, the Jardine-Matheson collection on Malaya and China, and the papers of Charles, 1st Baron Hardinge of Penshurst. Photostats and microfilms of original documents on colonial and international relations are included in the rapidly-increasing collection of such material in the University Library and the Seeley Library.

The papers of the Grey family are deposited with the University of Durham and lists of those of the 3rd Earl Grey will shortly be available.

The National Library of Scotland now has the papers of Lord Haldane and the official records of the various Presbyterian missions in Africa of the Church of Scotland.

In the University of London Library are papers of the Royal Africa Company. The School of Oriental and African Studies in the University has much original material relating to Rhodesia, East and West Africa, Uganda and Zanzibar, including papers of Sir William Mackinnon, first President of the Imperial British East Africa Company; also books, pamphlets and some manuscripts of the Anti-Slavery and Aborigines Protection Society. The papers of the Royal Niger Company have been inherited by its successor, the United Africa Company, Unilever House, Blackfriars, London, E.C. 4. Surveys of original materials for West African history, both in African and in European sources, are at present being undertaken.

The personal papers of many prominent persons are still in private hands; for instance those of Lord Beaconsfield, Lord Bryce, Sidney Buxton, Lord Carnarvon, Lord Derby, Lord Iddesleigh, Lord Kimberley, Lord Kindersley, Joseph Chamberlain, Lord Lansdowne, Lord Rosebery, Bonar Law, Lloyd George and Lord Curzon. Considerable use has already been made of these collections in biographies. Their whereabouts can usually be traced through the National Register of Archives.

The resources of philanthropic, religious and other societies have been briefly noted in *C.H.B.E.* vol. vii, pt. 1, pp. 604–5, and vol. viii, pp. 883–5. Especially important for the period covered by the present volume were the Church Missionary Society, the London Missionary Society and the Society for the Propagation of the Gospel. The Church Missionary Society (6 Salisbury Square, Fleet Street, London, E.C. 4) has a valuable manuscript collection accessible to accredited students. Its own archives date from the society's foundation in 1799 and comprise Minute Books, Incoming Letters, Missionaries' Journals and Annual Letters, Outgoing Letters and Mission Books. Indexes are kept to many of these. The Society also possesses the personal papers of several famous missionaries such as those of Archdeacon Walker of Uganda; also the journal of Alexander Mackay, the East African explorer, and Krapf's journals and sketch-maps.

The records of the London Missionary Society (Livingstone House, Westminster, S.W. 1) may be inspected by accredited research workers. Besides many Livingstone letters, there is much other material relating to Central Africa, also to Madagascar and Mauritius; the West Indies and the Far East are also represented by large collections. Typed calendars exist for many groups of records, which are, with few exceptions, open to the year 1905. The archives of the Society for the Propagation of the Gospel in Foreign Parts (15 Tufton Street, Westminster, S.W. 1) are well kept and arranged. *The Digest of the S.P.G. Records* (1900 edn.) and C. F. Pascoe's *Two Hundred Years of the S.P.G., 1701–1900* (1901) are still of use as guides to the collection, and typed recent lists and indexes are available at the Society.

Most of the nonconformist churches have had missions in the West Indies, Africa, India, Ceylon and the Far East. The Methodist Missionary Society (25 Marylebone Road, London, N.W. 1) has a large collection of missionary letters and journals, many relating to the West Indies, Ceylon and the South Sea Islands. The records of the Baptist Missionary Society (93 Gloucester Place, London, W. 1) are now partly accessible, and are likely to prove valuable, when reorganised after war damage. For the various Presbyterian Missions, the papers of the Church of Scotland are the most extensive. These are now in the National Library of Scotland. Other missionary societies, such as the Universities' Mission to Central Africa (35 Great Peter Street, London, S.W. 1), have well-kept archives. The *Directory of Foreign Missions* (International Missionary Council) gives some indication of other material available.

(c) IN THE COLONIES AND DEPENDENCIES

Since earlier volumes of this History were prepared the care and attention given to records in the dependent, or formerly dependent, countries of the Commonwealth have greatly increased. Efficient archive repositories have been set up in the West Indies, in West, Central and East Africa, in Ceylon, Malaya and even in some of the Pacific Islands. *Central African Archives in Retrospect and Prospect* (Salisbury, 1947) describes the pioneering work of this repository during its first twelve years, including the issue of the Oppenheimer series of texts. There are later annual reports and cumulations. K. O. Diké has made a *Report on the Preservation and Administration of Historical Records and Establishment of a Public Record Office in Nigeria* (Lagos, 1954). The exemplary *Bibliography of Mauritius, 1509–1954* (Port Louis, 1955), prepared by A. Toussaint and H. Adolphe, analyses manuscript sources as well as books, pamphlets and periodicals. Very little has as yet been published about most of the countries, but, in general, it should be noted that the records preserved in the colonies and dependencies themselves, besides duplicating series in the Colonial Office files, include papers not sent to London. For instance, at Fourah Bay College, Freetown, are the Letter-books and Minute Papers of the Native Affairs Department, Sierra Leone; at Entebbe are the Secretariat records of Uganda, and at Makerere College are the papers of the Uganda Company and other contemporary material.

3. SELECT LIST OF PARLIAMENTARY PAPERS

There is now available a clear and concise *Guide to Parliamentary Papers* (Oxford, 1955; 2nd edn. 1956), by P. and G. Ford. This explains "what they are, how to find them, how to use them". *The Colonial Office List*, 1877, contains classified lists of "Papers presented to Parliament relating to the Colonies since 1864", the *C.O. List*, 1887 contains those from 1877, and the *C.O. List*, 1948 those from 1887; unfortunately volume numbers are not given in the earlier lists.

Annual reports, known as the "Blue Book Reports", including statistical information, were issued for all colonies and dependencies during this period, e.g. *Reports on the Present State of Her Majesty's Colonial Possessions for 1868*. Part I, West Indies. Part II, North America, Africa, Australia and Mediterranean Possessions. Part III, Eastern Colonies. 1870, XLIX [C. 85], [C. 149], [C. 151]. From 1889–90 these annual colonial reports were also given serial numbers in a General series and in a Miscellaneous series. Other regular annual series were: *Africa* (from 1900), *Statistical Abstracts for the several British Self-Governing Colonies* (from 1851 to 1902) and *Statistical Abstracts for the British Empire* (from 1889), first issued in 1905.

Official indexes to Parliamentary Papers of the House of Commons were issued for each session and also decennially during the period covered by this volume. The following consolidated index omits references to all the Command and Sessional numbers of the papers: *General Index to the Bills, Reports, Estimates and Accounts and Papers, etc., 1852–99*. Parl. Pap. 1909. There is a consolidated *General Alphabetical Index* to House of Lords papers for the years 1871 to 1884–5, and sessional indexes for 1886 onwards.

The lists below are grouped under headings similar to those in the "Special Bibliographies" given later. The references indicate in each case the session during which a paper was printed, the volume for that session into which it has been bound by the House of Commons, or House of Lords, and the Sessional ( ) or Command [ ] number of the papers. The square brackets round the reference numbers of Command papers have been omitted on the title-pages of the papers themselves since 1922, but for earlier dates are the correct form. It should be noted that the sessional numbers of *Bills* are a separate series from those of *Reports, Accounts and Papers*. Unless otherwise indicated, references given below are to House of Commons Papers.

COLONIAL POLICY AND ADMINISTRATION IN GENERAL,
1870–1914

1870, XLIX [C. 24], [C. 51]. Proposed Conference of Colonial Representatives in London—Corresp. and papers.

1870, XLIX [C. 85], [C. 149], [C. 151]. Reports on Present State of Colonial Possessions [annual].

1870, XLIX [C. 139]. Colonial judges—Corresp. re renewals and suspensions.

1870, XLIX (297). Corresp. re Disposal of Colonial Crown Lands.

1871, H.L., XIV (318). Ballot System in Colonies—Papers.

1871, XLVII (106). Return re past Governors. [Thereafter annually.]

1871, XLVII [C. 334], [C. 407], [C. 415]. Reports on Colonial Possessions for 1869.

1872, XLII [C. 523], [C. 583], [C. 617]. Reports on Colonial Possessions for 1870.

1873, I (248). Bill for Relief of Colonial Clergy.

1873, XLVIII (259), (259–I), (259–II). Ecclesiastical Grants—Corresp. with Colonial Governors.

1873, XLVIII [C. 709], [C. 709–I], [C. 709–II]. Reports on Colonies for 1871.

1874, VII (245). Report from Select Comm. on Colonial Clergy Bill.

1874, XLIV [C. 882], [C. 1102]. Reports on Colonial Possessions for 1873.

1874, XLIV [C. 979]. Colonial Bishops—Corresp. re trust property.

1875, LI [C. 1183]. Papers relating to colonial possessions, Part I. 1874–5.

1875, LI [C. 1335], [C. 1336]. Reports on Colonial Possessions, II, III. 1874–5.

1876, LI [C. 1622], [C. 1622–I]. Reports on Colonial Possessions, 1875–6.

1877, LIX [C. 1825], [C. 1869]. Reports on Colonial Possessions, 1875–7.

1878, LV [C. 2149]. Reports on Colonial Possessions for 1876–7.

1878–9, L [C. 2273], [C. 2444]. Reports on Colonial Possessions, 1876–8.

1880, XLVIII [C. 2598], [C. 2730]. Reports on Colonial Possessions, 1877–79.

1881, XLIV [C. 3075]. Papers re functions of Crown Agents for the Colonies.

1881, XLIV [C. 2829], [C. 3094]. Reports on Colonial Possessions for 1879–80.

1882, XLIV [C. 3218], [C. 3388]. Reports on Colonies for 1879–81.

1883, XLV [C. 3642], [C. 3794]. Reports on Colonies for 1880–2.

1883, LIV [C. 3688]. Reports re legislative assemblies in colonies.

1884, XLVII (227). Colonial Office—Corresp. re Lower Division clerks.

1884, LIV [C. 4015], [C. 4193]. Reports on Colonies for 1881–4.

1884–5, LII [C. 4404], [C. 4583]. Reports on Colonies for 1883–5.

1884–5, LIV [C. 4290]. Berlin Conversations on colonial matters.

1886, XLV [C. 4842], [C. 4904]. Reports on Colonies for 1883–5.

1887, I (369). Bill on govt. of settlements.

1887, LVII [C. 5071], [C. 5239]. Reports on Colonial Possessions, 1884–6.

1888, LXXII [C. 5249]. Reports on Colonies for 1884–7.

1889, LIV [C. 5620]. Reports on Colonies for 1887–9.

1889, LV (70). Return re colonial representative assemblies.

1889, LV [C. 5828]. Corresp. re appointment of colonial governors.

1890, XLVIII [C. 5897]. Reports on Colonies for 1887–90.

1890, XLIX (194). Return re representative assemblies in Colonies.

1890–1, LV [C. 6269]. Colonial Reports, Annual series for 1889–90, nos. 1–15.

1890–1, LV [C. 6270]. Colonial Reports, Miscellaneous series, nos. 1–2.

1892, LV [C. 6563], [C. 6829]. Colonial Reports for 1889–92, nos. 16–49.

1893–4, II (484). Colonial Acts Confirmation Bill.

1893–4, LIX, LX [C. 6837]. Colonial Reports, nos. 50–101.

1893–4, LXXXIX (388). Return re payments of members of colonial legislatures.

1894, LVI [C. 7319]. Colonial Reports for 1892–3, annual series, nos. 102–116.

1894, LVI [C. 7553]. Colonial Conference at Ottawa—Report by Lord Jersey.

1895, LXIX [C. 7629], [C. 7847]. Colonial Reports, nos. 117–47.

1895, LXX [C. 7632], [C. 7824]. Colonial Conference, 1894. Further corresp.

1896, LVII [C. 7944]. Annual Colonial Reports for 1894–5, nos. 148–75.

1896, LVIII [C. 8143]. Resolutions and messages of loyalty from Canada, Australia and New Zealand.

1897, LIX [C. 8279]. Annual Colonial Reports for 1895–6, nos. 176–201.

1897, LIX [C. 8485]. Corresp. with Colonies on celebrating 60th anniversary of Queen's accession.

1897, LIX [C. 8596]. Conference between Colonial Secretary and Premiers of Self-Governing Colonies. Proceedings, 1897.

1898, LIX [C. 8650]. Annual Colonial Reports, for 1896–7, nos. 202–31.

1899, LXI [C. 9046]. Annual Colonial Reports, nos. 232–76.

1899, LXII [C. 9498]. Annual Colonial Reports, nos. 232–76.

1900, LIV [Cd. 3], [Cd. 354]. Annual Colonial Reports for 1899, nos. 277–307.

1901, I (209). Colonial Acts Confirmation Bill.

1901, IV (286). Royal Style and Title Bill.

1901, XLV [Cd. 431]. Annual Colonial Reports, nos. 308–29 (Bahamas, Barbados, Basutoland, Bermuda, British Guiana, British Honduras, British Solomon Islands, Christmas Island, Gambia, Grenada, Hong Kong, Jamaica, Lagos, Leeward Islands, Malta, St Helena (2), St Lucia, St Vincent, Sierra Leone, Southern Nigeria, Turks and Caicos Islands).

1901, XLVI (362). Return re Colonial Bills or Acts not receiving Royal Assent since 1894.

1901, XLVI [Cd. 708]. Royal Style and Title of Crown—Corresp. re proposed alteration.

1902, LXIV, LXV [Cd. 788]. Colonial Reports, nos. 330–75.

1902, LXVI [Cd. 846]. Court of Colonial Appeal—Corresp. re proposed establishment.

1902, LXVI [Cd. 1299]. Colonial Conference, 1902. Papers.

1903, XLIII [Cd. 1388]. Colonial Reports for 1902, Annual series, nos. 376–94.

1903, XLIV [Cd. 1597]. Colonial Conference, 1902—Memo. on Sea Power.

1903, XLIV [Cd. 1723]. Colonial Conference, 1902—Corresp. re publication of Proceedings.

1904, LVI [Cd. 1768]. Annual Colonial Reports, nos. 395–408.

1904, LVII [Cd. 1768]. Annual Colonial Reports, nos. 409–22.

1905, LI [Cd. 2238]. Annual Colonial Reports, nos. 423–53.

1905, LIII (142). Colonial Representative Institutions—Return re methods of conferring since 1837.

1906, LXXIII [Cd. 2648]. Annual Colonial Reports, nos. 454–512.

1906, LXXVII (184). Return re Colonial Acts, not receiving Royal Assent or disallowed, since 1901.

1906, LXXVII [Cd. 2785], [Cd. 2975]. Future Organisation of Colonial Conferences. Corresp.

1907, II (202). Evidence (Colonial Statutes) Bill.

1907, VI (244). Evidence (Colonial Statutes) Bill—Report from Standing Committee B, with Proceedings.

1907, LIII [Cd. 3285]. Annual Colonial Reports, nos. 513–24.

1907, LIV [Cd. 3285]. Annual Colonial Reports, nos. 525–35.

1907, LIV [Cd. 3337], [Cd. 3340]. Colonial Conference, 1907—Corresp. and papers.

1907, LV [Cd. 3404], [Cd. 3406]. Colonial Conference, 1907—Published Proceedings and Précis.

1907, LV [Cd. 3523], [Cd. 3524]. Colonial Conference, 1907—Minutes of Proceedings and Papers laid.

1908, LXVIII [Cd. 3729]. Annual Colonial Reports, nos. 536–90.

1908, LXX [Cd. 3795]. Colonial Office—Despatch re reorganisation.

1909, LVII, LVIII [Cd. 4448]. Annual Colonial Reports, nos. 591–608, 609–25.

1910, LXIV [Cd. 4964]. Annual Colonial Reports, nos. 626–63.

1910, LXV [Cd. 5135]. Report of Dominions Dept. of Colonial Office, 1909–10.

1910, LXV [Cd. 5273]. Further Corresp. *re* Imperial Conference.
1910, LXVI (129). Corresp. with Foreign Powers *re* constitutional position of Dominions and Colonies in treaties.
1911, LI, LII [Cd. 5467]. Annual Colonial Reports, nos. 664–99.
1911, LIII [Cd. 5582]. Report of Dominions Dept. of Colonial Office, 1910–11.
1911, LIV [Cd. 5513], [Cd. 5741], [Cd. 5745]. Imperial Conference—Corresp. précis and minutes of proceedings, and papers.
1911, LIV [Cd. 5746–I], [Cd. 5746–II]. Imperial Conference—Papers laid.
1912–13, XVI [Cd. 6515], [Cd. 6516], [Cd. 6517]. 1st Interim Report of Royal Comm. on Natural Resources, Trade and Legislation of Dominions.
1912–13, LVII [Cd. 6007]. Annual Colonial Reports, nos. 700–51.
1912–13, LX (131). Order by Secretary of State classifying Governorships.
1912–13, LX (160). Return *re* Colonial Bills or Acts not receiving Royal Assent since 1906.
1912–13, LX [Cd. 6091]. Report of Dominions Dept. of Colonial Office, 1911–12.
1913, XLV [Cd. 6667]. Annual Colonial Reports for 1912, nos. 752–8.
1913, XLV [Cd. 6863]. Report on the Dominions Dept. of Colonial Office, 1912–13.
1914, XVII [Cd. 7170], [Cd. 7171], [Cd. 7172]. Royal Comm. on Dominions—Evidence and Papers.
1914, XVIII [Cd. 7173], [Cd. 7351]. Royal Comm. on Dominions—Papers.
1914, XVIII [Cd. 7210]. 2nd Interim Report of Royal Comm. on Dominions.
1914, XVIII [Cd. 7505]. 3rd Interim Report of Royal Comm. on Dominions.
1914, LVII, LVIII [Cd. 7050]. Annual Reports on Colonies, nos. 751–808.
1914, LX [Cd. 7507]. Report on Dominions Dept., Colonial Office, 1913–14.
1914–16, XIII [Cd. 7706], [Cd. 7707], [Cd. 7710]. Royal Comm. on Dominions—Evidence and Papers.
1914–16, XIV [Cd. 7711], [Cd. 7898], [Cd. 7971], [Cd. 8123], [Cd. 8156]. 4th Interim Report of Royal Comm. on Dominions, Evidence and Papers.
1914–16, XLIII, XLIV [Cd. 7622]. Annual Reports on Colonies, nos. 809–73.
1916, XIX [Cd. 8172]. Annual Colonial Reports, nos, 874–912.
1917–18, VIII [Cd. 8457], [Cd. 8458]. 5th Interim Report of Royal Comm. on Dominions and Evidence.
1917–18, IX [Cd. 8459], [Cd. 8460], [Cd. 8461]. Royal Comm. on Dominions, Evidence and Papers.
1917–18, X [Cd. 8462]. Final Report of Royal Comm. on Dominions.
1917–18, XXII [Cd. 8434]. Annual Colonial Reports, nos. 913–50.
1918, XVII [Cd. 8973]. Annual Colonial Reports, nos. 951–76.
1919, XXXV [Cmd. 1]. Annual Colonial Reports, nos. 977–1006.
1920, XXXII [Cmd. 508]. Annual Colonial Reports, nos. 1017–56.
1921, XIV (195). Speech on League of Nations to the Imperial Conference by Lord President of the Council.
1921, XIV [Cmd. 1474]. Conference of Prime Ministers of U.K., Dominions and India—Summary of Proceedings and Documents, 1921.
1921, XXVI [Cmd. 1103]. Annual Colonial Reports, nos. 1057–71.

COLONISATION AND EMIGRATION, 1870–1918

1870, XVII [C. 196]. 30th Report of Land and Emigration Commissioners.
1870, XLIX (179). Emigration—Circular to Governors of Colonies.
1870, XLIX (297). Papers *re* Crown Lands in Colonies.
1871, XX [C. 369]. 31st Report of Emigration Commissioners.
1871, XLVII [C. 296]. Report from Murdoch on Emigration.
1871, XLVII [C. 335], [C. 335–I]. Emigration circular and corresp.
1871, XLVII [C. 403]. Emigration—Corresp. *re* Chinese coolies from Maçao.
1872, XVI [C. 562]. 32nd Report of Emigration Commissioners.

1872, XLIII (154). Return re Colonial Land and Emigration Commissioners and information on emigration to colonies.

1872, XLIII [C. 614]. Corresp. re emigration.

1873, XVIII [C. 768]. 33rd Report of Emigration Commissioners.

1875, LII (275). 1st Report of Select Comm. of Parliament of Canada on Immigration and Colonisation.

1881, LXXXII [C. 2995]. Reports on emigrant shipping accommodation.

1882, LXII (252), (279), (398), (404). Returns and reports on conditions in emigrant ships.

1883, LXII (261). Return re conditions in emigrant ships.

1886, XLV [C. 4751]. Corresp. re emigration and establishing of Emigrants' Information Office, 1884-6.

1888, H.L., xv (248). Report of Select Comm. on Emigration and Immigration (Foreign).

1888, LXXIII [C. 5361]. Replies from colonies re Kimberley's scheme of colonisation.

1888, LXXX [C. 5403]. Corresp. re crofters colonisation scheme.

1889, VI (327). Bill to amend Passengers Acts, 1855 and 1863.

1889, X (274). Report from Select Comm. on Colonisation.

1889, LV (106), (232), (314). Replies by colonial governments to memo. of Parliamentary Colonisation Committee, 1888.

1890, XII (354). Report of Select Committee on Colonisation.

1890, XLIX [C. 6064]. Report on Emigrants' Information Office for 1889-90.

1890-1, XI (152), Report from Select Comm. on Colonisation: proceedings, evidence and appendices.

1892, LVI [C. 6573]. Report on Emigrants' Information Office.

1893-4, LX [C. 6887], [C. 7269]. Report on Emigrants' Information Office for 1892 and 1893.

1896, LVIII [C. 7613], [C. 7979]. Report on Emigrants' Information Office for 1894 and 1895.

1897, LXI [C. 8360]. Report on Emigrants' Information Office for 1896.

1898, LIX [C. 8756]. Report on the Emigrants' Information Office, 1897.

1899, LVIII [C. 9196]. Report on the Emigrants' Information Office for 1898.

1900, LV [Cd. 90]. Report on the Emigrants' Information Office for 1899.

1900, LVII (383). Return re treatment of Indians in British Colonies.

1901, XLVI [Cd. 526]. Report on the Emigrants' Information Office for 1900.

1903, XLIV [Cd. 1464]. Report on the Emigrants' Information Office for 1902.

1904, LIX [Cd. 2105]. Immigration Papers re Colonial Laws and Regulations.

1905, LIII [Cd. 2396]. Report on Emigrants' Information Office, 1904.

1906, LXXVII [Cd. 2976]. Report on Emigrants' Information Office, 1905.

1907, LXVII [Cd. 3407]. Memo. on History and Functions of Emigrants' Information Office.

1908, LXX [Cd. 3918]. Report on the Emigrants' Information Office, 1907.

1909, LIX [Cd. 4526]. Report on Emigrants' Information Office, 1908.

1910, XXII [Cd. 5133], [Cd. 5134]. Report of Committee on Distressed Colonial and Indian Subjects, with Minutes.

1910, LXVI [Cd. 5101]. Report on Emigrants' Information Office, 1909.

1911, LX [Cd. 5580]. Report on Emigrants' Information Office, 1910.

1912-13, LX [Cd. 6088]. Report on Emigrants' Information Office, 1911.

1913, XLV [Cd. 6670]. Report on Emigrants' Information Office, 1912.

1914, LX [Cd. 7212]. Report on Emigrants' Information Office, 1913.

1914, LX [Cd. 7262]. Return showing Indian populations in Colonies.

1914-16, XXI [Cd. 7794]. Report on Emigrants' Information Office, 1914.

1917-18, X [Cd. 8672]. Report of Committee on settlement of ex-service men within the Empire.

1918, I (30). Bill to improve organisation for Emigration.

1918, XX [Cd. 9173]. Corresp. re Emigration Bill.

IMPERIAL FINANCE, TRADE AND COMMUNICATIONS, 1870–1921

(See also under the various Colonies)

1870, XLIX (80). Return of annual cost of Colonies, 1859–68 and 1869.

1871, XLVII (52). Cost of Colonies—Return for 1870.

1871, XLVIII (510). Colonies return re taxes and imposts in 1868. [Thereafter annually.]

1871, LXIX [C. 379]. Statistical Abstracts for Colonies (7th) for each year, 1855–69.

1872, XLIII (247). Return re taxes and impost in Colonies from 1868.

1872, XLIII [C. 591]. Corresp. on sale of intoxicating liquors in Colonies.

1872, LXIII [C. 616]. Statistical Abstracts for Colonies, 1856–70.

1873, XLVIII (36). Colonial loans—Return of imperial guarantees.

1873, LXIX [C. 834]. Statistical Abstracts for Colonies, 1857–71.

1874, XLIV (354). Taxes and Imposts (Colonies).

1874, LXX [C. 1037], [C. 1038]. Statistical Abstracts for Colonies, 1858–72.

1875, LI (32), (475). Return of taxes and imposts in Colonies, 1874–5.

1875, LI (194). Cost of Colonies, 1869–73.

1875, LXXX [C. 1304]. Statistical Abstracts for Colonies, 1859–73.

1876, LXXVII [C. 1545]. Statistical Abstracts for Colonies, 1860–74.

1877, LXXV [C. 1842]. Statistical Abstracts for Colonies, 1861–75.

1878, LXVIII (395). Memorials from British West Indies and from Bristol on sugar bounties.

1878, LXXVIII [C. 2029]. Statistical tables re Colonies, 1871–5.

1878, LXXVIII [C. 2093]. Statistical Abstracts for Colonies, 1862–76.

1878–9, I (278). Bill re colonial chartered banks.

1878–9, XIII (321). Report from Select Committee on Sugar Industries.

1878–9, L [C. 2197]. Analysis of returns re colonial timber.

1878–9, LXV (218). Colonial import duties—Return for years 1859–79.

1878–9, LXXIII [C. 2392]. Papers laid before select Committee on Sugar Industries.

1878–9, LXXV [C. 2306]. Statistical Abstracts for Colonies, 1863–77.

1880, I (4), (109). Chartered Banks (Colonial) Bill.

1880, VIII (115). Chartered Banks (Colonial) Bill, Report from Select Committee.

1880, XII (106), (332). Report from Select Committee on Home and Colonial Sugar Industries.

1880, XLIX (370). Chartered Banks—Treasury Minute.

1880, LXVII (120), (120–1). Foreign and Colonial Import Duties—Returns.

1880, LXXV [C. 2476]. Further corresp. re sugar question.

1880, LXXVI [C. 2520]. Statistical Abstracts for Colonies, 1864–78.

1881, LXIV (417). Return re advances to Colonies by imperial government.

1881, LXXV (421). Return listing Colonial Banks.

1881, XCII [C. 3051]. Representations of Chambers of Commerce re new French commercial treaty.

1881, XCIV [C. 2867]. Statistical Abstracts for Colonies, 1865–79.

1881, XCIV [C. 2936]. Statistical Tables for Colonies, 1876–8.

1882, H.L., v (164). Merchant Shipping (Colonial Courts of Inquiry)—Papers.

1882, XLIV [C. 3224]. Restriction of sale of intoxicating liquor in Colonies: Corresp.

1882, LXXIII [C. 3216]. Statistical Abstracts for Colonies, 1866–80.

1883, XLV [C. 3477]. Restriction of sale of intoxicating liquor in the Colonies—Corresp.

1883, LXXVI [C. 3502]. Statistical Abstracts for Colonies, 1867–81.

1884, LXXXIV [C. 3874]. Statistical Abstracts for Colonies, 1868–82.

1884–5, H.L., XII (247). Depression of trade and industry: memorandum by Lord Iddesleigh.

1884–5, LXXXIII [C. 4519]. Colonial Statistical Tables for 1879–81.

1884–5, LXXXIII [C. 4520]. Colonial Statistical Abstracts, 1869–83.
1886, XXI [C. 4621]. 1st Report of Royal Comm. on Depression of Trade and Industry.
1886, XXII [C. 4715–I]. 2nd Report on Depression of Trade.
1886, XXII [C. 4715–II]. Appendices to 1st Report on Depression of Trade.
1886, XXIII [C. 4893]. Final Report on Depression of Trade, with evidence and appendices.
1886, LX [C. 4779]. Diplomatic and consular assistance to British trade abroad: corresp.
1886, LXVIII [C. 4825]. Statistical Abstracts for Colonies, 1871–85.
1887, XX [C. 5083]. Report of Royal Comm. on Colonial and Indian Exhibition.
1887, LXXXVII [C. 5176]. Statistical Abstracts for Colonies, 1872–86.
1888, LXXIII [C. 5563]. Restriction of sale of intoxicating liquors in the Colonies —Further corresp.
1888, XCVIII [C. 5369]. Return re treaties of commerce precluding preferences in Colonies.
1888, CV [C. 5507]. Statistical Abstracts for Colonies, 1873–87.
1888, CV [C. 5508]. Statistical Tables for Colonies, 1882–4.
1889, LXXXII [C. 5863]. Statistical Abstracts for Colonies, 1874–88.
1890, LXXVIII [C. 1660]. Statistical Abstracts for Colonies, 1875–89.
1890–1, LVI [C. 6278]. Report of Departmental Committee on investment of trust funds in colonial stocks.
1890–1, LVI [C. 6348], [C. 6485]. Corresp. re Sunday labour in Colonies.
1890–1, XC [C. 6456]. Statistical Abstracts for Colonies, 1876–90.
1892, XXXVI, Pt. v [C. 6795–XI]. Report of Comm. on Labour. Vol. II. Colonies and Indian Empire.
1892, LXXXVII [C. 6719]. Statistical Abstracts for Colonies, 1877–91.
1893–4, LX [C. 7052]. Further papers on Sunday labour in Colonies.
1893–4, LXXI (467). Shareholders in British South Africa Co. and other companies: corresp.
1893–4, C [C. 7144]. Statistical Abstracts for Colonies, 1878–92.
1894, LX [C. 7313]. 1st Report of Royal Comm. on Opium.
1894, LXI [C. 7397]. Royal Comm. on Opium; further evidence and appendices.
1894, LXII [C. 7471], [C. 7473]. Royal Comm. on Opium: further evidence and appendices.
1894, XVI [C. 7400]. 1st Report of Royal Comm. on the Agricultural Depression, Parts I–III.
1894, XCII [C. 7526]. Statistical Abstracts for Colonies, 1879–83.
1894, XCII [C. 7527]. Statistical Tables for Colonies, 1888–90.
1895, XLII [C. 7723–I], [C. 7723–II]. Royal Commission on Opium: final report and historical appendices.
1895, LXX [C. 7824]. Trade and commercial treaties: despatches from the Colonial Secretary.
1896, LVIII [C. 7960]. Reports from Colonies on bounties.
1896, LVIII [C. 7989]. Return showing sugar production and export in Colonies, 1889–94.
1896, XCI [C. 8210]. Statistical Abstracts for Colonies, 1881–95.
1897, LX [C. 8449]. Despatch from Chamberlain and replies from Colonial Governors re British Empire trade and foreign competition.
1897, LXI [C. 8359]. Corresp. re sugar industry in West Indies.
1897, LXXIX (390). Return re colonial tariffs on imports from Britain.
1897, XCVII [C. 8605]. Statistical Abstract for Colonies, 1882–96.
1897, XCVII [C. 8606]. Statistical Tables for Colonies for 1891–3.
1898, I (302). Bill for Colonial Loans.
1898, L [C. 8655], [C. 8656], [C. 8657]. Report and papers of Royal Comm. on Sugar Industry in West Indies.

1898, LI [C. 8669], [C. 8799]. Royal Comm. on Sugar Industry—Further papers.
1898, XCII [C. 8780], [C. 8938]. Corresp. *re* Brussels Conference on sugar bounties.
1898, C [C. 8993]. Statistical Abstracts for 1883–97.
1899, I (98), (294). Bills for advance of Colonial Loans.
1899, LVIII (3-Sess. II). Return showing excise restrictions on spirits in Colonies.
1899, LVIII [C. 9439], [C. 9440]. Statement on loans and expenditure under Colonial Loans Bill, 1899.
1899, LIX [C. 9247], [C. 9283]. Report and corresp. *re* Pacific cable.
1899, CIV [C. 9459]. Statistical Abstracts for Colonies, 1884–98.
1900, LV [Cd. 46]. Corresp. *re* Pacific cable.
1900, LXXXVII [Cd. 324]. Return *re* trade, economic conditions, etc. in South East Asia.
1900, XCIX [Cd. 58]. Statistical Tables for Colonies, 1894–96 [thereafter annually].
1900, C [Cd. 307]. Statistical Abstracts for Colonies, 1885–99.
1901, XXXVII (94). Statements *re* advances under Colonial Loans Acts, 1899.
1901, XLVI [Cd. 614]. Selections from Colonial Medical Reports.
1901, LXXV (336). Return *re* colonial import duties on U.K. articles.
1901, LXXXVI [Cd. 751]. Statistical Abstracts for Colonies, 1886–1900.
1901, LXXXVII [Cd. 492]. Statistical Tables for Colonies, 1897–8.
1902, LXVI [Cd. 1328], [Cd. 1330]. Replies to circular despatch of 12 Dec. 1902 *re* representation of trading companies in colonial legislatures.
1902, CIV [Cd. 940]. Sugar Conference at Brussels, 1901–2—Corresp.
1903, XLIV (299). Return *re* colonial Import Duties and Population—1882, 1892 and last year published.
1903, XLIV [Cd. 1598]. Papers *re* Malaria and Schools of Tropical Medicine.
1903, LXVIII (262). Return *re* trade of Colonies, 1890–1900.
1903, LXX [Cd. 1638]. Statement *re* value of Colonial trade during 1901.
1903, LXXX [Cd. 1729]. Statistical Abstracts for Colonies, 1888–1902.
1903, LXXXI [Cd. 1728]. Statistical Tables for Colonies, 1901.
1904, LVIII [Cd. 1811], [Cd. 2185]. Returns *re* Colonial import duties in 1903 and 1904.
1904, LIX (118). Indentured Coolie Labour—Return *re* ordinances in Colonies.
1904, LIX [Cd. 1944]. Crown Agents' Office—Despatch *re* commercial business.
1904, LXII [Cd. 1956]. Convention respecting Employment of Chinese Labour in British Colonies and Protectorates.
1904, CIII [Cd. 1912]. Statistical Abstracts for Colonies, 1889–1903.
1904, CIV [Cd. 2184]. Statistical Tables for Colonies, 1902.
1905, LIII [Cd. 2326]. Papers *re* Resolutions of Colonial Legislatures since 1890 in favour of Preferential Trade Relations with the United Kingdom.
1905, LXIII [Cd. 2241]. Crown Agents' Office—Accounts of Funds for 1900–2.
1905, LXXXV [Cd. 2281]. Report on condition and prospects of British trade in Ohman, Bahrein and Arab posts in Persian Gulf.
1905, XCIV [Cd. 2395]. Statistical Abstracts for British Empire, 1889–1903. [1st no. of new annual series.]
1905, XCV [Cd. 2629]. Statistical Tables for Colonies, 1903.
1905, XCVI [Cd. 2679]. Statistical Abstracts for Colonies, 1889–1904.
1905, CIII [Cd. 2246]. Anglo-Chinese Convention on employment of Chinese Labour in British Colonies.
1906, LXXIII [Cd. 2684–No. 46]. 1st Annual Report of the Colonial Survey Committee.
1906, LXXVI [Cd. 2978], [Cd. 2979]. Report and papers of Departmental Committee on Rider Haggard's Report on Agricultural Settlements in British Colonies.
1906, LXXVII (357). Indentured Coolie Labour—Return *re* conditions.
1906, LXXVII [Cd. 2874], [Cd. 3095]. Statement of Colonial Contributions to Imperial Institute from foundation.

1906, cxxxi [Cd. 3107]. Statistical Tables for Colonies, 1904.
1906, cxxxii [Cd. 3253]. Statistical Abstracts for Colonies, 1891–1905.
1907, liv [Cd. 3567]. Report of Colonial Merchant Shipping Conference.
1907, lvi (4). Indentured Coolie Labour—Return re conditions.
1907, lvi (181). Crown Agents for the Colonies. Return re commissions charged in 1904–6.
1907, lvi [Cd. 3402]. Circular Despatch re Colonial ex-governors and companies.
1907, lvi [Cd. 3589]. Company Laws in the British Empire—Comparative analysis.
1907, xcv [Cd. 3706]. Statistical Tables for Colonies, 1905.
1907, xcvi [Cd. 3707]. Statistical Abstracts for Colonies, 1893–1906.
1908, cxviii [Cd. 3893]. Statistical Abstracts for British Empire, 1892–1906.
1908, lxx (20). Indentured Coolie Labour—Return re conditions.
1909, xvi [Cd. 4473], [Cd. 4474]. Crown Agents Office—Report from Committee of Enquiry and Minutes.
1909, lix [Cd. 4589]. Papers re mechanical transport in Colonies.
1909, c [Cd. 4486]. Statistical Abstracts for British Empire, 1893–1907.
1909, ci [Cd. 4881]. Statistical Tables for Colonies, 1907.
1909, cii [Cd. 4954]. Statistical Tables and Charts relating to British and Foreign Trade and Industry, 1854–1908.
1910, lxvi [Cd. 5215]. Memo. on Govt. action re cotton-growing in Crown Colonies.
1910, lxvi [Cd. 5391]. Accounts of the Crown Agents Office Funds for 1909.
1910, civ [Cd. 5094]. Statistical Abstracts for British Empire, 1894–1908.
1910, cvi [Cd. 4984]. Statistical Abstracts for Colonies, 1894–1908.
1910, cvi [Cd. 5420]. Statistical Abstracts for Colonies, 1895–1909.
1910, cvii [Cd. 5295]. Statistical Tables for Colonies, 1908.
1911, liii [Cd. 5744]. Accounts of the Crown Agents Office Funds for 1910.
1911, liii [Cd. 5864]. Comparative Analysis of Company Laws of U.K., India and Dominions.
1911, xcviii [Cd. 5552]. Statistical Abstracts for British Empire, 1895–1909.
1911, xcviii [Cd. 6003]. Statistical Abstracts for Colonies, 1896–1910.
1911, xcix [Cd. 5906]. Statistical Tables for Colonies, 1909.
1912–13, xlix (89), (331). Lists of Colonial Stocks available for trustee investment under Colonial Stock Act, 1900.
1912–13, lx (68). Return re Land-ownership in Crown Colonies and Protectorates.
1912–13, lx [Cd. 6279]. Accounts of the Crown Agents Office Funds for 1911.
1912–13, lx [Cd. 6429]. Corresp. re development of entomological research in British Colonies.
1912–13, lx [Cd. 6439]. Report on Anti-Trust Legislation in Self-Governing Dominions.
1912–13, lxxxiii [Cd. 6476]. Return re rates of colonial import duties.
1912–13, ciii [Cd. 6533]. Statistical Abstracts for Colonies, 1897–1911.
1912–13, civ [Cd. 6400]. Statistical Tables for Colonies, 1910.
1913, xli (91). Treasury List of Colonial Stocks complying with Colonial Stock Act, 1900.
1913, xlv [Cd. 4862]. Accounts of Crown Agents Office Funds, 1912.
1913, lx [Cd. 7035]. Tables showing progress of merchant shipping.
1913, lxviii [Cd. 6771]. Reports on British Trade in West Africa, Straits Settlements, British Guiana and Bermuda.
1913, lxxi [Cd. 7148]. Employment of Native Labour—Circular Despatch.
1913, lxxv [Cd. 7024]. Statistical Tables for Colonies, 1911.
1914, xcvi [Cd. 7165]. Statistical Abstracts for Colonies, 1898–1912.
1914, lx [Cd. 7510]. Accounts of the Crown Agents Office Funds for 1913.
1914, xcvi [Cd. 7241]. Statistical Abstracts for British Empire, 1896–1912.

1914–16, XLV [Cd. 7973]. Accounts of the Crown Agents Office Funds for 1914.
1914–16, LXXVIII [Cd. 7667]. Statistical Tables for Colonies, 1912.
1914–16, LXXVII [Cd. 7827]. Statistical Abstracts for British Empire, 1897–1913.
1914–16, LXXIX [Cd. 7786]. Statistical Abstracts for Colonies, 1899–1913.
1916, XX [Cd. 8307]. Accounts of the Crown Agents Office Funds for 1915.
1916, XXXII [Cd. 8329]. Statistical Abstracts for Colonies, 1900–14.
1917–18, XXIII [Cd. 8795]. Accounts of the Crown Agents Office Funds for 1916.
1918, XVII [Cd. 9186]. Accounts of the Crown Agents Office Funds for 1917.
1918, XXV [Cd. 9051]. Statistical Abstracts for Colonies, 1901–15.
1919, XXX [Cmd. 372]. Report of West Indian Shipping Committee.
1919, XXXVI [Cmd. 392]. Accounts of the Crown Agents Office Funds for 1918.
1920, XIII [Cmd. 730]. Report of Committee on staffing agriculture departments in Colonies.
1920, XIII [Cmd. 939]. Report of Committee on Colonial Medical Service.
1920, XXXIII [Cmd. 1027]. Accounts of the Crown Agents Office Funds for 1919.
1920, XLIX [Cmd. 664]. Statistical Abstracts for Colonies, 1903–17.
1921, XIX (204). Treasury list of Colonial stocks under Colonial Stock Act, 1900.
1921, X [Cmd. 1231]. Report of Imperial Customs Conference, 1921.
1921, XXIV [Cmd. 1144], [Cmd. 1472]. 1st Annual Report of Colonial Research Committee and of *ad hoc* Committee.
1922, XXII [Cmd. 1630]. Statistical Abstracts for Colonies, 1905–19.
1924, XXIV [Cmd. 2247]. Statistical Abstracts for Colonies, 1907–21.

THE BRITISH EMPIRE AND THE UNITED STATES OF AMERICA,
1870–1914

1870, LXIX [C. 22]. Alabama claims—Corresp., 1869–70.
1871, LXX [C. 262]. Treaty of Washington—Corresp. *re* appointment of Joint High Commission.
1871, LXX [C. 386]. United States—Treaty of Washington, 1871.
1872, VI (260). Bill to carry into effect Treaty of Washington.
1872, LXIX [C. 469], [C. 476], [C. 505], [C. 506], [C. 506–VII], [C.528], [C.531], [C. 545], [C. 548], [C. 566], [C. 570], [C. 571], [C. 594]. Treaty of Washington—Corresp. and Papers *re* British and American Case presented to Tribunal of Arbitration.
1873, XLIX [C. 702], [C. 750], [C. 774]. Treaty of Washington—corresp. with Canada.
1873, LXXIV [C. 688], [C. 689], [C. 690], [C. 691], [C. 692], [C. 693], [C. 694], [C. 695], [C. 696]. North America—Geneva Arbitration papers,
1873, LXXIV [C. 736], [C. 775]. Treaty of Washington—protocol and additional article.
1874, LXXV [C. 1012], [C. 1046], [C. 1047]. Report and Papers on Proceedings and Awards of Mixed Comm. under Treaty of Washington, 1871.
1875, VIII (218). Treaty of Washington, Claims Distribution Bill.
1875, LXXXII [C. 1131]. Corresp. *re* North West Boundary between Canada and U.S.
1876, LX (111). Memorial of Royal Colonial Institute *re* Royal Style.
1878, LXXX [C. 2056]. U.S.A.—Corresp. *re* Halifax Fisheries Comm.
1878–9, LXXVII [C. 2183], [C. 2184], [C. 2186]. Corresp. *re* award of Halifax Fisheries Comm.
1880, LXXVIII [C. 2717]. United States of America—Further corresp. *re* Fortune Bay, Newfoundland.
1881, LXXIV [C. 2984]. Reports *re* legislative assemblies in self-governing colonies.
1881, XCVIII [C. 2757], [C. 3059]. Further corresp. *re* Fortune Bay incidents, Newfoundland.
1882, LXXX [C. 3110], [C. 3446]. Corresp. *re* projected Panama Canal.

1883, XLVI [C. 3762]. Corresp. *re* Fortune Bay claims.

1884, LXXXVIII [C. 3854]. Panama Canal—Further corresp. *re* Clayton–Bulwer Treaty.

1887, XCI [C. 4937], [C. 4995]. Corresp. *re* North American fisheries, 1884–7.

1890, LXXXII [C. 6131]. Corresp. *re* Behring Sea seal fisheries.

1890–1, XCVI [C. 6334]. United States and Newfoundland—Corresp. *re* proposed convention on commerce and fisheries.

1892, XCVI [C. 6633], [C. 6634], [C. 6635], [C. 6639]. Corresp. and treaty *re* Behring Sea seal fisheries.

1893–4, VII (393). Behring Sea Seal Fishery Bill.

1893–4, CX [C. 6845]. Anglo-American Convention *re* Alaska boundary, 22 July 1892.

1893–4, CX [C. 6969], [C. 6918], [C. 6922], [C. 6920], [C. 6921]. Report and papers of Behring Sea Commission.

1893–4, CXI [C. 6949], [C. 6950], [C. 6951], [C. 7161], [C. 7107]. Papers of Behring Sea Arbitration Tribunal, United States Case, and Award.

1896, XCVII [C. 7926], [C. 8105]. Anglo-American corresp. *re* arbitration on Venezuela–British Guiana boundary.

1896, XCVII [C. 7972], [C. 8012], [C. 8016], [C. 8194], [C. 8195]. Corresp. and papers *re* Venezuela–British Guiana boundary.

1896, XCVII [C. 8101]. Anglo-American Convention for arbitration in Behring Sea Seal Fishery disputes.

1897, CII [C. 8331]. Despatch with Anglo-American Treaty of Arbitration, Jan. 1897.

1897, CII [C. 8393]. Corresp. *re* communicating rules of arbitration under Treaty of Washington, 1871.

1897, CII [C. 8439]. Treaty with Venezuela *re* boundary with British Guiana, 2 Feb. 1897.

1898, CV [C. 8662]. Anglo-American corresp. *re* Behring Sea seal fisheries.

1898, CV [C. 8702], [C. 8703]. Papers *re* Behring Sea seal fishery.

1899, CXI [C. 9336], [C. 9337], [C. 9338]. British Guiana–Venezuela Boundary Arbitration—British Case.

1899, CXI [C. 9499], [C. 9500]. British Guiana–Venezuela Boundary Arbitration —Venezuelan case.

1899, CXII [C. 9501], [C. 9533]. British Guiana–Venezuela Boundary Arbitration Award.

1900, CV [Cd. 6]. Anglo-American notes on boundary of Alaska and Canada.

1900, CV [Cd. 30]. Anglo-American Convention, supplementary to Nicaragua Canal Convention of 1850.

1901, XCI [Cd. 438]. Corresp. *re* Washington Convention of 1900 on Nicaragua Ship Canal Project.

1903, LXXXVII [Cd. 1400], [Cd. 1472]. Washington Convention on Alaska Boundary, 24 Jan. 1903.

1903, LXXXVII [Cd. 1528]. Anglo-Venezuelan Protocol for settlement of claims, 7 May 1903.

1904, CXI [Cd. 1877], [Cd. 1878]. Corresp. *re* Alaska boundary and map.

1906, CXXXVII [Cd. 3159]. Anglo-American Convention *re* Alaska boundary, 1906.

1906, CXXXVII [Cd. 3262]. United States—Corresp. *re* Newfoundland fisheries.

1908, CXXV [Cd. 3734], [Cd. 3754]. Newfoundland fisheries—Notes exchanged.

1909, CV [Cd. 4528]. Anglo-American Agreement *re* arbitration on North Atlantic fisheries.

1909, CV [Cd. 4558]. Anglo-American Treaty *re* boundary waters with Canada.

1910, LXXIV [Cd. 5396]. North Atlantic Fisheries Arbitration.

1911, CIII [Cd. 5803]. Anglo-American agreement for settlement of outstanding pecuniary claims.

1912–13, CXXII [Cd. 6451], [Cd. 6585], [Cd. 6645]. Anglo-American corresp. *re* U.S. Panama Canal Act, 1912.

IMPERIAL DEFENCE, 1870–1918

(see also under GIBRALTAR, MALTA AND CYPRUS and under EGYPT
AND SUDAN below)

1870, LX (949). Returns re shipping, 1869

1871, XXXVIII (7). Army Estimates (Colonies), 1871–2.

1872, XXXVII (46). Army Estimates (Colonies), 1872–3.

1873, XL (47). Army Estimates (Colonies), 1873–4.

1874, XXXVI (43). Army Estimates (Colonies), 1874–5.

1875, XLIII (36). Army Estimates (Colonies), 1875–6.

1876, XLIII (37). Army Estimates (Colonies), 1876–7.

1877, L (54). Army Estimates (Colonies), 1877–8.

1878, XLVII (38). Army Estimates (Colonies), 1878–9.

1878–9, XLIII (47). Army Estimates (Colonies), 1879–80.

1880, XLI (50). Army Estimates (Colonies), 1880–1.

1881, LVIII (51). Army Estimates (Colonies), 1881–2.

1882, XXXVIII (93). Army Estimates (Colonies), 1882–3.

1883, XXXIX (47). Army Estimates (Colonies), 1883–4.

1884, XLVIII (84). Army Estimates (Colonies and Egypt), 1884–5.

1884, XLVIII [C. 4186]. Corresp. re defence of colonial possessions and garrisons abroad.

1884–5, H.L., I (52). Offers of military aid from the Colonies.

1884–5, H.L., XII (125). Colonial naval forces: corresp. with Australian colonies.

1884–5, XLVI (69). Military expenditure in the Colonies and Egypt, and probable repayments, 1885–6.

1884–5, XLVI [C. 4226]. Defence of Colonies and Garrisons: further corresp.

1886, XXXIX (73). Military expenditure in the Colonies and Egypt, and probable repayments, 1886–7.

1887, I (74). Military expenditure in the Colonies and Egypt, and probable repayments, 1887–8.

1887, XV [C. 5062]. Report of Royal Commission on Warlike Stores and Ordnance Department.

1888, H.L., VII (277). National Defence Bill.

1888, III (346). Bill for carrying into effect provision for imperial defence.

1888, LXVI (67). Military expenditure in the Colonies and Egypt, and probable repayments, 1888–9.

1888, LXVII [C. 5304]. Orders in Council re War Department.

1889, V (186). Naval Defence Bill.

1889, XLVIII (55). Military expenditure in the Colonies and Egypt, and probable repayments, 1889–90.

1889, L [C. 5632]. Report of Committee on Naval Manœuvres of 1888.

1890, XIX [C. 5979]. Reports of Royal Commission on Administration of Naval and Military Departments.

1890–1, LI (284). Ascension Island—Return re cost of maintaining naval establishments.

1892, XLVIII (308—Sess. 1), (318—Sess. 1). Imperial Defence Act, 1888— accounts of expenditure, 1888–92.

1892, LI (123—Sess. 1), (105—Sess. 1). Naval Defence Act, 1889—accounts of expenditure, contracts, etc.

1893–4, VI (450). Naval Defence Bill.

1896, LI (483), (487). Orders in Council defining duties of Commander-in-Chief, etc.

1899, LIII (535). Orders in Council defining duties of principal officers in Army.

1901, XXXVII (166). Accounts of survey used under Imperial Defence Act, 1888.

1901, XL (580), (581). Report of Committee on War Office Organisation.

1901, XL (607). Report by Secretary of State on requirements from Army, 1891.

1901, XLII (80). Imperial Defence—Account under Naval Works Acts.

1904, VIII [Cd. 1932], [Cd. 1968], [Cd. 2002]. Report of War Office Reconstruction Comm., 1904.

1904, XXX [Cd. 2061], [Cd. 2062]. Report of Royal Comm. on Militia and Volunteers, 1904.

1904, XXXI [Cd. 2063], [Cd. 2604]. Report of Comm. on Militia, Evidence.

1904, XL [Cd. 1789], [Cd. 1790]. Report of Royal Comm. on South African War, 1903: Report and Evidence I.

1904, XLI [Cd. 1791]. Report on South African War, Evidence II.

1904, XLII [Cd. 1792]. Report on South African War, Appendices.

1907, LV [Cd. 3404], [Cd. 3406]. Colonial Conference, 1907. Committee of Imperial Defence.

1908, LXXXI [Cd. 4325]. Naval Defence of Australia and New Zealand—Corresp.

1909, I (304). Bill to amend Colonial Naval Defence Act, 1865.

1909, IV (305). Bill for better provision of Naval Establishments.

1909, LI [Cd. 4475]. Imperial General Staff—Corresp. re proposed formation.

1909, LIV [Cd. 4554], [Cd. 4555]. International Naval Conference—Corresp. and documents and proceedings.

1909, LIX [Cd. 4948]. Conference on Imperial Defence—Corresp. and Papers, 1909.

1912–13, LX [Cd. 6560]. Committee of Imperial Defence—Despatch re representation of self-governing Dominions.

1914, LX [Cd. 7347]. Corresp. re representation of Dominions on Committee of Imperial Defence and proposed Naval Conference.

1914, CI [Cd. 7607]. Corresp. re naval and military assistance from Oversea Dominions.

1917–18, XXIII [Cd. 8566], [Cd. 8673]. Imperial War Conference—Extracts from Minutes of Proceedings and Papers.

1918, XVI [Cd. 9177]. Imperial War Conference—Extracts from Minutes of Proceedings and Papers.

GIBRALTAR, MALTA AND CYPRUS

(See also the Annual Reports from the Colonies, 1870–1921, noted under COLONIAL POLICY above)

1870, XLIX (251). Malta—Corresp. re ecclesiastics in govt.

1871, XLVII (208). Gibraltar—Statement on revenues.

1872, XLIII (20). Malta—Corresp. on rejection of Education Bill.

1874, XLV (260). Malta—Papers re Education Bill.

1876, LIII (153). Malta—Corresp. on constitution of council.

1876, LIII [C. 1582]. Malta—Corresp. re grievances of nobility.

1877, LXI (322), (340). Malta—Further papers on grievances.

1877, LXI [C. 1783], [C. 1894]. Gibraltar—Papers re regulation of trade.

1878, LV [C. 2032]. Malta—Corresp. re taxation and expenditure.

1878, LV [C. 2044], [C. 2131]. Malta—Corresp. and report of Comm. on Maltese nobility.

1878, LV [C. 2145]. Gibraltar—Corresp. re Customs Ordinance.

1878–9, XLIII (151), (151–I), (169). Cyprus—Returns re forces employed in occupation, health, etc.

1878–9, LI (330). Malta—Return re occupations of inhabitants.

1878–9, LI [C. 2317]. Malta—Corresp. re riots in 1878.

1878–9, LIV [C. 2229], [C. 2244], [C. 2324]. [C. 2326], [C. 2351], [C. 2355], [C. 2394], [C. 2396], [C. 2398], [C. 2425], [C. 2427]. Cyprus—Corresp. and papers.

1880, XLIX [C. 2542], [C. 2544]. Cyprus—Return and report *re* public works, harbour of Famagousta, etc.

1880, XLIX [C. 2543]. Cyprus—Report of High Commissioner for 1879. [Thereafter annually.]

1880, XLIX [C. 2628], [C. 2629]. Cyprus—Returns and corresp. *re* finances.

1880, XLIX [C. 2684], [C. 2685]. Malta—Reports on civil establishment and education.

1880, XLIX [C. 2699]. Cyprus—Return of officials.

1880, XLIX [C. 2729]. Malta—Corresp. on constitution and administration.

1881, LXV [C. 2930], [C. 3091]. Cyprus—Corresp. *re* affairs.

1881, LXV [C. 2991], [C. 3005]. Cyprus—Papers *re* finances.

1881, LXV [C. 3092]. Cyprus—Report of High Commissioner for 1880.

1882, XLV [C. 3201], [C. 3213]. Corresp. and papers *re* installation of Dr Canilla as Vicar Apostolic.

1882, XLV [C. 3211]. Cyprus—Despatch *re* new legislative council.

1882, XLV [C. 3383]. Cyprus—Papers *re* finances.

1882, XLV [C. 3385]. Cyprus—Report of High Commissioner for 1881.

1883, H.L., XI (164). Malta, titles of nobility.

1883, XLVI [C. 3661], [C. 3662]. Cyprus—Papers *re* administration and finances.

1883, XLVI [C. 3772]. Cyprus—Report of High Commissioner for 1882.

1883, XLVI [C. 3791]. Cyprus—Papers *re* new Legislative Council.

1883, XLVII [C. 3524]. Malta—Corresp. *re* alterations of constitution.

1883, XLVII [C. 3812]. Malta—Report and corresp. on privileges of Maltese nobility.

1883, LXXXII [C. 3551]. Corresp. *re* maritime jurisdiction in Gibraltar waters.

1884, LIV [C. 3992]. Gibraltar—Order in Council *re* tariff and corresp.

1884, LIV [C. 4120]. Cyprus—Corresp. *re* reduced grant-in-aid.

1884, LIV [C. 4188]. Cyprus—Report of High Commissioner for 1883–4.

1884, LV [C. 3948], [C. 4165], [C. 4187]. Malta—Corresp. *re* constitution and administration.

1884–5, LIII [C. 4264]. Cyprus—Report on census, 1881.

1884–5, LIII [C. 4435], [C. 4585]. Cyprus—Papers *re* revenue funds.

1884–5, LIII [C. 4438], [C. 4471]. Cyprus—Papers *re* revenue and expenditure.

1884–5, LIII [C. 4586]. Malta—Corresp. *re* constitution and administration.

1886, XLVI [C. 4694]. Cyprus—Report of High Commissioner for 1885.

1886, XLVI [C. 4830]. Malta—Corresp. *re* currency.

1886, XLVI [C. 4831]. Cyprus—Corresp. *re* revenue reforms.

1887, LVIII [C. 4961]. Cyprus—Report of High Commissioner for 1886.

1888, LXXIII [C. 5251]. Cyprus—Report of Acting High Commissioner for 1887.

1888, LXXIII [C. 5308], [C. 5338]. Malta—Corresp. *re* constitution and administration.

1888, LXXIII [C. 5490]. Malta—Corresp. *re* nobility.

1888, LXXIII [C. 5523]. Cyprus—Corresp. *re* affairs and finances.

1889, LVI [C. 5749]. Cyprus—Report of High Commissioner for 1887–8.

1889, LVI [C. 5812]. Cyprus—Further corresp. *re* affairs and finances.

1890, XLIX [C. 6003]. Cyprus—Corresp. *re* affairs and finances.

1890, XLIX [C. 6189]. Cyprus—Report of High Commissioner for 1889.

1890–1, LVI [C. 6489]. Cyprus—Corresp. *re* affairs and finances.

1892, LVI [C. 6764]. Cyprus—Reports of High Commissioner for 1889–90 and 1890–1.

1893–4, LX [C. 7053]. Cyprus—Report of High Commissioner for 1891–2.

1894, LVII [C. 7411]. Cyprus—Report of High Commissioner for 1892–3.

1896, LVIII [C. 8076]. Cyprus—Annual report for 1894–5.

1897, LXI [C. 8580]. Cyprus—Annual reports for 1895–6.
1899, LIX (287). Malta—Corresp. *re* political conditions.
1899, LIX [C. 9288]. Cyprus—Annual Reports for 1897–8.
1899, LIX [C. 9289]. Cyprus—Report on agriculture.
1901, XLVI [Cd. 618]. Gibraltar—Report on recent improvements.
1901, XLVI [Cd. 715]. Malta—Corresp. *re* political condition.
1903, XLIV [Cd. 1455]. Gibraltar—Report on proposed Eastern Harbour.
1903, XLIV [Cd. 1465]. Cyprus—Report for 1901–2.
1903, XLIV [Cd. 1660]. Malta—Corresp. *re* political condition.
1904, LX [Cd. 1984]. Cyprus—Annual Report for 1902–3.
1904, LX [Cd. 2023]. Malta—Corresp. *re* political condition.
1905, LIV [Cd. 2327]. Cyprus—Annual Report for 1903–4.
1906, LXXVII [Cd. 2717]. Cyprus—Report and corresp. on agricultural resources, especially cotton.
1906, LXXVIII [Cd. 3024], [Cd. 3099]. Malta—Corresp. *re* Protestant Mission Services.
1908, LXXI [Cd. 3742], [Cd. 4199]. Cyprus—Annual Reports for 1906–7, 1907–8.
1908, LXXI [Cd. 3996]. Cyprus—Corresp. *re* affairs.
1909, LIX [Cd. 4905]. Cyprus—Annual report for 1908–9.
1910, LXVI [Cd. 5217]. Malta—Further corresp. *re* political condition.
1910, LXVI [Cd. 5372]. Cyprus—Annual Report for 1909–10.
1911, LIII [Cd. 5898]. Cyprus—Annual Report for 1910–11.
1912–13, XL [Cd. 6090], [Cd. 6280], [Cd. 6281]. Malta—Report of Royal Comm. on Finances, Economic Position and Judicial Procedure, with Evidence and Documents.
1912–13, LX [Cd. 6430]. Cyprus—Annual Report for 1911–12.
1914, LX [Cd. 7065]. Cyprus—Annual Report for 1912–13.
1914–16, XLVI [Cd. 7643]. Cyprus—Annual Report for 1913–14. [Thereafter in General series.]

EGYPT, SUDAN, ADEN AND SOMALILAND

(See also under IMPERIAL DEFENCE above)

1870, LXIX [C. 100]. Egypt—Corresp. with Turkey *re* Khedive's loan.
1876, XLII [C. 1579]. Suez Canal—Treasury Minute, 1876.
1876, XLV (77). Suez Canal—Return of Ships paying Dues, 1875.
1876, XLIX (14), (142). Suez Canal—Sums required for Purchase of Shares, Cave Mission, etc.
1876, LXVIII (176). Suez Canal—Annual Increments of Tonnage, 1870–5.
1876, LXXIII [C. 1391], [C. 1392], [C. 1393], [C. 1396], [C. 1415], [C. 1416], [C. 1425], [C. 1484], [C. 1525]. Egypt—Corresp. *re* Suez Canal, Judicial Reforms, Finances, etc.
1877, LXXXVIII [C. 1766], [C. 1797]. Corresp. *re* Suez Canal.
1877, LXXXVIII [C. 1769]. Corresp. *re* arrests at Massowah.
1878, XLVI (248). Suez Canal—Accounts *re* purchase of shares.
1878, LXXXVI [C. 2010], [C. 2012]. Corresp. *re* Suez Canal.
1878–9, XLII (239). Suez Canal—Accounts. [Thereafter annually.]
1878–9, LXXIII [C. 2399]. Suez Canal—Corresp. *re* affairs.
1878–9, LXXVIII [C. 2224], [C. 2233], [C. 2185], [C. 2352], [C. 2395], [C. 2397]. Egypt—Corresp. *re* finances and affairs.
1880, LIX [C. 2662]. Egypt—Despatch, with law of liquidation.
1880, LXXV [C. 2606]. Egypt—Circular reports on state of country.
1880, LXXV [C. 2715]. Suez Canal—Further corresp.
1880, LXXIX [C. 2549], [C. 2550]. Egypt—Corresp. *re* affairs.
1880, LXXV [C. 2715]. Corresp. *re* Suez Canal.

1881, LVII (300). Suez Canal accounts.

1881, XCI [C. 2805]. Corresp. re dues levied by Suez Canal Company.

1881, XCVIII [C. 2766]. Egypt: Corresp. re affairs.

1882, XXXVIII (402). Egypt—Extract from telegram of G.O.C. H.M. Troops.

1882, XL [C. 3305], [C. 3315]. Outbreak at Alexandria and naval bombardment.

1882, LXXII [C. 3105]. Egypt—Corresp. re affairs.

1882, LXXII [C. 3345]. Papers re Suez Canal.

1882, LXXXII [C. 3105], [C. 3106], [C. 3161], [C. 3230], [C. 3249], [C. 3251], [C. 3257], [C. 3258], [C. 3295], [C. 3298], [C. 3299], [C. 3330], [C. 3391], [C. 3401], [C. 3407]. Egypt—Corresp. re affairs.

1882, LXXXII [C. 3188], [C. 3237]. Egypt—Returns re foreigners in service of government.

1882, LXXXII [C. 3296]. Egypt—Corresp. re Constantinople Conference on Egyptian affairs.

1882, LXXXII [C. 3390]. Egypt—Corresp. re riots at Alexandria.

1882, LXXXIII [C. 3391], [C. 3401], [C. 3407]. Corresp. re affairs.

1882, LXXXIII [C. 3347]. Egypt—Corresp. re Anglo-French financial control.

1883, XXXVIII (26). Egypt—Treasury minute on cost of expedition.

1883, LXIV (249). Heads of agreement between Britain and President of Suez Canal Company.

1883, LXIV [C. 3474], (41). Suez Canal—Return of shipping and tonnage. [Thereafter annual.]

1883, LXXXIII [C. 3462], [C. 3529], [C. 3554], [C. 3696]. Egypt—Corresp. re re-organisation.

1883, LXXXIII [C. 3693], [C. 3461], [C. 3528], [C. 3802]. Egypt—Corresp. re affairs.

1883, LXXXIII [C. 3733]. Egypt—Dufferin's despatch re new political institutions.

1883, LXXXIV [C. 3463], [C. 3632], [C. 3668]. Egypt—Papers re Europeans in service of government, etc.

1883, LXXXIV [C. 3670]. Report on the Soudan.

1883, LXXXIV [C. 3672], [C. 3695]. Suez Canal—Reports and corresp. on provisional agreement, 1883.

1883, LXXXIV [C. 3697], [C. 3698], [C. 3728], [C. 3734], [C. 3805]. Suez Canal —Corresp. and papers.

1884, LXXXVIII [C. 3844], [C. 3852], [C. 3967], [C. 3969]. Egypt—Corresp. re affairs.

1884, LXXXVIII [C. 3845]. Egypt—Corresp. re Gordon's mission.

1884, LXXXVIII [C. 3850]. Suez Canal—Further corresp.

1884, LXXXVIII [C. 3851]. Egypt—Papers re Lord R. Churchill's charges against Khedive.

1884, LXXXVIII [C. 3878]. Egypt—Despatch, with instructions to Gordon.

1884, LXXXVIII [C. 3879], [C. 3881], [C. 3884]. Corresp. and papers re Soudan.

1884, LXXXIX [C. 3970], [C. 3997], [C. 3998], [C. 3999], [C. 4001], [C. 4003], [C. 4005], [C. 4042], [C. 4100], [C. 4105], [C. 4107], [C. 4132], [C. 4177]. Egypt—Further corresp. re affairs.

1884, LXXXIX [C. 4000], [C. 4047], [C. 4127], [C. 4130], [C. 4131]. Egypt— Corresp. and papers re finances.

1884, LXXXIX [C. 4002]. Soudan—Return re telegrams from Gordon.

1884, LXXXIX [C. 4045]. Agreement between Britain and Egypt re most-favoured nation treatments.

1884–5, H.L., IV (74). Egyptian loan—Papers.

1884–5, I (122). Egyptian Loan Guarantee Bill.

1884–5, XLVI (205). Report by Wilson on Khartoum expedition.

1884–5, XLVI [C. 4472]. Papers re withdrawal from Dongola.

1884–5, LXIX [C. 4591]. Suez Canal—Corresp. and revised regulations for navigation.

1884–5, LXXXVIII [C. 4204], [C. 4203], [C. 4278], [C. 4600]. Egypt—Corresp. re affairs.

1884–5, LXXXVIII [C. 4242], [C. 4337], [C. 4338], [C. 4447]. Egypt—Corresp. re finances.

1884–5, LXXXVIII [C. 4339]. Declaration by Britain, Germany and other powers re finances of Egypt and free navigation of Suez Canal.

1884–5, LXXXVIII [C. 4341]. Convention of London re finances of Egypt.

1884–5, LXXXIX [C. 4280], [C. 4281], [C. 4345], [C. 4392], [C. 4598]. Corresp. re military operations in Soudan.

1884–5, LXXXIX [C. 4417], [C. 4423]. Corresp. re ports in Red Sea and Gulf of Aden.

1884–5, LXXXIX [C. 4599]. Corresp. re Suez Canal International Comm.

1886, LXXIV [C. 4604], [C. 4611], [C. 4740], [C. 4769]. Egypt—Corresp. re affairs.

1886, LXXIV [C. 4768]. Egypt—Corresp. re finances.

1887, XCII [C. 4918], [C. 4942], [C. 5165]. Egypt—International Convention and corresp. re finances.

1887, XCII [C. 4941]. Egypt—Corresp. re affairs.

1887, XCII [C. 4994]. Egypt—Corresp. re slavery.

1887, XCII [C. 4996], [C. 5050], [C. 5110]. Egypt—Papers and corresp. re Sir Drummond Wolff's mission.

1887, XCII [C. 4997]. Egypt—Despatch re employment of Europeans.

1887, XCII [C. 5162]. Egypt—Corresp. with government re Soudan operations.

1888, CX [C. 5255]. Suez Canal—Corresp. re proposed international convention.

1888, CX [C. 5316], [C. 5319]. Egypt—Corresp. re affairs.

1888, CX [C. 5317], [C. 5318]. Egypt—Corresp. re finances.

1888, CX [C. 5580], [C. 5605]. Egypt—Corresp. re Suakin affairs.

1889, LII (63). Egypt—Adjustments of Accounts with Britain, 1888–9. [Thereafter annual statements.]

1889, LXXXVII [C. 5623]. International convention for free navigation of Suez Canal.

1889, LXXXVII [C. 5673]. Corresp. re Suez Canal Comm.

1889, LXXXVII [C. 5718], [C. 5668], [C. 5676]. Egypt—Corresp. re finances and affairs.

1890, LXXXIII [C. 5915]. Egypt—Corresp. re new commercial convention.

1890, LXXXIII [C. 5973], [C. 6135]. Egypt—Report and corresp. re finances and condition.

1890–1, XCVII [C. 6320]. Egypt—Reports on finances.

1890–1, XCVII [C. 6321]. Egypt—Report on administration and progress of reforms.

1892, LXXI [C. 6556]. Suez Canal—Corresp. re passage of petroleum.

1892, XCVI [C. 6559], [C. 6561], [C. 6589]. Egypt—Reports and papers on affairs.

1893–4, CXI [C. 6849], [C. 6956]. Egypt—Corresp. re affairs.

1893–4, CXI [C. 6957]. Egypt—Report on administration, finances and reforms.

1894, XCVI [C. 7308]. Egypt—Report on finance, administration and progress of reforms.

1896, XCVII [C. 7978]. Egypt—Report on finances, administration and condition.

1897, CII [C. 8306], [C. 8332], [C. 8427]. Egypt—Report and corresp. on finances, administration and condition.

1898, CVII [C. 8815]. Egypt—Report on finances and condition.

1899, CXII [C. 9054], [C. 9055]. Egypt—Corresp. with French government re Upper Nile Valley.

1899, CXII [C. 9133]. Despatches re conduct of British and Egyptian troops after Omdurman.

1899, cxii [C. 9231], [C. 9332], [C. 9424]. Reports on finances and condition of Egypt and Soudan.

1899, cxii [C. 9242]. Soudan—Return *re* expenditure on military operations since 1883.

1900, cv [Cd. 95]. Egypt and Soudan—Reports on finances and conditions in 1899.

1901, xlviii [Cd. 591], [Cd. 597]. Corresp. *re* military operations in Somaliland.

1901, xci [Cd. 441]. Egypt and Soudan—Report on finances, etc. in 1900.

1901, xci [Cd. 672]. Egypt—Report on irrigation of Upper Nile.

1902, lxix [Cd. 1006]. Somaliland—Papers *re* military operations, 1901–2.

1903, xlv [Cd. 1394], [Cd. 1500]. Corresp. *re* Mullah rising and operations of Somaliland Field Forces.

1903, lxxxvii [Cd. 1529]. Egypt and Soudan—Report on finances and condition in 1902.

1904, lxii [Cd. 1935]. Somaliland Protectorate—Report on trade and commerce, 1902–3.

1904, cxi [Cd. 1951]. Egypt and Soudan—Reports on finances, administration and condition.

1904, cxi [Cd. 2165]. Despatch and Report on Upper Nile Basin.

1905, lvi [Cd. 2254]. Somaliland—Despatches *re* military operations, 1902–4.

1905, ciii [Cd. 2384]. Anglo-French Declaration *re* Egypt and Morocco, 1904.

1905, ciii [Cd. 2409]. Egypt and Soudan—Reports on Finances, Administration and Condition, 1904.

1906, cxxxvii [Cd. 2817]. Egypt and Soudan—Reports on finances, administration and condition, 1905.

1906, cxxxvii [Cd. 3006]. Corresp. *re* Turco-Egyptian frontier in Sinai.

1906, cxxxvii [Cd. 3086], [Cd. 3091]. Egypt—Corresp. *re* attack on British officers at Denshawai.

1907, lxxxv [Cd. 3345]. Corresp. *re* Suez Canal dues.

1907, c [Cd. 3394]. Egypt and Soudan—Reports on Finances, administration and condition, 1906.

1907, c [Cd. 3397]. Egypt—Despatch from Cromer *re* water supply.

1907, c [Cd. 3451]. Egypt—Despatch from Cromer *re* proposals of General Assembly.

1908, cxxv [Cd. 3874]. Egypt—Agreement additional to Commercial Convention of 1889.

1908, cxxv [Cd. 3966]. Egypt—Reports on finances, administration and condition, 1907.

1909, cv [Cd. 4580]. Egypt—Reports on finances, administration and condition, 1908.

1910, lxvi [Cd. 5000], [Cd. 5132]. Somaliland—Corresp. *re* affairs.

1912–13, cxxi [Cd. 6149]. Reports on Egypt and Soudan for 1911.

1913, lxxxi [Cd. 6682]. Egypt and Soudan—Report for 1912.

1913, lxxxi [Cd. 6875], [Cd. 6878]. Egypt—Despatch, with translation of organic and electoral laws of 1913.

1914, lx [Cd. 7066], [Cd. 7566]. Somaliland—Corresp. *re* affairs.

WEST INDIES, BERMUDA, BRITISH HONDURAS AND BRITISH GUIANA

(See also the Annual Reports from the Colonies, 1870–1921, noted under Colonial Policy above)

1870, xlix (232). West Indies—Returns *re* immigrants and liberated Africans [similar later returns].

1870, l (196). West Indies and British Guiana—Return *re* ecclesiastical funds distributed.

1870, L (450). Trinidad—Papers re education.

1871, III (170). Act for federation of Leeward Islands.

1871, XX [C. 393], [C. 393–I], [C. 393–II]. British Guiana—Report of Comm. on Indian and Chinese Immigrants.

1871, XLVII (133). West Indies—Return re immigrants and liberated Africans since 1843.

1871, XLVII [C. 458]. British Guiana—Complaints of Portuguese residents.

1871, XLVIII (34). West Indies—Account of sums advanced for relief.

1871, XLVIII (269). West Indies—Despatches on ecclesiastical grants.

1871, XLVIII [C. 353]. West Indies—Corresp. re federation of Leeward Islands.

1871, LVI [C. 362]. Leprosy—Corresp. re alleged cure.

1872, XLIII (62). West Indies—Corresp. re ecclesiastical grants.

1872, XLIII [C. 641]. British Guiana—Corresp. on treatment of immigrants.

1873, XLIX [C. 879]. British Guiana—Disturbance among Indian immigrants.

1873, L (206). British West Indies—Return re immigrants and liberated Africans.

1873, L [C. 729]. British West Indies—Report on leprosy and yaws.

1874, XLIV (293). Papers re coolie traffic to West Indies.

1874, XLV (34). West Indies—Advances and repayments, 1873–4.

1874, XLVII (313). Coolie Traffic—Geoghegan's Report.

1875, LIII (23). West Indies—Sums advanced and repayments, 1874–5.

1876, VII (253). Bill for government of St Vincent, Tobago and Grenada.

1876, LIII (249). St Vincent—Corresp. re immigrant coolies, 1861–75.

1876, LIII [C. 1539], [C. 1559]. Barbados—Papers re disturbances.

1876, LIII [C. 1625]. Barbados—Annual Financial Reports by Auditor General, 1874, 1875.

1877, LXI (30). Jamaica—Return re coolies introduced since 1859.

1877, LXI [C. 1679], [C. 1687]. Barbados—Further papers re disturbances.

1877, LXI [C. 1893]. Jamaica—Draft criminal code.

1877, LXXVIII [C. 1861]. Reports re treatment of coolies in Surinam.

1878–9, VII (Bill 167). Bill for winding-up West Indian Relief Commission. [42/43 Vict. cap. 16.]

1878–9, LI [C. 2249]. Grenada—Papers re coolie immigrants.

1878–9, LI [C. 2437]. Jamaica—Corresp. re Indian coolie immigration.

1880, XLIX [C. 2545]. Barbados—Corresp. re constitution and administration, 1877.

1880, XLIX [C. 2602]. Grenada—Report on Indian immigrants.

1881, LXV (425). Jamaica—Corresp. re memorial on grievances.

1881, LXV [C. 2978]. British Honduras—Corresp. re administration.

1882, XLVI (285). Jamaica—Returns of revenue and expenditure, 1851–82.

1883, XLVII (271). Jamaica—Return re imports and exports, 1851–82.

1884, LV [C. 3854]. Jamaica—Corresp. on constitutional reform.

1884–5, XLVI [C. 3840]. British West Indian Islands—Report of Royal Commission on Finances.

1884–5, LIII [C. 4234]. Corresp. re West Indian Incumbered Estates.

1884–5, LIII [C. 4366]. Trinidad—Corresp. re coolie disturbance.

1884–5, LIII [C. 4482]. Papers re proposed union of Grenada, St Lucia, St Vincent and Tobago.

1884–5, LXXI [C. 4340]. West Indies—Corresp. re treaty regulating trade with United States.

1886, H.L., VI (115). West Indies—Incumbered Estates Bill.

1886, VI (233—Sess. 1). Bill re West Indian Incumbered Estates.

1887, VI (368). Bill to unite colonies of Trinidad and Tobago.

1890, XLIX (49). Jamaica—Return re area under sugar cane.

1892, LVI (25—Sess. 1). British Guiana—Return re immigration of coolies since 1871.

1892, LVI [C. 6680], [C. 6805]. West Indies and Guiana—Corresp. and papers re commercial arrangement with United States.

1893–4, LX [C. 6887]. Jamaica—Corresp. on reform of Legislative Council.

1897, LXI [C. 8359]. West Indies—Corresp. re sugar industry.

1898, L [C. 8655], [C. 8656], [C. 8657]. Report and papers of Royal Comm. on Sugar Industry in West Indies.

1898, LI [C. 8669], [C. 8799]. Royal Comm. on Sugar Industry—Further papers.

1899, LIX [C. 9177]. Jamaica—Corresp. re finances and resources.

1899, LIX [C. 9412], [C. 9413]. Jamaica—Reports by Barbour on finances.

1900, LIV [Cd. 3]. Bahamas—Report for 1898 [annual].

1900, LIV [Cd. 354]. Barbados—Report for 1899 [annual].

1900, LV [Cd. 125]. Jamaica—Further corresp. re finances and government.

1903, XLIV [Cd. 1661], [Cd. 1662]. Trinidad—Papers re disturbances at Port of Spain and Report of Commission.

1904, LIX [Cd. 1989]. Trinidad and Basutoland—Immigration Ordinances.

1904, LIX (185), [Cd. 1989]. British Guiana—Corresp. re ordinance of 1891 and other immigration ordinances.

1904, LX [Cd. 1985]. Bahamas—General Descriptive Report, including Annual Report for 1902.

1904, LX [Cd. 1987]. Return re exports of sugar and fruit from West Indies, 1899–1900 and 1902–3.

1904, LX [Cd. 1988]. Trinidad—Further papers re disturbances at Port of Spain.

1904, CX [Cd. 2166]. Award of King of Italy re boundary between British Guiana and Brazil.

1906, LXXVI [Cd. 2877]. Montserrat—Report on Agricultural Industries, by F. Watts.

1906, LXXVI [Cd. 3878]. Report on sugar industry in Antigua and St Kitts–Nevis, 1881–1905, by F. Watts.

1906, LXXVI [Cd. 2901]. West Indies—Report of Imperial Department of Agriculture.

1906, LXXVII [Cd. 2822], [C. 3026]. British Guiana—Corresp. re disturbances.

1906, LXXVIII (320). West Indies—Return of average annual exports to U.K. and U.S.A., 1889–1904.

1906, LXXVIII [Cd. 2775]. West Indian Inter-Colonial Sanitary Convention, 1904.

1907, LIV [Cd. 3307]. Report on the Cayman Islands.

1907, LII (160). Return re sugar production in West Indies and British Guiana.

1907, LVII [Cd. 3403]. Jamaica—Corresp. re Swettenham's resignation of governorship.

1907, LVII [Cd. 3527]. Trinidad and Tobago—Labour Contract for Panama Canal.

1908, LXX [Cd. 3766], [Cd. 4326]. Turks and Caicos Islands—Reports on Salt and Sisal Industries.

1908, LXXIII [Cd. 3827]. West Indies—Laws re emigration of labourers.

1908, CVII [Cd. 3960]. Despatches from Panama re West Indian labour in Canal Zone.

1910, XI [Cd. 5369], [Cd. 4991], [Cd. 5370], [Cd. 5371]. Report and Evidence of Royal Comm. on Trade relations between Canada and West Indies.

1911, LII [Cd. 5472]. St Vincent—Report on Administration of Roads and Land Settlement Fund.

1912–13, LX [Cd. 6092]. Agreement between Canada and West Indian Colonies, 9 April 1912.

1912–13, LX [Cd. 6282]. West Indies—Corresp. re Brussels Sugar Convention.

1913, XLV [Cd. 6674]. Ordinances of West Indian Colonies giving effect to Canadian–West Indian Preferential Tariff Agreement, 1912.

1913, XLV [Cd. 6861]. Trinidad and Tobago—Agreement with United British West Indies Petroleum Syndicate.

1914–16, XLV [Cd. 7876]. St Vincent—Report on Administration of Roads and Land Settlement Fund to 1914.

1922, XVI [Cmd. 1679]. Report by Parliamentary Under-Secretary on visit to West Indies and British Guiana, 1921–2.

TROPICAL AFRICA

i. In General

1878, LXXXIII [C. 2059], [C. 2081], [C. 2083], [C. 2108], [C. 2014]. Corresp. *re* Congress at Berlin, text of treaty, etc.

1886, XLVII [C. 4739]. Berlin Conference, General Act, 1885.

1888, LXXIV [C. 5432]. Acquisitions of territory on coasts of Africa since Berlin Conference, 1885.

1899, LXIII [C. 9223]. Reprint from *Board of Trade Journal* of articles on Africa.

1899, LXIII [C. 9335]. Corresp. *re* African Liquor Traffic Convention, 1899.

1900, CV [Cd. 103]. International Convention on Liquor Traffic in Africa, Brussels, 1899.

1903, XLV [Cd. 1635]. Memo. showing position of four African Protectorates under Foreign Office.

1904, LXII [Cd. 2163]. Memo. on state of African Protectorates under Foreign Office.

1905, LV [Cd. 2408]. Memo. on state of African Protectorates under Foreign Office.

1905, CIII [Cd. 2383]. Convention between U.K. and France respecting Newfoundland, West and Central Africa.

1905, CIII [Cd. 2486]. Anglo-French Convention on Commercial Relations with British Protectorates in Africa, 1903.

1906, LXXIX [Cd. 3189]. Corresp. *re* preservation of wild animals in Africa.

1906, CXXXVI [Cd. 3264]. Despatch, with Brussels Convention *re* liquor traffic in Africa, 1906.

ii. West Africa

(See the Annual Reports from the Colonies, noted under COLONIAL POLICY above, and also SLAVE TRADE below)

1870, L (444), [C. 264]. Gambia—Corresp. on proposed cession to France.

1872, XLIII (191). West Africa—Return *re* revenue and expenditure, 1865–70.

1872, LXX [C. 474]. West Africa—Convention with Netherlands for transfer of Guinea, 1871.

1873, XLIX (171). Cape Coast—Corresp. *re* Fanti Confederation.

1873, XLIX (266), (266–I). Gold Coast—Various papers.

1873, XLIX (307). West Africa—return of revenue and expenditure, 1871–3.

1873, XLIX [C. 801], [C. 802], [C. 804], [C. 819]. Gold Coast—Corresp. *re* Ashanti invasion.

1874, XXXVI (10), (11), (146). West Africa—Returns *re* costs of Ashantee Expedition.

1874, XLVI (192). West African settlements—Returns *re* Governors and administration since 1843.

1874, XLVI (398). Gold Coast—Corresp. *re* British Settlements and French occupation of Assinee.

1874, XLVI [C. 890], [C. 891], [C. 892], [C. 893], [C. 894], [C. 907], [C. 921], [C. 922], [C. 962], [C. 1009]. Gold Coast—Corresp. and papers *re* Ashantee Invasion.

1874, XLVI [C. 941]. West Africa—Return of revenue, expenditure, imports and exports for 20 years.

1874, XLVI [C. 962]. Gold Coast—Report on expedition against Ashanti.

1874, XLVI [C. 1007]. Gold Coast—Despatches re domestic slavery and introduction of slaves by Ashantee.

1875, XLIII (79). Gold Coast—Supplementary Estimate for Ashantee Expedition.

1875, LII [C. 1139], [C. 1140], [C. 1159]. Gold Coast—Corresp. on Queen's jurisdiction and abolition of slavery.

1875, LII [C. 1343]. West Africa—Papers re H.M. possessions.

1876, LII [C. 1402]. West Africa—Papers re Sierra Leone, Gold Coast and Lagos.

1876, LII [C. 1409], [C. 1498]. Gambia—proposed exchange of West African territory with France.

1877, LX [C. 1685], [C. 1694]. West Africa—Corresp. re financial condition of Sierra Leone, Gambia and St Helena.

1877, LX [C. 1827]. Gambia—Corresp. re limits of British jurisdiction.

1880, LXIX [C. 2538], [C. 2702]. Corresp. re bombardment of Onitsha and Batanga.

1881, LXV [C. 3064]. Gold Coast—Corresp. re threatened Ashantee Invasion.

1881, LXV [C. 3065]. Corresp. re expedition to Upper Gambia.

1882, XLVI [C. 3386]. Gold Coast—Corresp. re affairs.

1882, XLVI [C. 3420], [C. 3430]. Sierra Leone—Corresp. re Jong River and Onitsha incidents.

1883, XLVII [C. 3765]. British Sherbro—Corresp. re disturbances.

1883, XLVIII [C. 3531]. West Africa—Corresp. re territory between 5° 12″ and 8° South, 1847–77.

1883, XLVIII [C. 3687]. Gold Coast—Further corresp. re affairs.

1884, LVI [C. 3885], [C. 3886], [C. 4023]. Corresp. and papers re Congo treaty with Portugal.

1884, LVI [C. 3198]. Sierra Leone—Corresp. re disturbances.

1884, LVI [C. 4052]. Gold Coast—Further corresp.

1884–5, LV [C. 4284], [C. 4360], [C. 4205], [C. 4241]. West African Conference—Corresp.

1884–5, LV [C. 4361]. West African Conference—Protocols, General Act and corresp.

1884–5, LV [C. 4414]. Convention with Belgium, Berlin, 1884.

1884–5, LV [C. 4442]. Arrangement between Britain and Germany re spheres of influence in Africa.

1884–5, LV [C. 4477]. Gold Coast—Corresp. re affairs.

1886, XLVII [C. 4739]. Berlin West African Conference—General Act.

1886, XLVII [C. 4642], [C. 4840], [C. 4905]. Sierra Leone—Corresp. re disturbances.

1886, XLVII [C. 4906]. Gold Coast—Corresp. re affairs.

1887, LX [C. 4957]. Lagos—Negotiations with warring interior tribes.

1887, LX [C. 5236]. Sierra Leone—Corresp. re disturbances.

1888, LXXV [C. 5357], [C. 5615]. Gold Coast—Corresp. re affairs.

1888, LXXV [C. 5358]. Sierra Leone—Corresp. re Yonnie Expedition.

1888, LXXIV [C. 5365]. West Africa—Papers re opening trade.

1889, LVI [C. 5740]. Sierra Leone—Corresp. re disturbances in adjacent territories.

1890, XLVIII [C. 5897]. Gold Coast—Report on Economic Agriculture.

1890, LI [C. 5905]. Anglo-French West African Agreement, 1889—Corresp.

1890–1, LV [C. 6270]. Gold Coast—Further Reports on Economic Agriculture.

1892, LVI [C. 6687]. Sierra Leone—Report on Festing Mission to Bumban-Limbah.

1892, LVI [C. 7601]. West Africa—Papers re Anglo-French arrangements on frontiers and commercial interests.

1893–4, LX [C. 7225]. Gold Coast—Despatch forwarding memorial with complaints.

1893–4, LXII [C. 7163]. West Coast of Africa—Corresp.

1893–4, LXII [C. 7227]. Lagos—Report by Carter on Interior Expedition, 1893.

1893–4, CIX [C. 7026], [C. 7230]. Anglo-German agreements *re* boundaries in West Africa.

1893–4, CIX [C. 7108]. Gold Coast—Anglo-French boundary agreement, 1893.

1895, LXXI [C. 7916]. Niger Coast Protectorate—Report on administration, 1894–5.

1896, LVIII [C. 7917], [C. 7918]. Corresp. *re* affairs in Ashanti.

1896, LIX [C. 7977]. Niger Protectorate—Report by Kirk on disturbances at Brass.

1897, LXII [C. 8480]. West Africa—Papers relative to liquor trade.

1898, LIX [C. 8922]. Sierra Leone—Commission and instructions to Chalmers.

1898, LX [C. 8677]. Papers *re* massacre of British officials near Benin and punitive expedition.

1898, LX [C. 8775]. Niger Coast Protectorate—Report on administration, 1896–7.

1898, LX [C. 8854]. Despatch with Anglo-French Convention for delimitation of British and French possessions on Niger.

1899, VI (260). Bill providing for payments under Royal Niger Co. charter.

1899, LX [C. 9388], [C. 9391]. Sierra Leone—Report and papers of Royal Comm. on insurrection in Protectorate.

1899, LXIII [C. 9124]. Niger Coast Protectorate—Report on administration, 1897–8.

1899, LXIII [C. 9372]. Papers *re* Royal Niger Co. Charter, and other papers *re* government and finances, 1882–98.

1899, LXIII [C. 9529]. Benin Expedition—Corresp.

1899, CIX [C. 9334]. Anglo-French Convention delimiting possessions and spheres of influence east and west of Niger, 1898.

1901, XXXVII (39). Accounts of, and financial Reports on, Royal Niger Company.

1901, XLVIII [Cd. 501]. Corresp. *re* Ashanti War, 1900.

1902, LXVI [Cd. 1097]. Sierra Leone—Reports by King-Harman.

1903, XLV [Cd. 1433]. Nigeria—Corresp. *re* Kano.

1904, LXXII [Cd. 2101]. Statement of revenue, expenditure and trade of Gambia, Sierra Leone and the Gold Coast from 1895, and of Lagos, Southern and Northern Nigeria from 1900.

1905, LIII [Cd. 2244]. Reports on Rubber in Gold Coast and Sierra Leone.

1905, LVI [Cd. 2325]. Papers *re* construction of railways in Sierra Leone, Lagos and Gold Coast.

1905, LVI [Cd. 2564]. Returns of revenue and expenditure of West African Colonies and Protectorates, 1885 to 1905–6.

1906, LXXVI [Cd. 2875], [Cd. 2778]. Northern Nigeria—Reports on mineral survey and economic products.

1906, LXXVI [Cd. 2876]. Southern Nigeria—Reports on mineral survey.

1906, LXXVIII [Cd. 2787]. Nigeria—Corresp. *re* railway construction.

1906, CXXXVI [Cd. 3158]. Anglo-French Convention *re* frontiers east of Niger.

1907, LIV [Cd. 3309]. Northern Nigeria—Memorandum on taxation of natives.

1907, LVII [Cd. 3620]. Nigeria—Corresp. *re* Sokoto and Munshi country.

1907, XCIX [Cd. 3303]. Anglo-French Agreement *re* frontiers from Gulf of Guinea to Niger.

1907, XCIX [Cd. 3346]. Anglo-French Agreement *re* boundary between Gold Coast and French Soudan.

1908, LXX [Cd. 3999]. Southern Nigeria—Report on Forest Administration.

1909, LIX [Cd. 4719]. Northern Nigeria—Report on results of mineral survey, 1906–7.

1909, LX [Cd. 4523]. Nigeria—Further corresp. *re* railway construction.

1909, LX [Cd. 4906], [Cd. 4907]. Southern Nigeria—Report of Committee of Enquiry and Minutes.

1909, CV [Cd. 4699]. Anglo-German Exchange of Notes *re* protocols (1907) defining boundaries in Africa.

1910, XLIV [Cd. 5102], [Cd. 5103]. Report of Northern Nigeria Lands Committee and despatches, and Minutes.

1910, LXV [Cd. 4993]. Gold Coast—Report on Forests, by H. N. Thompson.

1910, LXVI [Cd. 5368]. Nigeria—Protocol and Supplementary Reports on boundary between Yola and Cross River, 1907-9.

1911, LII [Cd. 5899]. Report on Mineral Surveys of Northern Nigeria, 1907-8, 1908-9.

1911, LII [Cd. 5900]. Nyasaland—Report on Mineral Survey, 1908-9.

1911, LIII [Cd. 5743]. Gold Coast—Corresp. re alienation of tribal lands.

1912-13, XLVIII [Cd. 6426], [Cd. 6427]. West Africa—Departmental Committee Report and Minutes on Currency.

1912-13, LIX [Cd. 6089]. West Africa—Vital Statistics re non-native officials, 1911.

1912-13, LIX [Cd. 5278]. Gold Coast and Ashanti—Report on Alienation of Native Lands.

1912-13, LIX [Cd. 6512]. Bill in Gold Coast Legislature re palm oil concession.

1912-13, LIX [Cd. 6561]. West Africa—Corresp. re grant to Lever's of palm oil extractive rights.

1913, XLV [Cd. 6672]. West Africa—Vital Statistics of Non-Native Officials.

1913, XLV [Cd. 6673]. Gold Coast—Corresp. re lease of oil-palm lands.

1913, XLV [Cd. 6961]. Sierra Leone—Despatch re measures against unlawful societies.

1914, LX [Cd. 7263]. West Africa—Vital statistics of non-native officials, 1913.

1914-16, XLV [Cd. 7871]. West Africa—Vital statistics of non-native officials, 1914.

1916, IV [Cd. 8247], [Cd. 8248]. West Africa—Report of Committee on Nuts and Seeds.

1919, XXXVI [Cmd. 468]. Report by Lugard on amalgamation of Northern and Southern Nigeria and administration, 1912-19.

1920, XXXIII [Cmd. 920]. West Africa—Vital Statistics of non-native officials, 1919.

iii. *Central Africa*

1890, LI [C. 5904]. Action of Portugal in Mashonaland and Shire and Lake Nyasa Districts—Corresp.

1893-4, CIX [C. 7032]. Anglo-Portuguese Agreement re spheres of influence north of Zambesi.

1894, LVII [C. 7360]. Papers re Anglo-Belgian Congo Agreement.

1894, LVII [C. 7504]. British Central Africa—Report by Commissioner Johnston on first three years' administration of eastern portion.

1894, LVII [C. 7505]. Corresp. re independent state of Congo.

1894, XCVI [C. 7358], [C. 7390], [C. 7549]. Anglo-Belgian Congo Agreement re spheres of influence in East and Central Africa, and further papers.

1894, LVII [C. 7504]. Eastern British Central Africa—Report on first three years' administration.

1894, LVII [C. 7505]. Independence of Congo—Corresp.

1895, LXXI [C. 7637]. British Sphere of Influence North of Zambesi and Agreements with British South Africa Co.—Papers.

1896, LVIII [C. 7925], [C. 8013]. British Central Africa—Corresp. re operations against slave traders.

1896, LVIII [C. 8254]. British Central African Protectorate—Report on Trade and General Condition, 1895-6.

1897, LXII [C. 8438]. British Central Africa Protectorate—Report on Trade and General Condition.

1897, LX [C. 8683]. British Central Africa Protectorate—Report by Hardinge.

1899, LXIII [C. 9048]. Annual Report on British Central Africa Protectorate for 1897-8.

1899, LXIII [C. 9125]. British Central Africa Protectorate—Report by Hardinge, 1897–8.

1899, CXII [C. 9134]. Despatch with Declaration on British and French spheres of influence in Central Africa.

1903, XLV [Cd. 1536]. British Central Africa—Report from Commissioner on Anglo-Congolese Frontier.

1904, LXII [Cd. 1772]. British Central Africa Protectorate—Report on trade and general conditions. [Thereafter annually.]

1905, LVI [Cd. 2242]. British Central Africa Protectorate—Report on trade and general condition, 1903–4.

1906, LXXIX [Cd. 3002]. Corresp. re Report of Commission on Independent State of Congo.

1906, CXXXVI [Cd. 2920]. Agreement with Independent State of Congo modifying Brussels Treaty of 1894.

1906, LXXIX [Cd. 3002]. Corresp. re Report of Commission of Inquiry into Administration of Independent State of Congo.

1906, CXXXVI [Cd. 2920]. Agreement with Independent State of Congo, modifying Brussels Agreement, 1894.

iv. *East Africa*

(See the Annual Reports from the Colonies noted under COLONIAL POLICY above, and also SLAVE TRADE below)

1890, LI [C. 5903], [C. 5904]. Corresp. re Portuguese actions in East Africa and Delagoa Bay Railway.

1890, LI [C. 5906]. Corresp. re Stanley's expedition for relief of Emin Pasha.

1890, LI [C. 6043]. East Africa—Despatch to Malet.

1890, LI [C. 6046]. Corresp. re Anglo-German Agreement on Africa and Heligoland.

1890–1, LVII [C. 6212], [C. 6370], [C. 6495]. Corresp. and papers re Anglo-Portuguese Conventions of 1890 and 1891.

1890, LXXXI [C. 6130]. Anglo-French Declarations re Madagascar, Zanzibar and North Africa.

1890–1, LVII [C. 6495]. Great Britain and Portugal in East Africa—Corresp.

1890–1, XCVI [C. 6316]. Anglo-Italian Protocols re spheres of influence in Eastern Africa, 1891.

1892, LVI [C. 6555], [C. 6560], [C. 6817]. Papers re Mombasa Railway and Uganda.

1892, LVI [C. 6560], [C. 6555], [C. 6817]. Proposes Mombasa–Lake Victoria Nyanza Railway—Papers.

1893–4, LXII [C. 6725]. Proposes Mombasa–Lake Victoria Nyanza Railway—Further Papers.

1893–4, LXII [C. 6847], [C. 6848], [C. 6853], [C. 7109]. Uganda—Papers re affairs.

1893–4, LXII [C. 7025]. Uganda—Report on Mombasa–Lake Victoria Railway Survey.

1893–4, CIX [C. 7032]. Anglo-Portuguese agreement re spheres of influence north of Zambesi.

1893–4, CIX [C. 7203]. Anglo-German East African Boundaries Agreement.

1894, LVII [C. 7303], [C. 7351]. Uganda—Reports by Sir G. Portal and map.

1894, XCVI [C. 7358], [C. 7390], [C. 7549]. East and Central African Spheres of Influence—Papers re agreement between Great Britain and Belgium, 1894.

1894, XCVI [C. 7388]. Anglo-Italian Protocol re spheres of influence in Eastern Africa, 1894.

1895, LXXI [C. 7646]. Imperial East Africa Company—Corresp. re retirement.
1895, LXXI [C. 7708]. Uganda—Further Papers.
1895, LXXI [C. 7833]. Uganda Railway Committee Report.
1896, VII (305). Uganda Railway Bill.
1896, LIX [C. 8049]. Uganda Railway Bill—Memorandum.
1896, LIX [C. 8274]. British East Africa—Corresp. re recent rebellion.
1896, XCV [C. 7971]. Anglo-Portuguese Agreement re spheres of influence north of Zambesi.
1897, LXII [C. 8434]. Spheres of influence—Papers re interpretation of Article II of Anglo-Portuguese Treaty, 1891.
1897, LXII [C. 8435]. Report on progress with Uganda Railway.
1898, LII (188). Accounts re expenditure under Uganda Railway Act, 1896.
1898, LX [C. 8683]. East Africa Protectorate—Report by Hardinge on progress since establishment, 1897.
1898, LX [C. 8718], [C. 8941]. Uganda Protectorate—Papers on recent events.
1898, LX [C. 8942]. Uganda—Report on progress of railway.
1898, LX [C. 9027]. Uganda—Report on recent mutiny of Soudanese troops.
1899, LI (108). Accounts for Uganda Railway to 31 March 1898.
1899, LXIII [C. 9123], [C. 9232], [C. 9503]. Uganda Protectorate—Papers re Macdonald's expedition and other events.
1899, LXIII [C. 9125]. Report by Hardinge on British East Africa Protectorate for 1897–8.
1899, LXIII [C. 9331], [C. 9333]. Reports on Uganda Railway.
1900, V (182). Bill to provide further money for Uganda Railway.
1900, XLVII (109). Account of expenditure on Uganda Railway.
1900, XLVII (364). Expenditure under Royal Niger Co. Act, 1899.
1900, LVI [Cd. 97], [Cd. 355]. Report and memoranda on Uganda Railway.
1900, LVI [Cd. 256], [Cd. 361]. Uganda—Preliminary Report and maps of Protectorate.
1901, XXXVIII (153). Accounts for Uganda Railway.
1901, XLVIII [Cd. 434], [Cd. 670], [Cd. 674]. Uganda Railway—Return, Corresp. and Report.
1901, XLVIII [Cd. 571]. Uganda—Report by Special Commissioner. [Thereafter annually.]
1901, XLVIII [Cd. 590], [Cd. 671]. Uganda—Reports by Commissioner on Protectorate.
1901, XLVIII [Cd. 769]. East Africa Protectorate—Report of Commissioner. [Annual.]
1902, LXIX [Cd. 910]. Uganda—Instructions to Sadler as Commissioner.
1903, XXXVI (196). Expenditure under Uganda Railway Acts.
1903, XLV [Cd. 1534], [Cd. 1536], [Cd. 1626], [Cd. 1631]. East Africa Protectorate—Reports by Commissioner, by A. Whyte on travels, on slavery and free labour, on Congo frontier, etc.
1903, XLV [Cd. 1625]. Return re purchases for Uganda Railway.
1903, XLV [Cd. 1628]. Return of concessions in East Africa and Uganda Protectorates.
1904, XLIX (184). Uganda Railway Acts—Expenditure to 31 March 1903.
1904, LXII [Cd. 1770]. Uganda Railway Committee—Report on progress, 1902–3.
1904, LXII [Cd. 1839]. Uganda Protectorate—General Report, 1902–3.
1904, LXII [Cd. 2099]. East Africa Syndicate—Corresp. re Eliot's resignation and Concession.
1904, LXII [Cd. 2100]. East Africa and Uganda Protectorates—Return of concessions.
1904, LXII [Cd. 2164]. Uganda Railway Committee—Final Report.
1905, LVI [Cd. 2250]. Uganda Protectorate—General Report for 1903–4.

1905, LVI [Cd. 2312]. Report on Survey of new Frontier between British East Africa and Abyssinia.

1905, LVI [Cd. 2331]. East Africa Protectorate—Report for 1903-4.

1905, LVI [Cd. 2332]. Report on Uganda railway and steamboat service on Lake Victoria, 1903-4.

1905, LVI [Cd. 2406]. East Africa Protectorate—Report on possible cotton growing.

1905, LVI [Cd. 2410]. East Africa—Report on government farms, 1904.

1905, LVI [Cd. 2584]. Award of King of Italy on western boundary of Barotse Kingdom.

1906, LXV (113). Account of expenditure under Uganda Railway Acts, 1896 and 1902.

1906, LXXX [Cd. 2716]. Report on working of Uganda railway and steamboat service on Lake Victoria, 1904-5.

1906, LXXX [Cd. 2740]. East Africa Protectorate—Reports re administration.

1906, LXXX [Cd. 2902]. East Africa Protectorate—Grants of land, 1904-5.

1906, CXXXVI [Cd. 3260]. Anglo-German Agreement re boundary from Yola to Lake Chad.

1907, LIV [Cd. 3561]. Kenya—Report on the forests.

1907, LVII (312). British East Africa and Uganda—Return re sales of Government lands.

1907, LVII [Cd. 3562]. Kenya—Corresp. re flogging of natives at Nairobi.

1908, LXX [Cd. 3914], [Cd. 3915]. Northern Nigeria—2nd and 3rd Reports on Mineral Survey, 1904-6.

1908, LXX [Cd. 3916]. Nyasaland—Report on results of Mineral Survey, 1906-7.

1908, LXXI [Cd. 4117]. East Africa Protectorate—Corresp. re tenure of land.

1908, LXXI [Cd. 4122]. East Africa Protectorate—Corresp. re affairs.

1909, LIX [Cd. 4524]. Uganda—Report by Governor on tour through Eastern Province.

1909, LIX [Cd. 4908]. Nyasaland—Report on results of Mineral Survey, 1907-8.

1909, LIX [Cd. 4910]. Uganda—Report on Cotton Industry.

1909, LX [Cd. 4723]. East Africa—Report on Forests.

1911, LII [Cd. 5584]. East Africa—Corresp. re Masai tribe.

1913, XLV [Cd. 6939]. East Africa—High Court Judgment re Masai Case.

1914, II (122). Bill to authorise Loans to East African Protectorates.

1920, XXXIII [Cmd. 873]. East African Protectorate—Despatch and papers re native labour.

v. *Zanzibar*

(see also SLAVE TRADE AND SLAVERY below)

1886, XLVII [C. 4609]. Zanzibar—Corresp. re affairs.

1887, LIX [C. 4609], [C. 4917]. Zanzibar—Corresp. and treaty with Sultan.

1887, LIX [C. 4940]. Zanzibar—Further corresp.

1888, LXXIV [C. 5315]. Zanzibar—Further corresp.

1888, LXXIV [C. 5603]. Germany and Zanzibar—Corresp.

1889, LVI [C. 5822]. Germany and Zanzibar—Further corresp.

1890, LI [C. 6046]. Anglo-German Heligoland—Zanzibar Agreement—Corresp.

1890-1, LVII [C. 6254]. Zanzibar—Declaration re exercise of judicial powers, 1891.

1893-4, LXII [C. 6955]. Zanzibar—Report on Protectorate.

1893-4, CIX [C. 6851]. Zanzibar—Declaration re exercise of judicial powers.

1898, LX [C. 8701]. Report on Island of Pemba, 1896-7.

1906, CXXXVII [Cd. 2685]. Anglo-American Convention re extra-territorial jurisdiction in Zanzibar.

1909, LIX [Cd. 4816]. Zanzibar—Despatch with Report on finance, administration and condition.

SLAVE TRADE AND SLAVERY

1870, LXI (41). Slave trade—Return re vessels captured, 1864–9.

1870, LXI [C. 140], [C. 141], [C. 142]. Slave trade—Corresp. re West Africa, East Africa, Europe and America.

1870, LXI [C. 209]. East African Slave Trade—Report by committee.

1870, LXIX [C. 193]. Slave trade—Convention with U.S.A., 1870.

1871, XII (420). Slave trade—Report from Select Committee on East African traffic.

1871, LXII [C. 339], [C. 340], [C. 341]. Slave trade—Corresp. re West Africa, East Africa and elsewhere.

1871, LXII [C. 385]. Slave trade—Corresp. re East Africa.

1872, LXX [C. 470]. Slave trade—Convention with Portugal, 1871.

1873, V (236). Slave trade—East African Courts Bill.

1873, V (249). Slave trade—Suppression Consolidation Bill.

1873, LXI [C. 820]. Slave trade—Corresp. re Bartle Frere's mission.

1873, LXI [C. 867–I]. Slave trade in East Africa—Corresp.

1874, LXII [C. 887], [C. 889], [C. 903], [C. 904]. Treaties with Muscat, Zanzibar, Johanna and Maculla for suppression of slave trade.

1874, LXII [C. 946], [C. 1062], [C. 1064]. East African slave trade—Reports and corresp.

1875, LXXI (326). Slave trade—Return of vessels captured, etc.

1875, LXXI [C. 1168]. Corresp. with British representatives and Reports from naval officers on East African Slave Trade.

1876, VII (270). Bill for more effectually punishing slave trading.

1876, XXXVIII [C. 1516–I]. Report of Commission on Fugitive Slaves.

1876, LXX [C. 1521]. Zanzibar—Communications from Kirk re suppression of slave trade.

1876, LXXXIV [C. 1387]. Treaty with Zanzibar for suppression, 1875.

1876, LXX [C. 1413], [C. 1480], [C. 1588], [C. 1593]. Corresp. with Agents and Naval Officers on fugitive slaves, slave ships, etc.

1877, LXXVIII [C. 1800], [C. 1829], [C. 1862]. Slave trade—Corresp. with British representatives and naval officers, and other papers.

1878, LV [C. 2148]. Gold Coast—Report by Chalmers on abolition of slavery.

1878, LXVII [C. 1900]. Convention between Britain and Egypt for suppression of slave trade, 1877.

1878, LXVII [C. 1902]. Treaty with King of Dahomey, 1877.

1878, LXVII [C. 2139], [C. 2140]. Slave trade—Corresp. with British representatives and naval officers.

1878–9, LXVI (381). Return re slave vessels captured and slaves rescued, for five years.

1878–9, LXVI [C. 2422], [C. 2423]. Slave trade—Corresp. with British representatives and naval officers.

1880, LXIX [C. 2720]. Slave trade—Corresp. with British representatives and naval officers.

1880, LXXVIII [C. 2477]. Convention with German Empire for suppression of slave trade.

1881, LXXXV [C. 3052]. Slave trade—Corresp. with British representatives and naval officers.

1882, XLVI [C. 3285]. Slavery in Protected Malay States—Corresp.

1882, XLVI [C. 3285], [C. 3429]. Corresp. re slavery in Protected Malay States.

1882, LXV [C. 3160]. Corresp. with British representatives and naval officers.

1883, LXVI [C. 3547]. Corresp. with British representatives and agents abroad.

1883, LXVI [C. 3700]. Report on state of slave trade and slavery in Morocco.

1884, LV [C. 4192]. Slavery in Protected Malay States—Further corresp.

1884, LXXV [C. 3849]. Slave trade—Corresp. with British representatives and naval officers.

1884, LXXV [C. 3935]. Despatch *re* slavery in Egypt.

1884, LXXV [C. 4099]. Treaty with Abyssinia for suppression of slave trade.

1884–5, LXXIII [C. 4239]. Corresp. *re* execution of 1877 convention with Egypt.

1884–5, LXXIII [C. 4523]. Slave trade—Corresp. with British representatives and naval officers.

1886, LXII [C. 4776]. Slave trade—Corresp. with British representatives, naval officers, etc., 1885.

1887, LVIII [C. 4958]. Slavery in Protected Malay States—Further corresp.

1887, LXXVII [C. 5111]. Slave trade—Corresp. with agents, naval officers, etc., 1886.

1888, VII (42). Bill to consolidate laws *re* slavery.

1888, LXXIV [C. 5559]. Suppression of slave trade in East African waters—Corresp.

1888, LXXIII [C. 5566]. Slavery in Protected Malay States—Further corresp.

1888, LXXIV [C. 5578], [C. 5599]. Report and corresp. on East African slave trade, 1887–8.

1888, XCIII [C. 5428]. Slave trade—Further corresp.

1889, LXXII [C. 5821]. Slave trade—Further corresp.

1889, LVI [C. 5884]. Slavery in Protected Malay States—Further corresp.

1890, VIII (150). Slavery Law Amendment Bill.

1890, L [C. 6048]. Brussels Conference, 1889–90. General Act.

1890, L [C. 6049], [C. 6049–I]. Brussels Slave Trade Conference, 1889–90—Protocols and General Act.

1890–1, LVII [C. 6211]. Zanzibar—Anti-slavery decree by Sultan, 1890.

1890–1, LVII [C. 6354]. Gold Coast—Corresp. *re* administration of laws against slavery.

1890–1, LVII [C. 6373]. Papers *re* trade in slaves from East Africa.

1892, LXXIV [C. 6699]. Papers *re* suppression of slave-raiding in Nyasaland.

1892, LXXIV [C. 6702]. Zanzibar—Papers *re* slavery and slave trade.

1892, XCV [C. 6557]. General Act of Brussels Conference, 2 July 1890.

1892, XCV [C. 6592]. Anglo-Spanish treaty for suppression of slave trade, 1890.

1893–4, LXXXV [C. 7031]. Papers *re* suppression of slave-raiding in British Central Africa.

1893–4, LXXXV [C. 7035], [C. 7247]. Zanzibar—Papers *re* traffic in slaves and number freed.

1896, LVIII [C. 7925], [C. 8013]. British Central Africa—Corresp. *re* operations against slave traders.

1896, LIX [C. 8275]. Zanzibar—Corresp. *re* slavery.

1896, XCVII [C. 7929], [C. 8011]. Anglo-Egyptian Convention for suppression of slavery and slave trade, with annexures.

1897, LXII [C. 8394], [C. 8433]. Corresp. *re* abolition of slavery in Zanzibar and Pemba.

1898, LX [C. 8858]. Corresp. *re* abolition of legal status of slavery in Zanzibar.

1899, LXIII [C. 9502]. Corresp. *re* status of slavery in East Africa and Zanzibar.

1900, LVI [Cd. 96]. Corresp. *re* slavery and slave trade in East Africa and Zanzibar and Pemba.

1901, XLVIII [Cd. 593]. Corresp. *re* slavery and slave trade in East Africa, Zanzibar and Pemba.

1903, XLV [Cd. 1389]. Corresp. *re* slavery and slave trade in East Africa, Zanzibar and Pemba.

1905, LVI [Cd. 2330]. Corresp. *re* slavery in Zanzibar and Pemba.

1909, LIX [Cd. 4732]. Zanzibar—Despatch *re* Slavery Decree.

1914, VI (134). Bill to consolidate enactments *re* slave trade, slavery, peonage and forced labour.

MAURITIUS AND SEYCHELLES

(See also the Annual Reports from the Colonies, 1870–1921, noted under
COLONIAL POLICY above)

1870, XLIX (232). Mauritius—Return *re* immigrants.
1871, XLVII (133). Mauritius—Return *re* immigrants.
1873, L (206). Mauritius—Return *re* immigrants.
1875, XXXIV [C. 115]. Mauritius—Report of Comm. on immigrants.
1875, XXXIV [C. 115–I]. Mauritius—Report of Comm.: Appendices.
1875, L [C. 746]. Seychelles—Corresp. *re* liberated Africans.
1875, LIII [C. 1188]. Mauritius—Corresp. *re* Comm. on Indian immigrants.
1877, LXI [C. 1877]. Mauritius—Order in Council (1845) *re* English in law-courts.
1884, LV [C. 4064]. Mauritius—Corresp. *re* ecclesiastical and educational questions.
1884, LV [C. 4074]. Mauritius—Corresp. *re* constitution of council.
1884–5, LIV [C. 4318], [C. 4470]. Mauritius—Corresp. *re* salaries.
1884–5, LIV [C. 4436]. Mauritius—Corresp. *re* constitution of Government.
1884–5, LIV [C. 4455]. Mauritius—Communication on sugar crisis.
1886, XLVI [C. 4754]. Mauritius—Constitution of Council—Further correspondence.
1887, LVIII [C. 5101]. Mauritius: Royal Commission of Inquiry—Despatch on Report.
1892, IV (425). Mauritius—Bill to authorise payment of loan.
1910, XLII [Cd. 5185], [Cd. 5186], [Cd. 5187]. Mauritius—Report of Royal Commission on administrative and financial conditions and resources.

CEYLON

(See principally the Annual Reports listed under COLONIAL POLICY above)

1872, XLIII [C. 521]. Ceylon—Corresp. *re* deepening of Paumben Channel.
1876, LIV (154). Ceylon—Papers *re* ecclesiastical endowments.
1877, LXI (123). Ceylon—Corresp. *re* memorials against ecclesiastical subsidies.
1899, LVIII [C. 9370]. Ceylon—Corresp. *re* recent land legislation.
1905, LIII [Cd. 2341]. Ceylon—Reports on results of Mineral Survey, 1903–4.
1905, LVIII [Cd. 2484]. Ceylon—Papers *re* education of Tamil children on estates.
1906, LXXVI [Cd. 3190]. Ceylon—Reports on results of Mineral Survey, 1904–5.
1906, LXXVII [Cd. 2873]. Ceylon—Corresp. *re* elementary education.
1906, LXXVII [Cd. 2906]. Ceylon—Corresp. *re* lease of pearl fisheries.
1908, LXX [Cd. 3762]. Ceylon—Report on results of Mineral Survey, 1905–6.
1908, LXXI [Cd. 4000]. Ceylon—Corresp. *re* consumption of opium.
1910, LXVI [Cd. 5098]. Ceylon—Despatches *re* constitution of legislative council.

MALAYA AND HONG KONG

(See also the Annual Reports from the Colonies, 1870–1921, noted under
COLONIAL POLICY above)

1871, XLVII (379). Hong Kong—Corresp. *re* licensed gambling houses.
1872, XLIII (90). Straits Settlements—Corresp. *re* union of Oabuan.
1873, LXXV [C. 829]. Hong Kong—Measures against Macao coolie trade.
1875, LIII [C. 1189]. Hong Kong—Corresp. *re* Chinese revenue cargoes.
1875, LIII [C. 1320]. Native States in Malaya—Further corresp.

1876, LIV [C. 1505], [C. 1505–I], [C. 1510], [C. 1512]. Malaya—Corresp. re native states.

1876, LIV [C. 1628]. Hong Kong—Complaints against Chinese cruisers.

1877, LXI [C. 1709]. Straits Settlements—Corresp. re Malay chiefs.

1881, LXV (426). Hong Kong—Despatches from governor, 1877 and 1881, re restrictions on Chinese.

1881, LXV [C. 3095]. Papers re Protected Malay States.

1882, XLVI [C. 3428]. Protected Malay States—Further Papers.

1883, LXVI [C. 3702], [C. 3727]. Conventions with sultans of Mohilla and Johanna.

1886, XLVI [C. 4627]. Agreement with Sultan of Johore.

1887, LVIII [C. 4958]. Corresp. re Protected Malay States.

1888, LXXIII [C. 5253]. Straits Settlements—Agreement between Governor and Sultan of Pahang.

1888, LXXIII [C. 5566]. Corresp. re Protected Malay States.

1890–1, LVII (378). Corresp. re ex-Sultan Abdullah of Perak.

1890–1, LVII [C. 6222]. Protected Malay States—Papers.

1890–1, LVII [C. 6290]. Straits Settlements—Corresp. re increased military contribution.

1892, LVI [C. 6576]. Reports re Protected Malay States for 1890.

1893–4, LXI [C. 6858], [C. 7228]. Reports re Protected Malay States, 1891–2.

1895, LXX [C. 7784]. Straits Settlements—Further corresp. re increased military contribution.

1896, LVIII [C. 8257]. Protected Malay States—Report for 1895.

1897, LXI [C. 8367]. Papers relating to Cocos-Keeling and Christmas Islands.

1898, LIX [C. 8661]. Federated Malay States—Report for 1896. [Thereafter annually.]

1899, CIX [C. 9087]. Hong Kong—Anglo-Chinese Convention re extension of territory, 1898.

1900, LV [Cd. 382]. Federated Malay States—Reports for 1899.

1900, LV [Cd. 403]. Hong Kong—Report on New Territory.

1904, LX [Cd. 1819]. Report on Federated Malay States, 1902.

1906, LXXVIII [Cd. 2777], [Cd. 3186]. Reports on Federated Malay States, 1904, 1905.

1906, LXXVIII [Cd. 3249]. Straits Settlements—Corresp. re expropriation of Tanjong Pagar Col.

1907, LVII [Cd. 3287]. Straits Settlements—Return re opium trade, 1896–1905.

1909, LXI [Cd. 4471], [Cd. 4722]. Reports on Federated Malay States, 1907, 1908.

1910, LXVI [Cd. 5373]. Federated Malay States—Report for 1909.

1910, LXVI [Cd. 5389]. Report on Kedah and Perlis. [Thereafter annual.]

1911, LIII [Cd. 5902]. Federated Malay States—Report for 1910.

1912–13, LX [Cd. 6562], [Cd. 6563]. Report on Federated Malay States, Kedah, etc., 1911.

1914, LX [Cd. 7208]. Federated Malay States—Report for 1912.

1914–16, XLVI [Cd. 7709]. Federated Malay States—Report for 1913.

1914–16, XLVI [Cd. 8155]. Federated Malay States—Report for 1914.

1916, XX [Cd. 8377]. Federated Malay States—Report for 1915.

1917–18, XXIII [Cd. 8814]. Federated Malay States—Report for 1916.

1919, XXXVI [Cmd. 26], [Cmd. 469]. Federated Malay States—Reports for 1917, 1918.

1920, XXXIII [Cmd. 1094]. Federated Malay States—Report for 1919.

1921, XXIV [Cmd. 1135]. Report on Unfederated Malay States, 1919.

PACIFIC ISLANDS

(See also the Annual Reports from the Colonies, 1870–1921, noted under
COLONIAL POLICY above)

1871, XLVII (425). Fiji Islands—Corresp. *re* annexation.

1871, XLVIII [C. 399]. South Sea Islanders—Corresp. *re* deportation.

1872, III (45), (184). Pacific Islanders Protection Bill, with Lords' amendments.

1872, XLIII [C. 479], [C. 496], [C. 509]. Fiji—Corresp. *re* deportations of South Sea Islanders.

1873, XLII (76). Fiji Islands—Instructions to naval officers.

1873, XLIX (124). Fiji Islands—Corresp. with New South Wales.

1873, L (244). South Sea Islands—Communications *re* outrages.

1874, XLV (232). South Seas—Corresp. *re* outrages on natives.

1874, XLV [C. 983], [C. 1011]. Fiji Islands—Corresp. *re* cession.

1875, LII [C. 1114]. Fiji—Further corresp. *re* cession.

1875, LII [C. 1337]. Fiji—Corresp.

1876, LIV [C. 1404], [C. 1624]. Fiji—Corresp. *re* affairs.

1876, LIV [C. 1566]. New Guinea—Papers *re* annexation.

1877, LIX [C. 1826]. Fiji—Corresp. *re* outbreak by cannibal tribes.

1877, LXI [C. 1880]. Fiji—Corresp. *re* taxes on native produce.

1878, LV (111). Fiji—Ordinances and corresp. *re* Polynesian labourers and Indian coolies.

1881, XCIX [C. 2747], [C. 2748]. Samoa—Treaties with King and government, 1879.

1882, LXXXI [C. 3108], [C. 3109]. Affairs of Sulu and Brunei (Claims)—Papers.

1882, LXXXI [C. 3400]. Treaty of friendship with Tonga, 1879.

1883, XLVII [C. 3617], [C. 3691]. New Guinea—Corresp. *re* affairs.

1883, XLVII [C. 3641]. Corresp. *re* Pacific natives and labour traffic.

1883, XLVII [C. 3814]. Corresp. *re* New Guinea, New Hebrides and other Pacific islands.

1884, LV [C. 3863], [C. 3839]. Corresp. *re* Pacific Islands.

1884, LV [C. 3905], [C. 4126]. Reports on state of Pacific Islands.

1884–5, LIII [C. 4433]. Fiji—Corresp. *re* German landing claims.

1884–5, LIII [C. 4484]. Fiji—Corresp. *re* native population.

1884–5, LIV [C. 4217], [C. 4273], [C. 4584]. Corresp. *re* New Guinea and other Pacific islands.

1884–5, LIV [C. 4290]. Memo. of conversations at Berlin on Africa, New Guinea and Western Pacific.

1884–5, LIV [C. 4441]. New Guinea—Arrangement between Great Britain and Germany *re* spheres of influence.

1884–5, LXXXVII [C. 4276]. Samoa—Convention *re* Apia, 1883.

1886, XLVII [C. 4858]. Gulf of Guinea—Supplementary arrangement between Britain and Germany *re* spheres.

1886, LXXIII [C. 4656]. Western Pacific—Declarations by Britain and Germany *re* spheres.

1887, LVIII [C. 5039]. Fiji—Corresp. *re* native population.

1887, LVIII [C. 5106], [C. 5161]. Tonga—Report by High Commissioner on disturbances.

1887, LVIII [C. 5240]. Western Pacific—Corresp. on proposed international agreement *re* supply of arms, alcohol, etc. to natives.

1888, LXXIII [C. 5564]. New Guinea—Orders and instructions for government.

1888, LXXIII [C. 5617]. British North Borneo—Papers *re* agreements with Sarawak and Brunei.

1888, CIX [C. 5246]. Agreement with Brunei *re* New Hebrides, 1887–8.

1888, CIX [C. 5372]. Declaration concerning islands to leeward of Tahiti.

1889, LVI [C. 5883]. Further corresp. *re* New Guinea and other islands.

1890, LXXXI [C. 5907], [C. 5911]. Samoa—Corresp. and Final Act of Conference at Berlin.

1890–1, LVII [C. 6323]. British New Guinea—Corresp.

1892, XCV [C. 6553]. Borneo-Anglo-Dutch Convention defining boundaries.

1892, XCV [C. 6594]. Tonga—Agreement *re* trial of British subjects.

1893–4, CIX [C. 6973]. Samoa—Corresp. *re* affairs.

1894, LVII [C. 7546]. Report on Protected Malay States for 1893.

1895, LXX [C. 7679]. Fiji—Further corresp. *re* affairs.

1897, LIX [C. 8457]. British Solomon Islands—Report by Woodford.

1898, LIX [C. 8935]. British New Guinea—Corresp. *re* agreement with British New Guinea Syndicate.

1899, LIX [C. 9148]. Pitcairn Island—Corresp. *re* condition of islanders.

1899, CX [C. 9506]. Samoa—Report of Joint Commission and corresp.

1900, CV [Cd. 7], [Cd. 38], [Cd. 39], [Cd. 98]. Samoa—Despatch and conventions between Britain, Germany and U.S.A. on claims and other questions.

1901, XLVI [Cd. 754]. Pitcairn—Further corresp. *re* condition of islanders.

1902, LXVI [Cd. 807]. Gilbert and Ellis Islands—Reports for 1896–1900.

1904, LIV [Cd. 2240]. Fiji—Corresp. *re* taxation and communal system.

1905, LIII [Cd. 2397]. Pitcairn Island—Report on conditions.

1905, LIV [Cd. 2240]. Fiji—Corresp. *re* native taxation and communal system.

1906, LXXVIII [Cd. 2714]. New Hebrides—Report on trade.

1906, CXXXVI [Cd. 3160]. New Hebrides—Anglo-French Convention confirming Protocol of 27 Feb. 1906.

1907, LVI [Cd. 3288], [Cd. 3525]. New Hebrides—Corresp. with France *re* Convention, 1906.

1907, LVI [Cd. 3619]. Brunei—Report for 1906.

1907, LVII [Cd. 6289]. New Hebrides—Report on trade, 1905.

1907, LXXI [Cd. 3763]. Fiji—Corresp. *re* land tenure.

1908, LXXIII [Cd. 3456]. Gilbert and Ellice Islands Protectorate—Corresp. *re* administration.

1908, LXXI [Cd. 3763]. Fiji—Corresp. *re* tenure of land.

1908, LXXIII [Cd. 3741]. Report on the Federated Malay States.

1908, LXXIII [Cd. 4356]. Gilbert and Ellice Islands Protectorate—Corresp. *re* administration.

1908, CXXV [Cd. 3876]. New Hebrides—Anglo-French Exchange of Notes *re* Convention of 1906.

1910, LXVI [Cd. 4992]. Gilbert and Ellice Islands—Report on visit by Mahaffy.

1916, XX [Cd. 8379]. Brunei—Report on state, 1915.

1917–18, XXIII [Cd. 8813]. Brunei—Report on state, 1916.

1919, XXXVI [Cmd. 28]. Brunei—Report for 1918.

1919, XXXVI [Cmd. 201]. Fiji—Report on trade by R. W. Dalton.

4. SELECT LIST OF PARLIAMENTARY DEBATES

In 1870 *Hansard's Parliamentary Debates* was still a private venture, published at that time by Cornelius Buck, at 23 Paternoster Row, London. Since 1855, however, the Stationery Office had been directed by the Treasury to purchase 100 copies of each issue for public departments. In 1878 further official recognition was given by the grant of a subsidy out of the Stationery Office vote for the improvement of the system of reporting. Thenceforward the proprietors of Hansard employed their own reporters to supplement newspaper versions. A Select Committee of the House of Commons in 1888 reported in favour of an authorised report. This was achieved in 1892 when the name "Hansard" disappeared (until 1943) in favour of the title: *Parliamentary Debates, Authorised Edition*. Speeches were still summarised, however, to as little as one-third of the original, and in 1907 the subject was again reviewed by a Select Committee. The procedure they recommended has been that adopted since 1909, namely: a verbatim account by official reporters in the service of the House itself and printed under the direction of the Controller of His (Her) Majesty's Stationery Office.

The figures given in the references below indicate the series, volume and columns in which can be found the more important debates on imperial affairs in general from 1870 to 1918 and on the subjects discussed in the present volume of *C.H.B.E.* References to debates on the affairs of Commonwealth countries not included here will be found in volumes II, IV–VIII of the History. The debates are given in chronological order and unless otherwise indicated were in the House of Commons.

Lords. British Colonies. Carnarvon's Motion; 14 Feb. 1870. 3rd ser. CXCIX, 193–233.

Emigration as a remedy for distress in Britain—Motion; 1 March 1870. 3rd ser. CXCIX, 1002–77.

Supply—Army Estimates. Reduction in Colonial Establishments; 3 March 1870. 3rd ser. CXCIX, 1158–234.

Withdrawal of troops from New Zealand—Motion; 7 March 1870. 3rd ser. CXCIX, 1324–62.

Navy—African Squadron; 29 March 1870. 3rd ser. CC, 833–58.

Colonies—Motion for select committee; 26 April 1870. 3rd ser. CC, 1817–908.

East India—Opium Revenue; 10 May 1870. 3rd ser. CCI, 480–524.

East India—Council of State; 17 May 1870. 3rd ser. CCI, 825–53.

Lords. Singapore—Petition for judicial independence; 20 May 1870. 3rd ser. CCI, 1041–49.

Lords. Colonies—Russell's Address for a Commission; 20 June 1870. 3rd ser. CCII, 451–85.

Lords. Judicial Committee of the Privy Council—appellate business; 1 July 1870. 3rd ser. CCII, 1283–99.

Settlement of Gambia; 15 July 1870. 3rd ser. CCIII, 351–67.

British residents at Belize—Question; 21 July 1870. 3rd ser. CCIII, 632–33.

Lords. Judicial Committee Bill—2nd, 3rd readings; 18, 25 July 1870. 3rd ser. CCIII, 402–7, 865–67.

Judicial Committee Bill—3rd reading; 8 Aug. 1870. 3rd ser. CCIII, 1706–25.

Demerara Commission—Question; 4 Aug. 1870. 3rd ser. CCIII, 1526–27.

Dutch forts on Gulf of Guinea—Question *re* cession; 27 March 1871. 3rd ser. CCV, 657.

Armament of Gibraltar—Guest's Motion; 28 March 1871. 3rd ser. CCV, 771–81.

Relations between U.K. and Colonies—Macfie's Resolution; 12 May 1871. 3rd ser. CCVI, 750–70.

West Indies—Confederation of Leeward Islands; 31 March 1871. 3rd ser. CCV, 985–6.

West African settlements; 9 June 1871. 3rd ser. CCVI, 1806–23.

Sierra Leone—Question *re* Administrator; 12 June 1871. 3rd ser. CCVI, 1928–30.

Gambia—Question *re* transfer to France; 4 May 1871. 3rd ser. CCVI, 153–4.

Lords. Treaty with U.S.A.; 22 May 1871. 3rd ser. CCVI, 1101–8.

West Indies—Confederation of Leeward Islands; 25 May 1871. 3rd ser. CCVI, 1251–2.

Lords. Treaty of Washington; 12 June 1871. 3rd ser. CCVI, 1823–901.

Treaty of Washington—Question; 12 June 1871. 3rd ser. CCVI, 1903–5.

Lords. Privy Council—Appellate jurisdiction; 15 June 1871. 3rd ser. CCVII, 53–66.

Gibraltar—Revenue; 16 June 1871. 3rd ser. CCVII, 179–85.

Euphrates Valley Railway scheme; 23 June 1871. 3rd ser. CCVII, 525–40.

Lords. U.S.A. Treaty of Washington; 29 June 1871. 3rd ser. CCVII, 729–41.

Slave Trade in East Africa; 30 June 1871. 3rd ser. CCVII, 952–7.

U.S.A. Treaty of Washington; 4 Aug. 1871. 3rd ser. CCVIII, 861–925.

Mauritius—Question *re* Indian immigrants; 12 Feb. 1872. 3rd ser. CCIX, 208–9.

Dr Livingstone—Expedition to search for him; 12 Feb. 1872. 3rd ser. CCIX, 209–12.

West Africa—Acquisition of Dutch settlements; 13 Feb. 1872. 3rd ser. CCIX, 319–29.

Pacific Islands Protection Bill; 15 Feb. 1872. 3rd ser. CCIX, 522–3.

Chinese coolie traffic—Motion; 16 Feb. 1872. 3rd ser. CCIX, 529–48.

Aytoun's Resolution *re* transfer of Dutch possessions on West Coast of Africa. 3rd ser. CCIX (18 Feb. 1872), 319–29.

Emigration Commissioners—Functions of; 20 Feb. 1872. 3rd ser. CCIX, 773–86.

Lords. Debate on Responsible govt. at Cape Colony; 7 March 1872. 3rd ser. CCX, 1621–39.

Colonies—Macfie's Resolution *re* participation in imperial govt. 31 May 1872. 3rd ser. CCXI, 912–38.

East African slave trade—Question; 13 May 1872. 3rd ser. CCXI, 653–4.

Pacific Islanders Protection Bill, Committee stage; 22 April 1872. 3rd ser. CCX, 1665–74.

Lords. Pacific Islanders Protection Bill; 2nd reading; 3, 7 May 1872. 3rd ser. CCXI, 184–9, 368–70.

Lords. Protection of Fiji Islanders; 24 June 1872. 3rd ser. CCXII, 81–91.

Fiji Islands Protectorate—McArthur's Motion; 25 June 1872. 3rd ser. CCXII, 192–219.

East African slave trade; 23 July 1872. 3rd ser. CCXII, 1608–20.

Lords. Responsible govt. in Cape Colony. 3rd ser. CCXIII (29 July 1872), 24–34.

Lords. Kidnapping of South Sea Islanders; 10 Feb. 1873. 3rd ser. CCXIV, 185–92.

Colonies—Motion for Select Comm.; 28 Feb. 1873. 3rd ser. CCXIV, 1102–23.

Defence of the colonies—Resolution; 7 March 1873. 3rd ser. CCXIV, 1520–34.

Ashantee invasions, West Africa—Question; 2 May 1873. 3rd ser. CCXV, 1392–96.

Chinese coolie trade—Obs.; 23 May 1873. 3rd ser. CCXVI, 375–96.

Lords. Colonial Church Bill; 27 May 1873. 3rd ser. CCXVI, 484–93.

Protectorate of Fiji—Resolution; 13 June 1873. 3rd ser. CCXVI, 934–59.

Ecclesiastical Policy in Windward Islands and Trinidad—Motions; 15 July 1873. 3rd ser. CCXVII, 424–46.

East African Slave Trade—Motion; 28 July 1873. 3rd ser. CCXVII, 1068–76.

Lords. Future policy on Gold Coast—Question; 30 March 1874. 3rd ser. CCXVIII, 394–98.

Ashantee War—Vote of Thanks to forces; 30 March 1874. 3rd ser. CCXVIII, 412–31.

Gold Coast—Resolution *re* withdrawal; 27 April, 4 May 1874. 3rd ser. CCXVIII, 1204–25, 1592–663.

Lords. Suez Canal. Motion *re* neutralisation; 5 June 1874. 3rd ser. CXXIX, 1032–37.

Gold Coast. Resolution *re* slavery; 29 June 1874. 3rd ser. CCXX, 607–41.

Lords. Straits Settlements, Courts Bill; 17 July 1874. 3rd ser. CCXXI, 173–79.

Lords. Fiji Islands, Motion *re* cession; 17 July 1874. 3rd ser. CCXXI, 179–97.

Fiji Islands, Motion *re* annexation; 4 Aug. 1874. 3rd ser. CCXXI, 1264–301.

Lords. Pacific Islanders Protection Bill; 16 March 1875. CCXXII, 1857–60.

Suez Canal shares. Vote; 14 Feb. 1876. 3rd ser. CCXXIII, 266–99.

Circular *re* fugitive slaves; 22, 24 Feb. 1876. 3rd ser. CCXXXVII, 685–764, 820–902.

Lords. Circulars *re* fugitive slaves; 25 Feb., 7 March 1876. 3rd ser. CCXXXVII, 903–9, 1506–65.

Lords. Malay Peninsula—Address; 28 Feb. 1876. 3rd ser. CCXXVII, 1000–18.

East African Slave Trade—Resolution; 4 April 1876. 3rd ser. CCXXVIII, 1216–31.

Lords. Disturbances in Barbados—Observations; 28 April 1876. 3rd ser. CCXXVIII, 1817–28.

River Gambia policy—Motion; 2 May 1876. 3rd ser. CCXXVIII, 1998–2007.

Disturbances in Barbados—Observations; 5 May 1876. 3rd ser. CCXXIX, 144–65.
Malaya. Murder of Birch—Observations; 26 May 1876. 3rd ser. CCXXIX, 1290–309.
Lords. Malaya—Resolution; 3 July 1876. 3rd ser. CCXXIX, 824–46.
Barbados. Social and political conditions; 28 July 1876. 3rd ser. CCXXXI, 42–59.
Colonial Marriages Bill, 2nd Reading; 28 Feb. 1877. 3rd ser. CCXXXII, 164–94.
Slave Circulars, 1876—Resolution; 16 March 1877. 3rd ser. CCXXXIII, 69–79.
Lords. Coolie emigration—Hampton's Motion; 20 July 1877. 3rd ser. CCXXXIV, 1556–62.
Colonial Marriages Bill. 2nd Reading; 27 Feb. 1878. 3rd ser. CCXXXVIII, 406–39.
Lords. Military forces—Indian troops; 20 May 1878. 3rd ser. CCXXXIX, 187–253.
Military forces—Indian troops. Hartington's Resolution; 20, 21, 23 May 1878. 3rd ser. CCXXXIX, 264–348, 362–438, 499–614.
Egypt—Finance, observations; 21 Feb. 1879. 3rd ser. CCXLIII, 1619–38.
Occupation of Cyprus. Observations; 24 March 1879. 3rd ser. CCXLIV, 1509–87.
Administration of Cyprus. Resolution; 29 July 1879. 3rd ser. CCXLVIII, 1563–84.
Malta. Cost of police, Resolution; 1 Aug. 1879. 3rd ser. CCXLVIII, 1898–918.
Expenses of War in Afghanistan—Fawcett's Amendment to Address; 11 Feb. 1880. 3rd ser. CCL, 453–77.
Motion for Select Comm. on Commerce and Free Trade; 13 Feb. 1880. 3rd ser. CCL, 604–38.
Cyprus. Forced labour—Rylands's Motion; 1 June 1880. 3rd ser. CCLII, 897–929.
Lords. Cyprus, Famagousta Harbour. Observations; 2 July 1880. 3rd ser. CCLIII, 1380–83.
Central Africa—Missionaries in. Cameron's Motion; 2 July 1880. 3rd ser. CCLIII, 1424–43.
Lords. Queen's Speech; 6 Jan. 1881. 3rd ser. CCLVII, 3–8.
India and China—Observations re opium trade; 29 April 1881. 3rd ser. CCLX, 1451–514.
Power of Representatives Abroad—Resolution; 29 April 1881. 3rd ser. CCLX, 1424–50.
Cyprus. Famagusta Harbour—Question re purchase; 24 May 1881. 3rd ser. CCLXI, 1212–13.
Anglo-Turkish Convention—Motion for papers; 24 June 1881. 3rd ser. CCLXII, 1273–335.
Pacific Islands—Jurisdiction of High Commissioner—Observations; 5 Aug. 1881. 3rd ser. CCLXIV, 1018–27.
Foreign and Imperial Policy of Government—Bartlett's Motion; 23 Aug. 1881. 3rd ser. CCLXV, 768–92.
Lords. British North Borneo Company charter—Observations; 13 March 1882. 3rd ser. CCLXVII, 708–24.
Egypt. Resolution re international tribunals. 13 March 1882. 3rd ser. CCLXVII, 763–80.
British North Borneo Company charter—Resolution. 17 March 1882. 3rd ser. CCLXVII, 1148–230.
Slave trade in Asia and Africa—Motion by Labouchere; 28 April 1882. 3rd ser. CCLXVIII, 1711–28.
Egypt. Political affairs; 26 May 1882. 3rd ser. CCLXIX, 1711–32.
Egypt. Question re Anglo-French intervention; 16 June 1882. 3rd ser. CCLXX, 1418–22.
Egypt. Questions re military intervention; 18 July 1882. 3rd ser. CCLXXI, 893–922.
Lords. Egypt—Granville's statement; 24 July 1882. 3rd ser. CCLXXI, 1484–523.
Supply—Strengthening of forces in Mediterranean; 24, 25, 26, 27 July 1882, 3rd ser. CCLXXI, 1574–619, 1687–818, 1829–902, 1992–2108.
Egypt—Expense of Military Expedition; 27 July 1882. 3rd ser. CCLXXII, 2116–8.
Egypt—Expense of Military Expedition; 31 July 1882. 3rd ser. CCLXXIII, 255–307.

Egypt—State of public opinion; 10 Aug. 1882. 3rd ser. CCLXXIII, 1384–400.
Egyptian Political Affairs—Consolidated Fund (Appropriation) Bill; 15 Aug. 1882.
    3rd ser. CCLXXIII, 1875–959.
Lords. Debate on Address; 15, 16 Feb. 1883. 3rd ser. CCLXXVI, 7–64, 154–64.
Commons' Debate on Address; 15, 16 Feb. 1883. 3rd. ser., CCLXXIII, 90–154,
    178–250.
Egypt. Expense of military operations—Resolutions; 2 March 1883. 3rd ser.
    CCLXXVI, 1300–27.
Egypt. Grant-in-aid of Expedition; 2 March 1883. 3rd ser. CCLXXVI, 1327–63.
Africa. Bright's Resolution on Congo; 3 April 1883. 3rd ser. CCLXXVII, 1284–332.
Lords. British Possessions Abroad—Royal Commission; 4 May 1883. 3rd ser.
    CCLXXVIII, 202–59.
Lords. Defence of Colonies, Colonial Naval Forces—Motion; 10 July 1883. 3rd.
    ser. CCLXXXI, 932–50.
Suez Canal Company—Northcote's Motion; 30 July 1883. 3rd ser. CCLXXXII,
    962–1055.
Self-governing Colonies—Power of Raising Military and Naval Forces; 20 Aug.
    1883. 3rd ser. CCLXXXIII, 1345–6.
Government Policy—Debate on the Address; 5 Feb. 1884. 3rd ser. CCLXXXIV,
    40–94.
Egypt. Events in Soudan—Vote of censure; 12, 14, 15, 18, 19 Feb. 1884. 3rd ser.
    CCLXXXIV, 684–762, 896–979, 1025–114, 1208–47, 1353–462.
Lords. Egypt, Events in Soudan—Vote of Censure; 12 Feb. 1884. 3rd ser.
    CCLXXXIV, 567–658.
Egypt. Eastern Soudan, Military Operations; 15 March 1884. 3rd ser. CCLXXXV,
    1653–729.
Madagascar. Protection of British Interests and Subjects; 26 March 1884. 3rd ser.
    CCLXXXVI, 794–8.
Jamaica. Legislative Council, Constitutional Reform; 25 April 1884. 3rd ser.
    CCLXXXVII, 691–724.
Lords. Malta. Constitution and Administration; 29 April 1884. 3rd ser. CCLXXXVII,
    840–2.
Lords. Trade and Commerce—Motion for Select Committee; 6 Nov. 1884. 3rd
    ser. CCXCIII, 1044–82.
Lords. Defence of Colonial Possessions—Carnarvon's Observations; 13 Nov. 1884.
    3rd ser. CCXCIII, 1534–56.
Egypt. Soudan—Northcote's Censure Motion; 23, 24, 26, 27 Feb. 1885. 3rd ser.
    CCXCIV, 1052–144, 1193–263, 1425–519, 1627–719.
Lords. Egypt, Soudan—Salisbury's Censure Motion; 20, 26 Feb. 1885. 3rd ser.
    CCXCIV, 1311–94, 1523–97.
Heligoland. Proposed Cession to Germany—Gorst's Observations; 30 March
    1885. 3rd ser. CCXCVI, 1010–18.
Supply—Foreign and Colonial Office Votes; 17 Sept. 1886. 3rd ser. CCCIX, 892–
    934.
Debate on the Address; 31 Jan., 1, 3 Feb. 1887. 3rd ser. CCCX, 274–365, 394–530,
    557–735.
Supply—Foreign and Colonial Services; 6 Sept. 1887. 3rd ser. CCCXX, 1404–55.
Protection of the Empire—Observations; 5 March 1888. 3rd ser. CCCXXIII, 229–
    313.
Liquor Traffic in British Dependencies—Resolution; 24 April 1888. 3rd ser.
    CCCXXV, 391–431.
Lords. Imperial Defence; 29 June 1888. 3rd ser. CCCXXVII, 1677–711.
Lords. East Central Africa—Questions and Observations; 6 July 1888. 3rd ser.
    CCCXXVIII, 536–57.
Debate on the Address; 21, 22, 26 Feb. 1889. 3rd ser. CCXXXIII, 35–107, 140–212,
    269–480.

Lords. Colonial Conference of 1887—Motion; 25 March 1889. 3rd ser. CCCXXXIV, 657–79.

Slave Trade—S. Buxton's Motion; 26 March 1889. 3rd ser. CCCXXXIV, 886–927.

Lords. Liquor Traffic among Africans—Westminster's Observations; 6 May 1889. 3rd ser. CCCXXXV, 1194–219.

Lords. Egypt. Military Operations against Dervishes—Carnarvon's Observations; 12 Aug. 1889. 3rd ser. CCCXXXIX, 993–1005.

Debate on the Address; 12, 13 Feb. 1890. 3rd ser. CCCXLI, 123–64, 262–93.

Lords. Portugal and East Africa—Harrowby's Observations; 16 May 1890. 3rd ser. CCCXLIV, 1094–104.

Lords. Anglo-German Agreement Bill; 10 July 1890. 3rd ser. CCCXLVI, 1258–92.

Anglo-German Agreement Bill; 24, 25 July, 1890. 3rd ser. CCCXLVII, 743–835, 907–83.

Lords. Colonies, Conference on Imperial Trade and Defence—Motion; 12 Feb. 1891. 3rd ser. CCCL, 433–53.

Colonies. Conference on Imperial Trade and Defence—Vincent's Motion; 17 Feb. 1891. 3rd ser. CCCL, 908–44.

Supply—Army Estimates, Imperial Defence; 23 Feb. 1891. 3rd ser. CCCL, 1382–463.

Sea Commerce. British Colonies and Dependencies—Colomb's Motion; 2 March 1891. 3rd ser. CCCL, 1948–78.

Supply—Army Estimates, Imperial Defence; 5 March 1891. 3rd ser. CCCLI, 297–339.

Supply—Civil Service, South and West African Charges; 9 March 1891. 3rd ser. CCCLI, 532–69.

Supply—Foreign Office and Colonial Office Votes; 16 March 1891. 3rd ser. CCCLI, 1120–76.

Supply—Colonial Office Vote; 10 July 1891. 3rd ser. CCCLV, 935–62.

Lords. Debate on the Address; 9 Feb. 1892. 4th ser. I, 6–38.

Debate on the Address; 9 Feb. 1892. 4th ser. I, 43–154.

Supply—Civil Service Estimates, Imperial British East Africa Company; 3 March 1892. 4th ser. I, 1836–83.

Supply—Civil Service Estimates, Uganda Railway Survey Vote; 4 March 1892. 4th ser. II, 50–91.

Chartered Companies in Africa; 23 May 1892. 4th ser. IV, 1525–6.

Polynesian Labour in Queensland; 26 May 1892. 4th ser. IV, 1961–2000.

Lords. Disturbances in Uganda—Observations; 13 June 1892. 4th ser. V, 825–31.

Debate on the Address, 8, 11 Aug. 1892. 4th ser. VII, 195–304, 332–430.

Lords. Queen's Speech; 31 Jan 1893. 4th ser. VIII, 2–4.

Debate on the Address; 31 Jan., 2, 3, 6, 7, 8, 9, 10, 11 Feb. 1893. 4th ser. VIII, 6–48, 57–163, 256–351, 357–82, 429–500, 559–650, 691–770, 774–839, 915–1012, 1066–151, 1154–222.

Uganda—Labouchere's Motion; 20 March 1893. 4th ser. X, 539–605.

Supply—Egypt—Dilke's Motion for Evacuation; 1 May 1893. 4th ser. XI, 1634–81.

Supply—Foreign Office and Colonial Office Vote; 7, 8 Sept. 1893. 4th ser. XVII, 485–555, 676–706.

Matabeleland—Labouchere's Motion; 9 Nov. 1893. 4th ser. XVIII, 543–627.

Debate on the Address; 12, 13, 14 March 1894. 4th ser. XXII, 4–125, 163–254, 257–67.

Supply—Civil Service Estimates; 15 March 1894. 4th ser. XXII, 391–429.

Opium Commission—Pease's Motion; 1 June 1894. 4th ser. XXV, 181–270.

Supply. Civil Service Estimates—Uganda Vote; 1 June 1899. 4th ser. XXV, 181–270.

Debate on the Address—Imperial Customs Union; 5 Feb. 1895. 4th ser. XXX, 110–28.

Lords. Uganda; 14 Feb. 1895. 4th ser. XXX, 693–706.

Local Legislative Assemblies—Observations; 29 March 1895. 4th ser. XXXII, 523–60.

Opium Commission—Please's Motion; 24 May 1895. 4th ser. xxxiv, 278–324.
Supply—War Office Vote; 21 June 1895. 4th ser. xxxiv, 1673–712.
Supply—Colonial Office Vote; 22 Aug. 1895. 4th ser. xxxvi, 630–52.
Lords. Debate on the Address; 11 Feb. 1896. 4th ser. xxxvii, 9–61.
Commons' Debate on the Address; 11, 12, 13, 14, 17 Feb. 1896. 4th ser. xxxvii, 73–164, 168–216, 242–332, 361–436, 468–536, 569–628.
Supply—Supplementary Vote for Colonial Services; 28 Feb. 1896. 4th ser. xxxvii, 1406–20.
Army Supplementary Estimates, 1895–6—Ashanti Expedition; 12 March 1896. 4th ser. xxxviii, 785–849.
Occupation of Egypt—Motion; 13 March 1896. 4th ser. xxxviii, 894–8.
Defence of the Empire—Observations; 13 March 1896. 4th ser. xxxviii, 898–944.
Military Expedition to Dongola—Government Statement; 16 March 1896. 4th ser. xxxviii, 1027–60.
Supply—Civil Service, Egypt and Soudan; 20 March 1896. 4th ser. xxxviii, 1478–574.
Supply—Civil Service, East Africa; 27 March 1896. 4th ser. xxxix, 311–59.
Uganda Railway—Motion for grant from Consolidated Fund; 2 July 1896. 4th ser. xliii, 553–70.
Uganda Railway Bill. Committee stage; 30 July 1896. 4th ser. xliii, 1094–1109.
Lords. Debate on the Address; 19 Jan. 1897. 4th ser. xlv, 1–36.
Commons' Debate on the Address; 19, 20, 21, 22, 25, 26 Jan. 1897. 4th ser. xlv, 42–120, 123–71, 201–68, 305–76, 411–87, 517–98.
Supply—Egyptian Expedition, 1896–7; 5 Feb. 1897; 4th ser. xlv, 1439–522.
Supply—Maintenance of Military Forces for Defence of Empire; 8 Feb. 1897. 4th ser. xlv, 1565–636.
Supply—Africa and European Powers; 2 April 1897. 4th ser. xlviii, 425–50.
Supply—Vote, Colonial Services including Uganda, Central and East Africa; 24, 25 June 1897. 4th ser. l, 545–56, 626.
Supply—Colonial Office Vote; 19 July 1897. 4th ser. li, 479–506.
Lords. Debate on Address—Egypt and Empire Defence; 7 Feb. 1899. 4th ser. lxvi, 3–34.
Supply—Army Supplementary Estimates, Egypt and Soudan; 24 Feb. 1899. 4th ser. lxvii, 456–569.
Supply—Foreign Office and African colonies; 27 Feb. 1899. 4th ser. lxvii, 650–62, 700–47.
Civil Services (Supplementary Estimates)—East Africa; 10 March 1899. 4th ser. lxviii, 450–81.
Navy (Supplementary Estimates)—Imperial Defence; 10, 13, 16 March 1899. 4th ser. lxviii, 503–8, 573–659, 997–1106.
Supply—Colonial Vote; 20 March 1899. 4th ser. lxviii, 1348–93.
Supply—East Africa and Uganda; 10 April 1899. 4th ser. lxix, 693–725.
Supply—Soudan, grant to Lord Kitchener; 5 June 1899. 4th ser. lxxii, 327–406.
Lords. Motion of thanks to Lord Kitchener; 8 June 1899. 4th ser. lxxii, 599–610.
Lords. Debate on Address; 30 Jan. 1900. 4th ser. lxxviii, 5–44.
Commons' Debate on Address; 30, 31 Jan., 1, 2, 5, 6, 7, 8, 9 Feb. 1900. 4th ser. lxxviii, 71–156, 164–232, 295–400, 451–548, 590–684, 731–828, 830–96, 942–1016, 1066–1159.
Supplementary Estimates—Central and East Africa; 22 Feb. 1900. 4th ser. lxxix, 876–908.
Colonial representation in imperial Parliament—Resolution; 3 April 1900. 4th ser. lxxxi, 1131–54.
Uganda Railway Bill; 14 May 1900. 4th ser. lxxxiii, 105–46.
Imperial telegraphic communication—Resolution; 22 May 1900. 4tn ser. lxxxiii, 969–1011.

Supply—Foreign Office Vote, East Africa, Zanzibar, Slavery; 15 June 1900. 4th ser. LXXXIV, 216–42.

Supply—Colonial Office Vote; 15 June 1900. 4th ser. LXXXIV, 245–7.

Lords. Proposed Colonial Naval Reserve; 19 July 1900. 4th ser. LXXXVI, 435–48.

Colonial Office Vote, including Emigration Grant; 25 July 1900. 4th ser. LXXXVI, 1164–264.

Army. Supplementary Estimate, 1900–1. South Africa, China; 27 July 1900; 4th ser. LXXXVI, 1525–640.

Supply—Colonial Office vote, including Emigration Grant; 3 Aug. 1900. 4th ser. LXXXVII, 661–734.

Lords. Debate on the Address; 6 Dec. 1900. 4th ser. LXXXVIII, 19–54.

Commons' Debate on the Address; Colonial Affairs in General, British Interests in China, etc.; 6, 7, 10 Dec. 1900. 4th ser. LXXXVIII, 97–198, 221–322, 359–486.

Army. Supplementary Estimate, 1900–1—South Africa, China, Imperial Defence; 11, 12 Dec. 1900. 4th ser. LXXXVIII, 512–98, 612–60.

Civil Service Estimates—Foreign Office Vote; 26 July 1901. 4th ser. XCVIII, 247–332.

Pacific Cable—Enabling Resolution; 30, 31 July 1901. 4th ser. XCVIII, 681–96, 773–84.

Supply—Grant to Lord Roberts; 31 July 1901. 4th ser. XCVIII, 698–762.

Navy Estimates—Resolution *re* colonial contribution; 31 July 1901. 4th ser. XCVIII, 761–72.

Civil Service Estimates—Colonial Vote; 2 Aug. 1901. 4th ser. XCVIII, 1094–1196.

Pacific Cable Bill; 13 Aug. 1901. 4th ser. XCIX, 627–50.

Lords. Debate on Address; 16 Jan. 1902. 4th ser. CI, 2–42.

Commons' Debate on Address—Colonial Affairs; 16, 20, 21, 22 Jan. 1902. 4th ser. CI, 86–164, 323–436, 471–572, 574–643.

Commons' Debate on Address—English Language in Malta; 28 Jan. 1902. 4th ser. CI, 1168–208.

Anglo-Japanese Agreement—Motion; 13 Feb. 1902, 4th ser. CII, 1272–313.

Supply—Navy Estimates, Imperial Defence; 20 June 1902. 4th ser. CIX, 1257–326.

Supply—Colonial Office Vote, including expenses connected with Emigration; 29 July 1902. 4th ser. CXII, 23–91.

Supply—Supplementary Colonial Vote, including grant in aid of sugar industry in West Indies; 31 July 1902. 4th ser. CXII, 290–328.

Brussels Sugar Convention—Resolution for ratification; 24 Nov. 1902. 4th ser. CXV, 251–72.

Lords. School teaching of Empire history and geography—Proposed Empire Day; 1 Dec. 1902. 4th ser. CXV, 813–23.

Uganda Railway Grant—Resolutions in Committee; 9, 11 Dec. 1902. 4th ser. CXVI, 501–36, 923–58.

Lords. Debate on Address—Colonial and Foreign Affairs; 17 Feb. 1903. 4th ser. CXVIII, 2–34.

Commons' Debate on Address—British interests in China and Persia; 18 Feb. 1903. 4th ser. CXVIII, 203–47.

Lords. Venezuela and U.S.A.—Motion; 2 March 1903. 4th ser. CXVIII, 1043–88.

Civil Service Estimates—Grant in Aid of East Africa; 2 March 1903. 4th ser. CXVIII, 1186–204.

Committee of Imperial Defence—Motion; 5 March 1903. 4th ser. CXVIII, 1578–649.

British and Colonial Trade—Resolution; 17 March 1903. 4th ser. CXIX, 1069–84.

Supply—Colonial Office Vote; 19 March 1903. 4th ser. CXIX, 1240–93.

Consolidated Fund Bill—Native Labour in Africa; 24 March 1903. 4th ser. CXX, 67–118.

Great Britain and the Persian Gulf—Motion; 5 May 1903. 4th ser. CXXI, 1329–54.

Congo Free State—Motion; 20 May 1903. 4th ser. CXXII, 1289–1332.

Fiscal Policy of the Country—Motion; 28 May 1903. 4th ser. CXXIII, 141–98.

Lords. Fiscal Policy of the Country—Motion by Goschen; 15 June 1903. 4th ser. CXXIII, 837–921.

New South Wales and Preferential Tariffs—Motion; 17 June 1903. 4th ser. CXXIII, 1241–78.

Colonial Conference—Question *re* publication of proceedings; 22 June 1903. 4th ser. CXXIV, 63.

Colonial Conference—Further Question *re* publication of proceedings; 8 July 1903. 4th ser. CXXV, 22–23.

Lords. Preferential Tariffs, Position of India—Motion; 10 July 1903. 4th ser. CXXV, 272–302.

Lords. Fiscal Policy—Question; 13 July 1903. 4th ser. CXXV, 379–84.

Sugar Convention Bill; 28, 29 July, 4, 5 August, 1903. 4th ser. CXXVI, 587–668, 690–808, 1527–68, 1593–710.

Lords. Debate on Address; 2 Feb. 1904. 4th ser. CXXIX, 2–51.

Commons' Debate on Address—Colonial and Foreign Affairs; 2, 8 Feb. 1904. 4th ser. CXXIX, 106–82, 600–23.

Debate on Address—Fiscal Policy; 8, 9, 10, 11, 12, 15 Feb. 1904. 4th ser. CXXIX, 623–708, 735–840, 854–960, 1040–136, 1199–256, 1340–452.

Lords. Fiscal Policy—Motion; 18, 19 Feb. 1904. 4th ser. CXXX, 132–227, 348–442.

Lords. Crown Agents for the Colonies—Question; 25 Feb. 1904. 4th ser. CXXX, 946–61.

Brussels Sugar Convention—Motion; 2 March 1904. 4th ser. CXXX, 1545–84.

Fiscal Policy—Motion; 9 March 1904, 4th ser. CXXXI, 652–700.

Lords—Fiscal Question; 14 March 1904; 4th ser. CXXXI, 919–48.

Cotton growing in Africa—Motion; 27 April 1904. 4th ser. CXXXIII, 1367–404.

Anglo-French Convention Bill; 1 June 1904. 4th ser. CXXXV, 499–577.

Supply—Foreign Office Vote—conditions in tropical Africa; 9 June 1904. 4th ser. CXXXV, 1236–96.

Lords. Crown Agents for the Colonies—Motion; 10 June 1904. 4th ser. CXXXV, 1328–63.

Civil Service Estimates—Colonial Office Vote; 21 July 1904; 4th ser. CXXXVIII, 789–884.

Estimates—Expenses of Committee of Imperial Defence; 2 Aug. 1904. 4th ser. CXXXIX, 601–50.

Lords. Debate on Address—Fiscal Policy, etc.; 14 Feb. 1905. 4th ser. CXLI, 1–38.

Commons' Debate on Address—Fiscal Policy, Coolie Labour, etc.; 14, 15, 16, 17 Feb. 1905; 4th ser. CLXI, 108–68, 178–276, 329–428, 481–540.

Debate on Address—Brussels Sugar Convention; 28 Feb. 1905. 4th ser. CXLI, 1494–586.

Preferential Trading with the Colonies—Motion; 8 March 1905. 4th ser. CXLII, 805–56.

Estimates—Colonial Vote—Education of Tamil children in Ceylon, Trade with Marshall Islands, etc.; 20 March 1905. 4th ser. CXLIII, 541–82.

Estimates—Colonial Vote—Protectionist proposals; 22 March 1905. 4th ser. CXLIII, 881–918.

Free Imports and Shipping Trade—Motion; 29 March 1905. 4th ser. CXLIII, 1608–46.

Lords. Germany and British traders in Marshall Islands—Motion; 4 April 1905. 4th ser. CXLIV, 288–92.

Lords. Proposed Colonial Conference—Motion; 11 April 1905. 4th ser. CXLIV, 1159–244.

Estimates—Statement by Prime Minister on Defence; 11 May 1905. 4th ser. CXLVI, 61–129.

Lords. Indentured labourers in Colonies—Motion; 15 May 1905. 4th ser. CXLVI, 246–53.

West Indian Administration—Motion; 17 May 1905. 4th ser. CXLVI, 694–724.

Lords. Fiscal policy, Colonial Conference—Motion; 5 June 1905. 4th ser. CXLVII, 629–64.

Lords. Importation and sale of liquor in West Africa —Motion; 6 June 1905. 4th ser. CXLVII, 826–45.

Lords. Tariff Reform—Motion; 27 July 1905. 4th ser. CL, 471–78.

Lords. Colonial Appeals to Judicial Committee of Privy Council—Motion; 31 July 1905. 4th ser. CL, 893–6.

Lords. Debate on Address—Colonial Conference, Algeciras, etc.; 19 Feb. 1906. 4th ser. CLII, 21–66.

Commons' Debate on Address—Colonial and Fiscal Policy, etc.; 19, 20 Feb. 1906. 4th ser. CLII, 140–204, 217–82.

Lords. Fiscal Question—Motion; 22 Feb. 1906. 4th ser. CLII, 456–86.

Free trade and fiscal reform—Motion; 12, 13 March 1906. 4th ser. CLIII, 944–1052, 1124–88.

Lords. Cotton-growing in the Empire—Motion; 10 May 1906. 4th ser. CLVI, 1422–43.

Lords. Imperial Defence—Motion by Lord Roberts; 10 July 1906. 4th ser. CLX, 656–700.

Lords. Debate on Address—Imperial affairs, etc.; 12 Feb. 1907. 4th ser. CLXIX, 2–39.

Commons' Debate on Address—Imperial affairs—Coolie labour, etc.; 12, 13 Feb. 1907. 4th ser. CLXIX, 58–152, 160–270.

Debate on Address—Imperial defence; 15 Feb. 1907. 4th ser. CLXIX, 453–92.

Lords. Cabling to colonies of ministerial speeches; 19 Feb. 1907. 4th ser. CLXIX, 674–88.

Commons' Debate on Address—Colonial Conference and imperial trade; 19, 20 Feb. 1907. 4th ser. CLXIX, 723–812, 863–976.

Estimates—Organisation of the Colonial Conference, Africa, New Hebrides, etc. 11 March 1907. 4th ser. CLXX, 1278–376.

Consolidated Fund (No. 1) Bill—Colonial Affairs—Transvaal, Newfoundland Fisheries, Ceylon, Hong Kong, Malaya; 18 March 1907. 4th ser. CLXXI, 490–582.

Lords. British East Africa—Motion for papers; 27 June 1907. 4th ser. CLXXVII, 8–30.

Colonial Preference—Resolution; 15 July 1907; 4th ser. CLXXVIII, 363–464.

Lords. Fiji—Motion for papers; 16 July 1907; 4th ser. CLXXVIII, 473–83.

Commons' Debate on Address—Reform of Imperial Fiscal System; 18, 19 Feb. 1909. 5th ser. I, 237–326, 336–404.

Debate on Address—Congo; 25 Feb. 1909. 5th ser. I, 943–60.

Naval policy and defence of Empire—vote of censure; 29 March 1909. 5th ser. III, 39–150.

Motion on adjournment—International naval conference: Declaration of London; 7 April 1909. 5th ser. III, 1163–209.

Motion on adjournment—Colonial and Foreign Affairs—Native policy and protectorates; 27 May 1909. 5th ser. V, 1378–424.

Supply—Colonial Office Vote. East Africa, etc.; 27 July 1909. 5th ser. VIII, 1027–138.

Supply—Navy and Army Expenditure Imperial defence; 29 July 1909. 5th ser. VIII, 1367–432.

Consolidated Fund Bill—Egyptian administration; 13, 15 June 1910. 5th ser. XVII, 1103–63, 1366–76.

Supply—Colonial Office Vote—Relations with Dominions, India and Colonies; 29 June 1910. 5th ser. XVIII, 956–1072.

Consolidated Fund Bill—Colonial Preference; 21 July 1910. 5th ser. xix, 1453–525.

Appropriation Bill—Situation in Egypt; 21 July 1910. 5th ser. xix, 1554–93.

Commons Debate on Address—Canada and Imperial Preference; 8, 9 Feb. 1911. 5th ser. xxi, 293–398, 456–564.

Imperial Conference, constitution and procedure—Motion; 19 April 1911. 5th ser. xxiv, 957–1000.

Motion on Adjournment—Tariff Reform and trade with Dominions; 31 May 1911. 5th ser. xxvi, 1111–35.

Commons Debate on Address—Fiscal Reform and imperial relations; 22 Feb. 1912. 5th ser. xxxiv, 748–866.

Sugar duties—Motion; 15 May 1912. 5th ser. xxxviii, 1212–33.

Supply—Colonial Office Vote—Position and prospects of Crown Colonies and Protectorates; 27 June 1912; 5th ser. xl, 503–620.

Supply—Treasury vote: Committee of Imperial Defence; 25 July 1912. 5th ser. xli, 1384–502.

Supply—Colonial Services: East Africa, Cyprus, etc.; 29 July 1912. 5th ser. xli, 1671–720.

Tariff reform—Motion; 2 April 1913. 5th ser. li, 475–522.

Soudan Loan Guarantee—Motion; 23 April 1913. 5th ser. lii, 417–54.

Soudan Loan Guarantee—Resolution; 25 June 1913. 5th ser. liv, 1101–27.

Imperial Wireless Chain—Motion on adjournment; 16 July 1913. 5th ser. lv, 1342–92.

Supply—Colonial Office Vote—Export and production of raw materials in Crown Colonies; 31 July 1913. 5th ser. lvi, 777–868.

Supplementary Estimates—Events in Somaliland—Motion; 24 Feb. 1914. 5th ser. lviii, 1619–92.

Imperial defences—Motion; 17 March 1914. 5th ser. lix, 1967–2014.

Mediterranean—Political and strategic position—Motion; 18 March 1914. 5th ser. lix, 2154–99.

British citizens' rights and the Empire—Motion; 1 April 1914. 5th ser. lx, 1270–313.

East African Protectorates Loan Bill—Committee stage; 14, 15 April 1914. 5th ser. lxi, 33–156, 183–92.

Supply. Foreign Office Vote. Persian Gulf and imperial communications—Motion; 29 June 1914, 5th ser. lxiv, 53–129.

Supply—Colonial Office Vote—Defence of colonies during War; 21 July 1915. 5th ser. lxxiii, 1512–63.

Supply—Colonial Office Vote—Malaya, Ceylon, East and West Africa, etc.; 3 Aug. 1916. 5th ser. lxxxv, 529–640.

Nigeria—Sale of enemy property—Resolution; 8 Nov. 1916; 5th ser. lxxxvii, 249–368.

Supply—Colonial Office Vote—Administration of crown colonies and dependencies; 14 Aug. 1917. 5th ser. xcvii, 991–1057.

Supply—Foreign Office Vote—Affairs in Egypt; 15 May 1919. 5th ser. cxv, 1829–909.

PART II

OTHER WORKS

1. GENERAL BIBLIOGRAPHY

(a) BIBLIOGRAPHIES AND GUIDES

ADAM, M. I., EWING, J. and MUNRO, J. *Guide to the principal Parliamentary Papers relating to the Dominions, 1812–1911.* Edinburgh, 1913. Highly selective.

COLONIAL OFFICE LIBRARY. *Catalogue of the Printed Books in the Library of the Colonial Office.* 1896. *Supplement,* 1907. Appendix F, *Reports,* 1921.

—— *Catalogue of the Maps, Plans and Charts in the Library of the Colonial Office.* 1910. Most of those prior to 1885 have been transferred to the Public Record Office.

COMMONWEALTH RELATIONS OFFICE. *Guide to the India Office Library.* 1952.

CRAVEN, W. F. "Historical Study of the British Empire. (Bibliographical Article.)" *Jour. Mod. Hist.* vol. VI (1934), pp. 40–69.

FORD, P. and G. *Guide to Parliamentary Papers.* 2nd edn. Oxford, 1956.

FREWER, L. B. *Bibliography of Historical Writings published in Great Britain and the Empire, 1940–1945.* Oxford, 1947.

—— *Rhodes House, its function and resources.* Oxford, 1956. Offprint from *Bodleian Library Record,* vol. VI, no. 6 (Oct. 1956).

GIUSEPPI, M. S. *A Guide to the Manuscripts preserved in the Public Record Office.* 2 vols. 1923–4. Information regarding Colonial Office, Foreign Office and other relative material is in vol. II and in many ways supplements the printed and typed Public Record Office *Lists and Indexes.* The *Report of the Committee on Departmental Records* [Cmd. 9163], pt. II, gives information on the selection of "modern departmental records for preservation".

GREGORY, W. (Ed.). *List of the Serial Publications of Foreign Governments, 1815–1931.* New York, 1932. Includes those of Great Britain, Commonwealth countries and dependencies.

GRIFFIN, A. P. C. *List of Books, with References to Periodicals, relating to the Theory of Colonization.* 2nd rev. edn. Washington, 1901.

GRIFFIN, G. G. and others. *Writings on American History, 1902– .* Washington, etc.; 1904– . In progress. Annual bibliography, with sections devoted to Canada, the West Indies, foreign relations, etc.

HER MAJESTY'S STATIONERY OFFICE. *Government Publications. Sectional List,* no. 24. Record Publications. 3rd edn. H.M.S.O. 1956. Notes the series of Lists and Indexes of Public Record Office documents, calendars of state papers and other record publications. *See also* Horrocks, *The State as Publisher* (1952).

HEWITT, A. R. *Guide to Resources for Commonwealth Studies in London, Oxford and Cambridge.* Inst. of Commonwealth Studies, 1957.

HISTORICAL ASSOCIATION. *Annual Bulletin of Historical Literature,* no. 1 (1911)–1912– . In progress. Highly selective sections on British imperial history.

LEWIN, E. *Best Books on the British Empire: a Bibliographical Guide for Students.* (Royal Empire Soc. Bibliographies, No. 12.) 2nd edn. 1945.

—— *Subject Catalogue of the Library of the Royal Empire Society, formerly the Royal Colonial Institute.* Vols. I–IV. 1930–7. Much of the Society's library was destroyed in the War of 1939–45 and, although many works have been replaced, the catalogue is no longer a guide to the Library, but remains valuable as a bibliography, particularly for references to pamphlets and articles in periodicals.

LONDON SCHOOL OF ECONOMICS AND POLITICAL SCIENCE. *London Bibliography of the Social Sciences.* Vols. 1–9. 1931–55. Contents of the Library of the School, up to 1950. Much on imperial history, economics and political theory.

MARTINEAU, A. (Ed.). *Bibliographie d'histoire coloniale (1900–30).* Soc. de l'Hist. des Colonies françaises, 1932. Section on British works published during those years.

MAXWELL, L. F. *A Bibliography of the Law of British Colonies, Protectorates and Mandated Territories.* (Being vol. VII of Sweet and Maxwell's *Legal Bibliography.*) 1949. Supplement issued 1954.

MILNE, A. T. *Writings on British History, 1934–* . Royal Historical Society, 1937–. In progress. Comprehensive annual bibliography, including sections on relations with Commonwealth countries.

MINISTRY OF DEFENCE. JOINT INTELLIGENCE BUREAU. *Guide to Government Libraries and other Libraries and Information Bureaux.* 8th edn. 1955. Restricted in circulation; useful indication of resources of Colonial Office and other departmental libraries.

MORRELL, W. P. *A Select List of Books relating to the History of the British Commonwealth and Empire Overseas.* (Historical Association Pamphlet, no. 130.) 1944. Supersedes earlier editions prepared by A. P. Newton and others.

PERHAM, MARGERY. *Colonial Government. An annotated reading list.* Oxford, Nuffield College, 1950. Historical sections.

PUBLIC RECORD OFFICE. *List of Colonial Office Records* [to 1837] *preserved in the Public Record Office.* 1911. Supplemented by typescript lists (see above, p. 772).

PULLING, A. *The Law Reports. Index to Orders in Council, Proclamations, etc., 1880–83.* 1885.

RAGATZ, L. J. *A List of Books and Articles on Colonial History and Overseas Expansion published in the United States, 1900–1930.* Ann Arbor, 1939. Supplements for 1931–35. In progress.

—— *The Literature of European Imperialism, 1815–1939.* 3rd edn. Washington, 1947.

—— *A Bibliography for the Study of European History, 1815 to 1939.* Ann Arbor, 1942. Supplements 1–3 (1943–55). Sections on "European Imperialism in General", on "The British Empire" and on "International Relations".

RAGATZ, L. J. and J. E. *A Bibliography of Articles, Descriptive, Historical and Scientific, on Colonies and other Dependent Territories, appearing in American Geographical and Kindred Journals.* 2 vols. Washington, 1951.

ROYAL GEOGRAPHICAL SOCIETY. *Catalogue of the Library.* 1895. Supplements (quarterly). Index to Supplements, 1938.

SACKS, B. *Bibliography for the British Empire.* Albuquerque, 1946.

SCIENCE MUSEUM. *An Exhibition of Charts and Maps illustrating the Cartography of the British Empire.* 1928.

STAVELEY, R. (Ed.). *Government Information and the Research Worker.* Library Assoc., 1952. Chapter XXIV is on the "Colonial Office and Commonwealth Relations Office", by A. B. Mitchell.

STREIT, R. *et alt. Bibliotheca Missionum.* Vols. 18–20. *Afrikanische Missionsliteratur, 1809–1940.* Vol. 21. *Missionsliteratur von Australien und Ozeanien, 1525–1940.* Freiburg, 1953–6.

TAYLOR, C. R. H. *A Pacific Bibliography.* Wellington: Polynesian Soc., 1951.

WORK, M. N. *A Bibliography of the Negro in Africa and America.* New York, 1928.

(b) PERIODICALS

The following periodicals are those which have most frequently dealt with colonial affairs in general. Specialist journals are noted elsewhere. For British newspapers consult *The Times Tercentenary Handlist of English and Welsh Newspapers, Magazines and Reviews* [1620–1920], 2 vols. 1920. Newspapers most concerned with imperial matters were *The Times,* the *Standard,* the *Morning Post,* the *Daily Telegraph,* the *Daily Chronicle,* the *Daily Mail,* the *Daily News,* the *Financial Times,* the *Pall Mall*

Gazette, the *Westminster Gazette*, the *Birmingham Post*, the *Manchester Guardian*, the *Yorkshire Post*, the *South Wales Daily News*, the *Scotsman*, the *Glasgow Herald*, *The Irish Times* and the weekly *Sunday Times* and *Observer*.

American Historical Review. New York, etc. 1895– . In progress.
Annual Register, New Series. London, 1864– . In progress.
Archives. British Records Association, 1949– . In progress.
Blackwood's Magazine. Edinburgh, London, 1817– . In progress.
Board of Trade Journal. London, 1877– . In progress.
Bulletin of the Imperial Institute. London, 1903– . In progress.
Bulletin of the Institute of Historical Research. London, 1923– . In progress.
Bulletin of the School of Oriental and African Studies. London, 1917– . In progress.
Cambridge Historical Journal. Cambridge, 1923–57. Continued as *Historical Journal*, 1958– .
Canadian Historical Association. *Reports*: Ottawa, 1915– . In progress. *Canadian Historical Review*. Toronto, 1920– . In progress.
Chambers' Journal. Edinburgh, 1832–1955.
Colonial Office Journal. London, 1907–10. Continued as *Colonial Journal*, 1913–20.
Colonial Office List. London, 1862–1925. Continued as the *Dominions Office and Colonial Office List*, 1926–40. Resumed as *Colonial Office List*, 1946. H.M.S.O. 1946– . In progress.
Commonwealth and Empire Review. London, 1901– . Title varies; vols. 1–78 (1901–44) as *Empire Review*. In progress.
Commonwealth Relations Office List, 1951– . H.M.S.O. 1951– . In progress.
Contemporary Review. London, 1866– . In progress.
Cornhill Magazine. London, 1860–1956.
Corona: the Journal of H.M. Colonial Service. London, 1949– . In progress.
Crown Colonist. London, 1931– . In progress.
Dublin Review. London, Dublin, 1836– . In progress.
Edinburgh Review. Edinburgh and London, 1802–1932.
Empire. Fabian Society, 1938– . In progress.
Empire Review. London, 1923– . In progress.
English Historical Review. London, 1886– . In progress.
Foreign Office List. London, 1852– . In progress.
Fortnightly Review. London, 1865– . In progress.
Fraser's Magazine. London, 1830–82.
Gentleman's Magazine. 303 vols. London, 1731–1907.
Geographical Journal. Royal Geographical Society, 1893– . In progress.
Geographical Review. Washington, American Geographical Society, 1916– . In progress.
Geography. Geographical Association, 1901– . In progress.
Historical Studies, Australia and New Zealand. Melbourne, 1940– . In progress.
Historische Zeitschrift. Munich, etc., 1859– . In progress.
History, new series. Historical Association, 1916– . In progress.
History Today. London, 1950– . In progress.
International Affairs. Royal Institute of International Affairs, 1922– . In progress.
Irish Historical Studies. Dublin, Belfast, 1937– . In progress.
Journal of Modern History. Chicago, 1929– . In progress.
London Gazette. Oxford, London, 1665– . In progress.
Nation and Athenaeum, 48 vols. London, 1907–31.
National Review. London, 1883– . In progress.
New Statesman and Nation. London, 1913– . In progress. Title varies.
Nineteenth Century and After. 1877– . Title changed to *Twentieth Century*.
Notes and Queries. London, 1849– . In progress.
Pacific Historical Review. American Historical Association. Pacific Coast Branch, 1932– . In progress.

Politica. London School of Economics and Political Science, 1934– . In progress.
Political Science Quarterly. Boston, New York, 1886– . In progress.
Quarterly Review. London, 1809– . In progress.
Review of Reviews. London, 1890–1936. Later *World Review.*
Revue d'histoire des colonies. Paris, 1913– . In progress. Current title *Revue d'histoire coloniale.*
Revue historique. Paris, 1876– . In progress.
Round Table. London, 1910– . In progress.
Saturday Review. London, 1855–1937.
Scottish Historical Review, vols. 1–25, 26– . In progress. Edinburgh, 1903–28, 1946– . In progress.
Spectator, 1828– . In progress.
Statesman's Yearbook. London, 1864– . In progress.
Transactions of the Royal Historical Society. London, 1871– . In progress.
United Empire. London, 1909– . In progress. Supersedes *Journal and Proceedings of the Royal Colonial Institute* (1869–1909).
Whitaker's Almanack. London, 1868– . In progress.

(c) COLLECTED HISTORICAL RECORDS

For collections of printed sources relating to independent countries of the Commonwealth, see the bibliographies in *C.H.B.E.* vols. IV–VIII. Only the most comprehensive of these are given here.

BENNETT, G. (Ed.). *The Concept of Empire. Burke to Attlee, 1774–1947.* 1953.
COSTIN, W. C. and WATSON, J. S. (Eds.). *The Law and Working of the Constitution: Documents, 1660–1914.* 2 vols. 1952.
EGERTON, H. E. (Ed.). *Federations and Unions within the British Empire.* 2nd edn. Oxford, 1924.
FOREIGN OFFICE. *The Constitutions of all Countries.* Vol. I. *The British Empire.* H.M.S.O. 1938.
KEITH, (Sir) A. B. (Ed.). *Selected Speeches and Documents on British Colonial Policy, 1763–1917.* 2 vols. 1918. New edn. 1948.
—— *Speeches and Documents on the British Dominions, 1918–1931.* Oxford, 1932.
MADDEN, F. (Ed.). *Imperial Constitutional Documents, 1765–1952. A Supplement.* Oxford, 1953.
NEWTON, A. P. (Ed.). *Federal and Unified Constitutions.* 1923.
SIMMONS, J. (Ed.). *From Empire to Commonwealth. Principles of British Imperial Government.* [1942.] "Political anthology."
TREASURY. STATUTORY PUBLICATIONS OFFICE. Statutes revised. 3rd edn. 1950. 36 vols. [Complete collection of statutes to end of 1948, including *Index to the Statutes in Force at 31 Dec. 1948.*]
WIGHT, M. (Ed.). *British Colonial Constitutions.* Oxford, 1952.

(d) GENERAL HISTORIES AND DESCRIPTIVE WORKS

ADAMS, J. T. *Empire on the Seven Seas; the British Empire, 1784–1939.* New York, 1940.
CARRINGTON, C. E. *The British Overseas; Exploits of a Nation of Shopkeepers.* 1950.
CHEVALLIER, J. J. *L'Evolution de l'Empire britannique.* 2 vols. Paris, 1931.
CROKAERT, J. *Histoire du Commonwealth britannique.* Paris, 1949.
CURREY, C. H. *The British Commonwealth since 1815.* 2 vols. Sydney, 1950–1.
DEMANGEON, A. *The British Empire: a Study in Colonial Geography.* New York, 1925.
DOMVILLE-FIFE, C. W. (Ed.). *Encyclopaedia of the British Empire.* 3 vols. Bristol, 1924.
EGERTON, H. E. *Origin and Growth of Greater Britain.* Oxford, 1908. 2nd edn. 1920.
ELTON, O. (Lord). *Imperial Commonwealth.* 1940.
ENSOR, R. C. K. *England, 1780–1914.* Oxford, 1936. *Oxford History of England,* ed. G. N. Clark, vol. XIV.

FAIRGRIEVE, J. and YOUNG, E. *Human Geography: the Imperial Commonwealth.* 2 vols. 1931.

FAWCETT, C. B. *A Political Geography of the British Empire.* New York, 1933.

FORBES, A. H. *History of the British Dominions beyond the Seas, 1558–1910.* 1919.

GEORGE, H. B. *Historical Geography of the British Empire.* 7th edn. Revised by R. W. Jeffery. 1924.

GOOCH, G. P. *A History of our Time. 1885–1914.* 1946.

GRESSWELL, W. P. *The Growth and Administration of the British Colonies, 1837–97.* 1898.

GRETTON, R. H. *Modern History of the English People, 1880–1922.* 3 vols. 1912–29.

GUNN, H. (Ed.). *The British Empire. A Survey.* 12 vols. 1924.

HALÉVY, É. *A History of the English People in the Nineteenth Century.* Vol. IV, *Victorian Years, 1841–1895.* Vol. V, *Imperialism and the Rise of Labour, 1895–1905.* Vol. VI (2 parts), *The Rule of Democracy, 1905–14.* 2nd edn. 1951–2.

HALL, W. P. *Empire to Commonwealth. Thirty Years of British Imperial History.* New York, 1928. From 1890's.

HALL, W. P. and ALBION, R. G. *History of England and the British Empire.* Boston, 1937.

HANCOCK, (Sir) W. KEITH. *Survey of British Commonwealth Affairs.* 4 vols. Oxford, 1937–42.

HERBERTSON, A. J. and HOWARTH, O. J. R. (Eds.). *Oxford Survey of the British Empire.* 6 vols. Oxford, 1914.

HERBERTSON, A. J. and THOMPSON, R. L. *Geography of the British Empire.* 1912. 3rd edn. rev. by O. J. R. Howarth, Oxford, 1918.

HODSON, H. V. *Twentieth-century Empire.* 1948.

HUGHES, E. A. *Britain and Greater Britain in the 19th century.* Cambridge, 1920.

KEETON, G. W. (Ed.). *The British Commonwealth: the development of its laws and constitutions.* Vol. I. *The United Kingdom.* 1955. In progress.

KIRKMAN, F. B. B. *Growth of Greater Britain.* 1909.

KNAPLUND, P. *Britain: Commonwealth and Empire, 1901–1955.* New York, 1956.

—— *The British Empire, 1815–1939.* New York, 1942.

LEROY-BEAULIEU, P. *De la Colonisation chez les Peuples Modernes.* 2 vols. Paris, 1908.

LOW, Sir S. J., and SANDERS, L. C. *The History of England during the Reign of Victoria, 1837–1901.* 1913. Longman's *Political History of England*, ed. by W. Hunt and R. L. Poole, vol. XII.

LUCAS, Sir C. P. *Historical Geography of the British Empire.* 15 vols. Oxford, 1887–1923.

McCARTHY, J. *The History of Our Own Times.* 4 vols. 1899.

MacINNES, C. M. *The British Empire and Commonwealth, 1815–1949.* 1951.

MARRIOTT, Sir J. A. R. *The Evolution of the British Empire and Commonwealth.* 1939.

MAXWELL, Sir H. *A Century of Empire, 1801–1900.* 3 vols. 1909–11.

MORGAN DE BORNIER, J. *L'Empire britannique: son évolution politique et constitutionnelle.* Paris, 1930.

MUIR, R. *A Short History of the British Commonwealth.* Vol. II, *The Modern Commonwealth, 1763–1953.* 8th edn. 1954.

MULLETT, C. F. *The British Empire.* New York, 1938. Historical in treatment.

NEWTON, A. P. *A Hundred Years of the British Empire.* New edn. 1942.

NEWTON, A. P. and EWING, J. *The British Empire since 1783, its political, economic and social development.* New edn. 1939.

PAUL, H. *History of Modern England [1845–95].* 5 vols. 1904–6.

ROBERTSON, (Sir) C. G. and BARTHOLOMEW, J. G. *Historical and Modern Atlas of the British Empire.* New edn. 1924.

ROYAL INSTITUTE OF INTERNATIONAL AFFAIRS. *The British Empire. A Report...by a Study Group.* 2nd edn. Oxford, 1938.

SANDERSON, E. *The British Empire in the Nineteenth Century.* 6 vols. 1878–98.

SEELEY, Sir J. R. *The Expansion of England.* 1st edn. 1883. New edn. 1925.

SIMNETT, W. E. *The British Colonial Empire.* 2nd edn. 1949.

SOMERVELL, D. C. *The British Empire*. New edn. 1942.

SPENDER, J. A. *Great Britain—Empire and Commonwealth, 1886–1935.* 2 vols. 1936.

STEWART, J. I. *An Economic Geography of the British Empire Overseas.* 1933.

TILBY, A. WYATT. *English People Overseas*. 6 vols. 1908–14. 2nd edn. of vols. I–II, 1910.

TREVELYAN, G. M. *British History in the Nineteenth Century and After, 1789–1919.* New edn. 1937.

TROTTER, R. G. *The British Empire–Commonwealth: a Study in Political Evolution* [since 1783]. Toronto, 1932.

WALKER, E. A. *The British Empire, its Structure and Spirit.* 1943. New edn. 1956.

WILLIAMSON, J. A. "Phases of Empire History." *History*, vol. XXXIII (1948), pp. 49–71.

—— *A Short History of British Expansion.* Vol. II, *The Modern Empire and Commonwealth.* 4th edn. 1954.

ZIMMERMANN, A. *Die europäischen Kolonien.* 5 vols. Berlin, 1896–1903. Vols. II and III deal with *Die Kolonialpolitik Grossbritanniens* (1898–9).

ZIMMERN, Sir A. E. *The Third British Empire.* 3rd edn. Oxford, 1934.

(e) BIOGRAPHIES

For biographies relating to particular countries or subjects see *C.H.B.E.* vols. IV–VIII. Memoirs and correspondence are placed in the Special Bibliographies below.

COLLECTED BIOGRAPHY

BOASE, F. *Modern English Biography.* 6 vols. 1892–1921. Brief notes of persons, many not in the *D.N.B.*, who died after 1850.

DALTON, C. *Men of Malaya.* 1942.

DAVIDSON, J. M. *Eminent English Liberals.* 1880.

ESCOTT, T. H. S. *Pillars of the Empire. Sketches of living Indian and Colonial Statesmen, Celebrities and Officials.* 1879.

GIBB, A. D. *Scottish Empire.* 1937. Scottish builders of the Empire.

GUNN, H. *Makers of the Empire.* 1924. British Empire Survey, vol. VIII.

HILL, RICHARD (comp.). *A Biographical Dictionary of the Anglo-Egyptian Sudan.* 1951.

SCHOLEFIELD, G. H. *Dictionary of New Zealand Biography.* 2 vols. Wellington, 1940.

STEPHEN, L., LEE, Sir S. and others (Eds.). *Dictionary of National Biography.* Rev. edn. including 1901 Supplement. 22 vols. 1908–9. Second Supplement, 1901–13 (n.d.). Supplement, 1912–21 (1927), 1922–30 (1937), 1931–40 (1949). A reissue of the *Concise Dictionary of National Biography*, vol. I, to 1900 (1954), has an appendix of corrections.

STRIDE, W. K. *Empire-Builders; a course of lectures.* 1906.

WALLACE, W. S. (comp.). *Dictionary of Canadian Biography.* Toronto, 1926. A larger work is in preparation.

WARD, T. H. *Men of the Reign. A biographical dictionary of eminent persons of British and Colonial birth* [who died 1837–84]. 1885.

Who's Who, an annual biographical dictionary. 1849– . In progress.

Who was Who, 1897–1916. London, 1920. *1916–1920.* London, 1929. *1929–1940.* London, 1941.

WILLIAMSON, J. A. *Builders of the Empire.* Oxford, 1925.

Obituaries are to be found in the *New Annual Register*, the *Gentleman's Magazine* and *The Times*, for which see Palmer's Index and the later official index.

INDIVIDUAL STATESMEN

For convenience of reference the works which follow are arranged under the names of their subjects. Further biographies appear in the Special Bibliographies below.

ASQUITH. *Life of H. H. Asquith, Lord Oxford*. By J. A. Spender and C. Asquith. 2 vols. 1932.

BALFOUR, A. J., Lord. *Chapters of Autobiography*. 1930.
Arthur James Balfour, first Earl of Balfour. By B. Dugdale. 2 vols. 1936.

BRIGHT. *John Bright*. 1913. By G. M. Trevelyan. New edn. 1925.

CAMPBELL-BANNERMAN. *The Life of Sir Henry Campbell-Bannerman*. By J. A. Spender. 2 vols. 1923.

CARNARVON. *The Life of Henry Howard, fourth Earl of Carnarvon, 1831–90*. By Sir A. H. Hardinge. 3 vols. 1925.

CHAMBERLAIN. *Life of Joseph Chamberlain*. By J. L. Garvin and J. Amery. Vols. I–IV, 1923–4. 1951.
Joseph Chamberlain. By V. Halperin. Zürich, 1942.
Joseph Chamberlain. By Sir C. Petrie. 1940.

CHILDERS. *Life and Correspondence of H. C. E. Childers*. By E. S. C. Childers. 3 vols. 1901.

CHURCHILL. *Lord Randolph Churchill*. By (Sir) W. L. S. Churchill. 2 vols. 1906. New edn. 1952.

CLARENDON. *Life and Letters of the fourth Earl of Clarendon*. By Sir H. Maxwell. 2 vols. 1913.
A Vanished Victorian [4th Earl of Clarendon]. By G. Villiers. 1938.

CRANBROOK. *Gathorne Hardy*. By A. E. Gathorne Hardy. 2 vols. 1910.

CROMER. *Lord Cromer*. By Lord Zetland. 1932.

CURZON. *Life of Lord Curzon*. By Lord Zetland. 3 vols. 1928.

DERBY. *The Earl of Derby*. By G. Saintsbury. 1892.
Life of Lord Derby. By T. E. Kebbel. 1890.

DE VILLIERS. *Lord de Villiers and his times*. By E. A. Walker. 1925.

DEVONSHIRE. *Life of Spencer Compton, eighth Duke of Devonshire*. By B. Holland, 2 vols. 1911.

DILKE. *Life of Sir Charles W. Dilke*. By S. Gwynn and G. M. Tuckwell. 2 vols. 1917.

DISRAELI. *The Life of Benjamin Disraeli, Earl of Beaconsfield*. By W. F. Monypenny and G. E. Buckle. 6 vols. 1910–20.
Lord Beaconsfield. By J. A. Froude. 1890.
Disraeli. By A. Maurois. Trans. 1928. New English edn. 1947.

DUFFERIN. *Life of the Marquis of Dufferin and Ava*. By Sir A. Lyall. 2 vols. 1905.

EDWARD VII. *Life of King Edward VII*. By Sir Sidney Lee. 2 vols. 1925–7.
King Edward VII. By E. F. Benson. 1933.

FORSTER. *Life of W. E. Forster*. By T. Wemyss Reid. 2 vols. 1888.

FRERE. *Life and Correspondence of Sir Bartle Frere*. By J. Martineau. 2 vols. 1895.
Sir Bartle Frere. By W. B. Worsfold. 1913.

GALT. *The Life and Times of Sir A. T. Galt*. By O. D. Skelton. Toronto, 1920.

GLADSTONE. *Life of Gladstone*. By John, Lord Morley. 3 vols. 1903.
Gladstone: A Biography. By Sir P. Magnus. 1954.
The Life of W. E. Gladstone. By H. W. Paul. 1918.

GOLDIE. *Sir George Goldie, Founder of Nigeria*. By D. Wellesley, 1934.

GOSCHEN. *The Life of George Joachim Goschen, first Viscount Goschen*. By A. R. D. Elliot. 2 vols. 1911.
Lord Goschen and his Friends. The Goschen Letters. Ed. by P. Colson. 1946.

GRANVILLE. *The Life of Granville George Leveson Gower, second Earl Granville*. By Lord E. Fitzmaurice. 3rd edn. 2 vols. 1905.

GREY. *Grey of Fallodon*. By G. M. Trevelyan. 1937.

GREY. *Sir George Grey*. By J. Collier. Christchurch, N.Z., 1909.
Life of Sir George Grey. By W. L. Rees. 2 vols. 1892.

HALDANE, R. B., Lord. *Autobiography*. 1929.

HARCOURT. *Life of Sir William Vernon Harcourt*. By A. G. Gardiner. 2 vols. 1923.

HICKS BEACH. *The Life of Sir Michael Hicks Beach, Earl St Aldwyn*. By Lady V. Hicks Beach. 2 vols. 1932.

JOHNSTON, Sir H. H. *The Story of my Life.* 1923.
KEIR HARDIE. *J. Keir Hardie.* By W. Stewart. 1921.
KIPLING. *Rudyard Kipling.* By C. E. Carrington. 1955.
  Rudyard Kipling: a Study in Literature and Political Ideas. By E. Shanks. 1940.
LABOUCHERE. *The Life of Henry Labouchere.* By A. L. Thorold. 1913.
LANSDOWNE. *Lord Lansdowne.* By T. W. Legh, Lord Newton. 1929.
LAURIER. *Life and Letters of Sir Wilfrid Laurier.* By O. D. Skelton. 2 vols. 1922.
LAW. *The Unknown Prime Minister. The Life and Times of Andrew Bonar Law, 1858–1923.* By R. Blake. 1955.
LLOYD GEORGE. *Lloyd George, the Official Biography.* By M. Thompson. 1948.
  Lloyd George. By T. Jones. 1951.
  Tempestuous Journey. Lloyd George, his Life and Times. By F. Owen. 1955.
LUGARD. *Lcrd Lugard.* Vol. I, *The Years of Adventure, 1858–98.* By M. Perham. 1956.
LYONS. *Lord Lyons.* By T. W. Legh, Lord Newton. 2 vols. 1913.
MACDONALD. *John A. Macdonald.* By D. G. Creighton. 2 vols. 1952–5.
MILNER. *Lord Milner and the Empire.* By V. Halperin. 1952.
MOLTENO. *Life and Times of Sir J. C. Molteno.* By P. A. Molteno. 1900.
MUNDELLA. *A. J. Mundella, 1825–97: the Liberal Background to the Labour Movement.* By W. H. G. Armytage. 1951.
NORTHBROOK. *The Earl of Northbrook.* By B. Mallet. 1908.
NORTHCOTE (Lord Iddesleigh). *Life, Letters and Diaries of Sir Stafford Northcote.* By A. Lang. 2 vols. Edinburgh, 1891.
NORTON. *Life of C. B. Adderley, 1st Lord Norton.* By W. S. Childe-Pemberton. 1909.
PARKES. *Life of Sir Henry Parkes.* By C. E. Lyne. 1897.
PAUNCEFOTE. *Lord Pauncefote.* By R. B. Mowat. 1929.
RHODES. *The Life of Cecil John Rhodes, 1853–1902.* By Sir L. L. Michell. 2 vols. 1910.
  Life of Cecil Rhodes. By J. G. Lockhart. 1933.
  Cecil Rhodes. By S. G. Millin. New edn. 1952.
  Cecil Rhodes. By G. Oudard. 2nd edn. Paris, 1939.
  Cecil Rhodes. By B. Williams. 1921.
RIPON. *Life of the first Marquess of Ripon.* By L. Wolf. 2 vols. 1921.
ROSEBERY. *Lord Rosebery: his Life and Speeches.* By T. Coates. 2 vols. New York, 1900.
SALISBURY. *Life of Robert, Marquis of Salisbury.* By Lady Gwendolen Cecil. 4 vols. 1921–22.
  Lord Salisbury. By A. L. Kennedy. 1954.
SHERBROOKE. *Life and Letters of Robert Lowe, Viscount Sherbrooke.* By A. P. Martin. 2 vols. 1893.
SMITH. *Life of W. H. Smith.* By S. H. Maxwell. 1893.
SMUTS. *Smuts.* By S. G. Millin. 2 vols. 1936.
  Jan Christian Smuts. By J. C. Smuts. 1952.
STEAD. *The Life of W. T. Stead.* By F. Whyte. 2 vols. 1925.
TREVELYAN. *Sir George Otto Trevelyan.* By G. M. Trevelyan. 1932.
VICTORIA. *Queen Victoria.* By E. F. Benson. 1935.
  Queen Victoria. By Sir S. Lee. Rev. edn. 1904.
  Queen Victoria. By R. Fulford. 1951.
VINCENT. *Life of Sir Howard Vincent.* By S. H. Jeyes and F. D. How. 1912.
VOGEL. *The Life and Times of Sir Julius Vogel.* By R. M. Burdon. Christchurch, N.Z., 1948.

2. SPECIAL BIBLIOGRAPHIES

A. COLONIAL POLICY AND ADMINISTRATION, 1870–1921

(chapters I, II, V, X and XI)

(a) MANUSCRIPT SOURCES

See Part I, 1 and 2, particularly the following series in the Public Record Office: C.O. 30/6 (Carnarvon Papers), C.O. 30/29 (Granville Papers), C.O. 323 (Colonies General), C.O. 384, 385 (Emigration), C.O. 537 (Supplementary Correspondence). Many of the Colonial Office and Foreign Office series now open to public inspection as far as the end of 1902 were only partially available when previous volumes of this History were published, for instance, C.O. 201 (New South Wales), C.O. 209 (New Zealand), C.O. 224 (Orange River Colony), C.O. 234 (Queensland), C.O. 273 (Straits Settlements), C.O. 291 (Transvaal), C.O. 422 (New Guinea) and C.O. 427 (Zululand). Foreign Office correspondence bearing directly on imperial policy is contained in such series as F.O. 2 (Africa), F.O. 12 (Borneo), F.O. 27 (France and West Africa), F.O. 27/2414–8 (French encroachment in West Africa), F.O. 27/2843–3536 (Pacific Islands), F.O. 63/1129–32 (Portugal), F.O. 64/1101–6 (Annexation of Angra Pequeña), F.O. 64/1144–50 (Annexations in Pacific), F.O. 84 (Slave Trade), F.O. 107 (Zanzibar), F.O. 141 (Egypt and Sudan). Confidential Print now available in the Public Record Office includes the following series important for this period: C.O. 806/106–365 (African East, West and South, 1879–97), C.O. 807/28–84 (America, North, 1878–91), C.O. 808/27–129 (Australian, 1878–94), C.O. 809/19–63 (Eastern, 1879–96), C.O. 810/1–37 (Mediterranean, 1880–91), C.O. 811/8–44 (West Indies, 1877–99), C.O. 812/14–144 (Miscellaneous, 1879–1902). C.O. 812/111 contains the Report of the Conference between Chamberlain and the Premiers of Self-Governing Colonies at the Colonial Office in June and July 1897; C.O. 812/144 contains proceedings of the Conference between the Secretary of State for the Colonies and the Premiers of Self-governing Colonies, October 1902.

The Gladstone Papers in the British Museum are especially important for Liberal policy, e.g. B.M. Add. MSS. 44165–80, 44538, 44638, 44759. Miss A. Ramm has edited selections from these papers and those of Lord Granville for the Royal Historical Society—*The Political Correspondence of Mr Gladstone and Lord Granville, 1868–1876* (Camden 3rd ser., vols. 81, 82), (1952). The Kimberley Papers, including Lord Kimberley's Diary, are also being edited for the Society by Miss E. Drus. As pointed out above (p. 791), the papers of Joseph Chamberlain and many other statesmen of the period are still in private hands.

(b) OFFICIAL PUBLICATIONS

See Part I, 3 (a) and (b) and 4, particularly the following Parliamentary Papers: Proposed Colonial Conference, *Parl. Pap.* 1870, XLIX [C. 24], [C. 51]; Colonial Conference at Ottawa, 1894, *Parl. Pap.* 1894, LIV [C. 7553], *Parl. Pap.* 1895, LXX [C. 7632], [C. 7824]; Conference with Colonial Premiers, 1897, *Parl. Pap.* 1897, LIX [C. 8596]; Colonial Conference 1902, *Parl. Pap.* 1902, LXVI [Cd. 1299], 1903, LXIV [Cd. 1597]. Future organisation of Colonial Conferences, *Parl. Pap.* 1906, LXXVII [Cd. 2785], [Cd. 2975], Colonial Conference 1907, *Parl. Pap.* 1907, LIV [Cd. 3404], [Cd. 3340], 1907, LV [Cd. 3404], [Cd. 3406], [Cd. 3523], [Cd. 3524]; Imperial Conference, 1911, *Parl. Pap.* 1911, LIV [Cd. 5513], [Cd. 5741], [Cd. 5745], [Cd. 5746–I], [Cd. 5746–II]; Final Report of Royal Commission on Dominions, *Parl. Pap.* 1917–18, X [Cd. 8462].

Relevant papers concerning Canada, Australia, New Zealand and South Africa are contained in the lists given in *C.H.B.E.* vols. IV–VIII.

(c) CONTEMPORARY WRITINGS

ADDERLEY, Sir C. B. (Lord Norton). *Our Relations with the Colonies and Crown Colonies.* 1870.
—— *A Review of "The Colonial Policy of Lord John Russell's Administration", by Earl Grey, 1853; and of subsequent colonial history.* 1869.
ALLARDYCE, A. "A New View of Imperial Federation." *Blackwoods,* May 1890, pp. 708–20.
AMERY, L. S. *Union and Strength: a series of papers on imperial questions.* 1912.
ARNOLD-FORSTER, H. O. "The Liberal Idea and the Colonies." *Nineteenth Century,* Sept. 1883, pp. 385–401.
BAGEHOT, WALTER. *The English Constitution.* 2nd edn. 1872.
BARKER, J. ELLIS. *Great and Greater Britain: the Problems of Motherland and Empire.* 1909. 2nd edn. 1910.
BASSETT, A. TILNEY (Ed.). *Gladstone's Speeches.* 1916.
BERARD, V. *L'Angleterre et l'impérialisme.* Paris, 1900.
BOURINOT, Sir J. G. *Canada under British Rule, 1760–1900.* Cambridge, 1900.
BRYCE, JAMES (Lord). *Impressions of South Africa.* 2nd edn. 1898.
CARLYLE, J. E. *African Colonies and Colonization.* 1885.
CARNARVON, GEORGE (Lord). *Speeches on the Affairs of West Africa, etc.* 1903.
CHAMBERLAIN, J. *Foreign and Colonial Speeches.* 1897.
CHEVILLIARD, G. *Les Colonies anglaises.* Paris, 1899.
CLARK, G. B. *Transvaal and Bechuanaland.* 1885.
COLOMB, J. C. R. "Wanted, an Imperial Conference." *Nineteenth Century,* vol. XXXVI (Dec. 1894), pp. 936–46.
COLONIAL AND INDIAN EXHIBITION. *Her Majesty's Colonies.* 1886.
COOK, E. T. "The Colonial Conference." *Quarterly Rev.* July 1902, pp. 315–41.
COOPE, W. J. *Swaziland as an Imperial Factor.* 1895.
COTTON, J. S. and PAYNE, E. J. *The Colonies and Dependencies.* 1883.
CRAMB, J. A. *Reflections on the Origins and Destiny of Imperial Britain.* 1900. 2nd edn. 1915.
CREASY, Sir E. S. *The Imperial and Colonial Constitutions of the Britannic Empire.* 1872.
CROMER, EVELYN, Lord. *Ancient and Modern Imperialism.* 1910.
CUNINGHAM, G. C. *A Scheme for Imperial Federation.* 1895.
CURTIS, L. *The Problem of the Commonwealth.* 1917.
DICEY, E. "Mr Gladstone and our Empire." *Nineteenth Century,* Sept. 1877, pp. 292–308.
DILKE (Sir) C. W. *Greater Britain.* 1868. 2nd rev. edn. 1876.
—— *Problems of Greater Britain.* 2 vols. 1890.
DUBOIS, M. *Systèmes coloniaux et peuples colonisateurs.* Paris, 1895.
ELLIOT, A. R. D. "Confederation or Independence." *Edinburgh Rev.* April 1890, pp. 565–92.
FORSTER, W. E. *Our Colonial Empire.* Edinburgh, 1875.
FREEMAN, E. A. *Greater Greece and Greater Britain.* 1886.
—— "Imperial Federation." *Macmillan's Mag.* vol. LI (1885), pp. 430–45.
FRERE, Sir H. BARTLE. "Have we a Colonial Policy?" *National Rev.* Sept. 1883, pp. 385–401.
FROUDE, J. A. *The English in the West Indies.* 1888.
—— *Oceana; or England and her Colonies.* 1886.
—— *Short Studies on Great Subjects,* vol. II (1898 edn.). Contains reprints of articles on colonial questions from *Fraser's Magazine* and the *Quarterly Review.*
—— *Two Lectures on South Africa.* 1880.
GLADSTONE, W. E. *Foreign and Colonial Policy.* 1881.
—— "Kin Beyond the Sea." *North American Rev.* Sept. 1878. [Reprinted in *Gleanings of Past Years* (1879), I, 203–48.]
—— *Political Speeches in Scotland.* Rev. edn. Edinburgh, 1880.

GODARD, J. G. *Racial Supremacy: being Studies in Imperialism.* 1905.

GOOCH, G. P. "Imperialism." In *The Heart of the Empire.* 1901.

GORDON, A. *The Future of the Empire: or a brief statement of the case against Imperial Federation.* 1889.

GRESWELL, W. H. P. "England and France in West Africa." *Fortnightly Rev.* Dec. 1897, pp. 917–25.

—— *Our South African Empire.* 1885.

—— *The Outlines of British Colonisation.* 1893.

GUTHRIE, E. *Home Rule and Federation.* 1887.

HAGGARD, (Sir) H. RIDER. *Cetewayo and his White Neighbours.* 1882.

HOBSON, J. A. *Imperialism.* 1902. New edn. 1938.

—— *The Psychology of Jingoism.* 1901.

HOLLAND, B. H. "*Imperium et Libertas*": *a Study in History and Politics.* 1901.

HYTHE, Viscount (2nd Earl Brassey). *Problems of Empire: the Faith of a Federalist.* 1913. Earlier edn. 1904.

IRELAND, A. *The Far Eastern Tropics: Studies in the Administration of Tropical Dependencies.* Boston, 1905.

—— *Tropical Colonisation.* 1899.

JEBB, R. *Studies in Colonial Nationalism.* 1905.

JENKINS, A. *Discussions on Colonial Questions.* 1872.

JENKYNS, Sir H. *British Rule and Jurisdiction beyond the Seas.* Oxford, 1902.

Imperial Federation: journal of the Imperial Federation League. 8 vols. 1886–93.

IMPERIAL FEDERATION LEAGUE. "Fifty Years Progress" (Special number of *Imperial Federation*, June 1886.)

JOHNSTONE, H. A. MUNRO BUTLER. *Imperialism, Federation, and Policy.* 1902.

KIDD, B. *The Control of the Tropics.* 1898.

KIPLING, R. *Take up the White Man's Burden!* 1899.

DE LABILLIERE, F. P. *Federal Britain.* 1894. Imperial federation movement.

LEWIS, Sir G. C. *An Essay on the Government of Dependencies.* New edn. 1891. Introduction and notes by C. P. Lucas.

LUCAS, Sir C. P. *British Colonial Administration and its Agencies.* (Oxford Survey of the British Empire, vol. VI.) 1914.

LUCY, HENRY W. *A Diary of Two Parliaments.* 2 vols. 1886, 1892. Vol. I, *The Gladstone Parliament, 1880–85*; vol. II, *The Salisbury Parliament, 1886–92.*

MACDONALD, J. RAMSAY. *Labour and the Empire.* 1907.

MARCKS, E. *Die imperialistische Idee in der Gegenwart.* 1903.

MILNER, ALFRED, Lord. *Constructive Imperialism. Five Speeches* (Oct.–Dec. 1907). 1908.

—— *The Nation and the Empire. Being a Collection of Speeches and Addresses, with an Introduction.* 1913.

—— *Questions of the Hour.* 2nd edn. 1925.

MOCKLER-FERRYMAN, A. F. *Imperial Africa.* 1898.

MOLESWORTH, Sir W. *Selected Speeches on Questions regarding Colonial Policy.* Ed. by H. E. Egerton. 1903.

MONYPENNY, W. F. and others. *The Empire and the Century*: a series of essays. 1905.

MORLEY, J. (Lord). "The Expansion of England." *Macmillan's Mag.* XLIX (1884), pp. 241–58. Review of Seeley.

ORPEN, J. M. *Bechuanaland.* 1885.

PARKIN, Sir G. R. *Imperial Federation: the problem of national unity.* 1892.

PAYNE, E. F. *Colonies and Colonial Federation.* 1905.

PEARSON, C. H. *National Life and Character.* 1893.

REINSCH, P. S. *Colonial Administration.* New York, 1905.

ROBERTSON, J. M. *Patriotism and Empire.* 1899.

ROGERS, T. *The Colonial Question.* 1872.

SEELEY, Sir J. R. *The Expansion of England.* 1883.

—— *The Growth of British Policy.* 2 vols. 1895.

SHAW, G. B. (Ed.). *Fabianism and the Empire.* 1900.
SHERBROOKE, Lord. "Imperialism." *Fortnightly Rev.* Oct. 1878, pp. 453–65.
SMITH, GOLDWIN. *Commonwealth and Empire.* 1902.
SNOW, A. H. *The Administration of Dependencies.* New York, 1902.
SPENDER, H. "The Empire and the Colonies." *Edinburgh Rev.* Oct. 1902, pp. 464–86.
STEAD, W. T. *The Best or the Worst of Empires: Which?* 1906.
THORBURN, W. M. *The Great Game: a Plea for a British Imperial Policy.* 2nd edn. 1875.
THRING, Lord. "The Fallacy of 'Imperial Federation'." *Nineteenth Century,* Jan. 1886, pp. 22–34.
TODD, A. *Parliamentary Government in the British Colonies.* 1880. 2nd edn. 1894.
TROLLOPE, ANTHONY. *South Africa.* 1878.
VIALLATE, A. *La Crise anglaise: impérialisme et protection.* Paris, 1905.
WEDDERBURN, Sir D. *British Colonial Policy.* 1881.
WHITE, A. *Efficiency and Empire.* 1901.
WHITE, A. S. "The Partition of Africa." *Nineteenth Century,* July 1894, pp. 23–37.
WILSON, E. D. J. "What is a Colonial Governor?" *Nineteenth Century,* Dec. 1878.

Significant articles on colonial policy and administration were contributed to almost every number of the following periodicals: *Contemporary Review, Edinburgh Review, Fortnightly Review, Fraser's Magazine, Quarterly Review, Saturday Review, Spectator, Westminster Review;* also to many other magazines and newspapers.

(d) DOCUMENTS, MEMOIRS AND CORRESPONDENCE

AMERY, L. S. *My Political Life.* 2 vols. 1953–4.
ASQUITH, H. H., Earl of Oxford and Asquith. *Fifty Years of Parliament.* 2 vols. 1926.
BEACONSFIELD, Lord. *Letters of Disraeli to Lady Bradford and Lady Chesterfield.* Ed. by Lord Zetland. 2 vols. 1929.
BOWEN, Sir G. F. *Thirty Years of Colonial Government, 1859–88.* Ed. by S. L. Poole. 2 vols. 1889.
BRIGHT, JOHN. *Diaries.* Ed. by P. Bright. 1930.
BUTLER, Sir W. *Autobiography.* 1911.
CHAMBERLAIN, JOSEPH. *Mr Chamberlain's Speeches.* Ed. by C. W. Boyd. 2 vols. 1914.
—— *A Political Memoir.* Ed. by C. Howard. 1953.
CURTIS, LIONEL. *With Milner in South Africa.* Oxford, 1951.
EGERTON, H. E. *Federations and Unions within the British Empire.* Oxford, 1911. 2nd edn. 1924.
ESHER, Lord. *Journals and Letters of Viscount Esher.* Ed. by M. V. Brett. 2 vols. 1934.
EYBERS, G. W. (Ed.). *Select Constitutional Documents illustrating South African History, 1795–1910.* 1918.
GLADSTONE, H. J., Lord. *After Thirty Years.* 1928.
GLADSTONE, W. E. *Gladstone's Speeches.* Ed. by A. Tilney Bassett. 1916.
GREY, Sir E. (Lord). *Twenty-five Years, 1892–1916.* 2 vols. 1925.
GUEDALLA, P. (Ed.). *The Queen and Mr Gladstone.* 2 vols. 1933.
HAMILTON, Lord G. *Parliamentary Reflections and Reminiscences, 1868–1906.* 2 vols. 1917–22.
HATTERSLEY, A. F. (Ed.). *Later Annals of Natal.* 1938.
—— (Ed.). *The Natalians; further annals of Natal.* Pietermaritzburg, 1940.
HEADLAM, C. (Ed.) *The Milner Papers, 1897–1905.* 2 vols. 1931–33.
KEITH, A. B. (Ed.). *Select Speeches and Documents on British Colonial Policy, 1763–1917.* 1917. New edn. 1948.
KILBRACKEN, Lord. *Reminiscences.* 1931.

LANG, A. (Ed.). *Life, Letters and Diaries of Sir Stafford Northcote.* 2 vols. Edinburgh, 1891.

LORING, A. H. and BEADON, R. J. (Eds.). *Papers and Addresses by Lord Brassey.* 1895.

MACDONALD, Sir J. A. *Memoirs.* Ed. by J. Pope. Ottawa, London, 1894.

MARINDIN, G. E. (Ed.). *Letters of Frederic, Lord Blachford.* 1896.

MARTINEAU, J. *Life and Correspondence of Sir B. Frere.* 2 vols. 1895.

MILNER, ALFRED, Lord. *The Milner Papers.* Ed. by C. Headlam. 2 vols. 1931–3.

MORLEY, J., Lord. *Recollections.* 2 vols. 1917.

OLLIVIER, M. (Ed.). *The Colonial and Imperial Conferences, 1887–1937.* 3 vols. Ottawa, 1954. Abridgement of official proceedings.

PARKES, Sir H. *Fifty Years in the Making of Australian History.* 2 vols. 1892.

PONSONBY, Sir F., Lord Sysonby. *Recollections of Three Reigns.* Ed. by Colin Welch. 1951.

RODD, J. RENNELL, Lord Rennell. *Social and Diplomatic Memories, 1884–1893.* 1922.

RUSSELL, Lord. *Later Correspondence of Lord John Russell, 1840–78.* Ed. by G. P. Gooch. 2 vols. 1925.

SELBORNE, R. PALMER, Earl of. *Memorials, Personal and Political.* 4 vols. 1896–8.

SMITH, GOLDWIN. *Reminiscences.* Ed. by A. Haultain. 1910.

—— *A Selection from Goldwin Smith's Correspondence.* Ed. by A. Haultain [1913].

SPRING RICE, C. *Letters and Friendships of Cecil Spring Rice.* Ed. by S. Gwynn. 1929.

STANMORE, Lord. *Records of Private and of Public Life.* 4 vols. Privately printed, 1897.

TAYLOR, Sir HENRY. *Autobiography,* 2 vols. 1885.

—— *Correspondence.* Ed. by E. Dowden. 1888.

TUPPER, Sir CHARLES. *Life and Letters of Sir Charles Tupper.* Ed. by E. M. Saunders. 2 vols. 1916.

UNDERHILL, F. H. (Ed.). *The Dufferin–Carnarvon Correspondence, 1874–8.* (Champlain Soc. Pubns. XXXIII.) Toronto, 1955.

VICTORIA. *Letters of Queen Victoria.* Ed. by G. E. Buckle. 2nd series, 3 vols. 1921–8. 3rd series, 3 vols. 1930–2.

WEST, Sir A. E. *The Private Diaries of Algernon West.* Ed. by H. G. Hutchinson. 1922.

—— *Recollections, 1832–86.* 2 vols. 1899.

(e) LATER WORKS

For other biographies, see Section 1 (e), pp. 840–2 above.

ADAMS, G. B. "The Origin and Results of the Imperial Federation Movement in England." *Proc. Wisconsin State Hist. Soc.* 1899, pp. 93–116.

AGAR-HAMILTON, J. A. I. *The Road to the North: South Africa, 1852–1886.* 1937.

BARKER, Sir E. *Ideas and Ideals of the British Empire.* Cambridge, 1941.

BELL, Sir H. *Foreign Colonial Administration in the Far East.* 1928.

BENNETT, G. (Ed.). *The Concept of Empire. Burke to Attlee, 1774–1947.* 1953.

BERTRAM, Sir A. *The Colonial Service.* 1930.

BODELSEN, C. A. *Studies in Mid-Victorian Imperialism.* Copenhagen. 1924.

BRIE, F. *Imperialistische Strömungen in der englischen Literatur.* 1928.

BRUCE, Sir C. *The Broad Stone of Empire.* 2 vols. 1910. Crown Colony administration.

BURT, A. L. *Imperial Architects: being an Account of Proposals in the Direction of a Closer Imperial Union, made previous to the Opening of the First Colonial Conference of 1888.* Oxford, 1913.

CECIL, A. *Queen Victoria and Her Prime Ministers.* 1953.

CHENG, S. C. *Schemes for the Federation of the British Empire.* New York, 1931.

CLARK, C. *The Crown Colonies and their History.* 1939.

COUPLAND, Sir R. *The Exploitation of East Africa, 1856–1890.* 1939.

COUPLAND, Sir R. *Zulu Battle-Piece (Isandhlwana)*. 1948.

CRANKSHAW, E. *The Forsaken Idea: a Study of Viscount Milner*. 1952.

CREIGHTON, D. G. "The Victorians and the Empire." *Canadian Hist. Rev.* vol. XIX (June 1938), pp. 138–53.

CURREY, C. H. *British Colonial Policy, 1783–1915*. 1916.

DAWSON, R. M. (Ed.). *The Development of Dominion Status, 1900–1936*. Oxford, 1937.

DE KIEWIET, C. W. *British Colonial Policy and the South African Republics, 1848–72*. 1929.

—— *The Imperial Factor in South Africa*. Cambridge, 1937.

DRUS, E. "The Colonial Office and the Annexation of Fiji." *Trans. Royal Hist. Soc.* 4th ser. vol. XXXII (1950), pp. 87–110.

—— "The Question of Imperial Complicity in the Jameson Raid." *Eng. Hist. Rev.* vol. LXVIII (Oct. 1953), pp. 582–93.

EGERTON, H. E. *British Colonial Policy in the Twentieth Century*. 1922.

—— *A Short History of British Colonial Policy, 1606–1909*. Ed. by A. P. Newton. 1932.

—— "The System of British Colonial Administration of the Crown Colonies in the seventeenth and eighteenth centuries compared with the System prevailing in the nineteenth century." *Trans. Royal Hist. Soc.* 4th ser. vol. I (1918), pp. 190–217.

FABIAN SOCIETY. *Fabian Colonial Essays*. Ed. by R. Hinden. 1945.

FARR, D. M. L. *The Colonial Office and Canada, 1867–1887*. Toronto, 1955.

FIDDES, Sir G. V. *The Dominions and Colonial Offices*. 1926.

FINDLAY, J. G. *The Imperial Conference of 1911 from within*. 1912.

FITZMAURICE, Lord E. G. P. *The Life of Granville George Leveson Gower, Second Earl Granville*. 2 vols. 1905.

FOLSOM, A. *The Royal Empire Society*. 1933.

GRESWELL, W. P. *The Growth and Administration of the British Colonies, 1837–1897*. 1898.

GRETTON, R. H. *Imperialism and Mr Gladstone, 1876–1887*. 1923.

GUEDALLA, P. *The Queen and Mr Gladstone, 1876–1887*. 1923.

GWYNN, S. and TUCKWELL, G. M. *Life of Sir C. W. Dilke*. 2 vols. 1917.

HALL, H. L. *Australia and England*. 1934.

—— *The Colonial Office: a History*. 1937.

HALPERIN, V. *Lord Milner and the Empire. The Evolution of British Imperialism*. 1952.

HANCOCK, (Sir) W. KEITH. *Argument of Empire*. 1943.

—— *Colonial Self-Government*. Nottingham, 1956. Pamphlet.

HARDIE, F. *The Political Influence of Queen Victoria, 1861–1901*. 1935.

HARDINGE, Sir A. H. *Life of H. H. M. Herbert, 4th Earl of Carnarvon*. 3 vols. 1925.

HARRISON, H. *Parnell, Joseph Chamberlain and Mr Garvin*. 1938.

HARROP, A. J. *England and New Zealand*. 1926.

HATTERSLEY, A. F. "The Annexation of the Transvaal, 1877." *History*, vol. XXI (June 1936), pp. 41–47.

—— *The Colonies and Imperial Federation*. Pietermaritzburg, 1919.

HENDERSON, G. C. *Life of Sir George Grey*. 1907.

HICKS BEACH, Lady V. *Sir M. Hicks Beach*. 1932.

HOWARD, C. H. D. "Joseph Chamberlain and the Unauthorized Programme." *Engl. Hist. Rev.* vol. LXV (Oct. 1950), pp. 477–91.

—— "Lord Randolph Churchill." *History*, vol. XXV (1940), pp. 25–40.

HOWE, SUSANNA. *Novels of Empire*. New York, 1949.

JEBB, R. *The Empire in Eclipse*. 1926.

—— *The Imperial Conference*. 2 vols. 1911.

—— *Studies in Colonial Nationalism*. 1905.

JEFFRIES, Sir C. J. *The Colonial Empire and its Civil Service*. Cambridge, 1938.

KEITH, Sir A. BERRIEDALE. "Development of Colonial Self-Government in the 19th century." *Roy. Soc. of Arts Jour.* vol. LVI (1908), pp. 332–47.

KEITH, Sir A. BERRIEDALE. *Imperial Unity and the Dominions.* Oxford, 1916.
—— *Responsible Government in the Dominions.* 3 vols. Oxford, 1912. 2nd edn. 2 vols. Oxford, 1928.
KNAPLUND, P. *Gladstone and Britain's Imperial Policy.* 1927. Especially Pt. I, ch. 4, "The Colonial Policy of Gladstone's First Ministry, 1868–1874."
—— "Gladstone's Views on British Colonial Policy." *Canadian Hist. Rev.* vol. IV (1923), pp. 304–15.
LOVELL, R. I. *The Struggle for South Africa, 1875–1899.* New York, 1934.
LUGARD, F. J. D., Lord. *Representative Forms of Government and "Indirect Rule" in British Africa.* 1928.
MILLER, J. D. B. *Richard Jebb and the Problem of Empire.* Inst. of Commonwealth Studies, 1956. Pamphlet.
MOLTENO, P. A. *Life and Times of Sir J. C. Molteno.* 2 vols. 1900.
MOON, P. T. *Imperialism and World Politics.* 1928.
MORISON, J. L. "Imperial Ideas of Benjamin Disraeli." *Canadian Hist. Rev.* vol. I (1920), pp. 267–80.
MORRIS, E. E. *Memoir of George Higinbotham.* 1895
MORRIS, G. W. and WOOD, L. S. *English Speaking Nations: a Study in the Development of the Commonwealth Ideal.* Oxford, 1924.
O'BRIEN, R. B. *The Life of Charles Stewart Parnell, 1846–91.* 2 vols. 1898.
PARKES, Sir H. *Fifty years in the Making of Australia.* 2 vols. 1892.
PAUL, H. W. *Life of J. A. Froude.* 1905.
PETY DE THOZEE, C. *Théories de la colonisation au XIXe siècle.* Brussels, 1902.
PYRAH, G. B. *Imperial Policy and South Africa, 1902–10.* 1955.
RAGATZ, L. J. "Must we rewrite the History of Imperialism?" *Hist. Studies, Australia & New Zealand,* vol. VI (Nov. 1953), pp. 90–8.
REID, T. W. *Life of W. E. Forster.* 2 vols. 1888.
ROBERTS, P. E. *History of British India.* 2nd edn. Oxford, 1938.
SALOMON, F. *Der britische Imperialismus.* 1916.
SCHUYLER, R. L. "The Climax of Anti-Imperialism in England." *Political Science Quart.* vol. XXXVII (Sept. 1922), pp. 415–39.
—— *Parliament and the British Empire: some Constitutional controversies concerning imperial legislative jurisdiction.* New York, 1929.
SINCLAIR, K. *Imperial Federation: a Study of New Zealand Policy and Opinion, 1880–1914.* (Commonwealth Papers, No. 2.) Institute of Commonwealth Studies, 1955. Brief.
SNOW, A. H. *Administration of Dependencies: a Study of the Evolution of the Federal Empire.* 1902.
STRAUSS, W. L. *Joseph Chamberlain and the Theory of Imperialism.* Washington, 1942.
TYLER, J. E. *The Struggle for Imperial Unity, 1868–95.* 1938.
UYS, C. J. *In the Era of Shepstone.* 1933. Largely based on Shepstone's papers.
VAN DER POEL, JEAN. *The Jameson Raid.* Cape Town, 1951.
WALKER, E. A. "The Jameson Raid." *Cambridge Hist. Jour.* vol. VI (1940), pp. 283–306.
—— *Lord de Villiers and his Times. South Africa, 1842–1914.* 1925.
WARD, J. M. *British Policy in the South Pacific, 1786–1893.* 1948.
WIGHT, M. *The Development of the Legislative Council, 1606–1945.* 1945.
WINSLOW, E. M. *The Pattern of Imperialism.* New York, 1948.
WORSFOLD, W. B. *Sir Bartle Frere.* 1913.
—— "The Imperial Federation League, 1884–1893." *United Empire,* vol. VI (1915), pp. 263–73.
WRONG, E. M. "The Growth of Nationalism in the British Empire." *Amer. Hist. Rev.* vol. XXII (Oct. 1916), pp. 45–57.
WRONG, H. *The Government of the West Indies.* 1923.
ZIMMERMANN, A. *Die Kolonialpolitik Grossbritanniens* (Die europäische Kolonien, Bde. II, III). Berlin, 1898–9.

B. THE OPENING OF TROPICAL AFRICA, 1870–1914
(Chapters III, IV, etc.)

(a) Manuscript Sources

See Part I, 1 and 2, particularly the following series in the Public Record Office:
C.O. 87 (Gambia), C.O. 96 (Gold Coast), C.O. 147 (Lagos), C.O. 267 (Sierra
Leone), C.O. 444 (Niger Coast), C.O. 445 (West Africa), C.O. 446 (Nigeria,
Northern), C.O. 519 (East Africa), C.O. 520 (Nigeria, Southern), C.O. 525
(British Central Africa), C.O. 536 (Uganda), C.O. 583 (Nigeria), C.O. 806
(Confidential Print, Africa). Among the Foreign Office series, note especially
F.O. 2 (Africa), F.O. 367 (Africa, correspondence), F.O. 84 (Slave trade),
F.O. 107 (Zanzibar), F.O. 403 (Confidential Print, Africa and Slave Trade).

Among the private papers listed in Part I, 2, note especially those of Cawston,
Gladstone, Lugard, Mackinnon, Portal, Rennell of Rodd and Salisbury; also the
papers of the Church Missionary Society, the London Missionary Society and
other missions; the archives of the Royal Niger Company, the Imperial East Africa
Company and the Uganda Company. The papers of the Anti-Slavery Society are
now mostly in the Bodleian Library, Oxford. The Library of the Royal Geographical Society contains papers of Livingstone and other explorers, including maps,
itineraries, etc.

Reports of accessions are issued by the Central African Archives at Salisbury,
where there is already a large collection. V. W. Hiller has compiled the first volume
of a *Guide to the Public Records of Southern Rhodesia* (Salisbury, 1956). Nothing comparable yet exists for the archive offices recently established in Nigeria, Ghana
and East Africa.

(b) Official Publications

See Part I, 3 and 4, for Parliamentary Papers and Debates, also Part I, for the
Government Gazettes and other printed papers of colonial governments which are
open without restriction of date. Sir E. Hertslet: *Map of Africa by Treaty* (3 vols.
1894. 3rd edn., 1909) conveniently brings together agreements defining boundaries and other papers. The volumes of *British and Foreign State Papers* (1841– , in
progress) also include such material, together with extracts from despatches on
international negotiations, the slave trade and many other relevant matters.

(c) Bibliographies

African Abstracts, a quarterly review of ethnological, social and linguistic studies
　　appearing in current periodicals, vol. 1– . International African Institute, 1950–.
Central African Archives. *A Bibliography of Cecil John Rhodes*. Reprinted from
　　The Story of Cecil Rhodes (1953). Salisbury, Southern Rhodesia, 1952.
Du Bois, W. E. B. and Johnson, G. B. (Eds.). *Encyclopedia of the Negro. Preparatory
　　volume, with reference lists and reports*. New York, 1946. Includes "Bibliography
　　of Bibliographies dealing directly or indirectly with the Negro".
Heyse, T. "Centenary Bibliography of Publications concerning Henry Morton
　　Stanley." *Royal African Soc. Jour.* vol. XLII (April 1943), pp. 91–8.
International African Institute. *A Select Annotated Bibliography of Tropical
　　Africa*. 1956.
International Association for the Study of the History of Religions.
　　International Bibliography of the History of Religions. Vols. 1 (for 1952)– . Leiden,
　　1954– . In progress.
Lewin, E. *Annotated Bibliography of Recent Publications on Africa, South of the Sahara*.
　　(Royal Empire Soc. Bibliographies, No. 9.) 1945.
—— *Subject Catalogue of the Library of the Royal Empire Society*. Vol. 1, *The British
　　Empire generally, and Africa*. 1930.

MYLIUS, N. *Afrikabibliographie.* 1943–51. Vienna, 1954.
PENZER, N. M. *An Annotated Bibliography of Sir Richard Francis Burton.* 1923.
POWER, J. L. *Catalogue of Maps in the Intelligence Division, War Office.* Vol. III. *Africa.* 1891.
RAGATZ, L. J. *Bibliography for the Study of African History in the 19th and 20th Centuries.* Washington, 1943. Brief.
SOUTH AFRICAN INSTITUTE OF INTERNATIONAL AFFAIRS. *Africa Library,* List no. 1–. Johannesburg, 1951–.
SOUTH AFRICAN LIBRARY. *A Bibliography of African Bibliographies, covering territories South of the Sahara.* 3rd edn. (Grey Bibliographies, no. 6.) Cape Town, 1955.
STREIT, R. *et alt. Bibliotheca Missionum.* Vols. 18–20. *Afrikanische Missionsliteratur, 1809–1940.* Freiburg, 1953–4.
WOODSON, C. G. *The African Background outlined, or Handbook for the Study of the Negro.* Washington, D.C., 1936.
WORK, M. N. *A Bibliography of the Negro in Africa and America.* New York, 1928.

(d) GENERAL PERIODICALS

Africa. Journal of the International African Institute. 1928–. In progress.
African Affairs. Journal of the Royal African Society, 1901–. In progress.
African Studies. Johannesburg, 1942–. In progress. Formerly *Bantu Studies* (1927–41).
Bulletin de l'Institut d'Études Centrafricaines. Brazzaville, 1945–. In progress.
Bulletin de l'Institut Français d'Afrique Noire. Dakar, 1939–.
The East and the West: a Quarterly Review for the Study of Missionary Problems, 1902–. In progress.
International Review of Missions, vol. I–. Edinburgh, Oxford, 1912–. In progress. Includes bibliographies of current literature.
Journal of African Administration, 1949–. In progress, quarterly.
Oversea Education: a journal of educational experiment and research in tropical and subtropical areas. 1929–. In progress, quarterly.
Zaire, revue congolaise. Brussels, 1947–. In progress.

(e) CONTEMPORARY WRITINGS ON EXPLORATION, etc.

ARDEN-CLOSE, Sir C. "The Cross River Country in 1895." *Geog. Jour.* vol. XCVIII (1941), pp. 189–97.
BAKER, J. N. L. "Sir Richard Burton and the Nile Sources." *Eng. Hist. Rev.* vol. LIX (1944), pp. 49–61.
BATEMAN, C. J. L. *The first Ascent of the Kasai.* 1889.
BENTLEY, W. H. *Pioneering on the Congo.* 2 vols. 1900.
BINGER, L. G. *Du Niger au Golfe de Guinée par le pays de Kong et le Mossi, 1887–89.* Paris, 1892.
BURTON, Sir R. F. and others. *The Lands of Cazembe.* 1873.
BURTON, Sir R. F. and CAMERON, V. L. *To the Gold Coast for Gold.* 2 vols. 1883.
CAMERON, V. L. *Across Africa.* 2 vols. 1877.
—— "Slavery in its Relation to Trade in Tropical Africa." *Royal Soc. of Arts Jour.* vol. XXXVII (1889), pp. 299–309.
CAPELLO, H. and IVENS, R. *From Benguella to the Territory of Yacca.* 1882.
CARLYLE, J. E. *African Colonies and Colonization.* 1885.
CHAMBERLIN, D. (ed.). *Some Letters from Livingstone, 1840–1872.* 1940.
CHANLER, W. A. *Through Jungle and Desert: travels in East Africa.* 1896.
DARWIN, LEONARD. "British Expansion in Africa." *National Review,* vol. XXXIII (March–Aug. 1899).
DRUMMOND, H. *Tropical Africa.* 1888.
ELTON, J. F. *Travel and Researches among the Lakes and Mountains of East and Central Africa.* 1879.
FITZGERALD, W. W. *Travels in the Coastlands of British East Africa and the Islands of Zanzibar and Pemba.* 1898.

GESSI, R. *Seven Years in the Soudan.* 1892.

GIRAUD, V. *Les lacs de l'Afrique équatoriale: voyage d'exploration, 1883–5.* Paris, 1890.

GREGORY, J. W. *The Great Rift Valley, being a narrative of a journey to Mount Kenya and Lake Baringo.* 1896.

HARRIS, J. H. *Dawn in Darkest Africa.* 1912.

—— *Africa: Slave or Free?* 1919.

IRELAND, A. *Tropical Colonisation.* 1899.

JOHNSTON, (Sir) H. H. *The Kilimanjaro Expedition.* 1886.

JUNKER, W. *Travels in Africa.* 2 vols. 1890–2.

KINGSLEY, MARY. *Travels in West Africa.* 1897.

LIVINGSTONE, D. *Last Journals of David Livingstone.* 1874.

LUGARD, F., Lord. "Travels from the East Coast to Uganda, Lake Albert Edward and Lake Albert." *Proc. Royal Geog. Soc.* vol. XIV (1892), pp. 817–41.

MILUM, J. *Thomas Birch Freeman.* N.d.

MONTEIL, P. L. *De Saint-Louis à Tripoli par le lac Tchad.* Paris, 1895.

NEW, CHARLES. *Life, Wanderings and Labours in Eastern Africa.* 1883.

PATTERSON, J. H. *The Man-eaters of Tsavo and other East African Adventures.* 1907.

PETERS, K. *Die deutsch-ostafrikanische Kolonien.* 2nd edn. 1889.

—— *Die Gründung von Deutsch-Ostafrika.* 1906.

PINTO, A. S. *How I crossed Africa.* 1881.

READE, WINWOOD. *The African Sketch-Book.* 2 vols. 1873.

SCHWEINFURTH, G. A. *Heart of Africa.* Trans. by E. E. Frewer. 2 vols. 1878.

SOUTHERN RHODESIA. GOVERNMENT ARCHIVES. Oppenheimer series, No. 1–. 1945–. In progress. No. 2. *The Matabele Mission, 1858–78.* Ed. J. P. R. Wallis, 1945. No. 3. *The Northern Goldfields. Diaries of Thomas Baines.* 3 vols. 1946–.

STANLEY, Sir H. M. *Autobiography.* Ed. by D. Stanley. 1909.

—— *How I found Livingstone.* 1872.

—— *In Darkest Africa.* 2 vols. 1890.

THOMSON, J. "Notes on the Basin of the River Rovuma." *Proc. Royal Geog. Soc.* new ser. vol. IV (1882).

—— *Through Masai Land.* 2nd edn. 1885.

—— *To the Central African Lakes and Back*: the narrative of the Royal Geographical Society's East Central Africa Expedition. 2 vols. 1881.

TROUP, J. R. *With Stanley's Rear Column.* 1890.

WALLER, H. (ed.). *The Last Journals of David Livingstone.* 1874.

WHITE, A. S. *The Development of Africa.* 1892.

WHITFORD, J. *Trading Life in Western and Central Africa.* 1877.

WISSMANN, H. VON. *Unter deutscher Flägge quer durch Afrika von West nach Ost.* 1889.

—— *My Second Journey through Equatorial Africa, from the Congo to the Zambesi.* Trans. by M. J. A. Bergmann. 1891.

YOUNG, E. D. *Nyassa.* 1877.

Many British explorations were described, often by participants, in the *Journal of the Royal Geographical Society* and in the *Journal of the Royal Society of Arts.*

(f) LATER WORKS

For works on the Partition of Africa, see below Part II, 2 (D), INTERNATIONAL RELATIONS AND COLONIAL AFFAIRS.

ANDERSON-MORSHEAD, A. E. M. *History of the Universities Mission to Central Africa.* 1897.

ASBECK, F. M. VAN. *Sprongen en annlopen naar Zelfrieging in Brits Afrika.* Leiden, 1953. "Origin and development of self-government in British Africa."

BAKER, J. N. L. *History of Geographical Discovery.* 1931.

BEER, G. L. *African Questions at the Paris Peace Conference.* New York, 1923.

BLAKE, J. W. "The Study of African History." *Trans. Royal Hist. Soc.* 4th ser. vol. XXXII (1950), pp. 49–69.

Bovill, E. W. *Caravans of the Old Sahara.* 1933.

Brown, R. *The Story of Africa and its Explorers.* 5 vols. London, 1892–5. 4 vols. New York, 1911. Popular, but useful.

Buell, R. L. *Native Problems in Africa.* 2 vols. 1928. Vol. II contains important bibliog. and texts of international acts.

Burton, Lady Isabel. *Life of Sir Richard F. Burton.* 2 vols. 1893.

Coupland, Sir R. *The British Anti-Slavery Movement.* 1933.

Cust, R. N. *Africa Rediviva: or the Occupation of Africa by Christian Missionaries.* 1891.

Darcy, J. *France et Angleterre. Cent années de rivalité coloniale. L'Afrique.* 1904.

Du Plessis, J. *The Evangelisation of Pagan Africa.* Cape Town, 1929.

Evans, I. L. *The British in Tropical Africa, an historical outline.* Cambridge, 1929.

Findlay, C. J. and Holdsworth, W. W. *The History of the Wesleyan Methodist Missionary Society.* 5 vols. 1921–24.

Fortes, M. and Evans-Pritchard, E. E. (Eds.). *African Political Systems.* 1940.

Gibbons, H. A. *The New Map of Africa, 1900–1916: the History of European Colonial Expansion and Colonial Diplomacy.* 1917.

Giglio, C. *La politica Africana dell' Inghilterra.* Dadova, 1950.

Goodall, Norman. *A History of the London Missionary Society, 1895–1945.* 1954.

Groves, C. P. *The Planting of Christianity in Africa.* Vol. II, 1840–76. 1954.

Hailey, W. M., Lord. *An African Survey: a Study of problems arising in Africa south of the Sahara.* Oxford, 1938. 2nd edn. Oxford, 1945.

—— *Native Administration in British African Territories.* 1951.

Hannay, D. *The Great Chartered Companies.* 1926.

Herskovits, M. J. *The Myth of the Negro Past.* New York, 1941.

Hertslet, E. *Map of Africa by Treaty.* 3 vols. 1894. 3rd edn., 3 vols., 1909. 4th edn., 1911.

Hoskins, H. L. "British Policy in Africa, 1873–1877." *Geog. Rev.* Jan. 1942, pp. 140 *et seq.*

Johnston, Sir H. H. *History and Description of the British Empire in Africa.* 1910.

—— *History of the Colonisation of Africa by Alien Races.* 1899. Later edn. 1930.

—— *The Opening Up of Africa.* 1911. Later edn. 1937.

—— *The Story of My Life.* 1923.

Keltie, J. Scott. *The Partition of Africa.* 1893. 2nd edn. 1895.

Latourette, K. S. *A History of the Expansion of Christianity.* Vol. V, *The Great Century in the Americas, Australia, Asia and Africa, 1800–1914.* Vol. VI, *The Great Century in Northern Africa and Asia, 1800–1914.* New York, 1943–4.

League of Nations. *Slavery Convention, Geneva, September 25, 1926.* Geneva, 1926.

Lord, F. Townley. *Achievement: a Short History of the Baptist Missionary Society.* 1941.

Lovett, R. *History of the London Missionary Society.* 1899.

Lucas, Sir C. *Partition and Colonisation of Africa.* Oxford, 1922.

Lugard, F., Lord. *The Dual Mandate in British Tropical Africa.* 3rd edn. 1926.

—— "Slavery, Forced Labour and the League." *Nineteenth Century,* vol. XCIX (1926), pp. 76–85.

Mockler-Ferryman, A. F. *Imperial Africa.* 1898.

Morel, E. D. *The Black Man's Burden.* 1920. Slavery and forced labour.

Myers, J. B. (ed.). *The Centenary Volume of the Baptist Missionary Society, 1792–1892.* 1892.

Newlyn, W. T. and Rowan, D. C. *Money and Banking in British Colonial Africa.* 1954.

Noble, F. P. *The Redemption of Africa: a Story of Civilisation.* 2 vols. Chicago, 1899. Includes select bibliography on African missions.

Pascoe, S. P. *Two Hundred Years of the S.P.G.* 1901.

Perham, M. F. *Lugard.* Vol. I. *The Years of Adventure, 1858–98.* 1956.

Perham, M. F. and Simmons, J. (Eds.). *African Discovery.* 1942. Anthology of narratives by British explorers.

PIM, Sir A. W. *The Financial and Economic History of the African Tropical Territories.* 1941.

RAPHAEL, L. A. C. *The Cape-to-Cairo Dream. A Study in British Imperialism.* 1936.

SIMON, KATHLEEN, Lady. *Slavery.* 1929.

STOCK, E. *History of the Church Missionary Society.* 4 vols. 1899, 1916.

THOMPSON, H. P. *Into all Lands. The History of the S.P.G. in Foreign Parts, 1701–1950.* 1951.

WEIR, R. W. *A History of the Foreign Missions of the Church of Scotland.* 1900.

WESTERMANN, D. *Geschichte Afrikas.* Cologne. 1952.

WHITE, A. S. *The Development of Africa.* 1890. 2nd edn. 1892.

WIARTE, W. E. C. DE. *Les Grandes Compagnies coloniales anglais au XIXe siècle.* Paris, 1899.

WOOLF, L. *Empire and Commerce in Africa.* 1920.

WEST AFRICA IN GENERAL

See also under INTERNATIONAL RELATIONS below.

BAILLAUD, E. *La Politique indigène de l'Angleterre en Afrique occidentale.* Paris, 1912.

BAUER, P. T. *West African Trade.* 1954.

CARY, J. *Britain and West Africa.* 1947.

COLONIAL OFFICE. *West Africa Pocket Book: a Guide for newly-appointed Government officials.* 1905. Later edns.

CROWE, S. E. *The Berlin West Africa Conference, 1884–1885.* 1942.

FAGE, J. D. *Introduction to the History of West Africa.* 1955.

GEORGE, C. *The Rise of British West Africa.* 1904.

HERSKOVITS, M. J. *The Myth of the Negro Past.* New York, 1941.

—— "The Significance of West Africa for Negro Research." *Jour. of Negro History,* vol. XXI (1936), pp. 15–30.

KINGSLEY, MARY H. *The Story of West Africa.* [1899.]

—— *West African Studies.* 1899.

LUGARD, F., Lord. "West Africa." In *The Empire and the Century* (1905), pp. 835–60.

McPHEE, A. *The Economic Revolution in British West Africa.* 1926.

MEEK, M. and H. *Europe and West Africa.* 1940.

MOCKLER-FERRYMAN, A. F. *British West Africa.* 1900.

MONOD, J. L. *Histoire de l'Afrique occidentale française.* Paris, 1926.

PAYNE, J. A. D. *Payne's Lagos and West African Almanack and Diary for 1873–94.* 22 vols. 1873–94. Annual.

PROTHERO, Sir G. (Ed.). *West Africa.* 1920. Peace Handbooks, no. 90.

RUDIN, H. R. *The Germans in the Cameroons.* 1938.

WALLIS, C. B. *The Advance of our West African Empire.* 1903.

WAR OFFICE. *Diagram to illustrate the progress of the delimitation of British frontiers in Africa.* 1925.

—— *The Position of England and other European Powers on the West Coast of Africa and in the Hinterlands.* 1898.

West African Year-Book, 1901–. In progress.

SIERRA LEONE

(a) BIBLIOGRAPHY

LUKE, Sir H. C. *A Bibliography of Sierra Leone.* 2nd edn. 1925.

(b) PERIODICALS

Sierra Leone Studies, nos. 1–22, new ser. no. 1–, Freetown, 1919–39, 1953–. In progress.

(c) CONTEMPORARY WRITINGS

ALLDRIDGE, T. J. *The Sherbro and its Hinterland.* 1901.
BANBURY, G. A. L. *Sierra Leone, or White Man's Grave.* 1888.
BOURNE, H. R. Fox. "The Sierra Leone Troubles." *Fortnightly Rev.* (1898), pp. 216 *et seq.*
CHALMERS, J. A. "In Defence of Sir David Chalmers." *Nineteenth Century*, March 1900, pp. 485–97. Rising of 1899.
GARRETT, G. H. "Sierra Leone and the Interior, to the Upper Waters of the Niger." *Proc. Royal Geog. Soc.* vol. XIV (1892), pp. 433–55.
GRIFFITH, T. R. "Sierra Leone: past, present and future." *Proc. Royal Colonial Inst.* vol. XIII (1881–2), pp. 56–98.
INGHAM, E. G. *Sierra Leone after a Hundred Years.* 1894.
MADROLLE, C. *En Guinée.* 2nd edn. Paris, 1895.
PRINGLE, G. "White Man's Grave." *Westminster Rev.* Nov. 1899, pp. 565–70.
PROBYN, Sir L. "Sierra Leone and the Natives of West Africa." *African Soc. Jour.* vol. VI (1907), pp. 250–8.
SIERRA LEONE. *Ordinances*, etc. 1880–1904, 1905– . In progress. In parts to 1904, thereafter annually.
SLESSOR, A. K. "A Subaltern in the Bush." *Macmillan's Mag.* Aug. 1900, pp. 241–53.
TROTTER, J. K. *Niger Sources and the Borders of the New Sierra Leone Protectorate.* 1889.

(d) LATER WORKS

ALLDRIDGE, T. J. *A Transformed Colony: Sierra Leone as it was, and as it is.* 1910.
BIRTWHISTLE, A. *Thomas Birch Freeman.* 1950.
BUTT-THOMPSON, F. W. *Sierra Leone in History and Tradition.* 1926.
CROOKS, J. J. *Historical Records of the Royal Africa Corps.* Dublin, 1925.
GODDARD, T. N. *The Handbook of Sierra Leone.* 1925.
GWYNN, S. *The Life of Mary Kingsley.* 1932.
HARGREAVES, J. D. "The Establishment of the Sierra Leone Protectorate and the Insurrection of 1898." *Cambridge Hist. Jour.* vol. XII (1956), pp. 56–80.
—— "The Evolution of the Native Affairs Department." *Sierra Leone Studies*, new ser. no. 3 (Dec. 1954), pp. 168–84.
LUKE, Sir H. *Cities and Men: an Autobiography.* 3 vols. 1953–6. Vol. I, 1884–1914, has chapters on Sierra Leone, West Indies and Cyprus.
MIGEOD, F. W. H. *A View of Sierra Leone.* 1926.
NEWLAND, H. O. *Sierra Leone: its Peoples, Products and Secret Societies.* [1916.]
UTTING, F. A. J. *The Story of Sierra Leone.* 1931.

GAMBIA

(a) CONTEMPORARY WRITINGS

ARCHER, F. B. *The Gambia Colony and Protectorate: an official handbook.* 1906.
FITZGERALD, C. *The Gambia and its Proposed Cession to France.* 1875–6.
GAMBIA. *Ordinances, Rules, Regulations*, etc. 1901. Bathurst, 1901– . Issued in parts to 1920, thereafter annually. Collected and edited in 1916–17 and 1926.
YOUNG, Sir F. "Report on the Gambia Question." *Proc. Royal Colonial Inst.* vol. VII (1875–6), pp. 68–83, 122–24.

(b) LATER WORKS

ARMITAGE, Sir C. H. "Gambia Colony and Protectorate." *Royal Soc. of Arts Jour.* vol. LXXVI (1928), pp. 810–18.
GRAY, Sir J. M. *A History of the Gambia.* Cambridge. 1940.

HAMLYN, W. T. *A Short History of the Gambia.* Bathurst, 1931.
PROTHERO, Sir G. (Ed.). *Gambia.* 1920. Peace Handbooks, no. 91.
REEVE, H. F. *The Gambia: its History, Ancient, Medieval and Modern.* 1912.

GHANA

(a) BIBLIOGRAPHIES

CARDINALL, A. W. *A Bibliography of the Gold Coast.* Accra, 1932.
FULLER, Sir F. C. *Bibliography of the Gold Coast.* [1924.]

(b) PERIODICALS

Gold Coast Review. 1925– . In progress.
Transactions of the Gold Coast and Togoland Historical Society. Achimota, 1952– . In progress.
Transactions of the Cape Coast Historical Society, no. 1. Cape Coast, 1936.

(c) CONTEMPORARY WRITINGS

ALLEN, M. *The Gold Coast: or a cruise in West African waters.* 1874.
ARMITAGE, Sir C. H. and MONTENARO, A. F. *The Ashanti Campaign of 1900.* 1901.
BADEN-POWELL, Lord. *The Downfall of Prempeh.* 1896.
BELL, Sir H. H. J. *The History, Trade, Resources and Present Condition of the Gold Coast Settlement.* Liverpool, 1893.
BISS, H. C. V. *The Relief of Kumasi.* 1901.
BOYLE, F. *Through Fanteeland to Commassie: a diary of the Ashantee expedition.* 1874.
BRACKENBURY, Sir H. *The Ashanti War.* 2 vols. 1874.
BURTON, Sir R. F. and CAMERON, V. L. *To the Gold Coast for Gold: a personal narrative.* 2 vols. 1883.
BUTLER, Sir W. F. *Akim-foo: the history of a failure.* 1875.
ELLIS, A. B. *Tshi-Speaking Peoples of the Gold Coast.* 1887.
GLOVER, Sir J. H. *The Voyage of the Dayspring: being the Journal of the late Sir J.H.G.* Ed. by A. C. G. Hastings. 1926.
HAY, Sir J. D. *Ashanti and the Gold Coast.* 1874.
HENTY, G. A. *The March to Commassie.* 1874.
HODGSON, Lady. *The Siege of Kumasi.* 1901.
MACDONALD, G. *Gold Coast, Past and Present.* 1898.
MACDONNELL, Sir R. G. "Our Relations with the Ashantees." *Proc. Royal Colonial Inst.* vol. v (1873–4), pp. 71–102.
MAURICE, Sir J. F. *Ashantee War.* 1874.
MUSGRAVE, G. C. *To Kumassi with Scott.* 1896.
READE, W. W. *Story of the Ashantee Campaign.* 1874.
ROGERS, E. *Campaigning in West Africa and the Ashantee Invasion.* 1874.
STANLEY, Sir H. M. *Coomassie and Magdala: the story of two British Campaigns in Africa.* 1874.
SWANZY, A. *Trade on the Gold Coast.* 1874.

(d) LATER WORKS

BOURRET, F. M. *The Gold Coast. A Survey of the Gold Coast and British Togoland,* 1919–1951. 2nd edn. 1952. Chapters on earlier periods
CARDINALL, A. W. *In Ashanti and Beyond.* 1927.
CLARIDGE, W. W. *A History of the Gold Coast and Ashanti.* 2 vols. 1915.
DANQUAH, J. B. *Gold Coast.* 1928.
ELLIS, A. B. *History of the Gold Coast.* 1893.
FULLER, Sir F. C. *A Vanished Dynasty, Ashanti.* 1921.

GLOVER, Lady C. *Sir John Hawley Glover.* 1897.
HAYFORD, C. *Gold Coast Native Institutions.* 1903.
MIGEOD, F. W. H. "A History of the Gold Coast and Ashanti." *Jour. African Soc.* vol. xv (1916), pp. 234–43.
PROTHERO, Sir G. (Ed.). *Gold Coast.* 1920. Peace Handbooks, no. 93.
REYMAYNE, P. *The Gold Coast, Yesterday and Today.* 1938.
SARBAH, J. M. *Fanti Customary Laws.* 1897. 2nd edn. 1904.
SMITH, E. W. *The Golden Stool: some aspects of the conflict of cultures in modern Africa.* 1926.
SOUTHON, A. E. *Gold Coast Methodism.* 1934.
WARD, W. E. F. *A History of the Gold Coast.* 1949.
WEIMAN, C. W. *The Native States of the Gold Coast.* 1930.
WIGHT, M. *The Gold Coast Legislative Council.* 1947.
WILLCOCKS, Sir J. *From Kabul to Kumassi.* 1904.

NIGERIA

(a) BIBLIOGRAPHY

IBADAN. UNIVERSITY COLLEGE. *Nigerian Publications, 1950–.* *A list of works received under the Publications Ordinances.* Ibadan, 1953–. In progress.
NIGERIA. *The Preservation and Administration of Historical Records and the Establishment of a Public Record Office in Nigeria.* Lagos, 1954.

(b) PERIODICALS

Journal of the Historical Society of Nigeria. Ibadan, 1956–. In progress.
Nigeria. Lagos, Ibadan, 1933–. Title until 1936 *Nigerian Teacher.*
Nigerian Journal. Lagos, 1920–. In progress.
Proceedings of the Lagos Institute. Lagos, 1901–.

(c) CONTEMPORARY WRITINGS

BACON, Sir R. H. S. *Benin; the city of blood.* 1897.
BINDLOSS, H. *In the Niger Country.* 1898.
BOISRAGON, A. *The Benin Massacre.* 1897.
BURDO, A. *The Niger and the Benue.* 1880.
CALVERT, A. F. *Nigeria and its Tin Fields.* 1910.
CROUCH, A. P. *Glimpses of Feverland.* 1889.
CROWTHER, S. A. *Niger Mission: Bishop Crowther's report.* 1872.
DAWSON, A. J. *In the Bight of Benin.* 1897.
DELAFOSSE, M. *Haut Sénégal-Niger.* 3 vols. Paris, 1912.
ELLIS, A. B. *Yoruba-Speaking Peoples of the Slave Coast of West Africa.* 1894.
GOLDIE, H. *Calabar and its Mission.* 1890.
HAZZELDINE, G. D. *White Man in Nigeria.* 1904.
HIMBURY, Sir W. H. *Nigeria.* 1914.
LEONARD, A. G. *The Lower Niger and its Tribes.* 1906.
LUGARD, F., Lord. "England and France on the Niger: the Race for Borgu." *Nineteenth Century,* vol. xxxvii (June 1895), pp. 889–903.
—— "An Expedition to Borgu on the Niger." *Geog. Jour.* vol. vi (1895). Other articles by Lugard are noted in M. Perham, *Lugard,* vol. i (1956), pp. 722–23.
LUGARD, FLORA, Lady. *A Tropical Dependency.* 1905. Northern Nigeria.
MOCKLER-FERRYMAN, A. F. *Up the Niger: narrative of Major Claude Macdonald's mission.* 1892.
MOLONEY, Sir C. A. "Notes on Yoruba and the Colony and Protectorate of Lagos." *Proc. Royal Geog. Soc.* vol. xii (1890), pp. 596–614.

MOREL, E. D. *Affairs of West Africa.* 1902.
—— *Nigeria: its Peoples and Problems.* 2 vols. 1911.
PINNOCK, J. *Benin: the Surrounding Country, Inhabitants, Customs, Trade.* Liverpool, 1897.
ROBINSON, C. H. *Nigeria, our Latest Protectorate.* 1900.
ROE, H. *West African Scenes.* 1874.
ROTH, H. L. *Great Benin: its Customs, Art and Horrors.* Halifax, 1903.
ROYAL NIGER COMPANY. *Reports of the Directors,* etc., 1882–1914. London, 1883–1915.
SOMERSET, R. F. *Diary.* Privately printed, n.d.
THOMAS, N. W. *Anthropological Report on the Edo-Speaking Peoples of Nigeria.* 2 vols. 1910.
TREMEARNE, A. J. N. *The Niger and the West Sudan.* [1910.]
VANDELEUR, C. F. S. *Campaigning on the Upper Nile and Niger.* 1898.
VIARD, E. *Au Bas-Niger.* Paris, 1886.
WILLCOCKS, Sir J. *From Kabul to Kumassi.* 1904.

(d) LATER WORKS

ARNETT, F. J. *Rise of the Sokoto Fulani.* Kano, 1929.
BELL, E. M. *Flora Shaw, Lady Lugard.* 1948.
BURDON, (Sir) J. A. *Historical Notes on certain Emirates and Tribes.* 1909.
BURNS, Sir A. C. *History of Nigeria.* 5th edn. 1955.
COOK, A. N. *British Enterprise in Nigeria.* 1943.
CROCKER, W. R. *Nigeria: a critique of British administration.* 1936.
CROWTHER, D. C. *The Establishment of the Niger Delta Pastorate Church, 1864–1892.* Liverpool, 1907. Especially work of Bishop Crowther.
DIKÉ, K. O. *Trade and Politics in the Niger Delta, 1830–1885.* Oxford, 1956.
EPELLE, E. M. T. *The Church in the Niger Delta.* Aba, 1955.
GEARY, Sir W. M. N. *Nigeria under British Rule.* 1927.
HOGBEN, S. J. *The Muhammadan Emirates of Nigeria.* 1930.
HUBBARD, J. W. *The Sobo of the Niger Delta.* Zaria, 1953.
JOHNSON, S. *History of the Yorubas.* 1921.
LIVINGSTONE, W. P. *Mary Slessor of Calabar, Pioneer Missionary.* 1918.
LUGARD, F., Lord. *The Dual Mandate in British Tropical Africa.* 3rd edn. 1926.
MACLEOD, O. *Chiefs and Cities of Central Africa.* 1912.
MAXSE, F. I. "Acquisition of British Nigeria." *National Rev.* Jan. 1904, pp. 783–98.
—— "The Story of Nigeria." *National Rev.* Dec. 1903, pp. 607–23.
—— *Seymour Vandeleur.* 1905.
MEEK, C. K. *Northern Tribes of Nigeria.* 2 vols. Oxford, 1925.
NADEL, S. F. *A Black Byzantium: the Kingdom of Nupe in Nigeria.* 1942.
NIVEN, C. R. *Nigeria.* 1946.
ORR, C. W. J. *The Making of Northern Nigeria.* 1911.
PAGE, J. *The Black Bishop: Samuel Adjai Crowther.* 1907.
PERHAM, M. *Lugard.* Vol. I, *The Years of Adventure, 1858–98.* 1956.
—— *Native Administration in Nigeria.* Oxford, 1937.
PROTHERO, Sir G. (Ed.). *Nigeria.* 1920. Peace Handbooks, no. 94.
SCHULTZE, A. *The Sultanate of Bornu.* Trans. from German with additions...by P. A. Benton. 1913.
SCOTTER, W. H. "International Rivalry in the Bights of Benin and Biafra, 1815–85." *Bull. Inst. Hist. Research,* vol. XII (June 1934), pp. 63–66. Summary of unpublished thesis.
TALBOT, P. A. *Peoples of Southern Nigeria.* 4 vols. Oxford, 1926.
—— *Tribes of the Niger Delta.* 1932.
WALKER, F. D. *The Romance of the Black River.* 1930.
WELLESLEY, Lady D. *Sir George Goldie, Founder of Nigeria.* 1934.

EASTERN AND CENTRAL AFRICA

See also *C.H.B.E.* vol. II, pp. 993–7 and under TROPICAL AFRICA above.

(a) PERIODICALS

East African Historical Society Journal. Nairobi, 1954– . In progress.
Northern Rhodesia Journal. Livingstone, Northern Rhodesia Society, 1950– . In progress.
Reports of the Central Africa Archives, 1935– . Salisbury, S.R., 1947– . In progress.

(b) CONTEMPORARY WRITINGS

BAKER, Sir S. W. *Ismailia: a Narrative of the Expedition to Central Africa for the Suppression of the Slave Trade, organised by Ismail, Khedive of Egypt.* 2 vols. 1874.
CHESSON, F. W. *A Brief Reply to Sir Bartle Frere.* Aborigines Protection Society Pamphlet. 1881.
CHURCHILL, (Sir) W. L. S. *My African Journey.* 1908.
COOPER, J. *The Lost Continent, or Slavery and the Slave-Trade in Africa.* 1875.
CRAWFORD, O. "Slavery in East Central Africa." *Nineteenth Century,* Sept. 1888, pp. 439–50.
ELIOT, Sir C. N. E. *The East African Protectorate.* 1905.
FOSTER, H. J. *Handbook of British East Africa, including Zanzibar, Uganda and the Territories of the Imperial British East Africa Company.* 1893.
FRERE, Sir H. BARTLE. *East Africa as a Field for Missionary Labour.* 1874.
GESSI, R. *Seven Years in the Soudan…campaigns against the Arab slave hunters.* 1892.
Handbook for East Africa, Uganda and Zanzibar, 1905– . Mombasi, Nairobi, 1905– . Later edns. as *Red Book* (1919 etc.).
HORE, E. C. *Tanganyika, Eleven Years in Central Africa.* 1892.
HUTCHINSON, E. *The Slave Trade in East Africa.* 1874.
IMPERIAL BRITISH EAST AFRICA COMPANY. *Prospectus, Reports* [and other publications], 1888–95. 1888–97.
JOHNSTON, Sir H. H. *British Central Africa.* 1897.
—— *History of a Slave.* 1889.
—— *The Nile Quest.* 1903.
LONG, C. C. *Central Africa: naked truths of naked people.* 1876.
MCDERMOTT, P. L. *British East Africa or IBEA.* 1893. 2nd edn. 1895.
MACDONALD, J. R. L. *Soldiering and Surveying in British East Africa.* 1897.
MACKENZIE, J. *Austral Africa, losing it or ruling it.* 2 vols. 1887.
PETERS, CARL. *New Light on Dark Africa.* Trans. by H. W. Dulcken. 1891.
PURVIS, J. B. *Handbook of British East Africa and Uganda.* 1900.
STANLEY, Sir H. M. *The Congo and the Founding of its Free State.* 2 vols. 1885.
TORRENS, W. M. D. "The East Africa Slave-trade." *Fortnightly Rev.* May 1888, pp. 691–706.
TUCKER, A. R. *Eighteen Years in Uganda and East Africa.* 2 vols. 1908.
UNIVERSITIES MISSION TO CENTRAL AFRICA. *Reports,* 1909– . 1910– . In progress.
WALLER, H. "The Two Ends of the Slave-Stick." *Contemporary Rev.* vol. LV (April 1889), pp. 528–38.
WARD, G. *Letters from East Africa, 1895–97.* 1899.
WARD, H. F. and MILLIGAN, J. W. *Handbook of British East Africa.* Nairobi, 1912.
WAR OFFICE. *Précis of Information concerning the British East Africa Protectorate and Zanzibar.* 1901.
WASON, J. C. *East Africa and Uganda, or our last land.* 1905.

(c) LATER WORKS

ANDERSON-MORSHEAD, A. E. M. *The History of the Universities Mission to Central Africa, 1859–96.* 1909.

ANSTRUTHER, I. *I presume.* 1956. Biography of Sir H. M. Stanley.

BAKER, F. G. "Sir Richard Burton as I knew him." *Cornhill,* vol. LI (Oct. 1921), pp. 411–23.

BRADY, C. T. *Commerce and Conquest in East Africa.* Salem, Mass. 1950.

BRODE, H. *British and German East Africa: their Economic and Commercial Relations.* 1911.

—— *Tippoo Tib.* Trans. by H. Havelock. 1907.

CHIESI, G. *La colonizzazione europea nell'Est Africa.* Turin, 1909.

CLARKE, R. F. *Cardinal Lavigerie and the African Slave Trade.* 1889.

CORSI, A. *Colonie inglesi: el colonizzazione dell'Africa Orientale Inglese.* Rome, 1913.

COUPLAND, Sir R. *The Exploitation of East Africa, 1856–90.* 1939.

—— *Kirk on the Zambesi.* 1928.

—— *Livingstone's Last Journey.* 1945.

FROMENT-GUIEYSSE, G. *Brazza.* 1945.

GOYAU, G. *Un grand Missionnaire: le Cardinal Lavigerie.* 1925.

GREGORY, J. W. *Foundations of British East Africa.* 1901.

HANNA, A. J. *The Beginnings of Nyasaland and North-Eastern Rhodesia, 1859–95.* Oxford, 1956.

—— "The Role of the London Missionary Society in the Opening Up of East Central Africa." *Trans. Royal Hist. Soc.* 5th ser. vol. V (1955), pp. 41–59.

HANNAY, D. *The Great Chartered Companies.* 1926.

HARRIES, L. P. *Islam in East Africa.* 1954.

HENLEY, R. M. *A Memoir of Edward Steere.* 3rd edn. 1898.

HIEKE, E. *Zur Geschichte des deutschen Handels mit Ostafrika.* 1939.

HINDE, S. L. *The Fall of the Congo Arab.* 1897.

HOLE, H. M. *The Making of Rhodesia.* 1926.

HOWARD, C. and PLUMB, J. H. (Eds.). *West African Explorers.* Oxford, 1951.

JACKSON, Sir F. *Early Days in East Africa.* 1930.

JOELSON, F. S. *East Africa Today.* 1928.

JOHNSTON, A. *The Life and Letters of Sir Harry Johnston.* 1929.

JOHNSTON, Sir H. H. *George Grenfell and the Congo.* 2 vols. 1898.

—— *Livingstone and the Exploration of Central Africa.* 1891.

KIDNER, R. W. *The First Hundred Road Motors.* 1950.

KONDAPI, C. *Indians Overseas, 1838–1949.* New Delhi, Bombay, 1951. Particularly in Eastern and Southern Africa.

KURTZE, B. *Die Deutsch-Ostafrikanische Gesellschaft.* 1913.

LABOURET, H. *Monteil.* Paris, 1937.

LONDON MISSIONARY SOCIETY. *Register of Missionaries, Deputations, etc., from 1796 to 1923.* 4th edn. 1923.

LONG, B. K. *Drummond Chaplin: his life and times in Africa.* Oxford, 1941.

LUGARD, Lord. *The Rise of our East African Empire.* 2 vols. 1893.

MACKENZIE, W. D. *John Mackenzie: South African Missionary and Statesman.* 1902.

MACKINTOSH, C. W. *Coillard of the Zambesi.* 1907.

McNAIR, J. I. *Livingstone the Liberator.* 1941.

MAPLES, CHANNCY. *Journals and Papers.* Ed. by Ellen Maples. 1899.

MOIR, F. *After Livingstone.* 1923.

MURRAY, T. D. and SILVA WHITE, A. *Sir Samuel White: a Memoir.* 1895.

OLIVER, R. *The Missionary Factor in East Africa.* 1953.

—— *Sir Harry Johnston and the Scramble for Africa.* 1957.

—— "Some Factors in the British Occupation of East Africa, 1874–94." *Uganda Jour.* vol. XV (March 1951).

PERBANDT, C. VON, RICHELMANN, G. and SCHMIDT, R. *Hermann von Wissmann.* 1906.

PLAYNE, S. and GALE, F. H. *East Africa, British: its history, people, commerce, industry and resources.* 1909.

REEVES, J. S. *International Beginnings of the Congo Free State.* Baltimore, 1894.

ROBINSON, N. J. *The History of Smith Mackenzie and Company Limited.* 1938.

ROSCOE, J. *Twenty-five Years in East Africa.* Cambridge, 1921.

ROWLEY, H. "Story of the Universities' Mission to Central Africa." *Quarterly Rev.* Jan. 1889, pp. 229–48.

RUSHBROOK WILLIAMS, L. F. *Indian Emigration.* 1924.

RUSSEL, E. F. *Life of Charles Alan Smythies, Bishop of the Universities Mission to Central Africa.* 1898.

SCHONFIELD, H. J. *Richard Burton, Explorer.* 1936.

SCHWEINFURTH, G. *et alt. Emin Pasha in Central Africa.* 1888.

SCHWEITZER, G. *The Life and Work of Emin Pasha.* 2 vols. 1898.

SILLERY, A. *The Bechuanaland Protectorate.* 1952.

SIM, A. F. *Life and Letters of Arthur Fraser Sim.* 1897.

SIMMONS, J. *Livingstone and Africa.* 1955.

SMITH, E. W. *The Way of the White Fields in Rhodesia. A Survey of Christian Enterprise.* 1928.

SWANN, A. J. *Fighting the Slave-Hunters in Central Africa.* 1910.

THOMSON, J. B. *Joseph Thomson, African Explorer.* 1896.

TOZER, W. G. *Letters of Bishop Tozer and his Sister, together with some other records of the Universities Mission from 1863–1873.* Ed. by G. Ward. 1902.

VARIAN, H. F. *Some African Milestones.* 1953. Railway construction.

WALLIS, J. P. R. *Thomas Baines of King's Lynn, explorer and artist, 1820–1875.* 1941.

WEINTHAL, L. (Ed.). *Story of the Cape to Cairo Railway and River Route, 1877–1922.* 1923.

WEST, ALGERNON. *Private Diaries.* 1922.

WILSON, G H. *A History of the Universities Mission to Central Africa.* 1936.

BRITISH SOMALILAND

See also *C.H.B.E.* vol. II, p. 995.

(a) CONTEMPORARY WRITINGS

CAVENDISH, H. S. H. "Through Somaliland and around and South of Lake Rudolf." *Geog. Jour.* vol. XI (1898), pp. 372–96.

JAMES, F. L. *The Unknown Horn of Africa: an exploration from Berbera to the Leopard River.* 1888.

PEASE, Sir A. E. "Some Account of Somaliland." *Scottish Geog. Mag.* vol. XIV (1898), pp. 57–73.

SMITH, A. D. *Through unknown African Countries: the first expedition from Somaliland to Lake Lamu.* 1897.

WAR OFFICE. *Précis of Information concerning Somaliland.* 2 vols. 1902.

(b) LATER WORKS

BATTERSBY, H. F. P. *Richard Corfield of Somali.* 1914.

DRAKE-BROCKMAN, R. E. *British Somaliland.* 1912.

HAMILTON, J. A. L. M. *Somaliland.* 1911.

JARDINE, D. J. *The Mad Mullah of Somali.* 1923.

RAYNE, H. A. *Sun, Sand and Somals: leaves from the Note-Book of a district commissioner in British Somaliland.* 1923.

SCHWEIZER, G. *The Life and Work of Emin Pasha.* 2 vols. 1898.

WAR OFFICE. *Military Report on Somaliland.* 1907.

—— *Official History of the Operations in Somaliland, 1901–4.* 2 vols. 1907.

KENYA

See also *C.H.B.E.* vol. II, pp. 995–6, and EASTERN AND CENTRAL AFRICA above.

(a) PERIODICAL

Transactions of the Kenya Historical Society, 1956– . In progress.

(b) CONTEMPORARY WRITINGS

ANDERSON, A. G. *Our Newest Colony: being an account of British East Africa and its possibilities.* 1910.
BRONSON, E. B. *In closed Territory.* Chicago, 1910. Kenya.
CRANWORTH, Lord. *A Colony in the Making.* 1912.
HARDINGE, Sir A. H. "Legislative Methods in the Zanzibar and East African Protectorates." *Jour. Comp. Legis. and Internat. Law*, new ser. vol. 1 (1899), pp. 1–10.
HINDLIP, Lord. *British East Africa: Past, Present and Future.* 1905.
STIGAND, C. H. *Land of Zinj: being an account of British East Africa, its ancient history and present inhabitants.* 1913.
THOMSON, J. *Through Masai Land.* 1885.

(c) LATER WORKS

ADMIRALTY. *Handbook of Kenya Colony.* [1920.]
DILLEY, M. R. *British Policy in Kenya Colony.* 1937.
HILL, M. F. *Permanent Way. The Story of the Kenya and Uganda Railway.* Nairobi, 1949.
HINDE, S. L. and H. *Last of the Masai.* 1901.
HOBLEY, C. W. *Kenya: from chartered company to crown colony.* 1925.
HOLLIS, Sir A. C. *The Masai.* Oxford, 1905.
—— *The Nandi.* Oxford, 1909.
HOTCHKISS, W. R. *Then and now in Kenya: forty adventurous years in East Africa.* 1937.
HUXLEY, E. *Settlers of Kenya.* 1948.
—— *White Man's Country: Lord Delamere and the Making of Kenya.* New edn. 2 vols. 1953.
HUXLEY, E. and PERHAM, M. *Race and Politics in Kenya.* 1944.
LEYS, N. *Kenya.* 3rd edn. 1926.
ORDE-BROWNE, G. ST J. *Vanishing Tribes of Kenya.* 1925.
RAINSFORD, W. S. *Land of the Lion.* 1909. Kenya.
ROSS, W. M. *Kenya from within: a short political history.* 1927.
SALVADORI, M. *La colonisation européenne au Kenya.* Paris, 1938.
SMART, J. *Jubilee History of Nairobi, 1900–1950.* Nairobi, 1950.
WILSON, C. *Before the Dawn in Kenya.* Nairobi, 1952.

UGANDA

See also *C.H.B.E.* vol. II, pp. 993–4, and EASTERN AND CENTRAL AFRICA above.

(a) PERIODICALS

Bulletin of the Uganda Society, nos. 1–5. Kampala, 1943–45.
Uganda Journal. Kampala, Uganda Society, 1934– . In progress.

(b) CONTEMPORARY WRITINGS

ASHE, R. P. *Chronicles of Uganda.* 1894.
CATHOLIC UNION OF GREAT BRITAIN. *Notes on Uganda...the Late War between the I.B.E.A. Co. and the Catholics of the British Dependency.* 1893.

COLVILE, Sir H. E. *The Land of the Nile Springs*. 1895.
DILKE, Sir C. W. "The Uganda Problem." *Fortnightly Rev.* Feb. 1893, pp. 145–61.
FELKIN, R. W. and WILSON, C. T. *Uganda and the Egyptian Sudan.* 1882.
GOLDIE, Sir G. D. TAUBMAN. "Spheres of Influence." *Nineteenth Century*, Dec. 1892, pp. 984–90.
HATTERSLEY, C. W. *The Baganda at Home.* 1908.
JOHNSTON, Sir H. H. *The Uganda Protectorate.* 2 vols. 1904.
JONES, H. G. *Uganda in Transformation, 1876–1926.* 1926.
LLOYD, A. B. *Uganda to Khartoum: life and adventure on the Upper Nile.* 1906.
LUGARD, F., Lord. "British Officials and French Accusations" [about Uganda]. *Fortnightly Rev.* vol. LVIII (Nov. 1892), pp. 689–96. For Lugard's other writings see list in M. Perham: *Lugard*, vol. 1 (1956), pp. 722–3.
—— "East and West Africa in Parliament." *Blackwoods Mag.* vol. CLV (Jan. 1894).
MACKENZIE, Sir G. S. "Uganda and the East Africa Protectorates." *Fortnightly Rev.* Dec. 1894, pp. 882–94.
MERCUI, J. *L'Ougandia: La Mission Catholique et les Agents de la Compagnie Anglaise.* Paris, 1893.
Notes on Uganda. 1893.
PORTAL, Sir G. H. *The British Mission to Uganda in 1893.* Ed. by R. Rodd. 1894.
WOODWARD, E. M. *Précis of Information concerning the Uganda Protectorate.* War Office, 1902.

(c) LATER WORKS

ADMIRALTY. *Handbook of the Uganda Protectorate.* 1920.
BATTERSBY, C. F. H. *Pilkington of Uganda.* 1898.
GRAY, Sir J. "Early Treaties in Uganda, 1888–91." *Uganda Jour.* vol. XII (March 1948).
—— "Sir John Kirk and Mutesa." *Uganda Jour.* vol. XV (March 1951).
LOW, A. "British Public Opinion and the Uganda Question, October–December 1892." *Uganda Jour.* vol. XVIII (Sept. 1954).
THOMAS, H. B. "More Early Treaties in Uganda, 1891–96." *Uganda Jour.* vol. XIII (Sept. 1949).
THOMAS, H. B. and SCOTT, R. *Uganda.* 1935.
THOONEN, J. P. *Black Martyrs of Uganda.* 1941.
TUCKER, A. R. *Eighteen Years in Uganda and East Africa.* Vol. 1. 1908.

ZANZIBAR

See also *C.H.B.E.* vol. II, pp. 996–7, and EASTERN AND CENTRAL AFRICA above.

(a) CONTEMPORARY WRITINGS

BURTON, Sir R. F. *Zanzibar: city, island and coast.* 2 vols. 1872.
CAMERON, V. L. "Zanzibar, its past, present and future." *Revue des Colonies Internationales*, vol. 1 (1885), pp. 417–30.
COLOMB, P. H. *Slave-Catching in the Indian Ocean: a record of naval experience.* 1873.
CRASTER, J. E. E. *Pemba, the Spice Island of Zanzibar.* [1913.]
FIRMINGER, W. K. *Protectorate of Zanzibar.* British Empire series, vol. II (1899), pp. 259–78.
FITZGERALD, W. W. A. *Travels in the Coastlands of British East Africa and the Islands of Zanzibar and Pemba: their agricultural resources and general characteristics.* 1898.
FRERE, Sir H. BARTLE. "Zanzibar." *Macmillan's Mag.* 1875, pp. 183–92, 275–88.
LUGARD, F., Lord. "Slavery under the British Flag." *Nineteenth Century*, vol. XXXIX (Feb. 1896), pp. 335–55.
NEWMAN, H. S. *Banani, the transition from slavery: freedom in Zanzibar and Pemba.* [1898.]

SCHMIDT, K. W. *Sansibar.* Leipzig, 1888.
WALLER, H. *Case of our Zanzibar Slaves: why not liberate them?* 1896.
—— *Heligoland for Zanzibar, or one island full of free men for two full of slaves.* 1893.
YOUNGHUSBAND, E. *Glimpses of East Africa and Zanzibar.* 1910.

(*b*) LATER WORKS

ADMIRALTY. *Handbook of Kenya Colony and the Protectorate of Zanzibar.* 1920.
BRITISH EMPIRE EXHIBITION, WEMBLEY. *Zanzibar. An account of its People, Industries and History.* 1924.
COUPLAND, Sir R. *The Exploitation of East Africa, 1856–1890.* 1939.
CROFTON, R. H. *The Old Consulate at Zanzibar.* 1935.
—— *Zanzibar Affairs, 1914–1933.* 1953.
DE GROOT, E. "Great Britain and Germany in Zanzibar. Consul Holmwood's Papers, 1886–7." *Jour. Mod. Hist.* vol. xxv (1953), pp. 120–38.
HOLLINGSWORTH, L. W. *A Short History of the East Coast of Africa.* 1929.
—— *Zanzibar under the Foreign Office, 1890–1913.* 1953.
INGRAMS, W. H. *Zanzibar, its History and its People.* 1931.
LYNE, R. N. *Zanzibar in Contemporary Times: a short history.* 1905.
PEARCE, F. B. *Zanzibar: the island metropolis of East Africa.* 1919.
PROTHERO, Sir G. (Ed.). *Kenya, Uganda and Zanzibar.* 1920. Peace Handbooks, no. 96.
RODD, Sir J. R., Lord Rennell of Rodd. *Social and Diplomatic Memories, 1884–93.* 1922.
RUSSELL, C. E. B. *General Rigby, Zanzibar and the Slave Trade.* 1935.
SMITH, H. M. *Frank, Bishop of Zanzibar: life of Frank Weston, 1871–1924.* [1926.]
TAYLOR, A. J. P. *Germany's First Bid for Colonies.* 1938.
VAUGHAN, J. H. *The Dual Jurisdiction in Zanzibar.* 1935.

NYASALAND

See also *C.H.B.E.* vol. ii, p. 997.

(*a*) PERIODICAL

Nyasaland Journal. Blantyre, 1948– . In progress.

(*b*) CONTEMPORARY WRITINGS

COTTERILL, H. B. "Opening out of the District to the North of Lake Nyassa." *Soc. Arts Jour.* vol. xxvii (1879), pp. 242–7.
DAWSON, E. C. (Ed.). *The Last Journals of Bishop Hannington.* 1888.
ELMSLIE, W. A. *Among the wild Ngoni: being some chapters in the history of the Livingstonia Mission in British Central Africa.* 1899.
FOTHERINGHAM, L. M. *Adventures in Nyasaland: a two years' struggle with Arab slave-dealers in Central Africa.* 1891.
GEDDIE, J. *Lake Regions of Central Africa.* 1883.
Handbook of Nyasaland. 2nd edn. 1910.
HETHERWICK, A. *The Romance of Blantyre.* n.d.
JACK, J. W. *Daybreak in Livingstonia.* 1900.
KOLLMAN, P. *Victoria Nyanza: the land, the race and their customs.* 1899.
LUGARD, Lord. "The fight against slave-traders on Nyasa." *Contemporary Rev.* vol. lvi (Sept. 1889), pp. 335–45.
STEVENSON, J. *The Arabs in Central Africa and at Lake Nyasa.* Glasgow, 1888.
YOUNG, E. D. *Nyassa: a Journal of Adventures whilst exploring Lake Nyassa.* 1877.

(*c*) LATER WORKS

BARNES, B. H. *Johnson of Nyasaland.* 1933. [W. P. Johnson.]
DUFF, Sir H. L. *Nyasaland under the Foreign Office.* 1903. 2nd edn. 1906.

GEDDIE, J. *The Lake Regions of Central Africa: a record of modern discovery.* 1883.
HANNA, A. J. *The Beginnings of Nyasaland and North-Eastern Rhodesia, 1859–95.* Oxford, 1956.
LANGWORTHY, E. D. *This Africa was Mine.* 1952. Nyasaland in the 1890's.
LAWS, ROBERT. *Reminiscences of Livingstonia.* 1934.
LENFANT, G. *La découverte des grandes sources du centre de l'Afrique.* Paris, 1909.
LIVINGSTONE, W. P. *Laws of Livingstonia.* 1921. Dr Robert Laws.
MURRAY, S. S. *Handbook of Nyasaland.* 1932.
PERTHES, J. *Der Victoria-Njansa: eine monographische Studie auf Grund der vorhandenen Literatur.* Gottingen, 1913.
RANDOLPH, B. W. *Arthur Douglas, Missionary on Lake Nyasa.* 1912.

C. IMPERIAL FINANCE, TRADE AND COMMUNICATIONS, 1870–1914

(Chapters VI and XII)

(a) MANUSCRIPT SOURCES

See Part I, 1 and 2, especially Board of Trade returns on foreign and colonial trade (C.O. 442) and the various series of colonial government Gazettes and Miscellanea (for Shipping returns, etc.) preserved in the Colonial Office papers. The Treasury, Board of Trade and Customs House records noted contain much relevant material not yet examined by scholars.

(b) OFFICIAL PUBLICATIONS

See Part I, 3 and 4. The annual "Blue Book Reports" from the colonies, noted under PARLIAMENTARY PAPERS, 3 (a), contain essential statistical information on commerce. Under 3 (c) are listed the comparative statistics of imperial trade presented annually from 1865, for the years 1850 onwards. Besides these *Statistical Abstracts for the several Colonial and other Possessions of the United Kingdom,* the Colonial Office also prepared for Parliament annual *Statistical Tables regarding the British self-governing Dominions, Crown Colonies, Possessions and Protectorates, 1850–* (1865–). The Board of Trade issued a *Statistical Abstract for the British Empire, 1889–1913* (11 vols. 1904–15), and the Customs House has prepared since 1895 an *Annual Statement of the Trade of the United Kingdom with Foreign Countries and British Possessions, 1894–* (H.M.S.O. 1895–). In addition to the Statistical Abstracts, the following Parliamentary Papers may be specially noted: Report from Select Committee on Home and Colonial Sugar Industries, *Parl. Pap.* 1880, XII (106), (332); Papers on functions of Crown Agents for Colonies, *Parl. Pap.* 1881, XLIV [C. 3075]; Reports of Royal Commission on Depression of Trade and Industry, *Parl. Pap.* 1886, XXI [C. 4621], XXII [C. 4715–I], [C. 4715–II], XXIII [C. 4893]; Despatch from Chamberlain and replies from Colonial Governors re British Empire trade and foreign competition, *Parl. Pap.* 1897, LX [C. 8449]; Report and Papers of the Royal Commission on Sugar Industry in West Indies, *Parl. Pap.* 1898, L [C. 8655], [C. 8656], [C. 8657], LI [C. 8669], [C. 8675]; Despatch re business of Crown Agents' Office, *Parl. Pap.* 1904, LIX [Cd. 1944]; Statistical Tables relating to British and Foreign Trade and Industry, 1854–1908, *Parl. Pap.* 1909, CII [Cd. 4954]; Tables showing Progress of Merchant Shipping, *Parl. Pap.* 1913, LX [Cd. 7035]; Report of Committee on Edible and Oil-Producing Seeds in West Africa, *Parl. Pap.* 1916, IV [Cd. 8247]; Report to the Board of Trade on the Empire Cotton-Growers Association, *Parl. Pap.* 1920, XVI [Cmd. 523].

(c) BIBLIOGRAPHIES

See Part II, i (a) and the following special guides:

HEADICAR, B. M. and others. *A London Bibliography of the Social Sciences.* London School of Economics, 1931–7. 7 vols. Supplements, 1938– . In progress. Catalogue of the Library of the L.S.E., which is rich in books and pamphlet literature on imperial trade and economic doctrine.

MANN, J. DE L. and others. "List of Books and Articles on British Economic History, 1925" [etc.]. *Economic History Review,* 1927– . In progress. Latest list by W. M. Stern in vol. VIII, no. 3 (April 1956).

ROYAL EMPIRE SOCIETY. *Subject Catalogue of the Library.* Vol. I. 1930.

(d) PERIODICALS

See also Part II, i (b).

Agricultural History. Chicago, Baltimore, Agricultural History Society, 1927– . In progress.

Agricultural History Review. British Agricultural History Society, 1952– . In progress.

Bankers Magazine, 1844– . In progress.

Board of Trade Journal. London, 1877– . In progress.

Economic History (Supplement to the *Economic Journal*). Royal Economic Society, 1926– . In progress.

Economic History Review. Economic History Society, 1927– . In progress.

Economic Journal. Royal Economic Society, 1891– . In progress.

Economica. London School of Economics, 1921– . In progress.

Economist. London, 1843– . In progress, weekly.

IMPERIAL INSTITUTE. *Bulletin,* 1903– . In progress. Information on colonial products, trade, etc.

Institute of Bankers Journal, 1876– . In progress.

Institute of Transport Journal, 1920– . In progress.

Journal of Economic and Business History, vol. I– . Cambridge, Mass. 1928– .

Journal of Economic History. Economic History Association, New York, 1941– . In progress.

Journal of Political Economy. Chicago University, Chicago, 1892– . In progress.

Journal of Transport History. University of Leicester, 1955– . In progress.

Manchester Statistical Society Transactions. For 1853–4– . Manchester, 1854– . In progress.

Quarterly Journal of Economics. London, 1887– . In progress.

Review of Economic Studies, 1933– . In progress.

ROYAL STATISTICAL SOCIETY. *Journal.* London, 1838– . In progress.

Statist (The): a weekly journal for economists and men of business, 1866– .

(e) CONTEMPORARY WRITINGS

The following is only a small, representative selection of the vast polemical literature of the period.

AMERY, L. C. M. S. (Lord). *Union and Strength: a series of papers on imperial questions.* 1912.

ASHLEY, W. J. "The Argument for Preference." *Econ. Jour.* vol. XIV (1904), pp. 1–10.

—— (Ed.). *The British Dominions, their Present Commercial and Industrial Condition.* 1911.

—— *The Tariff Problem.* 2nd edn., 1904. 4th edn., 1920.

ASQUITH, H. H., Lord Oxford. *Trade and the Empire: Mr Chamberlain's Proposals examined in four speeches.* [1903.]

AUBRY, P. *Étude critique de la politique commerciale de l'Angleterre à l'égard de ses colonies.* Toulouse, 1904.

BADEN-POWELL, Sir G. S. "Colonial Government Securities." *Jour. Royal Col. Inst.* vol. xviii (1886–7), pp. 254–95.

—— "Financial Relations of the Empire: can they be improved?" *Jour. Royal Col. Inst.* vol. xxviii (1896–7), pp. 306–44.

—— *Protection and Bad Times, with special reference to the political economy of English colonization.* 1879.

BAGEHOT, W. *Lombard Street: a description of the money market.* 6th edn. 1875.

BERARD, V. *L'Angleterre et l'impérialisme.* Paris, 1900.

BOURNE, S. *Trade, Population and Food: a series of papers in economic statistics.* 1880.

BRASSEY, Lord. *Sixty Years of Progress and the new fiscal Policy.* 2nd edn. 1906.

BRIGHT, C. *Imperial Telegraphic Communication.* 1911.

BRITISH AND COLONIAL UNION. *Conference of Delegates from the various Chambers of Commerce of the British Colonies and Possessions on the Subject of British and inter-colonial Tariffs.* 1881.

BYLES, Sir J. B. *Sophisms of Free-Trade and Popular Political Economy Examined.* 1904.

CHAMBERLAIN, J. *Mr Chamberlain's Speeches.* Ed. by C. W. Boyd. 2 vols. 1914.

CLARKE, H. "On the Financial Resources of our Colonies." *Jour. Royal Col. Inst.* vol. iii (1872), pp. 130–47.

COOKE, E. C. "The Sugar Convention and the West Indies." *Econ. Jour.* vol. xvii (1907), pp. 315–29.

COWIE, A. G. *Sea Services of the Empire as Fields for Employment.* 1903.

COX, H. (Ed.). *British Industry under Free Trade: essays by experts.* 1903.

DAVIDSON, J. *Commercial Federation and Colonial Trade Policy.* 1900.

DENISON, C. T. *The Struggle for Imperial Unity.* 1909.

DILKE, Sir C. W. *Problem of Greater Britain.* 2 vols. 1890.

DRAGE, G. *The Imperial Organisation of Trade.* 1911.

FARRER, T. H., Lord. *Free Trade versus Fair Trade.* 3rd edn. 1886.

FLUX, A. W. "British Trade and German Competition." *Economic Jour.* vol. vii (1897), pp. 40–41.

GARVIN, J. L. "Lord Cromer and Free Trade." *National Rev.* Feb. 1908, pp. 981–99.

—— "The Maintenance of Empire: a Study of the Economic Basis of Political Power." *The Empire and the Century* (1905), p. 73.

GILMOUR, T. L. (Ed.). *All Sides of the Fiscal Controversy: speeches by Mr Chamberlain, Earl of Rosebery, and others.* 1903.

GISBORNE, W. "Colonisation." *Jour. Royal Col. Inst.* vol. xx (1888–9), pp. 53–88.

GRAHAM, W. *Free Trade and the Empire: a study in economics and politics.* 1904.

GREGORY, H. D. "Tariff Reform and Colonial Preference." *Empire Rev.* vol. xxi (1911), pp. 240–53.

GRESWELL, W. P. *The British Colonies and their Industries.* 1893.

GRICE, J. W. "The Oil Resources of the Empire." *United Empire,* vol. iv (Sept. 1913), pp. 745–53.

—— *The Resources of the Empire.* 1917.

GRIFFIN, M. I. J. "Colonies, Tariffs and Trade Treaties." *Blackwood's,* vol. cliii (June 1893), pp. 789–99.

HEATON, Sir J. H. "The Imperial Conference and our Imperial Communications." *Nineteenth Century,* vol. lxx (1911), pp. 265–78.

HIGGS, H. *The Financial System of the United Kingdom.* 1914.

HILLIER, A. P. *The Commonweal: a Study of the federal system of political economy.* 1909.

HIRST, F. W. and others. *Liberalism and the Empire.* 1900.

HIRST, Sir H. "The Organisation of Empire Trade." *Britannic Rev.* vol. i (1914), pp. 76–85.

HOLLAND, Sir T. "Trend of Mineral Development in India." *Jour. Royal Soc. Arts,* vol. lix (12 May 1911), pp. 642 *seqq.*

HOWARTH, O. J. R. "Some Aspects of Imperial Communications and Communication." In *Oxford Survey of the British Empire*, vol. VI (1914), pp. 342–62.

INTERNATIONAL FREE TRADE LEAGUE. *The Burden of Protection: an international repudiation of the gospel of artificial society.* 1912.

IRELAND, A. *Tropical Colonisation.* 1899.

KIRKALDY, A. W. *British Shipping: its history, organisation and importance.* 1914.

KIRKPATRICK, F. A. *Imperial Defence and Trade.* 1914.

KNOWLES, L. C. A. *The Economic Development of the British Overseas Empire.* 2nd edn. 2 vols. 1928.

LETHBRIDGE, R. *India and Imperial Preference.* 1907.

McCULLOCH, J. R. *A Dictionary of Commerce and Commercial Navigation.* New edn., ed. by A. J. Wilson. 1882. First pubd. 1832.

MAXWELL, H., PARKER, G. and TAYLOR, B. "Imperial Reciprocity." *Nineteenth Century*, June 1903, pp. 897–917. Three articles.

METHUEN, Sir A. M. M. *England's Ruin, discussed in 16 letters to the Rt. Hon. Joseph Chamberlain, M.P.* 3rd edn. [1905.]

MILNER, A., Lord. *Constructive Imperialism.* 1908.

MOLESWORTH, Sir G. L. *Our Empire under Protection and Free Trade.* 1902.

MULHALL, M. G. "The Trade of the British Colonies." *Contemporary Rev.* vol. LXXII (Nov. 1897), pp. 697–708.

MURRAY, K. B. "Mr Chamberlain and Colonial Opinion." *Econ. Jour.* vol. VII (1897), pp. 21–33.

NICHOLSON, J. S. *A Project of Empire: a critical study of the economics of imperialism.* 1909.

PAISH, G. "The Export of Capital and the Cost of Living." *Statist*, Supplement (14 Feb. 1914), p. iv.

—— "Great Britain's Capital Investments in Individual Colonial and Foreign Countries." *Jour. Royal Statistical Soc.* vol. LXXIV (Jan. 1911), pp. 176–200.

PORTER, G. R. *Progress of the Nation.* Ed. by F. W. Hirst. 1912. First pubd. 1836–43.

PRICE, L. L. "The Economic Possibilities of an Imperial Fiscal Policy." *Econ. Jour.* vol. XIII (1903), pp. 486–504.

—— "Economic Theory and Fiscal Policy." *Econ. Jour.* vol. XIV (1904), pp. 372–87.

PULSFORD, E. *Commerce and the Empire.* 1903.

RAWSON, Sir R. W. *Synopsis of the Tariffs and Trade of the British Empire.* 2 vols. Imperial Federation League, 1888.

ROOT, J. W. *Colonial Tariffs.* Liverpool, 1906.

—— *Tariff and Trade.* Liverpool, 1897.

ROSENBAUM, S. "The Trade of the British Empire." *Jour. Royal Statistical Soc.* vol. LXXVI (1913), pp. 739–74.

ROYAL COLONIAL INSTITUTE. *Official Report of the Emigration Conference*, 30, 31 May 1910. Ed. by H. E. Egerton. 1910.

SCHOOLING, J. H. *The British Trade Book, covering the years 1880–1907.* 3rd edn. 1908.

SCOTT, Sir G. *Burma. A Handbook of Practical Commercial and Political Information.* Rev. edn. 1921.

SCOTT, W. R. *Free Trade in relation to the Future of Britain and the Colonies: a plea for an imperial policy.* 1903.

SHAW, F. G. *Fiscal Facts and Fictions: a strictly commercial view of the tariff problem.* 1904.

SHAW, G. B. *Fabianism and the Fiscal Question: an alternative policy.* Fabian Soc., 1904.

SMITH, GOLDWIN. "Canada, the Empire, and Mr Chamberlain." *Monthly Rev.* Oct. 1903, pp. 38–54.

SPENDER, E. H. "Sir Robert Peel and Mr Chamberlain, 1845–1903; a contrast." *Fortnightly Rev.* Oct. 1903, pp. 598–613.

VINCENT, Sir C. E. H. "Inter-British Trade and its influence on the Unity of the Empire." *Jour. Royal Col. Inst.* vol. XXII (1890–1), pp. 265–303.

VOGEL, Sir J. "Colonies, Tariffs and Trade Treaties." *Edinburgh Rev.* June 1893, pp. 783–99.
—— "A Zollverein of the British Dominions." *Nineteenth Century*, Sept. 1892, pp. 498–508.
WATSON, J. F. "Character of the Colonial and Indian Trade of England contrasted with her Foreign Trade." *Jour. Royal Col. Inst.* vol. IX (1877–8), pp. 109–62.
WEBSTER, R. G. *Trade of the World: our present system of commerce examined.* 1880.
WILLIS, J. C. *Agriculture in the Tropics.* 3rd edn. 1922.
WILSON, A. J. *An Empire in Pawn: being lectures and essays on Indian, Colonial and domestic finance.* 1909.

(f) LATER WORKS

ALBION, R. G. "British Shipping and Latin America, 1806–1914." *Jour. Econ. Hist.* (Fall, 1951).
ALLIN, C. D. *A History of the Tariff Relations of the Australian Colonies.* Minneapolis, 1918.
ANSTEY, V. *The Economic Development of India.* 1929.
BAXTER, A. S. J. *The Imperial Banks.* 1929.
BELCHER, E. A. and WILLIAMSON, J. A. *Migration within the Empire.* (British Empire Survey, ed. by H. Gunn, vol. 12.) 1924.
BOGAARS, G. "The Effect of the Opening of the Suez Canal on the Trade and Development of Singapore." *Proc. Royal Asiatic Soc.*, Malayan Branch, vol. XXVIII, pt. 1 (1955), pp. 99–143.
BROWN, B. H. *The Tariff Reform Movement in Great Britain, 1881–95.* New York, 1943.
CAIRNCROSS, A. K. *Home and Foreign Investment, 1870–1913.* Cambridge, 1953.
CAMPBELL, P. C. *Chinese Coolie Emigration to Countries within the British Empire.* 1924.
CARROTHERS, W. A. *Emigration from the British Isles.* 1929.
CHALMERS, R. *History of Currency in the British Colonies.* 1893.
CLAPHAM, J. H. *An Economic History of Modern Britain.* 3 vols. 1932–38.
COLONIAL OFFICE. *An Economic Survey of the Colonial Empire, 1937.* H.M.S.O. 1940.
CROMLEY, C. H. *Protection in Canada and Australasia.* 1904.
CUNNINGHAM, W. *Growth of English Industry and Commerce in Modern Times.* 3rd edn. pt. 2, *Laissez Faire.* Cambridge, 1925. Previous edns. 1882, 1907.
—— *The Rise and Decline of the Free Trade Movement.* Cambridge, 1905.
DAVIDSON, J. "England's Commercial Policy towards her Colonies since the Treaty of Paris." *Polit. Science Quart.* vol. XIV (1899), pp. 39–68, 211–39.
DAY, C. *A History of Commerce.* 1917.
DEERR, N. *The History of Sugar.* 2 vols. 1949–50.
DWARKA NATH. *History of the Indians in British Guiana.* 1950.
ERICKSON, E. L. "The Introduction of East Indian Coolies into the British West Indies." *Jour. Mod. Hist.* vol. VI (June 1934), pp. 127–46.
FAY, C. R. *Great Britain from Adam Smith to the Present Day.* 1926.
—— *Imperial Economy and its Place in the Formulation of Economic Doctrine, 1600–1932.* Oxford, 1934.
FAYLE, C. E. *A Short History of the World's Shipping Industry.* 1933.
FEIS, H. *Europe, the World's Banker, 1870–1914.* New Haven, 1930.
FITZPATRICK, B. *The British Empire in Australia: an economic history, 1834–1939.* Melbourne, London, 1941.
FLUX, A. W. "The Commercial Supremacy of Great Britain." *Econ. Jour.* vol. IV (1894), pp. 457–67, 595–605; vol. IX (1899), pp. 173–83.
FRANKEL, S. H. *Capital Investment in Africa: its course and effects.* 1938.
FUCHS, C. J. *The Trade Policy of Great Britain and her Colonies since 1860.* Trans. from the German by Constance H. M. Archibald. 1905.
GRAHAM, G. S. "The Ascendancy of the Sailing Ship, 1850–85." *Econ. Hist. Rev.* 2nd ser. vol. IX (Aug. 1956), pp. 74–88.
GUILLET, E. C. *The Great Migration.* New York, 1937.
GULL, E. M. *British Economic Interests in the Far East.* 1943.

HANCOCK, (Sir) W. K. *Survey of British Commonwealth Affairs.* 4 vols. 1937–42.
—— *Wealth of Colonies.* 1950.
HANNAY, D. *The Great Chartered Companies.* 1926.
HENDERSON, W. O. "British Economic Activity in the German Colonies, 1884–1914." *Econ. Hist. Rev.* vol. xv (1945), pp. 56–66.
HITCHINS, F. H. *The Colonial Land and Emigration Commission* [1840–78]. Philadelphia, 1931.
HOBSON, C. K. *The Export of Capital.* 1914.
HOFFMAN, R. J. S. *Great Britain and German Trade Rivalry, 1875–1914.* Philadelphia, 1933.
HOSKINS, H. L. *British Routes to India.* Philadelphia, 1928.
HURD, Sir A. S. *The Sea Traders.* 1921.
—— *The Triumph of the Tramp Ship.* 1922.
HUTCHINSON, T. W. *Review of Economic Doctrines, 1870–1929.* 1953.
IMLAH, A. H. "British Balance of Payments and Export of Capital, 1816–1913." *Economic Hist. Rev.* 2nd ser. vol. v, no. 2 (1952), pp. 208–39.
—— "The Terms of Trade of the United Kingdom, 1798–1913." *Jour. Economic History*, vol. x, no. 2 (Nov. 1950), pp. 170–94.
JENKS, L. H. *The Migration of British Capital to 1875.* 1939.
JEUDWINE, J. W. *Studies in Empire and Trade.* 1923.
JOHNSON, S. C. *History of Emigration from the United Kingdom to North America, 1763–1912.* 1913.
JOHNSTON, Sir H. H. *History of the Colonisation of Africa by Alien Races.* Cambridge, 1899. New edn. 1930.
JONES, G. P. and POOL, A. G. *A Hundred Years of Economic Development in Great Britain, 1840–1940.* 1940.
JOURDAIN, W. R. *History of Land Legislation and Settlement in New Zealand.* 1925.
KAHN, A. E. *Great Britain in the World Economy.* 1946.
KIRKALDY, A. W. and EVANS, A. D. *The History and Economics of Transport.* 1915.
KNAPLUND, P. "Intra-Imperial Aspects of Britain's Defence Question, 1870–1900." *Canadian Hist. Rev.* III (June 1922), pp. 120–42.
KNOWLES, L. C. A. and C. M. *The Economic Development of the British Overseas Empire.* 3 vols. 1924–36.
KOEBNER, R. "The Concept of Economic Imperialism." *Econ. Hist. Rev.* 2nd ser. vol. II, no. 1 (1949), pp. 1–30.
KUCZYNSKI, J. *A Short History of Labour Conditions under Industrial Capitalism.* Vol. I, pt. 2. *The British Empire, 1800 to the present day.* 1946.
LONGHURST, H. C. *The Borneo Story: the history of the first hundred years of trading in the Far East by the Borneo Company Limited.* 1956.
LUBBOCK, B. *The China Clippers.* Glasgow, 1922.
—— *The Colonial Clippers.* Glasgow, 1921.
—— *The Last of the Windjammers.* 2 vols. Glasgow, 1927–9.
McLEOD, Sir C. C. and KIRKALDY, A. W. *The Trade, Commerce and Shipping of the Empire,* 1924.
McPHEE, A. *The Economic Revolution in British West Africa.* 1926.
MAIR, L. P. *Welfare in the British Colonies.* 1944.
MAIZELS. A. "The Oversea Trade, Statistics of the United Kingdom." *Jour. Royal Statistical Soc.* ser. A, vol. CXII, pt. 2 (1949), pp. 207–23.
MARAIS, J. S. *The Colonization of New Zealand.* 1927.
MASEFIELD, G. B. *A Short History of Agriculture in the British Colonies.* 1950.
MORRIS, Sir D. "The Imperial Development of Agriculture in the West Indies." *United Empire,* vol. II (1911), p. 78 *et seq.*
MURRAY, M. *Union-Castle Chronicle.* 1953.
NEWLYN, W. T. and ROWAN, D. C. *Money and Banking in British Colonial Africa.* Oxford, 1954.
PAGE, W. (Ed.). *Commerce and Industry: an Historical Review of the Economic Conditions of the British Empire from 1815 to 1914.* 2 vols. 1919.

PIM, Sir A. W. *The Financial and Economic History of the African Tropical Territories.* Oxford, 1940.

PLANT, G. F. *Oversea Settlement: Migration from the United Kingdom to the Dominions.* R.I.I.A., 1951. Chiefly on the period 1919–39.

PLUMTREE, A. F. W. *Central Banking in the British Dominions.* Oxford, 1940.

POLLARD, S. "The Economic History of British Shipbuilding, 1870–1914." Unpublished Ph.D. thesis, University of London, 1951.

PORRITT, E. *The Fiscal and Diplomatic Freedom of the British Oversea Dominions.* Oxford, 1922.

—— *Sixty Years of Protection in Canada.* 1908.

RAPHAEL, Mrs L. A. C. *Cape to Cairo Dream: a Study of British Imperialism.* 1936.

REID, W. S. *An Economic History of Great Britain.* New York, 1954.

ROBERTS, S. H. *History of Australian Land Settlement, 1788–1920.* Melbourne, 1924.

—— "History of the Contacts between the Orient and Australia." In *Australia and the Far East* (Sydney, 1935), p. 13.

ROSTOW, W. W. *The British Economy of the Nineteenth Century.* Oxford, 1948.

ROUSSEAUX, P. *Les mouvements du fond de l' économie anglaise, 1800–1913.* Louvain, 1938.

ROYAL INSTITUTE OF INTERNATIONAL AFFAIRS. *The Problems of International Investment: a Report by a Study Group.* 1937.

RUSSELL, R. S. *Imperial Preference.* 1947.

SCHLOTE, W. *British Overseas Trade, 1700 to the 1930's.* Trans. by W. O. Henderson and W. H. Chalmers. Oxford, 1952. First pubd. in German, 1938.

SCHUYLER, R. L. *The Fall of the Old Colonial System. A Study in British Free Trade, 1770–1870.* 1945.

SCOTT, Sir G. *Burma, a Handbook of Practical Commercial and Political Information.* Rev. edn. 1921.

SMITH, C. W. *Primal Root-causes of the Decline of the British Empire, 1876–1911.* 1911.

STAHL, K. M. *The Metropolitan Organisation of British Colonial Trade: four regional studies.* 1951.

THOMAS, B. *Migration and Economic Growth: a Study of Great Britain and the Atlantic Economy.* Cambridge, 1954.

VINER, J. *Canada's Balance of International Indebtedness, 1900–1913.* Cambridge, Mass. 1924.

WAGNER, D. O. "British Economists and the Empire." *Polit. Science. Quart.* XLVI (June 1931), pp. 248–76; XLVII (March 1932), pp. 57–74.

WARD, J. M. *British Policy in the South Pacific, 1786–1893.* 1948.

WOOLF, L. *Empire and Commerce in Africa.* 1920.

D. INTERNATIONAL RELATIONS AND COLONIAL AFFAIRS, 1869–1914

(Chapters IV, VIII, XIII and XIV)

(a) MANUSCRIPT SOURCES

See Part I, 1 and 2, for relevant lists of Colonial Office and Foreign Office papers, and for the private papers of statesmen. The captured German documents at present in Britain include valuable records of the Reichskanzlei from 1870. Many have been copied on microfilm or photostat, and these copies are available at the Public Record Office, London, where typed lists of them are kept. Most classes of French diplomatic documents are now open to 1900 at the Archives Nationales or the Ministère des Affaires Etrangères in Paris. Permission is occasionally granted for consultation of later documents. Useful guides to Belgian material on the Congo have been issued by the Institut Royal Colonial Belge, Brussels. For British material on the West Africa Conference of 1884–5, see especially F.O. 84/1809–22.

(b) COLLECTED HISTORICAL RECORDS

See Part I, 3 and 4, for the numerous Parliamentary Papers and Debates on international and colonial affairs, e.g. West African Conference, *Parl. Pap.* 1884–5, LV [C. 4205], [C. 4241], [C. 4284], [C. 4360], [C. 4361]. The General Act of the Conference is in *Parl. Pap.* 1884–5, LV [C. 4739]. Selected papers of the Conference were also issued as United States of America, *49th Congress, 1st Session, Senate Executive Document* No. 196 (1885). The following collections contain essential diplomatic documents for the whole period:

BITTNER, L., PRIBRAM, A. F. and others (Eds.). *Österreich-Ungarns Aussenpolitik von der bosnischen Krise 1908 bis zum Kriegsausbruch 1914.* 9 vols. Vienna, 1930.

FRANCE. COMMISSION DE PUBLICATION DES DOCUMENTS RELATIFS AUX ORIGINES DE LA GUERRE DE 1914. *Documents diplomatiques françaises, 1871–1914.* Ed. by E. Bourgeois, G. Pagès and others. First ser. 1871–1900. Second ser. 1901–11. Third ser. 1911–14. Paris, 1929– . In progress.

FRANCE. MINISTÈRE DES AFFAIRES ÉTRANGÈRES. *Documents diplomatiques. Affaires du Congo et de l'Afrique Occidentale, 1884 et 1885.* Paris, 1885.

GERMANY. REICHSTAG. *Stenographische Berichte über die Verhandlungen des Reichstages.* Berlin, 1870– . The series contains German White Books, e.g. *Angra Pequena,* 1884 and *Aktenstücke betreffend die Kongo Frage,* 1885.

GOOCH, G. P. and TEMPERLEY, H. W. V. (Eds.). *British Documents on the Origins of the War, 1898–1914.* 11 vols. in 13. H.M.S.O. 1927–38.

HERTSLET, Sir E. and others. (Eds.). *British and Foreign State Papers.* London, 1841– . In progress. *Treaties between Great Britain and Foreign Powers.* 31 vols. 1835–1926. After 1927 included in *B. & F.S.P.*

HERTSLET, Sir E. (Ed.). *The Map of Africa by Treaty.* 1894. Later edns., 3 vols. 1909 and 1911.

KAUTSKY, K. (comp.). *Die deutschen Dokumente zum Kriegsausbruch.* Ed. by M. Montgelas and W. Schücking. 4 vols. in 2. Charlottenburg, 1919. English translation: *The Outbreak of the War.* New York, 1924.

LEPSIUS, J., MENDELSSOHN-BARTHOLDY, A. and THIMME, F. (Eds.). *Die Grosse Politik der europäischen Kabinette, 1871–1914.* 40 vols. in 54. Berlin, 1922–7. (Selection in English, trans. by E. T. S. Dugdale under title: *German Diplomatic Documents, 1871–1914.* 4 vols. 1928–31.)

MACMURRAY, J. V. A. (Ed.). *Treaties and Agreements with and concerning China, 1894–1919.* 2 vols. New York, 1921.

MARCHAND, R. (Ed.). *Un Livre Noir. Diplomatie d'avant guerre d'après les documents des archives russes, 1910–17.* 3 vols. Paris, 1922–23.

PRIBRAM, A. F. (Ed.). *The Secret Treaties of Austria-Hungary, 1879–1914.* 2 vols. Cambridge, Mass., 1920–1.

SCHWERTFEGER, B. (Ed.). *Die belgischen Dokumente zur Vorgeschichte des Weltkrieges, 1885–1914.* 9 vols. Berlin, 1925.

SOCIETY OF COMPARATIVE LEGISLATION AND INTERNATIONAL LAW. *The Suez Canal: a selection of documents relating to the international status of the Suez Canal and the position of the Suez Canal Company, Nov. 30, 1854–July 26, 1956.* 1956.

TEMPERLEY, H. W. V. and PENSON, L. M. (Eds.). *A Century of Diplomatic Blue Books.* Cambridge, 1938.

—— (Eds.). *Foundations of British Foreign Policy from Pitt, 1792, to Salisbury, 1902.* Cambridge, 1938.

TREAT, P. J. (Ed.). *Diplomatic Relations between the United States and Japan.* Vol. III, 1895–1905. Stanford Univ., Cal., 1938.

(c) BIBLIOGRAPHIES

See above Part II, 1 (a) and the bibliographies in the *Cambridge Modern History,* vol. XII and in the *Cambridge History of British Foreign Policy,* vol. III (1923) for detailed lists up to the years of their publication. The classified lists of new works in each number of the *Journal of Modern History* are convenient.

ABBOTT, W. C. *An Introduction to the Documents relating to the International Status of Gibraltar, 1704-1934.* New York, 1934. Includes a general bibliography of official publications, books and articles on Gibraltar.

BEMIS, S. F. and GRIFFIN, G. G. *Guide to the Diplomatic History of the United States, 1775-1921.* Washington, 1935. Valuable for international relations in general as well as Anglo-American negotiations.

CONOVER, H. F. *Guide to Bibliographical Tools for Research in Foreign Affairs.* Washington, Library of Congress, 1956.

FOREIGN OFFICE. *Catalogue of the Printed Books in the Library of the Foreign Office.* 1926.

LANGER, W. L., ARMSTRONG, H. F. and others. *Foreign Affairs Bibliography. 1919-32, 1932-42, 1942-52.* 3 vols. New York, 1933, 1945, 1955.

WEGERER, A. VON. *Bibliographie zur Vorgeschichte des Weltkrieges.* Berlin, 1934.

WELTKRIEGSBUCHEREI. *Bibliographie zur Aussen und Kolonialpolitik des Deutschen Reiches, 1871-1914.* Stuttgart, 1943.

(d) PERIODICALS

See above, Part II, especially the *Cambridge Historical Journal, Current History, English Historical Review, Foreign Affairs, International Affairs, Journal of Modern History, Middle East, Pacific Affairs, Pacific Historical Review, Revue des Questions diplomatiques et coloniales, Revue d'histoire des colonies, Revue d'histoire moderne, Rivista Colonial.*

(e) CONTEMPORARY WRITINGS

Only a small selection of the vast polemical literature in book, pamphlet and article form is included here. On 'The Scramble for Africa', further material is given under Part II, B, pp. 850-65 above.

ALFORD, H. S. and SWORD, W. D. *The Egyptian Soudan: its Loss and Recovery.* 1898.

BAILLAUD, E. *La politique indigène de l'Angleterre en Afrique occidentale.* Paris, 1912.

BALFOUR, Lady BETTY. *Lord Lytton's Indian Administration.* 1899.

BANNING, E. *Le partage politique de l'Afrique.* Brussels, 1888.

BARING, E., Earl Cromer. *Modern Egypt.* 1908.

BRYCE, J. (Lord). *Impressions of South Africa.* 3rd edn. 1899.

BURROWS, M. *Imperial England.* [1880.] Foreign relations.

CHAMBERLAIN, J. *Foreign and Colonial Speeches.* 1897.

CHIROL, (Sir) V. *The Far Eastern Question.* 1896.

—— *The Middle Eastern Question.* 1903.

COLQUHOUN, A. R. *English Policy in the Far East.* 1885.

CURZON, G. N. (Lord). *Problems of the Far East.* Revised edn. 1896.

DERBY, EDWARD HENRY, Lord. *Speeches and Addresses.* Ed. by Sir T. H. Sanderson and E. S. Roscoe. 2 vols. 1894.

DEVILLE, V. *Le Partage de l'Afrique: exploration, colonisation, état politique.* Paris, 1898.

FELKIN, R. W. and WILSON, C. T. *Uganda and the Egyptian Sudan.* 1882.

FREYCINET, C. DE. *La Question d'Egypte.* Paris, 1914.

FULLERTON, W. M. *Problems of Power.* 2nd edn. 1914.

GESSI, R. *Seven Years in the Soudan.* 1892.

GORDON, C. G. *Letters of General C. G. Gordon to his sister, M. A. Gordon.* 1888.

HAKE, A. E. (Ed.). *The Journals of Major-General C. G. Gordon at Kartoum.* 1885.

IRELAND, A. *Colonial Administration in the Far East. Province of Burma.* 2 vols. Boston, 1907.

JOHNSTON, Sir H. H. *Common Sense in Foreign Policy.* 1913.

LEMONON, E. *L'Europe et la Politique Britannique, 1882–1909.* Paris, 1910.
MARTENS, T. T. *Russia and England in Central Asia.* 1879.
MILNER, Sir A. (Lord). *England in Egypt.* 1892.
MOREL, E. D. *Morocco in Diplomacy.* 1912.
NAPIER, M. (Ed.). *Selection from the Correspondence of Macvey Napier.* 1879.
POWER, P. *Letters from Khartoum.* 1885.
RAWLINSON, Sir H. *England and Russia in the East.* 1875.
ROUARD DE CARD, E. *Les territoires africains et les conventions franco-anglaises.* Paris, 1901.
SMITH, GOLDWIN. *Essays on Questions of the Day.* 2nd edn. New York, 1894.
STANLEY, Sir H. M. *The Congo and the Founding of its Free State.* 2 vols. 1885.
WINGATE, Sir F. R. *Mahdiism and the Egyptian Sudan.* 1891.
—— *Ten Years' Captivity in the Mahdi's Camp, 1882–1892.* 1892.

(f) CORRESPONDENCE, MEMOIRS AND BIOGRAPHIES

For other biographies of statesmen see above part II (e), where the arrangement is by subjects.

ASQUITH, H. H. (Lord Oxford). *The Genesis of the War.* 1923.
—— *Memories and Reflections, 1852–1927.* 2 vols. 1928.
BAINVILLE, J. *Bismarck et la France d'après les Mémoires du Prince Hohenlohe.* Paris, 1907.
BANNING, E. *Mémoires politiques et diplomatiques—comment fut fondé le Congo Belge.* Paris, 1927.
BISMARCK, O. VON, Prince. *Bismarck, the Man and the Statesman: being the Reflections and Reminiscences of Prince von Bismarck.* 2 vols. 1898.
BUCKLE, G. E. (Ed.). *Letters of Queen Victoria.* 2nd ser. 3 vols. 1926–28. 3rd ser. 3 vols. 1930–32.
BULOW, Prince von. *Memoirs.* 4 vols. 1931–32.
CECIL, Lady GWENDOLEN. *Life of Robert Marquis of Salisbury.* 4 vols. 1921–32.
CHAMBERLAIN, AUSTEN. *Down the Years.* 1935.
CHIROL, Sir V. *Fifty Years in a Changing World.* 1927.
CHURCHILL, (Sir) W. L. S. *Lord Randolph Churchill.* 2 vols. 1906.
CREWE, Lord. *Lord Rosebery.* 2 vols. 1931.
DENNETT, T. *John Hay.* New York, 1934.
DENNIS, A. L. P. *Adventures in American Diplomacy, 1896–1906.* New York, 1928.
DESCHANEL, P. *Gambetta.* 1920.
EDWARDS, H. SUTHERLAND. *Sir William White.* 1902.
EYCK, E. *Bismarck.* 3 vols. Zürich, 1946.
—— *Bismarck and the German Empire.* 1951.
FITZMAURICE, Lord E. *Life of the 2nd Earl Granville.* 2 vols. 1905.
FREYCINET, C. DE. *Souvenirs.* Paris, 1913.
GARDINER, A. G. *Life of Sir William Harcourt.* 2 vols. 1923.
GARVIN, J. L. and AMERY, J. *Joseph Chamberlain.* Vols. I–IV. 1932–4. 1951.
GREGORY, J. D. *On the Edge of Diplomacy.* 1929.
GREY, Sir E. (Lord Grey of Fallodon). *Twenty-five Years.* 2 vols. 1925.
GWYNN, S. and TUCKWELL, G. *Life of Sir Charles Dilke.* 2 vols. 1917.
GWYNN, S. *Letters and Friendships of Sir Cecil Spring Rice.* 2 vols. 1929.
HALDANE, R. B., Lord. *Before the War.* 1920.
HICKS BEACH, Lady V. *Life of Sir Michael Hicks Beach.* 2 vols. 1932.
KENNEDY, A. L. *Life of Lord Salisbury.* 1954.
LEE, Sir S. *King Edward VII.* 2 vols. 1925–27.
MAURICE, Sir F. D. *Haldane.* 1937.
MEYENDORFF, A., Baron (Ed.). *Correspondance diplomatique de M. de Staal, 1884–1900.* 2 vols. Paris, 1929.

MONYPENNY, W. F. and BUCKLE, G. E. *The Life of Benjamin Disraeli, Earl of Beacons-field.* 6 vols. 1910–20. Especially vols. V and VI, for the forward policy and Congress of Berlin.

MORLEY, JOHN, Lord. *Life of W. E. Gladstone.* 3 vols. 1903.

NEVINS, A. *Henry White: thirty years of American Diplomacy.* New York, 1930.

NEWBOLD, Sir DOUGLAS. *Life and Letters. The Making of the Modern Sudan.* Ed. K. D. D. Henderson, 1953.

NEWTON, Lord. *Lord Lansdowne.* 1929.

—— *Lord Lyons.* 2 vols. 1913.

NICOLSON, H. *Lord Carnock, a Study in the Old Diplomacy.* 1930.

POOLEY, A. M. (Ed.). *The Secret Memoirs of Count Hayashi.* 1915.

ROBERTS, Lord. *Forty-one Years in India.* 1897.

ROBERTSON, C. GRANT. *Bismarck.* 1918.

RONALDSHAY, Lord. *Life of Lord Curzon.* 3 vols. 1928.

RUSSELL, G. W. E. *Malcolm MacColl.* 1914.

SPENDER, J. A. *Life of Sir Henry Campbell-Bannerman.* 2 vols. 1923.

SPENDER, J. A. and ASQUITH, C. *Life of H. H. Asquith, Lord Oxford and Asquith.* 2 vols. 1932.

TAFFS, W. *Ambassador to Bismarck: Lord Odo Russell, first Baron Ampthill.* 1938.

TIRPITZ, A. VON. *My Memoirs.* 1919.

TREVELYAN, G. M. *Grey of Fallodon.* 1937.

WOLF, L. *Life of Lord Ripon.* 2 vols. 1921.

ZETLAND, Lord. *Lord Cromer.* 1932.

(g) LATER WORKS

See also Part II, 2 A and B above.

(i) *General Studies of Diplomacy*

ALBERTINI, L. *The Origins of the War of 1914.* Trans. from Italian by I. Massey. 3 vols. 1952–56.

BODELSEN, C. A. *Studies in Mid-Victorian Imperialism.* 1924.

BOURGEOIS, E. et PAGÈS, G. *Les origines et les responsabilités de la Grande Guerre.* Paris, 1922.

BRANDENBURG, E. *From Bismarck to the World War.* 1927.

BURROWS, M. *History of the Foreign Policy of Great Britain.* 1895. New edn. 1897.

CARRERE, J. *L'impérialisme britannique et le rapprochement franco-anglais, 1900–3.* Paris, 1917.

CECIL, A. *British Foreign Secretaries, 1807–1916.* 1927.

CRUTTWELL, C. R. M. *A History of Peaceful Change in the Modern World.* 1937.

ESCOTT, T. H. S. *The Story of British Diplomacy.* 1908.

FAY, S. B. *The Origins of the World War.* 2 vols. 2nd edn. New York, 1930.

FOOT, M. R. D. *British Foreign Policy since 1898.* 1956.

FRIEDJUNG, H. *Das Zeitalter des Imperialismus, 1884–1914.* 3 vols. Berlin, 1919–20.

FULLER, J. V. *Bismarck's Diplomacy at its Zenith* [1885–8]. Cambridge, Mass. 1922.

GLANVILLE, J. L. *Italy's Relations with England, 1896–1905.* Baltimore, 1934.

GLAZEBROOK, G. P. DE T. *Canadian External Relations: an Historical Study to 1914.* 1944.

—— "Canadian Foreign Policy in the Twentieth Century." *Jour. Mod. Hist.* vol. XXI (1949), pp. 44–55.

GOOCH, G. P. *Before the War: Studies in diplomacy.* 2 vols. 1936–8.

—— *Recent Revelations of European Diplomacy.* 4th edn. 1940.

—— *Studies in Diplomacy and Statecraft.* 1942.

—— *Studies in German History.* 1948.

GOSSES, F. *Het Bestuur des buitenlandsche betrekkingen in Engeland voor den Eersten Wereldoorlog hoofdzakelijk in de periode 1880 tot 1914.* Leyden, 1948. "The management of British foreign policy before the First World War, especially during the period 1880–1914."

HAGEN, M. VON. *Bismarcks Kolonial-politik.* Stuttgart, 1923.

HARDY, G. *La politique coloniale et le partage de la terre au XIXe et XXe siècles.* Paris, 1937.

HEADLAM-MORLEY, A. *Studies in Diplomatic History.* 1930.

HENDERSON, K. D. D. *The Making of the Modern Sudan: the Life and Letters of Sir Douglas Newbold.* 1953.

KENNEDY, A. L. *Old Diplomacy and New.* 1922.

KNAPLUND, P. *Gladstone and Britain's Imperial Policy.* 1927.

—— *Gladstone's Foreign Policy.* New York, 1935.

KOSCHITZKY, M. *Deutsche Kolonialgeschichte.* 2 vols. Leipzig, 1887–8.

LAFERLA, A. V. *British Malta.* 2 vols. 1938– .

LANGER, W. L. *The Diplomacy of Imperialism.* 2 vols. New York, 1935. 2nd edn. 1951.

—— *European Alliances and Alignments, 1871–90.* New York, 1930. 2nd edn. 1950.

—— *The Franco-Russian Alliance, 1890–94.* Cambridge, Mass. 1929.

LONDON. "THE TIMES" NEWSPAPER. *The History of "The Times", 1841–1921.* Vols. 2–4. 3 vols in 4 pts. 1939–52.

MARDER, A. J. *British Naval Policy, 1880–1905.* 1941.

MEDLICOTT, W. N. *The Congress of Berlin and After.* 1938.

—— "Diplomatic Relations after the Congress of Berlin." *Slavonic Rev.* vol. VIII (June 1929), pp. 66–79.

—— *Bismarck, Gladstone, and the Concert of Europe.* 1956.

MOON, P. T. *Imperialism and World Politics.* New York, 1928.

MORROW, I. F. D. "The Foreign Policy of Prince von Bülow, 1898–1909." *Cambridge Hist. Jour.* vol. IV (1932), pp. 63–93.

MURRAY, G. G. A. *The Foreign Policy of Britain, 1906–15.* Oxford, 1915.

PENSON, L. M. "The New Course in British Foreign Policy, 1892–1902." *Trans. Royal Hist. Soc.* 4th ser. vol. XXV (1943), pp. 121–38.

PRIBRAM, A. F. *Austria-Hungary and Great Britain, 1908–14.* 1951.

—— *England and the International Policy of the European Powers, 1871–1914.* Oxford, 1931.

—— *The Secret Treaties of Austria-Hungary, 1879–1914.* Cambridge, 1920.

RENOUVIN, P. "Les engagements de l'alliance franco-russe. Leur évolution de 1891 à 1914." *Rev. d'Histoire de la Guerre Mondiale,* vol. XII (1934), pp. 297–310.

ROBERTS, S. H. *The History of French Colonial Policy, 1870–1925.* 2 vols. 1929.

ROTHFELS, H. *Bismarcks englische Bündnispolitik.* Stuttgart, 1924.

SCHMITT, B. E. *The Coming of the War.* 2 vols. New York, 1930.

SETON-WATSON, R. W. *Britain in Europe, 1789–1914.* Cambridge, 1937.

SEYMOUR, C. *The Diplomatic Background of the War, 1870–1914.* New Haven, 1921.

SMITH, H. *Britain in Malta.* Vol. I, *Constitutional Development of Malta in the 19th century.* Vol. II, *Italian influence on British Policy in Malta, 1899–1903.* 2 vols. Valetta, 1953.

SONTAG, R. J. "British Foreign Policy, 1898–1912." *Jour. Mod. Hist.* vol. II (Sept. 1930), pp. 472–80. Review article.

—— "German Foreign Policy, 1904–6." *American Hist. Rev.* vol. XXXIII (1928), pp. 278–301.

—— *Germany and England: Background of Conflict, 1848–94.* New York, 1938.

SPENDER, J. A. *Fifty Years of Europe: a study in pre-War documents.* 1933.

STUART, G. H. *French Foreign Policy from Fashoda to Serajevo, 1898–1914.* New York, 1921.

TAYLOR, A. J. P. *Germany's First Bid for Colonies, 1884–5.* 1938.

TAYLOR, A. J. P. "Les premières années de l'alliance russe, 1842–95." *Rev. historique*, vol. CCIV (1950), pp. 62–76.
—— *The Struggle for Mastery in Europe, 1848–1918.* Oxford, 1954.
TEMPERLEY, H. W. V. "British Secret Diplomacy from Canning to Grey." *Cambridge Hist. Rev.* vol. VI (1938), pp. 1–32.
TEMPERLEY, H. W. V. and COLVILLE, A. (Eds.). *Studies in Anglo-French History.* Cambridge, 1935.
TOWNSEND, M. E. *Origins of Modern German Colonialism, 1871–1885.* New York, 1921.
—— *The Rise and Fall of Germany's Colonial Empire, 1884–1918.* New York, 1930.
TYLER, J. E. *The British Army and the Continent, 1904–14.* 1938.
—— "Campbell-Bannerman and the Liberal Imperialists, 1906–8." *History*, vol. XXIII (1938), pp. 254–62.
VALENTIN, V. *Bismarcks Aussenpolitik von 1871 bis 1890.* Berlin, 1922.
WARD, Sir A. W. and GOOCH, G. P. (Eds.). *Cambridge History of British Foreign Policy, 1783–1919.* 3 vols. Cambridge, 1922–3.
WOODWARD, E. L. *Great Britain and the German Navy.* 1935.
ZIMMERMANN, A. *Geschichte der deutschen Kolonialpolitik.* Berlin, 1914.

(ii) *The Mediterranean, Middle East and India*

BLAISDELL, D. C. *European Financial Control in the Ottoman Empire.* New York, 1929.
CHAPMAN, M. R. K. *Great Britain and the Bagdad Railway, 1888–1914.* Northampton, Mass. 1948.
CHOUBLIER, M. *La question d'orient depuis le traité de Berlin.* Paris, 1899.
DAVID, W. D. *European Diplomacy in the Near Eastern Question, 1906–1909.* Urbana, 1940.
DAVIES, C. C. *The Problem of the North-West Frontier, 1890–1908.* Cambridge, 1932.
DELONCLE, L. R. *Statut international du Maroc.* Paris, 1912.
DICKSON, H. R. P. *Kuwait and her Neighbours.* 1956.
EARLE, E. M. *Turkey, the Great Powers and the Bagdad Railway.* 1923.
EL-HAJONI, M. O. *Histoire diplomatique du Maroc, 1900–1912.* Paris, 1937.
FOREIGN OFFICE. *The Congress of Berlin, 1878.* 1920. Foreign Office Handbook, no. 154.
GARRATT, G. T. *Gibraltar and the Mediterranean.* 1939.
GAULD, W. A. "The *Dreikaiserbündnis* and the Eastern Question, 1877–78." *English Hist. Rev.* vol. XLII (1927), pp. 561–68.
GLANVILLE, J. L. *Italy's Relations with England, 1896–1905.* Baltimore, 1934. Maltese question, Somaliland, etc.
HARRIS, D. *Britain and the Bulgarian Horrors of 1876.* Chicago, 1939.
—— *A Diplomatic History of the Balkan Crisis of 1875–78. The First Year.* Stanford Univ., Cal. 1936.
HEADLAM-MORLEY, Sir J. W. *Studies in Diplomatic History.* 1930.
HILL, Sir G. *History of Cyprus.* Vol. IV. *The Turkish Province and Cyprus under British Rule.* Ed. by Sir H. Luke. 1952.
HYAMSON, A. *The British Consulate in Jerusalem in relation to the Jews of Palestine.* Part II. 1862–1914. 1941.
LANGER, W. L. "Russia, the Straits Question and the European Powers, 1904–8." *Eng. Hist. Rev.* vol. XLIV (1929), pp. 59–85.
LEE, D. E. (Ed.). "The Anglo-Austrian Understanding of 1877." *Slavonic Rev.* vol. X (1931), pp. 189–200. Note and texts of correspondence.
—— *Great Britain and the Cyprus Convention Policy of 1878.* Cambridge, Mass. 1934.
—— "The Proposed Mediterranean League of 1878." *Jour. Mod. Hist.* vol. III (1931), pp. 33–45.
MARDER, A. J. "British Naval Policy in 1878." *Jour. Mod. Hist.* vol. XII (1940), pp. 367–73.

MARRIOTT, Sir J. *The Eastern Question*. 1917.

MEDLICOTT, W. N. *The Congress of Berlin and After: a diplomatic history of the Near Eastern settlement, 1878–80*. 1938.

—— "Bismarck and the Three Emperors' Alliance, 1881–87." *Trans. Royal Hist. Soc.* 4th ser. vol. XXVII (1945), pp. 61–83.

—— "The Gladstone Government and the Cyprus Convention, 1880–85." *Jour. Mod. Hist.* vol. XII (June 1940), pp. 186–208.

—— "The Mediterranean Agreements of 1887." *Slavonic Rev.* vol. V (1926), pp. 66–88.

—— "Lord Salisbury and Turkey." *History*, vol. XII (1927), pp. 244–7.

MINTO, MARY, Lady. *India, Minto and Morley, 1905–10*. 1934.

MONROE, E. *The Mediterranean in Politics*. 1938.

MOREL, E. D. *Morocco in Diplomacy*. 1912.

SETON-WATSON, R. W. *Disraeli, Gladstone and the Eastern Question*. 1935.

—— *The Rise of Nationality in the Balkans*. 1917.

STUART, G. H. *The International City of Tangier*. Stanford, 1931.

SUMNER, B. H. *Russia and the Balkans, 1870–80*. Oxford, 1937.

TEMPERLEY, H. W. V. "Disraeli and Cyprus." *Eng. Hist. Rev.* vol. XLVI (1939), pp. 274–9, 457–60.

TYLER, M. W. *The European Powers and the Near East, 1875–1908*. Minneapolis, 1925.

WILLIAMSON, F. T. *Germany and Morocco before 1905*. Baltimore, 1937.

WOLF, J. B. *The Diplomatic History of the Bagdad Railroad*. New York, 1936.

(iii) *Egypt and The Sudan*

ABBAS, MEKKI. *The Sudan Question: the " Dispute" over the Anglo-Egyptian Condominium, 1884–1951*. 1952.

ALLEN, B. M. *Gordon and the Sudan*. 1931.

ARTHUR, Sir G. C. A. *Life of Lord Kitchener*. 1920.

—— (Ed.). *Letters of Lord and Lady Wolseley, 1870–1911*. 1922.

AURELES, J. D'. *Gordon Pacha*. Paris, 1945.

BLUNT, W. S. *My Diaries*. 2 vols. 1919–20.

CHURCHILL, (Sir) W. L. S. *The River War: an Account of the Reconquest of the Sudan*. 1899. 2nd edn. 1902.

CRABITES, P. *Gordon, the Sudan and Slavery*. 1933.

—— *The Winning of the Sudan*. 1934.

CROMER, Lord. *Abbas II*. 1915.

—— *Modern Egypt*. 2 vols. 1908. 2nd edn. 1911.

DUNDAS, L. J. L. *Lord Cromer*. 1932.

EGYPTIAN SOCIETY OF HISTORICAL STUDIES. *Proceedings*. Cairo, 1951– . In progress.

FREYCINET, CH. L. DE. *La Question d'Égypte*. Paris, 1905.

GIFFEN, M. B. *Fashoda*. Chicago, 1930.

HAGEN, M. VON. *England und Aegypten: Materialen zur Geschichte der britischen Okkupation mit besonderer Rücksicht auf Bismarcks Aegyptenpolitik*. Bonn, 1915.

HALLBERG, C. W. *The Suez Canal, its history and diplomatic importance*. New York, 1931.

HANOTAUX, F. *Fachoda*. Paris, 1909.

HANSON, L. and E. *Gordon*. 1953.

HENDERSON, K. D. D. *Survey of the Anglo-Egyptian Sudan, 1898–1944*. 1946.

—— *The Making of the Modern Sudan*. 1953.

HORNIK, M. P. "Mission of Sir Henry Drummond-Wolff to Constantinople, 1885–1887." *Eng. Hist. Rev.* vol. LV (1940), pp. 598–623.

HOSKINS, H. L. *British Routes to India*. New York, 1928.

—— "Some Recent Works on Mohamed Ali and Modern Egypt." *Jour. Mod. Hist.* vol. IV (March 1932), pp. 93–103.

KRAMER, W. *Die Koloniale Entwicklung des Anglo-aegyptischen Sudans*. Berlin, 1938.
LANDAU, J. M. "Notes on the Introduction of Ministerial Responsibility into Egypt." *Jour. Mod. Hist.* vol. XXVIII (March 1956), pp. 21–34.
LLOYD OF DOLOBRAN, G., Lord. *Egypt since Cromer*. 2 vols. 1933–4.
MacMICHAEL, H. *Sudan*. (Modern World Series.) 1954.
MARLOWE, J. *Anglo-Egyptian Relations, 1800–1953*. 1954.
MATTHEWS, J. J. *Egypt and the Formation of the Anglo-French Entente of 1904*. Philadelphia, 1939.
MAURICE, Sir F. B. and ARTHUR, Sir G. C. A. *The Life of Lord Wolseley*. 1924.
MILNER, Sir A. (Lord). *England in Egypt*. 1892.
RIFAAT BEY, M. *The Awakening of Modern Egypt*. 1947.
RIKER, T. W. "A Survey of British Policy in the Fashoda Crisis." *Polit. Science Quart.* vol. XLIV (1929), pp. 54–78.
ROYAL INSTITUTE OF INTERNATIONAL AFFAIRS. *Great Britain and Egypt, 1914–51*. (R.I.I.A. Information Papers, no. 19.) 3rd edn. 1952.
SABRY, MOHAMMED. *Episode de la question d'Afrique. L'empire égyptien sous Ismail et l'ingérence anglo-française, 1863–1879*. Paris, 1933.
—— *Le Soudan égyptien*. Cairo, 1947.
SAMMARCO, A. *Histoire d'Égypte moderne depuis Mohammed Ali jusqu'à l'occupation britannique, 1801–1882*. Cairo, 1937.
SANDWITH, F. M. "Egypt and the Egyptian Sudan, 1845–1907." In *Cambridge Modern History*, vol. XII, chapter 15. (Cambridge, 1911.)
SHIBEIKA, MEKKI EL. *British Policy in the Sudan, 1882–1902*. 1952.
SHUKRY, M. F. *Equatoria under Egyptian Rule*. Cairo, 1953. Includes correspondence of Gordon and Ismail, 1874–6.
STONE, J. *The Finance of Government Economic Development in the Sudan, 1899–1913*. Khartoum, 1954.
Sudan Notes and Records. Khartoum, Philosophical Society of the Sudan, 1918–. In progress.
TAYLOR, A. J. P. "Prelude to Fashoda: the Question of the Upper Nile, 1894–5." *Eng. Hist. Rev.* vol. LXV (Jan. 1950), pp. 52–70.
THEOBALD, A. B. *The Mahdiya: a History of the Anglo-Egyptian Sudan, 1881–1899*. 1951.
TRAILL, H. D. *England, Egypt and the Sudan*. 1900.
VELAY, E. *Les rivalités franco-anglaises en Egypte, 1876–1904*. Nîmes, 1904.
WILSON, Sir A. *The Suez Canal: its Past, Present and Future*. 1933.
WINGATE, Sir F. *Mahdiism and the Egyptian Soudan*. 1891.
WORTHAM, H. E. *Chinese Gordon*. Boston, 1933.
ZAGHI, C. *Gordon, Gessi e la Riconquista del Sudan, 1874–1881*. Florence, 1947.
ZETLAND, Lord. *Lord Cromer*. 1932.

(iv) *Africa*

See also under B. TROPICAL AFRICA, pp. 850–4 above.

ADAMS, M. "The British Attitude to German Colonisation, 1880–85." *Bull. Inst. Hist. Research*, vol. XV (1937), pp. 190–93. Summary of unpublished thesis.
ANDERSON, E. N. *The First Moroccan Crisis, 1904–6*. Chicago, 1930.
AYDELOTTE, W. O. *Bismarck and British Colonial Policy. The Problem of South West Africa, 1883–1885*. Philadelphia, 1937.
—— "The first German Colony and its Diplomatic Consequences." *Cambridge Hist. Jour.* vol. V, no. 3 (1937), pp. 291–313.
BAINS, I. "British Policy in relation to Portuguese Claims in West Africa, 1876–84." *Bull. Inst. Hist. Research*, vol. XIX (1941), pp. 94–96. Summary of unpublished thesis.
BEER, G. L. *African Questions at the Paris Peace Conference, with Papers on Egypt, Mesopotamia, and the Colonial Settlements*. New York, 1923.

BIXLER, R. W. *Anglo-German Imperialism in South Africa, 1880–1900*. Baltimore, 1932.
—— "Anglo-Portuguese Rivalry for Delagoa Bay". *Jour. Mod. Hist.* vol. VI (1934), pp. 425–40.
CROWE, S. E. *The Berlin West-African Conference, 1884–1885*. 1942.
CRUICKSHANK, E. F. *Morocco at the Parting of the Ways*. 1935. Madrid Conference, 1880.
DARCY, J. *France et Angleterre: cent années de rivalité coloniale: l'Afrique*. Paris, 1904.
DARMSTAEDTER, P. *Geschichte der Aufteilung und Kolonisation Afrikas*. 2 vols. Berlin, 1913, 1920.
DE GROOT, E. "Great Britain and Germany in Zanzibar: Consul Holmwood's Papers, 1886–1887." *Jour. Mod. Hist.* vol. XXV (1953), pp. 120–38.
DUBOIS, P. "Les négociations anglo-allemandes relatives aux colonies portugaises, 1912–14." *Rev. d'Hist. de la Guerre Mondiale*, vol. XVII (1939), pp. 353–68.
—— "Le traité anglo-allemand du 30 août 1898 relatif aux colonies portugaises." *Rev. d'Hist. de la Guerre Mondiale*, vol. XVII (1939), pp. 232–46.
GIBBONS, H. A. *The New Map of Africa, 1900–1916: the History of European Colonial Expansion and Colonial Diplomacy*. 1917.
HALLBERG, C. W. *The Suez Canal: its History and Diplomatic Importance*. New York, 1931.
HATTERSLEY, A. F. "The Annexation of the Transvaal, 1877." *History*, vol. XXI (June 1936), pp. 41–47.
HODGE, A. L. *Angra Pequéna*. Edinburgh, 1936.
HOLLINGSWORTH, L. W. *Zanzibar under the Foreign Office, 1890–1913*. 1953.
HORNIK, M. P. "The Anglo-Belgian Agreement of 12 May 1894." *Eng. Hist. Rev.* vol. LVII (April 1942), pp. 227–43.
JOHNSTON, Sir H. H. "International Interference in African Affairs." *Jour. Comparative Legislation*, vol. XL (1918), pp. 26–41.
KEITH, A. BERRIEDALE. *The Belgian Congo and the Berlin Act*. Oxford, 1919.
KONIGK, G. *Die Berliner Kongo Konferenz, 1884–5. Ein Beitrag zur Kolonialpolitik Bismarcks*. Essen, 1938.
LANGER, W. L. "The European Powers and the French Occupation of Tunis, 1878–81." *American Hist. Rev.* vol. XXXI (1925–6), pp. 55–78, 251–65.
LEBON, A. *La Politique de la France en Afrique, 1896–98*. Paris, 1901.
LEWIN, E. *The Germans and Africa*. 1915.
LONGRIGG, S. H. *A Short History of Eritrea*. 1945.
LOVELL, R. I. *The Struggle for South Africa*. New York, 1934.
MANGER, J. B. "Notes sur la crise marocaine de 1905." *Rev. d'Hist. de la Guerre Mondiale*, vol. XII (1934), pp. 311–40.
MURET, P. "La politique personnelle de Rouvier et la chute de Delcassé." *Rev. d'Hist. de la Guerre Mondiale*, vol. XVII (1939), pp. 209–31, 305–52.
NOWELL, C. E. "Portugal and the Partition of Africa." *Jour. Mod. Hist.* vol. XIX (March 1947), pp. 1–17.
PATZIG, C. A. *Die Afrikanische Konferenz und der Kongostaat*. Heidelberg, 1885.
PENNER, C. D. "Germany and the Transvaal before 1806." *Jour. Mod. Hist.* vol. XII (1940), pp. 31–58.
PYRAH, G. B. *Imperial Policy and South Africa, 1902–10*. 1955.
RAMM, A. "Great Britain and the Planting of Italian Power in the Red Sea, 1868–1885." *Eng. Hist. Rev.* vol. LIX (1944), pp. 211–36.
REEVES, J. S. *International Beginnings of the Congo Free State*. Baltimore, 1894.
RITCHIE, E. M. *The Unfinished War: the Drama of the Anglo-German Conflict in Africa*. 1940.
ROUARD DE CARD, E. *Les territoires africains et les conventions franco-anglaises*. Paris, 1901.
RUDIN, H. R. *Germans in the Cameroons*. New Haven, 1938.
SCOTT-KELTIE, J. *The Partition of Africa*. 1893.

SONTAG, R. J. "The Cowes Interview and the Kruger Telegram." *Polit. Science Quart.* vol. XL (1925), pp. 217–47.
STUART, G. H. *The International City of Tangier.* Stanford, 1931.
TAYLOR, A. J. P. "British Policy in Morocco, 1886–1902." *Eng. Hist. Rev.* vol. LXVI (July 1951), pp. 342–74. Reprinted in author's *Rumours of Wars* (1952).
—— *Germany's First Bid for Colonies, 1884–5.* 1938.
—— "Prelude to Fashoda: the Question of the Upper Nile, 1894–5." *Eng. Hist. Rev.* vol. LXV (1950), pp. 52–80. Reprinted in *Rumours of Wars* (1952).
THOMAS, M. E. "Anglo-Belgian Military Relations and the Congo Question, 1911–1913." *Jour. Mod. Hist.* vol. XXV (1953), pp. 157–65.
THOMSON, R. S. *Fondation de l'Etat Indépendant du Congo. Un chapitre de l'histoire du partage de l'Afrique.* Brussels, 1933.
TOWNSEND, M. E. *The Origins of Modern German Colonialism, 1871–85.* New York, 1921.
VAN DER POEL, J, *The Jameson Raid.* 1951,
WALKER, E. A. "The Jameson Raid." *Cambridge Hist. Jour.* vol. VI, no. 3 (1940), pp. 283–306.
YARNALL, H. E. *The Great Powers and the Congo Conference, 1884 and 1885.* Göttingen, 1934.

(v) *The Far East*

BARING-GOULD, S. *A History of Sarawak under two White Rajahs, 1839–1908.* 1909.
CLARKE, Sir A. *The Straits Settlements.* 1899.
DALLIN, D. J. *The Rise of Russia in Asia.* 1950.
DENNETT, J. *Roosevelt and the Russo-Japanese War.* New York, 1925.
DENNIS, A. L. P. *The Anglo-Japanese Alliance.* Berkeley, Cal. 1923.
EDWARDS, E. W. "The Far Eastern Agreements of 1907." *Jour. Mod. Hist.* vol. XXVI (1954), pp. 340–55.
HALL, D. G. E. *Burma.* 2nd edn. 1956.
HALL, D. G. E. "English Relations with Burma, 1587–1886." *History,* vol. XXVIII (Sept. 1943), pp. 182–200.
—— *A History of South-East Asia.* 1955.
HALL, L. J. "A Partnership in Peacemaking: Theodore Roosevelt and Wilhelm II." *Pacific Hist. Rev.* vol. XIII (1944), pp. 390–411.
HARRISON, B. *Southeast Asia, a Short History.* 1954.
HUDSON, G. F. *The Far East in World Politics.* 2nd edn. 1939.
INGRAMS, H. *Hongkong.* 1952.
JOSEPH, P. *Foreign Diplomacy in China, 1894–1900.* 1928.
KAWAI, K. "Anglo-German Rivalry in the Yangtze Region, 1895–1902." *Pacific Hist. Rev.* vol. VIII (Dec. 1939), pp. 413–33.
KENT, P. H. *Railway Enterprise in China.* 1907.
KIERNAN, E. V. G. "Britain, Siam and Malaya, 1875–1885." *Jour. Mod. Hist.* vol. XXVIII (March 1956), pp. 1–20.
—— *British Diplomacy in China, 1880–85.* Cambridge, 1939.
LOVAT, ALICE M., Lady. *Life of Sir Frederick Weld, pioneer of Empire.* 1914.
McCORDOCK, R. S. *British Far Eastern Policy, 1894–1900.* New York, 1931.
McNAIR, F. *Perak and the Malays.* 1878.
MAKEPEACE, W., BROOKE, G. E. and BRADDELL, R. St J. (Eds.). *One Hundred Years of Singapore.* 1921.
MAXWELL, Sir P. B. *Our Malay Conquests.* 1878.
MILLS, L. A. *British Rule in Eastern Asia: a study of comparative government and economic development in British Malaya and Hong Kong.* 1942. Institute of Pacific Relations, International Research series.
MORSE, H. B. (Ed.). *The International Relations of the Chinese Empire.* 3 vols. 1910–18.
PURCELL, V. *The Colonial Period in South-east Asia.* 1953.
RENOUVIN, P. *La question d'Extrême-Orient, 1840–1940.* Paris, 1946.

RUTTER, O. *British North Borneo.* 1922.
SWETTENHAM, Sir F. A. *British Malaya; an account of the origin and progress of British influence in Malaya.* 3rd edn. 1949. First pubd. 1906.
—— *Footprints in Malaya.* 1942. Autobiography.
TANSILL, C. C. *The Foreign Policy of Thomas F. Bayard, 1885–97.* New York, 1940.
THOMSON, J. *The Straits of Malacca, Indo-China and China.* 1875.
VAGTS, A. "William II and the Siam Episode." *American Hist. Rev.* vol. XLV (1940), pp. 834–41. Note and comments.
WINSTEDT, Sir R. *Malaya and its History.* 4th edn. 1956.
WINT, G. *The British in Asia.* 1947. 2nd edn. 1954.
WRIGHT, A. (Ed.). *Twentieth-century Impressions of British Malaya.* 1908.
WRIGHT, A. and REID, T. H. *The Malay Peninsula.* 1912.

(vii) *The Pacific*

BROOKES, J. I. *International Rivalry in the Pacific Islands, 1800–1875.* Univ. of California, 1941.
DRUS, E. "The Colonial Office and the Annexation of Fiji." *Trans. Royal Hist. Soc.* 4th ser. vol. XXXII (1950), pp. 87–110.
ELLISON, J. W. "The Partition of Samoa: a study in imperialism and diplomacy." *Pacific Hist. Rev.* vol. VIII (Sept. 1939), pp. 259–88.
FLETCHER, C. B. "Australia and the Pacific, 1788 to 1885," *Royal Australian Hist. Soc. Jour.* vol. XXVIII (1942), pp. 157–84.
JACOBS, M. G. "Bismarck and the Annexation of New Guinea." *Hist. Studies, Australia and New Zealand,* vol. V (Nov. 1951), pp. 14–26.
—— "The Colonial Office and New Guinea, 1874–84." *Hist. Studies, Australia and New Zealand,* vol. V (May 1952), pp. 106–18.
KEESING, F. M. *Modern Samoa.* 1934.
KOSKINEN, A. A. *Missionary Influence as a Political Factor in the Pacific Islands.* Helsinki, 1953.
MARTIN, K. L. P. *Missionaries and Annexations in the Pacific.* Oxford, 1924.
MASTERMAN, S. *The Origins of International Rivalry in Samoa, 1845–1884.* 1934.
SCHOLEFIELD, G. H. *The Pacific, its past and future, and the policy of the Great Powers from the 18th century.* 1919.
WARD, J. M. *British Policy in the South Pacific, 1786–1893.* 1948.
YOUNG, W. A. *Christianity and Civilisation in the South Pacific: the influence of missionaries upon European expansion in the Pacific during the 19th century.* Oxford, 1922.

E. THE BRITISH EMPIRE AND THE UNITED STATES OF AMERICA, 1870–1914

(Chapter IX)

(a) MANUSCRIPT SOURCES

See Part I, 1 (a) and (b) for lists of Colonial and Foreign Office records. The series most significant for this subject are: C.O. 807. Confidential Print, North America, 1677–1891; F.O. 5. General Correspondence, United States of America, 1793–1905; F.O. 115, Embassy and Consular Archives, United States of America, Correspondence, 1791–1929; F.O. 301, Americas, Archives of Commissions—Fisheries, Northwest Boundary, British and American Claims, Miscellaneous; F.O. 462, Confidential Print, United States of America; F.O. 548, Confidential Print, Settlements of Questions between the United States, Canada and Newfoundland, 1908–15. Among Gifts and Deposits at the Public Record Office, P.R.O. 30/6 Carnarvon Papers and P.R.O. 30/48 Granville Papers are valuable for Anglo-American Relations.

For papers of other statesmen, see Part I, 2 (*a*) and (*b*), particularly the Gladstone, Bright and Dilke Papers in the British Museum, and the Bryce, Salisbury and Lansdowne MSS. elsewhere. In the Public Archives at Ottawa are the papers of Laurier, Macdonald and Alexander Mackenzie, also the Baring family papers, of significance for Anglo-American relations at many points. Papers of many important American statesmen are in the Manuscript Department of the Library of Congress.

(*b*) Collected Historical Records

See Part I, 3 (*e*) and 4 for references to Parliamentary Papers and Hansard. On the American side, the main classes of printed Congressional Papers are: *Senate Executive Documents, Senate Miscellaneous Documents, Senate Reports, House (Executive) Documents, House Miscellaneous Documents, House Reports.* There is a *Checklist of United States Public Documents, 1789–1909* (3rd edn. Washington, Govt. Printing Office, 1911). Formal proceedings are recorded in the *Journal of the Senate, 1789–* (New York, Philadelphia, Washington, 1789– . In progress) and in the *Journal of the House of Representatives* (Washington, etc., 1789– . In progress). Debates during this period are in the *Congressional Globe,* 1833–73 (46 vols. in 111 vols. Washington, 1834–74), continued by the *Congressional Record,* vols. 1– (Washington, 1874– . In progress).

The following official U.S.A. publications are of special importance:

Papers relating to the Foreign Relations of the United States, 1861– . Washington, U.S.A., Dept. of State, 1872– . In progress. General index to vols. for 1861–99 (Washington, 1902).

Correspondence concerning Claims against Great Britain. 7 vols. Washington, U.S.A. Dept. of State, 1869–71.

Correspondence respecting the Geneva Arbitration. Washington, U.S.A. Dept. of State, 1872.

Papers relating to the Treaty of Washington. 6 vols. Washington, U.S.A. Dept. of State, 1872–4.

Correspondence in relation to the proposed Interoceanic canal between the Atlantic and Pacific Oceans, the Clayton-Bulwer Treaty and the Monroe Doctrine. Washington, Dept. of State, 1885.

Correspondence in relation to the Boundary Controversy between Great Britain and Venezuela. Washington, Dept. of State, 1896.

Reciprocity with Canada: a study of the Arrangement of 1911. Washington, U.S.A. Tariff Commission, 1920. One of a series of Tariff Commission Pamphlets.

Alaskan Boundary Tribunal Proceedings. *58th Cong. 2nd Sess. Senate Doc. 162.* 7 vols. Washington, 1904.

Boundaries of the United States and of the Several States and Territories. *58th Cong. 2nd Sess., House Document 678.* 3rd edn. Washington, 1904.

North American Conservation Congress. *60th Cong. 2nd Sess., Senate Document 742.* Washington, 1908.

The General Arbitration Treaties with Great Britain and France. *62nd Cong. 2nd Sess., Senate Document 353.* Washington, 1912.

The following collections are also indispensable:

Clyde, P. H. (Ed.). *United States Policy toward China. Diplomatic and Public Documents, 1838–1939.* Durham, N.C. 1940.

Gooch, G. P. and Temperley, H. W. V. (Eds.). *British Official Documents on the Origins of the War of 1914.* 11 vols. 1927–38.

Hackworth, G. H. *Digest of International Law.* 8 vols. Washington, 1940–44.

Hasse, A. R. *Index to United States Documents relating to Foreign Affairs.* 3 vols. Washington, 1914.

Hertslet, Sir E. and others (Eds.). *Treaties between Great Britain and Foreign Powers.* 31 vols. H.M.S.O., 1821–1925.

HYDE, C. C. (ed.). *International Law, chiefly as interpreted and applied by the United States.* 2 vols. 1923.

MOORE, J. B. *History and Digest of the International Arbitrations to which the United States has been a party.* (53rd Cong. 2nd Sess. House Misc. Doc. 212.) 6 vols. Washington, 1898.

—— *Digest of International Law.* 8 vols. Washington, 1906.

—— *International Adjudications.* New York, 1929– .

MILLER, HUNTER. *Treaties and Other International Acts of the United States of America.* 7 vols. Washington, 1932–42.

—— *Northwest Water Boundary: Report of the Experts summoned by the German Emperor* .... Seattle, 1942.

RICHARDSON, J. D. *A Compilation of the Messages and Papers of the Presidents, 1789– 1897.* 10 vols. Washington, 1896–99.

SCOTT, J. B. (Ed.). *The Proceedings of the Hague Peace Conferences* (translation of the official texts). New York, 1920–21.

—— (Ed.). *The Hague Court Reports.* 2 vols. New York, 1916, 1932.

TEMPERLEY, H. W. V. and PENSON, L. M. (Eds.). *A Century of Diplomatic Blue Books, 1814–1914.* Cambridge, 1938.

(c) BIBLIOGRAPHIES

See above, Part II, 1 (*a*) for general bibliographies and guides. More detailed lists on some aspects of Anglo-American relations are given in the *Cambridge History of British Foreign Policy*, vols. II and III (Cambridge, 1922–23) and in the *Cambridge Modern History*, vol. VII (Cambridge, 1903), pp. 823–9. Most important of all for this subject are the full critical bibliographies of sources, contemporary literature and later works given in S. F. Bemis and G. G. Griffin, *Guide to the Diplomatic History of the United States, 1775–1921* (Washington, 1935). Chapter XVI deals with "Anglo-American Relations, 1867–1914" and there are later sections on the Geneva Arbitration, the San Juan Boundary, the Alaskan and other boundary disputes, Isthmian diplomacy, Venezuela, and so on. The relevant portions of the following works are valuable:

BRADLEY, P. *Bibliography of the Monroe Doctrine.* London, 1929.

COLONIAL OFFICE. *Catalogue of the Printed Books in the Library of the Colonial Office.* 1896. *Appendix F*, Reports, 1921.

FOREIGN OFFICE. *Catalogue of the Printed Books in the Library of the Foreign Office.* London, 1926.

GRIFFIN, G. G. and others. *Writings on American History.* Washington, 1902– . Annual bibliography.

Handbook of Latin American Studies. Harvard University Press, 1936– . In progress, annually.

HUMPHREYS, R. A. *Latin America* (Chatham House Bibliographies). Oxford, 1941.

JONES, C. K. *A Bibliography of Latin American Bibliographies* (Library of Congress, Hispanic Foundation). Washington, 1924.

MEYER, H. H. B. *List of References on the Monroe Doctrine.* Washington, 1919.

(d) CONTEMPORARY WRITINGS

ARNOLD, MATTHEW. *Civilisation in the United States.* Boston, 1888.

BERESFORD, Lord CHARLES. *The Break-up of China.* 1899.

CUSHING, C. *The Treaty of Washington.* New York, 1873.

DAVIS, J. C. BANCROFT. *Mr Fish and the Alabama Claims.* New York, 1893.

DICEY, E. "The New American Imperialism." *Nineteenth Century*, vol. XLIV (1898), p. 500 *et seq.*

HACKETT, F. W. *The Geneva Awards Acts.* Boston, 1882.

LANSING, ROBERT. "The North Atlantic Coast Fisheries Arbitration." *American Jour. Internat. Law*, vol. V (1911), pp. 1–31.

MAHAN, A. T. "Hawaii and our Future Sea-Power." *Forum*, March 1893.
—— *The Interest of America in Sea Power, Present and Future.* Boston, 1900.
—— *Lessons of the War with Spain.* Boston, 1899.
—— *The Problem of Asia and Its Effect upon International Policies.* Boston, 1900.
MILLS, A. "Canada and the Treaty of Washington." *Contemporary Rev.* vol. XXI (1873), pp. 597–615.
MOORE, J. B. *The Interoceanic Canal and the Hay-Pauncefote Treaty.* Washington, 1900.
PIERANTONI, A. *Gli arbitrati internazionale e il trattato di Washington.* Naples, 1872.
PRITCHARD, G. *Queen Pomare and her Country.* 1878.
ROBINSON, E. E. and WEST, V. J. *The Foreign Policy of Woodrow Wilson.* New York, 1917.
SCOTT, J. B. *Argument of the Hon. Elihu Root on Behalf of the United States before the North Atlantic Fisheries Arbitration Tribunal at The Hague.* Boston, 1912.
STEVENSON, R. L. *Footnote to History—Eight Years of Trouble in Samoa.* New York, 1897.
TAFT, W. H. "Reciprocity with Canada." *Jour. Polit. Economy*, vol. XIX (1911), 513–26. Address delivered before the Western Economic Society, Chicago, 3 June 1911.

(*e*) BIOGRAPHIES, MEMOIRS AND CORRESPONDENCE

See also Part II, 1 (*e*), for other biographies, especially CECIL, CHAMBERLAIN, GALT, HARCOURT, LEVESON-GOWER, PALMER, PETTY-FITZMAURICE, RIPON.
ADAMS, H. *The Education of Henry Adams.* Boston, 1918.
ADLER, C. *Jacob H. Schiff.* 1929.
ALDERSON, B. *Arthur James Balfour.* 1903.
ALVERSTONE, Viscount. *Recollections of Bar and Bench.* (1914.) Behring Sea Arbitration, Venezuela Boundary, Alaska Boundary.
ARCHIBALD, E. J. (Ed.). *Letters of Sir E. M. Archibald.* Toronto, 1924. Consul-General, New York, 1857–83.
BAKER, R. S. *Woodrow Wilson: Life and Letters.* 8 vols. New York, 1927–39.
BALFOUR, A. J. (Lord). *Chapters of Autobiography.* 1930.
BANCROFT DAVIS, J. C. *Mr Fish and the Alabama Claims.* New York, 1893.
BARROWS, C. L. *William M. Evarts.* Chapel Hill, N.C., 1941.
BERESFORD, Lord CHARLES. *Memoirs.* 2 vols. 1914.
BLAINE, J. G. *Twenty Years of Congress.* 2 vols. Norwich, Conn., 1884–6.
BOWEN, H. W. *Recollections, Diplomatic and Undiplomatic.* New York, 1926.
BRYAN, W. J. *Memoirs.* Philadelphia, 1925.
BUNAU-VARILLA, P. *Panama.* Paris, 1913.
CHISHOLM, J. A. (Ed.). *Speeches and Public Letters of Joseph Howe.* 2 vols. Halifax, N.S., 1909.
CLEVELAND, GROVER. *Presidential Problems.* New York, 1904.
—— *The Venezuela Boundary Controversy.* Princeton University Press, 1913.
CREIGHTON, D. G. *Macdonald.* 2 vols. 1954–56.
CROLY, H. *William Straight.* New York, 1924.
DENNETT, T. *John Hay.* New York, 1933.
DYER, B. *The Public Career of William M. Evarts.* Berkeley, Cal., 1933.
FISHER, H. A. L. *James Bryce.* 2 vols. 1927.
FOSTER, J. W. *Diplomatic Memoirs.* 2 vols. Boston, New York, 1909.
GARDINER, A. W. *Life of Sir William Harcourt.* 2 vols. 1923.
GWYNN, S. L. (Ed.). *Letters and Friendships of Sir Cecil Spring Rice.* 2 vols. 1929.
HENDRICK, BURTON J. *The Life of Andrew Carnegie.* Garden City, New York, 1932.
HOPKINS, J. C. *Life and Works of Sir John Thompson.* Brantford, Canada, 1895.
JAMES, H. *Richard Olney and his Public Service.* Boston, New York, 1923.
JESSUP, P. C. *Elihu Root.* 2 vols. New York, 1938.

JOHNSON, A. and MALONE, D. (Eds.). *Dictionary of American Biography.* 22 vols. New York, 1928–44. Including Index and Supplement.

JUSSERAND, J. J. *What me Befell.* 1933.

KNAPLUND, P. (Ed.). *Sir Edward Grey. Speeches on Foreign Affairs, 1904–14.* 1931.

KNAPLUND, P. and LEWES, C. M. (Eds.). "Private Letters from the British Embassy in Washington to the Foreign Secretary, Lord Granville, 1880–5." *American Hist. Assoc. Ann. Rept. for 1941,* vol. 1 (1942), pp. 73–183.

LANG, A. *Life, Letters and Diaries of Sir Stafford Northcote, 1st Earl of Iddesleigh.* 2 vols. Edinburgh, 1890.

LEWIS, J. *George Brown.* 1906.

MACDONALD, Sir J. A. *Correspondence. Selections.* Toronto, 1921.

MACKENZIE, A. *The Life and Speeches of George Brown.* Toronto, 1882.

MACPHERSON, J. P. *Life of Sir John A. Macdonald.* 2 vols. St Johns, N.B. 1891.

MOWAT, R. B. *Life of Lord Pauncefote.* 1929.

NEVINS, A. *Letters of Grover Cleveland, 1850–1908.* Boston, 1933.

—— *Grover Cleveland.* New York, 1934.

—— *Hamilton Fish.* New York, 1937.

—— *Henry White: Thirty Years of American Diplomacy.* 1930.

PALMER, ROUNDELL, Earl of Selborne. *Memorials.* 2 vols. 1896–8.

PIERCE, E. L. (Ed.). *Memoirs and Letters of Charles Sumner.* 3 vols. Boston, 1893.

POPE, Sir J. *Memoirs of Sir John Alexander Macdonald.* 2 vols. 1894.

PRINGLE, H. F. *Theodore Roosevelt.* New York. 1931.

—— *The Life and Times of William Howard Taft.* 2 vols. New York, 1939.

REID, Sir T. W. (Ed.). *Memoirs and Correspondence of Lord Playfair.* 1899.

ROOSEVELT, THEODORE. *Autobiography.* New York, 1913.

RUSSELL, Lord JOHN. *Recollections and Suggestions, 1813–73.* 1875.

SAUNDERS, E. M. (Ed.). *Life and Letters of Sir Charles Tupper.* 2 vols. 1916. Supplement, ed. by Sir C. H. Tupper. Toronto, 1926.

SKELTON, O. D. *Life and Letters of Sir Wilfrid Laurier.* 2 vols. New York, 1922.

SMALLEY, G. M. *Anglo-American Memories.* 1st ser. 1910; 2nd ser. 1912.

SYKES, Sir P. *Sir Mortimer Durand.* 1926.

TAYLOR, C. C. *The Life of Admiral Mahan.* 1920.

THAYER, W. R. *The Life and Letters of John Hay.* 2 vols. Boston, New York, 1915.

—— *Theodore Roosevelt.* Boston, 1919.

TUPPER, Sir CHARLES. *Recollections of Sixty Years.* 1914.

VARG, P. A. *Open Door Diplomat: the Life of W. W. Rockhill.* Urbana, 1952.

WHITE, A. D. *Autobiography.* 2 vols. New York, 1905.

WILLIAMS, W. "Reminiscences of the Bering Sea Arbitration." *American Journ. Internat. Law.* vol. XXXVII (1943), pp. 562–84.

WILLISON, J. S. *Laurier.* 1903.

WILSON, F. M. HUNTINGTON. *Memoirs of an ex-Diplomat.* Boston, 1945.

(f) LATER WORKS

ADAMS, C. F. "The Treaty of Washington Before and After." In *Lee at Appomattox and Other Papers.* New York, 1903.

ADLER, S. "Bryan and Wilsonian Caribbean Penetration." *Hispanic American Hist. Rev.* vol. XX (1940), pp. 198–226.

ALEXANDER, F. *Australia and the United States.* (America Looks Ahead, No. 1.) Boston, 1941.

ALLEN, H. C. *Great Britain and the United States: a History of Anglo-American Relations, 1783–1952.* 1954.

ALVAREZ, A. *The Monroe Doctrine.* New York, 1924.

ARIAS, H. *The Panama Canal.* 1911.

ATWATER, E. *American Regulation of Arms Exports.* Washington, 1941.

BAILEY, T. A. "Japan's Protest against the Annexation of Hawaii." *Jour. Mod. Hist.* vol. III (1931), pp. 46–61.

—— "California, Japan, and the Alien Land Legislation of 1913." *Pacific Hist. Rev.* vol. I (1932), pp. 36–59.

—— "The World Cruise of the American Battleship Fleet, 1907–1909." *Ibid.* vol. I (1932), pp. 389–424.

—— "The Lodge Corollary to the Monroe Doctrine." *Political Science Quarterly*, vol. XLVIII (1933), pp. 220–39.

—— *Theodore Roosevelt and the Japanese-American Crises.* Berkeley, Cal. 1934.

—— "The North Pacific Sealing Convention of 1911." *Pacific Hist. Rev.* vol. IV (1935), pp. 1–14.

—— "Theodore Roosevelt and the Alaska Boundary Settlement." *Canadian Hist. Rev.* vol. XVIII (1937), pp. 123–30.

—— "Was the Election of 1900 a Mandate on Imperialism?" *Mississippi Valley Hist. Rev.* vol. XXIV (1937–8), pp. 43–52.

—— "Dewey and the Germans at Manila Bay." *American Hist. Rev.* vol. XLV (1939–40), pp. 59–81.

—— "The Root-Takahira Agreement of 1908." *Pacific Hist. Rev.* vol. IX (1940), pp. 19–35.

—— *A Diplomatic History of the American People.* 3rd edn. New York, 1948.

BALCH, T. W. *The Alabama Arbitration.* Philadelphia, 1900.

BAXTER, J. P. "British High Commissioners at Washington, 1871." *Proc. Massachusetts Hist. Soc.* vol. LXV (1940), pp. 334–57.

BEMIS, S. F. (Ed.). *The American Secretaries of State and their Diplomacy.* 10 vols. New York, 1927–9, covers 1781–1925. Vol. VII contains "Hamilton Fish, 1869–77", by J. V. Fuller. Vol. VIII has "Thomas Francis Bayard, 1885–89", by L. B. Shippee; "James Gillespie, 1889–92", by J. B. Lockey, "Richard Olney, 1895–97", by M. Schuyler. Vol IX has "John Hay, 1898–1905", by A. L. P. Dennis and "Elihu Root, 1905–9", by J. B. Scott.

—— (Ed.). *A Diplomatic History of the United States.* Rev. edn. New York, 1942.

—— (Ed.). *Latin-American Policy of the United States.* New York, 1943.

BISHOP, J. B. *The Panama Gateway.* New York, 1915.

—— *Theodore Roosevelt and his Time.* 2 vols. New York, 1920.

BLAKE, N. M. "Background of Cleveland's Venezuelan Policy". *American Hist. Rev.* vol. XLVII (1942), pp. 259–77.

—— "The Olney-Pauncefote Treaty of 1897." *American Hist. Rev.* vol. L (1945), pp. 228–43.

BREBNER, J. B. *North Atlantic Triangle: the Interplay of Canada, the United States and Britain.* New Haven, 1945.

BROWN, B. H. *The Tariff Reform Movement in Great Britain, 1881–1895.* New York, 1943.

BURRAGE, H. S. *Maine in the Northeastern Boundary Controversy.* Portland, 1919.

CALLAHAN, J. M. "Cuba and Anglo-American Relations." *Ann. Rept. American Hist. Assoc.* for 1897, pp. 195–215.

—— *Cuba and International Relations.* Baltimore, 1899.

—— *American Foreign Policy in Mexican Relations.* New York, 1932.

—— *American Foreign Policy in Canadian Relations.* New York, 1937.

CALLCOTT, W. H. *Caribbean Policy of the United States, 1890–1920.* Baltimore, 1942.

CAMERON, MERIBETH E. "American Recognition Policy towards the Republic of China, 1912–13." *Pacific Hist. Rev.* vol. II (1933), pp. 214–30.

CAMPBELL, C. S. *Special Business Interests and the Open Door Policy.* New Haven, 1951.

CECIL, A. *British Foreign Secretaries, 1807–1916.* 1927.

CHACKO, C. J. *The International Joint Commission between the United States of America and the Dominion of Canada.* New York, 1932.

CHADWICK, F. E. *Relations of the United States and Spain.* New York, 1911.

CHAMBERLAIN, D. H. *Charles Sumner and the Treaty of Washington.* Cambridge, Mass. 1902.

CLYDE, P. H. "Attitudes and Policies of George F. Seward, American Minister at Peking, 1876–1880: some Phases of the Co-operative Policy." *Pacific Hist. Rev.* vol. II (1933), pp. 387–404.

CORBETT, P. E. *The Settlement of Canadian-American Disputes.* New Haven, 1937.

CURTI, M. F. "Bryan and World Peace." *Smith College Studies in History,* vol. XVI, nos. 3 and 4 (1931), pp. 113–254.

DANIELS, J. *The Wilson Era: Years of Peace, 1910–1917.* Chapel Hill, North Carolina, 1944.

DENNETT, T. *Americans in Eastern Asia.* New York, 1922.

—— *Roosevelt and the Russo-Japanese War.* Garden City, New York, 1925.

—— "The Open Door Policy as Intervention." *Annals of the American Academy of Political and Social Science,* vol. CLXVIII (1933), pp. 78–83.

DENNIS, A. L. P. *The Anglo-Japanese Alliance.* Berkeley, California, 1923.

—— *Adventures in American Diplomacy, 1896–1906.* New York, 1928.

DEWEY, A. G. *The Dominions and Diplomacy: the Canadian Contribution.* 2 vols. 1929.

DOZER, D. M. "The Opposition to Hawaiian Reciprocity, 1876–1888." *Pacific Hist. Rev.* vol. XIV (1945), pp. 157–183.

DUBELOHN, G. R. *Principles of Foreign Policy under the Cleveland Administrations.* Philadelphia, 1941.

DULLER, F. R. *America in the Pacific.* Boston, 1932.

DUNNING, W. A. *The British Empire and the United States* [from 1815]. New York, 1914.

DUVAL, M. P. *Cadiz to Cathay.* Berkeley, Cal., 1940.

EGERTON, H. E. *British Colonial Policy in the Twentieth Century.* London, 1922.

ELLIS, L. E. *Reciprocity, 1911.* New Haven, 1939.

—— "The Northwest and the Reciprocity Agreement of 1911." *Mississippi Valley Hist. Rev.* vol. XXVI (1939–40), pp. 55–66.

ELLISON, J. W. *Opening and Penetration of Foreign Influence in Samoa to 1880.* Oregon State College Studies in History, 1938.

ELLISON, J. W. "The Partition of Samoa: A Study in Imperialism and Diplomacy." *Pacific Hist. Rev.* vol. VIII (1939), pp. 259–88.

EYRE, J. K., Jr. "Russia and the American Acquisition of the Philippines." *Mississippi Valley Hist. Rev.* vol. XXVIII (1941–2), pp. 539–62.

FAULKNER, H. U. *American Economic History.* 6th edn., New York, 1949.

FERGUSON, J. H. *American Diplomacy and the Boer War.* Philadelphia, 1939.

FINCH, G. A. "American Diplomacy and the Financing of China." *American Jour. Internat. Law,* vol. XVI (1922), pp. 25–42.

FITZGIBBON, R. H. *Cuba and the United States, 1900–1935.* Menasha, Wis. 1935.

FOSTER, J. M. V. "Reciprocity and the Joint High Commission of 1898–9." *Ann. Rept. Canadian Hist. Assoc.* (1939), pp. 87–98.

GELBER, L. M. *The Rise of Anglo-American Friendship.* 1938.

GLAZEBROOK, G. P. DE T. *Canadian External Relations: to 1914.* Toronto, 1942.

GOEBEL, J. *The Struggle for the Falkland Islands....* New Haven, 1927.

GORDON, G. S. *Anglo-American Literary Relations.* Oxford, 1942.

GRENVILLE, J. A. S. "Great Britain and the Isthmian Canal, 1898–1901." *American Hist. Rev.* vol. LXI (Oct. 1955), pp. 48–69.

GRISWOLD, A. W. *The Far Eastern Policy of the United States.* New York, 1938.

HACKETT, C. W. "The Mexican Revolution and the United States, 1910–1926." *World Peace Foundation Pubn.* vol. IX (1926), pp. 339–450.

HALL, L. J. "A Partnership in Peacemaking: Theodore Roosevelt and William II." *Pacific Hist. Rev.* vol. XIII (1944), pp. 390–411.

HANSON, S. G. *Argentine Meat and the British Market.* Stanford, 1938.

HARRINGTON, F. H. "The Anti-Imperialistic Movement in the United States, 1898–1900." *Mississippi Valley Hist. Rev.* vol. XXII (1935–6), pp. 211–30.

HARRINGTON, F. H. "Literary Aspects of American Anti-Imperialism, 1898–1902."
New England Quart. vol. x (1937), pp. 650–67.
—— *God, Mammon, and the Japanese: Dr Horace N. Allen and Korean-American Relations, 1884–1905.* Madison, Wis. 1944.
HART, A. B. *The Monroe Doctrine.* Boston, 1916.
HEINDEL, R. H *The American Impact on Great Britain, 1898–1914.* Philadelphia, 1940.
HERSHEY, A. "The Venezuelan Affair in the Light of International Law."
American Law Rev. vol. LI (1903), pp. 249–67.
—— "Calvo and Drago Doctrines." *American Jour. Internat. Law,* vol. I (1907), pp. 26–45.
HILL, H. C. *Roosevelt and the Caribbean.* Chicago, 1927.
HOLT, W. S. *Treaties Defeated by the Senate....* Baltimore, 1934.
—— "The United States and the Defense of the Western Hemisphere, 1815–1940." *Pacific Hist. Rev.* vol. x (1941), pp. 29–38.
HOWAY, F. N., SAGE, W. N., and ANGUS, H. F. *British Columbia and the United States.* Toronto, 1943.
HUTCHINSON, B. *The Struggle for the Border.* Toronto, 1955. Canadian–American relations.
IRELAND, G. *Boundaries, Possessions and Conflicts in Central and Northern America and the Caribbean.* Oxford, 1942.
JONES, C. L. *The Caribbean since 1900.* New York, 1936.
KEASBY, L. M. *Nicaragua Canal and the Monroe Doctrine.* New York, 1896.
KEENLEYSIDE, H. L. *Canada and the United States.* New York, 1929.
KELSEY, C. *The American Intervention in Haiti and the Dominican Republic.* Philadelphia, 1922.
KNAPLUND, P. A. *Gladstone and Britain's Imperial Policy.* 1927.
—— *Gladstone's Foreign Policy.* New York, 1935.
KRAUS, H. *Die Monroe-Doktrin....* Berlin, 1913.
LANGER, W. L. *The Diplomacy of Imperialism, 1890–1902.* 2 vols. New York, 1935.
LATANÉ, J. H. "The Diplomacy of the United States in regard to Cuba." *Ann. Rept. American Hist. Assoc. for 1897,* pp. 217–78.
—— *America as a World Power, 1897–1907.* New York, 1907.
—— "The Panama Canal and the British Protest." *American Journ. Internat. Law,* vol. VII (1913), pp. 17–26.
LINK, A. S. *Woodrow Wilson and the Progressive Era, 1910–17.* 1954.
LIVERMORE, S. W. "American Strategy Diplomacy in the South Pacific, 1890–1914." *Pacific Hist. Rev.* vol. XII (1943), pp. 33–51.
—— "American Naval-Base Policy in the Far East, 1850–1914." *Pacific Hist. Rev.* vol. XIII (1944), pp. 113–35.
—— "Battleship Diplomacy in South America, 1905–1925." *Jour. Med. Hist.* vol. XVI (1944), pp. 31–48.
—— "Theodore Roosevelt, the American Navy, and the Venezuelan Crisis of 1902–03." *American Hist. Rev.* vol. LI (1946), pp. 452–71.
LIVINGSTON, W. R. "Australasia in Conference, 1883–1887." *Pacific Hist. Rev.* vol. I (1932), pp. 60–81.
LONG, M. H. "Sir John Rose and the Informal Beginnings of the Canadian High Commissionership." *Canadian Hist. Rev.* vol. XII (1931), pp. 23–43. Treaty of Washington.
McCAIN, W. D. *The United States and the Republic of Panama.* Durham, N.C. 1937.
McINNIS, E. W. *The Unguarded Frontier: a History of American-Canadian Relations.* Toronto, 1942.
MACK, G. *The Land Divided.* New York, 1944.
MANCHESTER, A. K. *British Preëminence in Brazil: its rise and decline.* University of North Carolina Press, 1933.
MASLAND, K. W. "Missionary Influence upon American Far Eastern Policy." *Pacific Hist. Rev.* vol. x (1941), pp. 279–96.

MILLER, HUNTER. *San Juan Archipelago: A Study of the Joint Occupation of San Juan Island.* Bellows Falls, Vermont, 1943.

MINER, D. C. *The Fight for the Panama Route....* New York, 1940.

MOMMSEN, W. *Die letzte Phase des britischen Imperialismus auf dem amerikanischen Kontinent, 1880–96.* Berlin, 1933.

MONTAGUE, L. L. *Haiti and the United States, 1714–1938.* Durham, N.C. 1940.

MORISON, S. E. *Admiral Sims and the Modern American Navy.* Boston, 1942.

MORROW, R. L. "The Negotiation of the Anglo-American Treaty of 1870." *American Hist. Rev.* vol. XXXIX (1934), pp. 663–81.

MOWAT, R. B. *The Diplomatic Relations of Great Britain and the United States.* 1925.
—— *The American Entente.* 1939.

MUNRO, D. G. *The Five Republics of Central America.* New York, 1918.
—— *The United States and the Caribbean Area.* Boston, 1934.

NEALE, R. G. "British-American Relations during the Spanish-American War: some Problems." *Hist. Studies Australia and New Zealand,* vol. VI (Nov. 1953), pp. 72–89.

NEARING, S. and FREEMAN, J. *Dollar Diplomacy: A Study in American Imperialism.* New York, 1925.

NOTTER, H. *The Origins of the Foreign Policy of Woodrow Wilson.* Baltimore, 1937.

PADELFORD, N. J. *The Panama Canal in Peace and War.* New York, 1942.

PARKS, E. T. *Colombia and the United States, 1765–1934.* Durham, N.C., 1935.

PARKS, E. T. and RIPPY, J. F. "The Galapagos Islands: A Neglected Phase of American Strategy Diplomacy." *Pacific Hist. Rev.* vol. IX (1940), pp. 37–45.

PATTERSON, J. "Latin-American Reactions to the Panama Revolution of 1903." *Hispanic-American Hist. Rev.* vol. XXIV (1944), pp. 342–51.

PEFFER, N. "The United States in the Far East." *Polit. Science Quart.* vol. LIV (1939), pp. 1–14.

PERKINS, DEXTER. *The Monroe Doctrine, 1867–1907.* Baltimore, 1937.
—— *Hands Off! A History of the Monroe Doctrine.* Boston, 1941.

PRATT, J. W. "The Hawaiian Revolution; a Re-Interpretation." *Pacific Hist. Rev.* vol. I (1932), pp. 273–94.
—— "The 'Large Policy' of 1898." *Mississippi Valley Hist. Rev.* vol. XIX (1932–3), pp. 219–42.
—— *Expansionists of 1898.* Baltimore, 1936.

PROUDFOOT, M. *Britain and the United States in the Caribbean.* 1954.

QUINN, P. E. "The Diplomatic Struggle for the Carolines, 1898." *Pacific Hist. Rev.* XIV (1945), pp. 290–32.

REALE, EGIDIO. *Le règlement judiciaire du conflit de l'Alabama.* Geneva, 1929.

REID, J. G. *The Manchu Abdication and the Powers, 1908–1912.* Berkeley, Cal., 1935.

REUTER, B. A. *Anglo-American Relations during the Spanish-American War.* New York, 1924.

RHODES, J. F. *History of the United States from Hayes to McKinley.* New edn. New York, 1919.
—— *The McKinley and Roosevelt Administrations.* New York, 1927.
—— *A History of the United States from the Compromise of 1850.* Vols. V, VI (1904, 1906).

RIPPY, J. F. "Some Contemporary Mexican Reactions to Cleveland's Venezuelan Message." *Polit. Science Quart.* vol. XXXIX (1924), pp. 280–92.
—— *The United States and Mexico.* Rev. edn. New York, 1931.
—— *The Capitalists and Colombia.* New York, 1931.
—— *Latin America in World Politics.* 3rd edn. New York, 1938.
—— *America and the Strife of Europe.* Chicago, 1938.
—— *The Caribbean Danger Zone.* New York, 1940.
—— "The British Bondholders and the Roosevelt Corollary of the Monroe Doctrine." *Polit. Science Quart.* vol. XLIX (1934), pp. 195–206.
—— "The Initiation of the Customs Receivership in the Dominican Republic." *Hispanic American Hist. Rev.* vol. XVII (1937), pp. 419–57.

RIPPY, J. F. "Antecedents of the Roosevelt Corollary of the Monroe Doctrine."
  Pacific Hist. Rev. vol. IX (1940), pp. 267–79.
ROBERTSON, W. S. "Hispanic American Appreciations of the Monroe Doctrine."
  Hispanic American Hist. Rev. vol. III (1920), pp. 1–16.
ROOT, ELIHU. *Addresses on International Subjects.* Cambridge, Mass. 1916.
—— *The Military and Colonial Policy of the United States.* Cambridge, Mass. 1916.
—— *Latin America and the United States.* Cambridge, Mass. 1917.
—— *American Ideals during the Past Half Century.* New York, 1925.
ROWLAND, D. "The United States and the Contract Labor Question in Hawaii."
  Pacific Hist. Rev. vol. II (1933), pp. 249–69.
—— "The Establishment of the Republic of Hawaii." *Pacific Hist. Rev.* vol. IV
  (1935), pp. 201–20.
RUSS, W. A., Jr. "The Role of Sugar in Hawaiian Annexation." *Pacific Hist. Rev.*
  vol. XII (1943), pp. 339–50.
RYDEN, G. H. *The Foreign Policy of the United States in Relation to Samoa.* New Haven,
  1933.
SAGE, W. N. "The Historical Peculiarities of Canada with regard to Hemisphere
  Defense." *Pacific Hist. Rev.* vol. X (1941), pp. 15–27.
SCOTT, J. B. *The Declaration of London.* New York, 1919.
SEARS, L. M. *A History of American Foreign Relations.* New York, 1927.
SHIPPEE, L. B. *Canadian-American Relations, 1849–1874.* New Haven, 1939.
SMITH, GOLDWIN. *The Treaty of Washington, 1871: a Study of Imperial History.* Cornell,
  Oxford, 1941.
SMITH, T. C. "Secretary Olney's Real Credit in the Venezuelan Affair." *Proc.
  Massachusetts Hist. Soc.* vol. LXV (1940), pp. 112–47.
SPROUT, H. and M. *The Rise of American Naval Power, 1776–1918.* Princeton, 1940.
STACEY, C. P. "Fenianism and the Rise of National Feeling in Canada at the time
  of Confederation." *Canadian Hist. Rev.* vol. XII (1931), pp. 238–61.
TANSILL, C. C. *The Foreign Policy of Thomas F. Bayard, 1885–1897.* New York, 1940.
—— *Canadian-American Relations, 1875–1911.* New Haven, 1943.
TARKOW-NAAMANI, I. "The Abandonment of 'Splendid Isolation' by Great
  Britain." *Canadian Hist. Rev.* vol. XXVII (1946), pp. 163–88.
TATE, M. *The Disarmament Illusion.* New York, 1942.
TRAVIS, I. D. *The History of the Clayton–Bulwer Treaty.* Ann Arbor, Mich. 1900.
TREAT, P. J. *Diplomatic Relations between the United States and Japan, 1895–1905.*
  Stanford, 1938.
TRELLES, BARCIA. *La Doctrine de Monroe y la Cooperación International.* n.d.
TYLER, ALICE F. *The Foreign Policy of James G. Blaine.* Minneapolis, 1927.
VAGTS, A. *Deutschland und die Vereinigten Staaten in der Weltpolitik.* 2 vols. New York,
  1935.
—— "Hopes and Fears of an American-German War, 1870–1915." *Polit. Science
  Quart.* vol. LIV (1939), pp. 514–35; vol. LV (1940), pp. 53–76.
VAN ALSTYNE, R. W. *American Diplomacy in Action.* Stanford, 1944.
WALKER, L. M. "Guam's Seizure by the United States in 1898." *Pacific Hist. Rev.*
  vol. XIV (1945), pp. 1–12.
WEINBERG, A. K. *Manifest Destiny. A Study of Nationalist Expansionism in American
  History.* Baltimore, 1935.
WELLES, SUMNER. *Naboth's Vineyard, the Dominican Republic, 1844–1924.* New
  York, 1928.
WILGUS, A. C. (Ed.). *Studies in Hispanic American Affairs.* 4 vols. Washington,
  1933–6.
WILLIAMS, B. H. *Economic Foreign Policy of the United States.* New York, 1929.
WILLIAMS, M. W. *Anglo-American Isthmian Diplomacy, 1815–1915.* Washington, 1916.
WILSON, G. G. *The Hague Arbitration Cases.* Boston, London, 1915.
WOODWARD, E. L. *Great Britain and the German Navy.* Oxford, 1935.
WORLD PEACE FOUNDATION. *Arbitration and the United States.* Boston, 1926.

WRISTON, H. M. *Executive Agents in American Foreign Relations*. Baltimore and London, 1929.
YOUNG, G. B. "Intervention under the Monroe Doctrine: the Olney Corollary." *Polit. Science Quart.* vol. LVII (1942), pp. 247–80.
ZABRISKIE, E. H. *American-Russian Rivalry in the Far East*. Philadelphia, 1946.

F. IMPERIAL DEFENCE, 1870–1914

(Chapters VII and XV)

(a) MANUSCRIPT SOURCES

Some of the series of Admiralty and War Office records deposited in the Public Record Office and listed above (Part I, 1 and 2) are not open to public inspection beyond the year 1885; others only to 1902. A. J. Marder, *British Naval Policy, 1880–1905* (1940), mentions and quotes from a large number of important papers in the Admiralty not yet generally accessible. The work includes important policy reports of the Director of Naval Intelligence, which are printed in full, and extracts from the confidential volumes entitled *Naval Necessities*, prepared by Lord Fisher. Exact references to the Admiralty sources are not given. This author has also been able to use personal papers of Lord Spencer (First Lord of the Admiralty 1892–5), Lord Selborne (First Lord, 1900–5), Admiral Sir F. Richards (First Sea Lord, 1893–9) and Admiral Sir R. Constance (Director of Naval Intelligence, 1899–1902).

(b) OFFICIAL PUBLICATIONS

Since throughout the period the United Kingdom was almost entirely responsible for the "general defence" of the Empire, "imperial defence" as such was often subordinated to questions of War Office reform and technical progress in naval construction. Since, moreover, "general military policy", as viewed from Whitehall, was much concerned with anti-invasion measures, with protecting the Mediterranean and the routes to India, and eventually with the landing of an expeditionary force in Western Europe, the defence of the Empire (as apart from India) was also subordinated to these other, and seemingly more urgent, strategical problems. Hence, apart from the reports of the Colonial and Imperial Conferences, much of the official material necessary for an understanding of imperial defence must be looked for in places where the problem is only dealt with by implication. Thus the Hartington, Elgin and Esher Reports not only led to the creation of the Committee of Imperial Defence and the Imperial General Staff, but also produced a new form of War Office organisation under the Army Council, which served as a model for the self-governing Dominions.

The Colonial Office issued *Extracts from Proceedings of Colonial Conferences relating to Defence*, 1909. For Parliamentary Papers and Debates, see above, Part I, 3 and 4, especially the following papers (not all included above):

Returns *re* shipping, 1869, *Parl. Pap.* 1870, LX (349); Correspondence *re* Defence of Colonial Possessions and Garrisons Abroad, *Parl. Pap.* 1884, XLVIII [C. 4186] and 1884–5, XLVI [C. 4226]; Report of the Royal Commission on Warlike Stores and the Ordnance Department, 1887 (Sir James Fitzjames Stephens' Commission), *Parl. Pap.* 1887, XV [C. 5062]; Proceedings of the [first] Colonial Conference, 1887, *Parl. Pap.* 1887, LVI [C. 5091] and [C. 5091–I]; Imperial Defence Act, 1888 (51 & 52 Vict. cap. 32), *Parl. Pap.* 1888, III (346); Orders in Council *re* War Department, *Parl. Pap.* 1888, LXVII [C. 5304]; Naval Defence Act (1889), 52 & 53 Vict. cap. 8 (the original act), *Parl. Pap.* 1889, V (186); Report of the Committee on the Naval Manœuvres of 1888 (the report of the three Admirals), *Parl. Pap.* 1889, L [C. 5632]; Reports of the Royal Commission on the Civil and Professional Administration of the Naval and Military Departments (Hartington Report), *Parl. Pap.* 1890, XIX [C. 5979]; Naval Defence Bill (Second Act), 1894, *Parl. Pap.* 1893–4, VI

(450); Orders in Council of 21 Nov. 1895, defining Duties of the Commander-in-Chief, Adjutant-General, Quartermaster-General, Inspector-General of Fortifications, Inspector-General of Ordnance and the Financial Secretary of the War Office, *Parl. Pap.* 1896, LI (59) and Memo. on same [C. 7987]; Proceedings of the [second] Colonial Conference, 1897, *Parl. Pap.* 1897, LIX [C. 8596]; Orders in Council defining the Duties of the Principal Officers charged with Administration of the Army, *Parl. Pap.* 1899, LIII (113); Report of the Committee appointed to enquire into War Office organisation, 9 May 1901 (Dawkins Report), *Parl. Pap.* 1901, XL [Cd. 580], [Cd. 581]; Papers by the Secretary of State, laying down the Requirements from our Army, dated 1 June 1891 (Stanhope Memorandum—Note the ten years' delay in publication), *Parl. Pap.* 1901, XL [Cd. 607]; Proceedings of the [third] Colonial Conference, 1902, *Parl. Pap.* 1902, LXVI [Cd. 1299]; Report of the War Office (Reconstruction) Committee, 1904 (Esher Report), *Parl. Pap.* 1904, VIII [Cd. 1932], [Cd. 1968] and [Cd. 2002]; Report of the Royal Commission on the Militia and Volunteers, 1904 (Norfolk Report), *Parl. Pap.* 1904, XXX [Cd. 2061], [Cd. 2062] and XXI [Cd. 2063–4]; Report of the Royal Commission on the South African War, 1903 (Elgin Report), *Parl. Pap.* 1904, XL [Cd. 1789], [Cd. 1790], [Cd. 1791], [Cd. 1792]; Secretary of State for War, Summary of Speech, 14 July 1904, *Parl. Pap.* 1904, LI [Cd. 1907]; Army Statement showing basis on which the estimated cost for Conscription was made, *Parl. Pap.* 1904, LI [Cd. 1909]; Army: Summary of the Recommendations of the Inter-Departmental Committee, etc., on Reserves of Guns and Stores, and action taken (Mowatt Report), *Parl. Pap.* 1904, LI [Cd. 1908]; Particulars regarding the Proposed Army Organisation Scheme 1904, *Parl. Pap.* 1904, LI [Cd. 1910]; Memo. by the Secretary of State for War on the Army Estimates for 1906–7, *Parl. Pap.* 1906, LXVI [Cd. 2694]; Memo. by the Secretary of State for War on Army Reorganisation, 30 July, 1906, *Parl. Pap.* 1906, LXVII [Cd. 2993]; Army: Territorial and Reserve Forces Bill, Memo. by the Secretary of State for War, *Parl. Pap.* 1907, XLIX [Cd. 3366]; Memo. by the Secretary of State for War relating to the Army Estimates for 1907–8, *Parl. Pap.* 1907, XLVIII [Cd. 3293]; Proceedings of the [fourth] Colonial Conference, 1907 (including constitution of the Committee of Imperial Defence in 1907), *Parl. Pap.* 1907, LV [Cd. 3404], [Cd. 3406]; Correspondence *re* Naval Defence of Australia and New Zealand, *Parl. Pap.* 1908, LXXI [Cd. 4325]; Proceedings of the Imperial Defence Conference, *Parl. Pap.* 1909, LXIX [Cd. 4948]; Correspondence *re* proposed formation of an Imperial General Staff, *Parl. Pap.* 1909, LI [Cd. 4475]; Report of the Proceedings of the Imperial Conference 1911, *Parl. Pap.* 1911, LIV [Cd. 5513], [Cd. 5741], [Cd. 5745], [Cd. 5746–1 and 2]; Admiralty Memo. to Canadian Government (Churchill on command of the sea), *Parl. Pap.* 1912–13, LIII [Cd. 6513].

(c) BIBLIOGRAPHIES

See Part II, 1 (a) and following special guides:

WAR OFFICE. *Catalogue of the War Office Library.* Parts 1–3. 3 vols. 1906–12. Part 3 is a Subject Index (1912) and there are annual supplements to this for the years 1912 onwards. Headings such as "Colonies" and "Imperial Defence" note significant books and pamphlets. For articles in periodicals the appropriate headings in the *Catalogue of the Library of the Royal Empire Society*, vol. 1 (1930), may be consulted. There are useful select bibliographies in the works of Marder and Tyler noted below.

(d) PERIODICALS

Army Quarterly, London, 1920– . In progress.
Brassey's Naval Annual, London, 1886– . In progress.
Canadian Defence Quarterly, Ottawa, 1886– . In progress.
Journal of the Royal United Service Institution, London, 1857– . In progress.

Journal of the Society for Army Historical Research, 1921– . In progress.
Mariner's Mirror. Society for Nautical Research, 1911– . In progress.
Publications of the Navy Records Society, 1895– . In progress.
United Service Magazine. London, 1829–1920. Title varies.

Apart from the daily press, the following contemporary periodicals are of special importance:

Admiralty and Horse Guards Gazette, Army and Navy Gazette, Fortnightly Review, Monthly Review (especially for 1902–4), *National Review, Naval and Military Record, Navy League Journal, Nineteenth Century*.

(*e*) CONTEMPORARY WRITINGS

(Certain biographical works published since 1914 are included in this section)

AMERY, L. S. "Imperial Defence and National Policy." In *Union and Strength: a series of papers on imperial questions*. 1912.
—— *The Problem of the Army*. 1903.
ASQUITH, H. H. (Lord Oxford). *Genesis of the War*. 1923.
ASTON, Sir G. C. *Letters on Amphibious Wars*. 1911.
—— *Sea, Land and Air Strategy: a comparison*. 1914.
BARNABY, N. *Naval Development in the Century*. 1904.
BIDDULPH, Sir R. *Lord Cardwell at the War Office, 1868–74*. 1904.
BRASSEY, Lord. *The British Navy*. 4 vols. 1882.
—— "Imperial Federation for Naval Defence." *Nineteenth Century*, vol. XXXI (April 1892), pp. 90–100.
BRETTON, H. D. "Thoughts on Imperial Defence." *Blackwood's*, vol. XLVII (May 1895), pp. 665–88. See rejoinder by G. S. Clarke, *ibid*. (June 1895), pp. 962–9.
BRIDGE, Sir C. A. G. *Sea-power and other Studies*. 1910.
CALLWELL, Sir G. E. *Field Marshal Sir Henry Wilson, his Life and Diaries*. 1927.
CARNARVON, Lord. *Defence of the Empire: a selection from letters and speeches*. 1897.
CHURCHILL, W. S. *Lord Randolph Churchill*. 2 vols. 1906.
—— *The World Crisis*. Vol. I, 1923.
CLARKE, G. SYDENHAM. *Fortification: Its Past Achievements, Recent Developments and Future Progress*. 1890.
—— *Imperial Defence*. 1897.
COLOMB, Sir J. C. R. *The Defence of Great and Greater Britain: sketches of its naval, military and political aspects*. 1880.
—— *Our Ships, Colonies and Commerce in Time of War*. 1902.
COLOMB, Admiral P. H. *Essays on Naval Defence*. New edn. 1899.
CRAIG, G. C. *Federal Defence of Australia*. 1897.
D'EGVILLE, Sir H. *Imperial Defence and Closer Union: a short record of the life-work of the late Sir John Colomb*. 1913.
DILKE, Sir C. W. *Problems of Greater Britain*. 2 vols. 1890.
DILKE, Sir C. W. and WILKINSON, S. *Imperial Defence*. 1892.
ELLIOT, A. R. D. "Politics, Parties and Imperial Defence." *Edinburgh Rev.* vol. CLXXXII (Oct. 1895), pp. 524–44.
ESHER, Lord. *The Committee of Imperial Defence, its functions and potentialities*. 1912.
—— *Journals and Letters of Reginald Viscount Esher*, ed. by M. V. Brett. Vols. I and II, 1934.
FIENNES, G. *The Ocean Empire: its dangers and defence*. 1911.
FISHER, Lord. *Fear God and Dread Nought. The Correspondence of Admiral Lord Fisher*. Vols. I, II. Ed. by A. J. Marder. 1956.
—— *Memories*. 1919.
FOSTER, H. J. *War and the Empire: the principles of imperial defence*. 1914.
GRESWELL, W. H. P. "The Colonial Conference and Imperial Defence." *National Rev.* Jan. 1887, pp. 648–58.

GREY, E., Viscount Grey of Fallodon. *Twenty-five Years.* 1925.

HALDANE, Lord. *Before the War.* 1920.

HURD, Sir A. S. *The Command of the Sea: some problems of imperial defence.* 1912.

HURD, Sir A. S. and CASTLE, H. *German Sea-Power.* 1913.

IMPERIAL FEDERATION (DEFENCE) COMMITTEE. *Publications,* nos. 1–19. 1886–1902.

KIRKPATRICK, F. A. *Imperial Defence and Trade.* 1914.

LASCELLES, E. F. W. *The Colonies and Imperial Defence. The question of the provision of an Imperial Service Army Reserve.* 1906.

MAURICE, Sir F. D. *Haldane.* 1937.

MAY, E. S. *Principles and Problems of Imperial Defence.* 1903.

MONTGOMERY-CUNNINGHAME, Sir T. *Dusty Measure.* 1939.

MURRAY, S. L. "Some Strategic Problems of the Empire." *Nineteenth Century,* vol. LXXII (1942), pp. 206–20.

REPINGTON, C. A'C. *Imperial Strategy.* 1906.

—— *Foundations of Reform.* By the Military Correspondent of *The Times.* 1908. (Reprint of articles and addresses, 1906–8, with useful appendices.)

ROBERTS, Lord. *Speeches and Letters on Imperial Defence.* Oxford, 1906.

—— *Lord Roberts' Message to the Nation.* 1912.

—— *Lord Roberts' Campaign Speeches: a continuation of the "Message".* 1913.

ROBERTSON, Field-Marshal Sir W. *Soldiers and Statesmen.* 2 vols. 1926.

ROBINSON, C. N. *The British Fleet.* 1894.

SYDENHAM OF COMBE, Col. Lord. *My Working Life.* 1927. (See also CLARKE.)

WEST, C. *Canada and Sea Power.* Toronto, 1913.

WILKINSON, H. SPENSER. *Command of the Sea.* 2nd edn. 1894.

(*f*) LATER WORKS

AMERY, L. S. *My Political Life.* Vol. 1. 1953.

ARTHUR, Sir G. *The Life of Lord Kitchener.* 3 vols. 1920.

ASTON, Sir G. *The Committee of Imperial Defence: its Evolution and Prospects.* 1926.

—— *The Problem of Defence. Reminiscences and Deductions.* 1925.

BACON, Sir R. H. *Life of Lord Fisher of Kilverstone.* 2 vols. 1929.

BALLARD, C. R. *Kitchener.* 1930.

BOULGER, D. C. *Life of Gordon.* 1897.

BOYCOTT, A. G. *The Elements of Imperial Defence: a Study of the Geographic Features, Material Resources, Communications and Organisation of the British Empire.* 1936. 3rd edn. 1938.

CLOWES, Sir W. L. *The Royal Navy, a History from the earliest times to the present.* 7 vols. 1897–1903.

COLE, D. H. *Imperial Military Geography.* 3rd edn. 1925; 9th edn. 1939.

CORBETT, Sir J. S. *Some Principles of Maritime Strategy.* 1911.

—— *Naval Operations (Official History of the War).* Vol. 1, 1920.

CORNISH, V. *A Geography of Imperial Defence.* 1922.

CUNNINGHAM, A. B., Lord. *A Sailor's Odyssey: Autobiography.* 1951.

DUNFIELD, R. B. "British Defence Policy in Relation to the Development of Colonial Self-Government." (Unpublished thesis.)

DUNLOP, J. K. *The Development of the British Army, 1899–1914.* 2nd edn. Oxford, 1938.

—— *The Development of the British Army, 1904–14.* Oxford, 1924.

FORTESCUE, Sir J. W. *The Empire and the Army.* 1928.

—— *History of the British Army.* 12 vols. 1910–27.

FULLER, J. F. C. *Imperial Defence, 1588–1914.* 1926.

GIBBS, N. H. *The Origins of Imperial Defence.* (Inaugural Lecture.) Oxford, 1955.

GRAHAM, G. S. *The Maritime Foundations of Imperial History.* 1950. Inaugural lecture.

HANKEY, Lord. *Government Control in War.* 1945.

HANKEY, Lord. *Diplomacy by Conference.* 1946. (Includes chapter on the Committee of Imperial Defence, originally published in the *Army Quarterly*, 1927.)

HEARNSHAW, F. J. C. *Sea-power and Empire.* 1940.

JAMES, D. *Lord Roberts.* 1954.

LEWIS, M. *The Navy of Britain.* 1948.

LLOYD, C. *The Nation and the Navy: a History of Naval Life and Policy.* 1954.

LUCAS, Sir C. P. *The Empire at War.* Vol. 1. *Introductory volume to August 4th, 1914.* Oxford, 1921.

MARDER, A. J. *British Naval Policy, 1880–1905.* 1940. (See note on p. 892 above.)

—— *Portrait of an Admiral: the Life and Papers of Sir Herbert Richmond.* 1952.

MAURICE, Sir F. D. and ARTHUR, Sir G. C. A. *The Life of Lord Wolseley.* 1924.

RICHMOND, Admiral Sir H. R. *Statesmen and Sea Power.* 1946.

STACEY, C. P. *Military Problems of Canada.* Toronto, 1940.

—— *Canada and the British Army, 1846–71.* 1936.

TAYLOR, A. J. P. *Rumours of Wars.* 1952.

TUCKER, G. "Naval Policy of Sir Robert Borden." *Canadian Hist. Rev.* March 1947.

TYLER, J. E. *The British Army and the Continent, 1904–1914.* 1938.

UPLEGGER, F. *Die englische Flottenpolitik vor dem Weltkriege, 1904–1909.* Stuttgart, 1930.

WILKINSON, H. SPENSER. *Thirty-Five Years, 1874–1909.* 1910.

WOODWARD, E. L. *Great Britain and the German Navy.* 1935.

G. THE EMPIRE AT WAR, 1914–18

(Chapter XVI)

No attempt is here made to give even a selective bibliography of the First World War. For the vast literature on the subject reference may be made to the *Subject Index of the Books relating to the European War, 1914–1918, acquired by the British Museum, 1914–1920* (British Museum, Dept. of Printed Books, 1922), supplemented by relevant sections of the *Subject Index of Modern Works*, 1920– . (In progress.) Neither Sir G. W. Prothero, *A Select Analytical List of Books concerning the Great War* (1923) nor C. B. Falls, *War Books, a Critical Guide* (1930), take one very far. The most thorough bibliographies of the war were those issued under the dubious aegis of the Weltkriegsbucherei, Stuttgart. In addition to the periodicals on military and naval history noted above, special mention should be made of the *Revue d'histoire de la Guerre Mondiale* (Paris, 1923–), *Kriegsschuldfrage* (title varies) (Berlin, 1923–), and the *Journal of Modern History* (Chicago, 1929–), all of which note current publications in the field, and have special bibliographies on various aspects.

The books listed below are those which the student will find useful when studying the specific problems of the British Empire. French and German writers give them little attention, and are therefore, in general, omitted. This period is peculiarly rich in memoirs of statesmen and commanders, often composed in a controversial or justificatory style. The contentious questions of the higher direction of war, in so loose an organism as the British Empire, can be answered only by reference to these memoirs. State papers issued in London rarely give prominence to the point of view of the Dominions. State Papers issued in the Dominions are necessarily local in their outlook; for them the student is referred to *C.H.B.E.* volumes V–VIII.

(a) OFFICIAL PUBLICATIONS

See above, Part I, 3 and 4, for Parliamentary Papers and Debates, especially Published Proceedings and Précis of the Colonial Conference, 1907, *Parl. Pap.* 1907, LV [Cd. 3404] and [Cd. 3406]; Correspondence and Papers relating to a Conference with representatives of the self-governing Dominions on the Naval and Military Defence of the Empire, 1909, *Parl. Pap.* 1909, LIX [Cd. 4948]; Imperial

Conference (Minutes of Proceedings), 1911, *Parl. Pap.* 1911, LIV [Cd. 5745];
Imperial War Conference, Extracts from Minutes of Proceedings and Papers,
1917–18, *Parl. Pap.* 1917–18, XXIII [Cd. 8566], [Cd. 8673] and *Parl. Pap.* 1918, XVI
[Cd. 9172]; Reports of the War Cabinet, 1917, *Parl. Pap.* 1918, XIV [Cd. 9005], and
1918, *Parl. Pap.* 1919, XXX [Cmd. 325]; General Annual Reports of the British
Army, 1913–19, *Parl. Pap.* 1921, XX [Cmd. 1193]; *Statistics of the Military Effort of the
British Empire during the Great War, 1914–20* (War Office, 1922); and *India's Contribution to the Great War* (Calcutta, 1923). A few Parliamentary Papers relating to
campaigns are listed below.

(b) OFFICIAL HISTORIES

GOOCH, G. P. and TEMPERLEY, H. W. V. (Eds.). *British Documents on the Origins of
the War, 1898–1914.* 11 vols. in 13. H.M.S.O. 1927–38.
EDMONDS, Sir J. E. *History of the Great War Based on Official Documents, by direction of
the Historical Section of the Committee of Imperial Defence.* 1925– . In progress.
Military Operations. See below for separate campaigns under this heading.
Naval Operations, by Sir J. CORBETT and Sir H. NEWBOLT. 5 vols. 1920–31.
The War in the Air, by Sir W. RALEGH and H. A. JONES. 6 vols. 1922–37.
History of the Canadian Forces, 1914–18. Ottawa, 1935– . (See below for campaign in
France, under CANADIAN OFFICIAL HISTORY.)
Official History of Australia in the War of 1914–1918. 12 vols. Sydney, 1921–37. See
below for separate campaigns, under AUSTRALIAN OFFICIAL HISTORY.
Official History of New Zealand's Effort in the Great War. 4 vols. Wellington, 1919–23.
See below for separate campaigns, under heading NEW ZEALAND HISTORY.
Union of South Africa and the Great War. Pretoria, 1924. The South African official
history.
TEMPERLEY, H. W. V. *History of the Peace Conference of Paris.* 6 vols. 1920–4.

(c) OTHER GENERAL HISTORIES

See the following chapters in other volumes of the *Cambridge History of the British
Empire*: vol. V, *The Indian Empire, 1858–1918,* chapters 25, 26, 27, 32, 33; vol. VI,
Canada and Newfoundland, chapters 26, 28, 30, 31; vol. VII, Part i, *Australia,* chapters
17, 18, 19, 20; vol. VII, Part ii, *New Zealand,* chapters 10, 11; vol. VIII, *South Africa,*
chapters 26, 27, 28, 29.

BUCHAN, JOHN (Lord Tweedsmuir). *A History of the Great War.* 4 vols. 1921–2.
CRUTTWELL, C. R. M. *A History of the Great War.* Oxford, 1934.
HANKEY, Lord. *Government Control in War.* Cambridge, 1945.
KEITH, A. B. *War Government of two British Dominions* (Carnegie Endowment for
International Peace Pubn.). Oxford, 1921.
LIDDELL-HART, B. H. *The Real War, 1914–1918.* 1930. Contains useful biblio-
graphies.
LUCAS, Sir C. P. *The Empire at War.* Edited for the Royal Colonial Institute.
5 vols. London, 1921–6.

(d) MEMOIRS AND BIOGRAPHIES

BIRDWOOD, W. R. B., Lord. *Khaki and Gown: an autobiography.* 1941.
BORDEN, Sir R. L. *Memoirs.* 2 vols. 1938.
BOTHA. *General Louis Botha.* By EARL BUXTON. 1924.
General Louis Botha. By F. V. ENGELENBURG. 1929.
Botha, Smuts and South Africa. By A. F. BASIL WILLIAMS. 1946.
CALLWELL, Sir C. E. *Experiences of A Dugout, 1914–1918.* 1920.
CHURCHILL, WINSTON. *The World Crisis, 1911–1918.* 6 vols. 1923–31.
FISHER. *Life of Lord Fisher of Kilverstone.* By Sir R. H. S. BACON. 1929.
GODLEY, Sir A. J. *Reminiscences of an Irish Soldier.* 1939.

HALDANE, R. B. *Autobiography.* 1929.
　Before the War. 1920.
　Life of Haldane. By Sir F. D. MAURICE. 1937.
HUGHES, W. M. *The Splendid Adventure, a review of Empire Relations.* 1929.
KITCHENER. *Life of Lord Kitchener.* By Sir GEORGE ARTHUR. 3 vols. 1920.
LLOYD GEORGE, D. *War Memories.* 6 vols. 1933–6. Especially vol. IV.
LUKIN. *From Ulundi to Delville Wood.* By R. E. JOHNSTON. 1930.
MASSEY, W. F. *From Ploughboy to Premier.* By H. J. CONSTABLE. 1925.
OXFORD AND ASQUITH, Lord. *The Genesis of the War.* 1923.
RAWLINSON. *Lord Rawlinson of Trent.* By Sir F. MAURICE. 1928.
RIDDELL, G. A. R., Lord. *War Diary, 1914–1918.* 1933.
ROBERTSON, Sir W. *Soldiers and Statesmen.* 2 vols. 1926.
SMUTS. *General Smuts.* By S. G. MILLIN. 1936.
WESTER WEMYSS, Lord. *The Navy in the Dardanelles Campaign.* 1924.
WILSON. *Sir Henry Wilson, his Life and Diaries.* By Sir C. E. CALLWELL. 1927.

(*e*) CAMPAIGN HISTORIES

(i) *The Western Front. Official Publications*

Military Operations: EDMONDS, J. E. (Ed.). *France and Belgium: 1914*, 2 vols.
　(1923–5); 1915. 2 vols. (1927–8); 1916, 2 vols. (1932–8, incomplete); 1917,
　1 vol. (1940 incomplete); 1918, 4 vols. (1935–47, incomplete).
Australian Official History: BEAN, C. E. W. (Ed.). *The Australian Imperial Force in
　France.* 4 vols. Sydney, 1937–42.
Canadian Official History. DUGUID, A. FORTESCUE. Vol. I, August 1914–September
　1915. Ottawa, 1935.
New Zealand Official History. Vol. II. STEWART, H. *The New Zealand Division—
　France.* Wellington, 1921.
South African Official History. *The Union of South Africa and the Great War.* Pretoria,
　1924.
HAIG, Sir D. (Lord Haig). *Despatches.* Ed. by J. H. B. BORASTON. 2 vols. 1919.

(ii) *Western Front. General Works*

AITKEN, Sir M. (Lord Beaverbrook) and ROBERTS, C. G. D. *Canada in Flanders.*
　Vols. I and II. Ottawa, 1916–18.
BUCHAN, JOHN. *History of the South African Forces in France.* 1920.
LIVESAY, J. F. B. *Canada's Hundred Days* (August–November 1918). Toronto, 1919.
MACKENZIE, C. *Chronicles of the New Zealand Expeditionary Force.* 5 vols. Wellington,
　1916–19.
MEREWETHER, J. W. B. and SMITH, Sir F. E. *The Indian Corps in France.* 1917.
MONASH, Sir JOHN. *Australian Victories in France in 1918.* Melbourne, 1923.
SEELY, J. E. B. (Lord Mottistone). *Adventure* (for Canadian Cavalry Brigade).
　1930.
WILLCOCKS, Sir J. *With the Indians in France.* 1920.

(iii) *The Dardanelles, Gallipoli*

Military Operations:
ASPINALL-OGLANDER, C. F. *Gallipoli.* 2 vols. 1929–32.

Australian Official History:
BEAN, C. E. W. (Ed.). *The Story of Anzac.* 2 vols. Sydney, 1921–24.

New Zealand Official History:
WAITE, F. *The New Zealanders in Gallipoli.* Wellington, 1921.

Dardanelles Commission. Reports and Supplement: 1917–18. *Parl. Pap.* 1917–
　18, x [Cd. 8490], [Cd. 8502]; 1919, XIII [Cmd. 371].

HAMILTON, Sir I. *A Gallipoli Diary.* 2 vols. 1920.
KANNENGIESSER, H. *The Campaign in Gallipoli.* 1928. Translation.
MACKENZIE, C. *Chronicles of the New Zealand Expeditionary Force.* 5 vols. Wellington, 1916–19.
MASEFIELD, (Sir) JOHN. *Gallipoli.* 1916. A picturesque account.
MONASH, Sir JOHN. *War Letters.* Sydney, 1935.

(iv) *Egypt and Palestine*

Military Operations:
MACMUNN, Sir G. F. and FALLS, CYRIL. *Egypt and Palestine.* 2 vols. (Vol. II in 2 pts.) 1928–30.

Australian Official History:
GULLETT, H. S. *The Australian Imperial Force in Sinai and Palestine.* Sydney, 1923.

New Zealand Official History:
POWLES, C. GUY. *The New Zealanders in Sinai and Palestine.* Wellington, 1922.

South African Official History:
The Union of South Africa and the Great War. Pretoria, 1924. (Contains a meagre account of the Senussi Campaign.)

GULLETT, H. S., BARRETT, C. and BARKER, D. *Australia in Palestine.* Sydney, 1919.
MASSEY, W. T. *Allenby's Final Triumph.* 1920.
PRESTON, The Hon. R. M. P. *The Desert Mounted Corps.* 1921.
WAVELL, Lord. *The Palestine Campaign,* 1928.
—— *Allenby: A Study in Greatness.* 1940.

(v) *The Arab Revolt*

Military Operations:
MACMUNN, Sir G. F. and FALLS, C. *Egypt and Palestine.* 2 vols. 1928–30.
EDMONDS, C. *T. E. Lawrence,* 1935.
LAWRENCE, T. E. *Seven Pillars of Wisdom: a Triumph.* 1935. Also *Revolt in the Desert,* an abridged version of *Seven Pillars.*
LIDDELL HART, B. H. *T. E. Lawrence, in Arabia and After.* 1934.
YOUNG, Sir H. *The Independent Arab.* 1933.
STORRS, Sir R. *Orientations.* 2nd edn. 1945.

(vi) *Mesopotamia*

Military Operations:
MOBERLY, F. J. (Ed.). *The Campaign in Mesopotamia, 1914–18.* 4 vols. 1923–7.
Mesopotamia Commission. Report, 1917–18. *Parl. Pap.* 1917–18, XVI [Cd. 8610].
CALLWELL, Sir C. E. *Life of Sir Stanley Maude.* 1920.
DUNSTERVILLE, L. C. *Adventures of "Dunsterforce".* 1920.
HERBERT, AUBREY. *Mons, Anzac, and Kut.* By an M.P. 1919.
MARSHALL, Sir W. R. *Memories of Four Fronts.* 1929.
TOWNSHEND, Sir C. V. F. *My Campaign in Mesopotamia.* 1920.
WILSON, Sir ARNOLD T. *Loyalties: Mesopotamia, 1914–20.* 2 vols. 1930–1.

(vii) *Togoland and Cameroons*

Military Operations:
MOBERLY, F. J. *Togoland and the Cameroons.* 1931.
GEORGES, E. H. *The Great War in West Africa.* 1930.

(viii) *East Africa*

Military Operations:
HORDERN, C. *East Africa.* Vol. I. August 1914–September 1916. 1941.
South African Official History: The Union of South Africa and the Great War. Pretoria, 1924.

CROWE, J. H. V. *General Smuts' Campaign in East Africa.* 1918.
FENDALL, C. P. *The East African Force, 1915–1919.* 1921.
LETTOW-VORBECK, General VON. *My Reminiscences of East Africa.* (Translated.) 1920.
SMUTS. *General Smuts.* By S. G. Millin. 2 vols. 1936.
YOUNG, F. BRETT. *Marching on Tanga.* 1917.

(ix) *South African Rebellion, and South-West Africa.*

Report on the Outbreak of the Rebellion and Policy of the Government with regard to its Suppression. (U.G. No. 42.) Pretoria, 1916.
Report on the Rebellion. (U.G. No. 46.) Pretoria, 1916.
The Union of South Africa and the Great War. Pretoria, 1924.
BOTHA. *General Louis Botha.* By Earl Buxton, 1924.
HERTZOG. *General J. B. M. Hertzog.* By C. M. van den Heever. Johannesburg, 1946.
KEITH, A. B. *War Government of the British Dominions.* Oxford, 1921.
LUKIN. *From Ulundi to Delville Wood.* By R. E. Johnston. 1930.
SAMPSON, P. J. *Capture of De Wet with Conquest of German West Africa.* 1915.

(x) *New Guinea: Samoa*

Australian Official History:
MACKENZIE, S. S. *The Australians at Rabaul.* Sydney, 1927.

New Zealand Official History:
DREW, H. T. B. *The War Effort of New Zealand.* Wellington, 1923.

BURNELL, F. S. *Australia versus Germany, the story of the taking of German New Guinea.* 1915.
LEARY, L. P. *New Zealanders in Samoa.* Wellington, 1918.
MACKENZIE, C. *Chronicles of the New Zealand Expeditionary Force.* 5 vols. Wellington, 1916–19.
SMITH, S. J. *The Samoa Expeditionary Force.* Wellington, 1924.

H. THE BRITISH EMPIRE AND THE PEACE TREATIES, 1918–19
(Chapter XVII)

(a) OFFICIAL PUBLICATIONS

For discussions of imperial post-war policy see Reports of the War Cabinet, 1917 and 1918, *Parl. Pap.* 1918, XIV [Cd. 9005] and 1919, XXX [Cmd. 325]; also Canada, Parliament, Special Session, 1919: *Canada, Sessional Papers*, 1919, no. 41 J.

(b) COLLECTIONS OF DOCUMENTS

KEITH, Sir A. B. (Ed.). *Speeches and Documents on the British Dominions, 1918–1931.* 1932.
KENNEDY, W. P. M. (Ed.). *Statutes, Treaties and Documents on the Canadian Constitution.* 1930.

(c) BIBLIOGRAPHIES

See Part II 1 (*a*), especially LANGER, W. L. and others: *Foreign Affairs Bibliography* (3 vols. New York, 1933–55). The following bibliographical article is useful: R. C. BINKLEY, "Ten Years of Peace Conference History", *Jour. Mod. Hist.* vol. 1 (Dec. 1929), pp. 607–29. Later work can be traced in the relevant sections of the bibliographies in *International Affairs* and the *Journal of Modern History*.

(d) Contemporary and Later Works

Antonelli, E. *L'Afrique et la Paix de Versailles*. Paris, 1921.

Bailey, T. A. *Woodrow Wilson and the Lost Peace*. 1944.

Baker, R. S. *Woodrow-Wilson and World Settlement*. 3 vols. Garden City, N.Y., 1922.

Borden, H. (Ed.). *Robert Laird Borden: his Memoirs*. 2 vols. 1928.

Borden, Sir R. L. *Canada in the Commonwealth*. 1929.

—— *Canadian Constitutional Studies*. 1921.

Davey, A. C. *The Dominions in Diplomacy*. 2 vols. 1929.

Glazebrook, G. P. de T. *Canada at the Paris Peace Conference*. Oxford, 1942.

House, E. M. *The Intimate Papers of Colonel House*, ed. by C. Seymour. 4 vols. Boston, New York, 1926–28.

Hughes, W. M. *The Splendid Adventure*. 1929.

Keith, Sir A. B. *Responsible Government in the Dominions*. 2nd edn. 2 vols. 1928.

Kennedy, W. P. M. *The Constitution of Canada*. 2nd edn. 1938.

Keynes, J. M. *The Economic Consequences of the Peace*. 1920.

Lansing, R. *The Big Four and others of the Peace Conference*. Boston, 1921.

—— *The Peace Negotiations: a Personal Narrative*. Boston, 1921.

Lloyd George, D. *The Truth about the Peace Treaties*. 2 vols. 1938.

Mackenzie, N. and Laing, L. H. *Canada and the Law of Nations*. Oxford, 1938.

Marston, F. S. *The Peace Conference of 1919*. 1944.

Martin, C. (Ed.). *Canada in Peace and War: eight studies in national trends since 1914*. Oxford, 1941.

Miller, D. H. *My Diary at the Conference of Paris. With Documents*. 22 vols. Privately printed, 1924–26.

—— *The Drafting of the Covenant*. 2 vols. New York, 1928.

Millin, S. G. *General Smuts*. 2 vols. 1936.

Nicolson, H. *Peacemaking, 1919*. 1933.

Noel-Baker, P. J. *The Present Juridical Status of the British Dominions in International Law*. 1929.

Nowak, K. F. *Versailles*. New York, 1929.

Rudin, H. R. *Armistice, 1918*. 1944.

Shotwell, J. T. (Ed.). *The Origins of the International Labour Organisation*. 2 vols. 1934.

Temperley, H. W. V. (Ed.). *A History of the Peace Conference of Paris*. 6 vols. [Royal] Institute of International Affairs, 1920–4. See especially vol. 6.

Zimmern, Sir A. *The League of Nations and the Rule of Law*. 1936.

—— *The Third British Empire*. 3rd edn. 1934.

I. INTERNATIONAL LAW AND COLONIAL QUESTIONS, 1870–1914

(Chapter XVIII)

(a) Official Publications

See Part I, 3 and 4 for Parliamentary Papers and Debates, especially the following papers: Treaty of Washington, Correspondence and Papers, *Parl. Pap.* 1872, LXIX [C. 469], [C. 476], [C. 505], [C. 506], [C. 506–VII], [C. 531], [C. 545], [C. 548], [C. 566], [C. 570], [C. 571], [C. 594]; West African Conference, *Parl. Pap.* 1884–5, LV [C. 4361]; Behring Sea Arbitration, *Parl. Pap.* 1892, XCVI [C. 6639]; 1893–4, CX [C. 6918], [C. 6919], [C. 6920], [C. 6921]; 1893–4, CXI [C. 6949], [C. 6950], [C. 6951], [C. 7107], [C. 7161]; British Guiana Boundary Arbitration Award, *Parl. Pap.* 1899, CXI [C. 9336], [C. 9337], [C. 9338], [C. 9499], [C. 9500]; 1899, CXII [C. 9501], [C. 9533]; Correspondence on Alaska Boundary, *Parl. Pap.* 1904, CXI [Cd. 1877], [Cd. 1878]; 1906, CXXVII [Cd. 3159]; Proceedings of International Naval Conference, London, Dec. 1908–Feb. 1909; *Parl. Pap.* 1909, LIV

[Cd. 4554], [Cd. 4555]; North Atlantic Coast Fisheries Arbitration, *Parl. Pap.* 1910, LXXIV [Cd. 5396].

Other British official compilations on these arbitrations were:

FOREIGN OFFICE. *Behring Sea Arbitration.* 4 vols. 1890–3.
—— *British Boundary Arbitration with the United States of Venezuela.* 9 vols. 1898. American edn. 5 vols. New York, 1898.
—— *Alaska Boundary. Case. Counter-case,* etc. 7 vols. 1903.

Official American publications on the same subjects include the following:

U.S.A. CONGRESS. *Bering Sea Tribunal. Fur Seal Arbitration. Proceedings.* (53rd Cong. 2nd Sess. Senate Exec. Doc. 177.) 16 vols. Washington, 1895.
—— *Proceedings of the Alaska Boundary Tribunal.* (58th Cong. 2nd Sess. Senate Doc. 162.) 7 vols. Washington, 1904.
—— *Proceedings in the North Atlantic Coast Fisheries Arbitration before the Permanent Court of Arbitration at the Hague.* (61st Cong. 3rd Sess. Senate Doc. 870.) 12 vols. Washington, 1912–13.
U.S.A. DEPARTMENT OF STATE. *Correspondence in Relation to the Boundary Controversy between Great Britain and Venezuela.* Washington, 1896. Reprint of 50th Cong. 1st Sess. Senate Exec. Doc. 226 (1888) and 54th Cong. 1st Sess. Senate Doc. 31 (1895).
U.S.A. COMMISSION TO INVESTIGATE DIVISIONAL LINE BETWEEN VENEZUELA AND BRITISH GUIANA. *Report and Accompanying Papers.* 9 vols. Washington, 1896–7.

(b) BIBLIOGRAPHIES

BEMIS, S. F. and GRIFFIN, G. G. *Guide to the Diplomatic History of the United States.* Washington, 1935. Especially chap. xvi, "Anglo-American Relations, 1867–1917" and chap. xx, "International Arbitration and the Peace Movement".
HAGUE. PALACE OF PEACE LIBRARY. *Catalogue.* By P. C. Molhusen and E. R. Oppenheim. Leyden, 1916. Supplements, 1922– .
HAGUE. PERMANENT COURT OF INTERNATIONAL JUSTICE. *Bibliographical List of Official and Unofficial Publications concerning the Permanent Court.* Prepared by J. Douma. Hague, 1926. Supplements, 1927– .
HEADICAR, B. M. *Edward Fry Library of International Law. Catalogue.* 1923. Supplement, 1925. Subsequent additions in the London School of Economics and Political Science, *Bibliography of the Social Sciences.*
INSTITUTE OF ADVANCED LEGAL STUDIES. *Bibliographical Guide to the Law of the United Kingdom.* 1956. "International Law", pp. 146–54.
MYERS, D. P. *Manual of Collections of Treaties and of Collections relating to Treaties.* Cambridge, 1922.
SCHWARZENBERGER, G. *Manual of International Law.* 3rd edn. 1952. Contains useful "Study Outlines".
SWEET & MAXWELL, LTD. *A Legal Bibliography of the British Commonwealth.* 7 vols. New edn. 1955– . In progress.
WILSON, H. W., LTD. *Index to Legal Periodicals.* New York, 1908– . Annual.

(c) PERIODICALS AND PUBLICATIONS OF SOCIETIES

American Journal of International Law, vol. 1– . Washington, New York, American Society of International Law, 1907– . In progress. Supplements include diplomatic correspondence and other documents.
AMERICAN SOCIETY OF INTERNATIONAL LAW. *Proceedings.* Washington, 1907– . In progress.
British Yearbook of International Law, 1920/1– . Royal Institute of International Affairs, 1921– . In progress.
CARNEGIE ENDOWMENT FOR INTERNATIONAL PEACE. *Year Book,* 1911–47. Washington, 1911–47. Continued as *Annual Report.*

GROTIUS SOCIETY. *Transactions: Problems of Peace and War.* 1915– . In progress.
International and Comparative Law Quarterly. Society of Comparative Legislation, 1952– .
International Conciliation. New York, 1907– . In progress.
INTERNATIONAL LAW ASSOCIATION. *Reports of (Annual) Conferences.* 1873–1913; 1920– . In progress. *Transactions,* 1873–1924.
International Law Quarterly. London, 1947–51.
Journal of Comparative Legislation and International Law. Society of Comparative Legislation, 1896–1951.
Law Quarterly Review. London, 1895– . In progress.

(d) COLLECTIONS OF CASES AND OTHER SOURCES

BRIGGS, H. W. (Ed.). *The Law of Nations: Cases, Documents and Notes.* 5th edn. 1953.
CARNEGIE ENDOWMENT FOR INTERNATIONAL PEACE. DIVISION OF INTERNATIONAL LAW. *Autonomy and Federation within the Empire: the British self-governing dominions.* Washington, 1921.
COBBETT, PITT. *Leading Cases on International Law.* 4th edn. ed. H. H. L. Bellot. 2 vols. 1922–4. Latest edn. vol. I (1947), vol. II (1937).
DAWSON, R. M. (Ed.). *The Development of Dominion Status, 1900–1936.* 1937.
FOREIGN OFFICE. *Handbook of Commercial Treaties.* 4th edn. H.M.S.O. 1931.
—— *United Kingdom Treaty series.* H.M.S.O. 1892– .
HACKWORTH, G. H. (Ed.). *Digest of International Law.* 8 vols. Washington, 1940–44.
HERTSLET, Sir E. and others (Eds.). *Hertslet's Commercial Treaties: a complete collection of the treaties and conventions and reciprocal regulations subsisting between Great Britain and foreign powers.* 31 vols. H.M.S.O. 1820–1925.
HERTSLET, Sir E. (Ed.). *The Map of Africa by Treaty.* 3rd edn. 3 vols. 1909.
LAPRADELLE, A. G. DE. *Recueil des Arbitrages internationaux, 1798–1872.* 1905, 1924.
McNAIR, A. D., Lord (Ed.). *International Law Opinions.* Vols. I–III. Cambridge, 1956.
MAKAROV, A. N. and SCHMITZ, E. (Eds.). *Digest of the Diplomatic Correspondence of the European States, 1856–1871.* (*Fontes Juris Gentium* series.) 2 vols. 1932.
MARTENS, G. F. VON. *Nouveau recueil général de traités et autres actes relatifs aux rapports de droit international, continuation par Charles Samwer et Jules Hope.* 2nd ser. 1853–1907. 35 vols. Göttingen, 1876–1908. *Table générale,* Leipzig, 1910. *Continuation par Heinrich Triefel.* 3rd ser. 1894–1921. 10 vols. Leipzig, 1909–1921.
MOLLOY, W. M. (Ed.). *Treaties, Conventions, International Acts, Protocols and Agreements between the United States of America and other Powers.* (61st Cong. 2nd Sess. Senate Doc. 357.) 2 vols. Washington, 1910.
MOORE, J. B. *History and Digest of the Arbitrations to which the United States has been a Party.* (53rd Cong. 2nd Sess. House Misc. Doc. 212.) 6 vols. Washington, 1898.
—— (Ed.). *International Adjudications, Ancient and Modern.* 6 vols. 1929–33.
SCOTT, J. B. (Ed.). *The Hague Court Reports.* 1916. 2nd ser., 1932.
—— *The Hague Peace Conferences of 1899 and 1907.* 2 vols. Baltimore, 1909. French edn. trans. A. de Lapradelli, 3 vols. Paris, 1927. Vol. II (1909 edn.) and vols. II, III (1927 edn.) are documents.
SMITH, H. A. (Ed.). *Great Britain and the Law of Nations: a selection of documents.* 1932–5.

(e) OTHER CONTEMPORARY RECORDS

CARNEGIE ENDOWMENT FOR INTERNATIONAL PEACE. DIVISION OF INTERNATIONAL LAW. *The Declaration of London, Feb. 26, 1909: a collection of official papers and documents relating to the International Naval Conference held in London,* December 1908–February 1909. Ed. J. B. Scott. New York, 1919.

CARNEGIE ENDOWMENT FOR INTERNATIONAL PEACE. *The Proceedings of the Hague Peace Conference*. Trans. of the official texts. 5 vols. New York, 1920–1.

HAGUE. PERMANENT COURT OF ARBITRATION. *North Atlantic Coast Fisheries Tribunal of Arbitration*. The Hague, 1910.

ROOT, ELIHU. *Argument on Behalf of the United States before the North Atlantic Coast Fisheries Arbitration Tribunal*. Ed. by J. B. Scott. Boston, 1912.

SCOTT, J. B. (Ed.). *The Hague Conventions and Declarations of 1899 and 1907*. 3rd edn. New York, Carnegie Endowment, 1918.

—— (Ed.). *Reports to the Hague Conferences of 1899 and 1907*. Carnegie Endowment for International Peace, 1916.

(f) COMMENTARIES AND OTHER GENERAL WORKS

ANSON, Sir W. R. *Law and Custom of the Constitution*. 3 vols. 1907–35. Vol. I, 5th edn. Ed. Sir M. L. Gwyer, 1922; vol. II in two parts, 4th edn. Ed. A. B. Keith, 1935.

BRADY, A. *Democracy in the Dominions*. 2nd edn. Oxford, 1952.

BRIERLY, J. L. *The Law of Nations, an Introduction to the International Law of Peace*. 5th edn. 1955.

DUNNING, W. A. *The British Empire and the United States: a review of their relations during the century of peace following the treaty of Ghent*. 1915.

HALL, W. E. *A Treatise of International Law*. 8th edn. Ed. by A. Pearce Higgins. 1924.

HOLLAND, Sir T. E. *Studies in International Law*. Oxford, 1898.

JENNINGS, (Sir) W. I. and YOUNG, C. M. *The Constitutional Laws of the Commonwealth*. Oxford, 1952. Latest edn. of work first pubd. 1937.

KEETON, G. W. (Ed.). *British Commonwealth: the Development of its Laws and Constitutions*. Vol. I, *Commonwealth of Australia* (1951); vol. II, *Dominion of Ceylon* (1952); vol. IV, *New Zealand* (1954). In progress.

KEIR, Sir D. L. *Constitutional History of Modern Britain, 1485–1951*. 8th edn. 1952.

LORIMER, J. *The Institutes of the Law of Nations*. 2 vols. Edinburgh, 1883–4.

MAINE, Sir H. S. *International Law* (Whewell Lectures, Cambridge, 1887). 2nd edn. 1894.

OPPENHEIM, L. *International Law*. Ed. by H. Lauterpacht. Vol. I, Peace. 8th rev. edn., 1955; vol. II, Disputes, War and Neutrality. 7th edn. 1952.

PHILLIPS, O. HOOD and ELLENBOGEN, G. *Constitutional Law: the Constitutional Laws of Great Britain and the Commonwealth*. 1952.

SMITH, Sir F. E. (1st Earl of Birkenhead). *International Law*. 1899. 5th edn., revised by Coleman Phillipson. 1918.

SCHWARZENBERGER, G. *International Law*. Vol. I, *International Law as applied by international courts and tribunals*. 2nd edn. 1949; vol. III, "International Law as applied by Courts within the British Commonwealth and Empire" (not yet pubd. 1957).

TWISS, Sir T. *The Law of Nations in Time of Peace*. 2nd edn. 1884.

—— *The Law of Nations in Time of War*. 2nd edn. 1875.

WESTLAKE, J. *Collected Papers of John Westlake on Public International Law*, ed. L. Oppenheim. Cambridge, 1914.

—— *International Law*. 2nd edn. 2 vols. Cambridge, 1910–13.

WOOLSEY, T. D. *Introduction to the Study of International Law*. 6th edn. 1888.

(g) MONOGRAPHS AND ARTICLES

ANDRÉ, A. "Le traité anglo-américain d'arbitrage de 1897." *Rev. générale de droit international*, vol. XVIII (1911), pp. 654–66.

BALCH, T. W. *The Alaskan Frontier*. Philadelphia, 1930.

—— "The American-British Atlantic Fisheries Question." *Proc. Amer. Philosophical Soc.* vol. XLVII (1909), pp. 319–33.

BERNARD, M. *A Historical Account of the Neutrality of Great Britain during the American Civil War.* 1870.

BRIERLY, J. L. "International Law in England." *Law Quart. Rev.* vol. LI (1935), pp. 24–35.

CLEVELAND, GROVER. *The Venezuelan-Guiana Boundary Controversy.* Princeton, 1913.

CRAIES, W. F. "The Right of Aliens to enter British Territory." *Law Quart. Rev.* vol. VI (1890), pp. 27–41.

CUSHING, C. *The Treaty of Washington.* Washington, 1879.

FEILCHENFELD, E. H. *Public Debts and State Succession.* 1931.

FORSEY, E. A. *The Royal Power of Dissolution of Parliament in the British Commonwealth.* Oxford, 1943.

FRIEDMAN, S. *Expropriation in International Law.* Trans. I. C. Jackson. 1953.

HALL, H. D. *The British Commonwealth of Nations in War and Peace.* New York, 1943.

HIGGINS, P. *The Hague Peace Conference.* 1909.

HOLLS, F. W. *The Peace Conference at the Hague.* New York, 1900. 2nd edn. 1914.

HUDSON, M. O. *International Tribunals, past and future.* 1944.

JONES, J. MERVYN. *British Nationality, Law and Practice.* 1947.

KEITH, (Sir) A. BERRIEDALE. *Theory of State Succession: with special reference to English and colonial Law.* 1907.

LAUTERPACHT, H. *Private Law Sources and the Analogies of International Law.* 1927.
—— *Recognition in International Law.* 1947.

LINDLEY, M. F. *The Acquisition and Government of Backward Territory in International Law.* 1926.

McNAIR, Sir A. D. (Lord). *The Law of Treaties; British practice and opinions.* Oxford, 1938.

NEUENDORFF, G. *Studies in the Evolution of Dominion Status: the Governor-Generalship of Canada and the Development of Canadian Nationalism.* 1942.

NOEL-BAKER, P. J. *The Present Juridical Status of the British Dominions in International Law.* 1929.

NOEL-BAKER, P. J. and FAWCETT, J. E. S. *The British Commonwealth in International Law.* New edn. 1957.

O'CONNELL, D. P. *Law of State Succession.* Cambridge, 1956.

SMITH, Sir F. E. (Lord Birkenhead) and SIBLEY, N. W. *International Law as Interpreted during the Russo-Japanese War.* 2nd edn. 1907.

SPEYER, H. *La constitution juridique de l'empire coloniale britannique.* Paris, 1906.

STEWART, R. B. *Treaty Relations of the British Commonwealth of Nations.* New York, 1939.

TARRING, Sir C. J. *Chapters on the Law relating to the Colonies.* 3rd edn. 1906. 4th edn. 1913.

WESTLAKE, J. "The Muscat Dhows." *Law Quart. Rev.* vol. XXIII (1907), pp. 83–87.
—— "The Nature and Extent of the Title by Conquest." *Law Quart. Rev.* vol. XVII (1901), pp. 392–401.
—— "The South African Railway Case and International Law." *Law Quart. Rev.* vol. XXI (1905), pp. 335–39.

WHEARE, K. C. *The Statute of Westminster and Dominion Status.* 5th edn. 1953.

WIGHT, M. *The Development of the Legislative Council, 1606–1945.* 1946. Studies in Colonial Legislatures, vol. I.

J. THE COLONIAL OFFICE

(Chapter XIX)

There is no detailed study of the machinery of government in the nineteenth and early twentieth centuries. Miss E. W. Cohen, in *The Growth of the British Civil Service, 1780–1939* (1941), using printed sources only, has briefly traced the formal growth of the staff, and J. D. Kingsley in his *Representative Bureaucracy* (Antioch,

1944) has incorporated in what is properly a political study interesting, if tendentious, theories about its evolution. Professor K. B. S. Smellie's *A Hundred Years of English Government* (2nd edn. 1950) approaches the ideal, but cannot be claimed as a comprehensive survey. The absence of such a survey makes it hard for the historian of a single department to determine what was abnormal in its development.

Individual departments, the Colonial Office among them, have equally failed to attract competent historians. Dr H. L. Hall's *The Colonial Office, A History* (1937) is a mine of useful information. It is, however, rather a vindication of Imperial policy than the description of administrative processes and it is inconveniently arranged. It suffers from the fact that the author has not been bred up in the traditions of United Kingdom administration. Sir George Fiddes, *The Dominions and Colonial Office* (1926), has gathered together many historical facts. His book does not, however, purport to be a history but only a sketch of the work of the two offices at the time of publication. In *The Colonial Office from Within, 1909–1945* (1947) Sir Cosmo Parkinson has furnished some inside information on the Colonial Office as it was when the author entered it in 1909. In *Partners for Progress* Sir C. Jeffries is less revealing. The last three works are written with the reticence which characterizes the higher civil service at its traditional best.

The first half century of the Office's history has recently been surveyed in praiseworthy fashion in *Historical Studies, Australia and New Zealand* by J. Beaglehole ("The Colonial Office, 1782–1854") in vol. I and E. T. Williams ("The Colonial Office in the Thirties") in vol. II. These writers have fully used the material in Mrs H. T. Manning's *British Colonial Policy after the American Revolution* (New Haven, Conn., 1933), W. L. Burn's *Emancipation and Apprenticeship in the West Indies* (1937) and P. Knaplund's two articles on Stephen—"Sir James Stephen and British North American Problems" in the *Canadian Historical Review*, vol. V (1924) and "Mr Over-Secretary Stephen" in the *Journal of Modern History*, vol. I (1929)—without however rendering recourse to those works superfluous. D. M. Young has carried the early history of the Office much further in his attractive dissertation, at present unpublished, on "The Working of the British Colonial Office, 1812–1830" (University of London Ph.D. thesis, 1955). P. Knaplund in his *James Stephen and the British Colonial System* (Madison, Wis. 1953) has made a comprehensive study of Stephen's contribution to the formulation of Colonial policy. The introduction to K. N. Bell and W. P. Morrell's *Select Documents on British Colonial Policy, 1839–60* (Oxford, 1928) remains the most brilliant short sketch of Stephen at present available. The later history of the Office has not yet attracted so much attention, but D. M. L. Farr's *The Colonial Office and Canada, 1867–1887* (Toronto, 1955) contains a useful appraisement of Rogers, Herbert and their masters. A comparative study at an interesting point is A. L. Lovell and H. M. Stephen's *Colonial Civil Service: the selection and training of colonial officers in England, Holland and France* (New York, 1900). A recent survey of the British Civil Service during the whole period under consideration is R. K. Kelsall's *Higher Civil Servants in Britain from 1870 to the present day* (1955).

In the middle of the 19th century there begins a succession of official publications which form the most important printed sources for that period of the Office's history. Chief in importance are: "Copies of Correspondence...on the Appointment of an Assistant Secretary to the Colonies [and] of any Minute or Order in Council since...1833, relating to the Establishment of the Colonial Office", *Parl. Pap.* 1846, xxvii [455]; the Reports from the Select Committee on Miscellaneous Expenditure, *Parl. Pap.* 1847–8, xviii [543], pts. 1 and 2; and on Official Salaries (1850), *Parl. Pap.* xv [611]; the Reports from the Committee of Enquiry into Public Offices (1850–4), *Parl. Pap.* 1854, xxvii [1715]; the "Papers on the Reorganization of the Civil Service", *Parl. Pap.* 1854–5, xx [1870]; the Reports from the Select Committee on Civil Service Appointments, *Parl. Pap.* 1860, ix (440); the Third Report from the Select Committee on Civil Service Expenditure, *Parl. Pap.* 1873, vii (352); the Second Report of the Royal (Ridley) Commission on Civil Establishments, *Parl. Pap.* 1888, xxvii [C. 5545]; and the Appendices to the Second

Report of the Royal (MacDonnell) Commission on the Civil Service, *Parl. Pap.* 1912–13, xv [Cd. 6535]. The evidence of high officials in the Office contained in these documents, though intelligibly coloured by a desire on the witnesses' part to posture to good advantage before the world, probably furnishes a more credible picture of the actual operation of the Office machine than a student of today could derive from a lifetime's study of the records.

Such official documents, together with the semi-official *Colonial Office List*, are supplemented by the narratives of those who served in the Office. Sir Henry Taylor's delightful *Autobiography* (2 vols. 1885) and G. E. Marindin's edition of the *Letters of Lord Blachford* (1896) are the most useful (and the most readable) sources of this type. With them may be classed Lady Olivier's *Sydney Olivier: Letters and Selected Writings* (1948), Sir John Bramston's article "The Colonial Office from Within" in *The Empire Review*, vol. 1 (April 1901), pp. 279–87, Sir W. A. Baillie Hamilton's article "Forty-Four Years at the Colonial Office" in the *Nineteenth Century*, vol. LXV (April 1909), and Sir Edward Marsh's *A Number of People* (1939). To gain an insight into the outlook of Ministers and their dealings with the Cabinet and the Sovereign, the net must be more widely cast. The following standard works are, however, indispensable to the student of that subject: Sir A. Hardinge's *Life of Henry...Fourth Earl of Carnarvon* (3 vols. 1925), Lady V. Hicks Beach's *Life of Sir Michael Hicks Beach* (2 vols. 1932), John Morley's *Life of Gladstone* (3 vols. 1912), P. Knaplund's *Gladstone and Britain's Imperial Policy* (1927), S. Gwynn and G. M. Tuckwell's *Life of Dilke* (2 vols. 1917), J. L. Garvin's *Life of Joseph Chamberlain*, vol. III (1934) and all three series of *Queen Victoria's Letters*.

The voluminous archives of the Office have yet to be explored from the standpoint of administrative history. The class known as *Colonies General* (C.O. 323) contains the correspondence with the Treasury and therefore most of the papers about the establishment and office procedure. Every volume in this class deserves to be investigated with the aid of the appropriate registers. Thirteen volumes entitled "Office Minutes", 1836–1929, are an equally valuable source for the smaller points of official organization and routine. These are at present (1950) in the Colonial Office. In addition the future historian will need to make a selective study of the voluminous minutes written upon almost every file in order to determine the influence wielded by the respective officials and the amount of authority which they or some of them exercised upon their masters. Nor must minutes written in other departments be forgotten; for they should show the attitude of those departments towards the Colonial Office.

BIBLIOGRAPHY

A note added for the second impression

January 1967. No attempt has been made to revise the Bibliography for this re-issue but the following important corrections and additions should be noted.

p. 772.   Cabinet and departmental records, including those of the Colonial Office, are now open to the end of 1922. The Public Record Office has issued lists of Cabinet Papers of which it has copies from 1868: *List of Cabinet Papers, 1880–1914* (H.M.S.O., 1964); *1915 and 1916* (H.M.S.O., 1965).

pp. 772–86.   Further information is supplied in the *Guide to the Contents of the Public Record Office Vol. II, State Papers and Departmental Records* (H.M.S.O., 1963), in *Classes of Departmental Papers for 1906–1939* (P.R.O. Handbooks No. 10, H.M.S.O., 1966) and particularly in R. B. Pugh, *The Records of the Colonial and Dominions Offices* (P.R.O. Handbooks, No. 3, H.M.S.O., 1964).

p. 786.   CONFIDENTIAL PRINT.   There is now a *List of Colonial Office Confidential Print to 1916* (P.R.O. Handbooks, No. 8, H.M.S.O., 1965).

p. 790.   (*a*) *BRITISH MUSEUM, DEPARTMENT OF MANUSCRIPTS.* Add: *Catalogue of the Additions to the Manuscripts, 1926–30* (B.M., 1959). Add: Balfour Papers.

pp. 790–1.   (*b*) *OTHER BRITISH COLLECTIONS.* Asquith, Bryce and Goschen Papers are in the Bodleian Library, Chamberlain Papers in Birmingham University Library, Crewe Papers in Cambridge University Library, Lothian Papers in the Scottish Record Office.

pp.792–824.   SELECT LIST OF PARLIAMENTARY PAPERS.
p. 811, line 20 from foot: *for* LII *read* LVII.
p. 816, lines 15–18.   Delete duplicated entries.

PART II. OTHER WORKS

(a) BIBLIOGRAPHIES AND GUIDES

p. 835.   *Add:* HEWITT, A. R.   *Union List of Commonwealth Newspapers.* 1960.
p. 836.   *Substitute:* MORRELL, W. P.   *British Overseas Expansion and the History of the Commonwealth: a Select Bibliography.* Hist. Assoc., 1961.
p. 836.   *Add:* PUBLIC RECORD OFFICE. *Guide.* 2 vols. H.M.S.O., 1963–64. PUGH, R. B. *Records of the Colonial and Dominions Offices.* H.M.S.O., 1964.

(d) GENERAL HISTORIES AND DESCRIPTIVE WORKS

p. 839.   *Add:* HALL, H. D.   *The British Commonwealth of Nations.* London, 1920.
p. 840.   *Add:* THORNTON, A. P.   *The Imperial Idea and its Enemies.* 1959. WINKS, R. B. (Ed.).   *The Historiography of the British Empire-Commonwealth: Trends, Interpretations and Resources.* Durham, N.C., 1966.

(e) BIOGRAPHIES

p. 840.   *Add:* SIMPSON, D. H.   *Royal Commonwealth Society Library. Biography Catalogue.* 1961.
p. 841.   *Add:*
CHURCHILL. *Lord Randolph Churchill.* By R. R. James. 1959.
CHURCHILL. *Winston Churchill.* By R. Churchill. Vol. I. 1966.
DISRAELI. *Disraeli.* By R. Blake. 1966.
GOLDIE. *Sir George Goldie and the Making of Nigeria.* By J. E. Flint. 1960.

BIBLIOGRAPHY

p. 842. *Add:*
LUGARD. *Lord Lugard.* Vol. 2, *The Years of Authority, 1898–1945.* By M. Perham. 1960.
MILNER. *Alfred Lord Milner.* By Sir J. E. Wrench. 1958.
SMUTS. *Smuts.* Vol. 1, *The Sanguine Years.* By Sir W. Keith Hancock. 1962.
VICTORIA. *Queen Victoria.* By Lady Longford. 1965.

p. 843. End of first paragraph: *for* 'C.O. 812/111' [*etc.*] *read* A copy of C.O. Confidential Print in C.O. 885/6 no. 111 contains [*etc.*] and another in C.O. 885/8 no. 144 contains [*etc.*]

p. 847. (*d*) DOCUMENTS [*etc.*]
Add: NEWBURY, C. W. (Ed.). *British Policy towards West Africa. Select Documents 1786–1874.* 1965.

p. 851. (*d*) GENERAL PERIODICALS. *Add: Journal of African History, 1960–.* In progress.

p. 852. (*e*) CONTEMPORARY WRITINGS [*etc.*]
Add: PERHAM, MARGERY (Ed.). *The Diaries of Lord Lugard.* 4 vols. 1959–63.
(*f*) LATER WORKS
Add: ANSTEY, R. *Britain and the Congo in the 19th Century.* 1962.

p. 854. ROBINSON, R. and GALLAGHER, J. *Africa and the Victorians: the Official Mind of Imperialism.* 1961.

p. 855. (*c*) CONTEMPORARY WRITINGS
Add: FYFE, C. (Ed.). *Sierra Leone Inheritance.* 1964. [Documents]

p. 855. (*d*) LATER WORKS
Add: FYFE, C. *A History of Sierra Leone.* 1962.

p. 856. (*c*) CONTEMPORARY WRITINGS
Add: METCALFE, G. E. (Ed.). *Great Britain and Ghana. Documents of Ghana History, 1807–1957.* 1964.

p. 857. (*d*) LATER WORKS
Substitute: WARD, W. E. F. *A History of Ghana.* 2nd edn. 1958.
(*c*) CONTEMPORARY WRITINGS

p. 857. *Add:*
HODGKIN, T. (Ed.). *Nigerian Perspectives: an historical anthology.* 1960.
KIRK-GREENE, A. H. M. (Ed.). *The Principles of Native Administration in Nigeria. Selected Documents, 1900–1947.* 1965.

p. 858. (*d*) LATER WORKS
Substitute: BURNS. *Nigeria.* 6th edn. 1963.

p. 860. *Add:* INGHAM, K. *A History of East Africa.* 1962.

p. 863. *Add:* INGHAM, K. *The Making of Modern Uganda.* 1958.

p. 892. (F) IMPERIAL DEFENCE
Add: List of Papers of the Committee of Imperial Defence to 1914 (P.R.O. Handbooks No. 6). H.M.S.O., 1964.

p. 896. *Add:*
JOHNSON, F. A. *Defence by Committee: the British Committee of Imperial Defence, 1885–1959.* 1960.
MAGNUS, Sir P. *Kitchener: Portrait of an Imperialist.* 1958.

p. 897. (*c*) OTHER GENERAL HISTORIES
Add: TAYLOR, A. J. P. *English History, 1914–1945.* 1965.

p. 906. Lines 29–31: *for* dissertation . . . thesis, 1955 *read* book, *The Colonial Office in the Early Nineteenth Century* (1961)
Line 12 from foot: *after* history *insert* and access to which has been eased by R. B. Pugh's *The Records of the Colonial and Dominions Offices* (Public Record Office Handbooks No. 3) 1964.

p. 907. Line 8 from foot: *after* 1929, *insert* which form a part of the class called *Establishment, Miscellanea* (C.O. 873),
Lines 7 and 6 from foot: *delete the sentence* These . . . Office.

INDEX